November 5–7, 2014
Vancouver, BC, Canada

Association for
Computing Machinery

Advancing Computing as a Science & Profession

IMC'14

Proceedings of the 2014 ACM
Internet Measurement Conference

Sponsored by:

ACM SIGCOMM & ACM SIGMETRICS

Supported by:

National Science Foundation, Akamai, MLab, Verisign, Alcatel-Lucent, Facebook, Technicolor, & ThousandEyes

Association for
Computing Machinery

Advancing Computing as a Science & Profession

The Association for Computing Machinery
2 Penn Plaza, Suite 701
New York, New York 10121-0701

Notice to Past Authors of ACM-Published Articles
ACM intends to create a complete electronic archive of all articles and/or other material previously published by ACM. If you have written a work that has been previously published by ACM in any journal or conference proceedings prior to 1978, or any SIG Newsletter at any time, and you do NOT want this work to appear in the ACM Digital Library, please inform permissions@acm.org, stating the title of the work, the author(s), and where and when published.

ISBN: 978-1-4503-3213-2 (Digital)

ISBN: 978-1-4503-3385-6 (Print)

Additional copies may be ordered prepaid from:

ACM Order Department
PO Box 30777
New York, NY 10087-0777, USA

Phone: 1-800-342-6626 (USA and Canada)
+1-212-626-0500 (Global)
Fax: +1-212-944-1318
E-mail: acmhelp@acm.org
Hours of Operation: 8:30 am – 4:30 pm ET

Printed in the USA

Welcome from General Chair

Welcome to ACM IMC 2014 in Vancouver! IMC is a highly-regarded conference, co-sponsored by ACM SIGCOMM and ACM SIGMETRICS, that brings together networking researchers to advance the current state-of-the-art in the measurement and characterization of the Internet. It is an honour to host this event in Canada for the first time, and I thank you for being part of it.

The Program Chairs, Aditya Akella and Nina Taft, have an excellent technical program lined up for you. I thank them and their extensive Program Committee for doing the heavy lifting on this front. We hope that you enjoy the talks and have many stimulating discussions during your three days at the conference.

Many people helped make this conference a success. I would like to thank the IMC Steering Committee (Mark Allman, Jim Kurose, Ratul Mahajan, and Renata Teixera, plus former member Chen-Nee Chuah) for talking me into this role, and for handling industry sponsorships and the student travel grant program. Their collective knowledge provides an endless source of wisdom on conference finances and organizational logistics. Our many external supporters include Akamai, Alcatel-Lucent, Facebook, MLab, NSF, Technicolor, ThousandEyes, and Verisign. Their commitments to this event and the IMC conference series are appreciated, since they help keep our registration fees low, and allow many students to attend the conference. Shira Gordon and the team at MITACS Conference Services have been a pleasure to work with, helping with hotel selection, catering, AV, planning, and more. My hat is off to you for the fantastic service that you provide! My thanks to my local team members of Zongpeng Li as Proceedings Chair, and Mea Wang as Finance Chair, plus Canadian colleague Jianping Pan for his service as Publicity Chair. The assistance of our student volunteers (Michel Laterman, Sean Picard, Arsham Skrenes, and others) on site was much appreciated, as were the special touches provided by Sue Williamson. Last but not least, the staff at ACM (Diana Brantuas, Adrienne Griscti, Ann Lane, April Mosqus, and Stephanie Sabal), RegOnline, and Sheridan Communications helped keep all the paperwork moving to ensure smooth conference operations. My gracious thanks to you all!

Thank you all for attending ACM IMC 2014. I hope that you enjoy the conference, the hotel, the food, and the beautiful city of Vancouver!

Carey Williamson
ACM IMC 2014 General Chair
University of Calgary

Welcome from the Program Co-Chairs

It is our pleasure to welcome you to the 2014 Internet Measurement Conference. IMC has become the premier venue for measurement-based research into all kinds of networks that comprise the Internet ecosystem, and this year's program reflects that diversity of the IMC community.

IMC 2014 received 188 papers of which 103 were long and 85 were short. As usual, we solicited both long papers with deep treatment of topics and short papers that convey exciting work in progress, offer high-level visions, or present more succinct viewpoints. We accepted 43 papers, comprised of 32 long papers and 11 short papers. Unfortunately, one accepted long paper was withdrawn by the authors at the time of camera ready version preparation due to a reversed decision on publishing the material by the company of some of the authors. This was unfortunate and we wish to remind our community that those who need approval to publish must complete that process before submitting papers for review. Hence 42 papers are published in this year's proceedings.

As usual, we used a single-blind reviewing process, conducted over two rounds. In the first round, each paper was reviewed by three program committee (PC) members. The 115 papers selected for the second round were reviewed by at least one more PC member. In a few cases, we solicited 1-2 extra reviews from outside experts. The final decisions were based on all the reviews, extensive online discussions, and a day-long meeting. We wish to thank our talented, committed and hard working PC. Their rigorous reviewing and detailed insights were invaluable in this process. Many of our PC members made great efforts to attend the PC meeting, such as taking long international/overnight flights.

We discontinued the recent experiment of publishing a review summary along with each paper. We reached this decision after conducting a survey of a large and diverse subset of the IMC community. In short, most people found the utility of review summaries to be unclear. Details about our survey can be found on the IMC 2014 website.

We continued with the change made in 2012 for award papers, namely that of having two separate awards, one for the best paper and one for rewarding public release of datasets.

This year's program contains a special session integrated into the Community Feedback Session entitled "Ethics and Measurement". Our measurement techniques have greatly evolved in ways that facilitate interesting research but sometimes touch the borders of privacy best practices. To help both authors and future PCs navigate this ambiguous border, the ACM SIGCOMM Executive Committee is considering setting up guidelines for SIGCOMM sponsored conferences, including IMC. With this special session, we begin that process by discussing issues that are central to drafting such guidelines.

We would also like to thank the steering committee for their advice and responsiveness whenever we requested it, and our general chair, Carey Williamson, for help with logistics. Importantly, this conference is indebted to our generous sponsors whose contributions greatly benefit the experience of all participants.

Aditya Akella
University of Wisconsin-Madison, USA
akella@cs.wisc.edu

Nina Taft
Google, USA
nina.taft@google.com

Table of Contents

Session: Mobile Systems and Networks

Session: Theory Underpinnings

Session: Shedding Light on the Web

Session: Internet Censorship

Session: Insights into Networked System Operations

Session: Illuminating Malicious Behavior

Session: Measuring the Data and Control Planes

Session: Attacks: A Deeper Look

Session: SSL and Heartbleed

ACM IMC 2014 Conference Organizing Committee

General Chair: Carey Williamson *(University of Calgary, Canada)*

Program Chairs: Aditya Akella *(University of Wisconsin – Madison, USA)*
Nina Taft *(Google, USA)*

Finance Chair: Mea Wang *(University of Calgary, Canada)*

Publicity Chair: Jianping Pan *(University of Victoria, Canada)*

Proceedings Chair: Zongpeng Li *(University of Calgary, Canada)*

Local Arrangements Chair: Shira Gordon *(MITACS, Canada)*

Steering Committee: Mark Allman *(ICSI, USA)*
Jim Kurose *(University of Massachusetts – Amherst, USA)*
Ratul Mahajan *(Microsoft Research, USA)*
Renata Teixeira *(INRIA, France)*

Program Committee: Mark Allman *(ICSI, USA)*
Michael Bailey *(University of Michigan, USA)*
Hitesh Ballani *(Microsoft Research -- Cambridge, UK)*
Paul Barford *(University of Wisconsin – Madison, USA)*
Theophilus Benson *(Duke University, USA)*
David Choffnes *(Northeastern University, USA)*
Xenofontas Dimitropoulos *(FORTH and ETH Zurich, Switzerland)*
Vijay Erramilli *(Guavus, USA)*
Rodrigo Fonseca *(Brown University, USA)*
Phillipa Gill *(Stony Brook University, USA)*
Sharon Goldberg *(Boston University, USA)*
Saikat Guha *(Microsoft Research, India)*
Andreas Haeberlen *(University of Pennsylvania, USA)*
Arnaud Legout *(INRIA, France)*
Harsha Madhyastha *(University of California – Riverside, USA)*
Olaf Maennel *(Tallinn University of Technology, Estonia)*
Marco Mellia *(Politecnico di Torino, Italy)*
Jelena Mirkovic *(USC/ISI, USA)*
Alan Mislove *(Northeastern University, USA)*
Osnat Mokryn *(Haifa University, Israel)*
Thyaga Nandagopal *(NSF, USA)*
Vivek Pai *(Princeton University, USA)*
Michalis Polychronakis *(Columbia University, USA)*

Program Committee (continued):

Costin Raiciu *(U. Politehnica Bucuresti, Romania)*
Anmol Sheth *(A9, USA)*
Ramesh Sitaraman *(University of Massachusetts – Amherst, USA)*
Georgios Smaragdakis *(MIT/TU Berlin, Germany)*
Alex C. Snoeren *(University of California San Diego, USA)*
Oliver Spatscheck *(AT&T, USA)*
Darryl Veitch *(University of Melbourne, Australia)*
Shobha Venkataraman *(AT&T, USA)*
Zhi-Li Zhang *(University of Minnesota, USA)*

Additional Reviewers:

Mark Crovella *(Boston University, USA)*
Anna Gilbert *(University of Michigan, USA)*
Guy Leduc *(University of Liège, Belgium)*
Don Towsley *(University of Massachusetts—Amherst, USA)*
Walter Willinger *(Niksun, USA)*
Jun (Jim) Xu *(Georgia Tech, USA)*

ACM IMC 2014 Sponsors and Supporters

Sponsors: acm sigcomm; ACM SIGMETRICS

Platinum Supporter: NSF

Gold Supporters: Akamai; MLAB; VERISIGN

Silver Supporters: Alcatel·Lucent; facebook; technicolor; ThousandEyes

Inter-Domain Traffic Estimation for the Outsider

Mario A. Sanchez[†] Fabian E. Bustamante[†] Balachander Krishnamurthy[‡]
Walter Willinger[*] Georgios Smaragdakis[°] Jeffrey Erman[‡]
[†]Northwestern University [‡]AT&T Labs Research [*]Niksun, Inc. [°]MIT / TU Berlin

ABSTRACT

Characterizing the flow of Internet traffic is important in a wide range of contexts, from network engineering and application design to understanding the network impact of consumer demand and business relationships. Despite the growing interest, the nearly impossible task of collecting large-scale, Internet-wide traffic data has severely constrained the focus of traffic-related studies.

In this paper, we introduce a novel approach to characterize inter-domain traffic by reusing large, publicly available traceroute datasets. Our approach builds on a simple insight – the popularity of a route on the Internet can serve as an informative proxy for the volume of traffic it carries. It applies structural analysis to a dual-representation of the AS-level connectivity graph derived from available traceroute datasets. Drawing analogies with city grids and traffic, it adapts data transformations and metrics of route popularity from urban planning to serve as proxies for traffic volume. We call this approach *Network Syntax*, highlighting the connection to urban planning Space Syntax. We apply Network Syntax in the context of a global ISP and a large Internet eXchange Point and use ground-truth data to demonstrate the strong correlation (r^2 values of up to 0.9) between inter-domain traffic volume and the different proxy metrics. Working with these two network entities, we show the potential of Network Syntax for identifying critical links and inferring missing traffic matrix measurements.

Categories and Subject Descriptors

C.2.5 [**Communication Networks**]: Local and Wide-Area Networks—*Internet*; C.4 [**Performance of Systems**]: Measurement techniques

General Terms

Measurement, Traffic

IMC'14, November 5–7, 2014, Vancouver, BC, Canada.

ACM 978-1-4503-3213-2/14/11...$15.00.
http://dx.doi.org/10.1145/2663716.2663740.

Keywords

Traceroute; Inter-domain traffic; AS-level path

1. INTRODUCTION

Studies on the Internet inter-domain system have focused on network connectivity and dynamics and have ranged from exploring techniques to measure and generate AS-level graphs [10, 17, 48] to examining the properties of topology snapshots [23, 40]. There is, however, a growing consensus on the need to shift focus beyond connectivity towards understanding Internet traffic.

Knowledge of inter-domain traffic characteristics is important in a number of different contexts, from capacity planning to anomaly detection, and performance analysis. The major impediment to Internet traffic research has been the scarcity of publicly available traffic data. Researchers have typically had to choose between fine-grained data on a small slice of the network [7,11,14,33], or publicly available, but coarse-grained and sparse datasets [13]. While detailed studies of important network entities such as Internet eXchange Points (IXPs) [7] and Content Providers [6] can improve our understanding of the inter-domain traffic, enlisting the cooperation of Internet Service Providers (ISPs), Content Providers or IXPs requires personal connections and are thus hard to replicate or scale. On the other hand, analysis of individual networks for which traffic data is available, seriously limits researchers to a handful entities.

In this paper, we introduce a novel approach to characterize inter-domain traffic by reusing the many publicly available traceroute datasets. Our key observation is that the popularity of a route on the Internet can serve as an informative proxy for the volume of traffic it carries. While traceroute measurements allow us to draw the paths taken by packets when traversing the Internet, the routes identified by a large number of traceroutes can be used to infer the popularity of a path.

Building on this observation, we introduce a new abstraction of AS-level path and apply structural analysis to a dual-representation of the AS-level connectivity graph, derived from traceroute datasets. Drawing analogies with city grids and traffic, we adapt metrics of route popularity from urban planning to serve as *proxies* for network traffic. We call this approach *Network Syntax*, highlighting the connection to Space Syntax [26, 41], an urban-planning graph-based approach to study human and vehicular flows by leveraging the strong correlation between traffic and the morphological property of streets. Network Syntax (as the related Space Syntax) builds on known abstractions and techniques from graph theory, and adapts them to our problem domain to derive new insights on inter-domain traffic from traceroute data.

We leverage publicly available traceroute datasets and apply Network Syntax in the context of a global ISP and a large Internet eXchange Point (IXP).[1] To the best of our knowledge, our work is the first to point out and capitalize on the strong correlation between Internet route popularity and the volume of traffic it carries, showing how this popularity can be derived from easy-to-perform traceroute campaigns and available datasets. In this context, we present:

- An approach, Network Syntax, that leverages traceroute datasets to tackle a problem that can currently only be studied by a few researchers with access to proprietary data.
- A demonstration of the strong correlations between inter-domain traffic volumes and the different Network Syntax metrics applied to traceroute-based AS-level connectivity graphs (and, in contrast, the weak correlations that result from applying them to BGP-derived connectivity graphs).
- An analysis of the robustness of Network Syntax to inherent idiosyncrasies of the underlying traceroute data (e.g., IP alias resolution problem and inability to trace through layer 2 clouds) and the particulars of the measurement platform used (e.g., number and network location of the vantage points).
- An illustration of the potential of Network Syntax with two use cases – the prediction of missing traffic link volumes in a connectivity graph, and the ranking of AS-links based on traffic volume.

For validation we rely on traffic ground-truth data from an ISP and an IXP; the fact that, as in most Internet studies, we cannot reveal the sources or share this data, further motivates our approach.

2. BACKGROUND

There is a large body of work focused on generating, modeling and analyzing the inter-domain topology. These include efforts that examine graph properties of the AS topology as a logical construct [19, 23, 40], techniques to measure and infer AS-level connectivity [10, 17, 48], approaches to model and characterize the Internet topology [40], or concentrate on the IXP substrate and its topological importance [8, 48]. Other efforts have used traceroute measurements to augment intra-domain router-level ISP maps by deriving OSPF link weights that are consistent with routing [35].

Beyond topology, inter-domain traffic has been an active research topic given its importance in a wide range of contexts, from network engineering to application design. However, while some research projects have made selected network traffic traces available to vetted researchers [45], the nearly impossible task of collecting large-scale, Internet-wide traffic data has seriously restricted the focus of traffic-related studies. Previous efforts have thus investigated traffic estimation and characterization (e.g., [6,22,38,42,46]), but have to rely on close collaboration with ISPs, content providers or IXPs [16, 20–22, 33] to gain access to the necessary traffic data or be limited by the coarse-grained nature of publicly available datasets [13].

[1]We are making our own traceroute dataset and Network Syntax scripts publicly available.

Some related efforts have explored techniques and methodologies for inferring traffic matrix elements that are either not directly measurable [11,24] or missing [38,50–52]. What distinguishes our approach from these methods is their reliance, in one way or another, on link measurements obtained from either proprietary data or publicly available traffic measurements.[2]

3. NETWORK SYNTAX

In this section we expand on our descriptions of Network Syntax, its methodology and metrics. Network Syntax applies structural analysis to a dual-representation of the AS-level connectivity graph, derived from publicly available traceroute datasets, and uses different metrics to capture the popularity of a network path as a proxy for the volume of traffic it carries.

Drawing analogies with city grids and traffic, our approach adapts metrics of route popularity from urban planning's Space Syntax [26,41] for the analysis of inter-domain traffic. The following paragraphs presents a short overview of Space Syntax. We refer the reader to Hillier et al. [26] for a more in-depth description.

3.1 Space Syntax Overview

Space Syntax is a configurational analysis methodology first introduced in 1984 [25] for predicting pedestrian movement in urban settings based on an analysis of the urban grid. The key observation behind Space Syntax is that the configuration of space is the driving force behind how cities operate. Over the years, this observation has been leveraged to draw correlations between topological accessibility of spaces and urban features: from pedestrian and vehicular flows to land use, and the geographic distribution of various types of crime [27].

In Space Syntax, cities are represented as "axial maps" and then transformed into graphs. Axial maps of cities are obtained by drawing the smallest number of straight lines (called axial lines) that pass through all open spaces. These maps are then transformed into graphs by representing the axial lines as nodes and interconnecting the nodes that intersect in the map. This dual representation of the graph, where nodes are streets and edges are intersections, focuses on the connectivity of the streets irrespective of their width, length and location, and enables the identification of concrete metrics for each street. The centrality of a street or space in this graph is an indication of its importance in the city operation. Figure 1 shows an example of such a transformation.

Space Syntax introduces four core syntactic metrics, three of which can be mapped to an equivalent graph-theory metric but described using its own terminology. *(1) Connectivity* – also known as degree centrality in graph theory – is the simplest metric for assessing ranking of nodes within a connectivity graph, it equals the number of directly linked or neighboring nodes. A closely related metric *(2) Control value* measures the degree to which space controls access to its immediate neighbors by taking into account the number of alternative connections that each of

[2]From networks such as Internet2 or GEANT.

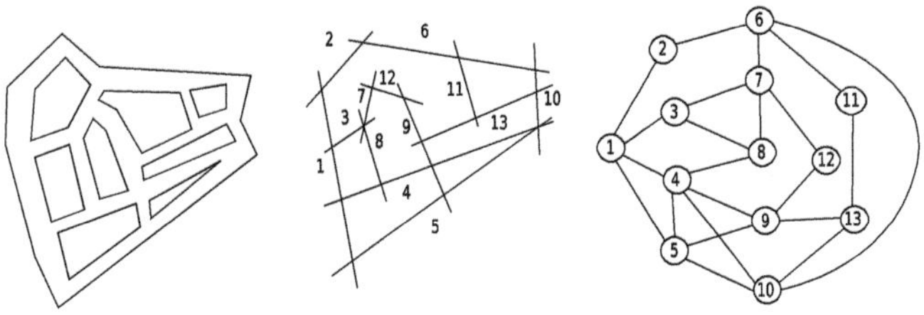

Figure 1: A sample urban system (a), its axial map (b) and connectivity graph (c).

these neighbors has [31]. It is calculated by summing the reciprocals of connectivities between neighbors. This metric can be linked to clustering coefficient in graph analysis. *(3) Global choice* – also known as betweenness centrality in graph theory – captures how often each line is used on topologically shortest paths from all lines to all other lines in the system. Finally, *(4) Integration* – a type of normalized closeness centrality metric in graph analysis – measures the mean distance between every segment and all other segments in the system [32]. The more integrated segments are those that are closest on average to all other segments, while the more segregated segments are those that are furthest on average from all other segments. Many empirical studies have shown that the integration metric is accurate in determining which segments are favored by the configuration [26,32].

3.2 Network Syntax

We argue that the construction of AS-level connectivity graphs as carved out by probes of large traceroute campaigns contain valuable information that can be leveraged through the use of similar metrics to those of Space Syntax. Carefully vetted traceroute measurements allow us to derive partial AS-level connectivity graphs that highlight the actual routes traversed by data packets. Given that the popularity of a route on the Internet can serve as an informative proxy for the volume of traffic it carries, we argue that by concentrating on all the AS-level paths that traverse a specific AS, the application of graph structural metrics can help us identify the popular links connected to those networks.

We would not expect, however, that the direct application of these metrics to just *any* undirected AS-level graph of the Internet (such as one derived from BGP data) would yield similar results. Indeed, as we show in Section 7.1, using a non-uniform line representation of AS-level connectivity and analyzing it by measures that are essentially topological ignores too much contextual information to be useful. The mere direct connectivity between two ASes says little about the utilization of those links for carrying traffic between different parts of the Internet, especially when many important deciding factors such as routing policy are ignored. After all, as has been pointed out, there are dangers in taking available data at face value while ignoring domain-specific context [47].

3.3 Connectivity Graphs and Metrics

At a high-level, Network Syntax metrics are applied to connectivity graphs generated for specific ASes by extracting the set of AS-level paths present in a traceroute dataset that traverse each individual AS. Each of the different AS-level paths is broken down into pairs of hops which represent a link between those ASes. The connectivity graph is generated by adopting a dual representation where each AS-link is transformed into a node, while the intersection between AS-links (the Autonomous Systems they interconnect) are represented as edges. Figure 2 shows a connectivity graph for a subset of important AS-links.

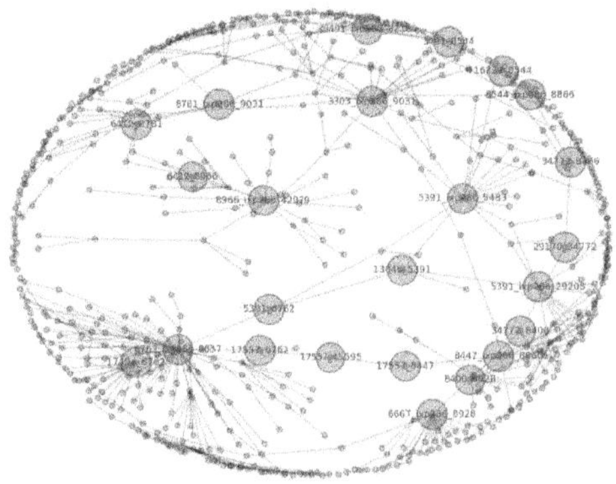

Figure 2: Dual representation of a partial AS-level connectivity graph. Each AS-link is represented by node, while the intersection between AS-links (the Autonomous Systems they interconnect) are represented as edges.

Metrics. The different metrics take a specific meaning in the context of the dual representation of the AS-level connectivity-graph.

Connectivity. In this context, captures the number of different AS-links that precede or succeed each AS-link in the graph. A high connectivity indirectly captures the diversity of the different end-to-end AS-level paths that traverse the link.

Control value of an AS-link is defined as the sum of the reciprocal of its neighbors' connectivity. Similar to connectivity, it captures the diversity of the AS-level paths that traverse the AS-link by considering the different AS-links that precede or follow its directly connected links.

Global choice measures the popularity of a link by looking at how likely it is to be passed through on all shortest paths from all other AS-links in the network. Important links will lie on a high proportion of paths between other AS-links in the network.

Integration attempts to capture link popularity by looking at the average distance from each AS-link to every other AS-link in the connectivity graph. Using this metric, important links are identified as those that are typically "close" (on average) to other AS-links in the network.

ALTP-frequency. In our context, the popularity of an AS-link can also be captured by the number of different end-to-end AS-level paths (discovered by the probes of a traceroute campaign) that traverse the particular link. That is, the frequency of AS-link Traversing Paths, or ALTP-frequency. This metric is specific to Network Syntax and seems to have no obvious or commonly known parallel in either graph theory or Space Syntax. We describe how to compute ALTP-frequency in Section 4.3.

Dataset	Unique VPs	Src ASes	Dst ASes	Probes
Ono 2011	116,978	2,095	12,010	12.9M
Ono 2013	51,884	1,351	12,592	13.8M

Table 1: Number of unique vantage points, unique source ASes and probes for each resulting dataset after applying the different heuristics described in Section 4.2.

4. FROM NETWORK SYNTAX TO INTER-DOMAIN TRAFFIC

In this section, we start with a description of our datasets: a collection of traceroutes launched from topologically diverse vantage points and the traffic datasets we rely on for ground truth. We describe then how we leverage the AS-level paths gathered by the probes of traceroute datasets to derive a connectivity graph upon which core Network Syntax metrics can be applied.

4.1 Datasets

We evaluate Network Syntax using a traceroute dataset and traffic data, our ground-truth, from two large network entities: a large European IXP and a global ISP.

Traceroutes. Our traceroute datasets consist of data collected in two difference campaigns by topologically diverse vantage points. It contains the probes launched towards randomly selected IP addresses from the Ono BitTorrent extension [18]. Ono peers perform measurements to randomly selected destinations from the set of connections established through BitTorrent. The datasets consist of all the measurements gathered between two 30-day periods in two different years – April 1 to 30, 2011 and April 1 to 30, 2013. Table 1 shows a summary of both datasets. The first one consists of ≈12.9 million probes launched by 116,978 distinct vantage points located in 2,143 unique ASes. The second dataset includes ≈13.8 million probes launched from 51,884 different vantage points located in 1,351 different networks.

Traffic. To validate our approach, we perform our analysis in the context of a large European IXP (IXP) and a global Tier-1 Internet Service Provider (ISP). Ground-truth traffic data for IXP consists of sFlow [30] records, collected over 1-week periods in April 2011 and April 2013, capturing the traffic exchanged over the public peering fabric of the IXP. Using a random sampling of $1/16K$ packets, the resulting *traffic matrix* contains the estimated number of bytes exchanged between pairs of ASes peering at the IXP. This detailed information allows us to rank the peerings based on the volume of (bi-directional) traffic they exchange.

The ground-truth data for ISP consists of the traffic exchanged between the ISP and all its customer ASes. The data contains per-customer link utilization from SNMP records for April 2011 and April 2013, and includes the 95th percentile utilization during the course of the month of the hourly port utilizations. Traffic data is summarized on a per-customer basis using link aggregation across different physical interfaces for customers with multiple links.

4.2 Methodology

We generate the partial connectivity graph for a particular ASX from the total set of AS-level paths that include ASX, i.e., paths that include AS-level links that connect to ASX. This traceroute-derived AS-level graph is "partial" in that it does not capture the complete connectivity graph. Since an AS-level path is a sequence of AS-level links, we call such AS-level paths ALTPs, for AS-link Traversing Paths.

The following paragraphs formally define ALTPs and describe how they are extracted from traceroute datasets and how they are used to generate a partial connectivity graph.

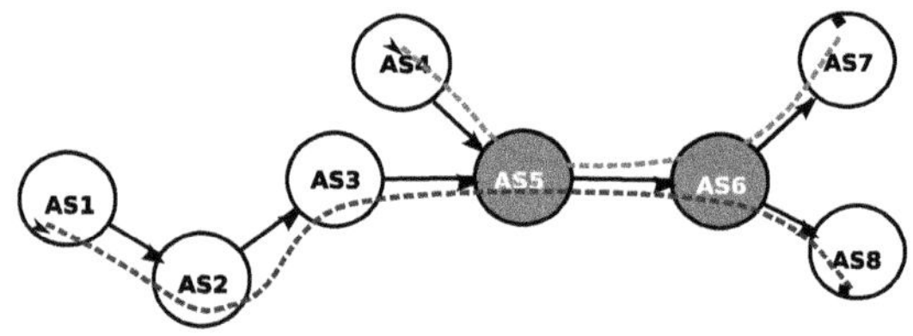

Figure 3: Two instances of AS-link Traversing ⟨Path $ALTP(5,6)$: $as_1, as_2, as_3, AS_5, AS_6, as_8\rangle$,$\langle as_4, AS_5, AS_6, as_7\rangle$

AS-link Traversing Paths (ALTPs). Formally, an AS-level path can be defined as a sequence of unique AS-level links, each connecting a pair of ASes. We denote an AS-level path as $\langle as_1, as_2, ..., as_k\rangle$. We define an $ALTP(x,y)$ as an AS-level path that traverses the AS-link $\langle x,y\rangle$, i.e., $\langle as_1, ..., x, y, ..., as_k\rangle$. Note that $\langle as_1, ..., x, y, ..., as_k\rangle$ and $\langle as_k, ..., y, x, ..., as_1\rangle$ are considered two different ALTPs. Figure 3 shows an example of such a path. The ALTP abstraction is directly applicable to paths that traverse an IXP whose presence is identified by the prefix assigned by the responsible Internet Registry. The set of all unique ALTPs found in a dataset that traverse a specific AS-link is called the ALTP-set of that link.

From probes to AS-level paths. We extract AS-level paths from different traceroute datasets using public IP-to-AS mapping and correcting for inconsistencies with BGP information [17]. For paths that traverse an IXP, we follow [10] to assign confidence levels to the discovered IXP-peerings.

We first prune our dataset by eliminating loops and cycles and filtering private and reserved IP ranges and remove the associated hops if they appear at the ends of the probe. We convert IP-level to AS-level paths using the AS mapping derived from publicly available BGP information. From the derived set we then conservatively remove any probes with unknown AS-hops in the path, probes for which the source or destination AS cannot be mapped[3], and probes for which the final AS-level path is too short (probes within the same AS).

We then apply known heuristics [17] to correct the set of AS-level paths, but preserving the IP addresses belonging to known IXP hops. IXP mapping requires a complete list of prefixes assigned to the different IXPs and the list of their AS members which we obtain from centralized databases like PCH [2], PeeringDb [3] and EuroIX [1], and websites maintained by the IXPs themselves. We remove obsolete

[3]Since the removed links appear only in the discarded paths, they are not popular and their removal has no impact on our findings.

records (inactive IXPs) and match IXPs with different names that represent the same entity. We assign confidence levels to the discovered IXP peerings following the approach in [10] labeling as high-confidence those peerings for which we have probes traversing the peering in both directions or those for which the ASes at both sides of the peering have been identified as members of the IXP from BGP data collected at the IXP. For our analysis we consider only these high-confidence peerings.

AS-Link connectivity graphs. To generate the connectivity graph for the various Autonomous Systems we extract the set of ALTPs present in the dataset that traverse links connected to each specific AS. As described in Section 3.2, each different ALTP is broken down into pairs of hops which represent a link between those ASes, and a dual-connectivity graph is generated where each AS-link is transformed into a node, while the intersection between links (the Autonomous Systems they interconnect) are represented as edges.

4.3 Computing ALTP-frequency

Having introduced partial connectivity graphs and formally defined ALTPs, we can now describe how to compute the Network Syntax ALTP-frequency metric. Using the derived set of AS-level paths, we compute the ALTP-sets for all the AS-links of interest found in those paths.

The relative cardinality of the ALTP-set of an AS-link, in a set S, is the cardinality of its ALTP-set divided by the sum of the cardinalities of the ALTP-sets of every AS-link in S. This relative cardinality is what we refer to as *ALTP-frequency*.

5. EVALUATION

In this section, we apply the approach outlined in Sections 3 and 4 to the links of *IXP* and *ISP* present in our 2011 and 2013 traceroute datasets, we then analyze the relation between the different Network Syntax metrics and the links' traffic volumes. Note that the idea of route popularity applies equally well to physical and logical AS-links between ASes. As a result, the Network Syntax approach can be applied in both our *IXP* and *ISP* scenarios for which the available measurements provide ground truth about traffic traversing physical and logical AS-links, respectively.

In our analysis, we rely on a number of statistical techniques that assume normally distributed variables. However, as we show next, this assumption does not necessarily hold for all the variables we are interested in. A well-known remedy for failure of normality expected by many parametric tests [9,28,44] is to apply appropriately-chosen transformations. In our analysis, whenever necessary, we use the most appropriate transformation for the different variables.

5.1 Traffic distribution

We first look at the traffic distribution for the subset of AS-links discovered by the different traceroute campaigns for both *ISP* and *IXP*. We extract from the corresponding traffic matrix (derived from the ground-truth traffic data) the amount of traffic each link carries, and generate a histogram of their traffic distribution. Figure 4 shows this histogram for the links of *IXP* discovered by the April 2011 traceroute campaign. As it is clear from the figure, the links' traffic follows a power-law distribution with several heaviest links carrying most of the traffic and the majority of the links carrying very little traffic.

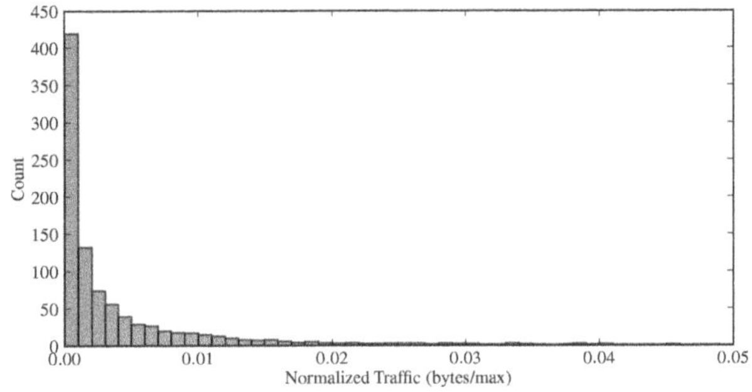

Figure 4: Distribution of traffic for all peerings in traffic matrix for *IXP*, April 2011.

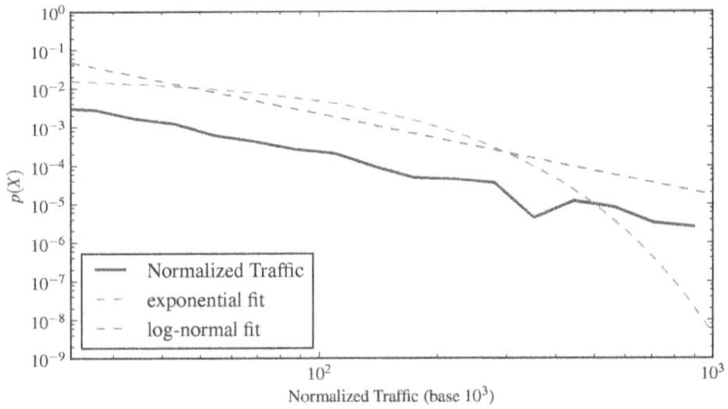

Figure 5: Comparing the goodness of fit of normalized traffic (blue line) with log-normal distribution. Dashed green line: log-normal fit starting from the optimal xmin=23.41, alpha=2.1. Dashed red line: exponential fit starting from the same xmin.

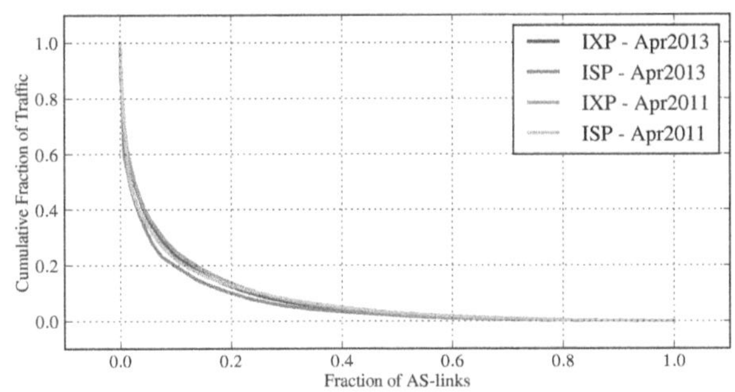

Figure 6: Complimentary CDF of the cumulative fraction of traffic for all AS-links of *ISP* and *IXP* discovered by our traceroute datasets.

Figure 5 shows the goodness of fit statistical confirmation that indeed the distribution of per-peering traffic (showed in blue) follows a log-normal distribution (represented by the dashed-green line), which is consistent with the previously observed property of intra-domain traffic matrix snapshots [13,39].

We observe similar distributions in the traffic carried by the links discovered by our April 2011 and April 2013 traceroute datasets for both *ISP* and *IXP*. This can be

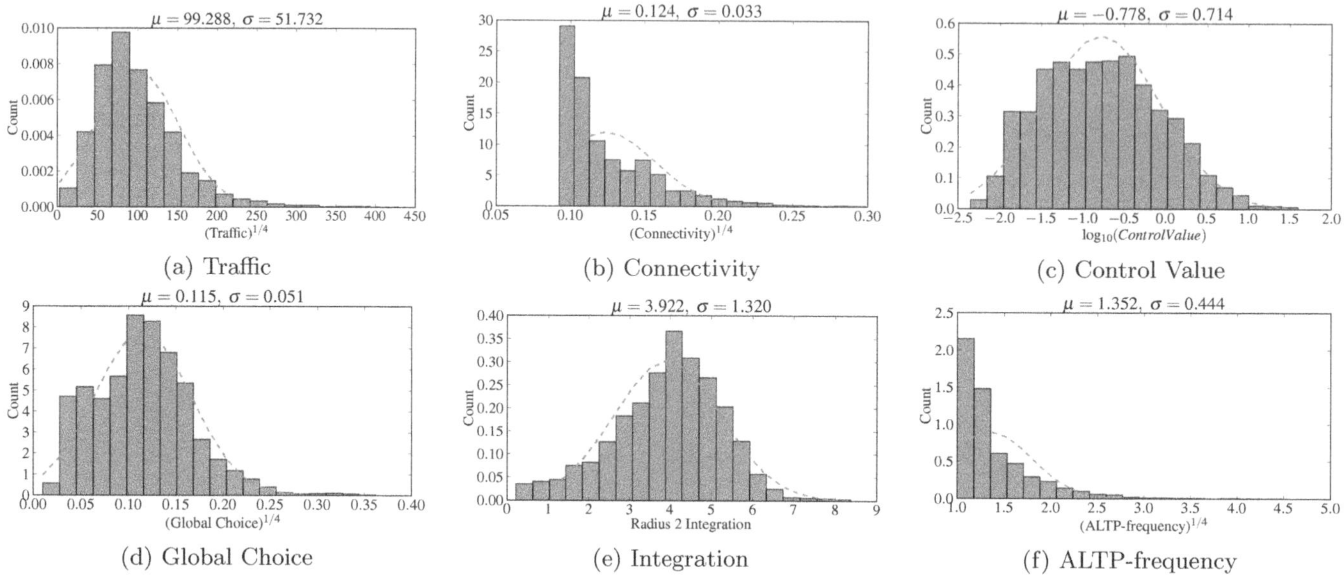

(a) Traffic (b) Connectivity (c) Control Value (d) Global Choice (e) Integration (f) ALTP-frequency

Figure 7: Distribution of the transformed different metrics and traffic volume for all AS-links discovered in the April 2011 traceroute datasets for *IXP*. Similar distributions are observed for the other datasets and the two studied network entities.

seen in Figure 6, the complimentary CDF of the cumulative fraction of traffic for all the discovered AS-links. In all cases, a small fraction of the links carries the majority of the traffic. To approximate normality in the cases where the dependent variable denotes traffic volume, we use the fourth root transformation for its highly skewed distribution (see Figure 7a).

5.2 Network Syntax analysis

We start by selecting, from our traceroute datasets, the ALTP-sets for all relevant AS-links that traverse *IXP* and *ISP*. We generate separate AS-link connectivity graphs for each dataset and compute the different Network Syntax metrics for each link present in the graph. Finally we plot each AS-link against the volume of traffic it carries as indicated by our traffic matrix.

To reduce the potential noise on the correlations introduced by particular AS-links (e.g., due to sampling issues), we use the different metrics to order AS-links, breaking ties based on connectivity, and cluster them in equal sized groups of ten links [4]. For each group, we compute its value for both the relative corresponding metric and carried traffic, as the average of the individual values of the AS-links within the group.

The different Network Syntax metrics present varied distributions. As shown in Figure 7e, the integration metric is already close to normal and is used without transformation. Furthermore, while the control metric (Figure 7c) is approximately normalized with the help of a logarithmic transformation, for the rest of the metrics, we achieve the desired approximate normality using the fourth root transformation (see Figures 7b, 7d and 7f). Having transformed the distributions of the dependent (i.e., traffic volume) as well as independent variables, we can study the relationships between traffic volume and the different Network Syntax metrics.

Figures 8 to 11 show the correlations between the five Network Syntax metrics and traffic volume for the links of *ISP* and *IXP* found in our traceroute datasets. The figures are presented side by side to facilitate horizontal and vertical comparisons between metrics and across datasets.

ALTP-frequency and connectivity have the strongest correlation coefficients, with the integration metric having the weakest one of all. The correlation with ALTP-frequency has r^2 values as high as 0.95 (*ISP* in April 2013) with the lowest value at 0.71 (for *IXP* in April 2013). We argue that this strong correlation comes from the fact that ALTP-frequency more directly captures the popularity of the high-traffic links.

The connectivity metric shows consistently strong correlations as well, with r^2 values ranging between 0.61 (for *IXP* April 2011) to 0.95 (for *ISP* April 2013). Recall that this metric captures the degree of each node in the connectivity-graph which correspond to a different AS-link in our dual representation of the AS-level connectivity-graph. As such, a large connectivity value captures the number of different AS-links that precede or succeeds it on the ALTPs identified. The connectivity metric, then, captures the diversity of the ALTPs that traverse through the link; it indirectly captures the ALTP-frequency of the link.

The correlation between traffic volume and the control value metric, while still strong, is comparably lower with a minimum r^2 value of 0.52 (for *IXP* April 2013) and a maximum value of 0.76 (for *ISP* April 2011). Although this metric is based on the connectivity values of a link's neighbors, it can overestimate the popularity of an AS-link given that the high connectivity of a neighbor can be partially due to AS-links traversed by paths that never cross the link in question.

The integration metric highlights the AS-links that have the shortest average path to every other AS-link in the

[4]Different clusters sizes yield similar trends.

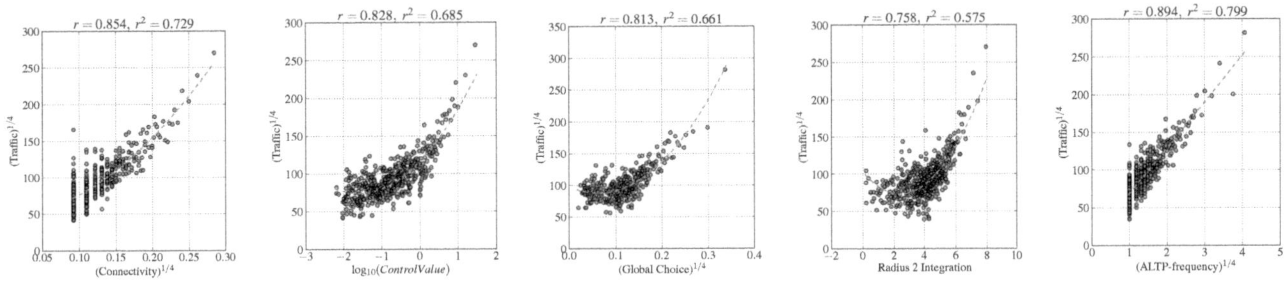

(a) Connectivity (b) Control Value (c) Global Choice (d) Integration (e) ALTP-frequency

Figure 8: Correlation between *connectivity*, *control value*, *global choice*, *local integration* metric (integration radius 2) and *ALTP-frequency* with traffic volume for *IXP* for April 2011.

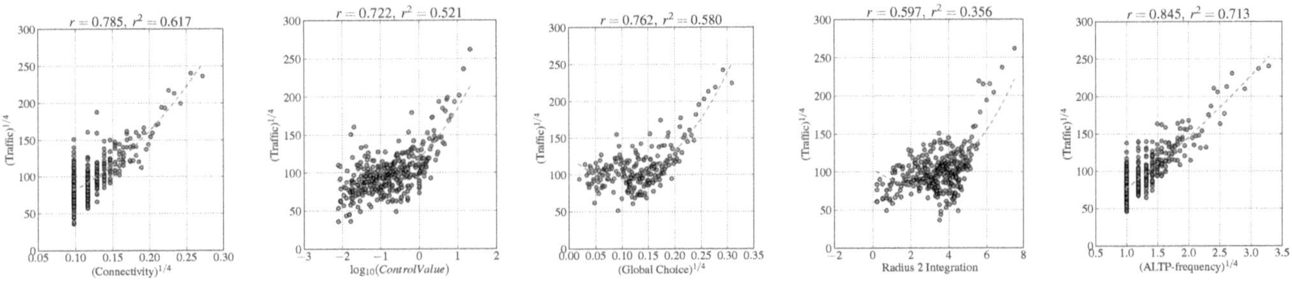

(a) Connectivity (b) Control Value (c) Global Choice (d) Integration (e) ALTP-frequency

Figure 9: Correlation between *connectivity*, *control value*, *global choice*, *local integration* metric (integration radius 2) and *ALTP-frequency* with traffic volume for *IXP* for April 2013.

network. The results for this metric present the largest variations in terms of correlation for the different datasets, ranging from 0.356 (for *IXP* April 2013) to 0.826 (for *ISP* 2011).

Finally, recall that global choice takes into account the relations between each node and the whole system. It indexes how often each line is used on topologically shortest paths from all lines to all other lines in the system. It thus, finds the AS-links that are necessary conduits for information that must traverse disparate parts of the network. The figures show that the correlation of this metric with traffic volume is also significant, with r^2 values between 0.58 (for *IXP* April 2013) and 0.90 (for *ISP* April 2013).

	IXP		*ISP*	
	Apr 2011	Apr 2013	Apr 2011	Apr 2013
Connectivity	0.729	0.617	0.789	0.954
Control Value	0.685	0.521	0.759	0.750
Global Choice	0.661	0.580	0.653	0.903
Integration	0.575	0.356	0.826	0.629
ALTP-freq	0.799	0.713	0.965	0.958

Table 2: r^2 values of the different metrics for *ISP* and *IXP*.

The values in Table 2 show that, although the different datasets vary in their degree of correlation, the regression lines are more or less coincident. While varying with context, a correlation coefficient greater than 0.5 is generally considered strong, and values greater than 0.8 as very strong correlation. The table shows the values of the coefficient of determination resulting from our regression analysis – nearly all (19/20) the r^2 values are above 0.5 and the ALTP-frequency values range between 0.7 and 0.96.

While the ALTP-frequency metric outperforms the rest of the metrics, there is a strong correlation between the different metrics and traffic. Exploring the relationship between different variables is part of future work.

6. USE CASES

In this section, we illustrate the potential uses of Network Syntax using two use-cases: (*i*) predicting missing traffic link volumes in a connectivity graph and, (*ii*) ranking AS-Links based on their traffic volume.

6.1 Predicting link traffic

We have shown in Section 5.2 that the fraction of traffic carried by the AS-links identified in massive traceroute datasets strongly correlates with the different Network Syntax metrics when those links are clustered in small groups. We now show that it is possible to leverage this strong correlation to estimate the traffic volume of arbitrary links, in the *absence* of ground-truth traffic data as long as we have information about the traffic for a subset of the remaining links in the connectivity graph. We do this using the April 2013 datasets for *ISP*; similar results were obtained using the remaining datasets.

In this analysis we employ a subset of the clusters of AS-links to compute the correlation and corresponding regression line between traffic volume and the Network Syntax metric with the strongest correlation: ALTP-frequency. We then use the computed parameters to estimate the traffic volume of the remaining clusters of links by using their ALTP-frequency as proxy.

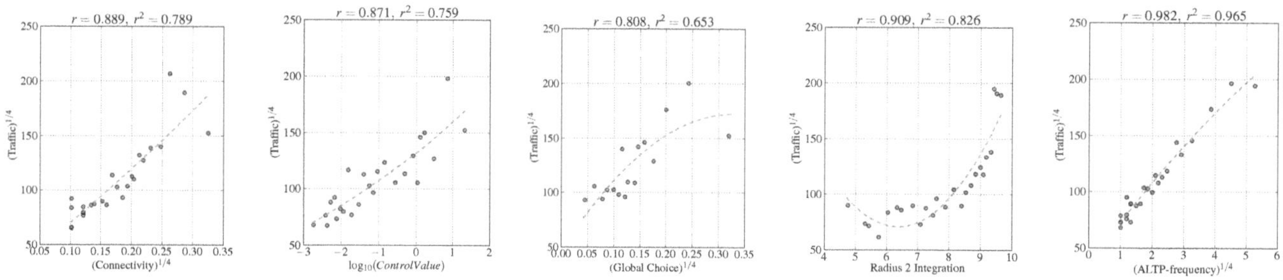

(a) Connectivity (b) Control Value (c) Global Choice (d) Integration (e) ALTP-frequency

Figure 10: Correlation between *connectivity, control value, global choice* , *local integration* metric (integration radius 2) and *ALTP-frequency* with traffic volume for *ISP* for April 2011.

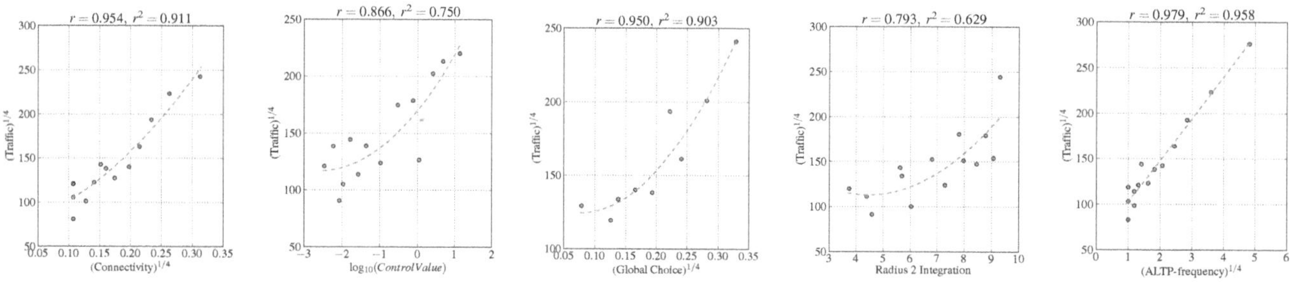

(a) Connectivity (b) Control Value (c) Global Choice (d) Integration (e) ALTP-frequency

Figure 11: Correlation between *connectivity, control value, global choice, local integration* metric (integration radius 2) and *ALTP-frequency* with traffic volume for *ISP* for April 2013.

To reduce the number of links per cluster as much as possible, we start by generating clusters of size ten as described in Section 5.2. We then remove, from each individual cluster, the AS-links that diverge from the median cluster ALTP-frequency by at least one standard deviation (a total of 25 links out of 147). This allows us to use the remaining links to generate clusters of half their original size while maintaining a similarly strong correlation.[5] Figure 12 shows this correlation and corresponding regression line for *ISP* for clusters of size five for the remaining 122 links.

We vary the fraction of clusters used to compute the regression line from 65% to 85% of the available clusters (in increments of 5%) and compute the difference, in orders of magnitude, between the median estimated traffic values and the actual traffic values (from the ground-truth) for the remaining clusters.[6] If the estimated and real value fall within the same order of magnitude (say, between 0 and 10MB or between 10 and 100MB), then the difference is zero. A difference between the estimated and real value of 1, on the other hand, means we may have under/over-estimated the traffic volume by one order of magnitude (e.g., declaring it to be in 50MB when it is closer to 5MB).

Figure 13 shows the result of our analysis after repeating our random selection for each percentage of clusters, 500 times. The figure plots the median difference between estimated and actual traffic volumes for each of the different fractions. For the median case, ≈80% of the estimated values fall within the same order of magnitude as the ground-truth values.

To characterize the size estimation errors for the link clusters with predicted and real values within the same order of magnitude, we compute the normalized mean absolute error between the median estimated and ground-truth traffic volumes. Figure 14 plots the mean estimation error for the different fractions of clusters used to compute the regression line. The figure shows the standard deviation logically varies depending on the fraction of clusters used. That is, increasing the number of points used to compute the fit decreases the number of clusters left for value estimation, making estimation errors more noticeable for smaller clusters. However, although for some clusters of links the traffic prediction estimates can be off by a large margin (e.g., predicting traffic to be 5MB when it was close to 1MB yields an error of 500%), the figure shows that the mean value remains relatively stable around 0.5, indicating that, on average, the median estimated traffic (in megabytes) differs from the cluster's real value by ≈50%. While we acknowledge that order of magnitude is a coarse approximation, we argue this is a valuable first step at inferring traffic volumes that are not directly measurable at scale or without access to a collection of proprietary data (e.g., Arbor Network's collection of inter-domain traffic data from some 110 commercial networks [33]). For instance, the approximate nature of alternative methods that formulate inter-domain traffic estimation as a matrix completion problem [24] is largely unknown.

[5] We observed similar results using clusters of size ten, without removing any links from the original sets.

[6] We considered the use of OC-based bucketing for this case study, but decided against it as our analysis compares groups of links rather than individual ones.

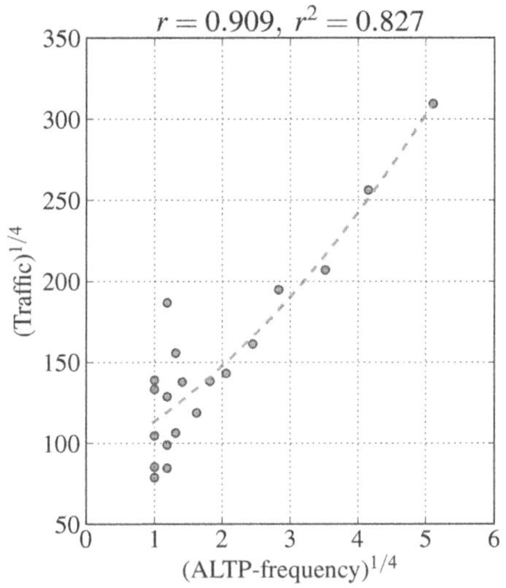

Figure 12: Correlation between ALTP-frequency and traffic volume for *ISP* for April 2013 with clusters of size 5.

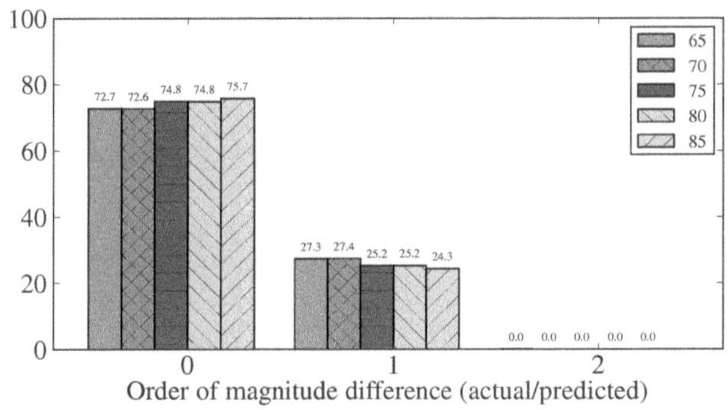

Figure 13: Traffic prediction using ALTP frequency.

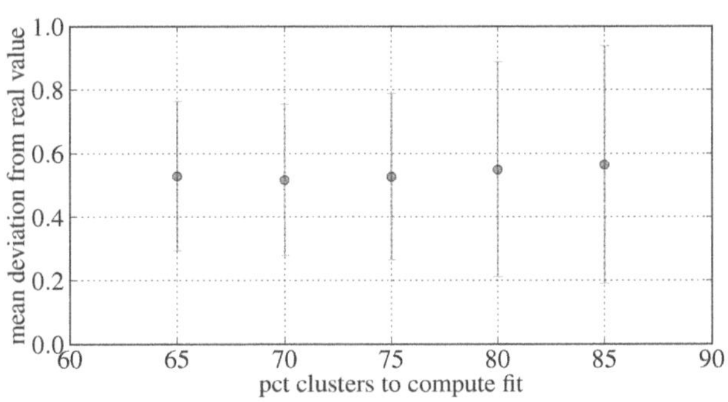

Figure 14: Traffic prediction using ALTP frequency.

6.2 Ranking AS-Links based on Traffic Volume

As our second use case, we show that ranking AS-links based on different Network Syntax metrics can be used as a proxy for the traffic-volume based ranking of those links.

For this analysis, we start by ranking the AS-links based on the amount of traffic they carry using our ground-truth traffic. We then select the subset of links identified on our traceroute dataset and rank those links a second time, based on the selected Network Syntax metric. As before, to reduce the potential noise introduced by the ranking of individual AS-links, we cluster them in equal-sized groups (ten in this case). For each group, we compute its ranking for both the relative Network Syntax metric and carried traffic, as the average of the individual rankings of the AS-links within the group. Given the strong correlation between the different Network Syntax metrics and traffic volume, potentially any of the metrics could be used to rank the links. For this analysis we select the two metrics with the highest degree of correlation: connectivity and ALTP-frequency, and compare their results.

Figures 15 and 16 show the correlation between traffic-based ranking and connectivity or ALTP-frequency respectively, for both *IXP* and *IXP*. The figures show strong r^2 for all four dataset using both Network Syntax metrics. However ALTP-frequency r^2 values are slightly higher than their connectivity counterpart, with values as high as 0.95 in the case of *ISP* and 0.75 in the case of *IXP*. Regardless, the results from this analysis show that using Network Syntax metrics to rank AS-links can be effectively used to rank links based on the amount of traffic they carry.

7. DISCUSSION

In this section, we elaborate on three critical issues: (*i*) wether the application of Network Syntax analysis to AS-level connectivity graphs derived from BGP data works as intended, (*iii*) the robustness of the approach to the known pitfalls of IP-to-AS level mapping for AS topology inference when using traceroute datasets, and (*iii*) the impact of different traceroute dataset characteristics on the results from Network Syntax metrics.

7.1 BGP-derived connectivity-graphs

As we discussed in Section 3.2, Network Syntax can not be applied to just any AS-level connectivity graph but depends on the information embedded in the graph inferred from traceroute datasets. To illustrate this we apply Network Syntax to the connectivity graph for *ISP* derived from the subset of AS-level paths contained in the public BGP view [5] for April 2011. Specifically, we extract all the BGP announcements that contain the AS number for *ISP*, derive their corresponding AS-level paths, and generate the connectivity-graph. We then compute the different Network Syntax metrics and evaluate our findings in the context of the ground-truth traffic data for *ISP* for same time period. As in Section 5, we first rank the links based on the corresponding metric and create clusters of ten links before examining the correlation.

Figure 17 shows the results of our analysis for the subset of 2,016 links identified in the dataset for the connectivity, control value, global choice and integration metrics. Since this analysis is based on AS-level paths extracted from BGP announcements, no traceroute probes were available to compute the ALTP-frequency metric.

The figure shows that, as anticipated, none of the metrics are strongly correlated with traffic volume. In most cases, links are clustered together either on the lower left side of the plot (corresponding to low traffic volume and nearly identical Network Syntax metric) as is the case in Figures 17c, 17b and 17c, or mostly grouped on the right lower side of the plot (which corresponds to high Network

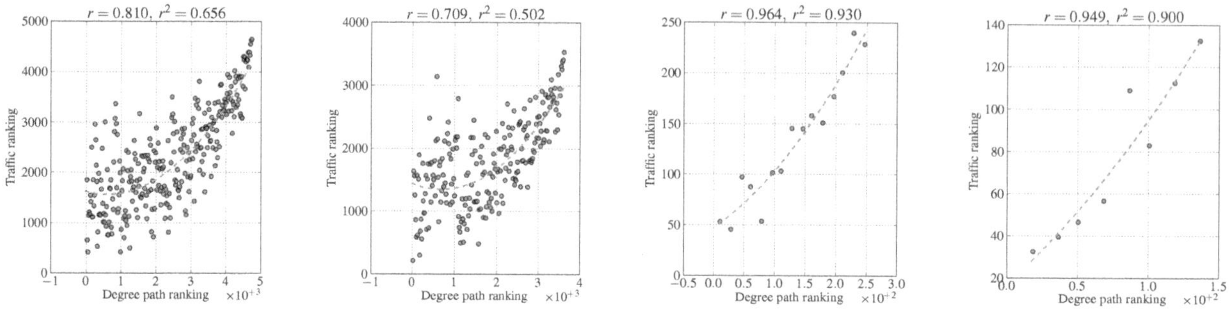

(a) *IXP* April 2011 (b) *IXP* April 2013 (c) *ISP* April 2011 (d) *ISP* April 2013

Figure 15: Ranking based on connectivity and traffic volume.

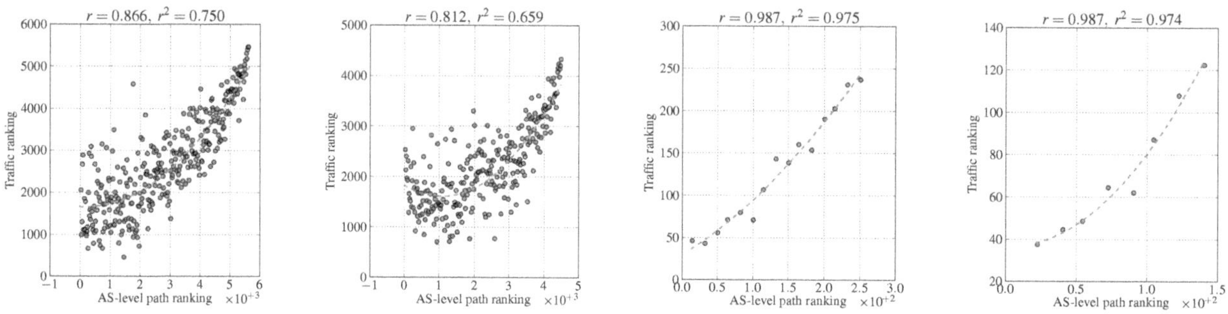

(a) *IXP* April 2011 (b) *IXP* April 2013 (c) *ISP* April 2011 (d) *ISP* April 2013

Figure 16: Ranking based on ALTP-frequency and traffic volume.

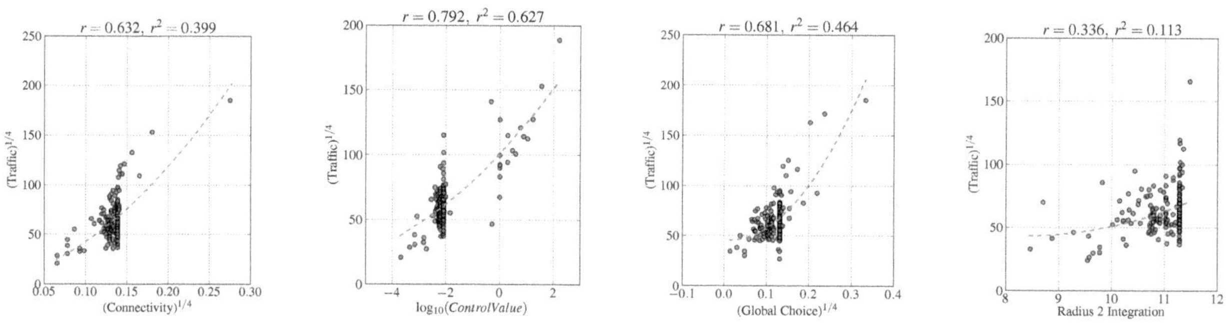

(a) Connectivity (b) Control Value (c) Global Choice (d) Integration

Figure 17: Correlation between Network Syntax metrics and traffic volume (BGP dataset) for *ISP* April 2011.

Syntax metric and low traffic volume) in the case of 17d. The seemingly moderately strong r^2 values are mostly driven by a few outliers, but it is apparently clear from the figures that the cluster of links are not cleanly distributed around the regression line (in contrast to Figures 10 and 11). This analysis shows that it is the data-plane and not the control-plane perspective that is relevant for Network Syntax.

7.2 Errors in traceroute-to-AS mappings

The pitfalls of IP-to-AS level mapping for AS topology inference are well-known. The common approach of using longest prefix matching to map the routers' IP addresses of a traceroute to AS numbers is known to generate potentially false AS links [49]. Several previous research efforts have studied these pitfalls [15,17,29,36,37] and identified common causes for the mismatch which range from the incompleteness of IP-to-AS mappings gathered from publicly available BGP feeds, to the constraints inherent to the traceroute measurement itself (e.g., routers silently dropping probes or not altering packets' TTL). We correct our datasets to avoid these pitfalls, as described in Section 4.2.

In this section we explore the robustness of Network Syntax when applied to traceroute datasets with some of these well known problems. We do this by computing the different Network Syntax metrics on the un-corrected April

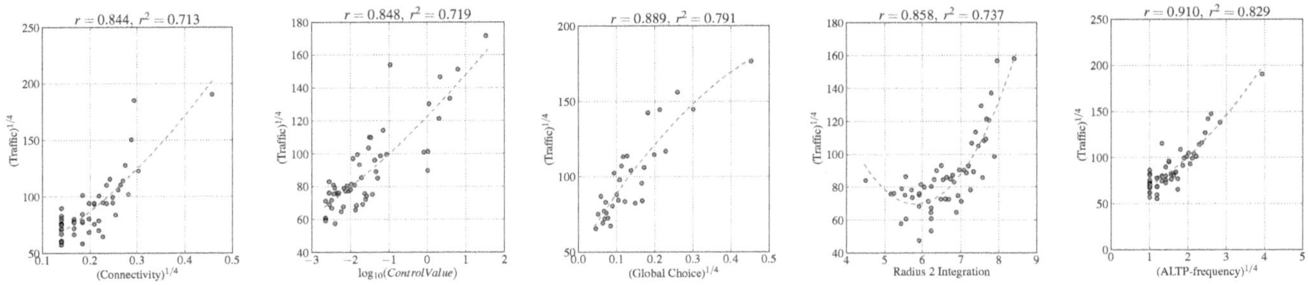

(a) Connectivity (b) Control Value (c) Global Choice (d) Integration (e) ALTP-frequency

Figure 18: Correlation between *connectivity, control value, global choice* , *local integration* metric (integration radius 2) and *ALTP-frequency* with traffic volume for *ISP* for April 2011 using the CAIDA traceroute dataset.

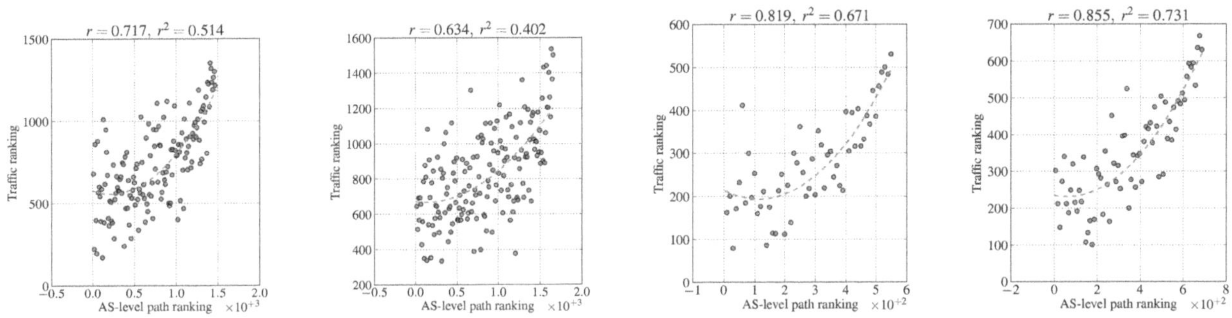

(a) *IXP* April 2011 (b) *IXP* April 2013 (c) *ISP* April 2011 (d) *ISP* April 2013

Figure 19: Correlation between ALTP-frequency and traffic volume for *IXP* and *ISP* using CAIDA datasets.

False AS links problems
Internet eXchange Points (IXPs)
Sibling ASes
Unannounced IP addresses
Using outgoing interface IPs
Private peering interface IPs

Table 3: Summary of problems within traceroute-inferred AS-level paths addressed by the filtering heuristics proposed in [17].

	Ono April 2011
1. Repeated Hop	19%
2. Unk Hop in Path	47%
3. Unk Src or Dst ASN	5%
4. Path too Short	30%

Table 4: Percentage of probes dropped by each of the extraction rules.

2011 traceroute dataset for *ISP* and comparing the resulting correlation with the corrected version.

To generate this alternative dataset we apply the same basic traceroute sanitation process described in Section 4.2 but stop before the application of the correction heuristics described in [17], wich we summarize in Table 3. The basic sanitation process conservatively discards ≈61% of our initial dataset and reduces the number of probes to 12.9M.

Table 4 presents a summary of the fraction of traceroutes dropped by each of our basic sanitation rules.

	Un-corrected	Corrected
Connectivity	0.759	0.789
Control Value	0.708	0.759
Global Choice	0.314	0.653
Integration	0.749	0.826
ALTP-frequency	0.919	0.965

Table 5: r^2 values of the different metrics for *ISP* using the April 2011 dataset.

Table 5 presents a comparison of the r^2 values for the different metrics when Network Syntax is applied to the connectivity graphs that result from both the un-corrected and corrected versions of the dataset. The results show that the application of the different correction heuristics does improve correlation between traffic volume an the different metrics, but most metrics (with the exception of global choice) still show significant r^2 values when computed using the un-corrected dataset.

When comparing both the corrected and un-corrected datasets, we note that the amount of traceroutes modified by the different correction heuristics accounts for ≈16% of the probes; which ultimately map to approximately 6% of the end-to-end AS-level in the dataset. The results from Table 5 highlight the robustness of Network Syntax when identifying popular AS-links in the presence of mis-mapped paths in the underlaying connectivity-graph.

7.3 Other datasets

We have shown that applying Network Syntax metrics to AS-level connectivity graphs using paths extracted from massive traceroute datasets reveals a strong correlation between traffic volume and the different metrics. We now apply the same technique to a different dataset, one collected from CAIDA's Ark monitors for the same time periods. This tracerotue dataset consist of probes launched towards randomly selected IP addresses from CAIDA's Ark monitors [12] which probe IP addresses from every routable IPv4 /24 prefix in cycles of approximately 48 hours. For this analysis, we combined data from three different probing cycles completed by different sets of Ark monitors between April 1-7, 2011 and April 1-7, 2013.

Figure 18 shows a comparison of the correlation between traffic volume and the different Network Syntax metrics for the CAIDA 2011 dataset for *ISP*[7]. The observed trends are similar to those seen in Section 5.2, where the amount of traffic carried by the clustered links strongly correlates with the different Network Syntax metrics. Additionally, Figure 19 shows a comparison of the correlation of AS-link ranking based on traffic volume versus ranking based on ALTP-frequency, using the CAIDA dataset for both *IXP* and *ISP*. The same trends as those seen in Section 6.2 can be observed for both network entities, with clusters of links carrying larger amounts of traffic corresponding to higher ALTP-frequency links.

Even though in both cases the correlations can still be observed, the r^2 values are smaller than their Ono-dataset counterpart. We argue that this is due to a fundamental difference on how the underlaying traceroutes were collected. As Table 6 shows, although the tracerotues of both the Ono and CAIDA datasets contain millions of traceroutes launched against a large number of different destination ASes; there is a *2-order of magnitude difference* in the number of source ASes from where the probes were launched.

Even though the correlation is still present, the r^2 values are smaller than their Ono-dataset counterpart. We argue that this is due to a fundamental difference on how the underlaying traceroutes were collected. As Table 6 shows, although the tracerotues of both the Ono and CAIDA datasets contain millions of traceroutes launched against a large number of different destination ASes; there is a *2-order of magnitude difference* in the number of source ASes from where the probes were launched.

As discussed in [34], one consequence of taking measurements using a small number of sources and relying on an end-to-end strategy, is that edges are selected disproportionately, so bias arises when edges incident to a node in the underlying graph are sampled disproportionately. Thus, an edge is much more likely to be visible if it is close to the vantage point that discovered them. To explore this potential issue, we focus our analysis on the CAIDA 2011 dataset and look at the discovered AS-links as the intersection of the number of probes that crossed through them vs the corresponding number of ALTPs that contain it. We concentrate on the top AS-link with the largest number of ALTPs which is seen by almost 10K ALTPs and was discovered by almost half a million probes. Closer inspection shows that the link connects AS195 (San Diego Supercomputer Center) and AS2152 (the California State University Network) at SD-NAP (an IXP located in San Diego, CA), and that all the probes responsible for discovering this link correspond to a CAIDA Ark monitor placed in the San Diego Supercomputer Center. A similar scenario was observed for the other top three links. This highlights that the location of the vantage points can lead to erroneous inferences about a link's popularity.

[7]Similar trends were observed for both *IXP* and *ISP* using CAIDA's 2011 and 2013 datasets.

Dataset	Unique VPs	Src ASes	Dst ASes	Probes
CAIDA 2011	53	52	36,034	26.9M
CAIDA 2013	65	60	42,440	48.9M

Table 6: Number of unique vantage points, unique source ASes and probes for each dataset.

8. CONCLUSIONS AND FUTURE WORK

We advance the state-of-the-art in traffic characterization by presenting a novel technique to infer traffic volumes from AS-level routing graphs carved out by massive traceroute campaigns. Our Network Syntax approach builds on the observation that the popularity of a route on the Internet can serve as an informative proxy for the volume of traffic it carries. Drawing analogies with city grids and traffic, Network Syntax applies structural analysis and metrics to predict with high accuracy the inter-domain traffic volume carried by different links. We demonstrated the effectiveness of our approach using two months of data (collected two years apart) from a Tier-1 Internet Service Provider and a large Internet eXchange Point, by identifying traffic-critical links and inferring missing traffic matrix measurements.

We evaluated four different publicly available traceroute datasets, but selected two for inclusion (due to space constraints) representing different standpoints with respect to type and location of vantage points. Multiple other datasets collected over the years could be leveraged by our technique, such as RIPE's Atlas project [4], or those collected from the DIMES project [43].

Going forward, Network Syntax opens a rich research agenda from specific methodological aspects (e.g., different metrics and datasets attributes) to applications of a better-understood flow of Internet traffic. Could we identify high-traffic links in the context of arbitrary AS-links on the Internet, i.e. can we establish the relative importance of a pair AS-links not tied to a specific network? This could be used, for instance, to augment existing AS-topology maps with the relative importance of links based on traffic carried. Could Network Syntax, perhaps in combination with existing techniques, be used to complete partial-traffic matrixes? Given our new ability to leverage long-available traceroute datasets, what could this approach tell us about the variability and evolution of the Internet over time?

Acknowledgements

We would like to thank our shepherd, Paul Barford, and the anonymous reviewers for their valuable feedback and assistance. Georgios Smaragdakis was supported by the EU Marie Curie International Outgoing Fellowship "CDN-H" (PEOPLE-628441). This work was supported in part by the National Science Foundation through Awards CNS

0644062, CNS 0917233 and CNS 0855253 and by a generous Google Faculty Research Award.

9. REFERENCES

[1] European Internet Exchange Association. `https://www.euro-ix.net/`.

[2] Packet Clearing House. `https://www.pch.net/`.

[3] PeeringDB. `https://www.peeringdb.com/`.

[4] Ripe. `http://www.ripe.net/project/ris`.

[5] University of Oregon Route Views Project. `http://www.routeviews.org/`.

[6] Adhikari, V. K., Jain, S., and Zhang, Z.-L. Youtube traffic dynamics and its interplay with a Tier-1 ISP: an ISP perspective. In *Proc. of IMC* (2010).

[7] Ager, B., Chatzis, N., Feldmann, A., Sarrar, N., Uhlig, S., and Willinger, W. Anatomy of a large european IXP. In *Proc. of ACM SIGCOMM* (2012).

[8] Ahmad, M. Z., and Guha, R. Understanding the impact of Internet eXchange Points on Internet topology and routing performance. In *Proc. of the ACM CoNEXT Student Workshop* (2010).

[9] Atkinson, A. *Plots, transformations, and regression.* Oxford science publications. Clarendon Press, Oxford, 1985.

[10] Augustin, B., Krishnamurthy, B., and Willinger, W. IXPs: Mapped? In *Proc. of IMC* (2009).

[11] Bharti, V., Kankar, P., Setia, L., Gürsun, G., Lakhina, A., and Crovella, M. Inferring invisible traffic. In *Proc. of ACM CoNEXT* (2010).

[12] CAIDA. The CAIDA UCSD IPv4 Routed /24 Topology Dataset - 1-7 April 2011 and 1-7 April 2013. `http://www.caida.org/data/active/ipv4_routed_24_topology_dataset.xml`.

[13] Cardona Restrepo, J. C., and Stanojevic, R. A History of an Internet eXchange Point. *SIGCOMM Comput. Commun. Rev. 42*, 2 (2012), 58–64.

[14] Chang, H., Jamin, S., Morley, Z., and Willinger, M. W. An empirical approach to modeling Inter-AS traffic matrices. In *Proc. of IMC* (2005).

[15] Chang, H., Jamin, S., and Willinger, W. Inferring AS-level internet topology from router-level path traces. In *Proc. of SPIE ITCom* (2001).

[16] Chatzis, N., Smaragdakis, G., Boettger, J., Krenc, T., and Feldmann, A. On the benefits of using a large IXP as an Internet vantage point. In *Proc. of IMC.*

[17] Chen, K., Choffnes, D. R., Potharaju, R., Chen, Y., Bustamante, F. E., Pei, D., and Zhao, Y. Where the sidewalk ends: Extending the Internet AS graph using traceroutes from P2P users. In *Proc. of ACM CoNEXT* (2009).

[18] Choffnes, D. R., and Bustamante, F. E. Taming the torrent: A practical approach to reducing cross-ISP traffic in peer-to-peer systems. In *Proc. of ACM SIGCOMM* (2008).

[19] Dhamdhere, A., and Dovrolis, C. Ten years in the evolution of the Internet ecosystem. In *Proc. of IMC* (2008).

[20] Fang, W., and Peterson, L. Inter-AS traffic patterns and their implications. In *Global Telecommunications Conference, 1999. GLOBECOM'99* (1999).

[21] Feldmann, A., Greenberg, A., Lund, C., Reingold, N., Rexford, J., and True, F. Deriving traffic demands for operational IP networks: Methodology and experience. *IEEE/ACM Transactions on Networking (ToN)* (2001).

[22] Feldmann, A., Kammenhuber, N., Maennel, O., Maggs, B., De Prisco, R., and Sundaram, R. A methodology for estimating interdomain web traffic demand. In *Proc. of IMC* (2004).

[23] Gao, L. On inferring autonomous system relationships in the internet. *IEEE/ACM TON 9*, 6 (2001).

[24] Gursun, G., and Crovella, M. On traffic matrix completion in the internet. In *Proc. of IMC* (2012).

[25] Hillier, B., and Hanson, J. *The Social Logic of Space.* Cambridge University Press, 1984.

[26] Hillier, B., Penn, A., Hanson, J., Grajewski, T., and Xu, J. Natural movement: or, configuration and attraction in urban pedestrian movement Environment and Planning B: Planning and Design, 1994.

[27] Hillier, B., and Sahbaz, O. High resolution analysis of crime patterns in urban street networks: an initial statistical sketch from an ongoing study of a London borough. In *Space Syntax Symposium* (2005), p. 451âĂŞ478.

[28] Howell, D. *Statistical Methods for Psychology.* Thomson Wadsworth, 2007.

[29] Hyun, Y., Broido, A., and claffy, k. On Third-party Addresses in Traceroute Paths. In *Proc. of PAM* (2003).

[30] InMon. Inmon sFlow. `http://sflow.org`.

[31] Jiang, B. A space syntax approach to spatial cognition in urban environments. In *Workshop on Cognitive Models of Dynamic Phenomena and Their Representations* (1998).

[32] Kostakos, V. Space Syntax and Pervasive Systems. *Geospatial Analysis and Modeling of Urban Structure and Dynamics* (2010), 21–52.

[33] Labovitz, C., lekel Johnson, S., Oberheide, J., and Jahanian, F. Internet inter-domain traffic. In *Proc. of ACM SIGCOMM* (2010).

[34] Lakhina, A., Byers, J. W., Crovella, M., and Xie, P. Sampling biases in IP topology measurements. In *Proc. Joint Conference of the IEEE Computer and Communications Societies* (2003).

[35] Mahajan, R., Spring, N., Wetherall, D., and Anderson, T. Inferring link weights using end-to-end measurements. In *Proc. ACM IMW* (2002).

[36] Mao, Z. M., Johnson, D., Rexford, J., Wang, J., and Katz, R. H. Scalable and accurate identification of AS-level forwarding paths. In *INFOCOM* (2004).

[37] Mao, Z. M., Rexford, J., Wang, J., and Katz, R. H. Towards an accurate as-level traceroute tool. In *Proc. of ACM SIGCOMM* (2003).

[38] Medina, A., Taft, N., Salamatian, K., Bhattacharyya, S., and Diot, C. Traffic matrix estimation: existing techniques and new directions. In *Proc. of ACM SIGCOMM* (2002).

[39] Nucci, A., Sridharan, A., and Taft, N. The problem of synthetically generating IP traffic matrices: Initial recommendations.

[40] Oliveira, R., Z. B., and Zhang, L. Observing the evolution of Internet AS topology. In *Proc. of ACM SIGCOMM* (2007).

[41] Penn, A., Hillier, B., Banister, D., and Xu, J. Configurational modelling of urban movement networks. *Environment and Planning B 25* (1998).

[42] Peterson, L. Inter-AS traffic patterns and their implications. In *in Proc. IEEE GLOBECOM* (1999).

[43] Shavitt, Y., and Shir, E. DIMES: Let the Internet measure itself. *ACM SIGCOMM Computer Communication Review 35*, 5 (October 2005).

[44] Tabachnick, B. G., and Fidell, L. S. *Using Multivariate Statistics (5th Edition)*. Allyn & Bacon, Inc., Needham Heights, MA, USA, 2006.

[45] The PREDICT Repository. Protected repository for the defense of infrastructure against cyber threats. `https://www.predict.org/`, Aug 2014.

[46] Uhlig, S., and Bonaventure, O. Implications of interdomain traffic characteristics on traffic engineering. *European Transactions on Telecommunications* (2002).

[47] Willinger, W., Alderson, D., and Doyle, J. C. Mathematics and the Internet: A Source of Enormous Confusion and Great Potential. *Notices of the AMS 56*, 5 (May 2009).

[48] Xu, K., Duan, Z., Zhang, Z.-L., and Chandrashekar, J. On properties of Internet eXchange Points and their impact on as topology and relationship. *Networking 3042* (2004).

[49] Zhang, Y., Oliveira, R. V., Zhang, H., and Zhang, L. Quantifying the pitfalls of traceroute in as connectivity inference. In *PAM* (2010), A. Krishnamurthy and B. Plattner, Eds., vol. 6032, Springer, pp. 91–100.

[50] Zhang, Y., Roughan, M., Duffield, N., and Greenberg, A. Fast accurate computation of large-scale ip traffic matrices from link loads. In *Proc. of ACM SIGMETRICS* (2003).

[51] Zhang, Y., Roughan, M., Lund, C., and Donoho, D. L. Estimating point-to-point and point-to-multipoint traffic matrices: An information-theoretic approach. *IEEE/ACM Trans. Netw.* (2005).

[52] Zhang, Y., Roughan, M., Willinger, W., and Qiu, L. Spatio-temporal compressive sensing and internet traffic matrices. In *Proc. of ACM SIGCOMM* (2009).

Challenges in Inferring Internet Interdomain Congestion

Matthew Luckie
CAIDA / UC San Diego
mjl@caida.org

Amogh Dhamdhere
CAIDA / UC San Diego
amogh@caida.org

David Clark
MIT
ddc@csail.mit.edu

Bradley Huffaker
CAIDA / UC San Diego
bradley@caida.org

kc claffy
CAIDA / UC San Diego
kc@caida.org

ABSTRACT

We introduce and demonstrate the utility of a method to localize and quantify inter-domain congestion in the Internet. Our Time Sequence Latency Probes (TSLP) method depends on two facts: Internet traffic patterns are typically diurnal, and queues increase packet delay through a router during periods of adjacent link congestion. Repeated round trip delay measurements from a single test point to the two edges of a congested link will show sustained increased latency to the far (but not to the near) side of the link, a delay pattern that differs from the typical diurnal pattern of an uncongested link. We describe our technique and its surprising potential, carefully analyze the biggest challenge with the methodology (interdomain router-level topology inference), describe other less severe challenges, and present initial results that are sufficiently promising to motivate further attention to overcoming the challenges.

Categories and Subject Descriptors

C.2.5 [**Local and Wide-Area Networks**]: Internet; C.2.1 [**Network Architecture and Design**]: Network topology

Keywords

Interdomain congestion; Internet topology

1. INTRODUCTION

Unlike traffic congestion on links within a single network (AS), where responsibility for resolving the congestion unambiguously belongs to that network, congestion on AS interconnection links (or *interdomain congestion*) may reflect a peering dispute, accompanied by finger-pointing over which network should pay to upgrade the link to handle the traffic demand. The two primary forms of interconnection are *transit*, when one AS sells another ISP access to the global Internet, and *peering*, when two ISPs interconnect to exchange customer traffic. The historical basis for settlement-free peering was a presumed balance of value to both parties.

IMC'14, November 5–7, 2014, Vancouver, BC, Canada.

http://dx.doi.org/10.1145/2663716.2663741.

Peering disputes arise when one party believes the exchange is no longer beneficial to them. Historically, peering disputes were between large transit networks (e.g. [5, 10, 32]) where one party would fall out of compliance with the agreement and be disconnected by the other party until a new agreement was reached. More recent peering disputes are fueled by exploding demand for high-bandwidth content (e.g., streaming video), and growing concentration of content among a few content distribution networks (e.g. [1, 3, 4, 6, 13, 14, 37]), some large and sophisticated enough to adjust loading (and thus congestion levels) on interconnection links [9, 15]. Many disputes do not lead to disconnection but stalled negotiation about who should pay for installation of new capacity to handle the demand, leaving the congested link as an externality for all users of the link until the dispute is resolved.

Unsurprisingly, there is growing public policy interest in the extent and scope of congestion induced by persistently unresolved peering disputes, and how harmful it is to consumers. Unfortunately, almost no data is available for researchers to study interconnection controversies. Traffic data and peering terms are almost always under NDA for newsworthy peering disputes; providers obfuscate network identities when they discuss congestion at all [35].

We provide three contributions to understanding the prevalence of interdomain congestion. First, we introduce and demonstrate the utility of a highly scalable probing method that allows us, from the edge of a given network to localize and characterize congestion on its interdomain links (section 2). Second, we analyze the many challenges associated with using this method to create a map of interdomain congestion, and how we have either started or plan to handle them (section 3). Third, we apply our method to illustrate evidence of persistent interdomain congestion involving large access and content providers (section 4). We compare our approach with related work in section 5 and identify ongoing future work in section 6.

2. TIME SEQUENCE LATENCY PROBES

The idea behind the time-sequence latency probes (TSLP) method is to frequently repeat round trip time (RTT) measurements from a vantage point (VP) to the *near* and *far* routers of an interdomain link. The measured RTTs are a function of the queue lengths of the routers on the forward and reverse paths: as queue lengths increase, so does RTT. When RTTs increase to the far router but not to the near router, we infer that a queue between these two routers induced the delay.

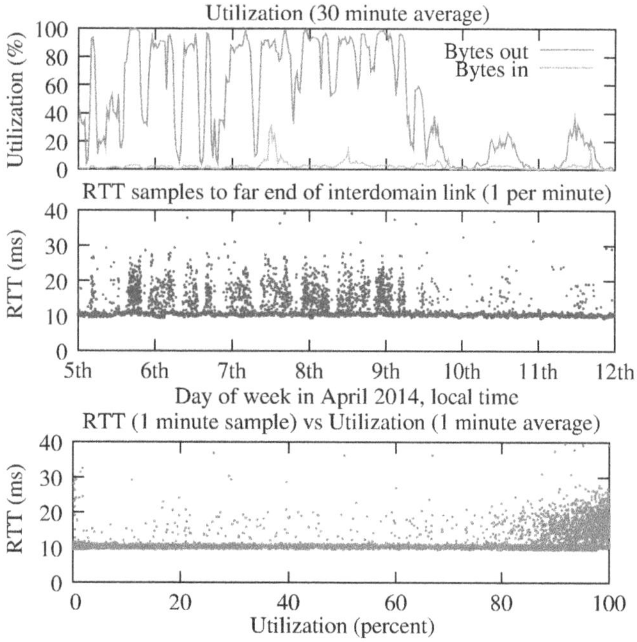

Figure 1: Comparing link utilization (top panel) with measured RTT (middle panel) on a 50Mbps customer link operated by a R&E network. The bottom scatterplot suggests that as the 1-minute average load exceeds ≈85%, increasing numbers of probes to the far side of the link encounter a queue, suggesting congestion at that moment.

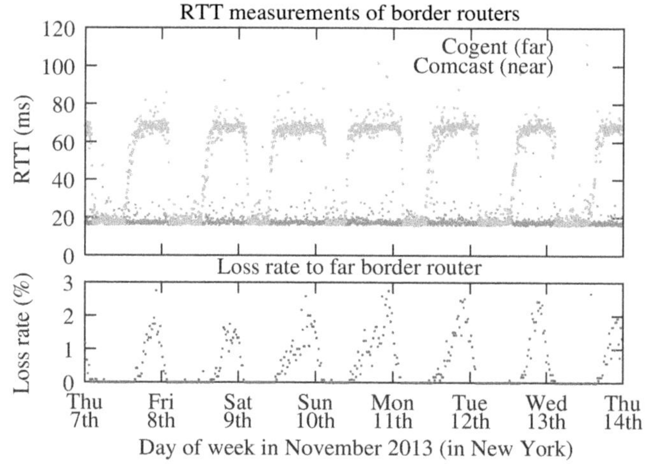

Figure 2: Congestion on an interdomain link between Comcast and Cogent, measured from a VP within Comcast. The RTT to the Cogent (far) router increases from 20ms to 70ms while the RTT to the Comcast (near) router is stable at 20ms. The approximate square wave indicates the queue is always close to full when the RTT increases to 70ms. The loss rate from the Cogent router increases after this level shift occurs, as the load on the link continues to increase.

Lending some confidence to this method, figure 1 plots a week of traffic (SNMP byte counters sampled per-minute) and RTT measurements across a research and education network link known by the operator to be well utilized. The 30-minute average utilization on the link (top graph) correlates with periods when some probes experience increased RTT to the far end of the interdomain link (middle graph). The bottom graph shows that most RTT measurements above 10ms occur when the average utilization is above 85%. To maximize the chance of observing RTT variation across a specific link, TSLP sends TTL-limited packets toward the same destination that expire at the near and far routers, rather than send packets addressed to the border routers.

If a link is so busy that a tail-drop queue is always close to full, a time series of RTT measurements to the far router will approximate a square wave, with the minimum RTT during the low state reflecting probes that did not experience delay, and the minimum RTT during the high state reflecting probes consistently encountering a queue close to full. Queue lengths are finite, limiting the delay contributed by any one queue, reflected by the top of the square wave. Figure 2 shows such an RTT pattern on a peering link between Comcast and Cogent; the minimum RTT measured every five minutes to the Cogent router increased from 20ms to 70ms for 14-18 hours per day. We also probed every second to observe packet loss across this link, which we only observed in periods where we also observed increased RTT. We hypothesize that the increasing loss rate correlates with increasing demand on the link, and that the width of the period with elevated delays reflects the length of time the link was congested. The height of the elevated period is not an indication of the *degree* of congestion, but rather the size of a queue in a router serving the interdomain link.

We asked the ISPs involved to validate our inferences of this and other links that exhibit this behavior, but they are generally blocked by NDAs from sharing traffic data. Informal feedback from content, transit, and access network operators has given us confidence in our observations.

We believe the TSLP approach is a relatively lightweight method for obtaining data to map which interdomain links attached to the local network are congested. Compared with available bandwidth measurement techniques, such as pathload which sends 12 streams of 100 packets in 15 seconds [21] and requires tomography to identify which is the constraining link, TSLP uses 2 packets every 5 minutes to sample a targeted interdomain link, and does not require a cooperative end-host at the other end of the path. However, TSLP does send enough traffic that it would not scale to deployment in video players for diagnostic purposes. Many concurrent TSLP flows would trigger router ICMP response rate-limiting which defeats the method. Furthermore, TSLP requires a delay history to detect level shifts, and consumer video devices tend to operate only when the user wants to view a video. The value of TSLP is not in its potential universal deployment, but the insight that a remarkably sparse deployment can provide to all users sending or receiving traffic over TSLP-measured interconnection links.

Tulip [27] sends ICMP timestamp messages directly to routers to infer per-hop queuing delay for routers in the forward path as part of a system for diagnosing and pinpointing faults in Internet paths. Compared with their work, we are focused on finding which interdomain links are consistently underprovisioned, and we do not sample an interdomain link by sending packets directly to routers.

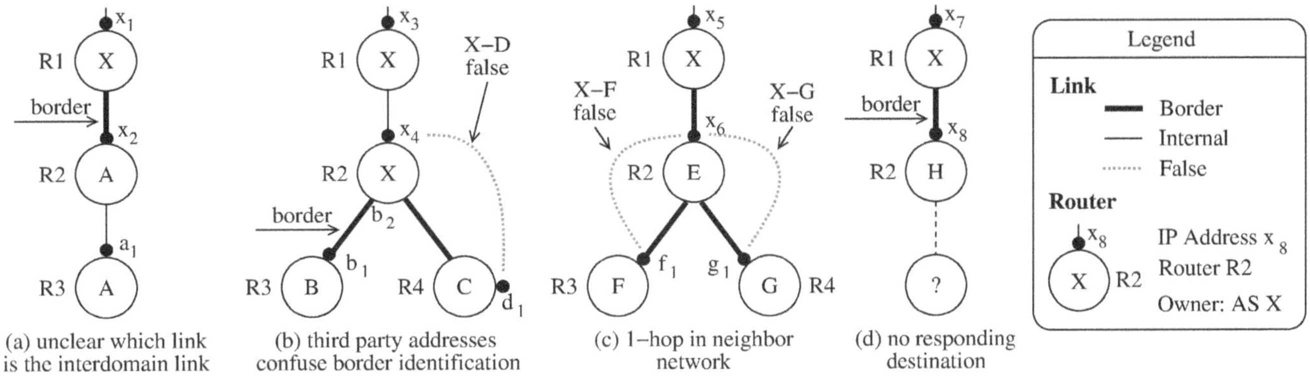

Figure 3: Challenges in AS boundary inference from traceroute for network X. In (a), it is unclear whether x_2, announced by X, or a_1 announced by A correspond to the far border router. In (b), X's peer C responds using an address d_1 originated by D, which could cause a false AS link inference X-D. In (c), we observe X's (unseen) peer with address x_6 originated by X, which could cause E's customers F and G to be incorrectly inferred as connected to X. In (d), we do not observe any responding address in H, which could cause us to not infer that x_8 represents H's border router.

3. METHODOLOGICAL CHALLENGES

While TSLP is a simple and surprisingly effective method for inferring congested links, there are many challenges to applying it effectively: identifying congestion on links with active queue management and/or weighted fair queueing policies; accurately finding and identifying all interdomain links involving the AS hosting a vantage point; proving the response from the far router returns over the targeted interdomain link; determining the direction of congestion; robustness to ICMP queuing behavior; adapting to path dynamics; and scaling processing to thousands of interdomain links.

3.1 AQM and WFQ

Active Queue Management (AQM) and Weighted Fair Queueing (WFQ) present challenges to TSLP. AQM techniques such as Random Early Detection [17] (RED) and successors try to maintain a small average queue size by discarding packets before a queue becomes full, as a function of the queue's current length. RED tries to prevent TCP global synchronization, where multiple senders experience packet loss at the same time and collectively reduce their transmission rate, resulting in an inefficient use of capacity. However, AQM techniques are not widely deployed [31], in part because operators traditionally provision links to meet forecasted demand; the only measurement study of RED deployment we know of was among access networks [12] rather than interdomain links. Where AQM techniques such as RED are deployed on congested links such as that in figure 2, we hypothesize that the level shift from low to high state will be more gradual as TCP connections encounter earlier loss, though we still expect to see the queue approach a state where it is nearly always full with this offered load.

A larger challenge is links that use a fair queueing strategy, where the router places packets in different queues according to some property, such as the incoming port or sender. TSLP cannot infer link congestion when our packets are placed in a queue that does not experience delay. From an interaction with one network operator, we learned that they had deployed WFQ on some of their persistently congested links; TSLP observed no level shift on these links, presumably due to the WFQ behavior.

3.2 Inferring Interdomain Links

If a public BGP view of the AS hosting a VP is provided to RouteViews or RIPE's RIS, then identifying interdomain links and paths where their border routers can be found is relatively simple. While some large access ISPs (including Verizon and AT&T) provide a public view, most large access ISPs (including Comcast, Time Warner, Cox, and RCN) do not, so we must infer AS links and corresponding border routers with traceroute, which is known to be difficult [8,39]. For each VP, we tracerouted to the first (.1) address in each of the 465,944 non-overlapping prefixes observed by RouteViews collector rv2, used BGP data to map the encountered IP addresses to ASes, and inferred an interdomain link when we observed the first address in a traceroute path that maps to an AS outside the VP's hosting network. However, this method may not correctly identify the border routers, or their owners, depending on how interfaces are numbered.

Figure 3 illustrates the variety of things that can go wrong. In figure 3a, when we observe traceroute path x_1, x_2, a_1, a simple IP-AS mapping incorrectly suggests the interdomain link is between R2 and R3, when it is between R1 and R2. More generally, the interdomain hop could be either the hop at which the IP-AS mapping changed, or one hop before. The convention in a customer-provider interconnection is to number the customer router interface from the provider's address space, which identifies R2 as the customer border router and the interdomain link as between R1 and R2, but there is no address assignment convention for peers.

It is usually simple to identify a border router connecting multiple peers as owned by the VP's network. However, some addresses observed after a border router may cause false interdomain link inferences because they map to *third-party* ASes, a well known challenge in AS topology mapping [39]. Figure 3b illustrates the danger: R4, owned by AS C, may respond with address d_1 which maps to AS D. We can improve the robustness of our inferences in the presence of third party addresses with two heuristics. First, if we require interface d_1 to have been observed in a traceroute path toward a prefix announced by D, d_1 is unlikely to be a third-party address. However, this filter discards many true adjacencies if no paths toward a prefix in B cross a specific interconnection with B. A second heuristic can retain some of these adjacencies by proving b_1 is not a third-party address: b_1 represents the incoming interface on R3 and a point-to-point interdomain link between X and B if b_2 is in the same /30 or /31 subnet and is an alias of x_4. We used this heuristic to prove that most addresses in a traceroute path represent the inbound interface on a point-to-point link [26]. Finally, if the interfaces used to infer an adjacency with D were x_4 and d_1, and address d_1 was probed, we have learned to be skeptical of the x_4 - d_1 adjacency, as a router with d_1 configured will reply to probes to d_1 with that address; d_1 might be configured on R3 and connect a subnet one hop away. When we receive a response directly from d_1, we try to discern the router it is connected to by probing another address in the same prefix as d_1 to solicit a TTL-exceeded response from the router on the path.

We have encountered related cases where we only observed the neighbor's border router and no further hops owned by the neighbor network. Figure 3c illustrates the implications of this challenge: R2 is owned by E, but we observe only x_6 on the router, and subsequent interfaces f_1 and g_1 could falsely imply interdomain links between X and F, G. We resolve these ambiguities by finding a *common provider AS* E for both F and G which we derive from CAIDA's AS relationship inferences [25].

In some cases we never observed an address in a neighbor network. Figure 3d illustrates this challenge: R2 is owned by H but R2's address x_8 is the last address we observed in the traceroute. To infer R2 is owned by H, we infer a *common origin AS* to the prefixes probed.

Chen *et al.* [8] used traceroute and BGP data to derive AS links from traceroute paths using heuristics more robust than a simple IP-AS mapping. Their work addressed the third-party address (figure 3b) and one-hop in neighbor network (figure 3c) problems by comparing AS paths inferred with traceroute to AS paths observed in BGP for the corresponding prefix. If they found an extra AS hop (D in X-D-C in figure 3b) they removed D from the traceroute-inferred AS path. If they found a missing AS hop (E in X-E-F in figure 3c) they added E to the traceroute-inferred path. However, they do not adjust IP-AS mappings or assign owners to routers. Integration of their techniques would likely improve our router ownership heuristics.

Mao *et al.* [29] adjusted IP-AS mappings by changing the owner of /24 prefixes to make traceroute-inferred AS paths congruent with BGP AS paths collected in the same AS. However, individual addresses (x_2 and x_8 in figure 3) are not mapped to different owner ASes. Zhang *et al.* [38] adjusted IP-AS mappings using the same approach as Mao *et al.* [29] but at /32 granularity; they did not use AS relationship data (customer relationships) to infer owners of border routers so did not adjust x_2 unless it made traceroute AS paths more congruent. Huffaker *et al.* [19] evaluated heuristics using router alias, AS relationships, and AS degrees. For routers with addresses from multiple ASes, assigning ownership to the AS with most addresses on the router yielded the most accurate results.

3.3 Asymmetric paths

A TTL-limited response from the far border router might not return via the near router, because the far router is operated by a different AS that might have a more preferred path toward our VP. In general, we hypothesize that a peer will respond via the near router, a provider will respond via the near router except in cases where the VP's AS (i.e., the customer) is doing traffic engineering, and a customer will respond via the near router unless it has a lower-cost path. We evaluated two methods to gain confidence that an increase in measured RTT from a near to a far router is due solely to traffic on the link connecting the two routers; that is, the link behavior was *isolated*. Katz-Bassett *et al.* used these two methods in reverse traceroute [22].

Pre-specified timestamps (PSTS): The PSTS IP option allows a host to request other hosts embed a timestamp in the packet. Using the notation in [33], G|BCDE denotes a probe to destination G that requests hosts with addresses B, C, D, and E to include timestamps. The option includes a pointer to the next timestamp slot in the packet, which advances when a router embeds a timestamp; if the packet visits C but not B first, then C will not embed a timestamp. Using the topology in figure 3a, to test if R3 returns packets to our VP via R2, we send an ICMP echo request packet in the form $a_1|a_1x_2$. If both a_1 and x_2 embed a timestamp, we infer the packet was returned across the R2-R3 link.

Record Route (RR): The RR IP option allows a host to request that up to nine hosts embed an IP address as they forward the packet. To test if R3 returns packets to our VP via R2, we send an ICMP echo request packet with the RR option set to R3. If we observe an address belonging to R3 in the RR option in the response, and an address belonging to R2 immediately after, we infer the packet returned across the R2-R3 link.

Preliminary Evaluation: Both the PSTS and RR options are known to have limitations due to routers that either do not implement the functionality, discard packets that contain options, or (in the case of RR) do not have sufficient space to embed the addresses of interest. Of the 599 interdomain router links involving Comcast that we assembled from our Ark VP (mry-us) deployed in Monterey, California we use either PSTS or RR to infer that 179 (29.9%) returned over the targeted link; 72 (12.0%) were isolated only with RR, and 78 (13.0%) were isolated with only PSTS. We could not isolate 71 (11.9%) because all nine slots were used, and the remainder (58.2%) were unresponsive to these IP options or inconclusive; different addresses in traceroute and RR may belong to the same router but resist alias resolution. We manually checked a few paths that RR suggests did not return over the targeted link; we observed, for example, Comcast's provider Tata forwarding packets that it received in Los Angeles to the San Jose interconnection.

3.4 Other challenges

ICMP queuing behavior: A concern with using ICMP TTL-exceeded responses is that routers may delay these responses (process them through the slow path), especially during periods of high load; we may thus measure load on the router and not congestion on a specific link. But it is unlikely that slow path processing would induce the same delay for each probe response, so using the minimum RTT during a given time window will more likely reflect the queue size, improving TSLP's robustness to potential idiosyncrasies in ICMP behavior. In some routers, the ICMP response generation delay spikes every 60 seconds due to periodic maintenance activity [27]. This behavior will mislead TSLP when our 5-minute samples synchronize with the maintenance activity. To avoid this problem we could randomize the send time of our probes in each 5-minute measurement round.

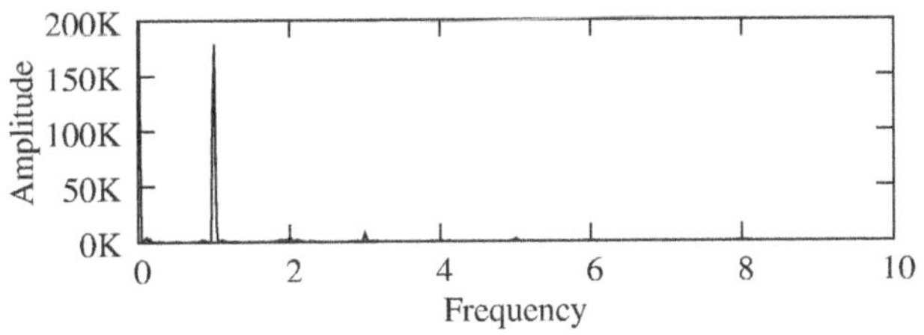

Figure 4: FFT analysis of time series data from the Comcast-Cogent interdomain link in figure 2. The sharp peak at f=1/day implies a strong diurnal pattern in the time series.

Determining the direction of congestion: Even when we are confident that the TTL-exceeded response from the far end of the router returns via the target link, we do not know whether the congestion on that link is in the forward or reverse direction (from the perspective of our VP). To determine the direction of congestion on the targeted link we could use the prespecified timestamp option, sending a sequence of probes toward the target link, soliciting timestamp t_n^1 from the near router, t_f from the far interface, and t_n^2 from the near router again. Clock skew between the routers prevents use of the difference in these timestamps to estimate queuing delay; however, if t_f - t_n^1 shows a diurnal pattern, then we can infer that the link is congested in the forward direction. If t_n^2 - t_f shows a diurnal pattern, then the link is congested in the reverse direction.

Adapting to change: Our probing setup infers interdomain links from traceroutes, and notes the distance from the VP at which each target is seen. However, network routing may change over time; the path to a destination may traverse a different interdomain link, or the same interdomain link may be seen at a a different distance from the VP. To adapt to change, each VP runs a topology discovery process in the background to continuously map interdomain links and their distance from the VP. We then adapt our probing to respond to changes in the measured topology.

Automated trace processing: A VP that tests every interconnection link out of its AS can yield hundreds (access) or thousands (tier-1) of interdomain links, requiring some automated method to detect evidence of congestion. In our initial study, a repeating diurnal pattern with a consistent duration of RTT change, such as that presented in the Comcast-Cogent interdomain link in figure 2, manifested clearly in a frequency domain transformation using a Fast Fourier Transform (FFT) with power density at f = 1/day in figure 4. A time series of RTT samples that contains a power density at 1 can be automatically identified as interdomain congestion. However, some RTT patterns imply congestion is present for only part of the week or weekend. In this case a wavelet transform may reveal the structure of frequencies across time. In the limit, there is a decision as to whether these cases represent noteworthy congestion, which is not an issue any classifier will resolve.

4. CASE STUDIES

We present five case studies showing the potential of the TSLP method to provide empirical data on peering disputes.

Evolution of congestion on Comcast links: A residential Ark monitor in Comcast's network in Monterey, California continuously performs ICMP Paris traceroutes toward randomly chosen destinations in all routed IPv4 /24

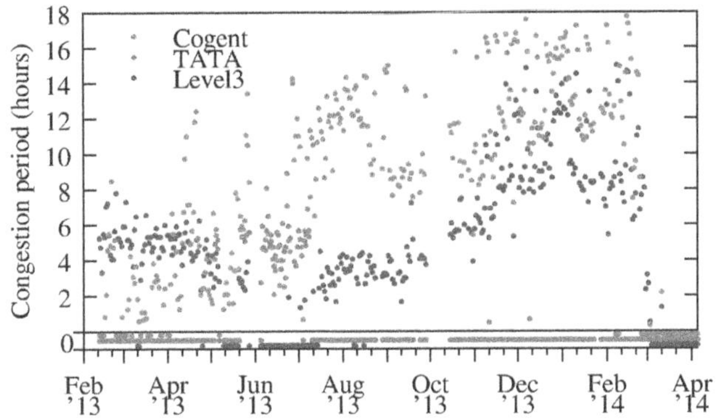

Figure 5: Inferred congestion duration (using CUSUM-based [36] level shift detection) for links connecting three major networks to Comcast. By February 2014, the Cogent and Level3 links were congested up to 18 and 14 hours per day, respectively. After Netflix and Comcast signed a peering agreement in February 2014, congestion on those links disappeared.

prefixes [20]. Large transit networks that are in the path to many destinations have their interdomain links sampled frequently. Our packets traversed interdomain links with Cogent, Level3, and Tata, which also transited Netflix traffic. To discover elevated RTTs in this data we used a level shift detection method that relies on the rank-based non-parametric statistical test CUSUM [36], which is robust to outliers and makes no assumptions about the distribution of underlying RTTs. Figure 5 shows the inferred duration of congestion on these links (in hours per day) from February 2013 to April 2014. Both the Cogent and Level3 links grow from being congested 4-6 hours per day in February 2013 to a maximum of 18 hours (Cogent) and 14 hours (Level3) in February 2014. From mid-May to mid-July, the congestion signal on the Level3 link is replaced with congestion on the TATA link, suggesting a significant volume of traffic was shifted from the Level3 to the TATA link. In late February 2014, Netflix and Comcast agreed to peer directly, and then congestion on the Cogent and Level3 links disappeared.

Netflix and Comcast direct peering: After the February 2014 agreement between Comcast and Netflix, our TSLP probes from the Comcast network started traversing direct peering links toward Netflix prefixes. For most interconnections, there was no level shift in RTT values that indicated a queue was always close to full. However, the peering link between Comcast and Netflix in San Jose, CA still appeared congested for 2-3 hours per day in April 2014 (figure 6a). We asked Netflix about it and learned that they had not fully deployed their peering with Comcast at San Jose.

Google and Free: Inspired by customer reports of poor performance of Youtube videos on Free's network [1], we used our Ark monitor in Free's network to measure the near and far end of a link between Google and Free with TSLP. Figure 6b shows a link that appears congested for 4-6 hours at peak time on weekdays, and more than 12 hours on the weekends (March 22nd and 23rd).

Level3 and AT&T, Verizon: In April 2014, Level3 published an article on their persistently congested links with six large broadband consumer networks: five were in the US and one in Europe [35]. They published an MRTG graph of their interconnect with an unnamed peer in Dallas,

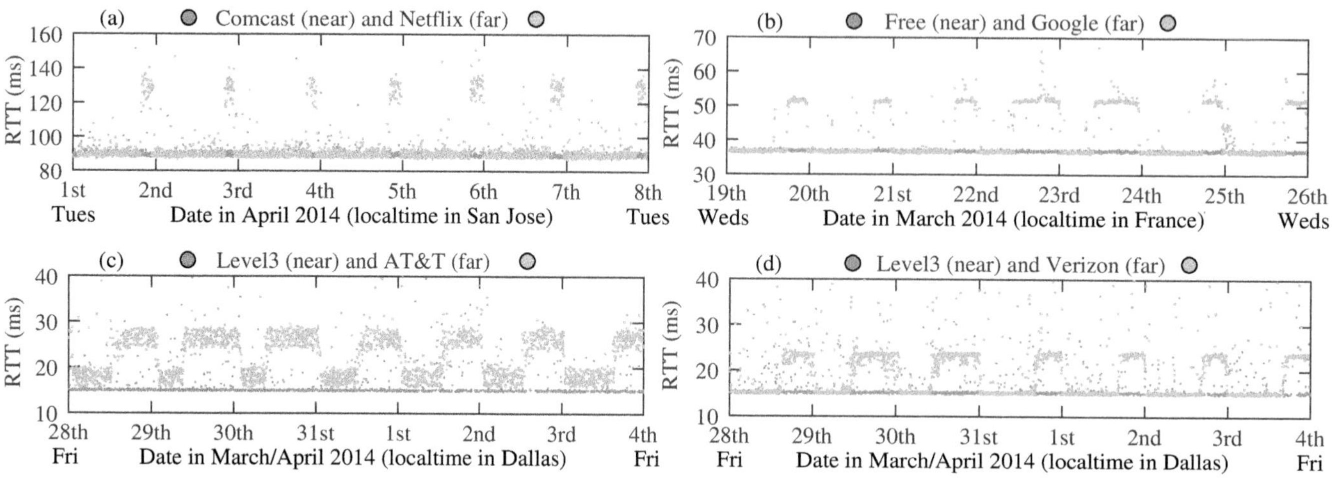

Figure 6: Case studies of four interdomain connections, discussed in section 4.

Texas. From our Ark monitor in Level3's network, we were able to observe congestion on Level3's interconnections with both AT&T and Verizon (we presume two of the broadband consumer networks) in Dallas (figures 6c and 6d). These links appear congested for 6 hours during weekdays and up to 16 hours during weekends in March/April 2014, and both are consistent with the anonymized MRTG graph published by Level3. While both time series are similar for this selected week (we chose to coincide with the MRTG graph in the Level3 article) we observe differences in the diurnal pattern on March 31st: AT&T was congested longer, and we believe it is the anonymized example [35]. For Verizon, the last day we observed the diurnal pattern was June 22nd. For AT&T, the last day we observed the pattern was July 14th; our Ark monitor was down until the 19th, and the signal was gone when the monitor restarted. This example illustrates the power of our technique to (1) provide independent evidence of specific congestion, (2) identify the parties involved where the parties themselves cannot do so because of their NDA agreements, and (3) inform the public debate.

5. OTHER RELATED WORK

Current methods of measuring systematic congestion require instrumentation at both ends of a path being measured [18, 30], but our TSLP method can potentially measure congestion from any VP hosted in an AS to any interdomain link involving that AS provided the link can be isolated. More recently researchers have studied in-home [7,11], and broadband access [2, 16, 23, 34] performance issues, and whether these components are the end-to-end performance bottlenecks for most users. Liu and Crovella used simulation to show that the *loss-pairs* methodology [24] can infer if a router uses AQM or tail-drop. Mahimkar *et al.* used a level shift detection algorithm to correlate changes in network performance with network upgrades [28].

6. CONCLUSION

We developed and tested a simple method of identifying congestion on interdomain links, and used it to study several incidents of reported congestion on interdomain links that correlate with reports of contested business negotiations between the ASes. The advantages of this method are its conceptual, implementation, and deployment simplicity. In contrast to experiments that produce broadband performance maps, which require VPs at many access points, we can measure interdomain links from a given serving area of an ISP with one VP. Most importantly, the TSLP method does not require a server on the other side of the link being probed. Approaches that depend on a server may reveal evidence of congestion from one measurement, but require either instrumentation in the right two places, and/or complex correlation and tomography to localize the point of congestion. Since the vast majority of links do not exhibit persistent congestion, being able to localize congestion deep in the network from a single endpoint has benefits that justify further attention by the research community to resolve the many challenges we have described.

The major challenge is not finding evidence of congestion but associating it reliably with a particular link. This difficulty is due to inconsistent interface numbering conventions, and the fact that a router may have (and report in ICMP responses) IP interface addresses that come from third-party ASes. This problem is well understood, but not deeply studied. Going forward we will study this problem, as well as focus on localizing the directionality of congestion.

We have reported early results from a new project to detect and measure congestion at Internet interconnection points, an issue of recent interest due to the changing nature of Internet traffic over the last decade. For the thousands of interconnection links we have probed thus far, we have not found evidence of widespread persistent congestion, which is good news, but also suggests the value of a lightweight technique that can locate interdomain congestion from a VP at the edge. We plan to deploy VPs in as many access networks as possible, to generate a global "congestion heat map" of the Internet, cross-validate with non-ICMP traffic, and publish evidence of congestion over time.

Acknowledgments

We thank the operators who discussed aspects of their network's operations, Ahmed Elmokashfi who provided an implementation of CUSUM-based level shift detection, and the anonymous reviewers and Ethan Katz-Bassett for their feedback. This work was supported by the U.S. NSF CNS-1414177 and CNS-1413905, by Comcast, and by Verisign, but the material represents only the position of the authors.

7. REFERENCES

[1] R. Andrews and S. Higginbotham. YouTube sucks on French ISP Free, and French regulators want to know why. *GigaOm*, 2013.

[2] S. Bauer, D. Clark, and W. Lehr. Understanding Broadband Speed Measurements. In *TPRC*, 2010.

[3] J. Brodkin. Time Warner, net neutrality foes cry foul over Netflix Super HD demands, 2013.

[4] J. Brodkin. Why YouTube buffers: The secret deals that make-and break-online video. *Ars Technica*, July 2013.

[5] S. Buckley. Cogent and Orange France fight over interconnection issues. *Fierce Telecom*, 2011.

[6] S. Buckley. France Telecom and Google entangled in peering fight. *Fierce Telecom*, 2013.

[7] K. L. Calvert, W. K. Edwards, N. Feamster, R. E. Grinter, Y. Deng, and X. Zhou. Instrumenting home networks. *ACM SIGCOMM CCR*, 41(1), Jan. 2011.

[8] K. Chen, D. R. Choffnes, R. Potharaju, Y. Chen, F. E. Bustamante, D. Pei, and Y. Zhao. Where the sidewalk ends: Extending the Internet AS graph using traceroutes from P2P users. In *ACM CoNEXT*, Dec. 2009.

[9] Y. Chen, S. Jain, V. K. Adhikari, and Z.-L. Zhang. Characterizing roles of front-end servers in end-to-end performance of dynamic content distribution. In *ACM SIGCOMM IMC*, Nov. 2011.

[10] S. Cowley. ISP spat blacks out Net connections. *InfoWorld*, 2005.

[11] L. DiCioccio, R. Teixeira, M. May, and C. Kreibich. Probe and Pray: Using UPnP for Home Network Measurements. In *PAM*, pages 96–105, 2012.

[12] M. Dischinger, A. Haeberlen, K. P. Gummadi, and S. Saroiu. Characterizing residential broadband networks. In *ACM SIGCOMM IMC*, Oct. 2007.

[13] J. Engebretson. Level 3/Comcast dispute revives eyeball vs. content debate, Nov. 2010.

[14] J. Engebretson. Behind the Level 3-Comcast peering settlement, July 2013. `http://www.telecompetitor.com/behind-the-level-3-comcast-peering-settlement/`.

[15] P. Faratin, D. Clark, S. Bauer, W. Lehr, P. Gilmore, and A. Berger. The growing complexity of Internet interconnection. *Communications and Strategies*, (72):51–71, 2008.

[16] FCC. Measuring Broadband America, 2011. `http://www.fcc.gov/measuring-broadband-america`.

[17] S. Floyd and V. Jacobson. Random early detection (RED) gateways for congestion avoidance. *IEEE/ACM Transactions on Networking*, 1(4):397–413, 1993.

[18] D. Genin and J. Splett. Where in the Internet is congestion?, 2013. `http://arxiv.org/abs/1307.3696`.

[19] B. Huffaker, A. Dhamdhere, M. Fomenkov, and kc claffy. Toward topology dualism: Improving the accuracy of AS annotations for routers. In *PAM*, Apr. 2010.

[20] Y. Hyun, B. Huffaker, D. Andersen, M. Luckie, and K. C. Claffy. The IPv4 Routed /24 Topology Dataset, 2014. `http://www.caida.org/data/active/ipv4_routed_24_topology_dataset.xml`.

[21] M. Jain and C. Dovrolis. End-to-end available bandwidth: Measurement methodology, dynamics, and relation with TCP throughput. *IEEE/ACM Transactions on Networking*, 11(4):537–549, 2003.

[22] E. Katz-Bassett, H. V. Madhyastha, V. K. Adhikari, C. Scott, J. Sherry, P. vas Wesep, T. Anderson, and A. Krishnamurthy. Reverse traceroute. In *USENIX NSDI*, Apr. 2010.

[23] C. Kreibich, N. Weaver, B. Nechaev, and V. Paxson. Netalyzr: Illuminating the Edge Network. In *ACM SIGCOMM IMC*, 2010.

[24] J. Liu and M. Crovella. Using loss pairs to discover network properties. In *ACM SIGCOMM IMW*, Nov. 2001.

[25] M. Luckie, B. Huffaker, A. Dhamdhere, V. Giotsas, and k claffy. AS relationships, customer cones, and validation. In *ACM SIGCOMM IMC*, 2013.

[26] M. Luckie and kc claffy. A second look at detecting third-party addresses in traceroute traces with the IP timestamp option. In *PAM*, 2014.

[27] R. Mahajan, N. Spring, D. Wetherall, and T. Anderson. User-level Internet path diagnosis. In *ACM SOSP*, Oct. 2003.

[28] A. A. Mahimkar, H. H. Song, Z. Ge, A. Shaikh, J. Wang, J. Yates, Y. Zhang, and J. Emmons. Detecting the performance impact of upgrades in large operational networks. In *ACM SIGCOMM*, Aug. 2010.

[29] Z. M. Mao, D. Johnson, J. Rexford, J. Wang, and R. Katz. Scalable and accurate identification of AS-Level forwarding paths. In *IEEE INFOCOM*, Mar. 2004.

[30] M. Mathis. Model Based Bulk Performance Metrics. `http://datatracker.ietf.org/doc/draft-ietf-ippm-model-based-metrics/`, Oct 2013.

[31] K. Nichols and V. Jacobson. Controlling queue delay. *ACM Queue*, 10(5), May 2012.

[32] M. Ricknas. Sprint-Cogent dispute puts small rip in fabric of Internet. *PCWorld*, Oct. 2008.

[33] J. Sherry, E. Katz-Bassett, M. Pimenova, H. V. Madhyastha, T. Anderson, and A. Krishnamurthy. Resolving IP aliases with prespecified timestamps. In *ACM SIGCOMM IMC*, Nov. 2010.

[34] S. Sundaresan, W. de Donato, N. Feamster, R. Teixeira, S. Crawford, and A. Pescapè. Broadband Internet performance: A view from the gateway. In *ACM SIGCOMM*, 2011.

[35] M. Taylor. Observations of an Internet Middleman, May 2014. `http://blog.level3.com/global-connectivity/observations-internet-middleman/`.

[36] W. A. Taylor. Change-point analysis: A powerful new tool for detecting changes, 2000. `http://www.variation.com/cpa/tech/changepoint.html`.

[37] Verizon. Unbalanced peering, and the real story behind the Verizon/Cogent dispute, June 2013. `http://publicpolicy.verizon.com/blog/`.

[38] B. Zhang, J. Bi, Y. Wang, Y. Zhang, and J. Wu. Refining IP-to-AS mappings for AS-level traceroute. In *IEEE ICCCN*, July 2013.

[39] Y. Zhang, R. Oliveira, H. Zhang, and L. Zhang. Quantifying the pitfalls of traceroute in AS connectivity inference. In *PAM*, 2010.

Inferring Complex AS Relationships

Vasileios Giotsas
CAIDA / UC San Diego
vgiotsas@caida.org

Matthew Luckie
CAIDA / UC San Diego
mjl@caida.org

Bradley Huffaker
CAIDA / UC San Diego
bradley@caida.org

kc claffy
CAIDA / UC San Diego
kc@caida.org

ABSTRACT

The traditional approach of modeling relationships between ASes abstracts relationship types into three broad categories: transit, peering, and sibling. More complicated configurations exist, and understanding them may advance our knowledge of Internet economics and improve models of routing. We use BGP, traceroute, and geolocation data to extend CAIDA's AS relationship inference algorithm to infer two types of complex relationships: hybrid relationships, where two ASes have different relationships at different interconnection points, and partial transit relationships, which restrict the scope of a customer relationship to the provider's peers and customers. Using this new algorithm, we find 4.5% of the 90,272 provider-customer relationships observed in March 2014 were complex, including 1,071 hybrid relationships and 2,955 partial-transit relationships. Because most peering relationships are invisible, we believe these numbers are lower bounds. We used feedback from operators, and relationships encoded in BGP communities and RPSL, to validate 20% and 6.9% of our partial transit and hybrid inferences, respectively, and found our inferences have 92.9% and 97.0% positive predictive values. Hybrid relationships are not only established between large transit providers; in 57% of the inferred hybrid transit/peering relationships the customer had a customer cone of fewer than 5 ASes.

Categories and Subject Descriptors

C.2.5 [**Local and Wide-Area Networks**]: Internet; C.2.1 [**Network Architecture and Design**]: Network topology

Keywords

AS relationships; complex routing policies

1. INTRODUCTION

Analysis and modeling of the Internet's AS topology requires accurate knowledge of AS relationships, which reflect often private negotiations between ASes. The details of these relationships are not comprehensively published anywhere, and many of them are subject to non-disclosure agreements, motivating many researchers to develop algorithms to heuristically infer AS relationships based on AS path information available in public BGP data [7–10, 12, 15, 22–24, 30, 32, 33]. To simplify the development of inference heuristics, researchers traditionally abstracted relationships into three (and sometimes only the first two) classes: provider-customer (p2c), peering (p2p) and sibling (s2s). In a p2c or transit relationship, a customer buys access to achieve global reachability. In a p2p relationship, two ASes share access to their networks and their customers' networks. In an s2s relationship, two ASes under common ownership may provide mutual transit to each other.

This oversimplification ignores more complex relationships and may introduce artifacts into the study of inter-domain routing [31], such as spurious relationship cycles [11], artificial policy violations [24, 30], and generally inaccurate AS path prediction [9, 23]. These problems have inspired the development of a relationship-agnostic AS topology model as an alternative [25, 26]. While BGP is a prefix-based routing protocol and AS relationships are a course-grained abstraction, operators themselves express their policies in terms of AS relationships, and understanding classes of relationships can help researchers predict routing decisions.

In this paper we propose an algorithm to infer the two most common types of complex AS relationships: *hybrid relationships*, where two ASes have different relationships at different interconnection points [28] (e.g. p2c in one location and p2p elsewhere), and *partial transit relationships*, which restrict the scope of a p2c relationship to the provider's peers and customers (but not providers) [10, 13, 22, 28, 29]. We can define these complex relationships as special cases of the traditional p2c and p2p types, which allows us to leverage CAIDA's relationship inference algorithm instead of designing an entirely new algorithm.

Section 2 provides an overview of Internet routing and related work. Section 3 describes the BGP, traceroute, and geolocation data we used in this study, and presents our methodology to infer complex AS relationships. Section 4 presents our inferences: 1,071 hybrid relationships and 2,955 partial transit relationships, used mostly by ASes with a small customer cone. Our data suggests that IXPs facilitate the establishment of hybrid relationships by stub ASes at diverse geographical locations. Using feedback from operators and relationships encoded in BGP communities and RPSL, we found that our hybrid and partial transit inferences had positive predictive values of 92.9% and 97.0%, respectively.

IMC'14, November 5–7, 2014, Vancouver, BC, Canada.

http://dx.doi.org/10.1145/2663716.2663743.

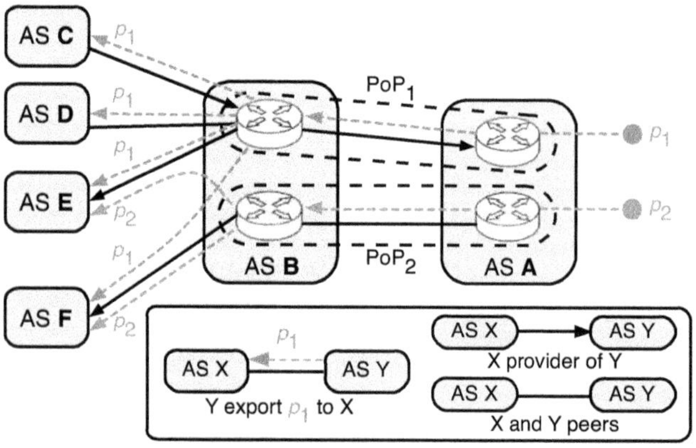

Figure 1: Hybrid relationship between ASes A and B at different points of presence (PoPs). In PoP_1, A is a customer of B, while in PoP_2 they are peers. B's export policy depends on the relationship between the ASes at each PoP; prefix p_1 is announced to all neighbors of B because A receives transit at PoP_1, while p_2 is only announced to customers of B because A receives peering at PoP_2.

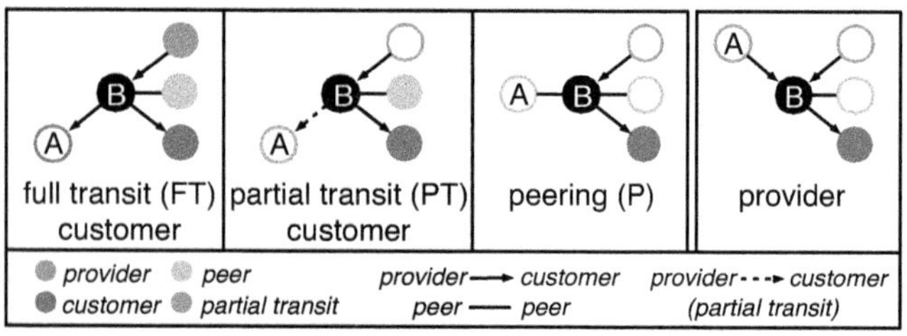

Figure 2: Partial transit compared with traditional relationship types. B's export policy to A changes based on B's relationship to A, with routes from the filled AS nodes exported to A in each scenario. In a partial transit relationship with A, B exports only customers and peers to A.

2. BACKGROUND

Interdomain routing is a collaborative effort among ASes, which interconnect and exchange routing information using the BGP protocol. Many ASes negotiate contractual agreements that impose technical restrictions on traffic exchange. The export policies that derive from relationships between ASes combined with traffic engineering largely define routing at the AS level. Unfortunately, operators are reluctant to publish their AS relationships which are often confidential. For more than a decade, researchers have studied how to infer the type of business relationships between networks through the analysis of AS-level paths [7,10,12,15,22,23,32].

Gao's seminal work [15] proposed a classification into three abstract relationship types; p2c, p2p, and s2s. Although these classifications capture the majority of AS interconnections, more complicated relationships exist. Norton defines two additional relationship types: *hybrid* and *partial transit* [28,29]. Hybrid relationships arise when two ASes agree to different relationship types at different inter-connection points of presence (PoPs); typically, the ASes will be peers in particular regions, but one AS will be a transit customer of the other AS elsewhere. Figure 1 illustrates the routing that results in such a relationship; B may advertise prefix p_1 to all of its neighbors, but B may only advertise p_2 to its customers. In some cases, B may only advertise p_2 to customers in the region served by PoP_2. Partial transit relationships arise when a provider sells access to its customers and peers but not to its providers. Figure 2 compares the routing differences between the traditional provider, peer, and customer relationships and the partial transit relationship; in the traditional customer relationship, A receives routes from B's customers, peers, and providers, but in the partial transit case A receives just customer and peer routes. Table 1 summarizes the four relationship types.

Type	Definition
Transit	An AS offers another AS access to its peers, customers, and providers.
Peering	Two ASes offer access to their customer routes to each other.
Partial transit	An AS offers another AS transit to its peers and customers, but not providers.
Hybrid	An AS offers another AS a combination of full transit, partial transit, or peering according to interconnection location.

Table 1: Relationship types that we inferred. This paper focuses on methods to infer hybrid and partial transit relationships.

Using only conventional transit and peering relationships to study the AS topology is problematic [31]. For example, in 2005 Mao *et al.* concluded that complex relationships may contribute to the inability to accurately predict AS-level paths [23]; in 2013 Deng *et al.* [9] reached a similar conclusion. Mühlbauer *et al.* proposed a relationship-agnostic AS topology model to capture complex BGP policies that cannot be modeled based on the conventional relationship abstraction [25,26].

A survey of operators by Dimitropoulos *et al.* in 2007 [10] confirmed the existence of relationships that vary across peering points and prefixes. In 2008, Faratin *et al.* suggested that AS relationships will become increasingly complex because the growth of Content Distribution Networks (CDNs) and eyeball networks change the perceptions of symmetry in traffic delivery costs [13]. Yet, there is little work that tackles the complicated challenges of inferring complex relationships, and little validation data available. In 2013, Neudorfer *et al.* proposed a method to infer complex relationships by examining policy violations (unconventional export policies) using the conventional transit and peering definitions at different Points-of-Presence (PoPs) [27]. However, they were only able to manually identify a single hybrid relationship, illustrating the difficulties involved in the inference of complex relationships.

In 2013, we presented and validated a new AS relationship inference algorithm that also only inferred conventional transit and peering relationships [22]. Our top-down approach began by inferring a Tier-1 clique, applied heuristics to infer c2p links based primarily on how neighbors were observed to export routes, and inferred the remainder to be p2p. That algorithm inferred hybrid and partial transit relationships as conventional transit relationships because at least some routes from the neighbor AS were exported to peers or providers. To account for the effect of hybrid relationships, we presented a new algorithm for inferring the *customer cone* – the set of ASes that can be reached by an AS using its customer links. Previous customer cone algorithms used a recursive model, inferring all customers of downstream customers to be in an AS's customer cone; complex relationships and traffic engineering behavior can distort such inferences. We addressed this limitation with the *provider/peer observed customer cone*, where we computed the customer cone of an AS using routes we observed from providers and peers of the AS. Because B will not export routes received from the peering portion of a hybrid relationship with customer C to provider A, we did not include these routes when computing the customer cone of A. Similarly, because B will not export routes from a partial transit customer C to provider A, we did not include these routes when computing the customer cone of A.

3. INFERENCE METHODOLOGY

Figure 3 shows a high-level overview of our process to infer complex relationships. First, we infer conventional transit and peering relationships and customer cones using our IMC 2013 algorithm [22] and publicly available BGP data. Because our IMC 2013 algorithm infers hybrid and partial transit relationships as conventional transit relationships, our new algorithm uses BGP data to infer per-prefix export policy for all conventional transit relationships, resulting in sets of partial transit and candidate hybrid relationships. Then, we use traceroute and geolocation data to infer if export policies of candidate hybrid relationships differ by geographic location. Our algorithm then classifies candidate hybrid relationships that have geographic characteristics as hybrid, with specific export policy classifications per geographic location.

3.1 Data

BGP data: We obtained routing information from BGP table snapshots collected by Route Views (RV) [5] and RIPE RIS (RIS) [4], which record BGP routing information by peering with globally distributed ASes. For each RV and RIS collector we downloaded one RIB file every five days for March 2014; we retained only paths that were observed in all files to reduce false positive complex relationship inferences. We extracted three attributes from each BGP route: the AS path, the prefix, and the communities string. We discarded AS paths with symptoms of misconfiguration or poisoning, e.g., loops, unassigned ASes, and non-adjacent Tier-1 ASes [22]. We also discarded prefixes longer than /24, which many ASes do not route. We used path and prefix attributes to identify partial transit and candidate hybrid relationships. We used available communities strings as a source of geographically-tagged interconnection points and to validate our complex relationship inferences.

Traceroute data: To derive the geographical footprint of AS relationships, we processed interface-level paths derived from two sources of traceroute data to infer the PoP-level AS connectivity. First, we used CAIDA's IPv4 Routed /24 Topology Dataset gathered by the Archipelago (Ark) [34] measurement infrastructure in March 2014 [19]. As of March 2014, Ark supports continual Paris traceroute measurements from 94 monitors in 84 different ASes distributed in 39 different countries, probing to one random IP address in each /24 of the entire routed IPv4 space approximately every three days. Second, we coordinated probing from thousands of public traceroute servers to expand coverage beyond what these existing Ark measurements capture. We developed

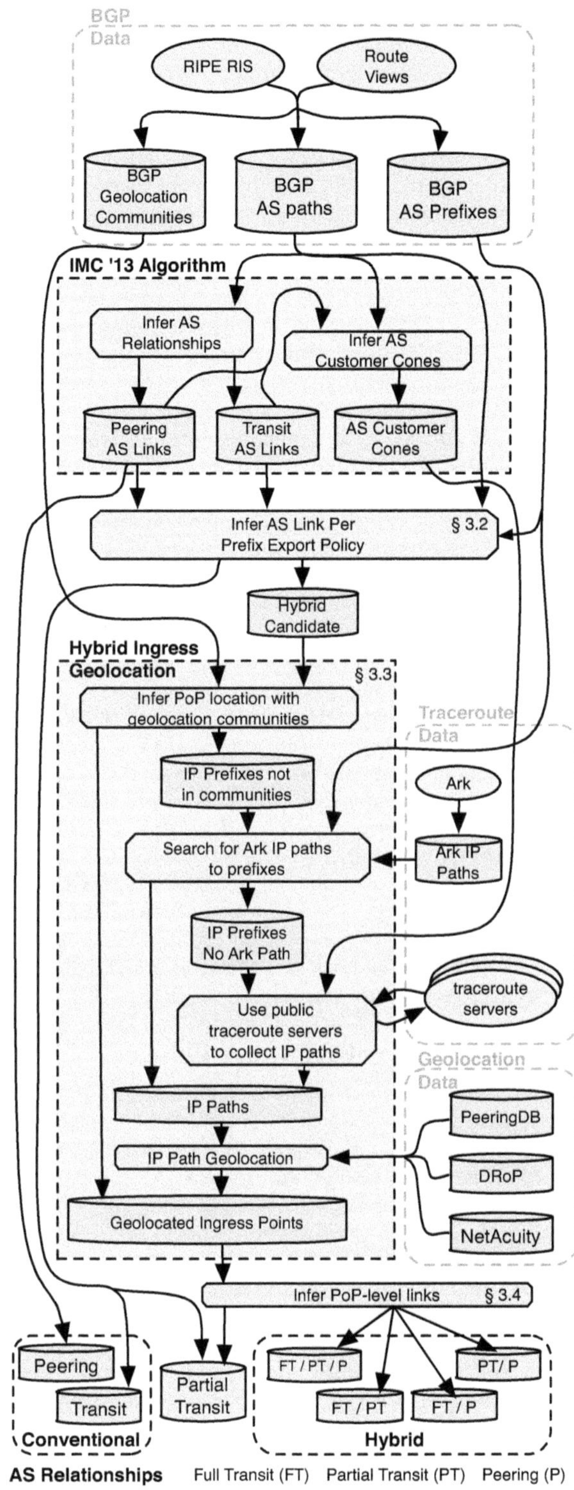

Figure 3: Overview of our process to infer complex AS relationships. We begin by inferring conventional peering and transit relationships and customer cones using AS paths from public BGP data. We infer partial transit and candidate hybrid relationships using paths and prefixes from BGP and conventional relationships. We use traceroute and geolocation data to infer hybrid relationships, and classify the arrangement by policy and location.

an overlay interface to interact with 2,509 public traceroute servers among 507 different ASes in 77 different countries. To avoid being blocked by traceroute servers for too frequent probing, we limited probing through this interface to one query every 10 seconds per server. We used customer cone data to inform target selection so that we would traceroute paths toward destinations most likely to cross a candidate hybrid relationship and therefore help with geolocation.

Geolocation data: To infer if export policies differ by geographic location, we used four sources of data, in order of preference: published BGP community information; PeeringDB's reverse DNS scan on IXP peering prefixes; strings found in DNS hostnames; and a commercial database.

Some ASes use communities to record the ingress location where a route entered their network. Community values and their corresponding meanings are not standardized, but many operators document their usage of communities in IRR records or network support pages, allowing us to compile a dictionary of values and their corresponding meanings. In total, we interpreted 1,533 values from 117 ASes that encoded the geographic location of AS interconnection points.

We used three data sources to map addresses observed in traceroute to geographic locations: PeeringDB's reverse DNS lookups of IXP prefixes [3], CAIDA's DNS-based Router Positioning (DRoP) [17], and Digital Envoy's NetAcuity [2]. We used PeeringDB's list to map addresses to IXP locations. We used DRoP to interpret DNS strings for geographic hints such as airport codes, city names, and CLLI codes (a geographic naming convention developed by the telecommunication industry [1]). If neither PeeringDB or DRoP reveals a location, we used NetAcuity, a commercial geolocation provider, to map the IP address to a geographic location. NetAcuity is more accurate at router positioning than other commercial geolocation databases, though it is optimized to infer edge host location (servers and end users) rather than router infrastructure IP addresses [18].

3.2 Inferring Prefix Export Policies

Hybrid relationships result in different export policies for different sets of prefixes across the same AS relationship. We therefore divide export policies into three types of increasingly restrictive policy: full transit (FT), partial transit (PT), and peering (P). To illustrate, in figure 2, FT is the only policy where the provider exports prefixes from its providers (in addition to peers and customers) to the customer. PT is more restrictive because the provider does not export provider routes, and P is the most restrictive because the provider exports only customer routes. We therefore annotate a PoP where two ASes interconnect with the most restrictive policy we observe in BGP for all prefixes we observe with traceroute to cross the link at that PoP.

Our algorithm begins by inferring the most restrictive export policy we observe in BGP for *link-prefix tuples*: for each link our IMC 2013 algorithm inferred to have a conventional transit relationship, we tag individual prefixes that propagate in BGP through the link. Figure 4 illustrates the approach; for a transit relationship between A and B where our IMC 2013 algorithm inferred A is a customer of B, we tag each prefix p_x that B exports to other neighbors it received from A. If we observe a triplet where B exports p_x to a provider, we tag the A-B p_x tuple with FT. If we do not observe an FT-triplet, but do observe a triplet where B exports p_x to a peer, we tag the tuple with PT. If we do not observe either FT or PT triplets, we tag the tuple with P. We use a similar process with each prefix p_y that B exports to A, and it is rare to BGP-observe B export the same prefix both to and from A, i.e., $p_x \neq p_y$ for any A-B link.

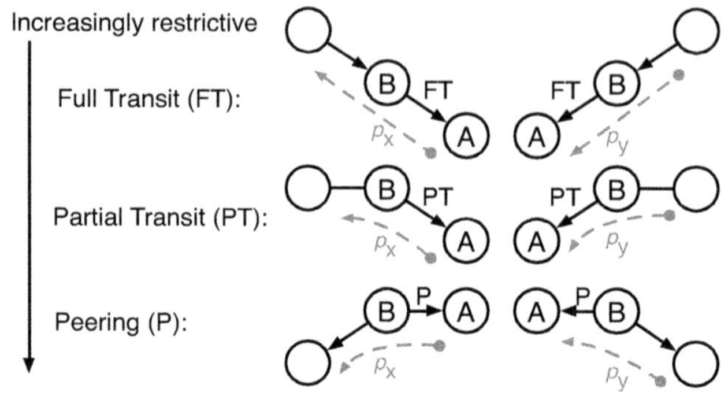

Figure 4: Tagging a link-prefix tuple between ASes A and B where our IMC 2013 algorithm infers A to be a customer of B. p_x is a prefix from A exported by B; p_y is exported by B to A. We tag a link-prefix tuple with the most restrictive export policy that could explain the observed routing for the prefix: FT if exported by B to (from) its providers; PT if exported by B to (from) its peers and customers but no further; P if exported by B to (from) its customers but no further.

If all tuples for a link are tagged FT, the relationship remains conventional provider-customer, and if all tuples are tagged PT, we classify the relationship as PT. However, if a given link has a mixture of FT, PT, or P tuples, we tag it as a candidate hybrid. At the end of this process, we infer 2,955 partial transit and 6,682 candidate hybrid relationships.

3.3 Candidate Hybrid Exploration

The presence of different export policies for different prefixes for the same AS link is an indication of a hybrid relationship, but it may also reflect traffic engineering practices that restrict the scope of route advertisements. To distinguish between hybrid relationships and traffic engineering, our technique relies on the ability to geolocate the ingress point of each link-prefix tuple. Depending on the combination of prefixes tagged as FT, PT, and P, a candidate hybrid relationship may fall into one of four categories; FT + PT + P, FT + PT, FT + P, or PT + P. We attempt to group prefixes with the same tag into mutually exclusive PoPs such that each PoP has a consistent BGP-observed export policy. For example, if all FT-tagged prefixes can be geolocated to paths that cross PoP_1 and all the P prefixes to PoP_2, then we infer the hybrid relationship to be FT + P. Conversely, if a prefix tagged as P crosses PoP_2, but so do prefixes tagged as FT or PT, then PoP_2 cannot represent a peering PoP, and we infer PoP_2 as FT or PT.

Therefore, given a candidate hybrid relationship with N_P prefixes tagged P, N_{PT} prefixes tagged PT, and N_{FT} prefixes tagged FT, we begin by inferring all interconnection PoPs for the P prefixes. We then try to rule out the PoPs as being peering PoPs by testing as many PT prefixes as necessary to find the same set of PoPs with a PT export policy; i.e., an AS cannot have a P policy at a PoP if it also exports PT prefixes at the PoP. Finally, we test as many FT prefixes as necessary to find the same set of PoPs as found for the P and PT cases.

We used a combination of BGP, traceroute, and geolocation data to infer PoPs for candidate hybrid relationships. For each candidate hybrid relationship's prefixes we searched BGP paths for a community that stores a geographic hint, which is our most trusted source of data. For each remaining prefix we tried to obtain a traceroute path toward the prefix that crosses the link. If a link is not observed with traceroute in any path toward a tagged prefix, we cannot infer the relationship as hybrid because we do not have adequate data to make a robust classification. In this case, the inferred relationship remains conventional transit to avoid misinterpreting traffic engineering as a complex relationship.

3.3.1 Obtaining traceroute paths

To minimize the workload we impose on public traceroute servers, we begin by using traceroute paths collected in existing Ark traces. For the set of prefixes and candidate hybrid relationships for which we find no usable Ark trace, we coordinate a distributed traceroute campaign using public traceroute servers. We traceroute only to prefixes that B exports from A, rather than the inverse, because in some cases B may export a complete routing table to A; i.e., in figure 4 we use p_x but not p_y. For each candidate hybrid link, we divide the available traceroute servers into two sets, depending on their relationship to the provider of the candidate hybrid relationship. The *full-visibility* set includes traceroute servers under the customer cone of the provider of the candidate relationship, which may be able to reach any of the targeted prefixes through the candidate hybrid relationship. The *limited-visibility* set includes traceroute servers in ASes that peer with the provider of the candidate relationship, or in ASes under whose customer cone the provider belongs. We consider traceroutes from these servers able to reach prefixes tagged either FT or PT through the candidate hybrid relationship, but not prefixes tagged P, since a peer should not export prefixes obtained from a peer to another peer. In figure 1, a traceroute server inside AS E would belong to the full-visibility set for the B-A relationship, a server inside AS C or AS D would belong to the limited-visibility set, and a server in a provider of D would not be used.

After classifying traceroute servers, we randomly select an IP address from each target prefix and traceroute it with the servers. Note that having a traceroute server in the full or limited-visibility groups does not imply that a traceroute will cross the targeted link, only that it could. Capturing possible peering PoP-level connectivity for a candidate hybrid relationship requires at least one traceroute server of full-visibility reaching the target prefixes through the link. For 97% of the candidate hybrid relationships we have at least one traceroute monitor of full-visibility, and for 85% of the of the links we have more than 10 full-visibility monitors. For 462 of our 6,682 candidate hybrid relationships, we could not identify ingress points due to lack of full-visibility traceroute servers and geographic communities.

3.3.2 Geolocation of Hybrid Links

If a traceroute toward a selected prefix crosses the candidate hybrid relationship, we use the path to geolocate the PoP. Identifying the interdomain link is difficult, since it is not clear who assigned the prefix used to establish routing. Consider the observed IP path a^0 a^1 b^0 in figure 5: changing the interdomain link from a^0–a^1 to a^1–b^0 has no effect on the IP path. Although it is not clear whether the interdomain

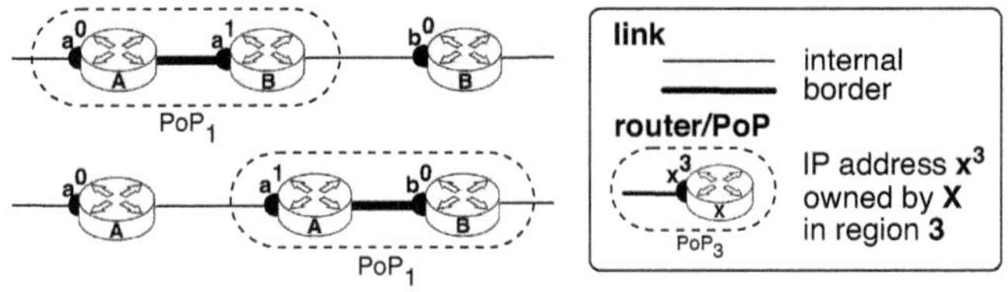

Figure 5: Regardless of which two routers form the interdomain link, interface a^1 is always part of the pair forming the interdomain link and so will be located in the same region.

Geolocation	Number	Percent
Communities	61,198	34.4%
PeeringDB	6,228	3.5%
DRoP	56,111	31.5%
Netacuity	54,590	30.6%

Table 2: The number of link-prefix tuples which were geolocated by each system, in the order they were geolocated.

link was just before or after the AS changed in the path, it does not matter for geolocation. The IP address just before the change will be on one of the two routers connected to the interdomain link and so will be in the same location as the target link. Therefore, we geolocate the IP address just before the AS changed, first using PeeringDB's reverse DNS scan, then by DRoP's inference given the hostname string, and then with Netacuity.

3.3.3 Classification of Hybrid Links

We use the BGP, traceroute, and geolocation data we collected and the logic in section 3.3 to infer which candidate hybrid links represent hybrid links. Table 2 shows which method geolocated each link-prefix tuple. For hybrid relationships where we find PoPs with a consistent export policy, we annotate the geolocated PoPs with specific FT, PT, and P classifications.

4. RESULTS

Of the 90,272 p2c relationships we inferred for March 2014, we inferred 4,026 (4.5%) of these relationships to be complex, including 1,071 hybrid AS relationships and 2,955 partial-transit relationships. The inferred hybrid relationships include 969 FT/P relationships, 72 PT/P relationships, 30 FT/PT relationships, and 4 FT/PT/P relationships. We found that hybrid relationships are not only established between large transit providers; in 57% of the hybrid transit/peering (T/P) relationships the customer had a customer cone size of less than 5 ASes. However, other metrics reflect network size differently than customer cone. For instance, we inferred 21 hybrid relationships that involve Akamai (AS 20940); although Akamai has no customers it is reported to be one of the top 10 networks in terms of inter-domain traffic volume [21]. For 34.6% of the hybrid T/P relationships the customers have traffic levels of at least 100 Gbps, according to traffic volumes self-reported in PeeringDB. The corresponding percentage for FT (customer relationships) in the whole BGP-observed graph is only 13.3%.

For 68.5% of the inferred hybrid T/P relationships, the peering link crossed a European IXP. Some ASes with open or selective peering policies are establishing peering relation-

	Hybrid			Partial		
	TP	FP	FN	TP	FP	FN
Direct report	33	2	1	2	0	0
Communities	124	10	4	158	5	0
RPSL	45	-	-	38	-	-
Validated	214 / 1,071: 20.0%			203 / 2,955: 6.9%		
Confirmed	202 / 1,071: 18.9%			198 / 2,955: 6.7%		
PPV	157 / 169: 92.9%			160 / 165: 97.0%		

Table 3: Validation results, showing true positives (TP), false positives (FP), and false negatives (FN). We validate 20.0% of our hybrid inferences and 6.9% of our partial transit inferences and found our inferences have 92.9% and 97.0% positive predictive values (PPV = TP/TP+FP), respectively.

ships with their customers over IXPs, sometimes unknowingly, as revealed by our discussions with some operators.

Partial transit relationships are also more frequently observed among European ASes. 88% of the inferred partial transit relationships were established in European PoPs. We believe that the dense peering connectivity among European ASes [6,16] makes partial transit more attractive, since partial transit providers can offer discounted access to a large fraction of their routing table through partial transit only. For instance, Init7 (AS13030), a large European provider, reports that 60% of their routing table is accessible through peering links [20] as of September 2014.

Despite the many complex relationships we inferred, and positive validation, we are limited by the well-known AS topology incompleteness problem [31], as our algorithm can only infer complex relationships where the peering component is revealed in public BGP data.

5. VALIDATION

We used three sources of validation data: direct e-mail feedback, BGP communities that signal relationship type, and relationship types expressed in different Routing Policy Specification Language (RPSL) objects.

Direct feedback: We obtained feedback from seven operators (of twelve contacted) that previously contributed AS relationship corrections through CAIDA's web interface [22]. We sent each operator our inferences for their ASes and asked them to specify if they were correct, and asked them if they were involved in other hybrid or partial-transit relationships not included in our inferences.

BGP communities: We compiled a dictionary of 1,502 communities defined by 281 ASes, which we used to extract a set of 40,820 relationships for March 2014, as explained in [22]. Relationship communities enable the implementation of sophisticated routing policies, so operators have a strong incentive to configure community values with correct relationship annotations [14]. We considered five types of relationship communities: customer, partial-customer, peer, partial-provider, and provider. We used the partial-customer and partial-provider communities to obtain validation data for partial transit relationships. We captured hybrid relationships when we observed that an AS tagged different inbound prefixes from the same neighbor with different community values depending on the ingress PoP. To mitigate transient misconfigurations we required that the same communities be observed in all BGP snapshots we collected.

RPSL: We used RPSL objects to evaluate only true positives, since RPSL objects are commonly expressed at a high level and in most cases do not encode complex relationships.

Table 3 summarizes our validation results. Overall, we were able to confirm 202 hybrid relationships (18.9% of the total hybrid inferences), and 198 partial-transit relationships (6.7% of the total partial-transit inferences). For the validation datasets that allowed us to test both true and false positives (directly reported and BGP communities) we had the correct inference for 157/169 (92.9%) of the inferred hybrid relationships, and for 160/165 (97.0%) of inferred the partial transit relationships. We failed to infer five hybrid relationships present in our validation dataset. For four, both the transit and the peering PoP were located in the same city, and our city-level geolocation granularity was too coarse to identify the different PoPs.

Via operator feedback we found that three of the inferred hybrid relationships were the result of misconfigurations, where the intended relationship was provider-customer. One operator followed up with a request for a semi-live system to alert operators of hybrid peering relationships, since they may be unintentional.

6. CONCLUSION

We presented a new algorithm to infer the two most common types of complex AS relationships: hybrid and partial transit using BGP, traceroute, and geolocation data. We inferred 1,071 hybrid and 2,955 partial-transit relationships for March 2014. We validated our inferences against direct feedback from operators, BGP communities, and RPSL data and found our hybrid and partial transit inferences have 92.9% and 97.0% positive predictive values, respectively. We have published our complex relationship inferences and validation data derived from BGP communities and RPSL at `http://www.caida.org/publications/papers/2014/complex`

We believe this is the first partly validated attempt to infer complex AS relationships. Our results reveal that complex relationships are more prevalent in the periphery of the AS topology than previously thought, while 61% of hybrid peering and 88% of partial transit relationships were inferred between European ASes that leverage Europe's extensive IXP ecosystem. Generally, unconventional relationships can have arbitrary complexity that may not be expressible in terms of relationship types, which is why we focused on the two most common types of complex relationships according to operator feedback and the existing literature, which are hybrid and partial transit. In the future we plan to expand our active measurements by integrating traceroute probes from RIPE Atlas, and we will continue to interact with AS operators for input and feedback to improve our inferences.

Acknowledgments

We thank the reviewers and Phillipa Gill for their feedback. The work was supported by CAIDA members, U.S. NSF grant CNS-1414177, DHS S&T Cyber Security Division BAA 11-02 and SPAWAR Systems Center Pacific via N66001-12-C-0130, by Defence Research and Development Canada (DRDC) pursuant to an Agreement between the U.S. and Canadian governments for Cooperation in Science and Technology for Critical Infrastructure Protection and Border Security. This work represents the position of the authors and not of CAIDA's members, NSF, DHS, or DRDC.

7. REFERENCES

[1] Common Language Location Identifier (CLLI) code. `http://en.wikipedia.org/wiki/CLLI_code`.

[2] NetAcuity. `http://www.digitalelement.com/our_technology/our_technology.html`.

[3] PeeringDB. `http://www.peeringdb.com`.

[4] RIPE RIS. `http://www.ripe.net/ris`.

[5] RouteViews. `http://www.routeviews.org/`.

[6] B. Ager, N. Chatzis, A. Feldmann, N. Sarrar, S. Uhlig, and W. Willinger. Anatomy of a large European IXP. In *ACM SIGCOMM*, pages 163–174, Aug. 2012.

[7] G. D. Battista, T. Erlebach, A. Hall, M. Patrignani, M. Pizzonia, and T. Schank. Computing the types of the relationships between autonomous systems. *IEEE/ACM Transactions on Networking*, 15(2):267–280, Apr. 2007.

[8] H. Chang, S. Jamin, and W. Willinger. To peer or not to peer: Modeling the evolution of the Internet's AS-level topology. In *INFOCOM*, pages 1–12, Apr. 2006.

[9] W. Deng, W. Muhlbauer, Y. Yang, P. Zhu, X. Lu, and B. Plattner. Shedding light on the use of AS relationships for path inference. *Communications and Networks*, 14(3):336–345, June 2013.

[10] X. Dimitropoulos, D. Krioukov, M. Fomenkov, B. Huffaker, Y. Hyun, k. claffy, and G. Riley. AS relationships: inference and validation. *ACM SIGCOMM CCR*, 37(1):29–40, Jan. 2007.

[11] X. Dimitropoulos, M. A. Serrano, and D. Krioukov. On cycles in AS relationships. *ACM SIGCOMM CCR*, 38(3):102–104, July 2008.

[12] T. Erlebach, A. Hall, and T. Schank. Classifying customer-provider relationships in the Internet. In *IASTED International Conference on Communications and Computer Networks*, Nov. 2002.

[13] P. Faratin, D. Clark, S. Bauer, W. Lehr, P. Gilmore, and A. Berger. The growing complexity of Internet interconnection. *Communications and Strategies*, (72):51–71, Dec. 2008.

[14] K. Foster. Application of BGP communities. *The Internet Protocol Journal*, 6(2):2–9, June 2003.

[15] L. Gao. On inferring autonomous system relationships in the Internet. *IEEE/ACM Transactions on Networking*, 9(6):733–745, Dec. 2001.

[16] V. Giotsas, S. Zhou, M. Luckie, and k claffy. Inferring multilateral peering. In *ACM CoNEXT*, pages 247–258, Dec. 2013.

[17] B. Huffaker, M. Fomenkov, and k. claffy. DRoP: DNS-based router positioning. *ACM SIGCOMM CCR*, 44(3):6–13, July 2014.

[18] B. Huffaker, M. Fomenkov, and k. claffy. Geocompare: A comparison of public and commercial geolocation databases. Technical report, CAIDA, May 2011. `http://www.caida.org/publications/papers/2011/geocompare-tr/`.

[19] Y. Hyun, B. Huffaker, D. Andersen, M. Luckie, and K. C. Claffy. The IPv4 Routed /24 Topology Dataset, 2014. `http://www.caida.org/data/active/ipv4_routed_24_topology_dataset.xml`.

[20] INIT7. Init7 partial transit. `http://www.init7.net/en/wholesale/partial-transit/`.

[21] C. Labovitz, S. Iekel-Johnson, D. McPherson, J. Oberheide, and F. Jahanian. Internet inter-domain traffic. In *ACM SIGCOMM*, pages 75–86, Aug. 2010.

[22] M. Luckie, B. Huffaker, A. Dhamdhere, V. Giotsas, and k claffy. AS relationships, customer cones, and validation. In *ACM SIGCOMM IMC*, pages 243–256, Oct. 2013.

[23] Z. M. Mao, L. Qiu, J. Wang, and Y. Zhang. On AS-level path inference. In *ACM SIGMETRICS*, pages 339–349, June 2005.

[24] R. Mazloum, M.-O. Buob, J. AugÃÍ, B. Baynat, D. Rossi, and T. Friedman. Violation of interdomain routing assumptions. In *PAM*, pages 173–182, Apr. 2014.

[25] W. Mühlbauer, A. Feldmann, O. Maennel, M. Roughan, and S. Uhlig. Building an AS-topology model that captures route diversity. In *ACM SIGCOMM*, pages 195–206, Aug. 2006.

[26] W. Mühlbauer, S. Uhlig, B. Fu, M. Meulle, and O. Maennel. In search for an appropriate granularity to model routing policies. In *ACM SIGCOMM*, pages 145–156, Aug. 2007.

[27] L. Neudorfer, Y. Shavitt, and N. Zilberman. Improving AS relationship inference using PoPs. In *IEEE INFOCOM Workshops*, pages 459–464, Apr. 2013.

[28] W. Norton. Dual Transit/Peering. `http://drpeering.net/white-papers/Art-Of-Peering-The-Peering-Playbook.html#4`.

[29] W. Norton. Partial Transit (Regional). `http://drpeering.net/white-papers/Art-Of-Peering-The-Peering-Playbook.html#7`.

[30] S. Qiu, P. McDaniel, and F. Monrose. Toward valley-free inter-domain routing. In *IEEE ICC*, pages 2009–2016, June 2007.

[31] M. Roughan, W. Willinger, O. Maennel, D. Perouli, and R. Bush. 10 lessons from 10 years of measuring and modeling the Internet's autonomous systems. *IEEE Journal on Selected Areas in Communications*, 29(9):1810–1821, Oct. 2011.

[32] U. Weinsberg, Y. Shavitt, and E. Shir. Near-deterministic inference of AS relationships. In *IEEE ConTEL*, pages 191–198, June 2009.

[33] H. Yihua, M. Faloutsos, S. Krishnamurthy, and M. Chrobak. Obtaining provably legitimate Internet topologies. *IEEE/ACM Transactions on Networking*, 20(1):271–284, Feb. 2012.

[34] Young Hyun. CAIDA: Archipelago Measurement Infrastructure. `http://caida.org/projects/ark`.

Peering at Peerings: On the Role of IXP Route Servers

Philipp Richter
TU Berlin
prichter@inet.tu-berlin.de

Georgios Smaragdakis
MIT / TU Berlin
gsmaragd@csail.mit.edu

Anja Feldmann
TU Berlin
anja@inet.tu-berlin.de

Nikolaos Chatzis
TU Berlin
nikolaos@inet.tu-berlin.de

Jan Boettger
TU Berlin
jan@inet.tu-berlin.de

Walter Willinger
Niksun
wwillinger@niksun.com

ABSTRACT

During the last few years, more and more of the medium-to-large Internet eXchange Points (IXP) around the world have started to operate a *route server* and offer its use as a free value-added service to their members. This service has greatly simplified inter-domain routing for those members and has made it easy for them to peer with possibly hundreds of networks at those IXPs from the get-go.

In this paper, we report on an empirical analysis that is based on a unique collection of IXP-provided datasets from two different European IXPs that operate a route server and gave us access to a wealth of route server-specific BGP data. Both IXPs also made the traffic datasets that they routinely collect from their public switching infrastructures available to us. Using this information, we perform a first-of-its-kind study that correlates a detailed control plane view with a rich data plane view to reason about the different peering options available at these IXPs and how some of the major Internet players make use of them. In the process, we highlight the important role that the IXPs' route servers play for inter-domain routing in today's Internet and demonstrate the benefits of studying IXP peerings in a manner that is not agnostic but fully aware of traffic. We conclude with a discussion of some of the ramifications of our findings for both network researchers and operators.

Categories and Subject Descriptors

C.2.3 [**Computer-Communication Networks**]: Network Operations—*Network Management*

Keywords

Internet Exchange Point (IXP); Peering; Routing; BGP.

1. INTRODUCTION

There are currently some 350+ Internet eXchange Points (IXP) worldwide, and some of the largest and most successful IXPs have more than 500-600 members and carry as much traffic as some of the global Tier-1 ISPs. With membership growth rates of 10-20% per year and annual traffic growth rates of 50-100%, these IXPs have emerged as key entities in the Internet infrastructure where a vast majority of today's peering connections are established. This growing importance of IXPs for the Internet peering ecosystem and the IXPs' increasing popularity with the full spectrum of Internet players have come in full view with recent studies such as [17, 21, 25, 36].

One of the main reasons for this emergence of IXPs as some of the most densely connected physical components in today's Internet has been the fact that many of them have started to offer the use of *route servers (RSes)*[1] as a free value-added service to their members. In essence, using an IXP's RS greatly simplifies routing for its members – a member AS has to set up just a single BGP session to connect to possibly hundreds of other member ASes. That is, most members use an IXP's RS to establish *multi-lateral* peerings (i.e., one-to-many) as compared to *bi-lateral* peerings (i.e., one-to-one). However, except for the fact that the peering fabrics of IXPs with RSes are significantly richer than of those that don't offer a RS, little is known in general about how IXPs operate RSes or how the members of such IXPs incorporate the use of RSes in their decision-making process that ultimately determines what sort of traffic is sent to/received from which of the other IXP members over what type of peering links.

The main contribution of this paper is an original and in-depth study of IXP RSes, from their architecture and deployment "in the wild" to their use by today's wide spectrum of Internet players. Our study combines a detailed control plane view of IXP-related peerings with a corresponding rich data plane view to examine how IXPs operate their RSes and, at the same time, reason about the different peering decisions that networks make when they connect with other networks at today's IXPs. To perform this analysis, we rely on our ongoing collaboration with an increasing number of European IXPs, which provided us access to a unique collection of datasets. Two of the IXPs operate a RS and gave us access to RS-specific BGP data and also made the traffic datasets that they routinely collect available to us.[2]

By correlating connectivity-related with traffic-specific aspects of peering at the level of individual links as well as routed prefixes, our analysis highlights the important role that the IXPs' RSes have started to play with respect to inter-domain routing in today's Internet. Among the key observations of our study are:

- RSes are key enablers for offering new and complex peering options to IXP members and also providing open access to a significant portion of Internet routes. At our IXPs, the

[1] Note, while the term "route server" often refers to a "route collector/monitor" or "Routeviews server", we use it exclusively to refer to an IXP route server [29, 31] as defined in Section 2.2.

[2] We also have data from a third, small European IXP; however, since this small IXP does not operate a route server, its data is not a focus of this paper.

IMC '14, November 05–07 2014, Vancouver, BC, Canada.

http://dx.doi.org/10.1145/2663716.2663757.

prefixes advertised via the RSes cover some 80-95% of the traffic and include many popular destinations.

- Due to the popularity of RSes, multi-lateral peering increasingly dominates classical bi-lateral peering in terms of number of peerings but not in terms of traffic; in fact, the majority of the traffic at our IXPs traverses bi-lateral peerings. Nevertheless, some of the top traffic contributors at each IXP use mainly multi-lateral peering.
- RS usage varies across IXPs and IXP members; while we observe certain patterns of RS usage among IXP members with similar business types, we illustrate the wide range of existing peering strategies with a number of case studies involving key Internet players as well as networks with interestingly complex peering setups.

These findings have ramifications for a number of recent developments that involve network operators and researchers alike. In particular, as many network operators are eagerly experimenting with and scrutinizing the wealth of peering alternatives that IXPs provide (e.g., to reduce transit costs, increase performance and robustness), a number of researchers are either exploring the evolution of the peering ecosystem as a whole or examine ways to innovate inter-domain routing. We contribute to each of these developments by providing an in-depth assessment of peering at IXPs with an emphasis on understanding and highlighting the role of IXP RSes in these different efforts.

For example, the recently launched Open-IX initiative [11] aims at establishing European-style IXPs in the USA. Its main objective is to increase the diversity in available peering options for networks in the US where the cost associated with the dominant form of interconnection (i.e., private peering or cross connects) is almost six times as much as in Europe [15], mainly because of limited competitive interconnection options. To understand the current Internet peering ecosystem and inform studies concerned with its evolution over time, our work provides a first in-depth look into a marketplace (i.e., Europe) where, thanks to the popularity of IXP RSes, networks have in general an abundance of interconnection options and have already acquired certain skills in using the available options strategically in support of their particular business.

At the same time, researchers have recently recognized the importance of the growing popularity of IXPs for trying to fundamentally improving inter-domain routing. In fact, the main premise of the work on Software Defined eXchanges (SDX) [27] is that IXPs are ideal venues for deploying new technologies such as Software Defined Networking (SDN) – only the mechanisms used at the IXP itself (e.g., RS operation) need to be changed while the rest of the Internet can remain unchanged. As a first account of practical RS usage "in the wild" that illustrates the innovative use of today's RSes for inter-domain routing, our work complements and informs these recent efforts. In particular, it contributes to the identification of new IXP service offerings that are beyond the capabilities of today's RSes but can be fully supported when relying on new technologies such as SDN.

Moreover, for the Internet measurement community, we demonstrate how our proprietary datasets can be used "for the good of science"; that is, calibrating the quality of the latest BGP measurements that are becoming publicly obtainable via Looking Glasses on some IXP RSes. By showing what parts of the ground truth of the peering fabrics of those IXPs are visible in these publicly available datasets and observing that the vast majority of the observed IXP traffic is destined to the RS prefixes, we significantly increase the value that these publicly available datasets will have for future studies by third parties.

The rest of the paper is structured as follows. Section 2 is an introduction to RS design and operation. In Section 3, we describe the different sets of control and data plane measurements that are available to us. We use this data in Section 4 to revisit connectivity-related issues and rely on it in Section 5 to study usage-related aspects of peerings. Moving beyond the traditional link perspective of peerings, we examine in Section 6 peering opportunities and traffic at the level of routed prefixes. We provide a longitudinal study of peering at IXPs in Section 7. We then study how different players implement peering in Section 8. We conclude in Section 9 and 10 with a discussion of trends in Internet peering and related open research problems.

2. TRENDS IN IXP OPERATIONS

IXPs offer a shared switching fabric where the members can exchange traffic with one another once they have established peering connections (public peering) between them. This generic service provided by IXPs is an example of a *(positive) network effect* (also known as *network externality* [34]) because the more members an IXP has, the more valuable that IXP is to each member. Especially in Europe where many IXPs operate on a not-for-profit basis [21], this observation has led to significant innovations at IXPs in the form of constantly expanding service offerings.

2.1 Background and motivation

An important example of a new IXP service offering has been the free use of IXP-operated RSes. With more IXPs operating RSes, the membership base of those IXPs keeps growing and more of their member ASes start using the RS service. The resulting proliferation of multi-lateral peerings creates new options for the member ASes to peer with one another which, in turn, causes them to reconsider their existing peering arrangements. At the same time, the ease with which networks can join IXPs and start using them has led to a trend whereby one and the same AS can be a member at multiple IXPs, often within the same city or geographic region.

In effect, offering the free use of their RSes has created a positive feedback loop for those IXPs. With more networks connecting to such an IXP, more member ASes use its RS and connect with most or all other members at the RS. This increases connectivity and typically also traffic, which in turn attracts yet more networks to join the IXP. Thus, while we are observing an Internet peering ecosystem in flux, a pre-requisite for studying the current system to ultimately reason about its evolutionary path is to have a basic understanding of "all things concerning RSes." Given the central role that IXP RSes play in this paper, we describe in this section the basic operations of an IXP RS and discuss the main reason for the observed bandwagon effect.

2.2 The IXP RS as enabler

The typical way to establish connectivity between two ASes is to establish a direct BGP session between two of their respective border routers. Initially, if two IXP member ASes wanted to exchange traffic via the IXP's switching fabric, they had to establish a *bi-lateral (BL)* BGP peering session at the IXP. However, as IXPs grew in size, to be able to exchange traffic with most or all of the other member ASes at an IXP and hence reap the benefits of its own membership, a member's border router had to maintain more and more individual BGP sessions. This started to create administrative overhead, operational burden, and the potential of pushing some router hardware to its limit.

To simplify routing for its members, IXPs introduced RSes and offered them as a free value-added service to their members. In short, an IXP RS is a process that collects routing information from

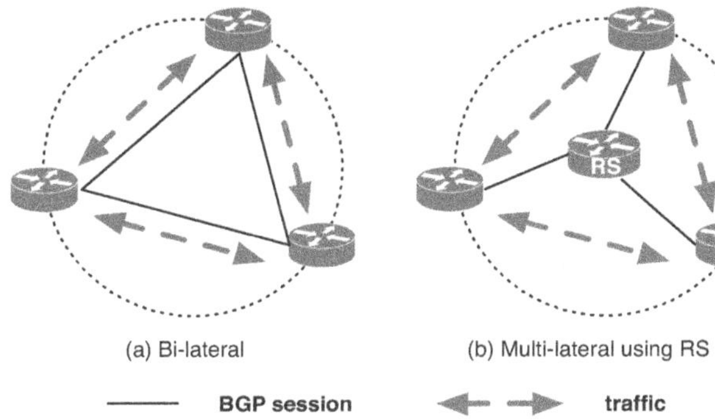

Figure 1: IXP peering options.

the RS's peers or participants (i.e., IXP members that connect to the RS), executes its own BGP decision process, and re-advertises the resulting information (i.e., best route selection) to all of the RS's peer routers. Figure 1 shows the flow of control plane information (BGP sessions) and data packets (data plane) for both traditional bi-lateral peering as well as peering via the RS at an IXP. The latter is referred to as *multi-lateral (ML)* peering because it typically involves more than two BGP partners.

A member AS just connects to the RS via a single BGP session to set up BGP peering with all other IXP members that peer with the RS.[3] Clearly, this lowers the maintenance overhead, in particular for small ASes. Note, however, that using the RS (i.e., ML peering) does not preclude BL peering by one and the same member AS. In particular, larger ASes can take advantage of the RS while still having the option to establish BL peerings with selectively-chosen IXP members. For example, if a large member AS finds the capabilities of the RS to be insufficient for its needs (e.g., with respect to traffic engineering or filtering) or prefers to have more control over the peerings with its most important peers, it can use BL peerings with the latter and ML peerings with those members that peer with the IXP's RS.

Note that the IXP RS is not involved in the data path. Moreover, it executes the BGP decision process based on the information it learns from its peers. Thus, there is no guarantee that the best route selected by the RS is the same as the one that the peer would have selected given a full set of BL peering sessions. In this sense, while using a RS solves a scalability problem, it has the potential of creating a new problem known as the *hidden path problem* [31]. For example, if different peers of the IXP's RS advertise routes for the same prefix, only one route will be selected and re-advertised to all other peers. If this route cannot be propagated to a certain peer (e.g., because of export filtering restrictions), that peer will not be able to receive any route for this prefix, even though an alternative path was advertised to the RS by a different peer. While this hidden path problem was an issue with earlier versions of RS software, recent advances have largely overcome the problem, and in Section 2.4, we describe a popular Internet routing daemon that addresses this problem by providing support for maintaining peer-specific routing tables. We recall that a similar problem also occurs in the context of large ISPs where *route reflectors* are used to redistribute routes to iBGP peers [20].

2.3 On the deployment history of RSes

The first RSes were designed and deployed in the US as part of the decommissioning of the NSFNET around 1995 [26]. However,

[3]For redundancy purposes, IXPs typically operate two RSes and encourage their members to connect to both RSes.

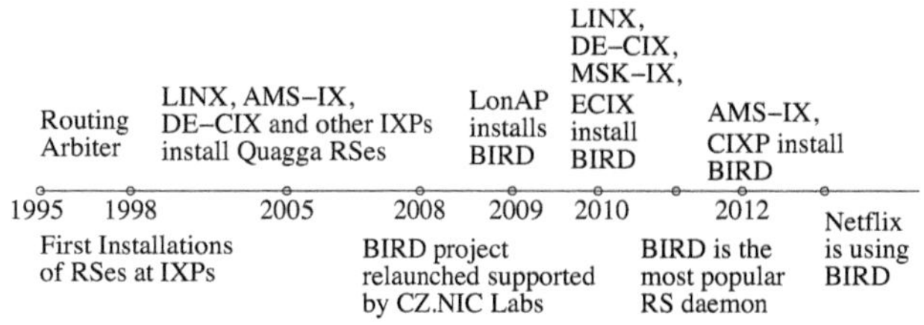

Figure 2: Route server deployment time line.

the service never took off due to the small size of the largest US IXPs at that time (i.e., MAE-East's membership approached some 20 ASes in mid-1990).[4]

Although some IXPs (e.g., DE-CIX in Frankfurt) offered the use of a route server as early as mid-1990, it took another 10 years and the increasing popularity of some European IXPs for the RS concept to re-emerge and gain momentum. In fact, around 2005 an increasing number of European IXPs already offered RS capabilities to their members. The de-facto RS at that time was Quagga [14]. However, early versions of Quagga suffered from the hidden path problem and had numerous operational problems (e.g., prefix filtering, resource consumption, performance limitations) [30, 32]. Later versions of Quagga and OpenBGPD [12] addressed most of these problems and started to be deployed around 2008. Difficulties with its maintenance prevented OpenBGPD from being widely adopted and deployed [38].

In 2008, the BIRD [16] project was relaunched (the initial project dates back to 1999), and it took just three years for BIRD to become the most popular IXP route server [4]. Figure 2 shows a time line when some of the larger IXPs migrated to BIRD. In fact, the success of BIRD goes beyond RSes. Since 2013, it is the core routing component of the Netflix Open Connect Appliance [10].

2.4 BIRD: A popular router daemon for RSes

BIRD is an open-source software routing daemon. The project was launched in 2008. The software was developed by CZ.NIC Labs and has been actively supported by the IXP community. In the following, we describe a BIRD configuration that has been abstracted from the Euro-IX RS example [4] and is the basis of the one in operational use by one of the IXPs with which we have an ongoing collaboration.

Like all routing daemons, BIRD maintains a Routing Information Base (RIB) which contains all BGP paths that it receives from its peers – the Master RIB. However, when using BIRD as RS, it can be configured to (i) maintain peer-specific RIBs and (ii) use them instead of the Master RIB for peer-specific BGP best path selection (see Figure 3). When configured this way, each member AS that peers with the RS maintains a BGP session with the RS, which results in a peer-specific RIB. When IXP member AS X advertises a prefix to the RS, it is first put into the AS X-specific RIB. Next, if this prefix passes the AS X-specific import filter, it is added to the RS' Master RIB. If the export filter of AS X allows it, then this prefix will also be added to each AS Y-specific RIB, where AS Y is any other IXP member that connects to the RS. Then the RS performs a peer-specific best path selection and exports the prefix by re-advertising it to each AS Y.

IXPs typically apply import filters to ensure that each member AS only advertises routes that it should advertise. To derive import filters, the IXPs usually rely on route registries such as IRR [7]. This policy limits the likelihood of unintended prefix hi-

[4]The RIPE RS [19] was a precursor of the RS proposed in [26].

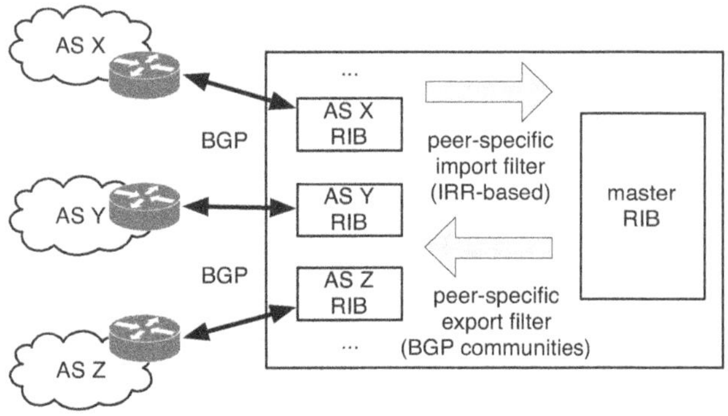

Figure 3: BIRD route server: Example setup with peer-specific RIBs and import/export filtering.

jacking and/or advertisements of bogon prefixes including private address space. With respect to export filters, they are typically triggered by the IXP members themselves to restrict the set of other IXP member ASes that receive their routes. The commonly used vehicle for achieving this objective is to tag route advertisements to the RS with RS-specific BGP community values [24]. These values are set on a per route basis and restrict to which members the route can be propagated. Thus, by using export filters, peers of the RS can express policies.

Using peer-specific RIBs overcomes the hidden path problem, because the BGP decision process is executed for each peer independently. If the best route for a certain prefix cannot be re-advertised to some particular members (e.g., because of export filters), the RS can still select and advertise an alternative route to those particular members – presuming that another, non-blocked route is available.[5] Maintaining separate RIBs for each RS peer has a cost in terms of memory requirements and processing capabilities. However, recent stress tests and real deployment performance reports for BIRD at large IXPs [22, 33, 32] show that maintaining about 400 RIBs, each with up to 100K prefixes, consumes roughly 4 GB of memory and can be achieved with commodity servers.

2.5 Looking glasses and RSes

The fact that network operators typically cannot see the results of their route announcements within their own network makes debugging BGP routing difficult. To address this problem, the community has set up BGP looking glasses (LGes) and route monitors (RMes) in many different locations across the Internet. LGes are user-interfaces, co-located on routers. Many of them are publicly accessible and can be used by anyone to execute a limited number of commands. On conventional LGes the commands include ping, traceroute, as well as some BGP commands. The latter provides details about all BGP sessions of the router. In the past, LGes have also been used by researchers to gain better visibility into the AS-level topology and IXP-specific peering fabrics [28, 18].

LGes can also be co-located with RSes at IXPs. In this case, the LGes act as proxies for executing commands against the Master RIB of the RS and are equipped with additional capabilities that may include commands which list (a) all prefixes advertised by all peers and/or (b) the BGP attributes per prefix. Such LGes (referred to as LG-RS below) are already available at some IXPs, including DE-CIX and LonAP, and they have recently been used to explore AS connectivity at IXPs [25].

[5]Also for iBGP route reflectors, the advantage of using peer-specific RIBs and independent decision processes is discussed [40].

IXP	L-IXP	M-IXP	S-IXP	L-IXP & M-IXP
Member ASes	496	101	12	50
Tier-1 ISPs*	12	2	1	2
Large ISPs*	35	4	1	4
Major Content/ Cloud Providers*	17	5	0	5
RS (IPv4/IPv6)	BIRD Multi-RIB	BIRD Single-RIB	No	/
Public RS-LG (IPv4/IPv6)	Yes	Yes, limited commands	No	/
Member ASes using the RS	410	96	/	43

Table 1: IXP profiles: members and RS usage.

3. DATA SOURCES

In this section, we describe the European IXPs with which we have fruitful ongoing collaborations and that have been very forthcoming with sharing their IXP-internal datasets with us. We provide details about these proprietary datasets as well as the public IXP-external datasets that are at our disposal for this study.

3.1 Profiles of our IXPs

We focus in the following on the two IXPs (denoted L-IXP and M-IXP) that operate a RS. These IXPs differ greatly in size (e.g., number of members and traffic) and service offerings that they provide for their members. For comparison, Table 1 that summarizes some key features of our IXPs and their members also includes some basic information about our third IXP (denoted S-IXP). This IXP is representative of the large number of smaller IXPs (i.e., less than 20 members) that do not operate a RS. However, for the remainder of this paper, we will only consider L-IXP and M-IXP and will not use the S-IXP.

Large IXP (L-IXP): With close to 500 members and peak traffic that exceeded 3 Tbps in late 2013, this IXP is one of the largest IXPs in Europe and worldwide. It operates a layer-2 switching fabric that is distributed over a number of colocations/datacenters within a metropolitan area. Members can connect on ports ranging from 1 to 100 Gbps. Its membership includes the full spectrum of networks, including CDNs, content providers, hosters and the whole range of ISPs (from Tier-1 to regional to local providers). This IXP provides arguably one of the richest and most advanced service offerings, including SLAs, remote peering,[6] and black-holing (mitigation of distributed denial of service attacks e.g., [8]). One of its key service offerings is the free use of its RS. It operates two (for redundancy) IPv4 and IPv6 RSes using a BIRD configuration similar to the one discussed in Section 2.4 with advanced LG support.

Medium IXP (M-IXP): This medium-sized IXP operates a layer-2 switching fabric, and is present in several locations. Half of its members are also members at the L-IXP. As of late 2013, this IXP had 101 members and its peak traffic exceeded 250 Gbps. It offers ports ranging from 1 to 100 Gbps. Among service offerings such as remote peering, it also offers the free use of its RS (again, two for each IPv4 and IPv6). However, this RS does not support peer-specific RIBs, and its LG allows the execution of only a limited set of commands.

[6]The router of the "remote peer" can be located anywhere in the world and is connected to the IXP typically via an Ethernet-over-MPLS connection e.g., [2].

3.2 IXP-internal data: Route server

For both IXPs that operate a RS (i.e., L-IXP and M-IXP), we have access to the data from their BIRD deployment. In the case of L-IXP, we have weekly snapshots of the peer-specific RIBs, starting in June 2013. For M-IXP, we have several snapshots of the Master-RIB, starting in December 2013. In addition, for L-IXP, we have all BGP traffic to and from its RS that is captured on the network interface via tcpdump.

The unique advantage of having access to these IXP-provided control plane measurements is that they are rich enough to accurately and completely reconstruct the "ground truth" in terms of connectivity at these IXPs that has been established with the help of the RS, i.e., the IXPs' multi-lateral peering fabrics.

3.3 IXP-internal data: Traffic

For each of our IXPs, we have access to data plane measurements in the form of traffic that is routinely collected from the IXPs' public switching infrastructures. More precisely, for each IXP, the available datasets consist of massive amounts of sFlow records [42], sampled from their public switching infrastructure. The measured sFlow records contain Ethernet frame samples that have been collected using random sampling (1 out of 16K). sFlow captures the first 128 bytes of each sampled frame. Thus, they contain full Ethernet, network- and transport-layer headers, as well as some bytes of payload for each sampled packet. For further details about relevant aspects of these collected sFlow records (e.g., absence of sampling bias, removal of irrelevant traffic), see [17].

We rely on 4 continuous weeks of collected sFlow for each IXP. For L-IXP we cover a 4-week period in August/September 2013, and for M-IXP we cover a 4-week period in December 2013.[7] In addition, we also use snapshots collected at the L-IXP that date back to 2011 and cover periods of two weeks.

Having access to these IXP-provided data plane measurements makes it possible to examine the connectivity that has been established without the use of the IXPs' RSes (i.e., bi-lateral peerings). However, more importantly, these measurements provide valuable but hard-to-obtain information about how the two parties of an IXP peering use that link and for what purpose.

3.4 Public IXP-specific data

In our work, we also rely on a number of widely-used public datasets, including BGP data from the route collectors from RIPE RIS, Routeviews, PCH [13], and Abilene [6]. We refer to them as RM BGP data. Moreover, we use the data from the RS-LG at the L-IXP in accordance with the method described in [25]. In addition, we rely on data obtained from several publicly accessible LGes which query the routing tables of routers that belong to members peering at the L-IXP.

4. CONNECTIVITY: BI-/MULTI-LATERAL

Relying on our IXP-provided measurements, we show in this section how we can get close to recovering the actual peering fabrics at the IXPs. We also illustrate what portions of those actual peering fabrics can and cannot be recovered when using the different public BGP data.

*The numbers reflect only the well-known and easy-to-identify networks by business type to illustrate the existence of common members. No attempt at a complete classification has been made.

[7]To assess a possible bias due to the holiday season, we performed our analysis also using only the first week in December and got consistent results.

Multi-lateral Peerings: RS RIBs				
	IPv4		IPv6	
	symmetric	asym.	symmetric	asym.
L-IXP	65,599	14,153	34,596	5,086
M-IXP	3,140	594	1,173	434
Bi-lateral Peerings: Inferred from Data-Plane				
	bi-/multi	bi-only	bi-/multi	bi-only
L-IXP	14,673	5,705	4,256	3,727
M-IXP	399	61	223	75
Total Peerings				
L-IXP	85,457 (70%)		43,409 (35%)	
M-IXP	3,795 (75%)		1,682 (33%)	
Visibility in the RS Looking Glass				
L-IXP	all multi-lateral		all multi-lateral	
M-IXP	none		none	

Table 2: Multi-lateral and bi-lateral peering links.

4.1 Connectivity: IXP-provided data

To determine if IXP members AS X and AS Y are using a ML peering at the IXP, we rely on the IXP-provided RS data. More specifically, for the L-IXP, we first check if AS X and AS Y peer with the RS. If so, we next check in the peer-specific RIB of AS Y for a prefix with AS X as next hop. If we find such a prefix, we say that AS X uses a ML peering with AS Y. If we also find AS Y in the peer-specific RIB of AS X as next hop, we say that the ML peering between AS X and AS Y is *symmetric or bi-directional*; otherwise, we say that the ML peering between AS X and AS Y is *asymmetric*.

Given that the RS at the M-IXP only uses the Master RIB but no peer-specific RIBs, we re-implement the per-peer export policies based upon the Master RIB entries to determine peerings via the RS. More specifically, if there is a route for a prefix in the Master RIB with AS X as next hop, we postulate a ML peering with all member ASes that peer with the RS, including AS Y, unless the community values associated with the route explicitly filter the route via the peer-specific export filter to AS Y.

To determine if IXP members AS X and AS Y are using a BL peering at the IXP, we rely on the IXP-provided traffic measurements. In particular, to conclude that AS X and AS Y established a BL peering at the IXP, we require that there are sFlow records in the IXP-provided traffic data that show that BGP data was exchanged between the routers of AS X and AS Y over the IXP's public switching infrastructure.[8] We cannot however differentiate between asymmetric and symmetric BL peerings with these data plane measurements.

Note that our methodologies yield a lower bound for BL peerings and an upper bound for ML peerings, but there is evidence that these bounds are in general very tight. For example, with respect to BL peerings, our method is not significantly biased by the sFlow sampling rate because the numbers are very stable once we use data from more than two weeks. Indeed, Figure 4 shows that for the L-IXP, the additional BL peerings seen in the third (fourth) week are less than 1% (0.5%). As far as ML peerings are concerned, our method does not account for the fact that some RS peers might reject the advertisements of the RS, which can result in some overcounting by our method. At the same time, we find member ASes that use one and the same link for ML as well as for BL peering.

Our best efforts to reconstruct the actual ML and BL peering fabrics of our IXPs is summarized in Table 2. We further break

[8]The routers' IP addresses have to be within the publicly known subnets of the respective IXP.

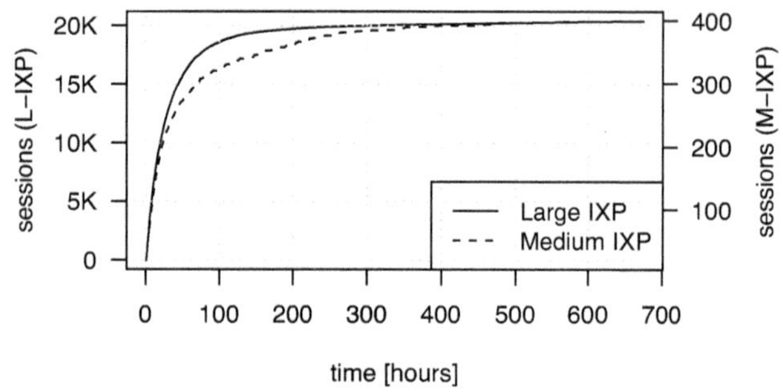

Figure 4: Inferred bi-lateral BGP sessions over time.

down (where possible) each of the ML and BL peering fabrics into links that are used for either IPv4 or IPv6 and in a symmetric or asymmetric manner. For each IXP, we also tally the total number of peerings along with the peering degree (percentage of established peering links compared to the number of possible peering links).

4.2 Connectivity: Public BGP data

To assess the ability of the various public BGP datasets to provide visibility into the peering fabrics of our IXPs and compare with our findings in Section 4.1 above, we first mine the RS-LG BGP data that has recently been considered and used in [25] and is publicly available. The results are shown in Table 2. There are three main take-aways. First, when restricting the study to the L-IXP that has an RS-LG with the capabilities listed in Section 2.5, the new methodology proposed in [25] is indeed successful in recovering the full-fledged ML peering fabric of that IXP. Second, as the example of the M-IXP shows, having a RS-LG that lacks the necessary querying capabilities is of no help for inferring the IXP's ML peering fabric.[9] Third, irrespective of the capabilities of the RS-LG, the RS-LG BGP data cannot be used to reveal any peerings of the L-IXP's and M-IXP's BL peering fabrics.

For completeness, we also obtained the number of peerings that can be discovered from mining the traditional and widely-used RM BGP data. The results confirm past findings that a majority of the peerings (i.e., some 70-80%) cannot be seen in those data [17, 18, 24, 41]. In addition, we also notice a significant bias in this data towards BL peerings. Interestingly, this data does produce peerings between IXP member ASes that we do not see even in our most complete peering fabrics discussed in Section 4.1. One possible explanation for seeing such peerings in the public but not in the IXP-provided BGP data is that the member ASes in question engage in *private peering* at the IXP[10] or peer in a different location.

Summary

We observe a dense peering mesh at our IXPs, with ML peerings outnumbering BL peerings by a ratio of 4:1 and 8:1 at the L-IXP and the M-IXP respectively. Thus, connectivity at these IXPs is clearly driven by their RSes and the resulting ML peerings. For IPv6 connectivity we note that at both IXPs, the number of IPv6 peerings is roughly half of the number of IPv4 peerings. LGes co-located with IXP RSes are able to uncover the full ML peering fabric, assuming they support an advanced set of commands. BL peerings remain hidden and can only partly be inferred using public RM BGP data.

5. FROM CONNECTIVITY TO TRAFFIC

In this section, we are mainly interested in how many of the established peerings reported in Table 2 are actually "used"; that is, see traffic. Furthermore, we are interested in the actual distribution of traffic when taking the type of the peering link into account.

5.1 Identifying traffic-carrying peerings

To identify a traffic-carrying peering between AS X and AS Y, we look for sFlow records that (i) contain MAC addresses which belong to AS X and AS Y, respectively, and (ii) have IP addresses that are not part of the IP address space assigned to the IXP. Thus, we only count the exchange of non-local IP traffic, which allows us to clearly separate control traffic (i.e., BGP sessions) and actual data traffic, thus we can distinguish between BL peerings with and without traffic. Once we identified a traffic-carrying peering link, we assign it to be either BL or ML, depending on our earlier introduced inference. For a small portion of the traffic (less than 0.5% for both IXPs) we did not find a corresponding BL or ML peering link. We discard this traffic from our analysis.[11]

In this context, for IXP member ASes that peer with other member ASes at the IXP both bi-laterally and multi-laterally, we are faced with the problem of determining whether the observed traffic between two such ASes is traversing the BL or ML peering link between them; that is, identifying the traffic-carrying peering(s). Taking a pragmatic approach, when two IXP member ASes peer with one another at the IXP both bi-laterally and multi-laterally, we tag the BL peering between them as the traffic-carrying peering and associate any observed traffic with it. Intuitively, our argument for this approach is based on the observation that compared to ML peering, establishing a BL peering requires work (e.g., manually setting up BGP sessions) and is an indication of joint incentives and needs between the involved parties. On the other hand, peering multi-laterally at the IXP (i.e., using the RS) is designed to be easy and informal, making it in general possible to exchange traffic with all the RS's peers from the get-go.

To provide empirical support for our argument, we manually searched for LGes that query the routing tables of member routers that peer both bi-laterally and multi-laterally with other members. We found six such LGes with sufficient capabilities to reason about the best path selected. In all cases, advertisements via BL sessions were selected as best path over advertisements from the RS.[12]

5.2 Traffic over ML and BL peerings

The results of our analysis of the traffic-carrying links are summarized in Table 3. When compared to Table 2, the first column in Table 3 shows that most peering links (i.e., more than 80% at both IXPs) are actually "used" in the sense of the binary attribute "carry traffic/no traffic". Moreover, we note that the ratio of traffic-carrying peerings is largest for BL peerings, followed by symmetric ML peering, followed by asymmetric ML peering.

Moving beyond this binary classification of peering links, this usage picture sharpens when examining the second column of Table 3. This column shows for each IXP the number of peerings that are responsible for 99.9% of the IXP's total traffic; that is, all

[9] Some portion of the ML peering fabric may be recovered but only with substantial additional efforts. For example, by using prefixes extracted from the RIPE RIS or Routeviews data, a portion of the IPv4 prefixes on the Master RIB of the M-IXP can be recovered and used to submit queries to this RS-LG.

[10] Private peerings at IXPs are handled completely separate from the IXP's public switching infrastructure and are not part of our study.

[11] Possible explanations for this traffic are either non-detected BGP sessions or peerings using protocols other than BGP (e.g., static routing).

[12] Selection of BL over ML was typically done by setting the local preference to a higher value for routes received via BL sessions. However, we point out that is not necessarily true for all peerings.

IPv4	L-IXP		M-IXP	
	all	99.9p	all	99.9p
% BL	92.4	55.6	93.5	47.7
% ML sym.	85.9	31.3	83.7	24.0
% ML asym.	23.8	5.43	38.5	7.89
links total	67,915	28,849	2,968	918

IPv6	L-IXP		M-IXP	
	all	99.9p	all	99.9p
% BL	76.2	4.92	74.9	7.17
% ML sym.	54.0	0.52	52.2	0.48
% ML asym.	30.4	0.04	25.3	0.07
links total	24,159	556	819	24

Table 3: Percentage of links that carry traffic (all traffic vs. top 99.9% of all traffic) and their corresponding type.

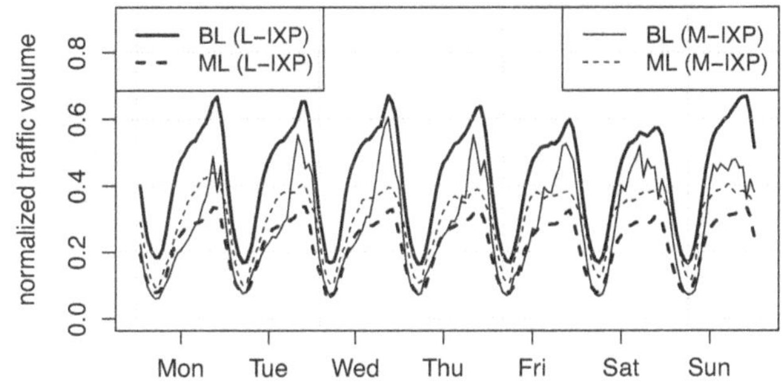

(a) Timeseries of traffic over BL/ML links.

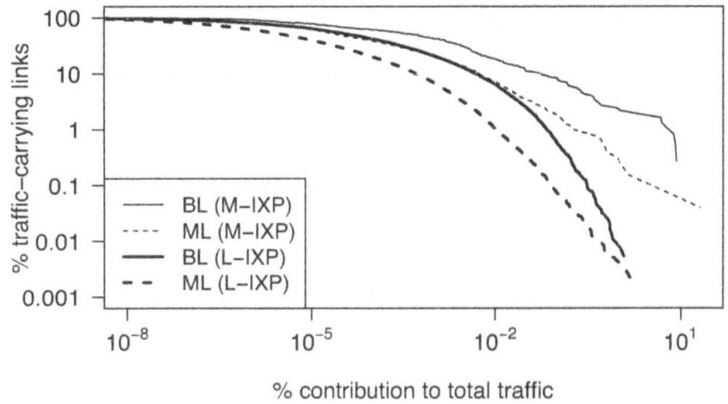

(b) CCDF: Traffic distribution over BL/ML links.

Figure 5: Traffic: bi-lateral (BL) and multi-lateral (ML).

peerings that collectively see less than 0.1% of the overall traffic are discarded.[13] When imposing such thresholds to eliminate peerings that carry only comparably little amounts of traffic, we observe a drastic reduction of the number of active peerings. Indeed, the main take-away from this thresholding exercise is that it puts the connectivity-related findings reported in Section 4.2 into proper perspective. Specifically, it demonstrates that while RSes increase connectivity and are responsible for the larger part of peerings, a majority of those ML peerings typically does not carry much traffic. At the same time, the smaller number of BL peerings that are established at IXPs carry in general the bulk of the traffic.

As a by-product of this thresholding, we also notice that essentially none of the large number of IPv6 peerings that have been established at our IXPs carry any significant traffic. Thus, while connectivity for IPv6 is there, traffic still ranges in the order of less than 1% at each of our IXPs. As a result, for the remainder of this paper, we will focus exclusively on IPv4 traffic that traverses the IXPs' switching infrastructures. Nevertheless, it is worthwhile to mention that some links are only present for IPv6 but not for IPv4.

To assess the overall contribution of BL and ML peerings, we map the total traffic of the L-IXP and M-IXP onto the BL and ML peerings that have been established at each of these IXPs. Figure 5(a) shows a time series for the traffic on BL and ML peerings at both IXPs over a one-week period. We observe that even though there are much fewer BL peerings than ML peerings at L-IXP, the total amount of BL traffic is more than twice the total amount of ML traffic. To contrast, for M-IXP, this BL:ML traffic ratio is more like 1:1.

Even though this traffic-centric picture of IXP peerings emphasizes the significance of BL peerings, ML peerings do play an important role. Figure 5(b) shows a CCDF of the distribution of traffic over BL/ML peerings. As far as the top traffic-contributing peerings are concerned, BL and ML peerings contribute similar amounts of traffic. In fact, for both the L-IXP and the M-IXP, the top traffic-contributing peering is a ML peering which highlights the critical role that the use of IXP RSes play in today's Internet.

Summary

While most peerings at our IXPs (e.g., some 80%) do carry traffic, BL peerings are more likely to carry traffic when compared to ML peerings. Taking traffic volumes into account, the small number of BL peerings clearly dominate the large number of ML peerings, with observed traffic ratios of 2:1 (L-IXP) and 1:1 (M-IXP). Thus, the majority of ML peerings only carry small amounts of traffic, but some of the top traffic-contributing links at both IXPs are ML peerings.

[13]Note that the corresponding thresholds still require a monthly traffic volume of some tens resp. hundreds of GBs at each IXP.

6. FROM TRAFFIC TO ROUTES: PREFIXES

In this section, we move beyond the link perspective of peerings and peering traffic and instead examine peerings at the level of routed prefixes. We show how this new perspective allows us to reason about peering opportunities at IXPs and the different peering options chosen by member ASes.

6.1 A prefix view of peering

An outward sign of the popularity of the RS service offering with the member ASes of the L-IXP and M-IXP is the large number of ML peerings that have been established at those IXPs. To further understand what set of routes RSes at popular IXPs offer – e.g., to understand the instant benefits that a new member AS can reap when connecting to the IXP's RS – we check each prefix that is advertised via the RS and count to how many of the RS's peers this prefix is exported. For the L-IXP, Figure 6(a) shows the resulting histogram (y-axis in log-scale) and reveals a striking bi-modality – either a prefix is exported to almost all members or to only a few selected ones. Focusing on the mode to the right, the sizable fraction of prefixes that is exported to almost all member ASes is a reflection of the very peering-friendly policies at the IXP. Summing up all the prefixes that are exported by the RS to more than 90% of its peers shows that a new IXP member will receive more than 65K routes from some 11K different origin ASes at the L-IXP and more than 12.5K routes from about 3K different origin ASes at the M-IXP (see Table 4) once connected to the RS.

As far as the mode to the left in Figure 6(a) is concerned, the sizable fraction of prefixes that are exported to fewer than 10% of the RS's peers is an indication that the strategy offered by the IXPs to restrict (block) the propagation of certain routes to certain members is effective and used. Upon closer inspection, we also observe that

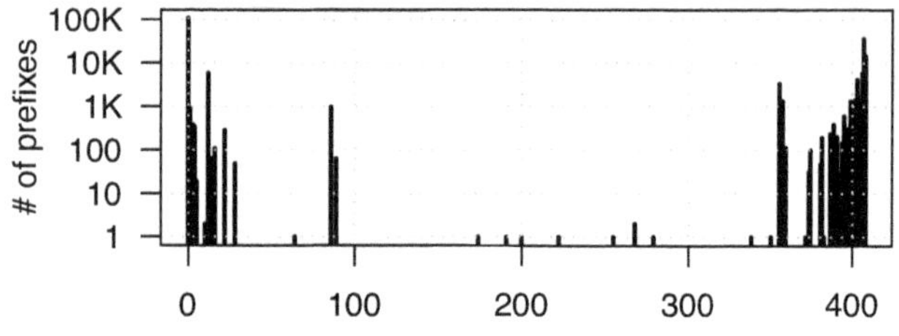

(a) Number of prefixes.

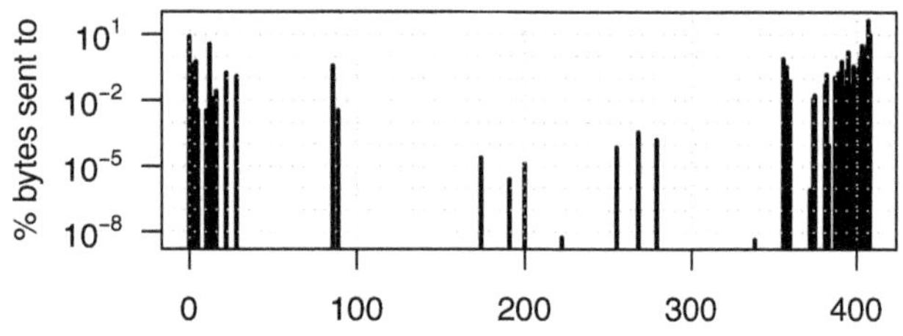

(b) Traffic share.

Figure 6: Prefixes advertised via the RS in relation to the number of member ASes they are exported to (L-IXP).

	L-IXP		M-IXP	
Export to % of peers	< 10%	> 90%	< 10%	> 90%
Prefixes	112.5K	68.0K	171	12.6K
/24 Equivalent	1.97M	819K	7.4K	337K
Origin ASes	13.06K	11.1K	44	3.0K

Table 4: Breakdown of advertised IPv4 address space.

the sets of reachable origin ASes for the mode to the left and mode to the right are largely disjoint. For M-IXP (not shown), we note that while the number of advertised prefixes and the corresponding reachable address space is much smaller, the vast majority of prefixes are exported to almost all peers.

To illustrate, of the 408 member ASes that connect to the L-IXP RS, we find that only some 24 limit the export of some or all of their prefixes. However, 371 members export their prefixes to more than 90% of the members participating in the RS. At M-IXP, we see an even more peering-friendly environment with only very few members applying strict export filtering for a small number of prefixes.

6.2 A prefix view of traffic

To complement the connectivity-centric prefix-level, we are now interested in how this corresponds to actual traffic exchanged. By matching all destination IP addresses of traffic exchanged (irrespective of the link type) on the aggregate of RS prefixes, we see that more than 80% of the overall traffic at L-IXP (95% at M-IXP) is sent towards RS prefixes. Hence, the prefixes advertised at RSes give significant insight into spatial aspects of its actual traffic components.

In view of Figure 6(a), we are especially curious about how much traffic is related to those prefixes that are exported to almost every peer of the RS and to those that are exported to only a few selected peers of the RS. We compute the percentage of traffic that each prefix at the RS is responsible for and plot in Figure 6(b) their sum as a function of the number of the RS's peers to which the RS exported the prefix. While we observe a similar bi-modality as in Figure 6(a), the openly-advertised prefixes are responsible for the

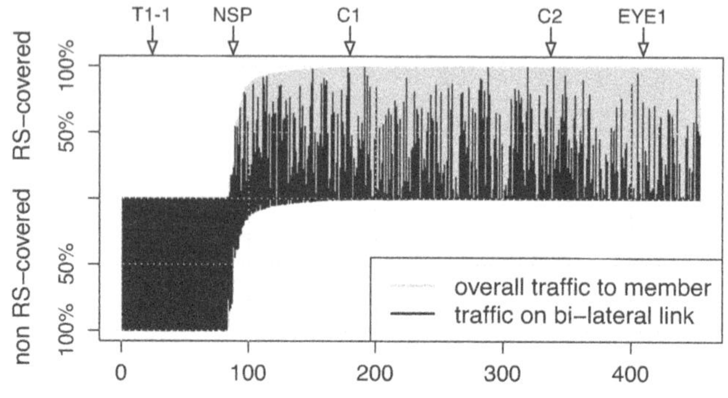

(a) L-IXP.

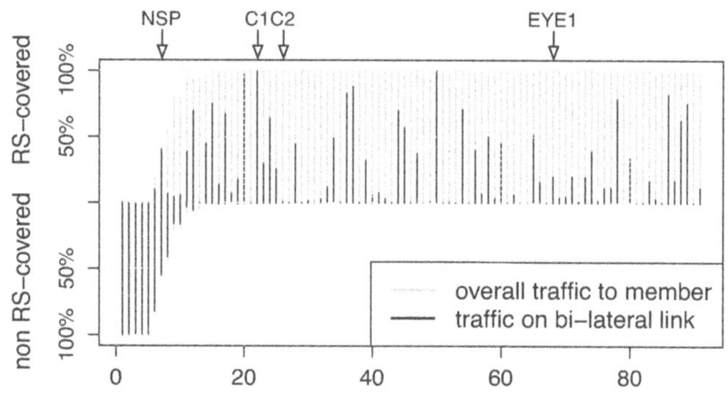

(b) M-IXP.

Figure 7: Traffic to member: to RS prefixes (upper half in each plot) / non-RS prefixes (lower half in each plot) with ML/BL traffic grey/black.

largest traffic share. While the percentage of traffic covered by the very selectively-advertised prefixes (exported to less than 10% of the member ASes using the RS) is about 9% of all traffic, the more openly-advertised prefixes (exported to more than 90% of the member ASes using the RS) cover the destination addresses of almost 70% of all exchanged traffic in terms of bytes.

6.3 A closer look at RS usage

To this point, we have mainly focused on the overall traffic at the IXPs and how it relates to the prefixes that are advertised via the IXP's RS. In particular, we have paid little attention to the per-member AS policies that determine which ASes advertise their prefixes to which other ASes and over what kind of IXP peering. On the one hand, a majority of members openly advertise their prefixes via the RS, and these prefixes cover a majority of the IXP traffic. At the same time, we see the bulk of traffic traversing BL links. Thus, we would like to know if members advertise different prefixes to the IXP's RS and over their BL peering session, i.e., what is the overlap in terms of routes advertised via both sessions.

The problem we face is that while we know the route set advertised over ML peerings, we only have binary information about the existence of BL peerings (i.e., we sampled BGP packets indicating an active BL session). To deal with this issue, we rely on properties of the actual traffic exchanged between members. In particular, we check for each IXP member if the traffic it receives is fully covered by the prefixes advertised via the RS or if there is traffic to a superset of RS prefixes. More precisely, to obtain Figure 7(a), we compute for each member AS of the L-IXP (x-axis) which fraction of the traffic sent to this member is (i) covered by the prefixes that this specific member advertises via the IXP's RS (shown in upper half of the plot) and (ii) not covered by the prefixes this member advertises to the RS (see lower part of the plot). Before plotting these values, we sort them in increasing order, starting with those members for which none of their traffic is covered by the RS prefixes. To minimize the impact of churn (new route advertisements, route withdrawals), we use one week of traffic, starting on the same day for which we have the corresponding RS dump.

Figure 7(a) shows that for the majority of members (to the right of $x \approx 120$), all traffic they receive is covered by the prefixes they advertise via the RS; that is, there is no traffic at the IXP destined to any addresses outside these prefixes – for these members, the RS is all there is! For another set of members (to the left of $x \approx 85$), we see that none of the traffic they receive is covered by the RS prefixes advertised by them. These members either do not connect to the RS at all or do not advertise any prefixes via the RS. Finally, there is a small group of member ASes in the middle (around $x = 100$) that use prefixes that they advertise via the RS as well as prefixes that they do not advertise via the RS. We discuss these cases in more detail in Section 8.2. In terms of numbers, about 67% of all traffic is sent to members on the right part of this figure and roughly 26% of the traffic is destined to the members in the cluster on the left. The members in the middle-section receive about 7% of all traffic – a significant share given the small number of members in the middle-section. For M-IXP, the members in the right part account for more than 95% of the traffic.

Figure 7 uses grey-shading to indicate which portion of a member's traffic is associated with BL or ML peerings. For example, the members that only peer bi-laterally are all black (the few exceptions are due to churn in route advertisements). Member ASes that only peer multi-laterally are all grey. In addition, some members are highlighted in terms of their main business type, and we will return to this cast of players in Section 8 below. Together, Figures 7(a) and 7(b) show that while most member ASes use BL and ML peerings, the majority of members only receive traffic for those prefixes that they also advertise via the RS. Thus, the need to advertise a different route set bi-laterally and multi-laterally can — in most cases — be ruled out as the reason for two member ASes to peer both bi-laterally and multi-laterally with each other at an IXP (following up on the discussion in Section 5.1). Instead, the reasons are more likely a question of control and trust (see discussion in Section 9.3), but more mundane reasons such as the ease with which ML peerings can be established and the lack of incentives to remove/block prefix advertisements via the RS once a BL peering has been established might also play a role.

Summary

Our IXP RSes provide access to a significant portion of the Internet's routes and networks and most member ASes provide open access to their RS-prefixes to all IXP RS participants. The routes advertised openly via the RS are indeed routes to popular destinations and they receive a majority of the traffic at both IXPs. In turn, the route set of an IXP RS is a good approximation of the popular destinations as seen from this IXP. Individual member ASes typically exhibit a binary behavior: either all routes for which traffic is received are advertised via the RS or none at all. Many member ASes that openly advertise their prefixes via the RS also establish BL sessions to selected other members ASes - without advertising a superset of prefixes on these sessions. This observation agrees with publicly-stated peering policies from large content providers (see, e.g., Google [5]), which state that BL peerings can be established once a significant amount of traffic is exchanged. We also see cases in which member ASes advertise a different route set on BL peerings than on ML peerings and discuss some of them in Section 8 below.

From To	04-2011 12-2011	12-2011 06-2012	06-2012 12-2012	12-2012 06-2013
# (ML ⇒ BL)	577	440	546	435
Δ Traffic	+86%	+230%	+82%	+204%
# (BL ⇒ ML)	172	175	189	242
Δ Traffic	+20%	-77%	-65%	-42%

Table 5: Number of peerings changed from BL type to ML type and vice versa and corresponding changes in traffic volumes carried over these peerings (L-IXP).

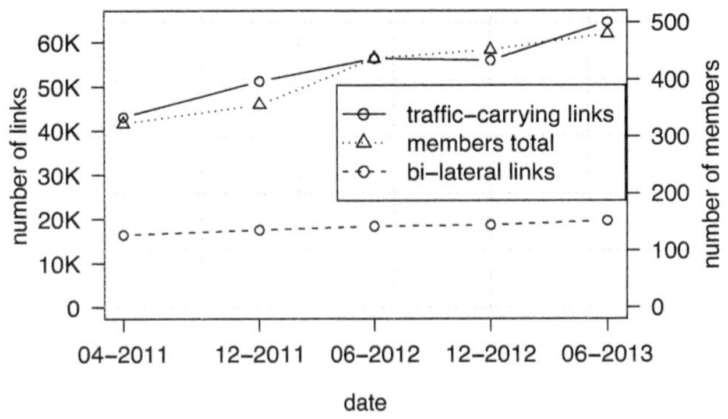

Figure 8: Number of peerings over time (L-IXP).

7. CHANGE CHANGES THINGS

With our IXP datasets, we are observing an Internet peering ecosystem in flux. With more IXPs operating RSes, more members peer multi-laterally and connect to more than one IXP. In this section, we examine in more detail how IXP peerings at the L-IXP change over time and how the common members at the L-IXP and the M-IXP use those IXPs.

7.1 Same IXP: IXP peerings over time

Taking advantage of our historical collection of sFlow records from L-IXP, we perform a longitudinal study of the IXP peerings at this IXP. To examine the relationship between BL and ML peerings during the last 2+ years, we focus on the traffic-carrying peerings and rely on the methodology described in the latter part of Section 4.1 to infer BL peerings. The results are depicted in Figure 8 and illustrate that while the total number of observed traffic-carrying links has increased noticeably during this time period, the number of BL peerings has only increased slightly. Thus, the observed increase in the number of traffic-carrying peerings is mainly due to the proliferation of ML peerings. Taking into account our earlier observation that only about 85% (24%) of symmetric (asymmetric) ML peerings do carry actual traffic, we can conclude that the number of established ML peerings exceeds the number of traffic-carrying ML peerings by some 5-10k links. At the same time, we find that the ratio of total BL peering traffic to total ML peering traffic has stayed constant at around 65–67% (not shown), a reminder that from a traffic perspective one has to consider both types of peerings.

To examine in more detail the dynamics of peerings over time, we consider next five different two-week snapshots of sFlow data, dating back to 2011. For each snapshot, we identify the traffic-carrying BL peerings and tag the remaining traffic-carrying links as

		L-IXP yes	L-IXP no
M-IXP	yes	67.9%	11.4%
	no	12.1%	8.6%

(a) Connectivity across IXPs.

		L-IXP yes	L-IXP no
M-IXP	yes	50.9%	13.6%
	no	22.8%	12.7%

(b) Traffic across IXPs.

		L-IXP BL	L-IXP ML
M-IXP	BL	27.8%	3.2%
	ML	22.6%	46.4%

(c) Peering type across IXPs.

Figure 9: Peerings between common members across L-IXP and M-IXP. Consistency regarding connectivity, traffic exchange and peering type.

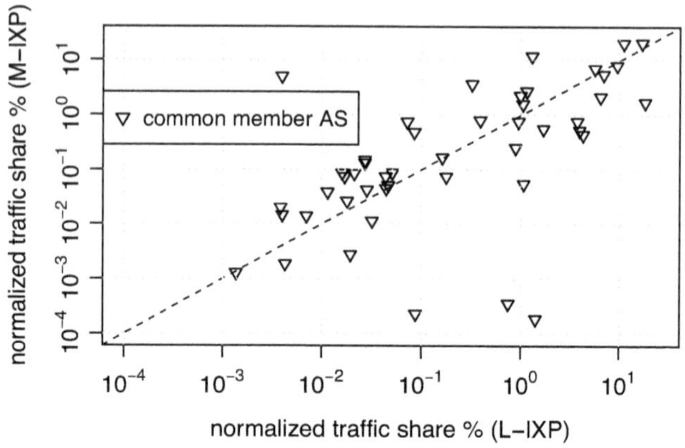

Figure 10: Common ASes: Normalized traffic share.

ML peerings. Then we check if the same traffic-carrying peerings that are present in two consecutive snapshots have changed their peering type or not (see Table 5). Although some small amount of churn could result from our inability to detect all BL sessions in a given snapshot (see Section 4.1), we observe that the number of changes from ML-to-BL and BL-to-ML, respectively, are relatively stable. The churn caused by ML peerings being replaced by BL peerings is consistently higher than the churn that is due to the peering types changing from BL to ML. We also notice that the traffic volume on these peerings increases substantially if the type changes from ML to BL. In contrast, a peering type change from BL to ML typically goes along with a significant decrease in the amount of traffic that gets exchanged. These observations support the argument that BL peerings are typically established and used if there is significant traffic volume that may or may not need additional BGP capabilities (see e.g., [5]). Another reason for encountering more ML-to-BL than BL-to-ML changes is that when new members join an IXP, they typically start with ML peerings and may switch later on to BL peerings with a subset of IXP member ASes.

7.2 Different IXPs: Common members

We next perform a comparative analysis and check how networks make use of the two IXPs that cover by and large the same geographic region. The two IXPs have 50 members in common (see Table 1). Figure 9 summarizes the results of our comparison with respect to connectivity (i.e., peerings and peering type) and traffic. Of these 50 common ASes, more than 75% use consistent peering setups in the sense that if they are peering/not peering with one another at one IXP, they also do so at the other IXP. At the same time, more than 20% do peer at one IXP but not at the other IXP. However, not all of these peerings see traffic, and the percentages of traffic-carrying peerings are reported in the second sub-table of Figure 9. As far a the types of these traffic-carrying peerings are concerned, we observe that in 46% of the cases ML peering is used at both locations and BL peering in 28% of the cases. This observation is consistent with the overall picture (not presented) and shows that while the member ASes at M-IXP use predominantly ML peerings, it is more often the case that the member ASes use BL peering at the L-IXP. In fact, the BL peerings common to both IXPs make up almost half of all traffic-carrying BL peerings at M-IXP.

To illustrate the common members' contributions to the traffic volume at the two IXPs, Figure 10 shows for all common member ASes that exchange traffic at the two IXPs how their normalized traffic shares compare. The scatter-plot shows for each common member AS the fraction of its traffic at the L-IXP (x-axis) vs. the fraction of its traffic at the M-IXP, where we normalize by all traffic over the common peerings. The observed clustering around the diagonal is an indication that the common member ASes' (relative) contributions to the respective overall peering traffic at the two IXPs are similar. A similar strong clustering can also be seen when examining the common members' contributions at the level of common peering links (not shown).

The overall picture that emerges from studying the common member ASes at the two IXPs and how they use the different IXPs is consistent with their profiles (see Section 3). For example, the ASes in the upper right corner of Figure 10 are the well-known big content providers/CDNs and make extensive use of both IXPs – they use the L-IXP because of its global role as a critical hub in today's Internet, and they are at M-IXP because of its mainly regional role as a place for small-medium eyeball networks to connect. On the other hand, the few outliers in Figure 10 (e.g., point in upper left and points in lower right) are typically smaller regional networks that prefer one IXP over the other for reasons such as location, reach, and needs. In addition, for the latter to establish connectivity at the two IXPs via the IXPs' RSes is very low overhead and justifies membership at the IXPs, irrespective of any imminent need to exchange traffic.

Summary

Our longitudinal analysis of the L-IXP shows that while its RS is clearly the main driver for increasing connectivity among member ASes at this IXP, the traffic ratio between BL and ML peering stays largely constant, with BL peerings accounting for twice as much traffic. Switch-overs from ML to BL peering typically occur when there is an increase of traffic carried over that link. For ASes that are members at two IXPs, we observe that peering links with other networks are largely consistent across the different IXPs. We also notice that the relative traffic contributions of members peering at our two IXPs exhibit strong correlations. This is also the case for common traffic-carrying peerings between the same ASes across IXPs.

AS	RS usage L/M IXP	Notes	# traffic links	# BL links	%BL traffic
C1	yes / yes	open peering	417 / 82	329 / 41	91 / 99
C2	yes / yes	open peering	392 / 73	138 / 2	35 / 0.5
OSN1	no /-	only BL	248 / -	256 / -	100 / -
OSN2	yes / -	open peering	337 / -	0 / -	0 / -
T1-1	no / no	very selective	3 / 0	22 / 0	100 / -
T1-2	yes / -	no-export	18 / -	19 / -	100 / -
EYE1	yes / yes	open peering	405 / 77	134 / 11	74 / 20
EYE2	yes / yes	open peering	401 / 77	198 / 41	84 / 72

Table 6: Case Studies: RS usage, number of traffic-carrying links, number of BL links, fraction of traffic seen on BL links at the L-IXP/M-IXP.

8. CASE STUDIES

In this section, we take a closer look at some of the well-known major players in today's Internet that send significant traffic over the public switching fabrics of either L-IXP or M-IXP. We are interested in understanding how they make use of these IXPs so that we can reason about their choices of peering options, and assess whether there are typical patterns for ASes of the same business type.

8.1 Our cast of big players

Our selection of "big players" was driven by the volume of traffic they exchange at L-IXP or M-IXP, by the type of businesses they represent, and by their geographic reach. To this end, we chose two ASes that are responsible for a significant share of content in today's Internet and are among the top traffic contributors at both IXPs where each of their traffic share is over 10% (C1 and C2). Moreover, we picked two popular Online Social Networks (OSN) that use the IXPs extensively (OSN1 and OSN2), two regional eyeball providers (EYE2 and EYE1), and two Tier-1s (T1-1 and T1-2).

There are two basic observations from our characterization work described in the previous sections. First, the big content providers and the regional eyeball networks are actively using the IXPs' RSes and peer openly, most likely to reduce transit cost and reduce latency. On the other hand, the Tier-1s which include some of the major eyeball networks with presence in Europe and overseas peer more restrictively and often do not use the RS. Our findings about the selected players are summarized in Table 6 and show some unexpected yet important differences.

In the case of the two major content providers, we note that C1 exchanges most of its traffic via BL peerings. However, this content provider actively markets the RS connectivity and maintains many ML peering sessions. On the other hand, C2 exchanges more than half of its traffic via the ML peerings and we notice an increasing tendency towards ML peerings for this player over the last two years. In both cases, their prefixes are openly advertised to all members and we see 100% resp. 99% of the traffic sent towards these members covered by the prefixes they advertise via the RS.

When examining the two OSNs, the most striking finding is that they approach peering completely different, choosing the two extremes of the spectrum of available peering options. On the one hand, OSN1 only offers BL peering and is not present at the IXPs' RS. A likely reason is that this OSN wants to have control over its traffic flows. On the other hand, OSN2 only does ML peering at IXPs like L-IXP that are outside of this OSN's home country. In fact, their publicly announced peering policy states that they try to avoid BL BGP sessions wherever peering using a RS is possible. A plausible reason to choose this option is to reduce the administrative overhead associated with BL peering.

As for the Tier-1s, in contrast to the US where Tier-1s typically do not use the IXPs' public switching fabrics, many Tier-1s connect at L-IXP, including our players T1-1 and T1-2. One of them also connects at M-IXP. Focusing on our two Tier-1s, they all use a selective peering policy which is often interpreted to mean that they do not use the RS. While this is true for most of them, we see some exceptions. T1-1, for example, does indeed not use the RS at all at either of the IXPs. While T1-2 connects to the L-IXP RS, it tags all of its routes with the NO-EXPORT community which implies that none of them are shared with any of the other ASes that are at the RS. Thus, this Tier-1 also solely relies on bi-lateral connections. The reason for its presence at the RS is unclear to us but might be a hint towards early exploration of RS usage.

The regional eyeball providers, EYE1 and EYE2 both peer openly utilizing the RS at both IXPs. We see all of the traffic sent to these members covered by their RS prefixes. While we notice a tendency towards more ML peerings at the M-IXP vs. the L-IXP, both eyeball networks also use BL peerings, with EYE2 relying mostly on BL sessions.

8.2 Players with hybrid peerings

Figure 7 (left lower part) clearly shows that some members only peer bi-laterally at L-IXP or M-IXP. The other large group of members consists of those that advertise all prefixes for which they receive traffic via the RS but receive varying amounts of traffic via BL peerings. However, the more intriguing cases are those members that occupy the small middle part in Figure 7 (e.g., around $x = 100$) and advertise some prefixes via the RS, but receive traffic for a superset of these prefixes. While this fraction of members is rather small compared to the overall number of members, we see some important players here, carrying significant traffic volumes. We select two cases, namely CDN, a mid-sized content delivery network and NSP, a large transit provider. We have seen that content providers typically advertise their prefixes openly and large transit providers advertise them more selectively. CDN and NSP differ from these typical cases by following a "hybrid" peering strategy by advertising some prefixes multi-laterally, some others only bi-laterally to selected member ASes.

In the case of CDN, we find that close to 90% of its incoming traffic is covered by the small number of openly advertised RS prefixes. However, this AS also has some 59 BL peering links, and on most of them we see traffic to a superset of the prefixes advertised via the RS.[14] We assume that this is as an example of complex traffic engineering performed by today's CDNs that, in this case, involves both using the vast connectivity provided by the RS, as well as the application of more fine-granular prefix advertisements for specific networks, e.g., to fulfill performance requirements for certain customers.

NSP advertises some 5K prefixes openly via the RS, and most of them contain subsequent ASNs in the AS path that are not other ASNs of the NSP. Nevertheless, most traffic is exchanged via BL peering sessions and only about 20% of NSP's incoming traffic is covered by its RS prefixes. While at L-IXP, NSP receives traffic from most members ASes, many of them peer bi-laterally with NSP and some of them send traffic to a large superset of the prefixes advertised via the RS. Interestingly, we see a very similar pattern for NSP also at M-IXP where it receives about 45% of its traffic for prefixes advertised via the RS and the other part for a super-

[14]We verified that a superset of prefixes is advertised on these sessions by using the LGes of IXP members. Moreover we note that the corresponding paths were prepended.

set. Again, we validated the advertisement of a superset of prefixes using LGes of IXP members having BL sessions with NSP. We assume that NSP's hybrid approach to peering is in support of its main business (e.g., transit provider), and hints towards growing diversification of models in the transit business (see e.g., [35], [23]). We note that NSP is present at many IXPs and thus might have more confidence and experience in making use of RS functionality, tailored to its business interests, than other transit providers.

Summary

Among the networks that have an open peering policy and utilize IXP RSes, we observe a diverse set of players ranging from content providers to eyeball networks. While many networks that utilize the RS also rely on additional BL peerings, some only use the RS (i.e., no BL peerings) and others (particularly larger transit networks) typically do not use RSes at all. We also observe networks with hybrid peering strategies in the sense that they advertise parts of their routes via the RS and others via BL peerings, hinting towards advanced usage of RSes.

9. DISCUSSION

Our empirical study of real-world IXP RS deployments and how IXP RSes are being used by a wide range of today's Internet players has implications for IXP and network operators as well as researchers.

9.1 On the benefits of connecting to an IXP

The success of the large European IXPs is an example of a (positive) network effect "in action." As these IXPs have been growing in size, their value for each of their members has increased, but managing and maintaining the ensuing bi-lateral peerings (i.e., large number of corresponding BGP sessions) has became a burden for many of these members. To alleviate this burden, these IXPs have started to offer their members the free use of their route servers, and this service has contributed to making those IXPs even more attractive to yet more networks.

To quantify this attractiveness, our empirical results suggest a concrete step that IXPs and network operators could take for effectively evaluating the instant benefits that a network can reap when connecting (either directly or remotely) to an IXP. In particular, we have seen that at our two IXPs, where a majority of the members connect to the RS (i.e., more than 80% of the L-IXP's members and more than 90% of the M-IXP's members), the prefixes advertised by each of the two IXPs' RSes cover some 80-95% of all traffic seen and include many of the most popular destinations. Thus, if IXPs provide the profile of routes that are advertised via their RSes (e.g., via adequately-supported LGes), network operators can immediately determine how much of their individual traffic would reach these destinations from "day one" (i.e., as soon as they start connecting to the IXP's RS). They can then compare the different available interconnection options in terms of costs, performance or other criteria to make an informed decision about which IXP(s) they want to connect to and how they want to make use of the IXP's RS (see Section 8).

Although we lack comparable data from the other large European IXPs that operate a RS, the fact that a majority of their members connect to the RS (e.g., some 70% at LINX, over 80% at AMS-IX) suggests that their RSes cover a similarly large portion of traffic seen at those IXPs as observed at the L-IXP and M-IXP. However, we caution against generalizing our RS-specific observations across the spectrum of IXPs worldwide. For example, even in Europe there are large regional IXPs (e.g., NL-IX) where the reported member participation at the RS is less than 50%. Looking beyond Europe, while many of the larger IXPs in North America operate a RS (e.g., Equinix, Any2), little is known about member participation in the RS[15] and typically no information is available about the portion of traffic covered by such an IXP's RS.

9.2 A peering ecosystem in flux

Our findings show that the popularity of the IXPs' RSes has led to a proliferation of ML peerings, but at this point, a majority of the traffic that is exchanged at a typical IXP is still exchanged via BL peerings. However, as more networks explore how to best use their many easy-to-establish and simple-to-maintain ML peerings (e.g., as back-up, as primary connection, only for certain traffic or particular peers) and try to incorporate them into their complex peering decision making processes, the current picture is bound to undergo constant changes, especially if the IXPs keep on innovating and improving RS functionalities and operations. Thus, new research efforts are required for developing and deploying appropriate monitoring infrastructures that yield reliable data for sensing the onset of possible "sea changes" in the future Internet peering ecosystem and also providing insight into the reasons for their occurrence.

In this context, although the IXP-provided data used in this study is proprietary, we show in Section 4 how it can be put to good use by increasing the value of certain publicly available datasets for future studies by other researchers. For example, proprietary data often enables a direct comparison between inferred connections (based on publicly available information) and actual connections (based on proprietary information), and we illustrate this capability in this paper by calibrating the quality of the BGP measurements that are becoming publicly available from RS-LGes in selective IXPs.

The use of such vetted public data would be of particular interest in the context of monitoring the impact (or lack thereof) of the recently launched *Open IX (OIX)* initiative [11]. This initiative's main objective is to bring more peering opportunities to the US interconnection marketplace that has historically been dominated by an inordinately small number of players whose main focus has been on private peering offerings (i.e., cross connects). As a result of this situation, prices for cross connects in the major metropolitan areas in the US are about six times as high as in the major European cities, where peering opportunities are abundant, especially in places with highly successful IXPs. Among the early developments related to the OIX initiative that was launched less than a year ago are the establishment of new European-style IXPs in the USA by the largest European IXPs (e.g., LINX in Northern Virginia [9], AMS-IX and DE-CIX in New York [1, 3]) and a formal certification process whereby the certified commercial data center and colocation provider companies explicitly agree to house certified IXPs in their facilities. Only time will tell if these early developments will bring about the "sea change" within the US peering ecosystem that the supporters of OIX are advocating, but our findings point to concrete data collection efforts that should be pursued to assess the actual impact of OIX in the US (e.g., encouraging the deployment of RS-LGes by the IXPs in the US and the continuous data collection from these emerging new vantage points).

9.3 Innovation in inter-domain routing

Based on our description of today's RSes, their popularity is understandable because establishing connectivity in the control plane via a RS is simple (i.e., requiring basically one BGP session setup), efficient (in terms of receiving routes to a significant part of the Internet), and quick (i.e., an ability to start exchanging traffic from the

[15] A noteworthy exception is SIX in Seattle, which started offering RS services in 2014 and provides a Looking Glass showing all members connecting to the RS and their advertised routes.

get-go). In this sense, the relatively recent RS offerings by IXPs can be viewed as a concrete example of an innovation in inter-domain routing, an area that is notorious for resisting changes to or deploying improvements over the status quo (i.e., BGP).

More importantly, our discussions of the design and operations of today's IXP RSes show that they do not forward any data traffic and adhere to a strict separation of control plane and data plane. This observation makes RS design and operations a prime candidate for Software Defined Networking (SDN) which, in turn, suggests that IXPs are natural places for harnessing SDN's power to improve if not revolutionize inter-domain routing. In fact, the concept of a software defined Internet exchange (SDX) is the topic of a recent paper [27] in which the authors consider novel approaches to innovation at the IXP RSes, including software support for a range of policies for inter-domain traffic engineering with BGP that are either difficult to perform using current RS capabilities or simply out of reach for today's RS implementations.

In fact, by describing how RSes are used in practice, our work is complementary to [27] and raises a number of questions that are mainly concerned with issues such as flexibility, trust, and security. Addressing these and related issues as part of the SDX effort would have far-reaching implications, mainly because they have prevented some of the larger players to rely and depend on the IXPs' RSes. For example, member ASes that want to control which prefixes are advertised to which other member ASes typically have the BGP know-how to peer bi-laterally to achieve the desired control over the traffic they receive. While the use of the RS does not preclude such control, peering bi-laterally offers a member AS additional opportunities for BGP traffic engineering, e.g., AS-path prepending, MED, scoped advertisements [39] etc., that are currently not fully supported by RSes. More generally, how to expand the effort described in [27] to also include bi-lateral peering as part of the proposed SDX approach looms as an interesting open problem.

With respect to trust-related issues, IXP operators are aware of concerns that some of their member ASes have about RS availability, RS operations, RS monitoring/debugging capabilities, and security at the RS.[16] For example, there currently exist no SLAs for the RS itself, but most of the IXPs operate redundant RSes.[17] From an operational perspective, there are numerous opportunities for misconfigurations at the RS (e.g., filter setup, mis-shapes with routing registries), and the monitoring capabilities at today's RSes are still in their infancy. In terms of security, an RS adds an additional middleman that has to be trusted with the proper handling of all route advertisements. In this context, large IXPs may be opportune places for future deployment of BGP security mechanisms such as sBGP [37].

10. CONCLUSION

Using a collection of IXP-provided datasets that offer unprecedented visibility into the control plane (i.e., BGP data from the RS) and data plane (i.e., sFlow measurements) as seen at two European IXPs, we report in this paper on an in-depth study of IXP RSes for the purpose of understanding an IXP's full-fledged public peering fabric; that is, the existence of peerings (i.e., connectivity) as well as their usage (i.e., traffic) and how they are used by which player and for what reasons. In the process, we obtain an accurate picture of the relative importance of ML peerings (large in numbers, but responsible for only a minority of the traffic) vs. BL peerings (small in numbers, but carrying the bulk of the traffic). More importantly, when moving beyond the traditional link-level perspective of peering and examining the correlation between the control and data plane views at the prefix-level, reasoning about which ASes peer with which other networks (e.g., how and for what reasons) becomes feasible. This, in turn, leads to new insight into how the IXPs' RSes are used by their member ASes and demonstrates that these RSes are quickly becoming critical enablers for connectivity and, as a result, integral entities of today's Internet inter-domain routing system that deserve the full attention of networking researchers.

Acknowledgments

We want to express our gratitude towards the IXP operators for their generous support and feedback. We thank our shepherd Phillipa Gill and the anonymous reviewers for their helpful feedback.

This work was supported in part by the EU project BigFoot (FP7-ICT-317858). Georgios Smaragdakis was supported by the EU Marie Curie International Outgoing Fellowship "CDN-H" (PEOPLE-628441).

11. REFERENCES

[1] AMS-IX New York. https://nynj.ams-ix.net/.

[2] AMS-IX Partner Program. https://ams-ix.net/connect-to-ams-ix/partner-program.

[3] DE-CIX New York. http://nyc.de-cix.net/.

[4] Euro-IX Resources: Traffic, Reports, and Best Practices. https://www.euro-ix.net/resources.

[5] Google Peering Policy. https://peering.google.com/about/peering_policy.html.

[6] Internet2 Network Research Data. http://noc.net.internet2.edu/i2network/research-data.html.

[7] IRR - Internet Routing Registry. http://www.irr.net.

[8] LINX: Black Holing Support for DDoS Attack. HotLINX 34, https://www.linx.net/files/hotlinx/hotlinx-34.pdf.

[9] LINX NoVA. https://www.linx.net/service/publicpeering/nova.

[10] Netflix Open Connect. https://signup.netflix.com/openconnect.

[11] Open-IX Association. http://www.open-ix.org/.

[12] OpenBGPD Border Gateway Protocol. http://www.openbgpd.org/.

[13] Packet Clearing House routing archive. https://www.pch.net/resources/data.php.

[14] Quagga Routing Suite. http://www.nongnu.org/quagga/.

[15] TeleGeography (press release on September 24, 2013): U.S., Europe Colocation Pricing Models Vary Significantly. http://www.telegeography.com/press/marketing-emails/2013/09/24/u-s-europe-colocation-pricing-models-vary-significantly/index.html.

[16] The BIRD Internet Routing Daemon. http://bird.network.cz.

[17] B. Ager, N. Chatzis, A. Feldmann, N. Sarrar, S. Uhlig, and W. Willinger. Anatomy of a Large European IXP. In *ACM SIGCOMM*, 2012.

[18] B. Augustin, B. Krishnamurthy, and W. Willinger. IXPs: Mapped? In *ACM IMC*, 2009.

[19] T. Bates. Implementation of a Route Server for Policy Based Routing across the GIX Project, 1993.

[16] Personal communication with IXP operators.

[17] The L-IXP reported zero downtime during 2013.

[20] M. O. Buob, S. Uhlig, and M. Meulle. Designing optimal iBGP route-reflection topologies. In *IFIP Networking*, 2008.
[21] N. Chatzis, G. Smaragdakis, A. Feldmann, and W. Willinger. There is More to IXPs than Meets the Eye. *ACM CCR*, 43(5), 2013.
[22] O. Filip. BIRD's flight from Lisbon to Prague. RIPE 60.
[23] P. Gill, M. Schapira, and S. Goldberg. A survey of interdomain routing policies. *ACM CCR*, 44(1), 2014.
[24] V. Giotsas and S. Zhou. Improving the Discovery of IXP Peering Links through Passive BGP Measurements. In *Glob. Internet*, 2013.
[25] V. Giotsas, S. Zhou, M. Luckie, and kc claffy. Inferring Multilateral Peering. In *ACM CoNEXT*, 2013.
[26] R. Govindan, C. Alaettinoglou, K. Varadhan, and D. Estrin. Route Servers for Inter-domain Routing. *Computer Networks*, 30, 1998.
[27] A. Gupta, Vanbever L, M. Shahbaz, S. P. Donovan, B. Schlinker, N. Feamster, J. Rexford, S. Shenker, R. Clark, and E. Katz-Bassett. SDX: A Software Defined Internet Exchange. In *ACM SIGCOMM*, 2014.
[28] Y. He, G. Siganos, M. Faloutsos, and S. V. Krishnamurthy. A systematic framework for unearthing the missing links: Measurements and Impact. In *NSDI*, 2007.
[29] N. Hilliard, E. Jasinska, R. Raszuk, and N. Bakker. Internet Exchange Route Server Operations. IETF draft, draft-ietf-grow-ix-bgp-route-srver-operations-01, 2013.
[30] M. Hughes. Route Servers at IXPs – Bugs and Scaling issues with Quagga. UKNOF 13.
[31] E. Jasinska, N. Hilliard, R. Raszuk, and N. Bakker. Internet Exchange Route Server. IETF draft, draft-ietf-idr-ix-bgp-route-server-03, 2013.
[32] E. Jasinska and C. Malayter. (Ab)Using Route Servers. NANOG 48.
[33] A. Labrinidis and E. Nguyenduy. Route Server Implementations Performance. 20th Euro-IX Forum, April 2012.
[34] S. J. Liebowitz and S. E. Margolis. Network Externality: An Uncommon Tragedy. *J. Econ. Perspectives*, 8(2), 1994.
[35] A. Lodhi, A. Dhamdhere, and C. Dovrolis. Open Peering by Internet Transit Providers: Peer Preference or Peer Pressure? In *IEEE INFOCOM*, 2014.
[36] A. Lodhi, N. Larson, A. Dhamdhere, C. Dovrolis, and kc claffy. Using PeeringDB to Understand the Peering Ecosystem. *ACM CCR*, 44(2), 2014.
[37] R. Lychev, S. Goldberg, and M. Schapira. Is the Juice Worth the Squeeze? BGP Security in Partial Deployment. In *ACM SIGCOMM*, 2013.
[38] C. Malayter. Route Servers, Mergers, Features, & More. NANOG 51.
[39] B. Quoitin, C. Pelsser, L. Swinnen, O. Bonaventure, and S. Uhlig. Interdomain traffic engineering with BGP. *IEEE Communications Magazine*, 2003.
[40] R. Raszuk, C. Cassar, E. Aman, B. Decraene, and S. Litkowski. BGP Optimal Route Reflection. IETF draft, draft-ietf-idr-bgp-optimal-route-reflection-06, 2013.
[41] M. Roughan, W. Willinger, O. Maennel, D. Pertouli, and R. Bush. 10 Lessons from 10 Years of Measuring and Modeling the Internet's Autonomous Systems. *IEEE J. on Sel. Areas in Comm.*, 29(9), 2011.
[42] InMon – sFlow. `http://sflow.org/`.

Measuring the Reliability of Mobile Broadband Networks

Džiugas Baltrūnas
Simula Research Laboratory
dziugas@simula.no

Ahmed Elmokashfi
Simula Research Laboratory
ahmed@simula.no

Amund Kvalbein
Simula Research Laboratory
amundk@simula.no

ABSTRACT

Mobile broadband networks play an increasingly important role in society, and there is a strong need for independent assessments of their robustness and performance. A promising source of such information is active end-to-end measurements. It is, however, a challenging task to go from individual measurements to an assessment of network reliability, which is a complex notion encompassing many stability and performance related metrics. This paper presents a framework for measuring the user-experienced reliability in mobile broadband networks. We argue that reliability must be assessed at several levels, from the availability of the network connection to the stability of application performance. Based on the proposed framework, we conduct a large-scale measurement study of reliability in 5 mobile broadband networks. The study builds on active measurements from hundreds of measurement nodes over a period of 10 months. The results show that the reliability of mobile broadband networks is lower than one could hope: more than 20% of connections from stationary nodes are unavailable more than 10 minutes per day. There is, however, a significant potential for improving robustness if a device can connect simultaneously to several networks. We find that in most cases, our devices can achieve 99.999% ("five nines") connection availability by combining two operators. We further show how both radio conditions and network configuration play important roles in determining reliability, and how external measurements can reveal weaknesses and incidents that are not always captured by the operators' existing monitoring tools.

Categories and Subject Descriptors

C.4 [**Performance of systems**]: Measurement techniques; C.4 [**Performance of systems**]: Reliability, availability, and serviceability

IMC'14, November 5–7, 2014, Vancouver, BC, Canada.

http://dx.doi.org/10.1145/2663716.2663725.

General Terms

Experimentation; Measurement

Keywords

Mobile broadband; reliability; robustness

1. INTRODUCTION

Cellular Mobile Broadband (MBB) networks are arguably becoming the most important component in the modern communications infrastructure. The immense popularity of mobile devices like smartphones and tablets, combined with the availability of high-capacity 3G and 4G mobile networks, have radically changed the way we access and use the Internet. Global mobile traffic in 2012 was nearly 12 times the total Internet traffic in 2000 [4]. MBB traffic is estimated to keep growing at a compound annual rate of 66% towards 2017. An increasing number of people rely on their MBB connection as their *only* network connection, replacing both a fixed broadband connection and the traditional telephone line.

The popularity of MBB networks has given them a role as *critical infrastructure*. The reliability of MBB networks is important for the daily routines of people and business, and network downtime or degradations can potentially impact millions of users and disrupt important services. More importantly, failures can also affect emergency services and people's ability to get help when they need it.

Given the importance of MBB networks, there is a strong need for a better understanding of their robustness and stability. Regulators need data in order to make informed policy decisions and determine where extra efforts are needed to improve robustness. Today, regulators are often left with a posteriori incident reports from the operators, and lack a true understanding of the many smaller events that affect the reliability of services. Providers of mobile services that run on top of MBB networks need reliable data on reliability in order to predict the performance of their own services. End users can use such information to compare different operators and choose the provider that best fills their needs.

The ambition of this work is to *measure the experienced reliability in MBB networks*, and to compare reliability between networks. We believe that reliability in MBB networks is too complex to be understood only through static analysis of the components involved, and that the most promising approach for assessing and predicting the reliability of the offered service is through long-term end-to-end measurements. We argue that reliability must be characterized at several levels, including the basic connection between the user equipment and the base station, the stability of the data plane, and the reliability of application level performance. In this work, these aspects of reliability are assessed through long-term active measurements from a large number of geographically distributed measurement nodes. By looking at measurements from individual connections, we are able to identify important differences between networks and to characterize the reliability of each network as a whole. In summary, this paper makes the following contributions:

1. We propose a *framework for measuring robustness in MBB networks.* The framework captures aspects of reliability on several layers, from a basic registration in the network to a stable application performance over time. Within this framework, we define metrics and measurement experiments that describe reliability on the connection level, the data plane level, and the application level.

2. We present the *first large-scale measurement study of MBB reliability*, from a dedicated measurement infrastructure. The measurement experiments are performed on Nornet Edge (NNE) [15]. NNE is the largest infrastructure of its kind, with dedicated measurement nodes distributed in over 100 Norwegian municipalities. The data used in this work is captured from a total of 938 MBB connections from 341 distinct nodes and 5 different operators over a period of 10 months. Through long-term monitoring of a large number of connections, we find that a significant fraction of connections (15-38% depending on the operator) lose their network attachment more than 10 minute per day. We also observe clear differences in reliability characteristics between networks. While one network experiences frequent but short-lived connection failures, other networks have a longer time between failures but a higher overall downtime.

3. By capturing a rich set of metadata that describes the context of the measurements, this study *increases the value of end-user measurement data.* The metadata allows us to explain measurement results by looking at factors such as signal quality, radio state, network attachment, connection mode, etc. In many cases, we are also able to distinguish between problems in the radio access network and the mobile core network. We find a clear correlation between signal conditions, connection failures and loss, but we also discover that many failures can not be explained by signal quality. We further find that the inability to obtain dedicated radio resources is a common cause of application failures in some networks.

4. Thanks to the multi-connected nature of NNE measurement nodes, we can directly compare the performance and reliability of different networks at the same location, and thereby *quantify the potential gain in robustness from end-device multi-homing.* We find that there is mostly good diversity in radio conditions between operators, and that downtime can be reduced significantly if multiple networks can be used in parallel. In fact, most measurement nodes can achieve 99.999% ("five nines") connection availability when combining two operators.

The rest of this paper is organized as follows. Section 2 introduces our framework for measuring reliability in MBB networks. Section 3 presents the measurement infrastructure and data that forms the basis for our analysis. Sections 4 - 6 analyses reliability at the connection-, data- and application layers respectively. Section 7 looks at correlations between the different networks, and discusses the potential gain in robustness through multi-homing in light of this. Section 8 discusses related work, and finally, section 9 sums up and discusses the lessons learned from this study.

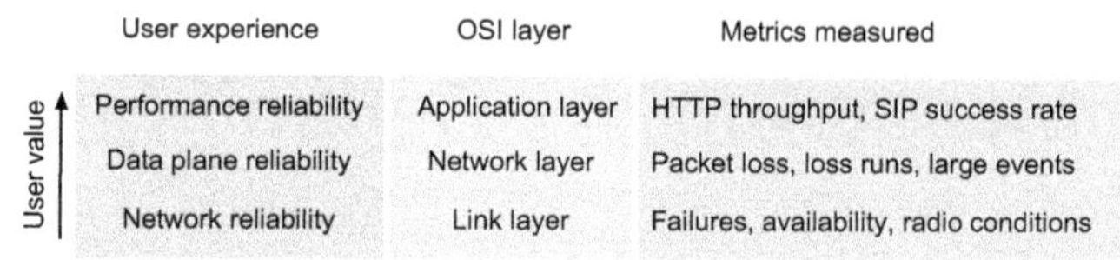

Figure 1: Framework for measuring experienced reliability in MBB networks.

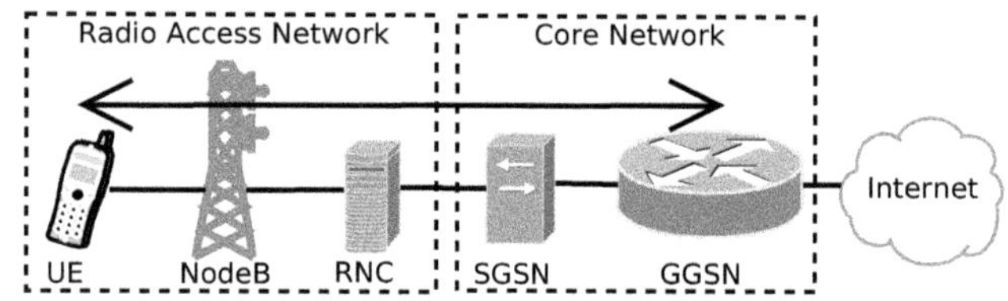

Figure 2: Simplified architecture of an UMTS MBB network.

2. A FRAMEWORK FOR MEASURING MOBILE BROADBAND RELIABILITY

Reliability is a complex notion, which relates to several stability and performance related metrics. Here, we propose a model where the reliability of a network is measured at different levels, reflecting increasing value for the user. A high level picture of the framework is shown in Fig. 1. The proposed model is a generic framework for describing the experienced reliability in MBB networks. In this work, we select a few relevant metrics at each level, and use these to characterize reliability of the measured networks. Other metrics can later be added to give an even more complete picture.

UMTS basics. Fig. 2 shows the main components of a UMTS network, divided into the Radio Access Network (RAN) and the Core Network (CN). Before any data can be transmitted, the User Equipment (UE), which can be a modem or a smartphone, must attach itself to the network and establish a Packet Data Protocol (PDP) context towards Gateway GPRS Service Node (GGSN). The PDP context is a data structure that contains the IP address and other information about the user session. This state is a prerequisite for any communication between the UE and the Internet. Once a PDP context is established, the Radio Network Controller (RNC) controls the Radio Resource Control (RRC) state of a user. Depending on the traffic pattern, RNC allocates a shared or dedicated radio channel for a user. If the user is not sending any data, RRC sets the state to IDLE or CELL_PCH. Otherwise, based on the bit rate, a user can be assigned a CELL_FACH state (shared channel, low bit rate, low power usage) or a CELL_DCH state (dedicated channel, high bit rate, high power usage). The principles are similar in networks based on the CDMA2000 architecture.

Connection level reliability. At the very basic level, the UE should have a reliable connection to the MBB network. By "connection" in this context, we mean that there is an established PDP context in the CN. The stability of the PDP context depends on both the RAN and the CN; the PDP context can be broken by loss of coverage, failures in base stations or transmission, or by failures or capacity problems in the central components such as SGSN or GGSN.

From the UE side, having a PDP context maps to having an assigned IP address from the mobile network. In Sec. 4, we measure reliability at the connection level by looking at the stability of the IP address assignment as a proxy for the PDP context. The metrics we look at are how often the connection is lost, and how long it takes before the node can successfully re-establish the PDP context. We also analyze how these metrics are related to underlying characteristics of the connections, such as signal strength and connection mode. The selected metric describes the stability of connections over time.

Data plane reliability. Having an established PDP context does not necessarily mean that the UE has well-functioning end-to-end connectivity to the Internet. Interference, drop in signal quality or congestion in either the wireless access or elsewhere in the mobile network may disrupt packet forwarding. This can cause periods of excessive packet loss, or "gaps" where no data comes through.

In Sec. 5, we measure data plane reliability by looking at loss patterns in long-lasting continuous probing streams. We describe loss patterns in each network, and discuss how loss must be seen in relation with the radio condition of the MBB connection. We also use packet loss to identify abnormal events where packet loss is higher than normal for a significant number of connections.

Application layer reliability. Reliability also involves a notion of stability and predictability in the performance an application achieves over the MBB network. This stability depends of course on both the connection level reliability and the data plane reliability. Application layer performance varies depending on the specific application requirements. Some applications will perform well under a wide range of network conditions, while others have stronger requirements on available bandwidth or delay. In MBB networks, the experienced network performance depends on the *state* of the connection, since radio resources are assigned depending on the traffic load. It is therefore difficult to predict the performance of an application based on generic measurement probes. Instead, application performance should be assessed through experiments with actual application traffic.

In Sec. 6, we report on measurements with two typical applications: HTTP download using curl and Voice over IP (VoIP) using SIP/RTP. These applications have been selected because they are popular in MBB networks, and because they represent two quite different application classes in terms of traffic load. We measure the success rate, i.e., how often the download or VoIP call can be successfully completed. We also report on the stability of the achieved download rate.

This paper takes an important first step towards measuring the reliability of MBB networks through end-to-end measurements. An important aspect that is missing from this study, is mobility. All measurement nodes used in this work are stationary, and we can therefore not use these to describe how the stability of the offered service varies as you move.

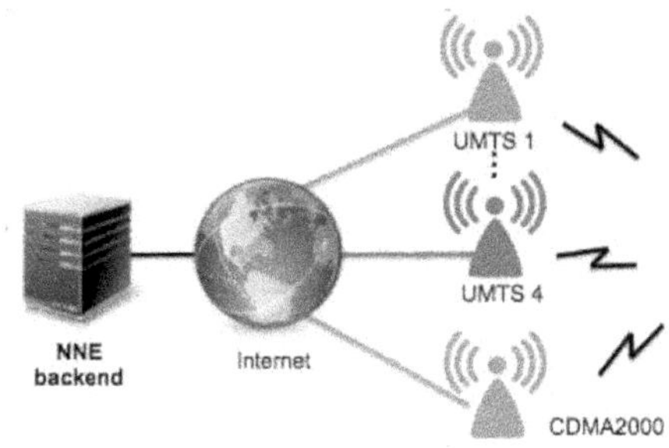

Figure 3: NNE overview.

There are, however, also advantages in doing measurements from fixed locations, since it removes a significant source of variation and uncertainty in the measurements. In future work, we plan to revisit MBB reliability in a mobile setting.

3. SYSTEM OVERVIEW AND DATA

This section presents the infrastructure that was used to run the measurement experiments described in this work, the MBB networks that were measured, the collected data, and how it is stored and post-processed.

3.1 The Nornet Edge measurement platform

NNE (Fig. 3) is a dedicated infrastructure for measurements and experimentation in MBB networks [15]. It consists of several hundred measurement nodes geographically distributed in more than 100 municipalities all over Norway, and a server-side infrastructure for management, processing and data storage. Figure 4 shows the placement of NNE nodes in Norway classified according to the number of MBB networks the node was connected to. NNE nodes are distributed to reflect the population density in Norway, with some bias towards urban areas. Nodes are placed indoors in small or large population centers, with a higher density of nodes in larger cities. More than half (177) NNE nodes are deployed in three largest cities, where 26.7%[1] of the coutry population lives.

An NNE node is a custom-made single-board computer, with a Samsung S5PV210 Cortex A8 microprocessor, one Fast Ethernet port, and 7 on-board USB ports. The node runs a standard Debian Linux distribution, giving large flexibility in the types of tools and experiments that can be supported. NNE also offers a set of tools for connection and configuration management, and a framework for deploying and managing measurement experiments. Each node is connected to 1-4 UMTS networks and 1 CDMA2000 1x Ev-Do network, using standard subscriptions. For the UMTS networks, connections are through Huawei E353 or E3131 3G USB modems. These modems support UMTS standards up to DC-HSPA and HSPA+ ("3.75G") respectively, but not LTE ("4G"). They are configured so that they always connect to the 3G network where available, and fall back to 2G elsewhere. The same modem model is always used for all networks on the same node, to avoid differences caused by different hardware. For the CDMA2000 network, we connect to the Internet via a CDMA home gateway device over the Ethernet port.

[1]http://www.ssb.no/en/beftett/

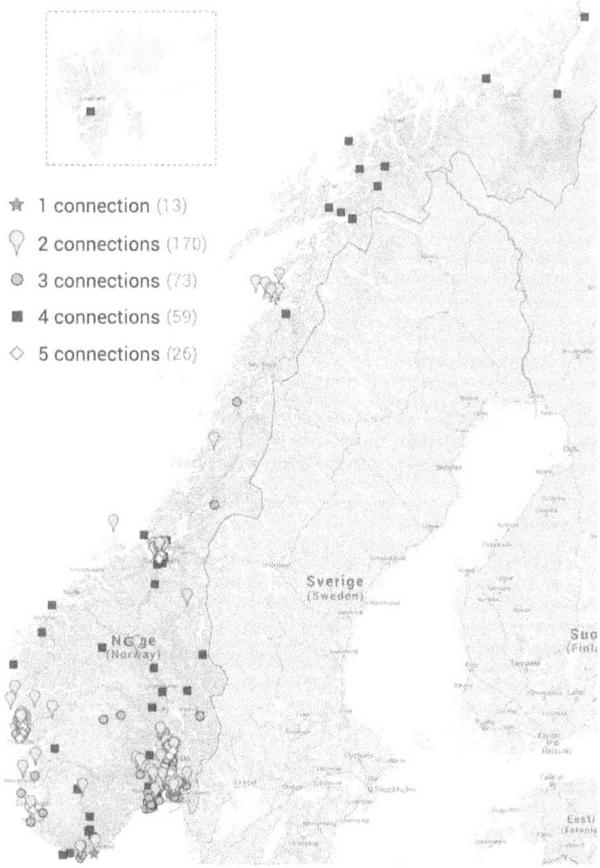

Figure 4: Placement of NNE nodes in Norway.

The NNE backend contains the server-side of the measurements, and is connected directly to the Norwegian research network UNINETT. The backend also contains servers for monitoring and managing the nodes, and for data processing.

3.2 Measured MBB networks

Nodes in the NNE platform are connected to up to five MBB networks. Four of these (Telenor, Netcom, Tele2 and Network Norway) are UMTS networks, while the last (Ice) is a CDMA2000 network operating in the 450 MHz frequency band. As shown in Fig. 5, Telenor and Netcom maintain their own nation-wide RAN. Tele2 and Network Norway are collaboratively building a third RAN, called Mobile Norway, which does not yet have nation-wide coverage. When outside of their home network, Tele2 customers camp on Netcom's RAN, while Network Norway customers camp on Telenor's RAN. This complex relation between the operators and RANs is an advantage for our measurement study. By looking at correlations between connections on the same RAN but in different operators (or vice versa), we can often determine whether an observed behavior is caused by the RAN or the CN.

3.3 Measurement experiments and data

The measurement experiments performed as part of this work are installed on the nodes using NNE's configuration

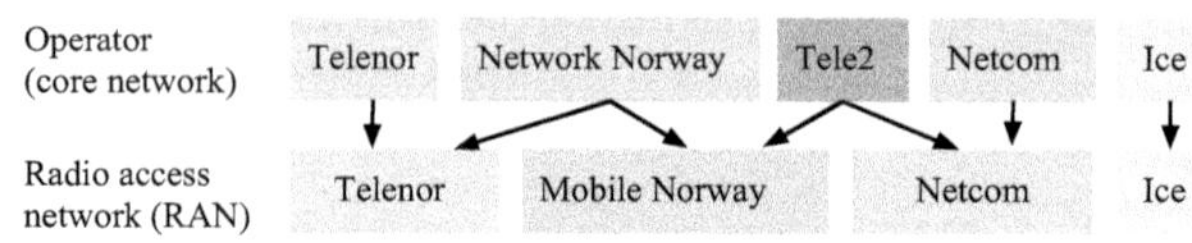

Figure 5: The operators and radio access networks measured in this study.

management system. Measurements are then performed against measurement servers that are part of the NNE backend. The measurement servers are well provisioned in terms of bandwidth and processing power, to make sure they are not a performance limiting factor. Data from the measurements are uploaded to the backend database periodically. The data is post-processed to calculate aggregates and also to filter out time periods from problematic connections, NNE maintenance windows or when NNE experienced problems at the server-side due to hardware problems or problems with their network provider.

3.4 Metadata collection

The mode and RRC state of an MBB connection directly impacts its performance. To better explain the observed behavior, it is therefore important to collect state changes along with measurement results. The CDMA2000 gateway device provides only very limited diagnostic data, therefore we collect state information only for UMTS networks. The state attributes that are the most relevant to our measurements are connection mode (GSM/GPRS, WCDMA, LTE), connection submode (e.g. EDGE, WCDMA, HSPA+), signal strength (RSSI) and signal to noise ratio (E_c/I_o), RRC state and camping network operator. In addition, we also record when a connection comes up or disappears, i.e., when the PDP context is established or lost. As will be shown in the sequel, results can be very different depending on the network state.

All in all, our dataset consists of 10.1 billion entries in the database, gathered from 938 distinct connections at 341 distinct nodes. 327 of these are Telenor connections, 142 are Netcom, 75 are Tele2, 66 are Network Norway, and 328 are Ice[2]. The number of simultaneously active measurement nodes has varied in the range between 108 and 253 through the measurement period.

4. CONNECTION RELIABILITY

Data can only be sent over an MBB connection when there is an established PDP context in the CN. To establish a PDP context, the UE signals its presence to the respective signaling gateway (SGSN in UMTS networks), which then establishes the PDP context and returns a data session with an allocated IP address. This data session is essentially a tunnel connecting the UE to the Internet through intermediate gateways (GGSN in UMTS networks). The PDP context can be broken either by problems in the RAN (e.g., poor signal quality), or in the CN (e.g., failures or capacity problems in the SGSN). Failures can also be caused by the complex interaction between the OS running on the measurement node, the node's USB subsystem, and the MBB

[2]The varying number of connections per operator is caused by practical and economical constraints.

USB modem itself. We conjuncture, however, that if the majority of failures are caused by such artifacts, the differences between operators would be minor and hard to spot. In this section, we measure the frequency of PDP context losses, the time it takes before the PDP context is successfully restored, and the resulting downtime when no PDP context is available. We further correlate with signal quality and connection mode to gain an insight into what may have triggered the failure. The discussion in this section is limited to the UMTS networks, since we do not have the necessary logs from the CDMA2000 network.

4.1 Measuring connection failures

An NNE node continuously monitors the status of the PDP context for all UMTS connections, and tries to re-establish it as soon as it is broken. If it fails in doing that, the node keeps retrying until it eventually succeeds; we log all these attempts. There is no hold time between these consecutive reconnection attempts, so a new attempt is immediately initiated after the failure of the preceding attempt. A failure will therefore trigger a varying number of reconnection attempts depending on its duration (each attempt takes tens of milliseconds).

In some cases, the node manages to re-establish the PDP context for a short period, before it is again broken. To build a time series of failure events, we group consecutive reconnection attempts spaced by less than M minutes into the same event. In other words, a connection must keep its PDP context for at least M minutes before the reconnection was deemed successful and the failure event ends. Setting M to a high value underestimates the connection stability, while a low value will report a flapping connection at partially available. We experiment with different values for M in the range from 1 to 5 minutes. We detect a total of 154772 failures when setting M to 1 minute. Varying M from 1 minute to 3 minutes has a negligible impact on the number of detected failures. This number only drops by 0.019% when we set M to 3 minutes. It, however, decreases by 3% and 4.9% when we set M to 4 minutes and 5 minutes respectively. Based on this, we set M to 3 minutes when identifying PDP context failures. We believe that this grouping captures well what the user perceives as a usable connection, since a connection is not worth much if it flaps at a high frequency. The result of this grouping is a sequence of connection failure events of varying duration for each connection.

We impose two conditions to avoid overestimating the number and duration of connection failures by including measurement artifacts. First, we discard all failure events that were rectified either by rebooting the node or actively resetting the USB modem, since these may be caused by effects in the measurement platform. Second, to compensate for absent log files and failures that are not rectified by the end of our study period[3], we consider only failures that have well defined starting and ending points.

4.2 Analyzing connection failures

The stability of the tunnel that connects the UE to the CN depends largely on the RAN. Hence, to capture the effect of the radio access, we group our connections based on their respective RANs. Recall that, the measured four UMTS operators use three RANs as illustrated in Fig. 5. This gives us five logical networks in total, which are Telenor, Netcom, Mobile Norway (which includes Network Norway and Tele2 connections that use Mobile Norway's RAN), Network Norway@Telenor (which includes Network Norway connections that camp on Telenor's RAN), and finally Tele2@Netcom (which includes Tele2 connections that camp on Netcom's RAN). We use the camping information we collect from the modems to identify the connections that belong to the last three logical networks. For example, we classify a Network Norway connection as Network Norway@Telenor if it spends more than half of the time camping on Telenor's RAN, otherwise we classify it as Mobile Norway.

The three plots in Fig. 6 show the cumulative distribution function of the mean time between failures (MTBF), the mean time to restore (MTTR), and downtime percentage (due to PDP failures) for each connection in our data set, grouped by the five logical networks. We record distinct differences between operators, and observe a strong dependency between connection stability and the RAN. The statistics of Telenor connections and Network Norway@Telenor connections resemble each other. The same is true for Netcom connections and Tele2@Netcom connections. Although Mobile Norway is Network Norway's home RAN, the statistics of Network Norway@Telenor clearly differs from Mobile Norway's. The same is true for Tele2 and Mobile Norway, albeit to a lesser extent. This confirms the dominating role of the RAN in determining connection stability.

Differences between operators. Telenor and Network Norway@Telenor connections are less stable compared to the other three operators. About half of Telenor and Network Norway@Telenor connections fail at least once every day. For the other three operators this is the case for between one fourth (Mobile Norway) to one third of connections (Tele2@Netcom and Netcom). Telenor and Network Norway@Telenor, however, have much shorter MTTR compared to the other networks. Only 19% and 20% of Telenor and Network Norway@Telenor connections respectively have MTTR more than five minutes. The same numbers jump to 54% for Mobile Norway, 57% for Netcom, and 64% for Tele2@ Netcom. These differences suggest that the MTTR values for Netcom, Tele2@Netcom and Mobile Norway connections are influenced by a set of long lasting failures. To investigate whether these failures are the main factor behind the observed differences, we compute the median time to repair for all connections. While the median values are naturally smaller than the mean, the differences between operators remain consistent. For example, less than 9% of Telenor connections have a median time to repair longer than one minute compared to 33% for Netcom. Note that there are also slight differences, especially in the MTTR, between Network Norway@Telenor and Telenor. These differences can be attributed to the fact that many Network Norway@Telenor connections, though mainly camping on Telenor's RAN, spend some time camping on their home network as well. There are similar differences between Tele2@Netcom and Netcom but less pronounced. To check whether the observed difference between operators stem from varying coverage levels we measure the average RSSI for all connections. Figure 7 shows the CDF of mean RSSI for each connection in all operators. All curves collapse onto each other indicating no systematic differences between operators. The same is true also for E_c/I_o (not shown here).

[3]In some cases, measurement nodes were lost for varying periods of time which resulted in gaps in the logged data.

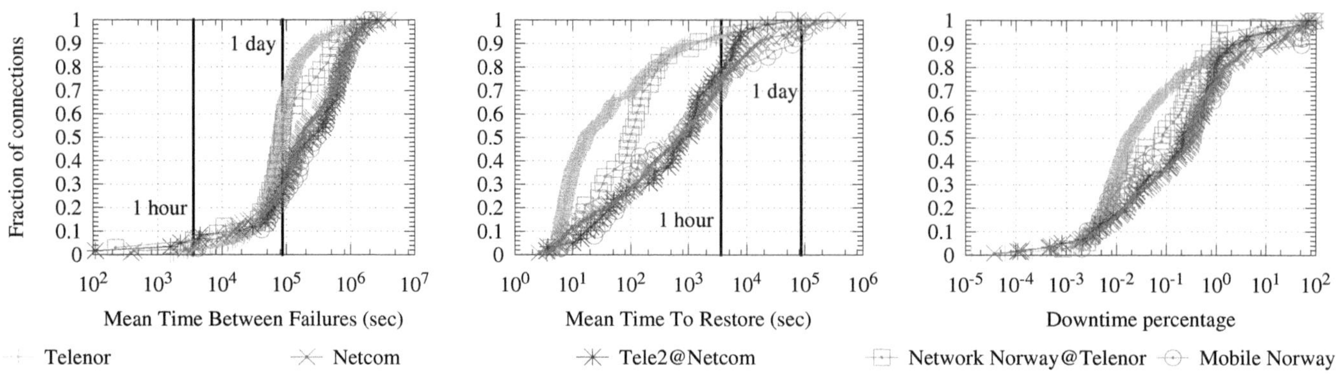

Figure 6: The statistics of connection failures.

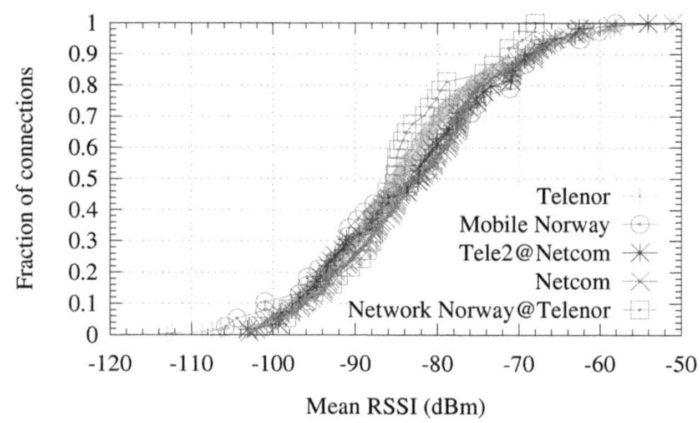

Figure 7: The CDF of the average RSSI per operator.

Failure properties. Telenor and Network Norway@Telenor are dominated by frequent but short-lived failures compared to the other three networks. About half of Telenor and Network Norway@Telenor connections have MTTR less than 17 seconds and 90 seconds respectively. Looking closer at these short failures, we find that they are related to the RRC state of the connection, and they happen when the connection fails to be promoted from a shared channel (CELL_FACH) to a dedicated channel (CELL_DCH). This triggers the modem to reset the connection. As we demonstrate in Sec. 6, these short failures can have a drastic impact on applications performance. Netcom and Tele2@Netcom, on the other hand, have more long-lived failures that last for tens of minutes or even up to several hours. To gain a better insight into these long lasting failures, we investigate 157 failures in 27 distinct Tele2@Netcom connections which lasted for more than 1 hour. These connections are from NNE nodes that also have both a Netcom connection and a Telenor connection. Almost half of these failures (48.4%) affected the corresponding Netcom connections at the same time. The Telenor connections, however, remained stable. Hence, we feel safe that these long-lasting failures are not artifacts of our measurements. They seem rather related to the radio access availability, coverage, and possibly the interaction between the modems and the network. We plan to investigate the root cause of these failures in our future work.

Downtime. Telenor and Network Norway@Telenor connections have less overall downtime compared to the other networks. The percentage of connections experiencing more than 10 minutes of downtime per day ranges from 38% for Tele2@Netcom to 15% for Network Norway@Telenor. Failures that last more than 10 minutes are between 5.1% and 13.5% of all failures depending on the operator. They are, however, responsible for between 96.4% and 98.7% of the overall downtime. Besides characterizing the overall connection downtime, we also investigate how connection stability has varied during our study period. To this end, we calculate the median daily downtime percentage per network measured as the median downtime across all connections available on each day. Figure 8 shows the time series of this metric for all networks throughout the study period. For all networks, the median daily downtime remains stable hinting at no significant changes in connection stability during our measurement period. Further, the time series are in line with the observations we made earlier in this section. Networks that share the same RAN exhibit similar median daily downtime. Also, Telenor and Network Norway@Telenor are a characterized by a frequently observed median daily downtime of $5e-5\%$, which corresponds to a single outage of 4.32 seconds. This higher downtime percentage for both networks is consistent with our observation that they suffer more frequent short-lived failures compared to the other networks.

4.3 Correlating with metadata

To understand what may trigger the connection to be broken, we correlate the downtime due to PDP failures in a certain hour with the connection mode (e.g., 2G or 3G), the average RSSI, and the average E_c/I_o in that hour. To correlate with the connection mode, we say that a connection is in 3G (2G) mode in a given hour if it stays in 3G (2G) mode for at least 70% of its available time. Further, to construct a meaningful correlation with the signal quality, we group the average RSSI values into five categories that correspond to the standard mobile phones signal bars: 1 bar (-103 dBm or lower), 2 bars (-98 dBm to -102 dBm), 3 bars (-87 dBm to -97 dBm), 4 bars (-78 dBm to -86 dBm), and 5 bars (-77 dBm or higher). We also group the average E_c/I_o values

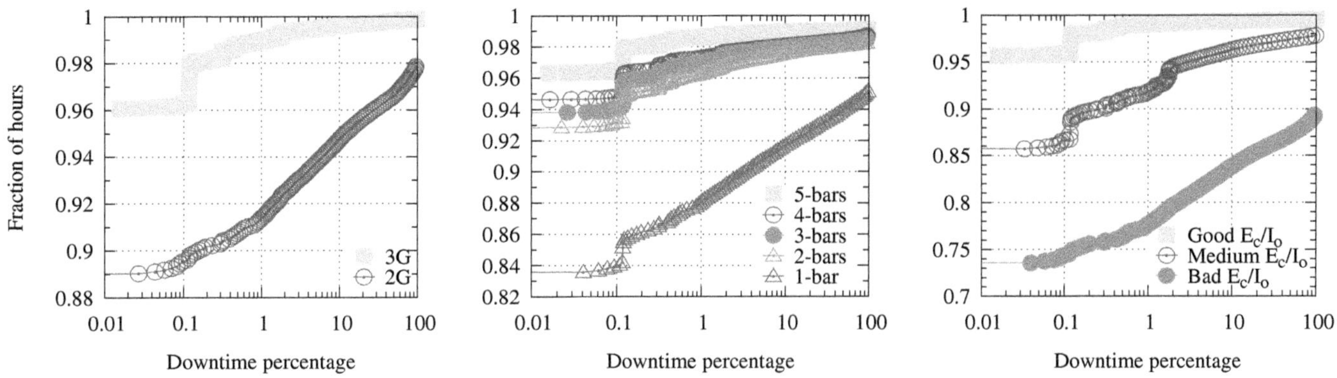

Figure 9: Downtime correlation with connection mode, RSSI and E_c/I_o.

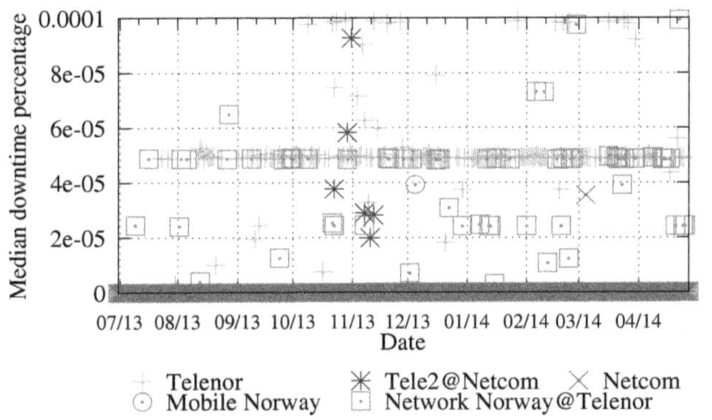

Figure 8: The daily mean downtime percentage for each MBB operator.

into three commonly used categories: Good (0 dB> E_c/I_o >-8 dB), Medium (-8 dB> E_c/I_o >-15 dB), Bad (-15dB> E_c/I_o <-33 dB) [10].

The left panel in Fig. 9 shows the CDF of the downtime percentage per hour, split according to the connection mode. This plot includes all connections from all operators. The center and right panels show the CDF of the downtime experienced at different RSSI levels and at different E_c/I_o levels respectively. The downtime is markedly higher for 2G connections than for 3G connections. We record 1% downtime or more in 1% of the hours with 3G connectivity compared to 9% of the hours with 2G connectivity. Further, as expected, downtime is influenced by the signal quality. Connections with an average RSSI equivalent to one signal bar have significantly higher downtimes. Beyond that, the differences between signal bar levels are less significant. Downtime also correlates strongly with E_c/I_o categories. We further observe that a sizable fraction of hours with downtime exists even when having good E_c/I_o or RSSI. For example, we experience downtime in 5% of the hours characterized by a good E_c/I_o. This indicates that radio quality can not alone explain all connection failures. To explain the stronger correlation between downtime and E_c/I_o as opposed to RSSI, we note that the RSSI measures the received signal strength which include all received components (i.e. signal and noise). Hence, a high RSSI does not necessarily translate into a good radio condition. E_c/I_o on the other hand measures the signal quality (i.e. the signal to noise ratio) capturing both interference with ambient and surrounding noise as well as interference from cross traffic at adjacent frequencies. We further correlate these three parameters to investigate whether a single measure is sufficient to describe the radio condition and consequently connection stability. Across operators, we do not observe clear correlation between RSSI and connection mode. Poor E_c/I_o, however, strongly correlates with RSSI of one bar as well as with 2G connectivity. This suggests that E_c/I_o can be picked as a predicator of connection stability.

The above explained correlations are visible in all operators, but the relation between downtime and metadata is not always linear. For instance, the correlation between different E_c/I_o categories and connection stability is more evident in Telenor and Network Norway@Telenor than in Netcom and Tele2@Netcom. This suggests that disconnects in Telenor and Network Norway@Telenor are more often caused by the radio conditions, matching well with the short MTTRs discussed above. While such failures also exist for Netcom and Tele2@Netcom, they are masked by the dominating long-lasting failures.

Summary of findings. The results presented in this section show that many connections have a downtime that can be problematic for critical applications, such as alarms or payment systems. 15-38% of connections are unavailable more than 10 minutes per day on average. There are also clear differences in connection stability between operators. While Telenor experiences relatively frequent but short-lived failures caused by the failure to acquire a dedicated radio channel, other operators have less frequent but longer lived failures giving a higher overall downtime. We further find that the connection level reliability is highly dependent on the RAN. In particular there is a high correlation between downtime and the signal-to-noise ratio of the connection. Still, there is also a significant number of connection failures that can not be explained by radio conditions. These may be caused by congestion or central failures in the network.

5. DATAPLANE RELIABILITY AND PERFORMANCE

This section looks at the networks' ability to deliver uninterrupted packet forwarding with an acceptable loss rate. Based on continuous end-to-end probing, we report on packet loss and on the duration of unavailable periods where no

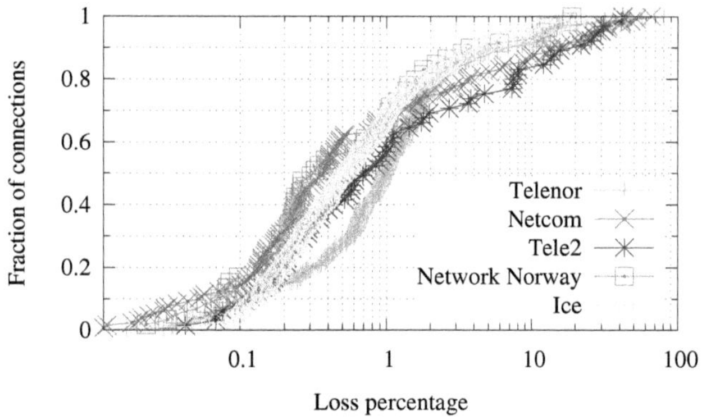

Figure 10: Loss rate for each MBB operator.

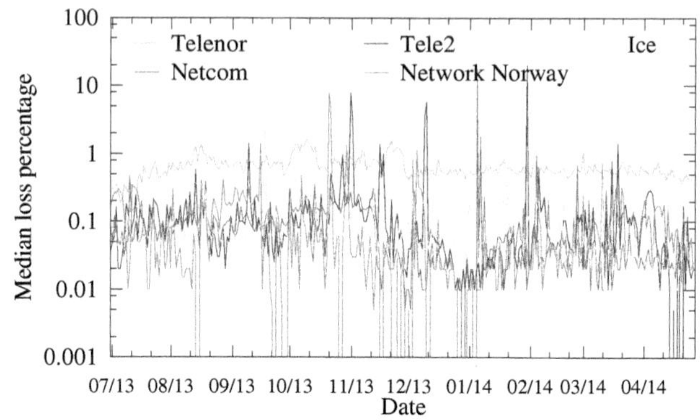

Figure 11: Median daily loss rate for each MBB operator.

packets come through. We look at how these metrics are related to mode, radio state and and signal quality. Finally, we identify particular events where a large fraction of connections simultaneously experienced abnormal packet loss rates.

5.1 Measurement description

Data plane reliability is measured by sending one 20 byte UDP packet to an echo server every second, and recording the reply packet from the server. A timestamp and an incremental sequence number is included in the packet payload for duplicate detection and round-trip time calculation. While the round-trip time normally is in the order of tens of milliseconds, we sometimes observe delays in the order of several seconds. Such high delays can sometimes be caused by excessive buffering [13]. We consider a packet to be lost if we do not receive a reply within 60 seconds.

This measurement test starts automatically on all network interfaces as they become active, and keeps running as long as the interface is up. When the connection is not available, the measurement script stops sending request packets and waits until the connection becomes available again. In total, more than 10 billion data points were collected from June 2013 to Apr. 2014. The measurement duration for each connection varies depending on how long the node was available and had working connections. In the following analysis, we require that we have at least 10 days of measurements to include a connection in the discussion. Due to space limitations we focus on packet loss in this section, and defer discussing delays and duplicates to future work.

5.2 Loss rate

The CDF in Fig. 10 shows the overall average loss rate for each connection in all operators. The loss rate is defined as (lost packets)/(sent packets) for the whole measurement period. Loss is relatively limited in all networks, and 50% of connections have less than 1% packet loss in all operators. We observe that relatively fewer Telenor connections have a very low packet loss rate compared to the other networks. 72% of Telenor connections have a loss rate higher than 0.5%, whereas this ratio is between 42 and 56% for the other networks. Telenor does not, however, have many connections with a high loss rate. Only 10% of connections have more than 5% loss, compared to 20% for Netcom and 23% for Tele2. Overall, Network Norway and Ice have the lowest packet loss rates.

There are diurnal patterns in packet loss in all networks, with higher loss rates in office hours when traffic is more intense. Ice, which has a larger fraction of home users, reaches their highest loss rates around 8PM. Packet loss in Telenor is consistently higher than in other networks throughout the day, also outside peak hours. We therefore believe that this higher packet loss is due to the RAN configuration rather than capacity limitations. To account for possible hardware, software or configuration changes over time in MBB networks, in Fig. 11 we plot the median daily loss rate for each MBB operator. We see that during the whole measurement period the median loss percentage remains stable and conforms with the results show in Fig. 10. Days with unusually high loss percentage are due to large events presented later in this section.

Networks differ in the thresholds they use to promote a connection from CELL_FACH to CELL_DCH. Telenor is more conservative than the other networks in such promotions [15], and hence the measured Telenor connections are more often in CELL_FACH. For instance, a Telenor connection spends on average 65% of its time in CELL_FACH compared to 34% for a Netcom connection. Unlike in the other networks, Telenor connections have a higher loss rate in CELL_FACH than in CELL_DCH, indicating that this channel is operating closer to its capacity limit[4]. Telenor does, however, have higher packet loss than other operators also when on CELL_DCH, so this can not alone explain the difference.

To further explain the observed differences, we have looked at loss rates combined with the metadata collected in parallel with the measurements. We first observe that loss rates are similar for 2G and 3G connections in all networks, with the exception of Netcom, where 2G loss is higher. A typical Netcom connection experiences more than 1% packet loss in 60% (25%) of all hours when it is on 2G (3G). Loss increases in periods when connections perform vertical handovers between 2G and 3G.

Not surprisingly, loss is higher in connections with poor signal quality. The Venn diagram in Fig. 12 shows that many

[4]Telenor has previously confirmed to us that they have had capacity issues in the FACH channel.

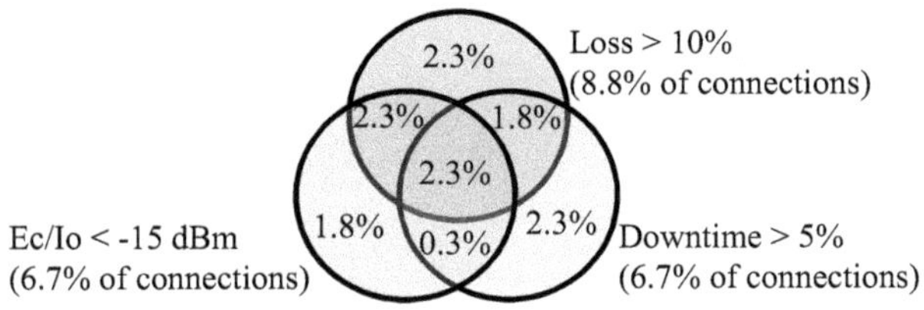

Figure 12: Loss, downtime and signal quality.

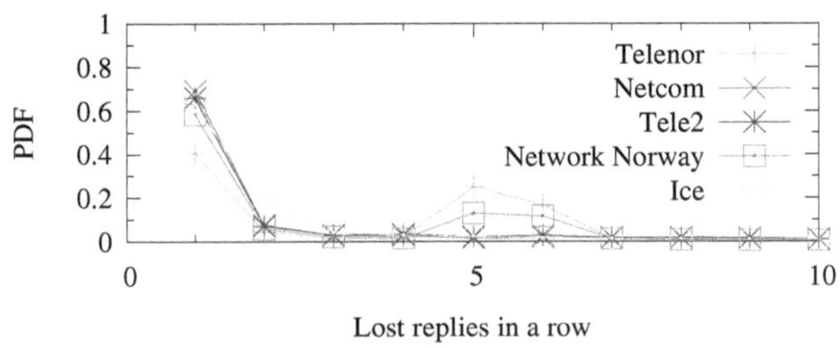

Figure 13: The distribution of loss run sizes across operators.

of the connections that experience a high loss rate also experience much downtime and have low E_c/I_o values. Out of the 341 connections where we have all the necessary metadata to make this comparison, 8.8% have an average loss rate higher than 10%. As seen in the figure, most of these (73%) have either a downtime ratio >5%, E_c/I_o <-15 dBm, or both. We can not identify any systematic differences between operators in the relation between loss, downtime and signal quality.

5.3 Loss runs

From our measurement data, we identify each sequence of packets that were lost in a row. We call such sequence a *loss run*. Loss runs are important for how packet loss will affect the user experience. Since we send one packet every second, the size of a loss run is approximately equal to the number of seconds when no downlink traffic is received.

The distribution of loss run sizes is shown in Fig. 13. Not surprisingly, the dominating size of a loss run is just one packet, accounting for 60% of loss runs for three of the networks. Telenor and Network Norway, however, also have many loss runs of size 5 and 6. As explained in Sec. 3, Network Norway connections sometimes camp on Telenor's RAN, and we have confirmed that this is the case for connections with many loss runs of size 5 or 6. There is no clear periodicity in occurrence of loss runs of size 5 or 6, nor any dependence on signal quality, time of day or geographical area. Looking at the connection state during such loss runs, we find that they are normally caused by an RRC state demotion from CELL_FACH to IDLE. Re-establishing the CELL_FACH radio state and resuming packet forwarding takes 5-6 seconds, which is longer than an ordinary promotion [17]. While we do not know the exact cause of these demotions, we note that demotions can some times be caused by a network-initiated revocation of the radio access bearer. Such revocations can be triggered when capacity needs to be made available for other connections.

5.4 Large events

Next, we discuss *large events*, where many connections in an operator experiences abnormal packet loss at the same time. Such events will normally be caused by failures in the CN. To identify and analyze large events, we first divide our measurement time series into 5 minute intervals, and calculate the loss rate for each connection in each interval. Additionally, to account for downtime periods, all 5 minute intervals when a connection was unavailable are assigned a 100% loss rate. We consider that a connection has an abnormal loss rate in a particular 5 minute interval if more than 10% of the packets are lost. A large event is defined as a period of one or more intervals when more than 10% of all connections in an operator has abnormal packet loss.

Figure 14 shows a visual representation of all large events recorded during our measurement period. Each event is represented by a circle (multiple events in the same day are merged). The diameter of the circle reflects the severity of the event, and can be thought of as the total volume of lost traffic. This is calculated as the product of the fraction of affected connections, the average loss rate in the affected connections, and the duration of the lossy period. The fraction of affected connections is also represented on the y-axis.

As seen in the figure, networks experience large events with varying severity and frequency. Short-lived events with limited loss and affecting 10-20% of connections happen on a weekly basis in all networks. These events might be attributed to short-lived congestion, and may be considered part of normal operation. There are, however, also a number of larger events that can severely influence the user experience.

The collected measurements can normally give a good idea about the underlying cause for the more severe large events. By looking at the geographical distribution of the affected connections, the affected RAN(s), loss intensity and other parameters, we can often pin the root cause to either the transmission network, the CN, or to the interconnection between operators.

For example, on Sept. 10 2013, most Tele2 connections experienced 20-50% packet loss for around 40 minutes. Similar behavior repeated itself on Oct. 28 and on Nov. 16. These failures happened outside of maintenance windows, and affected connections from all parts of the country, and were therefore likely related to a component in the CN. Tele2 has later informed us that these events were probably caused by a failure in a load balancer in their CN.

One of the largest events recorded in our measurement period took place in Tele2 on Nov. 1-2, when 86% of connections were unavailable for more than 6 hours. 41% of the affected connections lost the PDP context during this period, while the others maintained a valid IP address but could not send or receive any data. The failure affected only Tele2 connections camping on Netcom's RAN, and Tele2 has confirmed that the root cause of the failure was a failing component in the peering between these two networks.

An interesting event took place on Oct. 21-22, and affected all Network Norway connections camping on Telenor's RAN. These connections experienced around 50% packet loss for more than 11 hours. We also observe that the packet loss rate was higher at times when traffic volumes are higher,

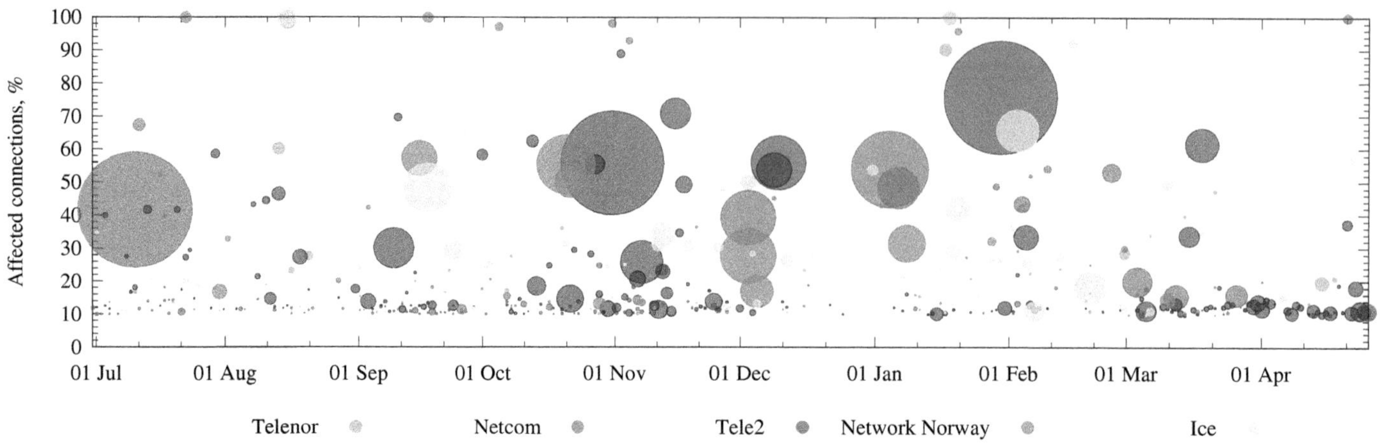

Figure 14: Large events since July 2013.

indicating a capacity problem in the connection between these two networks. Network Norway later confirmed that this event was caused by a routing problem that sent traffic through a roaming exchange point normally used for international roaming traffic only. This link is dimensioned for significantly lower traffic volumes, and could therefore not support the offered load.

In our discussions with the network operators, we have learned that several of the loss events identified in this study were not detected by their internal monitoring systems. These systems detect situations where many customers lose their Internet connections, but not necessarily situations where packet loss is less than 100%. This shows the potential of end-user measurements, and illustrates how they can help operators discover weaknesses and failures in their networks.

Summary of findings. In this section, we revealed clear differences in packet loss between operators. While Telenor has a non-negligible but low packet loss in most connections, other operators have higher variation in loss among connections. Telenor (and Network Norway@Telenor) also has a high number of loss runs of size 5 or 6, which tend to occur when connections lose their radio channel. Such short-lived gaps in packet forwarding can have a negative effect on applications such as interactive games, which often do not produce enough traffic to acquire a dedicated radio channel. Overall, the measured loss remains unexpectedly high since MBB networks rely heavily on link-layer retransmission to rectify errors. Our observations thus far, however, indicate that this unexpected loss is mainly related to state RRC transitions. We defer investigating the exact causes of loss to a followup study. Finally, we have used loss data to identify events that affect a significant fraction of connections in a single MBB network. An online alarm system based on end-to-end measurements that discovers such events can be useful for both operators and regulators.

6. APPLICATION LAYER RELIABILITY

An important aspect of reliability is a stable performance on the application layer. In this section, we look at the stability in performance of two representative applications: HTTP download and VoIP using the SIP protocol.

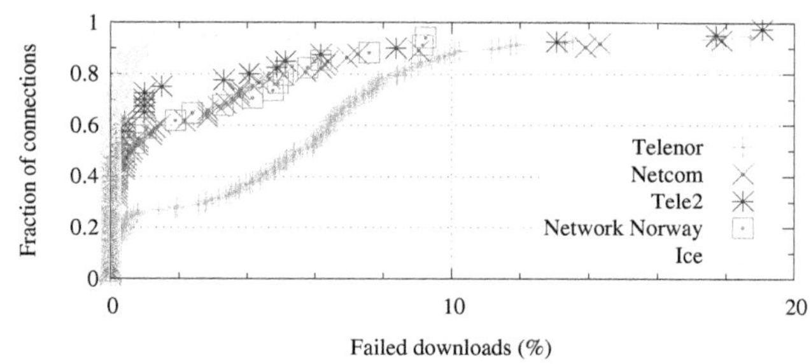

Figure 15: Failure rates in HTTP download tests.

6.1 HTTP download test

Much of the traffic in MBB networks goes over the HTTP protocol, which is used for both web browsing and streaming. Here, we report results from a simple experiment where a 1 MByte file is downloaded from a server using the HTTP GET method. For each test iteration, we record the time it took to start the data transfer, the total time to complete the download (if successful), throughput, and any error code. For each connection, the test was repeated once per hour for a duration of 3 weeks, giving a total of up to 504 runs per connection. Based on these measurements, we report on two different metrics: the probability of successfully completing the transfer, and the probability of achieving a download rate of at least 1 Mbps.

Note that our aim here is to look at the stability of the application layer performance, and not to measure the maximum achievable throughput in the connection, which would require a different approach.

Figure 15 shows the fraction of download attempts that could not be successfully completed. We observe that the fraction of failing attempts is significantly higher in Telenor than in the other networks. 55% of Telenor connections experience a failure rate higher than 5%, and 12% experience a failure rate higher than 10%. Ice, on the other hand, sees very few unsuccessful downloads, with only 9% of connections having a failure rate above 1%.

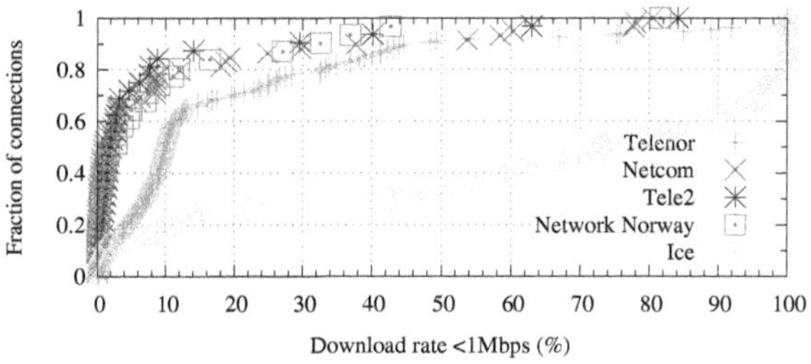

Figure 16: Probability of achieving less than 1Mbps HTTP throughput.

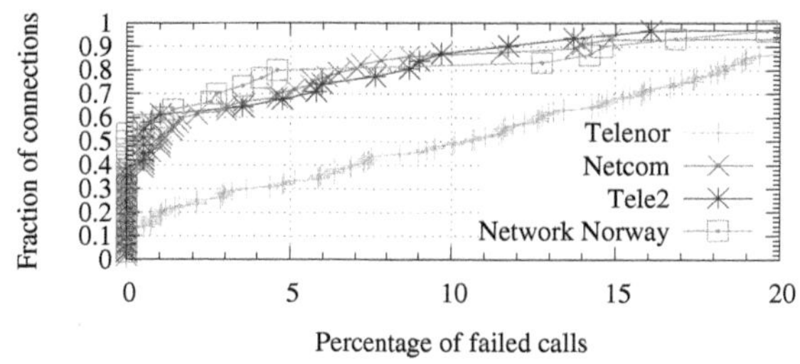

Figure 17: Failure rates in VoIP tests.

Looking at the error codes for the unsuccessful transfers, we find that the dominating reason for a failed download in all networks except Telenor is the failure to establish the connection. Correlating erroneous transfers with the data from our connectivity test we observed that these unsuccessful TCP handshakes happen during times with high packet loss. For Telenor, however, the connection broke *after* the initial TCP handshake in 74% of the failing attempts. Such errors are largely responsible for the difference between Telenor and the other networks. Looking closer at these events, we find that they happen when the connection can not be promoted from the CELL_FACH to the CELL_DCH state. The download traffic will normally trigger such a promotion, but when this does not happen, the modem responds by resetting the connection, and the download fails. There is a clear diurnal pattern in this type of failures, which makes it natural to believe that they are related to congestion in the FACH channel and/or insufficient resources for a promotion to CELL_DCH.

Figure 16 shows, for each connection, the fraction of runs where the achieved throughput was less than 1 Mbps. Only 3G connections are included in this plot. We observe that in all UMTS operators, most connections achieve this download rate most of the time. In Netcom, Tele2 and Network Norway, around 90% of connections achieve at least 1 Mbps 90% of the time or more. Telenor achieves this rate less often. We believe that this is caused by the higher loss rate observed in Telenor and how it interacts with TCP congestion control. Ice achieves far lower throughput than the UMTS operators. Around 20% of the connections never achieve the target download speed, while only 19% of connections meets the target in 90% of the cases. From Figs. 15 and 16, we conclude that Ice offers a slower but more stable download performance than the UMTS networks.

6.2 Voice-over-IP test

Initiating VoIP calls over MBB connections is becoming increasingly popular, thanks to the rise of applications such as Viber [24]. The ability to initiate and complete VoIP calls are therefore important aspects of the user-experienced reliability. To asses this ability we design a simple experiment that faithfully emulates a real VoIP call. Our test consists of a custom-made client that runs on the measurement node and an Asterisk PBX [6] hosted at the NNE backend. The client initiates a VoIP call to the PBX using SIP, then it uses RTP to play a one minute long audio file. Upon completion the PBX replays the same file back to the client and terminates the call. The audio file is encoded as G.711 [1] resulting in a sending rate of about 50 packets per second. For each connection, we run this experiment once per hour for one week, giving us 168 calls per connection.

Figure 17 illustrates the fraction of calls that could not be successfully completed. We observe that the failure rate is significantly higher for Telenor. 30% of Telenor connections have a failure rate higher than 15% compared to only 4% of Tele2 connections. 34% and 21% of the failures for Netcom and Tele2 respectively happened during the call initiation phase (i.e. the SIP INVITE fails). For Telenor and Network Norway, however, this percentage drops to 13% and 14.9% respectively. The remaining failures happened after the call started successfully. We believe that the explanation for these dropped calls is the same as for the unsuccessful HTTP downloads discussed above.

Summary of findings. This section has shown that short pauses in packet forwarding that are likely caused by the lack of available radio resources can lead to significant problems for applications, such as dropped calls and failed downloads.

7. ROBUSTNESS BY MULTI-HOMING

So far, our discussion has focused on the experienced reliability in each MBB network separately. A related question is how much reliability can be increased if an end device can be simultaneously connected to more than one MBB network. Such multi-homed devices are becoming increasingly popular, for example as mobile gateways that provide WiFi service on public transport.

The potential for increased reliability through end device multi-homing depends heavily on whether coverage and failure patterns are largely independent across operators. If connections to different operators tend to fail simultaneously due to the same underlying reasons, there is little to be gained from a redundant connection. Our discussion in this section focuses on three important aspects of cross-correlation between operators: coverage, connection failures and loss events.

7.1 Correlations in coverage

We first look at whether different operators are similar with respect to signal quality at a given location. NNE measurement nodes are distributed widely across Norway, and we believe they give a reasonable representation of the indoor signal quality that can be expected in each operator.

Figure 18 gives an overview of the E_c/I_o values for all UMTS connections in all nodes in our dataset. The values shown are averages across the whole measurement period (for most connections the variation is small). Since almost

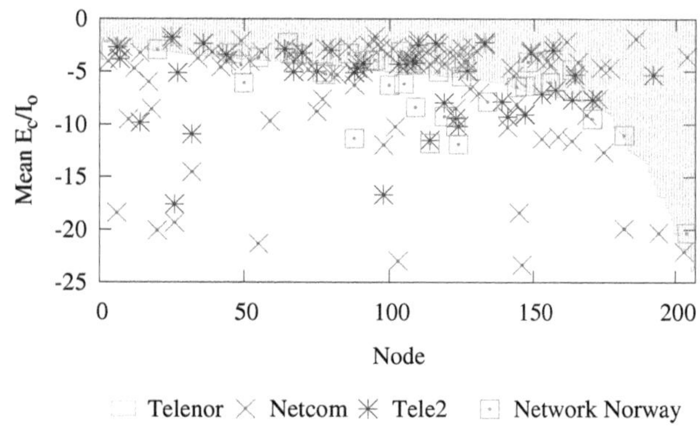

Figure 18: Average E_c/I_o values for connections in different operators.

all nodes have a Telenor connection, we sort the nodes based on the E_c/I_o of the Telenor connection, and plot E_c/I_o values for the other connections where available.

We observe that there does not seem to be a strong correlation between operators in general. As expected, we find that for some nodes, Netcom/Tele2 and Telenor/Network Norway have pairwise very similar E_c/I_o due to their national roaming arrangements. Calculating the Pearson correlation coefficient for each pair of operators confirms the visual impression from Fig. 18. The correlation coefficient for the pairs of operators that do not share the same RAN is between -0.10 (Netcom and Network Norway) and 0.25 (Telenor and Netcom). The correlation is evidently higher when the respective pair of operators share the same RAN, that is 0.47 for Tele2 and Netcom and 0.75 for Telenor and Network Norway. We also performed a similar analysis for RSSI values, which gave similar results. These findings are positive from a robustness perspective, since they indicate that there is a significant potential gain from provider multi-homing.

7.2 Correlations in downtime

Next, we revisit the connection failures discussed in Sec. 4, to see how downtime could be reduced if the end user is able to connect to more than one operator. For each pair of connections from the same node, we identify the time periods when both connections were unavailable (i.e., they had no PDP context). The resulting downtime represents a lower limit on the downtime that can be achieved if the end system is able to exploit both connections in parallel.

Figure 19 shows the downtime for three operators (repeated from Fig. 6), and the combined downtime for all pairs of connections from the same operators. Other operators and pairs are excluded from the graph for readability. For comparison, we also plot the expected combined downtime for connection pairs under the (false) assumption that they fail independently. This value is calculated by multiplying the downtime rates of each connection, and serves as a lower limit on the downtime we can expect by combining operators.

We make two main observations. First, there is a large potential for reducing downtime through multi-homing. 60% of the nodes achieve 99.999% uptime when combining Telenor and Tele2 connections; and 55% of the nodes achieve the same when combining Netcom and Telenor connections. These reductions in downtime are arguably surprisingly high, given that connection from different operators often share many potential sources of failures, such as local weather conditions, cell towers, power, or even transmission. We see that the measured combined downtime is not very different from the theoretical downtime assuming independence. Second, the reduction depends heavily on selecting the right pair of connections. As expected, operators that often camp on the same RAN show a much larger correlation in their failure pattern, and the gain from combining such connections is limited. As shown in Fig. 19, there is often little or no gain in combining connections from Netcom and Tele2.

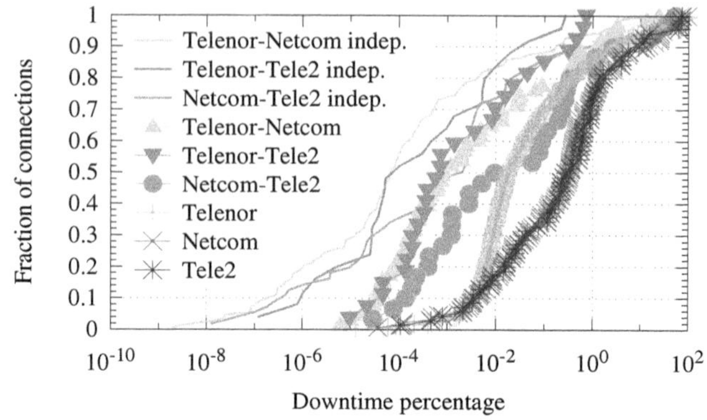

Figure 19: Common downtime across operators.

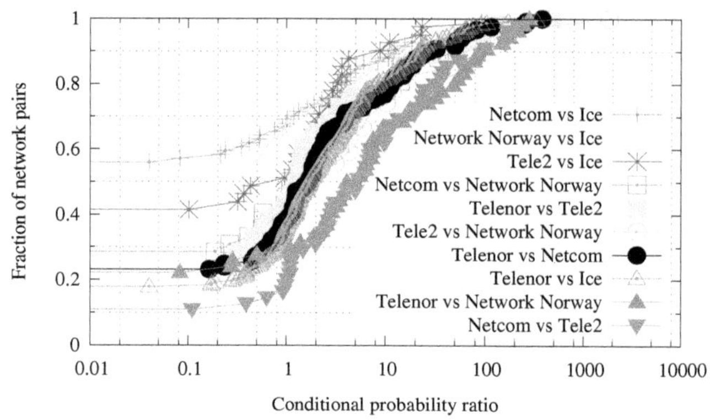

Figure 20: Conditional probability of loss events.

7.3 Correlations in loss

Finally, we look at correlations in loss between networks. We base our analysis on the same 5 minute intervals used in Sec. 5. Let $P(A)$ denote the (empirical) probability that a connection A has a loss rate higher than 10% in a given 5 minute interval, and $P(B)$ be the same for a connection B. We calculate the conditional probability $P(A|B)$ for each pair of connections from the same node, and compare it to the unconditional probability $P(A)$. If the conditional probability ratio $R = P(A|B)/P(A)$ is close to 1, it means that connection A and B fails largely independent, while a high R means that they tend to fail together. Note that by Baye's law, $P(A|B)/P(A) = P(B|A)/P(B)$.

Figure 20 shows R for all pairs of connections at the same node, grouped by operators. We require that A and B have at least one full week of overlapping measurements to be included in the analysis. Note that the number of events where both connections experience high loss may in some cases be very low, so the graph should be interpreted with some care. Some observations are still clear. First, connections from different networks are not completely independent. In between 25 and 70% of connection pairs, the likelihood of high packet loss in connection A more than doubles when connection B experiences high loss. In between 8 and 35% of the cases, the likelihood increases more than 10 times. There are, however, clear differences between operator pairs. Not surprisingly, the strongest pairwise dependence is for Netcom/Tele2 and Telenor/Network Norway. The weakest dependence is between Ice and the other operators. This might also be expected, since Ice operates with a different technology, a much lower frequency band, and has a different customer mix (and therefore traffic pattern) than the other operators.

Summary of findings. The results in this section indicate that there is a large potential for increased reliability through multi-homing to several MBB networks. There are generally clear differences between operators in signal quality at a given location, and exploiting two connections in parallel can potentially give 99.999% availability in many cases.

8. RELATED WORK

Mobile broadband measurement. During the past few years, there have been a growing interest by regulators, policy makers and the networking community in measuring the performance of home and mobile broadband networks. Several regulators have translated this into ongoing nationwide efforts, examples of such efforts include US FCC's Measuring Broadband America initiative [7] and an annual activity by the Communications Regulatory Authority of Lithuania for measuring MBB performance [5]. A study by Sundaresan et. al [23], partly based on the FCC data, demonstrated that the long-term continuous monitoring from the edge is indispensable for understanding and assessing home broadband performance. Our work is the first to present a country-wide assessment of MBB reliability filling an important gap in this area.

Approaches for measuring MBB networks can be classified into three categories:

1. Crowd-sourced user initiated measurements. The most prominent example in this respect is Mobiperf [2], an Android application that measure several performance metrics including throughput and latency. Nikravesh et al. [16] used an extensive data set contributed by the users of two apps, Mobiperf and Speedometer, and performed a longitudinal analysis of MBB performance. They highlighted significant performance differences across operators, access technologies, and regions. They also showed that the performance of MBB is not improving overtime, which necessitates the continuos monitoring of MBB performance. Sommers and Barford used crowd-sourced data from Speedtest.net to compare the performance of MBB to WiFi [21]. Approaches based on user-initiated tests can complement measurements from dedicated infrastructures such as NNE. It is difficult, however, to rely on such tests for the continuous monitoring of MBB networks stability.

2. Measurements collected using dedicated infrastructure. Examples of such studies include [18] and [14]. The former used a few laptops mounted on public buses to compare the performance of three MBB operators, while the latter used low cost notebooks for comparing the performance of four operators in seven locations in India. Our work falls into this category. It is, however, based on a much larger deployment in terms of the number measured operators, the number of connections, geographical distribution and duration.

3. Measurements based on network-side data. Several measurements used network side logs to assess various aspect of MBB performance. Examples include, assessing RRC state machine impact on performance [17], characterizing the properties of cellular traffic [20], HTTP performance [9], performance during crowded events [19], and TCP performance over LTE [11]. Such logs are however only available to operators. This line of work and ours complement each other. Network-side data gives more insights into the network internals, while end-to-end measurements can help operators detecting anomalies that are not easily identifiable by only using network-side monitoring, as we demonstrated in Sec. 5.

Measurement framework and metrics. Several ongoing efforts are aiming to standardize the task of performing large scale measurements [3] and to define meaningful performance metrics for IP networks in general [22] and MBB networks in particular [12]. Sundaresan et. al [23] investigated the suitability of different metrics in characterizing home broadband performance, while Goga and Teixeira explored several approaches for estimating broadband access speed [8]. This paper presents a framework for assessing MBB reliability using a large scale deployment. We believe that our work is a timely input to the ongoing efforts to defining approaches and metrics for measuring MBB networks.

9. DISCUSSION AND CONCLUSIONS

This work has presented a framework for measuring reliability in MBB networks, based on the position that end-to-end measurements can give useful insights about performance and stability problems in the network as a whole. The main argument in the proposed approach is that reliability must be measured at several levels, from the stability of the network connection to the reliability of the data plane and application layer performance. We believe that this framework gives a good basis for describing the overall reliability of an MBB network. In the future, this should also be extended with measurements that capture the effect of mobility on the experienced reliability. Efforts are ongoing to extend the NNE infrastructure with mobile nodes, which would allow such measurements.

Using the proposed framework, we have presented a large-scale study of reliability in 5 Norwegian MBB networks. We have focused on a few selected metrics at each level in the framework. There are still many other metrics that can be relevant for understanding reliability. On the connection level, the ability to *establish* a PDP context when needed is an important aspect of reliability, which is different than the ability to maintain the connection uninterrupted for a long time. On the data plane level, further analysis can be made to describe the pattern of packet loss and delay variations under varying network conditions. An important topic is also to look at the reliability and performance of various transport layer protocols in MBB networks.

The measurements presented here have demonstrated that there are clear differences in reliability between operators, and that these can be identified and characterized by end-to-end measurements. Networks vary in the stability of connections, in packet loss patterns, and in their ability to support popular applications. We have also shown how end-to-end measurements can be used to identify failures and performance problems that are not necessarily captured by the operators' monitoring systems.

This study was performed on the NNE infrastructure, with dedicated measurement nodes. The framework is, however, also applicable for studies based on crowd-sourced data from mobile phones. Such approaches will, nevertheless, often be more limited in the availability of metadata, and in the ability to gather long uninterrupted time series under stable conditions.

This study has some limitations that we hope to address in future work. First, only 2 different 3G modem models are used in this study. While this makes it possible to compare connections across operators and regions with the same equipment, it may also introduce effects that we would not see with other types of user terminals. In the future, we hope to include also a few other modem types in our studies. Further, the UMTS modems used in the NNE platform support 3G protocols up to DC-HSPA ("3.75G"), but not LTE/4G. As LTE becomes more widespread, it will be important to measure also these networks.

10. ACKNOWLEDGEMENTS

We thank Amogh Dhamdhere and the anonymous reviewers for their insightful comments on this draft. Nornet Edge is financed by the Research Council of Norway through the INFRASTRUKTUR program. Nornet Edge is realized with additional generous support from Tele2, Ice.net.

11. REFERENCES

[1] ITU-T recommendation G.711. Pulse code modulation (PCM) of voice frequencies, 1988.

[2] Mobiperf. http://www.mobiperf.com, 2014.

[3] M. Bagnulo, P. Eardley, T. Burbridge, B. Trammell, and R. Winter. Standardizing Large-scale Measurement Platforms. *SIGCOMM Comput. Commun. Rev.*, 43, 2013.

[4] Cisco Systems, Inc. *Cisco visual networking index: Global mobile data traffic forecast update, 2012 - 2017*, February 2013.

[5] Communications Regulatory Authority of the Republic of Lithuania. *Annual report of the Communications Regulatory Authority (RTT) of the Republic of Lithuania*, 2012.

[6] Digium. Asterisk. http://www.asterisk.org/.

[7] FCC. 2013 Measuring Broadband America February Report. Technical report, FCC's Office of Engineering and Technology and Consumer and Governmental Affairs Bureau, 2013.

[8] O. Goga and R. Teixeira. Speed Measurements of Residential Internet Access. In *Proc. of PAM*, 2012.

[9] E. Halepovic, J. Pang, and O. Spatscheck. Can you GET me now?: Estimating the time-to-first-byte of HTTP transactions with passive measurements. In *Proc. of IMC*, 2012.

[10] H. Holma and A. Toskala. *WCDMA for UMTS: HSPA Evolution and LTE*. John Wiley & Sons Ltd., 4th edition, 2007.

[11] J. Huang, F. Qian, Y. Guo, Y. Zhou, Q. Xu, Z. M. Mao, S. Sen, and O. Spatscheck. An In-depth Study of LTE: Effect of Network Protocol and Application Behavior on Performance. In *Proc. of SIGCOMM*, 2013.

[12] IEEE. P802.16.3 Project: Mobile Broadband Network Performance Measurements. http://www.ieee802.org/16/mbnpm/index.html.

[13] H. Jiang, Y. Wang, K. Lee, and I. Rhee. Tackling bufferbloat in 3g/4g networks. In *Proc. of IMC*, 2012.

[14] Z. Koradia, G. Mannava, A. Raman, G. Aggarwal, V. Ribeiro, A. Seth, S. Ardon, A. Mahanti, and S. Triukose. First Impressions on the State of Cellular Data Connectivity in India. In *Proceedings of the 4th Annual Symposium on Computing for Development*, ACM DEV-4 '13, 2013.

[15] A. Kvalbein, D. Baltrūnas, J. Xiang, K. R. Evensen, A. Elmokashfi, and S. Ferlin-Oliveira. The Nornet Edge platform for mobile broadband measurements. *Elsevier Computer Networks special issue on Future Internet Testbeds*, 2014.

[16] A. Nikravesh, D. R. Choffnes, E. Katz-Bassett, Z. M. Mao, and M. Welsh. Mobile Network Performance from User Devices: A Longitudinal, Multidimensional Analysis. In *Procs. of PAM*, 2014.

[17] F. Qian, Z. Wang, A. Gerber, Z. M. Mao, S. Sen, and O. Spatscheck. Characterizing Radio Resource Allocation for 3G Networks. In *Proc. of IMC*, 2010.

[18] S. Sen, J. Yoon, J. Hare, J. Ormont, and S.Banerjee. Can they hear me now?: A case for a client-assisted approach to monitoring wide-area wireless networks. In *Proc. of IMC*, 2011.

[19] M. Z. Shafiq, L. Ji, A. X. Liu, J. Pang, S. Venkataraman, and J. Wang. A first look at cellular network performance during crowded events. In *Proc. of SIGMETRICS*, 2013.

[20] M. Z. Shafiq, L. Ji, A. X. Liu, and J. Wang. Characterizing and Modeling Internet Traffic Dynamics of Cellular Devices. In *Proc. of SIGMETRICS*, 2011.

[21] J. Sommers and P. Barford. Cell vs. WiFi: On the Performance of Metro Area Mobile Connections. In *Proc. of IMC*, 2012.

[22] M. Stiemerling. IP Performance Metrics charter-ietf-ippm-05. http://datatracker.ietf.org/doc/charter-ietf-ippm/, 2013.

[23] S. Sundaresan, W. de Donato, N. Feamster, R. Teixeira, S. Crawford, and A. Pescapè. Broadband Internet performance: A view from the gateway. *SIGCOMM Comput. Commun. Rev.*, 41:134–145, 2011.

[24] Viber-Media. Viber. http://www.viber.com/.

Behind the Curtain – Cellular DNS and Content Replica Selection

John P. Rula
Northwestern University

Fabián E. Bustamante
Northwestern Univeristy

ABSTRACT

DNS plays a critical role in the performance of smartdevices within cellular networks. Besides name resolution, DNS is commonly relied upon for directing users to nearby content caches for better performance. In light of this, it is surprising how little is known about the structure of cellular DNS and its effectiveness as a client localization method.

In this paper we take a close look at cellular network DNS and uncover several features of cellular DNS, such as cellular network opaqueness and client to resolver inconsistency, that make it unsuitable for client localization in modern cellular networks. We study these issues in two leading mobile network markets – US and South Korea – using a collection of over 340 volunteer devices to probe the DNS infrastructure of each client's cellular provider.

We show the extent of the problem with regards to replica selection and compare its localization performance against public DNS alternatives. As a testament to cellular DNS's poor localization, we find surprisingly that public DNS can render equal or better replica performance over 75% of the time.

Categories and Subject Descriptors

C.2 [**Computer-Communication Networks**]: Distributed Systems—*Distributed Applications*; C.4 [**Performance of Systems**]: Measurement techniques

General Terms

Experimentation; Measurement; Performance

Keywords

Cellular DNS; Content Delivery Networks; Domain Name System

1. INTRODUCTION

Smartdevices are becoming the primary or only Internet point of access for an ever larger fraction of users. Nearly a quarter of current web traffic is mobile, and recent industry studies have estimated a fourfold increase in global mobile data traffic by 2018, mainly driven by data demands and the growing number of smart phones and tablets [7].

Content delivery networks (CDNs) are responsible for delivering most of today's Internet data. CDNs replicate popular content on servers worldwide and redirect users to "nearby" replica servers on demand. The Domain Name System (DNS) is instrumental in this process since CDN redirection, and thus the performance of content delivery, is typically based on the location of users' DNS resolvers [25].

Considering the importance of content and the critical role of DNS for both name resolution and localization in today's networks, it is somewhat surprising how little is known about the infrastructure and configuration of cell network DNS and its impact on content distribution. The 2011 study of Xu et al. [25] is today's most comprehensive analysis of (the US) cellular network infrastructure, combining data from DNS logs, smartphone users and server logs. For the radio technologies in their study – 3G UTMS and EVDO – the authors point out the dominant role of radio latency and the limited number of network ingress points. They conclude that, in that setting, the best option for content providers is to locate servers close to these ingress points and that, given the restricted routing in these cellular networks, choosing content servers based on local DNS servers is sufficiently accurate.

The recent growth of 4G access technologies [7, 12], such as LTE, radically changes the scene. Around the world service providers are busy rolling out 4G networks to meet users' increasing demand for faster, higher bandwidth connections. The most recent CISCO VNI report estimates that by 2018, the majority of North America devices and connections will have 4G capability. While 4G will be 15% of world-wide connections then, these connections will be responsible for 51% of traffic. When compared with 3G networks, 4G LTE presents a significantly different network, with a radically larger number of ingress points, and offers much lower radio access latency and variance. *We show that these changes make accurate content replica selection critical to the performance of end users in cellular networks.*

In this paper, we take a close look at cellular network DNS and replica selection in the two fastest growing 4G LTE markets – US and South Korea [12]. Using a collection of more than 280,000 experiments from over 340 globally distributed mobile devices, we probe the DNS infrastructure of each client's cellular provider and the content replicas they are redirected toward.

Our analysis shows the impact of network opaqueness and client-to-resolver inconsistency on the performance of content delivery in next generation mobile networks. As part of our study, we compare client/replica mappings through cellular DNS with those achieved through public DNS alternatives. We show that, in contrast to wired networks and despite providers' knowledge of clients'

IMC'14, November 5–7, 2014, Vancouver, BC, Canada

ACM 978-1-4503-3213-2/14/11 ...$15.00.
http://dx.doi.org/10.1145/2663716.2663734.

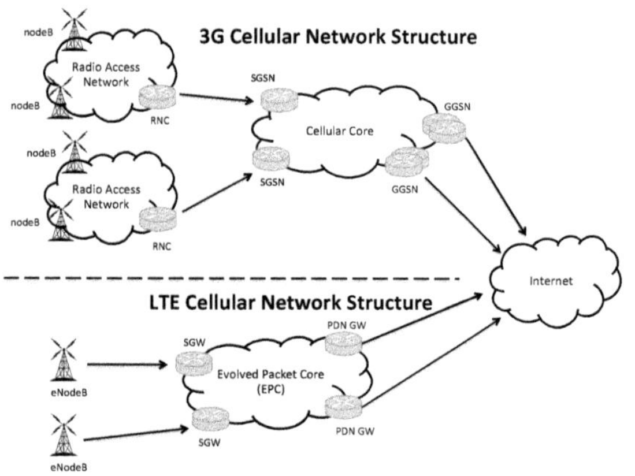

Figure 1: Network architecture changes cellular networks between 2/3G and LTE networks. LTE introduces a simpler, flatter network structure and an all-IP network.

locations, public DNS and the DNS of cell network providers yield comparable performance for replica selection.

In summary, our major contributions are:

- After describing our data sources and data collection methodology in Section 3, we detail the results of our investigation into cellular network DNS structure and behavior in Section 4.
- We present the first analysis of the interaction between cellular DNS and content replica selection in 4G networks in Section 5.
- We present the first comparison between cellular DNS and public DNS in resolution and replica selection performance in Section 6

We discuss the impact of cellular provider DNS and our finding's implications in content delivery networks in Section 7. We review closely related work in Section 8 and conclude in Section 9. We are making all our data available to the community from our project website.[1]

2. BACKGROUND AND MOTIVATION

In this section, we give an overview of current cellular infrastructure, the changes ongoing across cellular networks as they transition toward Long-Term Evolution (LTE) networks, and how these changes point toward the need for more intelligent replica selection for cellular devices.

2.1 Cellular Network Architecture

LTE has been growing rapidly since its entering the market in 2009. Service providers are busy rolling out 4G LTE networks to meet users' increasing demand for faster, higher bandwidth connections. LTE promises speeds up 150/75 Mbps of downstream/upstream throughput, significantly faster than what is possible in existing 3G networks. The 2014 CISCO VIN report estimates that, by 2018, the majority of North America devices and connections will have 4G capability. Transitioning to LTE technologies requires cellular operators to make substantial changes to their core networks, flattening their architectures and moving to an all-IP network. For example, LTE introduces an enhanced radio access component, the eNodeB, which removes the need for previous hierarchical structures such as the Radio Network Controller (RNC) by combining its functionality into a single node. These changes are illustrated in Figure 1. LTE also requires operators to switch over to the Evolved Packet Core (EPC), which requires an all-IP network [6], reducing the need for legacy, circuit based technologies.

Perhaps more relevant for content delivery, 4G LTE cellular networks are increasing the number of ingress/egress locations for cellular traffic. Prior work looking at cellular network structure concluded that CDNss had limited options from outside the cellular network to improve user experience [25]. The significant fraction of radio latency, combined with the limited number of ingress points into the cellular network, meant that CDNs had little control over user end-to-end latency. The significantly larger number of ingress points, a trend clear in Zarifis et al. [26] and in our own results (Section 5), means that CDNs have more options for placing and choosing content caches. These architectural changes and the radical improvements in radio access technology, suggest it is time to revisit the effectiveness of content delivery and the impact of DNS-based server selection in cellular networks.

2.2 Mobile Content Delivery

CDNs host and deliver the large majority of the mobile web content and, as in the wired Internet, most CDNs use the local DNS resolver (LDNS) of clients to locate them and find nearby replica servers for content delivery.

When a client requests an object hosted by a CDN, the client's local DNS resolver contacts the authoritative DNS (ADNS) of the domain name run by the CDN. The CDN uses the location of the client's DNS resolver as an approximate location for the client, and redirects the client to content servers nearby. In wired networks, this approach has been shown to be sufficiently accurate except when paired with certain ISP configurations or the use of public DNS services [18].

In cellular networks, however, CDNs have limited client network localization information. Firewall and NAT policies of cellular operators prohibit external entities like CDNs from probing clients or infrastructure in their network. Even if these policies did not exist, Balakrishnan et al. [3] showed the failure of IP-based identification and geolocation in cellular networks, due in part to the ephemeral and itinerant nature of mobile client's IPs – IPs assignment change rapidly and similar IPs are assigned to geographically distant devices.

Our experiments uncovered a wide range of performance results across the CDN replicas seen by clients in cellular networks. Figure 2 clearly shows this as the CDF of the differential performance of replica HTTP latency (time-to-first-byte) when accessing four different domains. The CDFs show, for various US and South Korean carriers, the difference between each replica observed by clients to their best seen replica.

While the degree of replica differential performance varies based on carrier and domain, we find replica latency increases ranging from 50% to 100% in all networks. In an extreme case, we find clients experiencing over 400% increases in latency in over 40% of the access to some key web sites.

3. METHODOLOGY OVERVIEW

Our analysis is based on data collected by end-user devices through two mobile apps sharing a common measurement exper-

[1]http://aqualab.cs.northwestern.edu/projects/atolls

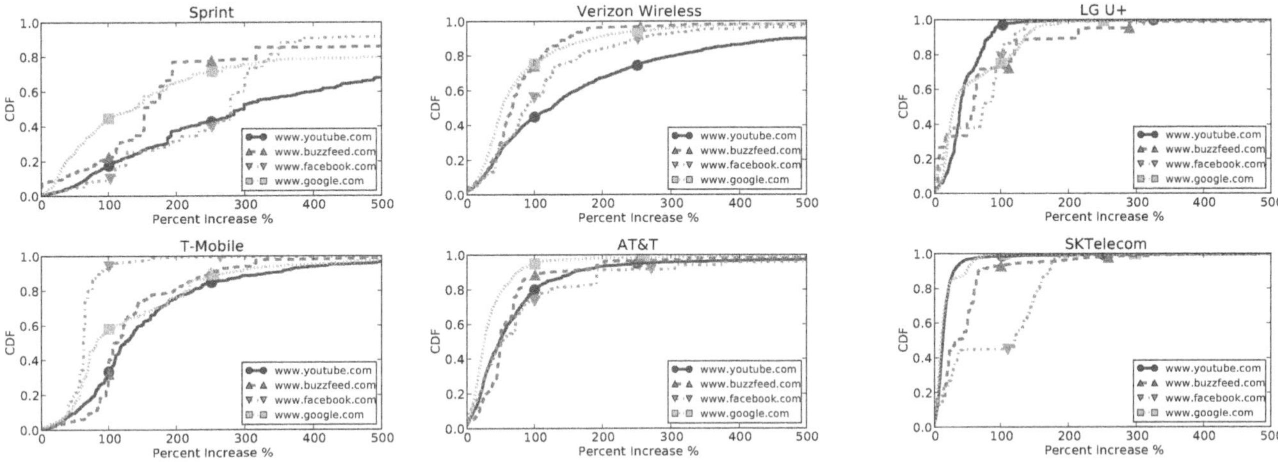

(a) US Carriers

(b) SK Carriers

Figure 2: Client observed performance of all replica servers seen. For each user in our dataset, each replica is represented as the percent increase in mean latency of each server compared to the "best" replica seen by that user. Users are consistently directed towards replica servers with latencies 100% greater than other existing replicas.

Carrier	# Clients	Country
AT&T	33	US
Sprint	9	US
T-Mobile	31	US
Verizon	64	US
SKTelecom	17	SK
LG U+	4	SK

Table 1: Distribution of measurement clients for the mobile operators profiled in our paper.

Mobile domains
m.yelp.com
www.youtube.com
www.facebook.com
www.google.com
www.yahoo.com
www.answers.com
www.buzzfeed.com
www.upworthy.com

Table 2: List of popular sites measured.

imentation library. The following paragraphs describe our measurement platform, experiments and measurement methodology.

3.1 Data Sources

The measurements used in this paper come from over 348 globally distributed Android mobile clients running our measurement application. The data was collected from two mobile applications posted to Google's Play Store, each packaged with the same network measurement library. For the purpose of this paper, we restricted our dataset to the 158 clients reporting to be in the top four cellular providers within the US, Sprint, Verizon Wireless, T-Mobile and AT&T, along with two large South Korean carriers, SK Telecom and LG U+. The number of clients distributed within each of these operators is given in Table 1. These markets were chosen due to the prevalence of LTE coverage, and the large volume of 4G traffic within their networks [12]. Our measurements cover a five month period between March 1, 2014, and August 1, 2014.

In all, our dataset consists of over 280,000 individual experiments, totaling over 8.1 million DNS resolutions, and 2.4 million pings, traceroutes and HTTP GET requests from mobile end hosts.

3.2 Experiment Description

Each device ran the specified experiment in the background, approximately once per hour. Taking into account the performance characteristics of different radio states in LTE devices [11], each experiment begins with a bootstrap ping to wake the radio up and mitigate any state promotion delay from the radio. Our experiment scripts are also designed to run continually and as quickly as possible to maintain the radio in a high power state. For the data presented in this paper, each experiment consist of the following:

- DNS resolutions for 9 popular mobile domains. The domains were chosen given their popularity and because their DNS resolution initially resulted in a canonical name (CNAME) record, indicating the use of DNS based load balancing and server selection. Table 2 list the different domains measured. These were conducted for the locally configured resolver, as well as public DNS services Google DNS and OpenDNS.

- Ping and traceroute probes to each replica server IP address returned from the previous resolutions. An HTTP GET request is also sent to each replica IP returned for the index page at that address.

- Resolution of clients' resolver IP addresses. The IPs are found, as in Mao et al. [16], by using an authoritative DNS (ADNS) for a subdomain of our research group's website. The IP address of the client's resolver is returned in the answer section of the response. These are conducted for locally configured resolver and public DNS resolvers for GoogleDNS and OpenDNS.

- Ping and traceroute probes to each IP address returned by our ADNS. In the case of the device's locally configured resolver, we ran additional probes to the IP address configured on the device as well as to the one returned by our ADNS, since they differed in *all* cases we measured.

3.3 Isolating Mobile Context and Performance Issues

We now describe some of the techniques used for mitigating device context and performance variation seen in network measurements from mobile devices [8]. Our comparison of content replicas is based on the latency from mobile devices to the content replicas they find. Each series of measurements described in the previous section are captured as a discrete *experiment*, with all measurements listed being taken at approximately the same time and within the device context.

We use ping latency, rather than throughput based measurements like page load time, to compare replica servers in light of previous work by Gember et al. [8] which showed that the former are more stable and less affected by changes in user context than the latter.

Current mobile devices are equipped with multiple radio technologies (i.e. LTE, HSPA, UTMS), each of which offer different levels of performance. For example, 7 different radio technologies were reported from users within both AT&T and T-Mobile, each showing different performance characteristics. Our focus on LTE and LTE's performance characteristics also helps control for these variations. LTE performance has been shown to provide much lower and more stable radio access latency than previous wireless technologies [11]. Figure 3 illustrates the performance and stability of LTE connections.

These figures show the performance of different radio technologies on domain name resolution performance for devices in four different US and two South Korean carriers. The different radio technologies present very distinct bands of performance, following the expected trend with newer generation radios offering lower resolution time. For example, we see a consistent performance differential between 4G technologies like LTE and 3G technologies like EHRPD and EVDO Rev. A, around 50ms at the median for both Sprint and Verizon CDMA networks. The figures also show the poor performance of 2G radio technologies like 1xRTT, taking nearly 1 second to complete a domain name resolution.

4. CELLULAR DNS CHARACTERIZATION

In this section, we present results of our characterization of the DNS infrastructure of four major US and two South Korean cellular providers. We find an indirect DNS resolver structure, with separate client-facing and external-facing resolvers, in all of the cellular networks we investigated. We evaluate the performance of cellular DNS resolution, and show that its performance under LTE is comparable to that of current residential broadband connections. We also examine the opacity of cellular LDNS resolvers, finding that cellular network opaqueness extends to their DNS resolvers, both in their external reachability and in their inconsistent mapping to clients.

Throughout the experiments described in Section 3, we used DNS resolutions to our ADNS servers to return the visible LDNS resolver IP address to clients. Looking at these IP addresses, and comparing them with the IP addresses configured as device resolvers, we find the use of *indirect* resolution techniques in *all* observed networks, where the LDNS resolver seen by the client (client-facing) differs from the resolver seen by other entities. One of the concerns with indirect LDNS resolution is that it can further distance end-hosts from their visible local DNS resolver, and obfuscate information for CDNs.

Indirect LDNS resolution takes the form of anycasted DNS resolvers, LDNS Pools [2], and tiered resolver infrastructure. In an anycast DNS resolver setup, each client keeps the same IP address for a DNS resolver, regardless of their location. DNS queries are directed toward nearby DNS resolvers within the cellular network through anycast routing.

Provider	Client	External	Pairs	Consistency %
Sprint	19	22	31	64.1
Verizon	27	28	27	100
T-Mobile	3	32	32	7.3
AT&T	5	43	43	12
SK Telecom	2	24	24	12
LG U+	5	80	80	6.2

Table 3: Number of LDNS Pairs seen by our mobile clients. Network structure and configuration varies by network in both the number of client facing and external facing resolvers, as well as the consistency of their pairings.

LDNS pools, as previously described by Azloubi et al. [2], consist of a collection of servers which load balance DNS requests within themselves. Unlike Azloubi et al., who detected the presence of LDNS pools by seeing different resolvers for consecutive queries responding to a CNAME entry, we were able to identify LDNS pools by directly comparing the configured resolver on the mobile device with the IP address seen by our ADNS.

Finally, we observed *tiered* DNS servers, which exist as two separate public IP addresses, yet with one client resolver and one external facing resolver. These paired resolvers also differ in latency and traceroute hops from client probes. For example, tiered resolvers in Verizon's network exist in entirely different ASes. Tiered resolvers may indicate a hierarchy of DNS resolvers within that operator's network, however, we are only able to observe the end points from our experiments.

We recorded the grouping of observed client- and external-facing resolvers to understand the configuration and dynamics of cellular infrastructure and their DNS resolvers. We refer to each grouping as an *LDNS Pair*. We calculate the consistency of these resolver pairings as the percentage of our measurements in which the client- and external-facing resolvers are paired. The consistency of pairings captures the stability of mappings between clients, their locally configured resolver, and the external facing resolver. For example, a client resolver equally load balanced between two external resolvers would have a consistency of 50%.

4.1 Cellular DNS Infrastructure

In our characterization, we find different DNS configurations within each of the cellular providers studied.

While every cellular provider measured employs indirect resolution techniques, their individual policies differ with regards to both the number of client-facing and external-facing DNS resolvers, and their consistency of pairings. Looking at the composition of LDNS pairings, we find several patterns emerging in DNS infrastructure configurations including the use of anycasted DNS, the presence of LDNS pools, and tiered DNS resolvers in separate ASes. A summary of each operator's DNS infrastructure is given in Table 3.

We observed the presence of LDNS pools within the Sprint's network and the network of the two South Korean carriers. In each of these cases, all resolvers are public IP addresses, and all have pairs in which a client facing resolver is observed paired with multiple external resolver addresses. In the case of Sprint, each resolver maintains a fairly consistent mapping between client and external resolvers, over 60% of the time.

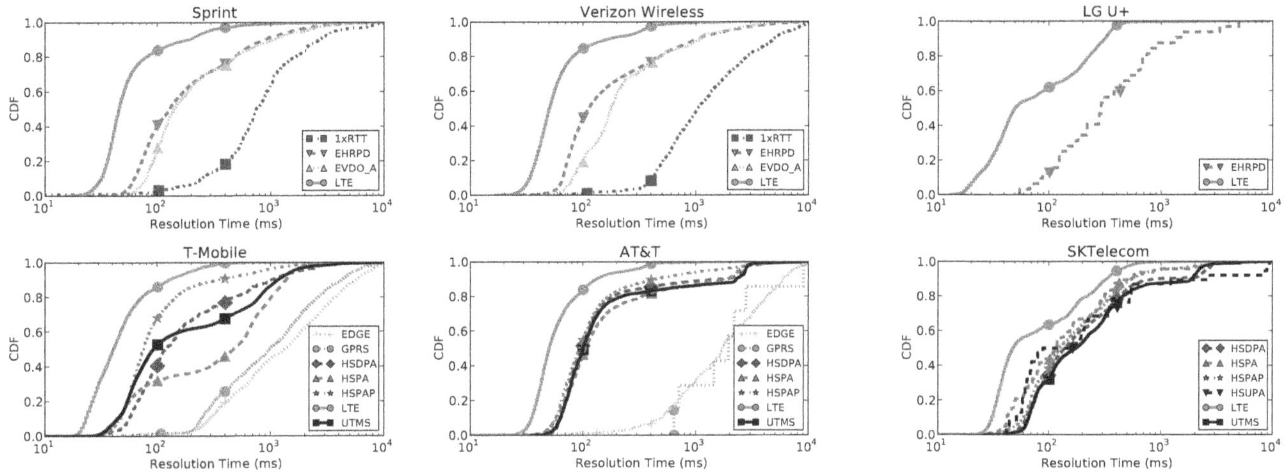

(a) US Carriers (b) SK Carriers

Figure 3: DNS resolution times for each cellular operator's DNS, grouped by the radio technology active during the domain resolution. We see very defined performance boundaries between different radio technologies.

For South Korean carriers SK Telecom and LG U+, we observed 2 and 5 client configured LDNS resolver addresses and 24 and 89 publicly visible addresses, respectively. For these carriers, each client and external pair are contained within the same /24 prefix. In Sprint, however, we find a high degree of load balancing between external resolvers in Sprint's network. We elaborate on the resolver consistency over time issue in Section 4.5.

Additionally, we found the use of anycasted DNS within AT&T's and T-Mobile's networks. Both carriers showed a limited number of configured DNS resolver addresses on client devices with a significantly larger number of publicly visible addresses indicating the use of IP anycast for resolvers. For example, a single AT&T address (172.26.38.1) in our measurements shows mapping to 40 external resolver addresses.

Verizon was the only cellular operator which maintained a 100% consistency between client and external facing resolvers. While both resolver locations were public IP addresses, we were unable to measure the distance between these resolver pairs due to unresponsive external resolver probes. However, each LDNS pair within Verizon exists in different ASes: 6167 for client facing resolvers and 22394 for external facing resolvers.

4.2 Cellular Resolver Distance

An important aspect of DNS in cellular networks is the network distance between clients and their corresponding resolver infrastructure. Distance to client facing resolvers is important for resolution performance, while distance to external facing resolvers has implications on content replica selection [18].

To capture the differences between both types of resolvers, clients were directed to issue *ping* probes to the sets of resolvers during each experiment. Figure 4 plots the cumulative distribution of latencies to clients' configured client facing resolver and external facing resolver. We see cases where both resolvers have nearly equal latencies indicating either identical machines or collocated resolvers, as is the case with SK Telecom. Resolvers in T-Mobile, Sprint and AT&T showed signs of distance between resolvers, revealing physical hierarchy of resolvers within their networks. We were unable to determine structural properties from latency measurements since only a minor fraction of external resolvers within Verizon and LG U+ networks responded to probes.

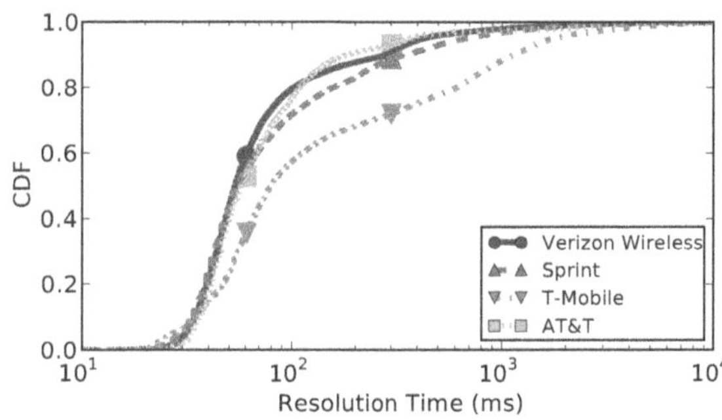

Figure 5: DNS resolution time for US carriers measured from client devices for the 4 major US cellular providers.

While we recorded traceroutes to each client and external facing resolver found, we observed the use of widespread tunnelling within each cellular network (e.g. VPN or MPLS). This rendered irrelevant much of the structural information, such as hop distance, gathered by these probes.

4.3 Cellular DNS Performance

We now look at the resolution performance of each mobile client's DNS provided from their cellular operator. We find DNS performance under LTE to be relatively consistent and comparable to DNS performance on wired broadband.

Figures 5 and 6 present, respectively, CDFs of resolution time for each of the four US carriers, and for the two South Korean carriers we studied. The figures show reasonable resolution performance for carriers in both markets, each having median resolution times between 30 and 50 ms. These numbers are comparable to resolution times within the wired Internet [1] for the lower 50th percentile.

Both South Korean carriers and T-Mobile exhibit bimodal behavior above their 50th percentile, and the remaining operators show a long tail of resolution times above the 80th percentile. To determine measure the impact of resolver cache on resolution time tails, we conducted back to back queries, measuring the difference between the first and second DNS queries. The results, presented

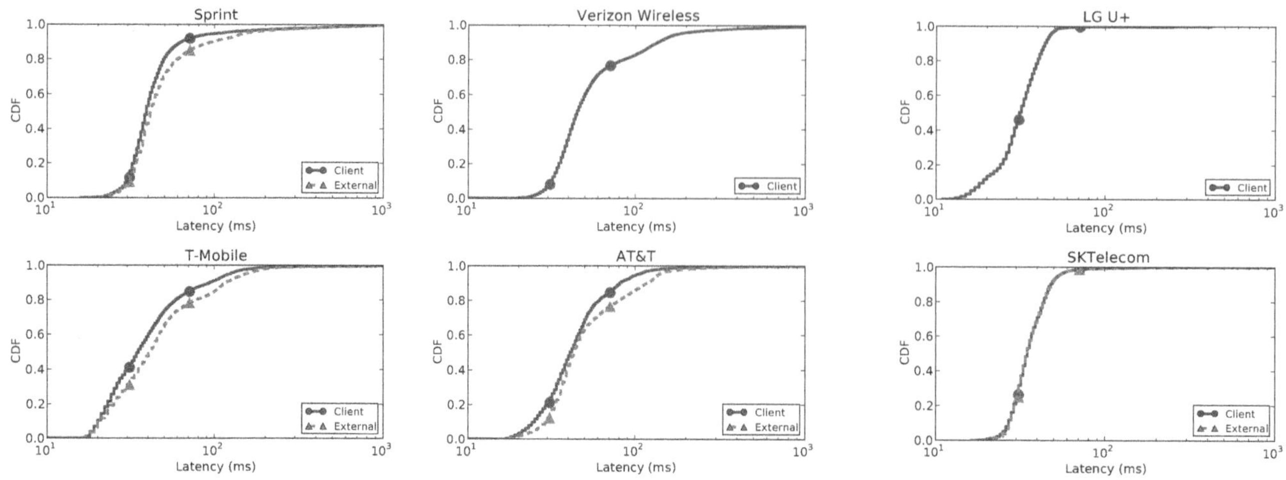

(a) US Carriers

(b) SK Carriers

Figure 4: Client latency to internal and external resolver locations. Ping latencies in Sprint, T-Mobile and AT&T reveal resolvers which are located in separate locations, with external resolvers located further away from clients. Although no external resolvers in either Verizon's or LG U+'s networks responded to probes, client and external resolvers exist in separate ASes in the case of Verizon.

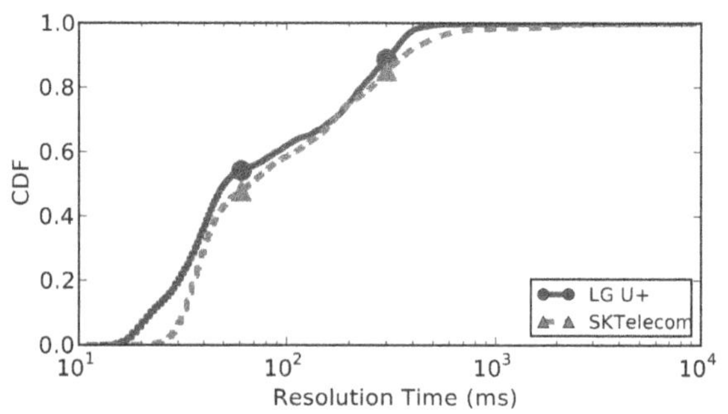

Figure 6: DNS resolution time for South Korean carriers measured from client devices for 2 major cellular providers.

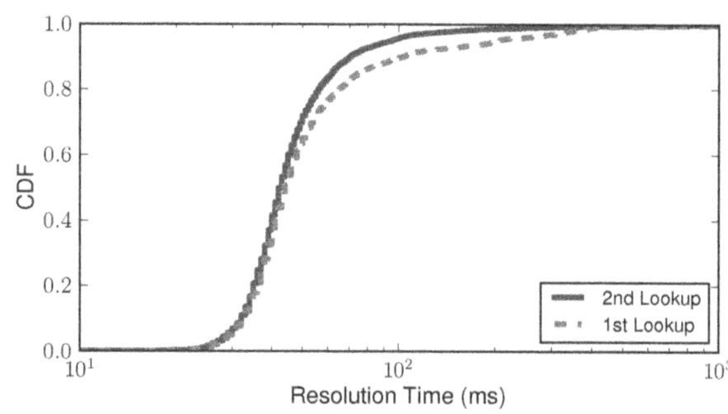

Figure 7: Cache performance for clients local DNS resolvers combined for each of the four US carriers. Although the hostnames we looked up were very popular, we see DNS cache misses for nearly 20% of DNS requests on cellular. This is due to the short TTLs used by CDNs, and explains the long tails of resolution times seen in Figure 5.

in Figure 7, show cache misses accounting for additional delays approximately 20% of the time, similar to the bimodal behavior seen in Figures 5 and 6.

4.4 Cellular Network Opaqueness

Unlike related studies characterizing the behavior and structure of wired networks DNS resolvers, measurement analysis of cellular DNS resolvers can only be carried from clients within their networks. This is because most, if not all, cellular operators employ NAT and firewall policies that prohibit externally generated traffic from their network [24].

We tested the external reachability of cellular network DNS resolvers by launching ping and traceroute probes from our university network to the observed external resolvers (Sec. 4.1). Table 4 presents a summary of our results. Of the six major cellular carriers we profiled, only Verizon and T-Mobile resolvers responded to a majority of ping requests, with a small fraction of AT&T's responding. None of the resolvers responded to our tracerotue probes on any of these networks and our probes were generally unable to penetrate the cellular network beyond the network's ingress points. In the case of Sprint and the two South Korean carriers we studied, none of the resolvers responded to any of our probes.

In contrast, all the probes launched by our mobile clients were able to measure the DNS infrastructure of these carriers. Clearly the known opaqueness of cellular networks extends to the cellular DNS infrastructure and, thus, any analysis of such infrastructure requires the participation of devices within each cellular network.

4.5 Client resolver inconsistency

In this section we analyze the consistency of LDNS resolvers for clients in each cellular provider. As the location of end-host's visible LDNS resolver are commonly used to approximate the actual end-host location, the consistency (or stickiness) of a device's LDNS resolver can significantly impact the effectiveness of services, such as CDNs, that rely on such approximation.

Our analysis revealed inconsistency between client and resolver mappings in all cellular providers investigated. These inconsistencies are not limited to the external resolver IP address, but include the /24 prefix of the external address. Figure 8 shows the LDNS

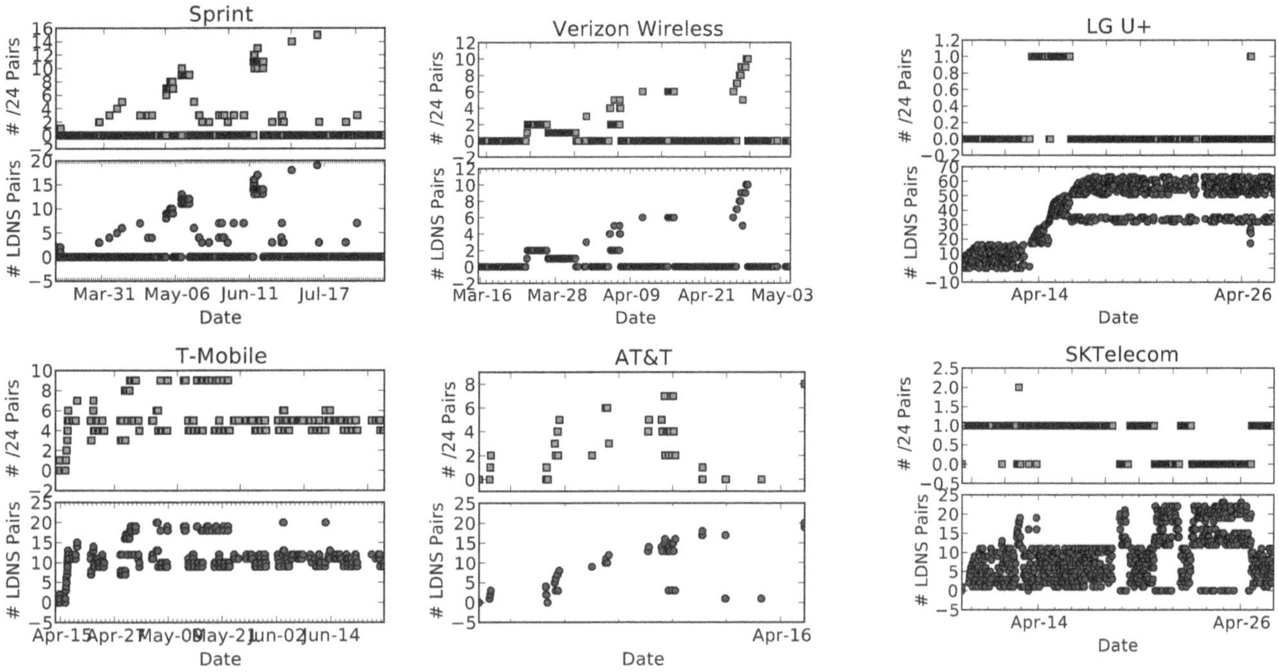

(a) US Carriers

(b) SK Carriers

Figure 8: Number of external resolvers observed by a client in each of the networks we looked at. Bottom: number of external resolver IP addresses. Top: number of unique /24 prefixes observed by resolvers. Client DNS resolvers change not just within localized clusters, but span multiple /24 prefixes over time.

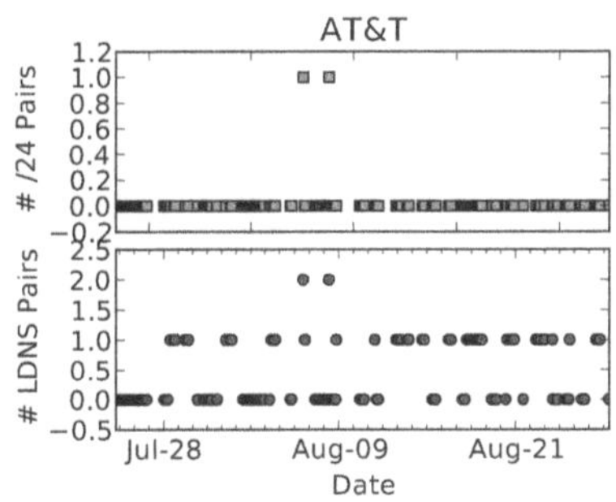

(a)

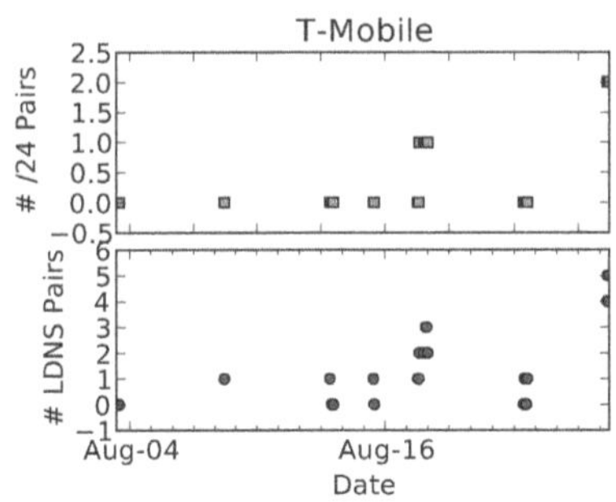

(b)

Figure 9: Client associations with enumerated LDNS resolvers for clients at a static location. Measurements were filtered to be within a 1 km radius of a chosen centroid. Even with relatively static location, clients still shift resolvers across IPs and /24 prefixes.

Provider	Total	Ping	Traceroute
Sprint	20	0	0
Verizon	34	32	0
AT&T	47	3	0
T-Mobile	40	40	0
SKTelecom	24	0	0
LG U+	80	0	0

Table 4: Number of external DNS resolvers able to be reached externally by either ping or traceroute probes.

pairs observed by each device over time, enumerated based on the order of appearance in our measurements.

The temporal stability of mapping between clients and external resolvers varies across carriers. Sprint and Verizon clients, for instance, show relatively stable mappings while the mappings for the remaining carriers appeared to be very unstable. Unstable mappings are not all the same, however, as can be seen when contrasting T-Mobile, AT&T and the two South Korean carriers. In the first two, changes in resolver IP addresses are typically accompanied by changes in the resolvers /24 prefix. In contrast, while clients in the two South Korean carriers experience more frequent changes in resolver IP addresses, the alternative resolvers are contained within one or two /24 prefixes. For example, a client within LG U+'s network witnessed over 65 external resolver IP addresses within a two week period, all of which were within only 2 /24 prefixes.

A possible reason for these unstable mappings is client mobility, with client-resolver mappings changing as devices move within the operator's network. To study this, we recorded a coarse client

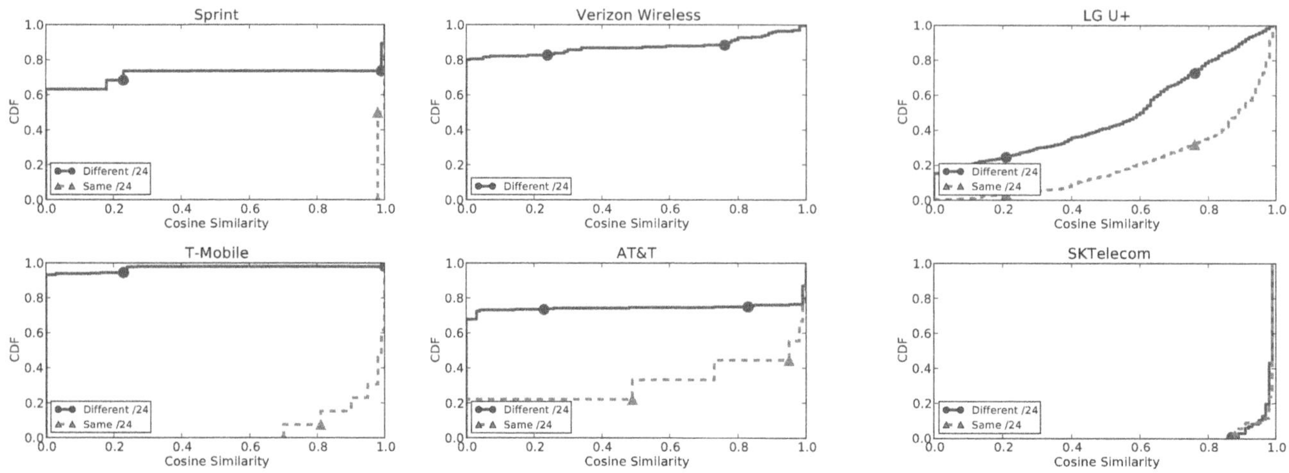

(a) US Carriers

(b) SK Carriers

Figure 10: Cosine similarity of replica servers for buzzfeed.com between resolvers within the same /24 prefix, and those in separate prefixes. Resolvers within the same /24 prefix see very similar sets of replicas (cosine similarity values close to one), and those in separate prefixes see high set independence (values close to zero). Clients changing resolver /24 prefixes are directed towards completely different sets of replica servers.

location for each experiment, rounded up to a 1000-meter radius area. We find that cellular clients experience changes to their DNS IP and /24 prefixes even when not moving. Figure 9 shows users on AT&T and T-Mobile's network, and their resolver consistency for a single location cluster.

To understand the potential impact of these inconsistencies consider that, as shown by Xu et al. [25], DNS resolvers tend to be clustered at egress points. A change of resolver can result in the association of a mobile client with a completely different (and distant!) egress point.

5. CELLULAR REPLICA SELECTION

We now explore the stability of replica server selection for different mobile websites across the different carriers in our study. For each hostnames in this set, we look at the number of replica IP addresses returned, and how often each replica is chosen.

For the selected DNS resolver, we construct a map of $< replicaIP, ratio >$ pairs capturing, for each replica server, the server IP address and the fraction of time that replica was used:

$$replica\_map =< (ip_1, \frac{ip_1 seen}{total\_seen}), ..., (ip_n, \frac{ip_n seen}{total\_seen}) >$$

We then us *cosine similarity* [5, 23] to quantify the similarity of replica servers mapped to each DNS resolver. The cosine similarity between two vectors A and B quantifies the degree of overlap between two vectors by computing the dot product of the vectors and dividing by the product of their lengths:

$$cos\_sim = \frac{A \cdot B}{\|A\|\|B\|}$$

Given our vectors of non-negative probabilities, cos_sim ranges from 0 to 1. When $cos\_sim = 0$, the sets of redirections have no clusters in common. Values greater than 0 indicate that some clusters are seen in both sets; $cos\_sim = 1$ means that the sets of clusters seen are equivalent.

5.1 Impact of Cellular DNS

CDNs typically aggregate client resolvers behind traceroute divergence points and map clients based on measurements to these points [15]. The opaqueness of cellular networks, restricting the reach of traceroutes (Sec. 4.4), calls into question the effectiveness of this approach.

This may explain the relatively small numbers of replica servers mapped to each cellular DNS resolver, particularly when compared to typical CDN-resolver mappings in wired networks.

Looking at the replica maps for each cellular operator and comparing cosine similarities, it appears that CDNs are grouping replica mappings by resolver /24 prefix. Figure 10 shows the cosine similarity (overlap) between replica sets for DNS resolvers in the same /24 prefix, and those in different prefixes. We see large degrees of independence between sets from differing /24 prefixes, with over 60% of sets having a cosine similarity of 0, meaning there is no overlap at all between replica vectors.

This high degree of replica set independence becomes a significant issue since, as we showed in Section 4.5, cellular clients change LDNS resolvers frequently and across /24 prefixes potentially leading to large performance variability.

5.2 Impact of network egress

A previous study of the structure of cellular networks identified the limited numbers of cellular ingress/egress points as a limiting factor to the performance of content delivery in mobile networks [25]. When their study was conducted the number of egress points in each cellular network numbered between 4 and 6, and their recommendation was to place replicas close to these egress points for best performance.

As cellular operators have continued to upgrade and evolve their infrastructure, they have increased the number of network egress points. Using our experiment dataset, we calculated the number of egress points observed by our clients by looking for the first traceroute hop outside a mobile operators network, taking the previous hop as the network egress point. Our results show a substantial increase (2-10x) in the number of network egress points across all US mobile operators, with 11 identified egress points

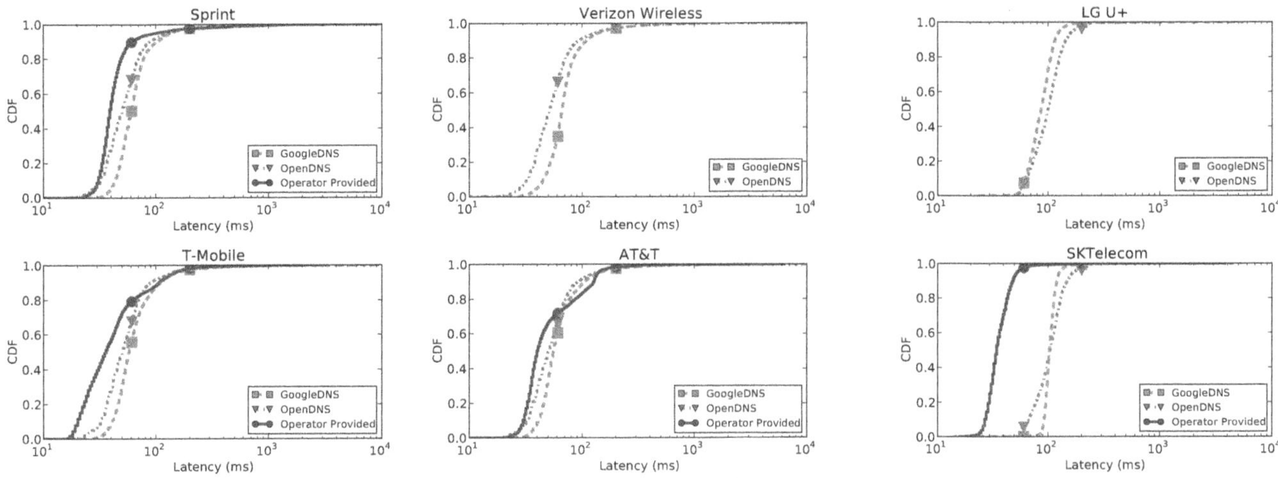

(a) US Carriers (b) SK Carriers

Figure 11: Ping latencies to public DNS resolvers GoogleDNS and OpenDNS. The external facing cellular operator provided LDNS is closer a significant majority of the time (with the exception of Verizon, in the US, and LG in SK, since those resolvers do not respond to probes).

in Sprint, 45 in AT&T, 62 in Verizon and 49 in T-Mobile. *It is this combination of significantly more egress points and radical improvements on the performance of radio access networks that makes client localization and replica selection critical for next generation cellular networks.*

6. PUBLIC DNS IN MOBILE NETWORKS

Considering the growth in public DNS services, in this section we investigate their performance on name resolution and its implications on CDN replica selection in cellular networks. Despite the fact that some cellular operators prohibit customers from configuring different DNS resolvers,[2] our characterization of public DNS services provides a valuable benchmark against which to compare the performance and localization effectiveness of different cellular operators DNS.

6.1 Public DNS Characterization

We characterize the number of resolvers seen from clients within each mobile provider. Table 5 shows the number of unique resolver IPs seen from our clients on each mobile provider. We see that the anycasted public DNS resolvers give significantly higher numbers of unique IP addresses to clients (GoogleDNS has over 4 times the IP addresses than the cellular DNS providers for US carriers). This is partly due to the architecture of these public DNS resolvers. For instance, according to their public documentation, GoogleDNS consists of 30 geographically distributed /24 subnetworks [9].

Accounting for the clustered nature of these public DNS resolvers, the bottom half of Table 5 shows the number of unique /24 subnetworks seen for each resolver. By aggregating by /24 subnetworks, we see relatively equal numbers for all three resolver types across each cellular provider, especially when compared to the large disparity in IP addresses shown above.

As in wired networks, the distance to public DNS resolvers could significantly impact the web performance experienced by clients [18]. Using the methods described in Section 4.1, we measure the distance to both public DNS resolvers, and compare it with that of the cellular operator provided DNS. Figure 11 present CDFs of these measured latencies for the different carriers in ours study.

Provider	Local	GoogleDNS	OpenDNS
Sprint (all IPs)	24	122	38
Verizon (all IPs)	37	135	41
T-Mobile (all IPs)	38	151	49
AT&T (all IPs)	47	160	38
SKTelecom	25	33	7
LG U+	80	47	6
Sprint (/24)	16	21	9
Verizon (/24)	37	13	7
T-Mobile (/24)	21	15	8
AT&T (/24)	27	15	6
SKTelecom (/24)	4	5	2
LG U+ (/24)	3	6	1

Table 5: Total number of DNS resolver IP addresses seen from our ADNS for each provider and resolver group. While public resolvers have more total IP addresses, most are located within the same /24 block. In addition we see more /24 blocks for local resolvers than public ones, with the exception of Sprint.

The figure shows that for the carriers whose resolvers responded to our probes, the cell DNS is commonly closer to clients than the public resolver. This is not surprising since all public DNS resolvers are outside of cellular networks, and resolution requests would have to leave the cellular network to complete. For the US carriers, the cell DNS resolvers is, at median, 10-25 ms closer than the best public DNS resolver. For South Korean operators, public DNS resolvers taken nearly twice for resolution as long at the median. On the other hand, the figure also shows the greater performance consistency of public DNS services and a long tail of resolution times from cell DNS. In the case of T-Mobile, public DNS resolvers performed equal or better over 40% of the time.

In addition to analyzing the observed structure of public DNS and its relative performance, we also explore the consistency of client-resolver mappings. We focus on Google Public DNS,

[2]Mobile devices must be "rooted" in order to change these settings; and, while no longer *illegal* in the United States, rooting voids the device's warranty in most cases.

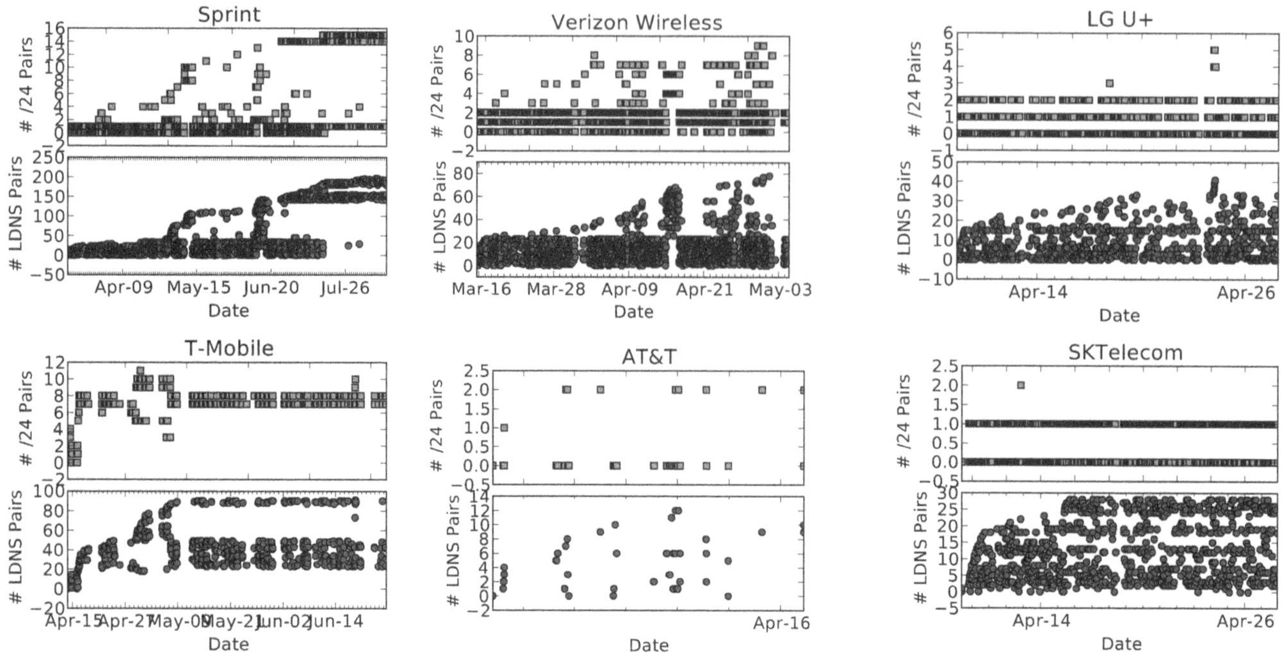

(a) US Carriers

(b) SK Carriers

Figure 12: Resolver consistency for GoogleDNS for users in each carrier. It is interesting to note that even though GoogleDNS's IP address (8.8.8.8) is anycast, users see large variability in the /24s they are sent to. Each /24 for GoogleDNS represents one of thirty distinct geographic locations for their services.

comparing the external resolver IP addresses assigned to a single client over time, in each of the carriers in our study. Figure 12 presents this both for DNS resolvers and their /24 prefix. As the figure shows, despite relying on anycast, Google users are directed toward multiple /24 blocks of resolvers at different geographic locations, given that each /24 block represents one of the 30 geographically distinct resolver clusters. This inconsistency could be the results of the widespread use of tunneling (e.g., via MPLS).

6.2 Public DNS Performance

Figure 13 shows domain resolution times for the device's locally configured DNS along with public DNS resolvers GoogleDNS and OpenDNS. Our results show that in a majority of cases, the locally configured resolver provides faster domain name resolutions. While the name resolution times are greater on average for public DNS resolvers, they exhibit lower variance in response times and have a shorter tail than all cellular operators we investigated.

In general, our results are consistent with those previously reported in [1,18], where public DNS resolvers were located further away from clients, and therefore incurred longer domain name resolution times due to the larger round trip times to the resolvers themselves.

6.3 Public DNS Replica Performance

We measured the performance of replicas selected by public DNS resolvers. For each experiment set described previously in Section 3, we calculated the difference in performance as a percentage change compared to the replica servers returned by the locally configured resolver. Figure 14 shows the cumulative distribution of percent difference between the replica servers returned by each public DNS resolver, and the locally configured one for all six providers. Replicas are aggregated by /24 prefix.

The aggregation shifts the results toward equal performance, as witnessed by the large percentage of experiments shown in the straight line down 0% in all carriers. For all providers in the US and South Korea, between 60 and 80% of the relative latency equals zero. The remainder falls evenly on both sides of the graph, indicating similar performance between cell networks and public DNS on average. Despite cellular network's knowledge of client location, and in contrast to wired networks, cell network provider's own DNS and public DNS yield comparable performance to selected replicas.

7. DISCUSSION

Our analysis reveals some critical problems with current cellular DNS infrastructures, and shows their impact on the performance of content distribution. We have mapped the problem with replica selection to the opaqueness of the cellular DNS infrastructure and the seemingly intended obfuscation of location information such as the inconsistency between mobile clients and the assigned resolvers.

This opaqueness, in an observed extreme case, show client- and external-facing DNS resolvers within a single operator (Verizon) within separate ASes. The opaqueness of cellular DNS means that even though many of the largest CDNs use DNS based replica selection for mobile clients [14], the CDNs themselves are unable to measure the distance from their replicas to these resolvers or place them in respective network coordinates outside of their network prefix. While previous work has shown the inconsistency of cellular device IP addresses, our work further demonstrates the inconsistency of client DNS resolvers within cellular networks.

Despite the public DNS results (Sec. 6.3), we are not particularly endorsing public DNS adoption. Cellular network DNS *should* be the preferred DNS for mobile users. Its resolvers offer lower

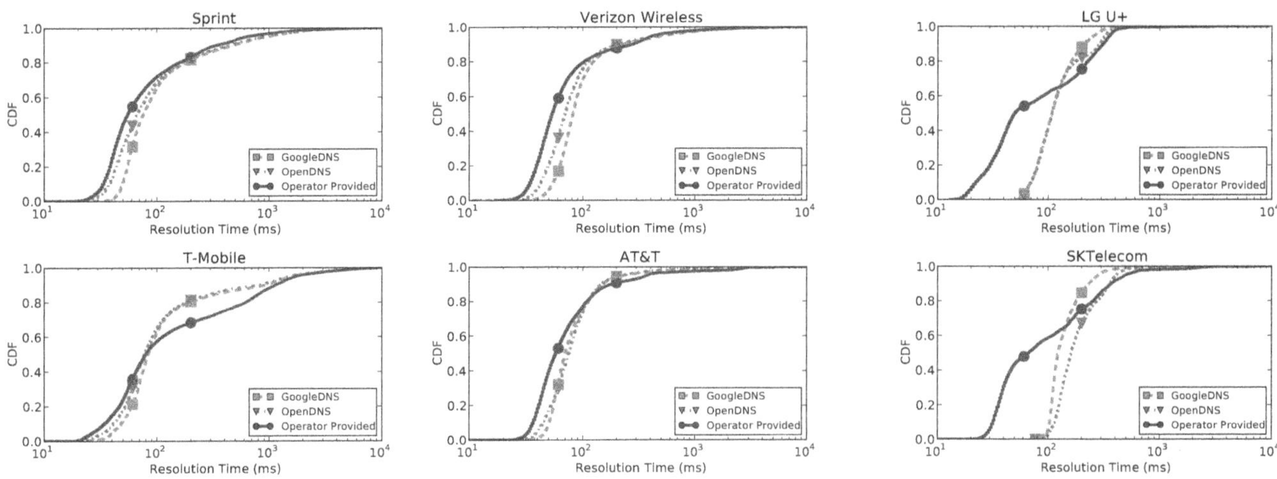

(a) US Carriers

(b) SK Carriers

Figure 13: Domain resolution times for the cellular operator's provided DNS compared with public DNS resolvers GoogleDNS and OpenDNS. Cellular operator DNS offers lower resolution times when compared to public DNS services.

resolution times than popular public DNS options, are closer to mobile users and can potentially offer a finer grained user localization. Rather, we use our analysis of public/provider DNS resolvers to better illustrate the overall inefficiencies of current cell networks and CDNs configurations. In light of these results, it is not surprising to see cellular operators taking steps to offer their own content delivery solutions [19].

8. RELATED WORK

Our work builds on the many previous efforts to explore mobile device performance within cellular networks, characterize client DNS infrastructure, and analyze the interplay between DNS and CDNs in replica selection. It represents the first analysis of cellular DNS infrastructure and its impact on content replica selection in 4G networks.

Several recent efforts have looked at the performance characteristics of mobile clients within cellular networks. Sommers et al. [22] compared the performance of mobile devices when they were in cellular networks or connected to 802.11 WiFi. Nikravesh et al. [17] looked at the longitudinal overall performance of mobile network performance from end devices, while Zarifis et al. [26] analyzed the increased latency experienced by mobile clients. With the exception of Zarifis et al., no paper considered the location of content replicas in their performance analysis.

Other work has investigated the impact of edge network effects such as client inaccessibility and IP address shuffling, and their impact on web services. Balakrishnan et al. [3] looks at the consistency of IP addresses within cellular networks as well as their geo-location accuracy. Casado et al. [4] studied how the opacity of edge networks and their stationarity of IP addresses can adversely affect network services. We continue this work with our observations of client LDNS resolver inconsistency, and its ill suited position as a client locator for CDNs.

Recently, Schomp et al. [20] and Alzoubi et al. [2] have performed large scale studies characterizing the structure and performance of client side LDNS resolvers. Our work is a natural complement as their investigation was limited to wired and broadband networks, because cellular network infrastructure can only be discovered from the end devices within the particular operator network given common firewall policies.

Krishnamurthy et al. [13] performed one of the earliest studies of content delivery networks and evaluated the effectiveness of replica selection for client performance. Our work naturally extends this, updating analysis with 4G cellular networks.

The effectiveness of DNS servers for content replica selection has been extensively explored before (e.g., [16, 21]). However most previous studies have been done under the assumption that client to resolver mappings remained constant. Huang et al. further investigated the replica selection mechanisms of a major CDN [10]. More recently Otto et al. [18] looked at the impact of using remote public DNS on replica selection for broadband connections. Here the authors show that using a client's ISP DNS servers yield the best performance a majority of the time, with public DNS services incurring significant performance of selected replicas. Our work shows that many times, the performance of replicas chosen by cellular operator DNS are in many cases no better than the publicly chosen ones, and offer worse performance in almost 25% of cases. The behavior of cellular DNS creates an entirely different environment for content replica selection, requiring its own set of localization techniques aside from client resolver.

Our work is closest to Xu et al. [25], which looked at the role cellular network structure plays in content placement. While the authors conducted initial investigations on DNS and content placement in cellular networks, our study includes longitudinal data from clients which allows us to monitor changes in DNS configuration from mobile end hosts. In addition, their work was conducted prior to major deployments of 4G technologies such as LTE which significantly decrease radio access latency and variance, as well as prior to the expansion of cellular network ingress points. Therefore, replica selection in modern networks represents a more important piece of mobile user performance than previously cited.

9. CONCLUSIONS AND FUTURE WORK

We presented a detailed analysis of cellular network DNS infrastructure and its implications on the effectiveness of CDN replica selection. Our work is motivated by the continued improvements in access latency and performance seen in next generation networks

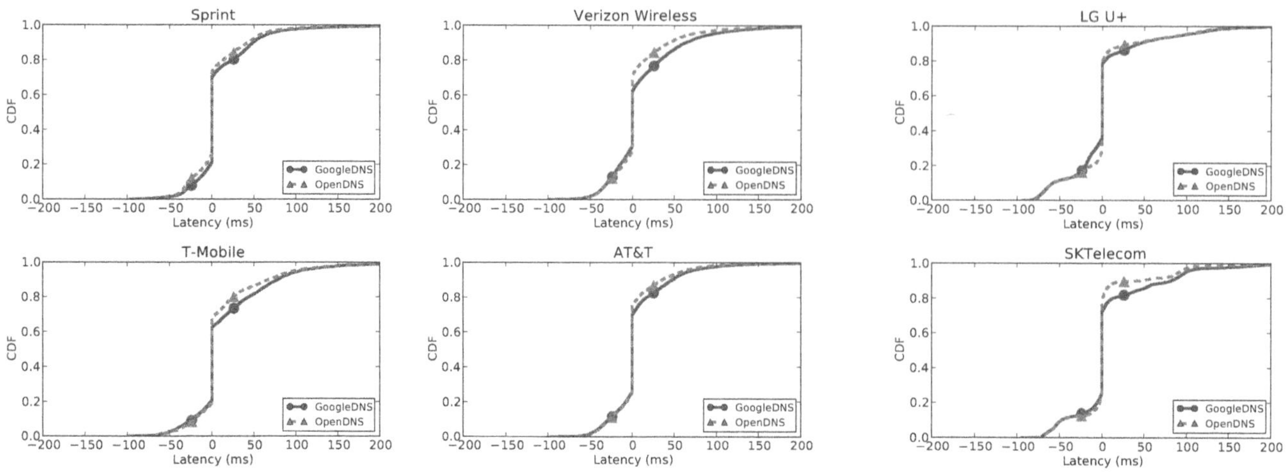

(a) US Carriers (b) SK Carriers

Figure 14: Relative replica latency performance for replicas given by cellular DNS and public DNS resolvers. In contrast to what has been observed in wired networks, replicas given from public DNS resolvers offer equal or better performance to those given from cellular DNS a majority of the time.

that, as we show, make accurate localization of clients critical to the mobile user experience. We explore these issues in the two fastest growing LTE markets – the US and South Korea – relying on data collected by over 340 distributed mobile devices across six carriers.

We found several issues that impact the performance of content delivery in modern cellular networks, including the opaqueness of the cellular networks, and the inconsistent mappings between mobile clients and cellular DNS resolvers. Our study, the first in the literature of public DNS performance from cellular networks, shows despite their greater distance from the associated mobile devices, that remote public resolvers yielded comparable performance in replica selection to that of cellular provider DNS.

Beyond extending our characterization of cellular networks to other markets, we have started to explore alternative approaches for improving CDN performance through better client localization.

Acknowledgements

We thank our shepherd Ramesh Sitaraman and the anonymous reviewers for their invaluable feedback. We are grateful to John Otto and Mario Sánchez for their early feedback on this work, and to Byungjin Jun for his help in application development. This work was supported in part by the National Science Foundation through Award CNS 1218287.

10. REFERENCES

[1] B. Ager, W. Mühlbauer, G. Smaragdakis, and S. Uhlig. Comparing DNS resolvers in the wild. In *Proc. IMC*, 2010.

[2] H. A. Alzoubi, M. Rabinovich, and O. Spatscheck. The anatomy of LDNS clusters: Findings and implications for web content delivery. In *Proc. WWW*, 2013.

[3] M. Balakrishnan, I. Mohomed, and V. Ramasubramanian. Where's that phone?: geolocating IP addresses on 3G networks. In *Proc. IMC*, 2009.

[4] M. Casado and M. J. Freedman. Peering through the shroud: The effect of edge opacity on ip-based client identification. In *Proc. USENIX NSDI*, 2007.

[5] D. R. Choffnes and F. E. Bustamante. Taming the torrent: a practical approach to reducing cross-isp traffic in peer-to-peer systems. *ACM SIGCOMM Computer Communication Review*, 38(4):363–374, 2008.

[6] CISCO. Architectural Considerations for Backhaul of 2G/3G and Long Term Evolution Networks. `http://www.cisco.com/c/en/us/solutions/collateral/service-provider/mobile-internet/white_paper_c11-613002.pdf`.

[7] CISCO. CISCO visual networking index: Global mobile data traffic forecast update 2013-2018. Technical report, CISCO Systems Inc., 2014.

[8] A. Gember, A. Akella, J. Pang, A. Varshavsky, and R. Caceres. Obtaining in-context measurements of cellular network performance. In *Proc. IMC*, 2012.

[9] Google. Frequently asked questions - Public DNS – Google Developers. `https://developers.google.com/speed/public-dns/faq`.

[10] C. Huang, A. Wang, J. Li, and K. W. Ross. Measuring and evaluating large-scale CDNs. In *Proc. IMC*, 2008.

[11] J. Huang, F. Qian, A. Gerber, Z. M. Mao, S. Sen, and O. Spatscheck. A close examination of performance and power characteristics of 4g lte networks. In *Proc. of MobiSys*, 2012.

[12] G. Intelligence. 4G driving data usage but not all markets reaping the rewards. Technical report.

[13] B. Krishnamurthy, C. Wills, and Y. Zhang. On the use and performance of content distribution networks. In *Proc. IMC*, 2001.

[14] B. Maggs. Personal Communication.

[15] B. Maggs. Challenges in engineering the world's largest content delivery networkstate of the union address.

[16] Z. M. Mao, C. D. Cranor, F. Douglis, M. Rabinovich, O. Spatscheck, and J. Wang. A precise and efficient evaluation of the proximity between web clients and their local DNS servers. In *Proc. USENIX ATC*, 2002.

[17] A. Nikravesh, D. R. Choffnes, E. Katz-Bassett, Z. M. Mao, and M. Welsh. Mobile network performance from user devices: A longitudinal, multidimensional analysis. In *Proc. PAM*, 2014.

[18] J. S. Otto, M. A. Sánchez, J. P. Rula, and F. E. Bustamante. Content delivery and the natural evolution of DNS: Remote DNS trends, performance issues and alternative solutions. In *Proc. IMC*, 2012.

[19] B. F. Rubin. Verizon to acquire content-delivery startup edgecast networks. *The Wall Street Journal*, 9 December 2013. Available: `http://online.wsj.com/article/BT-CO-20131209-703213.html`. [Last Accessed: 5 May 2014].

[20] K. Schomp, T. Callahan, M. Rabinovich, and M. Allman. On measuring the client-side dns infrastructure. In *Proc. IMC*, 2013.

[21] A. Shaikh, R. Tewari, and M. Agrawal. On the effectiveness of DNS-based server selection. In *Proc. IEEE INFOCOM* 2001.

[22] J. Sommers and P. Barford. Cell vs. wifi: on the performance of metro area mobile connections. In *Proc. IMC*, 2012.

[23] A.-J. Su, D. R. Choffnes, A. Kuzmanovic, and F. E. Bustamante. Drafting behind akamai (travelocity-based detouring). *ACM SIGCOMM Computer Communication Review*, 36(4):435–446, 2006.

[24] Z. Wang, Z. Qian, Q. Xu, Z. Mao, and M. Zhang. An untold story of middleboxes in cellular networks. *SIGCOMM Comput. Commun. Rev.*, 41(4):374–385, Aug. 2011.

[25] Q. Xu, J. Huang, Z. Wang, F. Qian, and A. G. Z. M. Mao. Cellular data network infrastructure characterization and implication on mobile content placement. In *Proc. ACM SIGMETRICS*, 2011.

[26] K. Zarifis, T. Flach, S. Nori, D. Choffnes, R. Govindan, E. Katz-Bassett, Z. M. Mao, and M. Welsh. Diagnosing Path Inflation of Mobile Client Traffic. In *Proc. PAM*, 2014.

Need, Want, Can Afford – Broadband Markets and the Behavior of Users

Zachary S. Bischof
Northwestern University

Fabián E. Bustamante
Northwestern University

Rade Stanojevic
Telefonica Research

ABSTRACT

We present the first study of broadband services in their broader context, evaluating the impact of service characteristics (such as capacity, latency and loss), their broadband pricing and user demand. We explore these relationships, beyond correlation, with the application of *natural experiments*. Most efforts on broadband service characterization have so far focused on performance and availability, yet we lack a clear understanding of how such services are being utilized and how their use is impacted by the particulars of the market. By analyzing over 23-months of data collected from 53,000 end hosts and residential gateways in 160 countries, along with a global survey of retail broadband plans, we empirically study the relationship between broadband service characteristics, pricing and demand. We show a strong correlation between capacity and demand, even though subscribers rarely fully utilize their links, but note a law of diminishing returns with relatively smaller increases in demand at higher capacities. Despite the fourfold increase in global IP traffic, we find that user demand on the network over a three year period remained constant for a given bandwidth capacity. We exploit natural experiments to examine the causality between these factors. The reported findings represent an important step towards understanding how user behavior, and the market features that shape it, affect broadband networks and the Internet at large.

Categories and Subject Descriptors

C.2.3 [**Computer Communication Networks**]: [Network Operations]; C.4 [**Performance of Systems**]: [Measurement techniques]

Keywords

Broadband access networks, User behavior, Causal inference, Natural experiments

IMC'14, November 5–7, 2014, Vancouver, BC, Canada.

ACM 978-1-4503-3213-2/14/11 ...$15.00.
http://dx.doi.org/10.1145/2663716.2663753 .

1. INTRODUCTION

As one of the most economically significant and fastest growing sectors of the Internet [19], broadband networks have attracted interest from researchers, network operators, and policy makers. Over the past decade, the number of broadband networks has increased rapidly. The latest "State of Broadband" reports that there are over 60 countries where fixed or mobile broadband penetration is above 25% and more than 70 countries where the majority of the population is online [4]. Providing broadband Internet access is known to be instrumental in social and economic development [35]. Several governments (including France, Finland and Spain) and the UN have even labeled broadband access a basic human right, similar to education and water.

While several recent and ongoing efforts have shed light on the performance and availability of broadband services [1, 2, 5, 12, 20, 28, 31, 33, 34], we lack a clear understanding of how these services are being used and how this use is impacted by the particulars of the market. The goal of our work is to examine broadband services in this broader context. How much bandwidth do people actually need? How does price affect usage? Do users in developing and developed countries impose different demands on their services? What is the impact of connection quality on usage?

We analyze over 23 months of information collected from 53,000 end hosts [30] and residential gateways [15] in 160 countries, along with a global survey of retail broadband plans [27]. We quantify the relationship between user demand on the network, retail price of available broadband services and the performance of the service to which the user subscribes. We observe a law of diminishing returns in the relationship between broadband capacity and the average/peak demand users put on their broadband link, implying that adding extra capacity on an already wide broadband line leads to a minor increment in user demand.

Looking at the longitudinal data, we find, somewhat surprisingly, that despite the fourfold increase in global IP traffic over the past five years [10], subscribers' demand in the same bandwidth capacity class remained constant, indicating that users "jump" to a higher service when their demand grows, rather than fully utilize their existing pipe. We study in depth the service upgrade dynamics and report our findings.

In a study such as this, controlled experiments are not feasible for studying the features of interest at scale. A key contribution of our work is thus a methodology for combining broadband measurement and retail price datasets along with the application of natural experiments to get to a problem otherwise impossible to tackle. We use natural experiments to examine the interaction between price, the quality of services available, and users' demands. We show that higher broadband prices increase demand when comparing users of similar capacities across markets. Additionally, we find that very high packet loss rates (over 1%) and latencies (above 500 ms) result in significantly lower usage.

Our study offers several insights on the interplay between user demand and broadband market features that are of value to the research community, network operators and policy makers. For network operators, an understanding of how user behavior changes with the network and broadband market can better inform network planning and operation. For policy makers, the work provides a firmer statistical footing for discussions on broadband incentives.

The rest of the paper is organized as follows. In Sec. 2, we explain our analysis methodology, describe our datasets, and summarize the performance of the broadband connections seen in our global dataset. We explore the impact of capacity on demand in Sec. 3, followed by a longitudinal study that investigates how demand changes over time in Sec. 4. In Sec. 5, 6, and 7 we study the impact of the price of broadband access, the cost of increasing capacity, and the connection quality on user demand, respectively. We then review related work in Sec. 8, summarize and discuss our findings in Sec. 9, and conclude in Sec. 10.

2. ANALYSIS METHODS AND DATASETS

In the following paragraphs we describe the three datasets we rely on for analysis, including a summary of key characteristics for the broadband connections they capture. We close the section with a brief discussion of the goals and methodology of our study.

2.1 Datasets

Our study builds on three datasets, two of broadband connections including: *(i)* measurements from residential gateways in the US, and *(ii)* detailed end-host collected data on broadband connections from around the world, and *(iii)* a compilation of retail broadband connectivity plans made available by Google [27]. We describe each of these in the following paragraphs.

Residential gateway data. Since 2010, the FCC, in collaboration with SamKnows, has publicly shared data collected from residential gateways distributed to broadband users around the US as part of the "Measuring Broadband America" effort [15]. Users that participate in this study were either selected to participate by their ISP or signed up through SamKnows' website. The data collected from these gateways includes measurements of link capacity, latency and packet loss as well as hourly recordings of the number of bytes sent and received over the WAN link.

End host data. Our end-host collected dataset comes from Dasu [30], a previously released network experimentation and broadband measurement client. Dasu is available as both an extension to BitTorrent and as a standalone client. As an incentive for adoption, Dasu informs users of their ISP's performance, providing detailed information on their home network configuration, the volume of network traffic sent and received by the localhost, the volume of detected cross traffic in the home network, and the results of performance measurements on their ISP (e.g. a comparison of their ISP's web browsing and DNS performance). Dasu records network usage data from the localhost and home network to account for cross traffic during characterization or the execution of network experiments.

Since its release, Dasu has been installed by over 100,000 users in over 160 countries, with the majority of clients using the BitTorrent extension. From this dataset, we select users that either have UPnP enabled on their home gateway device or those that were directly connected to their modem (thus their machine is the only device generating traffic). UPnP-enabled gateways provide byte counters that we use to measure activity on the link, taking into account issues with UPnP counters raised in other works [11,29]. For users directly connected to their modem, we use byte counters available from `netstat` to monitor network usage (available by default on most popular operating systems). Traffic byte counters are collected at approximately 30 second intervals with some variations due to scheduling.

As it is the case with all observational studies, there is a concern about potential biases in our datasets, coming either from P2P or SamKnow's users (e.g., uniquely demanding users, early-adopters or "geek-effect" [5,20,25]. We account for some of these issues throughout our analysis by, for instance, focusing on measurements gathered when users are not actively downloading/uploading content on BitTorrent, restricting our users to those directly connected to a modem or wirelessly connected to a UPnP-enabled one, using neighbor matching with a caliper to ensure close matches. On the potential biases with our P2P users' data, we show in Sec. 3.1 that the average demand of Dasu users in the US – when not actively using BitTorrent – is comparable to that of participants in the FCC's study.

Connectivity plans. Our third dataset is a compilation of international retail broadband connectivity plans, made available by Google on their "Policy by the Numbers" blog [27]. This data was compiled by Communications Chambers, a consultant group, by visiting the websites of broadband service providers around the world. The dataset covers 1,523 service plans across 99 countries. It includes information on the upload and download speeds of each plan, the monthly traffic limits, and monthly cost in the local currency. We selected this dataset over those provided by the FCC, OECD, or ITU given the breadth of countries included and the depth of plans listed. The FCC and OECD datasets focus on the US and members of the OECD while the ITU dataset only includes a single service plan for each country. In a few cases, we expanded this dataset by manually visiting the websites of ISPs in countries where we had users but no broadband price data.

To directly compare the price of broadband plans across different economies, we convert the monthly cost to US dollars. We account for differences in relative purchasing power in each country by using the purchasing power parity (PPP) to market exchange ratio. In most cases, this is included in the broadband service survey provided by Google. When that is not the case, we use publicly available data from the International Monetary Fund's website[1]. All monetary figures throughout this work are normalized by purchasing power parity, including the GDP per capita data provided by the International Monetary Fund that we use later in our case study.

[1]International Monetary Fund. `http://www.imf.org/`

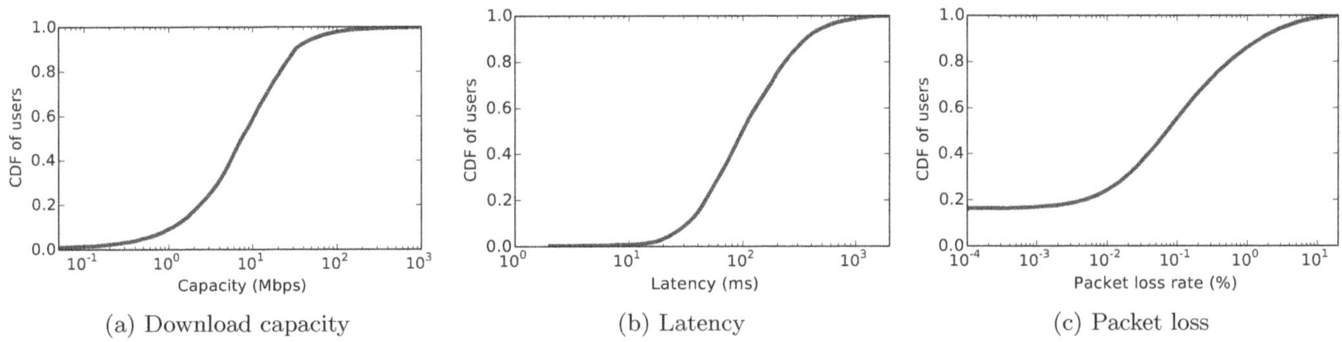

Figure 1: CDFs of the maximum download capacities, average latency to nearest available measurement server, and average packet loss rates measured for every network connections used throughout our analysis.

2.2 Broadband Networks Characteristics

We now describe the diversity of broadband connections in our global dataset, presenting distributions of their measured capacity, latency and packet loss. All the Dasu data were collected by running M-Lab's Network Diagnostic Tool (NDT) [23] within Dasu. NDT reports the upload and download capacity of a connection, as well as its end-to-end latency and packet loss rates.

Capacity. Figure 1a shows a CDF of the maximum download capacities, in Mbps, measured over each user's connection in our dataset. Our distribution has a median user download capacity of 7.4 Mbps and interquartile range of 14.3 Mbps (from 3.1 Mbps to 17.4 Mbps). Approximately 10% of users have download capacities below 1 Mbps, while the top 10% of users have capacities above 30 Mbps.

Latency. For latency, we measured the average latency to the closest NDT measurement server. Since measurement servers are hosted in a diverse set of networks of content providers (e.g. Google) and content distribution networks (e.g. Level 3), we believe such measurements provides a reasonable estimate of the latency to popular content. Figure 1b shows the distribution of measured latencies. We find that a "typical" user in our dataset has an average RTT of about 100 ms to the nearest NDT servers. The top 5% of users had an average latency above 500 ms. Based on the organization names that we found via `whois` lookups, the majority of connections with very high latencies appeared to be connecting over wireless modems or satellite providers.

Packet loss. Figure 1c shows the distribution of average packet loss rates reported by NDT tests. While the loss rate is relatively low for most users (less than 0.1%), approximately 14% of users saw an average loss rate above 1%. For the top 1% of users, average loss rates were above 10%. As was the case with high latency connections, the organization names of networks with very high packet loss rates indicated they were satellite or wireless (e.g. WiMAX, cellular) services.

2.3 Methodology

The main goal of our study is to provide insight into the impact of broadband service market characteristics on network usage. Specifically, we study the impact of the following market features: connection capacity, the price of broadband access, the cost of increasing capacity, and connection quality. While there are many other variables that can affect user behavior, this set covers the key characteristics of broadband service markets. Given the rapid pace of development in broadband and the reported growth in network traffic, we also conduct a longitudinal analysis of user demands on broadband services.

Beyond gathering a sufficiently large and diverse perspective of broadband connections, a key challenge for a macroscopic study such as ours is the nature of experiments one is able to conduct. Classical controlled experiments – where subjects in the study are randomly assigned to "treated" and "untreated" groups for comparison – are clearly not feasible at a global scale. It is also unlikely that the features we explore are independent, e.g., one would assume that price or service diversity can impact capacity and service quality. This has been a long, well understood problem in a range of fields, from epidemiology to sociology and economics. We address this challenge, as many studies do in those domains, by resorting to natural experiments in our analysis [14].

By using natural experiments [14] and related study designs, we remedy the fact that we cannot control the application of a treatment, Matching users in our treated group with similar users in the untreated group we simulate random or as-good-as-random assignment, manually ensuring that differences are evenly distributed between the two groups. This allows us to infer whether or not the relationship observed are likely to be causal. For example, to test if bandwidth capacity affects user demand, we pair users that are similar in terms of connection quality and broadband market. We then check if the user with higher capacity generates more traffic. If so, our hypothesis holds true for that pair. After testing this for each pair of similar users, we calculate the percentage of times that our hypothesis is correct.

If neither of the two variables under study – in this example, capacity and demand – have an impact on the other, then their interaction would be random. In our example this would mean, for instance, that lower capacity will result in lower (or higher) demand about 50% of the time. Significant deviations from this would suggest that a causal relationship is likely to exist between the two.

We use the one-tailed binomial test to measure the statistical significance of deviations from the expected distribution. As is common in many study designs, we consider a p-value that is less than 0.05 to be a strong presumption

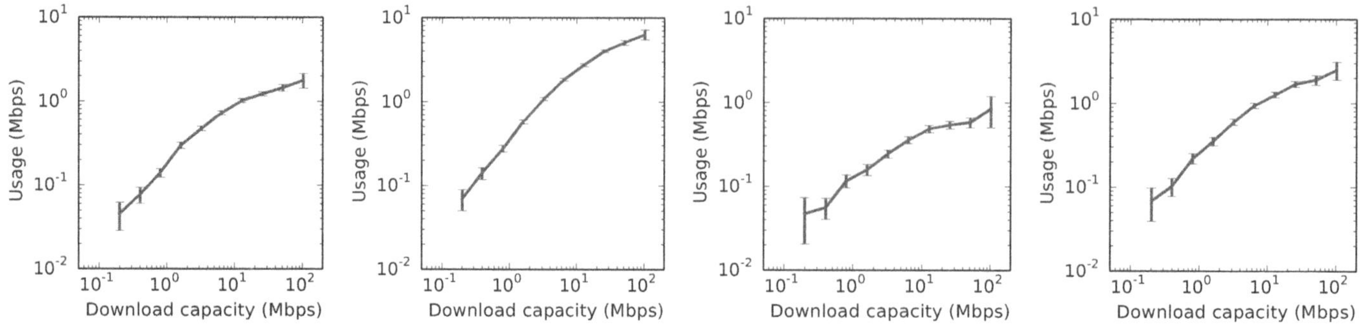

(a) Mean w/ BT ($r = 0.870$)

(b) 95th %ile w/ BT ($r = 0.913$)

(c) Mean no BT ($r = 0.885$)

(d) 95th %ile no BT ($r = 0.890$)

Figure 2: Volume of download traffic generated by users versus their download link capacity. Users are grouped by their download capacity and each bin is averaged. The error bars represent the 95% confidence interval of the mean. In each case, usage is strongly correlated with link capacity.

against the null hypothesis (H_0). One potential issue with our application of the binomial test in this context is the known problem that given a large enough dataset, the test will consider even minor deviations to be significant. That is, with a large enough sample of throws, an unbiased coin could fail to pass a χ^2 test for fitting the predicted binomial distribution [26]. To account for this issue, we only consider deviations larger than 2% to be practically important. In other words the hypothesis holds at least 52% of the time.

3. IMPACT OF CAPACITY

The interplay between broadband service characteristics and user demand is complex [36]. For instance, while subscribers cannot directly affect the cost of their service, they have some freedom in choosing what package (capacity) they purchase and how much traffic they generate. On the other hand, although they come with needs and budgets when choosing a broadband plan, once acquired, their usage patterns are shaped by their selection. In addition, there is the potential impact of seemingly irrational and biased choices by subscribers [16,32] that complicates any attempt at understanding and analytical modeling of the drivers of users' choices and demand. While we (or even most customers [17]) may not know the advertised service of a broadband connection, our study focuses on the impact of the actual maximum capacity provided to the user.

In this section, we begin to empirically explore the complex interactions between broadband service market features and user behavior by first studying the effects of capacity on user demand. When appropriate, we compare data collected from end hosts (via Dasu) and residential gateways (FCC/SamKnows).

3.1 Capacity vs. usage

We first explore the relationship between access link capacity and the demand users generate on the access network. To describe user demand, we rely on two metrics of usage: the average and peak volume of traffic generated. We define peak as the 95th-percentile value of the time series (sampled every 30-secs) of downlink demand for each user.

Figure 2 presents both the mean and peak demand, for different classes of users based on their measured downlink capacity. Given the range of services across the different markets we analyze, we split services into ten classes where every user in class (k) has a download capacity in the range of $(100Kbps * 2^{k-1}, 100Kbps * 2^k]$. We analyze usage both throughout the entire measurement period (Fig. 2a and 2b) and during periods when users are not actively uploading or downloading content on BitTorrent (Fig. 2c and 2d).

We also contrast Dasu' end-host collected data with that of users in the FCC study (gateway collected data), looking both at average and peak network usage. Figure 3 shows the mean and peak (95th percentile) demand of users, grouped by capacity, in the FCC and US-based Dasu dataset (when not using BitTorrent). Although the average usage is slightly higher for Dasu users, the peak usage is nearly identical for both groups. The difference in average demand is likely due to the fact that the FCC data is collected evenly throughout the 24-hour period, while Dasu usage (and thus our data) is partially biased towards peak usage hours.

We find that usage grows with capacity, as the plots of Fig. 2 and 3 clearly show. This is *despite* the fact that users rarely utilize their link (even at the 95th percentile, average utilization ranges between 10 and 48%). For both mean and 95th percentile usage, with and without BitTorrent traffic, we find that usage is strongly correlated with the group's link capacity ($r \geq 0.87$ for each).

Figure 2 also show that as capacity increases, usage begins to level off (related to the findings in Sundaresan et al. [34]). This would suggest that the relationship follows a law of diminishing returns: the relative increase in demand is greater for lower capacity connections than for higher capacity connections.

3.2 Inferring causality

While the access capacity and the demand users generate are strongly correlated, inferring the causality between these variables is significantly more challenging. For instance, demand might drive capacity (i.e. users sign up for faster services because they have access to applications with higher bandwidth needs, such as HD video streaming) or be driven by it, with users changing their behavior when given a higher

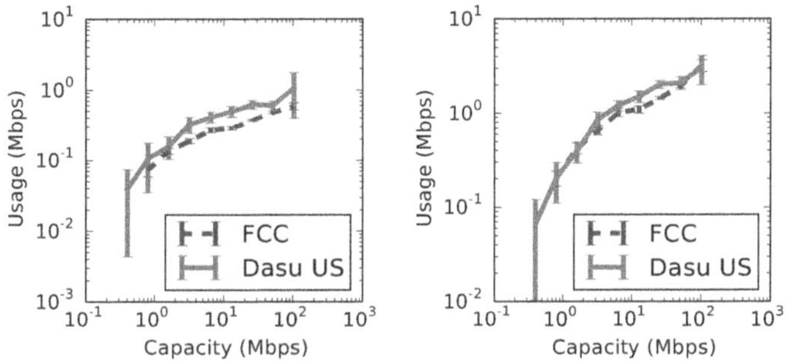

(a) Mean
($r = 0.915$)

(b) 95th %ile
($r = 0.905$)

Figure 3: Mean and peak (95th percentile) download traffic generated for FCC gateway users and Dasu users within the US when not using BitTorrent. The error bars represent the 95% confidence interval of the mean.

Metric	% H holds	p-value
Average usage	66.8%	1.94×10^{-25}
Peak usage	70.3%	1.13×10^{-36}

Table 1: Percentage of the time that an individual user's average and peak demand will increase when moving to a network with a higher capacity. In both cases, the control group is their behavior on the slower network and the treatment is their behavior on the faster network.

capacity and generating a higher demand. Additionally, there may be other factors that affect user demand such as the quality of the connection or the price of access.

To explore a causal relationship between access capacity and demand, we first design a natural experiment to see if the behavior of individual users changes when switching between networks of different capacities. This let us test the idea that when given a higher capacity link, users will increase their demand on the network. We then compare the demand of users that are similar in terms of price of broadband access, cost to upgrade, and link quality but differ in terms of service capacity.

User upgrades. To determine if their relationship between capacity and demand is causal, we need to account for differences in usage patterns between different users. We do this by looking at how individual users change their network demand when switching to faster services, allowing us to determine if the relationship between capacity and demand is likely causal.

Figure 4 presents the CDFs of mean and peak download link usage for users switching between a "slow" and "fast" network. Both average and peak volume of traffic are when the client is not active on BitTorrent. Each network is identified by a tuple *(ISP name, network prefix, geolocated city)*. For both average and peak demand, we see that usage tends to be considerably higher on the faster network. For example, at the median, average usage doubles from 95 kbps to 189 kbps and peak usage (95th percentile) more than triples, from 192 kbps to 634 kbps.

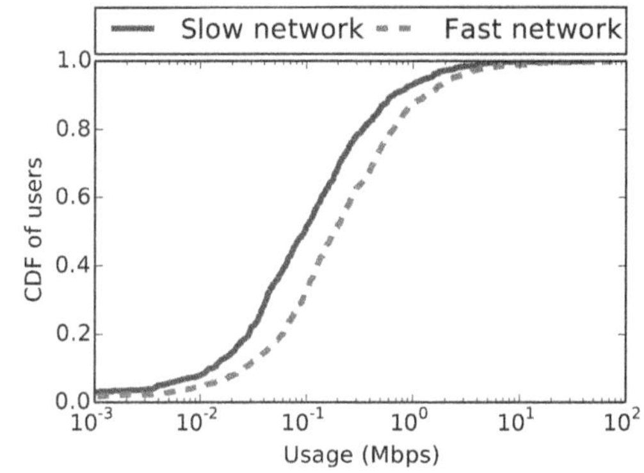

(a) Mean

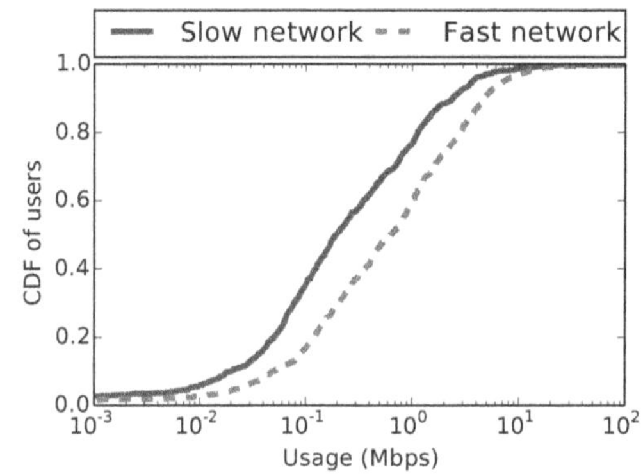

(b) 95th %ile

Figure 4: CDFs of the mean and peak download link usage for individual users on "slow" and "fast" networks when not using BitTorrent.

To validate this assertion we use a natural experiment. Our hypothesis (H) is that when a user moves from a slower to a faster service, demand will increase. As such, our null hypothesis (H_0) is that demand will not be affected by a change in capacity. We test this assertion for both the mean and peak demand and present our results in Table 1. As the table shows, our original hypothesis (H), is true 66.8% of the time when comparing average demand and 70.3% of the time for peak demand. For both metrics, we find very small p-values, leading us to reject the null hypothesis (H_0) that capacity does not affect the demand of individual users.

For these analysis we limit our data to that collected while the users were not generating BitTorrent traffic. Including BitTorrent traffic, we find an even higher increase in usage, and so is the percentage of the time that our hypothesis holds true. This is likely due to the fact that users are more likely to saturate their link for extended periods of time when using BitTorrent [9].

Impact of switching services. To further understand the interaction between capacity and demand, we explore the impact of service upgrades on demand, for different initial capacities of connections. Figure 5 shows the average change in demand, grouping upgrades by the "before" and "after" download capacities. The labels on the x-axis represent the capacity range of the initial service and each bar is the average change in demand when switching to a faster service in the respective capacity tier.

As the figure shows, for each metric, demand clearly increases when upgrading from slower services, particularly when looking at peak (95th percentile) usage. Increases in

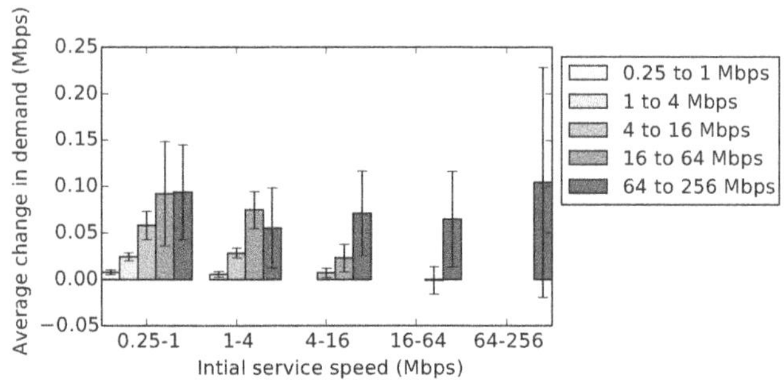

(a) Mean (w/ BT)

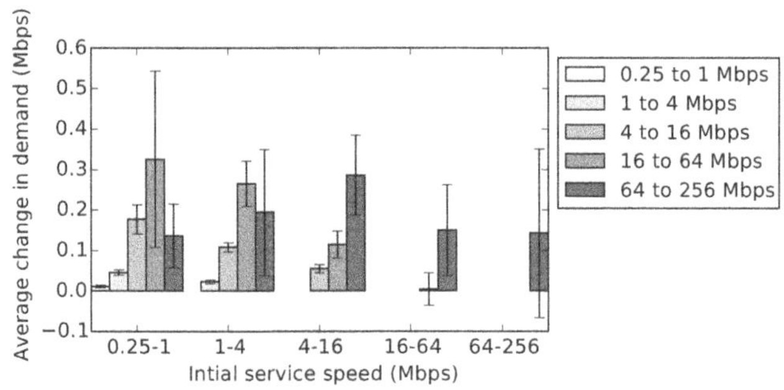

(b) 95th %ile (w/ BT)

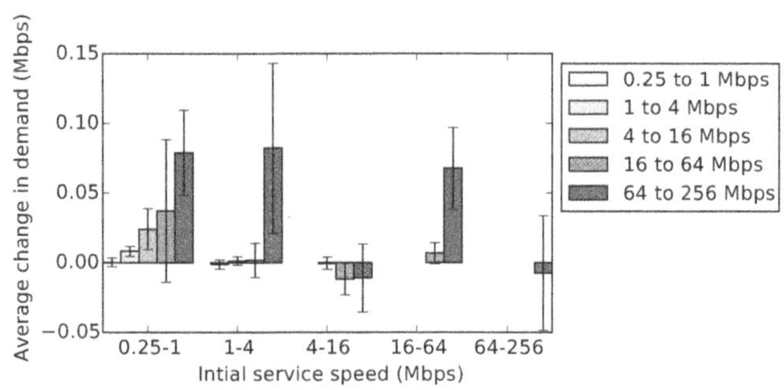

(c) Mean (no BT)

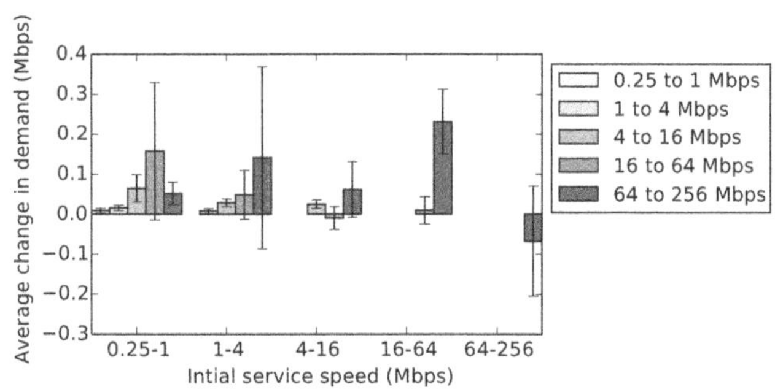

(d) 95th %ile (no BT)

Figure 5: Change in volume of traffic generated when switching to a faster connection. The x-axis corresponds to the initial service speed while each bar represents the average change for users switching to a faster service within that group. The error bars represent the 95% confidence interval.

Dasu data			
Control Group (in Mbps)	Treatment Group (in Mbps)	% H holds	p-value
$(0.1, 0.2]$	$(0.2, 0.4]$	75.2%	5.81×10^{-11}
$(0.2, 0.4]$	$(0.4, 0.8]$	63.4%	2.21×10^{-7}
$(0.4, 0.8]$	$(0.8, 1.6]$	59.9%	8.01×10^{-8}
$(0.8, 1.6]$	$(1.6, 3.2]$	59.3%	1.11×10^{-8}
$(1.6, 3.2]$	$(3.2, 6.4]$	53.3%	0.0166
$(3.2, 6.4]$	$(6.4, 12.8]$	57.5%	0.00707
$(6.4, 12.8]$	$(12.8, 25.6]$	56.8%*	0.0583
$(12.8, 25.6]$	$(25.6, 51.2]$	52.9%*	0.310
$(25.6, 51.2]$	$(51.2, 102.4]$	51.0%*	0.462
FCC data			
Control Group (in Mbps)	Treatment Group (in Mbps)	% H holds	p-value
$(0.4, 0.8]$	$(0.8, 1.6]$	66.4%	0.000223
$(0.8, 1.6]$	$(1.6, 3.2]$	58.1%	4.70×10^{-05}
$(1.6, 3.2]$	$(3.2, 6.4]$	56.2%	0.000487
$(3.2, 6.4$	$(6.4, 12.8]$	55.1%	0.00236
$(6.4, 12.8]$	$(12.8, 25.6]$	58.5%	2.54×10^{-7}
$(12.8, 25.6]$	$(25.6, 51.2]$	61.2%	6.76×10^{-17}
$(25.6, 51.2]$	$(51.2, 102.4]$	64.7%	0.00161

Table 2: Percentage of the time that increased capacity will increase demand when comparing similar users and each experiment's corresponding p-value. An asterisk denotes that a result was not statistically significant.

demand are less consistent when switching between already fast services, particularly above 16 Mbps, where there is a large variance on demand growth with capacity. In some cases, the large range in the 95% confidence interval shows that the upgrade likely had no significant impact on usage. These findings suggest that while capacities do drive demand, this is only true up to a certain point.

All users. We expand our comparison to all users in the datasets and use a matching study design to test the impact of increased capacity. As before, we place users into one of k bins, where $k = (100Kbps * 2^{k-1}, 100Kbps * 2^k]$. We then compare the usage of users in bins k and $k+1$. Our hypothesis (H) is that users in the "treated" group, $k+1$, will have a higher demand on the network due to their increased capacity. Our null hypothesis (H_0) is that the relationship is random and increased capacity will not result in higher demand.

To compare users from each group, however, we must ensure that each pair of users is similar in terms of connection quality (packet loss and latency), price of broadband access, and cost to upgrade capacity. For this and the remaining studies, we use nearest neighbor matching to pair similar users in "control" and "treatment" groups. We use a caliper to ensure that dissimilar users are not matched, requiring that users be within 25% of each other for each confounding factor. This means, for instance, that users with latencies of 50 and 62 ms and in regions where broadband Internet access costs \$25 and \$30 (USD) per month are considered to be sufficiently similar in terms of latency and cost of broadband access. Note the trade-off here, a tighter caliper will yield a potentially more accurate comparison, but will also reduced the number of comparisons we can perform.

Table 2 shows the experiment's results separated by the datasets used. For the Dasu data, increased capacity has the widest impact when comparing slower service groups. The increase in demand is statistically significant while comparing groups of users with capacities less or equal to 6.4 Mbps (though the achieved p-value when comparing groups $(6.4, 12.8]$ and $(12.8, 25.6]$ is very close to 0.05). When comparing users in bins above 12.8 Mbps, the difference tends to become random and our hypothesis holds about 50% the time. These results suggest that increasing capacity beyond $\approx$10 Mbps is less likely to have a significant impact on peak user demand.

For the FCC data, increased capacity tends to result in increased demand across all bins. We believe that this is largely due to the fact that the FCC vantage point set is comprised solely of users in the US, where higher capacity broadband services are available, but at a moderately higher price (this does not apply in many of the countries in our study). We also observed a similar trend of increased usage when studying Dasu users in the US, as we will show in Sec. 5.

4. LONGITUDINAL TRENDS IN USAGE

The last few years have witnessed a rapid growth on the capacity, coverage and affordability of broadband networks [4]. Concurrently, the volume of digital content and total IP traffic continue to grow at rapid pace. A recent Cisco report states that the total IP traffic has increased 18-fold since 2.4 exabytes in 2005 [10]. Meanwhile, the size of the "digital universe", the total amount of data created and replicated reported to be 2.8 zettabytes in 2012, doubles in size about every two years [18]. In this section, we look for changes in demand over time to see if these changes are reflected, and in what manner, in the network demand of broadband users.

To this end, we carry a longitudinal analysis of broadband connections in our dataset. We compare changing trends in usage relative to capacity, both average and peak, between 2011 and 2013. Figure 6 shows average and demand over this period, with and excluding BitTorrent traffic.

Trends in relative use are surprisingly different than what we expected. Despite the fourfold increase in global IP traffic, we find that subscribers' demand on the network remained constant at each speed tier. While we note a slight increase in demand for users with very fast connections (about 100 Mbps), overall the demand within the same broadband class has remained fairly consistent throughout the observation period.

Using a natural experiment, we are unable to find any significant change in demand at any given speed tier between 2011 and 2013. It would appear that growth in traffic is likely due to an increase in the number of broadband subscriptions and the increased capacity of available services.

5. PRICE OF BROADBAND ACCESS

This section examines the impact that the price of broadband access has on user demand. In recent years, we have seen significant growth in the number of people accessing the Internet [4]. While increased affordability has played a critical role in this growth, the price of broadband Internet access remains unaffordable in many parts of the developing world. In countries like Iran and Botswana, a 1 Mbps plan could cost as much as $150 USD per month, after accounting for purchasing power parity (PPP).

Control Group	Treatment Group	% H holds	p-value
(\$0, \$25]	(\$25, \$60]	63.4%	8.89×10^{-22}
(\$0, \$25]	(\$60, ∞)	72.2%	5.40×10^{-10}

Table 3: Percentage of the time that increased price results in increased usage for pairs of similar users and corresponding p-values.

Contrast this with countries like Germany, Japan, and the US, where a 1 Mbps plan (or faster) are available for less than $25 per month.

We have seen how, up to a point, demand increases with capacity. If price is a factor that affects a customers' decision when selecting a broadband plan, then we would expect that higher prices will result in users signing up for lower capacity services despite their needs. Similarly, if two services with similar speeds are available at different prices in two markets, we would expect that the service in the more expensive market would experience higher network demand since subscribers are willing to pay more for it.

We design the following study to test this idea. We define our hypothesis (H) such that users in markets where broadband Internet access is more expensive will have higher demands on the network than users in less expensive markets. Our null hypothesis (H_0) then, is that increased price does not have an affect on network demand.

For this experiment, we first need to group users based on price of broadband access in their region. We define the price of broadband access in a country as the monthly cost (USD PPP) of the cheapest service with a capacity of at least 1 Mbps. We grouped users by the cost of broadband access using the following bins: less than $25 per month, between $25 and $60 per month, and over $60 per month. Users in countries such as Germany, Japan, and the US fit in the first bin (< $25 per month). Countries such as Mexico, New Zealand, and the Philippines had prices between $25 and $60 per month, while prices in counties such as Botswana, Saudi Arabia, and Iran were above $60 per month.

After placing users into groups based on the monthly price of broadband access, we compared the demand of otherwise similar pairs of users in each group. In these experiments, we use peak usage (when not active on BitTorrent) to measure demand.[2] For this experiment, users are "treated" with an increased cost, which our hypothesis says will increase demand. The results are shown in Table 3. We find that indeed, as price increases, more users have a higher demand than those with a similar connection where access is cheaper.

Case study. We now illustrate the impact that price can have on usage with a concrete example using four markets: Botswana, Saudi Arabia, the US and Japan. We selected these four as examples of the diversity of markets in our dataset.

We chose Botswana and Saudi Arabia given that both countries were among those with the highest broadband access costs, but differed in terms of typical service capacities. Since its independence Botswana has enjoyed one of the highest GDP growth rates in the world.[3] In recent years, the country has seen rapid growth in the percentage of citizens

[2]Results of experiments with and without BitTorrent for both average and peak demand were all comparable.

[3]CIA World Factbook. `http://www.cia.gov/library/publications/the-world-factbook/geos/bc.html`

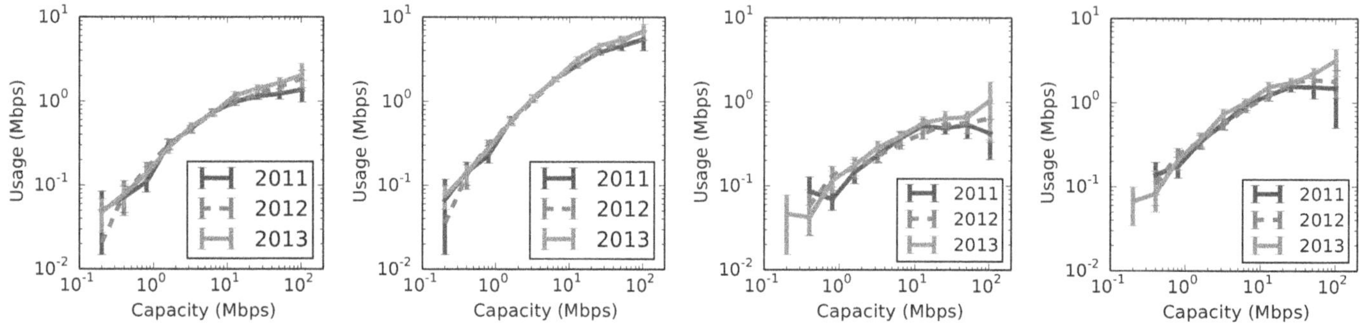

(a) Mean (w/ BT) (b) 95th %ile (w/ BT) (c) Mean (no BT) (d) 95th %ile (no BT)

Figure 6: Peak and average usage versus capacity, grouped by year. The error bars represent the 95% confidence interval.

Country	Number of users in dataset	Median capacity (Mbps)	Nearest tier (Mbps)	Price in USD (PPP)	Annual GDP per capita (PPP)	Cost of Internet access as percentage of monthly GDP per capita
Botswana	67	0.517	0.512	\$100	\$14,993	8.0%
Saudi Arabia	120	4.21	4	\$79	\$29,114	3.3%
US	3759	17.6	18	\$53	\$49,797	1.3%
Japan	73	29.0	26	\$37	\$34,532	1.3%

Table 4: The "typical" price of broadband in each country. The "Median capacity" column lists the maximum download capacity for the median user. We then matched the median capacity with the nearest speed tier in our set of Internet services available in a country. The "Price" column shows the price of that service (converted into US dollars using the purchasing power parity conversion factor). This price is used to calculate the monthly cost in each country as a percentage of monthly income.

with access to the Internet (from 3% in 2005 to 12% in 2013[4]). The cost of Internet access in Botswana, however, remains comparatively high. A 1 Mbps service, including a phone line, from Botswana Telecom costs about \$150 per month after accounting for purchasing power parity. In contrast, a 1 Mbps service in the US would cost about \$20 per month.

Over the past decade, Saudi Arabia has also experienced rapid growth in both GDP per capita (PPP) and the number of Internet subscribers. The percentage of the population using the Internet has tripled from just under 20% in 2007 to over 60% in 2013. However, according to the ITU only about 5% of the population with broadband subscriptions are on services faster than 10 Mbps (we see a similar percentage in our global dataset). A 1 Mbps connection is also relatively expensive in Saudi Arabia at about \$60 USD (PPP) per month, three times higher than a similar service in the US.

We include the US in our study as it presents another interesting case as one of the most diverse broadband service markets in terms of the available download capacities (from about 1 Mbps to over 100 Mbps). Japan, on the other hand, is one of the markets with widest availability of high-end broadband services. While the range of broadband service prices are similar to those in the US market, a larger fraction of users in Japan subscribes to high capacity services.

Table 4 summarizes the users and services seen in each market. We calculate the "typical" price of broadband in each of the country by matching the median capacity to the nearest service in our dataset. Compared to the US and Japan, customers in Botswana and Saudi Arabia are paying much more for slower services, especially as a fraction of monthly GDP per capita. Users in both Japan and the US appear to spend a similar fraction of monthly GDP per capita (1.3%). However, ISPs in Japan offered higher capacities at the same fraction of monthly income. As a result, users in Japan were more likely to subscribe to faster services.

Figure 7a shows the maximum download throughput rates measured for connections in each country. The typical maximum download capacity increases across these markets

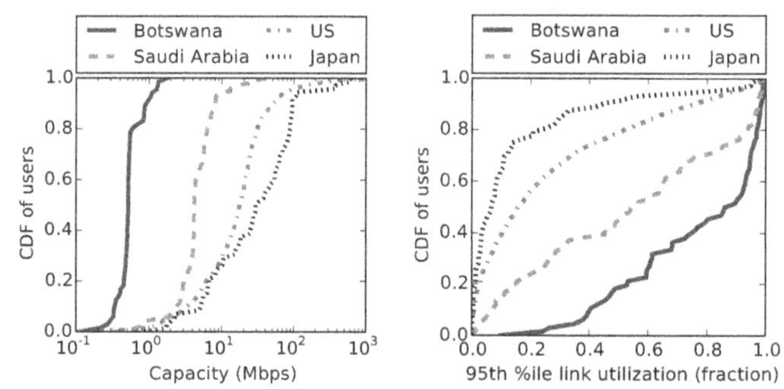

(a) Download capacities (b) 95th %ile utilization

Figure 7: CDF of the download capacities and peak utilization for all users in each of the four markets.

[4] All statistics on Internet access and growth are is from ITU. `http://www.itu.int`

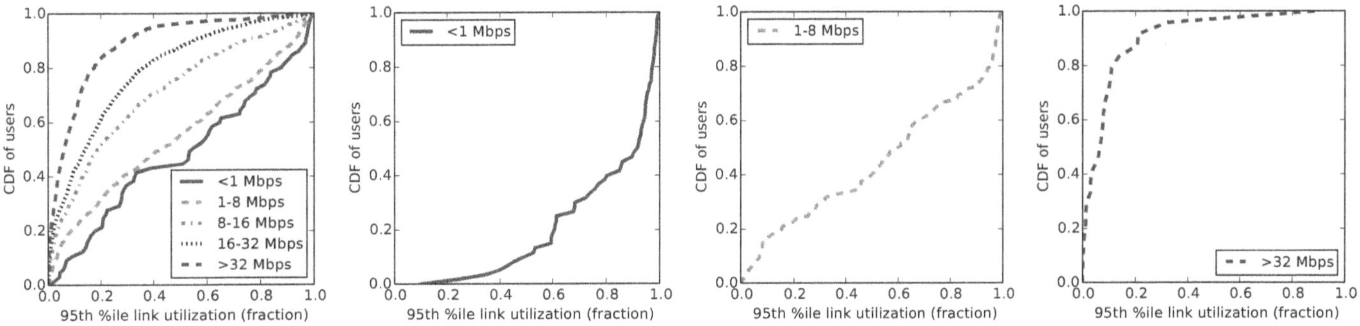

(a) US (b) Botswana (c) Saudi Arabia (d) Japan

Figure 8: CDF of the 95th percentile link utilization for users in each country. Users are split into five different groups depending on their maximum download capacity.

(Botswana, Saudi Arabia, the US, Japan). We find a large number of Botswana users on a $\approx$ 512 kbps service while users in Saudi Arabia are heavily clustered around 4 Mbps. Both the US and Japan show a wider distribution across different service levels. In Japan, however, a higher fraction of users are on high-end services. The majority of users in Japan (60%) have download speeds of at least 25 Mbps, compared with over 71% of users in the US who are on services slower than 25 Mbps.

It is interesting to contrast maximum download throughout rates with the fraction of the link utilized during peak usage for each user in these four countries (Fig. 7b). The countries appears in exactly reverse order. Botswana shows the highest peak utilization while Japan shows the lowest. In Japan, and to some extent in the US, links tend to be very underutilized, even at the 95th percentile.

Based on our earlier findings, we expect that users in Botswana and Saudi Arabia will have higher network demands than users with similar services in the US, due to increased costs. On the other hand, users in Japan should have lower demand on the network than users with similar services in the US, due to lower service costs for the same capacity.

Unfortunately, at this point it is difficult to directly compare user demand in each market due to the large differences in service capacities. Therefore, we group users into different tiers of service based on their service capacity. We then compare usage within the same tier across markets. For this analysis, we selected the following tiers: below 1 Mbps, 1 to 8 Mbps, 8 to 16 Mbps, 16 to 32 Mbps, and above 32 Mbps. The selection of tiers was based on the speeds common among the broadband technologies in our dataset and the range of capacities in each country. In the following plots, we do not include data on a particular tier for a country with less than 30 users in our dataset.

Figure 8 shows the 95th percentile utilization of users, categorized by the aforementioned speed tiers. Figure 8a represents the utilization for users in the US. In this case, as customers sign up for faster services, they tend to be using less of the link during peak usage.

Note the higher link utilization in Botswana (Fig. 8b) compared to the utilization on the same tier in the US. In Botswana, the average 95th percentile link utilization was 80%; in the US, the average peak utilization was about 52%.

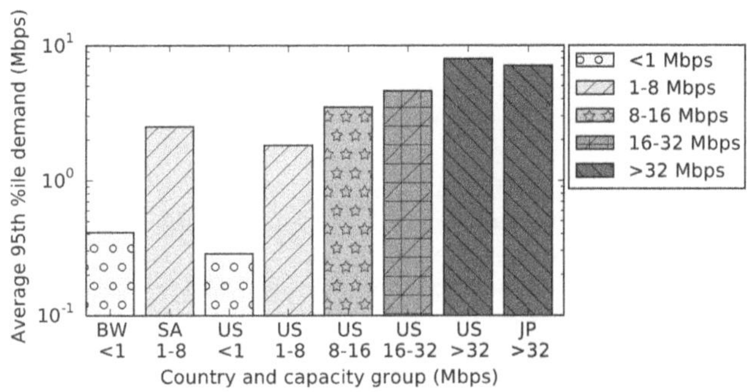

Figure 9: Average 95th percentile utilization for users in each country across each speed tier.

Such a significant difference could be explained by the much higher costs of faster service levels in Botswana where, for instance, a 2 Mbps plan costs about $200 (PPP) per month!

Figure 8c shows a similar, but less pronounced trend in Saudi Arabia. The large majority of users in Saudi Arabia have capacities around 4 Mbps, in the 1 to 8 Mbps download throughput-rate range. Compared to broadband users in the US on the same tier, we also find higher utilization of the link in Saudi Arabia,. Specifically, for users in the 1 to 8 Mbps group, the median link utilization increases from about 43% in the US to 60% in Saudi Arabia.

At the other end of the spectrum is Japan, shown in Fig. 8d. Here we find that, for the majority of users, links tend to be very under-utilized, with an average link utilization of 10%. Overall, the fraction of the link utilized is similar to the same tier in the US, though it is slightly higher, on average, in the US.

In Botswana, for example, users with less than 1 Mbps service used 410 kbps on average versus 286 kbps in the same tier in the US. Additionally, Fig. 9 shows that the demand on the network is 676 kbps (37%) higher in Saudi Arabia than on the same tier in the US. In fact, the average demand of the 8-16 Mbps tier in the US is only 39% higher than the 1-8 Mbps tier in Saudi Arabia, but is 90% higher than the 1-8 Mbps tier in the US. This difference supports our belief that the relatively high price of Internet access in the country, rather than user need, is preventing users in this market from signing up for faster services.

Similarly, users in the US with a service faster than 32 Mbps use 830 kbps more than users on the same tier in Japan. Despite the fact that the cost of broadband access is similar in both Japan and the US, the availability of faster services at a lower cost leads subscribers to sign up for services that will be less heavily used. We examine this trend in the next section. Figure 9 shows the average peak demand for different tiers in each country. We note that in the US, demand increases on each tier, despite the fact that the fraction of the link utilized decreased (shown in Fig. 8a). We also find that when comparing across markets at the same capacity tier, in addition to having higher link utilization, users in more expensive markets also tended to have a higher total demand.

6. COST OF INCREASING CAPACITY

Subscribers select broadband service based on their needs, the set of available plans and the plans' prices. Thus, given the diversity in service availability across markets, users with similar needs will end up choosing different broadband services, depending on what is available. In this section, we look at how the relative cost of alternative services impacts user demand.

Beyond price, broadband service markets differ in the relative cost of upgrading services. For example, according to our dataset of service plans, both Japan and the US have similar prices of broadband access with a connection of at least 1 Mbps costs less than $25 per month. The two markets differ, however, in service availability and the cost of upgrading. In Japan, a 100 Mbps plan is considerably less expensive than in the US ($40 per month instead of $115 per month). Furthermore, in contrast to the US, the broadband service market in Japan has more options with capacities above 50 Mbps and fewer fixed-line services below 10 Mbps.

It is clear that the cost of upgrading capacity, similar to the cost of a particular service level, can have an impact on a demand users impose on their service. To explore this, we begin by generalizing the cost of increased capacity. To this end, we collect all service plans for each country, perform a linear regression analysis on each market, and measure the correlation between capacity and price. We find that, in the majority of these markets (66%) there is a strong correlation (> 0.8) between price and capacity and in 81% there is at least moderate correlation (> 0.4).

In markets where there is weak or no correlation, price is often affected by other factors. For example, in Afghanistan, it is possible to sign up for a dedicated (not shared) DSL connection that is slower and more expensive than alternatives, lowering the correlation coefficient between price and capacity. Whether or not a service is wireless or has a monthly traffic cap would also affect the relationship between price and capacity.

For markets where price and capacity are at least moderately correlated ($r > 0.4$), we use the slope of the linear regression line to estimate the cost of upgrades (the slope is measured in monthly price per Mbps increase in capacity). Figure 10 presents a CDF of the cost of increasing capacity by 1 Mbps for all markets in our dataset.

For illustration, we note in the figure where a few representative markets fall in the distribution. At the lower end of the curve (less than $0.10 to upgrade), we find regions such as Hong Kong, Japan, and South Korea. Countries such as Canada and the US are at slightly above $0.50 per Mbps increase. The higher end of the distribution is largely comprised of countries in Africa and the Middle East, like Ghana and Uganda.

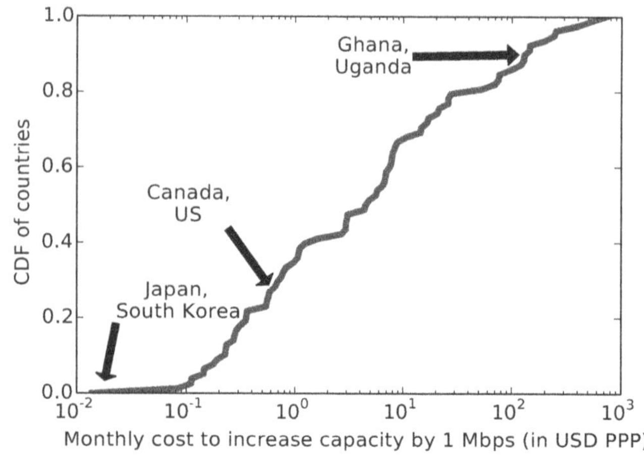

Figure 10: CDF of the monthly cost (after accounting for PPP) to increase broadband service capacity by 1 Mbps in a given country's broadband market. The arrows point out where the labeled countries were placed in the distribution.

Region	>$1	>$5	>$10
Africa	100%	84%	74%
Asia (all)	67%	47%	33%
Asia (developed)	0%	0%	0%
Asia (developing)	83%	58%	42%
Central America/Caribbean	100%	86%	14%
Europe	10%	0%	0%
Middle East	86%	57%	43%
North America	0%	0%	0%
South America	78%	55%	33%

Table 5: The percentage of countries in each region where increasing capacity costs more than $1, $5, and $10 per month for a 1 Mbps increase in capacity. We split Asia into two subgroups, developed and developing, given the diversity of economies within the area.[6]

As shown in Fig. 10, increasing capacity by 1 Mbps tends to cost less than $1 per month in developed countries but can be well above $100 (PPP) in some developing countries (e.g., Paraguay and Ivory Coast).[7] Table 5 summarizes this distribution by aggregated region, presenting the percentage of countries, per region, where the cost of increasing capacity by 1Mbps is above $1, $5 and %10 (PPP) per month. The trends are strikingly clear – for 74% of the countries in Africa and 43% of those in the Middle East, for instance, the costs of an additional 1Mbps is above $10 per month.

To test for the impact of service upgrade on user demand we define a new study. For this experiment, our hypothesis (H) states that as the cost to upgrade increases, users are less likely to upgrade and will have higher network demand than users in markets where upgrading is cheaper. Our

[6] As defined by the International Monetary Fund.

[7] Two exceptions in Asia are India and China, where upgrading capacity cost less than $1 per Mbps per month.

null hypothesis (H_0) is then that the price of upgrading will not affect demand. We use the cost of upgrade to split broadband markets into three classes: countries where the cost of increasing a service by 1Mbps is (*i*) below \$0.5, (*ii*) between \$0.5 and \$1 and (*iii*) above \$1.00 per Mbps.

Control Group	Treatment Group	% H holds	p-value
(\$0, \$0.50]	(\$0.50, \$1.00]	53.8%	0.00717
(\$0.50, \$1.00]	(\$1.00, ∞]	58.7%	0.0110

(a) Average demand w/ BitTorrent

Control Group	Treatment Group	% H holds	p-value
(\$0, \$0.50	(\$0.50, \$1.00]	52.2%*	0.0947
(\$0.50, \$1.00]	(\$1.00, ∞]	56.3%	0.0265

(b) Average demand w/o BitTorrent

Table 6: Percentage of the time that a higher cost to increase capacity (price per 1 Mbps increase) will result in higher network usage. An asterisk denotes that a result was not statistically significant.

We present the results of this experiment in Table 6, for average demand with and without including BitTorrent traffic. In general, increased upgrade prices do lead to higher demand. It is clear that users in developing countries tend to use more than similar users where faster service are more readily accessible. In cases where our results are statistically significant, we can reject the null hypothesis, and assert that the price of increasing capacity affects demand. Our results are inconclusive, i.e., p-value slightly higher than 0.05 when comparing demand (without BitTorrent) between markets where the cost of upgrade are (\$0, \$0.50] and (\$0.50, \$1.00].

We have already visited an example of the impact that the cost of increasing capacity can have on (Figs. 8 and 9). While both Japan and the US have similar monthly cost of broadband access, the costs of increasing capacity is over five times higher in the US explaining the observed higher demand in the US.

7. CONNECTION QUALITY

Previous works have shown that poor connection quality can have a negative impact on a user's quality of experience [13]. In this last section, we explore the potential impact that the quality of a connection, specifically latency and packet loss, has on user demand.

We hypothesize that a sufficiently poor quality of experience could lead to a decrease in demand on the broadband service. In the following paragraphs we test whether this is true by studying the impact of both long latencies and high packet loss rates. As we have done in our previous comparisons, we study the effects of these factors by comparing users that are similar in terms of link capacity and location. When testing the effects of increased latency, we require that average packet loss rates are similar between matched users and vice versa.

7.1 Latency

We first look at the impact of latency on user behavior. In this case, our hypothesis (H) is that decreasing latency will result in higher demand. Therefore, our null hypothesis

Control Group	Treatment Group	% H holds	p-value
(512, 2048]	(0, 64]	63.5%	0.00825
(512, 2048]	(64, 128]	63.4%	0.00620
(512, 2048]	(128, 256]	59.4%	0.00766
(512, 2048]	(256, 512]	56.3%	0.0330

Table 7: Percentage of the time that decreasing latency will result in higher 95th percentile usage (without BitTorrent). Very high latency (over 512 ms) to the nearest NDT server appears to result in lower demand than comparable users with lower latencies.

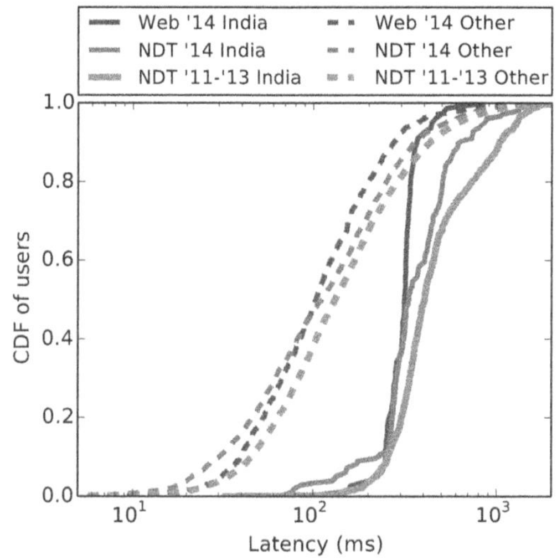

Figure 11: CDF of latency measurements for users in our dataset, grouped by location (India versus the rest of our sample population, labelled "Other"). "Web" represents each user's median latency to five of Alexa's Top Sites from our 2014 dataset. "NDT" represents the average latency to the nearest NDT server. We include NDT data from 2014 that was collected from the same set of users as the web 2014 data.

(H_0) is that decreasing latency does not affect demand and the interaction will be random.

We present the results of the study in Table 7. The table compares the peak demand (95th percentile usage when BitTorrent is not active) of users with problematically high latencies, above 512 ms in our dataset. Users are divided among exponentially increasing sized bins; our control and treatment groups in this case are the higher and lower latency groups, respectively. The results show that there is a significant increase in usage when switching from very high latency to any lower latency group, leading us to reject the null hypothesis.

While the case of latency impacting demand is visible in multiple countries, the impact of high-latency is clear when focusing on users in India. In our previous analysis broadband service plans, we find that the cost to increase capacity is similar in both the US and India (both are within 25% of each other). The cost of broadband access, however, is much higher in India (\$67 versus \$20). Thus, we would expect usage to be higher in India. When comparing

Control Group	Treatment Group	% H holds	p-value
(0.1%, 1%]	(0, 0.01%]	55.4%	5.85×10^{-6}
(0.1%, 1%]	(0.01%, 0.1%]	53.4%	8.55×10^{-4}
(1%, 15%]	(0, 0.01%]]	58.9%	2.16×10^{-5}
(1%, 15%]	(0.01%, 0.1%]	53.8%	0.0360

Table 8: Percentage of the time that decreasing packet loss will result in higher average usage (without BitTorrent). Very high packet loss (above 1%) appears to lead to lower demand than comparable users lower packet loss rates.

users in India to users with similar capacities in the US, we find, surprisingly, that users in India tend to impose lower demand 62% of the time (p-value < 0.001).

An analysis of NDT latencies shows that users in India report much higher latencies to NDT servers than users in other countries. The trends are not restricted to NDT servers but can also be seen when looking at latencies to the set of five globally popular websites: Facebook, Google, Windows Live, Yahoo, and YouTube. Four of these websites (Google, Facebook, YouTube, and Yahoo) accounted for the top five most popular websites in India[8] while Windows Live was ranked 26th.

Figure 11 describes these latency measurements, and compares them by user location (India versus the rest of our sample population). The lines labelled "Web" correspond to the median latency to the five popular websites while "NDT" is the average latency to the nearest NDT server (measured by NDT). We include data from two time periods – 2011 through 2013 (labelled "'11-'13") and from May 2014 to August 2014 (labelled "'14") to compare NDT and website latencies. [9]

Figure 11 shows that the distribution of latency measurements is similar for both NDT traces and the typical latency to the top Alexa sites. For the majority of users in India, we find much higher latencies to both NDT and popular websites compared to the rest of our sample population; nearly every user has a latency longer than 100 ms. Since we rejected the null hypothesis that latency does does not affect demand, we believe that the higher latency for users in India contributes to the fact that we see a decrease in network usage in India.

7.2 Packet loss

Next we examine the impact of packet loss on user demand. Our hypothesis (H) is that decreased packet loss rates result in higher demand. The results of this experiment are shown in Table 8. We find that when comparing users with very low packet loss rates to comparable users with very high packet loss rates, usage tended to be higher on connections with lower packet loss rates. This trend was most pronounced when comparing to connections with packet loss rates above 1%.

This impact of packet loss can be illustrated by looking at the behavior of users in India, as done in Sec. 7.1. We again found that users in India had much higher packet loss rates than the general population, as shown in Fig 12. As a result, we believe that the lower quality connections (both increased packet loss rates and latency) in India are the probable cause of lower demand on the network.

[8] Ranked by `http://www.alexa.com`

[9] We added the website latency experiment later in the study.

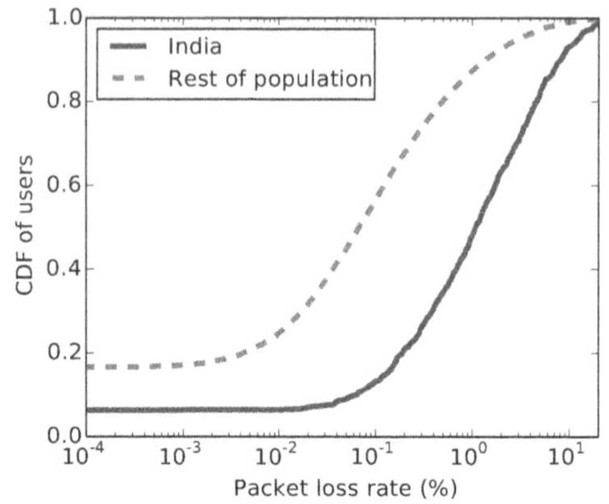

Figure 12: CDF of the average packet loss during measurements to the NDT servers for all users and users in India.

8. RELATED WORK

Broadband analysis has recently attracted much attention from the research community and the general public given its important business and policy implications. A number of efforts have focused on characterizing the availability and performance of broadband services around the world [1, 2, 5, 12, 20, 28, 31, 33]. The focus of our work is on exploring broadband services in their broader context, evaluating the complex interplay between broadband service characteristics, their market features and user demand.

Different aspects of the complex interplay between user behavior, network services and operation has been explore in previous work. Some recent studies have examined the relationship between user behavior, network services and the providers. In Dobrian et al. [13] the authors show that poor connection quality can have a negative impact on a user's quality of experience. Blackburn et al. [3] study how user behavior affects the economics of cellular operators. Chetty et al. [7] perform a user study to understand the effects of usage caps on broadband use. Other efforts have explored additional factors that may influence service demand, including the weather [6], service capacity [36] and the type of region [8].

The difficulty or outright impossibility of conducting controlled, randomized experiments of user behavior at Internet scale has been pointed out before. In his SIGCOMM 2011 Award presentation, Vern Paxson pointed to this issue and suggested the use of natural experiments to explore potential causal relationships with observational data. In a recent paper, Krishnan and Sitaraman [21] explore the use of related quasi-experimental design (QED) to evaluate the impact of video stream quality on viewer behavior and Oktay et al. [24] relies on it for causal analysis of user behavior in social media. We opted for natural experiments, rather than QED, as we consider the control and treatment groups to be sufficiently similar to random assignment.

9. SUMMARY AND DISCUSSION

The findings reported in this paper represent an import step towards understanding how user behavior, and the market features that shape it, affect broadband networks and the Internet at large. These findings should provide valuable insight to the research community, network operators and policy makers. For policy makers, there is a growing consensus that broadband access should be treated as a fundamental right and several efforts around the world are aimed at closing the digital gap. We believe that understanding digital inequality requires us to place broadband access in a broader context [22]. This work, to the best of our knowledge, is the first attempt to that end.

In our longitudinal study of usage between 2011 and 2013, we found that subscribers' demand remained relatively constant in a particular service class, despite the fourfold increase in global IP traffic over the past five years. Thus, we believe the growth in broadband traffic comes from a combination of increased service capacities and a rapidly increasing number of broadband subscribers, rather than higher demand at users' existing service levels.

We find a strong correlation between service capacity and user demand, despite the fact that users rarely fully utilize their links. We used two study designs to infer causality between capacity and usage by studying how individual users change behavior when switching to faster services and by comparing demand between users with different capacities that are otherwise similar. Their relationship also follows a law of diminishing returns; in both cases, we observed relatively lower increases in demand at higher capacities. This trend is particularly noticeable at approximately 10 Mbps, where usage begins to plateau for many users.

This suggest that as service capacities continue to increase, network operators can plan on higher over-provisioning rates. We did observe, however, larger increases in demand when including BitTorrent traffic in our analysis. Beyond capacity, we also showed the impact that the quality of a connection, in terms of latency and packet loss rates, has on user demand. For instance, we note that very long latencies (above 500 ms) and high packet loss rates (starting at 0.1%) clearly result in lower network usage. We speculate that the relationship between capacity, quality and demand will evolve with technology improvements and new applications with greater bandwidth requirements become widely available (e.g. 4k video streaming or telemedicine).

We examined how the price of broadband access affect user demand by comparing the behavior of users with similar broadband services located in different markets. We found that users in markets where broadband connections or additional capacity was more expensive, were more likely to impose higher bandwidth demands on their service than subscribers of comparable services in less expensive markets. For policy makers, this would imply that a focus on wider access to a medium, high-quality capacity service (around 10 Mbps) may have a more significant impact than a focus on increased service capacity. For operators, these trends may suggest a possible role for service pricing in network planning.

10. CONCLUSION

This paper is a first attempt at understanding broadband networks in their broader context, exploring the complex interplay between broadband service characteristics and user behavior. We combine data on broadband usage with relative broadband service pricing from around the world, and use alternative experimental designs to move beyond correlation analysis in our study of the relationship between user demand, broadband service retail prices, and connection characteristics.

There are a number of interesting research directions ahead, from further exploration of the interactions between market features and usage, to an expanded analysis capturing other contextual factors (from the weather and social events to economics). For instance, investigating the relative influence of levels of economic development or differences in broadband availability in rural and urban areas, will give us a more detailed understanding of the impact of different market features. Leveraging longitudinal data on broadband usage, it may be possible to explore the potential benefits of national broadband deployment plans [4], both on the market and on user behaviors. Finally, we have so far treated users as a homogeneous consumer group; it will be interesting to investigate how different categories of users (e.g., gamers, shoppers or movie-watchers) or more diverse households are impacted by different market and service features.

Acknowledgements

We thank our shepherd Vivek Pai and the anonymous reviewers for their invaluable feedback. This work was supported in part by the National Science Foundation through Award CNS 1218287 and by a generous Google Faculty Research Award.

11. REFERENCES

[1] Z. S. Bischof, J. S. Otto, and F. E. Bustamante. Up, down and around the stack: ISP characterization from network intensive applications. In *Proc. of W-MUST*, 2012.

[2] Z. S. Bischof, J. S. Otto, M. A. Sánchez, J. P. Rula, D. R. Choffnes, and F. E. Bustamante. Crowdsourcing ISP characterization to the network edge. In *Proc. of W-MUST*, 2011.

[3] J. Blackburn, R. Stanojevic, V. Erramilli, A. Iamnitchi, and K. Papagiannaki. Last call for the buffet: economics of cellular networks. In *Proc. of MobiCom*, 2013.

[4] Broadband Commission. The state of broadband 2013: Universalizing broadband. `http://www.broadbandcommission.org/Documents/bb-annualreport2013.pdf`.

[5] I. Canadi, P. Barford, and J. Sommers. Revisiting broadband performance. In *Proc. of IMC*, 2012.

[6] J. C. Cardona, R. Stanojevic, and R. Cuevas. On weather and Internet traffic demand. In *Proc. of PAM*, 2013.

[7] M. Chetty, R. Banks, A. Brush, J. Donner, and R. Grinter. You're capped: understanding the effects of bandwidth caps on broadband use in the home. In *Proc. of SIGCHI*, 2012.

[8] K. Cho, K. Fukuda, H. Esaki, and A. Kato. The impact and implications of the growth in residential user-to-user traffic. In *Proc. of ACM SIGCOMM*, 2006.

[9] D. R. Choffnes and F. E. Bustamante. Taming the torrent: A practical approach to reducing cross-ISP

traffic in peer-to-peer systems. In *Proc. of ACM SIGCOMM*, 2008.

[10] Cisco. Cisco visual networking index: Forecast and methodology 2012-2017.

[11] L. DiCioccio, R. Teixeira, M. May, and C. Kreibich. Probe and pray: Using UPnP for home network measurements. In *PAM*, 2012.

[12] M. Dischinger, K. P. Gummadi, A. Haeberlen, and S. Saroiu. Characterizing residential broadband networks. In *Proc. of IMC*, 2007.

[13] F. Dobrian, A. Awan, I. Stoica, V. Sekar, A. Ganjam, D. Joseph, J. Zhan, and H. Zhang. Understanding the impact of video quality on user engagement. In *Proc. of ACM SIGCOMM*, 2011.

[14] T. Dunning. *Natural experiments in the social sciences: a design-based approach.* Cambridge University Press, 2012.

[15] FCC. Measuring broadband America. `http://www.fcc.gov/measuring-broadband-america`.

[16] T. Gilovich, D. Griffin, and D. Kahneman. *Heuristics and biases: The psychology of intuitive judgment.* Cambridge University Press, 2002.

[17] J. Horrigan and E. Satterwhite. Americans' perspectives on online connection speeds for home and mobile devices. `http://www.fcc.gov/encyclopedia/broadband-speed`, 2010.

[18] IDC. The digital universe in 2020: Big data, bigger digital shadows, and biggest growth in the far east, 2013.

[19] ITU. The impact of broadband on the economy. `https://www.itu.int/ITU-D/treg/publications/bbreports.html`, 2012.

[20] C. Kreibich, N. Weaver, B. Nechaev, and V. Paxson. Netalyzr: Illuminating the edge network. In *Proc. of IMC*, 2010.

[21] S. S. Krishnan and R. K. Sitaraman. Video stream quality impacts viewer behavior: inferring causality using quasi-experimental designs. In *Proc. of IMC*, 2012.

[22] S. D. Meinrath, J. Losey, and B. Lennett. A growing digital divide: Internet freedom and the negative impact of command-and-control networking. *IEEE Internet Computing*, 2011.

[23] MLabs. Network diagnostic tool. `http://www.measurementlab.net/run-ndt/`.

[24] H. Oktay, B. J. Taylor, and D. D. Jensen. Causal discovery in social media using quasi-experimental designs. In *Proc. of the First Workshop on Social Media Analytics*, 2010.

[25] J. S. Otto, M. A. Sanchez, D. R. Choffnes, F. E. Bustamante, and G. Siganos. On blind mice and the elephant – understanding the network impact of a large distributed system. In *Proc. of ACM SIGCOMM*, 2011.

[26] V. Paxson. Strategies for sound Internet measurement. In *Proc. of IMC*, October 2004.

[27] Policy by the numbers. International broadband pricing study: Updated dataset. `http://policybythenumbers.blogspot.com/2013/05/international-broadband-pricing-study.html`.

[28] SamKnows. Accurate broadband information for consumers, governments and ISPs. `http://www.samknows.com/`.

[29] M. A. Sánchez, J. S. Otto, Z. S. Bischof, and F. E. Bustamante. Trying broadband characterization at home. In *Proc. of PAM*, 2013.

[30] M. A. Sánchez, J. S. Otto, Z. S. Bischof, D. R. Choffnes, F. E. Bustamante, B. Krishnamurthy, and W. Willinger. Dasu: Pushing experiments to the Internet's edge. In *Proc. of USENIX NSDI*, 2013.

[31] Speedtest.net. The global broadband speed test. `http://www.speedtest.net/`.

[32] R. Stanojevic, V. Erramilli, and K. Papagiannaki. Cognitive bias in network services. In *Proc. of HotNets*, 2012.

[33] S. Sundaresan, W. de Donato, N. Feamster, R. Teixeira, S. Crawford, and A. Pescapè. Broadband internet performance: a view from the gateway. In *Proc. of ACM SIGCOMM*, 2011.

[34] S. Sundaresan, N. Feamster, R. Teixeira, and N. Magharei. Measuring and mitigating web performance bottlenecks in broadband access networks. In *Proc. of IMC*, 2013.

[35] World Bank. IC4D 2009: Extending reach and increasing impact. `http://go.worldbank.org/NATLOH7HVO`.

[36] M. Zheleva, P. SChmitt, M. Vigil, and E. Belding. The increased bandwidth falacy: Performance and usage in rural Zambia. In *Proc. of ACM DEV*, 2013.

When the Internet Sleeps: Correlating Diurnal Networks With External Factors

Lin Quan[1,2] John Heidemann[1] Yuri Pradkin[1]
1: USC/Information Sciences Institute 2: Bank of China
{linquan, johnh, yuri}@isi.edu

ABSTRACT

As the Internet matures, policy questions loom larger in its operation. When should an ISP, city, or government invest in infrastructure? How do their policies affect use? In this work, we develop a new approach to evaluate how policies, economic conditions and technology correlates with Internet use around the world. First, we develop an adaptive and accurate approach to estimate *block availability*, the fraction of active IP addresses in each /24 block over short timescales (every 11 minutes). Our estimator provides a new lens to interpret data taken from existing long-term outage measurements, thus requiring no additional traffic. (If new collection was required, it would be lightweight, since on average, outage detection requires less than 20 probes per hour per /24 block; less than 1% of background radiation.) Second, we show that spectral analysis of this measure can identify *diurnal usage*: blocks where addresses are regularly used during part of the day and idle in other times. Finally, we analyze data for the entire responsive Internet (3.7M /24 blocks) over 35 days. These global observations show *when* and *where* the Internet sleeps—networks are mostly always-on in the US and Western Europe, and diurnal in much of Asia, South America, and Eastern Europe. ANOVA (Analysis of Variance) testing shows that diurnal networks correlate negatively with country GDP and electrical consumption, quantifying that national policies and economics relate to networks.

Categories and Subject Descriptors

C.2.3 [**Computer-Communication Networks**]: Network Operations—*Network Monitoring*; C.2.5 [**Computer-Communication Networks**]: Local and Wide-Area Networks—*Internet*; C.4 [**Performance of Systems**]: Reliability, availability, and serviceability

General Terms

Measurement

IMC'14, November 5–7, 2014, Vancouver, BC, Canada.

ACM 978-1-4503-3213-2/14/11 ...$15.00.
http://dx.doi.org/10.1145/2663716.2663721.

Keywords

Internet; Internet reliability; diurnal network usage

1. INTRODUCTION

The Internet is a large and complex combination of technology, policy, and human behavior. Separating these effects is difficult, yet businesses, governments, and individuals must make decisions every day, even with incomplete and contradictory information.

One metric of Internet maturity is network availability and the shift from on-demand on *always-on* network availability. Increasing use of broadband networks brings *always-on* networks. In fact, always-on is part of the U.S. Federal Communication Commission's *definition* of broadband [9]. Always-on networks have practical differences on how networks are used—the ease of not having to turn on a computer and connect is one enabler of the shift of home telephony and entertainment to IP. A similar shift is seen in the deployment of high-speed mobile phones, where always-on 3G and 4G networks are fast enough to take on data-intensive tasks like social media and streaming video. For many, an always-on phones is their primary interface to social media

Government policy makers and ISPs evaluate how the choices they make affect network usage. Until recently, tools to study the results of policy choices have been limited, with telephone-based surveys reaching a few thousand of randomly chosen people (for example, [40]), and in-home routers such as SamKnows [35] and BISmark [34] providing visibility to a few hundred, statically-chosen volunteers. While important, these studies consider a very sparse sample of individuals. A broader perspective would better quantify how policies and technologies affect Internet usage, and it is necessary to compare global differences and understand natural experiments that arise when different countries adopt different policies. For example, we know that some ISPs use network blocks on a diurnal basis because of economic constraints (saving power bills), or because of different access technologies (such as dial-up use with mandatory dynamic addressing [22]); in some countries these policies dominate use. To move beyond these anecdotes we would like to systematically explore what factors contribute different network usage.

To reach this goal, the first contribution of our work is to develop a new method to estimate *block availability*, the fraction of addresses in each /24 block that are in use and will reply to an ICMP probe. While the data collection is not new work, our *analysis* (§ 2) is completely new. We provide a new analytic tool to interpret existing long-term measurement studies of network outages [31]. We take this approach to leverage existing data, and because these outage measurements have already been shown to impose minimal cost (in probing traffic) on the subject networks. On average, outage detection requires less than 20 probes per hour, per /24, less than 1% of typically Internet background radiation observed in 2010 [39]. Even if our analysis required new data collection, its impact would be minimal.

Second, we show how this measurement can be interpreted to detect *diurnal* blocks. We use spectral analysis to identify blocks whose usage shows large daily changes. We also show that analysis of the *phase* of these changes relates to the longitude of blocks. We develop these two methods (§ 2) and validate them with controlled experiments (§ 3).

Our final contribution is to use these methods to study both diurnal behavior of 3.7M responsive blocks (each a /24 IPv4 prefix that replies to active probes) over more than one month (§ 4). While it is well known that network usage varies, our analysis provides the first *long-term, wide-scale* evaluation of diurnal use of the global Internet. Using ANOVA testing, we correlate these direct observations with economic and technical factors to *examine how external factors and national constraints* relate to Internet use, showing correlations by country and link technologies, as well as by economic factors (GDP and electricity consumption) (§ 5). Although we do not directly study policies of individual states, our methodology and data will enable future policy studies.

All data from this paper is currently available at no cost to other researchers [37].

2. METHODOLOGY

Our analysis begins with low-rate estimation of block-level availability (§ 2.1), allowing detection of diurnal blocks (§ 2.2). We then relate these measures to geolocation, organization, and link technologies (§ 2.3).

2.1 Dynamic Tracking of Block Availability

Our first new method estimates block *availability* [10], the probability that addresses in the block will respond to ICMP probes. We study the network in /24 blocks, since prior work has shown they are often homogeneous in use [3], and that larger aggregates are too coarse [31]. Although we track /24 blocks, we can detect diurnal activity that affects tens of addresses in a full block (§ 3.2.4). (As with other active probing, we cannot detect activity behind NATs or firewalls.)

While prior work defined availability A over the whole block, here we estimate three variants: short- and long-term estimates of the availability of the ever-active IP addresses ($\hat{A}_s$ and $\hat{A}_l$), and an *operational* ($\hat{A}_o$) value that is consistently designed to avoid overestimating A.

2.1.1 Problem Statement

Our goal is to derive an estimate $\hat{A}$ from analysis of probe data already taken as part of outage detection in Trinocular [31]. Trinocular already minimizes probes, with each observer sending on average to less than 1% of background radiation as of 2010 [39]. We wish to estimate A with *no* additional probes beyond what outage detection already requires.

We define the ground truth A as the fraction of addresses that respond when all our probed. While easy to define, a full measurement of ground truth is too expensive for operation.

There are several challenges that make A estimation difficult to add to outage detection. First, sampling in outage detection is *biased*. The goal of outage detection is to make the minimum number of probes to reduce stress on the target, so a few or even one positive response is usually sufficient to terminate probing. Probes are thus biased in favor of positive responses.

Second, outage detection itself depends on $\hat{A}$; we require an operational $\hat{A}_o$ estimate that is be *too high*. When $\hat{A}_o > A$, a few negative probes are a stronger indication that the block is down and Trinocular will produce false outages.

Two additional challenges are that observations are quantized, and that our initial A estimate may be quite inaccurate. Because we take from 1 to 15 observations per round, precision of a new A value is at most ± 0.07 and could be as coarse as 0.5 or 1. Short-term estimates therefore show significant jitter. Our initial estimates for A are based on historical data over several years. They may be off significantly if block usage has changed.

2.1.2 Approach

Each of our estimates use exponentially weighted moving average (EWMA) to smooth raw observations.

For each block, in each round of adaptive probing, we observe p positive responses and t total responses.

We first model short-term EWMA of positive and negative responses to quickly adapt to real values.

$$\hat{p}_s = \alpha_s p + (1 - \alpha_s)\hat{p}$$

$$\hat{t}_s = \alpha_s t + (1 - \alpha_s)\hat{t}$$

We use a gain of $\alpha_s = 0.1$ to quickly adapt to changes, and calculate the short-term availability $\hat{A}_s$:

$$\hat{A}_s = \hat{p}_s / \hat{t}_s$$

It is important that we estimate p and t separately. Because A is their ratio, applying EWMA directly to observations of A skews the data, for the same reason that one must use geometric mean to estimate normalized results [17]. (Our experiments in dataset A_{12w} use a variation on this approach, where short-term availability $\hat{A}'_s$ is tracked directly with EWMA, rather than tracking $\hat{p}_s$ and $\hat{t}_s$ separately. This method consistently over-estimates $\hat{A}$. While we accommodate for this variation in $\hat{A}_o$ and verify that it does not affect periodicity in $\hat{A}_s$, our current approach provides tighter results.)

An example of $\hat{A}_s$ is shown as a green line in Figures 1 through 3. Compared to the true A taken from complete survey data (the black line), we see that $\hat{A}_s$ is quite noisy (see Figure 1). However, this rapidly changing estimate is useful to understand diurnal block changes (§ 2.2).

We model long-term estimates of availability ($\hat{A}_l$) with the same process using a gain $\alpha_l = 0.01$.

Our goal in a conservative $\hat{A}_o$ is that it should not exceed the true value. To reflect this goal, we evaluate the absolute deviation of each sample from the estimate and then intentionally underestimate the operational value by a half of this amount. We model a deviation term d_l, and use it to compute a more conservative $\hat{A}_o$ (note that we limit $\hat{A}_o$ to a minimum of 0.1; very small values will result in excessive probes and Trinocular policy limits probes per round to do no harm):

$$\hat{d}_l = \alpha_l |\hat{A}_l - p/t| + (1 - \alpha_l)\hat{d}$$

$$\hat{A}_o = \max(\hat{A}_l - \frac{1}{2}\hat{d}_l, 0.1)$$

Our use of Trinocular works out well, since it provides lightweight probing. Once we accounting for Trinocular's policy of stopping on first positive response, its policy of walking all responsive addresses in a pseudorandom order is ideal for analysis of diurnal blocks.

2.2 Detecting Diurnal Blocks

Block availability relates to the number of *active IPs* in the block. Blocks that change diurnally will show regular daily changes to A as computers come and go. To identify diurnal blocks we estimate A as a timeseries of $\hat{A}_s$ observations taken each 11 minutes (following [10]). We then take the Fast-Fourier Transform of this timeseries to determine periodicity and phase.

Data cleaning: Spectral analysis typically requires an evenly sampled timeseries. We map our probing output to an 11-minute timeseries, but is not perfectly aligned with 11 minute rounds, sometimes we see missing or duplicate observations in a round (about 5% of rounds). Like previous work [30], we correct these by extrapolating single missing estimates, and trusting most recent observation when duplicates occur.

We trim our timeseries to start and end near midnight UTC. This approach ties phase to physical time, and it also reduces noise in FFT analysis of diurnal frequencies.

Detecting diurnal blocks: We use a Discrete Fast-Fourier transform to identify periodicity typical of diurnal use. Given a timeseries $A = a_m$, $m \in [0, n-1]$ of n input samples, we compute its $k \in [0, n-1]$ frequency-domain components as:

$$\alpha_k = \sum_{m=0}^{n-1} a_m e^{-2\pi i m k/n}$$

The magnitude of α_k shows the strength kth frequency component (sub-signal) of a_m. With our 11-minute ($R =$ 660 s) sampling period, α_k shows the frequency at $k/(Rn)$ Hz. To identify diurnal patterns for an experiment lasting N_d days we look in the $k = N_d$ component of α_k. To account for noise, we also consider the adjacent $k = N_d + 1$.

Diurnal activity in a block appears as strength in α_k corresponding to 24 hour intervals (and multiples of this frequency). For a *strictly diurnal* block, the strongest frequency occurs at 1 cycle per day (when $k = N_d$), *and* its strength is at least twice the next strongest, non-harmonic frequency, *and* greater than all harmonics.

We also consider *relaxed diurnal* blocks, where the strongest frequency is at 1 cycle per day or the first harmonic, without comparison to the second strongest frequency.

Block phase: In addition to the amplitude of the FFT (the "strength" of a given periodicity), spectral analysis also provides the phase (when the period occurs relative to the start of measurements). Phase is shown in the angle of the complex-valued FFT coefficients.

We examine phase in the 1-cycle-per-day component, and consider it valid only for strong or relaxed diurnal blocks. (For non-diurnal blocks, phase of this component is effectively random.)

Phases range from $[-\pi, \pi]$, with the exact value depending on when a measurement begins. We consider relative phases and compare them to physical location (§ 5.2); future work may tie phase to time-of-day.

Data appropriateness: FFT over data too short or non-stationary can distort analysis of periodic behavior. Our datasets are sufficiently long (two or more weeks) to capture many diurnal periods.

We verified our data is roughly stationary for our measurement periods by doing a linear fit of A over the observation and confirming slopes are near-zero. We confirmed with all 29,001 blocks in Survey S_{51w} that about 80.3% of these blocks are stationary, with a slope equivalent to less than 1 address changes per day.

2.3 Other Network Factors: Geolocation, Organizations, and Link Types

We analyze network behavior in /24 blocks, but to put these in context, we relate diurnal behavior to other factors: physical location, logical location (the organization operating the address), and last-mile link technology.

2.3.1 Geolocation

Different countries and regions have different policies and economics for networking. To understand these effects we use IP geolocation to get city-level physical locations. While there have been many approaches to IP geolocation (see for example [13,28]), we use MaxMind's city-level database [25] as a free and widely used source. Although this source is not the most accurate (claimed accuracy is 40 km), it is sufficient to demonstrate at least country-level correlation.

We map each /24 block to location. Although sometimes blocks span multiple locations, such instances are fairly rare. Our analysis of existing per-IP data [11] shows about 93% of /24 blocks have homogeneous locations, and our MaxMind dataset specifies location with at most /24 precision.

2.3.2 Organizations

To understand how the policies of different organizations affect how they use IP addresses, we map IP addresses to Autonomous System (AS) numbers, and ASes to organizations. (Ideally we would subdivide some ASes, perhaps into commercial and home networks, but we know of no such classification.)

We use Team Cymru's IP to AS number mapping [36]. We map each /24 to an AS based on its .0 address. Dividing ASes across /24s is rare, with only 0.005% of blocks in Team Cymru's data showing differing .0 and .128 ASes. Their data provides AS numbers and names for 99.41% of /24 blocks.

We map ASes to organizations using prior work that uses WHOIS and string-based clustering [4]. For a given organization or ISP P (for example, Time Warner Cable), we first use keyword matching (ex. "Time Warner") to find relevant clusters, then find all ASes within same cluster(s). Finally, for all ASes within P, we join with IP/AS mapping and find all relevant IP blocks for P.

The above method assumes good accuracy of IP/AS and AS/organization mappings. Future work may consider how accuracy of these mappings affects our correlations, or to compare the behavior of different ASes within the same organization.

2.3.3 Link Technology

We define the *link type* as the technology connecting the final hop to the destination. Identification of link types for blocks is difficult because such information is not readily available, and because in principle different parts of a /24 block could be connected differently (for example, a router at .1 and the rest of the addresses with dial-up). Previous work has shown one can often infer link types from reverse domain names [4, 16, 27, 33]. We build Thunderping's idea [33], but cannot reuse their data directly because their classification was done manually and only for the United States; we wish to study millions of international blocks. Other data is also sparse or old, so we identify block-level link types as follows.

First, we look up the reverse domain name of each address in each analyzable block. We then use string matching against pre-defined keywords to non-exclusively identify features (corresponding to link types, see § 5.5) for each address. For example, a reverse name of `dhcp-dialup-001.example.com` is marked as both DHCP and dial-up. Each block is therefore defined by a vector of 256 addresses, each with zero or more features. We suppress minor features in each block by filtering out features that are less than $\frac{1}{15}$th of the most frequent feature. Finally, we label the block with all remaining features that have non-zero counts.

We consider 16 keywords (sta, dyn, srv, rtr*, gw*, dhcp, ppp, dsl, dial, cable, ded*, res, client*, sql*, wireless*, wifi*). Of these, we discard the seven marked with asterisks because they are dominant in less than 1000 blocks. These keywords are all based on English; future work should explore non-English networking keywords and explore potential under-representation in countries where English is not the dominant language. We believe this approach works reasonable for ISPs serving homes; it is not designed to classify commercial providers (clouds or CDNs).

For our 3.7M blocks in dataset A_{12w}, and find that 46.3% of these blocks have some feature (4× more than Thunderping), and 11.4% have multiple features.

2.4 Factorial Analysis with ANOVA

To quantify the correlation of policies, places, and technologies on Internet usage, we need to weigh the factors that relate to network outcomes such as diurnal address usage and network reliability. While anecdotal and personal evidence suggests that individuals in some countries turn off computers at night to save power, we wish to measure these effects systematically.

To discover correlations between a range of possible factors and network outcomes we use analysis of variance or ANOVA, a form of statistical hypothesis testing. It tests the probability (p-value) of a factor or factors (separately or in combination) being correlated with an observation. A high p-value indicates that the factor has little correlation with outcome, while a low p-value indicates that correlation of the factor and outcome are unlikely to have been by chance alone. In practice, p-values less than a threshold (0.05 or 0.01) are typically considered statistically significant, because a low p-value (with high probability) rejects the null-hypothesis: that the input variable(s) and output variable are unrelated.

A full discussion of ANOVA is found in many textbooks (for example, [26]). We use the open source ANOVA package in *R* for our analysis.

2.5 Datasets

Our work draws on two active measurements: IPv4 surveys and Trinocular outage measurements.

To validate our results with complete information we re-evaluate *Internet IPv4 surveys* [10]. These datasets have probes to every address in about 2% of IPv4 /24 blocks, taken every 11 minutes for 2 weeks. With complete data for all IPs in the block, surveys provide ground truth. We primarily use Survey S_{51w}, starting 2012-11-16. To detect trends over the last three years (Figure 11), we analyze historical surveys taken since 2010 (Survey S_{31w} [37]).

Our new estimators to derive short-timescale block availability and diurnalness are based on data from Internet outage observation. We use outage data collected from Trinocular [31]. Our analysis here uses the A_{12w} dataset, taken from Los Angeles, California, USA [38] and covering 3.7 M Internet edge network blocks over 35 days, starting at 2013-04-24 17:18 UTC. We observe similar results from two other sites in Fort Collins, Colorado, USA, and Keio, Japan.

These datasets are publicly available [37]. We add new public datasets for link technology (§ 2.3.3) and our new availability and diurnal analysis.

3. VALIDATION

To validate our new measurement approaches we re-evaluate Internet surveys (summarized above § 2.5). We add controlled simulations of diurnal blocks to systematically investigate our sensitivity to variation in diurnal behavior. We also evaluate diurnal detection against blocks at USC that are or perhaps should be diurnal.

3.1 Tracking Block Availability

We first validate that we accurately estimate availability (A), since detection of diurnal blocks uses this estimate. We show our measure with examples and evaluation of all 29k blocks in S_{51w}.

3.1.1 Sample Blocks

To illustrate estimation of $\hat{A}$, we first compare $\hat{A}$ to true A for several representative sample blocks drawn from Survey S_{51w} (Figures 1 to 3). The survey provides complete data for all 256 addresses in the block for two weeks. We use the Trinocular algorithm to downsample this data, considering from 1 to 15 samples per round (shown as red dots on the graphs). We apply Trinocular's adaptive sampling to consider from 1 to 15 samples per 11 minute round. We then compare short-term and operational estimates ($\hat{A}_s$ and $\hat{A}_o$, the green and dark blue lines) and compare them to the true value (A, the black line) measured from complete data. Full data is shown in the image above each graph, with light green dots showing responses and black showing non-responses. We have examined hundreds of blocks; the examples we show here represent different conditions.

Figure 1 shows a block that is sparse, with only a few responding addresses (42 active over time), but relatively high availability ($A = 0.735$). The middle graph shows that the short-term estimate is noisy around the true value (the jagged green $\hat{A}_s$ line, compared to the steady black A line). We also see the operational value never overestimates once it leaves its inaccurate initial value ($\hat{A}_o < A$, the dark blue line is lower than the black line). Finally, we detect an outage at round 957.

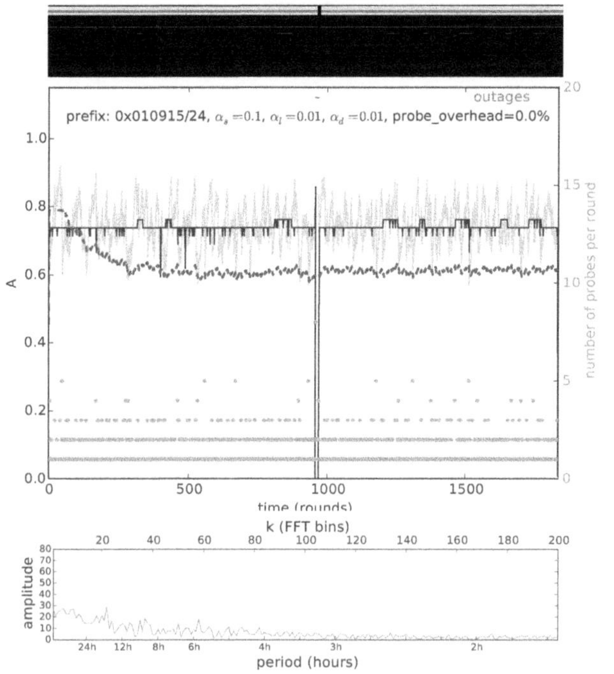

Figure 1: Block 1.9.21/24 from S_{51w}, a sparse but high availability block (42 every responding addresses, $A = 0.735$). Top: raw survey data: green is response, black is no response. Middle: compares true A (black, upper line with minimal variation), short-term estimate $\hat{A}_s$ (light green, upper line with larger variation), operational estimate $\hat{A}_o$ (dotted dark blue, lower line), and report the number probes per round (red dots at bottom and right scale). An outage occurs at round 957 (the magenta line). Probes-per-round (red dots, mostly along the bottom) use the right scale. Bottom: amplitude of FFT ($N_d = 14$) of $\hat{A}_s$, with no strong diurnal signals.

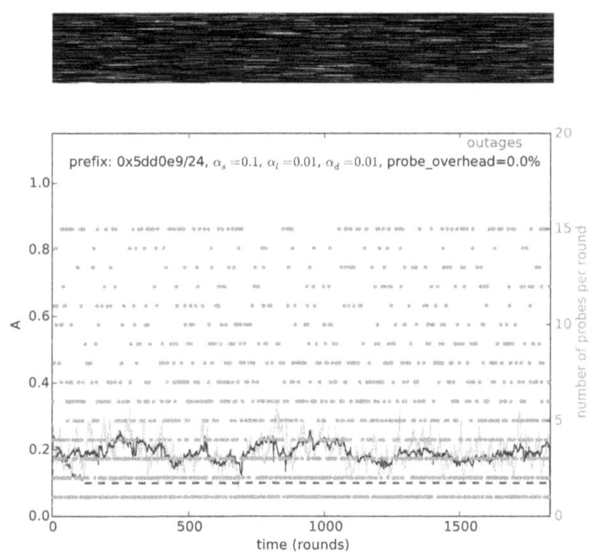

Figure 2: Block 93.208.233/24 from from S_{51w},$|E(b)| = 245$, $A = 0.191$. Dense but low availability block. (Block is non-diurnal, so FFT is omitted.) Lines described in Figure 1.

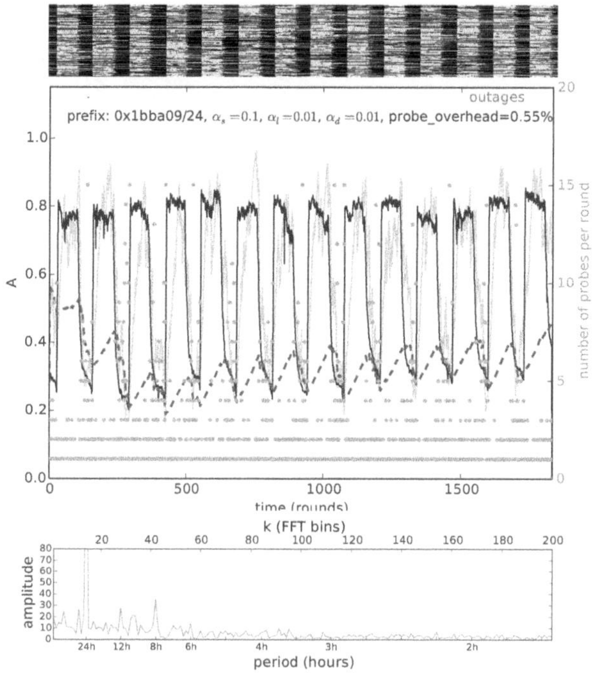

Figure 3: Block 27.186.9/24 from S_{51w}, $|E(b)| = 256$, $A = 0.598$. Diurnal block. Lines described in Figure 1. Bottom: amplitude of FFT ($N_d = 14$) of $\hat{A}_s$ showing strong diurnal amplitude.

Figure 2 shows a dense block where nearly all addresses in use ($|E(b)| = 245$), but availability is low ($A = 0.191$). Again, the short-term estimate tracks truth reasonably well, but with some noise, and the operational does not exceed the true value. The low availability of this block means several probes are often used per round (mean 5.08 probes/round). We conclude that our approach works on low-availability blocks as well.

Finally, Figure 3 shows a diurnal block. We count 14 "bumps" of A corresponding with the 14-days survey. The short-term estimate lags the truth slightly (compare green $\hat{A}_s$ to black A) , and the operational value ($\hat{A}_o$) is generally below the worst-case true A.

These samples show that our algorithms track A accurately, as we observe in many other blocks.

3.1.2 Comparison in Full Survey Blocks

To generalize from these examples we next systematically compare *all* 29k /24 blocks in Survey S_{51w}. We apply our availability tracking algorithm with sparse sampling and estimation to each block and compare to full data as ground truth.

Figure 4 compares our short-term estimates ($\hat{A}_s$) against ground truth (A) as a density plot. We normalize the density with the product of number of blocks and number of rounds. The dense cluster near the "perfect correlation" of $x = y$ line shows this correlation visually. Over the density plot, we plot the median (white line) and quartiles for all values in each group of 0.1 true A (white boxes), confirming our estimator is unbiased.

Figure 5 shows the same visualization for operational $\hat{A}_o$. Our goal is that the operational value not overestimate. This data shows our operational A_o values are almost always

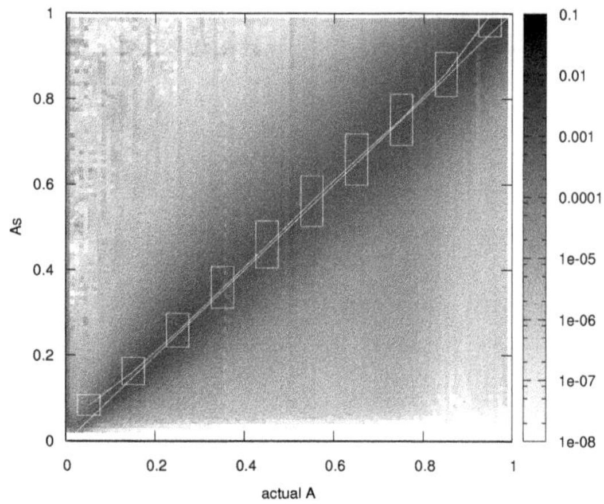

Figure 4: Correlation of actual (A) and estimated ($\hat{A}_s$) availability. Density is normalized by the product of number of blocks and rounds. Quartiles show A_s, binned by $0.1A$.

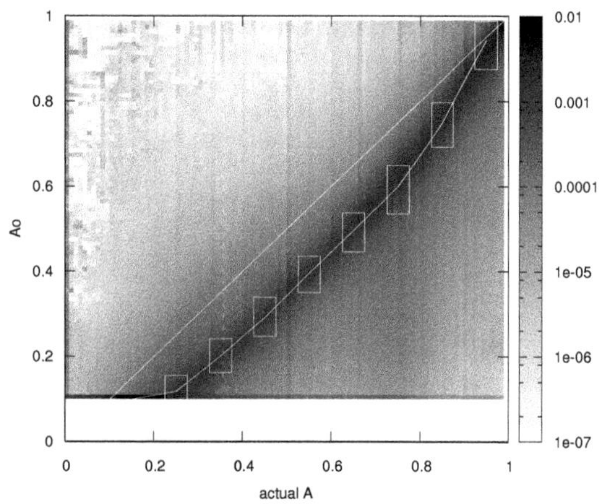

Figure 5: Correlation of actual (A) and operational ($\hat{A}_o$) availability. Density is normalized by the product of number of blocks and rounds. Quartiles show A_o, binned by $0.1A$.

(94% of the time) under true A. Since we do not probe very-sparse blocks, we omit cases where $\hat{A}_o < 0.1$.

Finally, we quantify the accuracy of our estimates by computing the correlation coefficient over true block availability A and estimated values. We find good correlation between true A value and estimated $\hat{A}_s$ with an overall correlation coefficient of 0.95685.

3.2 Diurnal Blocks

We next consider sample diurnal blocks, then systematically explore how different factors detect of diurnalness.

3.2.1 Sample Blocks

We first consider what spectral analysis (§ 2.2) reports about our sample blocks. In Figure 1, a few addresses are always used, and in Figure 2 all addresses are used intermittently. Both blocks show a flat spectrum, as illustrated by the bottom graph in Figure 1 (the second example is similar but omitted for space).

By contrast, the daily pattern in Figure 3 is visible in the raw data (top) and observed $\hat{A}_s$ (middle). It produces a strong peak corresponding to daily activity (bottom graph, here at $k = 17$). This sample block in our longer dataset A_{12w} also shows a strong daily peak in Figure 6 (at $k = 35$ due to the 35-day observation).

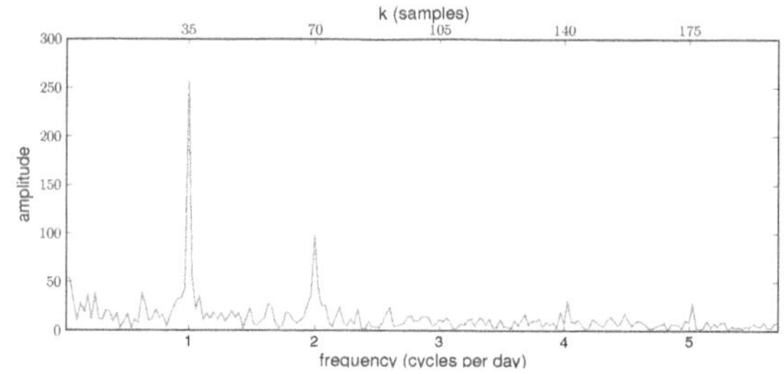

Figure 6: Amplitude of FFT for block 27.186.9/24, in 35-day A_{12w} ($N_d = 35$); shows strong diurnal pattern.

We have looked at many other example blocks; these cases are representative of diurnal and non-diurnal spectra. We report on diurnalness in A_{12w} in § 4. Of the 3.7M blocks we study in A_{12w} we classify 412k (11%) as strictly diurnal and 926k blocks (25%) as relaxed diurnal.

3.2.2 Controlled Diurnal Blocks with Simulation

We next turn to simulation to systematically study how easily we can detect diurnalness in the face of different kinds of variation and noise.

We simulate one /24 block (256 addresses) to provide exact ground truth against which to test our algorithm. Our simulation evaluates responses every 11-minutes for 4 weeks. In that block, 50 addresses are stable and always responding, and $n_d = 100$ addresses are diurnal, and the remaining addresses are not active. Diurnal addresses are responsive for 8 hours and down for 16 hours each day. Each diurnal address i turns on at a certain time during the day, the phase ϕ_i.

We evaluate the effects of three kinds of variation in this model. First, we vary phase, selecting ϕ_i for each address (once, at simulation start) uniformly from the range $[0, \Phi]$. We also add normally-distributed noise, either adding variance σ_s to the start time of the up period, or changing its duration with variance σ_d. In both cases, noise is drawn each day for each address. In each simulation below, we run 10 batches of experiments, each batch with 100 experiments to report accuracy: percentage of correct detection of diurnal blocks within the 100 experiments. The error bars show median and quartiles in the 10 batches.

For each simulation we observe $\hat{A}_s$ (§ 2.1) and diurnal detection (§ 2.2). We detect 100% of these simulated diurnal blocks in the simplest case when there is no noise ($\Phi = \sigma_s = \sigma_d = 0$).

Number of diurnal addresses: We first explore effects of *how many* addresses are diurnal. In Figure 7, we vary n_d, the number of diurnal addresses, from 1 to 100 (or 2% to 67% of responsive addresses). Our detection accuracy improves quickly. After 10 addresses (or 17% of responsive addresses), the accuracy is more than 85%. Examination of several cases shows the misses with $n_d < 10$ are because n_d is only a small fraction of the 50 always-on addresses, and our probing will usually pick an address within the stable ones and stop.

Varying phase: To vary phase we return to $n_d = 100$ but now select ϕ_i randomly, picking a value linearly dis-

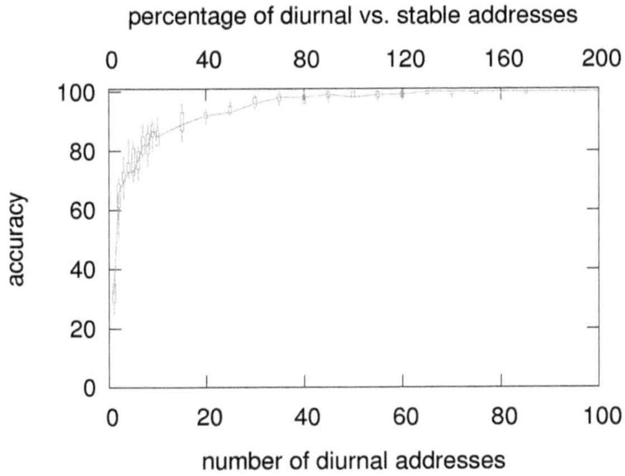

Figure 7: Accuracy of diurnal detection when the number of diurnal behavior addresses (n_d) per block varies from 2% to 67% of responsive addresses ($\Phi = \sigma_s = \sigma_d = 0$). Data: simulation.

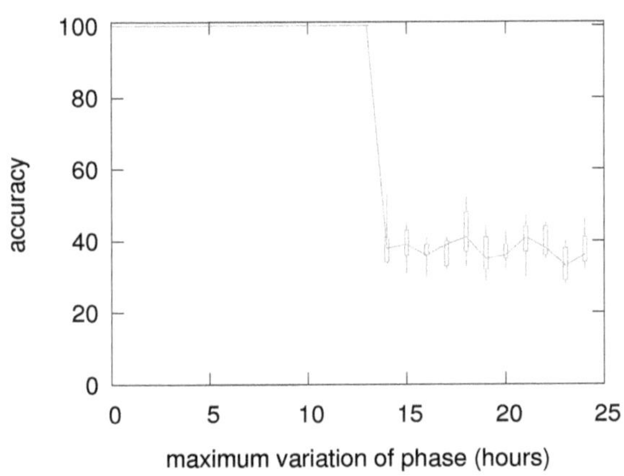

Figure 8: Accuracy of diurnal block detection when maximum Φ of diurnal addresses varies from 0 to 24 hours ($n_d = 100, \sigma_s = \sigma_d = 0$). Data: simulation.

tributed between 0 and Φ. to decide when it starts during the time of each day. Figure 8 shows a sharp drop when maximum Φ at 14 hours. This sharp threshold is due to the twice next strongest amplitude requirement of strict diurnalness; although variations in phase decay gradually, the signals from different addresses to blur together around this period, as confirmed in simulations where we vary maximum Φ from 0 to 24 hours (omitted due to space).

Varying duration: We vary duration by changing σ_d in Figure 9. We vary σ_d from 0 to 24 hours to evaluate our sensitivity to variations in up-time. We find that this variance only slightly affects accuracy for large σ_d (>10 hours). This is because we synchronize the up periods daily, similar to real world settings where people synchronize clocks and go to work. With a normal distribution, variations in uptime for the sub-signals will cancel each other out over time. Considering that ordinary people's schedules have variations within only a few hours, this shows that our algorithm works well for wide range of up-times.

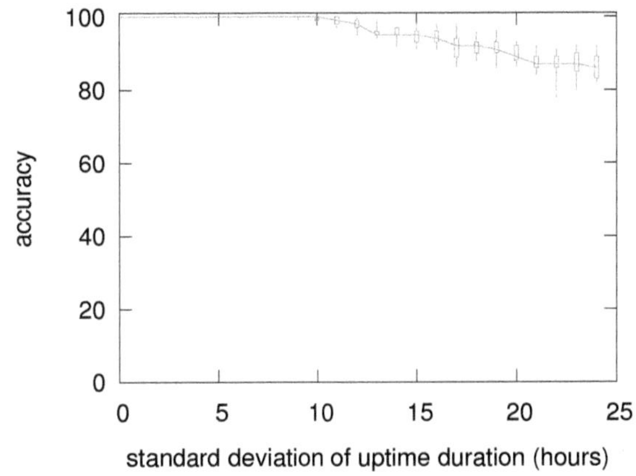

Figure 9: Accuracy of diurnal block detection when standard deviation of uptime duration (σ_d) varies from 0 to 24 hours ($n_d = 100, \Phi = \sigma_s = 0$). Data: simulation.

outcome		**dataset**	
with A	**with** $\hat{A}_s$	S_{51w}	
(correct) d	$\hat{d}$	2,890	9.97%
n	$\hat{n}$	23,497	81.02%
(error) d	$\hat{n}$	1,999	6.89%
n	$\hat{d}$	614	2.12%
precision: 82.48%; accuracy: 90.99%			

Table 1: Validation of diurnal blocks in Survey S_{51w} (29k blocks), using true availability (A) to compute ground truth, and Trinocular estimated availability ($\hat{A}_s$) to predict.

After studying sensitivity of n_d, ϕ, σ_d, we are confident with our availability tracking and diurnal detection algorithms. Because we can track blocks with small n_d (less than 20% of stable addresses), large Φ (typical human phase is less than 4 hours), and large σ_d (typical up time is 6 to 10 hours).

3.2.3 Comparison in Full Survey Blocks

We next evaluate diurnal behavior with and without estimated A. Following § 3.1.2, we define ground truth as diurnal detected with true availability (A) taken from full data in Survey S_{51w}; we cannot contact thousands of network operators to get actual ground truth. We compare that to diurnal computed from our lightweight estimate of availability ($\hat{A}_s$).

The comparison in Table 1 shows that our method has good precision (82.48%): we rarely falsely predict a wrong diurnal block. We also provide good overall accuracy (90.99%), which represents the ability to correctly track both positives and negatives. Our measurement is conservative in detecting diurnalness, with a fairly high false negative rate. For the comparisons we make in § 5, this bias seems preferable to false positives.

3.2.4 Validation with USC Ground Truth

We complement blind validation and controlled experiments by comparing our results to operator-provided ground truth at USC (we cannot obtain ground truth for thousands of ISPs in the general Internet). We next verify that the diurnal blocks we discover there are correct (no false positives) and evaluate completeness (false negatives).

True Positives: In A_{12w} we find four strictly diurnal blocks and 44 relaxed diurnal blocks. We evaluate block usage using both reverse DNS names and discussions with network operators. USC is large and network configuration is distributed and done partially on physical location, so DNS names provide the most precise information; we then confirm our results with operators.

Of the four strictly diurnal blocks, two are wireless blocks with dynamic address assignment. The other two have mixed use, mostly assigned to general use (assigned to buildings or departments). One block includes a range of 16 dynamically-assigned addresses. Examining the additional 40 relaxed diurnal blocks, keyword assignment identifies 20 as dynamic, 4 as wireless, and the other 16 are general use. In addition to hostnames, for 39 blocks (2 strong and 37 relaxed diurnal) we have full raw data from Survey S_{51w}.

False Positives are blocks detected as diurnal when survey shows consistent availability. Examination of all 39 blocks with full data shows clear diurnal trends in 38 blocks: A changes by at least 10% over multiple days in the two week survey. DNS data for the one block without diurnal trends shows a group of 15 dynamic addresses for mobile wired devices. We believe these addresses were activated in the four months between ground truth (S_{51w}) and detection (A_{12w}). We conclude that there are *at most 3% false positives* for USC.

False Negatives are diurnal blocks that we miss. At first glance, labeling only 20 dynamic and 6 wireless blocks as diurnal suggests a high false negative rate. (DNS at USC identify 32 blocks as dynamic and 142 as wireless, types that are often diurnal.)

Examination of these blocks shows that USC's wireless is *heavily* overprovisioned, with one wireless address for every student (142 blocks). *On average*, each block has around ten live addresses at any time (a load confirmed by operators), even though many addresses are used over months of observation. To avoid excessive per-address probing, by default Trinocular removes blocks with fewer than 15 active addresses, and it is difficult to detect diurnal trends in very sparse blocks (for example, see Figure 7). Thus, of the 142 wireless blocks, 119 were excluded from probing. Of the 23 blocks that are probed, we identify 6 as diurnal. We conclude that diurnal detection requires either moderately dense blocks (more than 15 active addresses) or tolerance for higher probing rates than 19 probes per hour per /24. These self-imposed *policy constraints* (constraining probing) result in false positives for USC's sparely operated wireless network.

Sparse blocks cause only false negatives, not false positives. We therefore claim that our Internet-wide measurements are a lower-bound on the fraction of diurnal blocks, and emphasize the correctness of diurnal claims (97% true positives).

Surprises: We found two surprising results examining USC. First, while DNS names show a few large, continuous areas that are diurnal (centralized wireless), decentralized address management also results in pockets of dynamic addresses in many /24 blocks. These dynamic addresses result in diurnal trends in otherwise general-use blocks. Second, while we expected diurnal usage of wireless and dynamically assigned addresses, we were surprised by the strong diurnal use in the 16 general-use blocks. We speculate that diurnal use reflect either broad use of laptop computers that are away from USC outside business hours, or a policy of turning off desktop computers at night.

	A_{12w}			
	diurnal	**either**	**non-diurnal**	**all**
A_{12j}	(d)	(e)	(N)	
d	297,080	341,919	4057	345,976
e	332,250	569,882	106,391	676,273
N	1898	122,173	1,996,653	2,118,826
all	334,148	692,055	2,103,044	2,795,099

Table 2: Comparing diurnal (d), diurnal and relaxed (e), and non-diurnal (N) for A_{12w} and A_{12j}.

3.3 Stability from Different Locations

To confirm that our approach is stable, we collected data from two other sites concurrent with A_{12w}: A_{12c} from Colorado State University, and A_{12j} from Keio University in Japan. We next compare A_{12w} against these datasets.

For each dataset, we define d as strongly diurnal blocks, r as relaxed diurnal blocks, e as either $d \cup r$, and N as neither. In Table 2 we compare d, e, and N for A_{12w} and A_{12j}. The first row shows that of the 345,976 diurnal blocks in A_{12w}, A_{12j} finds 85% as strongly diurnal and 98.8% as either strong or weakly diurnal, suggesting strong disagreement in only about 1.2% of blocks. We see similar results when we compare A_{12w} and A_{12c} after we account for a software bug (see [32]). We conclude that our approach is not sensitive to measurement location.

4. DIRECTLY OBSERVED RESULTS

In this section, we show direct observations of diurnal blocks in A_{12w}. We compare these observations with other factors to identify correlations in the next section § 5). We find 412k blocks (11%) that are strictly diurnal in A_{12w}, and 926k blocks (25%) that are relaxed diurnal of the 3.7M blocks we measure. These blocks are distributed all over the address space.

Daily or other periodicity? Our test for diurnalness looks strictly for regularity at 24 hours, requiring that to be the strongest periodicity in the block. We focus on daily patterns because they are likely to be related to human use of the Internet. There may be other sources of periodicity, for example related to DHCP lease cycles. If dynamic addresses are allocated for some period p, and given out sequentially across a region that spans multiple /24 blocks, then those blocks will see usage that changes with period p.

To understand the how prominent different periodicities are, Figure 10 shows the distribution of the strongest frequency for each of the 3.7 M blocks in A_{12w}. As expected, we observe a strong peak at 1 cycle per day (24 hours), about 25% of all the blocks. We only declare 11% to be strongly diurnal, where the 24-hour amplitude is twice the next strongest frequency; the remaining are relaxed diurnal. The second group (3%) is at about 4.3 cycles per day. This periodicity is a probing artifact, because we restart our probing software every 5.5 hours (4.3 times per day) to recover from possible prober failure. Our measurements starting in 2014-04 (A_{16all} [37]) use restart times around one week to reduce this effect.

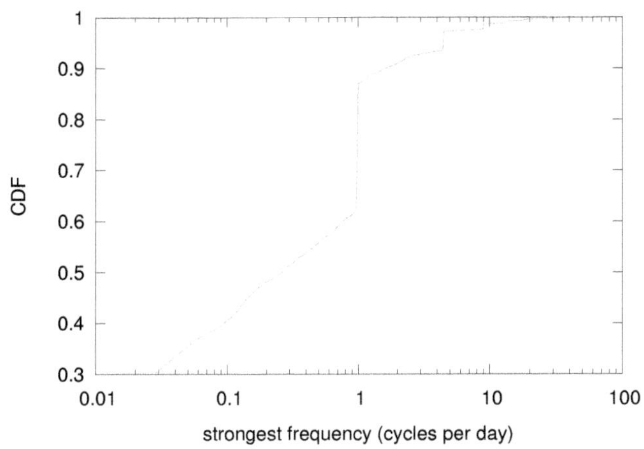

Figure 10: Cumulative distribution of the highest frequency in 35-day A_{12w}.

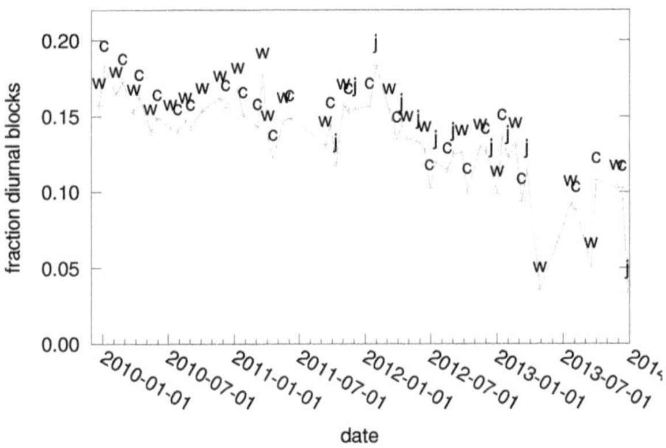

Figure 11: Fraction of diurnal blocks from long-term surveys. Uses 63 datasets, starting with S_{30w} in Dec. 2009, letters indicate location (w: Los Angeles, c: Colorado, j: Japan).

Long-term status: We next consider how block diurnalness changes over time. In Figure 11, we apply our spectral diurnal detection algorithm over more than 3 years of Internet surveys (each a sample of about 2% of IPv4 blocks). We observe that the percentage of diurnal blocks is relatively stable, but that it shows a marked decline since 2012. While we have observed in increasing trend in dynamic address allocation this downward trend may indicate that these dynamic addresses are slowly shifting to always-on activity (even if they move around). These results are generally consistent the 11% diurnal blocks in A_{12w}.

5. INDIRECTLY OBSERVED RESULTS

We next compare diurnal blocks to other factors: location, time-of-day, block allocation dates, economic factors, and link technologies.

5.1 Where Does the Internet Sleep? (Locating diurnal blocks)

Our first question is to identify *where diurnal Internet use is common*. We study this question using A_{12w} with MaxMind geolocation (succeeding for 3.45M of blocks, 93%). We first put our results in context by showing where the geolocatable blocks are located (Figure 12). In this world map, we count /24s blocks geolocated into a 2×2 degree grid. We see large numbers of addresses in North America and Europe, as well as concentrations in Japan, China, and several other countries. We also see some geolocation anomalies: when MaxMind knows only country, it locates the blocks in the geographic center of the country, falsely placing many networks away from population in Brazil, Russia, and Australia.

country code	region	blocks (/24s)	frac. diurnal	GDP (US$)
AM	W. Asia	1075	0.630	5900
GE	W. Asia	1395	0.546	6000
BY	E. Europe	1748	0.512	15900
CN	E. Asia	394244	0.498	9300
PE	S. America	4600	0.401	10900
KZ	Cent. Asia	3832	0.400	14100
RS	S. Europe	4429	0.393	10600
AR	S. America	20382	0.339	18400
TH	S.E. Asia	10986	0.336	10300
SV	Cent. America	1145	0.311	7600
UA	E. Europe	16575	0.289	7500
CO	S. America	9379	0.261	11000
MY	S.E. Asia	9747	0.247	17200
PH	S.E. Asia	5721	0.239	4500
IN	S. Asia	36470	0.225	3900
MA	N. Africa	2115	0.185	5400
BR	S. America	79095	0.185	12100
VN	S.E. Asia	8197	0.183	3600
ID	S.E. Asia	7617	0.166	5100
RU	E. Europe	53048	0.159	18000
...	...	...	...	
US	N. America	672104	0.002	50700

Table 3: Fraction of diurnal blocks, top 20 countries (with at least 1000 blocks in our study), and United States. Diurnal analysis data is from A_{12w}; Geolocation data is from MaxMind [25]; Per-capita GDP data is from CIA world factbook [5].

Of the 412k strictly diurnal blocks in this dataset, Figure 13 shows what percentage of blocks in each grid cell are diurnal. We see significant variation by country, with very few diurnal blocks in the U.S., western Europe, and Japan, but *many* diurnal blocks in Asia, Eastern Europe, and South America. Table 3 lists the countries with the most diurnal blocks.

These strong regional differences show the ability of our approach to identify global trends in Internet usage. In coming sections we explore how these differences correlate with of a combinations of cultural, policy, and economic causes.

5.2 When Does the Internet Sleep? (Phase of Diurnal Blocks)

Amplitude in spectral analysis of A shows *which* blocks are diurnal, and geolocation showed *where* these blocks are. We next show that *phase* in the FFT coefficients shows *when* these blocks are active.

We next look at the phase of geolocated diurnal blocks to see that it correlates strongly with longitude and therefore timezone. We measure how many blocks occur at each combination of longitude and phase. Since both phase and longitude are continuous, we count similar blocks by quantizing longitude and phase each into 100 bins ($\pm\pi$ and $\pm 180°$). Since both wrap around the circle, we "unroll" them by plot-

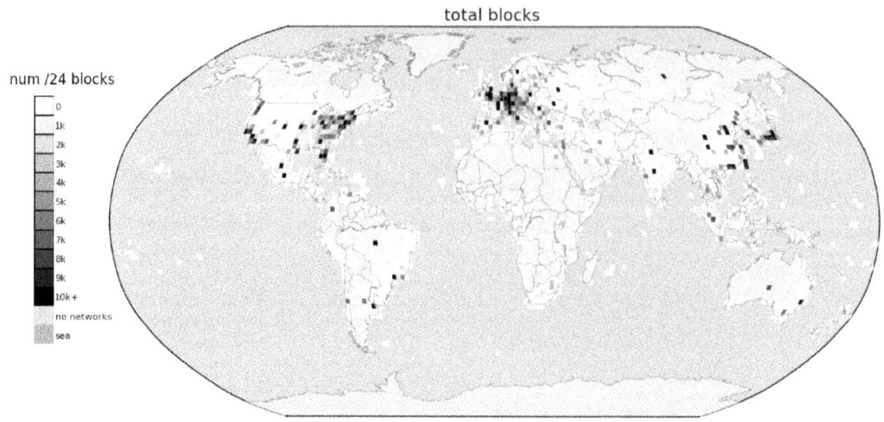

Figure 12: Number observable blocks (linear grayscale). Dataset: A_{12w}

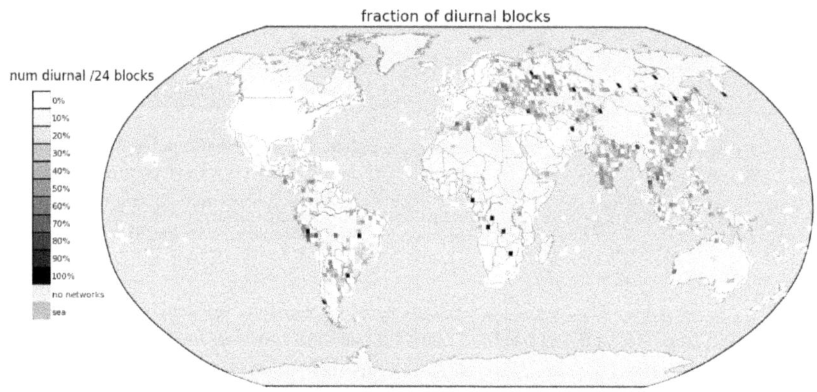

Figure 13: Percent of observable blocks that are diurnal. Dataset: A_{12w}.

region	blocks (/24s)	frac. diurnal
Northern America	721716	0.002
Southern Africa	11255	0.0108
W. Europe	275224	0.0109
Northern Europe	133911	0.0131
Caribbean	2174	0.016
Oceania	27206	0.0349
W. Asia	25570	0.0765
Northern Africa	9984	0.0992
Southern Europe	134933	0.124
Central America	44644	0.133
Eastern Europe	146552	0.135
Southern Asia	44524	0.200
South America	133493	0.208
South-Eastern Asia	48885	0.219
Eastern Asia	757352	0.279
Central Asia	3832	0.401

Table 4: Fraction of diurnal blocks grouped by regions. Diurnal analysis data is from A_{12w}; Geolocation data is from MaxMind [25].

ting phase in the range $[-\pi + L, \pi + L]$, where L is the longitude in radians.

Figure 14a shows a density plot of the 287k geolocatable, strictly diurnal blocks in A_{12w} as described above. We first observe that many blocks at longitude zero have phase near zero, and longitude and phase are strongly correlated—larger phases correspond with more eastward longitudes.

The correlation coefficient of unrolled phase against longitude is 0.835, showing they are strongly related. We did not attempt to align phase zero with longitude zero; their proximity is accidental and calibrating phase with local time of day is future work.

In Figure 14b we repeat this analysis with 590k blocks that are relaxed diurnal and geolocatable. The fit here is not quite as good (correlation coefficient is 0.763), but it is very close. This strong similarity suggests that our strict test for diurnal may be overly conservative.

In both Figure 14 we observe that the correlation between phase and longitude is fairly strong, except for longitudes between 100°E to 140°E. This range corresponds with Mongolia, China and southeast Asia. We believe this variation is primarily because our IP geolocation is not particularly accurate in China, and because it is a geographically wide country that uses a single timezone.

Finally, the relationship between phase and longitude suggests that phase may help geolocate diurnal blocks. Figure 14c shows mean and standard deviations when this mapping is derived from relaxed diurnal data. We see that the quality of the predictor varies significantly: a phase from -2 to 0 indicates only the hemisphere, while most other phases predict longitude within ± 20 degrees.

5.3 Correlating Block Diurnalness and Allocation Date

Policies for IP address allocation have evolved since IPv4 was introduced, with stricter requirements for density and reuse that encourage dynamic allocation through full alloca-

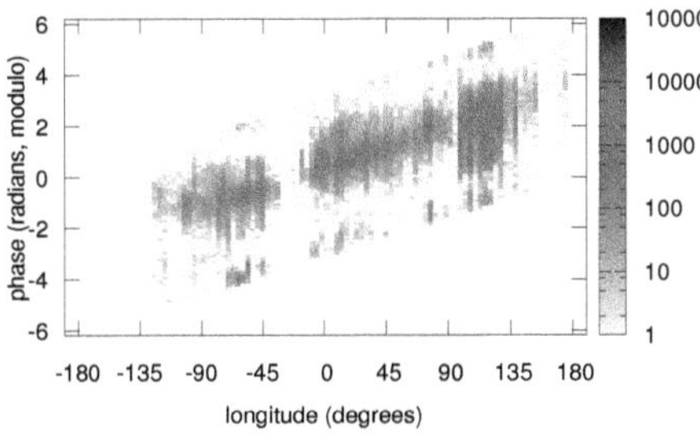

(a) Strictly diurnal blocks.

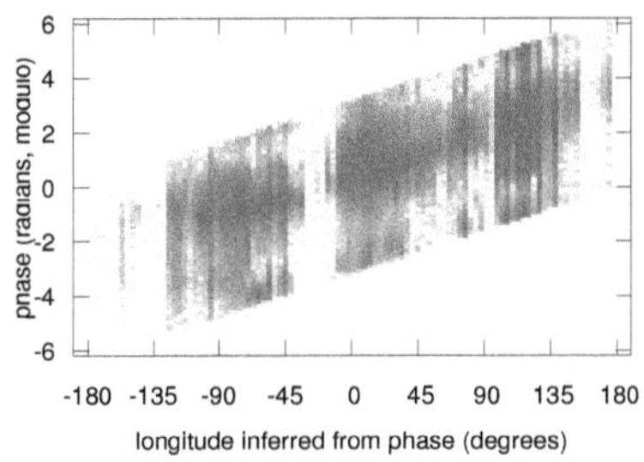

(b) Relaxed diurnal blocks.

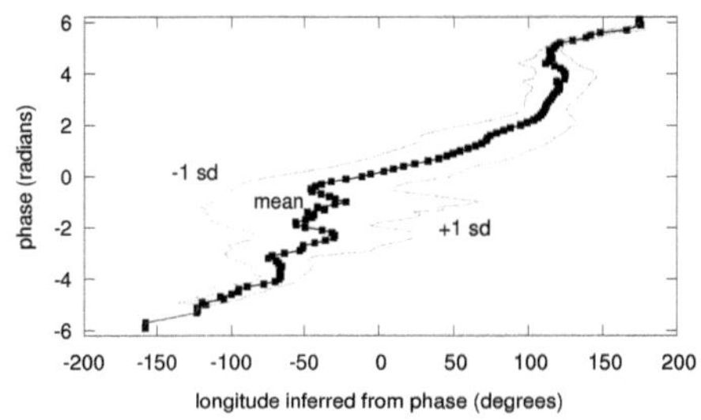

(c) Predicting longitude from phase (relaxed diurnal shown, strict is similar).

Figure 14: Comparing phase and longitude. Dataset: A_{12w}.

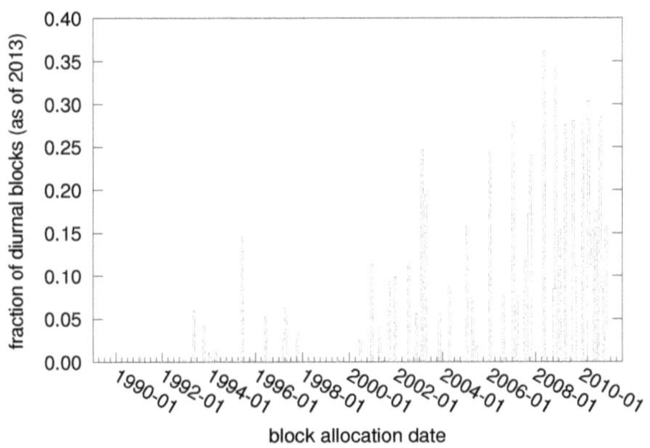

Figure 15: Percentage of diurnal blocks in each month, based on block allocation date. Dataset: 2013 diurnalness: A_{12w}; block allocation: IANA).

tion in May 2012 [15]. Prior work has documented increased dynamic addressing over time [3].

We can see how evolution in policies results in increased diurnal Internet blocks by correlate the fraction of diurnal blocks with the date when each /8 block was allocated to a regional registry by ICANN [14]. We show this relationship in Figure 15 by plotting a histogram of how many blocks are currently used diurnally, based on the date of allocation. The trend is for increased diurnal use as allocations proceed, corresponding with more careful policies in address use. (Linear regression shows a positive slope of 0.08% per month, with 0.609 correlation coefficient.) Even though the overall fraction of diurnal blocks shows a slight downward trend (Figure 11), this data shows that newer blocks are more often diurnal.

Changes in allocation policies have affected all countries, not just early adopters, and are independent of GDP (correlations between first allocation and mean allocation with GDP are both poor, $\rho < 0.27$).

5.4 Effects of Economic Conditions

We hypothesize that economic factors affect Internet use, since dynamic address assignment and turning devices off at night is more efficient than static or always-on dynamic assignment and always-on devices, and economic factors affect investment in telecommunications infrastructure. While one might suspect that economic factors correlate with diurnalness, our evaluation is able to quantify this relationship for the first time.

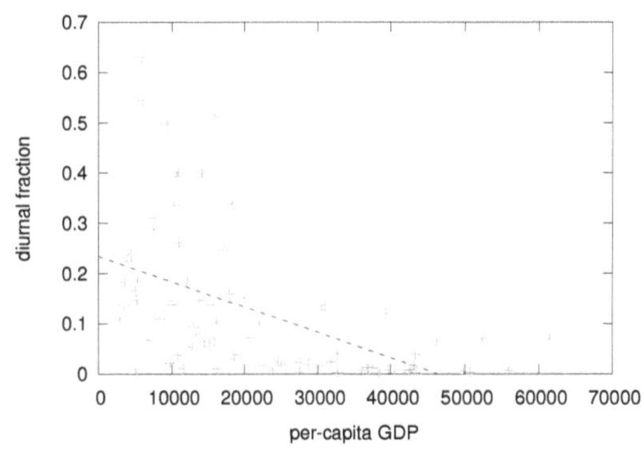

Figure 16: Scatter plot of diurnalness and per-capita GDP for all countries, for Table 3, with weak linear fit (dashed line). Dataset: A_{12w}, CIA.

5.4.1 Correlating Diurnal Blocks with Economics

Why do some countries have a greater fraction of diurnal blocks (§ 5.1)? Cultural differences across countries prompt different rates of savings, and different economic situations leave citizens different levels of disposable income. These difference and anecdotal evidence suggest that people of some countries, such as as China and India, to turn off their computers at night to save electricity bills.

Although we cannot directly model cultural differences, we can observe correlations between disposable income (measured in per-capita GDP, taken from the CIA World Factbook [5]) and diurnal network usage. Table 3 previously gave specific values. Figure 16 visualizes this correlation, including the weak linear fit (confidence coefficient: -0.526; such weak fits are common with coarse GDP data and few countries). The top 20 countries with diurnal fractions above 0.15 generally have a per-capita GDP less than USD $15,000, less than one-third of the United States. We conclude that economic factors correlate with differences in Internet use.

5.4.2 Non-GDP Factors: electricity and allocation age

GDP is one of many economic indicators. To understand correlations with other factors we carry out ANOVA factorial analysis (§ 2.4) comparing five factors: per-capita GDP,

	per-capita gdp	p.cpt. elec. cons.	I-net users/ host	age/ first alloc.	mean age/ alloc.
gdp	**6.61×10^{-8}**	0.306	0.822	0.789	0.995
elec.		0.703	0.609	—	**0.00148**
users/host			0.0366	0.959	0.849
first alloc.				0.830	—
mean alloc.					**0.0314**

Table 5: ANOVA showing correlations between diurnal and individual factors (the diagonal) and pairwise combinations of factors (off the diagonal). Bold combinations are statistically significant. Dataset: A_{12w}.

Internet users per host, electricity consumption per capita (each from the CIA factbook), and age of first (and mean) block allocation (from IANA) and fraction of diurnal blocks (from our analysis).

Table 5 shows this analysis for all one- and two-factor combinations. A p-value less than 0.05 suggests a strong correlation. We find there are three combinations meet this requirement: per-capita GDP, with p-value of 6.61×10^{-8}. The second is the combination of per-capita electricity consumption and mean age of allocation, with p-value of 0.001476. The third is mean age of allocation, with a p-value of 0.031354.

Our analysis with ANOVA supports our previous hypothesis that per-capita GDP is the main factor for diurnalness, and suggests that electrical usage and mean allocation age are also correlated. Electricity consumption is correlated with economic activity (and thus GDP), but ANOVA considers each combination o factors. Mean allocation age suggests that newer countries have more diurnal use, as shown in § 5.3.

5.4.3 *Independence and Relationship to Policies*

ANOVA shows correlations between diurnal networks and several individual and pairs of several measurable factors. Although ANOVA is a powerful technique, we must take care that factors not necessarily independent—low GDP may imply less developed infrastructure and less available power.

Future work is needed to show a causal relationship between these (or other) factors and network use, and to identify the how specific government and telecommunications policies relate to these measurable factors. Policy analysis is typically much more qualitative, since policies vary by country and region, and attribution of specific results to even a single policy requires significant effort (the U.S. Broadband Plan is more than 350 pages [9]). Our work suggests the potential to identify such relationships, is the first to describe specific measurements to assist this direction of study.

5.5 Effects of Access-Link Technology

We next consider correlations between access-link technology and diurnalness. National policies are often set to encourage new link technologies and promote always-on networks. In addition, while such policies and economic conditions are difficult for individuals to influence, users and ISPs often can choose different "last-mile" methods to connect to the Internet.

We infer link type (§ 2.3.3) for all blocks in A_{12w}, classifying 22.4% of those blocks. For these blocks, we correlate link type with diurnalness. Each of these link types have more than 30k blocks; we omit the wireless keyword because we see only 691 wireless/wifi blocks, not enough to provide statistically strong results.

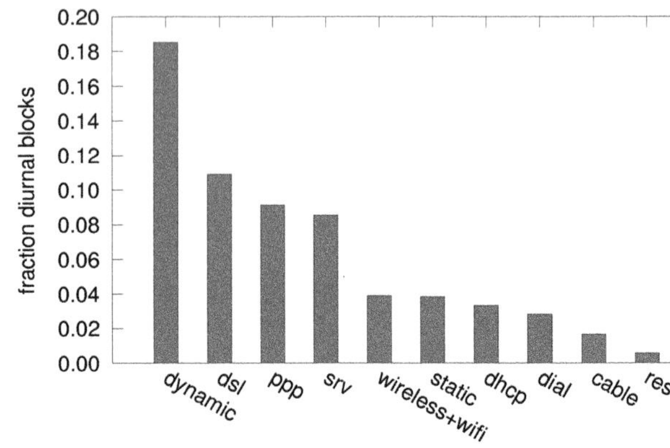

Figure 17: Fraction of diurnal blocks for 9 access keywords. Dataset: A_{12w}.

Figure 17 shows the fraction of diurnal networks for each different link type. As expected, dynamic addresses are strongly correlated with diurnal behavior, with *dynamic* at 19%. Somewhat surprisingly, *dialup* is not strongly diurnal (< 3%), while *dsl* is more diurnal (11%). These results suggest the importance of measuring network behavior rather than assuming.

5.6 Applications

This paper demonstrates that it is possible to identify diurnal network usage from active measurements, and that that diurnal networks correlate with GDP and other factors. A direct application of this work is to use it to explore the outcomes of government and telecommunications policy decisions (§ 5.4.3). For example, a goal of U.S. broadband deployment is always-on networking [9]; one can evaluate if new network technologies (fiber-to-the-home or cable modems) have are less diurnal (and so more always-on) than older technologies (dial-up, ISDN) by looking for correlations in access-link technology (§ 5.5). Comparisons of fraction of diurnal networks per country or state can be used to judge the progress of different areas towards the goal of always-on networking.

Information about blocks that are diurnal can also be used to calibrate other measurements. For example, one can scan the IPv4 space in tens of minutes to estimate the availability of each /24 block, but this near-snapshot will be representative only for non-diurnal blocks. For diurnal blocks, one needs several measurements at different times-of-day to determine the range of values.

Finally, information about diurnal networks is one component towards estimating the size of the Internet measured in active, public IP addresses [10].

6. RELATED WORK

ISP comparison: Several third-party systems exist to compare performance of ISPs, including Keynote [19], top ten reviews [19], and the popular speed test tool offered by OOKLA [29]. They share a common drawback: lack of scalability. Perhaps closest to our work is Netdiff [24], which measures performance of hundreds of paths for 18 backbone ISPs. They find that ISP performance depends on geographic properties of traffic and popularity of destinations. Our work is more focused on nodes instead of paths, and thus complements Netdiff.

Adaptive and pervasive sampling: Several prior studies have used adaptive probing techniques to find network faults (for example, [2]), and use simulations for validation. Similar to these, we use adaptive sampling inside network blocks to achieve accurate availability information ($\hat{A}_s$), with low probing cost.

Prior work has explored full enumeration of IPv4 [10]. We use some surveys from this work to validate our sampled results. Although we can do full enumeration quickly, as advocated by others [8], such effort is a poor match for long-term data collection: it is unnecessary and annoys target network operators. Instead, we build directly on the adaptive data collection methods of Trinocular [31], adding new analysis to identify diurnal networks.

Node-based studies: Barford et al. use node-based methods to detect network performance anomalies [1], with clever weighting algorithms to find which links to probe next; they simulate 15 types of topologies based on ns-2. Several other previous studies also use similar strategies, including Hubble [18] and iPlane [23]. Such node-based studies are precise in understanding performance on link paths between the node mesh. However, they usually "only" cover hundreds or thousands of nodes. We complement such systems with a much larger coverage (3.7M /24 blocks), and with measurements on a regular basis every 11 minutes.

Tomography studies: Network tomography is interested in finding the exact location of problems [6,7,12,20,21]. We correct for correlated error by removing outages near our probers. We are interested in tracking block-level network reachability in the whole Internet edge, but without exact localization of outages. Our work and tomography studies can benefit from each other. Our future work could be more precise by localizing problems. Tomography studies can use our system as a pre-step for finding symptoms.

7. CONCLUSIONS

In this paper, we develop an accurate adaptive approach to estimate network block availability over time. Based on this, we perform the first long-term, wide-scale analysis of diurnal network behavior and outages. We also begin to evaluate how policies, economic conditions and technologies affect Internet use in the world. With statistical analysis (ANOVA), we correlate diurnal usage and outages to economic factors such as GDP and power consumption.

Acknowledgments

This research is partially sponsored by the Department of Homeland Security (DHS) Science and Technology Directorate, HSARPA, Cyber Security Division, BAA 11-01-RIKA and Air Force Research Laboratory, Information Directorate under agreement number FA8750-12-2-0344, and via SPAWAR Systems Center Pacific under Contract No. N66001-13-C-3001. The U.S. Government is authorized to reproduce and distribute reprints for Governmental purposes notwithstanding any copyright notation thereon. The views contained herein are those of the authors and do not necessarily represent those of DHS or the U.S. Government.

This work was classified by USC's IRB as non-human subjects research (IIR00001648).

We thank Brian Yamaguchi (USC/ITS) for guidance about USC networks, and Christos Papadopoulos (CSU) and Rod Van Meter, Yohei Kuga, and Midori Kato (WIDE) for supporting data collection from their sites. We thank John Wroclawski, Alberto Dainotti, Georgios Smaragdakis (our shepherd), and the anonymous reviewers for comments on the paper.

8. REFERENCES

[1] P. Barford, N. Duffield, A. Ron, and J. Sommers. Network performance anomaly detection and localization. In *INFOCOM 2009, IEEE*, pages 1377–1385, 2009.

[2] M. Brodie, I. Rish, and S. Ma. Intelligent probing: A cost-effective approach to fault diagnosis in computer networks. *IBM Systems Journal*, 41(3):372 –385, 2002.

[3] Xue Cai and John Heidemann. Understanding Block-level Address Usage in the Visible Internet. In *Proc. of SIGCOMM*, 2010.

[4] Xue Cai, John Heidemann, Balachander Krishnamurthy, and Walter Willinger. Towards an AS-to-Organization map. In *Proceedings of the ACM Internet Measurement Conference*, pages 199–205, Melbourne, Australia, November 2010. ACM.

[5] CIA World Factbook. List of countries by GDP (PPP) per capita. `https://www.cia.gov/library/publications/the-world-factbook`.

[6] Ítalo Cunha, Renata Teixeira, Nick Feamster, and Christophe Diot. Measurement methods for fast and accurate blackhole identification with binary tomography. In *Proc. of 9thACM IMC*, 2009.

[7] Amogh Dhamdhere, Renata Teixeira, Constantine Dovrolis, and Christophe Diot. NetDiagnoser: troubleshooting network unreachabilities using end-to-end probes and routing data. In *Proc. of ACM Conference on Emerging Networking Experiments and Technologies*, pages 18:1–18:12. ACM, 2007.

[8] Zakir Durumeric, Eric Wustrow, and J. Alex Halderman. ZMap: Fast internet-wide scanning and its security applications. In *Proc. of USENIX Security Symposium*, pages 605–620, Washington, DC, USA, August 2013. USENIX.

[9] Federal Communication Commission. Collecting America: the national broadband plan. Technical report, FCC, March 2010.

[10] John Heidemann, Yuri Pradkin, Ramesh Govindan, Christos Papadopoulos, Genevieve Bartlett, and Joseph Bannister. Census and survey of the visible Internet. In *Proc. of ACM IMC*, pages 169–182, Vouliagmeni, Greece, October 2008. ACM.

[11] Zi Hu and John Heidemann. Towards geolocation of millions of IP addresses. In *Proceedings of the ACM Internet Measurement Conference*, pages 123–130, Boston, MA, USA, 2012. ACM.

[12] Yiyi Huang, Nick Feamster, and Renata Teixeira. Practical issues with using network tomography for fault diagnosis. *SIGCOMM Comput. Commun. Rev.*, 38:53–58, September 2008.

[13] Bradley Huffaker, Marina Fomenkov, and k. c. claffy. Geocompare: a comparison of public and commercial geolocation databases. Technical report, CAIDA, May 2011.

[14] Internet Assigned Numbers Authority. IANA IPv4 address space registry. web page http://www.iana.org/assignments/ipv4-address-space/ipv4-address-space.txt, May 2013.

[15] Internet Corporation for Assigned Names and Numbers. Global policy for post exhaustion IPv4 allocation mechanisms by the IANA, May 2012.

[16] Internet Software Consortium. Internet Domain Survey. web page http://www.isc.org/solutions/survey, January 2007.

[17] Philip j. Fleming and John J. Wallace. How not to lie with statistics: the correct way to summarize benchmark results. *Communications of the ACM*, 29(3):218–221, March 1986.

[18] Ethan Katz-Bassett, Harsha V. Madhyastha, John P. John, Arvind Krishnamurthy, David Wetherall, and Thomas Anderson. Studying black holes in the internet with Hubble. In *NSDI*, 2008.

[19] Keynote. Internet Health Report. http://www.internetpulse.net.

[20] Ramana Rao Kompella, Jennifer Yates, Albert Greenberg, and Alex C. Snoeren. IP fault localization via risk modeling. In *NSDI*, 2005.

[21] Ramana Rao Kompella, Jennifer Yates, Albert Greenberg, and Alex C. Snoeren. Detection and Localization of Network Black Holes. In *Proc. of IEEE Infocom*, 2007.

[22] LACNIC. LACNIC policy manual (v2.1), March 2014.

[23] Harsha V. Madhyastha, Tomas Isdal, Michael Piatek, Colin Dixon, Thomas Anderson, Arvind Krishnamurthy, and Arun Venkataramani. iPlane: An information plane for distributed services. In *Proc. of 7th OSDI*, pages 367–380, Seattle, WA, USA, November 2006. USENIX.

[24] Ratul Mahajan, Ming Zhang, Lindsey Poole, and Vivek Pai. Uncovering performance differences among backbone isps with netdiff. In *Proceedings of the 5th USENIX Symposium on Networked Systems Design and Implementation*, NSDI'08, pages 205–218. USENIX Association, 2008.

[25] MaxMind. GeoIP Geolocation Products. http://www.maxmind.com/en/city.

[26] Rupert G. Miller. *Beyond ANOVA: Basics of Applied Statistics (Texts in Statistical Science Series)*. Chapman & Hall/CRC, January 1997.

[27] P. Mockapetris. Domain names—concepts and facilities. RFC 1034, Internet Request For Comments, November 1987.

[28] James A. Muir and Paul C. Van Oorschot. Internet geolocation: Evasion and counterevasion. *ACM Computing Surveys*, 42(1), December 2009.

[29] OOKLA. Speedtest. http://www.speedtest.net.

[30] Lin Quan, John Heidemann, and Yuri Pradkin. Detecting internet outages with precise active probing (extended). Technical Report ISI-TR-2012-678, USC/ISI, February 2012.

[31] Lin Quan, John Heidemann, and Yuri Pradkin. Trinocular: Understanding internet reliability through adaptive probing. In *Proceedings of the ACM SIGCOMM Conference*, pages 255–266, Hong Kong, China, August 2013. ACM.

[32] Lin Quan, John Heidemann, and Yuri Pradkin. When the Internet sleeps: Correlating diurnal networks with external factors (extended). Technical Report ISI-TR-2014-691b, USC/Information Sciences Institute, May 2014. (updated August 2014).

[33] Aaron Schulman and Neil Spring. Pingin' in the rain. In *Proc. of ACM IMC*, pages 19–25, Berlin, Germany, November 2011. ACM.

[34] Srikanth Sundaresan, Sam Burnett, Nick Feamster, and Walter de Donato. BISmark: A testbed for deploying measurements and applications in broadband access networks. In *Proc. of USENIX Annual Technical Conference*. USENIX, June 2014.

[35] Srikanth Sundaresan, Walter de Donato, Nick Feamster, Renata Teixeira, Sam Crawford, and Antonio Pescapè. Broadband Internet performance: A view from the gateway. In *Proc. of SIGCOMM*, pages 134–145, Toronto, Ontario, Canada, August 2011. ACM.

[36] Team Cymru. IP to ASN Mapping. http://www.team-cymru.org/Services/ip-to-asn.html.

[37] USC/LANDER Project. LANDER: Los Angeles network data exchange and repository. web page http://www.isi.edu/ant/lander/, November 2007.

[38] USC/LANDER project. Internet address survey dataset, predict id usc-lander/internet_address_survey_adaptive_reprobing_a12w. web page http://www.isi.edu/ant/lander, April 2013.

[39] Eric Wustrow, Manish Karir, Michael Bailey, Farnam Jahanian, and Geoff Huston. Internet background radiation revisited. In *ACM IMC*, 2010.

[40] Kathryn Zickuhr and Aaron Smith. Home broadband 2013. Technical report, Pew Research Center, August 2013.

WhoWas: A Platform for Measuring Web Deployments on IaaS Clouds

Liang Wang†, Antonio Nappa*‡, Juan Caballero*, Thomas Ristenpart†, and Aditya Akella†
† University of Wisconsin – Madison, {liangw,rist,akella}@cs.wisc.edu
* IMDEA Software Institute, {antonio.nappa,juan.caballero}@imdea.org
‡ Universidad Politécnica de Madrid

ABSTRACT

Public infrastructure-as-a-service (IaaS) clouds such as Amazon EC2 and Microsoft Azure host an increasing number of web services. The dynamic, pay-as-you-go nature of modern IaaS systems enable web services to scale up or down with demand, and only pay for the resources they need. We are unaware, however, of any studies reporting on measurements of the patterns of usage over time in IaaS clouds as seen in practice. We fill this gap, offering a measurement platform that we call WhoWas. Using active, but lightweight, probing, it enables associating web content to public IP addresses on a day-by-day basis. We exercise WhoWas to provide the first measurement study of churn rates in EC2 and Azure, the efficacy of IP blacklists for malicious activity in clouds, the rate of adoption of new web software by public cloud customers, and more.

Categories and Subject Descriptors

C.2 [**Computer-Communication Network**]: Miscellaneous; C.4 [**Performance of Systems**]: Measurement Techniques

General Terms

Measurement

Keywords

Cloud Computing; EC2; Azure; Web Service; Active Measurement

1. INTRODUCTION

Public infrastructure-as-a-service (IaaS) clouds enable customers to launch virtual machine (VM) instances, with each instance assigned a publicly routable IP address and given access to other resources such as storage, memory, and CPU time. The customer can start and stop instances, and pays fixed rates per unit time (typically per hour). An important use case for such clouds is rapid, scalable deployment of web services: a study last year used active DNS interrogation to show that 4% of the Alexa most popular one million websites [1] were using IaaS clouds in some capacity [2].

IMC'14, November 5–7, 2014, Vancouver, BC, Canada.
Copyright © 2014 ACM 978-1-4503-3213-2/14/11 ...$15.00.
http://dx.doi.org/10.1145/2663716.2663742.

Unfortunately, little is known about the pattern of usage of IaaS clouds and whether peculiarities arise due to the new ways in which web systems are built. For example, an oft-advertised benefit of using IaaS clouds is elasticity, or the ability to scale up or down deployments as needed in response to load. We are unaware of any measurements that reveal the extent to which customers are taking advantage of elasticity. Such measurements can inform the design of future cloud provisioning and scaling algorithms. Relatedly, we do not know the level of churn of ownership of public cloud IPs, and whether it may cause problems for tools that assume IP ownership is relatively static (e.g., IP blacklists of malicious websites).

We build and exercise a platform for measuring web deployments on IaaS clouds over time. Our platform, called WhoWas, can be used to perform measurements over time of cloud address ranges. Unlike prior work that uses DNS interrogation, we provide direct measurements of what is running on cloud-associated IP addresses via lightweight network probing and HTTP requests. Analysts can then use the gathered data to perform lookups on particular IP addresses to receive a history of status and content for that IP address over time. We include various analysis tools, including a novel webpage clustering heuristic to associate webpages hosted on distinct IP addresses together.

We use WhoWas to measure web deployments on Amazon EC2 for a three month period and Microsoft Azure for a two month period, with a resulting dataset of size approximately 900 GB. To understand changes over time, we repeatedly probe provider-advertised IP ranges at an average rate of once per day. This enables a number of first-of-their-kind measurement results, including:

(1) Over the time periods reported, we see sizable growth in the number of servers running on EC2 (4.9% increase) and Azure (7.7% increase).

(2) The majority of web services appear to use a small number of servers, with more than three-quarters of all identified web services on each of EC2 and Azure using just a single IP address on average. There exist, however, very large services, in the most extreme case we identify a service associated with more than 30,000 EC2 IP addresses any given day.

(3) The change in status of an IP address (e.g., no longer hosting web content or appearing to change ownership) from one measurement to the next is low on both clouds: around 3% of all IP addresses scanned. Large deployments of webpages across many IPs are highly available as well as stable in terms of number of IPs used over time, but have significant turnover in terms of which IP addresses are used over the course of our measurements.

(4) We discover small amounts of malicious activity (mostly phishing and malware hosting) by comparing data from

WhoWas with blacklists. We summarize three IP usage behaviors of the discovered malicious webpages, and observe that the malicious webpages can stay up for a long time after being blacklisted.

(5) We find that a majority of web servers use dated versions of server and backend software, some of which have known vulnerabilities.

To facilitate future research, we have made the source code for WhoWas publicly available [3] and will make data available to researchers upon request.

The rest of this paper is structured as follows. We present background on IaaS clouds in §2, and related work in §3. We outline the WhoWas platform in §4, and its key analysis engines in §5. We describe how we collect data using WhoWas in §6, and the ethical and privacy considerations we take into account are discussed in §7. In §8, we show the broad utility of WhoWas via three usage cases: an analysis of the dynamics of cloud deployments, a study of malicious activity, and a characterization of in-use web software. We conclude in §9.

2. BACKGROUND

Infrastructure-as-a-Service (IaaS) systems allow users to rent virtual machines (VMs or instances) with flexible computing resources and operating systems. IaaS providers like Amazon EC2 and Azure typically provide a few default VM configurations with set resources (e.g., number of CPUs, storage, and memory), and many configuration options to adapt instances to the user's needs.

The most commonly offered instances are *on-demand*, which can be created by users as required, stopped when no longer needed, and are charged for the hours used. Azure only offers on-demand instances, while EC2 in addition offers *reserved* instances, which are rented for one or three years at lower cost.

Each instance has two associated IP addresses, a private IP that only works inside the cloud and a publicly routable IP. Both IPs are by default dynamic; they are released when an instance is stopped and can be reassigned to a different instance, possibly from a different customer. This creates IP churn, where the same public IP address may frequently change ownership.

In addition, EC2 and Azure provide up to 5 static public IP addresses to each account or service deployment[1]. These static IPs are not specific to an instance, but assigned to the user until explicitly released, and the user chooses the mapping between IP and instance. Both providers also offer load-balancing services to distribute requests to an IP across multiple instances.

In EC2, each instance is also assigned an externally resolvable DNS name, whose structure follows a provider-specific pattern: the prefix "ec2-" followed by a string that replaces the dots in the public IP with hyphens, and a region-specific suffix.

EC2 virtual networking. Amazon Virtual Private Cloud (VPC) allows users to create a fully-controllable and easy-to-customize virtual networking environment for their instances. Each VPC is a logically separate virtual network. We use the terms EC2-Classic and EC2-VPC to refer to classic networking and VPC networking, respectively. Compared to EC2-Classic, EC2-VPC provides extra features. For example, an EC2-VPC instance (also referred to as a VPC instance) can run on single-tenant hardware, while an instance launched with EC2-Classic (a classic instance) may run on shared hardware; a user can assign one or multiple specific private IP addresses to an EC2-VPC instance; classic instances can only have one public IP, while VPC instances can bind to multiple network interfaces and IP addresses (at most 240 IPs, the exact maximum depending on instance type) [4]. Because of the security and management benefits compared to EC2-Classic, Amazon has encouraged users to adopt VPC and announced that accounts created after Dec. 12, 2013 can only launch instances with VPC enabled.

3. RELATED WORK

Prior measurement studies of web usage in the cloud primarily used active DNS probing and packet capture [2]. Such an approach provides only a limited view of website availability and deployment changes over time. Packet captures (along with similar techniques such as passive DNS [5]) are also subject to sampling bias.

Closely related to our work is the Wayback Machine, which archives old versions of websites [6]. While we investigated using its data for our study, this would only provide information on sites submitted and, in particular, provide relatively poor coverage of cloud usage.

Active probing is a popular technique that has been used for a variety of applications. Two decades ago, Comer and Lin proposed active probing to identify differences between TCP implementations [7]. Internet-wide active probing has been used for identifying vulnerable SSH servers [8], compiling a Web census [9], finding DNS servers providing incorrect resolutions [10], detecting weak cryptography keys in network devices [11], for identifying malicious servers [12, 13], and more. In our work we do not scan the full Internet but only IP ranges from cloud hosting providers. Localized scans have also been used for detecting network-based malware [14] in a local network. In contrast we scan remote networks.

Other works study how to scan fast. Staniford et al. described techniques that malware can use to quickly spread through scanning [15]; Netmap [16] proposed a software framework for fast packet I/O, enabling a single core to saturate a 10Gbps link; and Durumeric et al. released Zmap [17], a horizontal scanner that can probe the Internet in 45 minutes from a single host. WhoWas does not aim to scan fast or wide. Rather, it periodically scans the same IP ranges to analyze temporal evolution.

The ethical issues of active probing and sharing measurement data are treated by several prior works. Leonard et al. [18] describe how to perform maximally polite Internet-wide horizontal scans. We use their recommendations as guidelines for our probing. Allman and Paxson [19] discuss issues when sharing network measurement data. Currently, we do not make our data publicly available on the Internet, but will release it to researchers upon request, after privacy issues have been evaluated.

Prior works have studied malicious activity in cloud services. Balduzzi et al. [20] investigate security issues in the sharing of virtual images among EC2 users. Canali et al [21] install web applications on shared hosting providers and issue abuse reports on them. In contrast, we measure malicious activity by cloud users renting virtual machines. Nappa et al. [22] show that attackers are abusing cloud instances to host drive-by exploit servers. Our work further quantifies this trend by including multiple types of malicious activity, and analyzing the effect of cloud IP churn on blacklists.

4. THE WHOWAS PLATFORM

To track website deployments on IaaS clouds over time, we design and build a system that can perform lightweight probing of clouds, process the results, and enable a programmatic interface for conducting analyses on the gathered data. The basic functionality we seek is to be able to associate a (cloud) IP address with its status and content at some point in time, where status means whether it

[1]Called Elastic IPs in EC2 and Reserved IPs in Azure.

is hosting a VM instance responding to network packets, running a web server, or otherwise.

To do so, WhoWas performs lightweight, active measurements over some user-specified time period and records the results for later analysis. A key design choice we faced involved how to balance the granularity of observations (how often we probe) of an IP address's status against not burdening customers of cloud services with many network requests. Another challenge is in identifying and extracting website features that may be useful for determining if two IP addresses are hosting the same web content. If successful, this would allow us to measure the "footprint" of a particular service: the number of IP addresses used by the service at a given period of time.

The main components of the WhoWas system are shown in Figure 1. They consist of a scanner, webpage fetcher, and feature generator, which are used in that order to populate a database with information about measurement results. WhoWas defines a Python library interface to allow programmatic access to the resulting data sets. This makes it easy to write analyses, and also to build extensions on top of the basic platform (see §5). All source code is publicly available [3].

We discuss each of the main components of WhoWas in turn.

Scanner. WhoWas is seeded with a list of IP address ranges to target. At the moment these must be manually gathered. Both EC2 and Azure make public the IP addresses used by their services [23, 24]. For clouds that do not, one could enumerate them via other means (e.g., via appropriate Whois interrogation) to seed a list. The scanner also takes a blacklist of IP addresses that should not be scanned. This enables users to avoid certain ranges, which enables operators to allow tenants to opt out from measurement studies.

The scanner translates these IP lists into a task list. The primary goal of the scanner is to ascertain what IP addresses are running typical services. In particular we focus on identifying instances running HTTP and/or HTTPS services. For each IP address, the scanner sends a TCP SYN (from now on, a probe) first to port 80 (HTTP default) and then to 443 (HTTPS default). If both probes fail to respond, then a probe is sent to port 22 (SSH). The SSH probe enables identifying live instances that are not hosting publicly accessible HTTP(S) servers.

The scanner times out a probe after two seconds and does not retry failed probes. The former increases speed of the scanner while the latter minimizes interaction with the cloud customers. To evaluate the effect of larger timeouts, we performed the following experiment. First, we randomly selected 5% of EC2 IPs from each /24 prefix used by EC2. This resulted in 235,070 IPs. For these IPs, we compared probes with timeouts of 2 s and 8 s. We observed an increase of only 0.61% in the number of IPs responding with the longer timeout. For the same set of IPs we also had the scanner probe with a 2 s timeout once, then again 200 s later and again three more times at intervals of 100 s for a total of 5 probes. Compared to the first round of scanning, only 0.27% more IPs responded if one took into account the additional 4 probes. We concluded that these failure rates will not unduly affect interpretation of scanner results.

By default, the scanner uses a global scan rate of 250 probes per second (pps) and only treats each IP once a day. This means that an IP address receives at most three probes (80/tcp, 443/tcp, 22/tcp) in a day. These scan rates are significantly smaller than those used in prior work that range from 1,000 pps up to 1.4 million pps [17, 18] (though we will admittedly be targeting smaller ranges). One round of scanning visits all the IP addresses input to WhoWas. We chose small defaults to balance burden on infrastructure with the temporal granularity of WhoWas measurements.

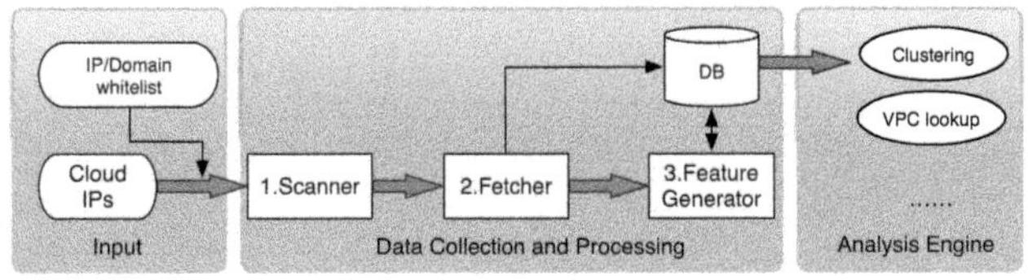

Figure 1: The main components of WhoWas.

We say an IP address is *responsive* if it responds to any of the network probes. Otherwise it is *unresponsive*.

HTTP requests. For any IP address that responds as being open on port 80 or port 443, the scanner submits the IP to the webpage fetcher, which will randomly pick up a worker process from a worker pool to gather further information from this IP. The worker generates a URL by concatenating the IP address to either "http://" (should port 80 and 443 have been seen as open) or "https://" (if only port 443 was open). A GET request is submitted to the resultant URL concatenating with "robots.txt". Then, a GET may be sent to the URL depending on the content of robots.txt. At most two GETs are made per round of scanning for a given IP address.

The fetcher records any received HTTP response code, response header, or error information in a MySQL database. Each round of scanning uses a distinct database table, with a timestamp in the table name to indicate the start of the round. If the type of the response content is "application/*", "audio/*", "image/*" or "video/*", the fetcher foregoes downloading the content as our analysis engine cannot yet process non-text data. For text content (e.g., HTML, JSON, XML) we store the first 512 KB of content into the database. The fetcher does not follow links in the collected content and does not execute active content. The fetcher is built using the Python Requests library [25].

An IP is *available* in a round if the HTTP(S) request for the URL without robots.txt succeeded, and *unavailable* otherwise. Note that unresponsive IPs are also unavailable.

Feature extraction. After a round of scanning is finished, WhoWas invokes a separate process to extract various features from the results. For each webpage successfully fetched, we extract and insert into the database: (1) the back-end technology from the "x-powered-by" field in HTTP response headers; (2) a description of a webpage from the "description" tag in the returned HTML; (3) a string that consists of all field names in the HTTP response header (sorted alphabetically and separated by "#"); (4) the length of the returned HTML; (5) the title string from the HTML; (6) the web template (e.g., Joomla!, WordPress, or Drupal) indicated by "generator" tags in the HTML; (7) the server type as reported in HTTP response headers; (8) the keywords as indicated in a keywords tag in the HTML; and (9) any Google Analytics ID found in the HTML. We mark entries as unknown when they are missing from the HTML or HTTP headers.

We additionally compute (10) a simhash [26–28] over the HTML of the returned webpage. This algorithm has been used previously for webpage comparison: two webpages are similar if their fingerprints have low Hamming distance. We use 96-bit hashes.

Limitations. We briefly highlight a few limitations of our platform. First, it can only detect a portion of web-facing instances hosted in the cloud. For example, the scanner fails to successfully discover a web server instance if the owner configures firewalls to only allow traffic from a given source; the instance is not bound to a public

IP address (e.g., instances in some EC2 VPC networks); and/or the ports used for SSH or web services are not set to the default.

A second limitation is that we can visit a website using only the IP address instead of the intended domain. PaaS providers or web hosting providers may use one instance for multiple websites or web applications, and not allow requests without specific URLs. In this case, they will return 404 pages or other customized pages to the fetcher. Even so, for some IPs, we can still identify their ownership by looking at unique features in the returned contents (e.g., if the 404 response contains the domain name of the website).

A third limitation is the granularity achieved by WhoWas. By only querying once per day, or even once per several days, we can only measure changes in status with that granularity. Network packet drops or other temporary failures will have WhoWas mark an IP as unresponsive or unavailable for the entire measurement period. More generally, EC2 and Azure (as well as other clouds) have per-hour charging models, meaning that we might expect an hourly granularity to better reflect the rapidity of changes.

Increasing the scan rate could be easily accommodated via parallelism. However, while fetching webpage content at such granularities might not represent a burden for large enterprise tenants (let alone the IaaS provider), it is impossible to know whether WhoWas is also interacting with tenants expecting very little, or even no, network traffic[2]. For these reasons we err on the side of having a relatively conservative scan rate.

5. ANALYSIS TOOLS

As described thus far, WhoWas can perform scans, fetch pages, and store them. To enable richer analyses, we build in extra tools to aid users. We first include a clustering algorithm to associate IP addresses that are likely to be hosting the same webpage or, at least, be operated by the same owner. We also build in some knowledge of the semantics associated with particular IP addresses by way of cloud cartography techniques.

Clustering. After collecting webpages for a period of time, we use clustering to help identify IP addresses that are likely to be hosting the same web applications. Features used for clustering are the title, template, server software, keywords, Google Analytics ID, and simhash. Other extracted features are not used for clustering because they are unstable (e.g., HTML length) or redundant. We then use a 2-level hierarchical clustering, using the features for IPs across all rounds of measurement. The clustering is run across all rounds, so that each entry in a cluster corresponds to an <IP, round> pair. In the first level clustering, we cluster solely on the first five features. At this level, strict equality is used for comparison, so each first-level cluster only has webpages with the same title, template, server, keywords, and Analytics ID.

In the second level clustering we use the simhashes. The distance measure here is the Hamming distance between two simhashes, which can take on a value from 0 (identical) to 96 (very dissimilar) since we use 96-bit hashes. We use a simple tuning procedure to pick a distance threshold for clustering based on the gap statistic, which is a common method for estimating the number of clusters when doing unsupervised clustering [29]. Each resulting second-level cluster is given a unique random identifier, and we associate to each IP's round record their cluster assignment.

If using this clustering approach to identify IPs belonging to the same website, an immediate limitation is that significant changes to the features (e.g., due to an update to the page or underlying server software) will result in IPs being placed into distinct clusters. We therefore provide some additional heuristics to help catch changes in features that may not be indicative of change of ownership of an IP address. In a post-processing step after clustering, we merge clusters using the following algorithm.

Consider two records in the database:
$DB[IP, T, simhash, cluster, f_a, f_b, f_c, f_d, f_e]$,
$DB[IP', T', simhash', cluster', f'_a, f'_b, f'_c, f'_d, f'_e]$
where we store the IP, the timestamp (T), the simhash of the content of the page and the cluster to which the IPs belong, and the other features (f_x) namely: title, server, template, keywords, and Google Analytics ID. We merge two records if the following conditions hold: the IPs are the same, the simhashes differ at most by 3 bits (used also in [30]), one feature is the same between the two records, and the two clusters are temporally ordered.

The 2-level clustering and merging heuristic above strive to identify web applications that are being used across distinct IPs or across time on the same IP address. It was the culmination of a manual refinement process, where we started with using just simhashes and then added top level features to help improve clustering results (as measured by manual inspection of samples). This was made easy by the programmatic WhoWas interface. The interface also makes it easy to modify, for example, the approach above to cluster with other goals in mind, such as simply finding related content (dropping the server feature) or only using Analytics IDs.

After merging, some clusters may still include IP addresses actually operated by different owners. For example, sites that lack a Google Analytics ID but reply with a default Apache page all end up in the same cluster. To not have such clusters bias analyses further in the paper, we perform some manual cleaning of the clusters. First, we write a script to remove the top-level clusters (and associated second-level clusters) whose title contains expressions indicating that WhoWas failed to fetch useful content. (e.g., "not found" and "error".) Then, for second-level clusters with over 20 IP addresses associated with them on average per day, we check the titles of their top-level clusters, and exclude them if they correspond to default server test pages. (e.g., with title "welcome-apache".)

Unless specified otherwise, from now on we refer to second-level clusters after merging and cleaning as simply clusters.

Cloud cartography. Previous work highlighted the utility of so-called cloud cartography, in which one uses measurements to associate cloud public IP addresses to types of infrastructure. For example, this has been used to estimate in EC2 the type [31] and availability zone [2,31] of a given instance. Different than previous works, we use cartography to help disambiguate distinct networking configurations associated with public EC2 IPs.

Recall that Amazon EC2 provides two ways to launch instances: classic and VPC. For classic instances, one public IP address represents one VM instance. VPC instances can instead have multiple public IPs associated to them. If we see a cluster of N IPs, if these IPs are VPC it may therefore be the case that these IPs are associated with fewer than N VM instances.

We would therefore like to have WhoWas be able to differentiate between VPC and classic instances. We use DNS interrogation to differentiate between public IP addresses used for classic instances and those used for VPC instances: Amazon's internal DNS always returns a public IP address when resolving the public domain name associated to a VPC IP address (c.f., [32]).

In more detail, we have the following procedure for a one-time measurement to label each public IP in a region with VPC or classic. In that region, we launch an instance in the classic network, and then perform a DNS query for each public IP in this region. For example, say the IP address is 1.2.3.4, then we

[2]Indeed, we received emails from a handful of tenants that did not realize their web servers were publicly accessible! See also §7.

Region	VPC prefixes	% all IPs in region
USEast	280	13.7
USWest_Oregon	256	36.4
EU	124	20.8
AsiaTokyo	98	32.0
AsiaSingapore	82	33.9
USWest_NC	72	22.5
AsiaSydney	64	33.3
SouthAmerica	56	31.9

Table 2: Breakdown of public IP prefixes in EC2 by VPC

form the EC2-style public domain name[3] "ec2-1-2-3-4.compute-1.amazonaws.com" and perform a DNS lookup from the instance. If the DNS response contains a start-of-authority (SOA) record (meaning no DNS information for that DNS name), then there is no active instance on this IP and also the IP is labeled as classic. If instead the response contains an IP address that is in EC2's public IP address space, then the IP is using VPC; otherwise, the IP is using classic networking.

After performing such queries for all EC2 public IP addresses (with a suitably low rate limit), we obtain a map of IP prefixes as being used for VPC or classic. Table 2 shows the results in terms of the number of /22 prefixes (c.f., [33]) used for VPC compared to all IPs associated to that region.

We include in WhoWas the resulting /22 map to add to any public EC2 IP address round record an indicator of whether the IP uses VPC or classic networking.

6. DATA COLLECTION

We seed WhoWas with the Amazon EC2 and Azure public IP address ranges as of Sep. 10, 2013 and use them as the target IP addresses [23, 24]. There are 4,702,208 target IP addresses in EC2 and 495,872 in Azure. The probing on EC2 began on Sep. 30, 2013 and lasted for 3 months, and the probing on Azure began on Oct. 31, 2013 and lasted for 2 months. In October and November, a round of measurements was performed every 3 days. We then increased the frequency to one round per day in December. The final round of measurement was on Dec. 31, 2013. In the end, we collected a total of 51 rounds of scanning in EC2 and 46 in Azure. The number of rounds are similar despite an extra month of probing on EC2 because of the slower rate in the first two months and because at the beginning we occasionally stopped the probing for updates on our infrastructure.

We run WhoWas from a pair of machines, one for EC2 and one for Azure. The machines had the same configuration: Ubuntu 12.10 i386 server, 8 core Intel i7 @ 3.40 GHz CPU, 32 GB memory, and 2 TB hard drive for storing data. The only software dependencies are Python Requests and Python MySQLdb libraries. The worker number for the crawler is set to 250 by default. The timeout for HTTP(S) connections is set to 10 seconds.

The resulting data set. We collected about 900 GB of data in total. Afterwards, we ran the analysis tools described in §5 to cluster the IP addresses and also label IP addresses as being VPC or classic. Recall that clusters contain <IP, round> pairs. As shown in Table 4, an average of 64.7% of the responsive EC2 IP addresses (60.6% for Azure) are available in each round of probing. Table 3 shows a break down of the ports open on responsive IPs. For the available IP addresses, Table 5 shows the top 5 text content types in the responses, as only text content is collected by WhoWas.

[3]Recall as per §2 that these differ slightly on a per-region and per-zone basis, but that it is easy to determine from looking at examples from one's own accounts.

provider \ port	22-only	80-only	443-only	80&443
EC2	25.9	38.0	5.5	30.6
Azure	9.3	45.8	16.5	28.4

Table 3: Average percentage of responsive IPs per measurement round that open a given port(s)

provider \ code	200	4xx	5xx	other
EC2	64.7	28.0	7.2	0.10
Azure	60.6	30.2	9.2	0.02

Table 4: Average percentage of responsive IPs per measurement round that respond with a given HTTP status code.

Table 6 summarizes the clustering for both datasets. First, it shows the number of responsive IP addresses. Then, the distinct simhashes for the content obtained from those IP addresses, which is larger than the number of IP addresses because the content collected from an IP address varies over time. Next, it shows the number of first-level and second-level clusters, which shows that some first-level clusters are split into multiple second-level clusters. The last row shows the final number of clusters, after merging and cleaning has been applied to the second-level clusters.

7. ETHICAL CONSIDERATIONS

The unsolicited nature of active probing can make some targets consider it offensive and can potentially place a burden on both the individual tenants and the cloud provider. We take this issue seriously in our study and seek a careful balance between the amount of interaction required and the merits of the obtained data. We guide our active probing on the recommendations of prior work [18].

Our scanner and fetcher are located at the premises of one of our institutions and their use was made in cooperation with the institution's IT staff. To minimize the impact on the EC2 and Azure networks we limit the probing to an average of once per day and constrain our probing to only 3 ports (80/tcp, 443/tcp, 22/tcp).

Our HTTP fetcher includes a brief note in the User-Agent string stating that the request is being made for a research project. The note includes an email address to contact in case of questions/concerns. This allows tenants to request opting out of future queries. We also exclude IPs that we have observed to disallow robots requesting the top-level content, as per the robots exclusion protocol [34]. In the course of operating WhoWas we received 84 emails from instance operators. Upon further explanation, most operators were happy to hear about our research project. Only 16 requested to have IPs excluded from future scans, which we promptly did. In total 67 IPs were excluded in the course of the experiment. In general, the reasons offered for requesting IPs be excluded were either: (1) the servers are not designed to be public, but with careless configurations, they are accidentally discovered by WhoWas; and (2) since IaaS providers charge tenants based on traffic, the traffic generated by WhoWas, though it is very small, is still unwelcome for some tenants.

While technically any data we obtain is public, in the sense that we are simply fetching webpages from publicly advertised IP addresses, it is clear that some cloud tenants inadvertently made accessible what should not be. So as to respect potential privacy issues, we will not make our data set publicly available on the In-

EC2		Azure	
text/html	95.9	text/html	97.8
text/plain	2.1	text/plain	1.0
application/json	1.0	application/xml	0.7
application/xml	0.3	application/json	0.2
text/xml	0.3	application/xhtml+xml	0.1
other	0.4	other	0.2

Table 5: Top 5 content-types in EC2 and Azure and the percentage of webpages of each content-type in all collected webpages.

	EC2	Azure
Responsive IPs	1,359,888	154,753
Unique simhashes	1,767,072	210,418
Top-level clusters	236,227	30,581
2nd-level clusters	256,335	39,183
Final clusters	243,164	31,728

Table 6: The number of responsive IPs and unique simhashes of their content, as well as the number of clusters output by the different steps of the clustering.

ternet. Interested researchers should contact the authors if they desire access to the data set, and we will evaluate the privacy issues of each request and use appropriate privacy safeguards (e.g., use anonymization tools [35]). The code and other tools that WhoWas consists of will however be released publicly, and in future work we may investigate making a public interface to our data set that provides appropriate privacy protections (e.g., only providing aggregate statistics).

8. ANALYSES USING WHOWAS

In this section we report on various analyses performed using WhoWas with the data sets gathered as discussed in §6. We start by using WhoWas to study usage and its change over time in EC2 and Azure. Then we use WhoWas to shed light on malicious activity in clouds, and finally we use WhoWas to describe the distribution of software in the web ecosystem in clouds.

8.1 Cloud Usage Dynamics

IP responsiveness and availability. Table 7 summarizes the usage statistics across all measurement rounds. The average number of responsive IPs is almost an order of magnitude larger in EC2 than in Azure, which illustrates their difference in popularity. The average IP address space usage is almost identical on both services and relatively low (23.7–23.9%), so both have ample room for growth. EC2 has on average 758 K available IPs, 7.6 times more than Azure with 99 K, which indicates that EC2 hosts a higher proportion of services running on ports other than 80/tcp and 443/tcp, which are less likely to be web services.

Figure 8 shows the IP responsiveness and availability over the two month measurement period. The variation of responsive and available IP addresses in both services over the two months is low, with a 0.3–0.5% standard deviation. On absolute numbers, EC2 grew more over this period, adding 36,414 responsive IPs by the end of the period, compared to 8,270 for Azure. However, the relative growth of Azure is larger, with an increase in 7.3% of responsive and 7.7% of available IPs, compared to 3.3% and 4.9% for EC2. Figure 8 shows several noticeable dips in the curves. In EC2, these dips correspond to the dates Oct. 4, Nov. 8, Nov. 30, Dec. 14, and Dec. 28, all in 2013. Interestingly, they are all Fridays or Saturdays. By appropriate queries to the WhoWas database, we found that 3,198, 2,767, 1,449, 983, and 1,327 clusters become unavailable on EC2 on these dates, respectively, and never return again. In Azure, the dips happened on Nov. 29 and Dec. 07, 2013, also Friday and Saturday. On these two days, 360 and 385 clusters become unavailable and never return again. A total of 15,295 IPs in EC2 and 775 IPs in Azure are associated with these clusters. These dips may be caused by web service maintenance, webpage update, web service migration (to other providers or to new added networks that we did not probe), or other reasons. It is possible that the servers that left the cloud were intended for other purposes instead of web services. Unfortunately, we could not figure out the exact reason for these departures.

Cluster number and size. The average number of clusters for a round of probing in EC2 is 185,701 and in Azure 27,048. Over the measurement period, the number of clusters increased by 3.3% in EC2 and by 6.2% in Azure.

We define the average size of a cluster to be the average number of IPs in a cluster per round of measurement. The average cluster size distribution for EC2 is: 78.8% have average size of one IP address; 20.8% between 2 and 20; 0.28% between 21 and 50; and only 0.07% greater than 50. For Azure the distribution is quite similar, with a slightly larger number of small clusters: 86.2% (1), 13.6% (2–20), 0.1% (21–50), and 0.1% (> 50). The numbers show that the vast majority of clusters in both clouds use just a small number of IPs.

The amount of overlap across the two clouds we study is small. We find 980 clusters are using both EC2 and Azure, and 85% (834) of them use the same average number of IPs in each cloud. These latter clusters all use a small number of IPs on average (at most 5 IPs). We also observe 110 clusters that use more IPs in EC2 than they use in Azure, on average. One of these clusters, a VPN service (cluster 3 in Table 15), uses over 2,000 IPs more in EC2 than it uses in Azure. We did not see any cluster migrations between EC2 and Azure during our measurement period.

The clustering heuristics we use can only provide estimates, and so we may be under- or over-counting cluster size in some cases. Web services may also be making use of other providers not included in our study, which would lead us to underestimate their overall resource usage. Indeed some larger services may use other hosting solutions such as content delivery networks, which are not included in our study. Despite these potential sources of error, the data still supports the conclusion that the majority of the services hosted in clouds are small. We delve more deeply into some of the largest clusters at the end of this section.

IP status churn. A key feature of WhoWas is our ability to estimate churn, meaning the quantity of change in status of IP addresses. The overall churn rate, meaning the number of IPs that change status in terms of responsiveness, availability, or which cluster they are associated to divided by the total number of IPs, is 3.0% for each of EC2 and Azure. Investigating individual types of status change, we have that for EC2 the average change in responsiveness was 2.5%, the average change in availability was 1.0%, and an average of 0.1% of IPs changed clusters between measurement rounds.[4] The same values for Azure are 2.2%, 1.7%, and 0.3%. A time series of churn rates is shown in Figure 9.

If one instead looks at percentages relative to all unique IP addresses that are responsive on either round $T-1$ or T, then overall churn rate becomes 11.9% in EC2 and 12.2% in Azure on average. The responsiveness, availability, and cluster change rates become

[4]Note that they do not sum to 3.0% since unavailable IPs include unresponsive IPs, as well as responsive but unavailable IPs.

	EC2			Azure		
	# Responsive IPs	**# Available IPs**	**# Clusters**	**# Responsive IPs**	**# Available IPs**	**# Clusters**
Minimum	1,061,834 (22.6%)	718,693 (15.3%)	179,870	111,851 (22.6%)	94,348 (19.0%)	25,903
Maximum	1,145,448 (24.4%)	773,832 (16.5%)	188,274	120,605 (24.3%)	102,953 (20.8%)	27,786
Average	1,113,599 (23.7%)	758,144 (16.1%)	185,701	118,290 (23.9%)	99,720 (20.1%)	27,048
Std. dev.	18,733 (0.4%)	13,232 (0.3%)	1,939	2,169 (0.4%)	2,640 (0.5%)	605
Overall growth	36,414 (3.3%)	35,442 (4.9%)	5,984	8,270 (7.3%)	7,299 (7.7%)	1,604

Table 7: Summary of overall usage of EC2 and Azure address spaces. Percentages are the fraction of the total number of IP addresses probed.

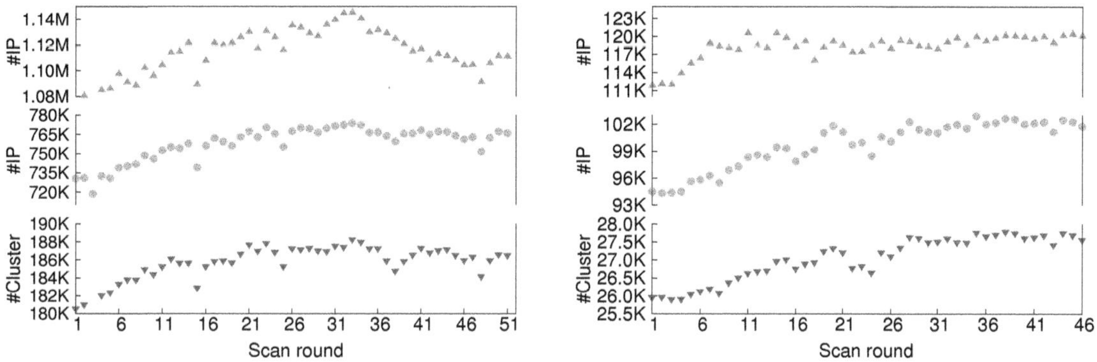

Figure 8: Change over time in responsive IPs, available IPs and clusters **(from top to bottom)** in **(left)** EC2 and **(right)** Azure. X-axis is the round of scanning and note that the Y-axes have gaps in the range covered.

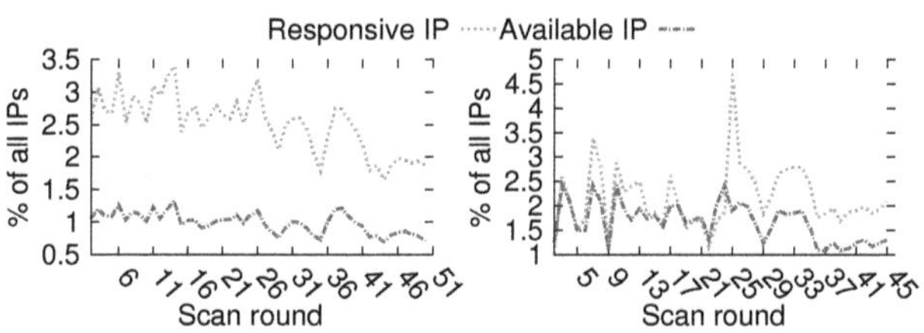

Figure 9: Change in status of responsive IPs and available IPs as a fraction of all IP addresses in **(left)** EC2 and **(right)** Azure.

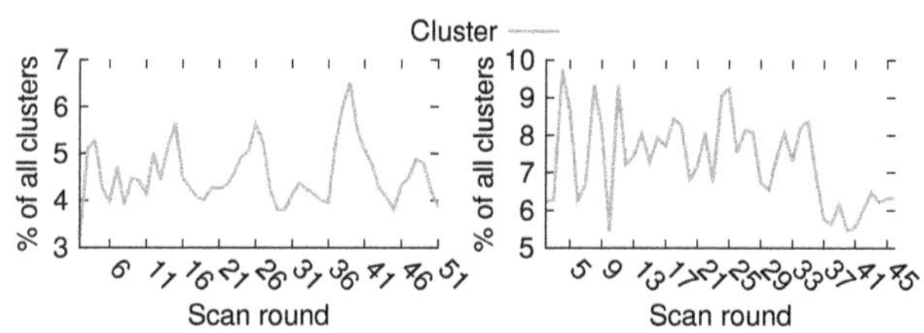

Figure 10: Change in availability of clusters as a percentage of the total number of clusters seen throughout the measurement period in **(left)** EC2 and **(right)** Azure.

10.1%, 4.0%, and 0.3% for EC2 and 8.7%, 6.8%, and 1.1% for Azure.

Even considering that these are just estimates (sources of error including incorrect clustering or transitory network failures), the per-round churn in these clouds appears quite small.

Cluster availability over time. A cluster is available in a given round if at least one of the IPs in the cluster is available in that round. Figure 10 plots for each round the fraction of clusters that changed from available to unavailable or vice versa, compared to the previous round, over the total number of unique clusters observed throughout the measurement period. On average across all rounds, the average percentage of cluster status changes is 4.6% on EC2 and 7.3% on Azure.

Cluster size over time. We now characterize the observed ways in which a cluster's size (the number of IPs associated to the cluster) changes over time. Table 11 shows the results of our analysis, in particular the top five size change patterns observed. Here a pattern of 0 means no change; 0,1,0 indicates an increasing trend; 0,-1,0 a decreasing trend; and so on. So about half of clusters are quite stable in terms of size. We now describe how we arrived at these patterns, and then discuss the results in further detail.

For each cluster, we first generate a vector D of the number of instances it used at each time point. So a vector of $(10, 3, 20)$ means that in time period one the cluster had 10 IPs associated to it, 3 in the next time period, etc. The dimension of the vector is the number of rounds of scanning. We reduce the dimensionality of the resulting vectors in order to more accurately compare and understand general usage patterns.

To do so we use piecewise aggregate approximation (PAA) [36], a method for reducing the dimensionality of time-series data. We divide the vector into frames and use the median value of a frame to represent the frame. Since the time interval of our data is not always constant, we could not simply use an equal number of data points in each frame. We use a 7-day window to generate frames. We use the 7-day time window because it can cover at least 3 data points and can catch more changes in IP usage. Each frame may contain different numbers of data points. For example, frame one may contain 3 data points from the first 7 days of scanning while frame two contains 4 data points from the next 7 days.

We therefore compute from D a new vector D' of dimension 13 for EC2 (since measurement lasts for 93 days) and 9 for Azure (62 days) whose values are the median of the values in each window. We use median so as to be robust in the face of outliers.

Using D', we then define a new vector D'', called the tendency vector, as shown in Algorithm 1. For example, and using smaller vector dimension for brevity, if $D' = (1, 2, 3, 1, 1, 1)$

pattern	description	# EC2 clusters	# Azure clusters
0		121,297 (49.9%)	17,092 (53.9%)
0,1,0		36,465 (15.0%)	4,406 (13.9%)
0,-1,0		33,400 (13.7%)	3,952 (12.5%)
0,1,0,-1,0		12,598 (5.2%)	1,189 (3.8%)
0,-1,1,0		9,857 (4.1%)	1,376 (4.3%)

Table 11: Top five size-change patterns observed in EC2 and Azure. Percentages in parentheses are with respect to total number of clusters.

Algorithm 1 Algorithm for computing tendency vector given D'

for $1 \le i \le |D'| - 1$ **do**
  if $D'[i+1] > D'[i]$ **then**
    set $D''[i] = 1$
  else if $D'[i+1] = D'[i]$ **then**
    set $D''[i] = 0$
  else
    set $D''[i] = -1$
  end if
end for

then $D'' = (1, 1, -1, 0, 0)$, or if $D' = (1, 10, 0, 5, 4, 2)$ then $D'' = (1, -1, 1, -1, -1)$. Finally we merge repeat values in D'', so for example, $(0, 1, 1, 0, -1, -1)$ becomes $(0, 1, 0, -1)$. The resulting merged tendency vector is the size-change pattern. Again the top five such patterns observed are given in Table 11.

As previously noted, about half the clusters in EC2 and Azure, respectively, follow pattern 0 (no change in cluster size). Clusters in pattern 0 can be further split into two groups:

(1) Ephemeral clusters: the median number of IPs they used is zero, because they just appeared in the cloud for a very short period of time. In EC2, 11.4% of all clusters are ephemeral while in Azure 13.1% are ephemeral. Of ephemeral clusters, 92.8% only use 1 IP, 99.1% use less than 3 IPs, and 24 clusters use more than 10 IPs. We arbitrarily chose 10 of these last 24 clusters for manual investigation, which revealed a few explanations that may generalize more broadly: (a) a website was under maintenance so it temporarily changed the top-level webpage; (b) a website just moved into the cloud and was under construction, and we caught the in-development webpage; or (c) the webpage was developed by tenants who may temporarily use the cloud for testing and left the cloud soon.

(2) Relatively stable clusters: The other 38.5% of clusters in EC2 (40.8% in Azure) instead use nearly the same number of IPs in each round over the entire measurement period. In this group, 38,466 (15.8%) clusters in EC2 and 7,789 (24.5%) in Azure haven't changed the number of IPs they used during measurement periods and are available in each scan round. Most of these clusters (92.7%) use the exact same IP addresses all the time.

Pattern 0,-1,1,0 represents clusters that have a drop in the instance usage, immediately followed by an increase. A short-term unavailability can cause such a drop. We define the lifetime of a cluster as the time period between the first time a cluster is available and the last time it was available. The cluster uptime is the fraction of time the cluster is available relative to its lifetime. For example, if a cluster was first observed on one day, and last observed 10 days later, and no IP associated with it responded on one of the days in between, then the lifetime is 10 days and the uptime is 90%. In EC2 54.3%'s of the singleton clusters have 100% uptime, 89.1% have $\geq$90% uptime, and 92.7% have $\geq$80%. Of clusters of

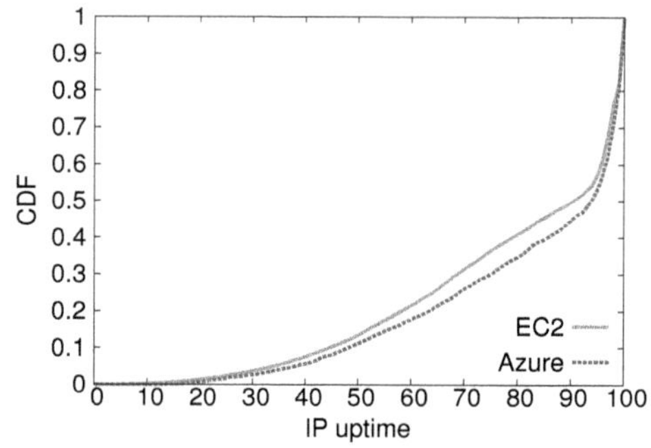

Figure 12: Distribution of average IP uptime of clusters of size two or larger.

size 2, 86.4% have a 100% uptime. The cluster uptime of all the clusters with size greater than or equal to 18 is 100%. Clusters in Azure show a similar pattern — in general, the more IPs a cluster uses, the higher cluster uptime it has. The cluster IP time of only a small fraction of clusters are less than 90% (9.4% of clusters in EC2 and 10.6% in Azure).

Churn within clusters. We turn now to measuring the amount of turnover in IPs used by a given cluster. Website deployments may be designed to have relatively high turnover, taking advantage of cloud elasticity to scale with demand. For example, EC2 includes an auto-scaling feature, and several third party companies advertise similar services. Alternatively, churn may be indicative of instability in deployments such as VM instance restarts caused by crashes or other failures. Our measurements cannot distinguish between such causes of churn, but can give an overall estimate of the amount of churn.

We define the uptime of an IP for a given cluster as the fraction of days the IP is available and associated to the cluster divided by the total amount of time the cluster is available. The average IP uptime of a cluster is the average of IP uptimes for all IPs associated to the cluster. Average IP uptime therefore provides a measure of how much a cluster experiences churn within the IPs that it uses. If a cluster uses the same IP addresses all the time, then the average IP uptime of this cluster will be 100%. Low average IP uptime indicates the cluster frequently changes IPs.

A total of 183,119 (75.3%) clusters in EC2 and 25,037 (78.9%) in Azure have a 100% average IP uptime. The bulk of these are singleton clusters, meaning clusters of size one. In EC2, 71.4% of all clusters are singletons, and in Azure 76.2% are singletons. For non-singleton clusters, we find more evidence of churn. Figure 12 gives a CDF of the average IP uptimes across all clusters of size two or larger. We see that about half of the clusters have average IP uptime greater than 90%, in either cloud. A large fraction in fact (27.2% and 30.1% of clusters in EC2 and Azure, respectively) have average IP uptime between 95% and 99%, indicative of low churn. For the other half of clusters having below 90% average IP uptime, we see quite a spread of uptimes.

When the cluster size increases, the average IP uptime becomes smaller. For clusters with cluster size 50 or greater, the average IP uptime is 62%. For the top 10 websites by cluster size, about 90% of the IPs being used in one measurement round, are still used in the next round, but less than 50% of the IPs have been used for the entire 3 months.

Region and VPC usage. Prior work [2] showed that the vast majority of websites use a single region. Our measurements are inline with this: 97.0% of all clusters use a single region. Even among

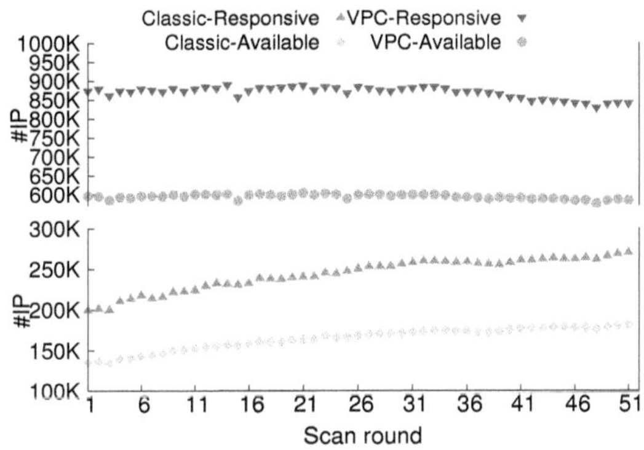

Figure 13: Change over time in responsive IPs, available IPs and clusters in EC2 VPC and classic instances. X-axis is the round of scanning. Note that Y-axes are different in each chart.

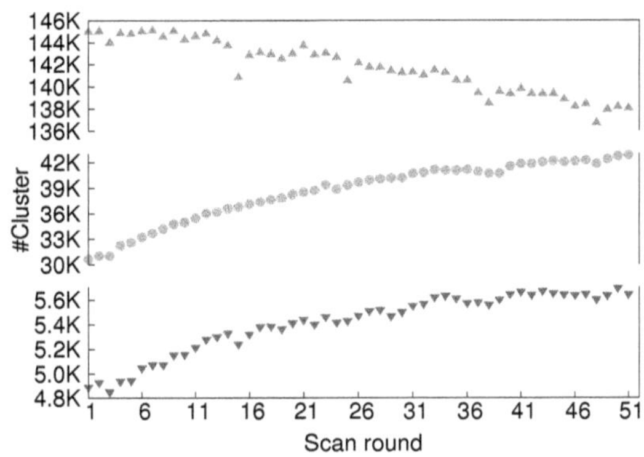

Figure 14: Change over time in classic-only, VPC-only, and mixed clusters **(from top to bottom)** in EC2.

the top 5% of all clusters (in terms of cluster size), only 21.5% use more than a single region. While most of the clusters use the same region(s) over time, a small number of them have a change in region usage. 98.37% of clusters use the same region(s), 0.7% use 1 extra region, 0.07% use 2 extra regions, 0.76% decrease by 1, and 0.07% decrease by 2 in EC2. In Azure, 97.33% use the same region(s), 1.28% use 1 extra region, 1.13% decreased by 1 and 0.09% decreased by 2.

For EC2, we can use the cartographic mechanisms described in §5 to examine the usage of VPC versus classic networking. This is particularly interesting as it shows the uptake of a newer feature, and one that is required for new accounts. Figure 13 shows a timeline of the number of responsive and available IPs as broken down by VPC/classic. We found in total 177,246 (72.9% of all clusters) use only classic IPs; 59,547 (24.5%) use only VPC IPs; and 6,371 (2.6%) use both classic and VPC IPs. As shown in Figure 14, the number of classic-only clusters is decreasing rapidly while VPC-only and mixed clusters are increasing. We also observed a total of 1,024 mixed clusters that transitioned from classic to VPC while 483 went in the other direction.

Large clusters. We found a number of very large clusters within the collected data. Table 15 gives details regarding the top ten clusters in EC2, by average cluster size (the clusters in Azure have relatively smaller sizes compared with those in EC2, so we did not examine them in detail). We manually investigated these ten clusters, and provide a categorization of the type of industry they are associated to. These clusters show a diversity of usage dynamics.

In the table, the total number of unique IPs associated to the cluster across the entire measurement period is "Total #IP", while "Mean/Median/Min/Max #IP" indicate the basic statistics of number of IPs used by a cluster across all rounds. The average IP uptime of these clusters varies greatly, and is generally lower than the uptime of smaller clusters. As noted previously, most IPs are stable for short periods of time, meaning if they are used by the cluster in one round of measurement they are likely to be used in the next. The column "Max IP departure" gives the maximum, across all rounds, of IPs leaving a cluster as a fraction of the number of IPs used by the cluster in that round. An IP leaves a cluster in a given round if it was not associated with the cluster in that round, but was in the previous round. The column "Stable IP" gives the ratio of the number of IPs that were used throughout the entire measurement period by the cluster over the total number of unique IPs used by the cluster. As can be seen, long-run stability is low except for cluster 9. Finally, we give the number of regions used and the average number of VPC IPs per round for each cluster.

8.2 Finding and Analyzing Malicious Activity

We turn to using WhoWas to investigate malicious activity on IaaS clouds. We use two sources for flagging malicious behavior, Google Safe Browsing and VirusTotal. We will show that WhoWas can help investigate, as well as discover new, malicious activity. We will also quantify the time between a website appearing and it being marked as malicious and the time an IP address remains malicious after being dropped from a blacklist.

Google Safe Browsing. The Google Safe Browsing API allows one to submit a URL and obtain a status report indicating a status of either "phishing", "malware" (hosting malicious software), or "ok". To make use of the API, we extracted all the URLs contained in top-level webpages gathered by WhoWas and queried each against the safe browsing API after each round of scanning. In each round, there were about 3.2 M distinct URLs across the entire set of pages fetched, only a small fraction of which end up marked as malicious by Safe Browsing.

For EC2, we found 196 unique IPs (149 in classic and 47 in VPC) that contain at least one link labeled as phishing or malware, for a total of 1,393 distinct malicious URLs. Many of the webpages contain multiple malicious URLs: nine had a total of 63 URLs marked as phishing and 187 of them had a total of 1,330 URLs marked as malware. These 196 IPs are associated to 51 distinct clusters. A total of 19 IPs hosting malicious links were associated to different clusters (over time), but upon manual inspection of the webpages it was clear that the different clusters were in fact just revisions of the same, significant enough to push them into a distinct cluster. All but 18 of the IPs that the malicious URLs resolved to are outside EC2. Interestingly, one IP address removed the malicious URL around 3 days after being detected, changed the webpage to include a different malicious URL, and then changed it later to again include the first malicious URL. The webpage on this IP in fact appears to be legitimate (upon manual inspection), so it could be that the hosting server is compromised.

For Azure, we found 14 malicious URLs hosted on 13 distinct IPs that are associated to 11 clusters. All of these URLs are malware URLs. The malicious URLs were resolved to 19 IPs, and 7 of these IPs are in Azure. We did not find any malicious URLs that were linked to by webpages in both clouds.

Below we say that an IP is malicious if it hosts a webpage including a malicious URL. We define the lifetime of a malicious IP as the number of days that an IP address has a malicious URL within its

Cluster	Total #IP	Mean #IP	Median #IP	Min #IP	Max #IP	Avg IP uptime (%)	Max IP departure (%)	Stable IP (%)	Regions used	Mean #VPC IP	Category
1	51,211	33,145	33,513	30,624	34,509	73.8	6.6	49.9	2	1	PaaS
2	15,283	5,597	5,601	5,435	5,785	49.1	8.1	22.2	8	1,344	Cloud hosting
3	3,869	2,029	2,050	1,724	2,228	65.9	8.9	36.2	8	1,346	VPN
4	22,226	1,167	1,077	179	2,501	13.1	85.4	0.1	6	5	SaaS
5	8,488	617	403	57	1,836	14.1	81.3	0.1	1	0	Game
6	919	529	625	169	738	78.1	62.0	1.4	1	0	Shopping
7	1,928	370	320	141	622	26.2	86.3	1.6	1	0	PaaS
8	1,207	366	367	338	419	50.1	18.7	14.3	2	366	Video
9	303	281	285	269	291	94.5	6.3	89.1	1	0	Marketing
10	3,263	255	253	132	478	16.6	68.3	0.6	5	0	Cloud hosting

Table 15: Top 10 websites based on average number of IPs used per round, all in EC2.

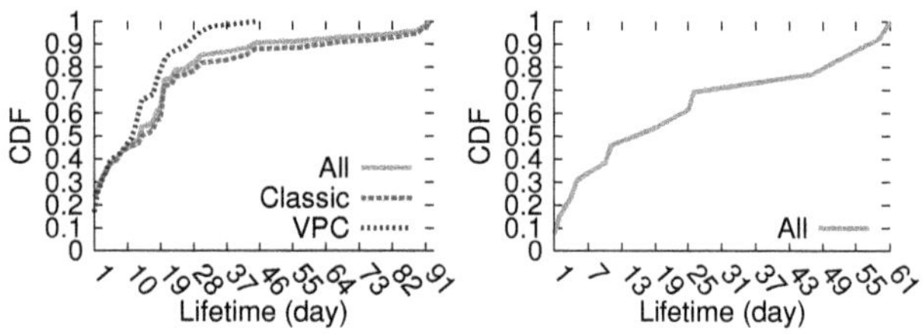

Figure 16: CDF of lifetimes of IPs hosting malicious content as indicated by Google Safe Browsing in **(left)** EC2 and **(right)** Azure.

HTML. We find the lifetime of malicious IPs to be relatively long; see Figure 16. In EC2, 62% of malicious IPs host malicious URLs for more than 7 days, and 46% host malicious URLs for over 14 days. The lifetime of malicious IPs in EC2-VPC is slightly shorter than in EC2-Classic. The longest availability of a malicious IP was 45 days in VPC and 93 days (the complete measurements period) for classic. In Azure, about 70% of malicious IPs host malicious URLs for more than 7 days, and 50% for at least 14 days.

We also find some IPs appear to serve as a "linchpin" for maliciousness. A linchpin IP hosts a webpage that aggregates many malicious URLs [37]. For example, we found at one point a particular IP address on EC2 contained 128 malware URLs (associated with different domains); all of these URLs linked to webpages that contained the Blackhole Exploit kit [38]. In our dataset, we identify five linchpin IPs that all host the same webpage. The malicious URLs in these webpages point to 23 different domains. The average lifetime of the IPs that host these malicious URLs is 20 days.

VirusTotal. VirusTotal aggregates information from multiple engines that detect malicious activity (e.g., AV products and blacklists). One service VirusTotal provides is to query an IP address to obtain a JSON report of malicious activity associated with the IP. Each report contains passive DNS information for the IP, and for each engine that detected malicious activity on that IP, the time and type of the malicious activity, e.g, malicious URLs and MD5 hashes of malware hosted on the IP. During Feb. 2014, we used this service to collect reports on all the IPs in EC2 and Azure.

VirusTotal aggregates information from the multiple engines without validating their detections, thus it is possible that an engine may (incorrectly) consider an IP address as malicious, when other engines do not. To reduce false positives, we only consider an IP address malicious when it is reported as malicious by two or more engines. Even with this constraint there could still be some false positives, which will be inherited by the following analysis.

After applying the above constraint, we find that from Sep. 30, 2013 to Dec. 31, 2013, there were 2,070 malicious IPs in EC2, hosting 13,752 malicious URLs. The malicious IPs represent 0.3% of the average available IPs in EC2. In contrast, no malicious IPs were found in Azure. Table 17 breaks down the malicious EC2 IPs by region and month, showing an overall increase of malicious activity over time.

Region	# Malicious IP Oct	Nov	Dec	Total
USEast	544	847	728	1,422
EU	60	106	107	200
USWest_Oregon	50	94	110	192
USWest_NC	18	56	44	91
SouthAmerica	8	28	32	57
AsiaSingapore	13	26	22	51
AsiaTokyo	7	19	23	35
AsiaSydney	5	14	6	22

Table 17: Number of IPs in each EC2 region labeled as malicious by two or more engines in VirusTotal.

Domain	# URLs
dl.dropboxusercontent.com	993
dl.dropbox.com	936
download-instantly.com	295
tr.im	268
www.wishdownload.com	223
dlp.playmediaplayer.com	206
www.extrimdownloadmanager.com	128
dlp.123mediaplayer.com	122
install.fusioninstall.com	120
www.1disk.cn	119

Table 18: Top 10 domains associated with malicious IPs in EC2 by VirusTotal.

We extract 2,888 unique domains from the 13,752 malicious URLs. Of these, 222 (7.7%) contain the substring "download" in their domain names. Table 18 shows the top 10 domains by number of URLs that include the domain. The results show that Dropbox (which runs on EC2) and other file hosting providers have become a popular platform for distributing malware. The VirusTotal reports show that 371 IPs belonging to Dropbox have been used to distribute malicious content (the domains of these IPs all resolved to "dl.dropboxusercontent.com" or "dl.dropbox.com".) These 371 IPs hosted 1,929 malicious URLs and 2,421 pieces of malware. Tr.im provides a URL-shortening service [39] that attackers sometimes use to hide malicious URLs. We observe some engines only detecting the shortened URL, so the malicious page remains accessible via the malicious long URL. The remaining URLs in the top 10 correspond to sites distributing adware and other potentially unwanted software.

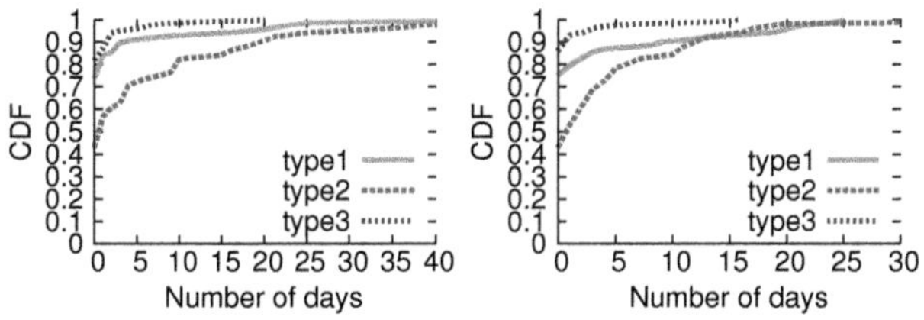

Figure 19: CDFs of the number of days an IP address hosts the same webpage **(left)** before first being labeled as malicious by VirusTotal and **(right)** after last being detected as malicious by VirusTotal.

WhoWas. We use WhoWas to analyze the content hosted over time by the malicious EC2 IPs obtained from VirusTotal. Only 98 of the malicious EC2 IP addresses appear in one of the final clusters in our analysis. The others return default webpages or errors. These 98 IPs are associated to 166 different clusters: 63 IPs are associated to only one cluster, 21 to two clusters, and five to three clusters. Two of the IPs are associated to 19 clusters. Among these 98 IPs, we observe three types of malicious behaviors over time. The first type corresponds to 34 IPs that host the same malicious webpage without any changes over time. The second type are 42 IPs where the same malicious webpage repeatedly appears and disappears. Once detected, the malicious webpage is temporarily removed from the IP, but returns several days later. The third type corresponds to 22 IPs that host multiple malicious webpages.

Next, we examine the lag time of the blacklists, defined to be the time a blacklist takes to detect a malicious website after it goes up. The engines in VirusTotal may scan an IP multiple times, generating multiple records, which may be associated with different malicious webpages. For our purposes, there are two import time points for any given webpage: (1) the first detection time, which is the first time an engine labels a webpage on an IP as malicious, and (2) the last detection time, which is the last time the malicious webpage on that IP was reported as being malicious by an engine. The last detection time also indicates when the engines believe the webpage has become benign.

Using WhoWas, we compare the lifetime of a cluster associated with a malicious IP address to those two time points. Figure 19 shows CDFs of the time between a webpage becoming available and being marked as malicious by the blacklist (left graph), and the time after being removed from blacklists that a malicious webpage remains active (right graph). Overall, about 90% of type 1 and type 3 webpages, and 50% of type 2 are detected within three days. Most of the type 1 and type 3 webpages are removed after the last detection. But in type 2, only about 40% of webpages are actually removed. There are some webpages that have a very long lifetime. For example, a particular type 1 IP hosted malware for at least 82 days (at the time of writing it is still available, in fact). Anecdotally, we also found that it frequently changes its domain name, presumably to avoid detection.

We can also use the clustering mechanism of WhoWas to find new malicious IP addresses, by labeling as malicious IP addresses in a cluster with a VirusTotal-labeled malicious IP address. In this way, we label an additional 191 IPs. As a breakdown, 15 VirusTotal-labeled IPs each had one additional IP; 10 IPs had 2 additional IPs, 6 had 3, and 16 had 4–13. We manually inspected the WhoWas records for these additional IPs, verifying the correctness of the approach in every case. All this shows that WhoWas can help find malicious activity.

8.3 Characterizing the Web Software Ecosystem on Clouds

As a final case study to exercise WhoWas, we study the software ecosystem of web services running the cloud. This includes the a census covering the kinds of web servers, back-end software languages, website templates, and third party-trackers running on top of EC2 and Azure.

In the rest of this section all the percentages reported are averages taken over all rounds of measurement; we omit repeatedly referring to them as averages for brevity.

Web servers and backend techniques. For EC2, we identified the server software running on 89.9% (682 K on average) of the available IPs. Apache (55.2%), nginx (21.2%), and Microsoft-IIS (12.2%) are the most popular web servers, accounting for over 88.6% of the identified servers. MochiWeb is also used (30,372 servers on average, 4.4%), but the servers running it are only associated with 47 clusters in total. Its use is almost entirely accounted for by a single PaaS provider. We further identify the backend techniques that support about 32% (215 K on average) of servers. Of these servers, 52.6% are using PHP, followed by ASP.NET (29.0%) and Phusion Passenger (8.1%). For the server usage and backend techniques, we did not see any significant difference between VPC and classic.

In Azure, we find, perhaps unsurprisingly, that the software ecosystem displays less diversity. Microsoft-IIS runs on 89% (about 86 K on average) of the identified servers in Azure. Only about 7.6 K IPs are running Apache and 1.7 K are running nginx, accounting for a total of 9.7% of identified servers. For back-ends in Azure, we found that 94.2% are using ASP.net, followed by PHP (4.3%) and Express (0.6%).

Examining the versions of commonly used servers, we find new versions of servers are not being adopted quickly. Of the Apache servers in EC2, 24.6% are using Apache/2.2.22, followed by Apache-Coyote/1.1 (15.0%) and Apache/2.2.25 (7.6%). More than 40% of identified Apache servers are using Apache/2.2.*. A few IPs (208 in total) in EC2 use Apache 1.3.*. The most recent version of Apache used in EC2 is Apache 2.4.7, and this is used by 147 IPs in the last round of measurement (the highest measured). Surprisingly, some of the websites that employ a large number of IPs are still using Apache/2.2.22.

In Azure, the top three IIS releases being used are 8.0 (39.0%), 7.5 (23.7%), and 7.0 (19.8%). Only 3.4% are using IIS 8.5.

The Security Engineering Research Term (SERT) reported the ten most vulnerable server versions as determined by a large-scale scan [40]. We find seven of the ten vulnerable servers are also being used in both clouds. For example, in EC2 in total across all rounds of measurement 2,641 IPs are running Microsoft-IIS/6.0, and 56 IPs are running ''Apache/2.2.24 (Unix) mod_ssl/2.2.24 OpenSSL/1.0.0-fips mod_auth_passthrough/2.1 mod_bwlimited/1.4 FrontPage/5.0.2.2635''. Most servers also use old releases of PHP. Of the servers that are using PHP in EC2, 60% are using PHP 5.3.*. PHP 5.3.10 (24.5%), 5.3.27 (16.22%) and 5.3.3 (9.7%) are the 3 top used PHP releases. The most recent version of PHP used in EC2 is PHP 5.4.23, used by 845 servers in the last round of measurement.

Website templates. We identify the template of webpages on an average of about 26 K IPs (3% of available IPs) running on EC2. The top 3 templates being used are: WordPress (71.1%), Joomla! (9.7%) and Drupal (4.1%). In Azure, we only find templates for an average of about 950 webpages. WordPress (55%) and Joomla! (12%) are still the most popular templates in this smaller set.

WordPress versions below 3.6 contain a series of known cross-site scripting (XSS) vulnerabilities [41]. More than 68% of the sites using WordPress are running vulnerable versions of WordPress. Checking the distribution of WordPress major versions we observed from Sep. 30, 2013 to Dec. 31, 2013, WordPress 3.5.* (6.5 K on average) and 3.6.* (5 K on average) are used by most of the identified WordPress-using webpages. We saw that one month after WordPress 3.7.* (released on Oct. 14, 2013) and 3.8.* (released on Dec. 12, 2013) were released, around 3,500 webpages and 2,500 webpages on average are using the new WordPress version, respectively, but 3.5.* and 3.6.* are still the most popular WordPress releases.

Third-party trackers. Many third party trackers work by having site owners embed a specific piece of JavaScript, called tracking code, into their webpage. We can determine if a website uses a given tracker by searching for the tracker's corresponding tracking code in the page's HTML contents. This method will miss trackers loaded dynamically or in the case that the code is modified by the site operator. Tracking code always contains a special URL which can serve as a fingerprint. Using MySQL regular expressions to search these fingerprints in the WhoWas database provides a lower bound on the number of websites using a given tracker. As a concrete example, for the tracker associated with scorecardresearch.com, we construct a query string

‘‘<script.*http:\\/\\/b\\.scorecardresearch \\.com.*\\//script>’’

which means search for ‘‘http://b.scorecardresearch.com’’ in the JavaScript section of a page. The URL is the link to the tracker's service extracted from its tracking code.

We search for use of the trackers previously identified by Mayer et al. [42]. Table 20 shows the Top 10 trackers used by websites in EC2 and Azure on Dec. 31, 2013 (the last round of our measurements). In both clouds, Google-Analytics, Facebook and Twitter sharing widgets, and doubleclick are the most widely used third-party trackers.

The Google Analytics service is the most popular tracker being used in EC2-hosted and Azure-hosted websites. In EC2, we can see on average 55 K clusters use this service. Using the service requires a user to apply for a Google Analytics ID and put that ID in her tracking code. We extract a total of 71,363 unique IDs from the webpages over 275,513 unique IPs in EC2. These IDs belong to 106,871 top-level clusters and 111,696 webpage clusters. In Azure, we collect 6,254 IDs from 11,840 IPs. We also find 166 IDs appeared in both clouds. According to Google [43], a Google Analytics ID can be split into two parts: user account and profile identifier. For example, in an ID "UA-0000-*", the "0000" is an ID for the user. The user might use "UA-0000-01", "UA-0000-02", and so on with different websites or applications. By checking IDs we can quickly estimate a lower bound on the number of unique websites in the two clouds, as well as the number of websites that belong to the same user. In EC2, the collected IDs belonging to 64,716 user accounts. Of these accounts, 93.5% use only one profile, 4.8% have two profiles, 1.6% have 3–11 profiles, and the rest (0.1%) use 14–35 profiles. In Azure, the IDs belong to 5,794 user accounts, 94.4% have one profile and 3.9% have two. An account in Azure is at most associated with 13 profiles.

Websites may use multiple trackers. We observed 77% of tracker-using webpages only use a single tracker, 16% use two trackers and 6% use three trackers in EC2. In Azure, 81% of tracker-using webpages use a single tracker, 15% use two trackers and 3.8% use three trackers.

EC2			Azure		
Tracker	**#IP**	**#Clust.**	**Tracker**	**#IP**	**#Clust.**
google-analytics	127,604	55,406	google-analytics	6,839	5,148
facebook	24,130	13,462	facebook	1,615	1,253
twitter	14,706	8,520	twitter	1,115	696
doubleclick	5,342	2,189	doubleclick	316	178
quantserve	2,243	742	atdmt	50	31
scorecardresearch	1,509	475	scorecardresearch	40	29
imrworldwide	474	95	quantserve	35	25
serving-sys	383	136	serving-sys	11	7
atdmt	275	69	adnxs	10	6
yieldmanager	188	54	imrworldwide	7	4
Total	176,852	81,147	Total	10,037	7,376

Table 20: Top 10 third party trackers in EC2 and Azure (on Dec. 31, 2013)

9. CONCLUSION

A growing number of web services are being hosted on public IaaS clouds such as EC2 and Azure. These cloud providers offer a variety of features, such as elastic scale in/out and pay-as-you-go payment models. Understanding how different tenants exercise these features can inform a variety of work on workload modeling, data center compute/network provisioning and placement, as well as on securing tenants' deployments. Unfortunately, however, very little is known about prevalent usage patterns and their evolution over time.

To shed light on this, we designed a measurement platform called WhoWas. Using carefully designed active probes, WhoWas enables direct measurements of what web services are running on cloud-associated IP addresses. This data can be used to perform lookups on particular IP addresses or web services, and retrieve a history of their activities over the period of measurement.

This paper presented the design of WhoWas and reported on using WhoWas to perform a first-of-its-kind measurement studies of usage patterns over time in EC2 and Azure, efficacy of blacklists for malicious activities in clouds, and adoption of new Web software by cloud customers.

Future work may include expanding WhoWas to analyze non-web services, evaluate improved clustering heuristics and provide more rigorous estimates of clustering error, provide deeper crawling of websites by following links in HTML, and correlate WhoWas data with other sources such as passive or active DNS interrogation. To facilitate such work, we have made the software underlying WhoWas public and open source [3].

Acknowledgements

The authors would like to especially thank the system administrators at the University of Wisconsin who helped ensure the experiments went smoothly. This work was supported in part by the National Science Foundation under grants CNS-1253870 and CNS-1330308. This research is also partially supported by the Spanish Government through Grant TIN2012-39391-C04-01 and a Juan de la Cierva Fellowship for Juan Caballero. Any opinions, findings, and conclusions or recommendations expressed in this material are those of the authors and do not necessarily reflect the views of the sponsors.

10. REFERENCES

[1] Alexa. Alexa. `http://alexa.com/`, 2014.

[2] Keqiang He, Alexis Fisher, Liang Wang, Aaron Gember, Aditya Akella, and Thomas Ristenpart. Next stop, the cloud: understanding

modern web service deployment in EC2 and Azure. In *IMC 2013*, pages 177–190. ACM, 2013.

[3] Whowas project. `http://www.cloudwhowas.org/`.

[4] Amazon. Amazon EC2 instance IP addressing. `http://docs.aws.amazon.com/AWSEC2/latest/UserGuide/using-instance-addressing.html#MultipleIP`, 2013.

[5] Farsight Security. Passive DNS data. `https://www.dnsdb.info/`, 2014.

[6] Wayback machine. `http://archive.org/web/`.

[7] Douglas E. Comer and John C. Lin. Probing TCP implementations. In *USENIX Summer Technical Conference*, Boston, MA, June 1994.

[8] Niels Provos and Peter Honeyman. Scanssh - scanning the internet for ssh servers. Technical Report CITI TR 01-13, University of Michigan, October 2001.

[9] Darcy Benoit and André Trudel. World's first web census. *International Journal of Web Information System*, 3, 2007.

[10] David Dagon, Chris Lee, Wenke Lee, and Niels Provos. Corrupted Dns resolution paths: The rise of a malicious resolution authority. In *Network and Distributed System Security Symposium*, 2008.

[11] Nadia Heninger, Zagir Durumeric, Eric Wustrow, and J.Alex Halderman. Mining your ps and qs: Detection of widespread weak keys in network devices. In *USENIX Security Symposium*, 2012.

[12] Antonio Nappa, Zhaoyan Xu, M. Zubair Rafique, Juan Caballero, and Guofei Gu. Cyberprobe: Towards internet-scale active detection of malicious servers. In *Network and Distributed System Security Symposium*, 2014.

[13] Zhaoyan Xu, Antonio Nappa, Robert Baykov, Guangliang Yang, Juan Caballero, and Guofei Gu. AutoProbe: Towards Automatic Active Malicious Server Probing Using Dynamic Binary Analysis. In *Proceedings of the 21st ACM Conference on Computer and Communication Security*, Scottsdale, AZ, November 2014.

[14] Zhaoyan Xu, Lingfen Chen, Guofei Gu, and Christopher Kruegel. Peerpress: Utilizing enemies' p2p strength against them. In *ACM Conference on Computer and Communications Security*, 2012.

[15] Stuart Staniford, Vern Paxson, and Nicholas Weaver. How to 0wn the internet in your spare time. In *USENIX Security Symposium*, San Francisco, CA, August 2002.

[16] Luigi Rizzo. Netmap: A novel framework for fast packet i/o. In *usenixatc*, 2012.

[17] Zakir Durumeric, Eric Wustrow, and J. Alex Halderman. ZMap: Fast Internet-wide scanning and its security applications. In *Proceedings of the 22nd USENIX Security Symposium*, August 2013.

[18] D. Leonard and D. Loguinov. Demystifying service discovery: Implementing an internet-wide scanner. In *Internet Measurement Conference*. ACM, 2010.

[19] M. Allman, V. Paxson, and J. Terrell. A brief history of scanning. In *Internet Measurement Conference*. ACM, 2007.

[20] Marco Balduzzi, Jonas Zaddach, Davide Balzarotti, Engin Kirda, and Sergio Loureiro. A security analysis of amazon's elastic compute cloud service. In *Proceedings of the 27th Annual ACM Symposium on Applied Computing*, pages 1427–1434. ACM, 2012.

[21] Davide Canali, Davide Balzarotti, and Aurelien Francillon. The Role of Web Hosting Providers in Detecting Compromised Websites. In *Proceedings of the 22nd World Wide Web Conference*, 2013.

[22] Antonio Nappa, M. Zubair Rafique, and Juan Caballero. Driving in the cloud: An analysis of drive-by download operations and abuse reporting. In *SIG SIDAR Conference on Detection of Intrusions and Malware & Vulnerability Assessment*, 2013.

[23] Amazon. Amazon EC2 public IP ranges. `https://forums.aws.amazon.com/ann.jspa?annID=1701`, 2013.

[24] Microsoft. Azure datacenter IP ranges. `http://msdn.microsoft.com/en-us/library/azure/dn175718.aspx`, 2013.

[25] Kenneth Reitz. Requests: Http for humans. `http://docs.python-requests.org/en/latest/`, 2014.

[26] Moses S Charikar. Similarity estimation techniques from rounding algorithms. In *Proceedings of the thiry-fourth annual ACM symposium on Theory of computing*, pages 380–388. ACM, 2002.

[27] Monika Henzinger. Finding near-duplicate web pages: a large-scale evaluation of algorithms. In *Proceedings of the 29th annual international ACM SIGIR conference on Research and development in information retrieval*, pages 284–291. ACM, 2006.

[28] Mat Kelcey. The simhash algorithm. `http://matpalm.com/resemblance/simhash/`, 2013.

[29] Robert Tibshirani, Guenther Walther, and Trevor Hastie. Estimating the number of clusters in a data set via the gap statistic. *Journal of the Royal Statistical Society: Series B (Statistical Methodology)*, 63(2):411–423, 2001.

[30] Gurmeet Singh Manku, Arvind Jain, and Anish Das Sarma. Detecting near-duplicates for web crawling. In *WWW 2007*, pages 141–150. ACM, 2007.

[31] Thomas Ristenpart, Eran Tromer, Hovav Shacham, and Stefan Savage. Hey, you, get off of my cloud: exploring information leakage in third-party compute clouds. In *CCS 2009*, pages 199–212. ACM, 2009.

[32] Amazon. Public IP addresses and external DNS hostnames. `http://docs.aws.amazon.com/AWSEC2/latest/UserGuide/using-instance-addressing.html`, 2014.

[33] Huan Liu. Amazon data center size. `http://huanliu.wordpress.com/2012/03/13/amazon-data-center-size/`, 2012.

[34] Robot exclusion. `http://www.robotstxt.org/faq/prevent.html`.

[35] Anonymization tools taxonomy. `http://www.caida.org/tools/taxonomy/anonymization.xml`.

[36] Eamonn Keogh, Kaushik Chakrabarti, Michael Pazzani, and Sharad Mehrotra. Dimensionality reduction for fast similarity search in large time series databases. *Knowledge and information Systems*, 3(3):263–286, 2001.

[37] Zhou Li, Sumayah Alrwais, Yinglian Xie, Fang Yu, and XiaoFeng Wang. Finding the linchpins of the dark web: a study on topologically dedicated hosts on malicious web infrastructures. In *S&P 2013*, pages 112–126. IEEE, 2013.

[38] Fraser Howard. Blackhole exploit kit analysis. `http://nakedsecurity.sophos.com/exploring-the-blackhole-exploit-kit/`, 2012.

[39] tr.im. tr.im. `http://tr.im`, 2013.

[40] SERT. Sert quarterly threat intelligence report q4 2013. Technical report, Solutionary Security Engineering Research Team, 2013.

[41] CVE. Cve-2013-4338. `http://web.nvd.nist.gov/view/vuln/detail?vulnId=CVE-2013-4338`, 2013.

[42] Jonathan R Mayer and John C Mitchell. Third-party web tracking: Policy and technology. In *Security and Privacy (SP), 2012 IEEE Symposium on*, pages 413–427. IEEE, 2012.

[43] Google. Accounts and views. `https://developers.google.com/analytics/resources/concepts/gaConceptsAccounts`, 2013.

Towards Network-level Efficiency for Cloud Storage Services

Zhenhua Li
Tsinghua University
Peking University
lizhenhua1983@tsinghua.edu.cn

Cheng Jin
University of Minnesota
Twin Cities
cheng@cs.umn.edu

Tianyin Xu
University of California
San Diego
tixu@cs.ucsd.edu

Christo Wilson
Northeastern University
Boston, MA, US
cbw@ccs.neu.edu

Yao Liu
State University of New York
Binghamton University
yaoliu@cs.binghamton.edu

Linsong Cheng
Tsinghua University
Beijing, China
chengls10@mails.tsinghua.edu.cn

Yunhao Liu
Tsinghua University
Beijing, China
yunhao@tsinghua.edu.cn

Yafei Dai
Peking University
Beijing, China
dyf@pku.edu.cn

Zhi-Li Zhang
University of Minnesota
Twin Cities
zhzhang@cs.umn.edu

ABSTRACT

Cloud storage services such as Dropbox, Google Drive, and Microsoft OneDrive provide users with a convenient and reliable way to store and share data from anywhere, on any device, and at any time. The cornerstone of these services is the *data synchronization* (sync) operation which *automatically* maps the changes in users' local filesystems to the cloud via a series of network communications in a *timely* manner. If not designed properly, however, the tremendous amount of data sync traffic can potentially cause (financial) pains to both service providers and users.

This paper addresses a simple yet critical question: *Is the current data sync traffic of cloud storage services efficiently used?* We first define a novel metric named ***TUE*** to quantify the ***T**raffic **U**sage **E**fficiency* of data synchronization. Based on both real-world traces and comprehensive experiments, we study and characterize the *TUE* of six widely used cloud storage services. Our results demonstrate that a considerable portion of the data sync traffic is in a sense wasteful, and can be effectively avoided or significantly reduced via carefully designed data sync mechanisms. All in all, our study of *TUE* of cloud storage services not only provides guidance for service providers to develop more efficient, traffic-economic services, but also helps users pick appropriate services that best fit their needs and budgets.

Categories and Subject Descriptors

C.2.4 [**Computer-communication Networks**]: Distributed Systems—*Distributed applications*; D.4.3 [**Operating Systems**]: File Systems Management—*Distributed file systems*

IMC'14, November 5–7, 2014, Vancouver, BC, Canada.

http://dx.doi.org/10.1145/2663716.2663747.

General Terms

Design, Experimentation, Measurement, Performance

Keywords

Cloud storage service; network-level efficiency; data synchronization; traffic usage efficiency

1. INTRODUCTION

Cloud storage services such as Dropbox, Google Drive, and Microsoft OneDrive (renamed from SkyDrive since Feb. 2014) provide users with a convenient and reliable way to store and share data from anywhere, on any device, and at any time. The users' data (*e.g.*, documents, photos, and music) stored in cloud storage are *automatically* synchronized across all the designated devices (*e.g.*, PCs, tablets, and smartphones) connected to the cloud in a *timely* manner. With multiplicity of devices – especially mobile devices – that users possess today, such "anywhere, anytime" features significantly simplify data management and consistency maintenance, and thus provide an ideal tool for data sharing and collaboration.

In a few short years, cloud storage services have reached phenomenal levels of success, with the user base growing rapidly. For example, Microsoft OneDrive claims that over 200 million customers have stored more than 14 PB of data using their service [9], while Dropbox has claimed more than 100 million users who store or update *1 billion* files every day [6]. Despite the late entry into this market (in Apr. 2012), Google Drive obtained 10 million users just in its first two months [7].

The key operation of cloud storage services is *data synchronization* (sync) which automatically maps the changes in users' local filesystems to the cloud via a series of network communications. Figure 1 demonstrates the general data sync principle. In a cloud storage service, the user usually needs to assign a designated local folder (called a "sync folder") in which every file operation is noticed and synchronized to the cloud by the client software developed by the service provider. Synchronizing a file involves a sequence of data sync events, such as transferring the data index, data content, sync notification, sync status/statistics, and sync acknowledgement. Naturally, each data sync event incurs network traffic. In this paper, this traffic is referred to as *data sync traffic*.

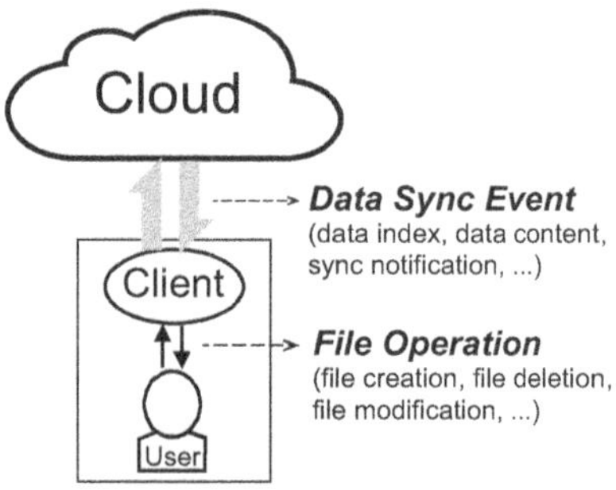

Figure 1: Data synchronization principle.

If not designed properly, the amount of data sync traffic can potentially cause (financial) pains to both providers and users of cloud storage services. From the providers' perspective, the aggregate sync traffic from all users is enormous (given the huge number of files uploaded and modified each day!). This imposes a heavy burden in terms of infrastructure support and monetary costs (*e.g.,* as payments to ISPs or cloud infrastructure providers). To get a quantitative understanding, we analyze a recent large-scale Dropbox trace [12] collected at the ISP level [25]. The analysis reveals: (1) The sync traffic contributes to more than 90% of the total service traffic. Note that the total service traffic is equivalent to one third of the traffic consumed by YouTube [25]; (2) Data synchronization of a file (sometimes a batch of files) generates 2.8 MB of *inbound* (client to cloud) traffic and 5.18 MB of *outbound* (cloud to client) traffic on average. According to the Amazon S3 pricing policy [1] (Dropbox stores all the data content in S3 and S3 only charges for outbound traffic), the Dropbox traffic would consume nearly \$0.05/GB $\times$ *5.18 MB* $\times$ *1 billion* = \$260,000 every day[1]. These costs grow even further when we consider that *all* cloud storage service providers must bear similar costs, not just Dropbox [4].

Data sync traffic can also bring considerable (and unexpected) financial costs to end users, despite that basic cloud storage services are generally free. News media has reported about user complaints of unexpected, additional charges from ISPs, typically from mobile users with limited data usage caps [8, 2]. As a consequence, some users have warned: *"Keep a close eye on your data usage if you have a mobile cloud storage app."* In addition, some cloud storage applications (*e.g.,* large data backup [3]) are also impaired by the bandwidth constraints between the user clients and the cloud. This limitation is regarded as the "dirty secrets" of cloud storage services [5]. Hence users likewise would also benefit from more efficient sync traffic usage.

This paper addresses a simple yet critical question: *Is the current data sync traffic of cloud storage services efficiently used?* Our goal is to quantify and optimize the *efficiency* of data sync traffic usage, *i.e.,* the pivotal network-level efficiency for cloud storage services. Without impairing user experience, providers would like to limit data sync traffic as much as possible to reduce operational costs. On the other side, users also desire more efficient traffic usage, which can save money and result in better quality of experience. Although several studies have measured cloud storage services [30, 33, 25, 20, 24, 36, 32, 48], none have addressed the issue of sync traffic efficiency using real-world, large-scale data from multiple cloud storage services.

[1]We assume that there is no special pricing contract between Dropbox and Amazon S3, so our calculation of the traffic costs may involve potential overestimation.

To answer the question thoroughly, we first define a novel metric named ***TUE*** to quantify the ***T****raffic* ***U****sage* ***E****fficiency* of data synchronization. Borrowing a term similar to *PUE* (*i.e.,* the *Power Usage Effectiveness* = $\frac{\text{Total facility power}}{\text{IT equipment power}}$ [14], a widely adopted metric for evaluating the cloud computing energy efficiency), we define

$$TUE = \frac{\text{Total data sync traffic}}{\text{Data update size}}. \quad (1)$$

When a file is updated (*e.g.,* created, modified, or deleted) at the user side, the *data update size* denotes the size of altered bits relative to the cloud-stored file [2]. From the users' point of view, the data update size is an intuitive and natural signifier about how much traffic *should* be consumed. Compared with the absolute value of sync traffic (used in previous studies), *TUE* better reveals the essential traffic harnessing capability of cloud storage services.

In order to gain a practical and in-depth understanding of *TUE*, we collect a real-world user trace and conduct comprehensive benchmark experiments of six widely used cloud storage services, including Google Drive, OneDrive, Dropbox, Box, Ubuntu One, and SugarSync. We examine key *impact factors* and *design choices* that are common across all of these services. *Impact factors* include file size, file operation, data update size, network environment, hardware configuration, access method, and so on. Here the "access method" refers to PC client software, web browsers, and mobile apps. *Design choices* (of data sync mechanisms) include data sync granularity, data compression level, data deduplication granularity, and sync deferment (for improved batching).

By analyzing these factors and choices, we are able to thoroughly unravel the *TUE* related characteristics, design tradeoffs, and optimization opportunities of these state-of-the-art cloud storage services. The major findings in this paper and their implications are summarized as follows:

- The majority (77%) of files in our collected trace are small in size (less than 100 KB). Nearly two-thirds (66%) of these small files can be logically combined into larger files for *batched data sync* (BDS) in order to reduce sync traffic. However, only Dropbox and Ubuntu One have partially implemented BDS so far.

- The majority (84%) of files are modified by users at least once. Unfortunately, most of today's cloud storage services are built on top of RESTful infrastructure (e.g., Amazon S3, Microsoft Azure, and OpenStack Swift) that typically only support data access operations at the *full-file* level [26, 17]. For these services, enabling the efficient *incremental data sync* (IDS) mechanism requires an extra mid-layer for transforming MODIFY into GET + PUT + DELETE file operations. Given that file modifications frequently happen, implementing IDS is worthwhile for improved network-level efficiency.

- 52% of files can be effectively compressed and 18% of files can be deduplicated. Nevertheless, Google Drive, OneDrive, Box, and SugarSync never compress or deduplicate data. Even for Dropbox and Ubuntu One, the effect of compression and deduplication is largely influenced by the access method.

- Implementing compression and block-level deduplication together is technically challenging. Based on our trace analysis, we suggest providers to implement compression and full-file deduplication because the combination of these two techniques is sufficient to provide efficient usage of sync traffic.

[2]If data compression is utilized by the cloud storage service, the *data update size* denotes the compressed size of altered bits.

- Frequent modifications to a file often lead to large *TUE*. For instance, for 8.5% of Dropbox users, more than 10% of their sync traffic is caused by frequent modifications [36]. Some services deal with this issue by batching file updates using a fixed sync deferment. However, fixed sync deferments are inefficient in some scenarios. We propose an *adaptive sync defer* (ASD) mechanism to overcome this limitation.

- In the presence of frequent file modifications, surprisingly, users with relatively "poor" hardware or Internet access save on sync traffic, because their file updates are naturally batched.

In a nutshell, our research findings demonstrate that for today's cloud storage services, a considerable portion of the data sync traffic is in a sense wasteful, and can be effectively avoided or significantly reduced through carefully designed data sync mechanisms. In other words, there is plenty of space for optimizing the network-level efficiency of these services. Our study of *TUE* provides guidance in two folds: (1) help service providers develop more efficient, traffic-economic cloud storage services; and (2) help end users select appropriate services that best fit their needs and budgets.

Roadmap. In the remainder of the paper, we first describe the common design framework of cloud storage services in § 2, and then introduce our research methodology in § 3. Next, we present research results and findings, broken down logically into three areas: simple file operations (§ 4), compression and deduplication (§ 5), and frequent file modifications (§ 6). Finally, we discuss the tradeoffs for cloud storage system design in § 7, review related work in § 8, and conclude the paper with future work in § 9.

2. COMMON DESIGN FRAMEWORK OF CLOUD STORAGE SERVICES

From the perspective of sync traffic usage, the common design framework of cloud storage services involves a number of *impact factors* and *design choices*, which can be on the client side, server (cloud) side, or network side. The *impact factors* refer to those (*objective*) factors such as the client location, hardware, file size, data update size, network environment, and so on that must be accounted for in the design and usage of cloud storage services. The *design choices* (of data sync mechanisms) refer to those (*subjective*) design decisions which the system designers make, such as the data sync granularity, data compression level, data deduplication granularity, and so forth.

Both the impact factors and design choices may influence the data sync *TUE*. To avoid being trapped by trivial or elusive issues, we select key impact factors and design choices according to the following two rules:

- *Rule 1: The impact factors should be relatively constant or stable, so that our research results can be easily repeated.*

- *Rule 2: The design choices should be measurable and service/implementation independent, so as to make our research methodology widely applicable.*

Following *Rule 1*, we do not study impact factors such as sync delay[3], cloud server location, etc. For example, we observe that uploading a 1-MB JPEG photo to Google Drive may incur an elusive sync delay varying between several seconds and several minutes (under different network environments). Instead, we choose to study the *sync traffic*, which is almost invariable in all cases.

[3] *Sync delay* measures how long the user client synchronizes a file to the cloud.

Table 1: Key impact factors and *design choices*.

Client side	Client location, Client hardware, Access method, File size, File operation, Data update size, Data update rate, *Data compression level*, *Sync deferment*
Server side	*Data sync granularity*, *Data deduplication granularity*, *(Data compression level)* *
Network side	Sync traffic, Bandwidth, Latency

* Note: The server-side data compression level may be different from the client-side data compression level.

Besides, we observe that the cloud server location serving a given file is not constant. This is because a cloud storage service usually hosts a user's files across multiple geographically dispersed data centers, and it often migrates or copies a file from one cloud server to another. Instead, we record the *bandwidth* and *delay* between the client and the cloud, as they can be reproduced using client-side methods (introduced in § 3.2).

Following *Rule 2*, we do not consider design choices such as the metadata structures, file segmentation and replication on the cloud side, because they require specific knowledge of the back-end cloud implementation. For example, the metadata structure (including the list of the user's files, their attributes, and indices to where the files can be found inside the cloud) cannot be extracted from the network communication packets, because almost all the commercial cloud storage services have encrypted their application-layer data in certain (unknown) ways.

In the end, ten key impact factors and four design choices are selected, as listed in Table 1. Some of them are self-explanatory or have been explained before. Below we further explain a few:

- *File operation* includes file creation, file deletion, file modification, and frequent file modifications.

- *Data update rate* denotes how often a file operation happens.

- *Sync deferment.* When frequent file modifications happen, some cloud storage services *intentionally* defer the sync process for a certain period of time for batching file updates.

- *Data sync granularity.* A file operation is synchronized to the cloud either in a *full-file* granularity or in an incremental, *chunk-level* granularity. When the former is adopted, the whole updated file is delivered to the cloud; when the latter is adopted, only those file chunks that contain altered bits (relative to the file stored in the cloud) are delivered.

- *Data deduplication granularity* denotes the *unit* at which data fingerprints are computed and compared to avoid delivering duplicate data units to the cloud. The unit can be either a full file or a file block. Note that data deduplication can be performed across different files owned by different users.

- *Bandwidth* is defined as the peak upload rate between the client and the cloud server. We measure it by uploading a large file to the cloud and meanwhile recording the network traffic with the Wireshark network protocol analyzer [18].

- *Latency* is defined as the round trip time (*RTT*) between the client and the cloud. We measure it by using the standard Ping command.

Table 2: Number of users and files recorded in our collected cloud storage trace.

	Google Drive	OneDrive	Dropbox	Box	Ubuntu One	SugarSync
Number of users	33	24	55	13	13	15
Number of files	32677	17903	106493	19995	27281	18283

Table 3: File attributes recorded in our collected trace.

User name	File name MD5	Original file size
Compressed file size	Creation time	Last modification time
Full-file MD5	128 KB/256 KB/512 KB/1 MB/2 MB/4 MB/ 8 MB/16 MB block-level MD5 hash codes	

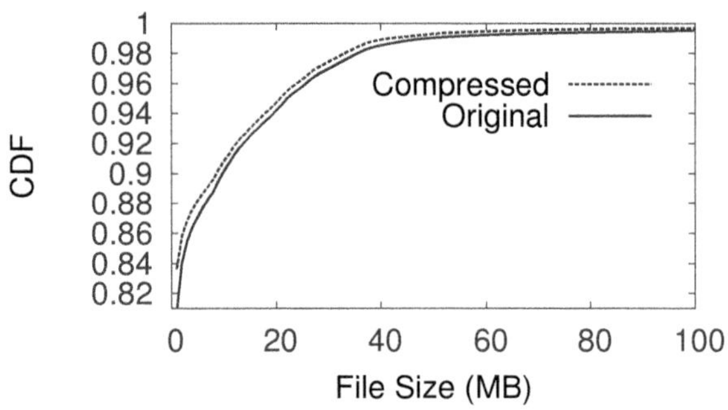

Figure 2: CDF (cumulative distribution function) of 1) original file size and 2) compressed file size, corresponding to our collected trace. For original files, the maximum size is 2.0 GB, the average size is 962 KB, and the median size is 7.5 KB. For compressed files, the maximum size is 1.97 GB, the average size is 732 KB, and the median size is 3.2 KB. Clearly, the tracked files can be effectively compressed on the whole, and the majority of them are small in size.

3. METHODOLOGY

This section describes our methodology for studying the *TUE* of cloud storage services. First, we introduce a real-world cloud storage trace collected to characterize the key impact factors. Next, we design a variety of benchmark experiments to uncover the key design choices of data sync mechanisms. Last but not the least, we provide an overview of the research results.

3.1 Real-world Cloud Storage Trace

Our measurement study takes advantage of a real-world user trace of cloud storage services. It is collected in several universities and companies in the US and China from Jul. 2013 to Mar. 2014, including 153 long-term users with 222,632 files inside their sync folders. Refer to Table 2 for the per service statistics. This trace is used to characterize the key impact factors with regard to the six widely used services. It is also used to guide the design of benchmark experiments and enable further macro-level analysis (in particular, the *TUE* related optimization opportunities of cloud storage services).

This cloud storage trace records detailed information of every tracked file in multiple aspects. Table 3 lists the concrete file attributes recorded. Figure 2 depicts the distributions of original file size and compressed file size corresponding to the trace. We have made this trace publicly available to benefit other researchers. It can be downloaded via the following link:

http://www.greenorbs.org/people/lzh/public/traces.zip.

3.2 Benchmark Experiments

To obtain an in-depth understanding of *TUE* and the key design choices of data sync mechanisms, we design a variety of benchmarks for performing comprehensive controlled experiments. The benchmarks span multiple commercial cloud storage services, involving diverse client machines locating at distinct locations and network environments.

Cloud storage services. Among today's dozens of commercial cloud storage services, our research focuses on the following six mainstream services: Google Drive, OneDrive, Dropbox, Box, Ubuntu One, and SugarSync, as they are either the most popular (in terms of user base) or the most representative (in terms of data sync mechanism). Other cloud storage services are also briefly discussed when necessary.

Client locations. Since the above cloud storage services are mainly deployed in the US, we select two distinct locations to perform each experiment: MN (*i.e.,* Minnesota, US) and BJ (*i.e.,* Beijing, China). In a *coarse-grained* manner, MN represents a location close to the cloud: the bandwidth is nearly 20 Mbps and the latency $\in (42, 77)$ msec, while BJ represents a location remote from the cloud: the bandwidth is nearly 1.6 Mbps the latency $\in (200, 480)$ msec.

Controlled bandwidth and latency. To tune the network environment in a *fine-grained* manner, we interpose a pair of packet filters in the communication channel between the client and the cloud in MN. These filters enable fine-grained adjustment of the bandwidth (the maximum possible speed is 20 Mbps) and latency in either direction. Specifically, the packet filters are interposed by using an intermediate proxy that runs the Linux Netfilter/Iptables tool, thus behaving like a common software firewall.

Controlled file operations. We synthetically generate almost all kinds of file operations appearing in the literature. Moreover, these operations are applied upon both compressed and compressible files. These controlled file operations will be elaborated in § 4, § 5, and § 6.

Client machine hardware. A total of eight client machines are employed in the experiments: four in MN (*i.e.,* M1, M2, M3, and M4) and four in BJ (*i.e.,* B1, B2, B3, and B4). Their detailed hardware information is listed in Table 4. M1/B1 represents a typical client machine at the moment, M2/B2 an outdated machine, M3/B3 an advanced machine with SSD storage, and M4/B4 an Android smartphone. M1–M3 and B1–B3 are installed with Windows 7-SP1 and the Chrome-30.0 web browser.

Benchmark software and access methods. For each cloud storage service, all the experiments regarding M1–M3 and B1–B3 are performed with the latest version (as of Jan. 2014) of the client software on Windows 7. For the M4 and B4 smartphones, we experiment with the latest-version Android apps (as of Jan. 2014). The corresponding sync traffic (*i.e.,* incoming/outgoing packets) are recorded using Wireshark. For the Android smartphones, we route the network traffic through a PC that promiscuously monitors the packets using Wireshark.

Table 4: Hardware information of the experimental client machines.

Machine	CPU	Memory	Disk Storage
M1 @ MN	Quad-core Intel i5 @ 1.70 GHz	4 GB	7200 RPM, 500 GB
M2 @ MN	Intel Atom @ 1.00 GHz	1 GB	5400 RPM, 320 GB
M3 @ MN	Quad-core Intel i7 @ 1.90 GHz	4 GB	SSD, 250 GB
M4 @ MN	Dual-core ARM @ 1.50 GHz	1 GB	MicroSD, 16 GB
B1 @ BJ	Quad-core Intel i5 @ 1.70 GHz	4 GB	7200 RPM, 500 GB
B2 @ BJ	Intel Atom @ 1.00 GHz	1 GB	5400 RPM, 250 GB
B3 @ BJ	Quad-core Intel i7 @ 1.90 GHz	4 GB	SSD, 250 GB
B4 @ BJ	Dual-core ARM @ 1.53 GHz	1 GB	MicroSD, 16 GB

Table 5: Our major findings, their implications, and locations of relevant sections.

Simple File Operations	Implications
Section 4.1 (File creation): The majority (77%) of files in our trace are small in size (<100 KB), which may result in poor *TUE*.	For providers, nearly two thirds (66%) of small files can be logically combined into larger files for *batched data sync* (BDS). However, only Dropbox and Ubuntu One have partially implemented BDS so far.
Section 4.2 (File deletion): Deletion of a file usually incurs negligible sync traffic.	For users, no need to worry about the traffic for file deletion.
Section 4.3 (File modification): The majority (84%) of files are modified by users at least once. Most cloud storage services employ *full-file sync*, while Dropbox and SugarSync utilize *incremental data sync* (IDS) to save traffic for PC clients (but not for mobile or web-based access methods).	Most of today's cloud storage services are built on top of RESTful infrastructure (*e.g.,* Amazon S3, Microsoft Azure, and OpenStack Swift) that only support data access operations at the *full-file* level. *TUE* can be significantly improved by implementing IDS with an extra mid-layer that transforms MODIFY into GET + PUT + DELETE file operations.
Compression and Deduplication	**Implications**
Section 5.1 (Data compression): 52% of files can be effectively compressed. However, Google Drive, OneDrive, Box, and SugarSync never compress data, while Dropbox is the only one that compresses data for every access method.	For providers, data compression is able to reduce 24% of the total sync traffic. For users, PC clients are more likely to support compression versus mobile or web-based access methods.
Section 5.2 (Data deduplication): Although we observe that 18% of files can be deduplicated, most cloud storage services do not support data deduplication, especially for the web-based access method.	For providers, implementing compression and block-level deduplication together is technically challenging. Based on the trace analysis, we suggest providers implement compression and full-file deduplication since the two techniques work together seamlessly.
Frequent File Modifications	**Implications**
Section 6.1 (Sync deferment): Frequent modifications to a file often lead to large *TUE*. Some services deal with this issue by batching file updates using a fixed sync deferment. However, we find that fixed sync deferments are inefficient in some scenarios.	For providers, we demonstrate that an *adaptive sync defer* (ASD) mechanism that dynamically adjusts the sync deferment is superior to fixed sync deferment.
Section 6.2 (Network and hardware): Suprisingly, we observe that users with relatively low bandwidth, high latency, or slow hardware save on sync traffic, because their file updates are naturally batched together.	For users, in the presence of frequent file modifications, today's cloud storage services actually bring good news (in terms of *TUE*) to those users with relatively "poor" hardware or Internet access.

3.3 Overview of Our Major Findings

Based on the above methodology, we are able to thoroughly unravel the *TUE* relevant characteristics, design tradeoffs, and optimization opportunities of the six mainstream cloud storage services. The detailed research results (from simple to complex) will be presented in the following three sections: simple file operations (§ 4), compression and deduplication (§ 5), and frequent file modifications (§ 6). As an overview and a roadmap of our research results, Table 5 summarizes the major findings and their implications.

4. SIMPLE FILE OPERATIONS

This section presents our major measurement results, findings, and implications on the *TUE* of simple file operations. For each measurement, we first introduce the experiment process and results, and then unravel several interesting findings and implications. In this section, we do not mention the client locations, network environments, and hardware configurations, because the *TUE* of simple file operations is independent to these impact factors.

4.1 File Creation

[Experiment 1] : We first study the simple case of creating a highly compressed file of Z bytes inside the sync folder (we will further study the data compression in detail in § 5.1). Thereby, calculating the *TUE* of file creation becomes straightforward (*i.e., TUE* $= \frac{\text{Total sync traffic}}{Z \text{ bytes}}$). According to Figure 2, most compressed files are small in size (several KBs), and the maximum compressed file size is below 2.0 GB. Therefore, we experiment with

$$Z \in \{1, 1\,K, 10\,K, 100\,K, 1\,M, 10\,M, 100\,M, 1\,G\}.$$

Table 6: Sync traffic of a (compressed) file creation.

Service	PC client sync traffic (Bytes)				Web-based sync traffic (Bytes)				Mobile app sync traffic (Bytes)			
	1	1 K	1 M	10 M	1	1 K	1 M	10 M	1	1 K	1 M	10 M
Google Drive	9 K	10 K	1.13 M	11.2 M	6 K	7 K	1.06 M	10.6 M	32 K	71 K	1.27 M	11.0 M
OneDrive	19 K	20 K	1.14 M	11.4 M	28 K	31 K	1.11 M	11.7 M	29 K	44 K	1.23 M	10.7 M
Dropbox	38 K	40 K	1.28 M	12.5 M	31 K	37 K	1.09 M	10.6 M	18 K	32 K	1.08 M	10.9 M
Box	55 K	47 K	1.10 M	10.6 M	55 K	58 K	1.10 M	10.5 M	16 K	34 K	1.29 M	10.8 M
Ubuntu One	2 K	3 K	1.11 M	11.2 M	37 K	39 K	1.20 M	11.3 M	20 K	24 K	1.08 M	10.9 M
SugarSync	9 K	19 K	1.17 M	11.4 M	31 K	32 K	1.10 M	10.7 M	31 K	47 K	1.22 M	10.9 M

Table 7: Total traffic for synchronizing 100 compressed file creations. Each file is 1 KB in size.

Service	PC client		Web-based		Mobile app	
	Sync traffic	(*TUE*)	Sync traffic	(*TUE*)	Sync traffic	(*TUE*)
Google Drive	1.1 MB	(11)	1.2 MB	(12)	5.6 MB	(56)
OneDrive	1.3 MB	(13)	2.2 MB	(22)	1.9 MB	(19)
Dropbox	**120 KB**	**(1.2)**	***600 KB***	**(6.0)**	***360 KB***	**(3.6)**
Box	1.2 MB	(12)	3.2 MB	(32)	3.2 MB	(32)
Ubuntu One	**140 KB**	**(1.4)**	***500 KB***	**(5.0)**	2.5 MB	(25)
SugarSync	0.9 MB	(9)	4.0 MB	(40)	1.5 MB	(15)

The second goal of **Experiment 1** is to get a quantitative understanding of the *overhead traffic*, as *TUE* heavily depends on the ratio of the overhead traffic over the total sync traffic. Synchronizing a file to the cloud always involves a certain amount of overhead traffic, which arises from TCP/HTTP(S) connection setup and maintenance, metadata delivery, etc. Specifically, the overhead traffic is equal to the total sync traffic excluding the payload traffic for delivering the file content, so in **Experiment 1**,

Overhead traffic $\approx$ Total sync traffic - Z bytes.

Table 6 lists the results of **Experiment 1** regarding the six concerned cloud storage services. We vary the file size from 1 B to 1 GB, but for brevity only list four typical sizes: 1 B, 1 KB, 1 MB, and 10 MB. The table records the sync traffic generated by the three typical service access methods: PC client, web (browser) based, and mobile app. In general, from Table 6 we have the following finding and implication:

- *TUE* for synchronizing a (compressed) file creation mainly depends on the file size. A *small* file results in big *TUE* up to 40000, while a *big* file incurs small *TUE* approaching 1.0. Therefore, for providers, a number of small files can be logically combined into a *moderate-size* file for *batched data sync* (BDS) to save traffic, in particular the overhead traffic.

This finding poses a key question: *What is a small size and what is a moderate size?* By plotting the *TUE vs.* File Size relationship (for PC clients) in Figure 3, we get an intuitive conclusion that a moderate size should be at least 100 KB and had better exceed 1 MB, in order to achieve small *TUE* – at most 1.5 and had better stay below 1.2. Here we only draw the curve for PC clients since the corresponding curves for web-based and mobile apps are similar.

As a consequence, small size is regarded as less than 100 KB, which together with Figure 2 reveals that the majority (77%) of tracked files are small in size (meanwhile, 81% in terms of compressed size). More importantly, by analyzing our collected trace, we find that nearly two-thirds (66%) of these small files can be created in batches and thus can effectively benefit from BDS.

[Experiment 1'] : Given that the BDS mechanism can effectively optimize *TUE*, a new question comes out: *Is BDS adopted by the*

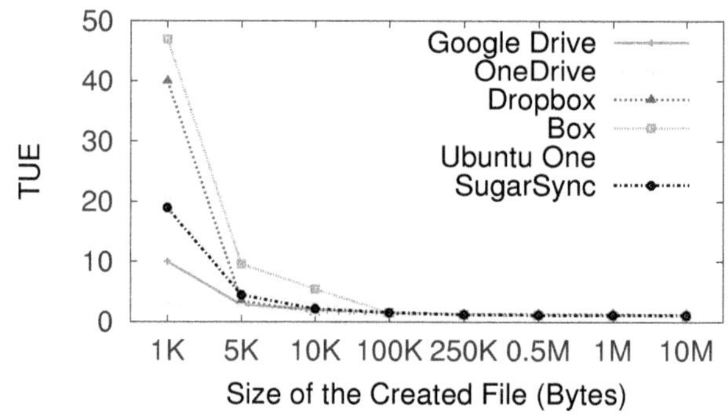

Figure 3: *TUE vs.* Size of the created file.

six mainstream cloud storage services? To get the answer, we first generate 100 (distinct) highly compressed files, and then move all of them into the sync folder in a batch. Each file is 1 KB in size, so $TUE = \frac{\text{Total sync traffic}}{\text{100 KB}}$. If BDS is adopted, the total sync traffic should be around 100 KB and *TUE* should be close to 1.0.

The results of **Experiment 1'** listed in Table 7 reveal that Dropbox and Ubuntu One have adopted BDS for PC clients. Further, it is possible that Dropbox has adopted BDS for web-based and mobile access methods, because the corresponding sync traffic (600 KB and 360 KB) is within an order of magnitude of the data update size (100 KB). Also, Ubuntu One may have used BDS in its web-based data synchronization, since the sync traffic (500 KB) lies between 600 KB and 360 KB. On the contrary, Google Drive, OneDrive, Box, and SugarSync have not adopted BDS yet.

4.2 File Deletion

[Experiment 2] : Each file created in **Experiment 1** is deleted after it is completely synchronized to the cloud, so as to acquire the sync traffic information of a file deletion.

The **Experiment 2** results indicate that deletion of a file usually generates negligible (< 100 KB) sync traffic, regardless of the cloud storage service, file size, or access method. The reason is straightforward: when a file f is deleted in the user's local sync fold-

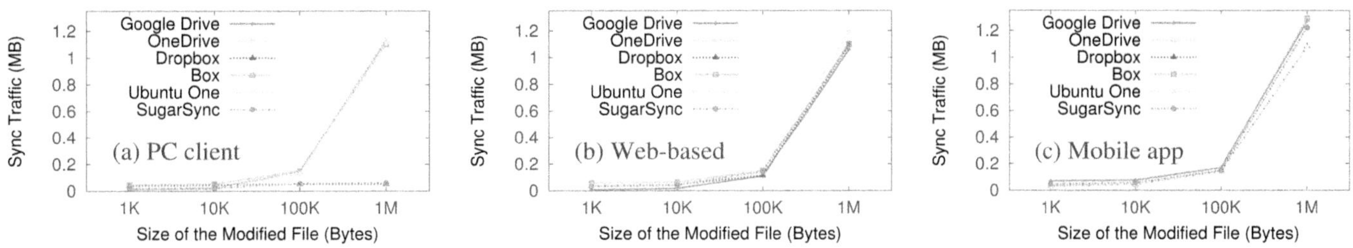

Figure 4: Sync traffic of a random byte modification, corresponding to the three typical service access methods: (a) PC client, (b) Web-based, and (c) Mobile app. By comparing the three subfigures, we discover that only the PC clients of Dropbox and SugarSync utilize the *incremental data sync* (IDS) mechanism for improved network-level efficiency.

er, the user client just notifies the cloud to change some attributes of f rather than remove the content of f. In fact, such "fake deletion" also facilitates users' data recovery, such as the version rollback of a file. Naturally, we get the following implication:

- Cloud storage service users do not need to worry about the sync traffic when deleting a file.

4.3 File Modification and Sync Granularity

[Experiment 3] : The analysis of our collected cloud storage trace reveals that the majority (84%) of files are modified by users at least once. That is to say, file modifications are frequently made by cloud storage users. This subsection studies a simple case of file modification, *i.e.*, modifying a random byte in a compressed file of Z bytes inside the sync folder. In this case, $TUE = \frac{\text{Total sync traffic}}{\text{1 Byte}}$. Similar as § 4.1, we experiment with

$$Z \in \{1, 1\,K, 10\,K, 100\,K, 1\,M, 10\,M, 100\,M, 1\,G\}$$

and plot the sync traffic of four typical sizes: Z = 1 K, 10 K, 100 K, and 1 M in Figure 4.

Figure 4 shows that today's cloud storage services generally utilize two kinds of data sync granularity: 1) full-file and 2) chunk-level. Accordingly, their data sync mechanisms are classified into *full-file sync* and *incremental sync* as follows:

- **Full-file sync.** Google Drive is an example to use the full-file sync mechanism. When a random byte is modified in a Z-byte compressed file, the resulting sync traffic is almost the same as that of creating a new Z-byte compressed file. In other words, Google Drive deals with each file modification by simply uploading the full content of the modified file to the cloud and then deleting the old file. Consequently, Google Drive is more suitable for hosting media files (like photos, music, and videos) which are rarely modified by users. The full-file sync mechanism is also employed by OneDrive, Box, Ubuntu One, Amazon Cloud Drive, and some popular cloud storage services in China like Kuaipan, Kanbox, Baidu CloudDisk, and 115 CloudDisk.

- **Incremental sync** (or **delta sync**). Dropbox (PC client) is an example to use the incremental data sync (IDS) mechanism. When a random byte modification happens, the resulting sync traffic stays around 50 KB, regardless of the size of the modified file. According to the working principle of the incremental sync algorithm: rsync [16], once a random byte is changed in a file f, in most cases the whole data chunk that contains this byte must be delivered for synchronizing f. Therefore, the sync granularity (*i.e.*, the chunk size C) can be approximately estimated as

$$C \approx \text{Total sync traffic} - \text{Overhead traffic}.$$

From the **Experiment 1** results, we understand that the overhead traffic of synchronizing a one-byte file with the Dropbox PC client is nearly 40 KB. Therefore, the data sync granularity of Dropbox PC client is estimated as: $C \approx 50\text{ KB} - 40\text{ KB} = 10\text{ KB}$. This is further validated by the recommended default chunk size (*i.e.*, from 700 B to 16 KB) in the original rsync implementation [15]. Moreover, we find that SugarSync, IDriveSync, and 360 CloudDisk also utilize the IDS mechanism for their PC clients.

On the contrary, as depicted in Figure 4 (b) and 4 (c), web-based apps and mobile apps for all the six services still use the full-file sync mechanism, probably because IDS is hard to implement in JavaScript (for web-based apps) or due to energy concerns (for mobile apps). Specifically, JavaScript is the most widely used script language for the development of web-based apps (including cloud storage apps). Nevertheless, for security concerns, JavaScript is unable to directly invoke file-level system calls/APIs like open, close, read, write, stat, rsync, and gzip [11]. Instead, JavaScript can only access users' local files in an indirect and constrained manner, which is of less efficiency in terms of implementing IDS.

In summary, we have the following finding about simple file modification and the data sync granularity:

- When a file modification is synchronized to the cloud, *TUE* is mostly affected by the data sync granularity which varies significantly among different cloud storage services. Most services simply use full-file sync, but some services (like Dropbox and SugarSync) utilize IDS to achieve improved network-level efficiency for PC clients.

Conflicts between IDS and RESTful infrastructure. Although enabling the IDS mechanism can help service providers reduce the data sync traffic, implementing IDS is not an easy job in practice. Most of today's cloud storage services (*e.g.*, OneDrive, Dropbox, and Ubuntu One) are built on top of RESTful infrastructure (*e.g.*, Amazon S3, Microsoft Azure, and OpenStack Swift). For simplifying both the providers' implementation complexities and the developers' programming complexities, RESTful infrastructure typically only supports data access operations at the *full-file* level, like PUT (upload a new file), GET (download a whole file), DELETE (delete a whole file), and so forth. Note that the PUT, GET, and DELETE operations may have aliases in other RESTful infrastructure.

Thus, enabling IDS usually requires an extra mid-layer for transforming MODIFY into GET + PUT + DELETE file operations in an *efficient* manner (like what Dropbox has done [25, 36]) [4]. Since file modifications frequently happen, implementing such a mid-layer is worthwhile for improved network-level efficiency.

[4]An alternative to enable IDS is to store every chunk of a file as a separate data object. When a file is modified, the modified chunks are deleted with the new chunks being stored as new objects; also, file metadata has to be updated (as what is used in Cumulus [43]).

Table 8: **Sync traffic of a 10-MB text file creation. UP: The user uploads the file to the cloud. DN: The user downloads the file from the cloud.**

Service	Sync traffic (MB)					
	PC client		Web-based		Mobile app	
	UP	DN	UP	DN	UP	DN
Google Drive	11.3	11.0	10.6	11.7	11.8	10.8
OneDrive	11.4	11.2	11.0	11.0	12.2	10.7
Dropbox	**6.1**	**5.5**	10.6	**5.5**	**8.1**	**5.5**
Box	10.6	11.2	10.5	11.3	10.4	11.1
Ubuntu One	**5.6**	**5.3**	10.9	**5.3**	**8.6**	10.6
SugarSync	11.3	11.5	10.4	10.7	11.6	11.8

5. COMPRESSION AND DEDUPLICATION

In a real-world storage system, compression and deduplication are the two most commonly used techniques for saving space and traffic. This section makes a detailed study of cloud storage compression and deduplication, from both the system designers' and users' perspectives.

5.1 Data Compression Level

[Experiment 4] : To study whether data updates are compressed before they are synchronized to the cloud, we create an X-byte text file inside the sync folder. As a small file is hard to compress, we experiment with $X = 1$ M, 10 M, 100 M, and 1 G. Each text file is filled with random English words. If data compression is actually used, the resulting sync traffic should be much less than the original file size. Furthermore, after each text file is completely synchronized, we download it from the cloud with a PC client, a web browser, and a mobile app, respectively, so as to examine whether the cloud delivers data updates in a compressed form.

As a typical case, the **Experiment 4** results corresponding to a 10-MB text file are listed in Table 8. First, in the file upload (UP) phase, among the six mainstream cloud storage services, only Dropbox and Ubuntu One compress data with PC clients and mobile apps. No service ever compresses data with web browsers. Further, we observe that the 10-MB text file can be compressed to nearly 4.5 MB using the highest-level WinZip compression on our desktop. Thus, for Dropbox and Ubuntu One, the compression level with PC clients seems moderate, while the compression level with mobile apps is quite low. The motivation of such a difference is intuitive: to reduce the battery consumption of mobile devices caused by the computation-intensive data compressions.

Next, in the file download (DN) phase, only Dropbox and Ubuntu One compress data with PC clients and web browsers, and the compression level is higher than that in the file upload phase. For mobile apps, only Dropbox compresses data.

By analyzing our collected cloud storage trace, we find that 52% of files can be *effectively compressed*. Here "effectively compressed" implies that $\frac{\text{Compressed file size}}{\text{Original file size}} < 90\%$ when the highest-level WinZip compression is applied. As a result, the total *compression ratio* ($= \frac{\text{Size of data before compression}}{\text{Size of data after compression}}$) regarding all the files recorded in the trace reaches 1.31. In other words, data compression is able to reduce 24% of the data sync traffic (compared with no compression). These observations lead to the following findings and implications:

- Data compression provides obvious benefits by reducing the sync traffic, but is not supported by every cloud storage service. Google Drive, OneDrive, Box, and SugarSync never compress data, while Dropbox is the only service that compresses data for every access method.
- Web browser typically *does not* compress a file when uploading it to the cloud storage, probably also due to the limitations of JavaScript or other web-based script languages (refer to § 4.3). Besides, using a mobile app is usually not as efficient as using a PC client.

Algorithm 1 : Iterative Self Duplication Algorithm

Set the lower bound: $L = 0$ bytes, and the upper bound: $U = +\infty$ bytes. Guess a deduplication block size: B_1;

Step 1:
  Generate a new compressed file f_1 of B_1 bytes;
  Upload f_1 to the cloud. When f_1 is completely synchronized to the cloud, record the total sync traffic: Tr_1;

Step 2:
  Generate another file f_2 by appending f_1 to itself, that is $f_2 = f_1 + f_1$ (the so-called "self duplication");
  Upload f_2 to the cloud. When f_2 is completely synchronized to the cloud, record the total sync traffic: Tr_2;

Step 3:
if $Tr_2 \ll Tr_1$ **and** Tr_2 is small ($\approx$ tens of KBs) **then**
  B_1 is actually the deduplication block size (B);
  exit;
else there are two cases
  case 1: $Tr_2 < 2B_1$ and Tr_2 is not small (implying that $B_1 > B$) **then**
  Set B_1 as the upper bound: $U \leftarrow B_1$, and decrease the guessing value of B_1: $B_1 \leftarrow \frac{L+U}{2}$;
  case 2: $Tr_2 > 2B_1$ (implying that $B_1 < B$) **then**
  Set B_1 as the lower bound: $L \leftarrow B_1$, and increase the guessing value of B_1: $B_1 \leftarrow \frac{L+U}{2}$;
goto Step 1;

5.2 Data Deduplication Granularity

[Experiment 5] : Data deduplication is another potential method to reduce data sync traffic, with the intuition that users often upload duplicated files with similar content. Inferring the deduplication granularity of a cloud storage service requires some efforts, especially when the deduplication block size B (bytes) is not a power of two (*i.e.*, $B \neq 2^n$, where n is a positive integer) [5]. To measure the deduplication granularity, we design and implement Algorithm 1 (named the "Iterative Self Duplication Algorithm"). It infers the deduplication granularity by iteratively duplicating and uploading one or multiple synthetic file(s) and meanwhile analyzing the incurred data sync traffic. It is easy to prove that the iteration procedure can finish in $O(\log(B))$ rounds.

First, we study inter-file data deduplication with respect to an identical user account. By applying **Experiment 5** to the six mainstream cloud storage services, we figure out their data deduplication granularity in Table 9 (the 2nd column). In this table, "Full file" (only for Ubuntu One) means that data deduplication only happens at the full-file level, "4 MB" (only for Dropbox) indicates that the deduplication block size $B = 4$ MB, and "No" shows that there is no deduplication performed. Note that block-level deduplication naturally implies full-file deduplication, but *not* vice versa.

Second, we study cross-user data deduplication. For each cloud storage service, we first upload a file f to the cloud, and then

[5] The deduplication block size B (bytes) is traditionally a power of two [39], but we still have to thoughtfully consider the exception when $B \neq 2^n$.

Table 9: **Data deduplication granularity. We do not list the web-based case because the web-based file synchronization typically *does not* apply data deduplication.**

Service	Same user	Cross users
	PC client & Mobile app	PC client & Mobile app
Google Drive	No	No
OneDrive	No	No
Dropbox	4 MB	No
Box	No	No
Ubuntu One	Full file	Full file
SugarSync	No	No

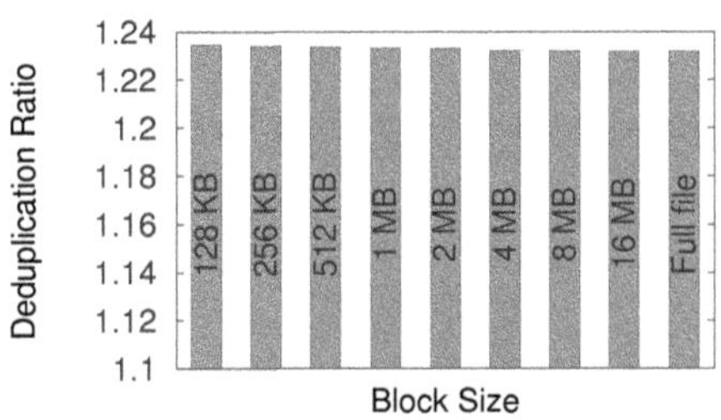

Figure 5: *Deduplication ratio* (cross-user) *vs.* Block size. Here the deduplication ratio = $\frac{\text{Size of data before deduplication}}{\text{Size of data after deduplication}}$.

use another user account to upload f to the cloud again. In this case, the sync traffic should be trivial if full-file deduplication is performed across users. If the cross-user full-file deduplication is confirmed, **Experiment 5** is run again to figure out the accurate cross-user deduplication granularity; otherwise, we can conclude that there is no cross-user data deduplication at all. The results are also shown in Table 9 (the 3rd column). Obviously, only Dropbox employs a different cross-user data deduplication granularity from the identical-user case.

From the above measurements, we get the following findings and implications:

- A cloud storage service usually adopts the same data deduplication granularity for PC clients and mobile apps, while the web-based data synchronization typically *does not* apply data deduplication.
- By analyzing our collected trace, we find that cross-user data (block) duplication pervasively exists: even the full-file level *duplication ratio* ($= \frac{\text{Size of duplicate files}}{\text{Size of all files}}$) reaches 18.8%. However, most cloud storage services do not support cross-user deduplication (perhaps for privacy and security concerns) or block-level deduplication at the moment, thus losing considerable opportunities for optimizing *TUE*.

Further, we compare the two types of deduplication granularity to answer a question: *Is the block-level deduplication much better (i.e., has a much larger deduplication ratio) than the full-file deduplication?* Since the computation complexity of block-level deduplication is much higher than that of full-file deduplication, the answer could help decide whether or not the block-level deduplication is worthwhile. Note that when referring to the "file blocks", we are dividing files to blocks *in a simple and natural way*, that is to say, by starting from the head of a file with a fixed block size. So clearly, we are not dividing files to blocks in the best possible manner [19, 39] which is much more complicated and computation intensive.

As our collected trace contains both the full-file hash codes and the block-level (128 KB – 16 MB blocks) hash codes of each tracked file (refer to § 3.1, Table 3), we perform the trace-driven simulation to figure out the (cross-user) deduplication ratio when each deduplication granularity is adopted. The simulation results demonstrate that the block-level deduplication usually exhibits *trivial superiority* to the full-file deduplication, as shown in Figure 5. Therefore, we have the following implication:

- For providers, in terms of deduplication granularity, supporting full-file deduplication is basically sufficient.

Conflicts between compression and block-level deduplication. Although data deduplication can reduce the sync traffic, we notice that it has a potential performance conflict with data compression. Implementing block-level deduplication and compression together is technically challenging.

For cloud storage service providers, though storing and delivering data in its compressed form can effectively save storage space and sync traffic, it may significantly increase the (computation and I/O) complexity of block-level deduplication. Specifically, after a file (f) is delivered to the cloud storage in its compressed form (f'), f' must be first uncompressed to calculate each block's fingerprint, so as to enable block-level deduplication. Then, the uncompressed file must be deleted from disk. Furthermore, the above operations must be re-executed (in part) as long as one block of f is modified. It is basically unwise for a service provider to shift these operations to its user clients, unless the service provider does not care about user experience.

In this subsection we have known that block-level deduplication exhibits trivial superiority to full-file deduplication. Meanwhile, full-file deduplication is not challenged by data compression, because full-file deduplication can be directly performed on compressed files. Therefore, we suggest that providers implement full-file deduplication and compression since these two techniques work together seamlessly.

6. FREQUENT FILE MODIFICATIONS

In addition to backing up and retrieving files, cloud storage services are also widely used for collaboration, such as collaborative document editing, team project building, and database hosting. All the above mentioned advanced functions involve a special kind of file operations: *frequent modifications* to a file.

In § 4 and § 5, we have studied various simple file operations that are each performed at once. On the contrary, frequent modifications imply that a file is modified in a frequent and incremental manner. Thus, they exhibit diverse data update patterns in terms of data update *size* and *rate*. The large-scale trace collected by Drago *et al.* [12] reveals that for 8.5% of Dropbox users, more than 10% of their sync traffic is caused by frequent modifications [36]. Further, frequent modifications may well incur abundant overhead traffic that far exceeds the amount of useful data update traffic sent by the user client over time, which is referred to as the *traffic overuse problem* [36]. Besides, in this section we will elaborate on client locations, network environments, and hardware configurations, because the *TUE* of frequent file modifications is largely influenced by these factors.

6.1 Sync Deferment

[Experiment 6] : To experiment with frequent file modifications, we append X random kilobytes to an empty file inside the sync folder every X seconds, until the total appended bytes reach a certain size C (typically $C = 1$ MB). This is denoted as the "X KB/X

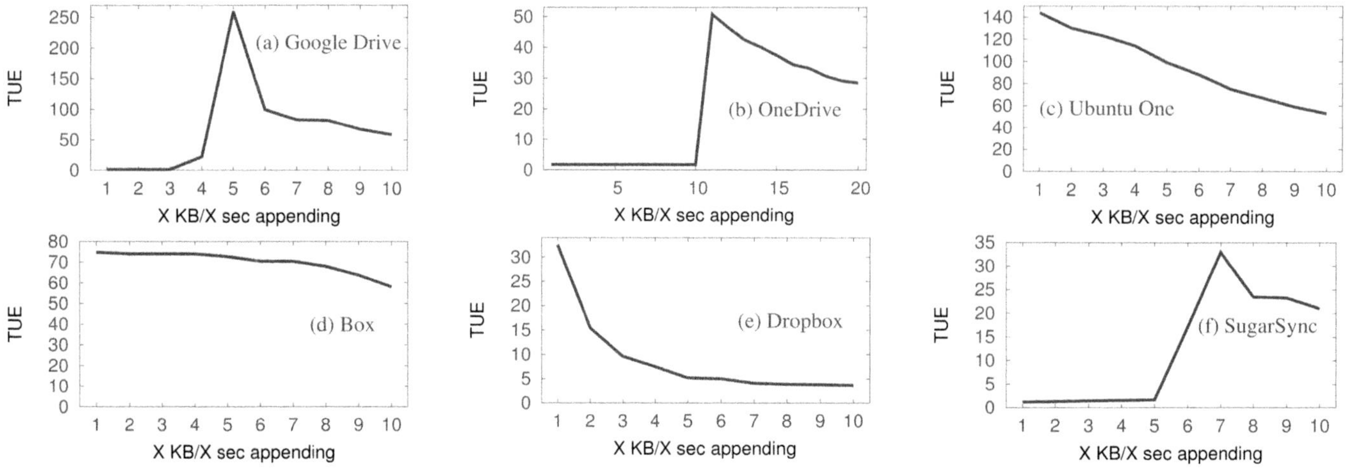

Figure 6: *TUE* of the six cloud storage services in response to controlled frequent file modifications. Note that the subfigures have distinct Y-axes, and the (b) OneDrive subfigure has a different X-axis.

sec" appending experiment. We use random bytes since they are difficult to compress, thus preventing file compression from influencing our measurements of *TUE*.

Our goal is three folds by doing this experiment: 1) We observe and understand the sync traffic and *TUE* in response to frequent modifications; 2) We aim to discover whether the cloud storage service has used the *sync deferment* in order to avoid or mitigate the traffic overuse problem; and 3) If the sync deferment is adopted, we want to measure how long the sync deferment is.

All the experiments in this section are performed using M1 @ MN (refer to Table 4) with 20 Mbps of bandwidth, and the latency (between M1 and each cloud) is between 42 msec and 77 msec. In terms of service access method, we only examine the PC client, because almost all the frequent modifications are generated from PC clients in practice [6]. Experiments with other benchmarks will be presented in § 6.2.

First, to investigate the impact of frequent file modifications on *TUE*, we examine the cases for $X \in \{1, 2, \cdots, 19, 20\}$. As depicted in Figure 6, the six mainstream cloud storage services exhibit diverse and interesting phenomena:

- Frequent modifications to a file often lead to large *TUE* (the aforementioned "traffic overuse problem"). As for the six mainstream services, the maximum *TUE* can reach 260, 51, 144, 75, 32, and 33, respectively.
- We observe (except in the sync defer cases: Figure 6 (a), 6 (b), and 6 (f)) that *TUE* generally decreases as the modification frequency ($= \frac{1024}{X}$) decreases. The reason is straightforward: though the total data update size is always $C = 1$ MB, a lower data update frequency implies fewer data sync events, and thus the overhead traffic is reduced.

A natural question is: *Why are the maximum* TUE *values of Google Drive (260), OneDrive (51), Ubuntu One (144), and Box (75) much larger than those of Dropbox (32) and SugarSync (33)?* The answer can be found from their data sync granularity (refer to § 4.3): Google Drive, OneDrive, Ubuntu One, and Box employ *full-file sync*, while Dropbox and SugarSync employ block-level *incremental sync* which significantly improves the network-level traffic efficiency.

On the other hand, there do exist a few cases (in Figure 6 (a), 6 (b), and 6 (f)) where *TUE* is close to 1.0. According to our observations, (a) Google Drive, (b) OneDrive, and (f) SugarSync deal with the traffic overuse problem by batching file updates using a *fixed* sync deferment: T seconds (which cannot be re-configured by users). Figure 6 (a), 6 (b), and 6 (f) indicate that $T_{GoogleDrive} \in (3, 5)$ sec, $T_{SugarSync} \in (4, 6)$ sec, and $T_{OneDrive} \in (10, 11)$ sec. Moreover, to figure out a more accurate value of T, we further tune X from integers to floats. For example, we experiment with $X = 3.1, 3.2, \cdots, 4.9$ for $T_{GoogleDrive}$, and then find that $T_{GoogleDrive} \approx 4.2$ sec. Similarly, we find that $T_{SugarSync} \approx 6$ sec and $T_{OneDrive} \approx 10.5$ sec.

One may have the following question: *Is it possible that the deferred data synchronization of (a) Google Drive, (b) OneDrive, and (f) SugarSync is triggered by a* byte counter *or an* update counter *rather than the* time threshold *(T)?* In other words, the three concerned services may trigger the data synchronization once the number of uncommitted bytes or updates exceeds a certain value. This question can be addressed in two cases:

- Case 1: If the data synchronization is triggered by a *byte counter*, the resulting *TUE* would be close to 1.0 according to our previous study on the byte-counter based "efficient batched synchronization" (UDS) [36]. This is clearly not true as illustrated by Figure 6 (a), 6 (b), and 6 (f).
- Case 2: If the data synchronization is triggered by an *update counter*, the resulting *TUE* in Figure 6 (a), 6 (b), and 6 (f) would *linearly* decrease as the modification period (X sec) increases. Obviously, this is not true, either.

Therefore, we conclude that the deferred data synchronization is not triggered by a byte counter or an update counter.

Unfortunately, fixed sync deferments are limited in terms of usage scenarios. As shown in Figures 6 (a), 6 (b), and 6 (f), the traffic overuse problem still occurs when $X > T$.

To overcome the limitation of fixed sync deferments, we propose an *adaptive sync defer* (ASD) mechanism. ASD adaptively tunes its sync deferment (T_i) to follow the latest (say, the i-th) data update. In other words, when data updates happen more frequently, T_i gets shorter; when data updates happen less frequently, T_i gets

[6]The UIs (user interfaces) of web browser and mobile apps for cloud storage services are usually not fit for performing frequent modifications to a file.

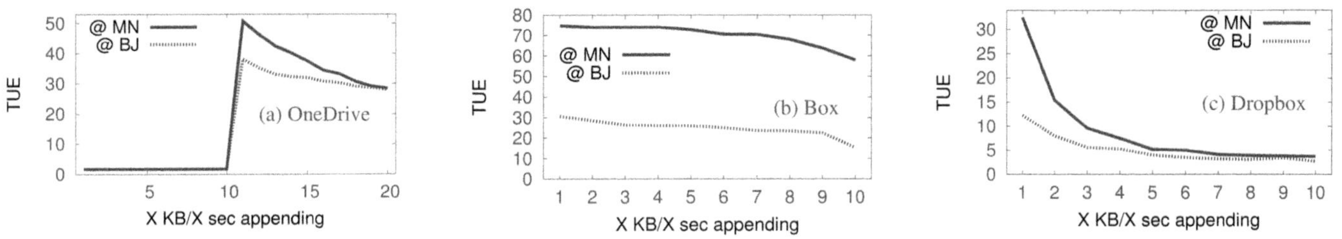

Figure 7: *TUE* of (a) OneDrive, (b) Box, and (c) Dropbox on handling the "X KB/X sec" appending experiment, in Minnesota (MN) and Beijing (BJ), respectively.

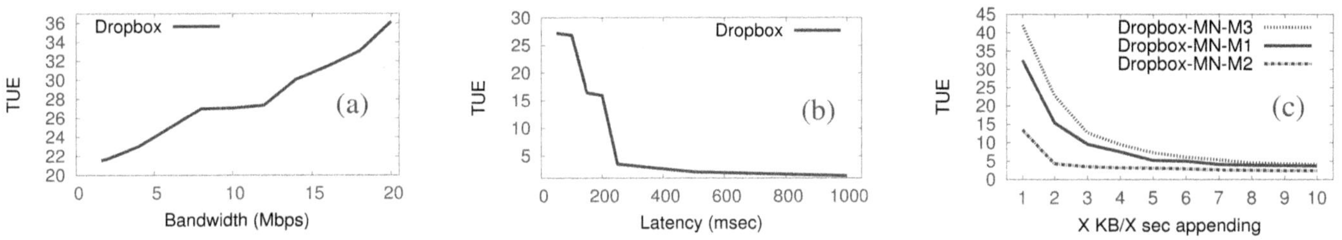

Figure 8: *TUE* of Dropbox on handling the (a) "1 KB/sec" appending experiment with variable bandwidths, (b) "1 KB/sec" appending experiment with variable latencies, and (c) "X KB/X sec" appending experiment with distinct hardware configurations.

longer. In either case, T_i tends to be slightly longer than the latest inter-update time, so that frequent modifications can be properly batched for synchronization (without harming user experience). Specifically, T_i can be adapted in such an iterative manner:

$$T_i = \min\left(\frac{T_{i-1}}{2} + \frac{\Delta t_i}{2} + \epsilon,\ T_{max}\right) \qquad (2)$$

where Δt_i is the inter-update time between the (i-1)-th and the i-th data updates, and $\epsilon \in (0, 1.0)$ is a small constant that guarantees T_i to be slightly longer than Δt_i in a small number of iteration rounds. T_{max} is also a constant representing the upper bound of T_i, as a too large T_i will harm user experience by bringing about intolerably long sync delay.

If Google Drive would utilize ASD on handling the "X KB/X sec" ($X > T_{GoogleDrive}$) appending experiments, the resulting *TUE* will be close to 1.0 rather than the original 260 ($X = 5$), 100 ($X = 6$), 83 ($X = 7$), and so forth. The situation is similar for OneDrive and SugarSync. More detailed performance evaluation of ASD can be found in our previous work [37].

6.2 Impact of Network and Hardware

In this subsection, we first study the impact of network and hardware on *TUE*, and then explore why they impact *TUE*.

[Experiment 7, Network environment] : To study the impact of network environment (including both bandwidth and latency) on *TUE*, we conduct the following two batches of experiments.

The first batch of experiments are performed on B1 @ BJ. It represents a relatively poor network environment: low bandwidth (nearly 1.6 Mbps) and long latency (between 200 msec and 480 msec) relative to the cloud, because the six mainstream cloud storage services are mainly deployed in US. After repeating **Experiments 1 – 6** in this network environment, we compare the results with the corresponding results by using M1 @ MN with abundant bandwidth (nearly 20 Mbps) and short latency (between 42 msec and 77 msec), which represents a good network environment.

The second batch of experiments are performed by using M1 @ MN with controlled bandwidth (between 1.6 Mbps and 20 Mbps) and latency (between 40 msec and 1000 msec), so that we are able to get fine-grained results about how the network environment impacts *TUE*.

From the two batches of experiments, we mainly get the following findings and implications:

- *TUE* of a simple file operation is usually not affected by network environment.
- However, in the case of frequent file modifications, a user client with relatively low bandwidth or long latency can save more sync traffic.

Specifically, for the first batch of experiments, we plot the *TUE* of (a) OneDrive, (b) Box, and (c) Dropbox on handling the "X KB/X sec" appending experiment in Minnesota and Beijing in Figure 7 (a), 7 (b), and 7 (c), respectively. The situation of Google Drive and SugarSync is similar to Figure 7 (a), and the situation of Ubuntu One looks like Figure 7 (b). In each subfigure, the two curves ("@ MN" *vs.* "@ BJ") clearly illustrate that poor network environment leads to smaller *TUE*, especially when the modification period (X sec) is short (excluding the sync defer cases).

For the second batch of experiments, as a typical example, we plot the *TUE* of Dropbox on handling the "1 KB/sec" appending experiment with variable bandwidths and latencies in Figure 8 (a) and Figure 8 (b), respectively. In Figure 8 (a), the latency is fixed to around 50 msec and the bandwidth is tuned from 1.6 Mbps to 20 Mbps. In Figure 8 (b), the bandwidth is fixed to around 20 Mbps and the latency is tuned from 40 msec to 1000 msec. Obviously, higher bandwidth or shorter latency leads to larger TUE.

[Experiment 7', Hardware configuration] : Next, we examine the impact of hardware configuration on *TUE* by repeating **Experiments 1 – 6** with distinct client machines: M1 (a typical machine), M2 (an outdated machine), and M3 (an advanced machine). Their detailed hardware information is listed in Table 4. All the experiments are performed in Minnesota with abundant bandwidth (nearly 20 Mbps) and short latency (between 42 msec and 77 msec).

Through the **Experiment 7'** results, we observe that *TUE* of a simple file operation generally has no relation with hardware configuration, but *TUE* of frequent file modifications is actually affected by hardware configuration. As a typical example, in Figure 8 (c) we plot the *TUE* of Dropbox on handling the "X KB/X sec" appending experiment with M1, M2, and M3. The three curves clearly demonstrate that slower hardware incurs less sync traffic.

Why do network environment and hardware configuration impact *TUE*? To explore the reason why network environment and hardware configuration impact *TUE*, we analyze the communication packets of data synchronization, in particular the TCP data flows. The analysis reveals that in the presence of frequent modifications to a file, the user client does *not* always synchronize every file modification to the cloud *separately*. Instead, the user client often batches multiple file modifications for data synchronization. Specifically, a new file modification (or a sequence of new file modifications) is synchronized to the cloud when at least the following two conditions are both satisfied:

- **Condition 1:** The previous file modification (or the previous batch of file modifications) has been completely synchronized to the cloud.
- **Condition 2:** The client machine has finished calculating the latest metatata of the modified file.

As to Condition 1, when the network environment is relatively poor, synchronizing the previous file modification (or the previous batch of file modifications) takes more time, so the client needs to wait for a longer period of time to synchronize the new file modification. As to Condition 2, when the client runs on top of slower hardware, calculating the latest metatata (which is computation-intensive) also requires a longer period of time. Because the failure of either condition will cause the new file modification (or the sequence of new file modifications) to be naturally batched, poor network environment or poor hardware increases the probability that a file modification gets batched, and thereby optimizes the *TUE*.

Finally, combining all the findings in this subsection, we get the following implication:

- In the case of frequent file modifications, today's cloud storage services actually bring good news (in terms of *TUE*) to those users with relatively poor hardware or Internet access.

7. DISCUSSION

While this paper mainly focuses on the *traffic costs* of cloud storage services, we keep in mind that the total costs of running a cloud storage service also involves the *computation costs*, *storage costs*, *operation costs*, and so forth. Therefore, we would like to further study and understand the traffic usage from an insider's point of view. In particular, we want to quantify the *tradeoff* between *TUE* and other system metrics. For example, regarding data sync granularity, incremental synchronization is a double-edge sword: It effectively saves traffic and storage compared with full-file synchronization, but it also puts more computational burden on both service providers and end users. Likewise, determining the best data compression level to achieve a good balance between traffic, storage, and computation deserves further research efforts.

Specifically, studying the aforementioned system tradeoffs would require at least the following three-fold information from cloud storage providers:

- *The user device composition* (*i.e.,* the percentages of PCs, tablets, and smartphones) is the most important information required. For PCs, it is generally fine to sacrifice computation, storage, and/or network-level efficiency for better service quality (*e.g.,* faster synchronization of file operations). For example, PC clients usually maintain a local sync folder that stores a copy for almost every synchronized file at the cloud side. On the other hand, smartphones are sensitive to computation cost, storage space, and sometimes network overhead (in 2G/3G/4G modes). Accordingly, mobile apps usually maintain a small-size local folder that caches only a few most recently accessed files.
- *The logical interfaces of the storage infrastructure* decides the implementation difficulty and working efficiency of IDS (incremental data sync) for file modifications. The logical interfaces mainly include the RESTful (full-file level) interfaces, file-level interfaces, and block-level interfaces. For example, Microsoft Azure, Amazon S3, and OpenStack Swift provide RESTful interfaces, and thus implementing IDS on top of them is not an easy job. On the contrary, implementing IDS on top of a NFS-based infrastructure (with file-level interfaces) is quite straightforward. In addition, as GFS and HDFS provide seemingly file-level interfaces based on block-level infrastructure, the corresponding implementation difficulty and working efficiency of IDS lie between those with RESTful and file-level interfaces. Finally, the logical storage interfaces also impact the working efficiency of BDS (batched data sync) for small files.
- *The physical devices of the storage infrastructure* have non-negligible influence on the working efficiency and implementation (monetary) costs of a cloud storage service. Obviously, a single SSD is faster while much more expensive than a single HDD, but up to now it is still not clear which is the most cost-effective among an SSD cluster, an HDD cluster, a hybrid SSD+HDD cluster, or even a tape-based cluster [41]. Moreover, the performance of *the filesystem* can affect the working efficiency of a cloud storage service. For instance, OpenStack Swift works better with XFS than EXT3/EXT4, as pointed out by the official OpenStack development document [13]. In addition, even those seemingly independent infrastructure components may share deep, hidden dependencies that lead to unexpected *correlated failures*, thus undermining the redundancy efforts and working efficiencies of cloud storage services [46, 47].

We hope cloud storage service providers to release their proprietary traces to promote future research in this field.

8. RELATED WORK

As cloud storage services are becoming more pervasive and changing the way people store and share data, a number of research efforts have been made in academia, including the design and implementation of the service infrastructure [22, 43, 44, 31], integration services with various features and functionalities [29, 28, 23, 42, 36, 35, 34], performance measurement [33, 25, 24, 20, 45], as well as privacy and security issues [40, 21, 38, 27, 32]. While the previous work covers the data sync mechanism as one of the key operations and the resulting traffic usage, none of them tries to understand the *efficiency* of the traffic usage *comprehensively*. Due to the system complexity and implementation difference, one can hardly form a general and unified view of the traffic usage efficiency, not to mention the further improvement.

Our work is different from and complementary to previous studies by quantifying and optimizing traffic usage efficiency, the pivotal network-level efficiency for cloud storage services. Based on the measurements and analysis of six state-of-the-art cloud storage services, we unravel the key impact factors and design choices that may significantly affect the traffic usage efficiency. Most importantly, we provide guidance and implications for both service providers and end users to economize their sync traffic usage.

Dropbox is one of the earliest and most popular cloud storage services, and its data sync mechanism has been studied in depth in [25, 36]. Through an ISP-level large-scale measurement, Drago *et al.* first uncover the performance bottlenecks of Dropbox due to both the system architecture and the data sync mechanism [25]. They suggest a bundling sync scheme with delayed sync ACK to improve the sync performance of Dropbox. In addition, Li *et al.* identify a pathological issue that may lead to the "traffic overuse problem" in Dropbox by uploading a large amount of unnecessary (overhead) traffic [36]. They propose an efficient batched sync algorithm (named UDS) to address this issue. Complementary to these studies, our results are not limited to Dropbox. Instead, we unravel the general factors that may significantly affect the data sync traffic. In consequence, our results are more general and applicable for designing network-level efficient cloud storage services, rather than improving one particular service.

Some measurement studies have partially covered the traffic usage of cloud storage services. Hu *et al.* examine "the good, the bad and the ugly" of four cloud storage services by comparing their traffic usage, delay time, and CPU usage of uploading new files [30]. They observe that the sync traffic usage varies substantially with factors such as file size, data compressibility, and data duplication levels. Drago *et al.* further compare the system capabilities of five cloud storage services, and find that each service has limitations with regard to data synchronization [24]. Both of these two studies confirm the importance of sync traffic usage, and the possibility of further optimizing the sync traffic usage.

In this paper, we zoom into the problem towards a comprehensive understanding of traffic usage efficiency. Different from the simplified benchmarks used in the above mentioned studies [36, 30, 24], we consider the diversity of access methods, client locations, hardware configurations, and network conditions to match the real-world usage. Indeed, we discover that these factors lead to different traffic usage patterns, some of which are even not expected. Last but not the least, different from previous studies that never consider mobile usage, one of our focus is the mobile usage of sync traffic – mobile users are those who mostly suffer from traffic overuse.

9. CONCLUSION AND FUTURE WORK

The tremendous increase in data sync traffic has brought growing pains to today's cloud storage services, in terms of both infrastructure support and monetary costs. Driven by this problem, this paper quantifies and analyzes the data sync traffic usage efficiency (*TUE*) of six widely used cloud storage services, using a real-world trace and comprehensive experiments. Our results and findings confirm that much of the data sync traffic is unnecessary and can be avoided or mitigated by careful design of data sync mechanisms. In other words, there is enormous space for optimizing the network-level efficiency of existing cloud storage services. We sincerely hope that our work can inspire the cloud storage designers to enhance their system and software, and meanwhile guide the users to pick appropriate services.

In Jun. 2014, Apple Inc. announced its cloud storage service, iCloud Drive, in its annual WWDC conference. iCloud Drive is planned as an important component of iCloud, the popular cloud service provided by Apple that has amassed over 300 million users. Therefore, in the near future, iCloud Drive may be ranked higher than several cloud storage services studied in this paper (*e.g.*, Dropbox and Box). To our knowledge, multiple groups of researchers (including us) have been anxious to investigate the network-level efficiency of iCloud Drive, in the hopes of harvesting novel and interesting discoveries. Unfortunately, up to now (Aug. 2014), the iCloud Drive service is still unavailable to common users [10]. In general, we believe that the network-level efficiency of iCloud Drive would be a promising research topic, as iCloud Drive lives in a unique and closed ecological system fully operated by Apple.

10. ACKNOWLEDGEMENTS

This work is supported by the High-Tech Research and Development Program of China ("863 – China Cloud" Major Program) under grant SQ2015AAJY1595, the National Basic Research Program of China ("973") under grant 2011CB302305, the China NSF (Natural Science Foundation) under grants 61232004 and 61471217, the China Postdoctoral Science Fund under grant 2014M550735, and the US NSF under grants CNS-1054233, CNS-1017647, CNS-1017092, CNS-1117536 and CRI-1305237.

We would like to thank our shepherd Theophilus Benson and our team member He Xiao for the valuable help. We thank every volunteer who contributes their data and makes our research possible.

11. REFERENCES

[1] Amazon S3 pricing policy (Jan. 2014). *http://aws.amazon.com/s3/#pricing*.

[2] Bandwidth costs for cloud storage. *http://blog.dshr.org/2012/11/bandwidth-costs-for-cloud-storage.html*.

[3] Bandwidth limitations are a concern with cloud backup. *http://searchdatabackup.techtarget.com/video/Bandwidth-limitations-are-a-concern-with-cloud-backup*.

[4] Cisco Global Cloud Index: Forecast and Methodology, 2012-2017. Trend 3: Remote Data Services and Storage Access Services Growth. *http://www.cisco.com/en/US/solutions/collateral/ns341/ns525/ns537/ns705/ns1175/Cloud_Index_White_Paper.html*.

[5] Dirty Secrets: 5 Weaknesses of Cloud Storage Gateways. *http://www.nasuni.com/blog/28-dirty_secrets_5_weaknesses_of_cloud_storage*.

[6] Dropbox Is Now The Data Fabric Tying Together Devices For 100M Registered Users Who Save 1B Files A Day. *http://techcrunch.com/2012/11/13/dropbox-100-million*.

[7] Google Drive Now Has 10 Million Users: Available on iOS and Chrome OS. *http://techcrunch.com/2012/06/28/google-drive-now-has-10-million-users-available-on-ios-and-chrome-os-offline-editing-in-docs*.

[8] Hidden Costs of Cloud Storage. *http://www.onlinefilestorage.com/hidden-costs-of-cloud-storage-1756*.

[9] How fast is SkyDrive (OneDrive) growing? *http://www.liveside.net/2012/10/27/how-fast-is-skydrive-growing*.

[10] iCloud Drive features preview. *http://www.apple.com/ios/ios8/icloud-drive*.

[11] JavaScript Tutorials, Refernces, and Documentation. *http://developer.mozilla.org/en-US/docs/Web/javascript*.

[12] Large-scale Dropbox trace collected at the ISP level. *http://traces.simpleweb.org/wiki/Dropbox_Traces*.

[13] OpenStack Installation Guide for Ubuntu 12.04/14.04 (LTS). *http://docs.openstack.org/icehouse/install-guide/install/apt/content*.

[14] PUE (Power Usage Effectiveness). *http://en.wikipedia.org/wiki/Power_usage_effectiveness.*

[15] A question about the default chunk size of rsync. *http://lists.samba.org/archive/rsync/2001-November/000595.html.*

[16] rsync web site. *http://www.samba.org/rsync.*

[17] Why RESTful Design for Cloud is Best. *http://www.redhat.com/promo/summit/2010/presentations/cloud/fri/galder-945-why-RESTful/RestfulDesignJBWRH2010.pdf.*

[18] Wireshark network protocol analyzer. *http://www.wireshark.org.*

[19] B. Aggarwal, A. Akella, A. Anand, A. Balachandran, P. Chitnis, C. Muthukrishnan, R. Ramjee, and G. Varghese. EndRE: An End-system Redundancy Elimination Service for Enterprises. In *Proc. of NSDI*, pages 419–432. USENIX, 2010.

[20] A. Bergen, Y. Coady, and R. McGeer. Client Bandwidth: The Forgotten Metric of Online Storage Providers. In *Proc. of PacRim*, pages 543–548. IEEE, 2011.

[21] A. Bessani, M. Correia, B. Quaresma, F. André, and P. Sousa. DepSky: Dependable and Secure Storage in a Cloud-of-clouds. *ACM Transactions on Storage (TOS)*, 9(4):12, 2013.

[22] B. Calder, J. Wang, A. Ogus, N. Nilakantan, A. Skjolsvold, S. McKelvie, Y. Xu, et al. Windows Azure Storage: A Highly Available Cloud Storage Service with Strong Consistency. In *Proc. of SOSP*, pages 143–157. ACM, 2011.

[23] Y. Chen, K. Srinivasan, G. Goodson, and R. Katz. Design Implications for Enterprise Storage Systems via Multi-dimensional Trace Analysis. In *Proc. of SOSP*, pages 43–56. ACM, 2011.

[24] I. Drago, E. Bocchi, M. Mellia, H. Slatman, and A. Pras. Benchmarking Personal Cloud Storage. In *Proc. of IMC*, pages 205–212. ACM, 2013.

[25] I. Drago, M. Mellia, M.M Munafò, A. Sperotto, R. Sadre, and A. Pras. Inside Dropbox: Understanding Personal Cloud Storage Services. In *Proc. of IMC*, pages 481–494. ACM, 2012.

[26] R.T. Fielding. *Architectural Styles and the Design of Network-based Software Architectures*. PhD thesis, University of California, Irvine, 2000.

[27] S. Halevi, D. Harnik, B. Pinkas, and A. Shulman-Peleg. Proofs of Ownership in Remote Storage Systems. In *Proc. of CCS*, pages 491–500. ACM, 2011.

[28] D. Harnik, R. Kat, D. Sotnikov, A. Traeger, and O. Margalit. To Zip or Not to Zip: Effective Resource Usage for Real-Time Compression. In *Proc. of FAST*, pages 229–242. USENIX, 2013.

[29] D. Harnik, B. Pinkas, and A. Shulman-Peleg. Side Channels in Cloud Services: Deduplication in Cloud Storage. *IEEE Security & Privacy*, 8(6):40–47, 2010.

[30] W. Hu, T. Yang, and J.N. Matthews. The Good, the Bad and the Ugly of Consumer Cloud Storage. *ACM SIGOPS Operating Systems Review*, 44(3):110–115, 2010.

[31] Y. Huang, Z. Li, G. Liu, and Y. Dai. Cloud Download: Using Cloud Utilities to Achieve High-quality Content Distribution for Unpopular Videos. In *Proc. of ACM Multimedia*, pages 213–222. ACM, 2011.

[32] D. Kholia and P. Wegrzyn. Looking Inside the (Drop) box. In *Proc. of the 7th USENIX Workshop on Offensive Technologies (WOOT)*, 2013.

[33] A. Li, X. Yang, S. Kandula, and M. Zhang. CloudCmp: Comparing Public Cloud Providers. In *Proc. of IMC*, pages 1–14. ACM, 2010.

[34] Z. Li, Y. Huang, G. Liu, F. Wang, Z.-L. Zhang, and Y. Dai. Cloud Transcoder: Bridging the Format and Resolution Gap between Internet Videos and Mobile Devices. In *Proc. of NOSSDAV*, pages 33–38. ACM, 2012.

[35] Z. Li and J. Li. Deficiency of Scientific Research behind the Price War of Cloud Storage Services. *Communications of China Computer Federation (CCCF)*, 10(8):36–41, 2014.

[36] Z. Li, C. Wilson, Z. Jiang, Y. Liu, B.Y. Zhao, C. Jin, Z.-L. Zhang, and Y. Dai. Efficient Batched Synchronization in Dropbox-like Cloud Storage Services. In *Proc. of Middleware*, pages 307–327. Springer, 2013.

[37] Z. Li, Z.-L. Zhang, and Y. Dai. Coarse-grained Cloud Synchronization Mechanism Design May Lead to Severe Traffic Overuse. *Elsevier Journal of Tsinghua Science and Technology*, 18(3):286–297, 2013.

[38] P. Mahajan, S. Setty, S. Lee, A. Clement, L. Alvisi, M. Dahlin, and M. Walfish. Depot: Cloud Storage with Minimal Trust. *ACM Transactions on Computer Systems (TOCS)*, 29(4):12, 2011.

[39] D.T. Meyer and W.J. Bolosky. A Study of Practical Deduplication. *ACM Transactions on Storage (TOS)*, 7(4):14, 2012.

[40] M. Mulazzani, S. Schrittwieser, M. Leithner, M. Huber, and E. Weippl. Dark Clouds on the Horizon: Using Cloud Storage as Attack Vector and Online Slack Space. In *Proc. of USENIX Security*, 2011.

[41] V.S. Prakash, X. Zhao, Y. Wen, and W. Shi. Back to the Future: Using Magnetic Tapes in Cloud Based Storage Infrastructures. In *Proc. of Middleware*, pages 328–347. Springer, 2013.

[42] P. Shilane, M. Huang, G. Wallace, and W. Hsu. WAN-optimized Replication of Backup Datasets using Stream-informed Delta Compression. *ACM Transactions on Storage (TOS)*, 8(4):13, 2012.

[43] M. Vrable, S. Savage, and G.M. Voelker. Cumulus: Filesystem Backup to the Cloud. *ACM Transactions on Storage (TOS)*, 5(4):14, 2009.

[44] M. Vrable, S. Savage, and G.M. Voelker. Bluesky: A Cloud-backed File System for the Enterprise. In *Proc. of FAST*. USENIX, 2012.

[45] G. Wallace, F. Douglis, H. Qian, P. Shilane, S. Smaldone, M. Chamness, and W. Hsu. Characteristics of Backup Workloads in Production Systems. In *Proc. of FAST*. USENIX, 2012.

[46] E. Zhai, R. Chen, D.I. Wolinsky, and B. Ford. An Untold Story of Redundant Clouds: Making Your Service Deployment Truly Reliable. In *Proc. of HotDep*. ACM, 2013.

[47] E. Zhai, R. Chen, D.I. Wolinsky, and B. Ford. Heading Off Correlated Failures through Independence-as-a-Service. In *Proc. of OSDI*. USENIX, 2014.

[48] Y. Zhang, C. Dragga, A. Arpaci-Dusseau, and R. Arpaci-Dusseau. ViewBox: Integrating Local File Systems with Cloud Storage Services. In *Proc. of FAST*, pages 119–132. USENIX, 2014.

Paying for Likes?
Understanding Facebook Like Fraud Using Honeypots

Emiliano De Cristofaro
University Colege London
London, U.K.

Arik Friedman
NICTA
Sydney, Australia

Guillaume Jourjon
NICTA
Sydney, Australia

Mohamed Ali Kaafar
NICTA & INRIA
Sydney, Australia

M. Zubair Shafiq
The University of Iowa
Iowa City, IA, U.S.A.

ABSTRACT

Facebook pages offer an easy way to reach out to a very large audience as they can easily be promoted using Facebook's advertising platform. Recently, the number of likes of a Facebook page has become a measure of its popularity and profitability, and an underground market of services boosting page likes, aka like farms, has emerged. Some reports have suggested that like farms use a network of profiles that also like other pages to elude fraud protection algorithms, however, to the best of our knowledge, there has been no systematic analysis of Facebook pages' promotion methods.

This paper presents a comparative measurement study of page likes garnered via Facebook ads and by a few like farms. We deploy a set of honeypot pages, promote them using both methods, and analyze garnered likes based on likers' demographic, temporal, and social characteristics. We highlight a few interesting findings, including that some farms seem to be operated by bots and do not really try to hide the nature of their operations, while others follow a stealthier approach, mimicking regular users' behavior.

Categories and Subject Descriptors

C.2.4 [**Computer-Communication Network**]: Distributed Systems—*Distributed applications*

Keywords

Online Social Networks; Malicious Activities; Honeypots

1. INTRODUCTION

Online Social Networks (OSNs) such as Facebook have become one of the primary outlets for businesses and enterprises to advertise and communicate with their customers. Just in 2013, Facebook's net ad revenue amounted to $6.7B, i.e., 5.64% of the global market [12]. One feature offered by Facebook is the concept of *pages*, which business can create, e.g., to display information about products and events. Users can *like* them to receive updates, post messages, or connect with other customers. Page likes also become part of the user's profile. The number of likes for a given page is often considered a measure of its popularity: ChompOn estimates the expected revenue from each like to be $8, while other estimates range between $3.60, $136.38, and $214.81 [6].

To reach out to their potential audience, businesses can *promote* their Facebook page using targeted ads, via *page like* ads. Based on the advertiser's preferences, ads can be targeted to users from a specific age or location group, or to users who have certain interests. As per Facebook's guidelines, this is the only legitimate way to collect page likes [13]. However, a growing underground industry has emerged that provides paid services, aka *like farms*, to inflate the number of Facebook page likes. Some recent press articles [3, 7, 14, 18] have started to look into Facebook page promotion methods and speculated that like farms use fake profiles trying to imitate real users' behavior. As these likes – which we call *fake likes* – do not correspond to a genuine interest in the advertised page, they are less valuable to businesses in terms of potential customer engagement and revenue. Other reports [19, 20, 22] have suggested that promoting pages using legitimate Facebook ad campaigns may also garner significant amounts of fake likes. One possible explanation is that fake profiles attempt to diversify their liking activities to avoid Facebook's fraud detection algorithms. To do so, they need to click on ads and like pages other than those they are paid for. However, to the best of our knowledge, there has been no systematic analysis of Facebook pages' promotion methods, even though the understanding of fake likes is arguably crucial to improve algorithms for fraud detection/mitigation in OSNs.

In this paper, we start addressing this gap with a comparative measurement study of Facebook likes garnered by means of legitimate Facebook page like ads and by using a few underground like farms. We set up thirteen Facebook *honeypot* pages and promote them using both methods. We monitor the likes garnered by these pages, collect information about the likers (e.g., gender, age, location, friend list, etc.), and perform a comparative analysis based on demographic, temporal, and social characteristics of the likers.

Our study highlights a few interesting findings. When targeting Facebook users worldwide, we obtain likes from only a few countries. Likers' profiles also seem to be skewed toward male profiles. We found evidence that different like farms (with different pricing schemes) garner likes from a similar set of users and may be managed by the same operator. We also identified two main *modi operandi* of the like farms. Our results suggest that a first set of farms is operated by bots and do not really try to hide the nature of their operations, delivering likes in bursts and forming disconnected social sub-graphs. Other farms follow a stealthier approach, mimicking regular users' behavior, and rely on a large and well-connected network structure to gradually deliver likes while

IMC'14, November 5–7, 2014, Vancouver, BC, Canada.

http://dx.doi.org/10.1145/2663716.2663729.

keeping a small count of likes per user. The first strategy reflects a "quick and dirty" approach where likes from disposable fake users (as also indicated by the number of terminated accounts) are delivered rapidly, as opposed to the second one, which exhibits a stealthier approach that leverages the underlying social graph, where real users (or well-masked fake users) trickle their likes.

We did not find direct evidence that the likes garnered by the Facebook campaigns also originate from like farms. However, when comparing profiles attracted by the Facebook campaigns to those associated with like farms, we did identify a noticeable overlap in the pages they liked overall. We also observed that likers from Facebook campaigns liked a lot more pages than typical Facebook users, and much closer to that observed for like farm users.

2. RELATED WORK

Prior work has studied and detected sybil and/or fake OSN accounts by relying on tightly-knit community structures [5, 10, 28, 29, 30]. Findings revealed by our work also highlight several characteristics about the social structure and activity of fake profiles attracted by the honeypot pages, e.g., their interconnected nature or the activity bursts. In fact, our analysis does not only confirm a few insights used by sybil detection algorithms but also reveals new patterns that could complement them. A few *passive* measurement studies have also focused on characterizing fake user accounts and their activity. Nazir *et al.* [21] studied phantom profiles in Facebook gaming applications, while Thomas *et al.* [25] analyzed over 1.1 million accounts suspended by Twitter. Gao *et al.* [15] studied spam campaigns on Facebook originating from approximately 57,000 user accounts. Yang *et al.* [27] performed an empirical analysis of social relationships between spam accounts on Twitter, and Dave *et al.* [11] proposed a methodology to measure and fingerprint click-spam in ad networks. Our work differs from these studies as they all conduct passive measurements, whereas we rely on the deployment of several honeypot pages and (paid) campaigns to actively engage with fake profiles.

Stringhini *et al.* [23] and Lee *et al.* [17] created honeypot profiles in Facebook, MySpace, and Twitter to detect spammers. Their work differs from ours in that (1) their honeypot profiles were designed to look legitimate, while our honeypot pages explicitly indicated they were not "real" (to deflect real profiles), and (2) our honeypot pages *actively* attracted fake profiles by means of paid campaigns, as opposed to passive honeypot profiles. Also, Thomas *et al.* [26] analyzed trafficking of fake accounts in Twitter. They bought fake profiles from 27 merchants and developed a classifier to detect these fake accounts. In a similar study, Stringhini *et al.* [24] analyzed the market of *Twitter followers*, which, akin to Facebook like farms, provide Twitter followers for sale. Note that Twitter follower markets differ from Facebook like farms as Twitter entails a *follower-followee* relationship among users, while Facebook friendships imply a bidirectional relationships. Also, there is no equivalent of liking a Facebook page in the Twitter ecosystem.

Beutel *et al.* [4] proposed a technique to detect fake likes based on identifying groups of users who liked a set of pages within a given time period. However, their technique does not rely on ground truth data, so it is unclear whether or not the detection mechanism blocks all fake likes, or actually only those exhibiting a certain pattern. By contrast, we focus on actively measuring like fraud activities by means of honeypots, i.e., attracting fake likes to empty pages, through payment. We elicit and study ground truth data, and highlight how some like farms actually try to emulate behavior of regular users and thereby stay below the detection radar. Nonetheless, our work serves as the starting point for improved fake like detection and can complement techniques from [4].

Finally, a few investigative press reports [3, 7, 14, 20] have also looked into Facebook page ads and underground like farms, however, without any systematic analysis of Facebook pages' promotion methods.

3. METHODOLOGY

This section presents the methodology used to deploy and monitor Facebook honeypot pages and to promote them using both Facebook page like ads and like farms.

Honeypot Pages. We created 13 Facebook pages called "Virtual Electricity" and intentionally kept them empty (i.e., no posts or pictures). Their description included: *"This is not a real page, so please do not like it."* 5 pages were promoted using legitimate Facebook (FB) ad campaigns targeting users, respectively, in USA, France, India, Egypt, and worldwide. The remaining 8 pages were promoted using 4 popular like farms BoostLikes.com (BL), SocialFormula.com (SF), AuthenticLikes.com (AL), and MammothSocials.com (MS), targeting worldwide or USA users.

In Table 1, we provide details of the honeypot pages, along with the corresponding ad campaigns. All campaigns were launched on March 12, 2014, using a different administrator account (owner) for each page. Each Facebook campaign was budgeted at a maximum of \$6/day to a total of \$90 for 15 days. The price for buying likes varied across likes farms: BoostLikes charged the highest price for "100% real likes" (\$70 and \$190 for 1000 likes in 15 days from, respectively, worldwide and USA). Other like farms also claimed to deliver likes from "genuine", "real", and "active" profiles, but promised to deliver them in fewer days. Overall, the price of 1000 likes varied between \$14.99–\$70 for worldwide users and \$59.95–\$190 for USA users.

Data Collection. We monitored the "liking" activity on the honeypot pages by crawling them, using Selenium web driver [2], every 2 hours to check for new likes. At the end of the campaigns, we reduced the monitoring frequency to once a day, and stopped monitoring when a page did not receive a like for more than a week. We used Facebook's reports tool for page administrators, which provides a variety of aggregated statistics about attributes and profiles of page likers. Facebook also provides these statistics for the global Facebook population. Since a majority of Facebook users do not set the visibility of their age and location to public [8], we used these reports to collect statistics about likers' gender, age, country, home and current town.[1] Later, in Section 4, we will use these statistics to compare distributions of our honeypot pages' likers to that of the overall Facebook population. We also crawled public information from the likers' profiles, obtaining the lists of liked pages as well as friend lists, which are not provided in the reports. Overall, we identified more than 6.3 millions total likes by users who liked our honeypot pages and more than 1 million friendship relations.

We acknowledge that our limited budget allows us to only monitor 13 honeypots for a few weeks. Note, however, that our work is a first-of-a-kind, exploratory study of like fraud practices – as it will become clear in the rest of the paper, our methodology actually allows us to derive several interest findings (which could be further explored, in future work, with larger/more diverse campaigns).

Campaign Summary. In Table 1, we report the total number of likes garnered by each campaign, along with the number of days we monitored the honeypot pages. Note that the BL-ALL and MS-ALL campaigns remained inactive, i.e., they did not result in any

[1]As stated in [1], Facebook uses public *and* private attributes to provide aggregated statistics about users who clicked on page like ads, e.g., current location is determined based on IP address.

Campaign ID	Provider	Description	Location	Budget	Duration	Monitoring	#Likes	#Terminated
FB-USA	Facebook.com	Page like ads	USA	$6/day	15 days	22 days	32	0
FB-FRA	Facebook.com	Page like ads	France	$6/day	15 days	22 days	44	0
FB-IND	Facebook.com	Page like ads	India	$6/day	15 days	22 days	518	2
FB-EGY	Facebook.com	Page like ads	Egypt	$6/day	15 days	22 days	691	6
FB-ALL	Facebook.com	Page like ads	Worldwide	$6/day	15 days	22 days	484	3
BL-ALL	BoostLikes.com	1000 likes	Worldwide	$70.00	15 days	-	-	-
BL-USA	BoostLikes.com	1000 likes	USA only	$190.00	15 days	22 days	621	1
SF-ALL	SocialFormula.com	1000 likes	Worldwide	$14.99	3 days	10 days	984	11
SF-USA	SocialFormula.com	1000 likes	USA	$69.99	3 days	10 days	738	9
AL-ALL	AuthenticLikes.com	1000 likes	Worldwide	$49.95	3-5 days	12 days	755	8
AL-USA	AuthenticLikes.com	1000 likes	USA	$59.95	3-5 days	22 days	1038	36
MS-ALL	MammothSocials.com	1000 likes	Worldwide	$20.00	-	-	-	-
MS-USA	MammothSocials.com	1000 likes	USA only	$95.00	-	12 days	317	9

Table 1: Facebook and like farm campaigns used to promote our Facebook honeypot pages.

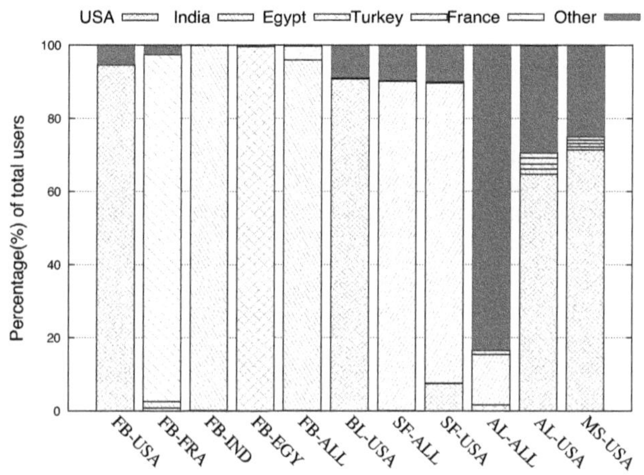

Figure 1: Geolocation of the likers (per campaign).

Campaign ID	Gender % F/M	Age Distribution (%) 13-17	18-24	25-34	35-44	45-54	55+	KL
FB-USA	54/46	54.0	27.0	6.8	6.8	1.4	4.1	0.45
FB-FR	46/54	60.8	20.8	8.7	2.6	5.2	1.7	0.54
FB-IND	**7/93**	52.7	43.5	2.3	0.7	0.5	0.3	**1.12**
FB-EGY	**18/82**	54.6	34.4	6.4	2.9	0.8	0.8	**0.64**
FB-ALL	**6/94**	51.3	44.4	2.1	1.1	0.5	0.6	**1.04**
BL-USA	53/47	34.2	54.5	8.8	1.5	0.7	0.5	0.60
SF-ALL	37/63	19.8	33.3	21.0	15.2	7.2	2.8	0.04
SF-USA	37/63	22.3	34.6	22.9	11.6	5.4	2.9	0.04
AL-ALL	42/58	15.8	52.8	13.4	9.7	5.2	3.0	0.12
AL-USA	31/68	7.2	41.0	35.0	10.0	3.5	2.8	0.09
MS-USA	26/74	8.6	46.9	34.5	6.4	1.9	1.4	0.17
Facebook	46/54	14.9	32.3	26.6	13.2	7.2	5.9	–

Table 2: Gender and age statistics of likers.

likes even though we were charged in advance. We tried to reach the like farm admins several times but received no response. Overall, we collected a total of 6,292 likes (4,523 from like farms and 1,769 from Facebook ads). The largest number of likes were garnered by AL-USA, the lowest (excluding inactive campaigns) by FB-USA.

Ethics Considerations. Although we only collected openly available data, we did collect (public) profile information from our honeypot pages' likers, e.g., friend lists and page likes. We could not request consent but enforced a few mechanisms to protect user privacy: all data were encrypted at rest and not re-distributed, and no personal information was extracted, i.e., we only analyzed aggregated statistics. We are also aware that paying farms to generate fake likes might raise ethical concerns, however, this was crucial to create the honeypots and observe the like farms' behavior. We believe that the study will help, in turn, to understand and counter these activities. Also note that the amount of money each farm received was small ($190 at most) and that this research was reviewed and approved by the NICTA legal team.

4. ANALYSIS

We now compare the characteristics of the likes garnered by the honeypot pages promoted via legitimate Facebook campaigns and those obtained via like farms.

4.1 Location and Demographics Analysis

Location. For each campaign, we looked at the distribution of likers' countries: as shown in Figure 1, for the first four Facebook campaigns (FB-USA, FB-FRA, FB-IND, FB-EGY), we mainly received likes from the targeted country (87–99.8%), even though FB-USA and FB-FRA generated a number of likes much smaller than any other campaign. When we targeted Facebook users worldwide (FB-ALL), we almost exclusively received likes from India (96%). Looking at the like farms, most likers from SocialFormula were based in Turkey, regardless of whether we requested a US-only campaign. The other three farms delivered likes complying to our requests, e.g., for US-only campaigns, the pages received a majority of likes from US profiles.

Other Demographics. In Table 2, we show the distribution of likers' gender and age, and also compare them to the global Facebook network (last row). The last column reports the KL-divergence between the age distribution of the campaign users and that of the entire Facebook population, highlighting large divergence for FB-IND, FB-EGY, and FB-ALL, which are biased toward younger users. These three campaigns also appear to be skewed toward male profiles. In contrast, the demographics of likers from SocialFormula and, to a lesser extent, AuhtenticLikes and MammothSocials, are much more similar to those of the entire network, even though male users are still over-represented.

4.2 Temporal Analysis

We also analyzed temporal patterns observed for each of the campaigns. In Figure 2, we plot the cumulative number of likes observed on each honeypot page over our observation period (15 days). We observe from Figure 2(b) that all the like farm campaigns, except BoostLikes, exhibit a very similar trend with a few bursts of a large number of likes. Specifically, for the SocialFormula, AuthenticLikes, and MammothSocials campaigns, likes were garnered within a short period of time of two hours. With Authen-

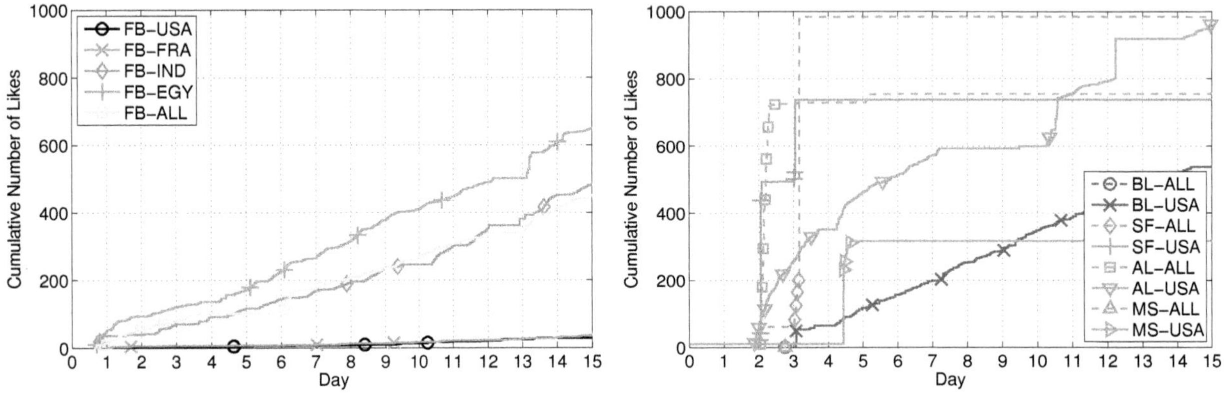

(a) Facebook Campaigns

(b) Like Farms

Figure 2: Time series of cumulative number of likes for Facebook and like farms campaigns.

ticLikes, we observed likes from more than 700 profiles within the first 4 hours of the second day of data collection. Interestingly, no more likes were observed later on. On the contrary, the BoostLikes campaign targeting US users shows a different temporal behavior: the trend is actually comparable to that observed in the Facebook Ads campaigns (see Figure 2(a)). The number of likes steadily increases during the observation period and no abrupt changes are observed.

This suggests that two different strategies may be adopted by like farms. On the one hand, the abrupt increase in the cumulative number of likes happening during a short period of time might likely be due to automated scripts operating a set of fake profiles. These profiles are instrumented to satisfy the number of likes as per the customer's request. On the other hand, BoostLikes's strategy, which resembles the temporal evolution in Facebook campaigns, seems to rely on the underlying social graph, possibly constituted by fake profiles operated by humans. Results presented in the next section corroborate the existence of these two strategies.

4.3 Social Graph Analysis

Next, we evaluated the social graph induced by the likers' profiles. To this end, we associated each user with one of the like farm services based on the page they liked. Note that a few users liked pages in multiple campaigns, as we will discuss in Section 4.4. A significant fraction of users actually liked pages corresponding to both the AuthenticLikes and the MammothSocials campaigns (see Figure 4): we put these users into a separate group, labelled as ALMS. Table 3 summarizes the number of likers associated with each service, as well as additional details about their friendship networks. Note that the number of likers reported for each campaign in Table 3 is different from the number of campaign likes (Table 1), since some users liked more than one page.

Many likers kept their friend lists private: this occurred for almost 80% of likers in the Facebook campaigns, about 75% in the BoostLikes campaign, and much less frequently for the other like farm campaigns (~40–60%). The number and percentage of users with public friend lists are reported in Table 3. The fourth column reports the average number of friends ($\pm$ the standard deviation) for profiles with visible friend lists, and the fifth column reports the median. Some friendship relations may be hidden, e.g., if a friend chose to be invisible in friend lists, thus, these numbers only represent a *lower bound*. The average number of friends of users associated with the BoostLikes campaign (and to a smaller extent, the AuthenticLikes campaign) was much higher than the average number of friends observed elsewhere.

To evaluate the social ties between likers, we looked at friendship relations between likers (either originating from the same campaign provider or not), ignoring friendship relations with Facebook users who did not like any of our pages. Table 3 (sixth column) reports, for each provider, the overall number of friendship relationships between likers that involved users associated with the provider.

In Figure 3(a), we plot the social graph induced by such friendship relations (likers who did not have friendship relations with any other likers were excluded from the graph). Based on the resulting social structure, we suggest that:

1. Dense relations between likers from BoostLikes point to an interconnected network of real users, or fake users who mimic complex ties to pose as real users;
2. The pairs (and occasionally triplets) that characterize SocialFormula likers might indicate a different strategy of constructing fake networks, mitigating the risk that identification of a user as fake would consequently bring down the whole connected network of fake users; and
3. The friendship relations between AuthenticLikes and MammothSocials likers might indicate that the same operator manages both services.

We also considered indirect links between likers, through mutual friends. Table 3 reports the overall number of 2-hop relationships between likers from the associated provider. Figure 3(b) plots the relations between likers who either have a direct relation or a mutual friend, clearly pointing to the presence of relations between likers from the same provider. These tight connections, along with the number of their friends, suggest that we only see a small part of these networks. (In fact, like farms sell packages of as many as 50k likes.) For SocialFormula, AuthenticLikes, and MammothSocials, we also observe many isolated pairs and triplets of likers who are not connected. One possible explanation is that farm users create fake Facebook accounts and keep them separate from their personal accounts and friends. In contrast, the BoostLikes network is well-connected.

4.4 Page Like Analysis

We then looked at the *other* pages liked by profiles attracted to our honeypot pages. In Figure 4(a) and 4(b), respectively, we plot

Provider	# Likers	# Likers with Public Friend Lists	Avg (± Std) #Friends	Median #Friends	# Friendships Between Likers	# 2-Hop Friendship Relations Between Likers
Facebook.com	1448	261 (18.0%)	315 ± 454	198	6	169
BoostLikes.com	621	161 (25.9%)	1171 ± 1096	850	540	2987
SocialFormula.com	1644	954 (58.0%)	246 ± 330	155	50	1132
AuthenticLikes.com	1597	680 (42.6%)	719 ± 973	343	64	1174
MammothSocials.com	121	62 (51.2%)	250 ± 585	68	4	129
ALMS	213	101 (47.4%)	426 ± 961	46	27	229

Table 3: Likers and friendships between likers.

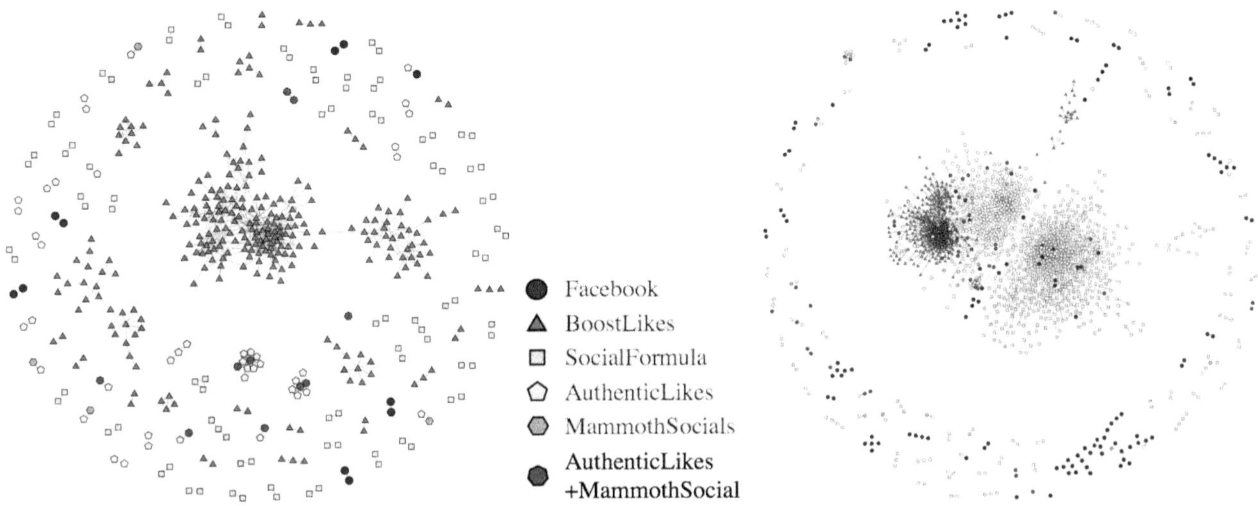

(a) Direct friendship relations

(b) 2-hop friendship relations

Figure 3: Friendship relations between likers of different campaigns.

the distribution of the number of page likes for Facebook ads' and like farm campaigns' users. To draw a baseline comparison, we also collected page like counts from a random set of 2000 Facebook users, extracted from an unbiased sample of Facebook user population. The original sample was crawled for another project [9], obtained by randomly sampling Facebook public directory which lists all the IDs of searchable profiles.

We observed a large variance in the number of pages liked, ranging from 1 to 10,000. The median page like count ranged between 600 and 1000 for users from the Facebook campaigns and between 1200 and 1800 for those from like farm campaigns, with the exception of the BL-USA campaign (median was 63). In contrast, the median page like count for our baseline Facebook user sample was 34. The page like counts of our baseline sample mirrored numbers reported in prior work, e.g., according to [16], the average number of pages liked by Facebook users amounts to roughly 40. In other words, our honeypot pages attracted users that tend to like significantly more pages than regular Facebook users. Since our honeypot pages both for Facebook and like farm campaigns explicitly indicated they were not "real", we argue that a vast majority of the garnered likes are fake. We argue that these users like a large number of pages because they are probably reused for multiple "jobs" and also like "normal" pages to mimic real users.[2]

To confirm our hypothesis, for each pair of campaigns, we plot their Jaccard similarity. Specifically, let S_k denote the set of pages liked by a user k: the Jaccard similarity between the set of likes by likers of two campaigns A and B, which we plot in Figure 5(a), is defined as $|A \cap B|/|A \cup B|$, where $A = \bigcup_{\forall i \in A} S_i$ and $B = \bigcup_{\forall j \in B} S_j$. We also plot, in Figure 5(b), the similarity between $A' = \bigcup_{\forall i \in A} i$ and $B' = \bigcup_{\forall j \in B} j$, i.e., the similarity between the set of likers of the different campaigns.

Note from Figure 5 that FB-IND, FB-EGY, and FB-ALL have relatively large (Jaccard) similarity with each other. In addition, the SF-USA and SF-ALL pair and the AL-USA and MS-USA pair also have relatively large Jaccard similarity. These findings suggest that the same fake profiles are used in multiple campaigns by a like farm (e.g., SF-ALL and SF-USA). Moreover, some fake profiles seem to be shared by different like farms (e.g., AL-USA and MS-USA), suggesting that they are run by the same operator.

5. CONCLUDING REMARKS

This paper presented a comparative measurement study of Facebook page promotion methods, aiming to shed light on like farms' activities. We identified two main *modi operandi*: (1) some farms, like SocialFormula and AuthenticLikes, seem to be operated by bots and do not really try to hide the nature of their operations, as demonstrated by large bursts of likes and the limited number of friends per profile; (2) other farms, like BoostLikes, follow a much stealthier approach, aiming to mimic regular users' behavior, and rely on their large and well-connected network structure to disseminate the target likes while keeping a small count of likes per user. For the latter, we also observed a high number of friends per profile and a "reasonable" number of likes.

A month after the campaigns, we checked whether or not likers' accounts were still active: as shown in Table 1, only one account associated with BoostLikes was terminated, as opposed to 9,

[2]Facebook does not impose any limit on the maximum number of page likes per user.

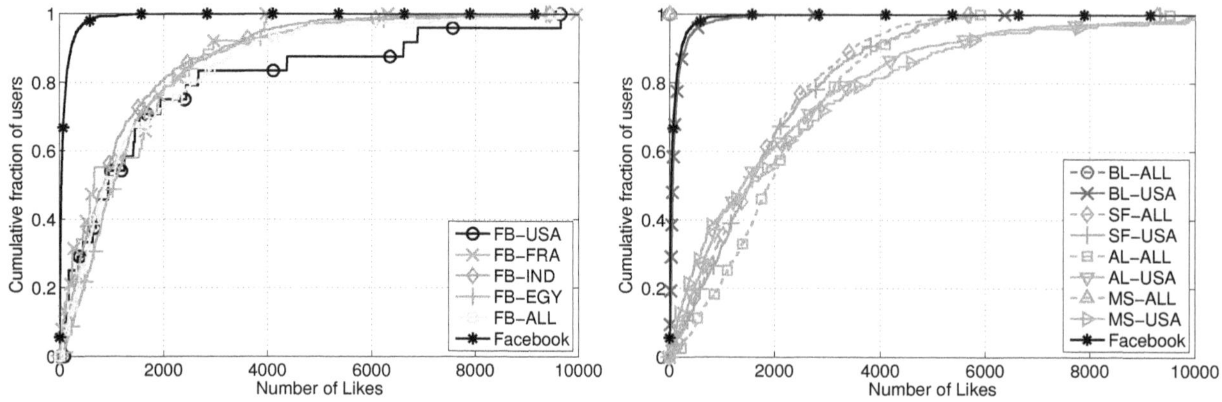

(a) Facebook Campaigns (b) Like Farms

Figure 4: Distribution of the number of likes by users in Facebook and like farm campaigns.

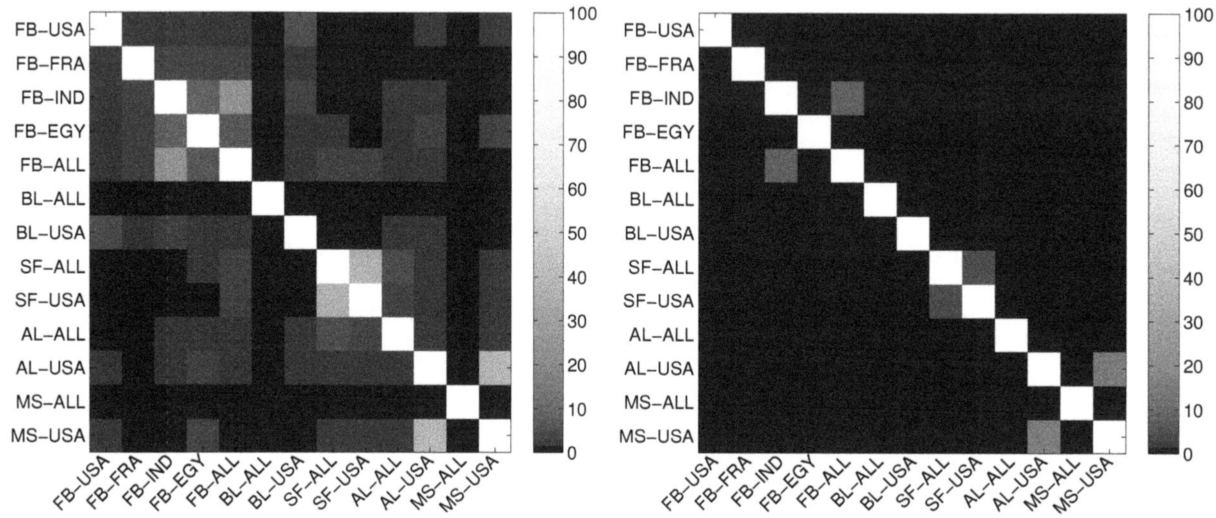

(a) Page Like (b) User

Figure 5: Jaccard index similarity ($\times 100$) matrices of page likes and likers across different campaigns

20, and 44 for the other like farms. 11 accounts from the regular Facebook campaigns were also terminated. Although occurring not so frequently, the accounts' termination might be indicative of the disposable nature of fake accounts on most like farms, where "bot-like" patterns are actually easy to detect. It also mirrors the challenge Facebook is confronted by, with like farms such as BoostLikes that exhibit patterns closely resembling real users' behavior, thus making fake like detection quite difficult.

We stress that our findings do not necessarily imply that advertising on Facebook is ineffective, since our campaigns were specifically designed to avert real users. However, our work provides strong evidence that likers attracted on our honeypot pages, even when using legitimate Facebook campaigns, are significantly different from typical Facebook users, which confirms the concerns about the genuineness of these likes. We also show that most fake likes exhibit some peculiar characteristics – including demographics, likes, temporal and social graph patterns – that can and should be exploited by like fraud detection algorithms.

Besides the design of detection techniques, items for future work include larger and more diverse honeypots measurements as well as longer observation of removed likes. Also, as suggested in prior work [4], fake likes might be generated via fake accounts, malware, malicious browser extensions, credential stealing, and social engineering, thus prompting the need for further investigation of fake likes' origin.

Acknowledgments. We would like to thank the reviewers and our shepherd for their feedback and useful comments. We are also grateful to Gianluca Stringhini for reviewing a draft of the paper.

6. REFERENCES

[1] Facebook Ads Optimization. http://weigend.com/files/teaching/stanford/2009/homeworks/ad_optimization_final.pdf.

[2] Selenium WebDriver: Browser Automation. http://docs.seleniumhq.org/projects/webdriver/.

[3] C. Arthur. How low-paid workers at 'click farms' create appearance of online popularity. http://www.theguardian.com/technology/2013/aug/02/click-farms-appearance-online-popularity, August 2013.

[4] A. Beutel, W. Xu, V. Guruswami, C. Palow, and C. Faloutsos. CopyCatch: Stopping Group Attacks by Spotting Lockstep Behavior in Social Networks. In *WWW*, 2013.

[5] Q. Cao, M. Sirivianos, X. Yang, and T. Pregueiro. Aiding the Detection of Fake Accounts in Large Scale Social Online Services. In *NSDI*, 2012.

[6] B. Carter. *The Like Economy: How Businesses Make Money with Facebook*. Que Publishing, 2013.

[7] R. Cellan-Jones. Who 'likes' my Virtual Bagels? http://www.bbc.co.uk/news/technology-18819338, July 2012.

[8] A. Chaabane, G. Acs, and M.-A. Kaafar. You Are What You Like! Information Leakage Through Users' Interests. In *NDSS*, 2012.

[9] T. Chen, A. Chaabane, P. U. Tournoux, M.-A. Kaafar, and R. Boreli. How Much is too Much? Leveraging Ads Audience Estimation to Evaluate Public Profile Uniqueness. In *PETS*, 2013.

[10] G. Danezis and P. Mittal. SybilInfer: Detecting Sybil Nodes using Social Networks. In *NDSS*, 2009.

[11] V. Dave, S. Guha, and Y. Zhang. Measuring and Fingerprinting Click-Spam in Ad Networks. In *SIGCOMM*, 2012.

[12] eMarketer. Mobile Growth Pushes Facebook to Become No. 2 US Digital Ad Seller. http://preview.tinyurl.com/mq6vu3u, December 2013.

[13] Facebook. Can I buy likes for my Facebook Page? http://www.facebook.com/help/281084665319172.

[14] J. Filan. Facebook Ads: What Are You Really Paying For? http://www.searchenginejournal.com/facebook-ads-what-are-you-really-paying-for/46194/, July 2012.

[15] H. Gao, J. Hu, C. Wilson, Z. Li, Y. Chen, and B. Y. Zhao. Detecting and Characterizing Social Spam Campaigns. In *IMC*, 2010.

[16] J. Lafferty. How Many Pages Does The Average Facebook User Like? http://allfacebook.com/how-many-pages-does-the-average-facebook-user-like_b115098, 2013.

[17] K. Lee, J. Caverlee, and S. Webb. Uncovering social spammers: Social honeypots + machine learning. In *SIGIR*, 2010.

[18] M. Mendoza. How Facebook Likes Get Bought And Sold. http://www.huffingtonpost.com/2014/01/05/buy-facebook-likes_n_4544800.html, 2014.

[19] R. Metzger. Facebook: I Want My Friends Back. http://dangerousminds.net/comments/facebook_i_want_my_friends_back, October 2012.

[20] D. Muller. Facebook Fraud. https://www.youtube.com/watch?v=oVfHeWTKjag, February 2014.

[21] A. Nazir, S. Raza, C.-N. Chuah, and B. Schipper. Ghostbusting Facebook: Detecting and Characterizing Phantom Profiles in Online Social Gaming Applications. In *WOSN*, 2010.

[22] J. Schneider. Likes or lies? How perfectly honest businesses can be overrun by Facebook spammers. http://thenextweb.com/facebook/2014/01/23/likes-lies-perfectly-honest-businesses-can-overrun-facebook-spammers/, January 2014.

[23] G. Stringhini, C. Kruegel, and G. Vigna. Detecting Spammers on Social Networks. In *ACSAC*, 2010.

[24] G. Stringhini, G. Wang, M. Egeley, C. Kruegel, G. Vigna, H. Zheng, and B. Y. Zhao. Follow the Green: Growth and Dynamics in Twitter Follower Markets. In *ACM IMC*, 2013.

[25] K. Thomas, C. Grier, V. Paxson, and D. Song. Suspended Accounts in Retrospect: An Analysis of Twitter Spam. In *IMC*, 2011.

[26] K. Thomas, D. McCoy, C. Grier, A. Kolcz, and V. Paxson. Trafficking Fraudulent Accounts: The Role of the Underground Market in Twitter Spam and Abuse. In *USENIX Security Symposium*, 2013.

[27] C. Yang, R. Harkreader, J. Zhang, S. Shin, and G. Gu. Analyzing SpammersŠ Social Networks for Fun and Profit. In *WWW*, 2012.

[28] Z. Yang, C. Wilson, X. Wang, T. Gao, B. Y. Zhao, and Y. Dai. Uncovering Social Network Sybils in the Wild. In *IMC*, 2011.

[29] H. Yu, P. B. Gibbons, M. Kaminsky, and F. Xiao. SybilLimit: A Near-Optimal Social Network Defense against Sybil Attacks. In *IEEE Security & Privacy*, 2008.

[30] H. Yu, M. Kaminsky, P. B. Gibbons, and A. Flaxman. SybilGuard: Defending Against Sybil Attacks via Social Networks. In *SIGCOMM*, 2006.

Whispers in the Dark: Analysis of an Anonymous Social Network

Gang Wang, Bolun Wang, Tianyi Wang, Ana Nika, Haitao Zheng, Ben Y. Zhao
Department of Computer Science, UC Santa Barbara
{gangw, bolunwang, tianyi, anika, htzheng, ravenben}@cs.ucsb.edu

ABSTRACT

Social interactions and interpersonal communication has undergone significant changes in recent years. Increasing awareness of privacy issues and events such as the Snowden disclosures have led to the rapid growth of a new generation of anonymous social networks and messaging applications. By removing traditional concepts of strong identities and social links, these services encourage communication between strangers, and allow users to express themselves without fear of bullying or retaliation.

Despite millions of users and billions of monthly page views, there is little empirical analysis of how services like *Whisper* have changed the shape and content of social interactions. In this paper, we present results of the first large-scale empirical study of an anonymous social network, using a complete 3-month trace of the Whisper network covering 24 million whispers written by more than 1 million unique users. We seek to understand how anonymity and the lack of social links affect user behavior. We analyze Whisper from a number of perspectives, including the structure of user interactions in the absence of persistent social links, user engagement and network stickiness over time, and content moderation in a network with minimal user accountability. Finally, we identify and test an attack that exposes Whisper users to detailed location tracking. We have notified Whisper and they have taken steps to address the problem.

Categories and Subject Descriptors

J.4 [**Computer Applications**]: Social and Behavioral Sciences; K.6 [**Management of Computing and Information Systems**]: Security and Protection

General Terms

Measurement; Design; Security

Keywords

Anonymous Social Networks; Graphs; User Engagement; Privacy

IMC'14, November 5–7, 2014, Vancouver, BC, Canada.

http://dx.doi.org/10.1145/2663716.2663728 .

1. INTRODUCTION

Over the last decade, online social networks (OSNs) such as Facebook, LinkedIn, and Twitter have revolutionized the way we communicate. By formalizing our offline social relationships into digital form, these networks have greatly expanded our capacity for social interactions, both in volume and frequency.

Yet the industry landscape is changing. Content posted on Facebook is now commonly used to vet job candidates, support divorce litigation, and terminate employees. In addition, studies have observed a significant growth in privacy-seeking behavior, even despite changes in social networks to encourage broader information sharing [34]. Finally, these trends have only been accelerated by recent revelations following the Snowden disclosures, with numerous headlines reminding Internet users that their online behavior is under constant scrutiny by NSA and other entities.

All these have contributed to the rapid rise of a new wave of privacy-preserving communication and social networking tools. These fast-growing services are pseudo-anonymous messaging mobile applications: *SnapChat* made headlines for ensuring that photos self-destruct in a few seconds; *Whisper* allows users to anonymously post their thoughts to a public audience; and *Secret* allows users to share content with friends without revealing their own identity. This is just the tip of the iceberg, as many similar services are popping up with increasing frequency, *e.g.*, Tinder, Yik-yak, and Wickr.

The anonymous nature of these communication tools has drawn both strong supporters as well as vocal critics. Supporters believe that they provide valuable outlets for whistleblowers avoiding prosecution, and allow users to express themselves without fear of bullying or abuse [40,41]. Critics argue that the lack of accountability in these networks enables and encourages negative discourse, including personal attacks, threats, and rumor spreading [2,4]. Yet all parties agree that these tools have had a dramatic impact on how users interact and communicate.

In this paper, we describe our experience and findings in our effort to study pseudo-anonymous social networks, through a detailed measurement and analysis of *Whisper*. Whisper is a mobile app that allows users to post and reply to public messages on top of an image (*e.g.* Internet memes), all using anonymous user identifiers. Whisper does not associate any personal identifiable information with user IDs, does not archive any user history, and does not support persistent social links between users. These design choices are the polar opposite of those in networks such as Facebook. Yet they have made Whisper one of the most popular new social networks, with more than 3 billion page views per month[1]. As our working dataset, we captured 100% of the Whisper data stream for a 3-month period starting in February 2014, including more than 24

[1]To our knowledge, there is no public data on Whisper user counts.

million whispers and replies written by more than 1 million unique users.

We focus our study on the net impact of anonymity in Whisper, compared to traditional social media with verified identities and social links. Given the large differences between Whisper and current leaders such as Facebook and LinkedIn, our analysis can have significant implications on future infrastructures for social networks, issues of user privacy in messaging networks, and our understanding of social behavior. More concretely, our study also sheds light on the long-term sustainability of anonymous communication networks, given the removal of persistent social links, often considered key to the "stickiness" of today's networks.

Our analysis provides several key findings.

- First, we seek to understand user interactions in the absence of social links. We build interaction graphs and compare them with those of traditional social networks like Twitter and Facebook. Not surprisingly, we find that user communication patterns show high dispersion, low clustering, significantly different from prior systems. Per user, we observe that "friends" are highly ephemeral, and strong, long-term friendships are rare.
- Second, our study of user activity over time shows that a constant stream of new users contribute significantly to content generation, and users bifurcate clearly into short-lived (1-2 days) and long-term users. We demonstrate that users can be accurately classified into either group by applying ML techniques to only 1 week's worth of activity history.
- Third, we study the question of abusive content through analysis of "deleted whispers." We show that most deleted whispers focus on adult content, and Whisper's moderation team usually deletes offensive whispers within a short time after initial posting.
- Finally, we identified a significant attack that exposes current Whisper users to detailed location tracking. We describe the attack in detail and our experiments. Note that we have already notified Whisper of this vulnerability, and they are taking active steps to mitigate the problem.

To the best of our knowledge, our work is the first detailed study on Whisper and pseudo-anonymous messaging systems as a group. Their rapid user growth on mobile platforms suggests they may offer a real challenge to today's established OSNs. We believe our initial work sheds light on these systems as new platforms for interpersonal communication, and provides insight into designs for network infrastructures to support Whisper and similar services.

2. BACKGROUND AND GOALS

In this section, we briefly describe background information about the Whisper network, followed by a high level summary of the goals of our study.

2.1 Background: the Whisper Network

Whisper.sh is a two-year old smartphone app that has become a leader in a new wave of pseudo-anonymous messaging and social communication services, including *Snapchat*, *Secret*, *Tinder*, *Yik-yak*, *Ether* and *Wickr*. While detailed functionality may vary, these services generally provide ways for users to make statements, share secrets or gossip, all while remaining anonymous and untrackable.

As a mobile-only service, Whisper allows users to send messages, receive replies using anonymous nicknames. It has grown tremendously in popularity since launching in 2012, and averages more than 3 billion monthly page views as of early 2014 [16]. The

Figure 1: Screenshot of a sample whisper message (left) and the public stream of latest whispers (right).

functionality is very simple: the app overlays each user's short text message on top of a background image based on keywords from the message (Figure 1). The resulting *whisper* is posted to the public with the user's random or self-chosen nickname. Others can *heart* (Whisper's version of "like") a message anonymously, or post a public followup reply with their own whisper. In addition, users can send *private messages* to the author of a whisper to start a chat, and private messages are only visible to the participants.

User Anonymity. Whisper's focus on anonymity breaks some of the core assumptions made in traditional social networks like Facebook or Google+. First, Whisper users are identified only by randomly assigned (or user-chosen) nicknames, not associated with any personal information, *e.g.*, phone numbers or email addresses[2]. Second, Whisper servers only store public Whispers, and users' private messages are only stored on their end user devices. There is no functionality to search or browse a specific user's historical whispers or replies. Third, there is no notion of a persistent social link between users (*e.g.*, friends on Facebook, followers on Twitter). Thus users are encouraged to interact with a wide range of strangers instead of a known group of "friends."

Public Feeds. Without social links, users browse content from several public lists instead of the news feed of their friends (or followees). These lists include a *latest* list which contains the most recent whispers (system-wise); a *nearby* list which shows whispers posted in nearby areas (about 40 miles of radius range); a *popular* list which only shows top whispers that receive many likes and replies; and *featured* list which shows a subset of popular whispers that are hand-picked by Whisper's content managers. All these lists sort content by most recent first.

2.2 Goals

In its current form, Whisper represents an ideal opportunity to study the impact of pseudo-anonymity on social networks. Three key properties make it ideal for study and analysis. First, Whisper is centralized, *i.e.* there is a single stream of data accessible to all users. Second, Whisper is amenable to periodic data gathering, *i.e.* content is unencrypted and persistent for a moderate amount of time. Third, we were able to meet Whisper's management team, and received permission to gather and analyze Whisper's public data stream.

[2]On the server side, Whisper associates new users with a globally unique identifier (GUID), and binds it to the DeviceID of user's phone. Users can transfer their accounts (private message history) when switching to new phones via iCloud.

At a high level, our primary goals are to understand how users communicate on pseudo-anonymous social networks, how anonymity affects user behavior, and its consequences on user interactions, long term user engagement, and network stability. Beyond basic analysis of the Whisper network structure, we can solidify our goals into several specific questions. First, how do whisper users interact in an anonymous environment, and do they form communities similar to those in traditional social networks? Second, does Whisper's lack of identities eliminate strong ties between users, and does it eliminate the stickiness critical to long term user engagement in traditional social networks? And given the lack of user-specific network effects, is it possible to model and predict user engagement using short term history cues? Finally, what are the implications of pseudo-anonymity on user content and user privacy?

3. DATA AND INITIAL ANALYSIS

Before diving into our analysis of Whisper, we first describe our data collection methodology and collected datasets. We then describe some high level analyses of our dataset.

3.1 Data Collection

Our goal is to collect whispers and their replies posted in the entire network. Given that Whisper does not archive historical data, our method is to keep crawling newly posted whispers over a long period (February to May 2014). We focus on the "latest" list, which is a public stream of the latest whispers from all Whisper users. Unlike other public lists *e.g.*, "nearby" and "popular", the "latest" list provides access to the entire stream of whispers in the network. Since Whisper does not provide a third-party API, we crawl the "latest" list by scrapping Whisper's website.

Each downloaded whisper includes a whisperID, timestamp, plain text of the whisper, author's GUID, author's nickname, a location tag, and number of received likes and replies. An author's GUID was not intended to act as a persistent ID for each user, but was implemented that way due to Whisper's dependency on a third-party service for private messages. Authors' GUIDs make it possible to track a user's posts over time. After we reported this issue to Whisper's management team, they removed the GUID field in June 2014. The location tag shows user location at the city and state level (*e.g.*, Los Angeles, California), and is available only if the whisper author enabled location sharing permission. Replies to a whisper are similar, the only difference is that replies are also marked with the whisperID of the previous whisper in the thread.

Crawling. We implemented a distributed web crawler with two components, a main crawler that pulls the latest whisper list, and a reply crawler that checks past whispers and collects all sequences of replies associated with an existing whisper. We observe that Whisper servers keep a queue of the latest 10K whispers. Running the main crawler every 30 minutes ensures that we capture all new whispers. In contrast, crawling for replies is more computationally intensive. We crawl for replies every 7 days, and check for new replies for all whispers written in the last month. In practice, we observe that whispers usually receive no followup replies 1 week after being posted.

We ran our crawler from February 6 to May 1, 2014. During this period of roughly 3 months, we collected 9,343,590 total Whispers with 15,268,964 replies and 1,038,364 unique GUIDs. Thanks to server side queues, we collected a continuous data stream despite a small number of interruptions to update crawler code. The only point of note is that, at Whisper's request on April 20, we shifted our crawlers to crawl a different Whisper server using a new set of API calls. The shift reduced load for Whisper, but produced whispers without location tags. Since this only affected 10 days of data, we believe this has little impact on our analysis of location-based features.

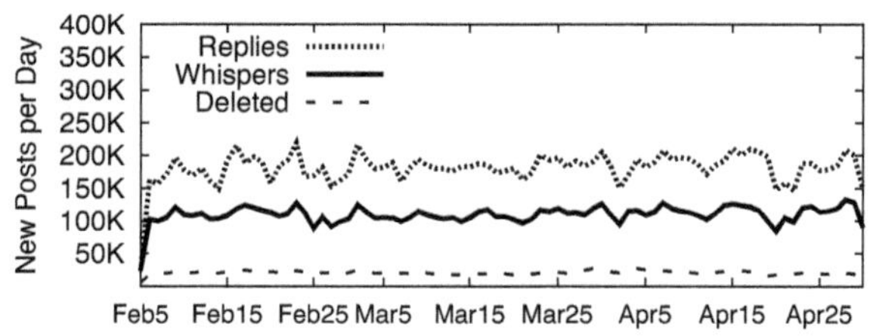

Figure 2: Number of new whispers, new replies and deleted whispers each day.

Validating Consistency. We further verify the completeness of the "latest" stream using a small experiment. We use HTTP requests to simultaneously crawl the "nearby" streams of 6 locations near different cities: Seattle, Houston, Los Angeles, New York, San Francisco and Chicago. We capture these streams for 6 hours, and confirm that the 2000+ whispers from 6 locations were all present in the "latest" stream during the same timeframe.

Limitations. There are two types of data our measurements do not capture. First, we do not capture users who only read/consume whispers but never post any content. Since these passive users do not generate visible user interactions, they are unlikely to affect the majority of our conclusions. Second, our data is limited to visible public data, and we do not have access to private messages between users. Thus our results represent a lower bound on user interactions in the system. As we discuss later, we believe there should be strong correlation between public interactions and private messages.

3.2 Preliminary Analysis

Next we present some high level results on our dataset of whispers, replies and users. Our results in this section set the context for more detailed analysis on user behavior and anonymity in later sections.

Whispers Over Time. We begin by looking at whisper posts over time. Figure 2 shows number of new whispers and replies posted every day during our study. As shown, new content in Whisper is relatively stable, averaging 100K new whispers and 200K replies per day. One interesting observation is that in any time frame, there are significantly more replies than there are original whispers.

During our data collection, we found that a significant portion of whispers is deleted by either the author or Whisper moderators. As far as we can determine, old Whispers do not "expire" and stay on Whisper servers, and can be referenced by following a chain of replies. For deleted whispers, however, we receive an "the whisper does not exist" error when we try to re-crawl their replies. Among the 100K new whispers posted every day, roughly 18% are eventually deleted. We analyze deleted whispers in detail later in §6.

Replies. Users can post replies to a new whisper or other replies. Multiple replies can generate their own replies, thereby forming a tree structure with the original whisper as the root. Figure 3 and Figure 4 show total replies per whisper and the longest chain length (maximum tree depth) per whisper. Unsurprisingly, 55% of whispers receive no replies. Since all whispers are posted to the same public lists, each whisper only has a short time window

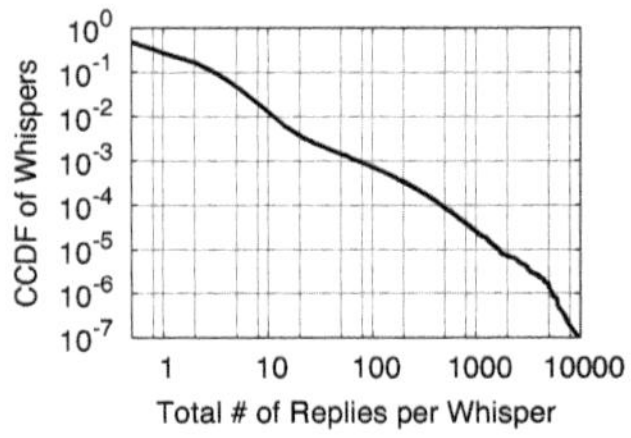

Figure 3: Total number of replies per whisper.

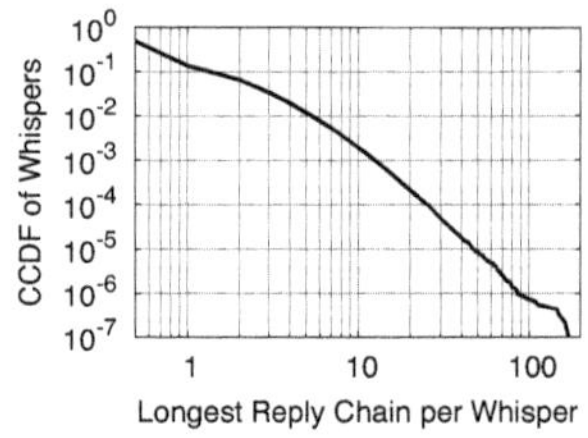

Figure 4: Length of longest reply chain per whisper.

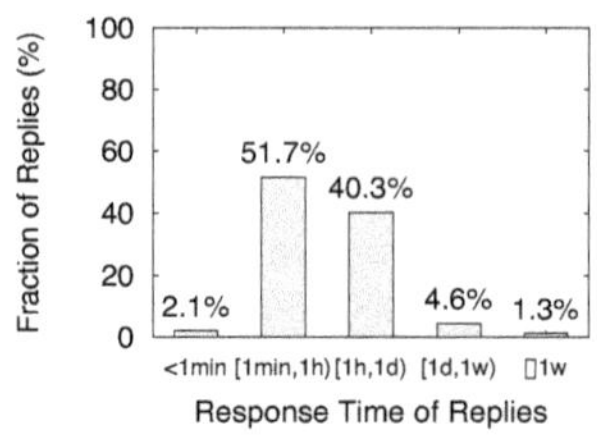

Figure 5: Time gap between reply and original whisper.

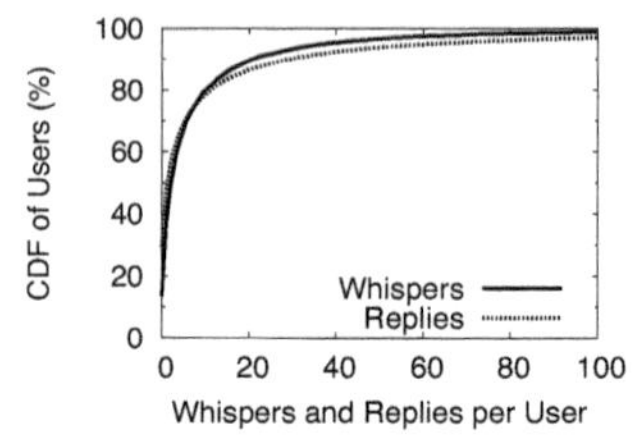

Figure 6: Whispers and replies posted per user.

to attract users' attention. Among whispers with replies, roughly 25% have a chain of at least 2 replies. These essentially become threads of conversations between users.

Figure 5 plots the distribution of reply arrival time, which is the time gap between each reply and the original whisper. 54% of replies arrive within an hour of the original whisper, and more than 94% of replies arrive within a day. Only 1.3% of replies arrive a week or more after the whisper. This confirms our intuition—if a whisper does not get attention shortly after posting, it is unlikely to get attention later.

Users. We look at content-generated per user based on unique GUID. Figure 6 plots the number of whispers and replies posted by each user. Most users (80%) post less than 10 total whispers or replies. Roughly 15% of users only post replies but no original whispers, and 30% of users only post whispers but no replies.

Content Analysis. A high-level analysis of the contents of whispers shows that users post highly personal content. A search of singular first-person pronouns (*e.g.*, I, me, my, myself) hits about 62% of all whispers. We also find a heavy usage of emotional key words. Specifically, 40% of whispers contain one of the 1,113 human mood related key words provided by WordNet Affect [33]. Finally, people often ask questions seeking advice or empathy. About 20% of whispers are questions, based on the usage of question marks and interrogatives (*e.g.*, what, why, which). These three categories effectively cover 85% of all whispers. It is clear that the anonymity provided by Whisper encourages users to post personal and intimate content without privacy concerns. We will take a closer look at "topics" of whispers in §6.

4. USER INTERACTIONS

Our study begins with user interactions on Whisper. The fact that Whisper users cannot construct persistent social links between them fundamentally changes how users interact and develop friendships. In this section, we study the bidirectional interactions built from whispers and their replies, and seek to understand user interactions from three different levels. First, we study interactions at a global network level, by comparing structural properties of the Whisper interaction graph to those of traditional OSNs, *e.g.*, Facebook and Twitter. Second, we study user communities in the Whisper graph and explore key factors driving their formation. Finally, we look at interactions at per-user level to understand if users still develop strong ties (frequently interacted friends) in Whisper.

4.1 Whisper Interaction Graph

We first compare the interaction graph of Whisper with those of traditional online social networks (Facebook and Twitter). Our goal is to understand whether the lack of social links in Whisper fundamentally changes users' interaction patterns at an aggregate network level. We build a Whisper interaction graph based on whispers and replies, and compare its structure to those of graphs constructed from Facebook wall posts and Twitter retweets.

Building Interaction Graphs. We build the Whisper interaction graph based on whispers and followup replies, which are the primary publicly visible interactions in Whisper. The result is a directed interaction graph, where nodes are users and edges represent reply actions. For example, if user A posts a reply whisper to B's whisper, we build a directed edge from A to B. Only direct replies are used to build edges. We remove disconnected singleton nodes from the graph. We produce a main interaction graph from our 3 month dataset (*Whisper-all*).

For comparison, we also build interaction graphs for Facebook and Twitter, based on anonymous datasets from our prior work [39, 42]. Both datasets crawled historical data that covers user interactions over at least 3 months. We built a directed interaction graph using Facebook wall post data: if user A posts on user B's wall, we create a directed edge from A to B. For Twitter, we built the graph based on retweet interactions: if user A retweets a tweet from B, we create a directed edge from A to B. To match the 3-month time coverage of Whisper graph, we build similar Facebook and Twitter graphs each using data covering 3 month periods. Table 1 shows the key statistics of all three interaction graphs.

Degree Distribution and Fittings. Users in Whisper show much higher average degree than users in Facebook and Twitter, meaning users interact with a larger sample of other users. We determine the best fitting function for each graph's degree distribution using 3 commonly used fitting functions for social graphs, power law ($P(k) \propto k^{-\alpha}$), power law with exponential cutoff ($P(k) \propto k^{-\alpha}e^{-\lambda k}$) and lognormal ($P(k) \propto e^{\frac{(lnx-\mu)^2}{2\sigma^2}}$) [14,39]. We follow the fitting method in [10] and use Matlab to compute fitting parameters and accuracy (R-squared values), and show the results in Figure 7. For both the Whisper and Facebook graphs, the out-degree distribution looks similar to the in-degree distribution. For brevity, we only show the in-degree distribution for each graph. Intuitively, Facebook was designed to emulate offline social relationships, and the prevalent bidirectional interactions lead to symmetric in- and out-degree distributions. For Whisper, user interactions are largely random between users. In contrast, Twitter's in-degree and out-degree distributions are significantly different. It's well known that Twitter is more of an information dissemination medium than a social network, and interactions are highly asymmetric [25].

Clustering Coefficient. Clustering coefficient is the ratio of the number of connections that exist between a node's immediate neighbors over all possible connections that could exist. It measures the level of local connectivity between nodes. Clustering coefficient in the Whisper graph (0.033) is much smaller than that of Facebook (0.059) and Twitter (0.048). The cause is clear: Whisper

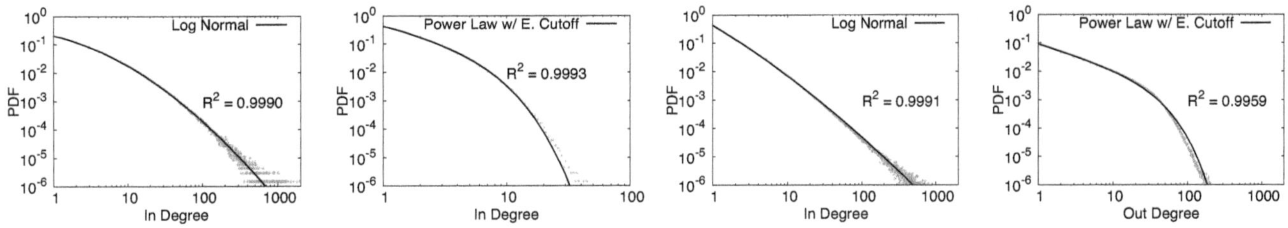

(a) Whisper In (b) Facebook In (c) Twitter In (d) Twitter Out

Figure 7: Degree distribution and fitting result.

Graph	# of Nodes	# of Edges	Avg. Degree	Clustering Coef.	Avg. Path Length	Assortativity Coef.	Largest SCC	Largest WCC
Whisper	690K	6,531K	9.47	0.033	4.28	-0.011	63.3%	98.9%
Facebook	707K	1,260K	1.78	0.059	10.13	0.116	21.2%	84.8%
Twitter	4,317K	16,972K	3.93	0.048	5.52	-0.025	14.2%	97.2%

Table 1: High level statistics of different interaction graphs.

users are highly likely to interact with complete strangers, who are highly unlikely to interact with each other.

Average Path Length. Average path length is the average of all pairs of shortest paths in the graph. Given the size of our graphs, it's impractical to compute the shortest path for all node pairs. Instead, we randomly select 1000 nodes in each graph and compute the average shortest path from them to all other nodes in the graph. The result shows that Whisper graph has the shortest average path length of the 3 networks. This is again intuitive, since the formation of interactions between random strangers creates numerous shortcuts in the graph, thereby shrinking the average path length. Considering Whisper's high average degree, low clustering level and short average path length, Whisper exhibits more properties of a random graph [38] than those of a "small-world" network like Facebook and Twitter.

Assortativity. Assortativity coefficient measures the probability for nodes in a graph to link to other nodes of similar degrees. Assortativity > 0 indicates that nodes tend to connect with other nodes of similar degree, while assortativity < 0 indicates that nodes connect to others with dissimilar degrees. Our result shows the assortativity coefficient of Whisper graph is very close to zero (-0.011), which closely resembles a random graph [29]. In contrast, similar users tend to flock together in social networks with bidirectional links (*e.g.*, Facebook), producing positive assortativity (0.116). In Twitter, large numbers of normal users follow celebrities and notable figures, thus producing a more negative assortativity (-0.025).

4.2 Communities in the Interaction Graph

Next, we analyze the presence of community structures in Whisper's interaction graph. Communities are defined as groups of nodes that are densely connected within but sparsely connected to the rest of the network, *i.e.* high modularity. We seek to answer two key questions. First, without persistent social links, do Whisper users still form communities in the interaction graph? Second, if so, what's the key factor driving the formation of user communities?

Community Detection. We start by applying community detection algorithms to Whisper graphs to examine whether community structures exist. We choose two widely used community detection algorithms Louvain [7] and Wakita [37]. We compute the *modularity* of the resulting communities. Modularity [28] is a well accepted metric used for community detection, which measures the difference between the fraction of links within the communities and

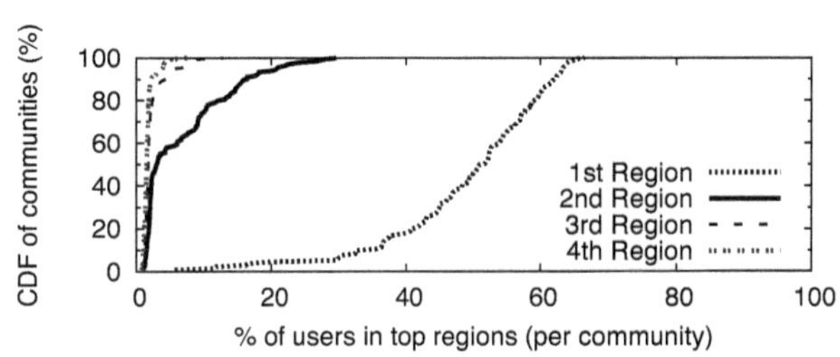

Figure 8: % of users in top regions per community. Users within a community are highly skewed to one region.

Community (size)	Top 4 Region (% of users)
C_1 (61,686)	NY (11), NJ (10), CT (4.8), CA (4.2)
C_2 (39,824)	England (61), Wales (3.5), CA (1.1), TX (0.9)
C_3 (28,342)	CA (62), TX(1.5), England (1.2), AZ (0.9)
C_4 (22,010)	IL (37), WI (21), IN (4.5), CA (1.5)
C_5 (16,017)	CA (64), England (1.4), TX (1.3), NY (0.8)

Table 2: Top 5 biggest communities and their top regions.

the expected fraction when links are randomly connected. Modularity ranges from -1 to 1, and higher values represent stronger communities in the graph.

To capture user interactions using the graph, we weigh graph edges based on the number of interactions between the two nodes. Also we focus this analysis on the biggest weakly connected component, which contains 99% of all nodes. Applying Louvain produces average modularity of communities of 0.4902 for Whisper. In practice, modularity > 0.3 indicates significant community structure in a graph [24]. We confirm our results using the Wakita community detection algorithm, and find a resulting modularity of 0.409 (also above 0.3). As a point of reference, modularity scores of existing social graphs include Facebook (0.63), Youtube (0.66) and Orkut (0.67) [24]. Not surprisingly, the relatively weak communities in Whisper match other observations including low clustering activities and weak ties.

User Communities vs. Geolocation. The natural followup question is, why are there any communities in Whisper at all? If user interactions are random, then shouldn't all interactions be uniform? Our hypothesis is that this is due to the "nearby" functionality in Whisper, which allows users to browse (and likely reply to) whispers posted by people in nearby areas. Our intuition is that the nearby stream drives users to interact more often with others

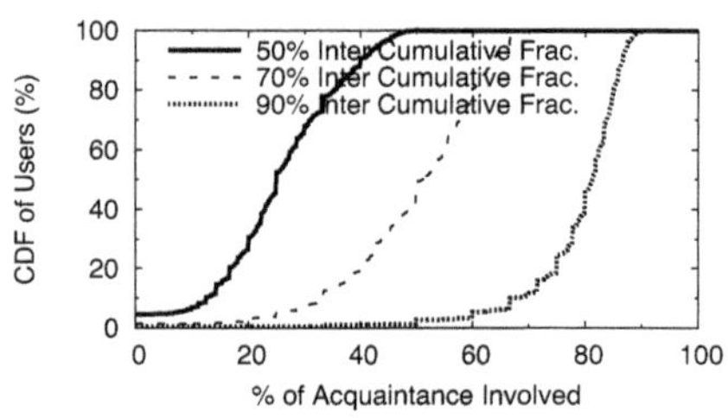

Figure 9: The distribution of users' interaction among their acquaintances, for different % of interactions.

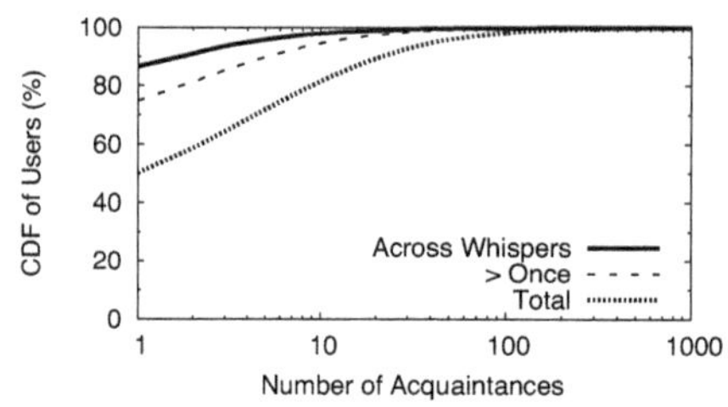

Figure 10: Number of user's acquaintances, and those that users interact > once and across whispers.

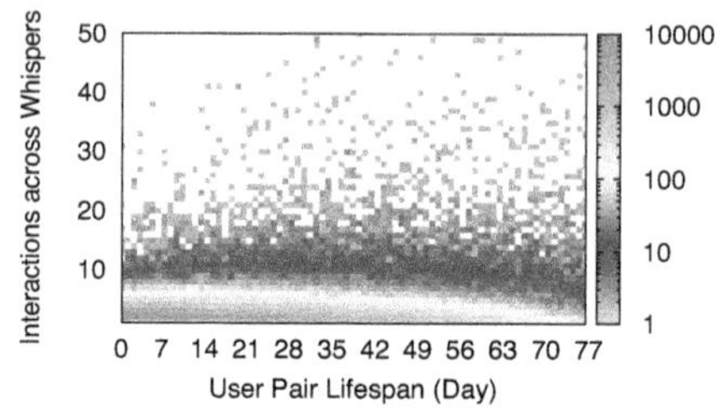

Figure 11: Users pairs with interaction across whispers: lifespan vs. # of interactions.

in the same geographic locale, thus helping geographically driven communities form in the interaction graph.

To test this idea, we examine the most prevalent geographic regions for users in each community. If geo-factor is the key driving force to form communities, then the community should be dominated by users from the same location. Table 2 shows the top 5 Whisper communities generated by Louvain and their corresponding top regions. Here we use "state" or "province" level location tags. We find that the top 5 communities all confirm this: the majority of users are skewed to a single region or several geographically adjacent regions (*e.g.* NY, NJ and CT for C_1).

To quantify this phenomenon across all communities, we plot in Figure 8 the fraction of users in the top four geographic regions per community. Louvain produces 912 communities with varying sizes, and we only consider the largest 150 communities which together cover >90% of users. Again the results confirm our hypothesis, community membership is dominated by the top region or top 2 regions. This strong geographic locality in interactions confirms that the "nearby" stream plays an important role in the formation of Whisper communities. While other factors may contribute to the formation of user communities (*e.g.*, users' shared topics and interests, time zones), we leave their analysis to future work.

4.3 User Interactions and Strong Ties

Finally, we analyze user interactions and implicit social links at the per-user level. Recall that Whisper's lack of persistent identities and social links encourages users to interact with strangers. In the following, we seek the answers to two key questions. First, do users have a fixed set of "friends" that they frequently interact with? Such friendships could have formed despite the anonymous nature of Whisper nicknames. Second, how likely are any strong ties the result of offline friendships?

Per-user Interaction. We search for potential friendships (*i.e.* strong ties) by looking for pairs of users who interact more frequently with each other than with others. For convenience, we call the set of people that a user interacts with (regardless of direction) as her *acquaintances*. For each user, we compute a distribution of her interactions across her top acquaintances, and look for *skew* in her interactions with all acquaintances. We select several points (50-, 70- and 90-percentiles) from each user's distribution and aggregate them in a CDF to show the percentage of top acquaintances involved (Figure 9). To avoid statistical outliers, we only include users with at least 10 interactions.

We find user's interactions are distributed rather evenly across acquaintances. Take the 90-percentile line for example, for nearly all the users (~90%), more than 70% of their acquaintances are responsible for 90% of their interactions. This relatively low skew in Whisper is exactly the opposite of traditional OSNs like Facebook, where a small fraction of friends (strong ties) are responsible for the vast majority of user's interactions [39].

Interaction across Whispers. Across a user's acquaintances, we look for potential strong ties, *i.e.* acquaintances with whom the user interacts often. Figure 10 shows user's number of total acquaintances, acquaintances that users interacted more than once, and acquaintances that users interact more than once *using multiple whisper threads*. In Whisper, it's common for people to interact more than once under the same whisper. However, it's rare to talk with the same person across different whispers, because keeping track of a particular user via their anonymous nickname is difficult. As shown in Figure 10, only 13% of users have acquaintances that they interact with across whispers.

We then select those user pairs who have interacted across whispers for further analysis. In total, there are 503K such user-pairs. Figure 11 presents the heat map of these user-pairs' lifespan (timespan between their first and last interaction) and their number of interactions across whispers. Note that the color palette is log-scale—the vast majority of user pairs are stacked at the left bottom corner, indicating short-lived, low-interaction relationships. Only a very small fraction of outliers (right top corner) achieved long-term and frequent interactions.

Friends or Random Encounters? Even though the strong ties are outliers, it is interesting to explore how could these user-pairs constantly interact with each other *across whispers*: Are these pairs of offline friends who actively track each other in the public feeds (using nicknames), or are these simply users who bump into each other often by chance? We realize this is a very hard question to answer deterministically. But we have a key intuition: if these interactions are truly random, then it is highly likely that these two users are co-located in same geographic area, particularly areas with a sparse population of Whisper users. Then as long as the two users actively post whispers, they have a good chance to see each other in the nearby list.

Now we use our data to test this intuition. For user-pairs with cross-whisper interactions, we first examine their geographic distances[3]. We find that among 503K user pairs, 90% have two users co-located in the same "state" and 75% have their distance <40 miles which is the maximum range of the nearby stream. Figure 12 shows the correlation between geo-distance and the interaction frequency of user pairs. Each stacked bar adds up to 100%, and each category represents user pairs with different interaction level (*i.e.* number of interactions across whispers). It shows that frequent interactions are more skewed to users that are geographically close to each other.

[3]This is the distance between two user's city-level tags. The GPS coordinates of each city are obtained from Google Geocoding API.

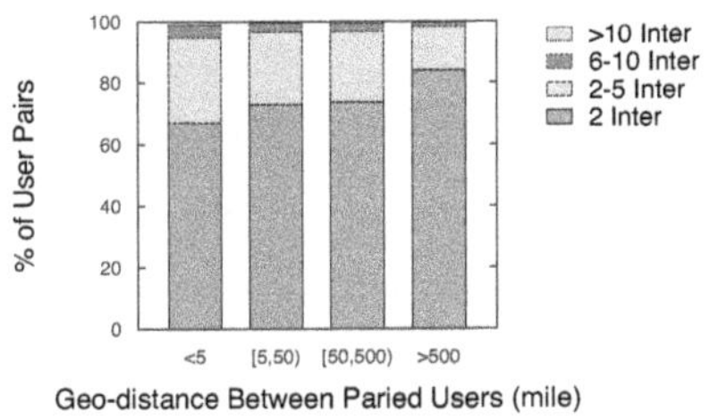

Figure 12: For all user pairs, distance between two users vs. # of interactions of the user pair.

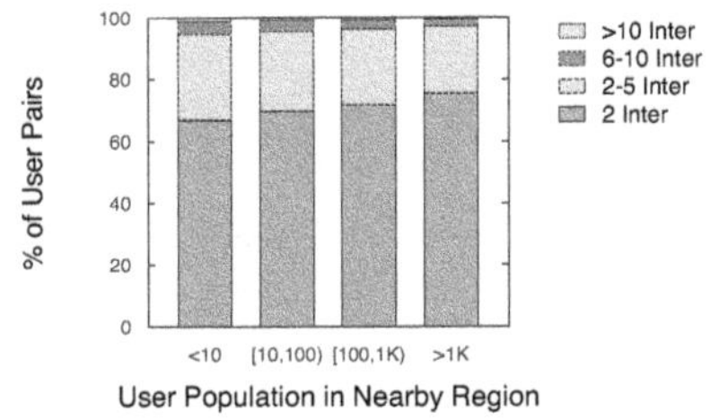

Figure 13: For nearby user pairs, user population in nearby areas vs. # of interaction of the user pair.

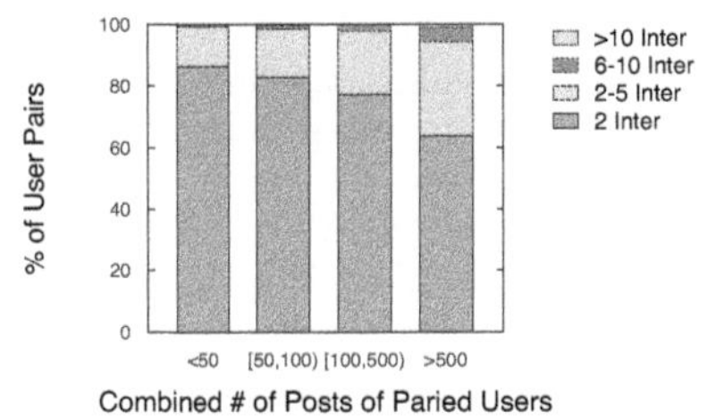

Figure 14: For nearby user pairs, total # of whispers vs. # of interactions of the user pair.

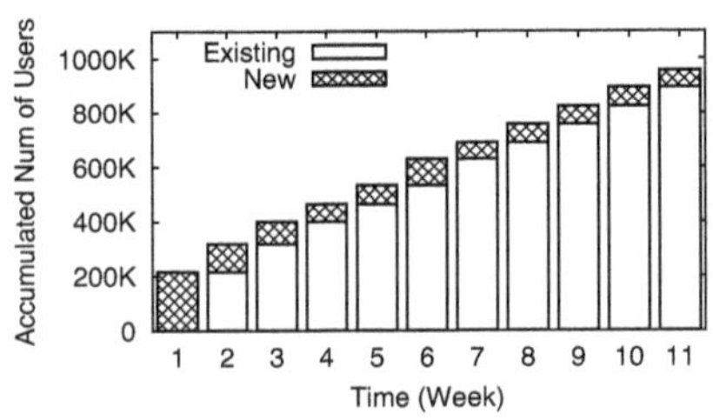

Figure 15: The growth of user population in our dataset over time.

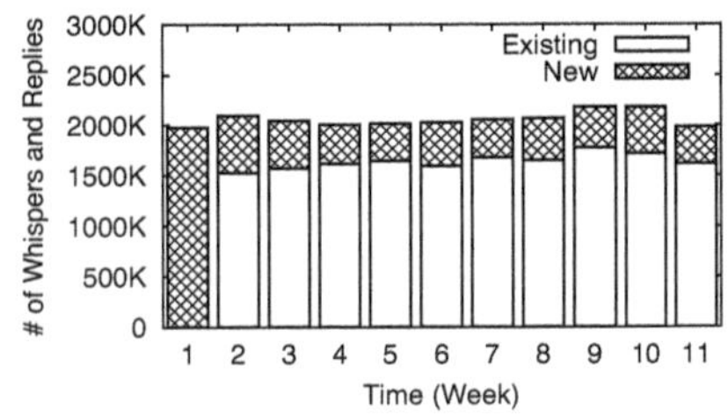

Figure 16: # of whispers and replies by new and old users per week.

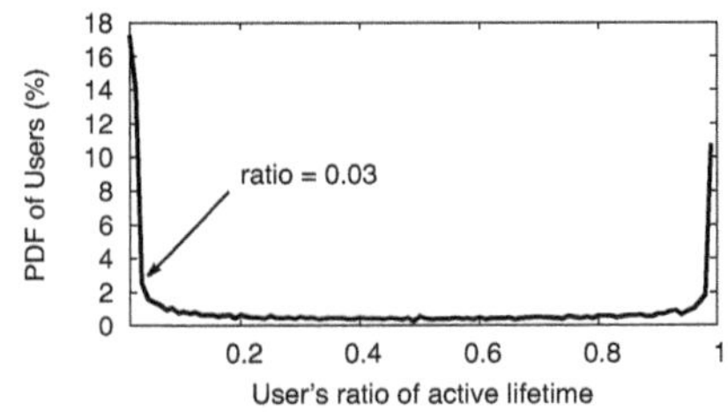

Figure 17: User's active lifetime over staying time in our dataset.

Then we further examine these pairs co-located in nearby areas (*i.e.* distance <40 miles). More specifically, we analyze two factors that potentially impact users' likelihood of chance encounters—the user population in the geographic area and total number of whispers posted by the two users (Figure 13 and Figure 14). Intuitively, the smaller user population in the same nearby area, the higher chance to encounter the same person in the nearby list again and again. Similarly, the more whispers two users post, the more likely they encounter each other and form interactions. Here the user population is estimated by the total number of unique users that have the same city-level location tags with the paired users. Both results confirm our intuition. As user population density decreases and as the number of user posts increases, the probability of more frequent user-pair interactions also increases.

In summary, our analysis suggests strong ties are extremely rare in Whisper. We also find strong ties are skewed to user-pairs who have a higher chance to encounter each other (*i.e.* active users that are co-located in areas with sparse user population). Thus while it is possible to develop strong relationships from Whisper interactions, such relationships are likely heavily influenced by geographic density and user whisper frequency. Note that our analysis relies on only public interactions and do not include private messages. Intuitively, we believe users' private interactions should correlate with their public interactions, and we can predict user pairs with private interactions from their public interactions. Prior work also confirms that public interactions are more informative when modeling strength of ties than private communications [13,22].

5. USER ENGAGEMENT

Thus far our analysis shows Whisper users tend to interact with strangers rather than stable friends. The negative consequence is that a lack of strong ties usually produces a less "sticky" network, *i.e.* fewer disincentives to prevent users from leaving [11]. This raises a natural question: without strong ties, can Whisper users stay engaged in the network in the long run?

In this section, we seek to consider this question by looking at *per-user* engagement. First, we examine user engagement over time to understand user attrition in the 3 month period of our dataset. Second, we evaluate a machine learning classifier and show that we can accurately predict whether users stay engaged in the system using only a short history of their actions after their first post. We use experiments to determine key signals that indicate a user's intention to leave. Note that our analysis is limited to "active" users who have posted at least 1 whisper or reply, and does not include passive users who consume but do not contribute content.

5.1 User Engagement Over Time

We start with basic analysis of user activity over time using three metrics: user population growth, content contribution by new versus existing users, and the distribution of users' active lifetime.

User Population Growth. Figure 15 shows the total number of users over time (11 weeks) in our dataset. Each bar shows a breakdown of new users who just joined that week (new) and the existing users we observed before that week (existing). We observe a stable arrival rate of new users to the network, roughly 80K new users per week. Recall that the daily new posts (whispers and replies) in the entire network remain roughly stable (see Figure 2), despite the growth in users. This indicates there are an ongoing number of users who "disengage," *i.e.* stop posting whispers or replies.

Content by New and Existing Users. This motivates us to look at the relative contribution of content by new and existing users. Figure 16 shows the breakdown of posts (whispers plus replies) by users who showed up for the first time in the current week (new) and users who showed up before this week (existing). We find that new users make significant contributions to the overall whisper stream (> 20%). However, as more and more users transition from new to "existing users," content generation by existing users does not grow significantly over time. This confirms our intuition that a certain portion of users are disengaging over time.

Per-user Active Period. Next, we focus on individual users and examine how long users stay active before they disengage. More specifically, we compute their active "lifetime" (timespan between their first and last posts) over their staying time in the dataset (timespan between a user's first post and the last date of our data collection). Given our focus on long-term activity, we exclude users who just recently joined during the last the month of our data collection. Thus for Figure 17, we only consider users who have been in our dataset for at least one month (70.3% of all users).

Figure 17 shows the distribution of user's ratio of active lifetime (PDF). Users are clearly clustered into two extremes: one major cluster around an extremely low ratio (0.03), representing those who quickly turned inactive in 1 or 2 days after their first post; another major cluster around 1.00, representing users who remain active for their entire time in the dataset (at least 1 month). Similar patterns have also been observed in other user generated content (UGC) networks, such as blogs and Q&A services [17]. If we set a threshold for active ratio at 0.03, these "try and leave" users account for 30% of all users. This explains our observation in Figure 16—because a significant portion of users become inactive quickly, the overall content posting rate remains stable despite a significant number of new users joining the network.

5.2 Predicting User Engagement

A key observation of the above analysis is that Whisper users tend to fall into one of two behavioral extremes—either staying active for a long time, or quickly turning inactive (Figure 17). The bimodal nature of the distribution hints at the potential to classify users into the two clusters.

Here, we experiment with machine learning (ML) classifiers to determine if we can predict long term user engagement based on their early behavior after their first post (in our dataset). We seek to answer three key questions: First, is this prediction even possible? Second, what ML models produce the most accurate predictions? Third, what early-day signals can most strongly indicate a user's intention to leave?

We take three steps to answer the above questions. First, we collect a set of behavioral features based on users' activities in their first X days on Whisper, ideally with a small value for X. Second, we use these features to build different machine learning classifiers to predict long term user engagement. Finally, we run feature selection to determine the features that provide the best early signals indicating which users might disengage.

Features. We explore multiple different classes of features (20 features in all) to profile users' behavior during their first X days. Out of these, we will select the most essential features.

- *Content posting features (F1-F7).* 7 features: user's number of total posts, number of whispers, number of replies, number of deleted whispers, and number of days with at least one post/whisper/reply.
- *Interaction features (F8-F15).* 8 features: ratio of replies in total posts, number of acquaintances, number of bi-directional acquaintances, outgoing replies over all replies, maximum number of interactions with the same user, ratio of whispers with replies, and average number of replies and likes per whisper.
- *Temporal features (F16-F17):* 2 features: average delay before first reply to user's whisper; average delay of user's replies to other users' whispers.
- *Activity trend (F18-F20):* 3 features: we equally split each user's first X days into three buckets and record the number of posts in each bucket ($First$, $Middle$ and $Last$). We compute 2 features as $\frac{Middle}{First}$ and $\frac{Last}{First}$. Finally, whether the number of posts decreases monotonically across the three buckets.

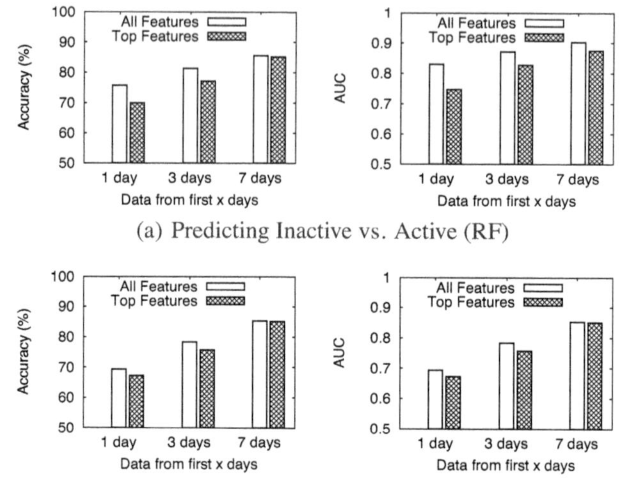

(a) Predicting Inactive vs. Active (RF)

(b) Predicting Inactive vs. Active (SVM)

Figure 18: Prediction result using Random Forests and SVM. The model performance is evaluated by accuracy (left) and Area under ROC curve (right) .

Classifier Experiments. To build a training set for our classifiers, we focus on users that have at least a month's worth of activity history in our dataset (730K users). We select a set of "short-term" users who tried the app for 1-2 days and quickly disengaged (no more posts). Using results from Figure 17, we randomly sample 50K users from those whose active lifetime ratio < 0.03 as the *Inactive* set. We then choose a random sample of 50K users whose active lifetime ratio > 0.03 to form the *Active* set.

Our goal is to classify the two sets of users solely based on users' activities in their first X days, and we use $1, 3$ and 7 as values of X. We build multiple machine learning classifiers including Random Forests (RF), Support Vector Machine (SVM) and Bayes Network (BN), using implementations of these algorithms in WEKA [19] with default parameters. For each experiment, we run 10-fold cross validation and report classification accuracy and area under ROC curve (AUC). Accuracy refers to the ratio of correctly predicted instances over all instances. AUC is another widely used metric, with higher AUC indicating stronger prediction power. For instance, AUC > 0.5 means the prediction is better than random guessing.

The experiment results with Random Forests and SVM are shown in Figure 18. The Bayesian results closely match those of SVM, thus we omit them for brevity. We make two key observations. First, behavioral features are effective in predicting future engagement. The accuracy is high (75%) even when only using users' first-day data (RF). This confirms that users' early actions can act as indicators of their future activity. If we include a week's worth of data, we can achieve accuracy up to 85%. Second, we find different classifiers achieve similar performance given 7 days of data. However, their results diverge when they are constrained to using less data (*e.g.*, 1-day). With less data, Random Forests produce more accurate predictions than SVM and Bayesian networks.

Feature Selection. Finally, we seek to identify the most powerful signals to predict a user's long-term engagement. To find the answer, we perform feature selection on the 20 features. More specifi-

Rank	Observation Time Frame		
	1 day	3 days	7 days
1	Interact-F9 (0.15)	Post-F5 (0.27)	Post-F5 (0.46)
2	Interact-F11 (0.12)	Trend-F19 (0.18)	Post-F6 (0.31)
3	Interact-F10 (0.11)	Post-F6 (0.18)	Trend-F19 (0.28)
4	Interact-F12 (0.11)	Interact-F9 (0.16)	Post-F1 (0.27)
5	Trend-F18 (0.05)	Post-F1 (0.16)	Post-F7 (0.23)
6	Interact-F15 (0.04)	Post-F7 (0.13)	Trend-F20 (0.21)
7	Post-F1 (0.04)	Interact-F15 (0.12)	Interact-F15 (0.21)
8	Interact-F8 (0.04)	Interact-F11 (0.12)	Post-F2 (0.19)

Table 3: The top 8 feature and its categories ranked by information gain (values shown in parentheses).

cally, we rank features based on *Information Gain* [18], which measures feature's distinguishing power over the two classes of data. We list the top 8 features in Table 3. As expected, prediction power varies significantly, and information gain drops off quickly (particularly for 1 day) after the top 4 features. To validate their prediction power, we repeat each experiment with only their top 4 features. The results in Figure 18 show that the top 4 features achieve most of the accuracy of the entire classifier, but with much less complexity.

Then we take a closer look at the top features. First, we note that the 1-day classifier relies on different set of features compared with 3- and 7-day classifiers. The 1-day models rely heavily on *interaction features*. Intuitively, the model predicts whether a user will stay engaged based on how actively the user participates in social interactions. If a user received many replies or actively replied to others on her first day, there's a high chance for this user to stay longer. For 3- and 7-day models, we find that the key features shift to user's *content posting* and *activity trend* features. This means once we monitor the users for a longer period, the user's intention to stay or leave can be more accurately reflected in her posting frequency and volume, and whether that activity is declining over time.

Engaging Users with Notifications. Stimulating user engagement is a key goal for any new service. One tool Whisper has already deployed is push notifications that deliver the "whisper of the day" to users' mobile device every evening between 7 and 9pm. The exact notification time varies each day and between Android and iOS devices. To examine the impact of these notifications, we conduct a small experiment. We monitor the notification time on 5 different phones every day for 6 days. We look at user activity in the Whisper stream for 5 minute and 10 minute intervals following the notifications, and find no statistically significant increase in new replies or whispers compared to other 5 or 10 minute windows between 7 and 9pm. This means that while these notifications may serve to engage users to read popular whispers, there is no significant increase in new whispers or replies as a result.

6. CONTENT MODERATION IN WHISPER

Anonymity facilitates free speech, but also inevitably fosters abusive content and behavior [21,35]. Like other anonymous communities, Whisper faces the same challenge of dealing with abusive content (*e.g.*, nudity, pornography or obscenity) in their network. In addition to a crowdsourcing-based user reporting mechanism, Whisper also has dedicated employees to moderate whispers [16]. Our basic measurements (§3.2) also suggest this has a significant impact on the system, as we observed a large volume of whispers (>1.7 million) has been deleted during the 3 months of our study. The ratio of Whisper's deleted content (18%) is much higher than traditional social networks like Twitter (<4%) [1,30].

Topic	Top 50 Keywords Most Related to Deleted Whispers
Sexting (36)	sext, wood, naughty, kinky, sexting, bj, threesome, dirty, role, fwb, panties, vibrator, bi, inches, lesbians, hookup, hairy, nipples, freaky, boobs, fantasy, fantasies, dare, trade, oral, takers, sugar, strings, experiment, curious, daddy, eaten, tease, entertain, athletic
Selfie (7)	rate, selfie, selfies, send, inbox, sends, pic
Chat (7)	f, dm, pm, chat, ladys, message, m
Topic	**Top 50 Keywords Least Related to Deleted Whispers**
Emotion (17)	panic, emotions, argument, meds, hardest, fear, tears, sober, frozen, argue, failure, unfortunately, understands, anxiety, understood, aware, strength
Religion (10)	beliefs, path, faith, christians, atheist, bible, create, religion, praying, helped
Entertain. (8)	episode, series, season, anime, books, knowledge, restaurant, character
Life story (6)	memories, moments, escape, raised, thank, thanks
Work (5)	interview, ability, genius, research, process
Politics (1)	government
Others (3)	exactly, beginning, example

Table 4: Topics of top and bottom 50 keywords related to whisper deletion.

In this section, we take a closer look at content deletions in Whisper. First, we analyze the content of deleted whispers to infer the reasons behind deletions. Second, we analyze the lifetime of deleted whispers to understand how fast do whispers get deleted. Third, we focus on authors of deleted whispers and compare their behavior to the norm.

Before we begin, we note that while users can delete their own whispers, we believe server-side content moderation is responsible for the large majority of missing whispers in our data. Intuitively, users who reconsider and later delete their own whispers are likely to do so within a relatively short time frame. In contrast, our "deleted" dataset comes from our followup crawl for replies, which runs once a week. In fact, since our main crawler on the latest stream runs every 30 minutes, we expect most self-deleted whispers will not even show up in our core dataset.

Content Analysis of Deleted Whispers. To explore the reasons behind deletion, we analyze the content of deleted whispers. Since whispers are usually very short, Natural Language Processing (NLP) tools do not work well (we confirmed via experiments). Thus we take a keyword-based approach: we extract keywords from all whispers and examine which keywords correlate with deleted whispers. First, before processing, we exclude common stopwords[4] from our keyword list. Also to avoid statistical outliers, we exclude low frequency words that appear in less than 0.05% of whispers. Then for each keyword, we compute a *deletion ratio* as the number of deleted whispers with this keyword over all whispers with this keyword. We rank keywords by deletion ratio, and examine the top and bottom keywords.

We run this analysis on all 9 million original (not including replies) whispers in our dataset, 1.7M of which are later deleted. This produces 2324 keywords ranked by deletion ratio. We list the top and bottom 50 keywords in Table 4 and classify them manually into topic categories. Not surprisingly, many deleted whispers violate Whisper's stated user policies on sexually explicit messages and nudity. In contrast, topics related to personal expression, religion, and politics are least likely to be deleted.

[4]`http://norm.al/2009/04/14/list-of-english-stop-words`

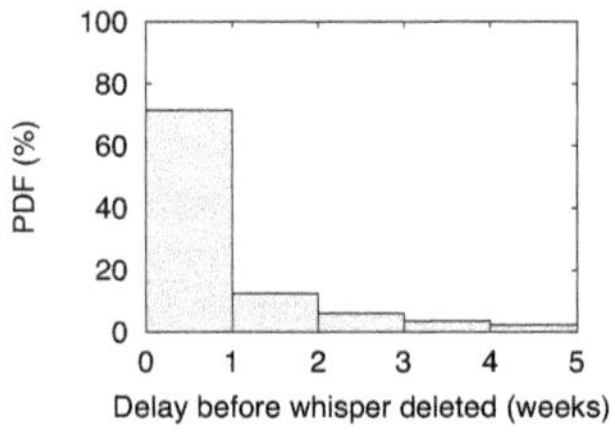

Figure 19: Deletion speed (coarse-grained).

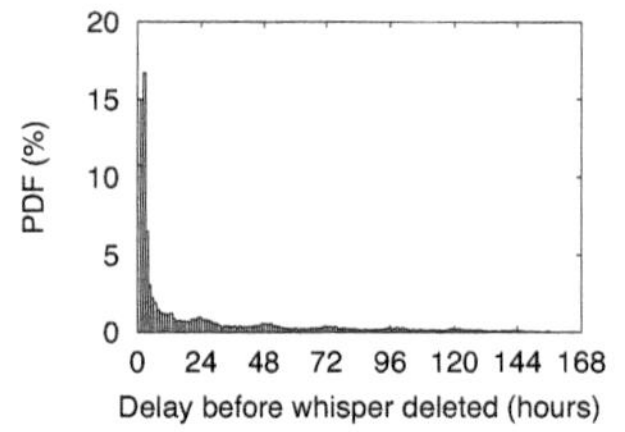

Figure 20: Deletion speed (fine-grained).

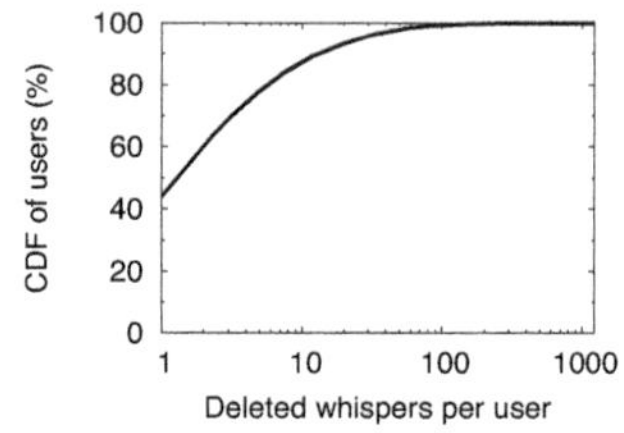

Figure 21: # of Deleted whispers per user.

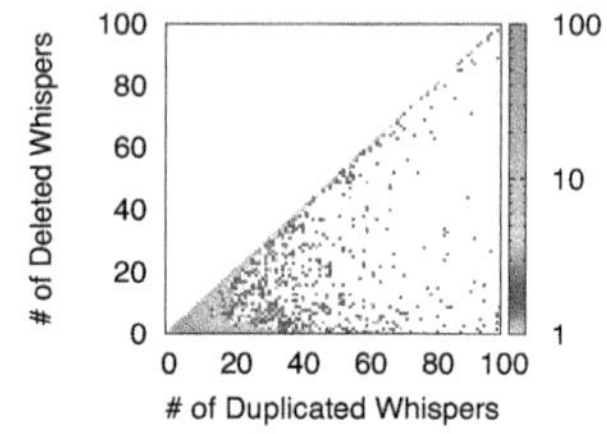

Figure 22: Duplicated vs. deleted whispers.

Deletion Delay. Next we analyze the deletion delay of whispers, *i.e.* how long do whispers stay in the system before they are deleted? Recall that our reply crawler works once a week, and thus detects deleted whispers on the granularity of once a week. As shown in Figure 19, the majority (70%) of deleted whispers are "deleted" within one week after posting. A small portion (2%) of whispers have stayed for more than a month before deletion. Since most whispers lose user attention after one week (Figure 5), we believe these deletions are not the results of crowdsourcing flagging, but deleted by Whisper moderators.

To get a more fine grain view of whisper deletions, we perform a period of frequent crawls on a small set of whispers. On April 14, 2014, we select 200K new whispers from our crawl of the latest whisper stream, and check on (recrawl) these whispers every 3 hours over a period of 7 days. Of the 200K whispers, 32,153 whispers are deleted during our monitoring period (a week). The more fine-grained distribution of the lifetime (hourly) of these whispers is shown in Figure 20. We find the peak of whisper deletion to be between 3 and 9 hours after posting, and the vast majority of deletions happen within 24 hours of posting. This suggests that the moderation system in Whisper works quickly to flag and remove offensive whispers. However, it is unclear whether this level of responsiveness is sufficient, since user page views focus on the most recent whispers, and moderation after 3 hours is possibly too late to impact the content most users see.

Characterizing Authors of Deleted Whispers. Finally, we take a closer look at the authors of deleted whispers to check for signs of suspicious behavior. In total, 263K users (25.4%) out of all users in our dataset have at least one deleted whisper. The distribution of deleted whispers is highly skewed across these users: 24% of users are responsible for 80% of all deleted whispers. The worst offender is a user who had 1230 whisper deleted during the time period of our study, while roughly half of the users only have a single deletion (Figure 21).

We observed anecdotal evidence of duplicate whispers in the set of deleted whispers. We find that frequently reposted duplicate whispers are highly likely to be deleted. Among our 263K users with at least 1 deleted whisper, we find 25K users have posted duplicate whispers. In Figure 22, we plot each user's number of duplicated whispers versus the number of deleted whispers. We observe a clear clustering of users around the straight line of $y = x$. This indicates that when users post many duplicated whispers, there's a higher chance that most or all duplicated whispers are deleted.

We also observe that authors of deleted whispers change their nicknames more often than the average user. Figure 23 shows the distribution of total number of nicknames used by each user. We categorize users based on how many deletions they have, and also include a baseline of users with 0 deletions. We find users with no deletion rarely change their nicknames, if ever, but nickname changes occur far more frequently for users with many deleted whispers. We speculate that perhaps users change their nickname to avoid being flagged or blacklisted. Since users cannot see their own GUID when using the app, they may assume the system identifies them using only their nickname.

7. TRACKING WHISPER USERS

In the final component of our Whisper study, we take a close look at a vulnerability that exposes detailed location of Whisper authors to the system. In practical terms, this attack allows a Whisper user to accurately track (or potential stalk) another Whisper user through whispers they've written, by writing simple scripts that query Whisper servers. This attack demonstrates the inherent risks to user privacy in mobile applications, even for apps that target user anonymity as a core goal. Note that we met the Whisper team in person and informed them of this attack. They are supportive of this work, and have already taken steps to remove this vulnerability.

In this section, we describe details of this location tracking attack. The attack makes use of Whisper's "nearby" function, which returns a list of whispers posted nearby, attaching a "distance" field to each whisper. The attack generates numerous "nearby" queries from different vantage points, and uses statistical analysis to reverse engineer the whisper author's location. We validate the efficacy of this attack through real-world experiments.

7.1 Pinpointing User Locations

We start by describing the high-levels of the attack: when a user (*i.e.* the victim) posts a new whisper, he exposes his location to the Whisper server. An attacker in an nearby area can query the nearby list to get their "distance" to the whisper author. The methodology is simple: the attacker can move to different (nearby) locations and query the nearby list for the distance to the victim. Using multiple distance measurements, the attacker can *triangulate* the whisper author's location. The fact that Whisper does not authenticate location in its queries makes this easier, an attacker can issue numerous distance queries from different locations all while sitting in the comfort of her living room.

With a bit more effort, an attacker can even track the victim's movement over time, by triangulating his location every time he posts a whisper. In practice, this means the attacker can physically go and stalk the victim. While the effective error is roughly 0.2 miles (details below), it is more than sufficient to infer the victim's movement to specific points of interest. Considering most Whisper users are young adults or teenagers [4], this attack can lead to severe consequences.

Distance Granularity and Errors. Implementing this attack is nontrivial. Whisper's design team has always been aware of location tracking risks to its users, and built in basic defense mechanisms into the current system. First, they apply a distance offset to every whisper, so the location stored on their servers is always

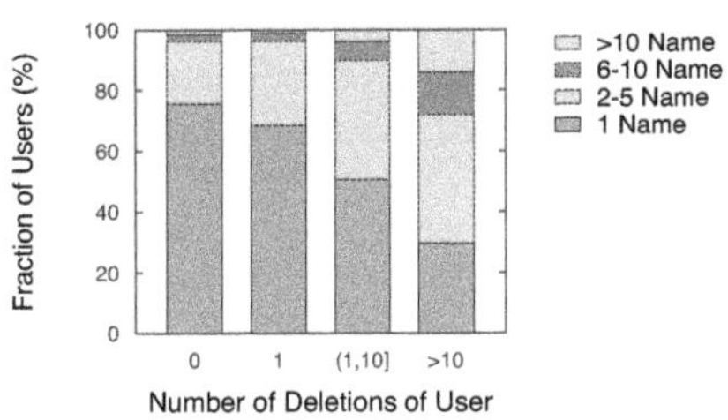

Figure 23: User's number of deletions vs. number of nicknames.

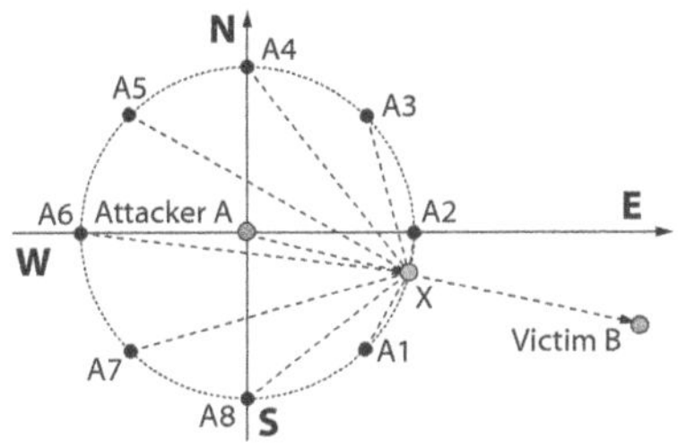

Figure 24: Estimating the distance and direction to the victim.

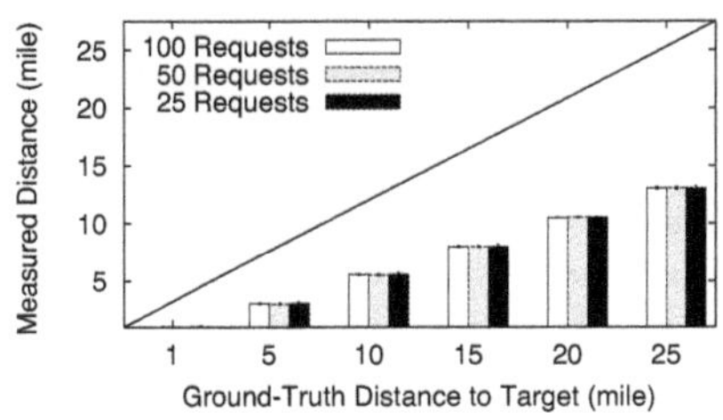

Figure 25: True distance vs. measured average distance (>1 mile).

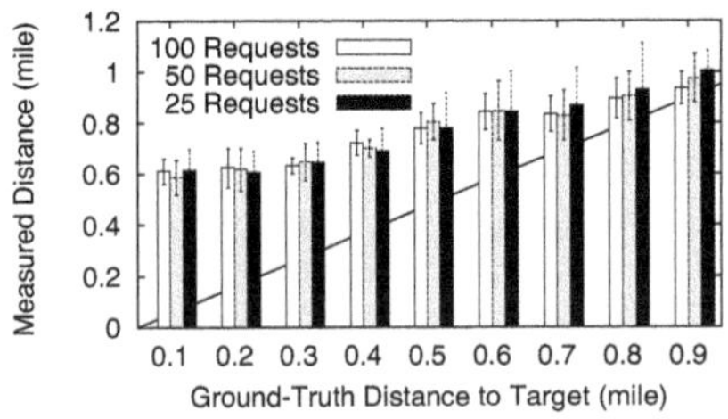

Figure 26: True distance vs. measured average distance (within 1 mile).

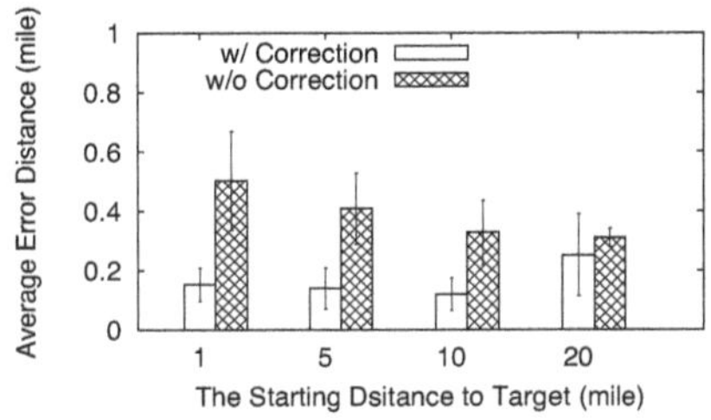

Figure 27: The final error distance of the attack.

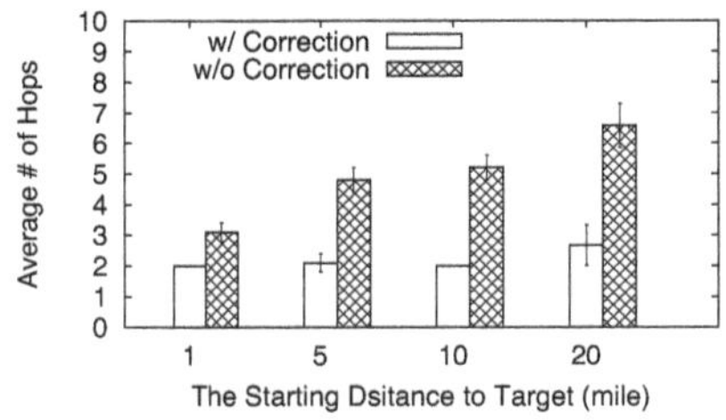

Figure 28: Number of hops to approach the victim.

off by some distance to the actual author location. Second, the distance field returned by the nearby function is a coarse-grained integer value (in miles). This was a recent change made by Whisper in February 2014, before which the nearby function returned distances with decimal values. Third, Whisper server adds a random error to the answer to each query, *i.e.* when we query the nearby list repetitively from the same location, each query returns a different distance for the same whisper. The specific error function is unknown.

Attack Details. To accurately pinpoint a user location, our approach is to extensively measure the "distance" from different vantage points, and use large-scale statistics to infer user's location. Specifically, our attack exploits a key property of Whisper: servers allow anyone to query the nearby list with arbitrarily self-reported GPS values as input, and impose no rate limits on such queries. This effectively helps us to overcome the limitations (*i.e.* random error, coarse granularity) on the returned distance. First, we can reduce or eliminate per-query noise by taking the average distance across numerous queries from the same observation location. Second, even though the absolute distance is still not accurate, we can estimate the *direction* to the victim based on the measurements from different locations. Then with distance and direction, an attacker can repeat the measurement from a location closer to the victim, thus iteratively deducing the victim's real location.

We use a simple example to illustrate how this works. Suppose user A (attacker) finds user B (victim)'s whisper in the nearby list, and A wants to pinpoint B's location:

1. A queries the nearby list to get its current distance (d) to victim B (averaged across multiple queries).
2. To estimate the direction, A needs additional observation points. We pick 8 points $\{A_1, A_2, ...A_8\}$ evenly distributed on a circle centered at A with radius d (Figure 24). From each point, A queries the nearby list to measure its distance to victim $\{d_1, d_2, ..., d_8\}$. Suppose X is a dot on the circle, then objective function $Obj = \sqrt{\frac{\sum_{i=1}^{8}(|\overrightarrow{A_iX}|-d_i)^2}{8}}$ reaches the minimum if $\overrightarrow{AX}$ is the right direction to the victim.
3. Then the attacker moves to the next location using $\overrightarrow{AX}$ and d, and repeats step 1 and 2. The algorithm terminates if $d < Thre_1$, or the distance d from two consecutive rounds differs $< Thre_2$.

In practice, the attacker can script all queries with forged GPS values and does not need to physically move.

Distance Error Correction. Finally, we introduce a final step that uses physical measurements to calibrate and add an additional "correction" factor to location data.

We first post a target whisper at a predefined physical location L (on UCSB campus). Then we measure distances to L using the nearby list from a set of observation points, each with known ground-truth distances to L. The ground-truth distance ranges cover from 1 to 25 miles (in 5 mile increments) and again from 0.1 to 0.9 miles (in 0.1-mile increments). At each increment, we use 8 observation points (as specified above) and use each to query the nearby list 100 times. Figure 25 and Figure 26 plot the ground-truth distance versus the measured distance (for 25, 50 and 100 requests per location). For distances greater than 1 mile, we find that our estimates underestimate true physical distance to the victim. Within 1 mile, it clearly overestimates. This mapping between true and measured distance serves as a guide for generating our "correction factor," which is applied to the final estimate.

7.2 Experimental Validation of the Attack

A Single-target Experiment. We first post a whisper at a pre-defined location on UCSB campus as the target (victim). Then we run the attack algorithm starting from distances of 1, 5, 10 and 20 miles away from the victim. Our algorithm takes the average distance over 50 queries per location, and terminates when the estimated distance from consecutive rounds differ < 0.1 mile or when estimated distance < 0.5 mile (based on Figure 26). We repeat each experiment 10 times and test the performance with and without our distance *error correction factor*. Results are shown in Figure 27 and Figure 28.

We make two key observations. First, the algorithm is very accurate. The final error distance, *i.e.* distance from the estimated victim location to the ground-truth location, is only 0.1 to 0.2 miles. With a radius of 0.2 miles, attackers can already effectively identify user's significant points of interest (*e.g.*, home, work, shopping mall) and reconstruct a victim's daily routine using mobility traces [3]. Second, the results show that distance error correction improves algorithm accuracy significantly and reduces the number of iterations needed to determine the victim's location.

Geographically Diverse Targets. To make sure our results are not biased and specific to a single location, we apply the correction factor computed from local measurements (Figure 25 and Figure 26) to carry out attacks in different cities. More specifically, we post target whispers in Santa Barbara and Seattle Washington, Denver Colorado, New York City, New York and Edinburgh Scotland. All whispers are posted via an Android phone with forged GPS coordinates. Then we run the algorithm with distance error correction. We find the final error distances are consistently less than 0.2 miles, and that our correction factor can be generalized to improve estimation accuracy regardless of geographic region.

7.3 Countermeasures

This type of statistical attack cannot be mitigated simply by adding more noise into the system. Attackers can always apply increasingly sophisticated statistical and data mining tools to eliminate noise and determine the true location of a whisper. Instead, the key is to restrict user access to extensive distance measurements. This means putting more constraints (*e.g.*, rate limits) on queries to the nearby list. For instance, one approach is to enforce per-device rate limits. Another is detect fake GPS values, either by relying on client hardware (difficult) or by detecting "unrealistic" movement patterns by potential attackers. Finally, the ultimate defense is to simply remove the "distance" field altogether. While the Whisper engineering team has already addressed this issue, we are not aware of the specific steps they took to do so.

8. RELATED WORK

Online Social Networks. Over the last few years, researchers have performed measurement studies on online social networks (OSNs) including Facebook [36,39], Twitter [8,25], Pinterest [12], and Tumblr [9]. Today's OSNs have stored large volumes of sensitive data about users (*e.g.*, personal profile, friending information, activity traces), all of which pose potential privacy risks. Various techniques have been proposed to compromise user anonymity and infer users' sensitive information from social network data [5,26, 27,44]. Our study focuses on anonymous social networks, which prioritize user privacy at the cost of eliminating persistent identities as well as social links.

Anonymous Online Communities. Anonymous online services allow users to post content and communicate without revealing their real identity. Researchers have studied various anonymous platforms including anonymous forums [32], discussion boards [6, 23] and Q&A sites [21]. Most earlier works study user communities focusing on content and sentiment analysis. More recently, anonymous social networks have emerged, particularly on mobile platforms. A recent work [31] conducted a user survey on SnapChat to understand how they used the anonymous social app. In comparison, our study is the first to quantitively study user interaction, user engagement, and security implications in the anonymous Whisper network.

Device Localization. Our attack algorithm to localize Whisper users is inspired by existing techniques used for device localization in wireless (mobile) networks [15,20,43]. We differ from existing techniques in our approach to deal with the random errors injected by Whisper server. Also, our contribution is more on identifying and validating the security vulnerability instead of the localization algorithm itself.

9. CONCLUSION AND FUTURE WORK

Anonymous, mobile-only messaging apps such as Whisper mark a clear shift away from traditional social networks and towards privacy-conscious communication tools. To the best of our knowledge, our study is the first large data-driven study of social interactions, user engagement, content moderation and privacy risks on the Whisper network. We show that without strong user identities or persistent social links, users interact with random strangers instead of a defined set of friends, leading to weak ties and challenges in long-term user engagement. We show that even in anonymous messaging apps, significant attacks against user privacy are very feasible. We believe that this shift towards privacy in communication tools is here to stay, and insights from our study on Whisper provides value for developers working on next generation systems in this space.

Whisper is not only a social communication tool, but also a network for sharing anonymous content. Analysis and modeling of topics and sentiments in Whisper would be interesting topics for future work. For example, whether and how do users establish communities around "topics" or "themes"? How can anonymous posts and conversations impact user sentiment and emotions? How does user behavior on Whisper compare to those of existing content networks such as Digg and Quora?

Acknowledgments

We would like to thank our shepherd Alan Mislove and the anonymous reviewers for their comments. This project was supported in part by NSF grants IIS-1321083, CNS-1224100, IIS-0916307, by the DARPA GRAPHS program (BAA-12-01), and by the Department of State. Any opinions, findings, and conclusions or recommendations expressed in this material are those of the authors and do not necessarily reflect the views of any funding agencies.

10. REFERENCES

[1] ALMUHIMEDI, H., WILSON, S., LIU, B., SADEH, N., AND ACQUISTI, A. Tweets are forever: a large-scale quantitative analysis of deleted tweets. In *Proc. of CSCW* (2013).

[2] ANDREESEN, M. Public tweets. Twitter, March 2014.

[3] ASHBROOK, D., AND STARNER, T. Using gps to learn significant locations and predict movement across multiple users. *Personal Ubiquitous Comput. 7*, 5 (2003), 275–286.

[4] ASSOCIATED PRESS. Whispers, secrets and lies? anonymity apps rise. USA Today, March 2014.

[5] BACKSTROM, L., DWORK, C., AND KLEINBERG, J. Wherefore art thou r3579x?: anonymized social networks, hidden patterns, and structural steganography. In *Proc. of WWW* (2007).

[6] BERNSTEIN, M. S., MONROY-HERNÁNDEZ, A., HARRY, D., ANDRÉ, P., PANOVICH, K., AND VARGAS, G. G. 4chan and/b: An analysis of anonymity and ephemerality in a large online community. In *Proc. of ICWSM* (2011).

[7] BLONDEL, V. D., GUILLAUME, J.-L., LAMBIOTTE, R., AND LEFEBVRE, E. Fast unfolding of communities in large networks. *JSTAT 2008*, 10 (2008).

[8] CHA, M., HADDADI, H., BENVENUTO, F., AND GUMMADI, K. Measuring User Influence in Twitter: The Million Follower Fallacy. In *Proc. of ICWSM* (2010).

[9] CHANG, Y., TANG, L., INAGAKI, Y., AND LIU, Y. What is tumblr: A statistical overview and comparison. *CoRR abs/1403.5206* (2014).

[10] CLAUSET, A., SHALIZI, C. R., AND NEWMAN, M. E. Power-law distributions in empirical data. *SIAM review 51*, 4 (2009), 661–703.

[11] GARCIA, D., MAVRODIEV, P., AND SCHWEITZER, F. Social resilience in online communities: The autopsy of friendster. In *Proc. of COSN* (2013).

[12] GILBERT, E., BAKHSHI, S., CHANG, S., AND TERVEEN, L. "i need to try this!": A statistical overview of pinterest. In *Proc. of CHI* (2013).

[13] GILBERT, E., AND KARAHALIOS, K. Predicting tie strength with social media. In *Proc. of CHI* (2009).

[14] GONG, N. Z., XU, W., HUANG, L., MITTAL, P., STEFANOV, E., SEKAR, V., AND SONG, D. Evolution of social-attribute networks: measurements, modeling, and implications using google+. In *Proc. of IMC* (2012).

[15] GONZALEZ, M. A., GOMEZ, J., LOPEZ-GUERRERO, M., RANGEL, V., AND OCA, M. M. GUIDE-gradient: A guiding algorithm for mobile nodes in wlan and ad-hoc networks. *Wirel. Pers. Commun. 57*, 4 (2011).

[16] GROVE, J. V. Secrets and lies: Whisper and the return of the anonymous app. CNet News, January 2014.

[17] GUO, L., TAN, E., CHEN, S., ZHANG, X., AND ZHAO, Y. E. Analyzing patterns of user content generation in online social networks. In *Proc. of KDD* (2009).

[18] GUYON, I., AND ELISSEEFF, A. An introduction to variable and feature selection. *JMLR 3* (2003), 1157–1182.

[19] HALL, M., FRANK, E., HOLMES, G., PFAHRINGER, B., REUTEMANN, P., AND WITTEN, I. H. The weka data mining software: an update. *SIGKDD Explor. Newsl. 11*, 1 (2009).

[20] HAN, D., ANDERSEN, D. G., KAMINSKY, M., PAPAGIANNAKI, K., AND SESHAN, S. Access point localization using local signal strength gradient. In *Proc. of PAM* (2009).

[21] HOSSEINMARDI, H., HAN, R., LV, Q., MISHRA, S., AND GHASEMIANLANGROODI, A. Analyzing negative user behavior in a semi-anonymous social network. *CoRR abs/1404.3839* (2014).

[22] JONES, J. J., SETTLE, J. E., BOND, R. M., FARISS, C. J., MARLOW, C., AND FOWLER, J. H. Inferring tie strength from online directed behavior. *PLoS ONE 8*, 1 (2013), e52168.

[23] KNUTTILA, L. User unknown: 4chan, anonymity and contingency. *First Monday 16*, 10 (2011).

[24] KWAK, H., CHOI, Y., EOM, Y.-H., JEONG, H., AND MOON, S. Mining communities in networks: a solution for consistency and its evaluation. In *Proc. of IMC* (2009).

[25] KWAK, H., LEE, C., PARK, H., AND MOON, S. What is Twitter, a social network or a news media? In *Proc. of WWW* (2010).

[26] MISLOVE, A., VISWANATH, B., GUMMADI, K. P., AND DRUSCHEL, P. You are who you know: inferring user profiles in online social networks. In *Proc. of WSDM* (2010).

[27] NARAYANAN, A., AND SHMATIKOV, V. Robust de-anonymization of large sparse datasets. In *Proc. of IEEE S&P* (2008).

[28] NEWMAN, M. E. Modularity and community structure in networks. *PNAS 103*, 23 (2006), 8577–8582.

[29] NEWMAN, M. E. J. Assortative mixing in networks. *Physical Review Letters 89*, 20 (2002), 208701.

[30] PETROVIC, S., OSBORNE, M., AND LAVRENKO, V. I wish i didn't say that! analyzing and predicting deleted messages in twitter. *CoRR abs/1305.3107* (2013).

[31] ROESNER, F., GILL, B. T., AND KOHNO, T. Sex, lies, or kittens? investigating the use of snapchat's self-destructing messages. In *Proc. of FC* (2014).

[32] SCHOENEBECK, S. Y. The secret life of online moms: Anonymity and disinhibition on youbemom.com. In *Proc. of ICWSM* (2013).

[33] STRAPPARAVA, C., AND VALITUTTI, A. Wordnet affect: an affective extension of wordnet. In *Proc. of LREC* (2004).

[34] STUTZMAN, F., GROSS, R., AND ACQUISTI, A. Silent listeners: The evolution of privacy and disclosure on facebook. *Journal of Privacy and Confidentiality 4*, 2 (2013).

[35] SULER, J., AND PHILLIPS, W. L. The bad boys of cyberspace: Deviant behavior in a multimedia chat community. *Cyberpsy., Behavior, and Soc. Networking 1*, 3 (1998), 275–294.

[36] UGANDER, J., KARRER, B., BACKSTROM, L., AND MARLOW, C. The anatomy of the facebook social graph. *CoRR abs/1111.4503* (2011).

[37] WAKITA, K., AND TSURUMI, T. Finding community structure in mega-scale social networks: [extended abstract]. In *Proc. of WWW* (2007).

[38] WATTS, D. J., AND STROGATZ, S. Collective dynamics of 'small-world' networks. *Nature*, 393 (1998), 440–442.

[39] WILSON, C., BOE, B., SALA, A., PUTTASWAMY, K., AND ZHAO, B. User Interactions in Social Networks and Their Implications. In *Proc. of EuroSys* (2009).

[40] WORTHAM, J. New social app has juicy posts, all anonymous. NY Times, March 2014.

[41] WORTHAM, J. Whatsapp deal bets on a few fewer 'friends'. NY Times, February 2014.

[42] XU, T., CHEN, Y., JIAO, L., ZHAO, B. Y., HUI, P., AND FU, X. Scaling microblogging services with divergent traffic demands. In *Proc. of Middleware* (2011).

[43] ZHANG, Z., ZHOU, X., ZHANG, W., ZHANG, Y., WANG, G., ZHAO, B. Y., AND ZHENG, H. I am the antenna: Accurate outdoor AP location using smartphones. In *Proc. of MobiCom* (2011).

[44] ZHELEVA, E., AND GETOOR, L. To join or not to join: the illusion of privacy in social networks with mixed public and private user profiles. In *Proc. of WWW* (2009).

QoE Doctor: Diagnosing Mobile App QoE with Automated UI Control and Cross-layer Analysis

Qi Alfred Chen, Haokun Luo, Sanae Rosen, Z. Morley Mao,
Karthik Iyer[†], Jie Hui[†], Kranthi Sontineni[†], Kevin Lau[†]
University of Michigan, [†]T-Mobile USA Inc.[1]
{alfchen,haokun,sanae,zmao}@umich.edu,
[†]{karthik.iyer,jie.hui,kranthi.sontineni1,kevin.lau}@t-mobile.com

ABSTRACT

Smartphones have become increasingly prevalent and important in our daily lives. To meet users' expectations about the Quality of Experience (QoE) of mobile applications (apps), it is essential to obtain a comprehensive understanding of app QoE and identify the critical factors that affect it. However, effectively and systematically studying the QoE of popular mobile apps such as Facebook and YouTube still remains a challenging task, largely due to a lack of a controlled and reproducible measurement methodology, and limited insight into the complex multi-layer dynamics of the system and network stacks.

In this paper, we propose *QoE Doctor*, a tool that supports accurate, systematic, and repeatable measurements and analysis of mobile app QoE. QoE Doctor uses UI automation techniques to replay QoE-related user behavior, and measures the user-perceived latency directly from UI changes. To better understand and analyze QoE problems involving complex multi-layer interactions, QoE Doctor supports analysis across the application, transport, network, and cellular radio link layers to help identify the root causes. We implement QoE Doctor on Android, and systematically quantify various factors that impact app QoE, including the cellular radio link layer technology, carrier rate-limiting mechanisms, app design choices and user-side configuration options.

Categories and Subject Descriptors

C.4 [**Performance of Systems**]: [Measurement techniques]; C.2.1 [**Computer-Communication Networks**]: Network Architecture and Design—*Wireless communication*

General Terms

Design, Measurement, Performance

Keywords

Quality of Experience (QoE); UI Automation; Cross-layer Analysis; Mobile Applications; Cellular Network

[1]The views presented in this paper are as individuals and do not necessarily reflect any position of T-Mobile.

IMC'14, November 5–7, 2014, Vancouver, BC, Canada.

http://dx.doi.org/10.1145/2663716.2663726.

1. INTRODUCTION

As smartphones become more prevalent, mobile applications (apps) become increasingly important to our daily lives, providing access to information, communication, and entertainment. Users would like apps to respond quickly to their requests, consume less mobile data to reduce their monthly bill, and consume less energy to ensure sufficient battery life. The degree to which apps meet these user expectations is referred to as QoE (Quality of Experience). Ensuring good QoE is crucial for app developers, carriers, and phone manufacturers to sustain their revenue models; thus it is essential to obtain a comprehensive understanding of app QoE and the critical factors that affect QoE.

However, it remains a challenging task to effectively and systematically study the QoE of popular mobile apps, such as Facebook and YouTube. Prior work were relied on user studies or app logs to evaluate QoE through *subjective* metrics such as user experience scores and user engagement [20, 24, 23, 18, 17], but these experiments are either costly in human effort or less able to control user behavior variations. To overcome these limitations, Prometheus [15] measures *objective* QoE metrics, such as the video rebuffering ratio, to eliminate the dependence on user behavior, but it requires the application source code to log UI events, limiting its applicability. Besides the methodology, another challenge is that mobile app QoE is affected by factors at many layers of the system and the network. For example, on cellular networks, the radio link layer state machine transition delay can lead to longer round-trip times, and thus increase user-perceived latency [35, 34]. These multi-layer dynamics and their inter-dependencies further complicate QoE analysis.

To address these challenges, we design a tool called QoE Doctor to support more accurate, systematic, and repeatable measurements and analysis of mobile app QoE. QoE Doctor uses UI automation techniques to replay user behavior such as posting a status on Facebook, and at the same time measures the application-layer user-perceived latency directly through UI changes on the screen. Our tool does not require access to the application source code, or modifications to the app logic or the underlying system, making it applicable to QoE measurements of popular apps. In addition to QoE measurements, QoE Doctor supports cross-layer analysis covering the application layer, transport layer, network layer, and radio link layer, in order to understand the root causes of poor QoE caused by network activities and device-specific operations.

We implement QoE Doctor on the Android platform, and systematically measure and analyze various QoE metrics in popular Android apps, including Facebook's post upload time and pull-to-update time, the initial loading time and rebuffering ratio in YouTube videos, and the web page loading time in popular Android browsers. We quantitatively evaluate the important factors impacting these QoE metrics, for example network conditions, application and carrier. Some of our key findings are:

- Network latency is not always on the critical path of the end-to-end user-perceived latency, such as when posting a status on Facebook.
- Changing one Facebook default configuration can reduce over 20% of mobile data and energy consumption.
- Carrier rate limiting policies can increase video loading time by more than 30 seconds (15×) and increase the rebuffering ratio from almost 0% to 50%.
- YouTube ads reduce the initial loading time of the main video, but on cellular networks the total loading time is doubled.
- The ListView version Facebook reduces device latency by more than 67% (compared to the WebView version), network latency by more than 30%, and downlink data consumption by more than 77%.
- Simplifying the 3G RRC state machine can reduce web page loading time by 22.8% for web browsing apps.

Our contributions in this paper are summarized as follows:

- To enable automated and repeated QoE data collection for mobile apps, we design a QoE-aware UI controller, which is able to replay QoE-related user interaction sequences on popular Android apps and directly measure user-perceived latency through UI changes.
- We design a multi-layer QoE analyzer, which provides visibility across the application layer, transport layer, network layer, and radio link layer, helping us systematically diagnose QoE problems and identify the root causes.
- We use QoE Doctor to measure QoE metrics in popular Android apps, and quantify how various important factors impact these QoE metrics.

For the rest of the paper, we first provide background information in §2 and a overview of QoE Doctor in §3. In §4 and §5, we describe two major parts of QoE Doctor: a QoE-aware UI controller and a multi-layer QoE analyzer respectively, and §6 summarizes the current tool limitations. In §7 we use QoE Doctor to systematically study various factors impacting mobile app QoE. We summarize related work in §8, and conclude the paper in §9.

2. BACKGROUND

Subjective and objective QoE metrics. QoE (Quality of Experience) refers to the metrics end users use to judge the quality of services they receive, such as web browsing, phone calls or TV broadcasts. There is a strong incentive for these services to maintain and improve QoE, as it is essential to their continued financial success. To assess the QoE perceived by the end users, one approach is to ask users to score the service experience, which we call a *subjective QoE metric*. Another approach is to directly measure service performance metrics that are related to user satisfaction, such as the number of stalls when watching a video, which we call *objective QoE metrics*. Much of the previous work in this area [20, 42, 17, 24, 18] has focused on subjective metrics. However, subjective evaluations usually require user studies that are hard to repeat and automate, and may be hard to reproduce due to varying user behavior. Thus, in this paper we focus on objective QoE metrics.

RRC/RLC. In order to understand the root causes of QoE problems on mobile devices, it is important to understand how various performance problems in the network stack can affect app QoE. Of particular interest are the RRC (Radio Resource Control) radio link layer control plane messages used by the base station[1] to coordinate with the device. RRC state behavior has a significant impact on app performance and power consumption [22, 33, 40, 41].

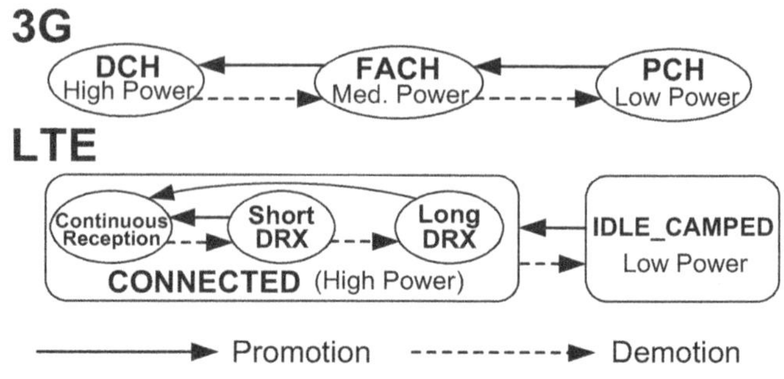

Figure 1: 3G and LTE RRC state machine overview.

Typically, 3G has three main RRC states: DCH, FACH and PCH; and LTE has CONNECTED and IDLE_CAMPED as shown in Fig. 1. DCH and CONNECTED are high-power, high-bandwidth states with dedicated communication channels, and PCH and IDLE_CAMPED are low-power states with no data-plane radio communication. FACH is an intermediate state with a lower-bandwidth shared communication channel. The device promotes from a low-power state to a high-power state if there is a data transfer, and demotes from high-power state to low-power state when a demotion timer expires.

We also examine the layer 2 data plane protocol, RLC (Radio Link Control) [14] . The smallest data transmission unit in RLC is called a PDU (Protocol Data Unit). For 3G uplink traffic, the PDU payload size is fixed at 40 bytes, while for 3G downlink traffic and all LTE traffic the size is flexible and usually greater than 40 bytes. As shown in Fig. 2, an ARQ (automatic repeat request) mechanism is used for reliable data transmission, which is similar to the TCP group acknowledgement mechanism but triggered by a polling request piggybacked in the PDU header.

3. OVERVIEW

In this paper, we develop a tool named *QoE Doctor* to support automated and repeated measurements of objective QoE metrics for popular mobile apps directly from the user's perspective, as well as systematically study various factors influencing these QoE metrics across multiple mobile system and network layers. In this section, we first introduce the target QoE metrics, and then provide an overview of the tool design.

3.1 QoE Metrics

In this paper, we study three important objective mobile app QoE metrics that directly influence user experience:

- **User-perceived latency.** This application-level QoE metric is defined as the time that users spend waiting for a UI response from the app. This includes the web page loading time in web browsers, the post upload time in social apps, and the stall time in video streaming apps.
- **Mobile Data consumption**. On mobile platforms, cellular network data can be expensive if a data limit is exceeded. Thus, for end users mobile data consumption is an important component of mobile app QoE [23].
- **Energy consumption**. Smartphones are energy-constrained devices, thus energy efficiency is a desired feature in mobile

[1]known as the *Node B* for 3G and the *eNodeB* for LTE

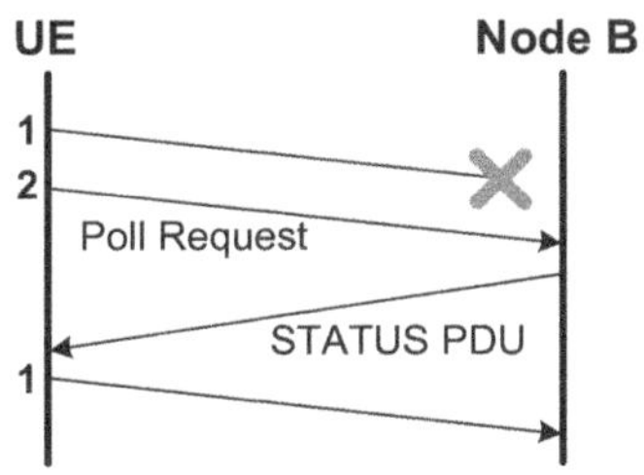

Figure 2: RLC PDU transmission with ARQ-based group acknowledgment mechanism

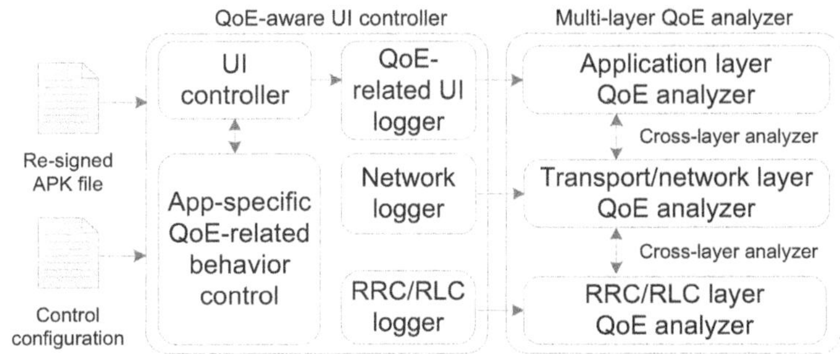

Figure 3: QoE Doctor design overview

apps [23]. In particular, we focus on the network energy consumption of mobile apps since it consumes a large share of the total device energy [19] and it is strongly influenced by app design choices [35, 32].

Among these 3 metrics, user-perceived latency is the most direct way for mobile end users to judge app performance. Thus, it is the main focus of this paper. Unlike previous work [39, 15, 47], our measurement approach (described in §4) directly calculates the latency from user's perspective — the UI layer, without requiring application source code or any OS/application logic instrumentation, which enables us to study this QoE metric broadly on any popular mobile apps of interest.

The other two QoE metrics, mobile data and energy consumption, are more mobile platform specific. Unlike previous work [43, 30, 35, 34], our analysis is driven by automatically replaying user behavior from the application layer. This enables us to study these QoE metrics from the user's perspective, and repeat experiments in a controlled manner.

3.2 Tool Design Overview

Fig. 3 shows the design of QoE Doctor. It includes 2 major components: a QoE-aware UI controller and a multi-layer QoE analyzer.

QoE-aware UI controller. This component runs online on the mobile device, and uses UI control techniques to drive Android apps to automatically replay user behavior traces, while collecting the corresponding QoE data at the application layer, the transport layer, the network layer, and the cellular radio link layer. This allows us to efficiently collect QoE data, and enables controlled QoE measurements without depending on varying user behavior. Unlike previous work [15], our UI control technique does not require access to application source code. Thus, QoE Doctor is able to support QoE analysis for popular Android apps such as Facebook and YouTube. At the UI layer, to accurately collect user-perceived latency data, our UI controller supports direct access to the UI layout tree. UI layout tree describes the app UI on the screen in real time and thus can be used to accurately record the time a UI change is made. We use `tcpdump` to collect network data, and a cellular radio link layer diagnosing tool from Qualcomm to collect radio link layer control plane (RRC) and data plane (RLC) data.

Multi-layer QoE analyzer. The collected QoE data are processed and analyzed offline in this component with multi-layer visibility. At the UI layer, user-perceived latency is calculated using the timestamps of each QoE-related UI event. At the transport and network layers, TCP flow analysis is used to separate network behaviors from different apps based on DSN requests and TCP flow data content. TCP flow analysis is also used to compute mobile data consumption corresponding to the QoE-related user behavior in the application layer. Mobile energy consumption is estimated based on the cellular network behavior according to the RRC state recorded in the radio link layer tool log. To more deeply analyze the QoE measurement results, our analyzer supports cross-layer mapping between the UI layer and the transport/network layer, and between the transport/network layer and the RRC/RLC layer. This allows us to better understand how user actions in the UI layer are delayed by the network traffic, and helps us identify the potential bottleneck in the cellular radio link layer that limits the TCP/IP data transmission speed.

4. QOE-AWARE UI CONTROLLER

In this section, we describe how QoE-related user behavior is automatically replayed and how the corresponding data is collected in QoE Doctor's QoE-aware UI controller.

4.1 Application control

As shown in Fig. 3, the QoE data collection in QoE Doctor is driven by a UI controller. This component initiates UI interactions such as button clicks, and thus controls the app automatically to perform user behaviors of interest. It eliminates human effort, and allows the same set of standardized user interactions to be replayed each time. In our implementation on Android, we control the app UI through the InstrumentationTestCase API [2] provided by the Android system for UI testing during app development. It allows UI interaction events to be sent to the app during testing, and the only requirement is to re-sign the binary APK file by our debugging key. Our work is the first to use the InstrumentationTestCase API for the purpose of automated QoE analysis.

UI control paradigm. The UI control in QoE Doctor follows a *see-interact-wait* paradigm. After launching the app, the *see* component first parses the app UI data shown on the screen, then the *interact* component chooses a UI element to interact with (*e.g.*, by clicking a button or scrolling a page). After the interaction, the *wait* component waits for the corresponding UI response. This paradigm follows natural user-app interaction behavior, allowing us to replay real user behavior. Using the InstrumentationTestCase API, the controller is launched in the same process as the controlled app, allowing direct access to the UI data as needed for the *see* and *wait* components. Unlike prior work which require system instrumentation or Android UI dump tools [21, 26, 29, 36], direct UI data sharing enables convenient and accurate latency measurements (described next).

The *Wait* component and accurate user-perceived latency measurement. In our *see-interact-wait* paradigm, the *wait* component measures the user-perceived latency: the time between triggering a UI interaction event and receiving the corresponding UI response. Thus, in our controller we log the start and end timestamps of the waiting process to measure user-perceived latency. The waiting process can either be triggered (1) by the user (*e.g.*, uploading a post in Facebook), or (2) by the app (*e.g.*, a video stall). To log the start timestamp, for (1) we log the time when the controller triggers the user action, and for (2) we log the time when the waiting process indicator (*e.g.*, a progress bar) shows up. For the end timestamp, we log the time when the wait-ending UI indicator occurs (*e.g.*, the progress bar's disappearance). As the controller shares the same process as the app, these UI element events can be monitored directly.

User behavior replay. We select several popular Android apps and identify critical QoE-related user behavior, along with the corresponding user interaction sequence. Based on the interaction sequences, control specifications are written for the UI control logic implementation. To write the specification, only some familiarity with Android UI View classes is required, so the average Android app developer should be able to do so. In our design, we support replaying the user interaction sequences both with and without replaying the timing between each action. In §7 we use both according to the experiment requirements.

To ensure the user interactions are sent to the right UI elements during replay, we design a View signature describing the View characteristics in the UI layout tree. This signature includes the UI element class name, View ID, and a description added by the developer. To support different Android devices, the Vew element coordinates are not included in this signature.

4.2 App-specific Control Design and User-perceived Latency Collection

According to a recent report [6], social networking app Facebook and video app Youtube are the top 2 mobile applications used in North America during peak periods, and web browsing is ranked the third in the amount of aggregate mobile traffic globally. Thus, we focus on these applications. Table 1 summarizes the QoE-related user behavior that QoE Doctor replays and the associated user-perceived latency metrics.

4.2.1 Facebook

For Facebook, we measure the following two user actions:

Upload post. One of the most common user actions on Facebook is to post an update: posting a status, check-in, or uploading a photo. For these actions, the user-perceived latency is the time from when the "post" button is clicked to the time when the posted item is shown on the news feed list. To measure this ending time, we put a timestamp string in the post, and after the "post" button is clicked, the *wait* component repeatedly parses the UI layout tree and logs the end timestamp as the time when the item with the timestamp string appears in the news feed.

Pull-to-update. Another common user action on Facebook is to pull the news feed list down to update it. This can be generated either by: (1) a pulling gesture, or (2) passively waiting for Facebook to update the news feed list by itself. To replay the former, our controller generates a scrolling down gesture. For the latter, the controller just waits on the Facebook news feed list, and uses the *wait* component to log the appearance and disappearance time of the loading progress bar for the news feed list.

4.2.2 YouTube

For YouTube, we replay searching for a video by name and then watching it.

Watch video. To replay this user behavior, the controller takes as input a list of video names. It searches for the video and plays it until it finishes. There are two user-perceived latency metrics the *wait* component monitors: the initial loading time, and the rebuffering ratio. The rebuffering ratio is the ratio of time spent stalling to the sum of total play and stall time after the initial loading. For the initial loading time, we start measuring when the controller clicks on a video entry in the search results, and finish measuring when the loading progress bar disappears. For the rebuffering ratio, the controller parses the UI layout tree after the video starts playing, and logs when the progress bar appears and disappears as the video rebuffering start and end timestamps.

When an advertisement (ad) is shown before the video, we measure the initial loading time and rebuffering ratio for the ad and the actual video respectively. We configure the controller to skip any ads whenever users are given that option, as a recent study shows that 94% of users skip these ads [1].

4.2.3 Web Browsing

For web browsing apps, we choose Google Chrome and Mozilla Firefox, which both have more than 50 million downloads in Google Play, along with the default Android browser (named "Internet"). For these browsers, we replay loading a web page.

Load web page. For web browsing, the most important performance metric is the web page loading time. To replay page loading, our controller takes a file with a list of URL strings as input, and enters each URL into the URL bar of the browser app line by line before sending an ENTER key. The *wait* component logs the ENTER key sending time as the start time, and monitors the progress bar in the UI layout tree to determine when the loading completes. A more accurate way of determining the loading complete time would be to log the time when the visible parts on the page are loaded, for example by capturing a video of the screen and then analyzing the video frames as implemented in Speed Index metric for WebPagetest [8]. We plan to support this in our future work by adding a screen video capturing into the controller, and supporting video frame analysis in the application layer analyzer.

4.3 Data Collection

While replaying user behavior to measure QoE, the UI controller collects data at multiple layers.

4.3.1 Application Layer Data Collection

Application layer QoE data is collected by the *wait* component during the user behavior replay. The controller generates a log file, called `AppBehaviorLog`, which records each user interaction event sent to the controlled app, in particular the start and end timestamps to calculate the user-perceived latency. The user interaction for each app and the corresponding UI elements for user-perceived latency measurements are described in §4.2, and summarized in Table 1.

4.3.2 Transport/Network Layer Data Collection

To measure mobile data consumption and help identify the root causes of QoE problems for other layers, our controller collects traffic logs at the transport and network layers using `tcpdump` [9] during the user behavior replay.

4.3.3 RRC/RLC Layer Data Collection

To collect RRC/RLC layer data, we use QxDM (Qualcomm eXtensible Diagnostic Monitor), a cellular network diagnosis tool from Qualcomm [12]. This tool provides real-time access to both RRC and RLC layer information for all commercial handsets with a

Application	User behavior to replay	User-perceived latency to measure	UI events to monitor for latency measurement	
			Measurement start time	Measurement end time
Facebook	Upload post	Post uploading time	Press "post" button	Posted content shown in ListView
	Pull-to-update	News feed list updating time	Progress bar appears	Progress bar disappears
YouTube	Watch video	Initial loading time	Click on the video entry	Progress bar disappears
		Rebuffering time	Progress bar appears	Progress bar disappears
Web browsing	Load web page	Web page loading time	Press ENTER in URL bar	Progress bar disappears

Table 1: Replayed user behavior and user-perceived latency metrics for Facebook, YouTube and web browsers

Qualcomm chipset, including popular Android phone models such as Samsung Galaxy S3/S4. Recent work [44] exposes RRC state on Intel/Infineon XGold chipsets by instrumenting the system, but it cannot access RLC data, which is critical in our cross-layer analysis in §5.4.2. To collect this data, we need to connect the mobile devices to a Windows PC, and configure the QxDM software for the corresponding network technology, either 3G or LTE. QxDM saves all radio link layer information to a file on the PC. By parsing this information, we isolate the RRC state transitions and RLC PDUs with corresponding timestamps.

QxDM limitations. There are two major limitations of the QxDM tool. First, as mentioned earlier, it requires a PC connection in order to collect real-time user data outside the laboratory. QoE Doctor helps reduce the impact of this limitation as we can replay real user behavior using the UI controller. Second, the QxDM tool is not designed to provide complete RLC PDU payload information. Perhaps to reduce logging overhead, the RLC PDUs only contain 2 payload bytes, which makes the cross-layer mapping between RLC PDUs and network packets non-trivial. We explain in §5.4.2 how we use a technique we call *long-jump mapping* to overcome this limitation.

5. MULTI-LAYER QOE ANALYZER

In this section, we describe how QoE metrics are calculated at each layer using the data collected by the UI controller, and what multi-layer analysis is supported to help study these QoE metrics.

5.1 Application Layer Analyzer

At the application layer, we can simply calculate the user-perceived latency metrics based on the start and end timestamps logged in the `AppBehaviorLog` by the UI controller. Unlike previous work [22, 31], we calculate UI latency directly rather than inferring it from network traces, which can capture the ground truth, and also enables us to analyze apps having encrypted traffic such as Facebook.

User-perceived latency calibration. We measure user-perceived latency by observing app-generated UI events by periodically parsing the UI layout tree. Fig. 4 shows the process for measuring a Facebook post upload, where the start timestamp is measured from a UI controller action and the end timestamp is measured from the UI layout tree. In QoE Doctor we want to measure t_{ui}, but due to overhead in parsing the UI tree, the actual measured latency is $t_m = t_{ui} + t_{offset} + t_{parsing}$. To accurately calculate t_{ui}, we need to subtract t_{offset} and $t_{parsing}$ from t_m. Assuming the end time of the UI data update falls uniformly in the parsing time interval, the expected value of offset time is $\bar{t}_{offset} = \frac{1}{2}t_{parsing}$. We calibrate the user-perceived latency by subtracting $\frac{3}{2}t_{parsing}$ from t_m. This calibration is used to correct the post uploading time, the web page loading time, and the initial loading time in Table 1. For the other two latency metrics, the start timestamp is measured by parsing the UI tree, which is the same as the end timestamp measurement, so the average offset time is $\bar{t}_{offset} = 0$. For these, we just subtract $t_{parsing}$ from t_m in the calibration.

5.2 Transport/Network Layer Analyzer

In the transport and network layers, we calculate the mobile data consumption QoE metric from data collected by `tcpdump`. Our analyzer parses the raw packet trace and extracts TCP flows, defined by the tuple {srcIP, srcPort, dstIP, dstPort}, and then associates each TCP flow with the server's URL by parsing the DNS lookups in the trace. Over repeated experiments, we identify the TCP flows with common server URLs to associate the replayed user behavior, and then calculate its network data consumption. We also calculate the number of data retransmissions, the RTT (Round-Trip Time), and the throughput for the TCP flows.

5.3 RRC/RLC Layer Analyzer

We obtain RRC state change information from QxDM logs. Using the Monsoon Power Monitor [7], we obtain the power level for each RRC state, and thus can calculate the network energy consumption for the entire mobile device using a technique from previous work [22]. To get the network energy consumed by the controlled app only, we remove all other apps on the device and log out all system app accounts to ensure that the network energy calculation is not affected by unrelated traffic. We also calculate tail energy as defined in previous work [34], and count all other network energy as non-tail energy.

First-hop OTA RTT. QxDM logs both uplink and downlink RLC PDUs, which include polling PDUs and the corresponding STATUS PDUs, as mentioned in §2. Based on this feedback loop, we calculate the first-hop OTA (Over The Air) RTT, which is the time from when the device transmits a polling request until when it receives the STATUS PDU. However, because of the group acknowledgement mechanism, we may not find a corresponding polling PDU for each STATUS PDU. Thus, we estimate the first-hop OTA RTT for a PDU by finding the nearest polling PDU to a STATUS PDU.

5.4 Cross-layer Analyzer

Besides analyzing data at individual layers, QoE Doctor also supports cross-layer analysis across the application, transport, network, and RRC/RLC layers to help perform root cause analysis.

5.4.1 *Cross Application, Transport/Network Layers*

To help identify root causes of QoE problems in the application layer, we examine the transport and network layer behavior to identify the critical path of the application layer delay and pinpoint the bottlenecks. We first identify the start and end time of a user-perceived latency problem logged in the `AppBehaviorLog`, which forms a *QoE window*. Then we focus our analysis on the network traffic which falls into this QoE window, and use flow analysis to identify the TCP flows responsible for the application layer delay. Through this cross-layer analysis, we can study fine-

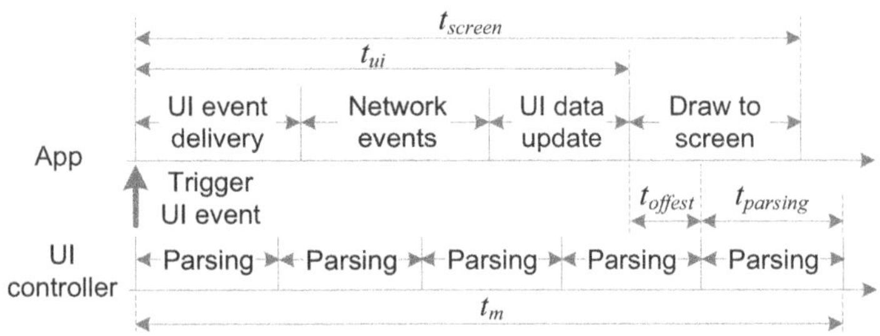

Figure 4: User-perceived latency measurement for uploading a post on Facebook

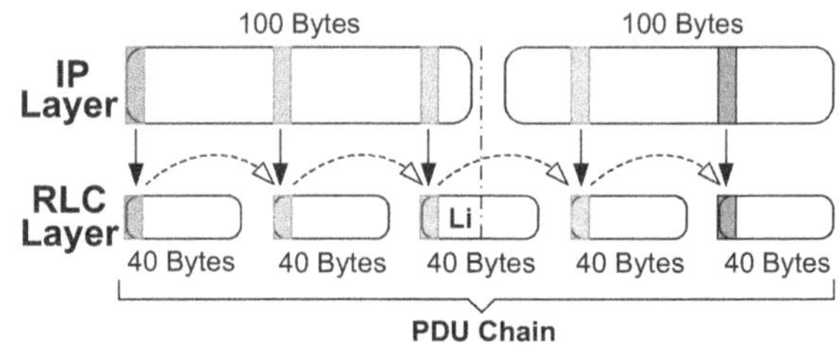

Figure 5: *Long-jump mapping* algorithm for cross-layer mapping from IP packets to a RLC PDU chain. The payload of the third PDU is a combination of the tail of the first IP packet and the head of the second IP packet.

grained QoE metrics such as the initial loading time for Youtube, which is otherwise indistinguishable from rebuffering events if only analyzing network data, as done in previous work [18, 42].

5.4.2 *Cross Transport/Network, RRC/RLC Layers*

To understand the impact of the interaction between the transport/network and the cellular radio link layers, QoE Doctor supports cross-layer analysis between them.

Transport/network layer and RRC layer. From the RRC state information logged by QxDM, we obtain the RRC state change information. By finding an overlap between the QoE window (defined in §5.4.1) and the RRC state transition window, we can pinpoint cases where RRC state transitions occur during the period of the user-perceived latency, which may help reveal the impact of RRC state transitions on the user-perceived latency.

Transport/network layer and RLC layer. To understand how network packets are transmitted in the lower layer, our analyzer supports the mapping from IP packets to RLC PDUs using the fine-grained RLC transmission information provided by QxDM. More specifically, we map complete IP packets to the corresponding fragmented RLC payload data bytes spreading among several PDUs. Due to the limitation of QxDM mentioned in §4.3.3, for each PDU only the first 2 payload bytes are logged, which provides us with limited information to identify the corresponding IP packet.

To ensure an accurate mapping, we design an algorithm which handles these limitations we have mentioned. As only 2 payload bytes are captured, after matching these 2 bytes we skip over the rest of the PDU, and try to match the first 2 payload bytes in the next PDU as shown in Fig. 5, which we call *long-jump mapping*. Since some PDUs may contain the payload data belonging to two consecutive IP packets, according to the 3G specification [14] we use the LI (Length Indicator) to map the end of an IP packet. If the cumulative mapped index equals the size of the IP packet, we have found a mapping successfully; otherwise no mapping is discovered.

We evaluate this mapping, and find that the percentage of mapped IP packets is 99.52% for uplink and 88.83% for downlink. The reason that we cannot achieve 100% accuracy is that occasionally a small fraction of RLC PDUs are not captured by QxDM, causing missing mappings for the corresponding IP packets. In our cross-layer analysis, we only consider the IP packets with successfully mapped RLC PDUs.

6. TOOL LIMITATIONS

The limitations of QoE Doctor are summarized as follows.

Manual efforts involved in the replay implementation. In order to replay user behavior, QoE Doctor currently requires manual identification of critical QoE-related user behavior, and some familiarity with Android UI View classes for writing control specifications. These manual efforts are necessary, as measuring the QoE metric of interest requires identifying the natural way a user interacts with the app. In future work, we will consider using learning algorithms to automatically generate common user behavior from user study logs.

Latency measurement imprecision. As shown in Fig. 4, although we are directly measuring the UI data changes (t_{ui}), the result may differ from the UI changes on the screen (t_{screen}), mostly due to the UI drawing delay. In §7.1 we find the measurement error is less than 4%.

Lack of fine-grained application layer latency breakdown. In our latency measurements, only the end-to-end latency is reflected in the UI layout data changes, and we cannot break down the latency into more fine-grained operations such as the transaction task delay and the inter-process communication delay. Without the ability to track detailed UI operation sequences, it is hard to confirm whether the network activity is asynchronous, which may mislead the cross-layer analysis. In our design, we do not support it because providing this information requires system or application logic instrumentation [39, 47], which may limit the tool's applicability.

Limitation related to RRC/RLC layer logger. Our analysis about layer 2 data plane (RLC) information may not be 100% accurate due to QxDM limitations as described in §4.3.3 and §5.4.2.

7. EXPERIMENTAL EVALUATION

In this section, we first evaluate the QoE measurement accuracy and overhead of QoE Doctor, and then use QoE Doctor to systematically and quantitatively study various factors which may have impact on our 3 QoE metrics. In this paper, we consider three factors potentially impacting QoE: (1) the network type and quality, for WiFi and 3G and LTE cellular networks; (2) the app's design and configuration; and (3) the carrier, in particular carrier rate limiting mechanisms for throttling. These factors are identified based on either our experiences with the apps or practical problems from real user experience identified by the authors at T-Mobile. We summarize our experiment goals in Table 2. In this section, 2 carriers are involved in our experiments, which we denote as C1 and C2.

7.1 Tool Accuracy and Overhead

In this section, we report our evaluation results of the accuracy and overhead of QoE Doctor. Table 3 summarizes the results in the section along with the IP packet to RLC PDU mapping performance reported in §5.4.2.

Section	Experiment goal	Relevant factor	Application
§7.2	Device and network delay on the critical path for user-perceived latency	Network condition, app	Facebook
§7.3	Data and energy consumption during application idle time	Network condition, app	Facebook
§7.4	Impact of app design choices on user-perceived latency	Network condition, app	Facebook
§7.5	Impact of carrier throttling mechanisms on user-perceived latency	Network condition, carrier	YouTube
§7.6	Impact of video ads on user-perceived latency	Network condition, app	YouTube
§7.7	Impact of the RRC state machine design on user-perceived latency	Network condition, carrier	Web browsers

Table 2: Experiment goals and mobile applications studied in §7.

Item	Value
User-perceived latency measurement error	≤40 ms (t_d)
	≤4% (t_d/t_{screen})
Transport/network to RLC data mapping ratio	99.52% (uplink)
	88.83% (downlink)
CPU overhead	6.18%

Table 3: Tool accuracy and overhead summary of QoE Doctor.

QoE measurement accuracy. The mobile data consumption metric is a precise value, calculated directly from data in the transport/network layer. The network energy consumption is calculated directly from RRC/RLC layer information using a well-established model [22, 48]. For the user-perceived latency metric, however, the UI data changes in the UI layout tree may not precisely correspond to screen changes due to UI drawing delays (Fig. 4). We evaluate the measurement accuracy by recording a video of the screen at 60 frames per second for each of the user-perceived latency tests we perform. Each experiment is repeated 30 times. The result shows that for all actions, the average time difference t_d between t_{screen} and the measurement result from QoE Doctor is under 40 milliseconds. We determine how the user-perceived latency measurements are affected by calculating the ratio of t_d to t_{screen} for each metric, as shown in Fig. 6. As t_d is not proportional to t_{screen}, the ratio differences between the 5 metrics are due to t_{screen}. To calculate an upper bound on this ratio, for each metric we use the shortest t_{screen} among all the experiments in this section in Fig. 6. As shown, for all experiment results the latency measurement error is less than 4%.

QoE measurement overhead. We use DDMS [3] to compare the CPU time when manually inputting the target user behavior with the CPU time when using QoE Doctor. We find the upper bound of this overhead by running the most compute-intensive operation, parsing the UI tree (Fig. 4), on the most computation-intensive app operation: uploading a Facebook post. We run this test 30 times, and find the average worst-case CPU computation overhead introduced by QoE Doctor is 6.18%.

7.2 Facebook: Post Uploading Time Breakdown Analysis

In this section, we focus on the action of uploading a post to Facebook, leveraging our multi-layer analysis to break down the roles the device and the network play in the user-perceived latency.

Experiment setup. We run the experiments on Facebook version 5.0.0.26.31 on a Samsung Galaxy S3 device with Android 4.3. We use QoE Doctor to post status, check-in, and 2 photos every 2 seconds for C1 3G and C1 LTE network. Each action is repeated 50 times.

Finding 1: The network delay is not always on the critical path. To understand the role of the device and the network in the end-to-end delay, we break down the device and network latency according to the steps of uploading a post shown in Fig. 4. To separate out the network latency portion, we first identify the TCP flows which are responsible for the post uploading using techniques described in §5.4.1. Even though the trace is encrypted, it is not hard to identify the flow with high confidence since in most cases only one flow has traffic during the QoE window (defined in §5.4.1). We then calculate the network latency as the timestamp difference between the earliest and latest packet of this TCP flow, and calculate the device latency by subtracting the network latency from the user-perceived latency.

Fig. 7 shows the breakdown results for posting 2 photos, status and check-in for C1 3G and C1 LTE network. In the figure, the standard deviation values of the latencies for posting 2 photos are all less than 0.7 seconds, and those for posting a check-in and a status are all less than 0.25 seconds. Surprisingly, we find that the network delay contributes little to the check-in and status uploading latency. We double-checked the network trace, and found that the corresponding TCP ACK packets for both actions are actually outside the QoE window. This indicates that showing these posts on the news feed list doesn't depend on the response from Facebook server. In other words, the *Facebook app pushes a local copy of status and check-in posts directly onto the news feed list to remove the network delay from the critical path, which ensures low user-perceived latency.* Note that this only happens to posting a status and a check-in; for posting 2 photos, the network latency always falls inside the QoE window, suggesting that it is very likely to be on the critical path, which is the case described in Fig. 4.

Finding 2: 3G RLC transmission delay contributes more than expected in the end-to-end photo posting time. Unlike status and check-in posting, Fig. 7 shows that for 2 photo uploading action the network latency has more than 65% share in the end-to-end latency. Using our cross-layer analysis between the application and transport/network layers, we always see a clear pattern of uploading then downloading two large chunk of data in the TCP flow inside QoE Window. Interestingly, for this action 3G has around 50% more network latency than LTE, while their device latencies are similar. To find out the reason, we further break down the network latency using our cross-layer analyzer between the transport/network layer and the RRC/RLC layer as described in §5.4.1.

In this more fine-grained network latency breakdown, we target four metrics: *IP-to-RLC delay* (t_1), *RLC transmission delay* (t_2), the *first-hop OTA delay* (t_3), and *other delay* (t_4) as shown in Fig. 9. *The IP-to-RLC delay* is the time difference between an IP packet and its first mapped RLC PDU when no other RLC PDUs are transmitted. For the *RLC transmission delay*, we first identify the periods where the device is "busy" transmitting RLC PDUs using a burst analysis for RLC PDUs. We implement this analysis by checking whether the inter-PDU time is less than the estimated first-hop OTA RTT defined in §5.3. Then, the *RLC transmission delay* is calculated by summing up all the inter-PDU time within

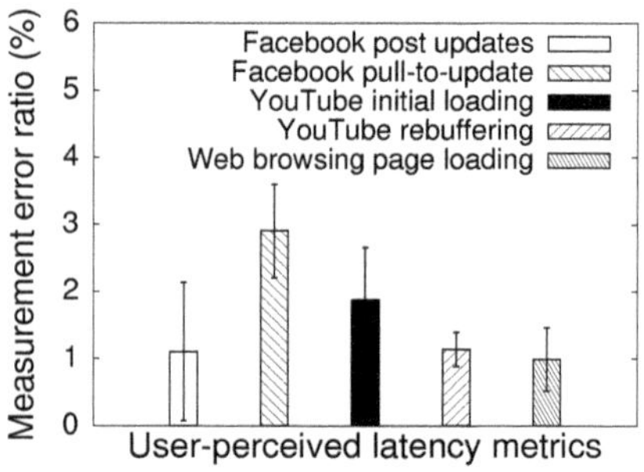

Figure 6: Error ratio of user-perceived latency measurements for each action.

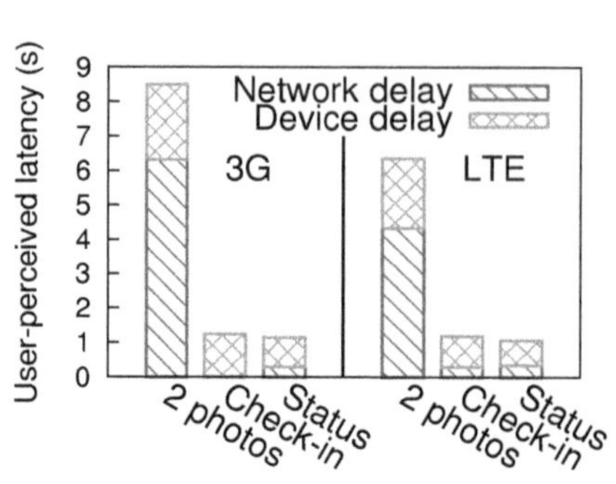

Figure 7: Device and network delay breakdown for different post uploads.

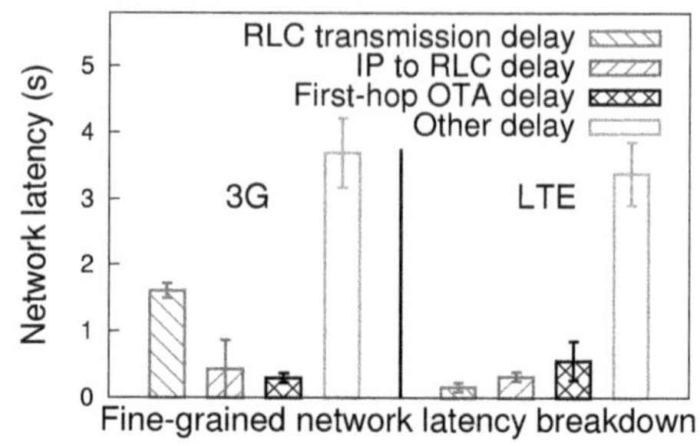

Figure 8: Fine-grained network latency breakdown for 2 photo uploading.

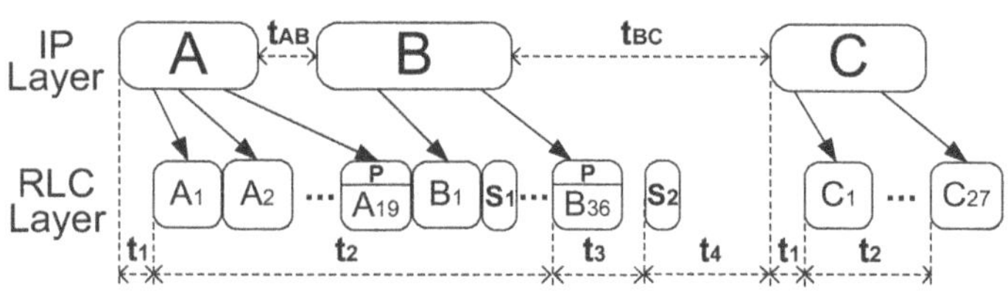

Figure 9: Example cross-layer network latency breakdown. t_{AB} and t_{BC} are the inter-IP packet times. Although $t_{AB} > 0$, A and B are transmitted back-to-back within one PDU burst in the RLC layer. PDUs with letter P are polling PDUs. S_1 and S_2 are STATUS PDUs.

each RLC burst. For the *first-hop OTA delay*, we notice that not all the first-hop OTA RTTs are on the critical path. For example, the RTT from A_{19} to S_1 is not on the critical path but the RTT from B_{36} to S_2 is, because for the former the device is busy transmitting B_1 but not explicitly waiting for S_1. Therefore, we define the *first-hop OTA delay* as the summation of the first-hop OTA RTTs which the device explicitly waits for. *Other delay* is calculated by subtracting the end-to-end time by the *IP-to-RLC delay*, the *RLC transmission delay*, and the *first-hop OTA delay*. The *IP-to-RLC delay*, the *RLC transmission delay*, and the *first-hop OTA delay* are all within one hop range from the local devices, so *other delay* consists of the latencies outside of the one-hop range, for example the latency in the switch/router, server processing delay, *etc.*

The breakdown results are shown in Fig. 8. In the figure, the RLC transmission delay in C1 3G is significantly greater than that in C1 LTE. We manually inspect the traces of posting 2 photos, and find that there are on average 270 IP packets transmitted within the QoE window, corresponding to 10553 RLC PDUs for C1 3G and 4132 RLC PDUs for C1 LTE. Such 2.55× additional number of RLC PDUs implies significant RLC PDU header processing overhead, which could be the potential reason of the higher RLC transmission delay in C1 3G.

7.3 Facebook: Background Traffic Data Consumption and Energy Analysis

To ensure that users can get interesting content from their social network at any time, Facebook app keeps communicating with the server even when it is not in the foreground. How much mobile data and energy are consumed by these background network events? How can we as users reduce cost and battery power usage while still getting timely updates? In this section, we use QoE Doctor to explore the answers.

Experiment setup. We use two devices, a Samsung Galaxy S3 device with Android 4.3 (referred as device A) and a Samsung Galaxy S4 device with Android 4.3 (referred as device B), and configure the accounts on device A and B to be mutual and exclusive friends with each other. Then, we use QoE Doctor's controller on device A to post statuses with texts of identical lengths, causing device B to receive these status updates. We change the settings of the account in device B so that it receives a notification for every news feed post from device A. Thus, device A simulates Facebook friends or public pages from which the user with device B wants to get updated with no delay. We consider these content to be *time-sensitive*. On device B, we only use the data collection functionality of QoE Doctor controller. Since our target is Facebook background traffic, we use flow analysis and only analyze TCP flows which talk to Facebook DNS domain names. For energy consumption, we use QxDM RRC state machine logs as described in §5.3.

Finding 3. Facebook's non-time-sensitive background traffic adds non-negligible overhead to users' daily mobile data and energy consumption. To see how uploading frequency impacts mobile data and energy consumption, we set the uploading frequency on device B to be every 10 minutes, 30 minutes, 1 hour, and no uploading. We run the experiment for 16 hours, and the results are shown in Fig. 10 and Fig. 11. For uploading every 10 minutes, 30 minutes and 1 hour, the results are expected: data and energy consumptions are strictly proportional to the upload frequency of device A. These content is time-sensitive for device B, so these overhead is acceptable. However, to our surprise, when device A's only friend, device B, posts nothing, device A still has around 200 Kilobytes mobile data consumption and around 300 J mobile network energy every day! We repeat the experiment and check the news feed content on device B, and find out that this traffic mainly comes from Facebook friends and page recommendations in the news feed list. Compared to the posts of device B's friends or public pages (simulated by device A), for which device B wants to get updated with no delay, we consider this traffic to be *non time sensitive*. For these content, even if it is not updated in the background, only a few seconds of waiting time is needed to update the list after the app launches. From our experiment results, if device B has time-sensitive updates every 1 hour, around half of the data and energy is spent on non-time-sensitive traffic, doubling the mobile data and energy overhead.

Finding 4. Changing one Facebook configuration can reduce mobile data and energy consumption caused by non-time-sensitive background traffic by 20%. In Facebook app's settings, an item called "refresh interval" determines how frequently the news feed list is refreshed in the background, which controls the

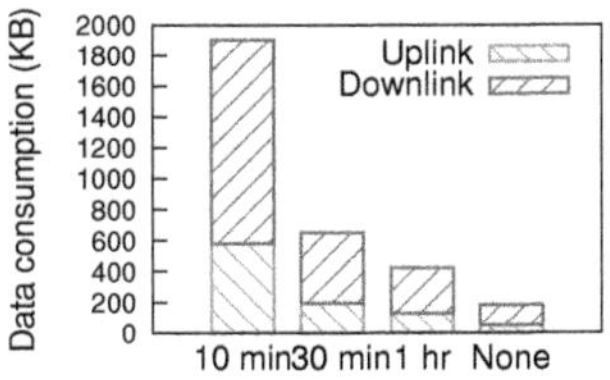

Figure 10: Per-flow mobile data consumption breakdown by post upload frequency.

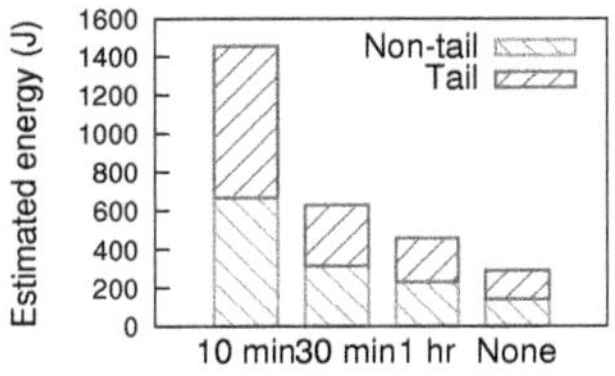

Figure 11: Estimated energy consumption breakdown by post upload frequency.

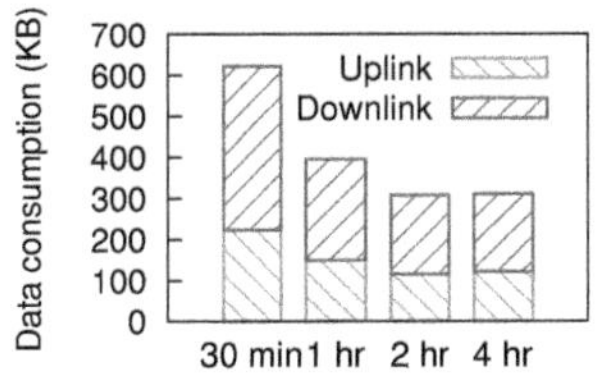

Figure 12: Per-flow mobile data consumption by refresh interval configuration.

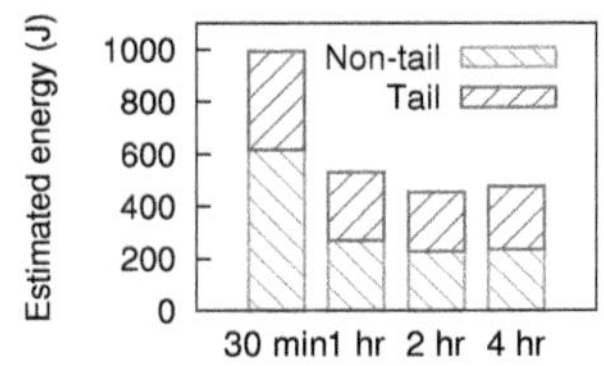

Figure 13: Estimated energy consumption by refresh interval configuration.

refresh frequency of the non-time-sensitive background traffic. In Fig. 10 and Fig. 11, the refresh interval we use is the default value, 1 hour. To explore how to configure the refresh interval, we fix the device A uploading frequency to 30 minutes to simulate the activity of its friend on device B, and change device B's refresh interval to 30 minutes, 1 hour, 2 hours and 4 hours. We collect data for 16 hours for each configuration. The results are shown in Fig. 10 and Fig. 11. As shown, the 2-hour configuration reduces mobile data consumption by 25% and mobile network energy consumption by 20% compared to the default 1-hour configuration. Another observation is that the data and energy consumptions are similar between the 2-hour and 4-hour configurations. After inspecting the traces closely, we find that the network traffic is mainly generated by status upload notifications from device A every 30 minutes, which are time-sensitive for device B. Thus, for users who think that delaying non-time-sensitive information for a while is acceptable, changing the refresh interval from 1 hour to 2 hours is likely to be a good balance between content timeliness and data, and energy consumption: it reduces mobile data and energy consumption by more than 20%, while only delaying non-time-sensitive content by 1 hour.

7.4 Facebook: Application Design Impact on News Feed Update Latency

In this section, we leverage QoE Doctor to study the impact of app design choices on user-perceived latency. We compare Facebook app version 1.8.3 and version 5.0.0.26.31. The major difference between them is that Facebook app changed the way of showing news feed list from an Android WebView to a ListView. The goal of our comparison is to identify and quantify impact of this change on QoE. We choose to relay pull-to-update action using QoE Doctor, which is an updating process related only to the news feed list.

Experiment setup. All experiments are launched on the same Samsung Galaxy S4 device with Android 4.2.2. Like §7.3, we use 2 devices, denoted by A and B. Their Facebook accounts are mutual and exclusive friends. Using QoE Doctor we have device A posting a status every 2 minutes for 6 hours. Device B passively waits for the news feed list to update by itself, which is also every 2 minutes, and measures the update latency. Facebook app version 1.8.3 does not self-update every 2 minutes, so we generate a scrolling gesture every 2 minutes to trigger the updating. We launch the experiment under both C1 LTE and WiFi. For all the experiments, we choose the same time period of a day to avoid time-of-day effect. We also choose the same place to run the experiments to ensure that the cellular and WiFi signal strengths in the comparison are the same.

Finding 5. The ListView design reduces device latency by more than 67% , network latency by 30%, and download data consumption by more than 77% compared to the WebView design. Fig. 14 shows the news feed list updating time distribution for both the WebView design and the ListView design under C1 LTE and WiFi. Under both network conditions, the user-perceived latency is greatly affected by the design – the average latency of the WebView design is more than 100% longer than that of the ListView. At the same time, the latency of the ListView has less variance. To understand the root cause, we break down the device and network delay using the same technique as in §7.2. As for posting photos in §7.2, in this experiment the network latency for news feed list updating is always inside the QoE window. As shown in Fig. 15, both network and device latency are improved by at least 67% and 30% respectively after changing the WebView design to the ListView design. We hypothesize that the reason for the device latency improvement is that WebView updating is quite complex compared to the ListView since it involves iterated content fetching and HTML parsing, which leads to a less responsive UI. For the network latency improvement, we further calculate the network uplink and downlink data consumption for the TCP flow responsible for the news feed list updating, which is shown in Fig. 16. For both C1 LTE and WiFi, the only difference is that the amount of downlink TCP data in the WebView design is more than 77% more than that in the ListView design. Thus, the network latency improvement in the ListView design is caused by much less network data to download. We think the reason is that WebView needs to display HTML content, thus compared to ListView it requires extra data to specify layout, structure, CSS, *etc.* Note that these results just suggest that using the ListView may lead to lower user-perceived latency compared to using the WebView, but the actual amount of improvement also depends on other factors such as app traffic characteristics.

7.5 YouTube: Carrier Throttling Mechanism Analysis

Most mobile users have limited monthly data plan contracted by different carriers. Normally users will be charged for over-limit data usage, while C1 uses another policy: users are still provided free data services even after exceeding the data limit [13], and the penalty is that carrier will throttle the network bandwidth on the base station. In this section, we use QoE Doctor to study how this policy may impact app QoE.

Experiment setup. To study the throttling mechanism's impact on QoE, we use QoE Doctor to play videos in YouTube app version 5.2.27 on a Samsung Galaxy S4 device with Android 4.3, with a throttled and an unthrottled SIM card for both C1 3G and C1 LTE.

Video dataset. We use "a" to "z" as keywords to search for videos in YouTube app, and choose the top 10 videos for each keyword to form our video dataset of 260 videos. This dataset is quite diverse in both the video length (1 minute to half an hour) and video popularity (several thousand views to more than 10 billion views). In this dataset the total video length is about 34.6 hours.

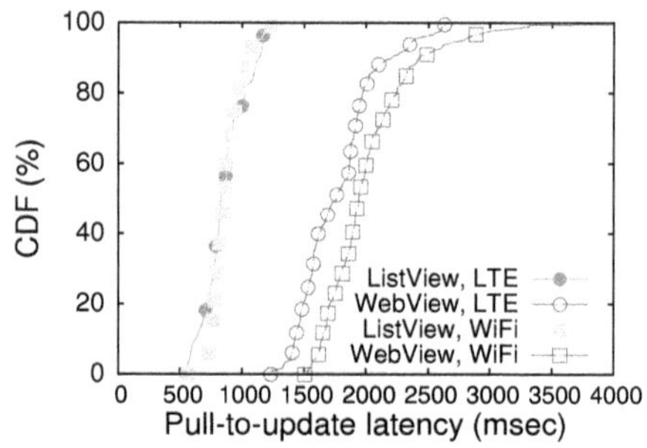

Figure 14: The news feed list updating time for WebView and ListView under C1 LTE and WiFi.

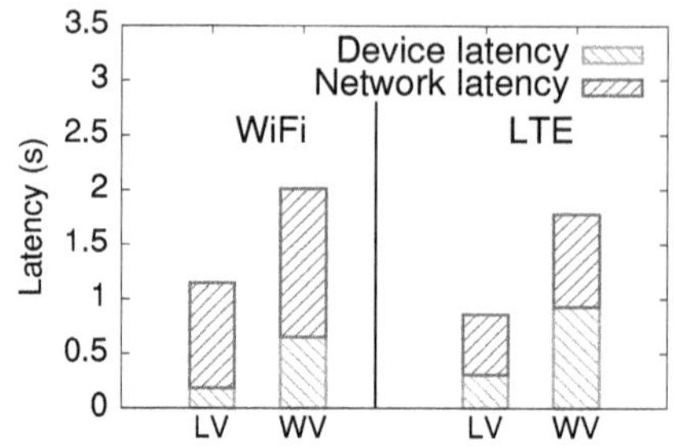

Figure 15: Breakdown of the news feed updating time for the WebView (WV) and ListView (LV) Facebook versions

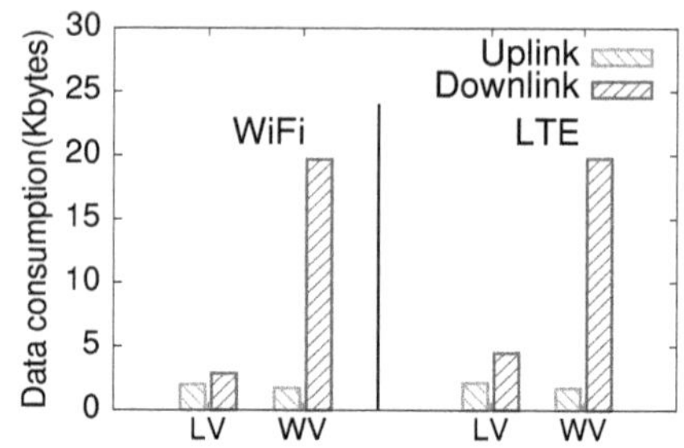

Figure 16: Network data consumption for the news feed updating for WebView (WV) and ListView (LV) Facebook versions

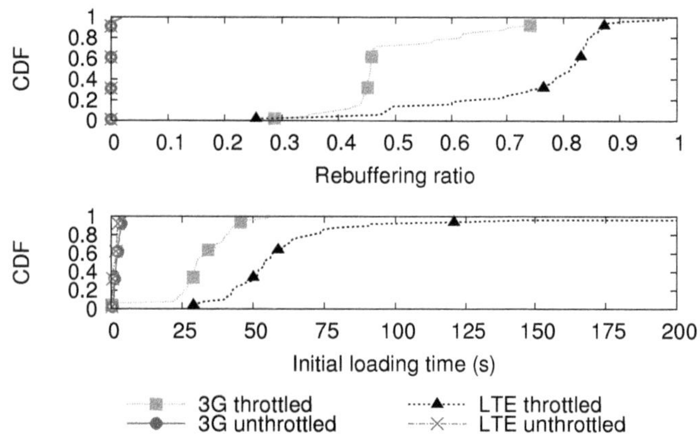

Figure 17: The video rebuffering ratio and the initial loading time distribution under throttled and unthrottled conditions for both C1 3G and C1 LTE.

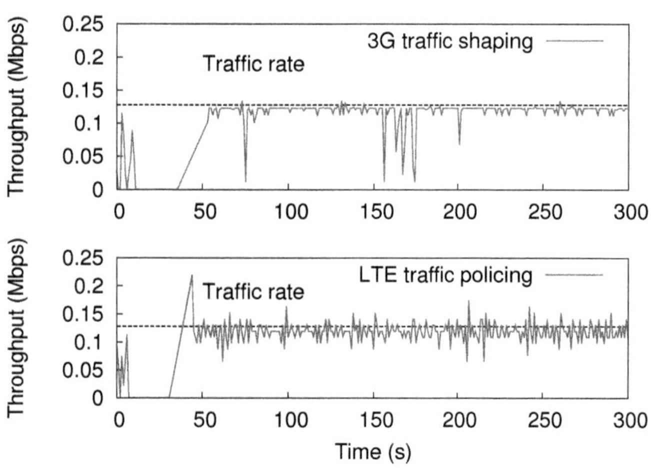

Figure 18: Throughput comparison between C1 3G traffic shaping and C1 LTE traffic policing.

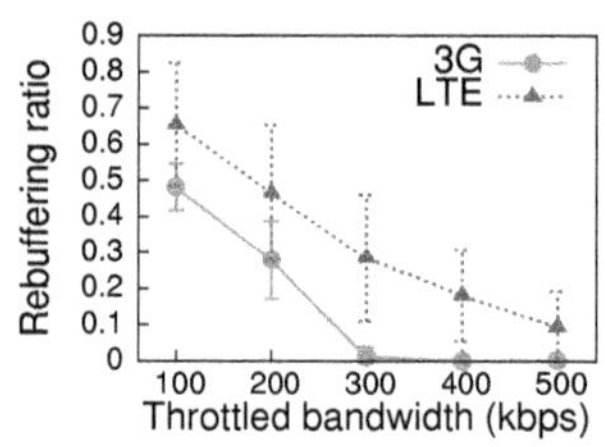

Figure 19: Rebuffering ratio for C1 LTE is consistently greater than that for C1 3G

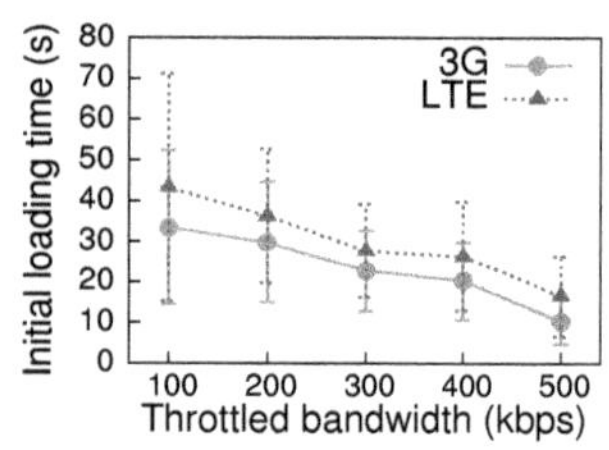

Figure 20: Initial loading time for C1 LTE is consistently greater than that for C1 3G

Finding 6. Network bandwidth throttling causes more than 30 seconds (15×) more initial loading time and increases the rebuffering ratio from around 0% to 50% on average. We randomly play 100 videos from our video dataset under both throttled and unthrottled conditions in C1 3G and C1 LTE, and the results are shown in Fig. 17. For C1 3G, the initial loading time increases by 30 seconds after the bandwidth throttling, which is 15× more compared to the unthrottled case. For C1 LTE, it is even worse: the increased initial loading time is more than 1 minute, which is 48× more! For the rebuffering ratio, without throttling there are nearly no rebuffering events, but with throttling, more than 50% and 75% of the total playback time is spent in rebuffering for C1 3G and C1 LTE respectively, which makes the user experience highly negative.

Besides the effect of bandwidth throttling, from Fig. 17 we have another interesting observation: both the value and the variance of the initial loading time and the rebuffering ratio for throttling in C1 3G are much smaller than those for throttling in C1 LTE. Next, we use QoE Doctor to further investigate the root cause.

Finding 7. The throttling mechanism choice causes more variance in the initial loading time and the rebuffering ratio in C1 LTE. By contacting carrier C1, we find out that C1 3G and C1 LTE actually adopt different throttling mechanisms: C1 3G uses traffic shaping, and C1 LTE uses traffic policing. Both throttling mechanisms use the token bucket algorithm for rate limiting, but when the traffic rate reaches the configured maximum rate, traffic policing drops excess traffic while traffic shaping retains excess packets in a queue and then schedules the excess for later transmission [11]. Using our application layer and transport/network layer analyzer, we compare the C1 3G and C1 LTE throttling impact in Fig. 18. In the network trace, compared with C1 LTE, in C1 3G there are relatively fewer TCP retransmissions, which implies less TCP packet drops on 3G base station. Thus, the average throughput variance for C1 3G is smaller than that for C1 LTE. These are consistent with the more bursty traffic pattern expected in traffic policing [11], which is very likely the reason for more variance in the initial loading time and the rebuffering ratio in C1 LTE.

Finding 8. A simple video resolution adaptation in YouTube increases the initial loading time by 50% and doubles the rebuffering ratio in C1 LTE compared to C1 3G. Throttling mechanism choice can explain the QoE variance differences between C1 3G and C1 LTE, but it does not explain the value differences. To understand the relationship between throttling bandwidth and the video QoE with rebuffering events, we utilize a Linux traffic control tool `tc` [10]. We select a small video set (26 videos) randomly from the videos with less than 90 seconds lengths in our video dataset, and automatically play them using QoE Doctor. We repeat the bandwidth limits of 100 kbps, 200 kbps, 300 kbps, 400 kbps, and 500 kbps for both C1 3G and C1 LTE network, and the results are shown in Fig. 19 and Fig. 20. In these figures, for all bandwidth limits, the rebuffering time ratio and initial loading time for C1 LTE is consistently much higher than that of C1 3G. Using our cross-layer analyzer, we find that the root cause lies in the total downloaded video data: in C1 LTE around 96.6% ($\sim$ 40 MB) more data is downloaded than that in C1 3G. From the MediaPlayer log [5] in Android logcat [4], we find out the reason: the default video resolution is 320$\times$180 px for 3G and 640$\times$360 px for C1 LTE. Due to this default adaptation, in Fig. 17 YouTube videos on throttled C1 LTE have 50% higher initial loading time and double the rebuffering ratio than on throttled C1 3G. LTE has better maximum throughput than 3G, but it does not imply that the throughput in LTE is always better in any network conditions. We suggest that *to improve its video QoE, YouTube should adapt the video resolution based on more fine-grained real-time network performance instead of simply based on network type information.*

7.6 YouTube: Advertisement Impact on Initial Loading Time

Ads that play in the video stream before the actual video (known as "pre-roll ads") are a popular monetization approach for major video providers. Previous work [25] has studied the effectiveness of video ads as measured by their completion and abandonment rates. We instead focus on the impact of pre-roll ads on the initial loading time for YouTube.

Experiment setup. We use the same experimental setup and video data set as §7.5. We use QoE Doctor to play 100 random videos from the dataset (in total 13.5 hours) under C1 3G, C1 LTE and WiFi. In our experiments, the cellular signal strength for C1 3G and C1 LTE is around -95 to -105 dbm. Note that the ad loading latency in the results in this section might be shorter in areas with better network condition.

Finding 9. Advertisements reduce the initial loading time of the actual video, but double the total initial loading time. Fig. 21 shows the distribution of initial loading time under C1 3G, C1 LTE and WiFi. We measure four values: "video after ad" refers to the time to load the video after a pre-roll ad; "video, no ad" refers to the time to load a video in the absence of a pre-roll ad; "ad" refers to the ad loading time, and "ad + video" refers to the combined loading time for both ad and video in the presence of a pre-roll ad. Interestingly, *the ad loading time is longer than the actual video loading time for every network.* We use the cross-layer analyzer to examine the network traffic inside the QoE Window, and find that the video appears to be pre-loading while the ad is loading as well. Despite this pre-loading, *the total initial loading time is roughly doubled.* Most interestingly, on WiFi the video loading time is largely masked by the ad loading time, but on cellular networks there is still a substantial loading delay for the actual video. By examining network traffic, the root cause is that the ad loading process often has to compete with traffic to analytics

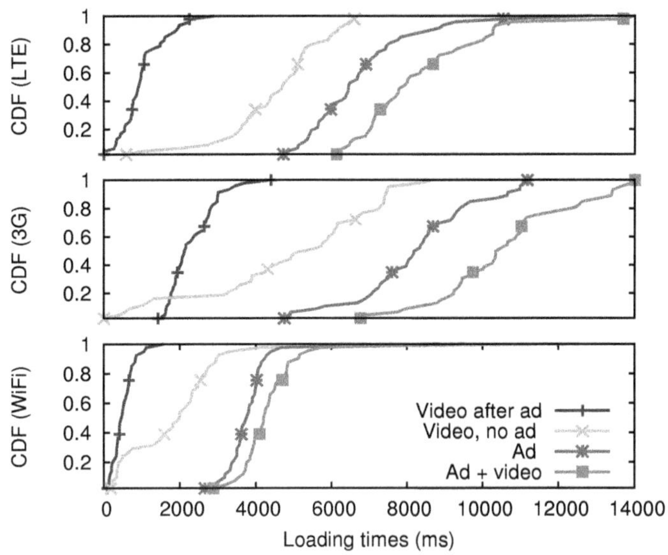

Figure 21: CDFs of video loading times for different network types, in the presence and absence of ads

services. Overall, cellular network has an additional delay of 4-6 seconds of loading time when an ad is played, on top of the 5 seconds the user must spend in watching an ad before skipping it.

7.7 Web Browsing: RRC State Machine Impact on Web Page Loading Time

As described by a previous study [33], the RRC state machine in 3G network generally consists of 3 states shown in Fig. 1. Surprisingly, during our experiment we find from QxDM that C2 has simplified its 3G RRC state machine into a 2-state model, which is shown in Fig. 22. This finding makes us curious about the possible influence this RRC state machine model change may have on mobile app QoE. In this section, we use QoE Doctor to study the impact of different RRC state machine models on the web page loading time in Android Google Chrome web browser version 18.0.1025469.

Experiment setup. In order to evaluate over real user experiences, we conducted a user study with 20 students from University of Michigan for 9 months. We installed `tcpdump` on 20 Samsung Galaxy S3 devices to collect network traces, and we anonymized device identities to protect user privacy. Using TCP and HTTP analysis, we separate the traffic generated by the Chrome browser app, and then filter out the the URLs visited by the real users along with the inter-request timings. In this filtering process, we first parse the traces to extract the links inside the HTTP requests, and then clean up the links manually to make sure that they are delivering web pages with meaningful content instead of downloading objects such as images, icons and scripts. QoE Doctor takes the filtered URL list in and replays the web browsing behavior in Google Chrome app on the C1 3G network and C2 3G network. C1 uses the 3-state model and C2 uses the simplified 2-state model in Fig. 22. As RRC state machine behavior is sensitive to the timing between network-related actions, in the experiment we not only replay the sequence of user actions, but use the URL visiting time intervals as well to ensure that the timings between user actions are also replayed.

In the experiments, the generated URL list for replay is 4 hours in length and has 597 URLs belonging to 71 different sites with a

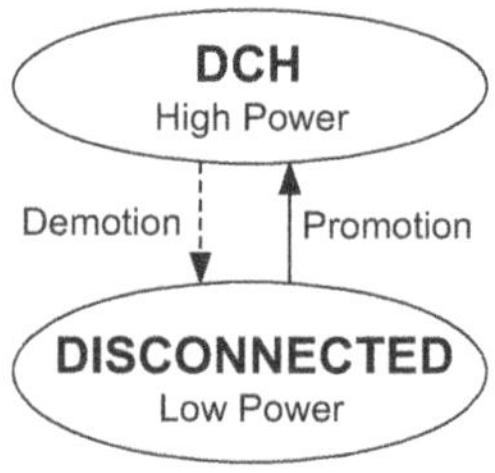

Figure 22: C2's RRC state machine has only two states, omitting FACH.

RRC transition	C1	C2
DCH	76.6 %	93.5 %
DCH→FACH→DCH	3.2 %	—
FACH→DCH	16.0 %	—
PCH→FACH→DCH	4.2 %	—
DCH→Disconnected→DCH	—	0.2 %
Disconnected→DCH	—	6.3 %

Table 4: RRC state transition distribution in the user study trace. C1 experiences a RRC state transition 23.4% of the time, while C2 only experiences 6.5%.

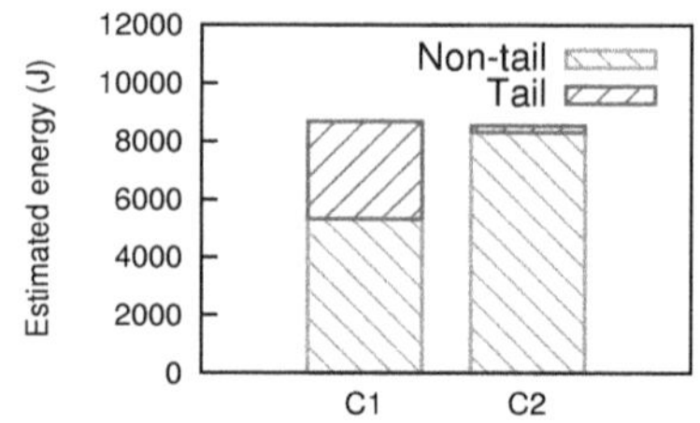

Figure 23: Tail energy contributes 35.68% of the total energy for C1, but only 2.88% for C2.

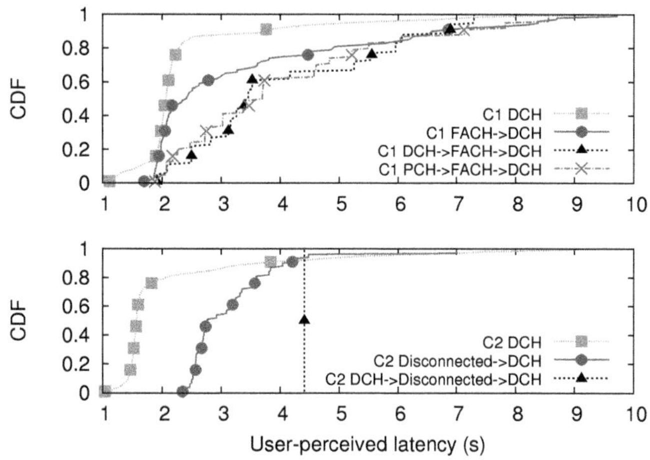

Figure 24: RRC state transitions introduce additional delay for the user-perceived web page loading time. There is only one data point for C2 DCH→DISCONNECTED→DCH.

wide range of content types, including news, movies, sports, social networking, google search results, and travel guides. Between the experiment for C1 and the experiment for C2, the average relative download data size difference is only 1.94%, which is mainly caused by changes in the HTTP metadata such as time, encoding mechanism, *etc.* instead of the web page content.

Finding 10. The 2-state RRC state machine model has a 16.9% lower chance to experience RRC state transitions, which causes 22.8% lower web page loading time than the 3-state RRC state machine model. To understand the impact of different types of RRC state machine transitions, we classify the loading time based on the RRC promotion and demotion events that happen inside the QoE Window. Fig. 24 shows the web page loading time distribution for different types of transitions for C1 and C2's 3G networks, and Table 4 shows the percentage of different types of transitions. Consistent with previous work [35, 34], the loading time in Fig. 24 for C1 and C2's 3G networks becomes longer when it involves RRC state machine transitions. The situation is the worst if the loading time involves both the state promotion and demotion – the page loading time at least doubles. In Table 4, between the 2-state model of C2 and 3-state model of C1, the web page loading in the 2-state model has a 16.9% lower chance to involve RRC state transitions. Based on QxDM logs, for C1 the DCH→FACH and FACH→PCH demotion timers are 3 seconds and 6 seconds, while for C2 the DCH→Disconnected timer is 10 seconds, which is roughly equal to the sum of the demotion timers in the 3-state model. Thus, the main cause for fewer state transitions in C2 is the simplified state machine design which removes the middle state: it stays in DCH most of the time, and once it promotes, it is very unlikely to demote. This results in 22.8% lower loading time in the 2-state model of C2 compared to the model of C1. We also calculate the energy consumption using the technique described in §5.3. As shown in Fig. 23, although the overall energy is similar, due to the lower chance of demotion, C2 has 92.5% lower tail energy compared to C1 according to the definition of tail energy in previous work [34]. For these results, we believe that they are generalizable to other apps besides web browsing apps, since the root cause lies in the RRC state machine design.

8. RELATED WORK

UI automation. UI automation tools are a common approach for dynamically analyzing applications for various purposes. **Application bug detection** is the most common application. In this category, Dynodroid [29], A3E [16], VanarSena [37], and ContextualFuzzing [27] are designed to uncover application bugs and crashes by automatically exploring all possible internal states, and exposing them to various external contexts. **Accessibility policy checking** is also a popular target. AMC [26] automatically explores app UI states to check for violations of UI requirements for vehicular apps. DECAF [28] uses UI automation to detect ad fraud. UI automation is also used for **security and privacy** purposes. For example, AppsPlayground [36] provides a framework using fuzz testing for malware analysis. Finally, PUMA [21] generalizes the common procedures for all the systems above, and provides a generic programmable framework. Unlike PUMA, QoE Doctor in this paper does not aim to expose abnormal behavior in mobile apps, but instead aims to analyze the QoE for normal mobile application usage. For example, we have a specially designed *wait* component in our UI automation (detailed in §4) for the accurate measurements of user-perceived latency, which in previous work was usually implemented using heuristic waiting timers.

QoE measurement. Previous work have measured application QoE using subjective evaluations from users such as evaluation scores. D. Joumblatt et. al. [24], Chen et. al. [20], and Ickin et. al. [23] define a target QoE metric based on user satisfactions and dissatisfactions. Schatz et. al. [42] and Balachandran et. al. [17, 18] use user engagement as the target QoE to predict. Unlike them, we focus on objective QoE metrics, which are reproducible and can be measured repeatedly and automatically. Like us, Prometheus [15], AppInsight [38], Timecard [39], and Panappticon [47] measure objective QoE metrics, but they either require access to app source code, or require instrumentation of the app logic or the underlying system, which QoE Doctor does not.

Rather than directly measuring subjective and objective QoE, QoE estimation from network traffic is also a popular approach. D. Joumblatt et. al. [24] predicts the QoE of network applications from network metrics. Schatz et. al. [42] and Balachandran et. al. [17, 18] build a predictive framework to find the relationships between measurable user engagement metrics and actionable video delivery mechanisms in the network (*e.g.,* the bit rate, initial loading time, and buffering ratio). Prometheus [15] predicts objective QoE metrics such as the buffering time with passive network measurements. Unlike them, QoE Doctor does not predict or estimate QoE metrics, but rather directly measures the ground truth values of QoE metrics.

QoE improvement. There has also been work on improving the QoE of mobile apps. Timecard [39] instruments a mobile OS to ensure that user-perceived delays can meet deadline requirements. Proteus [46] predicts future network performances over cellular networks in real time, and increases QoE for RTC applications. Sprout [45] builds a UDP-based end-to-end protocol for mobile apps such as video conferencing which requires both low latency and high throughput. Our work is complementary: QoE Doctor can be used to automatically and repeatedly collect and analyze QoE data for validating these systems, and can potentially uncover root causes of new QoE problems, shedding light on future areas for QoE improvement.

Cross-layer analysis. Cross-layer analysis has been less extensively explored. RILAnalyzer [44] uses cross-layer analysis approach to uncover how RRC states affect app performances. Compared to it, QoE Doctor supports automatically collecting objective QoE values from UI changes directly, instead of relying on user studies and studying network layer performance metrics such as TCP operations which are less directly related to user-perceived latency. ARO [35] analyzes `tcpdump` traces to uncover app performance issues. However, compared to QoE Doctor, their work mainly focuses on radio resource efficiency problems rather than app QoE.

9. CONCLUSION

In this paper, we built a tool, QoE Doctor, which automatically replays user interaction sequences of interest to measure mobile app QoE, record relevant QoE metrics, and allow the root causes of QoE problems to be analyzed across multiple layers, covering both the system and network stacks. Using this tool, we systematically study various QoE metrics for popular apps, and quantitatively evaluate the impact of various QoE-related factors on these QoE metrics. With QoE Doctor, we uncover several significant QoE problems along with the potential root causes of them for major applications and carriers.

Acknowledgments

We would like to thank Yihua Ethan Guo, Ashkan Nikravesh, the anonymous reviewers, and our shepherd, Anmol Sheth, for providing valuable suggestions and feedback on our work. We would also like to thank Warren McNeel, John Murphy, Pete Myron, Isaac Robinson, Samson Kwong, Jeffery Smith, the Device Development and QoE Lab team at T-Mobile for their assistance. This research was supported in part by the National Science Foundation under grants CNS-1059372, CNS-1039657, CNS-1345226, and CNS-0964545.

10. REFERENCES

[1] 94% Users Skip Pre-roll Ads. https://econsultancy.com/blog/63277-pre-roll-video-ads-is-it-any-wonder-why-we-hate-them#i.9gohovetnegyqcc.
[2] Android Activity Testing. http://developer.android.com/tools/testing/activity_testing.html.
[3] Android DDMS. http://developer.android.com/tools/debugging/ddms.html.
[4] Android Logcat. http://developer.android.com/tools/help/logcat.html.
[5] Android MediaPlayer. http://developer.android.com/reference/android/media/MediaPlayer.html.
[6] Global Internet Phenomena. https://www.sandvine.com/trends/global-internet-phenomena/.
[7] Monsoon Power Monitor. http://www.msoon.com/LabEquipment/PowerMonitor/.
[8] Speed Index metric for WebPagetest. https://sites.google.com/a/webpagetest.org/docs/using-webpagetest/metrics/speed-index.
[9] TCPDUMP. http://www.tcpdump.org/.
[10] Traffic Control HOWTO. http://tldp.org/HOWTO/Traffic-Control-HOWTO/.
[11] Comparing Traffic Policing and Traffic Shaping for Bandwidth Limiting. http://www.cisco.com/c/en/us/support/docs/quality-of-service-qos/qos-policing/19645-policevsshape.html, 2005.
[12] QxDM Professional Proven Diagnostic Tool for Evaluating Handset and Network Performance. http://www.qualcomm.com/media/documents/files/qxdm-professional-qualcomm-extensible-diagnostic-monitor.pdf, 2012.
[13] T-Mobile's next move: Shame AT&T and Verizon into ditching data overage fees. http://bgr.com/2014/04/09/t-mobile-vs-att-vs-verizon-data-overage-fees, 2014.
[14] T. 3rd Generation Partnership Project. 3GPP TS 25.322: Radio Link Control (RLC) - UMTS, 2013.
[15] V. Aggarwal, E. Halepovic, J. Pang, S. Venkataraman, and H. Yan. Prometheus: Toward Quality-of-Experience Estimation for Mobile Apps from Passive Network Measurements. In *HotMobile*, 2014.
[16] T. Azim and I. Neamtiu. Targeted and Depth-first Exploration for Systematic Testing of Android Apps. In *Proc. OOPSLA*, 2013.
[17] A. Balachandran, V. Sekar, A. Akella, S. Seshan, I. Stoica, and H. Zhang. A quest for an internet video quality-of-experience metric. In *ACM HotNet*, 2012.
[18] A. Balachandran, V. Sekar, A. Akella, S. Seshan, I. Stoica, and H. Zhang. Developing a predictive model of quality of experience for internet video. In *ACM SIGCOMM*, 2013.
[19] A. Carroll and G. Heiser. An analysis of power consumption in a smartphone. In *USENIX ATC*, 2010.
[20] K. Chen, C. Huang, P. Huang, , and C. Lei. Quantifying Skype user satisfaction. In *Proc. ACM SIGCOMM*, 2006.
[21] S. Hao, B. Liu, S. Nathy, W. G. Halfond, and R. Govindan. PUMA: Programmable UI-Automation for Large Scale Dynamic Analysis of Mobile Apps. In *Proc. ACM MobiSys*, 2014.
[22] J. Huang, F. Qian, A. Gerber, Z. M. Mao, S. Sen, and O. Spatscheck. A close examination of performance and

power characteristics of 4G LTE networks. In *Proc. ACM MobiSys*, 2012.
[23] S. Ickin, K. Wac, M. Fiedler, L. Janowski, J.-H. Hong, and A. K. Dey. Factors influencing quality of experience of commonly used mobile applications. *Communications Magazine, IEEE*, 50(4):48–56, 2012.
[24] D. Joumblatt, J. Chandrashekar, B. Kveton, N. Taft, and R. Teixeira. Predicting user dissatisfaction with internet application performance at end-hosts. In *INFOCOM, 2013 Proceedings IEEE*, 2013.
[25] S. S. Krishnan and R. K. Sitaraman. Understanding the effectiveness of video ads: a measurement study. In *Proc. ACM IMC*, 2013.
[26] K. Lee, J. Flinn, T. Giuli, B. Noble, and C. Peplin. AMC: Verifying User Interface Properties for Vehicular Applications. In *Proc. ACM MobiSys*, 2013.
[27] C.-J. M. Liang, N. Lane, N. Brouwers, L. Zhang, B. Karlsson, R. Chandra, and F. Zhao. Contextual Fuzzing: Automated Mobile App Testing Under Dynamic Device and Environment Conditions. Technical report, Microsoft Research, 2013.
[28] B. Liu, S. Nath, R. Govindan, and J. Liu. DECAF: Detecting and Characterizing Ad Fraud in Mobile Apps. In *Proc. NSDI*, 2014.
[29] A. Machiry, R. Tahiliani, and M. Naik. Dynodroid: An Input Generation System for Android Apps. In *Proc. ACM FSE*, 2012.
[30] A. Pathak, Y. C. Hu, and M. Zhang. Where is the energy spent inside my app?: fine grained energy accounting on smartphones with eprof. In *EuroSys*, 2012.
[31] F. Qian, S. Sen, and O. Spatscheck. Characterizing Resource Usage for Mobile Web Browsing. In *MobiSys*, 2014.
[32] F. Qian, Z. Wang, Y. Gao, J. Huang, A. Gerber, Z. Mao, S. Sen, and O. Spatscheck. Periodic transfers in mobile applications: network-wide origin, impact, and optimization. In *WWW*, 2012.
[33] F. Qian, Z. Wang, A. Gerber, Z. M. Mao, S. Sen, and O. Spatscheck. Characterizing radio resource allocation for 3G networks. In *Proc. ACM IMC*, 2010.
[34] F. Qian, Z. Wang, A. Gerber, Z. M. Mao, S. Sen, and O. Spatscheck. Top: Tail optimization protocol for cellular radio resource allocation. In *ICNP*, 2010.
[35] F. Qian, Z. Wang, A. Gerber, Z. M. Mao, S. Sen, and O. Spatscheck. Profiling resource usage for mobile applications: a cross-layer approach. In *MobiSys*, 2011.
[36] V. Rastogi, Y. Chen, and W. Enck. AppsPlayground: automatic security analysis of smartphone applications. In *CODASPY*, 2013.
[37] L. Ravindranath, S. Nath, J. Padhye, and H. Balakrishnan. Automatic and Scalable Fault Detection for Mobile Applications. Technical report, Microsoft Research, 2013.
[38] L. Ravindranath, J. Padhye, S. Agarwal, R. Mahajan, I. Obermiller, and S. Shayandeh. AppInsight: Mobile App Performance Monitoring in the Wild. In *Proc. Operating Systems Design and Implementation*, 2012.
[39] L. Ravindranath, J. Padhye, R. Mahajan, and H. Balakrishnan. Timecard: controlling user-perceived delays in server-based mobile applications. In *Proc. ACM SOSP*, 2013.
[40] S. Rosen, H. Luo, Q. A. Chen, Z. M. Mao, J. Hui, A. Drake, and K. Lau. Discovering Fine-grained RRC State Dynamics and Performance Impacts in Cellular Networks. In *Proc. ACM MobiCom*, 2014.
[41] S. Rosen, H. Luo, Q. A. Chen, Z. M. Mao, J. Hui, A. Drake, and K. Lau. Understanding RRC State Dynamics through Client Measurements with Mobilyzer. In *ACM MobiCom S3 Workshop*, 2014.
[42] R. Schatz, T. Hossfeld, and P. Casas. Passive YouTube QoE Monitoring for ISPs. In *Proc. IEEE IMIS*, 2012.
[43] G.-H. Tu, C. Peng, C.-Y. Li, X. Ma, H. Wang, T. Wang, and S. Lu. Accounting for roaming users on mobile data access: Issues and root causes. In *Proc. ACM MobiSys*, 2013.
[44] N. Vallina-Rodriguez, A. Auçinas, M. Almeida, Y. Grunenberger, K. Papagiannaki, and J. Crowcroft. RILAnalyzer: a comprehensive 3G monitor on your phone. In *Proc. ACM IMC*, 2013.
[45] K. Winstein, A. Sivaraman, H. Balakrishnan, et al. Stochastic forecasts achieve high throughput and low delay over cellular networks. In *Proc. NSDI*, volume 13, 2013.
[46] Q. Xu, S. Mehrotra, Z. Mao, and J. Li. PROTEUS: network performance forecast for real-time, interactive mobile applications. In *Proc. ACM MobiSys*, 2013.
[47] L. Zhang, D. R. Bild, R. P. Dick, Z. M. Mao, and P. Dinda. Panappticon: event-based tracing to measure mobile application and platform performance. In *CODES+ ISSS*, 2013.
[48] L. Zhang, B. Tiwana, Z. Qian, Z. Wang, R. Dick, Z. M. Mao, and L. Yang. Accurate Online Power Estimation and Automatic Battery Behavior Based Power Model Generation for Smartphones. In *CODES+ ISSS*, 2010.

A First Look at Performance in Mobile Virtual Network Operators

Fatima Zarinni†, Ayon Chakraborty†, Vyas Sekar°, Samir R. Das†, Phillipa Gill†
† Stony Brook University ° Carnegie Mellon University

ABSTRACT

Recent industry trends suggest a new phenomenon in the mobile market: mobile virtual network operators or MVNOs that operate on top of existing cellular infrastructures. While MVNOs have shown significant growth in the US and elsewhere in the past two years and have been successful in attracting customers, there is anecdotal evidence that users are concerned about cellular performance when choosing MVNOs over traditional cellular operators. In this paper, we present the first systematic measurement study to shed light on this emerging phenomenon. We study the performance of 3 key applications: web access, video streaming and voice, in 2 popular MVNO families (a total of 8 carriers) in the US, where each MVNO family consists of a major base carrier and 3 MVNOs running on top of it. We observe that some MVNOs do indeed exhibit significant performance degradation and that there are key differences between the two MVNO families.

Categories and Subject Descriptors

C.2.1 [**Network Architecture and Design**]: Wireless Communication; C.2.2 [**Network Protocols**]: Applications; C.4 [**Performance of Systems**]: Measurement Techniques.

Keywords

MVNO; Mobile measurements; Mobile performance; Cellular Measurements; Cellular performance; QoE; Applications.

1 Introduction

A new trend has been emerging in the last few years in the cellular market both in the US and in Europe—the rise of mobile virtual network operators or *MVNOs* [12, 14, 15]. At a high-level, MVNOs use the existing cellular infrastructures that are owned by the traditional cellular operators. MVNOs do not incur significant infrastructure or spectrum licensing costs and offer services that are different from traditional cellular operators (e.g., better pre-paid plans and multiple quotas).

While MVNOs started to appear in the market in the early 2000s, they have only recently become more mainstream in terms of market share. The growth is a culmination of several factors: increasing prices of traditional cellular providers for consumers, users' preference in avoiding contractual lock-ins, the popularity of "pre-paid" services, regulatory intervention to ensure competition and market segmentation focusing on niche demographics (e.g., tween markets) [22]. As of Q1 2014, there are 20, 23, 11 and 35 MVNOs running on top of the AT&T, T-Mobile, Verizon and Sprint networks in the US, respectively [5].

Even as MVNOs grow in market share, there are concerns among users about their performance. For example, a quick sampling of popular consumer complaints forums shows significant concerns related to both cost, billing, and service issues (e.g., poor coverage/signal, 3G/4G promised but getting 2G, poor application performance, and frequent disconnections). Shown below are some actual quotes from user forums about MVNOs:

> *[11]: I know that AIO is capped at 8mbps download speed. Are all the other MVNOs like Straight Talk, Net10 and Air-Voice also limited to 8mbps download speeds? Do they suffer from higher latency?*
> *[9]: I have been throttled every day since last week so each day I lose my 4g/E symbol and once I regain it Im throttled ... I've used 1.4gb and I have only 3 days left on my 30 plan.*
> *[13]: Does Sprint have means of degrading service to Ting (and other MVNO) customers in favor of Sprint customers in a particular crowded cell?*
> *[10]: My only concern is if the service quality of the service. With Straight Talk, for example, I'd be on AT&T's GSM network in Boston, I think ... but I wonder if as an MVNO customer I'd get second-tier access or service.*

Motivated by the growth of MVNOs and the aforementioned user concerns, this paper presents a first study to shed light on the performance of different MVNOs. While there is a lot of previous work in analyzing mobile performance (e.g., [25, 20, 21, 3]), they have not systematically analyzed performance in MVNOs. To address this gap, we study two major MVNO families in the US. In our study, each family includes the base carrier and three popular MVNOs running on top of the base carrier. While this sample study does not cover all base carriers in US or all MVNOs atop any base carrier, the carrier/MVNO choices have been done systematically, based on popularity (Section 2). In the performance analysis, we hide the actual names of the carriers and MVNOs to protect their business interests. To simplify presentation, we refer to the two base carriers as carrier `A` and `B`. We refer to the MVNOs within the carrier `A` as `A1`, `A2` and `A3`, and within the carrier `B` as `B1`, `B2` and `B3`. The base carrier along with its MVNOs (e.g., `A`, `A1`, `A2`, `A3`) are refered to as 'MVNO family' or just 'family.'(e.g., MVNO family `A`)

As a starting point, we analyze the performance for three dominant usage modes: web access, video streaming and voice calls.

IMC'14, November 5–7, 2014, Vancouver, BC, Canada.

ACM 978-1-4503-3213-2/14/11 ...$15.00.
http://dx.doi.org/10.1145/2663716.2663752.

Using over 13,000 measurements collected across 11 locations over a period of 3 months, we address the following questions:

- Does the performance vary across the MVNOs running atop the same base carrier? (e.g., is MetroPCS worse than Straight Talk given that they are both MVNOs running on T-Mobile network?)
- Do MVNOs perform worse compared to the base carrier in each case? (e.g., is H20 Wireless, an MVNO on AT&T network, worse than AT&T)?
- Are there differences across different MVNO families? (e.g., do all MVNOs in a family, say the T-Mobile family, show significantly worse performance than those in another family, say the AT&T family?)

We analyze application-specific quality-of-experience (QoE) metrics to address these questions. We also perform factor analysis to correlate the observed application-level performance with network-level performance, such as, TCP throughput, round-trip times (RTTs), packet loss rates, DNS look up times, and PHY-layer characteristics to attribute the observed performance differences (if any) to structural differences across the operators.

Our key findings are:

- The base carrier often performs better than the MVNOs and sometimes significantly so. For instance, some MVNOs over base carrier B fail to load a non-trivial ($\geq$10%) fraction of YouTube video requests and can have up to 6$\times$ worse page load time.
- There is significant diversity across MVNOs within the same MVNO family, for both the A and B MVNO families. For instance, often B2 performs considerably worse than B1 and B3 in MVNO family B.
- There are non-trivial differences between the two MVNO families; overall the MVNOs running atop A have better performance w.r.t the base carrier compared to their B counterparts.
- Finally, we see key differences across applications as well. While voice quality is largely similar across all MVNOs and base carriers, there is huge discrepancy in data performance both for web access as well as video streaming.

We hope that this paper serves as a motivation for future large-scale measurement studies in this direction, that would span wider areas, larger number of MVNOs and wider variety of data plans.

2 Measurement Setup

In this section, we begin by describing the choice of phone, carriers, and cellular plans. Then, we describe our data collection methodology.

Choice of phone: To ensure we do not have phone-specific effects (e.g. CPU speed/memory access latency/cache size) in our measurements, we use the same phone model for all carriers – Google's Nexus 4 with 2GB RAM, Quad-core CPU and 2G/3G/4G support (i.e., EDGE/UMTS/HSPA/HSPA+). All of our phones run the Android 4.2.2 (JellyBean) OS. Since Nexus 4 only supports GSM-based carriers, this study is limited to such carriers and their MVNOs only. We leave the investigation of performance in CDMA-based carriers and their MVNOs for future work.

Choice of carriers and plans: We chose popular and widely-used MVNOs that run atop two major base carriers in the U.S. We call them carriers A and B, respectively. We used Google Trends [4] and the list of all the available MVNOs [5] to find the top 3 MVNOs for each of these base carriers. The 6 MVNOs are summarized in Table 1. A1, A2 and A3 run atop A; B1, B2 and B3 run atop B. Cellular providers offer a range of plans with different prices. Hence, to provide a fair comparison between carriers, we select *similar* plans for all the carriers (as summarized in Table 1), in terms of features.When the exact plan was not available we picked the closest comparable plan.

Carrier	Type	Plan (all pre-paid except B)	$/Mo.
A	Base	Unlimited talk/text, 2.5GB data @ 4G	60
A1	MVNO	Unlimited talk/text, 2.5GB data @ 4G	45
A2	MVNO	Unlimited talk/text, 3GB data @ 4G	50
A3	MVNO	Unlimited talk/text, 2.5GB data @ 4G	60
B	Base	Unlimited talk/text, 2GB data @ 4G	65
B1	MVNO	Unlimted talk/text, 2.5GB data @ 4G	50
B2	MVNO	Unlimited talk/text, 2GB data @ 4G	50
B3	MVNO	Unlimited talk/text, 2GB data @ 4G	50

Table 1: Mobile carriers and plans used in our study.

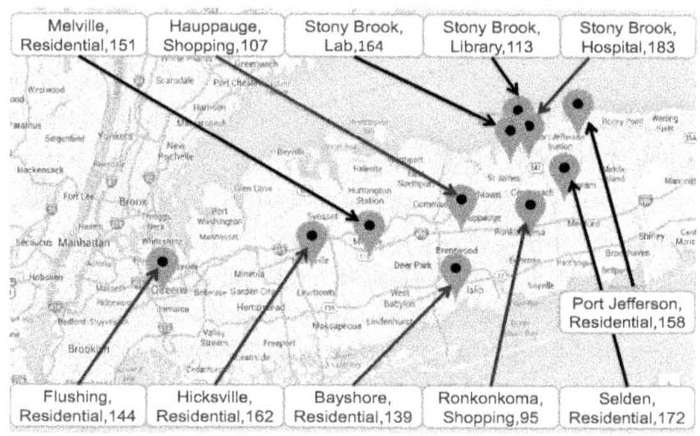

Figure 1: We conduct measurements at 11 different locations spanning across a 3000 km^2 wide area. The annotations show the names of the measurement locations along with the type of location, and the number of measurement sets.

Data collection: We selected 11 reasonably diverse locations spanning different usage scenarios: urban/suburban, shopping areas, residential, office/lab and hospital. Figure 1 shows the geographical spread of our measurement locations. We acknowledge a potential limitation, that all our measurements occurred in the Long Island/New York region. However, this region is a major population hotspot, covering part of New York city metro area and associated suburbs.

We developed a suite of custom scripts and mobile applications for web browsing, video streaming, and voice calls, representing common usage modes. Our custom tools collect relevant user quality-of-experience (QoE) metrics, and we defer application-specific details to the following sections.

At each location, we use four identically configured Nexus 4 phones (one for base and three for MVNO carriers) to run the same suite of experiments concurrently at that location. Our scripts run these applications at each location typically hourly or half-hourly for most of the day – often starting at early morning and going until late night – over different days of the week modulo practical constraints (e.g., shop/mall closures).

On average, we conducted about 150 sets of measurements for each carrier, across different locations, during Jan-Mar 2014, on different days. Each measurement set consists of a series of application runs, e.g., web page access for a set of chosen web sites, video streaming, voice calls, TCP upload throughput test, etc.

Concurrent with the QoE measurements, we also log packet traces using the `tcpdump` tool and a range of relevant phone characteristics using the Android API (e.g., radio stats), to enable further factor analysis. We verified separately via the `top` utility, that this additional monitoring adds only a modest CPU overhead ($\approx$ 5%). This does not bias our measurements. Prior to conducting actual measurements, we performed tests over WiFi, where we ran our apps with and without additional logging, and we measured the performance for web, video and voice applications, as well as, network tests. The attained results showed negligible difference in performance with this logging enabled or disabled.

Our analysis did not reveal any significant location, time-of-day or day-of-week specific change in terms of performance of carriers with respect to each other. Thus, we present only aggregate statistics (over all locations, times and days) and focus on performance differences across carriers and MVNO families. Since the experiments for base and MVNO carriers are always colocated in both space and time, we believe it is a fair characterization of the performance issues we describe in the rest of the paper.

3 Application Performance

In this section, we analyze the performance of the MVNOs and the base carriers for three common modes of mobile usage: web access, video streaming, and voice calls. In each case, we describe the application-specific setup, and the relevant QoE metrics we measure. We also correlate the observations to key network-level and PHY-layer characteristics.

3.1 Web Browsing

Setup and QoE Metric: We choose six popular websites with diverse characteristics: Youtube, Amazon, Wikipedia, Twitter, Bing, and CNN. All of these sites had an overall Alexa rank $\leq$ 20 in April 2014. We developed a custom browser application using Android WebViewClient. At each measurement site, the app visits each website's mobile landing page (in random order across carriers) and records the *page load time* QoE metric. We measure page load time as the difference between the time the URL is requested from the browser and the time when all the web objects (html text, images, etc.) are fetched and the `onPageFinished` event [7] is triggered.

Note that the set of webpages accessed is diverse in terms of structure and content size, with CNN and Amazon constituting the two largest median content sizes in the set ($\approx$ 570 KB and 400 KB, respectively) and Twitter and Bing having the smallest ($\approx$ 89 KB and 100 KB, respectively).

Evaluation of Page Load Times: Figure 2 shows the distribution of page load time across all runs for the six websites.[1] There are three key observations here. First, typically the carriers in MVNO family A perform better than their B counterparts; e.g., for CNN all carriers in MVNO family A perform better than all carriers in MVNO family B, and sometimes significantly so. Second, while the differences between base carrier A and its MVNOs are only modest, we see significant differences between base carrier B and some of its MVNOs; e.g., B2 is almost 6$\times$ worse than B for CNN. Finally, we see non-trivial variability across MVNOs within the same MVNO family; e.g., B2 is often considerably worse than other MVNOs in MVNO family B, and A1 is slightly worse than other MVNOs in MVNO family A. We confirmed that these differences between carrier page load times are statistically significant using the Kolmogrov-Smirnov (K-S) [8] statistical test, but do not show these results for brevity.

[1]Note that, >10 sec page load times are not surprising on a mobile platform, as seen in prior work [38, 19, 36]. For example, Welsh reports 75 seconds page load time for a webpage over a cellular link [38].

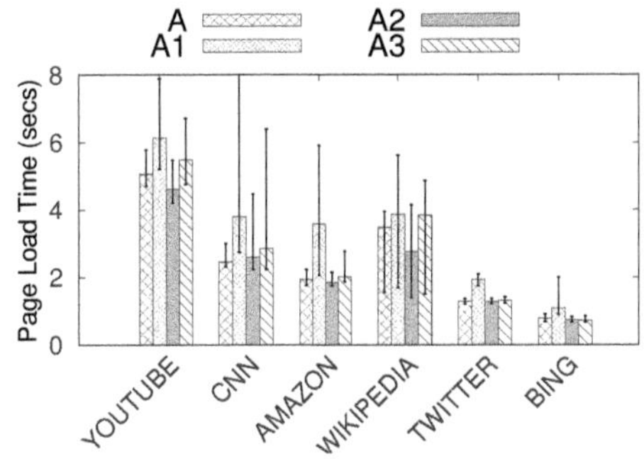

(a) MVNO family A

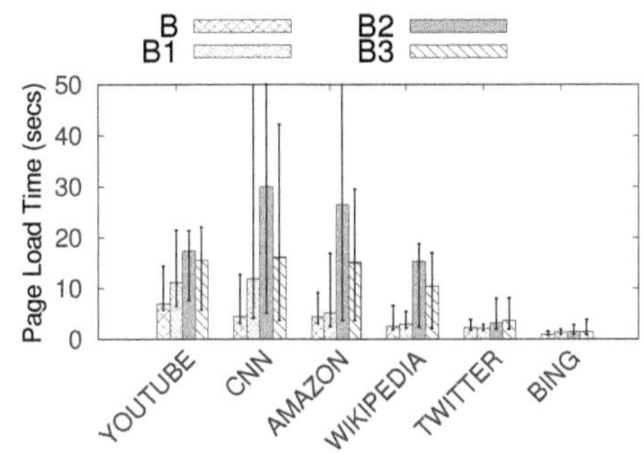

(b) MVNO family B

Figure 2: Distribution of page load times (median, 25th and 75th percentiles): We see that (a) MVNO family A usually performs better than MVNO family B; (b) within each MVNO family one or more MVNOs is worse than the base carrier; and (c) some MVNOs (e.g., B2, B3) suffer more than others).

Factor Analysis: To understand the causes of these performance differences, we looked at lower-layer metrics such as DNS lookup time, RTT, TCP retransmission rates, and signal strength. We computed the Pearson's correlation between the difference of page load times for the base carrier and the MVNOs and that of different lower-layer metrics, for every website. Based on this analysis, we zoom in on two key factors – RTT and TCP retransmissions (Figure 3). First, we can see that MVNO family A has generally lower RTTs and retransmission rates than MVNO family B. As prior studies have shown, lower RTTs imply lower page load times, which is consistent with our observations that A and its MVNOs have lower page load times [18]. Second, we see in Figure 3a that within the MVNO family A, A1 which had higher page load times, indeed has higher RTTs.[2] Finally, Figure 3d shows that the MVNOs in MVNO familyB (B2 and B3) with the highest page load times see very high retransmission rates.

We also observe that B1 has the lowest retransmission rates in its MVNO family, however, still higher RTTs than B, thus resulting in B1 having a lower page load time than B2 and B3, but, higher than B. However, this still does not explain some of the very high (> 30s) page load times for B1 (e.g., CNN in Figure 2b). Further analysis of the packet traces showed significant TCP idle times as shown in one example timeseries in Figure 4a. Figure 4b breaks down the page load measurements in the B MVNO family in two

[2]Higher RTTs for both Twitter and Bing, as compared with other webpages, could be due to the content-server locations that were accessed for these sites, or due to the path from carrier A's gateway routers to these servers [35, 39].

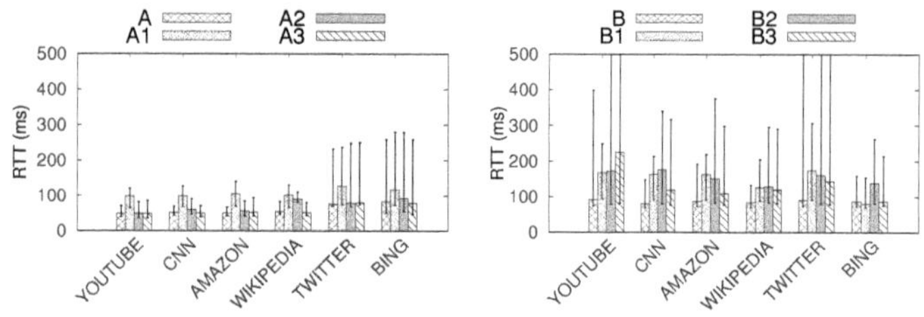

(a) RTT (MVNO family A) (b) RTT (MVNO family B)

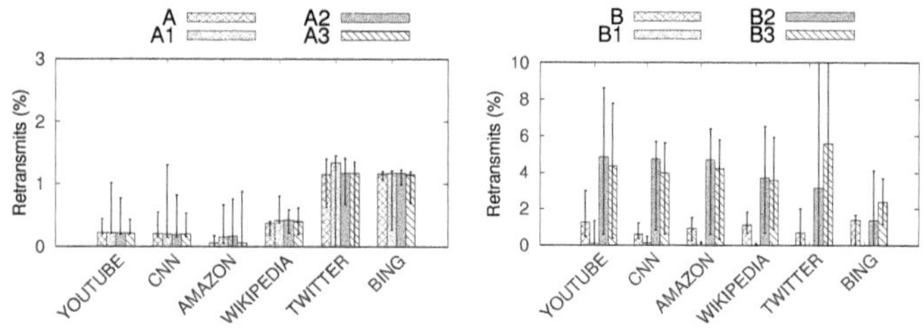

(c) Retransmissions (MVNO family A) (d) Retransmissions (MVNO family B)

Figure 3: Focusing on the key observed factors shows that generally speaking the MVNOs in family A with higher page load times have higher RTT and the MVNOs in family B with higher page load times tend to have high retransmission rates.

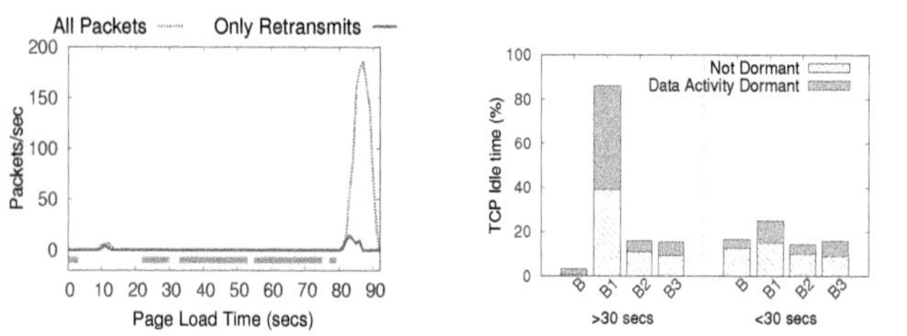

(a) Timeseries of one high page load (b) High dormancy impacts load times for B1

Figure 4: Higher page load times for B1 relative to B are not due to retransmissions but rather due to high radio dormancy periods. The red line in (a) shows intervals when data activity is dormant.

bins (< 30s and > 30s) and shows that these TCP idle periods have non-trivial influence on the page load times. This is specifically true for B1 where the long page load times have about 80% idle periods.

Further inspection reveals that many (but not all) of these idle periods are actually due to physical link being dormant, (as revealed by the DATA_ACTIVITY_DORMANT flag [1]). We suspect that this is influenced by the RRC state machine at the radio layer as defined in the 3GPP standard [24], but we do not have visibility to actual RRC states using the commodity Nexus 4 phone to examine this further. Prior work (e.g., [19, 34]) has also shown that inappropriately tuned RRC states impact web access performance. Overall, this suggests some potential misconfiguration or service differentiation at the radio layer for the MVNO B1 running over carrier B. In contrast, TCP idle/dormancy issues are negligible for MVNO family A and are not shown.

We also analyzed signal strengths, handoffs and the pool of cell-ids that the carriers are associating with and found no significant differences between carriers within the same MVNO family. This implies that these radio-layer aspects did not play a significant role in the performance difference observed between MVNOs. Some prior work (e.g., [23, 29]) also noticed little correlation between signal strengths and performance when analyzing their collected measurements. This is likely due to the signal strengths usually falling above a certain threshold.

Our investigation in this section also revealed interesting information about the structural differences across the A and B MVNO families. In MVNO family B, all web traffic goes through an explicit proxy server that terminates TCP connections while MVNO family A appears to use a transparent proxy that relays the connections to the webservers.[3]

3.2 Video Streaming

Setup: We choose a 3-minute YouTube video available in both high/low quality and play it in a custom app. We use the Android YouTube APIs [2] to extract player states (paused, playing, buffering) to compute the QoE metrics described below. Similar to the web experiments, we run measurements for both the base carrier and associated MVNOs, simultaneously, at multiple locations and at different times of the day.

QoE metrics and Evaluation: The key video QoE metrics are: (1) *video resolution* being delivered;[4] (2) *startup delay* or the time between the user clicking on the play button and the time the video starts playing; (3) *buffering ratio* or the percentage of the session duration spent in buffering state; and (4) *load failures*, where the video fails to load. Figure 5 summarizes the distribution of these metrics.

First, we observe that, with respect to resolution quality, carrier B and its MVNOs always use the high-resolution version of the video. On the other hand, carrier A and its MVNOs play a mix of resolutions, except for A3 that always plays the lower resolution video. Second, in terms of startup delay, MVNO family B overall shows a higher startup delay than MVNO family A, for the higher-resolution cases. Also, consistent with the web measurements, we find that in MVNO family B, the base carrier outperforms its MVNOs in terms of startup delay, and amongst the MVNOs, B2 performs the poorest with a median startup delay of 23 seconds. Third, we see that MVNO family A outperforms MVNO family B in terms of buffering ratio as well, and B2 again performs the worst amongst the MVNOs in its family. Finally, we find a non-trivial number of video load failures for the MVNOs in the B family; e.g., B1 fails ≈ 20% of the time.

Factor Analysis: As before, we use the correlation coefficients to zoom in on key network-level factors. The startup delay and buffering states are (unsurprisingly) mostly influenced by *TCP throughput*. Figure 6 shows the difference in the measured TCP throughput across the carriers and confirms the earlier observations about video QoE. Surprisingly, MVNO family B chooses the higher quality video even though it has lower TCP throughputs than MVNO family A (and hence incurs more buffering). We suspect that this is related to the explicit proxy described earlier; i.e., the bitrate negotiation at the beginning of the session is done by the proxy and does not account for the actual "last hop" throughput achievable by the client.

To further understand the load failures, we analyzed the packet-level traces and find two reasons behind these failures: (1) the proxy *blocks* the video requested by the client by sending an HTTP

[3]We were able to detect the transparent proxy using Netalyzr which showed HTTP header modifications [6].

[4]The YouTube API does not perform dynamic video resolution adaption on mobile. It selects a resolution that it considers suitable for the current connection at the start and uses it for the entire session.

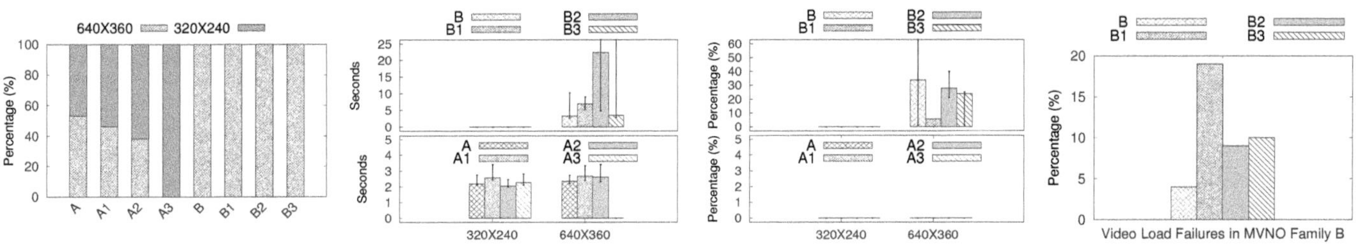

(a) Resolution of played video (b) Startup Delay (c) Buffering Ratio (d) Load failures

Figure 5: Video quality-of-experience metrics for the MVNOs and base carriers. Note that MVNO family B always plays the high-quality resolution and suffer significant buffering, startup delay, and video load failures.

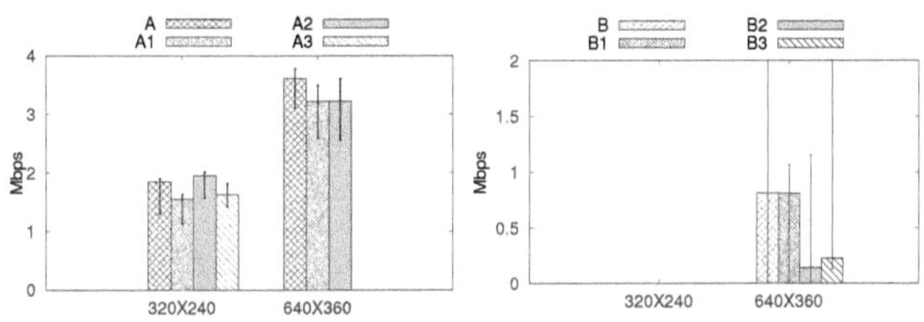

(a) MVNO family A (b) MVNO family B

Figure 6: TCP throughput influences video quality

response with the status code 403 ('access forbidden') and (2) the proxy does not respond to the initial request from the client causing the client to timeout. Specifically, B1 experiences the largest number of type (2) video load failures; this is related to radio dormancy issues discussed in Section 3.1.

3.3 Voice calls

Setup and QoE metrics: We created a custom *auto dial* application that is scripted to automatically call a number. This application runs on all 4 phones at different locations and times of the day. We also setup a recipient phone in the lab, and we build and run another custom application on this phone to log the time of the first ring, accept the call, and then immediately end the call. Because the Android top-level framework does not allow us to automatically answer/end a call, we mimicked a Bluetooth Headset request to automatically answer the call and used lower-layer APIs for ending the call. With this setup we compute the *Call Setup Time* or the time elapsed between the time the caller makes a call and when the callee receives it. To ensure that the caller/receiver are in sync, we use the ClockSync [16] Android app. We separately verified that the synchronization error was $\leq$ 10 ms (not shown); this suffices for our analysis as we look for user-perceivable (e.g., $\geq$ 100ms) differences in performance.

To measure the *audio quality*, we establish calls between each of the 4 phones and a Google Voice number on a laptop. We play a 3 minute (based on average audio call durations) audio file on the laptop and record the incoming audio to the phone.To minimize background noise we direct the audio output from the phone to the recorder via a standard 3.5mm cable. We compute the cross-correlation of the Mel-frequency Cepstral Coefficients (MFCCs), (recommended in the audio/speech processing literature [27]), between the reference audio file and the recorded audio file. We normalize this value by dividing it by the score attained when cross-correlating the MFCCs of the original file with itself, and we call this normalized value the *Call Quality Score*.

Evaluation: Figure 7a shows the distribution of the call setup time for the different carriers. MVNO family A showed fairly similar

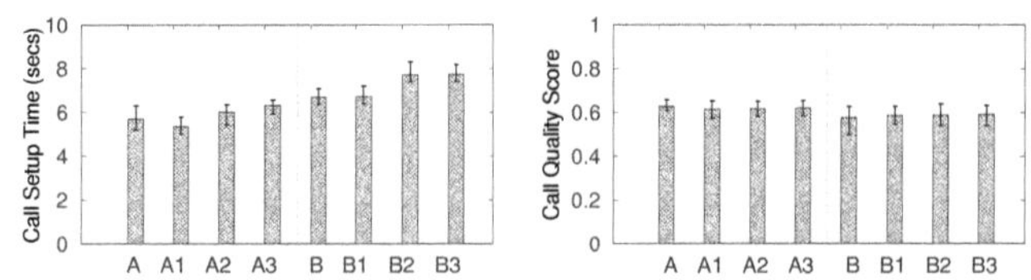

(a) Setup time (b) Audio quality

Figure 7: Call quality in terms of setup time and the audio quality. While there is no significant difference in the call quality, we do observe that some of the MVNOs in MVNO family B have a higher call setup time.

values for call setup times (median of 5-6 seconds). With MVNO family B, we notice that B2 and B3 have a 1.5 second higher median call setup time. However, this difference cannot be attributed to any client-side metric we collected. Figure 7b shows the Call Quality Score for the two MVNO families. In this case, we do not observe significant differences across the providers.[5] Since the discrepancy in quality is low, unlike the data experiments, we do not perform any further factor analysis.

4 Other Applications

In addition to the three usage scenarios discussed in the previous section, we also conduct smaller-scale measurements to capture other common user concerns. We briefly summarize the main observations from these experiements.

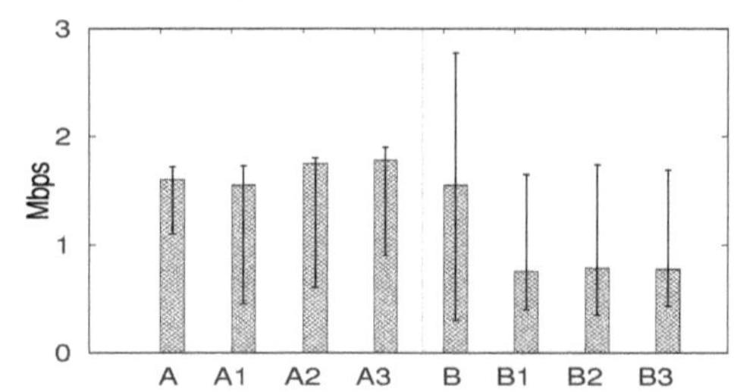

Figure 8: TCP Uplink Throughputs.

Uploads: Web and video workloads are largely download-bound. Users are increasingly using phones to upload content (e.g., Instagram, Vine). To understand the impact on such applications, we

[5] Note that Nexus 4 phones do not support VoLTE (Voice over LTE). Hence, audio voice calls are sent over a channel separate from the data channel, and thus voice is not impacted by differences on the data channel.

measure the upload speeds obtained by different carriers to a reference campus server in Stony Brook. Figure 8 shows similar characteristics to our previous experiments— MVNOs in MVNO family B perform significantly worse than base carrier B, whereas base carrier A and its MVNOs perform roughly similarly.

Video Chat (Google Hangout): We pick a popular video chat application – Google Hangout and evaluate its performance across carriers. We establish a chat (5 minutes long) from the phone to a well-provisioned laptop and play a video in front of the phones and the laptop using another screen. We collect packet traces at both ends. We repeat our experiments at 3 different locations, lab and two residential areas. We analyze frames/sec received at the laptop as well as the sending and receiving UDP throughputs. We did not observe any significant difference between the base carrier and their MVNOs for both A and B MVNO families. One interesting observation is that video chat shows no performance differences on MVNOs in MVNO family B, which is unlike the case of video streaming (Section 3.2). We speculate that this is due to a combination of two reasons: (1) chat traffic uses UDP and does not go through the explicit proxy and (2) unlike the YouTube video which chooses a static bitrate at the start, Hangout uses dynamic bitrate adaptation. (Recall that most of the problems in MVNO family B was the poor choice of initial bitrate via the proxy.)

Traffic Shaping and Port Blocking: Users like to know if MVNOs throttle or block less common applications. This is particularly relevant as we have seen use of proxies (Section 3.1) and use of middleboxes in cellular networks [37] is well-known. We use two tools, Bonafide [17] and Netalyzr [6], as they provide complementary coverage over the set of application tests. We used this to study 3 different types of applications: (1) BitTorrent, (2) VoIP-H323 and (3) RTSP-based apps. We found no evidence of application-specific traffic shaping for these protocols, in both MVNO families. Additionally, Netalyzr reveals that while MVNO family A does not exhibit any port blocking, MVNO family B exhibits more diverse blocking behavior. For example, B blocks TCP-based SIP and UDP access to NetBIOS-NS servers. While B3 and B2 do not block any ports, B1 blocks many application ports (FTP, PPTP, NTP, NetBIOS-NS, NetBIOS-DGM, IKE Key Exchange).

Coverage: As seen in our user quotes, users want to know if MVNOs get the same coverage/treatment as the base carriers (e.g., [10]). As discussed earlier, we logged relevant lower-layer information—serving cell-id, signal strength (RSSI/RSCP/RSRP), link layer technology used (e.g., EDGE, HSPA, HSPA+). In addition, we did a number of driving experiments covering major routes within the map in Figure 1. We found that in general, the carriers in each MVNO family connect to a similar set of cell-ids in a given location and that there was no statistically significant difference in signal strength or link-layer technology used.

Quota usage: Another common concern for users is whether carriers start throttling before the actual usage quotas are reached (e.g., [9]). We correlated the performance for different applications vs. the data usage amount for every billing cycle. We did not observe throttling behavior for either MVNO family. A detailed study of this subject via more controlled experiments is an interesting direction of future work, especially in light of known accounting discrepancies (e.g., [32]).

5 Related Work

With the growth of mobile traffic, there are several prior and ongoing efforts in mobile measurement. While the tools and techniques they use are similar to our work, the key difference is that these have not focused on the MVNO phenomenon to characterize differences across MVNOs or MVNOs vs. base carriers.

Mobile measurements: Previous studies have measured mobile performance from the infrastructure-side [26, 28, 31, 33] and the client-side [20, 21]. These focus primarily on characterizing traffic usage patterns, which is orthogonal to our work. Wang et al. showed how middlebox effects (e.g., timing out idle TCP connections) can have a huge impact on the mobile application performance [37]. Huang et al. compare different carriers on a range of applications across different smartphone hardware [25]. However, their study did not cover MVNOs. More recent studies analyze performance variability within carriers [30] and diagnose causes of high latency in cellular networks [39]. These are interesting factors to further dissect MVNO performance.

Tools and datasets: Several crowd-sourced solutions gather mobile measurements; e.g., FCC's broadband measurement tool [3], OpenSignal (`www.opensignal.com`), Mobiperf (`www.mobiperf.com`), OOKLA Speed Test (`www.speedtest.net`). These focus mostly on network-level metrics (e.g., latency, throughput, signal strength) and do not measure user-perceived QoE metrics which is our primary focus. Bashko et al. developed the Bonafide tool to detect traffic shaping and service differentiation [17]. Netalyzr is also a powerful tool for detecting port blocking, proxies, and DNS issues [6]. We leverage these two tools and apply them to study MVNOs.

6 Conclusions

In this paper, we presented a first attempt to shed light on a recent and growing trend in the mobile market: mobile virtual network operators or MVNOs. While these have been growing in market share, there are natural concerns about their performance and there has been little work done on systematically understanding this area. To fill this gap, we conducted a systematic measurement study with two major MVNO families in the US. Our analysis shows that while the MVNOs share the network infrastructure of the base carriers, there is visible performance degradation in quality of experience metrics for common mobile phone applications for some MVNOs. Further, MVNOs in the same MVNO family do not perform equally, and the two MVNO families behave differently. Deeper analysis reveals a range of structural and lower-layer differences across MVNO families and MVNOs, including use of proxy, varying latencies and loss rates, data activity dormancy issues and various forms of blocking/denials. We hope that our observations motivate and trigger future deeper and large-scale studies, across larger regions, more MVNOs and more variety of data plans, perhaps by using mobile measurement platforms being deployed in the wild.

7 Acknowledgements

We thank Gaurav Dugar, Su'aad Zaman, Naila Kabiraj, and Jihoon Ryoo for their help with data collection. We also thank Bashko et al., for sharing their BonaFide tool [17] with us. This research was partially supported by NSF grant CNS-1117719.

8 References

[1] Android TelephonyManager Class. http://developer.android.com/reference/android/telephony/TelephonyManager.html#DATA_ACTIVITY_DORMANT.

[2] Android YouTube Player API. https://developers.google.com/youtube/android/player/.

[3] FCC - Measuring Broadband America. http://www.fcc.gov/measuring-broadband-america.

[4] Google Trends. http://www.google.com/trends/.

[5] List of MVNOs in the U.S. http://en.wikipedia.org/wiki/List_of_United_States_mobile_virtual_network_operators.

[6] Netalyzer, HTTP proxy detection through HTTP header or content modification. http://n1.netalyzr.icsi.berkeley.edu/info_httpproxy_header.html.

[7] onPageFinished method: Android WebViewClient. http://bit.ly/1loeaVP.

[8] The K-S Statistical Test. http://en.wikipedia.org/wiki/Kolmogorov-Smirnov_test.

[9] Straight Talk has upped the ante on throttling users! http://www.howardforums.com/showthread.php/1773165-Straight-Talk-has-upped-the-ante-on-throttling-users!, 2012.

[10] Is there a catch to MVNOs? http://ask.metafilter.com/235587/Is-there-a-catch-to-MVNOs, 2013.

[11] AT&T vs. other MVNO's on latency, capped download speeds . http://www.howardforums.com/showthread.php/1813979-AT-amp-T-vs-other-mvno-s-on-latency-capped-download-speeds, 2013.

[12] M2M and MVNOs driving US connections growth. https://gsmaintelligence.com/analysis/2013/08/m2m-and-mvnos-driving-us-connections-growth/397/, 2013.

[13] Roaming, Regional, Mobile to Mobile, and Other Questions. https://help.ting.com/entries/21227328-roaming-regional-mobile-to-mobile-and-other-questions, 2014.

[14] Sprint, T-Mobile execs explain the MVNO explosion. http://www.fiercewireless.com/special-reports/mvno-explosion-will-latest-wave-virtual-operators-survive-0, 2014.

[15] Western Europe-Evolution of MVNO Business Models-Market Growth, Trends and Opportunities. http://www.releasewire.com/press-releases/western-europe-evolution-of-mvno-business-models-market-growth-trends-and-opportunities-493894.htm, 2014.

[16] S. Baranov. Android ClockSync Application. https://play.google.com/store/apps/details?id=ru.org.amip.ClockSync&hl=en.

[17] V. Bashko, N. Melnikov, A. Sehgal, and J. Schonwalder. Bonafide: A traffic shaping detection tool for mobile networks. In *IFIP/IEEE IM*, 2013.

[18] M. Belshe. More Bandwidth Doesn't Matter (much). http://bit.ly/1rNCOlC, 2010.

[19] J. Erman, V. Gopalakrishnan, R. Jana, and K. Ramakrishnan. Towards a SPDY'ier mobile web ? In *ACM CoNext*, 2013.

[20] H. Falaki, D. Lymberopoulos, R. Mahajan, S. Kandula, and D. Estrin. Diversity in smartphone usage. In *ACM MobiSys*, 2010.

[21] H. Falaki, D. Lymberopoulos, R. Mahajan, S. Kandula, and D. Estrin. A first look at traffic on smartphones. In *IMC*, 2010.

[22] K. Fitchard. Why are MVNOs so hot right now? Thank the carriers. http://gigaom.com/2012/06/25/why-are-mvnos-so-hot-right-now-thank-the-carriers/, 2012.

[23] A. Gember, A. Akella, J. Pang, A. Varshavsky, and R. Caceres. Obtaining in-context measurements of cellular network performance. In *Proceedings of IMC 2012*.

[24] I. Grigorik. *High Performance Browser Networking*. Chapter 7, O'Riley, 2013.

[25] J. Huang, Q. Xu, B. Tiwana, Z. M. Mao, M. Zhang, and P. Bahl. Anatomizing application performance differences on smartphones. In *ACM Mobisys*, 2010.

[26] Y. Lee. Measured TCP Performance in CDMA 1x EV-DO Network. In *PAM*, 2006.

[27] M. Lindasalwa, M. Begam, and I. Elamvazuthi. Voice recognition algorithms using Mel Frequency Cepstral Coefficient (MFCC) and Dynamic Time Warping (DTW) techniques. In *arXiv preprint arXiv:1003.4083*, 2010.

[28] G. Maier, F. Schneider, and A. Feldmann. A first look at mobile hand-held device traffic. In *PAM*, 2010.

[29] J. Manweiler, S. Agarwal, M. Zhang, R. Roy Choudhury, and P. Bahl. Switchboard: A matchmaking system for multiplayer mobile games. In *Proceedings of ACM Mobisys*, 2011.

[30] A. Nikravesh, D. Choffnes, E. Katz-Bassett, Z. M. Mao, and M. Welsh. Mobile network performance from user devices: A longitudinal, multidimensional analysis. In *PAM*, 2014.

[31] U. Paul, A. Prabhu Subramanian, M. Buddhikot, and S. Das. Understanding traffic dynamics in cellular data networks. In *INFOCOM*, 2011.

[32] C. Peng, C. yu Li, G. hua Tu, S. Lu, and L. Zhang. Mobile Data Charging: New Attacks and Countermeasures . In *Proc. CCS*, 2012.

[33] X. Qiang, J. Erman, A. Gerber, Z. Mao, J. Pang, and S. Venkataraman. Identifying diverse usage behaviors of smartphone apps. In *IMC*, 2011.

[34] S. Rosen, H. Luo, Q. A. Chen, Z. M. Mao, J. Hui, A. Drake, and K. Lau. Discovering Fine-grained RRC State Dynamics and Performance Impacts in Cellular Networks. In *Proceedings of ACM Mobicom*, 2014.

[35] J. P. Rula and F. E. Bustamante. Behind the curtain: The importance of replica selection in next generation cellular networks. In *Proceedings of ACM SIGCOMM*, 2014.

[36] A. Sivakumar, V. Gopalakrishnan, S. Lee, S. Rao, S. Sen, and O. Spatscheck. Cloud is Not a Silver Bullet: A Case Study of Cloud-based Mobile Browsing. In *Proceedings of ACM HotMobile*, 2014.

[37] Z. Wang, Z. Qian, Q. Xu, Z. Mao, and M. Zhang. An untold story of middleboxes in cellular networks. In *ACM SIGCOMM*, 2011.

[38] M. Welsh. Why Mobile Performance is Hard. ACM Mobicom Indutsrial Paper Session . http://www.sigmobile.org/mobicom/2013/MobiCom2013_IndustrialTalks_MattWelsh.pdf, 2013.

[39] K. Zarifis, T. Flach, S. Nori, D. Choffnes, R. Govindan, E. Katz-Bassett, Z. Mao, and M. Welsh. Diagnosing path inflation of mobile client traffic. In *PAM*, 2014.

OS Fingerprinting and Tethering Detection in Mobile Networks

Yi-Chao Chen[†], Yong Liao[‡], Mario Baldi[‡], Sung-Ju Lee[‡], Lili Qiu[†]
[†]The University of Texas at Austin, [‡]Narus Inc.

ABSTRACT

Fingerprinting the Operating System (OS) running on a device based on its traffic has several applications, such as NAT detection, policy enforcement in enterprise networks, and billing for shared access in mobile networks. In this paper, we propose to utilize several features in TCP/IP headers for OS identification, and use real traffic traces to evaluate the accuracy of fingerprinting. Our trace-driven study shows that several techniques that successfully fingerprint desktop OSes are not effective for fingerprinting mobile devices. Therefore, we propose new features for fingerprinting OSes on mobile devices. We also consider NAT/tethering detection, an important application of OS fingerprinting. We use the presence of multiple OSes from the same IP address along with TCP timestamp, clock frequency, and boot time to detect tethering. Evaluation shows that our approach effectively detects tethering and outperforms existing schemes.

Categories and Subject Descriptors

C.2.3 [**Computer-Communication Networks**]: Network Operations – Network monitoring

General Terms

Algorithms, Measurement, Performance

Keywords

OS Fingerprint; Tethering Detection; TCP/IP

1. INTRODUCTION

Identifying the Operating System (OS) running on an end device based on its traffic is valuable in many contexts. For example, an enterprise network may restrict the usage of specific OSes for security reasons. Moreover, OS fingerprinting can be used to detect NAT/tethering (*i.e.*, multiple devices sharing the Internet connection of a mobile device), since the presence of multiple OSes sharing the same IP address is an indication of tethering, which may be prohibited by a wireless network due to resource usage concerns.

IMC'14, November 5–7, 2014, Vancouver, BC, Canada.
Copyright 2014 ACM 978-1-4503-3213-2/14/11 ...$15.00.
http://dx.doi.org/10.1145/2663716.2663745.

Motivated by this need, we examine a series of features in network traffic to understand their effectiveness in detecting the OS running on an end device. In particular, we consider IP Time-to-Live (TTL), IP ID monotonicity, TCP window size scale option, TCP timestamp, clock frequency, and boot time. Among them, TTL, IP ID, TCP timestamp option, and boot time have been considered in other contexts, including machine fingerprinting [2, 9, 29, 35, 39, 43]. We also propose several new features: the stability of the clock frequency, presence of TCP timestamp option, and the default set of TCP window size scale factors.

Next we apply OS fingerprinting to detect tethering using a simple probabilistic approach. It consists of two steps: (i) identifying the OS running on a device (*i.e.*, iOS, Android, or Windows) based on a combination of features, and (ii) determining if there is a tethering based on the number of OSes along with the number of distinct TTLs, TCP timestamp monotonicity, standard deviation of clock frequency, and standard deviation of boot time.

We evaluate our approach using traces we collected in 2013, as well as publicly available traces [15] collected during OSDI'06 [14] and SIGCOMM'08 [7]. We find that Apple iOS can be accurately identified, while Android and Windows are identified with 1.0 precision (*i.e.*, the fraction of traffic our scheme detected as a given OS is indeed that OS) and 0.8 recall (*i.e.*, the fraction of traffic from a given OS is correctly detected by our scheme). Tethering detection has 0.78∼0.89 recall when the target precision is 0.8.

Our main contributions are as follows:

- We identify new features for OS fingerprinting, such as the presence of TCP timestamp, TCP window size scale factor, and standard deviation of clock frequency.
- We quantify the effectiveness of various individual features, including both new and previously proposed features. We show that clock skew, a feature proposed before for fingerprinting desktops in wired networks, does not work well in mobile networks. Existing work assumes that significant clock skew indicates different machines, but it is ineffective in a mobile context due to highly variable clock frequency in iOS devices and increased estimation error due to short transfers and unstable connectivity.
- We develop a probabilistic scheme that combines multiple features to detect OSes and tethering, and show it outperforms decision tree and linear regression.

2. TRACE DESCRIPTION

We use three packet traces in our study. The first two are WiFi packet traces captured during SIGCOMM'08 [7] and OSDI'06 [14], available from CRAWDAD [15]. We also collect our lab trace by setting up an AP in an office, recruiting users to use the AP for In-

Table 1: Summary of the traces.

Trace	Time	Duration	# IPs	# pkts	# flows
OSDI06 Trace	2006/11	1 day	292	1,408K	3,404
SIGCOMM08 Trace	2008/08	1 day	223	1,107K	2,586
Lab Trace	2013/10	2 hours	56	193K	741

ternet access, and capturing packet headers on the AP. Altogether, we had 14 captures from 4 different Android phone and tablet devices; 10 captures from iOS devices, including iPhone, iPod touch, and iPad; and 32 captures from laptops running Windows. Each capture lasts $10 \sim 30$ minutes. Table 1 summarizes the three traces.

3. OS FINGERPRINTING

We introduce a list of relevant features and describe how these features are used for OS fingerprinting. In this paper, we focus on identifying Windows, iOS, and Android, since recent market research [23,32] reports that Windows, iOS, and Android account for 12%, 43%, and 44% of the laptop/phone/tablet OSes, respectively. Our methodology is general and can be easily extended to cover more OSes.

3.1 Features

We identify the following features for OS fingerprinting.

IP Time-To-Live: The TTL value in the IP header specifies the maximum number of hops a packet can traverse. Different OSes set different initial TTL values; Windows uses 64 or 128, while iOS and Android use 64 by default.

IP ID Monotonicity: The identification field in the IP header is primarily used in IP de-fragmentation. We observe that IP IDs in packets from Windows machines consistently increase monotonically over time. iOS devices always randomize the IP ID of each packet. Interestingly, some Android devices completely randomize the IP IDs, while others monotonically increase them for some time and periodically reset to random values.

TCP Timestamp Option: The TCP timestamp option [25] is used for measuring roundtrip time and protecting against wrapped sequence numbers. Most packets from Windows do not have TCP timestamp options, whereas packets from iOS and Android usually do [13].

TCP Window Size Scale Option: This option allows increasing TCP receiver window size beyond 65,535 bytes. The scale value is negotiated during the TCP three-way handshake. Our traces reveal that the scale values vary across OSes: Windows uses 1, 4, or 256; iOS uses 16; and Android uses 2, 4, or 64.

Clock Frequency: The clock frequency of a machine should be relatively stable. We observe that this holds true mostly for Windows and Android machines. Interestingly, the clock frequency of iOS varies over time. From the trace we collected from multiple iOS devices, we see that their clock frequency varies between 920Hz to 1000Hz. We suspect that iOS might dynamically adjust the clock frequency for power saving.

We estimate the clock frequency as follows. Let t_1 and t_2 denote the capturing time of two packets from the same device, and T_1 and T_2 be the logic timestamps (*e.g.*, TCP timestamp) embedded in those two packets. We compute clock frequency as $\frac{T_2-T_1}{t_2-t_1}$.

If the standard deviation of the estimated clock frequency from a flow is large (*i.e.*, ≥ 3 in our evaluation), it implies the estimation frequency is unstable and is likely to be an iOS machine. Note that for OS detection, this heuristic may not be accurate since large standard deviation could be caused by multiple machines instead of one iOS machine. We will quantify the error through evaluation later.

Table 2: Probability of identifying OS witch each feature. $thresh_{v1}$=0.05, $thresh_{v2}$=0.40, $thresh_t$=0.05, and $thresh_c$=3. OS_a is Android; OS_i is iOS; and OS_w is Windows. We examine the distribution of values of each feature for different OSes and select the threshold yielding less than 10% false positive.

Feature f_i	$Pr(OS_a\|f_i)$	$Pr(OS_i\|f_i)$	$Pr(OS_w\|f_i)$
TTL = 128	0	0	1
TTL $\neq$ 128	0.43	0.30	0.27
IP ID monotonicity violation ratio $< thresh_{v1}$	0.18	0	0.82
IP ID monotonicity violation ratio $\in [thresh_{v1}, thresh_{v2}]$	0.75	0	0.25
IP ID monotonicity violation ratio $\geq thresh_{v2}$	0.22	0.78	0
TCP TS Opt ratio $< thresh_t$	0	0	1
TCP TS Opt ratio $\geq thresh_t$	0.59	0.41	0
TCP WS Opt = 4	0.1	0	0.9
TCP WS Opt = 16	0	1	0
TCP WS Opt = 64	0.82	0	0.18
TCP WS Opt = 256	0	0	1
clock freq std $< thresh_c$	0.67	0.27	0.07
clock freq std $\geq thresh_c$	0	1	0

Interestingly, this heuristic has better accuracy for tethering detection. When the large estimated frequency variation is due to multiple OSes instead of iOS, our scheme wrongly identifies iOS in the tethered traffic. However, because other OS fingerprinting features (*e.g.*IP TTL, TCP timestamp option, and TCP window size scale option) can still identify the correct OS, our scheme will identify iOS and non-iOS devices by combining results from all features. Since two or more OSes implies tethering usage, our scheme can still detect tethering correctly.

3.2 Using the Features

Exploiting each feature f_i listed in Section 3.1 to detect OSes requires an important probability $Pr(OS_x \mid f_i)$, *i.e.*, the probability of being OS x when feature f_i is present. We use Bayes' rule to derive $Pr(OS_x \mid f_i) = \frac{Pr(f_i|OS_x)Pr(OS_x)}{Pr(f_i)}$, where $Pr(f_i \mid OS_x)$ and $Pr(f_i)$ are empirically computed using our lab trace; $Pr(OS_x)$ is the probability of OS_x derived from the training traces. $Pr(f_i)$ denotes the fraction of IP addresses having feature f_i. An IP is considered to have feature f_i if its feature value exceeds the corresponding threshold (*e.g.*, the fraction of packets with TCP timestamp exceeds a threshold).

We divide each trace into a training set and a testing set. Below we describe how we empirically determine the threshold for each feature using the training set. We later use the testing trace to evaluate the accuracy of our detection in Section 5.

IP Time-To-Live: From our training set, we learn that Android and iOS use 64 as the default TTL, while Windows uses 64 or 128. We can thus use the TTL value to identify Windows (*i.e.*, an initial TTL of 128) with high confidence. This rule accurately catches all Windows machines as shown in row 1 of Table 2. When the default TTL is not 128, it could be any OS. Because only a small number of packets from Windows set TTL other than 128 and there are more Android than iOS in the training set, the probability of being an Android is higher as shown in row 2 of Table 2.

IP ID Monotonicity: In our training set, we observe that Windows devices increase IP ID monotonically, iOS devices use random IP IDs, and their violation ratio (*i.e.*, the current packet's IP ID is smaller than the previous IP ID) is around 50%. There are

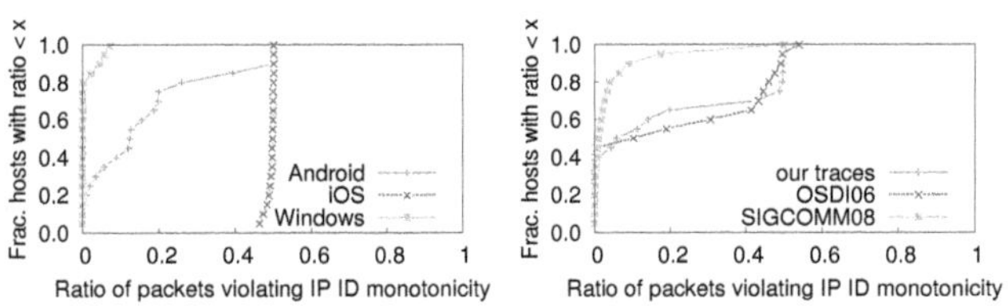

(a) Violation ratios across OSes (b) Violation ratios in the traces

Figure 1: CDF of ratio of packets violating IP ID monotonicity.

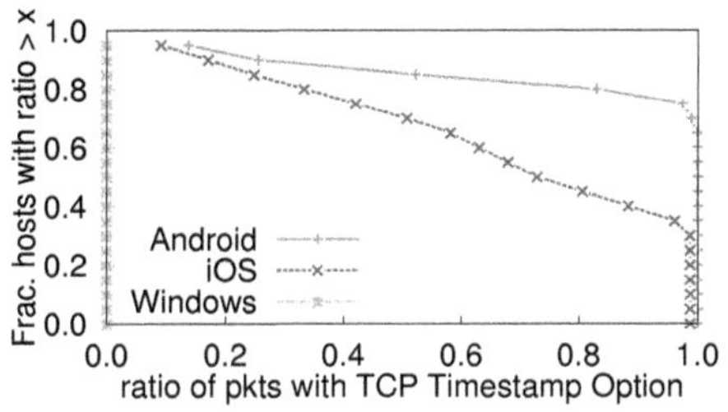

Figure 2: CCDF of ratio of packets with the timestamp option.

about 20% of Android devices randomizing the IP IDs. But 80% of Android devices have 40% or lower violation ratio. Figure 1(a) shows the ratio of packets violating IP ID monotonicity for three types of OSes in our training set.

Rows 3∼5 in Table 2 show that requiring IP ID monotonicity identifies Windows machines fairly accurately while significant violations of IP ID monotonicity can be used to identify iOS. So we derive the following rule. When the violation ratio is less than 5%, most likely it is a Windows device. When the violation ratio is greater than 40%, it is iOS. When the violation ratio is in between (*e.g.*, $5\% \le ratio < 40\%$), it is likely to be Android.

Figure 1(b) shows that the violation ratios are smaller than 5% on 72% of machines in SIGCOMM'08 trace. This implies that a large number of machines are likely to be Windows. In our lab trace and OSDI'06 trace, violation ratios are smaller than 5% on 42% and 44% of machines, respectively. These machines are likely Windows machines, as well.

TCP Timestamp Option: As shown in Figure 2, the ratios of packets with TCP Timestamp option are more than 10% and 14% for iOS and Android devices, respectively. For Windows machines, the ratio is smaller than 5%. Hence, 5% is a good threshold to distinguish Windows machines from others. If the ratio of packets with TCP Timestamp option is smaller than 5%, we conclude that it is a Windows device. Rows 6 and 7 in Table 2 show the coverage of using the presence of TCP timestamp option for identifying the OS: it accurately identifies Windows. The accuracy for detecting Android and iOS is lower.

TCP Window Size Scale Option: The scale factor is determined by the maximum receiving buffer space and cannot be changed after the connection is opened. Figure 3(a) shows the scale factors selected by different OSes. We observe that only iOS uses 16; Windows and Android use 2, 4, 64 and 256. Figure 3(b) shows that no scale factor is set to 16 in OSDI'06 dataset. Since iOS was first released in 2006, it implies that 16 is unique for iOS devices. Hence we derive the following rule: a TCP window scale factor of 16 is iOS, 64 is Android, and 256 is Windows. Rows 8∼11 in Table 2 show it is fairly accurate for determining the OSes.

Clock Frequency and Boot Time Estimation: Figure 4 shows that the standard deviation of clock frequency in 90% of Windows machines is less than 1, and that of 90% of Android devices is less than 3. Therefore when the clock frequency exceeds 3, we conclude it is iOS. Row 13 in Table 2 shows that we identify all iOS correctly based on unstable clock frequency.

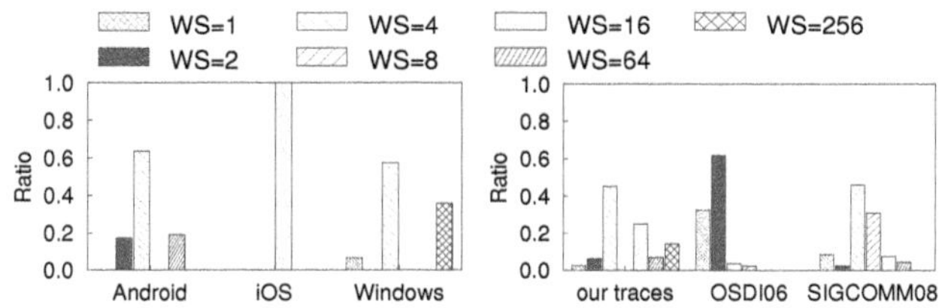

(a) Ratio in OSes (b) Ratio in data sets

Figure 3: Ratio of selected TCP window scale option.

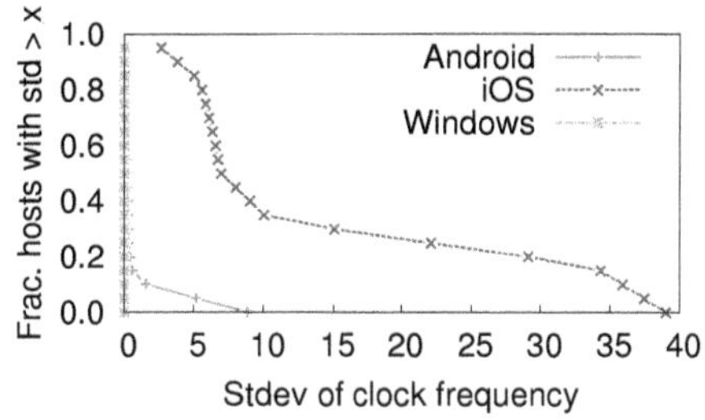

Figure 4: CCDF of clock frequency std in OSes.

3.3 Combining Features

So far, we have focused on using individual features. As we observed in Section 3.2, different features may work well in different scenarios. This motivates us to develop a technique to leverage multiple features to improve accuracy. We design a probability-based technique by applying the navïe Bayes classifier to effectively combine multiple features. Specifically, given the set of observed features $f_1 \sim f_k$, the probability of being OS_x can be computed as Equation (1) if features $f_1 \sim f_k$ are independent.

$$Pr(OS_x \mid f_1, ..., f_k) = Pr(OS_x)\frac{Pr(f_i, ..., f_k \mid OS_x)}{Pr(f_i, ..., f_k)} = Pr(OS_x)\frac{\prod_{i=1}^{k} Pr(f_i \mid OS_x)}{\prod_{i=1}^{k} Pr(f_i)}. \quad (1)$$

$Pr(OS_x)$ and $Pr(f_i|OS_x)$ are learned from the training traces. We then compute $Pr(f_i)$ based on all packets from an IP address in the testing trace and use Equation 1 to compute the probability that the IP uses OS_x. The OS is then identified as the one with the highest probability.

4. TETHERING DETECTION

The OS fingerprinting result can be used for tethering detection. To that end, we present a few more features specifically related to tethering detection and how tethering detection is conducted.

4.1 Features

If multiple types of OSes are detected from the traffic coming from an IP address, it is considered as tethering. In addition, the following features can also be used for tethering detection.

Number of TTL Values: If packets from an IP address has different TTL values, it is likely to be tethering.

TCP Timestamp Monotonicity: Packets generated by the same machine tend to monotonically increase TCP timestamp values, whereas packets from different machines usually have mixed TCP timestamp due to different clock offsets across machines.

Clock Frequency: If the standard deviation of clock frequency estimated using the packets from an IP address is too large, it is likely to be tethering.

Boot Time: Machine boot time can be inferred from TCP timestamp values in packets sent from that machine. Most OS implemen-

Table 3: **Probability of having tethering when the feature is observed (*i.e.*, $Pr(T|f_i)$), where all thresholds are derived from the training traces. $thresh_v = 0$, $thresh_c = 35$, and $thresh_b = 1455$.**

Feature f_i	lab trace	osdi06	sigcomm08
# distinct TTL = 1	0.33	0.24	0.24
# distinct TTL > 1	0.96	0.95	0.92
TCP TS monotonicity violation ratio $\leq thresh_v$	0.33	0.40	0.29
TCP TS monotonicity violation ratio $> thresh_v$	1	1	1
clock freq std $< thresh_c$	0.18	0.53	0.55
clock freq std $\geq thresh_c$	1	1	0.67
boot time std $< thresh_b$	0.1	0.36	0.66
boot time std $\geq thresh_b$	1	1	0.88

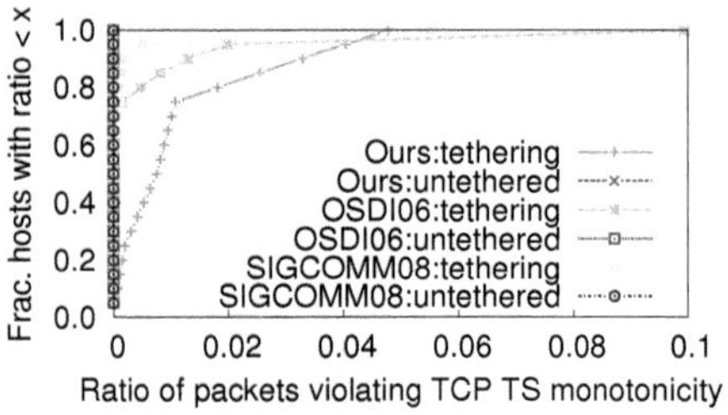

Figure 5: CDF of ratio of packets that violate TCP timestamp monotonicity.

tations use a random number as the starting value of TCP timestamps after booting. Hence the estimated boot time is not the real one. However, the value can still quite uniquely identify a machine because different machines have distinct boot times and distinct initial TCP timestamp values [39].

Note that TCP TS monotonicity, clock frequency, and the boot time are effective even when the tethered devices use the same OS, as the feature values vary across devices instead of OSes.

4.2 Using the Features

We describe how to use each feature for tethering detection. Similar to Section 3.2, we use the Bayes' rule to empirically compute $Pr(T|f_i)$ (*i.e.*, the probability of tethering under feature f_i) according to the training traces. To facilitate the empirical study, we simulate tethering activities in each trace by randomly mixing packets from different IPs and modifying the source IP address to make them look like from the same IP address. We assume that there is no tethering in the original traces. This assumption should hold in our lab trace due to the way in which they are collected. For OSDI'06 and SIGCOMM'08 traces, it is likely to be true since there is no reason for tethering when free WiFi is available (other literature [34] also makes a similar observation). For each trace, we select packets from 80% of the source IPs as the training traces to derive the threshold and use the remaining 20% as testing to quantify the accuracy of tethering detection in Section 5.3.

IP TTL: Based on the TTL analysis in Section 3.2, we conclude that there is tethering if the number of distinct TTLs in all packets from an IP address is more than one. From our training set, we find that this heuristic accurately identifies tethering: its coverage (*i.e.*, the fraction of traffic our scheme detected as tethering is indeed tethering) ranges from 0.92 to 0.96 in three different traces.

TCP Timestamp Monotonicity: Figure 5 shows the ratio of packets that violate TCP timestamp monotonicity. We see that untethered traffic have no violations, while 95% (our lab trace), 20% (OSDI), and 41% (SIGCOMM) of tethering machines have violation ratios larger than zero. Therefore, we conclude that the probability of tethering is one if the violation ratio of TCP timestamp monotonicity is larger than zero. When there is no violation of TCP timestamp monotonicity, the tethering probabilities are 0.33, 0.40, and 0.29 in our lab trace, OSDI'06 trace, and SIGCOMM'08 trace, respectively. The false negative cases are mainly due to two reasons. First, TCP timestamp option is not available in most of Windows devices. Second, sometimes flows from tethered devices do not overlap in time, and thus no violation is observed.

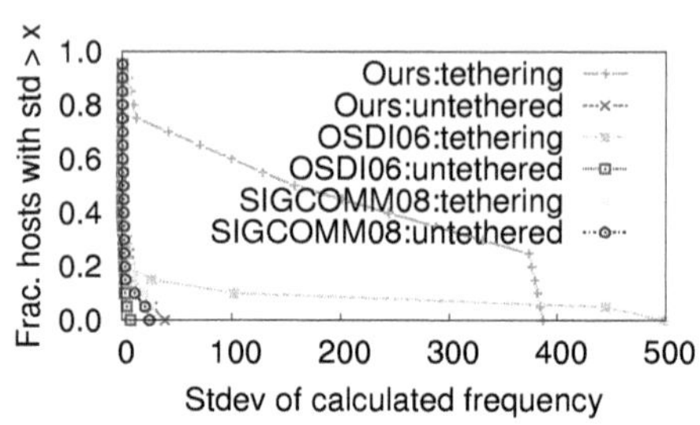

Figure 6: CCDF of clock frequency standard deviation in tethering/untethered devices.

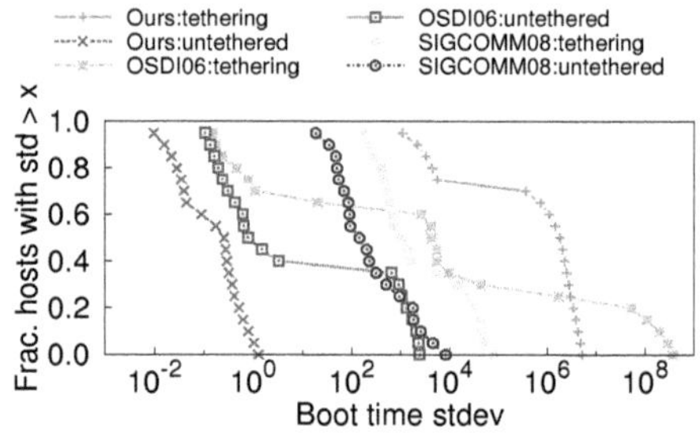

Figure 7: CCDF of boot time std in tethering and untethering traffic.

Clock Frequency: Figure 6 shows that the standard deviation in 90% of untethered traffic is smaller than 35 (lab trace), 9 (OSDI), and 12 (SIGCOMM). Therefore we conclude that there is tethering if the standard deviation is larger than 35.

Boot Time: Figure 7 shows standard deviation of estimated boot time. Using a large standard deviation of boot time can reliably detect tethering. When the standard deviation of boot time is larger than 1455, the probabilities of tethering are 1 for our lab trace and OSDI'06 trace, and 0.88 for the SIGCOMM'08 trace.

Table 3 is a summary of $Pr(T|f_i)$, *i.e.*, the probabilities of tethering we learned from our training data sets. Note that while the probabilities reported here may not always hold for other traces, the features we use and our methodology of deriving the thresholds for the features can be applied in general to other traces.

4.3 Combining the Features

We use two steps to compute tethering probability. First, we use features f'_i for OS fingerprinting to derive the probability of having multiple OSes from an IP address, $Pr(multiOS|f'_1, ..., f'_k)$, as

$$Pr(multiOS|f'_1, .., f'_k)$$
$$= 1 - \sum_{x=1}^{m} Pr(OS_x|f'_1, ..., f'_k) \prod_{y=1..m}^{y \neq x} (1 - Pr(OS_y|f'_1, ..., f'_k)),$$

where m is the number of different OSes, and probability $Pr(OS_x|f'_1, ..., f'_k)$ can be computed from Equation (1).

We then treat $Pr(multiOS|f'_1, .., f'_k)$ as one of the features for tethering detection, denoted as g, and use it along with the additional features presented in Section 4.2 to compute $Pr(T|f_1, ..., f_n, g)$ based on the Bayes' rule similar to Section 3.3.

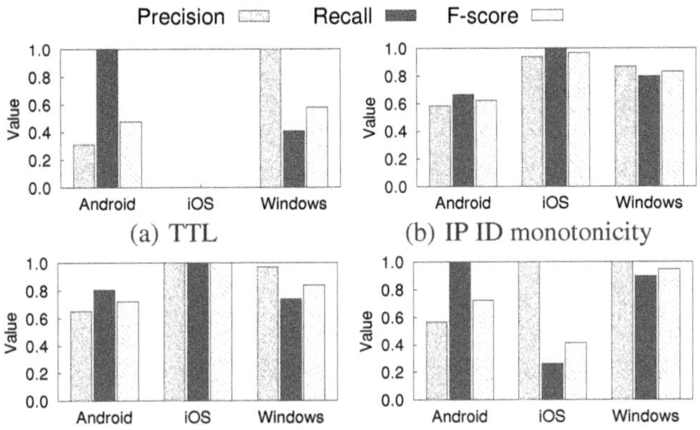

(a) TTL (b) IP ID monotonicity

(c) TCP window scale (d) Clock frequency stability

Figure 8: Accuracy of detecting OSes via individual features.

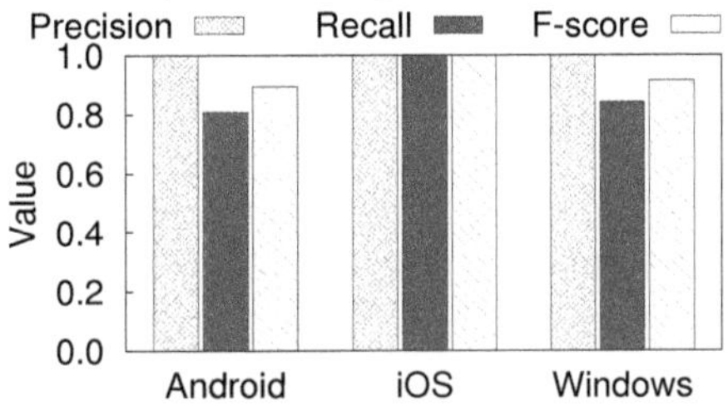

Figure 9: OS detection using combined method.

5. EVALUATION

5.1 Evaluation Metrics

We quantify the detection accuracy using three metrics: (i) *precision, i.e.*, the fraction of traffic our scheme detected as tethering (or have a given OS) is indeed tethering (or have that OS), (ii) *recall, i.e.*, the fraction of tethered traffic (or traffic from a given OS) are correctly detected by our scheme, and (iii) *F-score*, which is the harmonic mean of precision and recall (*i.e.*, $F-score = \frac{2}{1/\text{precision}+1/\text{recall}}$). For all three metrics, larger values indicate higher accuracy.

5.2 OS Detection Accuracy

We first evaluate how effective each individual feature is in detecting OSes using our lab trace, in which we have the ground truth on which OS generated each capture. We consider four OS specific features in this evaluation: TTL, IP ID monotonicity, TCP window scale, and clock frequency stability.

From Figure 8(a), we see that the precision of identifying Windows via TTL feature is high, because only Windows sets default TTL to 128. However, since Windows can also use 64 as its TTL, the recall is low. Android and iOS do not use 128 as the default TTL. When the TTL is not 128, the device is identified as Android because the probability of being Android is highest as shown in Table 2. Therefore, the recall of Android is one while recall and precision of iOS are both zero.

iOS has unique behaviors for IP ID monotonicity and TCP window scale, and thus we see from Figure 8(b) and 8(c) that both features identify iOS accurately. Although iOS devices are also distinguishable by having unstable clock frequency, some of the iOS packet captures in our lab trace are too short to reliably compute clock frequency. Therefore, we see from Figure 8(d) that the recall of identifying iOS via clock frequency is low.

The benefit of combining multiple features via our probability-based classifier is depicted in Figure 9. We see that our approach accurately identifies the OSes of most machines. The improvement is especially significant for identifying Android.

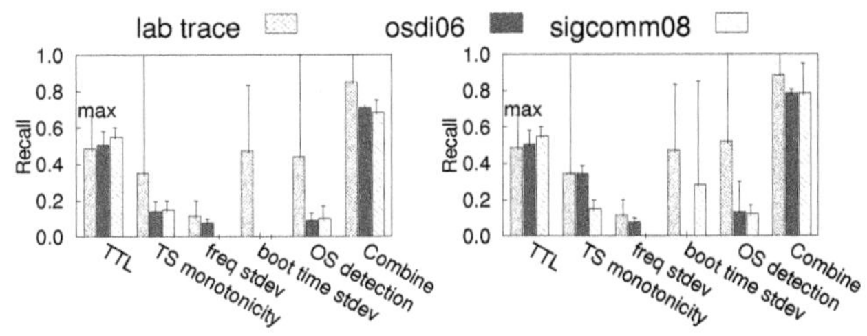

(a) Precision > 0.95 (b) Precision > 0.8

Figure 10: The recall of individual and combined technique when the precision is fixed to 0.95 and 0.8.

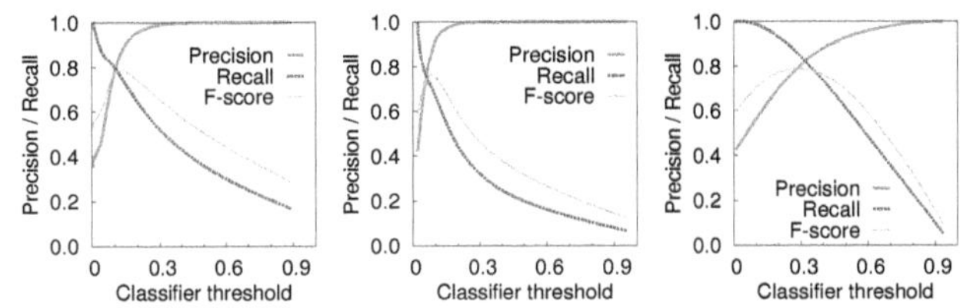

(a) our lab trace (b) OSDI'06 (c) SIGCOMM'08

Figure 11: Average detection accuracy as the classifier threshold is varied in our probability-based classifier.

5.3 Tethering Detection Accuracy

Next we evaluate the accuracy of applying the OS fingerprinting technique to tethering detection. Figure 10 shows combining multiple features using our probability-based classifier. We fix the targeted precision to be 0.95 and 0.80, and evaluate the average and maximal recall of detecting tethering via individual features and our probability-based classifier (depicted as "combine" in Figure 10).

Figure 10 provides a few interesting insights. First, our probability-based classifier consistently outperforms the schemes using individual features. Second, the clock frequency and boot time features are not effective in OSDI'06 and SIGCOMM'08 traces, because (i) the ratios of packets with TCP timestamps in two traces are small, and thus the clock frequency and boot time can be estimated in only a small number of devices, and (ii) the two traces have mostly short flows, which increase the error in clock frequency estimation. Moreover, we observe that OS detection is very effective in our traces but not in the other two. The main reason is that we do not have the ground truth on which OSes were used in OSDI'06 and SIGCOMM'08 traces and the probabilities learned from our lab trace may not work well for other traces.

The results shown in Figure 10 also demonstrate the trade-off between precision and recall in detecting tethering via our probability-based classifier. When we relax the target precision to 0.8, the recall of our probability-based classifier increases from 0.68∼0.85 to 0.78∼0.89. As we expect, the recall measurement will be higher when a lower precision is targeted.

In addition, Figure 11 shows the trade-off between precision and recall by varying the classification threshold. The probability-based classifier detects tethering when the probability is larger than a classification threshold. Determining the threshold itself is a challenging problem [12,34]. A higher threshold implies higher confidence on whether the device is tethering. Therefore, when we increase the classifier threshold, the precision becomes higher while the recall becomes lower.

Next we compare our probability-based classifier with two well-known classifiers: linear regression and decision tree. In linear regression, each feature takes its actual value (*e.g.*, the number of distinct TTL, clock frequency standard deviation), and tethering

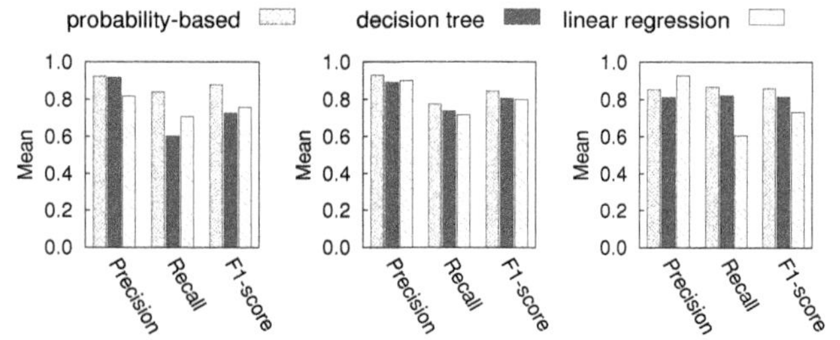

(a) our lab trace (b) OSDI'06 (c) SIGCOMM'08

Figure 12: Comparison between decision tree and regression-based classifiers.

is presented as a binary indicator. The linear regression classifier learns the weight of each feature from the training data such that the weighted sum of all features best approximates the binary tethering indicator. We estimate the weight by solving a linear inverse problem using min $L2$, which performs the least square fit. For the decision tree, we use an existing implementation from Weka [21]. For all three schemes, we select the classifier thresholds to maximize their F-scores. As we see from Figure 12, our probability-based classifier consistently outperforms decision tree by 5∼21% and linear regression by 6∼18% in the F-score measurement.

6. DISCUSSION

Other Features: Different OSes adopt different TCP congestion avoidance algorithms, referred to as *TCP flavors*. For example, OSX and iOS use New Reno [22] by default; Android and Linux use CUBIC [20] since kernel 2.6.19; Linux up to kernel 2.6.18 uses BIC [40]; Windows XP and earlier versions use New Reno; and Windows Server 2008 uses Compound TCP [38]. TCP flavors can be inferred by estimating the congestion window and how it changes in response to losses and RTT [26, 33]. It can be incorporated into our probability-based approach by adding another feature: $Pr(OS_x|flavor_y)$ from the training data. It is challenging to accurately infer TCP flavor from mobile network traces, because most flows are short and the throughput is usually limited by the lack of data to send [26] instead of congestion control algorithms.

The destination of the connection can also be used to identify OSes. For example, if a device connects to a Windows Update server, it is likely to be Windows. Similarly, connecting to Google Play or Apple App Store can also suggest Android and iOS devices.

Network Time Protocol (NTP) can also reveal the OS and tethering usage. The intervals between NTP messages vary from $64s$ to $1024s$ [3]. An interval less than $64s$ or changing dramatically can imply tethering. Besides, the default NTP servers are different across OSes and can be used to identify OSes (*e.g.*, `time.windows.com` or `time.apple.com`).

Tracking intervals between DNS queries sent from an IP address to the same hostname may be useful for tethering detection. NTP and DNS queries have not been considered for OS and device fingerprinting in the existing work. We will explore their effectiveness in the future work.

Hiding the Tethering Usage: Some tethering tools (*e.g.* tetherway [36], MyWi [1], PdaNet [4], etc.) camouflage the tethered traffic by changing packet headers, manipulating flow behaviors, or using VPN. The cost of camouflaging includes slowing down the traffic and consuming more power. Its cost will be higher as we identify more features.

In addition, some features are hard to be camouflaged, such as TCP flavors. Although we do not include this feature in our evaluation, our probability-based method is flexible and can easily incorporate new features.

Evaluation with a Larger Data Set: We apply our probability-based tethering detection method in a one week long campus trace. The trace includes 297,000 flows collected from 12,600 users at the beginning of 2013. We use the first day trace for training and trace of remaining days for testing. The tethering detection results are similar to those reported in Section 5.3: the precision is 0.86, the recall is 0.74, and the F-score is 0.8.

7. RELATED WORK

TCP/IP fingerprinting has been an active research area. Active probing of targeted system is adopted by [2,5,19,27,30,33,41,43]. Passive and hybrid schemes are studied as well [18,26]. Inferring tethering via exploiting different TCP/IP fingerprinting features has been extensively studied [2, 9, 13, 28, 29, 31, 35, 39, 43]. Combining multiple features improves the inferring accuracy. The `p0f` tool [43] includes five features in TCP/IP header as its signatures in OS detection. The `Nmap` tool [2] uses a set of nine tests to detect different OSes from network packets. Further optimization techniques to combining multiple features are studied [10, 37]. Our work complements the previous efforts by (i) providing the first comprehensive quantitative study on the effectiveness of passive TCP/IP fingerprinting to OS and tethering detection; (ii) identifying new features for OS fingerprinting and tethering detection; and (iii) designing a method to effectively combine multiple features.

There are other techniques for detecting OSes or tethering activities, which utilize information in high level protocols, such as application layer features [11,24] and web browser fingerprints [8,16,17, 42]. Unlike TCP/IP fingerprinting, those techniques require Deep Packet Inspection (DPI). DPI not only has non-negligible overhead in packet processing, but also raises privacy concerns when adopted by service providers [6]. Besides, increasing adoption of encryption makes high level protocol information unavailable to use. Due to those practical issues, our study focuses on the features in TCP/IP headers.

8. CONCLUSION

This paper develops and evaluates a methodology that uses several features in network traffic for identifying the OS on the sending device. This OS fingerprinting can be used for detecting tethering and more generally deployment of network address translation. The proposed methodology includes a probabilistic approach to combine multiple features to enhance detection accuracy. We evaluate the effectiveness of individual features and find TTL, TCP timestamp, and TCP window size scale factor are more accurate, while clock frequency and boot time are less accurate. Furthermore, the proposed probabilistic approach significantly improves the accuracy over using individual features. It can detect iOS systems deterministically, and detect Android and Windows with 100% precision and 0.8 recall. The recall of tethering detection is 0.68∼0.85 when the target precision is 0.95, and 0.78∼0.89 when the target precision is 0.8.

Acknowledgements

We are grateful to our shepherd Theophilus Benson and anonymous reviewers for their constructive feedback.

9. REFERENCES

[1] MyWi. http://intelliborn.com/mywi.html.

[2] Nmap Security Scanner. http://nmap.org/.

[3] ntpd(8) - Linux man page. http://linux.die.net/man/8/ntpd.

[4] PdaNet+. http://pdanet.co/.

[5] Snacktime: A Perl Solution for Remote OS Fingerprinting. http://www.planb-security.net/wp/snacktime.html.

[6] British Internet provider drops online tracking plans, 2009. http://goo.gl/FHtct2.

[7] CRAWDAD data set umd/sigcomm2008. Downloaded from http://crawdad.org/umd/sigcomm2008/, Mar. 2009.

[8] G. Acar, M. Juarez, N. Nikiforakis, C. Diaz, S. Gürses, F. Piessens, and B. Preneel. FPDetective: dusting the web for fingerprinters. In *Proc. of ACM CCS*, 2013.

[9] S. M. Bellovin. A technique for counting NATted hosts. In *Proc. of ACM IMW*, 2002.

[10] R. Beverly. A Robust Classifier for Passive TCP/IP Fingerprinting. In *Proc. of PAM*, 2004.

[11] J. Bi and J. Wu. Application Presence Information based Source Address Transition Detection for Edge Network Security and Management. *IJCSNS International Journal of Computer Science and Network Security*, 7(1), Jan. 2007.

[12] V. Brik, S. Banerjee, M. Gruteser, and S. Oh. Wireless device identification with radiometric signatures. In *Proc. of ACM MobiCom*, 2008.

[13] E. Bursztein. Time has something to tell us about network address translation. In *Proc. of NordSec*, 2007.

[14] R. Chandra, V. Padmanabhan, and M. Zhang. CRAWDAD data set microsoft/osdi2006 (v. 2007-05-23). Downloaded from http://crawdad.org/microsoft/osdi2006/, May 2007.

[15] CRAWDAD. http://crawdad.cs.dartmouth.edu.

[16] P. Eckersley. How unique is your web browser? In *Proc. of PETS*, 2010.

[17] E. Flood and J. Karlsson. Browser Fingerprinting. Master's thesis, University of Gothenburg, May 2012.

[18] F. Gagnon and B. Esfandiari. A Hybrid Approach to Operating System Discovery Based on Diagnosis. *Int. J. Netw. Manag.*, 21(2):106–119, Mar. 2011.

[19] L. G. Greenwald and T. J. Thomas. Toward undetected operating system fingerprinting. In *Proc. of USENIX WOOT*, 2007.

[20] S. Ha, I. Rhee, and L. Xu. CUBIC: A new TCP-friendly high-speed TCP variant. *ACM SIGOPS Operating Systems Review*, 42(5), July 2008.

[21] M. Hall, E. Frank, G. Holmes, B. Pfahringer, P. Reutemann, and I. H. Witten. The weka data mining software: An update. *SIGKDD Explor. Newsl.*, 11(1):10–18, Nov. 2009.

[22] T. Henderson, S. Floyd, A. Gurtov, and Y. Nishida. The NewReno modification to TCP's fast recovery algorithm, 2012. RFC 6582: http://tools.ietf.org/html/rfc6582.

[23] Ingrid Lunden. Gartner: Device shipments break 2.4b units in 2014, tablets to overtake PC sales in 2015. http://goo.gl/1kUHwm.

[24] Y. Ishikawa, N. Yamai, K. Okayama, and M. Nakamura. An Identification Method of PCs behind NAT Router with Proxy Authentication on HTTP Communication. In *Proc. of IEEE SAINT*, 2011.

[25] V. Jacobson, R. Braden, and D. Borman. TCP extensions for high performance, 1992. RFC 1323: http://tools.ietf.org/html/rfc1323.

[26] S. Jaiswal, G. Iannaccone, C. Diot, J. Kurose, and D. Towsley. Inferring TCP Connection Characteristics through Passive Measurements. In *Proc. of IEEE INFOCOM*, 2004.

[27] A. Khakpour, J. Hulst, Z. Ge, A. Liu, D. Pei, and J. Wang. Firewall Fingerprinting. In *Proc. of IEEE INFOCOM*, 2012.

[28] T. Kohno, A. Broido, and K. Claffy. Remote Physical Device Fingerprinting. In *IEEE Symposium on Security and Privacy*, 2005.

[29] G. Maier, F. Schneider, and A. Feldmann. NAT Usage in Residential Broadband Networks. In *Proc. of PAM*, 2011.

[30] J. P. S. Medeiros, A. M. Brito, and P. S. M. Pires. A new method for recognizing operating systems of automation devices. In *Proc. of IEEE ETFA*, 2009.

[31] S. B. Moon, P. Skelly, and D. Towsley. Estimation and removal of clock skew from network delay measurements. In *Proc. of IEEE INFOCOM*, 1999.

[32] NetMarketShare. Operating system market share. http://www.netmarketshare.com/operating-system-market-share.aspx.

[33] J. Pahdye and S. Floyd. On Inferring TCP Behavior. In *Proc. of ACM SIGCOMM*, 2001.

[34] J. Pang, B. Greenstein, R. Gummadi, S. Seshan, and D. Wetherall. 802.11 user fingerprinting. In *Proc. of ACM MobiCom*, 2007.

[35] P. Phaal. Detecting NAT devices using sflow. http://www.sflow.org/detectNAT/.

[36] S. Schulz, A.-R. Sadeghi, M. Zhdanova, H. Mustafa, W. Xu, and V. Varadharajan. Tetherway: a framework for tethering camouflage. In *Proc. of ACM WISEC*, 2012.

[37] K. Straka and G. Manes. Passive Detection of NAT Routers and Client Counting. *Advances in Digital Forensics II*, 222:239–246, 2006.

[38] K. Tan, J. Song, Q. Zhang, and M. Sridharan. A compound TCP approach for high-speed and long distance networks. In *Proc. of IEEE INFOCOM*, 2006.

[39] A. Tekeoglu, N. Altiparmak, and A. S. Tosun. Approximating the Number of Active Nodes Behind a NAT Device. In *Proc. of IEEE ICCCN*, 2011.

[40] L. Xu, K. Harfoush, and I. Rhee. Binary Increase Congestion Control for Fast, Long Distance Networks. In *Proc. of IEEE INFOCOM*, 2004.

[41] P. Yang, W. Luo, L. Xu, J. Deogun, and Y. Lu. TCP Congestion Avoidance Algorithm Identification. In *Proc. of IEEE ICDCS*, 2011.

[42] T.-F. Yen, Y. Xie, F. Yu, R. P. Yu, and M. Abadi. Host fingerprinting and tracking on the web: Privacy and security implications. In *Proc. of NDSS*, 2012.

[43] M. Zalewski. P0f. http://lcamtuf.coredump.cx/p0f3/.

WiFi, LTE, or Both? Measuring Multi-Homed Wireless Internet Performance

Shuo Deng, Ravi Netravali, Anirudh Sivaraman, Hari Balakrishnan
MIT Computer Science and Artificial Intelligence Lab
Cambridge, Massachusetts, U.S.A.
{shuodeng, ravinet, anirudh, hari}@csail.mit.edu

ABSTRACT

Over the past two or three years, wireless cellular networks have become faster than before, most notably due to the deployment of LTE, HSPA+, and other similar networks. LTE throughputs can reach many megabits per second and can even rival WiFi throughputs in some locations. This paper addresses a fundamental question confronting transport and application-layer protocol designers: which network should an application use? WiFi, LTE, or Multi-Path TCP (MPTCP) running over both?

We compare LTE and WiFi for transfers of different sizes along both directions (i.e. the uplink and the downlink) using a crowd-sourced mobile application run by 750 users over 180 days in 16 different countries. We find that LTE outperforms WiFi 40% of the time, which is a higher fraction than one might expect at first sight.

We measure flow-level MPTCP performance and compare it with the performance of TCP running over exclusively WiFi or LTE in 20 different locations across 7 cities in the United States. For short flows, we find that MPTCP performs worse than regular TCP running over the faster link; further, selecting the correct network for the primary subflow in MPTCP is critical in achieving good performance. For long flows, however, selecting the proper MPTCP congestion control algorithm is equally important.

To complement our flow-level analysis, we analyze the traffic patterns of several mobile apps, finding that apps can be categorized as "short-flow dominated" or "long-flow dominated". We then record and replay these patterns over emulated WiFi and LTE links. We find that application performance has a similar dependence on the choice of networks as flow-level performance: an application dominated by short flows sees little gain from MPTCP, while an application with longer flows can benefit much more from MPTCP — if the application can pick the right network for the primary subflow and the right choice of MPTCP congestion control.

CATEGORIES AND SUBJECT DESCRIPTORS

C.2.3 [**Computer-Communication Networks**]: Network Operations—*Network Management*; C.2.1 [**Computer-Communication Networks**]: Network Architecture and Design—*Wireless Communication*; C.4 [**Performance of System**]: Measurement techniques, Performance attributes

IMC'14, November 5–7, 2014, Vancouver, BC, Canada.

http://dx.doi.org/10.1145/2663716.2663727.

KEYWORDS

Multi-Network, Mobile Device, LTE, Multi-Path TCP

1. INTRODUCTION

Access to WiFi and cellular wireless networks are *de rigueur* on mobile devices today. With the emergence of LTE, cellular performance is starting to rival the performance of WiFi. Moreover, when WiFi signal quality is low or in crowded settings, the anecdotal experience of many users is that cellular performance may in fact be considerably better than WiFi performance.

But just how good are LTE and WiFi networks in practice and how do they compare with each other? Should applications and transport protocols strive to select the best network, or should they simply always use Multi-Path TCP (MPTCP) [21]? This paper seeks to answer these questions empirically.

To answer these questions, we implemented a crowd-sourced network measurement tool (Section 2) to understand the flow-level performance of TCP over WiFi and LTE in the wild from 16 different countries over a 6-month period, encompassing 3624 distinct 1-MegaByte TCP flows. We used this data to measure transfer times for different amounts of data transferred.

MPTCP isn't widely deployed yet on most phones[1]. As a result, we manually measured flow-level MPTCP performance and compared it with the performance of TCP running over exclusively WiFi or LTE in 20 different locations, in 7 cities in the United States (Section 3). Finally, to complement our empirical flow-level analysis, we used an existing record-and-replay tool to analyze (Section 4) and run (Section 5) mobile apps on emulated cellular and WiFi links, using it to study the impact of network selection on application performance.

Our key findings are as follows:

1. Cellular networks outperform WiFi around 40% of the time in our data set (Figure 3), a proportion considerably higher than we had hypothesized.
2. For short flows (100 KB or lower), MPTCP performs worse than TCP (Figure 7b). Further, it is crucial to select the proper network for the primary MPTCP subflow[2]. For instance, on a 10 KB flow, we found that the choice of the network for the primary subflow can affect MPTCP throughput by upto 60% (Figure 8). For long flows, selecting the proper congestion control algorithm is also important: for a 1 MB flow, for instance, modifying only the congestion control algorithm, while keeping the network used by the primary subflow fixed changes MPTCP throughput by 34% (Figures 13 and 14). On the other hand, modifying only the network used by the pri-

[1] The Apple iOS is an exception [13].

[2] For a description of subflow and other MPTCP-related terms, we refer the reader to Section 3.1

Figure 1: *Cell vs WiFi* User Interface.

mary subflow, while keeping the congestion-control algorithm fixed, changes throughput by 25%. (Figure 14)

3. Mobile app traffic patterns largely fall into two groups (Figure 17). We refer to apps that tend to open several connections, each transferring small amounts of data, as *short-flow dominated* apps, and we refer to apps that have fewer number of connections but transfer large amounts of data on each as *long-flow dominated* apps.
4. For *short-flow dominated* apps, MPTCP does not outperform the best conventional "single-path" TCP (over either Wi-Fi or LTE) (Figures 18 and 19). However, it is important to choose the correct network for standard TCP. Our emulation shows that selecting the proper network for single-path TCP can reduce response time by 50% compared to the minimum of the single-path TCP throughputs on LTE and WiFi. On the other hand, using MPTCP reduces application response time by only 35%.
5. For *long-flow dominated* apps, MPTCP does help markedly, provided the appropriate congestion-control algorithm is used and the two links have roughly comparable speeds: our emulation shows that using single path TCP with the correct choice of network reduces application response time by 42%, while using MPTCP with the proper congestion control can also reduce response time by about 50% (Figures 20 and 21).

Our crowd-sourced network measurement tool, *Cell vs WiFi*, is available for Android in the Google Play Store. All our measurement data and analysis tools are available at `http://web.mit.edu/cell-vs-wifi/`.

2. CELL VS WIFI MEASUREMENT

In September 2013, we published an Android app on Google Play, called *Cell vs WiFi* (`http://web.mit.edu/cell-vs-wifi`). *Cell vs WiFi* measures end-to-end WiFi and cellular network performance and uses these measurements to tell smartphone users if they should be using the cellular network or WiFi at the current time and location. The app also serves as a crowd-sourced measurement tool by uploading detailed measurement data to our server including packet-level traces. Over a nine-month period since the app was published, it attracted over 750 downloads. We collected over 10 GB of measurement data from 3632 distinct TCP connections over this duration from these users.

2.1 Cell vs WiFi App

Figure 1 shows the user interface of *Cell vs WiFi*. Users can choose to measure network performance periodically, or once per click. Users can also set an upper bound on the amount of cellular data that the app can consume; especially for devices on a limited cellular data plan.

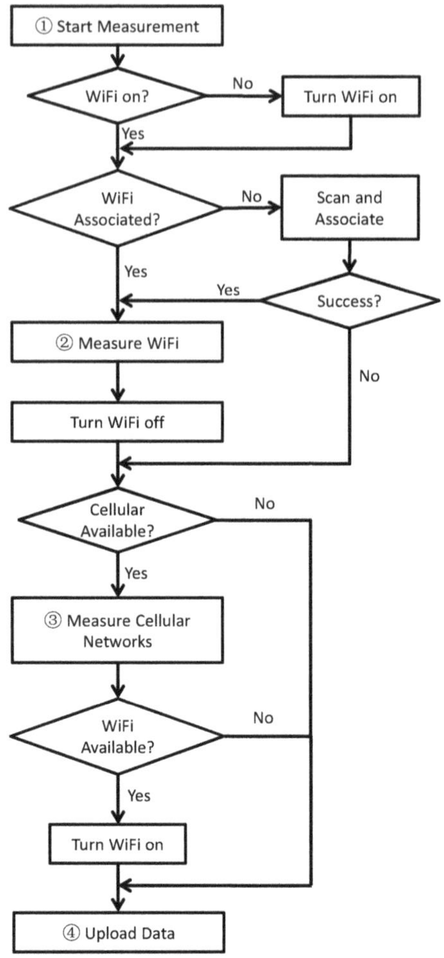

Figure 2: *Cell vs WiFi*: single measurement collection run.

The flow chart in Figure 2 shows a single measurement-collection run. When the user clicks the `Start` button or the pre-set periodic measurement timer expires, one run of measurement collection starts, shown as Step ① in the figure. If WiFi is available and the phone successfully associates with an Access Point (AP), *Cell vs WiFi* collects packet-level tcpdump traces for a 1 Mbyte TCP upload and a 1 Mbyte TCP download between the mobile device and our server at MIT.

After measuring WiFi, *Cell vs WiFi* turns off the WiFi interface on the phone and attempts to automatically connect to the cellular network. If the user has turned off the cellular data network, *Cell vs WiFi* aborts the cellular measurement. If *Cell vs WiFi* successfully connects to the cellular network, then in Step ③, it collects a similar set of packet-level tcpdump traces for both an upload and a download. Once both WiFi and cellular network measurements are finished, in Step ④, *Cell vs WiFi* uploads the data collected during this measurement run, together with the user ID (randomly generated when a smartphone user uses the app for the first time), and the phone's geographic location, to our server at MIT.

More information about *Cell vs WiFi* can be found at `http://web.mit.edu/cell-vs-wifi`.

2.2 Results

Location Name	(Lat, Long)	# of Runs	LTE %
US (Boston, MA)	(42.4, -71.1)	884	10%
Israel	(31.8, 35.0)	276	55%
US (Portland)	(45.6, -122.7)	164	45%
Estonia	(59.4, 27.4)	124	71%
South Korea	(37.5, 126.9)	108	66%
US (Orlando)	(28.4, -81.4)	92	35%
US (Miami)	(26.0, -80.2)	84	52%
Malaysia	(4.24, 103.4)	76	68%
Brazil	(-23.6, -46.8)	56	4%
Germany	(52.5, 13.3)	40	20%
Spain	(28.0, -16.7)	40	80%
Thailand (Phichit)	(16.1, 100.2)	40	80%
US (New York)	(40.9, -73.8)	24	33%
Japan	(36.4, 139.3)	16	25%
Sweden	(59.6, 18.6)	16	0%
Thailand (Chiang Mai)	(18.8, 99.0)	16	75%
US (Chicago)	(42.0, -88.2)	16	25%
Hungary	(47.4, 16.8)	8	0%
Italy	(44.2, 8.3)	8	0%
US (Salt Lake City)	(40.8, -111.9)	8	0%
Colombia	(7.1, -70.7)	4	0%
US (Santa Fe)	(35.9, -106.3)	4	0%

Table 1: Geographical coverage and diversity of the crowd-sourced data collected from 16 countries using *Cell vs WiFi*, ordered by number of runs collected. The last column shows the percentage of runs where LTE throughput is higher than WiFi

Cell vs WiFi collected network-performance data from locations in five continents: North America, South America, Europe, Africa, and Asia. We observed that some users use this app to measure only WiFi or LTE performance, but not both. We do not consider these measurement runs in this section because our goal is to compare LTE and WiFi performance at nearly the same place and time. To ensure that we only measure performance of LTE or an equivalent high-speed cellular network, such as HSPA+, we use the Android network-type API [2] and pick only those measurement runs that used LTE or HSPA+. When using the term LTE in this section, we mean LTE/HSPA+. After these filtering steps, our dataset contains over 1606 complete runs of measurement, i.e., both LTE and WiFi transfers in both directions.

In Table 1, we group nearby runs together using a k-means clustering algorithm, with a cluster radius of $r = 100$ kilometers; i.e., all runs in each group are within 200 kilometers of each other. For each location group, we also list the percentage of measurement runs where LTE has higher throughput than WiFi.

Figure 3 shows the CDF of difference in throughput between WiFi and LTE on the uplink and the downlink. We can see that the throughput difference can be larger than 10 Mbits/s in either direction. The grey region shows 42% (uplink) and 35% (downlink) of the data samples whose LTE throughput is higher than WiFi throughput. If we combine uplink and downlink together, 40% of the time LTE outperforms WiFi. Figure 4 shows the CDF of ping RTT difference between LTE and WiFi. During our measurement, we send 10 pings and take the average RTT value. The shaded area shows that in 20% of our measurement runs, LTE has a lower ping RTT than WiFi, although the cellular network is commonly assumed to have higher delays.

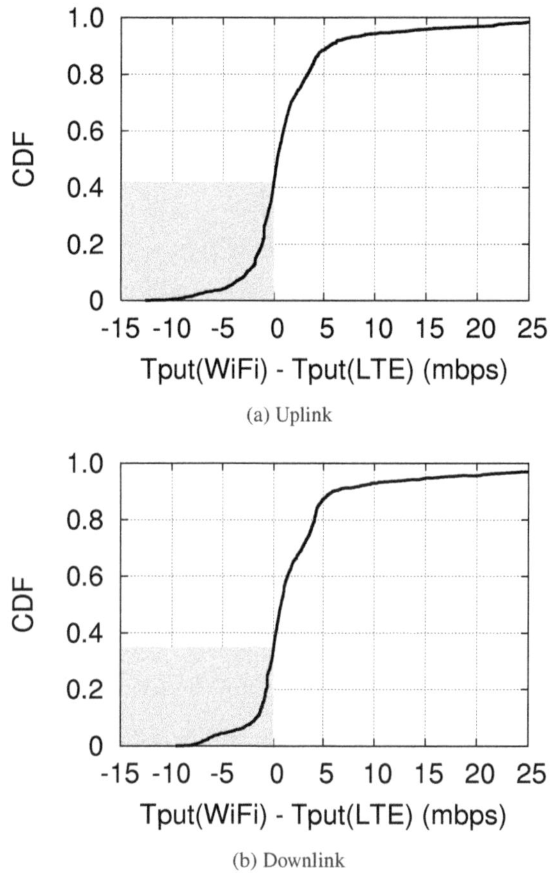

Figure 3: CDF of difference between WiFi and LTE throughput. The grey region shows 42% (uplink) and 35% (downlink) of the data samples whose LTE throughput is higher than WiFi throughput.

The simple network selection policy used by mobile devices today forces applications to use WiFi whenever available. However, our measurement results indicate that a more flexible network selection policy will improve the network performance of mobile applications.

3. MPTCP MEASUREMENTS

When WiFi and cellular networks offer comparable performance, or when each varies significantly with time, it is natural to use both simultaneously. Several schemes transmitting data on multiple network interfaces have been proposed in the past [22, 17, 15, 21]. Among these, the most widespread is MPTCP [21]. MPTCP can be used in two modes [16]: *Full-MPTCP* mode, which transmits data on all available network interfaces at any time and *Backup* mode, which transmits data on only one network interface at a time, falling back to the other interface only if the first interface is down. Unless stated otherwise, all experiments in this section use MPTCP in *Full-MPTCP* mode. For completeness, we compare the two modes in Section 3.6. We use a modified version of *Cell vs WiFi* to carry out MPTCP measurements. We observe the following:

1. We find that MPTCP throughput for short flows depends significantly on the network selected for the primary subflow[3] in MPTCP: for example, changing the network (LTE or WiFi)

[3] We define subflows in Section 3.1

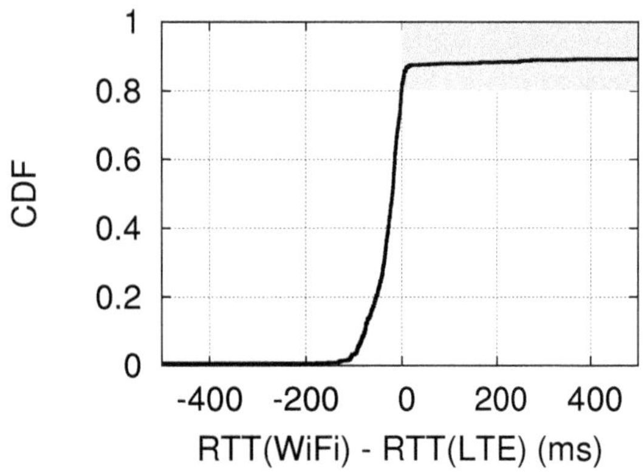

Figure 4: CDF of the difference between average Ping RTT with WiFi and LTE. The grey region shows 20% of the data samples whose LTE RTT is lower than WiFi RTT.

for the primary subflow changes the average throughput of a 10 KByte flow by 60% in the median (Figure 8 in Section 3.4).

2. For long flows, selecting the proper congestion control algorithm is also important. For example, using different congestion-control algorithms (coupled or decoupled) changes the average throughput of a 1 MByte flow by 34% in the median (Figure 13 in Section 3.5).
3. MPTCP's backup mode is typically used for energy efficiency: keeping fewer interfaces active reduces energy consumption overall. However, we find that for MPTCP in *Backup Mode*, if LTE is set to the backup interface, very little energy can be saved for flows that last shorter than 15 seconds (Section 3.6).

3.1 MPTCP Overview

MPTCP initiates a connection in a manner similar to regular TCP: it picks one of the available interfaces and establishes a TCP connection using a SYN-ACK exchange with the server over that interface. Every TCP connection that belongs to a MPTCP connection is called an MPTCP *subflow*. The first established subflow is called the *primary subflow*.

We used the Linux MPTCP implementation for our measurements [14] (Ubuntu Linux 13.10 with Kernel version 3.11.0, with the MPTCP Kernel implementation version v0.88). In this implementation, MPTCP initiates the primary subflow on the interface used as the default route on the machine. Once the primary subflow is established, if there are other interfaces available, MPTCP creates an additional subflow using each new interface, and combines the new subflow with the existing subflows on the same MPTCP connection.[4] For example, a mobile device can establish an MPTCP primary subflow through WiFi to the server, and then add an LTE subflow to the server. To terminate the connection, each subflow is terminated using four-way FIN-ACKs, similar to TCP. In Section 3.4, we study the effect of choosing different interfaces for the primary subflow on MPTCP performance.

There are two kinds of congestion-control algorithms used by MPTCP: *decoupled* and *coupled*. In decoupled congestion control, each subflow increases and decreases its congestion window independently, as if they were independent TCP flows [5]. In coupled congestion control, each subflow in an MPTCP connection increases its congestion window based on ACKs both from itself and from other subflows [21, 10] in the same MPTCP connection. In Section 3.5, we compare the coupled and decoupled algorithms and find that using different congestion-control algorithms has less impact on throughput compared with selecting the correct interface for primary subflows for short flows. However, for long flows, changing congestion-control algorithms results in a substantial throughput difference.

[4]For simplicity, here we only explain how MPTCP works when the server is single-homed (like the server in our experiments), and the client alone is multi-homed.

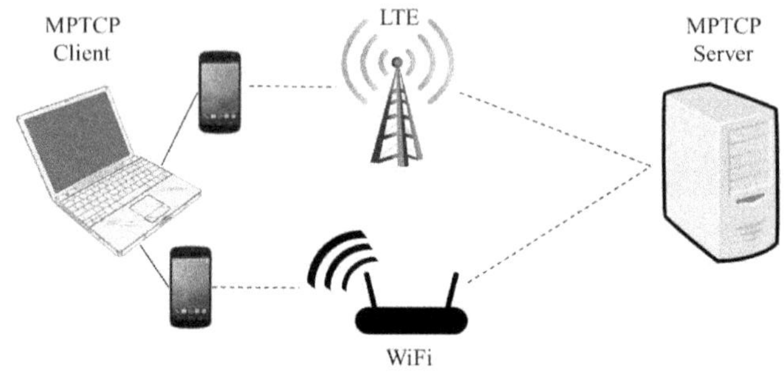

Figure 5: Setup of MPTCP measurement.

3.2 Measurement Setup

Figure 5 shows the MPTCP measurement setup. The MPTCP Client is a laptop running Ubuntu 13.10 with MPTCP installed. We tethered two smartphones to the laptop, one in "airplane" mode with WiFi enabled, and the other with WiFi disabled but connected to LTE (either the Verizon or the Sprint LTE network). The MPTCP server is located at MIT, with a single Ethernet interface, also running Ubuntu 13.10 with MPTCP installed.

We installed a modified version of *Cell vs WiFi* on both phones. The phone with WiFi enabled only measures WiFi performance, i.e., Step ② in Figure 2. The phone connected to LTE only measures cellular network performance, i.e., Step ③ in Figure 2.

The experimental setup also allows us to measure the energy consumption separately for each interface, which we present in Section 3.6.

Each measurement run comprises the following:

1. Single path TCP upload and download using modified *Cell vs WiFi* through LTE.
2. Single path TCP upload and download using modified *Cell vs WiFi* through WiFi.
3. MPTCP upload and download in *Full-MPTCP* mode with LTE as the primary subflow.
4. MPTCP upload and download in *Full-MPTCP* mode with WiFi as the primary subflow.

We conducted the measurements at 20 different locations on the east and west coasts of the United States, shown in Table 2. At each city, we conduct our measurement at places where people would often use mobile devices: cafes, shopping malls, university campuses, hotel lobbies, airports, and apartments. At 7 of the 20 locations, we measured both Verizon and Sprint LTE networks, using both MPTCP congestion-control algorithms: decoupled and coupled. At the other 13 locations, we were able to measure only the Verizon LTE network with coupled congestion control.

In Figure 6, we compare the WiFi and LTE throughput distributions for the data we collected at these 20 locations and the data collected from *Cell vs WiFi* in Section 2. We can see that for both upload and download, the "20-Location" CDF curves are close to the CDF curve from Section 2, implying that the 20 locations that were selected have similar variability in network conditions as the

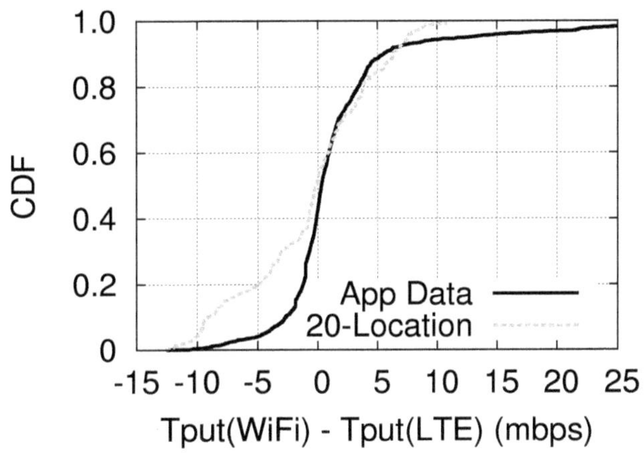

(a) Uplink

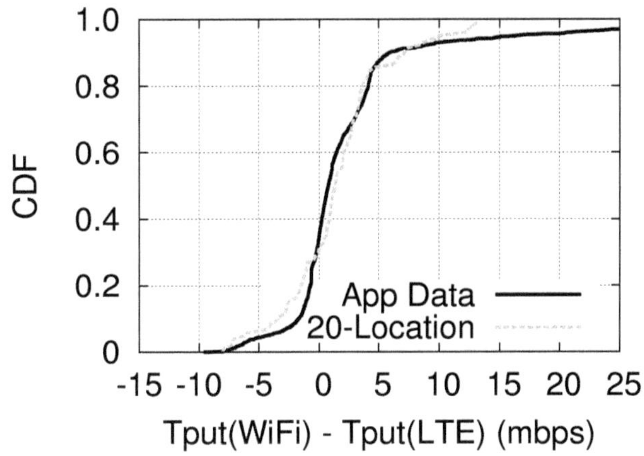

(b) Downlink

Figure 6: CDF for WiFi and LTE throughput measured using regular TCP at 20 locations (shown as "20-Location") comparing with the CDF in Figure 3(shown as "App Data").

ID	City	Description
1	Amherst, MA	University Campus, Indoor
2	Amherst, MA	University Campus, Outdoor
3	Amherst, MA	Cafe, Indoor
4	Amherst, MA	Downtown, Outdoor
5	Amherst, MA	Apartment, Indoor
6	Boston, MA	Cafe, Indoor
7	Boston, MA	Shopping Mall, Indoor
8	Boston, MA	Subway, Outdoor
9	Boston, MA	Airport, Indoor
10	Boston, MA	Apartment, Indoor
11	Boston, MA	Cafe, Indoor
12	Boston, MA	Downtown, Outdoor
13	Boston, MA	Store, Indoor
14	Santa Babara, CA	Hotel Lobby, Indoor
15	Santa Babara, CA	Hotel Room, Indoor
16	Santa Babara, CA	Conference Room, Indoor
17	Los Angeles, CA	Airport, Indoor
18	Washington, D.C.	Hotel Room, Indoor
19	Princeton, NJ	Hotel Room, Indoor
20	Philadelphia, PA	Hotel Room, Indoor

Table 2: Locations where MPTCP measurements were conducted

Cell vs WiFi dataset. For simplicity, in the rest of Section 3, we only show results of downlink flows from the server to the client.

3.3 TCP vs. MPTCP

A natural question pertaining to MPTCP is how the performance of MPTCP compares with the best "single-path" TCP performance achievable by an appropriate choice of networks alone. To answer this, we look at all four MPTCP variants (two congestion-control algorithms times two choices for the network used by the primary subflow) and both single-path TCP variants (WiFi and LTE) as a function of flow size. Figure 7 illustrates two qualitatively different behaviors.

Figure 7a shows a case where the performance of MPTCP is always worse than the best single-path TCP regardless of flow size.

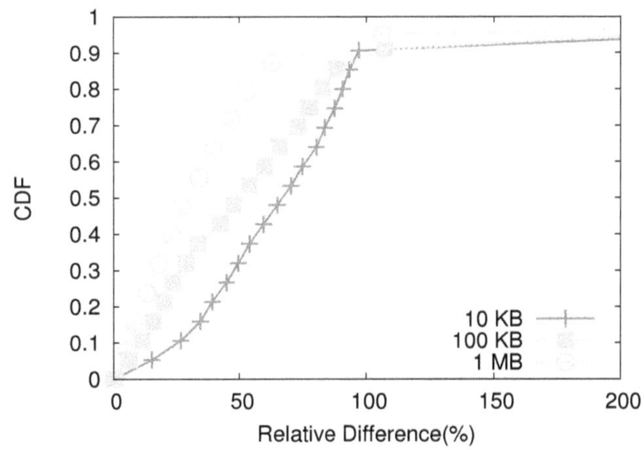

Figure 8: CDF of relative difference between $MPTCP_{LTE}$ and $MPTCP_{WiFi}$, for different flow sizes. The median relative difference for each flow size: 60% for 10 KBytes, 49% for 100 KBytes and 28% for 1MByte. Thus, throughput for smaller flow sizes is more affected by the choice of the network for the primary subflow.

This occurs in a particularly extreme scenario where a large disparity in link speeds between the two networks (LTE and WiFi) leads to degraded MPTCP performance irrespective of flow size. On the other hand, Figure 7b shows an alternative scenario where MPTCP is better than the best single-path TCP at larger flow sizes. In both cases, however, picking the right network for single-path TCP is preferable to using MPTCP for smaller flows. These results suggest that it may not always be advisable to use both networks, and an adaptive policy that automatically picks the networks to transmit on and the transport protocol to use would improve performance relative to any static policy.

3.4 Primary Flow Measurement

We then study how the choice of the network for the primary subflow can affect MPTCP throughput for different flow sizes. To show this quantitatively, we calculate the relative throughput difference as:

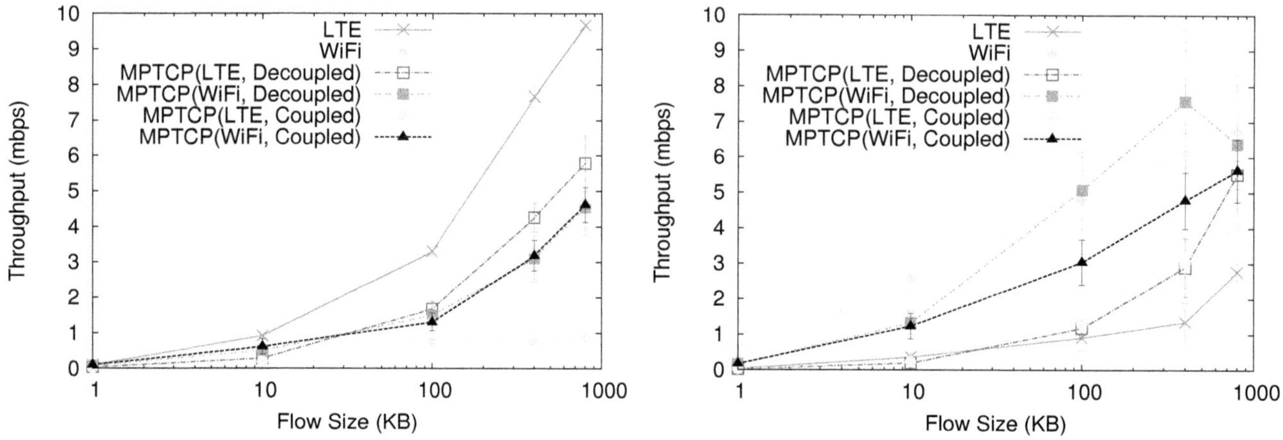

(a) MPTCP performs worse than single TCP.

(b) MPTCP performs better than single TCP.

Figure 7: MPTCP throughput vs single path TCP throughput at 2 representative locations. Figure 7a shows a case where MPTCP throughput is lower than the best throughput of single path TCP. Figure 7b shows a case where MPTCP throughput (in this case, MPTCP(WiFi, decoupled)) is higher than that of single-path TCP for large flow sizes.

$$\frac{|MPTCP_{LTE}-MPTCP_{WiFi}|}{MPTCP_{WiFi}}.$$

Here, $MPTCP_{LTE}$ is the throughput achieved by MPTCP using LTE for the primary subflow, and $MPTCP_{WiFi}$ is the throughput achieved by MPTCP using WiFi for the primary subflow (in this subsection, we only run MPTCP using *decoupled* congestion control). Figure 8 shows the CDF of the relative throughput difference for three flow sizes: 10 KBytes, 100 KBytes, and 1 MBytes. We see that using different networks for the primary subflow has the greatest effect on smaller flow sizes.

3.4.1 MPTCP Throughput Evolution Over Time

To understand how using different networks for the primary subflow affects MPTCP throughput evolution over time, we collected `tcpdump` traces at the MPTCP Client during the measurement. From the traces, we calculate the average throughput from the time the MPTCP session is established, to the current time t. In Figure 10 and 9, we plot the average throughput as a function of time. Each sub figure shows the throughput of the entire MPTCP session (shown as MPTCP) and the throughput of the individual WiFi and LTE subflows.

Figure 9 shows traces collected at a location where LTE has much higher throughput than WiFi. At time 0, the client sent the SYN packet to the server. In Figure 9a, it took the client 1 second to receive the SYN-ACK packet from the server over WiFi. MPTCP throughput is the same as the throughput of the WiFi subflow until the LTE subflow is established. Because LTE has much higher throughput at this location and time, once the subflow is established on LTE, it quickly increases its throughput (and therefore MPTCP's throughput). By contrast, in Figure 9b, the client receives the SYN-ACK faster, and MPTCP throughput increases more quickly because the first subflow is on the higher-throughput LTE network. Because of the smaller SYN-ACK RTT and higher throughput on the first primary subflow, the MPTCP connection using LTE for the primary subflow (Figure 9b) has a higher average throughput than the MPTCP connection using WiFi for the primary subflow (Figure 9a).

Similarly, Figure 10 shows traces collected at a location where WiFi has higher throughput than LTE. Here, using WiFi as the primary subflow for MPTCP results in higher throughput.

3.4.2 MPTCP Throughput as a Function of Flow Size

Figures 11a and 12a show how MPTCP throughput changes as the flow size increases. The flow size is measured using the cumulative number of bytes acknowledged in each ACK packet received at the MPTCP client. Figures 11b and 12b show the relative throughput ratio change as flow size increases. The relative throughput ratio is defined as:

$$\frac{MPTCP_{LTE}}{MPTCP_{WiFi}}.$$

Although the absolute value of the difference in throughputs is smaller for small flow sizes (Figures 11a and 12a), the relative throughput ratio, is larger (Figure 11b and 12b). Thus, for a connection with a given flow size, using the correct interface for MPTCP primary subflow can reduce the flow completion time, and the relative reduction can be significant for smaller flow sizes. For example, in Figure 11a, the absolute throughput difference between LTE and WiFi is 0.5 mbps for a 100 KB flow, and about 3 mbps for a 1 MB flow. But in Figure 11b, the relative throughput ratio is 2.2x for 100 KB flow, larger than the 1.5x for a 1 MB flow.

3.5 Coupled and Decoupled Congestion Control

To understand how the choice of congestion-control algorithm within MPTCP affects its throughput, at 7 of the 20 locations, we measured the following different MPTCP configurations on the Verizon LTE network and each location's dominant WiFi network:

1. LTE for primary subflow, *coupled* congestion control.
2. LTE for primary subflow, *decoupled*[5] congestion control.
3. WiFi for primary subflow, *coupled* congestion control.
4. WiFi for primary subflow, *decoupled* congestion control.

At each location, we measured 10 runs for each of the 4 configurations, along both the uplink and the downlink. Thus, each of the four configurations has 140 data points $((10+10)\times 7)$.

To quantify the throughput difference between configurations, we compute:

$$r_{network} = \frac{|MPTCP_{LTE,coupled}-MPTCP_{WiFi,coupled}|}{MPTCP_{WiFi,coupled}}, \text{ or}$$

[5]Here, the decoupled congestion control uses TCP Reno for each subflow.

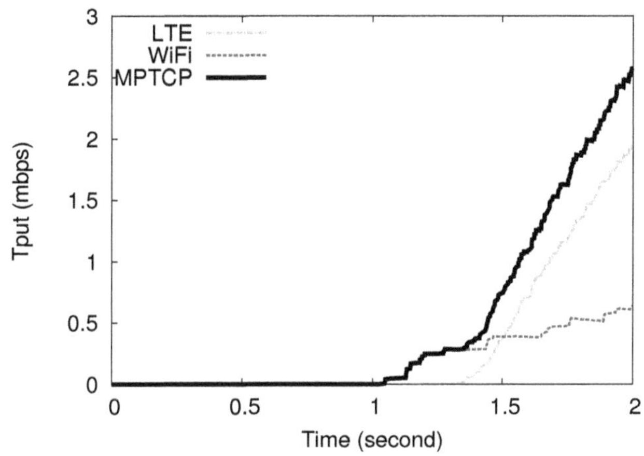

(a) Using WiFi for the primary subflow

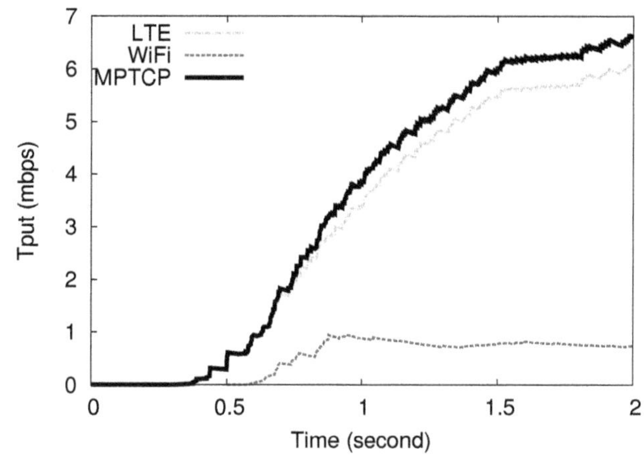

(b) Using LTE for the primary subflow

Figure 9: MPTCP throughput over time, measured at a location where LTE has higher throughput than WiFi. MPTCP throughput grows faster over time when using LTE for the primary subflow.

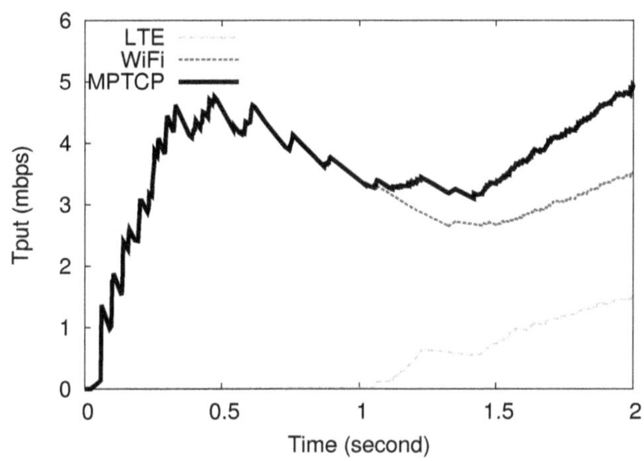

(a) Using WiFi for the primary subflow

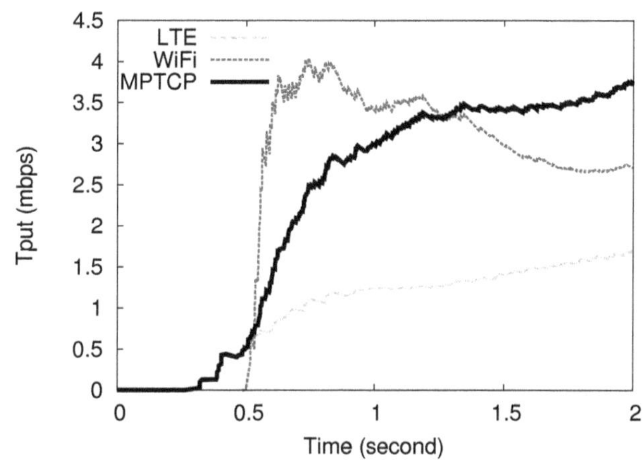

(b) Using LTE for the primary subflow

Figure 10: MPTCP throughput over time, measured at a location where WiFi has higher throughput than LTE. MPTCP throughput grows faster over time when using WiFi for the primary subflow.

$$r_{network} = \frac{|MPTCP_{LTE,decoupled} - MPTCP_{WiFi,decoupled}|}{MPTCP_{WiFi,decoupled}}.$$

Here, $r_{network}$ is the relative throughput difference when using different networks for primary subflow. $MPTCP_{n,c}$ is the throughput measured when using network n for primary subflow and using congestion control algorithm c. We also compute:

$$r_{cwnd} = \frac{|MPTCP_{LTE,decoupled} - MPTCP_{LTE,coupled}|}{MPTCP_{LTE,coupled}}, \text{ or}$$

$$r_{cwnd} = \frac{|MPTCP_{WiFi,decoupled} - MPTCP_{WiFi,coupled}|}{MPTCP_{WiFi,coupled}}.$$

Here, r_{cwnd} is the relative throughput difference when using different congestion-control algorithms.

Figure 13 shows the CDF of the relative throughput difference between using coupled and decoupled congestion control for three flow sizes: 10 KBytes, 100 KBytes, and 1 MByte. The rightmost CDF curve corresponds to the relative difference for 1 MByte, while the left-most one is for 10 KBytes. Thus, using different congestion control algorithms has a greater effect on larger flow sizes. In Figure 14, a pair-wise comparison between using different networks (labeled with"Network") and using different congestion control algorithms (labeled with "CC") for each flow size shows the following:

1. For small flow sizes, throughput is more affected by the choice of network for the primary subflow. For example, in Figure 14a and 14b, "Network" is to the right of "CC".
2. For large flow sizes, throughput is more affected by the choice of congestion control (decoupled or coupled) algorithms. For example: in Figure 14c, "CC" is to the right of "Network". However, the choice of network for the primary subflow is also important.

In practice, selecting the best network for the primary subflow is more feasible than changing congestion control algorithms for each MPTCP connection, since the primary flow can be defined solely by the MPTCP endpoint initiating the connection, while the congestion-control algorithm requires support at both endpoints.

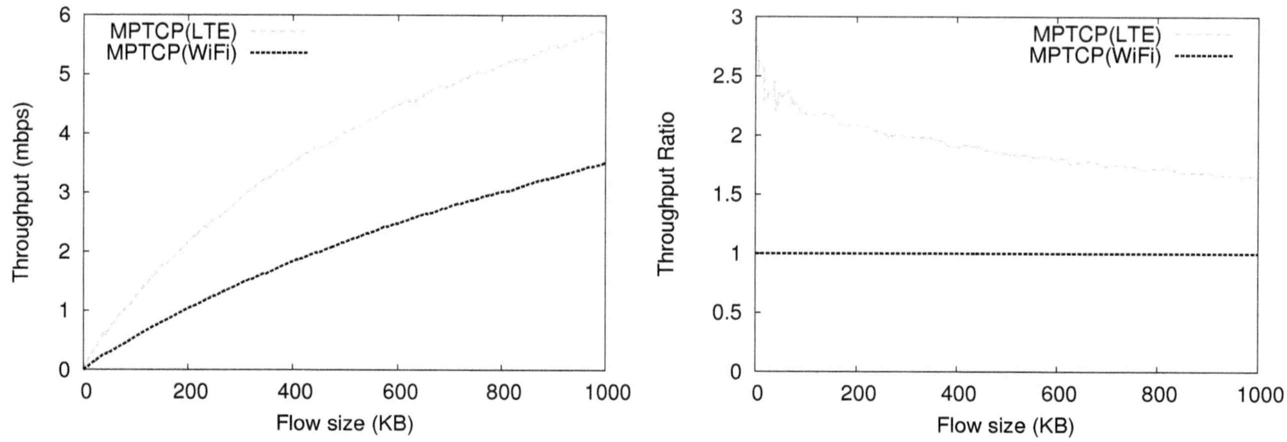

(a) Absolute throughput difference: larger difference between WiFi and LTE for larger flow sizes.

(b) Relative throughput ratio: larger difference between WiFi and LTE for smaller flow sizes.

Figure 11: Absolute throughput difference and relative throughput ratio as a function of flow size when LTE has higher throughput than WiFi.

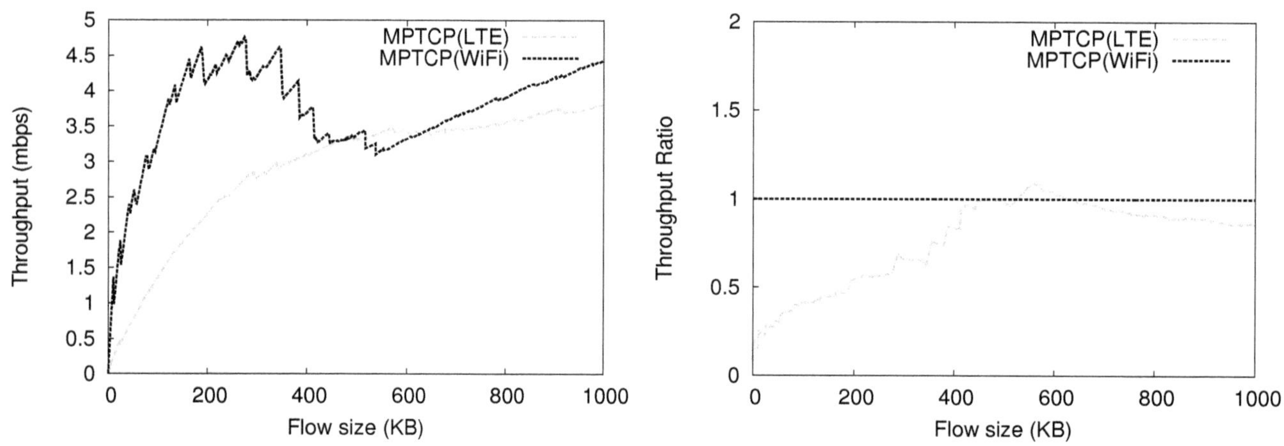

(a) Absolute throughput difference: larger difference between WiFi and LTE for larger flow sizes.

(b) Relative throughput ratio: larger difference between WiFi and LTE for smaller flow sizes.

Figure 12: Absolute throughput difference and relative throughput ratio as a function of flow size when WiFi has higher throughput than LTE.

3.6 Full-MPTCP and Backup Mode

In Sections 3.4 and 3.5, all measurements were done using *Full-MPTCP* mode, since our focus was on how MPTCP's throughput changes under different configurations, when all paths are fully utilized. *Backup Mode* is an MPTCP mode where only a subset of paths are used to save energy, especially on power-constrained mobile devices. In this section, we first show how *Backup Mode* differs from *Full-MPTCP* at the per-packet level. Then we discuss the energy efficiency of both *Full-MPTCP* and *Backup Mode*.

3.6.1 *Packet-Level Behavior of Full-MPTCP and Backup Mode*

Figure 15 shows the packet-transmission pattern over time for a long flow employing MPTCP, using *Full-MPTCP* and *Backup Mode*. We use `tcpdump` at the MPTCP client to log packet transmission and ack reception times. In Figure 15, we plot a vertical line at time t if there is a packet sent or ack received at time t in the `tcpdump` trace. $t = 0$ is the time when the first SYN packet is sent.

Each sub-figure contains the packet-transmission patterns on both the WiFi and LTE interfaces for one MPTCP flow. Sub-figures on the left column are packet transmission (sending and receiving) patterns captured when using LTE for the primary subflow, while sub-figures on the right are for using WiFi for the primary subflow.

Figures 16a and 16b show that in *Full-MPTCP* mode, packets are transferred through both WiFi and LTE during the entire MPTCP connection.

Figures 15c and 15d illustrate the backup mode where one network is set to be the backup interface. For example, in Figure 15c, when WiFi is set to backup, we only see the SYN and SYN ACK packets transferred during the 3-way handshake procedure at $t = 1$, when the connection establishes a WiFi subflow, as well as FIN and FIN-ACK packets at $t = 19$, when the connection ends. A similar pattern is shown in Figure 15d, when LTE is set to be the backup interface.

Figures 15e and 15f show packet transmissions in backup mode, when the primary network is disabled mid-flow. We disable the interface by setting the interface to "multipath off" in `iproute`. In Figure 15e, WiFi is set to backup. When the connection starts, it

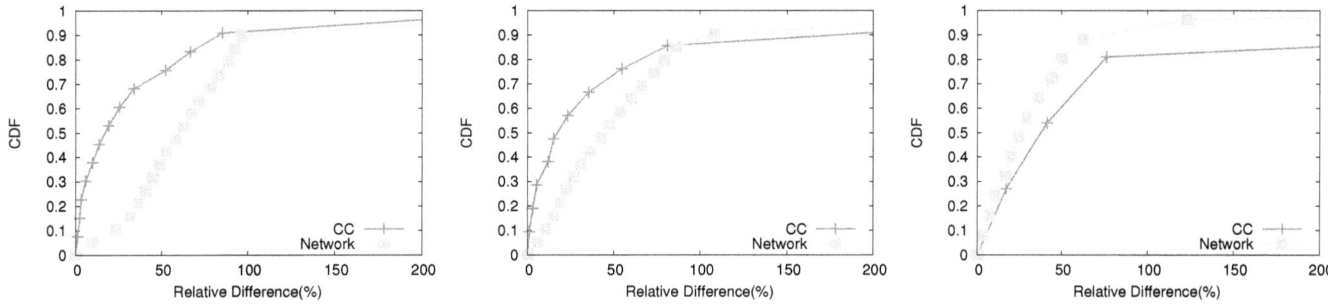

(a) 10 KB (b) 100 KB (c) 1 MB

Figure 14: CDF of relative difference for using different networks for primary subflow (labeled as "Network") vs using different congestion control algorithms (labeled as "CC"), across 3 flow sizes. Median values for CC curves: 16% for "10 KB", 16% for "100 KB", and 34% for "1 MB". Thus, using different congestion control algorithms has more impact on larger flows. Median values for Network curves: 60% for " 10 KB", 43% for "100 KB" , and 25% for "1 MB". Thus, using a different network for the primary subflow has the greatest impact on smaller flows.

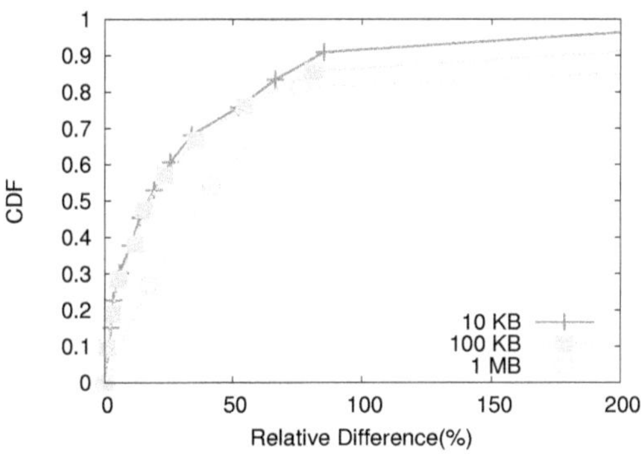

Figure 13: CDF of relative difference between $MPTCP_{coupled}$ and $MPTCP_{decoupled}$, for different flow sizes. The median relative difference for each flow size: 16% for 10 KBytes, 16% for 100 KBytes and 34% for 1MByte. Thus, throughput for larger flow sizes is most affected by the choice of congestion control.

transfers data through LTE. At $t = 7$, we disable LTE, so no data can be transferred over that interface. We see that the subflow over WiFi is brought up and transfers data until the flow ends. A similar behavior is seen in Figure 15f.

In Figures 15g and 15h, we disable one network by unplugging the USB cable connecting the phone to the laptop instead of disabling it using `iproute`. Interestingly, we observe different behaviors in this experiment. Figure 15h shows that when LTE is set to backup and we unplug WiFi in the middle of the transfer (at $t = 6$), the LTE path is brought up immediately to finish transferring the rest of the data. This behavior is similar to when WiFi was disabled by changing `iproute`. However, in Figure 15g, when WiFi is set to backup and we unplug the LTE network in the middle of the transfer (at $t = 3$), the client only transfers one `TCP Window Update` packet to the server through the WiFi subflow and then halts. At $t = 68$, we re-connect the phone with the laptop. Then the connection resumes, transfers the rest of the data through the LTE subflow, and ends the session by sending FIN packets on both path.

The reason why disabling paths by physically disconnecting them can cause different behaviors from disabling them in software is still under investigation.

3.6.2 *Energy Efficiency in Backup Mode*

As shown in Figure 15c and 15d, if MPTCP is set to *Backup Mode*, the backup interface still transfers SYN and FIN packets when a connection starts and ends. In Figure 16, we show that in certain configurations, these SYN/FIN packets can consume excessive amounts of energy on a mobile device. Here, we measure the power level of the tethered phones using a power monitor [12], when each phone serves as the backup or non-backup interface. In all sub-figures of Figure 16, the base power consumed is 1 Watt. This is the power consumed when the network interfaces are not active. It is the total power consumed by the other parts of the phone, such as the screen and the CPU.

Figure 16a shows the power level of LTE when it is actively transmitting data, i.e., WiFi is set as a backup interface. Similarly, Figure 16b shows the power level of WiFi when it is active. We can see that the WiFi power level is much lower than that of LTE. Also, in Figure 16a, after the FIN packet is sent, there is a 15-second period in which the LTE power level stays at 2 Watts, instead of the 1-Watt base power level. The energy consumed in this 15-second period is called the "Tail Energy" [3, 7].

Figures 16c and 16d show the power level when WiFi or LTE is set to be the backup interface. In Figure 16d, the energy consumed by WiFi is negligible. However, in Figure 16c, when a SYN or a FIN packet is transmitted through LTE, the power level stays high for about 15 seconds due to the "Tail Energy" effect. Thus, even if only SYN and FIN packets are transferred through LTE, the LTE interface still consumes an excessive amount of energy. For flows shorter than 15 seconds, little energy can be saved if the LTE interface is set to be the backup interface. To actually reduce energy consumption in this case, *fast dormancy* [9] should be used to quickly put the LTE interface in the low-power mode after a SYN and FIN. Alternatively, the *Backup Mode* should be implemented in a *break-before-make* manner. Prior work [16] has proposed *Single-Path Mode*, which establish a new MPTCP subflow only after the current subflow is inactive, at the expense of two more round-trip times compared with the current *Backup Mode*.

4. MOBILE APP TRAFFIC PATTERNS

So far, our measurements have looked at the flow-level performance of TCP over WiFi or LTE, and of MPTCP over both WiFi and LTE. We next turn to how the choice of networks for a multi-homed mobile device affects application-level performance as perceived by

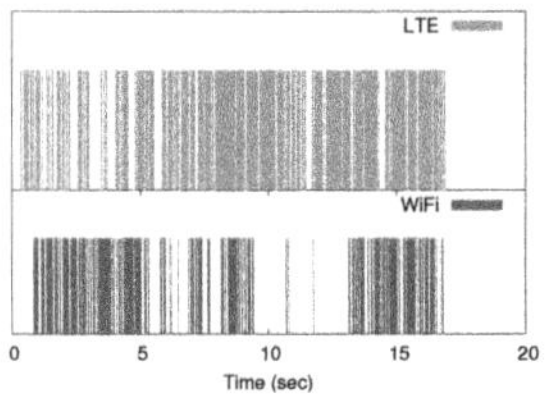

(a) *Full-MPTCP*, using LTE for primary subflow.

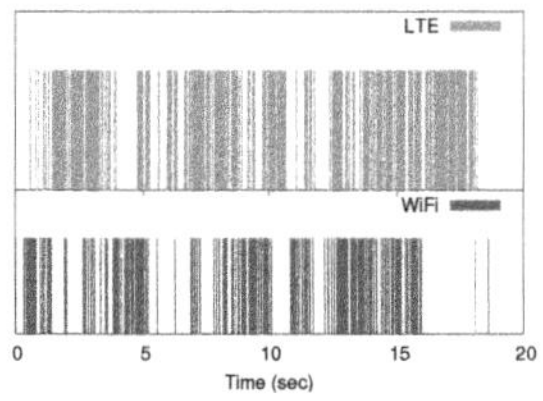

(b) *Full-MPTCP*, using WiFi for primary subflow.

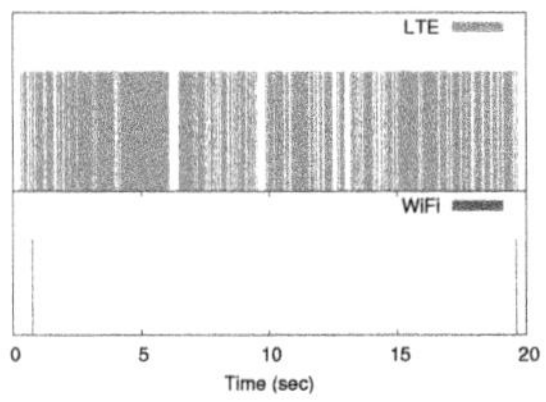

(c) *Backup Mode*, using LTE for primary subflow, WiFi for backup.

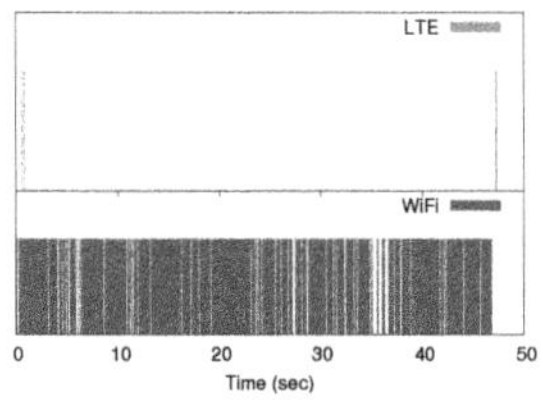

(d) *Backup Mode*, using WiFi for primary subflow, LTE for backup.

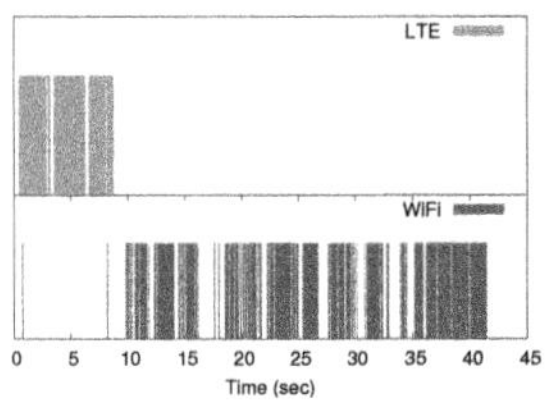

(e) *Backup Mode*, using LTE for primary subflow, WiFi for backup. Then set LTE to "multipath off" at $t = 9$ sec.

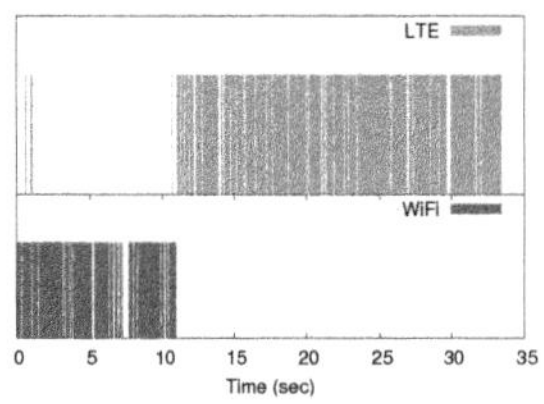

(f) *Backup Mode*, using WiFi for primary subflow, LTE for backup. Then set WiFi to "multipath off" at $t = 11$ sec.

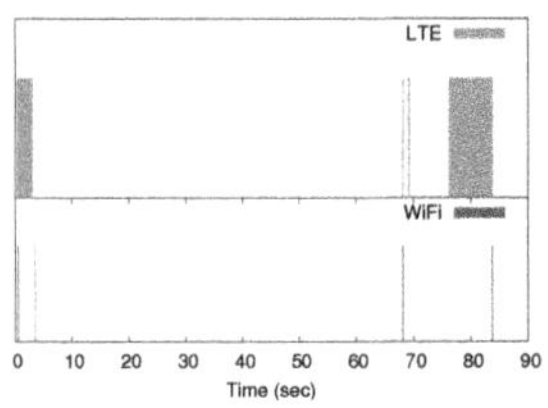

(g) *Backup Mode*, using LTE for primary subflow, WiFi for backup. Unplug LTE at $t = 3$ sec. *But WiFi does not continue transferring the rest of the data.* Plug LTE back at $t = 68$ sec.

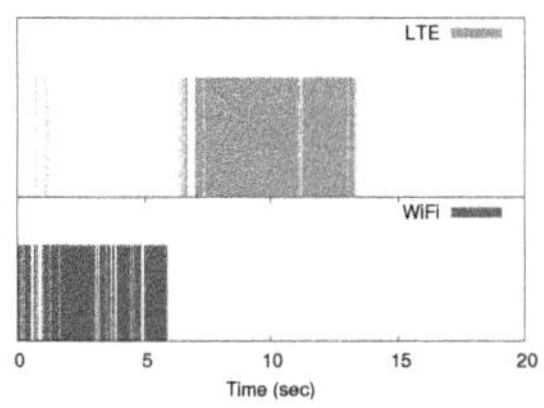

(h) *Backup Mode*, using WiFi for primary subflow, LTE for backup. Unplug WiFi at $t = 6$ sec.

Figure 15: *Full-MPTCP* and *Backup Mode*.

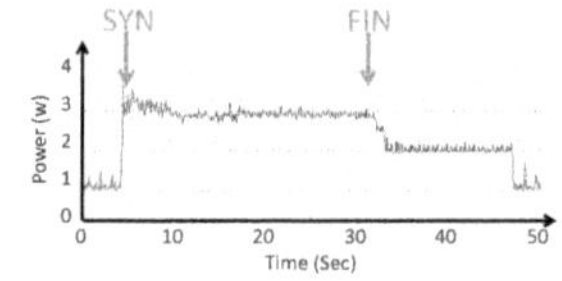

(a) LTE power level when used for non-backup subflow.

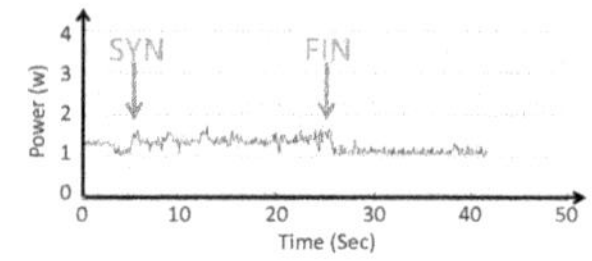

(b) WiFi power level when used for non-backup subflow.

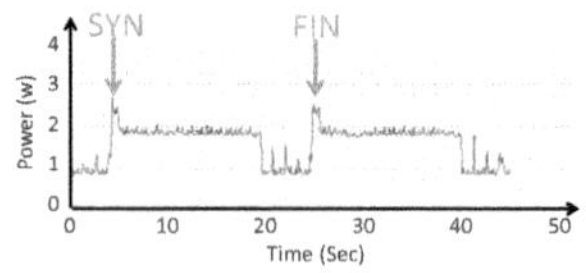

(c) LTE power level when used for backup subflow.

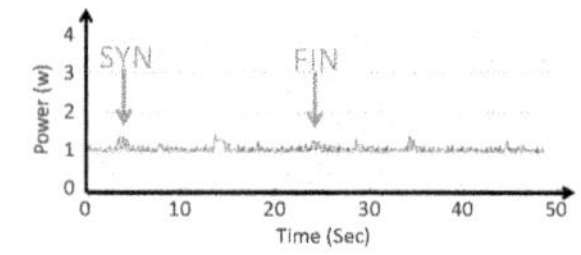

(d) WiFi power level when used for backup subflow.

Figure 16: Power level for LTE and WiFi when used as non-backup subflow. LTE has a much higher power level than WiFi in non-backup mode. LTE also consumes excessive amount of energy even in backup mode.

a mobile app that uses one or more of these networks. To measure performance at the level of a mobile app, we first record (Section 4.1) and analyze traffic (Section 4.2) originating from a mobile app, and then replay it under emulated link conditions (Section 5).

4.1 Record-Replay Tool

Mahimahi [11] is a record-and-replay tool that can record and replay client-server interactions over HTTP. Mahimahi's RecordShell is a UNIX shell that records HTTP traffic and stores it as a set of request-response pairs. Later, during replay, Mahimahi's ReplayShell—another modified UNIX shell—matches incoming requests to stored requests, ignoring time-sensitive fields in the request header (eg. If-Modified-Since) that have likely changed since recording.

Mahimahi also includes shells to emulate network delays and fixed-rate and variable-rate network links using packet-delivery traces. We extend these capabilities and develop a new shell, MpShell, to emulate multiple links along with their associated link delays. This allows us to mimic a multi-homed mobile phone that can use both cellular and WiFi links. We use a trace-driven approach, as Mahimahi does, to emulate both the cellular and WiFi links.

Because Mahimahi is agnostic to the specific client or server that generates the HTTP traffic, we use it to record all HTTP traffic to and from a mobile app running inside an Android emulator. Later, using ReplayShell and MpShell, we run the same mobile app within the Android emulator under appropriately emulated network conditions. This enables us to evaluate how MPTCP—or any other multipath-capable transport—affects application performance of a real mobile app.

4.2 Traffic Patterns of Mobile Apps

Figure 17 shows typical traffic patterns we observed across different mobile apps run inside RecordShell. We observe that apps tend to initiate multiple TCP connections when launched or in response to a user interaction. Most of these connections only transfer a small amount of data (eg. connection ID 2 in Figure 17c). Some connections, such as connection ID 2 in Figure 17a, persist after small data transfers.

A few connections, such as connection ID 30 in Figure 17d and connection ID 8 in Figure 17f, transfer significant amounts of data, lasting several seconds. The first example (ID 30) occurred when the user clicked a link to play a movie trailer. The app downloaded the entire trailer in one HTTP request. The second example (ID 8) occurred when the user clicked a PDF file in their Dropbox folder and the app downloaded the whole file.

In summary, we can categorize app traffic patterns as *short-flow dominated* and *long-flow dominated*. *short-flow dominated* apps have only short connections or long-lived connections with little data transferred. *long-flow dominated* apps have one or multiple long-lasting flows transferring large amounts of data.

5. MOBILE APP REPLAY

We feed the app traffic patterns described in Section 4 into Mahimahi's ReplayShell for subsequent replay. To accurately emulate different network conditions, we use the recorded single-path TCP packet traces on both WiFi and LTE as a proxy for the true packet-

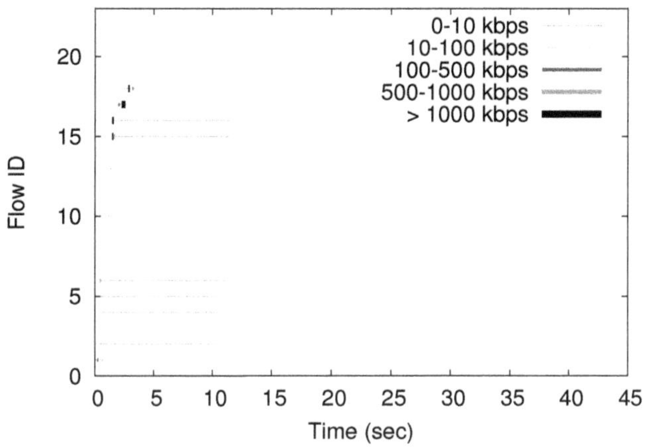

(a) CNN launch.

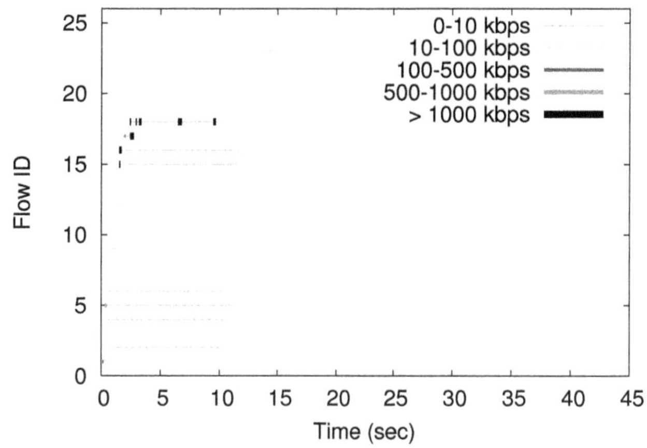

(b) CNN click.

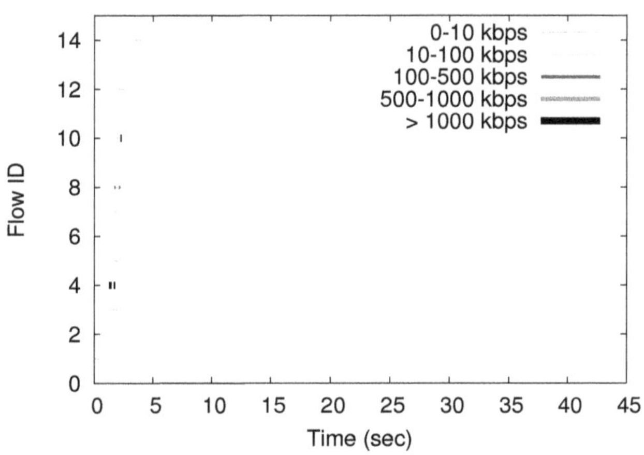

(c) IMDB launch.

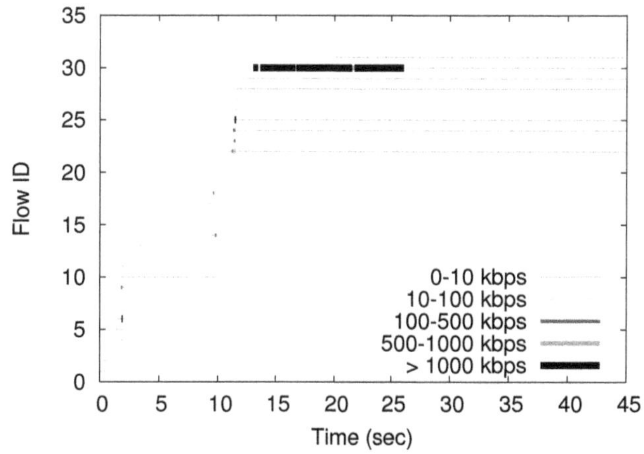

(d) IMDB click.

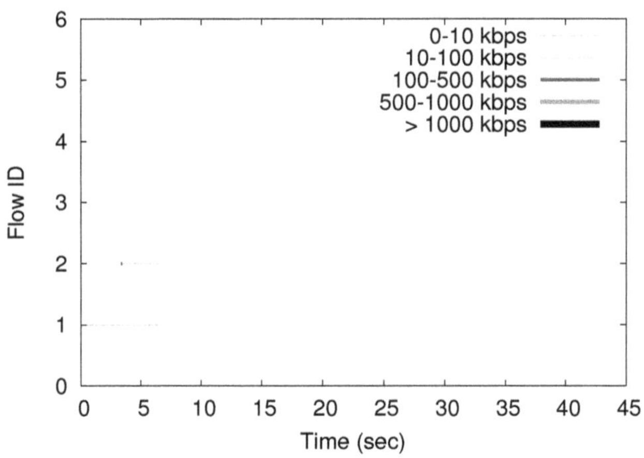

(e) Dropbox launch.

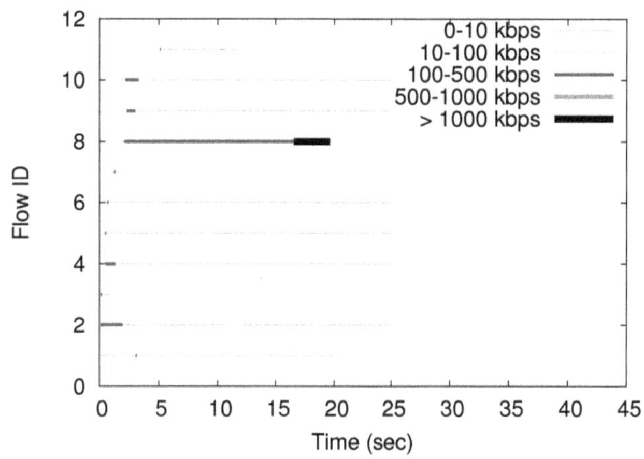

(f) Dropbox click.

Figure 17: Traffic patterns for app launching and user interacting. Figures 17d and 17f show the "long-flow dominated' traffic pattern, the other figures show the "short-flow dominated" pattern.

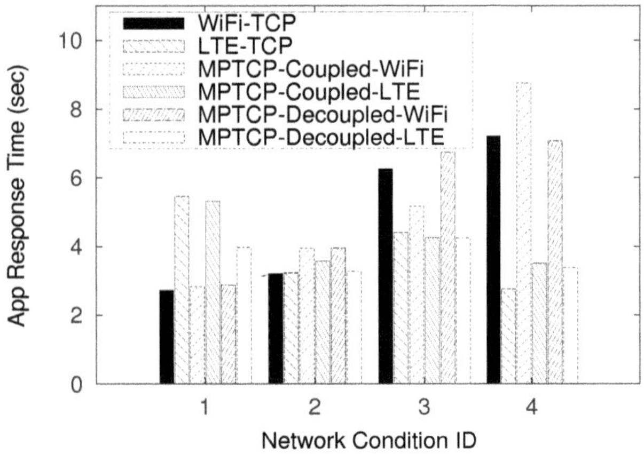

Figure 18: CNN app-response time under different network conditions.

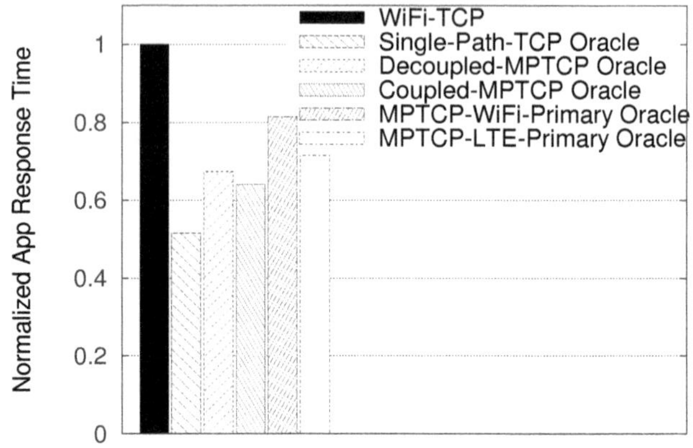

Figure 19: CNN normalized app-response reduction by different oracle schemes.

delivery trace for WiFi and LTE[6]. We use these TCP traces to emulate the WiFi and LTE links within MpShell. We emulate 20 distinct network conditions using the WiFi and LTE TCP data previously collected at 20 locations (Section 3.2).

We present results from replaying two traffic patterns. We refer to the first as the *short-flow dominated app* where, as shown in Figure 17a (CNN launch), an app initiates several connections but only transfers a small amount of data on each connection. We refer to the second as the *long-flow dominated app*, where, as shown in Figure 17f (Dropbox user click), an app initiates several connections and transfers a large amount of data for a few seconds over a small subset of the connections. We run each app pattern over the 20 different network conditions (we only show the results from 4 representative conditions due to space limitations). For each network condition, we emulate 6 configurations:

1. WiFi-TCP: Single-path TCP running on WiFi.
2. LTE-TCP: Single-path TCP running on LTE.
3. MPTCP-Coupled-WiFi: MPTCP with coupled congestion control using WiFi for the primary subflow.
4. MPTCP-Coupled-LTE: MPTCP with coupled congestion control using LTE for the primary subflow.
5. MPTCP-Decoupled-WiFi: MPTCP with decoupled congestion control using WiFi for the primary subflow.
6. MPTCP-Decoupled-LTE: MPTCP with decoupled congestion control using LTE for the primary subflow.

Using `tcpdump` during the emulation, we collect the timestamp at the start and end of each HTTP connection. Then we calculate the *app response time*: the time between the start of the first HTTP connection and the end of the last HTTP connection[7].

5.1 Short-Flow Dominated App Replay

Figure 18 shows the app-response time for the CNN app launching in different configurations under different network conditions. For clarity, we only show the emulation results for 4 representative network conditions out of the 20 we emulated; results for other conditions are similar.

Network Condition IDs 1 and 2 emulate locations where WiFi has a much higher bulk TCP throughput than LTE, and in Network Condition IDs 3 and 4, LTE outperforms WiFi. In Figure 18, we observe that:

1. Selecting the proper network to transmit for single-path TCP significantly affects app-response time. For example, in Network Condition 1, the app response time for WiFi-TCP is 2.7 seconds while LTE-TCP has an app response time of 5.5 seconds, implying that using the proper network for single-path TCP can reduce the app response time by about 2.0x. For a network condition in which LTE has better performance, such as Network Condition ID 4, the app-response times for TCP over WiFi (shown as "TCP-WiFi" in Figure 18) and TCP over LTE (shown as "TCP-LTE" in Figure 18) are 7.2 seconds and 2.8 seconds, respectively. In this case, using LTE can reduce the app response time by 2.6x.
2. Using MPTCP does not provide much improvement for the *short-flow dominated* app pattern. For instance, in Network Condition 1, MPTCP-Coupled-LTE and MPTCP-Decoupled-LTE have app response times of 5.3 and 4.0, respectively. Compared to TCP over LTE, these MPTCP schemes only reduce the app response time by 4% and 15%, much smaller improvements than the 2x improvement seen when using TCP over WiFi compared to TCP over LTE.

In summary, Figure 18 shows that the choice of network for the primary subflow has a strong impact on app response time. This result is consistent with the results we show in Section 3.5.

We also study the extent to which app response times can be reduced if we had access to an optimal network selection algorithm: an oracle that knew the right network to use, given a particular congestion control strategy (coupled vs decoupled) and another oracle that knew the right congestion control strategy to use given a particular choice for the network used by the primary subflow. Figure 19 shows the app-response time with different oracle schemes, averaged across all 20 network conditions and normalized by the app-response time with single-path TCP over WiFi (the default on Android today). The oracle schemes are:

1. Single-Path-TCP Oracle: Uses single-path TCP and knows which network minimizes app response time.
2. Decoupled-MPTCP Oracle: Uses MPTCP decoupled conges-

[6]This approach does underestimate the true packet-delivery trace of the underlying network because TCP takes a finite duration to reach the link capacity due to Slow Start.

[7]This metric doesn't account for computation time that might be spent in the app itself after the last HTTP connection ends, but this is impossible to measure without instrumenting or rewriting existing applications to report these numbers.

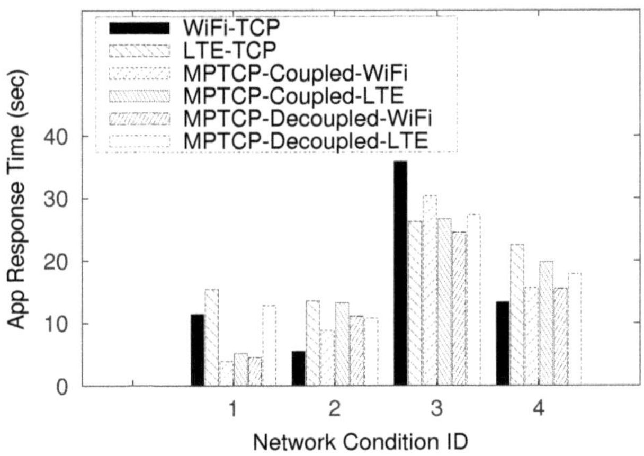

Figure 20: Dropbox app-response time under different network conditions.

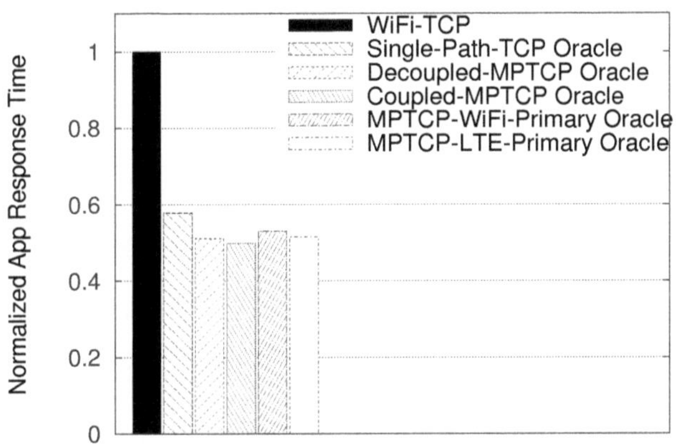

Figure 21: Dropbox normalized app-response reduction by different oracle schemes.

tion control and knows which network to use for the primary subflow to minimize app response time.

3. Coupled-MPTCP Oracle: Uses MPTCP coupled congestion control and knows which network to use for the primary subflow to minimize app response time.
4. MPTCP-WiFi-Primary Oracle: Uses MPTCP with WiFi for primary subflow and knows which congestion-control algorithm to use to minimize app response time.
5. MPTCP-LTE-Primary Oracle: Uses MPTCP with LTE for primary subflow and knows which congestion-control algorithm to use to minimize app response time.

We can see in Figure 19 that the 50% reduction in app response time with Single-Path-TCP Oracle is the most substantial, while the reductions with the MPTCP Oracles range from 15% to 35%. This suggests that MPTCP does not reduce app response time as significantly as selecting the right network for single-path TCP does.

5.2 Long-flow Dominated App Replay

Figures 20 and 21 show emulation results for the *long-flow dominated* traffic pattern, using the same data analysis methods and oracles as used in the previous subsection.

In Figure 20, Network Condition IDs 1 and 2 emulate places where WiFi has a much higher TCP throughput than LTE, and Network Condition IDs 3 and 4 represent places where LTE outperforms WiFi. We observe that:

1. Using MPTCP helps to reduce app response-time. For example, at Network Condition 1, when using single-path TCP, the app response time is 10 seconds for WiFi and 15 seconds for LTE. When using MPTCP, the app response time is 5 seconds.
2. Selecting the proper network is important: for example, at Network Condition ID 2, the app response time for MPTCP-Coupled-WiFi is 8 seconds, but if LTE is used for the primary flow, response time increases to 14 seconds.
3. Selecting the proper congestion control algorithm also affects app response time. For example, at Network Condition ID 1, when using LTE for the primary subflow, the app response time for coupled congestion control is 4 seconds, while the response time with decoupled congestion control is 13 seconds.

In Figure 21, we can see that:

1. MPTCP Oracles reduce the app response time by up to 50%, while the Single-Path-TCP Oracle only reduces app response time by 42%. So using MPTCP can help improve performance for "long-flow dominated" apps.
2. For MPTCP Oracles, both selecting the proper network for the primary flow and selecting the appropriate congestion control can reduce the normalized app response time by about 50%, implying that both mechanisms are almost equally beneficial to "long-flow dominated" apps.

6. RELATED WORK

We discuss related work under two headings: prior work comparing WiFi with cellular network performance and Multi-Path TCP.

6.1 WiFi-Cellular Comparison

Several prior papers compare cellular network performance with WiFi. Sommers et al. [20] analyzed crowd-sourced data from `SpeedTest.net`. Each data sample represents one run of a TCP upload/download test triggered by a mobile phone user, when the phone is connected to the Internet through either WiFi or a cellular network. We also collect our data in a crowd-sourced manner. However, our mobile app, *Cell vs WiFi*, measures both WiFi and cellular network performance on the same device at (almost) the same time. Thus, our dataset reflects the performance difference observed from a single device at almost the same time. Deshpande et al. [8] measured both 3G and WiFi performance simultaneously using a single device, but their measurement was focused on a vehicular setting and they only measured 3G, not LTE. Our dataset focuses on LTE measurements instead. In our app, we used an activity-recognition API provided by Google [1], which shows that most of our measurements happen when users are still. Moreover, our data is collected in a crowd-sourced manner, allowing it to capture a wide diversity of conditions.

6.2 Multi-Path TCP

Multipath TCP (MPTCP) [21], and its recent implementation in iOS 7 [13] allow a single TCP connection to use multiple paths. MPTCP provides TCP's reliable, in-order bytestream abstraction while taking advantage of multiple paths for increased throughput and fault tolerance. Previous work has looked at MPTCP in a mobile context: Raiciu et al. studied mobility with MPTCP [19]. Pluntke et al. designed a scheduler that picks radio interfaces with a view to reduce mobile energy consumption [18]. Paasch et al. proposed different MPTCP modes to be used by mobile devices for Mobile/WiFi handover [16]. Barlow-Bignell et al. [4] studied MPTCP performance in the presence of WiFi interference where multiple devices connected to the same AP could interfere with each other if they transmitted packets simultaneously. Closest to our work is the work of Chen et al., who measured MPTCP performance over cellular networks and WiFi [6]. Their measurement focuses on using different number of subflows, and fine-grained statistics, such as out-of-order delivery and round trip times. Instead, our focus is on studying the choice of networks for the primary subflow, the choice of congestion-control modes, MPTCP's energy consumption, and MPTCP's effect on higher-level metrics such as flow completion times and app-response times.

7. CONCLUSION AND FUTURE WORK

We presented a measurement study of single-path TCP and MPTCP over LTE and WiFi networks. For single-path TCP, we found that LTE outperforms WiFi 40% of the time – a higher fraction than one might expect at first sight. We also find that MPTCP offers no appreciable benefit over TCP for shorter flows, but it does improve performance for longer flows. For MPTCP, we found that, especially for short flows, it is crucial to select the correct network for the primary subflow. For long flows, it is equally important to select the proper congestion control algorithm. To understand how TCP and MPTCP over LTE and WiFi can affect mobile app performance, we analyzed mobile apps' traffic patterns and categorized apps as either *short-flow dominated* or *long-flow dominated*. For each category, we emulated app traffic patterns and the results we observed match our MPTCP measurement findings.

Our findings also bring up new research questions: how can we automatically decide when to use single path TCP and when to use MPTCP? How should we decide which network to use for TCP, or which network to use for a subflow with MPTCP? We think these are non-trivial questions due to the high mobility of devices and rapidly-changing network conditions. Also, with energy consumption being a major concern for mobile devices, how can we make the decisions when trying to minimize energy consumption? We plan to explore each of these future directions.

8. ACKNOWLEDGMENTS

We are grateful to the IMC reviewers, and our shepherd, Dr. Arnaud Legout in particular, for many helpful comments. We thank Katrina LaCurts, Lenin Ravindranath, and Amy Ousterhout for their thoughtful suggestions. This work was also supported in part by NSF grants 1407470 and 1161964. We also thank the members of the MIT Center for Wireless Networks and Mobile Computing (Wireless@MIT), including Amazon.com, Cisco, Google, Intel, Mediatek, Microsoft, ST Microelectronics, and Telefonica, for their support.

REFERENCES

[1] Recognizing the user's current activity. `http://developer.android.com/training/location/activity-recognition.html`.

[2] Android telephony manager api. `http://developer.android.com/reference/android/telephony/TelephonyManager.html`.

[3] N. Balasubramanian, A. Balasubramanian, and A. Venkataramani. Energy consumption in mobile phones: a measurement study and implications for network applications. In *IMC*, 2009.

[4] J. Barlow-Bignell, C. da Silva, J. Gjengset, and P. Oliha. Wireless interference and multipath tcpreducing 3g energy consumption on mobile devices, 2013.

[5] S. Barré, C. Paasch, and O. Bonaventure. Multipath tcp: from theory to practice. In *NETWORKING 2011*, pages 444–457. Springer, 2011.

[6] Y.-C. Chen, Y. Lim, R. J. Gibbens, E. M. Nahum, R. Khalili, and D. Towsley. A measurement-based study of multipath tcp performance over wireless networks. In *IMC*, 2013.

[7] S. Deng and H. Balakrishnan. Traffic-aware techniques to reduce 3g/lte wireless energy consumption. In *Proceedings of the 8th international conference on Emerging networking experiments and technologies*, pages 181–192. ACM, 2012.

[8] P. Deshpande, X. Hou, and S. R. Das. Performance comparison of 3g and metro-scale wifi for vehicular network access. In *Proceedings of the 10th ACM SIGCOMM conference on Internet measurement*, pages 301–307. ACM, 2010.

[9] UE "Fast Dormancy" behavior, 2007. 3GPP discussion and decision notes R2-075251.

[10] R. Khalili, N. Gast, M. Popovic, U. Upadhyay, and J.-Y. Le Boudec. Mptcp is not pareto-optimal: performance issues and a possible solution. In *CoNEXT*, 2012.

[11] Mahimahi. `http://mahimahi.mit.edu`.

[12] Monsoon power monitor. `http://www.msoon.com/LabEquipment/PowerMonitor/`.

[13] Apple ios 7 surprises as first with new multipath tcp connections. http://www.networkworld.com/news/2013/091913-ios7-multipath-273995.html.

[14] Multipath tcp - linux kernel implementation. http://www.multipath-tcp.org/.

[15] S. Nirjon, A. Nicoara, C.-H. Hsu, J. Singh, and J. Stankovic. MultiNets: Policy Oriented Real-Time Switching of Wireless Interfaces on Mobile Devices. In *RTAS*, 2012.

[16] C. Paasch, G. Detal, F. Duchene, C. Raiciu, and O. Bonaventure. Exploring mobile/wifi handover with multipath tcp. In *CellNet*, 2012.

[17] C. E. Perkins. Mobile ip. *Communications Magazine, IEEE*, 1997.

[18] C. Pluntke, L. Eggert, and N. Kiukkonen. Saving mobile device energy with multipath tcp. In *MobiArch*, 2011.

[19] C. Raiciu, D. Niculescu, M. Bagnulo, and M. J. Handley. Opportunistic mobility with multipath tcp. In *MobiArch*, 2011.

[20] J. Sommers and P. Barford. Cell vs. wifi: on the performance of metro area mobile connections. In *IMC*, 2012.

[21] D. Wischik, C. Raiciu, A. Greenhalgh, and M. Handley. Design, implementation and evaluation of congestion control for multipath tcp. In *NSDI*, 2011.

[22] X. Zhao, C. Castelluccia, and M. Baker. Flexible network support for mobility. In *MobiCom*, 1998.

Node Failure Localization via Network Tomography *

Liang Ma
IBM T. J. Watson Research
Yorktown Heights, NY, USA
liang.ma@ieee.org

Ting He
IBM T. J. Watson Research
Yorktown Heights, NY, USA
the@us.ibm.com

Ananthram Swami
Army Research Laboratory
Adelphi, MD, USA
a.swami@ieee.org

Don Towsley
University of Massachusetts
Amherst, MA, USA
towsley@cs.umass.edu

Kin K. Leung
Imperial College
London, UK
kin.leung@imperial.ac.uk

Jessica Lowe
DSTL
Salisbury, UK
jjlowe@dstl.gov.uk

Abstract

We investigate the problem of localizing node failures in a communication network from end-to-end path measurements, under the assumption that a path behaves normally if and only if it does not contain any failed nodes. To uniquely localize node failures, the measurement paths must show different symptoms under different failure events, i.e., for any two distinct sets of failed nodes, there must be a measurement path traversing one and only one of them. This condition is, however, impractical to test for large networks. Our first contribution is a characterization of this condition in terms of easily verifiable conditions on the network topology with given monitor placements under three families of probing mechanisms, which differ in whether measurement paths are (i) arbitrarily controllable, (ii) controllable but cycle-free, or (iii) uncontrollable (i.e., determined by the default routing protocol). Our second contribution is a characterization of the maximum identifiability of node failures, measured by the maximum number of simultaneous failures that can always be uniquely localized. Specifically, we bound the maximal identifiability from both the upper and the lower bounds which differ by at most one, and show that these bounds can be evaluated in polynomial time. Finally, we quantify the impact of the probing mechanism on the capability of node failure localization under different probing mechanisms on both random and real network topologies. We observe that despite a higher implementation cost, probing along controllable paths can significantly improve a network's capability to localize simultaneous node failures.

*Research was sponsored by the U.S. Army Research Laboratory and the U.K. Ministry of Defence and was accomplished under Agreement Number W911NF-06-3-0001. The views and conclusions contained in this document are those of the authors and should not be interpreted as representing the official policies, either expressed or implied, of the U.S. Army Research Laboratory, the U.S. Government, the U.K. Ministry of Defence or the U.K. Government. The U.S. and U.K. Governments are authorized to reproduce and distribute reprints for Government purposes notwithstanding any copyright notation hereon.

IMC'14, November 5–7, 2014, Vancouver, BC, Canada.
Copyright 2014 ACM 978-1-4503-3213-2/14/11 ...$15.00.
http://dx.doi.org/10.1145/2663716.2663723.

Categories and Subject Descriptors

C.2.3 [**Computer-communication Networks**]: Network Operations—*Network monitoring*; G.2.2 [**Discrete Mathematics**]: Graph Theory—*Network problems*

Keywords

Network Tomography; Node Failure Localization; Identifiability Condition; Maximum Identifiability

1. INTRODUCTION

Effective monitoring of network performance is essential for network operators in building a reliable communication network that is robust against service disruptions. In order to achieve this goal, the monitoring infrastructure must be able to detect network misbehaviors (e.g., unusually high loss/latency, unreachability) and localize the sources of the anomaly (e.g., malfunction of certain routers) in an accurate and timely manner. Knowledge of where problematic network elements reside in the network is particularly useful for fast service recovery, e.g., the network operator can migrate affected services and/or reroute traffic. However, localizing network elements that cause a service disruption can be challenging. The straightforward approach of directly monitoring the health of individual elements is not always feasible due to traffic overhead, access control, or lack of protocol support at internal nodes. Moreover, built-in monitoring agents running on network elements cannot detect problems caused by misconfigured/unanticipated interactions between network layers, where end-to-end communication is disrupted but individual network elements along the path remain functional (a.k.a. *silent failures*) [1]. These limitations call for a different approach that can diagnose the health of network elements from the health of end-to-end communications perceived between measurement points.

This different approach is generally known as *network tomography* [2], where a canonical application is inferring internal network characteristics by measuring end-to-end performance from a subset of nodes with monitoring capabilities, referred to as *monitors*. Unlike direct measurement, network tomography only relies on end-to-end performance (e.g., path connectivity) experienced by data packets, thus addressing issues such as overhead, lack of protocol support, and silent failures. In cases where the network characteristic of interest is binary (e.g., *normal* or *failed*), the problem is known as *Boolean network tomography* [3].

In this paper, we study an application of Boolean network tomography to localize node failures from measurements of path states. Assuming that a measurement path is normal if and only if all nodes on this path behave normally, we formulate the problem as a system of Boolean equations, where the unknown variables are the binary node states, and the known constants are the observed states of measurement paths. The goal of Boolean network tomography is essentially to solve this system of Boolean equations.

Because the observations are coarse-grained (path normal/failed), it is usually impossible to uniquely identify node states from path measurements. For example, if two nodes always appear together in measurement paths, then upon observing failures of all these paths, we can at most deduce that one of these nodes (or both) has failed but cannot determine which one. Observing that there are often multiple explanations for given path failures, existing work mostly focuses on finding the most probable explanation that involves the minimum set of failed nodes. There is, however, no guarantee that nodes in this minimum set have failed or that nodes outside the set have not. Generally, to distinguish between two possible failure sets, there must exist a measurement path that traverses one and only one of these two sets. There is, however, a lack of understanding of what this requires in terms of observable network settings such as topology, monitor placement, and measurement routing.

In this paper, we consider two closely related problems: In a network with any given monitor placement, (1) if the number of simultaneous node failures is bounded by k, then under what conditions can one uniquely localize failed nodes from path measurements? (2) what is the maximum number of simultaneous node failures (i.e., the largest value of k) that can be uniquely localized in this network? We study both problems in the context of the following families of probing mechanisms: (i) *Controllable Arbitrary-path Probing (CAP)*, where measurement paths are arbitrarily controllable, (ii) *Controllable Simple-path Probing (CSP)*, where measurement paths are controllable but cycle-free, and (iii) *Uncontrollable Probing (UP)*, where measurement paths are determined by the default routing protocol. These probing mechanisms assume different levels of control over the routing of probing packets and are feasible in different network scenarios (see Section 2.3); answers to the above two problems under these probing mechanisms thus provide insights on how the level of control bestowed on the monitoring system affects its capability in failure localization.

In the sequel, we assume that node failures are persistent, i.e., a failed node remains failed throughout the measurement process and leads to failures of all paths traversing it.

1.1 Related Work

Based on the number of simultaneously failed elements, existing work can be broadly classified into single failure localization and multiple failure localization. Single failure localization assumes that multiple simultaneous failures happen with negligible probability. Under this assumption, [4,5] propose efficient algorithms for monitor placement such that any single failure can be detected and localized. To improve the resolution in characterizing failures, range tomography in [6] not only localizes the failure, but also estimates its severity (e.g., congestion level). These works, however, ignore the fact that multiple failures occur more frequently than one may imagine [7]. In this paper, we consider the general case of localizing multiple failures.

Multiple failure localization often faces inherent uncertainty in the number of failures. Most existing works address this uncertainty by attempting to find the minimum set of network elements whose failures can explain the observed path states. Under the assumption that failures are low-probability events, this approach generates the most probable failure set among all possibilities. Using this approach, [8,9] propose solutions for networks with tree topologies, which are later extended to general topologies by [1]. Similarly, [11] proposes to localize link failures by minimizing false positives; however, it cannot guarantee unique failure localization. In a Bayesian formulation, [12] proposes a two-staged solution which first estimates the failure (loss rate above threshold) probabilities of different links and then infers the most likely failure set for subsequent measurements. Augmenting path measurements with (partially) available control plane information (e.g., routing messages), [13,14] propose a greedy heuristic for troubleshooting network unreachability in multi-AS (Autonomous System) networks that has better accuracy than benchmarks using only path measurements.

Little is known when we insist on *uniquely* localizing network failures. Given a set of monitors known to uniquely localize failures on paths between themselves, [15] develops an algorithm to remove redundant monitors such that all failures remain identifiable. If the number of failed links is upper bounded by k and the monitors can probe arbitrary cycles or paths containing cycles, [16] proves that the network must be $(k+2)$-edge-connected to identify any failures up to k links using one monitor, which is then used to derive requirements on monitor placement for general topologies. However, the condition remains unknown if the failures are associated with nodes instead of links, or constraints (e.g., cycle-free) are imposed on measurement paths by the routing protocols (see discussions in Section 4.1 for why the results of [16] do not apply to our problem). In this paper, we investigate the fundamental relationships between node failure identifiability and explicit network settings such as topology, placement of monitors, and probing mechanism, with focus on developing efficient algorithms to characterize the capability of failure localization under given settings.

1.2 Summary of Contributions

We study, for the first time, the fundamental capability of a network with arbitrarily given monitor placements to uniquely localize node failures from binary end-to-end measurements between monitors. Our contributions are five-fold:

1) We propose a novel measure, referred to as *maximum identifiability*, to characterize a network's capability in failure localization as the maximum number of simultaneous node failures it can uniquely localize.

2) We establish abstract necessary/sufficient conditions for uniquely localizing a bounded number of failures, which are applicable to all probing mechanisms.

3) We translate the abstract conditions into more concrete conditions in terms of network topology, placement of monitors, and measurement paths under three different probing mechanisms (CAP, CSP, and UP), which can be tested in polynomial time.

4) We show that a special relationship between the above necessary/sufficient conditions leads to tight upper and lower bounds on the maximum identifiability that narrows its value to at most two consecutive integers. The bounds are polynomial-

Table 1: Graph-related Notations

Symbol	Meaning
V, L	set of nodes/links
M, N	set of monitors/non-monitors ($M \cup N = V$, $\mu := \lvert M\rvert$, $\sigma := \lvert N\rvert$)
$\mathcal{N}(M)$	set of non-monitors that are neighbors of at least one monitor in M
$\mathcal{L}(V, W)$	$\mathcal{L}(V, W) = \{\text{link } vw : \forall v \in V, w \in W, v \neq w\}$
$\mathcal{G} - L'$	delete links: $\mathcal{G} - L' = (V, L \setminus L')$, where "\" is setminus
$\mathcal{G} + L'$	add links: $\mathcal{G} + L' = (V, L \cup L')$, where the endpoints of links in L' must be in V
$\mathcal{G} - V'$	delete nodes: $\mathcal{G} - V' = (V \setminus V', L \setminus L(V'))$, where $L(V')$ is the set of links incident to nodes in V'
$\mathcal{G} + V'$	add nodes: $\mathcal{G} + V' = (V \cup V', L)$

time computable under CAP and CSP; while they are NP-hard to compute under UP, we give a greedy heuristic to compute a pair of relaxed bounds that frequently coincide with the original bounds in practice.

5) We extensively compare the maximum identifiability under different probing mechanisms on random and real topologies. Our comparison shows that although controllable probing, especially CAP, is more difficult to implement, it significantly improves the capability of failure localization in terms of maximum identifiability.

Note that the proposed model captures network state at a small time scale (time for conducting probing) and all above results are valid as long as node failures are persistent during probing. Moreover, we have limited our observations to binary states (normal/failed) of measurement paths. It is possible in some networks to obtain extra information from probes, e.g., rerouted paths after a default path fails, in which case our solution provides lower bounds on the maximum identifiability. Furthermore, we do not make any assumption on the distribution or correlation of node failures across the network. In some application scenarios (e.g., datacenter networks), failures of some nodes may be correlated (e.g., all routers sharing the same power/chiller). We leave the characterization of maximum identifiability in the presence of such additional information to future work.

The rest of the paper is organized as follows. Section 2 formulates the problem. Section 3 presents abstract conditions for identifying node failures, followed by concrete, verifiable conditions for specific families of probing mechanisms in Section 4. Based on the derived conditions, Section 5 presents bounds on the maximum identifiability that can be efficiently evaluated. The bounds are evaluated on various synthetic/real topologies in Section 6 to study the impact of the probing mechanism on the capability of node failure localization. Finally, Section 7 concludes the paper.

2. PROBLEM FORMULATION

2.1 Models and Assumptions

We assume that the network topology is known and can be modeled as an undirected graph[1] $\mathcal{G} = (V, L)$, where V and L are the sets of nodes and links. In $\mathcal{G}$, the number of neighbors of node v is called the *degree* of v. Note that graph $\mathcal{G}$ can represent a logical topology where each node in $\mathcal{G}$ corresponds to a physical subnetwork. Without loss of generality, we assume $\mathcal{G}$ is connected, as different connected components have to be monitored separately.

A subset of nodes M ($M \subseteq V$) are *monitors* that can initiate and collect measurements. The rest of the nodes, denoted by $N := V \setminus M$, are *non-monitors*. Let $\mu := |M|$ and $\sigma := |N|$ denote the numbers of monitors and non-monitors. We assume that monitors do not fail during the measurement process, as failed monitors can be directly detected and filtered out within the monitoring system. Non-monitors, on the other hand, may fail, and a failure event may involve simultaneous failures of multiple non-monitors. Depending on the adopted probing mechanism, monitors can measure and determine the states of nodes by sending probes along certain paths. Let P denote the set of all *possible measurement paths* under a given probing mechanism; for given $\mathcal{G}$ and M, different probing mechanisms can lead to different sets of measurement paths, which will be specified later. We use *node state* (*path state*) to refer to the state, failed or normal, of nodes (paths), where a path fails if and only if at least one node on the path fails. To avoid trivial cases, we assume that each non-monitor is traversed by at least one measurement path, as otherwise the non-monitor is unobservable to the monitoring system and has to be excluded in failure localization. Table 1 summarizes graph-related notations used in this paper (following the convention of [10]).

Let $\mathbf{w} = (W_1, \ldots, W_\sigma)^T$ be the binary column vector of the states of all non-monitors and $\mathbf{c} = (C_1, \ldots, C_\gamma)^T$ the binary column vector of the states of all measurement paths. For both node and path states, 0 represents "normal" and 1 represents "failed". We can relate the path states to the node states through the following Boolean linear system:

$$\mathbf{R} \odot \mathbf{w} = \mathbf{c}, \tag{1}$$

where $\mathbf{R} = (R_{ij})$ is a $\gamma \times \sigma$ *measurement matrix*, with each entry $R_{ij} \in \{0, 1\}$ denoting whether non-monitor v_j is present on path $\mathcal{P}_i$ (1: yes, 0: no), and "$\odot$" is the Boolean matrix product, i.e., $C_i = \vee_{j=1}^{\sigma}(R_{ij} \wedge W_j)$. The goal of Boolean network tomography is to invert this Boolean linear system to solve for $\mathbf{w}$ given $\mathbf{R}$ and $\mathbf{c}$. Intuitively, node failures are identifiable if and only if (1) has a unique solution.

2.2 Definitions

Let a *failure set* F be a set of non-monitors ($F \subseteq N$) that may fail simultaneously. The challenge in failure localization is that the solution to (1) is usually not unique, i.e., there are multiple possible failure sets leading to the observed path states. To reduce ambiguity, we limit the solution space to a predetermined collection Ψ of likely failure sets and only seek to ensure uniqueness within this collection. Let P_F denote the set of all measurement paths affected by a failure set F (i.e., traversing at least one node in F). We now formally define the notion of identifiability in node failure localization.

DEFINITION 1. *Given a network $\mathcal{G}$, a set of measurement paths P, and a collection Ψ of likely failure sets in $\mathcal{G}$:*

1. *Two failure sets F_1 and F_2 in Ψ can be* distinguished *from each other if and only if $P_{F_1} \neq P_{F_2}$, i.e., $\exists$ a path that traverses one and only one of F_1 and F_2.*
2. *In Ψ, failure set F is* identifiable *if and only if F can be distinguished from every other failure set in Ψ.*
3. *Ψ is* identifiable *if and only if every failure set in Ψ is identifiable.*

[1] We use the terms *network* and *graph* interchangeably.

It is clear from the definition that whether a failure set is identifiable or not depends on the collection of potential failure sets it is compared against. Furthermore, Ψ being identifiable means that we can always uniquely localize node failures as long as the set of failed nodes falls into Ψ. Since a failure set may contain more than one node, we define the following notions to characterize network capability in localizing simultaneous node failures.

DEFINITION 2. *Given a network $\mathcal{G}$ and a set of measurement paths P in $\mathcal{G}$:*

1. *We say $\mathcal{G}$ is* k-identifiable *($0 \leq k \leq \sigma$) if the collection Ψ of all subsets of N with cardinality bounded by k is identifiable, i.e., any failure of up to k nodes can be uniquely localized.*
2. *The* maximum identifiability *of $\mathcal{G}$, denoted by $\Omega(\mathcal{G})$, is the maximum value of k such that $\mathcal{G}$ is k-identifiable.*

The maximum identifiability of a network characterizes its capability to localize failures in the worst case. That is, no matter where the failures occur, as long as the number of failed nodes is bounded by Ω, we can uniquely localize the failures from observed path states. Note that it is possible to uniquely localize a larger number of failures when they occur at a particular set of nodes, but localization cannot be guaranteed if the failures occur elsewhere. Both k-identifiability and maximum identifiability are defined with respect to a given P, which will be clear from the context.

2.3 Classification of Probing Mechanisms

Given the topology $\mathcal{G}$ and the monitor locations M, the probing mechanism plays a crucial role in failure localization by determining the set of measurement paths P. Depending on the flexibility of probing and the cost of deployment, we consider three families of probing mechanisms:

1. *Controllable Arbitrary-path Probing (CAP):* P includes any path/cycle, allowing repeated nodes/links, as long as each path/cycle starts and ends at monitors.
2. *Controllable Simple-path Probing (CSP):* P includes any *simple* path between distinct monitors, not including repeated nodes.
3. *Uncontrollable Probing (UP):* P is the set of paths between monitors determined by the routing protocol used by the network, not controllable by the monitors.

In particular, although CAP allows probes to traverse each node/link an arbitrary number of times, it suffices for probes to traverse each link at most once in either direction for the sake of localizing node failures.

These probing mechanisms clearly provide decreasing flexibility to the monitors and therefore decreasing capability to localize failures. Further, they also offer decreasing deployment cost. At the IP layer, CAP is feasible only if *(strict) source routing* (an IP option) [17] is enabled at all non-monitors, which allows them to modify the source and the destination addresses in packet headers hop by hop to probe a path prescribed by the monitor initiating the measurement probe[2]. If implemented at the application layer (e.g., to localize failures in overlay networks), CAP requires equivalent "source routing" to be supported by the application. Similarly, CSP is feasible under source routing (or equivalent capability at the application layer). It is also feasible under an emerging networking paradigm called software-defined networking (SDN) [18], where monitors can instruct the SDN controller to set up arbitrary cycle-free paths for the probing traffic. Note that the cycle-free constraint is crucial in SDN, as data forwarding is performed in a distributed manner by switches according to forwarding tables configured by the controller during route setup, which will encounter forwarding loops if the path has cycles. In contrast, UP only requires basic data forwarding and is generally feasible.

[2] The probe can follow the reverse path to return to the original monitor, thus effectively probing any path with *at least* one end at a monitor.

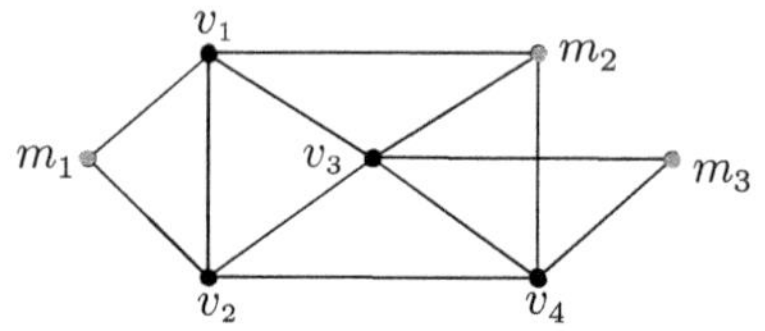

Figure 1: Sample network with three monitors: m_1, m_2, and m_3.

In this paper, we quantify how the flexibility of probing schemes affects the network's capability in failure localization. Although concrete results are only provided for the above families of probing mechanisms, our framework and our abstract identifiability conditions (see Section 3) can also be used to evaluate the failure localization capability of other probing mechanisms.

2.4 Objective

Given a network topology $\mathcal{G}$, a set of monitors M, and a probing mechanism (CAP, CSP, or UP), we seek to answer the following closely-related questions: (i) Given a bound k on the number of simultaneous failures, can we uniquely localize up to k failed nodes from observed path states? (ii) What is the maximum number of simultaneous failures we can localize? Clearly, answers to these questions require algorithms that can efficiently test for k-identifiability and determine the maximum identifiability.

2.5 Illustrative Example

Consider the sample network in Fig. 1 with three monitors (m_1–m_3) and four non-monitors (v_1–v_4). Clearly, the monitors' capability to identify failures of the non-monitors depends on the probing mechanism, i.e., which paths are measurable between the monitors. In this example, we will examine this capability and how it can be improved by relaxing constraints on measurement paths. Under UP, suppose that the default routing protocol only allows the monitors to probe the following paths: $\mathcal{P}_1 = m_1v_2v_1m_2$, $\mathcal{P}_2 = m_1v_2v_4m_3$, and $\mathcal{P}_3 = m_2v_3m_3$, which form a measurement matrix $\mathbf{R}^{\mathrm{UP}}$:

$$\begin{array}{l} \mathcal{P}_1 = m_1v_2v_1m_2 \\ \mathcal{P}_2 = m_1v_2v_4m_3 \\ \mathcal{P}_3 = m_2v_3m_3 \end{array} \Rightarrow \mathbf{R}^{\mathrm{UP}} = \begin{array}{c} \begin{array}{cccc} W_1 & W_2 & W_3 & W_4 \end{array} \\ \left(\begin{array}{cccc} 1 & 1 & 0 & 0 \\ 0 & 1 & 0 & 1 \\ 0 & 0 & 1 & 0 \end{array}\right) \end{array}, \quad (2)$$

where $R^{\mathrm{UP}}_{ij} = 1$ if and only if node v_j is on path $\mathcal{P}_i$. Then we have $\mathbf{R}^{\mathrm{UP}} \odot \mathbf{w} = \mathbf{c}$, where $\mathbf{c}$ is the binary vector of path states observed at the destination monitors. Based on Definition 1, we can verify that any single node failure is identifiable, as for every two non-monitors, there is a measurement path traversing one and only one of them. However, these three paths cannot identify simultaneous failures of two nodes. This is because if node v_2 fails, then we cannot determine if v_1 (or v_4) fails or not. Identifiability can be improved if more measurement paths are allowed. For example, under CSP, besides the three paths in (2), we can probe three additional paths: $\mathcal{P}_4 = m_1v_2v_3m_2$, $\mathcal{P}_5 = m_1v_1m_2$, and $\mathcal{P}_6 = m_2v_4m_3$, yielding an expanded measurement matrix in (3):

$$\begin{array}{l} \mathcal{P}_1 = m_1v_2v_1m_2 \\ \mathcal{P}_2 = m_1v_2v_4m_3 \\ \mathcal{P}_3 = m_2v_3m_3 \\ \mathcal{P}_4 = m_1v_2v_3m_2 \\ \mathcal{P}_5 = m_1v_1m_2 \\ \mathcal{P}_6 = m_2v_4m_3 \end{array} \Rightarrow \mathbf{R}^{\mathrm{CSP}} = \begin{array}{c} \begin{array}{cccc} W_1 & W_2 & W_3 & W_4 \end{array} \\ \left(\begin{array}{cccc} 1 & 1 & 0 & 0 \\ 0 & 1 & 0 & 1 \\ 0 & 0 & 1 & 0 \\ \hline 0 & 1 & 1 & 0 \\ 1 & 0 & 0 & 0 \\ 0 & 0 & 0 & 1 \end{array}\right) \end{array} \left.\begin{array}{c} \\ \\ \\ \end{array}\right\} \mathbf{R}^{\mathrm{UP}} \tag{3}$$

Using the six paths in (3), we can identify up to three failed nodes, a notable improvement over UP. However, if v_1, v_3, and v_4 all fail, then there is no measurement path under CSP that can be used to determine the state of v_2. Nevertheless, if CAP is supported, then we can send probes along a cycle $\mathcal{P}_7 = m_1v_2m_1$. In conjunction with the paths in (3), this yields the measurement matrix in (4):

$$\begin{array}{l} \mathcal{P}_5 = m_1v_1m_2 \\ \mathcal{P}_7 = m_1v_2m_1 \\ \mathcal{P}_3 = m_2v_3m_3 \\ \mathcal{P}_6 = m_2v_4m_3 \end{array} \Rightarrow \mathbf{R}^{\mathrm{CAP}} = \begin{array}{c} \begin{array}{cccc} W_1 & W_2 & W_3 & W_4 \end{array} \\ \left(\begin{array}{cccc} 1 & 0 & 0 & 0 \\ 0 & 1 & 0 & 0 \\ 0 & 0 & 1 & 0 \\ 0 & 0 & 0 & 1 \end{array}\right) \end{array} \tag{4}$$

Since the paths in (4) can independently determine the state of each non-monitor, CAP achieves full identifiability for the network in Fig. 1.

This example shows that in addition to the network topology and the monitor placement, the probing mechanism also significantly affects a network's capability to localize failures. In the rest of the paper, we will study this relationship both theoretically and algorithmically.

3. ABSTRACT IDENTIFIABILITY CONDITIONS

The definitions of identifiability in Definitions 1 and 2 are based on the enumeration of all possible failure scenarios and does not directly allow efficient testing and characterization of identifiability. To address this issue, we need more explicit identifiability conditions that can support efficient algorithm design. In this section, we will establish abstract sufficient/necessary conditions for k-identifiability under an arbitrary probing mechanism, which will later be developed into more concrete conditions for specific families of probing mechanisms.

Our sufficient condition is inspired by a result known in a related field called *combinatorial group testing* [19]. In short, group testing aims to find abnormal elements in a given set by running tests on subsets of elements, each test indicating whether any element in the subset is abnormal. This is analogous to our problem where abnormal elements are failed nodes and tests are conducted by probing measurement paths. A subtle but critical difference is that in our problem, the subsets of elements that can be tested together are limited by the set of measurement paths P, which are in turn limited by the topology, probing mechanism, and placement of monitors.

Most existing solutions for (nonadaptive) group testing aim at constructing a *disjunct testing matrix*. Specifically, a testing matrix R is a binary matrix, where $R_{i,j} = 1$ if and only if element j is included in the i-th test. Then R is called k-*disjunct* if the Boolean sum of any k columns does not "contain" any other column[3] [20]. In our problem, the existence of a disjunct testing matrix translates into a sufficient identifiability condition as follows.

LEMMA 3 (ABSTRACT SUFFICIENT CONDITION). *Any set of up to k failed nodes is identifiable if for any non-monitor v and failure set F with $|F| \le k$ ($v \notin F$), there is a measurement path going through v but no node in F.*

PROOF. Consider two distinct failure sets F and F', each containing no more than k nodes. There exists a node v in only one of these sets; suppose $v \in F' \setminus F$. By the condition in the lemma, $\exists$ a path p traversing v but not F, thus distinguishing F from F'. □

Our necessary condition is based on the simple observation that to identify k failures, we must be able to identify the remaining $k - s$ ($1 \le s \le k-1$) failures after identifying and removing s of the failed nodes from the network, which leads to the following necessary condition.

LEMMA 4 (ABSTRACT NECESSARY CONDITION). *Any set of up to k failed nodes is identifiable only if for any set V' of non-monitors with $|V'| < k$, any set of up to $k - |V'|$ node failures is identifiable in $\mathcal{G} - V'$.*

PROOF. Suppose that $\exists$ two non-empty sets V' and V'' of non-monitors, with $V' \cap V'' = \emptyset$ and $|V'| + |V''| = k$, such that V'' is not identifiable in $\mathcal{G} - V'$. Then the union $F = V' \cup V''$ must be unidentifiable in $\mathcal{G}$, as even if we have identified failures in V', we still cannot identify the rest of the failures. □

Although neither of the above conditions directly lead to efficient testing algorithms, the significance of these conditions is that they are valid without relying on the probing mechanism being used. Moreover, we will show in the next section that these conditions provide theoretical foundations for efficient testing under specific families of probing mechanisms (CAP, CSP, and UP). Efficient testing for other families of probing mechanisms can also be explored using these abstract conditions.

4. VERIFIABLE IDENTIFIABILITY CONDITIONS

In this section, we develop the abstract conditions in Section 3 into concrete conditions suitable for efficient testing for the three families of probing mechanisms in Section 2.3.

4.1 Conditions under CAP

Under CAP, we can essentially "ping" any node from a monitor along any path. In the face of failures, this implies that a monitor's ability to determine the state of a node depends on its connectivity to the monitors after removing nodes that are known/hypothesized to have failed. This observation allows us to translate the abstract conditions in Section 3 into more concrete identifiability conditions as follows.

THEOREM 5 (k-IDENTIFIABILITY UNDER CAP). *Network $\mathcal{G}$ is k-identifiable under CAP:*

a) if for any set V' of up to k non-monitors, each connected component in $\mathcal{G} - V'$ contains a monitor;

[3]That is, for any subset of k column indices S and any other column index $j \notin S$, there exists a row index i such that $R_{i,j} = 1$ and $R_{i,j'} = 0$ for all $j' \in S$.

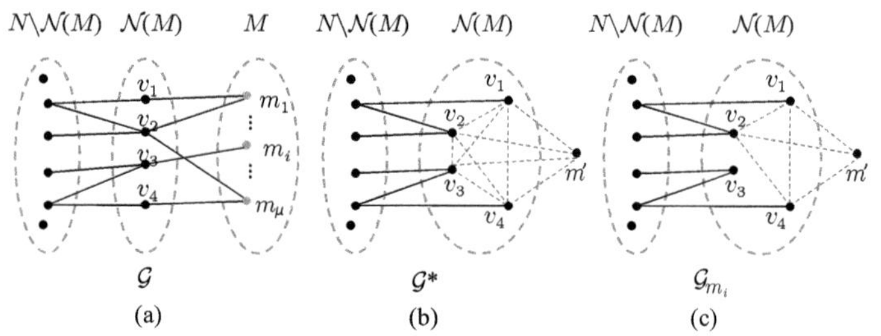

Figure 2: Auxiliary graphs: (a) Original graph $\mathcal{G}$; (b) $\mathcal{G}^*$ of $\mathcal{G}$; (c) $\mathcal{G}_{m_i}$ of $\mathcal{G}$ w.r.t. monitor m_i.

b) only if for any set V' of up to $k-1$ non-monitors, each connected component in $\mathcal{G}-V'$ contains a monitor.

PROOF. Suppose condition (a) holds, and consider a candidate failure set V' and a non-monitor v ($v \notin V'$). Since the connected component in $\mathcal{G}-V'$ that contains v has a monitor, there must exist a path connecting v to a monitor that does not traverse any node in V'. Following this path from the monitor to v and then back to the monitor then gives a path measurable under CAP that satisfies Lemma 3. Thus, condition (a) is sufficient.

Suppose condition (b) does not hold, i.e., there exists a non-monitor v that is disconnected from all monitors in $\mathcal{G}-V'$ for a set V' of up to $k-1$ non-monitors ($v \notin V'$). Then if nodes in V' fail, no remaining measurement path can probe v, and thus it is impossible to determine whether v has failed or not. This violates the condition in Lemma 4, and thus condition (b) is necessary. □

Simple as they look, these conditions still cannot be tested efficiently because they enumerate over a combinatorial number of sets V'. Fortunately, we are able to reduce them into explicit conditions on the vertex-connectivity of a related topology, which can then be tested in polynomial time. We use the following notions from graph theory.

DEFINITION 6. *[10] Graph $\mathcal{G}$ of $|V|$ vertices is said to be* k-vertex-connected *if $k \leq |V|-1$ and deleting any subset of up to $k-1$ vertices does not disconnect $\mathcal{G}$. The* vertex-connectivity *of $\mathcal{G}$, denoted by $\delta(\mathcal{G})$, is the maximum k such that $\mathcal{G}$ is k-vertex-connected.*

In our problem, the key observation is that requiring each connected component in $\mathcal{G}-V'$ to contain a monitor is equivalent to requiring each connected component in $\mathcal{G}-M-V'$ (i.e., after removing all monitors) to contain a neighbor of a monitor. Thus, if we add *virtual links* between these neighbors, the resulting graph $\mathcal{G}-M-V'+\mathcal{L}(\mathcal{N}(M), \mathcal{N}(M))$ should be connected. However, this does not mean the conditions are equivalent, because if $\mathcal{G}-M-V'$ is already connected, $\mathcal{G}-M-V'+\mathcal{L}(\mathcal{N}(M), \mathcal{N}(M))$ will certainly be connected but $\mathcal{G}-M-V'$ may not contain any neighbors of monitors. This special case can be avoided by introducing a *virtual monitor m'* connected to all neighbors of monitors via virtual links, resulting in an *auxiliary graph* $\mathcal{G}^* := \mathcal{G}-M+\{m'\}+\mathcal{L}(\mathcal{N}(M), \mathcal{N}(M))+\mathcal{L}(\{m'\}, \mathcal{N}(M))$ as illustrated in Fig. 2 (b). We will show that requiring at least one monitor per connected component in $\mathcal{G}-V'$ is equivalent to requiring $\mathcal{G}^*-V'$ to be connected.

The beauty of this new condition is that it reduces the tests over all possible V' to a single test of the vertex-connectivity of $\mathcal{G}^*$, as stated below.

LEMMA 7. *Each connected component in $\mathcal{G}-V'$ contains a monitor for any set V' of up to s ($s \leq \sigma-1$) non-monitors if and only if $\mathcal{G}^*$ is $(s+1)$-vertex-connected.*

PROOF. We first show the equivalence between the first condition and the connectivity of $\mathcal{G}^*-V'$. If the first condition holds, then each connected component in $\mathcal{G}-M-V'$ contains a neighbor of a monitor. Since these neighbors are connected with each other and also with m' in $\mathcal{G}^*-V'$, $\mathcal{G}^*-V'$ is connected. If the first condition is violated, i.e., there exists a connected component in $\mathcal{G}-M-V'$ without any neighbor of any monitor, then this component must be disconnected from m', and hence $\mathcal{G}^*-V'$ must be disconnected.

We then show that requiring $\mathcal{G}^*-V'$ to be connected for any V' of up to s non-monitors is equivalent to requiring it to be connected for any V' of up to s nodes in $\mathcal{G}^*$, including m', i.e., requiring $\mathcal{G}^*$ to be $(s+1)$-vertex-connected. It suffices to show that $\mathcal{G}^*-V'$ being connected for any V' of up to s non-monitors implies the connectivity of $\mathcal{G}^*-\{m'\}-V''$ for any V'' of up to $s-1$ non-monitors. Fixing a V'' of up to $s-1$ non-monitors, we assert that each connected component of $\mathcal{G}^*-\{m'\}-V''$ must contain a neighbor of a monitor, as otherwise $\mathcal{G}^*-V''$ will be disconnected. Since all these neighbors are connected via virtual links, $\mathcal{G}^*-\{m'\}-V''$ must be connected. □

Lemma 7 allows us to rewrite the identifiability conditions in Theorem 5 in terms of the vertex-connectivity of $\mathcal{G}^*$.

COROLLARY 8. *Network $\mathcal{G}$ is k-identifiable under CAP:*
a) if $\mathcal{G}^*$ is $(k+1)$-vertex-connected ($k \leq \sigma-1$);
b) only if $\mathcal{G}^*$ is k-vertex-connected ($k \leq \sigma$).

A special case not covered by this corollary is the case of $k=\sigma$ (the total number of non-monitors), i.e., if we wish to know whether the failure of *any* subset of non-monitors is identifiable. We address this case separately in the following proposition.

PROPOSITION 9. *Network $\mathcal{G}$ is σ-identifiable under CAP if and only if each non-monitor is the neighbor of a monitor.*

PROOF. If each non-monitor has a monitor as a neighbor, then their states can be determined independently through 1-hop probing, and hence any failure set is identifiable. On the other hand, if there exists a non-monitor v that is only reachable by monitors via other non-monitors, then the state of v cannot be determined in the case that all the other non-monitors fail, and hence $\mathcal{G}$ is not σ-identifiable. □

Discussion: A previous study [16] has provided necessary and sufficient conditions for a related problem of *link failure localization*, under the assumption that probes can traverse paths/cycles with possibly repeated nodes but no repeated links. Although the problem is analogous to node failure localization, the results of [16] do not apply to our problem[4].

Testing algorithm: A key advantage of the newly derived conditions over the abstract conditions in Section 3 is that they can be tested efficiently. Given a value of k, we

[4]Solving node failure localization using the results of [16] requires a topology transformation that maps each node to a link while maintaining adjacency between nodes and feasibility of measurement paths. To our knowledge, no such transformation exists whose output satisfies the assumptions of [16] (undirected graph, measurement paths not containing repeated links).

can evaluate the vertex-connectivity of $\mathcal{G}^*$, $\delta(\mathcal{G}^*)$, by the algorithm for determining network vertex connectivity in [21] in $O(\sigma^{3.75})$ time and compare the result with $k+1$ or k to test the conditions in Corollary 8.

4.2 Conditions under CSP

Under CSP, we restrict measurement paths P be the set of *simple paths* between monitors, i.e., paths starting/ending at distinct monitors and containing no cycles. As in the case of CAP, our goal here is again to translate the abstract conditions in Section 3 into concrete sufficient/necessary conditions that can be efficiently verified. We first give the following result analogous to Theorem 5.

THEOREM 10 (k-IDENTIFIABILITY UNDER CSP). *Network $\mathcal{G}$ is k-identifiable under CSP:*

a) if for any node set V', $|V'| \leq k+1$, containing at most one monitor, each connected component in $\mathcal{G}-V'$ contains a monitor;

b) only if for any node set V', $|V'| \leq k$, containing at most one monitor, each connected component in $\mathcal{G}-V'$ contains a monitor.

PROOF. Suppose condition (a) holds, and consider a candidate failure set F, $|F| \leq k$ and a non-monitor $v \notin F$. We argue that v must have two simple *vertex disjoint* paths to monitors in $\mathcal{G}-F$, and thus concatenating these paths provides a monitor-monitor simple path that traverses v but not F, satisfying the abstract sufficient condition in Lemma 3. Indeed, if such paths do not exist, i.e., $\exists$ a (monitor or non-monitor) node w ($w \neq v$) that resides on all paths from v to monitors in $\mathcal{G}-F$, then v will be disconnected from all monitors in $\mathcal{G}-F-\{w\}$, i.e., the connected component containing v in $\mathcal{G}-V'$, where $V' = F \cup \{w\}$, has no monitor, contradicting condition (a).

Suppose condition (b) does not hold, i.e., there exists a non-monitor v, a (monitor or non-monitor) node w, and a set of up to $k-1$ non-monitors F ($v \neq w$ and $v, w \notin F$) such that the connected component containing v in $\mathcal{G}-V'$, $V' = F \cup \{w\}$, contains no monitor. Then any path from v to monitors in $\mathcal{G}-F$ must traverse w, which means no monitor-monitor simple path in $\mathcal{G}-F$ will traverse v (as any monitor-monitor path traversing v must form a cycle at w). This violates the necessary condition in Lemma 4 because if node v fails, the failure cannot be identified in $\mathcal{G}-F$. $\square$

As expected, due to the restriction to simple paths, the identifiability conditions in Theorem 10 are stronger than those in Theorem 5. As with Theorem 5, the conditions in Theorem 10 do not directly lead to efficient tests, and we again seek equivalent conditions in terms of topological properties. Each condition in the form of Theorem 10 (a–b) covers two cases: (i) V' only contains non-monitors; (ii) V' contains a monitor and $|V'|-1$ non-monitors. The first case has been converted to a vertex-connectivity condition on an auxiliary topology $\mathcal{G}^*$ by Lemma 7; we now establish a similar condition for the second case using similar arguments.

Fix a set $V' = F \cup \{m\}$, where m is a monitor in M and F a set of non-monitors. Again, the key observation is that each connected component in $\mathcal{G}-V'$ containing a monitor is equivalent to each connected component in $\mathcal{G}-M-F$ containing a neighbor of a monitor other than m (i.e., a node in $\mathcal{N}(M \setminus \{m\})$). To capture this, we introduce another *auxiliary graph* $\mathcal{G}_m := \mathcal{G} - M + \{m'\} + \mathcal{L}(\mathcal{N}(M \setminus \{m\}), \mathcal{N}(M \setminus \{m\})) + \mathcal{L}(\{m'\}, \mathcal{N}(M \setminus \{m\}))$ with respect to (w.r.t.) monitor m as illustrated in Fig. 2 (c), where m' is again a virtual monitor. We will show that the last condition is equivalent to requiring $\mathcal{G}_m - F$ to be connected, and thus the following holds.

LEMMA 11. *The following two conditions are equivalent:*

(1) Each connected component in $\mathcal{G}-V'$ contains a monitor for any set V' consisting of monitor m ($m \in M$) and up to s ($s \leq \sigma - 1$) non-monitors;

(2) $\mathcal{G}_m$ is $(s+1)$-vertex-connected.

PROOF. The proof is similar to that of Lemma 7. If the first condition holds, then each connected component in $\mathcal{G}-M-F$ for $F := V' \setminus \{m\}$ contains a node in $\mathcal{N}(M \setminus \{m\})$, and thus $\mathcal{G}_m - F$ is connected. If the first condition is violated, then there is a connected component in $\mathcal{G}-M-F$ that does not contain any node in $\mathcal{N}(M \setminus \{m\})$. This component must be disconnected from m' in $\mathcal{G}_m - F$, and thus $\mathcal{G}_m - F$ must be disconnected. Hence, the first condition is equivalent to $\mathcal{G}_m - F$ being connected for any set F of up to s non-monitors. Moreover, $\mathcal{G}_m - F$ being connected for any set F of up to s non-monitors implies that $\mathcal{G}_m - \{m'\} - F'$ (m' is the virtual monitor in $\mathcal{G}_m$) is connected for any F' of up to $s-1$ non-monitors, because otherwise $\mathcal{G}_m - F'$ will be disconnected. Therefore, the first condition is equivalent to $\mathcal{G}_m - F$ being connected for any set F of up to s nodes in $\mathcal{G}_m$, i.e., the first and second conditions in Lemma 11 are equivalent. $\square$

Based on Lemmas 7 and 11, we can rewrite Theorem 10 as follows.

COROLLARY 12. *Network $\mathcal{G}$ is k-identifiable under CSP:*

a) if $\mathcal{G}^*$ is $(k+2)$-vertex-connected, and $\mathcal{G}_m$ is $(k+1)$-vertex-connected for each monitor $m \in M$ ($k \leq \sigma-2$);

b) only if $\mathcal{G}^*$ is $(k+1)$-vertex-connected, and $\mathcal{G}_m$ is k-vertex-connected for each monitor $m \in M$ ($k \leq \sigma-1$).

Special cases left out by this corollary are the cases of $k = \sigma$ and $k = \sigma - 1$, which are addressed separately as follows.

PROPOSITION 13. *Network $\mathcal{G}$ is σ-identifiable under CSP if and only if each non-monitor has at least two monitors as neighbors.*

PROOF. If each non-monitor has at least two monitors as neighbors, then their states can be determined independently by cycle-free 2-hop probing between monitors, and thus the network is σ-identifiable. On the other hand, suppose $\exists$ a non-monitor v with zero or only one monitor neighbor. Then $\nexists$ simple paths going through v without traversing another non-monitor, and hence the state of v cannot be determined if all the other non-monitors fail. $\square$

PROPOSITION 14. *Network $\mathcal{G}$ is $(\sigma-1)$-identifiable under CSP if and only if all but one non-monitor, denoted by v, have at least two monitors as neighbors, and v either has (i) two or more monitors as neighbors, or (ii) one monitor and all the other non-monitors (i.e., $N \setminus \{v\}$) as neighbors.*

PROOF. *a) Necessity:* Suppose that $\mathcal{G}$ is $(\sigma-1)$-identifiable under CSP. If it is also σ-identifiable, then each non-monitor must have at least two monitors as neighbors according to Proposition 13. Otherwise, we have $\Omega(\mathcal{G}) = \sigma - 1$. In this case, $\exists$ at least one non-monitor, denoted by v, with at most one monitor neighbor. Let $\mathcal{N}(v)$ denote all neighbors of v

including monitors. Suppose that v has λ neighbors (i.e., $|\mathcal{N}(v)| = \lambda$). Then there are two cases: (i) $\mathcal{N}(v)$ contains a monitor, denoted by $\widetilde{m}$; (ii) all nodes in $\mathcal{N}(v)$ are non-monitors. In case (i), the sets $F_1 = \mathcal{N}(v) \setminus \{\widetilde{m}\}$ and $F_2 = F_1 \cup \{v\}$ are not distinguishable because $\nexists$ monitor-to-monitor simple paths traversing v but not nodes in F_1. In case (ii), the sets $F_1 = \mathcal{N}(v) \setminus \{w\}$ (where w is an arbitrary node in $\mathcal{N}(v)$) and $F_2 = F_1 \cup \{v\}$ are not distinguishable as all monitor-to-monitor simple paths traversing v must go through at least one node in F_1. Based on (i–ii), we conclude that $\Omega(\mathcal{G}) \leq \lambda - 1$, where λ is the degree of any non-monitor with at most one monitor neighbor. For $\Omega(\mathcal{G}) = \sigma - 1$, we must have $\lambda \geq \sigma$, which can only be satisfied if all such non-monitors have one monitor and all the other non-monitors as neighbors. Moreover, if there are two such non-monitors v and u, then the sets $F \cup \{v\}$ and $F \cup \{u\}$, where $F = N \setminus \{v, u\}$, are not distinguishable as all monitor-to-monitor simple paths traversing v must go through F or u and vice versa. Therefore, such non-monitor must be unique.

b) Sufficiency: If each non-monitor has at least two monitors as neighbors, then $\mathcal{G}$ is σ-identifiable (hence also $(\sigma-1)$-identifiable) according to Proposition 13. If all but one non-monitor v have at least two monitors as neighbors, and v has one monitor $\widetilde{m}$ and all the other non-monitors (i.e., $N \setminus \{v\}$) as neighbors, then for any two failure sets F_1 and F_2 with $|F_i| \leq \sigma - 1$ $(i = 1, 2)$, there are two cases: (i) F_1 and F_2 differ on a non-monitor other than v; (ii) F_1 and F_2 only differ on v. In case (i), since the states of all non-monitors other than v can be independently determined, F_1 and F_2 are distinguishable. In case (ii), suppose that $F_1 = F \cup \{v\}$ and $F_2 = F$ for $F \subseteq N \setminus \{v\}$. Since $|F_1| \leq \sigma - 1$, $|F| \leq \sigma - 2$ and $\exists$ a non-monitor $w \in (N \setminus \{v\}) \setminus F$. We know that v is a neighbor of w (as v is a neighbor of all the other non-monitors) and w is a neighbor of a monitor m other than $\widetilde{m}$ (as it has at least two monitor neighbors). Thus, $\widetilde{m}vwm$ is a monitor-to-monitor simple path traversing v but not F, whose measurement can distinguish F_1 and F_2. Therefore, $\mathcal{G}$ is $(\sigma - 1)$-identifiable under CSP. □

Testing algorithm: Similar to the case of CAP, we can use the algorithm in [21] to compute the vertex-connectivities of the auxiliary graphs $\mathcal{G}^*$ and $\mathcal{G}_m$ ($\forall m \in M$), and then compare the results with $k+2$ and $k+1$ (or $k+1$ and k) to test the conditions in Corollary 12 for any given k. The overall complexity of the test is $O(\mu\sigma^{3.75})$.

4.3 Conditions under UP

Under UP, monitors have no control over the paths between monitors, and the set of measurement paths P is limited to the paths between monitors predetermined by the network's native routing protocol. In contrast to the previous cases (CAP, CSP), identifiability under UP can no longer be characterized in terms of topological properties. We can, nevertheless, establish conditions more explicit than the abstract conditions in Section 3. The idea is to examine how many non-monitors need to be removed to disconnect all measurement paths traversing a given non-monitor v. If the number is sufficiently large (greater than k), then we can still infer the state of v from some measurement path when a set of other non-monitors fail; if the number is too small (smaller than or equal to $k - 1$), then we will not be able to determine the state of v as the failures of all paths traversing v can already be explained by the failures of other non-monitors. This intuition leads to the following results.

In the sequel, $P_v \subseteq P$ denotes the set of measurement paths traversing a non-monitor v, and $\mathcal{S}_v := \{P_w : w \in N,\ w \neq v\}$ denotes the collection of path sets traversing non-monitors in $N \setminus \{v\}$. We use MSC(v) to denote the *minimum set cover* of P_v by $\mathcal{S}_v$, i.e., MSC(v) $:= |V'|$ for the minimum set $V' \subseteq N \setminus \{v\}$ such that $P_v \subseteq \bigcup_{w \in V'} P_w$. Note that covering is only feasible if v is not on any 2-hop measurement path (i.e., monitor-v-monitor), in which case we know $P_v \subseteq \bigcup_{w \in N, w \neq v} P_w$ and thus MSC(v) $\leq \sigma - 1$. If v is on a 2-hop path, then we define MSC(v) $:= \sigma$.

THEOREM 15 (k-IDENTIFIABILITY UNDER UP). *Network $\mathcal{G}$ is k-identifiable under UP with measurement paths P:*

a) if MSC(v) $> k$ for any non-monitor v;

b) only if MSC(v) $> k - 1$ for any non-monitor v.

PROOF. Suppose condition (a) holds. Then for any candidate failure set F with $|F| \leq k$ and any other non-monitor v ($v \notin F$), there must be a path in P_v that is not in $\bigcup_{w \in F} P_w$, i.e., traversing v but not F, which satisfies the abstract sufficient condition in Lemma 3.

Suppose condition (b) does not hold, i.e., there exists a non-monitor v and a set of non-monitors V' with $|V'| \leq k-1$ and $v \notin V'$, such that $P_v \subseteq \bigcup_{w \in V'} P_w$. Then given failures of all nodes in V', the state of v has no impact on observed path states and is thus unidentifiable, violating the abstract necessary condition in Lemma 4. □

Testing algorithm: The conditions in Theorem 15 provide an explicit way of testing the k-identifiability under UP, using tests of the form MSC(v) $> s$. Unfortunately, evaluating such a test, known as the decision problem of the *set covering problem*, is known to be NP-complete. Nevertheless, we can use approximation algorithms to compute bounds on MSC(v). The best-known algorithm with approximation guarantee is the *greedy algorithm*, which iteratively selects the set in $\mathcal{S}_v$ that contains the largest number of uncovered paths in P_v until all the paths in P_v are covered (assuming that v is not on any 2-hop path).

Let GSC(v) denote the number of sets selected by the greedy algorithm. This immediately provides an upper bound: MSC(v) $\leq$ GSC(v). Moreover, since the greedy algorithm has an approximation ratio of $\log(|P_v|) + 1$ [22], we can also bound MSC(v) from below: MSC(v) $\geq$ GSC(v)/($\log(|P_v|) + 1$). Applying these bounds to Theorem 15 yields a pair of relaxed conditions:

- $\mathcal{G}$ is k-identifiable under UP if $k < \lceil \min_{v \in N} \frac{\mathrm{GSC}(v)}{\log(|P_v|)+1} \rceil$;
- $\mathcal{G}$ is *not* k-identifiable under UP if $k > \min_{v \in N} \mathrm{GSC}(v)$.

These conditions can be tested by running the greedy algorithm for all non-monitors, each taking time $O(|P_v|^2\sigma) = O(|P|^2\sigma)$, and the overall test has a complexity of $O(|P|^2\sigma^2)$ (or $O(\mu^4\sigma^2)$ if there is a measurement path between each pair of monitors). However, we point out that it is unlikely that one can obtain stronger conditions based on Theorem 15 that are polynomial-time verifiable, as the greedy algorithm is known to give the best approximation for MSC(v).

4.4 Special Case: 1-identifiability

In practice, the most common failure event consists of the failure of a single node. Thus, a question of particular interest is whether $\mathcal{G}$ is 1-identifiable under a given placement of monitors and a given probing mechanism. Although our previous results (Corollaries 8 and 12, Theorem 15) provide an answer to the above question if the sufficient condition is satisfied or the necessary condition is violated for $k = 1$, the answer remains unknown if $\mathcal{G}$ satisfies the necessary condition but violates the sufficient condition. To address this case, we develop explicit methods to test the 1-identifiability.

4.4.1 Conditions for 1-identifiability

We start with a generic necessary and sufficient condition that applies to all probing mechanisms. Recall that P_v denotes the set of measurement paths traversing a non-monitor v. By Definition 1, we have the following claim:

CLAIM 16. *$\mathcal{G}$ is 1-identifiable if and only if:*
(1) $P_v \neq \emptyset$ for any $v \in N$, and
(2) $P_v \neq P_w$ for any $v, w \in N$ and $v \neq w$.

In Claim 16, the first condition guarantees that any nonempty failure set is distinguishable from the empty set (i.e., no failure), and the second condition guarantees that the observed path states can uniquely localize the failed node. An efficient test of these conditions, however, requires different strategies under different probing mechanisms.

4.4.2 Test under CAP

Under CAP, we know from Corollary 8 that for $\mathcal{G}$ to be 1-identifiable, the auxiliary graph $\mathcal{G}^*$ must be connected. Below, we will show that this condition is also sufficient.

LEMMA 17. *Network $\mathcal{G}$ is 1-identifiable under CAP if and only if $\mathcal{G}^*$ is connected, i.e., $\mathcal{G}$ has at least one monitor.*

PROOF. It suffices to show that $\mathcal{G}^*$ being connected is sufficient for the 1-identifiability of $\mathcal{G}$, which we prove by construction. First, it is easy to see that $\mathcal{G}^*$ is connected if and only if $\mathcal{G}$ has at least one monitor, denoted by m (recall that $\mathcal{G}$ is assumed to be connected). We build a spanning tree of $\mathcal{G}$ rooted at m, and sequentially probe each non-monitor in a breadth-first or depth-first order until (i) finding a first failure or (ii) completing probing without any failure. As each non-monitor is only probed after all its predecessors in the tree have been probed, we know in case (i) that the last probed non-monitor has failed, and in case (ii) that no node has failed. Therefore, $\mathcal{G}$ is 1-identifiable. □

Testing for 1-identifiability under CAP is therefore reduced to determining if the network has a monitor.

4.4.3 Test under CSP

Under CSP, we derive conditions that are equivalent to those in Section 4.4.1 but easier to test.

Condition (1) in Claim 16 requires that every non-monitor reside on a monitor-monitor simple path. While an exhaustive search for such a path will incur exponential complexity, we can test for its existence efficiently using the following observation. The idea is to construct an *extended graph* $\mathcal{G}' := \mathcal{G} + \{m'\} + \mathcal{L}(\{m'\}, M)$, i.e., by adding a virtual monitor m' and connecting it to all the monitors; see an illustration in Fig. 3. We claim that a non-monitor v is on a monitor-monitor simple path if and only if the size of the minimum vertex cut between v and m' in $\mathcal{G}'$ is at least two.

Indeed, by Menger's Theorem [10], the size of the *minimum vertex cut between v and m'* (minimum v-m' vertex cut) equals the maximum number of *vertex-independent*[5] simple paths between them. Therefore, a minimum v-m' vertex cut of size at least two implies the existence of two vertex-independent simple paths between v and m', illustrated as paths vm_2m' and vm_im' in Fig. 3. Truncating these two paths (vm_2m' and vm_im') at the first monitors (along the way from v to m') and concatenating the remaining two path segments gives a monitor-to-monitor simple path traversing v, i.e., m_2vm_i in Fig. 3. On the other hand, if $\exists$ a monitor-to-monitor simple path traversing v, then it can be split into two simple paths connecting v to two distinct monitors, which implies a minimum v-m' cut of at least two vertices in the extended graph $\mathcal{G}'$ as each of these two distinct monitors connects to m' by a virtual link.

Condition (2) in Claim 16 is violated if and only if there exist two non-monitors $v \neq w$ such that all monitor-to-monitor simple paths traversing v must traverse w (i.e., $P_v \subseteq P_w$) and vice versa. Since $P_v \subseteq P_w$ means that there is no monitor-to-monitor simple path traversing v in $\mathcal{G} - \{w\}$, by the above argument, we see that $P_v \subseteq P_w$ if and only if the size of the minimum vertex cut between v and m' in a new graph $\mathcal{G}'_w := \mathcal{G} - \{w\} + \{m'\} + \mathcal{L}(\{m'\}, M)$ is smaller than two. Therefore, condition (2) in Claim 16 is satisfied if and only if for every two distinct non-monitors v and w, either the minimum v-m' cut in $\mathcal{G}'_w$ or the minimum w-m' cut in $\mathcal{G}'_v$ has a size of at least two.

In summary, the necessary and sufficient condition for 1-identifiability under CSP is ($C_{v,w}$ denotes the minimum vertex cut between v and w):

i) $|C_{v,m'}| \geq 2$ in $\mathcal{G}'$ for each $v \in N$, and
ii) $|C_{v,m'}| \geq 2$ in $\mathcal{G}'_w$ or $|C_{w,m'}| \geq 2$ in $\mathcal{G}'_v$ for all $v, w \in N$ and $v \neq w$.

Since for a graph $\mathcal{G}$ of $|V|$ nodes and $|L|$ links, $|C_{v,w}| \geq 2$ can be tested in $O(|V| + |L|)$ time[6], the overall test takes $O(\sigma^2(|V| + |L|)) = O(\sigma^2(\mu + \sigma)^2)$ time.

4.4.4 Test under UP

Under UP, the total number of measurement paths $|P|$ is reduced to $O(\mu^2)$ (from exponentially many as in the case of CAP/CSP) since the measurable routes are predetermined. This reduction makes it feasible to directly test the generic conditions (1–2) in Claim 16 by testing condition (1) for each non-monitor and condition (2) for each pair of non-monitors. The overall complexity of this test is $O(\sigma^2\mu^2)$, dominated by the testing of condition (2) in Claim 16.

5. CHARACTERIZATION OF MAXIMUM IDENTIFIABILITY

Although it is challenging to determine the exact value of the maximum identifiability $\Omega(\mathcal{G})$ without a (polynomial-time verifiable) necessary *and* sufficient condition for testing k-identifiability (it remains open as to whether it is NP-hard to determine the value of $\Omega(\mathcal{G})$), we will show that the conditions derived in Section 4 have a nice structure that allows us to provide tight upper and lower bounds on $\Omega(\mathcal{G})$.

5.1 Maximum Identifiability under CAP

Observing that both the sufficient and the necessary conditions in Corollary 8 are imposed on the same property, i.e., vertex-connectivity of the auxiliary graph $\mathcal{G}^*$, we obtain a

[5]Two paths are vertex-independent if they have no common vertex except for the endpoints.

[6]For example, we can compute the biconnected component decomposition [23] and test if v and w belong to the same biconnected component.

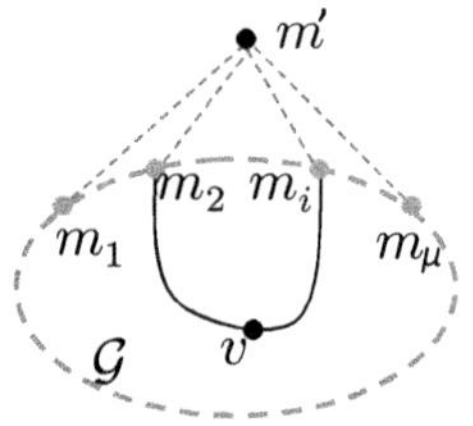

Figure 3: Extended graph $\mathcal{G}'$.

tight characterization of the maximum identifiability under CAP as follows. Here $\delta(\mathcal{G})$ is the vertex connectivity of $\mathcal{G}$ defined in Definition 6.

THEOREM 18 (MAXIMUM IDENTIFIABILITY UNDER CAP). *If $\delta(\mathcal{G}^*) \leq \sigma - 1$, the maximum identifiability of $\mathcal{G}$ under CAP, $\Omega^{CAP}(\mathcal{G})$, is bounded by $\delta(\mathcal{G}^*) - 1 \leq \Omega^{CAP}(\mathcal{G}) \leq \delta(\mathcal{G}^*)$.*

PROOF. Given $\delta(\mathcal{G}^*)$, we know that $\mathcal{G}^*$ is $\delta(\mathcal{G}^*)$-vertex-connected but not $(\delta(\mathcal{G}^*)+1)$-vertex-connected. By Corollary 8, this means that $\mathcal{G}$ is $(\delta(\mathcal{G}^*)-1)$-identifiable but not $(\delta(\mathcal{G}^*)+1)$-identifiable, which yields the above bounds on the maximum identifiability. Note that applying Corollary 8 requires $\delta(\mathcal{G}^*) \leq \sigma - 1$. □

Remark: In the special case of $\delta(\mathcal{G}^*) = \sigma$ (note that $\delta(\mathcal{G}^*) \leq \sigma$ by definition), $\mathcal{G}^*$ must be a clique, which means that all non-monitors must be neighbors of monitors. By Proposition 9, this implies that $\Omega^{\text{CAP}}(\mathcal{G}) = \sigma$.

Evaluation algorithm: Using the algorithm for determining network vertex connectivity in [21], we can compute $\delta(\mathcal{G}^*)$ and evaluate $\Omega^{\text{CAP}}(\mathcal{G})$ by the bounds in Theorem 18 in $O(\sigma^{3.75})$ time. The special case of $\Omega^{\text{CAP}}(\mathcal{G}) = \sigma$ can be checked separately in $O(\sigma)$ time using the condition in Proposition 9.

5.2 Maximum Identifiability under CSP

As in the case of CAP, we can leverage the analogy between the sufficient and the necessary conditions in Corollary 12 to bound the maximum identifiability under CSP from both sides. Specifically, let $\delta_{\min} := \min_{m: m\in M} \delta(\mathcal{G}_m)$ be the minimum vertex-connectivity for auxiliary graphs $\mathcal{G}_m$. Then the maximum identifiability is bounded as follows.

THEOREM 19 (MAXIMUM IDENTIFIABILITY UNDER CSP). *If $\min(\delta_{min}, \delta(\mathcal{G}^*) - 1) \leq \sigma - 2$, the maximum identifiability of $\mathcal{G}$ under CSP, $\Omega^{CSP}(\mathcal{G})$, is bounded by $\min(\delta_{min} - 1, \delta(\mathcal{G}^*) - 2) \leq \Omega^{CSP}(\mathcal{G}) \leq \min(\delta_{min}, \delta(\mathcal{G}^*) - 1)$.*

PROOF. By definition of vertex-connectivity, $\mathcal{G}^*$ is $\delta(\mathcal{G}^*)$-vertex-connected, and $\mathcal{G}_m$ is $\delta_{\min}$-vertex-connected for each monitor $m \in M$. This satisfies the condition in Corollary 12 (a) for $k = \min(\delta_{\min} - 1, \delta(\mathcal{G}^*) - 2)$, and thus $\Omega^{\text{CSP}}(\mathcal{G}) \geq \min(\delta_{\min} - 1, \delta(\mathcal{G}^*) - 2)$. Meanwhile, since $\mathcal{G}^*$ is not $(\delta(\mathcal{G}^*) + 1)$-vertex-connected, and $\mathcal{G}_m$ is not $(\delta_{\min} + 1)$-vertex-connected for some $m \in M$, the condition in Corollary 12 (b) is violated for $k = \min(\delta_{\min} + 1, \delta(\mathcal{G}^*))$ (which requires $\min(\delta_{\min} + 1, \delta(\mathcal{G}^*)) \leq \sigma - 1$). Thus, $\Omega^{\text{CSP}}(\mathcal{G}) \leq \min(\delta_{\min}, \delta(\mathcal{G}^*) - 1)$. □

Remark: Because the set of links in $\mathcal{G}_m$ is a subset of those in $\mathcal{G}^*$ while the nodes are the same, we always have $\delta_{\min} \leq \delta(\mathcal{G}^*)$. Therefore, the above bounds simplify to:

- $\delta_{\min} - 2 \leq \Omega^{\text{CSP}}(\mathcal{G}) \leq \delta_{\min} - 1$ if $\delta_{\min} = \delta(\mathcal{G}^*)$;
- $\delta_{\min} - 1 \leq \Omega^{\text{CSP}}(\mathcal{G}) \leq \delta_{\min}$ if $\delta_{\min} < \delta(\mathcal{G}^*)$.

In particular, if $\delta(\mathcal{G}^*) = 1$ (i.e., there is a cut-vertex in $\mathcal{G}^*$), then $\Omega^{\text{CSP}}(\mathcal{G}) = 0$, i.e., even single-node failures cannot always be localized.

The only cases when $\min(\delta_{\min}, \delta(\mathcal{G}^*) - 1) \leq \sigma - 2$ is violated are: (i) $\delta_{\min} = \delta(\mathcal{G}^*) = \sigma$, or (ii) $\delta_{\min} = \sigma - 1$ and $\delta(\mathcal{G}^*) = \sigma$. In case (i), $\mathcal{G}_m$ is a clique for all $m \in M$, i.e., each non-monitor still has a monitor as a neighbor after removing m; by Proposition 13, this implies that $\Omega^{\text{CSP}}(\mathcal{G}) = \sigma$. In case (ii), Corollary 12 (a) can still be applied to show that $\Omega^{\text{CSP}}(\mathcal{G}) \geq \sigma - 2$, and one can verify that the condition in Proposition 13 is violated, which implies that $\Omega^{\text{CSP}}(\mathcal{G}) \leq \sigma - 1$. In fact, we can leverage Proposition 14 to uniquely determine $\Omega^{\text{CSP}}(\mathcal{G})$ in this case. If condition (ii) in Proposition 14 is satisfied, then $\Omega^{\text{CSP}}(\mathcal{G}) = \sigma - 1$; otherwise, $\Omega^{\text{CSP}}(\mathcal{G}) = \sigma - 2$.

Evaluation algorithm: Evaluating $\Omega^{\text{CSP}}(\mathcal{G})$ by Theorem 19 involves computing the vertex-connectivities of the auxiliary graphs $\mathcal{G}^*$ and $\mathcal{G}_m$ ($\forall m \in M$) using the algorithm for determining network vertex connectivity in [21], which altogether takes $O(\mu\sigma^{3.75})$ time.

5.3 Maximum Identifiability under UP

Let $\Delta := \min_{v\in N} \text{MSC}(v)$ be the minimum set cover over all non-monitors. The conditions in Theorem 15 imply the following bounds on the maximum identifiability under UP.

THEOREM 20 (MAXIMUM IDENTIFIABILITY UNDER UP). *The maximum identifiability of $\mathcal{G}$ under UP, $\Omega^{UP}(\mathcal{G})$, with measurement paths P is bounded by $\Delta - 1 \leq \Omega^{UP}(\mathcal{G}) \leq \Delta$.*

PROOF. Since $\text{MSC}(v) > \Delta - 1$ for all $v \in N$, $\mathcal{G}$ is $(\Delta - 1)$-identifiable by Theorem 15 (a). Meanwhile, since there exists a node $v \in N$ with $\text{MSC}(v) = \Delta$, $\mathcal{G}$ is not $(\Delta + 1)$-identifiable by Theorem 15 (b). Together, they imply the bounds on $\Omega^{\text{UP}}(\mathcal{G})$. □

Remark: Recall that $\Delta \leq \sigma$ by definition. In the special case of $\Delta = \sigma$, we know that all non-monitors are on 2-hop measurement paths, whose states can be determined independently. Thus, $\Omega^{\text{UP}}(\mathcal{G}) = \sigma$ in this case.

Evaluation algorithm: The original bounds in Theorem 20 are hard to evaluate due to the NP-hardness of computing $\text{MSC}(\cdot)$. As in Section 4.3, we resort to the greedy algorithm, which implies the following relaxed bounds:

$$\left\lceil \min_{v\in N} \frac{\text{GSC}(v)}{\log(|P_v|) + 1} \right\rceil - 1 \leq \Omega^{\text{UP}}(\mathcal{G}) \leq \min_{v\in N} \text{GSC}(v). \quad (5)$$

Evaluating these bounds involves invoking the greedy algorithm for each non-monitor, with an overall complexity of $O(|P|^2\sigma^2)$ (or $O(\mu^4\sigma^2)$ if all monitors can probe each other).

6. IMPACT OF PROBING MECHANISM

Given the above results, we are now ready to quantify the impact of the probing mechanism on node failure localization. We aim to quantify this impact by evaluating, using our bounds on the maximum identifiability, the number of simultaneous failures we can uniquely localize in a given network with a given monitor placement under each of the three probing mechanisms (CAP, CSP, UP). In this study, we assume (hop count-based) shortest path routing as the default routing protocol under UP, i.e., the measurement paths under UP are the shortest paths between monitors, with ties broken arbitrarily.

6.1 Topologies for Evaluation

We evaluate the proposed metrics on both synthetic and real network topologies detailed as follows.

6.1.1 Synthetic Topologies

We first consider synthetic topologies generated according to four widely used random graph models: Erdös-Rényi (ER) graphs, Random Geometric (RG) graphs, Barabási-Albert (BA) graphs, and Random Power Law (RPL) graphs. We randomly generate graph realizations of each model[7], with each realization containing 20 nodes (i.e., $|V| = 20$). The generated graphs are then used to evaluate the impact of probing mechanisms. We now describe the models and present the corresponding results separately.

Erdös-Rényi (ER) graph: The ER graph [24] is generated by independently connecting each pair of nodes by a link with a fixed probability p. The result is a purely random topology where all graphs with an equal number of links are equally likely to be selected (note that the number of nodes is a predetermined parameter).

Random Geometric (RG) graph: The RG graph [25] is frequently used to model the topology of wireless ad hoc networks. It generates a random graph by first randomly distributing nodes in a unit square, and then connecting each pair of nodes by a link if their distance is no larger than a threshold d_c, which denotes the node communication range. The resulting topology contains well-connected sub-graphs in densely populated areas and poorly-connected sub-graphs in sparsely populated areas.

Barabási-Albert (BA) graphs: The BA model [26] provides a random power-law graph generated by the following preferential attachment mechanism. We begin with a small connected graph $\mathcal{G}_0 := (\{v_1, v_2, v_3, v_4\}, \{v_1v_2, v_1v_3, v_1v_4\})$ and add nodes sequentially. For each new node v, we connect v to $n_{\min}$ existing nodes, where $n_{\min}$ specifies (a lower bound on) the minimum node degree, such that the probability of connecting the new node to existing node w is proportional to the degree of w. If the number of existing nodes is smaller than $n_{\min}$, then v connects to all the existing nodes. The BA graph has been used to model many naturally occurring networks, e.g., citation networks, and social networks.

Random Power Law (RPL) graphs: The BA model introduces an artifact that all node degrees are lower bounded by $n_{\min}$. Alternatively, the RPL graph [27] provides another way of generating power-law graphs by directly specifying a sequence of expected node degrees $(d_1, ..., d_{|V|})$ according to the power law, i.e., $d_i = i^{\alpha}$ ($\alpha > 0$). The generation of a RPL graph is similar to that of an ER graph, except that instead of connecting each pair of nodes with the same probability, nodes i and j in a RPL graph are connected by a link with probability $p_{ij} = d_i d_j / \sum_{k=1}^{|V|} d_k$.

Remark: Our motivation for performing evaluations on random topologies is that they allow comprehensive evaluation without artifacts of specific network deployments, which are common in real topologies. Moreover, the selected graph models can provide insights on how the topological property affects node failure localization.

6.1.2 Real Topologies

For real topologies, we use the *Autonomous System* (AS) topologies collected by the Rocketfuel [28] and the CAIDA [29] projects, which represents IP-level connections between backbone/gateway routers of several ASes from major *Internet Service Providers (ISPs)* around the globe.

[7]All realizations are guaranteed to be connected, as we discard disconnected realizations in the generation process.

Algorithm 1: Enhanced Random Monitor Placement (ERMP)

input : Network topology $\mathcal{G}$, all possible measurement paths Q under UP, number of monitors μ
output: Set of monitors M
1 $M \leftarrow$ {all degree-1 nodes} $\cup$ {one in every two neighboring degree-2 nodes};
2 **if** $M = \emptyset$ **then**
3 | $M \leftarrow$ {endpoints of the longest path in Q};
4 **end**
5 $U \leftarrow V \setminus (\bigcup_{m,m' \in M} V_{mm'})$; // uncovered nodes
6 **while** $U \neq \emptyset$ **do**
7 | $m = \arg\max_{w \in V \setminus M} |U \cap \mathcal{V}(w, M)|$;
8 | $U \leftarrow U \setminus \mathcal{V}(m, M)$;
9 | $M \leftarrow M \cup \{m\}$;
10 **end**
11 **if** $|M| < \mu$ **then**
12 | $M \leftarrow M \cup \{\mu - |M|$ nodes randomly selected from $V \setminus M\}$
13 **end**

6.2 Placement of Monitors

Since the maximum identifiability Ω depends on the given placement of monitors, we want to randomize this given monitor placement for a comprehensive evaluation. A purely random placement, however, is likely to lead to trivial Ω, since $\Omega = 0$ whenever there is a non-monitor not traversed by any measurement path. Specifically, Ω^{CSP} and Ω^{UP} will be zero if any degree-1 node or any two neighboring degree-2 nodes are non-monitors; moreover, Ω^{UP} will also be zero if not all non-monitors lie on shortest paths between monitors. To avoid these trivial cases, we adopt an *Enhanced Random Monitor Placement (ERMP)* strategy, which consists of the following two steps.

Step (i): place monitors to avoid the obvious cases of zero-maximum identifiability mentioned above;

Step (ii): place additional monitors, if available, randomly.

See Algorithm 1 for the pseudo code of ERMP. It is assumed that the total number of monitors is sufficient for step (i) above. Note that ERMP is only used for evaluating Ω, while our bounds established in Section 5 are valid under arbitrary monitor placements, i.e., the expression of our bounds does not depend on the choice of monitor placement algorithm or the fraction of monitors ($\mu/|V|$). The optimization of monitor placement to achieve a desired level of identifiability will be pursued separately in a future work.

Specifically, it suffices to consider the most restrictive probing mechanism UP. Given the set of all *potentially* measurement paths Q under UP (here it is the set of all-pair shortest paths), let V_{vw} denote the set of nodes covered by the path between nodes v and w (inclusive). Given a set of existing monitors $M \subseteq V$ and a candidate monitor $w \in V \setminus M$, define $\mathcal{V}(w, M) := \bigcup_{m \in M} V_{wm}$ as the set of nodes covered by the paths between w and the existing monitors. We perform step (i) above by a greedy heuristic. We first jump-start the monitor placement with an initial set of monitors required to achieve a non-zero value for Ω^{CSP} (line 1); if this initial set is empty, we select the two monitors covering the maximum number of nodes (line 3). We then enlarge this set by selecting a new monitor in each iteration whose paths to the existing monitors cover the maximum number of *uncovered* nodes (line 7), until all nodes are covered by at least one

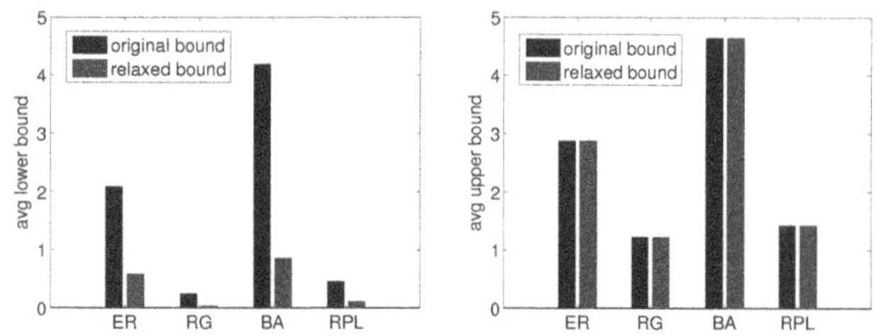

(a) Average lower bound (b) Average upper bound

Figure 4: Original and relaxed bounds on the maximum identifiability Ω^{UP} under UP for sparsely-connected random topologies ($|V| = 20$, $\mu = 10$, $\mathbb{E}[|L|] = 51$, 100 graph instances per model).

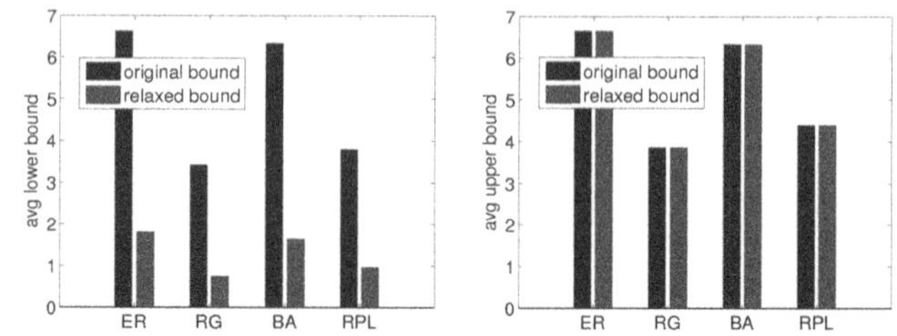

(a) Average lower bound (b) Average upper bound

Figure 5: Original and relaxed bounds on the maximum identifiability Ω^{UP} under UP for densely-connected random topologies ($|V| = 20$, $\mu = 10$, $\mathbb{E}[|L|] = 99$, 100 graph instances per model).

measurement path under UP (line 10). Finally, extra monitors, if any, are placed randomly among the remaining nodes.

6.3 Impact on Identifiability

6.3.1 *Tightness of Bounds*

To measure the impact of probing on the maximum identifiability Ω, we need tight bounds on Ω under all probing mechanisms. Although we have achieved this theoretically by deriving upper and lower bounds that differ by at most one (Theorems 18, 19, 20), only the bounds under CAP and CSP can be evaluated efficiently, and the bounds under UP have to be relaxed by a logarithmic factor to be computable in polynomial time (see (5)). The first question is therefore how tight the relaxed bounds are.

To this end, we compare the original bounds (Theorem 20) and the relaxed bounds (5) on a variety of topologies synthetically generated from the models in Section 6.1.1 in two scenarios, i.e., sparsely-connected and densely-connected topologies. To make the models comparable in each scenario, we have tuned each model to generate graphs with the same number of nodes and (average) number of links. We evaluate both bounds on multiple graph instances per model, each with a fixed number of monitors placed by ERMP, and present the average lower/upper bounds in Fig. 4 and Fig. 5. As expected, in both scenarios, the relaxed lower bounds are quite loose due to the logarithmic factor, but the relaxed upper bounds coincide with the original bounds for all graph instances. This indicates that although the relaxed upper bound $\min_{v\in N} \text{GSC}(v)$ can be a logarithmic-factor larger than the original upper bound Δ in the worst case, this worst case rarely occurs, and we can approximate Δ by $\min_{v\in N} \text{GSC}(v)$ to apply Theorem 20. This provides a tight characterization of Ω^{UP} for large networks, where computing the original bounds is infeasible.

6.3.2 *Comparison of Probing Mechanisms*

We are now ready to compare[8] Ω^{CAP}, Ω^{CSP}, and Ω^{UP}.

Comparison Using Random Topologies: Similar to Section 6.3.1, Ω^{CAP}, Ω^{CSP}, and Ω^{UP} are compared on both sparsely-connected and densely-connected topologies generated from the four random graph models. Under each scenario, we generate multiple graph instances from each of the four models and sequentially place monitors in each instance using ERMP such that the set of monitors grows strictly monotonically as the number of monitors increases.

[8]In the case of $0 \le \Omega \le 1$, we use the tests in Section 4.4 to uniquely determine the value of Ω.

We then evaluate our bounds on the maximum identifiability Ω^{CAP}, Ω^{CSP}, and Ω^{UP} for each graph instance under each monitor placement.

The average results in sparsely-connected networks are shown in Fig. 6. The results show large differences in the maximum identifiabilities of the different probing mechanisms: while UP can barely localize a single node failure even if half of the nodes are monitors, CAP can provide unique localization even if up to 90% of the non-monitors simultaneously fail. We also observe that the maximum identifiability is larger for ER graphs and smaller for BA graphs. Intuitively, this is because while nodes in ER graphs have uniform connectivity, those in BA graphs have highly variable connectivity, which creates poorly connected subgraphs whose node failures are more difficult to localize. Note that Ω eventually decreases as the number of monitors μ increases, as the maximum identifiability is always upper bounded by the total number of non-monitors ($\sigma = |V| - \mu$); we have verified that the *normalized maximum identifiability* Ω/σ increases monotonically with μ.

The average results for densely-connected networks are reported in Fig. 7. In comparison to Fig. 6, both CAP and CSP achieve greater maximum identifiability in densely-connected networks; in particular, CAP uniquely localizes arbitrary node failures, i.e., $\Omega^{\text{CAP}} = \sigma$, for all the graph models when $\mu/|V| \ge 45\%$. Meanwhile, as Fig. 7 shows, increasing the number of links (and hence the density of the graphs) hardly affects the maximum identifiability under UP. Intuitively, this is because densely-connected graphs yield more measurement paths between each pair of monitors under controllable probing mechanisms (CAP and CSP), thus enabling them to identify more simultaneous failures. In contrast, there is only one measurement path (the shortest path) between each pair of monitors under UP, independent of the number of links in the network. Therefore, UP exhibits similar maximum identifiability for both sparsely-connected and densely-connected topologies.

Comparison Using AS Topologies: For AS topologies, we first compute the minimum number of monitors required by step (i) of ERMP, denoted by μ_c, and then vary the fraction of monitors $\mu/|V|$ such that $\mu \ge \mu_c$ for all the topologies. To facilitate comparison, we use the same range of values for $\mu/|V|$ for each dataset. For each topology, we independently select 20 sets of monitors using ERMP (only $\mu - \mu_c$ monitors in each set are randomly placed), under which Ω^{CAP}, Ω^{CSP}, and Ω^{UP} are evaluated.

Fig. 8 shows bounds on the maximum identifiability averaged over different monitor placements for the Rocketfuel AS topologies. In the selected Rocketfuel topologies (Fig. 8),

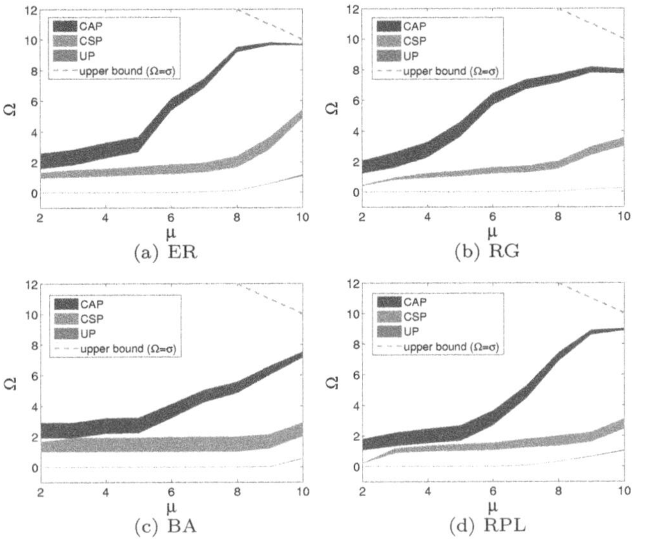

(a) ER (b) RG

(c) BA (d) RPL

Figure 6: Bounds on the maximum identifiability Ω under CAP, CSP, and UP for sparsely-connected random topologies ($|V| = 20$, $\mu = 2, \ldots, 10$, $\mathbb{E}[|L|] = 51$, 50 graph instances per model).

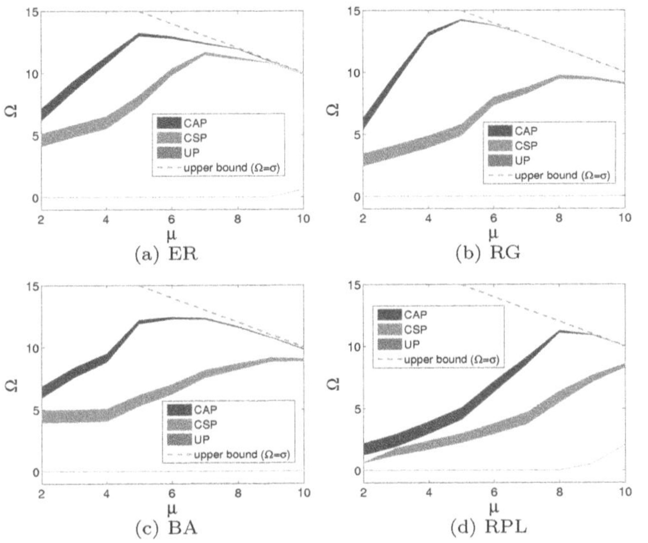

(a) ER (b) RG

(c) BA (d) RPL

Figure 7: Bounds on the maximum identifiability Ω under CAP, CSP, and UP for densely-connected random topologies ($|V| = 20$, $\mu = 2, \ldots, 10$, $\mathbb{E}[|L|] = 99$, 50 graph instances per model).

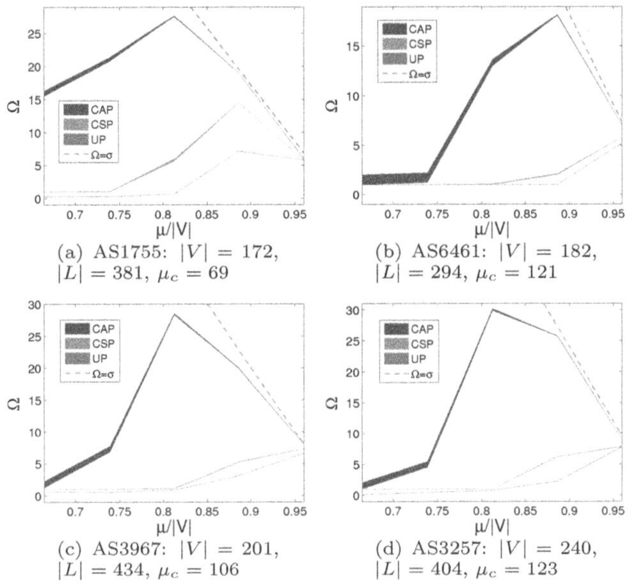

(a) AS1755: $|V| = 172$, $|L| = 381$, $\mu_c = 69$

(b) AS6461: $|V| = 182$, $|L| = 294$, $\mu_c = 121$

(c) AS3967: $|V| = 201$, $|L| = 434$, $\mu_c = 106$

(d) AS3257: $|V| = 240$, $|L| = 404$, $\mu_c = 123$

Figure 8: Bounds on maximum Identifiability for Rocketfuel AS Topologies.

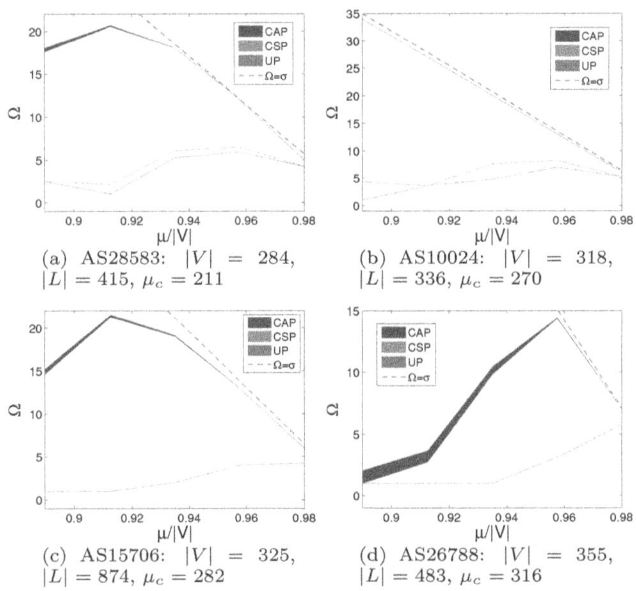

(a) AS28583: $|V| = 284$, $|L| = 415$, $\mu_c = 211$

(b) AS10024: $|V| = 318$, $|L| = 336$, $\mu_c = 270$

(c) AS15706: $|V| = 325$, $|L| = 874$, $\mu_c = 282$

(d) AS26788: $|V| = 355$, $|L| = 483$, $\mu_c = 316$

Figure 9: Bounds on maximum Identifiability for CAIDA AS Topologies.

AS6461 has the maximum ratio $\mu_c/|V|$ of approximately 0.665. Thus, we start the simulation from $\mu/|V| = 0.665$. Similar to the case of random topologies, the results show clear differences between the maximum identifiability under different probing mechanisms, especially between Ω^{CAP} and the other two. For most of the networks, UP and CSP only guarantee unique localization of single-node failures, while CAP can handle multi-node failures for all the networks. We also observe a much larger gap between Ω^{CAP} and Ω^{CSP} than the gap between Ω^{CSP} and Ω^{UP}, as the AS topologies are relatively sparse, leaving monitors little flexibility in selecting probing paths under cycle-free constraints (i.e., CSP). Across the networks, we observe that the ordering of the normalized maximum identifiability Ω/σ is roughly consistent with the minimum monitor fraction of monitors $\mu_c/|V|$ required by ERMP: the larger $\mu_c/|V|$, the smaller Ω/σ.

Because ISP topologies have evolved since the Rocketfuel project, we repeat the above evaluation on a recent dataset obtained by the CAIDA project; see results in Fig. 9. Compared with the Rocketfuel ASes, we observe that the CAIDA ASes require more monitors (computed by step (i) of ERMP), e.g., the largest fraction $\mu_c/|V|$ is 0.89 for AS26788 while the smallest is 0.74 for AS28583. Hence, we start from $\mu/|V| = 0.89$ in Fig. 9. Similar to Fig. 8, we again observe a huge gap between Ω^{CAP} and the other two, and Ω/σ is inversely related to $\mu_c/|V|$. In addition, Fig. 9 also shows that under the minimum monitor placement, even the most flexible probing mechanism, CAP, can only localize failures of a couple of nodes. Our results suggest that without control of probing paths (i.e., UP), randomly placed monitors are unlikely to guarantee unique failure localization; therefore, optimized monitor placement is needed to handle simultaneous failures of multiple nodes. Moreover, these results also imply that in the absence of deploying monitors at the vast majority of nodes, implementing controllable probing is an effective way to guarantee unique failure localization.

7. CONCLUSION

We have studied the fundamental capability of a network to localize failed nodes from the health condition of end-to-end paths between monitors. We proposed a novel measure, called the maximum identifiability, to quantify this capability as the maximum number of simultaneous failures that can be uniquely localized. We studied this measure in detail for three representative families of probing mechanisms that offer different tradeoffs between the controllability of probes and the cost of implementation. For each family of probing mechanisms, we established necessary/sufficient conditions for unique failure localization based on the network topology, the placement of monitors, the constraints on measurement paths, and the maximum number of simultaneous failures. We further showed that these conditions lead to tight upper/lower bounds on the maximum identifiability that differ by at most one. We showed that both the conditions and the bounds can be evaluated efficiently using polynomial-time algorithms. Our evaluations on random and real network topologies reveal that although incurring a higher implementation cost, giving the monitors more control over the routing of probes can significantly improve their capability to localize simultaneous failures.

8. REFERENCES

[1] R. R. Kompella, J. Yates, A. G. Greenberg, and A. C. Snoeren, "Detection and localization of network black holes," in *IEEE INFOCOM*, 2007.

[2] M. Coates, A. O. Hero, R. Nowak, and B. Yu, "Internet tomography," *IEEE Signal Processing Magazine*, vol. 19, pp. 47–65, 2002.

[3] D. Ghita, C. Karakus, K. Argyraki, and P. Thiran, "Shifting network tomography toward a practical goal," in *ACM CoNEXT*, 2011.

[4] Y. Bejerano and R. Rastogi, "Robust monitoring of link delays and faults in IP networks," in *IEEE INFOCOM*, 2003.

[5] J. D. Horton and A. López-Ortiz, "On the number of distributed measurement points for network tomography," in *ACM IMC*, 2003.

[6] S. Zarifzadeh, M. Gowdagere, and C. Dovrolis, "Range tomography: Combining the practicality of boolean tomography with the resolution of analog tomography," in *ACM IMC*, 2012.

[7] A. Markopoulou, G. Iannaccone, S. Bhattacharyya, C.-N. Chuah, and C. Diot, "Characterization of failures in an IP backbone," in *IEEE INFOCOM*, 2004.

[8] N. Duffield, "Simple network performance tomography," in *ACM IMC*, 2003.

[9] ——, "Network tomography of binary network performance characteristics," *IEEE Transactions on Information Theory*, vol. 52, pp. 5373–5388, 2006.

[10] R. Diestel, *Graph theory.* Springer-Verlag Heidelberg, New York, 2005.

[11] H. Zeng, P. Kazemian, G. Varghese, and N. McKeown, "Automatic test packet generation," in *ACM CoNEXT*, 2012.

[12] H. Nguyen and P. Thiran, "The boolean solution to the congested IP link location problem: Theory and practice," in *IEEE INFOCOM*, 2007.

[13] A. Dhamdhere, R. Teixeira, C. Dovrolis, and C. Diot, "Netdiagnoser: Troubleshooting network unreachabilities using end-to-end probes and routing data," in *ACM CoNEXT*, 2007.

[14] Y. Huang, N. Feamster, and R. Teixeira, "Practical issues with using network tomography for fault diagnosis," *ACM SIGCOMM Computer Communication Review*, vol. 38, pp. 53–58, 2008.

[15] H. X. Nguyen and P. Thiran, "Active measurement for multiple link failures diagnosis in IP networks," in *Passive and Active Measurement*, 2004.

[16] S. Ahuja, S. Ramasubramanian, and M. Krunz, "SRLG failure localization in all-optical networks using monitoring cycles and paths," in *IEEE INFOCOM*, 2008.

[17] [Online]. Available: http://www.ietf.org/rfc/rfc0791.txt

[18] "Open networking foundation." [Online]. Available: http://www.opennetworkingfoundation.org

[19] R. Dorfman, "The detection of defective members of large populations," *The Annals of Mathematical Statistics*, vol. 14, 1943.

[20] H.-G. Yeh, "d-Disjunct matrices: Bounds and Lovasz local lemma," *Discrete Math*, vol. 253, pp. 97–107, 2002.

[21] H. Gabow, "Using expander graphs to find vertex connectivity," *Journal of the ACM*, vol. 53, no. 5, pp. 800–844, September 2006.

[22] V. Chvatal, "A greedy heuristic for the set-covering problem," *Mathematics of Operations Research*, vol. 4, pp. 233–235, 1979.

[23] R. Tarjan, "Depth-first search and linear graph algorithms," *SIAM Journal on Computing*, vol. 1, pp. 146–160, 1972.

[24] P. Erdös and A. Rényi, "On the evolution of random graphs," *Publications of the Mathematical Institute of the Hungarian Academy of Sciences*, vol. 5, pp. 17–61, 1960.

[25] P. Gupta and P. Kumar, "Critical power for asymptotic connectivity in wireless networks," *Stochastic Analysis, Control, Optimization and Applications*, pp. 547–566, 1999.

[26] R. Albert and A.-L. Barabási, "Statistical mechanics of complex networks," *Reviews of Modern Physics*, vol. 74, pp. 47–97, Jan. 2002.

[27] F. Chung and L. Lu, *Complex Graphs and Networks.* American Mathematical Society, 2006.

[28] "Rocketfuel: An ISP topology mapping engine," University of Washington, 2002. [Online]. Available: http://www.cs.washington.edu/research/networking/rocketfuel/

[29] "Macroscopic Internet Topology Data Kit (ITDK)," The Cooperative Association for Internet Data Analysis (CAIDA), April 2013. [Online]. Available: http://www.caida.org/data/active/internet-topology-data-kit/

Efficient Large Flow Detection over Arbitrary Windows: An Algorithm Exact Outside An Ambiguity Region

Hao Wu
University of Illinois at Urbana-Champaign

Hsu-Chun Hsiao
Carnegie Mellon University
National Taiwan University

Yih-Chun Hu
University of Illinois at Urbana-Champaign

ABSTRACT

Many networking and security applications can benefit from *exact* detection of large flows over *arbitrary windows* (i.e. any possible time window). Existing large flow detectors that only check the average throughput over certain time period cannot detect bursty flows and are therefore easily fooled by attackers. However, no scalable approaches provide exact classification in one pass. To address this challenge, we consider a new model of exactness outside an *ambiguity region*, which is defined to be a range of bandwidths below a high-bandwidth threshold and above a low-bandwidth threshold. Given this new model, we propose a deterministic algorithm, EARDET, that detects *all* large flows (including bursty flows) and avoids false accusation against *any* small flows, regardless of the input traffic distribution. EARDET monitors flows over arbitrary time windows and is built on a frequent items finding algorithm based on average frequency. Despite its strong properties, EARDET has low storage overhead regardless of input traffic and is surprisingly scalable because it focuses on accurate classification of large flows and small flows only. Our evaluations confirm that existing approaches suffer from high error rates (e.g., misclassifying 1% of small flows as large flows) in the presence of large flows and bursty flows, whereas EARDET can accurately detect both at gigabit line rate using a small amount of memory that fits into on-chip SRAM.

Categories and Subject Descriptors

C.2.3 [**Computer-Communication Networks**]: Network Operations—*Network monitoring*; C.2.0 [**Computer-Communication Networks**]: General—*Security and protection*

Keywords

Large Flow Detection; Flow Classification; Ambiguity Region; Arbitrary Windows

IMC'14, November 5–7, 2014, Vancouver, BC, Canada.

ACM 978-1-4503-3213-2/14/11 ...$15.00.
http://dx.doi.org/10.1145/2663716.2663724.

1. INTRODUCTION

Being able to identify large flows[1] over any possible time window (referred to as the *arbitrary window model*) is of great importance for a wide variety of networking and security applications such as traffic engineering, accounting, anomaly detection, and Denial-of-Service (DoS) defense. The arbitrary window model monitors time windows on all time-scales, starting at each instant in time and ending at the current time, and can thus detect bursty flows and outperform models that are based on fixed-length windows. Given the high traffic volumes in today's Internet, no scalable approaches provide exact classification in one pass.

Thus, we consider a novel model of exactness outside a small *ambiguity region*, which contains flows that use bandwidth between two configurable thresholds. Our model classifies flows as either large, medium, or small. A flow is defined to be a large flow if there exists a time window in which the bandwidth of the flow exceeds the high-bandwidth threshold. A small flow is defined to be a flow whose volume is consistently lower than a low-bandwidth threshold function over all arbitrary window. The rest are defined as medium flows, or the flows in the ambiguity region. Exactness outside an ambiguity region guarantees perfect detection of large flows (including bursty flows) and no false accusation against any small flows. This model is reasonable because it limits the damage caused by large flows and allows existing techniques to handle the medium flows statistically. Prior work [17] [16] adopts a similar concept, yet they can only provide probabilistic bounds outside a region. The ambiguity region between the high-bandwidth and low-bandwidth thresholds allows us to trade the level of exactness for scalability, so that we can maintain state small enough to fit into limited on-chip memory for link-speed update.

The new models of exactness and arbitrary window benefit many applications. For example:

- *Detecting various DoS flows*: Denial-of-Service (DoS) attacks use a combination of large attack flows and bursty attack flows. Flows that are only bursty are hard to catch due to their low average traffic bandwidth. However, using the arbitrary window model, a detector can instantly detect DoS attempts that use bursty flows [25].
- *Bandwidth guarantees*: To enforce bandwidth allocation, schemes such as IntServ make impractical

[1]Large flows are flows that consume more than a threshold amount of bandwidth. They are also called elephant flows in the literature.

assumptions that either every router keeps per-flow state [33] or first-hop routers are trusted to regulate traffic on a per-flow basis [36] on behalf of intermediate routers [34]. Although a scalable and robust approach was proposed [28], it causes collateral damage due to the detection delay. Moreover, it cannot catch bursty flows. Our efficient detector built upon these two new models can help enforce bandwidth limits on flows because it enables fast detection with no false accusation on the legitimate small flows and no missed detection on large flows including bursty flows.

To the best of our knowledge, none of the existing algorithms provide exactness outside an ambiguity region under the arbitrary window model. Prior algorithms monitoring average throughput (e.g., algorithms based on fixed window and sliding window models) cannot detect bursty attacks. For example, in a large-flow detection system that resets state and starts a new measurement interval periodically [17], a large bursty flow can bypass detection by staying lower than the threshold of throughput across this whole interval, or even by deliberately spreading its burst across two consecutive intervals. Although randomization of measurement intervals can mitigate the problem of a burst spread across a measurement interval, randomized algorithms may be unable to provide strong deterministic guarantees.

In addition to lacking exactness and the arbitrary window model, the storage overhead of existing algorithms may grow unboundedly with the size of the input traffic in the presence of malicious inputs. For example, an adversary can perturb his traffic patterns (e.g., by varying the size and timing of packets) so as to cause algorithmic complexity attacks [11] because many algorithms bound their storage and computational overhead by assuming that the flow sizes follow a certain distribution, such as Zipfian.

To identify large flows over arbitrary windows with low storage overhead, we explore deterministic algorithms with a new model of exactness considering a small ambiguity region. We propose EARDet (**E**xact-Outside-**A**mbiguity-**R**egion **Det**ector), a simple, efficient, and no-per-flow-state large-flow detector which is exact outside an ambiguity region regardless of the input traffic distribution. Built on the Misra-Gries algorithm (a two-pass frequent items finding algorithm based on average frequency) [31], EARDet is a one-pass streaming algorithm with simple operations: it only keeps a small array of counters which are increased or decreased as each new packet arrives. A flow is identified as a large flow if its associated counter exceeds a threshold.

Surprisingly, despite EARDet's strong guarantees, we show in our analysis that EARDet requires extremely small amounts of memory that fit into on-chip SRAM for line-speed packet processing. We discuss implementation details to further demonstrate EARDet's efficiency. EARDet is highly scalable because it focuses on the accurate classification of large and small flows; unlike prior approaches, it does not aim to estimate flow volumes or identify the medium flows. In addition to our theoretical analysis, we also evaluate EARDet using extensive simulations based on real traffic traces. We demonstrate that existing approaches suffer from high error rates under DoS attacks, whereas EARDet can effectively detect large flows in the face of both flooding and burst DoS attacks [22,25].

Our main contributions are as follows.

- We propose a deterministic streaming algorithm that is exact outside an ambiguity region regardless of the input traffic. Two novel settings distinguish EARDet from previous work: it monitors flows over arbitrary windows, and it supports exact detection outside an ambiguity region.
- We rigorously prove the two guarantees—catching all large flows and preventing false accusation on any small flows—without making assumptions about the flow size distribution.
- Our numerical analysis shows that EARDet can operate at 40 Gbps high-speed links using only hundreds of bytes of on-chip SRAM, which is substantially smaller than the memory consumption in many existing systems. We also provide guidelines on how to configure EARDet to satisfy application-specific requirements.
- We compare EARDet with two closely related proposals [16, 17] via comparative analysis and extensive simulations based on real and synthetic traffic traces. The results confirm that these two are vulnerable to attack flows that manipulate the input traffic, while EARDet consistently catches all large flows without misclassifying small flows.

2. PROBLEM DEFINITION

Our goal is to design an efficient arbitrary-window-based algorithm which is exact outside an ambiguity region. In this section, we present the system model, formulate the large flow problem over arbitrary windows, and summarize our design goals.

2.1 System Model

Flow identifiers. Generally, packets are classified into flows based on the *flow identifiers* (or flow IDs) derived from the packet header fields.[2] Because our approach to large-flow detection is generic, we make no assumption on the definition of flow IDs. As in prior traffic monitoring work, we assume flow IDs are unforgeable, which is achievable by ingress filtering [19] and source authentication [4,24,27,32].

Packet streams. Let $\mathcal{X}$ be the packet space. We consider a packet stream $X = \langle x_1, \cdots, x_k \rangle$ coming through a link of capacity ρ, where $x_i \in \mathcal{X}\ \forall i = 1 \cdots k$. Packets in X are processed in sequence by a detection algorithm for identifying large flows. The algorithm can only make one pass over the packet stream due to the high link capacity and limited memory.

For a packet x, we denote by $\mathsf{time}(x)$ the time at which the detection algorithm observes the packet, by $\mathsf{size}(x)$ the size of the packet, and by $\mathsf{fid}(x)$ the flow ID of the packet. The traffic volume of a flow f during a time window $[t_1, t_2)$ is defined as $\mathsf{vol}(f, t_1, t_2) \triangleq \sum_{x \in \mathcal{X}, \mathsf{fid}(x)=f, t_1 \leq \mathsf{time}(x) < t_2} \mathsf{size}(x)$.

Synopses. A traffic synopsis is a data structure that summarizes flows and can be used to answer queries regarding certain flow statistics. When a new packet x arrives, the algorithm updates its traffic synopsis based on x's flow

[2]While the flow definitions vary depending on the applications, in most applications a flow consists of packets that share one or more header fields, such as the source IP, destination IP, source port, destination port, and the protocol number.

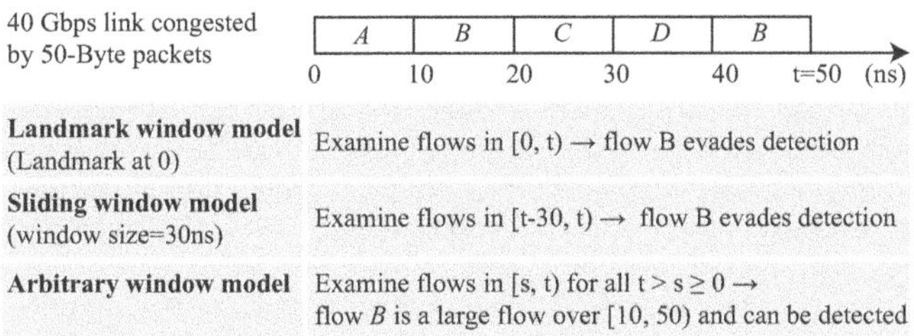

Figure 1: In this example, a flow is large if it sends more than $40Mbps \cdot w + 500kb$ for any time window of size w. Although flow B violates the limit over the time window $[10, 50)$, it can only be caught in the arbitrary window model.

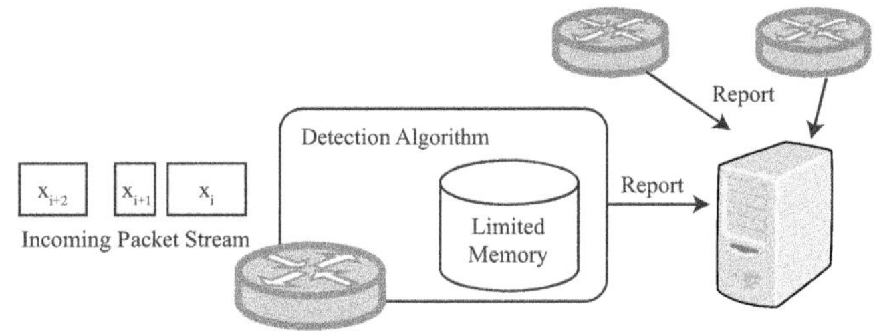

Figure 2: A general framework for a large-flow-detection algorithm. The detection algorithm processes incoming flows and keeps limited state in memory. Results may be reported to a remote server for further analysis.

ID, size, and arrival time. Formally, a large-flow detection algorithm supports three operations over a synopsis S:

- $\mathsf{Init}(params) \rightarrow S_0$. The initialization operation takes as inputs the large-flow definitions and desired detection accuracy, etc.
- $\mathsf{Update}(S_{i-1}, x_i) \rightarrow S_i$. The update operation outputs an updated synopsis S_i by incorporating the new packet x_i into the previous synopsis S_{i-1}. For convenience, we denote $\mathsf{Update}(S_i, \langle x_{i+1}, \cdots, x_{i+j}\rangle) = \mathsf{Update}(S_{i+1}, \langle x_{i+2}, \cdots, x_{i+j}\rangle) = S_{i+j}$.
- $\mathsf{Detect}(S_i, x_i) \rightarrow b \in \{0, 1\}$. The detection operation evaluates S_i to determine if x_i belongs to a large flow.

Time window models. Prior approaches to large-flow detection can be classified into three main categories based on the type of time window they monitor: landmark window [10, 14, 17, 18, 23, 29–31], sliding window [5, 21, 26], and arbitrary window [16].

In the landmark window model, each time window starts at the closest landmark in the past (e.g., a landmark is placed every five seconds) and ends at the current time. In the sliding window model, recent traffic is considered more important than old traffic, so the time window begins at some recent time in the past. The window slides as new packets arrive, such that the measurement incorporates the new packets and excludes the oldest packets. Finally, the arbitrary window model monitors every time window ending at the current time. It is more difficult to evade detection in this model than in others, as illustrated in Figure 1. Note that while the arbitrary window model covers every possible window, flows can still evade detection if the detection algorithm is inaccurate.

2.2 Large-Flow Problem Over Arbitrary Windows

Small, medium, and large flows. A flow f is a *large flow* if there exists a time window $[t_1, t_2)$ over which its volume $\mathsf{vol}(f, t_1, t_2)$ exceeds a high-bandwidth threshold function $\mathsf{TH_h}(t_2 - t_1)$. A flow is a *small flow* if its volume $\mathsf{vol}(f, t_1, t_2)$ is lower than a low-bandwidth threshold function $\mathsf{TH}_\ell(t_2 - t_1)$ over all possible time windows $[t_1, t_2)$. The rest are defined as medium flows, i.e. flows in an ambiguity region.

In this paper we define the two threshold functions in the form of leaky bucket descriptors: $\mathsf{TH_h}(t) = \gamma_h t + \beta_h$ and $\mathsf{TH}_\ell(t) = \gamma_\ell t + \beta_\ell$, where $\gamma_h > \gamma_\ell > 0$ and $\beta_h > \beta_\ell > 0$.[3] Although selecting appropriate parameters largely depends on the targeted application, we provide guidelines for selecting these parameters in Section 4.

Exact-outside-ambiguity-region large-flow problem. As exact solutions are inefficient, we consider a relaxed notion of exactness:

Definition 1. *Given a packet stream, the exact-outside-ambiguity-region large-flow problem returns a set of flows $\mathcal{F}$ such that (1) $\mathcal{F}$ contains every large flow, and (2) $\mathcal{F}$ does not contain any small flow.*

Because the number of large flows can increase indefinitely over time, $\mathcal{F}$ may become too large to fit into the limited on-chip memory. Hence, such an algorithm often reports to a remote server with mass storage that keeps a complete copy of $\mathcal{F}$, as illustrated in Figure 2. The algorithm must therefore operate correctly even without a complete copy of $\mathcal{F}$.

A *positive* is when a flow is added to $\mathcal{F}$, and a *negative* is when a flow is not added to $\mathcal{F}$. Hence, a False Positive of small flow (FP_s) occurs when the detection algorithm wrongly adds a small flow, and a False Negative of large flow (FN_ℓ) occurs when it fails to include a large flow.

The exact-outside-ambiguity-region large-flow problem is reasonable for two reasons: (1) It confines the damage by large flows and allows existing techniques (e.g., Sample and Hold [17]) to handle the medium flows statistically. (2) Prior work [17] [16] also involves a region similar to our ambiguity region, but they only provide probabilistic bounds outside the region.

2.3 Design Goals

Our main goals are as follows:

Exactness outside an ambiguity region. To achieve exactness outside an ambiguity region in traffic monitoring, we desire a deterministic monitor algorithm which identifies every large flow including bursty flow (i.e., no FN_ℓ)and

[3]Instead of using leaky bucket descriptors, prior work in the landmark window model often defines the high-bandwidth threshold to be a fraction of the link bandwidth, e.g., $\gamma_h = 0.01$ and $\beta_h = 0$. However, it is infeasible to adopt this fraction-based definition when it comes to the arbitrary window model because every flow will violate the threshold over a sufficiently small time window (e.g., a window containing only one packet).

protects every small flow (i.e., no FP_s) with no assumption on the input traffic or attack pattern. Hence, the high-bandwidth and low-bandwidth thresholds are also called the no-FN_ℓ and no-FP_s thresholds in this paper, respectively.

Scalability. Although using per-flow leaky buckets enables exact and instantaneous detection of large flows, keeping per-flow state is impractical due to the large number of flows in the Internet. Hence, the algorithm should require few per-packet operations and maintain small router state that fits in fast yet scarce storage devices (e.g., on-chip SRAM or even registers) regardless of input traffic or attack pattern, such that the detection algorithm can operate at line rate.

Fast detection. Fast detection of large flows minimizes collateral damage. Hence, for a large flow violating the high-bandwidth threshold over $[t_1, t_2)$, the algorithm should detect the flow no later than $t_2 + t_{process}$, where $t_{process}$ is the time it takes to process a packet.

3. ALGORITHM

In this section, we first investigate and prove the *no-FP_s* and *no-FN_ℓ relationships* between landmark and arbitrary window models because they are useful for constructing large-flow algorithms over arbitrary windows. Based on these relationships, we present EARDET, a streaming algorithm that efficiently addresses the large-flow problem over arbitrary windows (as defined in Definition 1) with exactness outside an ambiguity region. Finally, we discuss the implementation and optimization techniques in detail, and numerically demonstrate that EARDET can operate at high-speed links while using only hundreds bytes of on-chip SRAM.

It is important to investigate the relationships between landmark and arbitrary window models because they enable us to draw on the rich experience of research on the large-flow problem over landmark windows [10,14,17,18,23,29–31] for designing arbitrary-window algorithms. Particularly, we are interested in knowing whether and to what extent we can leverage existing landmark-window algorithms to build arbitrary-window ones. The technical contributions of this paper include proving two theorems that shed light toward a systematic approach applying existing landmark-window algorithms to arbitrary-window algorithms.

EARDET leverages the Misra-Gries (MG) algorithm [31], which finds all frequent items in a data stream in one pass but may falsely include non-frequent items. The MG algorithm works over landmark windows in the sense that the landmark is at the beginning of the data stream. The research challenges here include (1) how to preserve MG's no-FN_ℓ property (over landmark windows) when porting it to the arbitrary window model, and (2) how to achieve the no-FP_s property when processing packets in one pass. EARDET modifies the MG algorithm in several novel ways to effectively address the above challenges. Interestingly, despite these simple modifications, we prove that EARDET achieves both no-FP_s and no-FN_ℓ properties over arbitrary windows, thereby providing strong guarantees regardless of input traffic.

3.1 Relationships Between Landmark and Arbitrary Windows

Here is a straightforward yet inefficient solution to the exact-outside-ambiguity-region large-flow problem over arbitrary windows: the algorithm divides the problem into multiple sub-problems that each can be handled by a landmark-window algorithm, $\mathcal{L}$. More concretely, let L^i be a copy of $\mathcal{L}$ that monitors a time window starting from packet x_i and ending at the current time. For every newly arrived packet x_i, the algorithm initiates L^i, and adds x_i to the new as well as all previous copies, $L^1, L^2, \cdots, L^i$. Then the algorithm combines the answers returned by $L^1, L^2, \cdots, L^i$. This straightforward solution is correct, but requires space linear in the length of the traffic stream, which is prohibitively expensive.

To make it more efficient, the key idea is to eliminate redundant copies of $\mathcal{L}$. To show why this is possible, we formally state two relationships between landmark windows and arbitrary windows.

No-FP_s relationship. We observe that only one copy of $\mathcal{L}$ is needed to achieve the no-FP_s property over arbitrary window. Specifically, Theorem 2 states that if an algorithm ensures (L1) no FP_s in the landmark window model, then it also ensures (A1) no FP_s in the arbitrary window model.

THEOREM 2. *If an algorithm satisfies*

- L1: *For all t, it never reports a flow whose volume is below $\gamma'_\ell t + \beta'_\ell$ over time interval $[0, t)$.*

then it must also satisfy

- A1: *It never reports a flow whose volume is below $\gamma_\ell(t_2 - t_1) + \beta_\ell$ over time interval $[t_1, t_2)$ for all $t_2 > t_1$.*

when $\gamma'_\ell = \gamma_\ell$ and $\beta'_\ell = \beta_\ell$.

Proof sketch: L1 implies A1 because if a flow sends less than $\gamma_\ell(t_2-t_1)+\beta_\ell$ for all intervals $[t_1, t_2)$, it must also send less than $\gamma'_\ell t + \beta'_\ell$ for all intervals $[0, t)$ when $\gamma'_\ell = \gamma_\ell$ and $\beta'_\ell = \beta_\ell$. ■

No-FN_ℓ relationship. The no-FN_ℓ relationship is more challenging to prove. We observe that only one copy of $\mathcal{L}$ is needed to achieve the no-FN_ℓ property if *$\mathcal{L}$'s traffic synopsis is "similar" to the initial state* throughout the execution of the algorithm, as checking such a synopsis is roughly equivalent to checking all of $L^1, L^2, \cdots, L^i$. In other words, we can keep only one synopsis which somehow approximates the synopsis in each sub-problem.

Formally, we define a distance metric $\mathsf{dis}(S, S')$ quantifying the similarity between two synopses:

$$\mathsf{dis}(S, S') \triangleq \min_{X, S' = \mathsf{Update}(S, X)} \mathsf{tspan}(X)$$

where the time span of a packet sequence is defined as $\mathsf{tspan}(X) = \max_{x \in X} \mathsf{time}(x) - \min_{x \in X} \mathsf{time}(x)$. S is defined as a snapshot of the algorithm's internal state and thus does not depend on time. The distance between two snapshots is the shortest time it takes to convert one to the other given a link capacity.

Theorem 3 states if an algorithm ensures (L2) no FN_ℓ in the landmark window model and (L3) its synopsis is bounded, it also ensures (A2) no FN_ℓ in the arbitrary window model.

THEOREM 3. *If an algorithm satisfies*

- L2: *For all t, it reports all flows whose volume exceed $\gamma'_h t + \beta'_h$ over time interval $[0, t)$.*
- L3: *Throughout the execution of $\mathcal{L}$, $\mathsf{dis}(S_0, S_i) \leq \Delta$, where Δ is a small constant and $S_i = \mathsf{Update}(S_0, \langle x_1, \cdots, x_i \rangle)$.*

then it must also satisfy

- A2: *It always reports a flow whose volume exceeds* $\gamma_h(t_2 - t_1) + \beta_h$ *over time interval* $[t_1, t_2)$ *for some* $t_2 > t_1$.

when $\gamma_h(t_2 - t_1) + \beta_h \geq \gamma'_h(t_2 - t_1 + \Delta) + \beta'_h$.

Proof sketch: Let $\mathcal{L}$ be an algorithm satisfying L2 and L3. Let f be a flow that sends more than $\gamma_h(t_2 - t_1) + \beta_h$ over some time interval $[t_1, t_2)$, and t_2 is the smallest among all possible values if the flow f violates the spec multiple times. To prove this No-FN$_\ell$ relationship, in the following we show that $\mathcal{L}$ can catch any f when $\gamma_h = \gamma'_h$ and $\beta_h \geq \beta'_h + \gamma_h\Delta$, thus satisfying A2 as well.

For convenience, we denote by X_a^b the incoming packet stream between time interval $[a, b)$. Since $\mathcal{L}$ satisfies L3 (i.e., the synopsis state of $\mathcal{L}$ is always bounded), $\mathsf{dis}(S_0, S^{t_1}) \leq \Delta$ where S^{t_1} is its synopsis state at t_1.

Based on the definition of the distance function, there exists a packet sequence X' with a time span less than Δ and $\mathsf{Update}(S_0, X') = S^{t_1}$. In other words, from the algorithm's perspective, $\mathsf{Update}(S_0, X_0^{t_2}) = \mathsf{Update}(S_0, \mathcal{X}' \| X_{t_1}^{t_2})$,[4] i.e., the two packet sequences produce identical synopses. As a result, if the algorithm $\mathcal{L}$ can detect f in $X' \| X_{t_1}^{t_2}$ then it can also detect f in $X_0^{t_2}$ because the output of the detection function, Detect, solely depends on the synopsis.

Moreover, by construction, f sends more than $\gamma_h(t_2 - t_1) + \beta_h$ in the new sequence $X' \| X_{t_1}^{t_2}$, whose time span is $t_2 - t_1 + \Delta$. Therefore, $\mathcal{L}$ can detect f in the new sequence because $\gamma_h(t_2 - t_1) + \beta_h \geq \gamma'_h(t_2 - t_1 + \Delta) + \beta'_h$ holds when $\gamma_h = \gamma'_h$ and $\beta_h \geq \beta'_h + \gamma_h\Delta$. Hence, $\mathcal{L}$ can also detect f in the original stream, $X_0^{t_2}$. ■

We note that L1 and A2 contradict each other for any parameter selection: for any $\gamma'_\ell, \beta'_\ell, \gamma_h$, and β_h, consider an interval $[t_1, t_2)$ satisfying $t_1 = t_2 - \epsilon$ and $t_2 > \frac{\beta_h - \beta'_\ell + \gamma_h\epsilon + 1}{\gamma'_\ell}$. Then a flow sending $\gamma_h(t_2 - t_1) + \beta_h + 1$ over $[t_1, t_2)$ will violate the high bandwidth threshold over $[t_1, t_2)$ but comply with $\gamma'_\ell t_2 + \beta'_\ell$ over $[0, t_2)$. That is, no algorithm can satisfy (A2, L2, L3) and (A1, L1) at the same time.

The above two theorems can be viewed as guidelines for designing new arbitrary-window algorithms based on existing landmark-window algorithms.

3.2 Algorithm Construction

Several existing landmark-window approaches [10, 14, 17, 23, 29–31] satisfy L2 when β'_h is set to zero. Among these approaches, we observe that the MG algorithm [31] can be made to satisfy L2 in a general setting (i.e., β'_h can be non-zero) as well as L3 with slight modifications. As a result, we choose to leverage the MG algorithm for designing EARDet.

We prove in the next section that EARDet's design ensures L2 and L3, and therefore achieves the no-FN$_\ell$ property (i.e., catching every large flow) based on Theorem 3. We also prove that EARDet achieves the no-FP$_s$ property (i.e., protecting every small flow), whereas the MG algorithm requires a second pass to remove false positives in the landmark window model.

Background of the MG algorithm. We briefly review the MG algorithm, which inspires our design. The MG algorithm finds the exact set of frequent items (defined as items that appear in a stream of m items for more than $\frac{m}{n+1}$ times) in two passes with only n counters. This algorithm generalizes the Majority algorithm [6, 20], which focuses on the case when $n = 2$. The same generalization was rediscovered by Demaine et al. [14] and Karp et al. [23].

The MG algorithm assumes an associative array of counters indexed by items. Counters are initialized to zeros. We say that an item is stored if its counter is above zero. For each incoming item e, the MG algorithm works as follows: (1) If e is stored (i.e., $ctr[e] > 0$), increase $ctr[e]$ by 1; (2) Else if the number of non-zero counters is less than n, $ctr[e] = 1$; and (3) Otherwise, decrease all non-zero counters by 1.

Since there are at most n non-zero counters kept at any time, the storage overhead is $O(n)$. This can be easily extended to items with positive weights. After the first pass, the MG algorithm guarantees that every frequent item is associated with a non-zero count, and a second pass is required to remove falsely included infrequent items.

The correctness of this algorithm can be shown intuitively as follows: Suppose an item e appears more than $\frac{m}{n+1}$ times, but is not stored at the end. The total count would have been reduced by more than $\frac{m}{n+1} \cdot (n+1) = m$ counts during the execution, which is impossible since it is more than the total number of items.

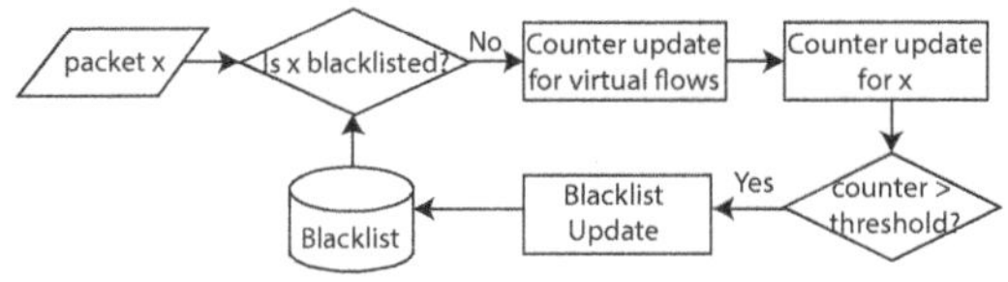

Figure 3: EARDet's decision diagram.

EARDet Overview. Figure 3 illustrates EARDet's decision diagram for each incoming packet. At a high level, EARDet works similarly to the MG algorithm except three crucial distinctions:

- **Blacklist:** EARDet keeps a local blacklist $\mathcal{L}$ that stores recently identified large flows. Counters are updated only if the flow ID of the packet is not blacklisted. The main purpose of keeping the blacklist is to avoid increasing a flow's counter when the counter value has already exceeded a *counter threshold*, β_{TH}. Additionally, we can avoid spending unnecessary resources on accounting blacklisted flows. We bound the blacklist's size in Section 3.3.
- **Counter threshold:** A flow is added to the blacklist if its associated counter value exceeds a threshold β_{TH}. Setting a counter threshold together with blacklisting ensures that counter values are always confined, i.e., $\leq \beta_{TH} + \alpha$, where α is the maximum packet size.
- **Virtual traffic:** In contrast to the frequent-item problem, the large-flow problem has to take the idle time between two consecutive packets into account so as to accurately detect large flows with respect to the link capacity. EARDet handles this by virtually filling the unused bandwidth with virtual traffic. Virtual traffic consists of multiple virtual flows, each of which is crafted purposely to comply with the low-bandwidth threshold, thus avoiding unnecessary alarms.

Algorithm description. Algorithm 1 describes how EARDet works. As the MG algorithm, EARDet keeps

[4] $\|$ denotes concatenating two packet sequences into one sequence.

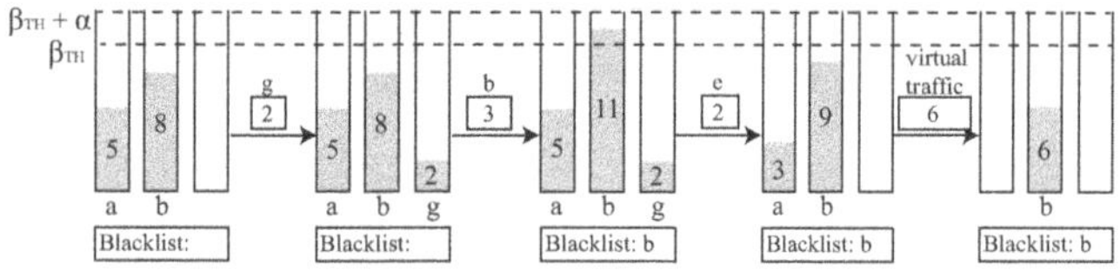

Figure 4: Example of EARDet's counter update.

n counters, each initialized to zero. Counters are stored in an associative array indexed by flow IDs, and the number of non-zero counters never exceeds n. EARDET counters are increased and decreased by the size of the packets, since a packet of size w can be viewed as w uni-sized items. We denote by C the set of non-zero counters. We discuss how to implement EARDET efficiently in Section 3.3.

Algorithm 1 EARDET

1: Initialization ($S \leftarrow$ Init(n), Line 8-9)
2: **for** each packet x in the stream **do**
3:   **if** x's FID f is not blacklisted ($f \notin \mathcal{L}$) **then**
4:     Update counters for virtual traffic (Line 18-22)
5:     Update counters for x ($S \leftarrow$ Update(S, x), Line 10-17)
6:     **if** detect violation (Detect(S, x) $== 1$, Line 21-22) **then**
7:       Add f to blacklist ($\mathcal{L} \leftarrow \mathcal{L} \cup \{f\}$)

8: **Initialization,** Init(n)
9: initialize all counters to zeros, $\mathcal{L} \leftarrow \emptyset$, $C \leftarrow \emptyset$

10: **Update counters for packet** x**,** Update(S, x)
11: **if** x's FID f is kept ($f \in C$) **then**
12:   Update f's counter by the packet size w ($c_f \leftarrow c_f + w$)
13: **else if** less than n counters are kept ($|C| < n$) **then**
14:   Set f's counter to w ($c_f \leftarrow w$, $C \leftarrow C \cup \{f\}$)
15: **else**
16:   Decrease all counters by $d = \min\{w, \min_{j \in C} c_j\}$
17:   Set c_f to $w - d$, and $\forall j$ remove j from C if $c_j = 0$

18: **Update counters for virtual traffic between** x_i **and** x_{i-1}
19: Compute the virtual traffic size, v ($v = \rho t_{idle} -$ size(x_{i-1}), and $t_{idle} =$ time(x_i) $-$ time(x_{i-1}))
20: For each unit u in the virtual traffic, update counters as if u belongs to a new flow (e.g., unit is 1 byte)

21: **Detect violation,** Detect(S, x)
22: Return whether x's flow counter exceeds threshold ($c_f > \beta_{TH}$)

Figure 4 gives an example showing how to update counters when $n = 3$, $\beta_{TH} = 10$, and $\alpha = 3$, where α is the maximum packet size. First, since there is an empty counter, flow g is added and its counter value becomes 2, the size of the new packet. Then, since flow b is stored already, its counter is increased by 3. The new value of $ctr[b]$ exceeds β_{TH}, and thus flow b is blacklisted. The next flow, e, is not stored yet and there is no empty counter, so all counters are decreased by the packet size. Finally, the virtual traffic is divided into single-unit packets with new flow IDs, resulting in the final state.[5]

Despite EARDET's simple operations, work remains to prove the no-FP$_s$ and no-FN$_\ell$ properties and to devise practical parameters. We answer these in Section 4.

---

[5]Conceptually, the counter values are updated as follows: $[3, 9, 0] \rightarrow [3, 9, 1] \rightarrow [2, 8, 0] \rightarrow [2, 8, 1] \rightarrow [1, 7, 0] \rightarrow [1, 7, 1] \rightarrow [0, 6, 0]$. Section 3.3 discusses techniques to accelerate this process.

3.3 Data Structure and Optimization

While EARDET requires very little memory state, its processing delay may be high in a naive implementation where EARDET accesses every counter for each decrement operation (i.e., Line 16 in Algorithm 1). We now present several optimization techniques to reduce the number of memory accesses and the processing time.

Reducing number of memory accesses. We minimize the number of memory accesses per packet via the following technique. First, we keep counters in a data structure that allows insertion, deletion, and finding the minimum in logarithmic time. Data structures such as balanced search trees and heaps can satisfy our requirements. Moreover, counter values are not absolute but relative to a *floating ground*, c_{ground}. Hence, the decrement operation, which requires decreasing all counters previously, can now be achieved by elevating the floating ground. The detection function becomes $c_f - c_{ground} > \beta_{BF}$.

The increment operation on Line 12 takes $O(1)$ time using an associative array. Adding a value to an empty counter as described on Line 14 takes $O(\log n)$ time because we have to insert the counter to the data structure. To prevent counter overflow, EARDET periodically resets the floating ground to zero and deducts all counters accordingly.

Efficient counter update for virtual traffic. Virtual traffic ensures accurate accounting of unused bandwidth, but efficient implementation is needed to handle virtual traffic at line speed. We now discuss how to efficiently update EARDET's counters for virtual traffic. Particularly, we aim to divide virtual traffic into multiple virtual flows in a way to minimize the time to process such virtual flows. The only constraint is that each virtual flow should comply with the low-bandwidth threshold to avoid triggering false alarms.

As Line 20 of Algorithm 1 shows, for each unit u of the virtual traffic, EARDET updates its counters (i.e., Update(S, u)) as if the traffic unit belongs to a new flow. We can minimize the number of updates by maximizing the unit size. To avoid false detection, the maximum size per unit is β_{TH} bytes. As β_{TH} must be larger than the minimum packet size (i.e., 40 bytes) for practical use, the overhead of using β_{TH}-byte virtual flows is bounded by the worst-case scenario where the link is congested by minimum-sized packets.

We can further optimize this task based on the following observation: Once all counters become empty, they should stay empty until the next real packet comes. Furthermore, since the maximum counter value is $\beta_{BF} + \alpha$, counters will all be empty if the size of the virtual flow $\geq (\beta_{BF} + \alpha) \cdot n$. (A tighter condition is if the virtual traffic size $\geq (\max_j c_j) * n - \sum_j c_j$, but this requires keeping track of the sum of all counters.) In other words, EARDET can simply reset all counters to zeros and avoid any update if the virtual traffic size exceeds a certain threshold.

Counter implementation. For efficiency, counters are implemented as integers (e.g., in bytes) rather than non-integer numbers. While packet sizes are always multiples of bytes, the size of virtual traffic may be non-integer, which introduces biases on EARDET's guarantees. For example, given a 800Mbps link and a nanosecond time precision at the router, the size of a 1-ns virtual traffic is 0.1 bytes.

We bound such biases with a slightly modified algorithm that adjusts virtual traffic. Let us denote by $\{v_1, v_2, \cdots\}$ the sizes of a sequence of virtual traffic and by $\{v'_1, v'_2, \cdots\}$ the adjusted sizes. We maintain an extra field called "carryover", co, which keeps the amount of uncounted virtual traffic. co is initialized to zero, and we ensure that $-0.5 \leq co < 0.5$ for all time. Virtual flows are adjusted such that $v'_i \leftarrow [v_i + co_i]$ and $co_{i+1} \leftarrow co_i + v_i - v'_i$ where co_i is the value of co before proceeding v_i. By construction, v'_is are all integers, and for any a, b, $|\sum_a^b v_i - \sum_a^b v'_i| = |co_{b+1} - co_a| \leq 1$. In other words, the adjusted virtual traffic differs from the original one by at most 1 unit for any time interval. Consequently, the modified algorithm guarantees to catch flows violating $\mathsf{TH_h}(t) = \gamma_h t + (\beta_h + 1)$ and guarantees not to catch any flow conforming to $\mathsf{TH}_\ell(t) = \gamma_\ell t + (\beta_h - 1)$.

Bounding the blacklist. EARDet keeps in memory not only counters but also a local blacklist storing recently detected large flows.

We propose a simple mechanism to bound $|\mathcal{L}|$ and thus prevent algorithmic complexity attacks to overflow the blacklist as follows. Since the blacklist's main purpose is to avoid increasing a flow's counter when the counter value has already exceeded a counter threshold, once a counter value has dropped below the threshold, the flow can be removed from the blacklist. In this way, the size of $\mathcal{L}$ will always be bounded by n because only flows that are currently stored can be blacklisted.

The key observation here is that flows that are not currently stored can be removed from the blacklist because such removal will not affect EARDet's no-FN$_\ell$ and no-FP$_s$ guarantees, as in EARDet whether a flow will be caught or not does not depend on other flows' behavior. The detector can periodically report the current blacklist to a remote administrator, such that the administrator keeps a complete list of detected large flows, while the detector maintains a small blacklist that helps avoid increasing a flow's counter when the counter value has already exceeded β_{TH}. The only tradeoff of this mechanism is that EARDet may spend unnecessary resources on accounting flows that have been identified as large flows.

Parallelizing EARDet. A common way to reduce processing time is parallelization. EARDet can be parallelized at both the algorithm and instruction levels. At the algorithm level, we can randomly distribute the flows (thus the workload) among multiple copies of EARDet. At the instruction level, we can access and update multiple counters in parallel using multi-port SRAM when the operations are order insensitive. We note that special-purpose SRAMs (i.e., multi-port SRAMs) can support multiple read/write simultaneously [38].

3.4 Storage and Computational Complexity

Given the above optimization techniques, we analyze EARDet's storage and computational overhead.

To operate at line rate on OC-768 (40 Gbps) high-speed links, a typical 3.2 GHz processor has to process 40 million medium-sized (1000 bits) packets per second, which means the per-packet processing time should be at most 32 ns or 76 CPU cycles. In this analysis, we consider the following memory model for commodity routers: CPU has 32 KB L1 cache, 256 KB L2 cache, 20 MB L3 cache, and gigabytes main DRAM memory. Accessing L1, L2, and L3 caches takes 4, 12, and 30 CPU cycles, respectively; accessing the main memory is as slow as 300 cycles.

Storage complexity. EARDet keeps an extremely small traffic synopsis, a blacklist of detected flows, and storage of flow ID keys (i.e. unique keys consist of IP address and port number) for flow identifier. The synopsis consists of n counters and a constant number of additional variables for optimization such as the floating ground. In IPv4, a flow ID key is 48 bits, and for IPv6, it is 144 bits. By implementing the tree map using a red-black tree [8], each counter needs store only one flow ID key. In most applications the synopsis and flow ID keys will be small enough to fit entirely in the router's L1 cache. For instance, in IPv4, using 100 32-bit counters and 100 48-bit key variables requires only 960 bytes; even in IPv6, the same case requires only 2200 bytes, which can fit in the L1 cache. (Guided by our analysis in Appendix A, we use 100 counters as a representative example.) If the number of counters is much larger than 100 in some configuration, we can also use L2 cache with some performance cost. In practice, a special-purpose device with more fast memory can also be installed for large flow detection. Moreover, we can flexibly tune the counter size to further reduce the memory requirement at the cost of a wider ambiguity region between the no-FP$_s$ and no-FN$_\ell$ thresholds.

Computational complexity. For each packet, EARDet looks up and updates one or more counters, and adjusts the internal data structure (e.g., a heap) of counters. In EARDet, locating and updating a counter requires an average of $O(1)$ memory access in a hash-map-based associative memory. Adjusting the data structure of n counters requires $O(\log n)$ memory accesses.

Since EARDet's state is small enough to fit into the L1 cache as we discussed, the per-packet processing time can be as low as tens of nanoseconds, which is suitable for processing packets at 40Gbps high-speed links. Even when all of EARDet's data is in the L2 cache, EARDet can still process packets at line speed on 13Gbps.

4. ANALYSIS

In this section, we prove the no-FP$_s$ and no-FN$_\ell$ properties. Furthermore, we analyze the incubation period of large flows, discuss EARDet's tradeoffs, and present practical guidelines for EARDet configuration. Finally, we compare EARDet with closely related proposals [16, 17] to demonstrate that it outperforms prior work in terms of both efficiency and detection accuracy.

We consider a network link with a capacity of ρ, and a EARDet detector with n counters. The counter threshold is β_{TH}. Once the value of a counter exceeds β_{TH}, the associated flow will be judged as a large flow and cut off immediately. Hence, the maximum value of each counter is $\beta_{TH} + \alpha$, where α is the maximum packet size. Table 1 summarizes the notations used in this section. We will discuss the relationship among parameters and how to set them in the Section 4.6.

4.1 Large-Flow False-Negative Analysis

THEOREM 4. ***No-FN$_\ell$ property.*** EARDet *detects every flow violating the high-bandwidth threshold $TH_h(t) =$*

Table 1: Table of Notations.

Network management parameters:		
ρ	$\triangleq$	Rate of link capacity
α	$\triangleq$	Maximum packet size
t_{upincb}	$\triangleq$	Upper bound of t_{incb} for any large flows
TH_ℓ	$\triangleq$	Low-bandwidth threshold
TH_h	$\triangleq$	High-bandwidth threshold
γ_ℓ, β_ℓ	$\triangleq$	Rate and burst for low-bandwidth threshold
γ_h	$\triangleq$	Rate for high-bandwidth threshold
Tunable parameters:		
n	$\triangleq$	Number of counters in EARDET
β_{TH}	$\triangleq$	Threshold of counters($> \beta_\ell$)
Parameters that depend on tunable parameters:		
β_h	$\triangleq$	Burst for high-bandwidth threshold
β_Δ	$\triangleq$	$\beta_{TH} - \beta_\ell$
Other notation:		
$R(t_1, t_2)$	$\triangleq$	Average flow rate in $[t_1, t_2)$
t_{incb}	$\triangleq$	Incubation period of large flows
R_{NFN}	$\triangleq$	No-FN$_\ell$ rate
R_{NFP}	$\triangleq$	No-FP$_s$ rate

$\gamma_h t + \beta_h$ *over a time window of length* t*, when* $\gamma_h \geq R_{NFN} = \frac{\rho}{n+1}$ *and* $\beta_h \geq \alpha + 2\beta_{TH}$.

Proof sketch: Firstly, we prove that EARDET satisfies L3 in Theorem 3. According to Algorithm 1, the maximum value of each counter c_i is $\beta_{TH} + \alpha$, and there are at most n non-zero counters at any time. Also, given any valid synopsis $S = \{c_i\}$ we can construct a packet stream X consisting of c_i bytes for flow i and no space between packets, and by construction $S = \mathsf{Update}(S_0, X)$. Combining the above two arguments and the definition of the distance function, we conclude that $\mathsf{dis}(S_0, S) \leq \frac{\mathsf{size}(\mathcal{X})}{\rho} \leq \frac{(\beta_{TH}+\alpha)n}{\rho}$. That is, setting $\Delta = \frac{(\beta_{TH}+\alpha)n}{\rho}$ satisfies L3.

Next we prove that EARDET satisfies L2 in Theorem 3 as well when setting $\gamma'_h = R_{NFN} = \frac{\rho}{n+1}$ and $\beta'_h = \beta_{TH}$. We prove by contradiction and assume there were a flow f violating $\gamma'_h + \beta'_h$ in the landmark window model at time t but not being detected (i.e., $c_f < \beta_{TH}$). This assumption implies that more than $\gamma'_h t + \beta'_h - \beta_{TH}$ amount of flow f would have been canceled out[6] during the decrement step, or equivalently, more than $(\gamma'_h t + \beta'_h - \beta_{TH}) \cdot (n+1) = \gamma'_h t \cdot (n+1) = \rho t$ amount of traffic would have been canceled out. This statement, however, contradicts the setting where the maximum traffic for t units of time is ρt. Thus, f cannot escape from EARDET, and L2 is satisfied by EARDET.

Based on Theorem 3, we conclude that EARDET satisfies A2 when $\gamma_h = \gamma'_h = \frac{\rho}{n+1}$ and $\beta_h \geq \beta'_h + \gamma_h \Delta = \beta_{TH} + \frac{\rho}{n+1}\frac{(\beta_{TH}+\alpha)n}{\rho} = \beta_{TH} + \frac{n}{n+1}(\beta_{TH} + \alpha)$. In particular, EARDET catches every flow violating the threshold $TH_h(t) = \gamma_h t + \beta_h$ when $\gamma_h \geq R_{NFN}$ and $\beta_h \geq \alpha + 2\beta_{TH}$. That is, EARDET catches all large flows in the arbitrary window model. ■

4.2 Small-Flow False-Positive Analysis

As discussed in Section 3.1, no algorithm can satisfy A2 in Theorem 3 and L1 in Theorem 2 at the same time. Hence, rather than applying Theorem 2, we have to take a different approach in proving the no-FP$_s$ property.

[6]A packet byte is canceled out if it does not contribute to the corresponding counter.

To analyze EARDET's no-FP$_s$ property, we consider how EARDET increases and decreases its counter values. Firstly, let us examine all cases based on the types of incoming flows. We say a flow is old if it is stored in the counters currently; otherwise the flow is new.

1. When the incoming flows are virtual flows and there are l empty counters, in a time window t, the decrement is $\frac{\rho}{l+1}t$ on all counters, and the increment is 0. $(l = 0, 1, 2, 3, ..., n)$
2. When the incoming flows are new real flows and there is no empty counter, in a time window t, the decrement is ρt on all counters and the increment is 0 (which is the same as the first case when $l = 0$).
3. When the incoming flows are old real flows, or new real flows and there are some empty counters, in time interval t, the decrement is 0 and the increment is ρt on one counter.

Thus, in the first and second cases, when there are l empty counters in the detector, the decrement is always $\frac{\rho}{l+1}t$ in the interval of t; and in the third case, the increment is always ρt on one counter in the interval of t. Finally, the increment and decrement cannot happen at the same time.

LEMMA 5. *For any small flow f that complies with the low-bandwidth threshold (i.e., $TH_\ell(t) = \gamma_\ell t + \beta_\ell$), once the flow f is associated to a counter at t_1, this counter will be always lower than β_{TH} after time $t_1 + t_{\beta_\ell}$, if the counter is occupied by the same flow as the flow f, where $t_{\beta_\ell} = \frac{(n-1)\alpha + (n+1)\beta_\ell}{[1-(n+1)\gamma_\ell/\rho]\rho}$.*

Due to space limitations, the detailed proofs are in our technical report [37].

THEOREM 6. ***No-FP$_s$ property.*** *EARDET will not catch any flow complying with the low-bandwidth threshold $TH_\ell(t) = \gamma_t + \beta_\ell$ for all time windows of length t, when $0 < \beta_\ell < \beta_{TH}$, $\gamma_\ell < R_{NFP}$, where $R_{NFP} = \frac{\beta_\Delta}{(n-1)\alpha + (n+1)\beta_\ell + (n+1)\beta_\Delta} \cdot \rho$.*

Proof sketch: According to Lemma 5, to avoid catching a small flow f, the counter should be smaller than β_{TH} before t_{β_ℓ}. Hence, we choose a γ_ℓ to achieve $\gamma_\ell t_{\beta_\ell} + \beta_\ell < \beta_{TH}$. Then, $\frac{(n-1)\alpha + (n+1)\beta_\ell}{[1-(n+1)\gamma_\ell/\rho]\rho} < \frac{\beta_{TH} - \beta_\ell}{\gamma_\ell}$,

$$\Leftrightarrow \gamma_\ell < \frac{\beta_\Delta}{(n-1)\alpha + (n+1)\beta_\ell + (n+1)\beta_\Delta} \cdot \rho \qquad (1)$$

The theorem is proved. ■

Interestingly, Theorem 6 shows that γ_ℓ approaches $\frac{\rho}{n+1}$ as β_Δ increases, but cannot go beyond $\frac{\rho}{n+1}$.

4.3 Relationship between Low-Bandwidth and High-Bandwidth Thresholds

Before the discussion, let us define two concepts:

Rate Gap: The ratio between γ_h and γ_ℓ (i.e. γ_h/γ_ℓ);

Burst Gap: The ratio between β_h and β_ℓ (i.e. β_h/β_ℓ).

Based on Theorems 4 and 6, the minimum rate gap is: $(\gamma_h/\gamma_\ell)_{min} = \frac{R_{NFN}}{R_{NFP}} = \frac{(n-1)\alpha + (n+1)(\beta_\ell + \beta_\Delta)}{\beta_\Delta(n+1)}$

Given $\beta_\Delta = \beta_{TH} - \beta_\ell$ and $n + 1 \doteq n \doteq n - 1$, we get

$$(\gamma_h/\gamma_\ell)_{min} \doteq 1 + \frac{2\alpha/\beta + 2}{\beta_h/\beta_\ell - (\alpha/\beta_\ell + 2)} \qquad (2)$$

Thus, the minimum possible rate gap $(\gamma_h/\gamma_\ell)_{min}$ is mainly influenced by the burst gap β_h/β_ℓ. Equation (2) tells us a) β_h/β_ℓ cannot be lower than $\alpha/\beta_\ell + 2$. b) EARDET only needs a low β_h/β_ℓ to achieve small enough $(\gamma_h/\gamma_\ell)_{min}$. For example, to achieve $(\gamma_h/\gamma_\ell)_{min} = 10$, we only need $\beta_h/\beta_\ell = 2.53$. c) $(\gamma_h/\gamma_\ell)_{min}$ cannot be lower than 1. $(\gamma_h/\gamma_\ell)_{min}$ approaches to 1 as β_h/β_ℓ grows.

4.4 Incubation Period of Large Flows

To define the incubation period, we first consider a large flow that violates the high-bandwidth threshold over $[t_1, t_2)$, and the packet at t_a triggers the detection. Because of EARDET's no-FN$_\ell$ property, $t_a \leq t_2$. The incubation period is defined as $t_a - t_1$, representing the time duration for which the large flow remains under the radar. We bound the incubation period as follows.

THEOREM 7. *For the flow f which violates $TH_h(t)$ over some time window $[t_1, t_2)$, if its average rate $R(t_1, t_a)$ is larger than R_{atk} in time interval of $[t_1, t_a)$ (R_{atk} is a constant rate larger than $R_{NFN} = \frac{\rho}{n+1}$), then f's incubation period is bounded by*

$$t_{incb} < \frac{\alpha + 2\beta_{TH}}{R_{atk} - \frac{\rho}{n+1}}. \tag{3}$$

Proof sketch: Because $R(t_1, t_a) > R_{atk}$, intuitively the t_{incb} of flow with average rate of $R(t_1, t_a)$ must be shorter than the t'_{incb} of flow with rate of R_{atk}. That is, $t_{incb} < t'_{incb}$.

Assume a flow f' with rate R_{atk} will violate $TH_h(t)$ over time window $[t'_1, t'_2)$, then

$$R_{atk}(t'_2 - t'_1) = \frac{\rho}{n+1}(t'_2 - t'_1) + \alpha + 2\beta_{TH}$$

$$\Rightarrow t_{incb} < t'_{incb} = t'_a - t'_1 \leq t'_2 - t'_1 = \frac{\alpha + 2\beta_{TH}}{R_{atk} - \frac{\rho}{n+1}} \tag{4}$$

Thus, the theorem is proved. ■

From Theorem 7, the bound of the incubation period decreases as R_{atk} increases. In other words, if R_{atk} is fixed, the bound of the incubation period decreases with increasing n, which implies we can reduce the upper bound by adding extra counters. To guarantee detection of flows whose rate is over R_{atk} ($R_{atk} > \frac{\rho}{n+1}$), the minimum number of counters is $\frac{\rho}{R_{atk}} - 1$, and the upper bound on the incubation period can be lowered significantly by adding a few counters. The details will be discussed in Section 4.6.

4.5 Tradeoff Analysis

We discuss three tradeoffs in EARDET: (1) memory consumption (i.e., the number of counters) vs. the rate gap, (2) the rate gap and burst gap, and (3) the rate gap and the upper bound on the incubation time.

First, since the rate gap can be expressed as $\gamma_h/\gamma_\ell > R_{NFN}/\gamma_\ell = \frac{\rho/\gamma_\ell}{n+1}$, we can see that the rate gap decreases with increasing n. Second, Equation (2) shows that the minimum rate gap γ_h/γ_ℓ is mainly influenced by β_h/β_ℓ, namely the burst gap, and the minimum rate gap decreases as the burst gap increases. Finally, Theorem 7 shows that a large burst gap results in a long incubation period. Hence, a small rate gap results in a big burst gap, and a high incubation period.

4.6 How To Engineer The Detector

To engineer our detector, we first identify parameters that are often known or given in a priori. Usually, users want a detector for a specific link capacity, ρ, to protect small flows which comply with the low-bandwidth threshold: $TH_\ell(t) = \gamma_\ell t + \beta_\ell$, and to detect attack flows that violate the high-bandwidth threshold: $TH_h(t) = \gamma_h t + \beta_h$. However, as discussed in Section 4.5, there is a tradeoff between the rate gap and burst gap, so their requirements cannot be both fulfilled. Thus, we choose to satisfy the rate requirement of γ_h, and then set β_h according to γ_h because it is more important to limit the flow rate than the burst size. Furthermore, since we want to minimize the incubation period of large flows, there is an upper bound of the incubation period, t_{upincb}.

We set $\beta_h = \alpha + 2\beta_{TH}$ and $\gamma_h > \frac{\rho}{n+1}$ to guarantee no FN$_\ell$ according to Theorem 4. Since $\beta_{TH} = \beta_\ell + \beta_\Delta$, we only need to decide the number of counters n and β_Δ. Hence, the problem can be simplified as follows. Given ρ, γ_ℓ, β_ℓ, γ_h, α, and t_{upincb}, we aim to calculate n and β_Δ such that the parameters satisfy the constraints in Theorems 4, 6 and 7. The detailed solution and analysis are in Appendix A. The detailed analysis shows that the tunable parameters depend on only the thresholds and are independent of the input traffic.

5. EVALUATION

To evaluate EARDET, we compare EARDET with two closely related proposals, which we refer to as FMF [17] and AMF [16]. Both of our theoretical comparison and trace-based simulations demonstrate that EARDET performs better than prior work in terms of both exactness[7] outside an ambiguity region and efficiency. The simulation results using real and synthetic traffic traces are consistent with the analysis in the theoretical evaluation.

5.1 Theoretical Comparison

Multistage filters. *Fixed-window-based Multistage Filters* (FMF) identify large flows in a fixed measurement interval. A FMF consists of parallel stages, each of which is an array of counters initialized to zeros at the beginning of a measurement interval. Each stage is assigned a hash function that maps a packet's flow identifier to a counter in the stage. For each incoming packet, its flow identifier is hashed to one counter in each hash stage, and the counter value increments by the size of the packet. A flow is considered a large flow if all of its corresponding counters exceed a pre-specified threshold.

Arbitrary-window-based Multistage Filters (AMF) identify large flows over arbitrary windows. To work in the arbitrary window model, AMF replaces each counter in FMF with a leaky bucket of a bucket size u and a drain rate r. A flow is considered a large flow if the corresponding leaky buckets are all violated.

Performance Comparison. Table 2 presents a numerical comparison of EARDET, FMF and AMF, where the high-bandwidth rate is 1% of the link capacity, and the low-bandwidth rate is 0.1% of link capacity. The results of FMF and AMF are derived based on the authors' original analysis

[7]The comparison in this section uses our definition of exactness.

Table 2: A numerical example given the requirements in Section 4.6. γ_h is 1% of the link capacity, and γ_ℓ is 0.1% of link capacity.

Scheme	# of counters	FP_s rate	FN_ℓ rate
EARDET	101	0	0
FMF	101/1000	*no guarantee* / ≤ 0.04*	0*
AMF	101/2000	*no guarantee* / ≤ 0.04	0

*FMF's results are derived in the landmark window model, and thus FMF's FP_s and FN_ℓ rates may be higher in the arbitrary window model.

Table 3: Summary of comparison of three schemes.

Scheme	FP_s	FN_ℓ	Memory	Input Traffic
EARDET	no	no	low	independent
FMF	yes	yes	high	dependent
AMF	yes	no	high	dependent

that assumes a specific number of active flows for the input traffic.

EARDET outperforms the other two approaches in several aspects: 1) EARDET guarantees no false detection of small flows, whereas it is unclear how FMF and AMF can achieve this property. Even with ten times or more extra storage, FMF and AMF still have error rates as high as 0.04. 2) Both EARDET and AMF can detect all large flows. However, FMF has FN_ℓ on bursty flows. 3) EARDET requires much less memory compared with multistage filters. 4) EARDET's performance is independent of the input traffic, because the error rate is always zero. On the contrary, to keep the same false positive rate, multistage filters require more stages as the number of active flows increases. Table 3 summarizes the comparison, which suggests that EARDET is exact outside an ambiguity region and more efficient than prior works.

Although EARDET presents several advantages compared with multistage filters, EARDET cannot estimate the size of a detected flow, which multistage filters achieve.

5.2 Experiment Settings

Datasets. Table 4 summarizes the characteristics of the two datasets used in the experiments. The Federico II dataset contains traces collected at the TCP port 80 of a 200 Mbps link [3, 12, 13]. The CAIDA dataset contains anonymized passive traffic traces from CAIDA's equinix-sanjose monitors on 10 Gbps backbone links [2]. For each dataset, we use the first 30 seconds for the experiments. We define flows based on the source and destination IP addresses.

Table 4: Dataset Information.

Dataset	Link capacity	Avg link rate	# of flows	Avg flow size
Federico II	$200Mbps$	$1.85MB/s$	2911	$19.9KB$
CAIDA	$10Gbps$	$279.65MB/s$	2517099	$3.3KB$

Attack scenarios. As stated in the theoretical analysis in Section 5.1, EARDET is exact outside an ambiguity region and efficient comparing to prior algorithms. The theoretical analysis focuses on the worst-case behaviors. To investigate how EARDET performs in reality, we conduct experiments and compare EARDET with FMF and AMF in the face of common attacks.

In particular, we generate attack flows using two simple strategies—*flooding attacks* and *Shrew DoS attacks* [22,25]—and then mix real traces with artificially generated attack flows to simulate an attack environment. In a flooding attack, the adversary sends high-rate flows with a specified rate γ_{large} (e.g. γ_h). Each high-rate flow is generated as follows. We randomly choose a 1-second time slot within the 30-second stream as the first second of the flow. Starting from that second, we randomly generate $\gamma_{large}/packetSize$ packets in each 1-second interval to make the flow size in each interval equal to that specified rate. In this experiment, we set the packet size to 1518 bytes, the maximum packet size. In a Shrew attack, the attacker sends periodic bursts in an attempt to cut off TCP traffic by exploiting TCP's congestion control mechanism. To generate a bursty flow with a period T, burst duration L, and bursty flow rate γ_{burst}, we randomly choose a time point from $[0, 29)$ second as the start time, and then randomly generate $\gamma_{burst} \cdot L$ packets in each L-length burst that occurs every T seconds. We then evaluate (1) how many malicious large flows can evade detection, and (2) how many small benign flows are falsely caught because of these coexisting attack flows.

We configure EARDET based on the guidelines in Section 4.6, such that it can detect large flows violating $TH_h(t) = \gamma_h t + \beta_h$, where $\gamma_h = 0.01\rho$, and $\beta_h = 2\beta_{TH} + \alpha$. β_{TH} will be calculated according to our technical report [37]. We also consider small flows that comply with $TH_\ell(t) = \gamma_\ell t + \beta_\ell$, where $\beta_\ell = 6072$ bytes and $\gamma_\ell = 0.01\rho$. Also, we require t_{upincb} to be smaller than 1 second. Table 5 summarizes the value of each parameter used in our experiments. In a "non-congested link" setting, a fixed number of attack flows are mixed with the real trace. We also consider a "congested link" setting, where we fill the link with attack flows, for the small dataset (i.e., the Federico II dataset) only. We leave it as future work to scale our attack flow generation tool to work for larger datasets.

To configure the two multistage filters (FMF and AMF), we set FMF's window size to 1 second, number of stages $d = 2$, number of counters in each stage $b = 250$, threshold of FMF $T = \gamma_h \cdot 1$ second, threshold of AMF $u = \beta_h$, and drain rate $r = \gamma_h$. We are also interested in the performance of FMF and AMF when their memory is as small as EARDET's. Hence, we run additional experiments in which the number of counters in each stage is 55. The details of these values are shown in the Table 6.

For each experiment environment, we design two sets of experiments to test the performance of these three filters in the presence of flooding attacks and Shrew attacks. We repeat each experiment for 10 times and present the average. In the case of flooding attacks, we randomly generate k_1 attack flows for each attack rate. In the case of Shrew attacks, we randomly generate k_2 bursty flows with $1.2 * \gamma_h$ burst rate and 1-second period for each burst duration L. We set $k_1 = k_2 = 50$ for the non-congested link setting, and set the k_1 and k_2 as large as possible to congest the link in the congested-link setting.

Table 6: Multistage Filter Parameters.

Dataset	$b * d$	T	u	r
Federico II	$55 * 2, 250 * 2$	$250KB$	$15.5KB$	$250KB/s$
CAIDA	$55 * 2, 250 * 2$	$12.5MB$	$15.4KB$	$12.5MB/s$

Table 5: **Parameters of Experiment Environment.**

Dataset	γ_h	β_h	γ_ℓ	β_ℓ	ρ	α	link status	β_{TH}	n	t_{upincb}
Federico II	$250KB/s$	$15.5KB$	$25KB/s$	$6072B$	$25MB/s$	$1518B$	congested/non-congested	$6991B$	107	$0.8370s$
CAIDA	$12.5MB/s$	$15.4KB$	$1.25MB/s$	$6072B$	$1.25GB/s$	$1518B$	non-congested	$6925B$	100	$0.1242s$

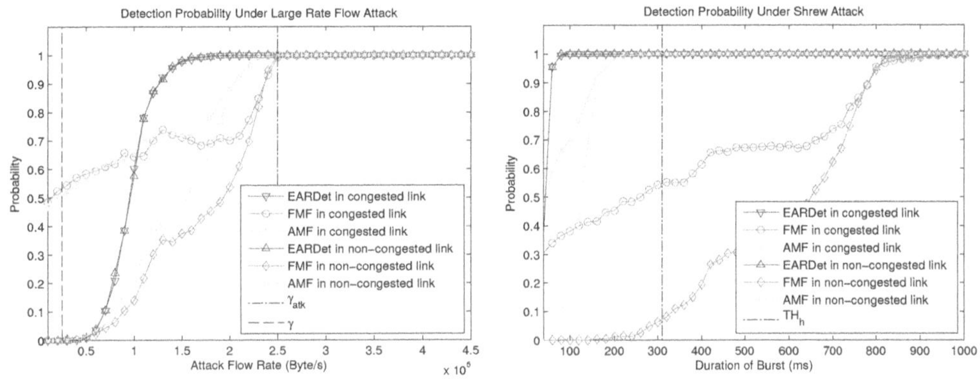

(a) Flooding DoS Attack (b) Shrew DoS Attack

Figure 5: Detection Probability in Experiment with 55*2 counters in Multistage Filter.

Evaluation metrics. We consider three evaluation metrics: detection probability, false positive probability on small flows, and incubation period. Detection probability is the probability to successfully detect a generated attack flow. False positive probability on small flows is the probability to wrongly catch a small flow when the link is attacked by attack flows of a certain rate. Incubation period represents the time needed to catch a generated attack flow since it is generated.

5.3 Experimental Comparison

Since the results for the two datasets are similar, we omit CAIDA's results due to space constraints.

Figure 5(a) and 5(b) shows the detection probability in the face of different types of attack flows. We focus on the scenario of using $55 * 2$ counters in FMF and AMF, as the results of $250 * 2$ counters are similar. In Figure 5(b), the TH_h line indicates whether a bursty flow exceeds the high-bandwidth threshold. The results show that EARDET detects attack flows with a 100% detection probability, which confirms Theorem 4. On the contrary, Figure 5(b) shows that FMF cannot catch most of the Shrew flows. Moreover, EARDET can catch most of the attack flows in the ambiguity region (between $TH_\ell(t)$ and $TH_h(t)$).

Figure 6(a) to Figure 6(h) show the results of FP_s rates. While EARDET has zero FP_s in any case as expected, Figure 6(a) to Figure 6(d) shows that both FMF and AMF have high FP_s rates in both attack scenarios when using very limited memory as EARDET. That is, the attacker can successfully incriminate benign small flows. Worst yet, when the link is congested by attack flows, the FP_s rate can be as high as 4% for FMF and 1% for AMF under flooding attacks, and for FMF, the FP_s rate is also extremely high under Shrew attacks. An interesting observation is that, in Figure 6(a), both FMF and AMF have a higher FP_s rate when the link is congested by malicious small flows. As Figure 6(e) to 6(h) show, using more counters in FMF and AMF can reduce, but not eliminate, the FP_s rates. The results of the CAIDA dataset exhibit similar trends.

Also, in our experiments, EARDET always produces similar results no matter whether the link is congested. In contrast, the results of AMF and FMF are much different between the congested-link version and non-congested-link version. This supports the conclusion in Section 5.1 that AMF and FMF rely on the number of active flows but EARDET does not. This advantage makes EARDET stable in any networking environment.

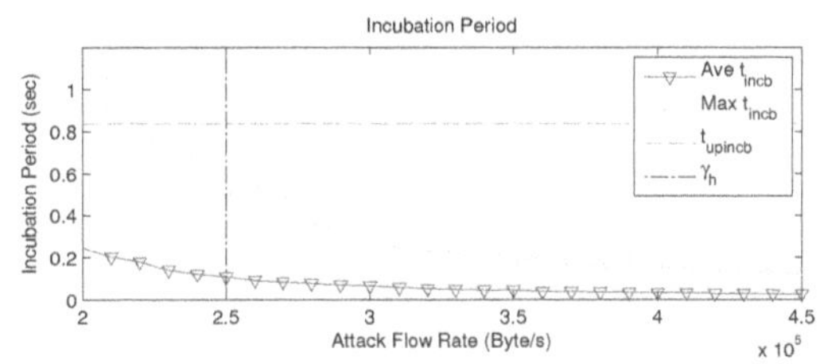

Figure 7: Incubation Period.

Figure 7 describes the maximum and average incubation period of high-rate flows with different rates in flooding attacks. We can find that the maximum incubation period for flows whose rate is over γ_h is always below the theoretical upper bound for the incubation period, t_{upincb}, which supports Theorem 7. Moreover, the average incubation period is much lower than the theoretical upper bound, which shows EARDET's incubation period is much shorter in practice.

6. RELATED WORK

Section 2.1 classifies prior work on detecting large flows and its closely related problem of finding frequent items based on the types of monitoring windows. Cormode and Hadjieleftheriou [9] present a thorough survey and comparison of algorithms for finding frequent items. This section reviews prior approaches based on the techniques used. Most

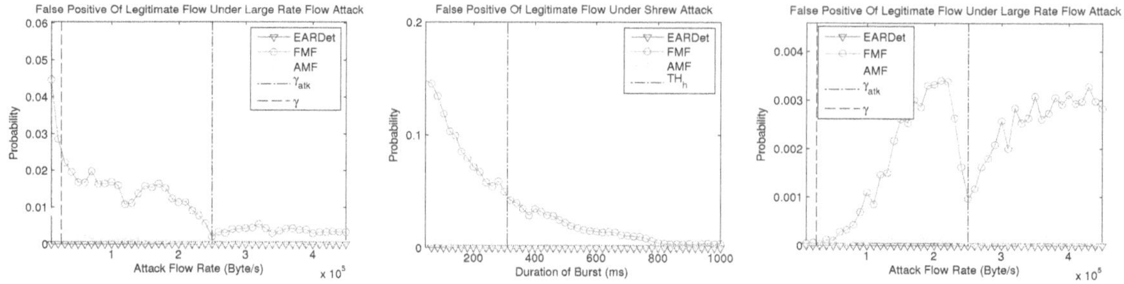

(a) 55*2 counters - Congested Link (b) 55*2 counters - Congested Link (c) 55*2 counters - Non-congested Link

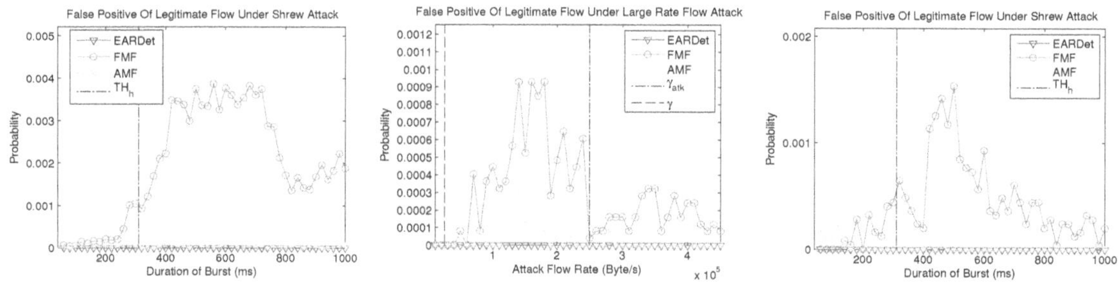

(d) 55*2 counters - Non-congested Link (e) 250*2 counters - Congested Link (f) 250*2 counters - Congested Link

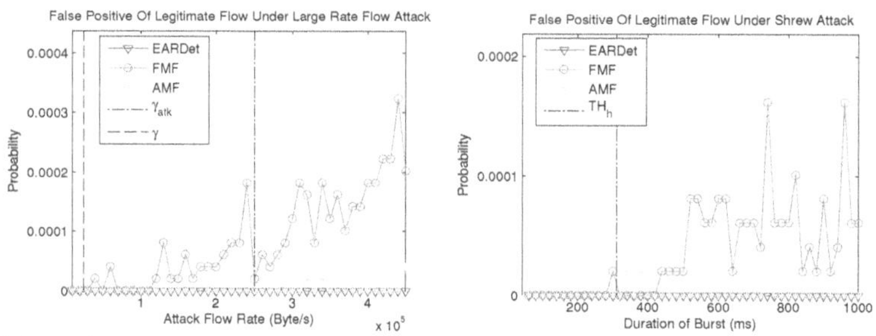

(g) 250*2 counters - Non-congested Link (h) 250*2 counters - Non-congested Link

Figure 6: False Positive on Small Flows.

of the prior work does not consider the arbitrary window model.

Counter-based techniques. Counter-based techniques maintain a small number of counters, each of which associated with a flow or an item. Manku and Motwani [29] present another well-known counter-based technique called Lossy Counting. For each stored item, Lossy Counting maintains and updates the upper bound and lower bound on the count of the item. The algorithm stores every new item and periodically removes items whose upper bound is less than the threshold. Similar to the MG algorithm discussed in Section 3.2, the Space Saving algorithm [30] proposed by Metwally et al. maintains k (item, counter) pairs and increases the corresponding counter of each incoming item. If the new item e is not stored currently, the stored item with the lowest count is replaced by the new item, and the counter increases accordingly.

Sketch-based techniques. Multistage filters identify large flows over fixed time windows [17] and over arbitrary windows [16]. Fang et al. [18] propose a similar multistage algorithm but their algorithm requires more than one pass over the input stream. Cormode and Muthukrishnan [10] present a novel data structure called count-min sketch, which summarizes an input stream and can answer several queries including finding frequent items. As pointed out in their paper, despite the fact that the construction is similar to that of multistage filters, count-min sketches can flexibly support negative weights and require only pairwise independence hash functions rather than fully independent ones. In general, sketches can support a richer set of queries with a higher memory overhead compared with counter-based techniques.

Sampling-based techniques. Sampled NetFlow [1] maintains a generic traffic summary of sampled packets. With a sampling rate $1/r$, the frequency estimate is derived by multiplying the count by r. To improve the accuracy of the estimates, both Sticky sampling [29] and Sample and Hold [17] examine every incoming item and increase the corresponding count if the item is being monitored. If the new item is not being monitored, it is sampled and added to the monitoring list with a certain probability. Sampling-based techniques in general cannot achieve high accuracy due to the lack of per-packet information. Duffield [15] studies how to perform fair sampling in traffic flow measurements.

Calders et al. [7] define a new frequency measure as the maximum frequency over all possible windows ending at the current time. Although their core idea is the same as the arbitrary window model, their algorithm focuses on accurately estimating the frequency based on the new frequency measure, whereas we seek to accurately identify large flows.

7. CONCLUSION

EARDET is a deterministic streaming algorithm that robustly catches all large flows and protects all small flows regardless of the traffic distribution. The core ideas differentiating EARDET from prior work are that it monitors flows over arbitrary windows and provides exactness outside an ambiguity region. We believe that EARDET can aid emerging applications such as detecting DoS attacks by bursty flows [25] and enforcing QoS-based SLA compliance [35], which require robust monitoring for high assurance. One future direction is to explore the design space of large-flow algorithms in the arbitrary window model by applying the no-FP and no-FN theorems to existing landmark-window-based algorithms. Another interesting future work is to formally examine the robustness of EARDET and prior algorithms against malicious inputs.

8. ACKNOWLEDGMENTS

We gratefully thank our shepherd Darryl Veitch and the anonymous reviewers for their valuable feedback. This research was supported in part by NSF under grants CNS-0953600, CNS-1248080, and CNS-1040801.

9. REFERENCES

[1] Random Sampled NetFlow. http://www.cisco.com/en/US/docs/ios/12_0s/feature/guide/nfstatsa.html.

[2] The CAIDA UCSD Anonymized Internet Traces 2012 - 1220. http://www.caida.org/data/passive/passive_2012_dataset.xml.

[3] Traces 1 of TCP port 80 traffic traces from Federico II. http://traffic.comics.unina.it/Traces/ttraces.php.

[4] D. G. Andersen, H. Balakrishnan, N. Feamster, T. Koponen, D. Moon, and S. Shenker. Accountable Internet Protocol (AIP). In *Proceedings of ACM SIGCOMM*, 2008.

[5] A. Arasu and G. S. Manku. Approximate Counts and Quantiles over Sliding Windows. In *Proceedings of ACM PODS*, 2004.

[6] B. Boyer and J. Moore. A Fast Majority Vote Algorithm. Technical report, ICSCA-CMP-32, Institute for Computer Science, University of Texas, 1981.

[7] T. Calders, N. Dexters, and B. Goethals. Mining Frequent Items in a Stream Using Flexible Windows. *Intelligent Data Analysis*, 12(3):293–304, 2008.

[8] T. H. Cormen, C. E. Leiserson, R. L. Rivest, and C. Stein. *Introduction to Algorithms*, chapter 13: Red-Black Trees. MIT Press and McGraw-Hill, 2001.

[9] G. Cormode and M. Hadjieleftheriou. Finding Frequent Items in Data Streams. *Proc. VLDB Endow.*, 1(2):1530–1541, 2008.

[10] G. Cormode and S. Muthukrishnan. An Improved Data Stream Summary: The Count-Min Sketch and its Applications. *Journal of Algorithms*, 55(1):58–75, 2005.

[11] S. A. Crosby and D. S. Wallach. Denial of Service via Algorithmic Complexity Attacks. In *Proceedings of USENIX Security*, 2003.

[12] A. Dainotti, A. Pescapè, P. Salvo Rossi, F. Palmieri, and G. Ventre. Internet Traffic Modeling by means of Hidden Markov Models. *Computer Networks (Elsevier)*, 52:2645–2662, 2008.

[13] A. Dainotti, A. Pescapè, and G. Ventre. A Cascade Architecture for DoS attacks Detection based on the Wavelet Transform. *Journal of Computer Security*, 17(6/2009):945–968, 2009.

[14] E. D. Demaine, A. López-Ortiz, and J. I. Munro. Frequency Estimation of Internet Packet Streams with Limited Space. In *Proceedings of ESA*, 2002.

[15] N. Duffield. Fair Sampling Across Network Flow Measurements. In *Proceedings of ACM SIGMETRICS*, 2012.

[16] C. Estan. *Internet Traffic Measurement: What's Going on in my Network?* PhD thesis, 2003.

[17] C. Estan and G. Varghese. New Directions in Traffic Measurement and Accounting: Focusing on the Elephants, Ignoring the Mice. *ACM Transactions on Computer Systems (TOCS)*, 21(3):270–313, 2003.

[18] M. Fang and N. Shivakumar. Computing Iceberg Queries Efficiently. In *Proceedings of VLDB*, 1999.

[19] P. Ferguson and D. Senie. Network Ingress Filtering: Defeating Denial of Service Attacks which employ IP Source Address Spoofing. RFC 2827 (Best Current Practice), May 2000. Updated by RFC 3704.

[20] M. Fischer and S. Salzberg. Finding a Majority Among N Votes: Solution to Problem 81-5. *Journal of Algorithms - JAL*, 3(4):362–380, 1982.

[21] L. Golab, D. DeHaan, E. D. Demaine, A. López-Ortiz, and J. I. Munro. Identifying Frequent Items in Sliding Windows over On-Line Packet Streams. In *Proceedings of ACM IMC*, 2003.

[22] M. Guirguis, A. Bestavros, and I. Matta. Exploiting the Transients of Adaptation for RoQ Attacks on Internet Resources. In *Proceedings of IEEE ICNP*, 2004.

[23] R. M. Karp, S. Shenker, and C. H. Papadimitriou. A Simple Algorithm for Finding Frequent Elements in Streams and Bags. *ACM Transactions on Database Systems*, 28(1):51–55, 2003.

[24] T. Kim, C. Basescu, L. Jia, S. B. Lee, Y.-C. Hu, and A. Perrig. Lightweight Source Authentication and Path Validation. In *Proceedings of ACM SIGCOMM*, 2014.

[25] A. Kuzmanovic and E. Knightly. Low-Rate TCP-Targeted Denial of Service Attacks and Counter Strategies. *IEEE/ACM Transactions on Networking*, 14(4):683–696, 2006.

[26] L. Lee and H. Ting. A Simpler and More Efficient Deterministic Scheme for Finding Frequent Items over Sliding Windows. In *Proceedings of ACM PODS*, 2006.

[27] X. Liu, A. Li, X. Yang, and D. Wetherall. Passport: Secure and Adoptable Source Authentication. In *Proceedings of USENIX/ACM NSDI*, 2008.

[28] S. Machiraju, M. Seshadri, and I. Stoica. A Scalable and Robust Solution for Bandwidth Allocation. In *Proceedings of IEEE International Workshop on Quality of Service*, volume 00, 2002.

[29] G. Manku and R. Motwani. Approximate Frequency Counts over Data Streams. In *Proceedings of VLDB*, 2002.

[30] A. Metwally, D. Agrawal, and A. El Abbadi. Efficient Computation of Frequent and Top-k Elements in Data Streams. In *Proceedings of ICDT*, 2005.

[31] J. Misra and D. Gries. Finding Repeated Elements. *Science of Computer Programming*, 2(2):143–152, 1982.

[32] J. Naous, M. Walfish, A. Nicolosi, D. Mazieres, M. Miller, and A. Seehra. Verifying and Enforcing Network Paths with ICING. In *Proceedings of ACM CoNext*, 2011.

[33] S. Shenker, C. Partridge, and R. Guerin. Specification of Guaranteed Quality of Service. RFC 2212 (Proposed Standard), Sept. 1997.

[34] I. Stoica, S. Shenker, and H. Zhang. Core-Stateless Fair Queueing: A Scalable Architecture to Approximate Fair Bandwidth Allocations in High-Speed Networks. *IEEE/ACM Transactions on Networking*, 11(1):33–46, Feb. 2003.

[35] D. M. Turner, V. Prevelakis, and A. D. Keromytis. A Market-Based Bandwidth Charging Framework. *ACM Transactions on Internet Technology*, 10(1):1–30, 2010.

[36] J. Turner. New Directions in Communications (Or Which Way to the Information Age?). *IEEE Communications Magazine*, 24:8–15, 1986.

[37] H. Wu, H.-C. Hsiao, and Y.-C. Yu. Efficient Large Flow Detection over Arbitrary Windows: An Algorithm Exact Outside An Ambiguity Region. Technical report, CMU-CyLab-14-006, CyLab, Carnegie Mellon University, 2014.

[38] M. Yu, L. Jose, and R. Miao. Software Defined Traffic Measurement with OpenSketch. In *Proceedings of USENIX NSDI*, 2013.

APPENDIX

A. ENGINEERING THE DETECTOR: SOLUTION AND ANALYSIS

We give a detailed solution and analysis to the problem defined in Section 4.6. The problem can be expressed by the inequality set (5):

$$\begin{cases} \dfrac{\alpha + 2\beta_{TH}}{\gamma_h - \frac{\rho}{n+1}} < t_{upincb} \\ \dfrac{\beta_\Delta}{\alpha(n-1) + (n+1)\beta_\ell + (n+1)\beta_\Delta} \cdot \rho > \gamma_\ell \\ \dfrac{\rho}{n+1} < \gamma_h \end{cases} \tag{5}$$

$$\Leftarrow \begin{cases} \dfrac{2(\alpha + \beta_{TH})}{\gamma_h - \frac{\rho}{n+1}} \leq t_{upincb} \\ \dfrac{\beta_\Delta}{\alpha + \beta_\ell + \beta_\Delta} \cdot \dfrac{\rho}{n+1} \geq \gamma_\ell \\ \dfrac{\rho}{n+1} < \gamma_h \end{cases} \tag{6}$$

$$\Leftrightarrow \begin{cases} \beta_\Delta \leq \dfrac{t_{upincb}(\gamma_h - \frac{\rho}{n+1}) - 2(\alpha + \beta_\ell)}{2} \\ \beta_\Delta \geq \dfrac{\gamma_\ell(\alpha + \beta_\ell)}{\frac{\rho}{n+1} - \gamma_\ell} \\ n > \dfrac{\rho}{\gamma_h} - 1 \end{cases} \tag{7}$$

$$\Rightarrow \begin{cases} \dfrac{\gamma_\ell(\alpha + \beta_\ell)}{\frac{\rho}{n+1} - \gamma_\ell} \leq \dfrac{t_{upincb}(\gamma_h - \frac{\rho}{n+1}) - 2(\alpha + \beta_\ell)}{2} \\ n > \dfrac{\rho}{\gamma_h} - 1 \end{cases} \tag{8}$$

We can assert that there must exist a solution pair of (n, β_Δ) which fulfills the inequality set (7), if and only if there is a n satisfying $n_{min} \leq n \leq n_{max}$, where

$$\begin{cases} n_{min} = \lceil \rho / \dfrac{M + \sqrt{M^2 - 4\gamma_h\gamma_\ell}}{2} \rceil - 1 \\ n_{max} = \lfloor \rho / \dfrac{M - \sqrt{M^2 - 4\gamma_h\gamma_\ell}}{2} \rfloor - 1 \\ M = \gamma_h + \gamma_\ell - \dfrac{2(\alpha + \beta_\ell)}{t_{upincb}} \geq 0 \end{cases} \tag{9}$$

Figure 8 illustrates the solution space. In this figure, the (n, β_Δ) solution pairs are in the space between the two lines of the lower bound curve and the upper bound curve. Note that the inequality sets (5) and (7) are not totally equal, so there may be additional solutions outside this space.

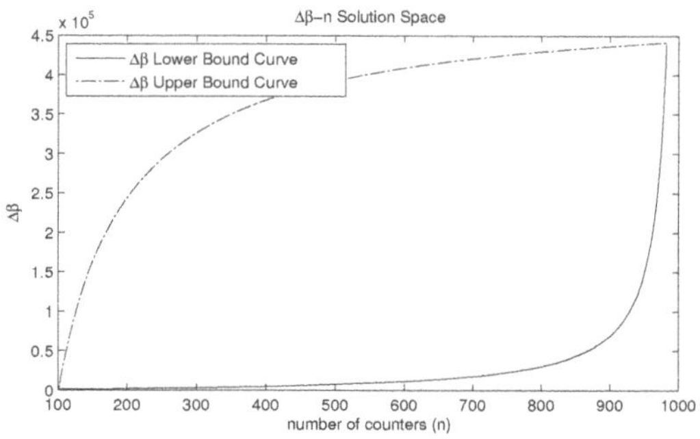

Figure 8: Curve of the lower bound of β_ℓ. ($\gamma_\ell = 100{,}000$ byte/s $\gamma_h = 1{,}000{,}000$ byte/s, $\rho = 100{,}000{,}000$ byte/s, $\alpha = 1518$ bytes, $\beta_\ell = 6072$ bytes, $t_{upincb} = 1$ second.)

According to the inequality set (7), the lower bound of β_Δ is $\beta_{\Delta\, min} = \frac{\gamma_\ell(\alpha+\beta_\ell)}{\frac{\rho}{n+1} - \gamma_\ell}$. We can see $\beta_{\Delta\, min}$ increases with n, as Figure 8 shows. Since we can reduce memory consumption and the burst gap by using a smaller n and β_Δ, we choose

$$\begin{cases} n = n_{min} = \lceil \rho / \dfrac{M + \sqrt{M^2 - 4\gamma_h\gamma_\ell}}{2} \rceil - 1 \\ \beta_{TH} = \beta_\ell + \beta_{\Delta\, min} = \beta_\ell + \dfrac{\gamma_\ell(\alpha + \beta_\ell)}{\frac{\rho}{n_{min}+1} - \gamma_\ell} \end{cases} \tag{10}$$

as our final answer to the design problem.

We give a numerical example showing how to configure EARDET based on the result above. Suppose the administrator of the detector chooses $\gamma_\ell = 100KB/s$, $\gamma_h = 1MB/s$, $\rho = 100MB/s$, $\alpha = 1518$ bytes, $\beta_\ell = 6072$ bytes, $t_{upincb} = 1$ second. Then using Equation (10), we choose $n = 101$ and $\beta_\Delta = 863$ bytes. With these two parameters, the incubation period is 0.7848 seconds which is smaller than $t_{upincb} = 1$ second, and the no false positive rate is 100450 byte/s which is larger than $\gamma_\ell = 100000$. The ratio between no false negative rate $\frac{\rho}{n+1}$ and low-bandwidth threshold rate γ_ℓ is $\frac{\rho}{n+1}/\gamma_\ell = 9.80$. The results show that to achieve quick reaction to large flows and a small rate gap, the detector only needs a small number of extra counters compared with the minimum number of required counters (i.e. $\frac{\rho}{\gamma_h} - 1 = 99$) and a low burst gap.

We obtain this particular solution by choosing the minimum n and minimum β_Δ. We can also solve the inequality set (5) for different requirements, such as minimizing the rate gap between $\frac{\rho}{n+1}$ and $\frac{\beta_\Delta}{\alpha(n-1)+(n+1)\beta+(n+1)\beta_\Delta} \cdot \rho$.

However, the inequality set (7) may be unsolvable for some $\rho, \gamma_\ell, \beta_\ell, \gamma_h, \alpha, t_{upincb}$. To make it solvable, we need to make sure $M^2 - 8\gamma_h\gamma_\ell$ and M are not negative in the inequality set (9). Namely,

$$\gamma_h + \gamma_\ell - \frac{2(\alpha + \beta_\ell)}{t_{upincb}} \geq \sqrt{4\gamma_h\gamma_\ell} \tag{11}$$

$$\Leftarrow t_{upincb} \geq \frac{2(\alpha + \beta_\ell)}{\gamma_h + \gamma_\ell - 2\sqrt{\gamma_h\gamma_\ell}} \tag{12}$$

Moreover, according to Section 4.3, $\gamma_h > \gamma_\ell$ is necessary to make the inequality set (7) solvable.

Crossroads: A Practical Data Sketching Solution for Mining Intersection of Streams*

Zhenglin Yu
Georgia Tech
Atlanta, GA, USA
yzhenglin@gatech.edu

Zihui Ge
AT&T Labs - Research
Florham Park, NJ, USA
gezihui@research.att.com

Ashwin Lall
Denison University
Granville, OH, USA
lalla@denison.edu

Jia Wang
AT&T Labs - Research
Florham Park, NJ, USA
jiawang@research.att.com

Jun (Jim) Xu
Georgia Tech
Atlanta, GA, USA
jx@cc.gatech.edu

He Yan
AT&T Labs - Research
Florham Park, NJ, USA
yanhe@research.att.com

ABSTRACT

The explosive increase in cellular network traffic, users, and applications, as well as the corresponding shifts in user expectations, has created heavy needs and demands on cellular data providers. In this paper we address one such need: mining the logs of cellular voice and data traffic to rapidly detect network performance anomalies and other events of interest. The core challenge in solving this problem is the issue that it is impossible to predict beforehand where in the traffic the event may appear, requiring us to be able to query arbitrary subsets of the network traffic (e.g., longer than usual round-trip times for users in a specific urban area to connect to FunContent.com using a particular model of phone). Since it is infeasible to store all combinations of such data, especially when it is collected in real-time, we need to be able to summarize the traffic data using succinct sketch data structures to answer these queries.

The major contribution of this paper is the introduction of a scheme, called Crossroads, that can be used to compute the intersection of the measurements between two overlapping streams. For instance, in the above example, it is possible to compute the intersection of all the data going between the downtown area and FunContent.com with all the data generated by the model of phone to detect anomalous RTT behavior. In effect, this gives us a way to essentially "square root" the number of sketches that we need to maintain, transforming a prohibitively expensive problem to one that is tractable in practice. We provide rigorous analysis of our sketch and the trade-offs between memory footprint and accuracy. We also demonstrate the efficacy of our solution via simulation on data collected at a major cellular service carrier in the US.

*This work has been supported in part by the collaborative NSF project that includes awards CNS 1218092 and CNS 1217758.

IMC'14, November 5–7, 2014, Vancouver, BC, Canada.
Copyright 2014 ACM 978-1-4503-3213-2/14/11 ...$15.00.
http://dx.doi.org/10.1145/2663716.2663733.

Categories and Subject Descriptors

C.2.3 [**Computer-Communication Networks**]: Network monitoring; C.4 [**Performance of Systems**]: Measurement techniques

General Terms

Algorithms; Networking

Keywords

Traffic analysis; Algorithms; Data Streaming

1. INTRODUCTION

The past several years have seen an explosive growth of mobile network technologies and services in all conceivable dimensions. The amount of cellular network traffic has dramatically increased year over year. Today a large percentage of the population on this planet – especially young people – spend a large chunk of their daily lives on mobile devices such as smartphones and tablets. More and more mobile services are provided through smartphone apps, allowing people to send/receive emails and text messages, watch videos, or play online games using their smartphones.

However, this growth also poses a significant challenge to cellular network providers in that it makes the performance anomalies in cellular networks and services hard to measure, detect, and diagnose. Cellular service providers do have sophisticated monitoring of network elements for faults and performance. However, services have gotten dramatically more complicated over recent years, with a plethora of sophisticated devices (phones, tablets) and a tremendous variety of apps and online services. Knowing when a single type of device app or device/app combination is having performance problems requires comprehensive service monitoring and sophisticated problem detection and trouble isolation, and yet is critical to being able to rapidly resolve such issues. Given the complexity of this network ecosystem, issues may be introduced by the device (e.g., software), network, application server, or by some complex interaction between different combinations of these. So simply monitoring the network or overall service performance will not detect all possible issues.

1.1 Problem Statement

In this work, we identify a challenging data mining problem that is critical for automatically detecting anomalies and degradation of performance, and propose a data sketching solution for it. The type of event we are looking for in this network environment is a set of cellular calls or data sessions whose performance is negatively impacted by a common cause. An example event could be that more than 100 sessions/calls (say during a five-minute measurement interval) from customers in a "Metropolis" (a fictitious city name) downtown location to FunContent server using "Magic Phone 7" (a fictitious device name) that run on "Magic OS 88.8" (a fictitious OS name) have longer-than-usual round-trip times (RTT) during a 5-minute time window τ. In this case, network operators will be asked to look into possible root cause(s) of the event which could include Magic Phone 7 operating systems software issues (e.g., the "Magic OS" version is too recent for the old model phone), routing problems along the path from that Metropolis location to San Francisco bay area (where Facebook servers are located), or software problems with the FunContent app or at the server side (e.g., incompatibility with an old version of the app used by many Metropolis-area customers).

If we were able to record every cellular packet and store it in a traditional static database, identifying such performance anomaly events becomes a variant of the association-rule mining problem. For example, our task would be looking for the following association rule in the abovementioned scenario:

"Device = Magic Phone 7" &
"OS = Magic OS 88.8" &
"Application = FunContent.app" &
"Source = Metropolis downtown location" &
"Destination = FunContent.com" &
"Time = τ"
$\Rightarrow$ "unusually long RTT".

Our problem here is much more challenging because in a major cellular network the raw traffic comes in too fast to be saved into a database and is too large to be stored for an extended period of time. In other words, we need to identify such association rules on the fly while the packets stream in. For the "streaming version" of the abovementioned problem, a naive solution is to maintain, for every possible value combination of the attributes "Device", "OS", "Application", "Source", "Destination", and "Time", a few statistics counters for tracking the average RTT of the set of packets that matches the value combination. While this solution may barely work today, when the total number of possible value combinations of these attributes is still in the tens or hundreds of millions, it will not work in the near future, as the explosive growth in the number of applications, devices, and content providers (destinations) will soon drive the total number of such value combinations to billions or even trillions, making it impossible to fit all these counters in main memory (DRAM). While disks (or solid state drives) are still large enough to store complete summaries, they are too slow to allow for per-packet updates (to the counters) in such a high-speed cellular network.

In this work, we propose a general memory-efficient technique for performing association-rule mining over high-speed data streams, of which the abovementioned scenario is a specific case. Data streaming is concerned with processing a long stream of data items in one pass using a small working memory in order to approximately answer a query regarding the stream. The key challenge is to "remember," in this small memory, as much information pertinent to the query as possible. Such information is often organized as a synopsis data structure referred to as a *sketch* and different sketch data structures are usually needed to answer different types of queries over the data stream. These sketches are inherently lossy, greatly reducing the storage cost of the data at the cost of some accuracy – there are well-understood analytical tradeoffs between the space savings and accuracy of such sketches. Our solution reduces the amount of working space needed to (approximately) track all possible attribute value combinations (say there are N of them) from $O(N)$ to $O(\sqrt{N})$, without significantly degrading the monitoring accuracy for major performance anomalies. This allows the working space to reside entirely in the main memory (DRAM), and thereby allows for the processing of each and every data item (in this case a packet) in the stream – and the updating of the corresponding sketches – on the fly.

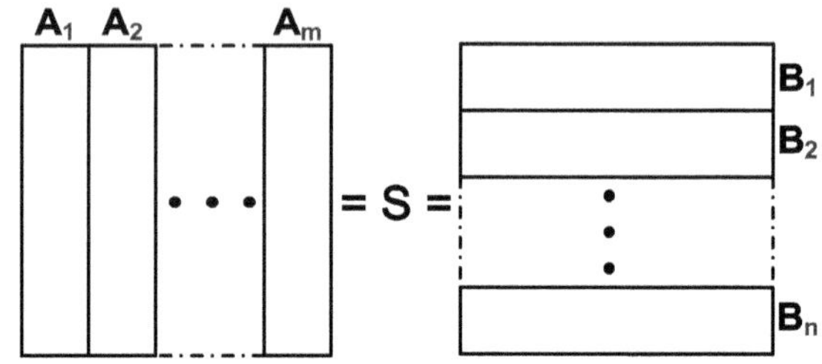

Figure 1: Two different partition scenarios of the same set. We partition the identical set S as subsets A_1, A_2... A_m and as subsets B_1, B_2... B_n

1.2 The "Crossroads" Approach

Our solution consists of three steps. The first step is to partition the set of attributes that needs to be mined for associations into two subsets so that the number of value combinations of attributes in each subset is much smaller than – and ideally close to the square root of – that of all attributes. As shown in Fig. 1, each subset of attributes can be viewed as a dimension along which the data set S (in our case consisting of all packets in a cellular network) is partitioned. For example, in the abovementioned scenario, one dimension could include all possible "Source" and "Destination" combinations, and the other "Device type", "OS", and "Application" (including its version number) combinations; while the number of joint value combinations of all these attributes in the future could be in trillions ($\sim 10^{12}$), that of each subset may only be in millions ($\sim 10^6$). In this way, the data set S can be partitioned into (data) subsets A_i for $i = 1, 2, ..., m$ along one dimension, each of which corresponds to the subset of data that takes a certain value combination along that dimension, and similarly into (data) subsets B_j for $j = 1, 2, ..., n$ along the other. In the abovementioned application scenario, the set of packets that match ("Source = the Metropolis downtown location" & "Destination = FunContent.com") could be one such A_i, and the set of packets that match ("Device = Magic Phone 7" & "OS = Magic OS 88.8" & "Application = FunContent.app" & "Time = τ") could be one such B_j. Then the set of packets that match the filter ("Device = Magic Phone 7" & "OS = Magic

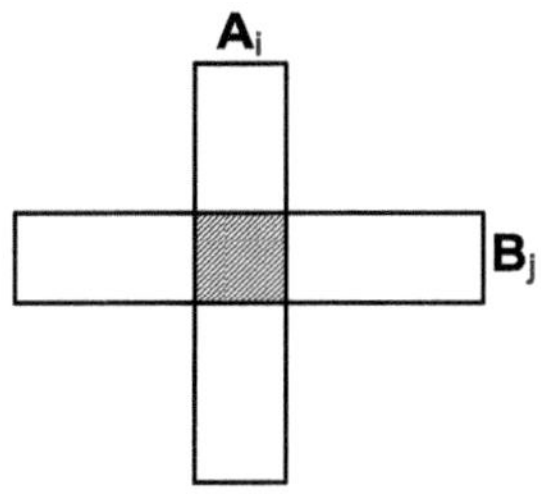

Figure 2: We can compute functions on the intersection of arbitrary sets A_i and B_j

OS 88.8" & "Application = FunContent.app" & "Source = the Metropolis downtown location" & "Destination = FunContent.com" & "Time = τ") – of which we would like to measure and monitor the performance metrics (e.g., average RTT) – is precisely the intersection of A_i and B_j, as illustrated in Fig. 2. As will become clear shortly, we will estimate these performance metrics by taking such intersections, and hence the name "Crossroads."

In the second step, for each set A_i, a sketch is constructed to succinctly summarize the performance metrics (e.g., average RTT) of all data items in it. The same is done for each B_j. We will talk about the sketch data structures suitable for this purpose later in Section 3. The novelty of this approach lies mainly in the third step, which is to derive the performance metrics of the data inside each $A_i \cap B_j$ by intersecting the sketches constructed for A_i and that constructed for B_j.

The potential further loss of accuracy in this intersection process aside, one may be tempted to take intersection on three or more such sketches. This is however provably impossible, if the Tug-of-War sketch is used as the underlying sketch data structure [1]. The Tug-of-War sketch is in general preferred over other types of sketches due to its lower space and computational complexities, and the much better numerical stability of the Gaussian distribution used by it. Slightly disappointing as this impossibility result might be, it serves as a somber reminder that we should count our blessings that we are able to perform even the two-way intersection after all.

It is assumed, in the above example, that the full data set is available to the association-rule mining (ARM) algorithm – that is, all attribute value combinations are stored. The contribution of this work is to significantly reduce the amount of data stored so that it can be performed over a high-speed data stream. We do not propose any new ARM algorithms, but give a way to reduce the amount of data that such an algorithm would need to use. Although we believe our technique could be used to reduce the space-complexity of many ARM algorithms, that is outside the scope of this paper.

2. PRELIMINARIES

In this section, we give a formal description of the problem and illustrate it with some examples.

For the problem of detecting anomalies and other events in a cellular network, we would like to estimate some useful quantities such as the *moments* of some important metrics (e.g., RTT) of the data stream. The kth moment of a packet stream is defined as: $M_k = \sum_i v_i^k$, where v_i is the value (e.g., RTT) of the ith packet in a stream. In particular, the moments $M_0 = \sum_i v_i^0 = \sum_i 1$ and $M_1(v) = \sum_i v_i$ give the number of packets and the sum of such values in all the packets in the stream, respectively. These quantities together allow us to estimate the mean of such values in the stream. The second moment ($M_2 = \sum_i v_i^2$) is even more interesting, since, normalized by the total number of packets M_0 in the stream, it can be decomposed into the sum of two quantities: (1) the square of the empirical mean v value, and (2) the empirical variance of the v values, across all packets in the stream (i.e., $\frac{M_2(v)}{M_0(v)} = E(v)^2 + Var(v)$). Any significant increase in either the mean or the variance, both constituting a performance anomaly, will be reflected in the second moment.

Here is a simple example of a stream containing 3 different packets. Let the RTT values of the 3 packets be 50, 100, 100. For this stream, the number of distinct elements will be $M_0(RTT) = 3$, the sum of RTT values in the stream will be $M_1(RTT) = 50 + 100 + 100 = 250$, and the second moment will be $M_2(RTT) = 50^2 + 100^2 + 100^2 = 22,500$.

Note that in the data streaming literature, we are usually concerned with the *frequency moments* of the stream, that is, moments based on the frequency with which each unique identifier appears. In the networking context, this identifier is usually that of a transport-layer (TCP or UDP) flow, i.e., the five-tuple consisting of source and destination IP addresses and port numbers, and the protocol. In our case, however, we consider every packet to have a unique identifier, or to be a singleton "flow" itself. In other words, we are interested in the much easier-to-compute moments of the (RTT) values of individual singleton flows. For a single stream this can trivially be computed using a single counter that is incremented with each new (RTT) value. The reason why our problem is challenging, and deserves this effort, is that we are interested in efficiently computing the moments of the *intersection* of two massive data streams. More precisely, we would like to compute the moments of the (RTT) values associated with the set of data items that appear in both data streams (i.e., their "intersection").

3. INTERSECTION ALGORITHM

In this section, we first describe the algorithm for sketching the data. We then explain how our intersection algorithm can be used for estimating the second frequency moment of a traffic feature. We use RTT as a concrete example, though we emphasize that any numeric feature can be used. Next, we formalize our M_2 intersection algorithm and provide theoretical guarantees and rigorous statistical analysis for it. Finally, we describe the design of our M_0 and M_1 algorithms and explain how they work. Once again, the sketch data structures are not novel, but the way in which they are used for computing intersections is the main contribution of our work.

3.1 Sketching Algorithm

As explained before and shown in Fig. 2, we would like to be able to estimate certain metrics (e.g., RTT) associated with data items that belong to the intersection of any A_i, $i = 1, 2, ..., m$ with any B_j, $j = 1, 2, ..., n$. We do so by maintaining a total of $m+n$ sketches, namely, one for each set A_i, $i = 1, 2, ..., m$ and one for each set B_j, $j = 1, 2, ..., n$. In our application scenario, the data are simply a massive stream of cellular network packets. We identify four important attributes I, J, V, and ID in each packet. The abovementioned partitioning of the whole stream into $A_i's$ and $B_j's$ is based on the value a packet takes on attribute I and J respectively. The V attribute is the metric (say RTT) that is of interest to us. The ID attribute is essentially the set of bits in a packet that uniquely identifies the packet. We emphasize this ID attribute is not the flow identifier (the abovementioned five tuple) although the latter could be a part of the former, since we consider each packet a "singleton flow" for the purpose of the second moment estimation, as we explained earlier.

Let us denote the sketches for A_i and B_j as $S(A_i)$ and $S(B_j)$, respectively, and let $M(v)$ be a function that computes the moments for a certain value v (e.g., $M(v) = v^2$ for M_2). Then our goal is to estimate $\sum_{pkt \in A_i \cap B_j} M(pkt.V)$, which denotes the moment of the values of all packets in the intersection of the sets A_i and B_j, from the sketches $S(A_i)$ and $S(B_j)$. Therefore, as shown in Algorithm 1, with the arrival of each packet pkt, we need to update both sketches $S(A_{pkt.I})$ and $S(B_{pkt.J})$ with its contribution $pkt.V$. We will explain in the next section how this contribution to both sketches are "linked" by the identifier of the packet $pkt.ID$ so that it can be accounted for and later retrieved from their intersection.

Algorithm 1 Processing algorithm

UPDATE:
1: Upon the arrival of a packet *pkt*
2: v:=*pkt*.V
3: i:=*pkt*.I
4: j:=*pkt*.J
5: Update(S(A_i), v, *pkt*.ID)
6: Update(S(B_j), v, *pkt*.ID)

As conventional data sketches weren't designed to handle such intersection operations, our work is focused on how to do that. We choose the *Tug-of-War sketch* as the underlying sketch data structure and build the intersection capability on top of it. Alon et al. [2] proposed this remarkable sketch, later named the "tug-of-war" sketch in [1], for estimating the second moment of a data stream using only logarithmic space. For all ϵ, $\lambda > 0$, the tug-of-war sketch uses only $O(\frac{\log(1/\epsilon)}{\lambda^2})$ counters to sketch the second moment of a stream with the guarantee that the probability with which the relative error is larger than λ is at most ϵ. The sketch allows arbitrary and efficient updates for the values. Let $\overrightarrow{s} = \{s_1, s_2, ...s_n\}$ be a vector of length n, where each entry s_i takes on value $+1$ or -1 with equal probability $\frac{1}{2}$, and $\overrightarrow{v} = \{v_1, v_2, ...v_n\}$ where $\{v_1, v_2, ...v_n\}$ are the respective V values of the n packets in the stream. Then the value of a counter in the sketch is $\overrightarrow{v} \cdot \overrightarrow{s} = v_1 s_1 + v_2 s_2 + \ldots + v_n s_n$ [2]. It was shown in [2] that the square of this counter value is an unbiased estimator for the second moment of the v_i values, and a small number of such estimators (i.e., squares of the values in multiple counters) can be combined to provide an accurate estimation of the second moment, as characterized by the abovementioned space-accuracy tradeoff.

One key property of the tug-of-war sketch is that if two sketches have the same size and use the same vector $\overrightarrow{s}$, then we can add up the two sketches to get the direct sum which is equivalent to taking the union of the original streams. This feature of allowing the computation of the union of two sketches is a vital property that we will later leverage in our algorithm design.

Algorithm 2 The Tug-of-War algorithm

PRE-PROCESSING:
1: Fix K independent hash functions $h_k : \boldsymbol{U} \rightarrow \{+1, -1\}$, $k = 1, 2, ..., K$, each of which is four-wise independent
2: Initialize $Z[k] := 0$ for $k = 1, 2, ..., K$

ALGORITHM:
1: Upon the arrival of a packet *pkt*
2: For $k := 1$ to K
3: $Z[k] := Z[k] + pkt.V * h_k(pkt.ID)$
4: Return $\left(\sum_{k=1}^{K} Z[k]^2\right) / K$

3.2 Intersection algorithm for estimating M_2

Recall that our data are a long stream of packets, and for each packet pkt, we identify four important attributes I, J, V, and ID. In this section, we explain how we compute the M_2 of the V values (RTTs in this case) for the intersection of a certain pair of sub-streams A_i and B_j. The sub-stream A_i consists of all packets whose I attribute value is equal to i, and the sub-stream B_j consists of all packets whose J attribute value is equal to j. To simplify the notation, we drop the subscripts in A_i and B_j in the sequel, referring to them as A and B respectively. With the streaming context of A and B being clear, we will call them sets rather than sub-streams in the sequel.

3.2.1 Algorithm Overview

We use the tug-of-war technique to sketch both A and B. Each sketch – $S(A)$ or $S(B)$ – is made up of K counters $\{Z[k]\}$, $k = 1, 2, ..., K$. For convenience of notation, we will write $S(A)$ or $S(B)$ as S_A or S_B in the sequel. Each counter $Z[k]$ is paired with a hash function h_k that generates the above-mentioned random vector $\overrightarrow{s}$ (now called $\overrightarrow{s_k}$ to distinguish them from one another) with which the V values of the packets in the stream, viewed as a vector, will take an inner product. The "Update(S(*), v, pkt.ID)" procedure inside Algorithm 1, when the underlying sketch is the tug-of-war, is shown in Algorithm 2. Upon the arrival of a packet *pkt* that belongs to the sub-stream, the update to to the kth counter is simply $Z[k] := Z[k] + pkt.V * h_k(pkt.ID)$, where each h_k is a hash function that deterministically outputs $+1$ or -1 with equal probability given any input value. As mentioned earlier, there is a tradeoff between the accuracy of the estimation and the number of counters K used. When we refer to the size of the sketch, we mean the number of counters K.

The tug-of-war technique has a useful property that, when two tug-of-war sketches $S(A)$ and $S(B)$ employ the same number of counters and set of hash functions, $S_{A \bigcup B}$, the sketch for the union of two sets, is simply the component-wise addition of S_A and S_B (i.e., their corresponding counters added up). Making use of this property by doing exactly so, we define $S_{A \oplus B}$ as the component-wise sum of S_A and S_B. Our estimation of the M_2 of $A \bigcap B$ is simply $\widehat{M_2}(S_{A \bigcap B}) = \frac{1}{2} \cdot \{M_2(S_{A \oplus B}) - M_2(S_A) - M_2(S_B)\}$, where $M_2(S_{A \oplus B})$, $M_2(S_A)$, and $M_2(S_B)$ can be obtained using the standard estimation procedures for the tug-of-war sketch.

3.2.2 Theoretical Guarantees

In this section, we derive the variance of the estimator $\widehat{M_2}(S_{A\bigcap B})$ when only one (instead of K) hash function and counter is used in sketching. We define two parameters $\gamma_A, \gamma_B \leq 1$ as $\sum_{A\cap B} v_i^2 = \gamma_A \sum_A v_i^2$ and $\sum_{A\cap B} v_i^2 = \gamma_B \sum_B v_i^2$. In other words, γ_A and γ_B represent the proportion of the intersection part respectively in set A and set B. Intuitively, this is the amount of overlap the intersection has with either set and we will need it to be large enough because otherwise the "signal" (M_2 of the intersection) will be drowned out by the noise (errors in estimating M_2's of A and B from their respective sketches). The following theorem demonstrates that such an estimator is unbiased and has reasonably low variance. Note this variance can be further reduced by about a factor of K, when K counters (and hash functions) are used.

Theorem 1 *The M_2 Intersection Algorithm produces an unbiased estimator for $M_2(S_{A\bigcap B})$, and the variance of the estimator is* $(\sum_{A\cap B} v_i^2)^2(\frac{1}{\gamma_A\gamma_B} - 1)$

Proof Let $\widehat{Y}$ denote the estimator for $M_2(S_{A\bigcap B})$ and recall that v_i denotes the value for the element with ID i. The estimator for the sketch S_A is $\widehat{M_2}(S_A) = (\sum_A v_i s_i)^2$ and that for sketch S_B is $\widehat{M_2}(S_B) = (\sum_B v_i s_i)^2$. In both sketches, every choice of $s_i \in \{+1, -1\}$ is identical as both use the same hash function $h : \boldsymbol{U} \rightarrow \{+1, -1\}$. The estimator $\widehat{M_2}(S_{A\oplus B})$ for the second frequency moment of $S_{A\oplus B}$ is then $\widehat{M_2}(S_{A\oplus B}) = (\sum_A v_i s_i + \sum_B v_i s_i)^2$.

Now we prove that our algorithm can produce an unbiased estimator for $M_2(S_{A\cap B})$. From the above algorithm, our estimator is:

$$
\begin{aligned}
\widehat{Y} &= \frac{1}{2}\cdot\{\widehat{M_2}(S_{A\oplus B}) - \widehat{M_2}(S_A) - \widehat{M_2}(S_B)\} \\
&= \frac{1}{2}\cdot\{(\sum_A v_i s_i + \sum_B v_i s_i)^2 \\
&\quad -(\sum_A v_i s_i)^2 - (\sum_B v_i s_i)^2\} \\
&= (\sum_A v_i s_i)(\sum_B v_i s_i).
\end{aligned}
$$

Then, the expected value of this estimator is

$$
\begin{aligned}
E[\widehat{Y}] &= E[(\sum_A v_i s_i)(\sum_B v_i s_i)] \\
&= E[\sum_{A\cap B} v_i^2 s_i^2 + \sum_{i\in A-B, j\in B-A} v_i s_i v_j s_j + \\
&\quad \sum_{i\in A\cap B, j\in B-A} v_i s_i v_j s_j + \sum_{i\in A-B, j\in A\cap B} v_i s_i v_j s_j] \\
&= \sum_{A\cap B} v_i^2 = M_2(S_{A\bigcap B}).
\end{aligned}
$$

In the second equality, for all $i \neq j$ we know that s_i and s_j are independent, so $E[s_i s_j] = E[s_i]\cdot E[s_j] = 0$ and all but the first term disappear. Also note that $s_i^2 = 1$ as each $s_i \in \{1, -1\}$, leading to the simplification of the first term. Thus, $\widehat{Y}$ is an unbiased estimator for $M_2(S_{A\cap B})$.

Now we will analyze the variance of our estimator in the algorithm. First, we compute

$$
\begin{aligned}
E[\widehat{Y}^2] &= E[(\sum_A v_i s_i)^2\cdot(\sum_B v_i s_i)^2] \\
&= E[(\sum_{A\cap B} v_i s_i + \sum_{A-B} v_i s_i)^2 \\
&\quad \cdot(\sum_{A\cap B} v_i s_i + \sum_{B-A} v_i s_i)^2] \\
&= \sum_{A\cap B} v_i^4 + 2\sum_{A\cap B, i<j} v_i^2 v_j^2 + (\sum_{A\cap B} v_i^2)(\sum_{B-A} v_i^2) \\
&\quad +(\sum_{A\cap B} v_i^2)(\sum_{A-B} v_i^2) + (\sum_{A-B} v_i^2)(\sum_{B-A} v_i^2).
\end{aligned}
$$

In the last equality we once again drop terms that include $s_i s_j$ where $i \neq j$ as their expectation is equal to 0.

From the derivation of the expectation, we know that:

$$(E[\widehat{Y}])^2 = \sum_{A\cap B} v_i^4 + 2\sum_{A\cap B, i<j} v_i^2 v_j^2.$$

so the variance of the estimator is

$$
\begin{aligned}
Var[\widehat{Y}] &= E[\widehat{Y}^2] - (E[\widehat{Y}])^2 \\
&= (\sum_{A\cap B} v_i^2)(\sum_{B-A} v_i^2) + (\sum_{A\cap B} v_i^2)(\sum_{A-B} v_i^2) \\
&\quad +(\sum_{A-B} v_i^2)(\sum_{B-A} v_i^2) \\
&= (\sum_{A\cap B} v_i^2)^2(\frac{1}{\gamma_B} - 1) + (\sum_{A\cap B} v_i^2)^2(\frac{1}{\gamma_A} - 1) \\
&\quad +(\sum_{A\cap B} v_i^2)^2(\frac{1}{\gamma_A} - 1)(\frac{1}{\gamma_B} - 1) \\
&= (\sum_{A\cap B} v_i^2)^2(\frac{1}{\gamma_A\gamma_B} - 1).
\end{aligned}
$$

Numerical Illustration: For instance, assume that the intersection of the two streams only has 1% of the value of both A and B (i.e., $\gamma_A = \gamma_B = 0.01$). Then, if we use just 100,000 counters per sketch, the variance-to-mean-square ratio is 0.1 – small enough to get under 10% error with high probability.

3.3 Intersection Algorithms for estimating M_0 and M_1

The zero-th moment M_0 indicates the number of distinct elements in a stream. Ordinarily, this quantity can be trivially tracked using just one counter for a single stream, but this trivial solution does not allow for the estimation of M_0 of the intersection of two streams. However, the above-mentioned intersection technique for estimating M_2 can be modified slightly to estimate M_0 of the intersection of two streams. We simply replace the term "*pkt*.V" in line 3 of the second routine in Algorithm 2 by the value 1. The M_0 estimator for the intersection is simply $\widehat{M_0}(S_{A\bigcap B}) = \frac{1}{2}\cdot\{M_0(S_{A\oplus B}) - M_0(S_A) - M_0(S_B)\}$. Note this simple modification works for M_0 estimation only in this special case, where every packet is a "singleton" flow.

To estimate the average RTT, we need also to estimate the first moment M_1, which is the sum of all the *RTT* values of the packets in a stream. It turns out that the M_2 intersection technique can again be slightly modified to suit our need. We simply replace the term "*pkt*.V" by its square root and the estimator remains the same as in the M_2 case.

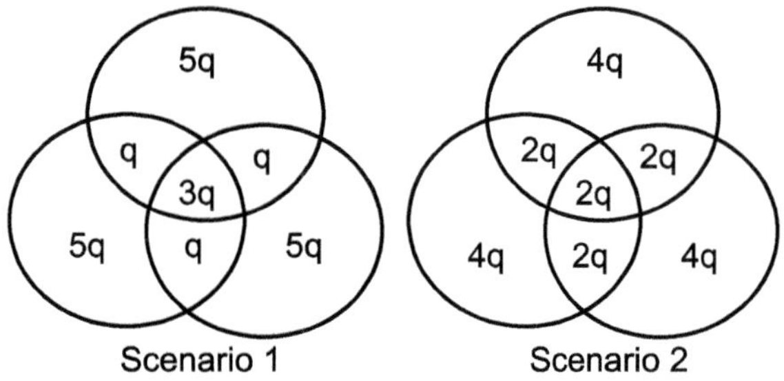

Figure 3: Two scenarios for intersection of 3 sketches.

Again, this simple modification works only in this special case, where every packet is a "singleton" flow. Otherwise, we would have to resort to much more expensive techniques such as the Cauchy distribution sketch proposed by Indyk [10]. The algorithms and analysis are very similar to the case for M_2 and are omitted here for brevity.

4. AN IMPOSSIBILITY RESULT ON 3-WAY INTERSECTION

In this section, we prove a claim stated earlier that, with Tug-of-War algorithm, it is impossible to generalize this 2-way intersection scheme to a 3-way (or higher) scheme. Note that in the Tug-of-War sketch, the final value of each counter is the result of a long random walk, which is known to be very close to Gaussian. This property will be used in the proof. Recall that our scheme uses Tug-of-War for estimating all three quantities (M_0, M_1, M_2) of interest, and is therefore governed by this impossibility result. Although it is possible to circumvent this impossibility using other types of sketches (e.g., the stable distribution sketches [10] other than the Gaussian one), they are in general much more expensive than the Tug-of-War sketch.

Intriguing as our claim is, its proof is in fact quite straightforward. Suppose three Tug-of-War sketches S_A, S_B, and S_C – each of which consists of the same number of counters – are used to summarize three data sets A, B, and C respectively. Since counter values in each sketch is i.i.d., without loss of generality it suffices to prove the case in which there is only one counter in each sketch (i.e., one random variable in each random vector). In the following, we will create two sets (of data sets) $\{A_1, B_1, C_1\}$ and $\{A_2, B_2, C_2\}$ so that the random vectors $\langle S_{A_1}, S_{B_1}, S_{C_1}\rangle$ and $\langle S_{A_2}, S_{B_2}, S_{C_2}\rangle$ have identical joint (approximately Gaussian) distributions, but $|A_1 \cap B_1 \cap C_1|$ and $|A_2 \cap B_2 \cap C_2|$ are very different in value. However, since any estimator of the 3-way intersection is necessarily a function of the joint distribution of these three sketches, this estimator cannot estimate both 3-way intersections accurately.

First consider scenario 1 in Figure 3. All three sets, A, B, and C, contain $10q$ packets each. Note that though their sizes are the same, A, B and C are distinct sets of packets. Let us assume that all the values for all packets have the same value T. In this scenario, the sketches produced from the three sets are three random variables (there is only one counter in each sketch as explained earlier) S_A, S_B, S_C. As explained before, when q is large, the marginal distribution of each random variable is Gaussian, and they have a joint Gaussian distribution. The variance of the three sketches are all $10T^2$, and their pairwise covariances $Cov[S_A, S_B]$, $Cov[S_B, S_C]$, $Cov[S_A, S_C]$ are all equal to $4qT^2$. Note that $4q$ is exactly the size of pairwise intersections $|A \cap C|$, $|A \cap B|$ and $|B \cap C|$. Thus these 3 random variables S_A, S_B, S_C have a joint Gaussian distribution with the covariance matrix:

$$\Sigma = \begin{bmatrix} 10T^2 & 4qT^2 & 4qT^2 \\ 4qT^2 & 10T^2 & 4qT^2 \\ 4qT^2 & 4qT^2 & 10T^2 \end{bmatrix}. \quad (1)$$

It can be easily verified that in scenario 2 these 3 random variables also have a joint Gaussian distribution, and have the same covariance matrix. Since the covariance matrix uniquely determines a joint Gaussian distribution, these two random vectors have the same joint probability distribution in both scenarios. However, the size of 3-way intersection in these two scenarios are $3qT^2$ and $2qT^2$ respectively. This means that there is at least 33% relative error in estimating one of these values.

5. IMPLEMENTATION ISSUES

In this section, we describe several important implementation issues with the data sketches and their cost and performance ramifications if applicable.

1. **Intersection Ratio.** We define the intersection ratio (IR) of the sets A and B as follows:

$$IR_A = \frac{size(A \cap B)}{size(A)}, IR_B = \frac{size(A \cap B)}{size(B)}, \quad (2)$$

where $size()$ denotes the number of packets contained in a set. IR_A and IR_B are equivalent respectively to γ_A and γ_B defined earlier, if the V values of all the packets are identical.

This IR has a great influence on the relative errors of our estimations, for M_0, M_1, and M_2, over the intersection $A \cap B$. For example, if $IR_A = IR_B = 0.01$, which means the intersection constitutes only 1% of the size of A or B, then these relative errors will be approximately 100 times larger than the relative errors of our estimations over A or B alone. When IR_A and IR_B are both very small (e.g., 10^{-4}), $A \cap B$ is so small compared to A and B that our approach will not produce accurate estimations over the intersection without consuming an excessive amount of counter memory. In our implementations, we dimension just enough counter memory for the cases in which IR_A and IR_B are both around or above 0.005.

2. **The ID attribute.** It has been shown that the first invariant (i.e., not including fields that are modified hop by hop by routers such as TTL) 28 bytes in an IP packet header suffice to uniquely identify a packet [21]. In the spirit of that, a similar set of bytes is used as the aforementioned ID attribute for the cellular network packets (different from IP). Our approach can also be extended to flow-level by using the unique identifier of each flow instead of each individual packet.

3. **Sketch resource allocation.** In this work, we are interested in estimating the average RTT, or equivalently $\frac{M_1(RTT)}{M_0(RTT)}$, from the underlying Tug-of-War sketches. However, since $M_0(RTT)$ is the denominator, its estimation accuracy affects the overall accuracy more than

the numerator $M_1(RTT)$. Therefore, we allocate more sketch memory, in terms of the number of counters and hash functions, for measuring M_0 than for measuring M_1.

4. **No median and all averaging.** The original Tug-of-War sketch used a median of mean of the counters [1] mainly for proving accuracy bounds rigorously. The number of different counters used is usually $s = s_1 \cdot s_2$, where s_1 represents the number of counters we average to improve the accuracy and s_2 represents the number of such averages we take the median of to improve the confidence. In this work, we decided to simply average all s counters together to arrive at our estimator, instead of also taking median, because our experiments show no improvement in empirical accuracy by doing so. Note that upon the arrival of each packet, all s counters must be updated no matter how s splits into s_1 and s_2, so unlike the bucketing issue described below, this decision does not affect the computational complexity of the per-packet update procedure.

5. **Tug-of-War bucketing.** Since the computational complexity of the update procedure of the original Tug-of-War algorithm can be quite high, especially when a large number of counters and hash functions are used, a bucketing technique first introduced in [26] is used in our implementations to reduce this complexity. Bucketing works by partitioning the available memory into several disjoint buckets of counters and introducing a new hash function. For every arriving packet, we map it to a bucket by hashing its packet ID using this new hash function. Counters in this bucket will then be updated in the same way as in the original Tug-of-War sketch. The second moment of the stream can be estimated by first obtaining the second moments of the sub-streams encoded by the buckets, and then adding them up. The computational complexity of each update can thus be reduced by a factor of the number of buckets. The accuracy loss due to bucketing is negligible, as shown in [26].

6. **Intersection overhead.** While the update of the sketches are optimized to be possible online, the intersection of pairs of sketches can be done offline as needed. There is a small computational overhead of $O(K)$ operations, where K is the sketch size used (a few thousand counters in the following experimental section). This overhead is small enough to be negligible, and well worth the savings in storage cost.

6. EVALUATION

In this section, we evaluate the accuracy and efficiency of our estimation algorithms using two types of data: real-world cellular network data from a major cellular service carrier in the US and synthetic traffic data. The cellular network data was collected during a one month period across the entire United States and was anonymized and aggregated. No personally identifiable information was gathered or used in conducting this study. We also generated synthetic data statistically similar to the real data so that we had more control over various parameters such as the sizes of the sets A and B to be intersected and the amount of overlap between them. Our results on real data show that our approach uses a memory space about 170 times smaller than the naive full-table approach (i.e., devoting one or a few statistics counters to each $A_i \bigcap B_j$) while suffering only about 10% loss in estimation accuracy.

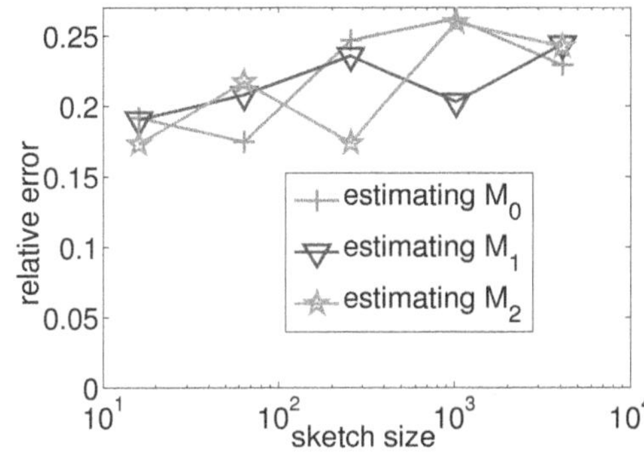

Figure 4: Synthetic results for M_2 intersection relative errors when the total memory is fixed to 4096 counters while the sketch size and the number of buckets are varied

6.1 Results for Synthetic Data

In our synthetic data, all RTTs were randomly generated values between 0 and 100 milliseconds, similar to the values we found in the real data set. For each experiment, we generated data according to whether we would like to vary the full data size (number of packets or unique combinations) or the size of the intersection compared with the size of the individual sets (i.e., intersection ratio).

We first evaluate the effect of bucketing on estimation accuracy by comparing estimation outcomes without bucketing (viewed as having one bucket containing all counters) with those with bucketing. In all cases, an identical number (4096) of counters are used. For this experiment, we fix the sizes (number of packets) of the intersecting sets A and B to be 0.1M and both intersection ratios to be 0.05. As we can see from Fig. 4, when the total number of counters we use in each sketch is set, and we vary the bucket size, defined as the number of counters in each bucket, and the number of buckets while keeping the total number of counters per sketch constant, the results do not vary substantially. This means that bucketing does not negatively impact the estimation accuracy while reducing computational complexities of the update procedure. We got similar results with various other total counter counts (not shown here in the interest of space). As there seems to be no marked performance benefit to avoid bucketing, we fixed the number of counters per bucket 16 in subsequent experiments. This means that each packet only triggers 16 counter updates, which is affordable computationally even for processing high-speed cellular network traffic.

Next, we vary the number of buckets, while fixing the bucket size to 16 (counters per bucket), to see how it affects the relative mean intersection estimation error and the relative mean sketch error in Fig. 5. Again the sizes (packets number) of both intersecting sets A and B are set to 0.1M and both intersection ratios 0.05. We found that the results for M_2, M_1 and M_0 were comparable. The reason for this is that the 3 frequency moment estimation processes all use the

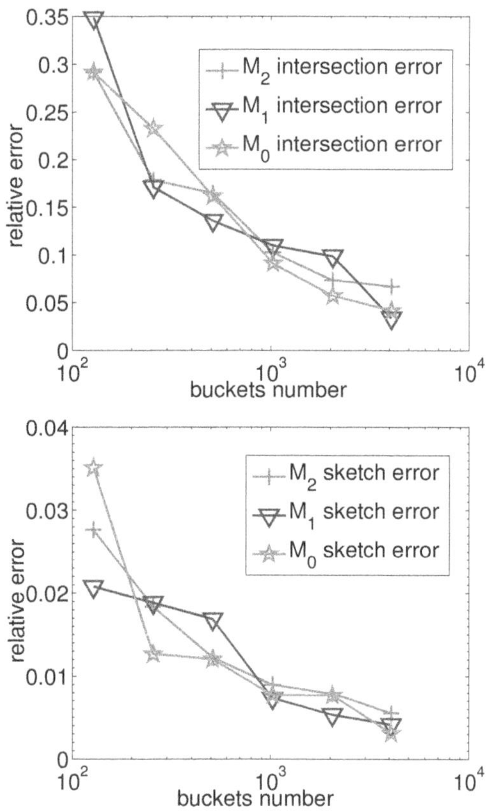

Figure 5: Synthetic results for mean intersection relative errors and sketch relative errors when varying (the number of) buckets. Bucket size set to 16 counters and the total memory usage is bucket size × buckets

same Tug-of-War sketch. In both figures, as the number of buckets gets larger, both relative sketch estimation error and intersection estimation error decrease, but with diminishing returns.

Next, we study the situation in which the intersection ratios IR_A and IR_B are varied simultaneously. The results are shown in Fig. 6. As IR increases, mean relative error decreases very quickly. The effect of increasing IR is quite notable for decreasing relative error. When IR is quite small (e.g., 10^{-5}), getting an accurate estimation for the intersection part is very difficult. As the intersection ratio gets larger, we get increasingly accurate estimates of the intersection. Note that the intersection ratio will not affect our sketch estimating errors; it affects only the intersection estimation error.

We also varied the size of A and B (with $size(A) = size(B)$) while keeping their IR constant. The results are shown in Fig. 7. We found that the mean relative error increases only slightly with the size of both sets. This suggests that the sizes of both sets do not significantly affect the relative intersection error as long as the intersection ratio remains constant. Hence, our method can be used for even larger data sets (i.e., larger packet streams) with little degradation in estimation accuracy.

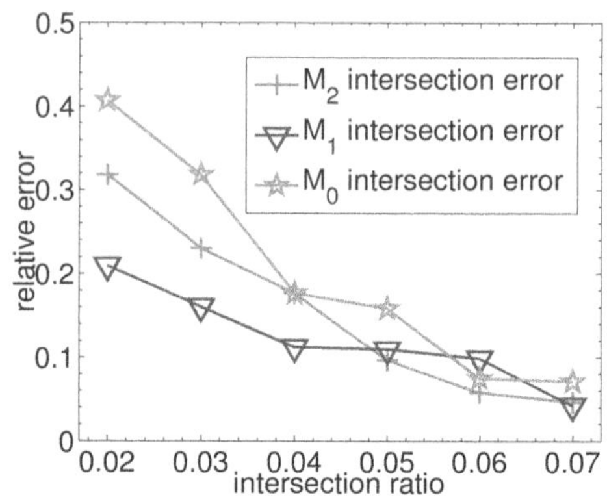

Figure 6: Synthetic results for mean intersection relative errors when varying intersection ratio. Bucket size set to 16 counters and the number of buckets to 1024

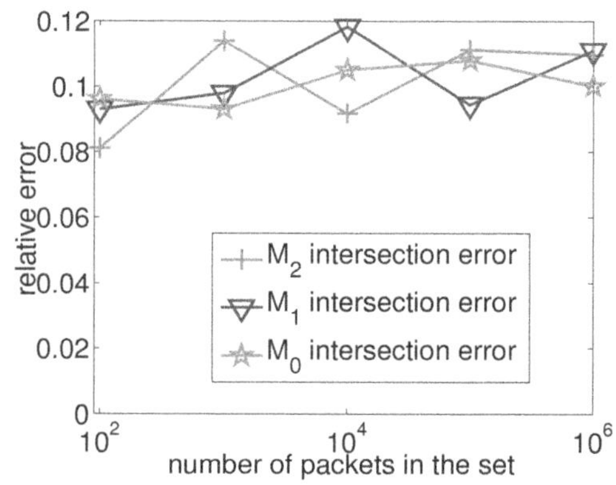

Figure 7: Synthetic results for mean intersection relative errors when varying the number of packets in the set. Bucket size set to 16 and buckets to 1024

6.2 Data Sets for Real Data

Our real-world data was collected from a major cellular service carrier in the US over the month of January 2014. It consists of anonymized TCP flow level data collected from the core network for the 3G data service provided by the cellular service carrier.

Figure 8 illustrates the architectural overview of the core network, which consists of two main types of nodes: the Serving GPRS Support Node (SGSN) and the Gateway GPRS Support Node (GGSN). The GGSN is the root node in the hierarchy of the cellular data network and responsible for sending and receiving Internet traffic to and from the cellular network. SGSN is an intermediate node that connects the lower level nodes to the GGSN through the G_n interface. Typically, a single SGSN is connected to multiple Radio Network Controllers (RNCs) and each RNC serves a geographical region through cell towers.

The raw data is collected at the G_n interface which connects the SGSNs to the GGSNs. Specifically, for each TCP flow, we first measure its end-to-end round trip time (RTT) by comparing the timestamps of IP packets during the TCP

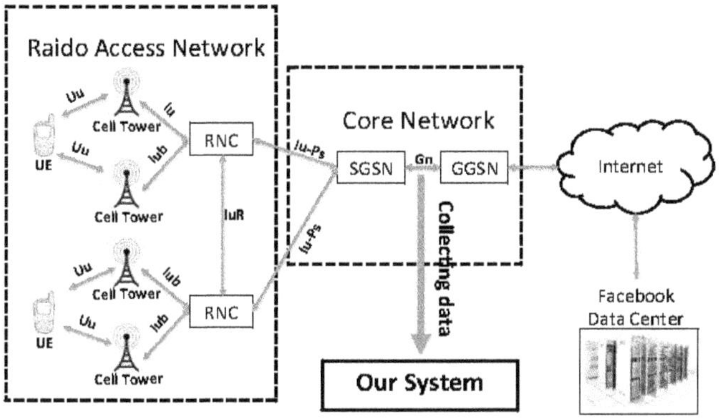

Figure 8: Data Collection Architecture

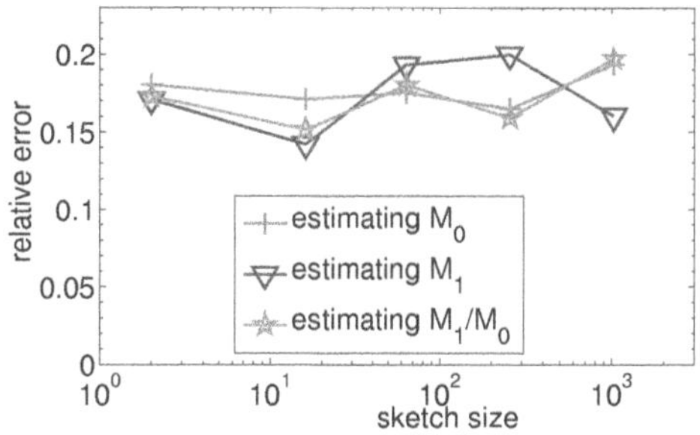

Figure 9: Results of mean intersection relative errors with fixed memory to 4096 counters and varying bucket size and the number of buckets

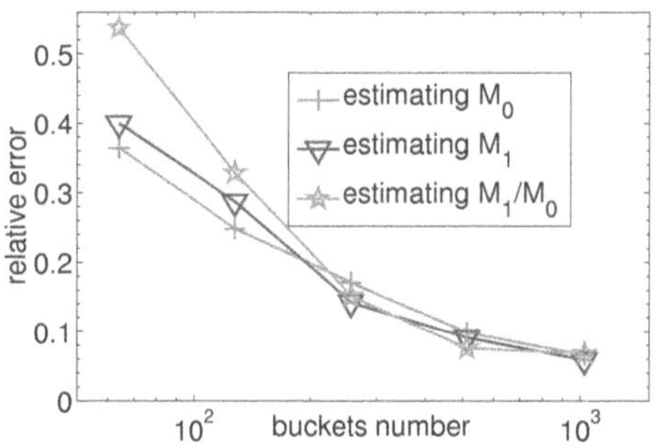

Figure 11: Results of mean intersection relative errors when varying buckets for real data. Bucket size set to 16

handshake and then associate the RTT value with various flow attributes such as standard coordinated universal time (UTC), the serving RNC that describes the user access point, the handheld device type, the application type, the content provider being accessed, etc. Due to the sheer amount of traffic volume, instead of storing the raw data for all individual flows, we only store the hourly total number of RTT measurements, the hourly summation of the RTT measurements and the hourly average RTT (computed as the sum divided by the total number) over eight different flow attributes: serving RNC, handheld device manufacturer/model, handheld device speed category, service category, content provider, day of week, hour and access point network (APN). No personally identifiable information is retained in the aggregate statistics. Being able to query these statistics for an arbitrary cross-section of the eight different flow attributes is critical for service providers to manage their service performance. In order to be able to perform a query for any arbitrary 8-tuple of these quantities, we divided these attributes into two groups. The results of some preliminary measurements showed that making serving RNC, service category, handheld device speed category and day of week as a group, and handheld device manufacturer/model, content provider, access point network and hour as another group, would minimize the total number of sketches that we would need to perform a query for an arbitrary slice of the data.

There are about 1.4 million distinct combinations for the former group described above and about 1.5 million for the latter. Thus, the cost of maintaining the value of each and every combination (a table with one counter per combination) would result in a space usage of 1.4M × 1.5M × 4 bytes, or more than 7.5 TB of storage capacity. In contrast, if we use 4096 counters in each sketch, our method needs only $(1.4M + 1.5M) \times 4096 \times 4$ bytes, or less than 45 GB. This is a savings of over two orders of magnitude that is paid for with a small loss in estimation error. Note that working with even larger data sets (for instance, monitoring a year's worth of data) will give even greater savings.

Since the data we get is already aggregated by hour, we were unable to perform per-packet processing. Instead, we updated our sketch data structures using the measurement count and measurement values for each tuple aggregated at each hour across 36 sub-regions that span the United States. A limitation of this aggregated data was that we were unable to compute the second moment values for the RTTs since we did not have these individual values available to us. In the future, when our algorithm is deployed directly at each RNC, we will be able to measure the second moment as well to estimate the variance of the RTT (or other) values. Since it was infeasible to measure estimates for all possible combinations of tuples, we instead sampled one hundred tuples at random and computed the average relative error for these combinations. The variance of these measurements was found to be small.

6.3 Results for Real Data

We tested our algorithms on the cellular traffic data described above. For anomaly detection and other change detection problems, it suffices to have a relative estimation error that is within 15% since we are only interested in detecting significant changes from the normal values. For instance, we may not want to sound an alarm until the RTT has nearly doubled from its usual value. Of course, in other applications we may want to bound the error to under a few percent; our evaluation extends to this range as well.

Unlike the experiments on synthetic data, we did not have the ability to change all parameters (e.g., relative set size or intersection ratio). Also note that it was infeasible to compute M_2 for the real data because they had already been aggregated into flow records. Therefore, we focused on M_0 and M_1, which can be computed from the aggregated data, and the average $(Avg = M_1/M_0)$.

We first investigated what parameters work well for our sketch on the real data. In Figure 9 we show the result when the number of buckets and the bucket size are simultaneously

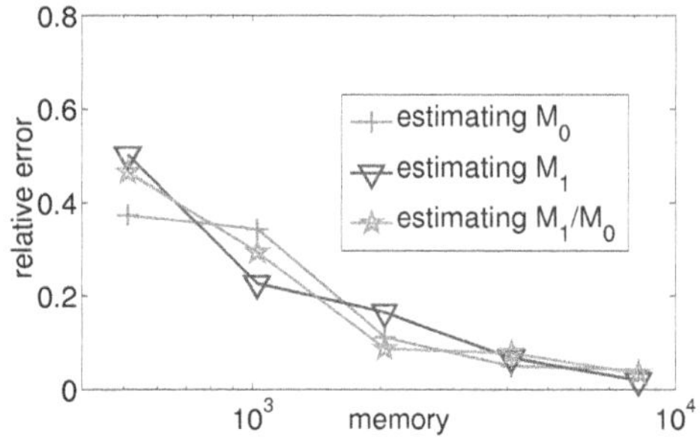

(a) 0.01 i.r.

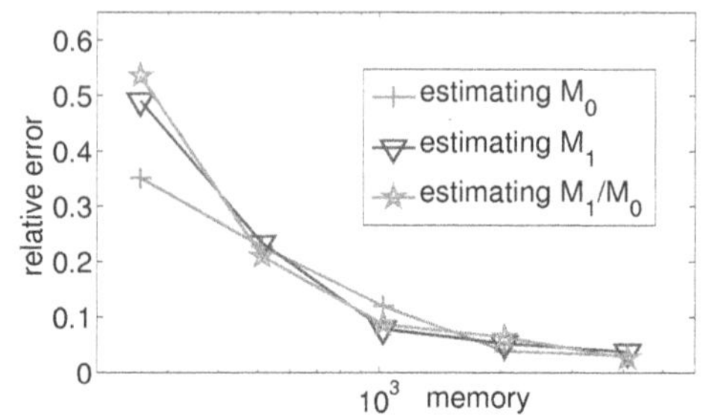

(b) 0.02 i.r.

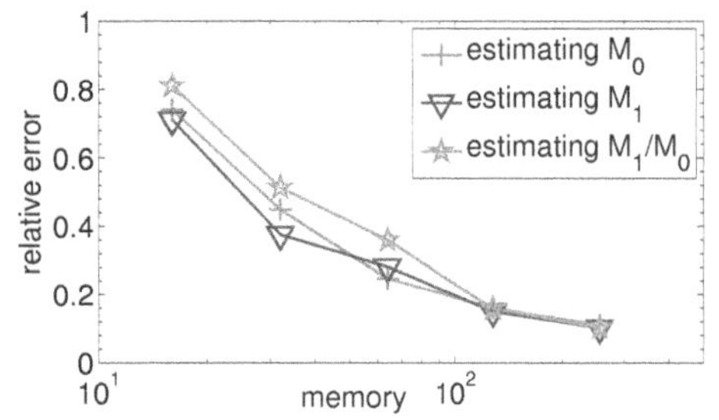

(c) 0.05 i.r.

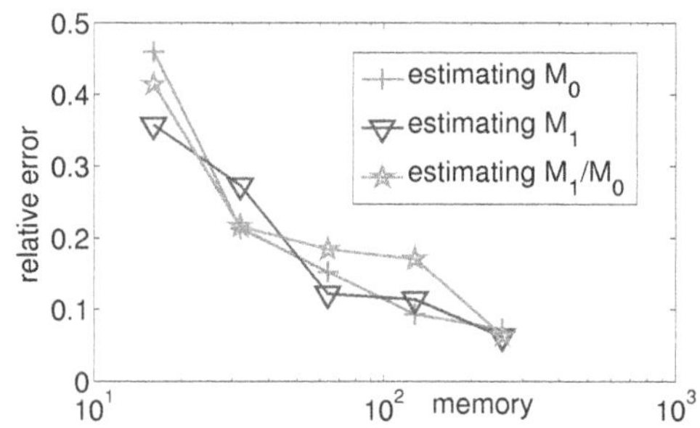

(d) 0.10 i.r.

Figure 10: Results of mean intersection relative errors when varying memory (buckets) for real data. Bucket size set to 16

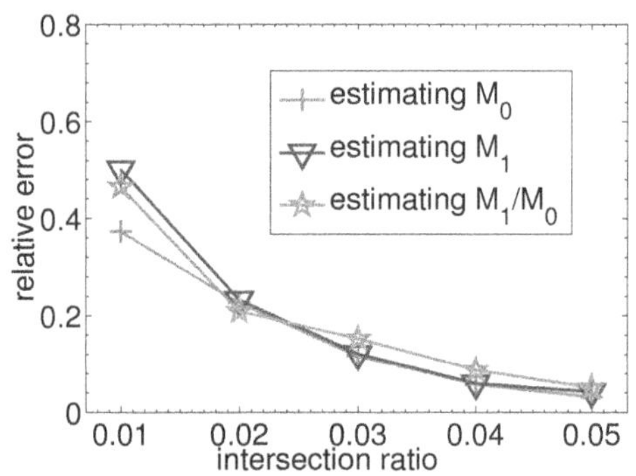

Figure 12: Results of mean intersection relative errors when varying intersection ratio for real data. Bucket size set to 16 and buckets to 32

varied, keeping the total number of counters fixed to 4096. As before, while keeping total memory usage fixed there is no significant change when varying the number of buckets and the bucket size, though we found that the results are slightly better if we make the bucket size smaller and number of buckets bigger. Hence, just as in the synthetic simulations, we chose to make the number of buckets as large as possible. For the remaining experiments we set the bucket size to 16.

In Fig. 11 we plotted the effect of varying the number of buckets on the relative error of the estimate when fixing the bucket size to 16. In this case there was a clear trend in the relative error of the measurement. From the plot, we can see that using memory of just $1024 \times 16 = 16384$ (buckets number $\times$ bucket size) is sufficient to retain high fidelity in the sketched data—under 5-10% relative error. We also found that using $256 \times 16 = 4096$ counters is sufficient to keep the error small enough for anomaly detection. Note that these results will only get better as the data sets available to us grow in size since the size of the data will not greatly affect the accuracy of the sketch. In particular, we foresee being able to maintain sketches of similar size even for packet-level data traces of several terabytes.

The results in Fig. 11, while satisfying, did not quite match up to those in our synthetic data. On closer examination, it turned out that there were several pairs for which the intersection ratio was considerably smaller than the 0.01-0.1 regime that we have been studying and are interested in studying. Recall that if the intersection ratio is very small (e.g., 0.001 or less), then it is not of significant interest in our application since it indicates a negligible-sized pairing. To focus our attention on the more interesting pairs, we re-ran the experiments sampling pairs from ones that had intersection ratio in the desired range. The corresponding plots for intersection ratios of at least 0.01, 0.02, 0.05 and 0.10 are shown in Fig. 10. For these data, we see that there is a considerable drop in the average relative error. In fact, for intersection ratio of 0.10 we see that even with $16 * 16 = 256$ counters we are able to reduce the relative error to well under 10%. As expected, the performance of the algorithm is considerably improved when the intersection ratio is higher.

Finally, to visualize the effect of intersection ratio on the accuracy of the sketch, we fixed the bucket size to 16 and measured the average relative error when sampling pairs that have at least some minimum intersection ratio. This is shown in Fig. 12. Once again, we see a substantial drop in the relative error within the 0.01 to 0.05 intersection ratio range that we are aiming for. This indicates that we can use considerably smaller sketch sizes (e.g., in the 10-100 KB range) if we are interested only in the pairs that have significant intersection ratio.

In summary, we were able to run our algorithm on data collected by a major cellular carrier over a one-month period and shrink the memory footprint by more than two orders of magnitude while introducing under ten percent error on the estimate of the average RTT value. We found that if the intersection ratio is high, as is expected in most of the target applications, we can use even smaller sketches or achieve smaller error, or both.

7. RELATED WORK

Our work falls at the intersection of data streaming algorithms, cellular network performance, and association rule mining.

Data streaming algorithms. The seminal work of Alon et al. [2] for estimating the frequency moments of a stream opened up the research field of data streaming algorithms. In particular, the Tug-of-War sketch, which originated in [2] and was given that name in [1], is a simple but elegant tool for estimating M_2 of a stream that we take advantage of in this paper. Other work on mining data streams used a variety of techniques. For instance, Lakhina et al. [14, 12, 13] studied the diagnosis and characterization of feature distributions of network-wide anomalies in streams. Liu et al. [15] proposed PCA- and sketch-based streaming algorithms for network traffic anomaly detection. Yang et al. [25] studied the computational partitioning method between mobile devices and the cloud to achieve optimal speeds for processing streaming data.

Cellular network performance. Various techniques have been studied in recent years for measuring and analyzing cellular network metrics and performance. Shafiq et al. proposed characterizing M2M traffic patterns in cellular networks and studied that RTT measurements for TCP flows in [19]. They also analyzed Internet traffic dynamics of cellular network devices in [20]. Wang et al. implemented a tool that can unveil carriers' NAT and firewall policies by conducting intelligent measurement and thus help inform developers optimizing mobile applications and network configurations [23]. They also characterized the geospatial dynamics of application usage in 3G cellular networks in [18] and studied cellular network issues in [17] by quantifying aggregate network load and characterizing user-level traffic sessions. Falaki et al. [7] studied the detailed components of smartphone traffic and packet loss. Trestian et al. [22] showed how the relationship of mobile network users to their locations can benefit cellular network providers and location-based services. Balasubramanian et al. [3] provided a measurement study of the three types of mobile network technologies: 3G, GSM, and WiFi. Xu et al. [24] focused on identifying diverse usage patterns of smartphone apps in spatial, temporal, user, and device dimensions in cellular networks. Erman et al. [6] studied caching techniques for video stream traffic generated by smartphones in cellular network. Gember et al. [8] studied in-context network performance when users interact with their mobile devices.

Association Rule Mining. There is much literature on the topic of association rule mining; for example, see [5, 9] and references therein. Jin and Agrawal [11] in particular study ARM in the context of streaming data. ARM techniques have also been used for network troubleshooting. For example, Qiu et al. [16] used standard ARM techniques to mine router syslogs for network performance anomalies. Brauckhoff et al. [4] used ARM for detecting anomalies in backbone networks. As noted earlier, rather than proposing new ARM algorithms, this work reduces the amount of storage needed by an existing ARM algorithm for processing a massive data stream.

8. CONCLUSIONS

Change and anomaly detection are tasks essential for all cellular network providers these days. In this paper, we tackle this problem by proposing a novel scheme, which we call Crossroads, to find the anomalous events such as longer-than-usual RTT in cellular network data. To do this, we introduced the technique of intersecting pairs of network data stream digests of overlapping streams. In particular, we provide intersection algorithms for estimating the M_2, M_1, and M_0 of values in a data stream, which allow us to reduce the storage cost of this diagnostic data drastically, from $O(n)$ to $O(\sqrt{n})$. Our evaluations on synthetic and real-world data from a major cellular service carrier in the US generate very accurate and rapid estimates for detecting anomalies or other changes, demonstrating that our algorithms are quite reliable in practice.

9. REFERENCES

[1] ALON, N., GIBBONS, P. B., MATIAS, Y., AND SZEGEDY, M. Tracking join and self-join sizes in limited storage. In *Proceedings of the eighteenth ACM SIGMOD-SIGACT-SIGART symposium on Principles of database systems* (1999), ACM, pp. 10–20.

[2] ALON, N., MATIAS, Y., AND SZEGEDY, M. The space complexity of approximating the frequency moments. In *Proceedings of the twenty-eighth annual ACM symposium on Theory of computing* (1996), ACM, pp. 20–29.

[3] BALASUBRAMANIAN, N., BALASUBRAMANIAN, A., AND VENKATARAMANI, A. Energy consumption in mobile phones: a measurement study and implications for network applications. In *Proceedings of the 9th ACM SIGCOMM conference on Internet measurement conference* (2009), ACM, pp. 280–293.

[4] BRAUCKHOFF, D., DIMITROPOULOS, X., WAGNER, A., AND SALAMATIAN, K. Anomaly extraction in backbone networks using association rules. In *Proceedings of the 9th ACM SIGCOMM Conference on Internet Measurement Conference* (New York, NY, USA, 2009), IMC '09, ACM, pp. 28–34.

[5] CHENG, J., KE, Y., AND NG, W. A survey on algorithms for mining frequent itemsets over data streams. *Knowledge and Information Systems 16*, 1 (2008), 1–27.

[6] ERMAN, J., GERBER, A., RAMADRISHNAN, K., SEN, S., AND SPATSCHECK, O. Over the top video: the gorilla in cellular networks. In *Proceedings of the 2011 ACM SIGCOMM conference on Internet measurement conference* (2011), ACM, pp. 127–136.

[7] FALAKI, H., LYMBEROPOULOS, D., MAHAJAN, R., KANDULA, S., AND ESTRIN, D. A first look at traffic on smartphones. In *Proceedings of the 10th ACM*

SIGCOMM conference on Internet measurement (2010), ACM, pp. 281–287.

[8] Gember, A., Akella, A., Pang, J., Varshavsky, A., and Caceres, R. Obtaining in-context measurements of cellular network performance. In *Proceedings of the 2012 ACM conference on Internet measurement conference* (2012), ACM, pp. 287–300.

[9] Han, J., Cheng, H., Xin, D., and Yan, X. Frequent pattern mining: Current status and future directions. *Data Min. Knowl. Discov. 15*, 1 (Aug. 2007), 55–86.

[10] Indyk, P. Stable distributions, pseudorandom generators, embeddings and data stream computation. In *Foundations of Computer Science, 2000. Proceedings. 41st Annual Symposium on* (2000), IEEE, pp. 189–197.

[11] Jin, R., and Agrawal, G. An algorithm for in-core frequent itemset mining on streaming data. In *Proceedings of the Fifth IEEE International Conference on Data Mining* (Washington, DC, USA, 2005), ICDM '05, IEEE Computer Society, pp. 210–217.

[12] Lakhina, A., Crovella, M., and Diot, C. Characterization of network-wide anomalies in traffic flows. In *Proceedings of the 4th ACM SIGCOMM conference on Internet measurement* (2004), ACM, pp. 201–206.

[13] Lakhina, A., Crovella, M., and Diot, C. Diagnosing network-wide traffic anomalies. In *ACM SIGCOMM Computer Communication Review* (2004), vol. 34, ACM, pp. 219–230.

[14] Lakhina, A., Crovella, M., and Diot, C. Mining anomalies using traffic feature distributions. In *ACM SIGCOMM Computer Communication Review* (2005), vol. 35, ACM, pp. 217–228.

[15] Liu, Y., Zhang, L., and Guan, Y. Sketch-based streaming pca algorithm for network-wide traffic anomaly detection. In *Distributed Computing Systems (ICDCS), 2010 IEEE 30th International Conference on* (2010), IEEE, pp. 807–816.

[16] Qiu, T., Ge, Z., Pei, D., Wang, J., and Xu, J. What happened in my network: Mining network events from router syslogs. In *Proceedings of the 10th ACM SIGCOMM Conference on Internet Measurement* (New York, NY, USA, 2010), IMC '10, ACM, pp. 472–484.

[17] Shafiq, M. Z., Ji, L., Liu, A. X., Pang, J., Venkataraman, S., and Wang, J. A first look at cellular network performance during crowded events. In *Proceedings of the ACM SIGMETRICS/international conference on Measurement and modeling of computer systems* (2013), ACM, pp. 17–28.

[18] Shafiq, M. Z., Ji, L., Liu, A. X., Pang, J., and Wang, J. Characterizing geospatial dynamics of application usage in a 3g cellular data network. In *INFOCOM, 2012 Proceedings IEEE* (2012), IEEE, pp. 1341–1349.

[19] Shafiq, M. Z., Ji, L., Liu, A. X., Pang, J., and Wang, J. A first look at cellular machine-to-machine traffic: large scale measurement and characterization. In *ACM SIGMETRICS Performance Evaluation Review* (2012), vol. 40, ACM, pp. 65–76.

[20] Shafiq, M. Z., Ji, L., Liu, A. X., and Wang, J. Characterizing and modeling internet traffic dynamics of cellular devices. In *Proceedings of the ACM SIGMETRICS joint international conference on Measurement and modeling of computer systems* (2011), ACM, pp. 305–316.

[21] Snoeren, A. C., Partridge, C., Sanchez, L. A., Jones, C. E., Tchakountio, F., Kent, S. T., and Strayer, W. T. Hash-based ip traceback. In *ACM SIGCOMM Computer Communication Review* (2001), vol. 31, ACM, pp. 3–14.

[22] Trestian, I., Ranjan, S., Kuzmanovic, A., and Nucci, A. Measuring serendipity: connecting people, locations and interests in a mobile 3g network. In *Proceedings of the 9th ACM SIGCOMM conference on Internet measurement conference* (2009), ACM, pp. 267–279.

[23] Wang, Z., Qian, Z., Xu, Q., Mao, Z., and Zhang, M. An untold story of middleboxes in cellular networks. *ACM SIGCOMM Computer Communication Review 41*, 4 (2011), 374–385.

[24] Xu, Q., Erman, J., Gerber, A., Mao, Z., Pang, J., and Venkataraman, S. Identifying diverse usage behaviors of smartphone apps. In *Proceedings of the 2011 ACM SIGCOMM conference on Internet measurement conference* (2011), ACM, pp. 329–344.

[25] Yang, L., Cao, J., Yuan, Y., Li, T., Han, A., and Chan, A. A framework for partitioning and execution of data stream applications in mobile cloud computing. *ACM SIGMETRICS Performance Evaluation Review 40*, 4 (2013), 23–32.

[26] Zhao, H. C., Lall, A., Ogihara, M., Spatscheck, O., Wang, J., and Xu, J. A data streaming algorithm for estimating entropies of od flows. In *Proceedings of the 7th ACM SIGCOMM conference on Internet measurement* (2007), ACM, pp. 279–290.

OFSS: Skampling for the Flow Size Distribution

Paul Tune
School of Mathematical Sciences
University of Adelaide, Australia
paul.tune@adelaide.edu.au

Darryl Veitch
Melbourne School of Engineering
University of Melbourne, Australia
dveitch@unimelb.edu.au

ABSTRACT

We introduce a new method for flow size estimation, the *Optimised Flow Sampled Sketch*, which combines the optimal properties of Flow Sampling with the computational advantages of a counter array sketch. Using Fisher Information as a definitive basis of comparison, we show that it is superior to alternatives in both model and traffic based comparisons.

Categories and Subject Descriptors

C.2.3 [**Computer Communications Networks**]: Network operations—*Network monitoring*; G.3 [**Mathematics of Computing**]: Probability and statistics—*Probabilistic algorithms*

Keywords

Fisher information; flow size distribution; network measurement; OFSS; skampling

1. INTRODUCTION

The distribution of *flow size*, the number of packets in a flow, is an important metric for numerous applications including traffic modelling, management, and attack detection. In resource constrained environments such as within core Internet routers however, accurate measurement of flow size can be challenging.

The traditional approach to fast approximate measurement has been traffic *sampling*. For example flow size estimation within Cisco's *Netflow* [1] is based on a simple pseudo-random per-packet sampling. In our prior work [6, 10, 11] we examined available sampling techniques in depth and showed that *flow sampling* (FS), where the random sampling decision is made directly on flows, has optimal properties. This conclusion was based on a rigorous evaluation, in terms of Fisher Information, of the inherent abilities of the sampling methods as information collectors. Unfortunately, FS requires a *flow table* supporting collision resolution, which incurs costs in memory (entries must store a flow key in addition to a counter), and in processing and latency (key comparison needed on all insertions). Such costs translate to bottlenecks, for example 'heavy hitter' flows generating unsustainable insertion rates.

Sketches are compact data structures with fast update rules that are used to approximately measure properties over data streams. Sketches have been proposed to measure many metrics including set membership [2], entropy [14], heavy hitters [4], and flow sizes [7].

In this paper we present a hybrid *skampling* approach to data collection for flow size measurement, called the OFSS or *Optimised Flow Sampled Sketch*. The FSS consists of a front-end sampling component, namely FS, feeding a sketching component 'Sk', the counting array sketch of [7]. It includes FS and Sk as special cases. The OFSS is an FSS tuned according to an optimal tradeoff between the information gathering strengths and weaknesses of the FS and Sk components. The result is FS-like statistical performance without flow table costs and bottlenecks. In designing OFSS we build on and extend the Fisher analysis of FS and Sk presented in [12].

It is natural, since OFSS is a 'Sample then Sketch' method, to compare against 'Sketch then Sample'. We accordingly compare against the 'Sketch Guided Sampling' approach of Kumar et al. [8] (SGS). We find SGS to have much worse performance than OFSS, both in terms of information gathering, and implementation. We also compare against an enhanced counter array based method of Ribeiro et al. [9] which also, in an implicit sense, incorporates sampling. We show that this *Eviction Sketch* (ESk) underperforms OFSS by a wide margin at meaningful sampling rates unless it is calibrated very differently than in [9], resulting in considerably higher memory use. For each of SGS and ESk we provide the first Fisher-based analysis.

The goal of this paper is to introduce the OFSS scheme, to give its key properties, and to demonstrate its effectiveness. To that end, we forgo proofs (these will appear elsewhere [13]), and focus on providing the underlying intuition. We do not provide a detailed implementation model, however with only a single hash and a single counter array, OFSS is very simple, cheap enough to implement alongside existing packet sampling based systems. Software will be made publically available to facilitate use of the method, in particular for the calculation of the optimal parameter value p_f^* of OFSS.

The paper is organised as follows. Section 2 gives background on the Fisher Information framework, and defines, recalls and derives key results for FS and Sk, SGS and ESk. Section 3 defines FSS then OFSS and describes their key properties. Section 4 gives the statistical performance com-

IMC'14, November 5–7, 2014, Vancouver, BC, Canada.

ACM 978-1-4503-3213-2/14/11 ...$15.00.
http://dx.doi.org/10.1145/2663716.2663732.

parisons on both model based and real data. We conclude in Section 5.

2. BACKGROUND

We assume that a unique flow key can be extracted from each incoming packet, and that the first packet of a flow (and hence the number of flows) can be identified (e.g. SYN packet in the case of TCP flows).

We write (column) vectors in bold lower-case, matrices in bold upper case, $\mathbf{A}^{\mathrm{T}}$ denotes the transpose of $\mathbf{A}$, and $\mathbf{diag}(\mathbf{x})$ an $m \times m$ diagonal matrix whose diagonal entries are taken from the vector $\mathbf{x} \in \mathbb{R}^m$. We denote the set $\{1, 2, \ldots, S\}$ by $[S]$.

2.1 Modelling Framework, Fisher Information

Consider a measurement interval of duration T containing N_f flows. Of these flows, M_k have size k packets, $1 \le k \le W$, where $W < \infty$ is the maximum flow size. The average flow size is $D = \sum_{k=1}^{W} kM_k/N_f$.

The flow size distribution, the unknown vector parameter we seek information on, is $\boldsymbol{\theta} = [\theta_1, \theta_2, \ldots, \theta_W]^T$ where $\theta_k = M_k/N_f$, and obeys

$$0 < \theta_k < 1 \ , \ k \in [W], \quad \sum_{k=1}^{W} \theta_k = 1 \ . \tag{1}$$

This is a deterministic model of the data over the measurement interval: randomness enters later through the action of the measurement method itself.

Any estimator of $\boldsymbol{\theta}$ is based on an underlying observable which summarises the traffic, where it here takes the form of a packet count random variable C. The discrete density $c_j(\boldsymbol{\theta})$ of C, $j \ge 0$, depends on the details of the summary method. Viewed as a function of $\boldsymbol{\theta}$ for a fixed value j of the observed data, it is known as the *likelihood*: $f(j, \boldsymbol{\theta}) = c_j(\boldsymbol{\theta})$.

The *Fisher Information* (FIM) is a measure of the information the observable holds about the unknown parameters. The unconstrained FIM is defined as

$$\begin{aligned}\mathbf{J}(\boldsymbol{\theta}) &= \mathbb{E}[(\nabla_{\boldsymbol{\theta}} \log f(j; \boldsymbol{\theta}))(\nabla_{\boldsymbol{\theta}} \log f(j; \boldsymbol{\theta}))^{\mathrm{T}}] \\ &= \sum_{j \ge 0} (\nabla_{\boldsymbol{\theta}} \log f(j; \boldsymbol{\theta}))(\nabla_{\boldsymbol{\theta}} \log f(j; \boldsymbol{\theta}))^{\mathrm{T}} c_j. \end{aligned} \tag{2}$$

The importance of $\mathbf{J}$ lies in the fact that $\mathbf{J}^{-1}$ is the *Cramér–Rao Lower Bound* (CRLB), which lower bounds the covariance matrix $\boldsymbol{\Sigma}_{\boldsymbol{\theta}}$ of **any** unbiased estimator of $\boldsymbol{\theta}$, i.e. $\boldsymbol{\Sigma}_{\boldsymbol{\theta}} \ge \mathbf{J}^{-1}$ in the positive semidefinite sense.

The constraints on $\boldsymbol{\theta}$ in (1) increase available information. The constrained FIM is given in [5] by

$$\boldsymbol{\mathcal{I}}^{+} = \mathbf{J}^{-1} - \mathbf{J}^{-1}\mathbf{G}\left(\mathbf{G}^{\mathrm{T}}\mathbf{J}^{-1}\mathbf{G}\right)^{-1}\mathbf{G}^{\mathrm{T}}\mathbf{J}^{-1}. \tag{3}$$

Here the constraint *gradient* matrix is $\mathbf{G}(\boldsymbol{\theta}) = \nabla_{\boldsymbol{\theta}}(\mathbf{1}_W^{\mathrm{T}}\boldsymbol{\theta} - 1) = \mathbf{1}_W$, where $\mathbf{1}_W$ is a $W \times 1$ vector of ones.

Of chief interest are the diagonal entries of $\boldsymbol{\mathcal{I}}^{+}$, since $\mathrm{Var}(\hat{\theta}_k) \ge (\boldsymbol{\mathcal{I}}^{+})_{kk}$ for any unbiased estimator. Comparison of these between methods corresponds to comparing the best performance the schemes are capable of supporting, thus reflecting their *comparative efficiency in extracting information from the traffic stream.*

The methods we study involve multiple identically distributed counters, which are approximately independent if N_f is large. The Fisher information arising from the entire measurement interval is then just that of a single counter C multiplied by the number of counters.

2.2 Four Methods and their FIMs

We define four existing methods and describe their FIM and $\boldsymbol{\mathcal{I}}^{+}$ matrices. FS is the statistical method of choice, and Sk a canonical implementation approach. SGS and ESk are alternative skampling methods.

Flow Sampling (FS)

In flow sampling flows are sampled (dropped) independently with probability p_f (resp. q_f). Sampling a flow means that each packet within it is sampled, or none.

Here C represents the size of a randomly selected (typical) flow. For a flow of size k, its density is given by $c_0 = q_f$, $c_k = p_f$, and $c_i = 0$ for all $i \neq \{0, k\}$. From [10, 11], an explicit expression for per-flow $\mathbf{J}$ is given by

$$\mathbf{J}_{\mathrm{FS}} = p_f \, \mathbf{diag}(\theta_1^{-1}, \theta_2^{-1}, \ldots, \theta_W^{-1}) + q_f \mathbf{1}_W \mathbf{1}_W^{\mathrm{T}}, \tag{4}$$

and $\boldsymbol{\mathcal{I}}^{+} = \mathbf{J}^{-1} - \boldsymbol{\theta}\boldsymbol{\theta}^{\mathrm{T}} = \frac{1}{p_f}\left(\mathbf{diag}(\boldsymbol{\theta}) - \boldsymbol{\theta}\boldsymbol{\theta}^{\mathrm{T}}\right)$, and so

$$(\boldsymbol{\mathcal{I}}_{\mathrm{FS}}^{+})_{kk} = \frac{\theta_k(1 - \theta_k)}{p_f} \ , \ k \in [W]. \tag{5}$$

The great strength of FS compared to other methods is that estimators based on it do not have to try to correct distortions: collected flows are perfect.

Counter Sketch (Sk)

The counter sketch, introduced by Kumar et al. [7], consists of an array of A packet counters, each initialised to zero at the beginning of the measurement interval. Incoming packets are mapped independently and uniformly over the counters, using a hash function mapping a flow key, so that each packet in a flow maps to the same counter, but collisions can occur so that a given counter may sum the packet counts from two or more flows. We define $\alpha = N_f/A$ to be the *flow load factor*, the average number of flows per counter.

Here C is the final packet count in a *typical counter*, at the end of the measurement interval when all N_f flows are in the sketch. By using a Poisson assumption for C, the density can be shown to be (see [13])

$$c_j = \left(\sum_{\mathbf{x} \in \Omega_j} \prod_{k=1}^{W} \frac{\lambda_k^{x_k}}{x_k!} \right) e^{-\sum_{k=1}^{W} \lambda_k}, \quad j \ge 0 \tag{6}$$

where x_k is the number of flows of size k in the counter, $\lambda_k = M_k/A = \alpha\theta_k$, $\mathbf{x} = [x_1, x_2, \cdots, x_W]$ denotes a *collision pattern*, and Ω_j is the set of flow collision patterns with packet count $C = \sum_{k=1}^{W} kx_k = j$. It follows that the per-counter Fisher matrix is given by

$$(\mathbf{J})_{ik} = \alpha^2 \Big(-1 + \sum_{j=\max(i,k)}^{\infty} (c_{j-i}c_{j-k})/c_j \Big), \tag{7}$$

and the per-flow information is $\mathbf{J}_{\mathrm{Sk}} = A\mathbf{J}/N_f = \mathbf{J}/\alpha$. The constrained per-flow CRLB, $\boldsymbol{\mathcal{I}}_{\mathrm{Sk}}^{+}$, is given by substituting $\mathbf{J}_{\mathrm{Sk}}$ into (3).

The strength of Sk is that all packets of all flows are efficiently collected, but as the sketch becomes increasingly full as α increases, we expect information-destroying flow collisions to become severe.

Sketch Guided Sampling (SGS)

Traditional *Packet Sampling* (PS) simply samples packets independently with fixed probability p, and is known to destroy information about $\boldsymbol{\theta}$ with remarkable efficiency [10,

11]. Sketch Guided Sampling, introduced in [8], is at heart a generalised packet sampling method indexed by a sampling probability function $p(k)$, $k \in [W]$. A packet will be sampled with probability $p(k)$ if it is the k-th packet encountered so far in its flow. Of course, we do not know the in-flow position of packets, if one did $\boldsymbol{\theta}$ would be already known! The innovation in [8] was to estimate this quantity by a coarse counter sketch, hence SGS is a skampling method.

To simplify comparisons, we assist SGS by replacing its sketch component with oracular knowledge of each packet's in-flow position. Assisted SGS is then a pure sampling method, whose per-flow counter density is characterised by its *sampling matrix* $\mathbf{B}$ as

$$c_j = \sum_{k=1}^{W} b_{jk}\theta_k, \quad 0 \le j \le W, \tag{8}$$

where b_{jk}, is the probability that if the original flow had k packets, only j remain after sampling. The matrix element b_{jk} can be calculated via the recursion $b_{j,k+1} = p(k+1)b_{j-1,k} + q(k+1)b_{j,k}$.

From general sampling results from [11], we can write

$$\mathbf{J} = \mathbf{B}^{\mathrm{T}}\mathbf{D}\mathbf{B}, \tag{9}$$

where $\mathbf{D} = \mathbf{diag}(\mathbf{B}\boldsymbol{\theta})$, and $\boldsymbol{\mathcal{I}}^{+} = \mathbf{J}^{-1} - \boldsymbol{\theta}\boldsymbol{\theta}^{\mathrm{T}}$.
Following [8], we use

$$p(k) = p(k;\beta,\epsilon) = \frac{1}{1+\epsilon^2 k^{(2\beta-1)}}, \; 1/2 \le \beta \le 1, \tag{10}$$

a monotonically decreasing function of k. The idea is that this creates a bias toward short flows which counteracts the strong large-flow bias of traditional PS, which corresponds to $\beta = 1/2$.

Note that (true) SGS requires both a flow table and a sketch, and so is more costly to implement than FS.

Eviction Sketch (ESk)
The data collection method proposed in [9] physically enhances Sk by associating to each of its A counters an *ownership* variable taking values in $[L]$, all initialised to L. An incoming packet is given a random priority class $\ell \in [L]$. If ℓ equals the value of the associated ownership variable its counter is incremented as normal, but if it is larger (lower priority than it) the counter is unchanged, and if smaller (higher priority) the counter is reset to 1, and the ownership variable is set to ℓ recording the fact that class ℓ now 'owns' the counter. This random eviction of lower class packets is an implicit packet sampling, reducing the input load α to an effective load $\alpha' < \alpha$, hence ESk is a skampling method.

It is not hard to show that the counter density is

$$c_0 = e^{-\alpha}, \tag{11}$$
$$c_j = F(L)\, c_{\mathrm{Sk},j}(\alpha/L), \quad j \ge 0 \tag{12}$$

where $F(L) = (1-e^{-\alpha})/(1-e^{-\alpha/L})$ and $c_{\mathrm{Sk},j}$ is the density (6) with load α/L. It follows that the per-counter Fisher matrix based on C is given by

$$(\mathbf{J})_{ik} = \frac{\alpha^2}{L^2}\Big(-1 + \sum_{j=\max(i,k)}^{\infty} (c_{j-i}c_{j-k})/c_j\Big), \tag{13}$$

and the per-flow information is $\mathbf{J}_{\mathrm{ESk}} = A\mathbf{J}/N_f = \mathbf{J}/\alpha$. The constrained per-flow CRLB, $\boldsymbol{\mathcal{I}}^{+}_{\mathrm{ESk}}$, is given by substituting $\mathbf{J}_{\mathrm{ESk}}$ into (3).

The degree of sampling offered by ESk, $p = \alpha'/\alpha = F(L)/L$, is only coarsely controllable via the choice of L, and is limited: p hits a limit of $1/L$ for $\alpha \gg L$. For a given α and k, the CRLB of θ_k is minimized at $L = \infty$. Here ESk reduces to FS with $\min(A, N_f)$ sampled flows, however this requires infinite memory. For $L = 1$ ESk reduces to Sk, a pure sketch with $p = 1$.

3. FSS AND OFSS

We define the *Flow Sampling Sketch* (FSS), a family of skampling methods indexed by an internal parameter p_f, describe its properties and derive its Fisher Information. We then introduce the *Optimised Flow Sampling Sketch* (OFSS), which is FSS with p_f chosen to maximise its Fisher Information gathering ability.

3.1 FSS

We begin by contrasting the nature of FS and Sk. The central issue is that of collision resolution. Allowing multiple flows to map to the same counter is the origin of the high speed implementation advantages of Sk, but also of its statistical weakness: collisions create complex ambiguities which literally destroy information (see below). In contrast, the information loss in FS is due solely to the fact that not all flows are used, but the requirement of strict collision resolution makes FS, for any p_f, computationally onerous at high speed.

The key idea of FSS is the following: if α could be kept low, then Sk could work at an 'operating point' with low information loss. A natural way to achieve this is to perform a thinning of the incoming flows to reduce the input α to an effective $\alpha' < \alpha$ seen by the sketch, set to a suitable value which trades off the need for low ambiguity (α' not too big), against adequate data collection as well as not under-utilising expensive memory (α' not too small). It is useful to keep in mind that when $\alpha' = 1$, a proportion $1 - c_0 = 1 - e^{-1} \approx 0.632$ of counters are used.

Definition: FSS(p_f;A) *Each flow is sampled with probability p_f. Packets of sampled flows are inserted into a counter sketch with A counters.*

Thus FSS has an 'FS front end' which sends sampled flows through to an unmodified counter sketch, which sees a reduced *effective* average flow load of

$$\alpha' = p_f\alpha.$$

In information terms, FSS combines the loss of information arising from FS's flow thinning, with a loss due to Sk's collision-induced flow ambiguity.

In terms of implementation, the key advantage of FSS is that the FS component does not require any flow table or collision resolution. Only the flow selection itself remains, but this can be easily implemented in deterministic time on a per-packet basis by hashing flow keys. As described in [12], the hash function can be simultaneously used to index into the sketch.

From the above, we expect FSS to behave exactly as Sk with load α'. However, whereas the number of flows N_f entering FSS is a known constant, the number reaching the counter array is, unlike for Sk, a random variable. Remarkably, it turns out (see [13]) that the counter density nonetheless takes the same form as for Sk (Equation (6)), with the λ_k replaced by $\lambda'_k = \alpha'\theta_k = p_f\lambda_k$. Since the dependence on $\boldsymbol{\theta}$

is unchanged, the per-counter information for FSS is just as for Sk with parameter α', and therefore the information per-incoming-flow is $\mathbf{J}_{\text{FSS}}(\alpha) = p_f \mathbf{J}_{\text{Sk}}(\alpha')$. The per-flow CRLB is therefore

$$\mathcal{I}^+_{\text{FSS}}(\alpha) = \frac{\alpha}{\alpha'}\mathcal{I}^+_{\text{Sk}}(\alpha') = \frac{1}{p_f}\mathcal{I}^+_{\text{Sk}}(\alpha'). \quad (14)$$

FSS inherits FS's flexibility in adapting to varying traffic levels. If α suddenly increases then p_f could be simply decreased to keep α' in a target range.

3.2 OFSS

The parameters considered fixed in a given measurement are the counter array size A, the number of flows N_f, and $\boldsymbol{\theta}$. The input load to the FSS is therefore fixed at $\alpha = N_f/A$, whereas p_f is an internal parameter free to be tuned to any value in $[0, 1]$.

In defining OFSS our aim is to select p_f to maximise the **total** amount of information captured by FSS, or equivalently, to minimise the CRLB when using all A counters. Thus, for each $\alpha > 0$, we seek to minimise the diagonal elements of

$$\mathcal{I}_T(p_f) = \frac{\mathcal{I}^+_{\text{FSS}}(\alpha)}{N_f} = \frac{\mathcal{I}^+_{\text{FSS}}(\alpha)}{A\alpha} = \frac{1}{A\alpha'}\mathcal{I}^+_{\text{Sk}}(\alpha') \quad (15)$$

over $p_f \in [0, 1]$, or equivalently, $\alpha' \in [0, \alpha]$.

Equation (15) is a product of two competing terms, each a function of p_f through $\alpha' = p_f\alpha$. The scalar $1/(A\alpha')$ depends on the number of flows delivered to the sketch by the FS component and is monotonically **decreasing** with p_f. The matrix $\mathcal{I}^+_{\text{Sk}}(\alpha')$ corresponds to the information stored per-flow in the counter array. It is monotonically **increasing** with p_f in a positive semidefinite sense [13]. The key question is whether an optimal point exists for any α, that is, if there is a maximum amount of information that can be stored in the sketch, so that excessive load is not just a matter of diminishing returns but actually results in information destruction. To answer it, let $I_k(x) = (\mathcal{I}^+_{\text{Sk}}(x)/x)_{kk}$. From (15), $(\mathcal{I}_T(p_f))_{kk} = I_k(\alpha')/A$.

THEOREM 1. *For each k, $I_k(x)$ has a global minimum at finite $x = \alpha_k^{**} > 0$ for any $\boldsymbol{\theta}$ with $W > 3$.*

The proof is based on the fact that the largest eigenvalue of $\mathcal{I}^+_{\text{Sk}}(x)$ is $O(x^{W-2})$, which defeats the $1/x$ factor for large x if $W > 3$ [13].

The existence of the global minimum implies the existence of a first local minimum $\alpha_k^* > 0$ obeying $\alpha_k^* \le \alpha_k^{**}$. We are now ready to define OFSS.

Definition: OFSS(k; A) *OFSS(k; A) is FSS(p_f^*; A), where $p_f^*(k;\alpha) \in (0, 1]$ is the value that minimises $(\mathcal{I}_T(p_f))_{kk}$, subject to $\alpha' = \alpha p_f^* \le \alpha_k^*$.*

Apart from the trivial case of $W = 2$, we do not know of any examples where the first local minima is not equal to the global minimum, and conjecture that $\alpha_k^* = \alpha_k^{**}$ in all cases with $W > 3$.

Even if there are cases when α_k^* is not optimal, it is advantageous to base a definition on it because

$$p_f^*(k;\alpha) = \begin{cases} 1, & \alpha < \alpha_k^*, \\ \frac{\alpha_k^*}{\alpha}, & \alpha \ge \alpha_k^*. \end{cases} \quad (16)$$

In other words, if $\alpha > \alpha_k^*$, select p_f to cut back the input so that $\alpha' = \alpha_k^*$, otherwise let all flows in. The significance of this property is that one only needs to calculate α_k^* to know $p_f^*(k;\alpha)$ for all α, a significant practical advantage when adapting $p_f^*(k;\alpha)$ to changing traffic conditions, or different resource allocation (A value). Calculation details for α_k^* can be found in [13].

4. PERFORMANCE COMPARISON

We compare the CRLB performance of OFSS against that of FS, Sk, and enhanced versions of our skampling competitors SGS and ESk. For SGS(β, ϵ), we use the assisted form as described above, and also test using $\beta = 0.75$ in addition to the $\beta = 1$ value used in [8]. For ESk(L), we compare not only against the $L = 2$ favoured in [9], but also larger values adapted to α, and ignore the additional memory required to maintain the ownership variables. In data estimation comparisons, we use ML estimators for all methods. Previously a sub-optimal estimator was used to test SGS and ESk.

We compare on a basis of equal counter memory. The methods Sk, FSS, OFSS, ESk are each given an array with A counters, whereas the sampling methods FS, SGS are given flow tables with A entries. This means that if $N_f > A$, only $N_f' = \min(N_f, A)$ flows will actually be delivered to the methods (we ignore flow expiry).

With A and N_f (or equivalently $\alpha = N_f/A$) fixed, methods Sk, ESk(2) and FS($p_f{=}N_f'/N_f = \min(1, 1/\alpha)$) are determined, as are OFSS(k) given the target θ_k. For SGS, for each of $\beta = \{0.75, 1\}$ we set ϵ to match the average number of captured packets to that of FS. For ESk, at larger α values we select two values of $L > 2$ to bracket OFSS (at the chosen k^*). Finally, we also compare against FS(1), that is perfect flow collection.

We compare over an operating range of $1 < \alpha \le 100$, since $\alpha \approx 1$ is theoretically important, and $\alpha = 100$ corresponds to a commonly quoted sampling probability of 0.01. Values as high as $\alpha = 10000$ are now typical in big data contexts. The structure of OFSS is such that its performance will be unaffected by higher loads, whereas other methods suffer in information or implementation terms, or both, as load increases.

Since A enters in only as a multiplicative factor, we plot per-counter variance rather than total variance. Here the objective is to compare methods, the absolute CRLB values depend on θ and are not important.

4.1 CRLB Comparisons

We evaluate $(\mathcal{I}_T(p_f))_{kk}$ numerically from the exact expressions given earlier, initially using a truncated geometric model TG(W, R) for $\boldsymbol{\theta}$, where $R = \theta_1/\theta_W$. The $R = 1$ case is a uniform distribution, which has a heavier tail than any (truncated) Pareto distribution.

Consider Figure 1 where $\boldsymbol{\theta}$ is uniform, $W{=}50$. In plot(a) $\alpha \approx 1$, a load so light that results are close to degenerate: OFSS(p_f^*) $\approx$ FSS(1) = Sk $\approx$ ESk(2), FS(p_f) $\approx$ FS(1). Despite this SGS already shows poor behavior. At $\alpha = 2$ it is already orders of magnitude worse than other methods for $k > 3$, and becomes almost impossible to calculate for $\alpha = 100$. This is consistent with the poor behaviour of packet sampling [11], whose structure SGS generalises, but does not fundamentally change. For small α ESk(2) outperforms OFSS, however as α increases both Sk and ESk(2) also have variances orders of magnitude beyond OFSS for all k, and then become difficult to calculate. At $\alpha = 100$ the field therefore narrows to ESk(L) for well chosen $L \gg 2$ versus OFSS. For each of plots (c) and (d) L values are used so that

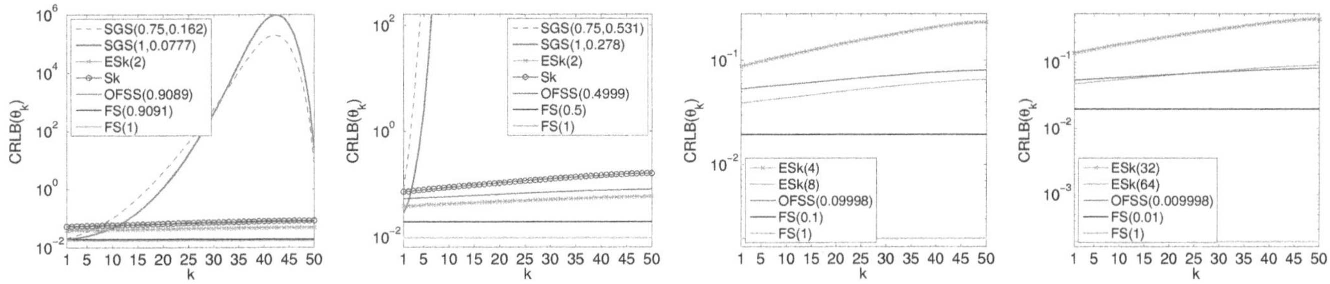

(a) $\alpha = 1.1$ (b) $\alpha = 2$ (c) $\alpha = 10$ (d) $\alpha = 100$

Figure 1: CRLB Comparisons with uniform $\boldsymbol{\theta}$, $W = 50$. We plot SGS(β, ϵ) when possible; ESk(2) and Sk for $\alpha \leq 2$, else ESk(L) for values bracketing OFSS($p_f^*(1)$), and FS($1/\alpha$). Here $p_f^* \approx 1/\alpha$. since $\alpha_1^* \approx 1$.

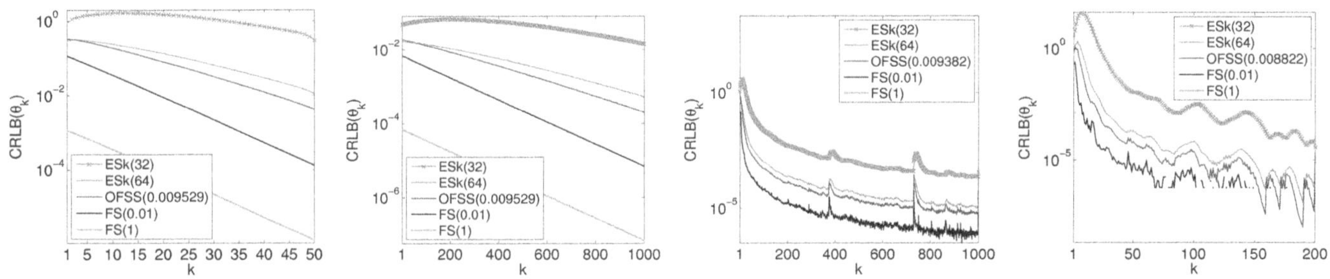

(a) $\boldsymbol{\theta}$ from TG(50, 1000) (b) $\boldsymbol{\theta}$ from TG(1000, 1000) (c) $\boldsymbol{\theta}$ from Abilene-III (d) $\boldsymbol{\theta}$ from Leipzig-II

Figure 2: CRLB Comparisons, $\alpha = 100$. [Abilene, Leipzig] truncated at $W = [1000, 200]$.

ESk brackets OFSS. In plot(d) we see that OFSS is within a constant factor of, and the same order of magnitude as, the benchmark FS($1/\alpha$). We see that to (just) defeat OFSS requires ESk with $L = 64$. Assuming a generous 32 bits per counter, this means that $\approx$19% extra memory is needed to achieve this, more for larger α.

Comparing plot(d) with Figure 2(a) shows that similar conclusions hold even after changing the distribution shape quite radically from uniform to TG(50, 1000). For TG(W, R) with $R = \{10, 1000\}$, $W = \{50, 1000\}$, similar results were found. Changing from optimising for θ_1 to other θ_k changes variance values somewhat for OFSS(k) and the matching L slightly for ESk(L), but not the conclusions.

Figure 2 provides a bridge from models to data with load fixed at $\alpha = 100$. From plots(a) to (b) we increase W from $W = 50$ to a more realistic $W = 1000$. The picture is remarkably unchanged. From plot(b) to (c) we move from a very rough traffic model, TG(1000, 1000), to data from the Abilene-III dataset (see Table 1), truncated at $W = 1000$. Again the same model-comparison conclusions hold. Finally, plot(d) uses $\boldsymbol{\theta}$ from the Leipzig-II dataset where $\theta_k = 0$ for many k, resulting in zeros manifesting as gaps in the FS and FS(1) curves. Associated 'spiky' far-tail estimates for OFSS and ESk are a sign of the need for truncation, here we used $W = 200$.

4.2 Estimation Comparisons

We now compare $\hat{\boldsymbol{\theta}}$ estimates, again for $\alpha = 100$, for FS, OFSS, SGS($1, \epsilon$), and ESk(64) using maximum likelihood estimation (see [13] for MLE derivations).

Trace	Link Capacity	N_f	Duration (hh:mm:ss)	D
Leipzig-II	50 Mbps	2,277,052	02:46:01	19.76
Abilene-III	10 Gbps	23,806,285	00:59:49	16.12

Table 1: Summary of the data traces used.

The datasets, summarised in Table 1, are old but adequate for testing the methods. We extract TCP flows according to the standard 5-tuple (with no timeout).

Figure 3 plots $\hat{\boldsymbol{\theta}}$ for Abilene-III, truncated at $W = 2000$, which is approximately the largest value for which $\theta_k > 0$ for all k. The grey curve, FS(1), corresponds to $\boldsymbol{\theta}$ itself. The estimate for SGS: $\hat{\boldsymbol{\theta}}_1 = 1$, and $\hat{\boldsymbol{\theta}}_k = 0$ for all $k > 1$, is as expected very poor, in fact degenerate. All other methods appear to perform quite well, however it is very difficult to assess performance reliably from such plots, in particular

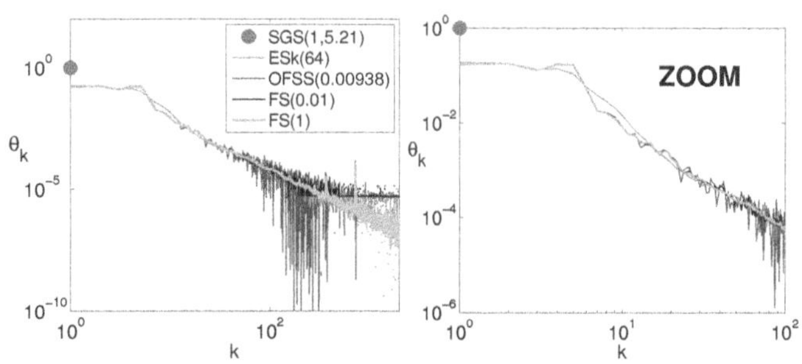

Figure 3: $\hat{\boldsymbol{\theta}}$ for Abilene, $W = 2000$. Here $\alpha = 100$, and OFSS and ESk are optimised for θ_1.

Trace	k^*	p_f^*	L	FS	OFSS	ESk	SGS
Abilene	1	0.009	64	1.6e-3	5.6e-3	7.8e-2	8.9e-1
Leipzig	1	0.009	64	9.4e-2	**2.1e-2**	2.5e-1	**2.8e-1**
Abilene	W	0.005	64	1.6e-3	4.1e-3	7.8e-2	8.9e-1
Leipzig	W	0.013	64	9.4e-2	**2.1e-2**	2.5e-1	**2.5e-1**

Table 2: ℓ_2 error: Abi. (W=2000), Leip. (W=200).

in the far tail because of the high variablility inherent in single point estimates as the data 'runs out'. Smoothing is typically used to improve behaviour in such cases [3].

For a more objective assessment, we employ the ℓ_2 error $\|\hat{\boldsymbol{\theta}} - \boldsymbol{\theta}\|_2 = (\sum_{k=1}^{W}(\hat{\theta}_k - \theta_k)^2)^{1/2}$ to summarise performance of each method over all k. Overall, for each trace the results of Table 2 reflect the variance pecking order FS<OFSS<ESk(64)≪SGS from the CRLB analysis averaged over all k, both when optimised for θ_1 and θ_W. Four exceptions are noted in bold. In two of these OFSS is seen to defeat FS. This is due to an implicit smoothing of the sketch component of OFSS improving the fit over the tail where for many indices $\theta_k = 0$ for Leipzig. In the other two cases SGS appears comparable to ESk for Leipzig when $k^* = W$ instead of much worse. This results from the fact that θ_1, θ_2 are fairly large and SGS is able to give rough estimates for them given its deliberate small flow bias, while setting $\hat{\boldsymbol{\theta}}_k = 0$ for all $k > 2$. Note that these exceptions are in part due to the limitations of ℓ_2 as a summary metric. Leipzig-II provides an instructive example of difficulties (for all methods) which arise when the assumption of $\theta_k > 0$ is violated. Abilene-III avoids this by a suitable, and larger, choice of W.

5. CONCLUSION

We have introduced OFSS, a hybrid 'skampling' method for flow size estimation. Its Fisher information gathering ability is of the same order as Flow Sampling (the optimum), but its sketch data structure allows its use in resource constrained applications. It is clearly superior to the alternative SGS and ESk in implementation terms, and in information terms, except for ESk for large enough L. However ESk is more complex and requires supplementary memory which increases both with L and hence with load. OFSS(k^*) is tuned to minimise the CRLB of θ_{k^*}, but for any k^*, it performs well for all θ_k.

Acknowledgment

Partially supported by Australian Research Council's Discovery Projects funding schemes # DP120102834 and # DP110103505.

6. REFERENCES

[1] Cisco NetFlow. http://www.cisco.com/en/US/products/ps6601/products_ios_protocol_group_home.html.

[2] B. H. Bloom. Space-time trade-offs in hash coding with allowable errors. *Communications of the ACM*, 13(7):422–426, 1970.

[3] N. Duffield, C. Lund, and M. Thorup. Estimating flow distributions from sampled flow statistics. *IEEE/ACM Transactions on Networking*, 13(5):933–946, 2005.

[4] C. Estan and G. Varghese. New directions in traffic measurement and accounting. *ACM Transactions on Computer Systems*, 21(3):270–313, August 2003.

[5] J. D. Gorman and A. O. Hero. Lower bounds for parametric estimation with constraints. *IEEE Trans. Info. Th.*, 36(6):1285–1301, Nov. 1990.

[6] N. Hohn and D. Veitch. Inverting Sampled Traffic. In *Proc. 2003 ACM SIGCOMM Internet Measurement Conference*, pages 222–233, Miami, Oct. 2003.

[7] A. Kumar, M. Sung, J. Xu, and J. Wang. Data streaming algorithms for efficient and accurate estimation of flow size distribution. In *Proceedings of ACM SIGMETRICS / IFIP WG 7.3 Performance 2004*, New York, June 2004.

[8] A. Kumar and J. Xu. Sketch Guided Sampling: Using online estimates of flow size for adaptive data collection. In *Proceedings of IEEE Infocom 2006*, Barcelona, Spain, April 2006.

[9] B. Ribeiro, D. Towsley, and T. Ye. A Resource-minimalist Flow Size Histogram Estimator. In *Proc. ACM/SIGCOMM Internet Measurement Conf.*, pages 285–290, Vouliagmeni, Greece, Oct. 20-22 2008.

[10] P. Tune and D. Veitch. Towards Optimal Sampling for Flow Size Estimation. In *Proc. ACM SIGCOMM Internet Measurement Conf.*, pages 243–256, Vouliagmeni, Greece, Oct. 20-22 2008.

[11] P. Tune and D. Veitch. Fisher Information in Flow Size Distribution Estimation. *IEEE Transactions on Information Theory*, 57(10):7011–7035, Oct. 2011.

[12] P. Tune and D. Veitch. Sampling vs Sketching: An Information Theoretic Comparison. In *IEEE Infocom 2011*, pages 2105–2113, Shanghai, China, April 10-15 2011.

[13] P. Tune and D. Veitch. OFSS: Skampling for the Flow Size Distribution: Technical Report. Technical report, Dept. E&EE, The University of Melbourne, 2014. copy available upon request.

[14] H. Zhao, A. Lall, M. Ogihara, O. Spatscheck, J. Wang, and J. Xu. A data streaming algorithm for estimating entropies of OD flows. In *Proc. 7th ACM SIGCOMM Internet Measurement Conf.*, pages 279–290, New York, NY, USA, 2007. ACM.

Dissecting Web Latency in Ghana

Yasir Zaki, Jay Chen
New York University Abu Dhabi, UAE
yasir.zaki@nyu.edu
jchen@cs.nyu.edu

Thomas Pötsch
University of Bremen
Bremen, Germany
thp@comnets.uni-bremen.de

Talal Ahmad, Lakshminarayanan Subramanian
CS, NYU and CTED, NYUAD
{ahmad, lakshmi}@cs.nyu.edu

ABSTRACT

Web access is prohibitively slow in many developing regions despite substantial effort to increase bandwidth and network penetration. In this paper, we explore the fundamental bottlenecks that cause poor web performance from a client's perspective by carefully dissecting webpage load latency contributors in Ghana. Based on our measurements from 2012 to 2014, we find several interesting issues that arise due to the increasing complexity of web pages and number of server redirections required to completely render the assets of a page. We observe that, rather than bandwidth, the primary bottleneck of web performance in Ghana is the lack of good DNS servers and caching infrastructure. The main bottlenecks are: (a) Recursive DNS query resolutions; (b) HTTP redirections; (c) TLS/SSL handshakes. We experiment with a range of well-known end-to-end latency optimizations and find that simple DNS caching, redirection caching, and the use of SPDY can all yield substantial improvements to user-perceived latency.

Categories and Subject Descriptors

C.2.2 [**Computer-Communication Networks**]: Network Protocols; C.4 [**Performance of Systems**]: Measurement techniques

Keywords

Web; HAR; DNS; Developing countries

1. INTRODUCTION

Web access in developing regions suffers from a continually widening content-connectivity gap: the rate of growth in connectivity is outstripped by the growth in the complexity of web pages. Despite lagging broadband and latency statistics relative to the Organisation for Economic Co-operation and Development (OECD) countries, Internet infrastructure in developing regions has been improving steadily over the past decade [1]. For example, Accra (the capital of Ghana) has several major undersea cable landing sites including: ACE, Main One, Glo1, and WACS [5]. Although this appears promising, the web has seen a 30 to 50-fold increase in average page complexity over the same decade [4, 11, 15, 19], which significantly outpaces the growth in connectivity.

Recent works have explored facets of slow Internet in developing regions from different perspectives, geographic locations, and infrastructural contexts. Some works find that high latency, buffer bloat, and packet loss are the central causes of poor performance [25]. Other works examine problems caused by the interaction between low bandwidth links and high network contention by TCP flows [16]. Yet other research cites routing protocols and architectural issues such as Content Distribution Networks (CDN) server placement among the central problems [4].

In this paper, we aim to understand the causes of user-perceived web latency in Ghana as it represents one of the most well connected developing countries in the world [5]. Unlike prior work in developing regions [16, 18, 25] that focus on access link performance in developing regions, our measurements detail the core infrastructural issues that lead to a poor web browsing experience. A number of works study similar web performance issues in fixed/wired or mobile environments such as [14, 31], but our unique context results in a different set of issues.

In our measurement driven approach, we collected download traces of Alexa's [2] top webpages from different locations in Ghana from 2012 to 2014. We also collected similar measurements in three different well-connected locations around the world over the same time period for comparison. We found the following key results: bandwidth is less of a bottleneck than several other factors, the actual time spent downloading content represents only a small fraction of the end-to-end page download time, and the main culprit of user-perceived web latency is actually DNS resolution. Specifically, DNS caching along with placement of the root and top level domain DNS servers play the most significant role in the overall web performance. We find that caching DNS records can decrease page load times in Ghana by five times. We also observe that other important factors for high end-to-end latency include HTTP redirections and TLS/SSL handshakes for secure pages. Caching HTTP redirects can enhance the page load time by 20%, and long TLS/SSL handshakes are present in 15% of Alexa page requests. Finally, to understand the effects of flow contention, we experimented with SPDY and found that depending on the server locations, SPDY can reduce some page load times in Ghana by up to 30%.

IMC'14, November 5–7, 2014, Vancouver, BC, Canada.

ACM 978-1-4503-3213-2/14/11 ...$15.00.
http://dx.doi.org/10.1145/2663716.2663748.

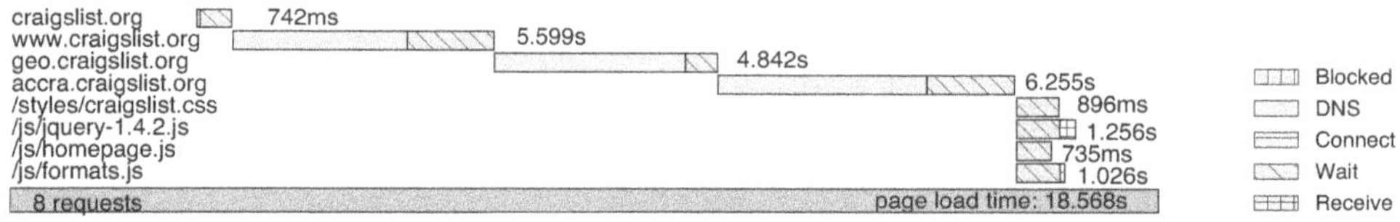

Figure 1: HAR trace visualization of `craigslist.com` from Accra, Ghana cellular in 2012

2. MOTIVATION

Information and Communication Technologies (ICTs) have been linked to development [26], where in the last four years, developing nations have experienced a significant increase in the number of Internet users, which is a promising trend. Between 2009 and 2011, Ghana experienced a huge increase in the number of Internet users from 5.4% to 14.1% [12], which is the largest increase in the country's history. A similar trend is being reflected in other developing countries, resulting in millions of new Internet users every year. However, the Internet that these users encounter is often extremely slow and cannot take advantage of all available content on the web.

Very little effort has been expended on understanding and solving the Internet problems in developing regions relative to the number of people these issues affect. Even very basic questions like why the Internet is so slow is a challenging question to answer due not only to the myriad of difficulties in collecting data in these regions, but also due to the multitude of answers depending on the context. Interestingly, when these problems are investigated, findings range widely from the relatively obvious, e.g. low bandwidth, high latency, unreliability, and loss, to the esoteric, e.g. mis-routing due to lack of peering points, small-packet regimes, etc. [20, 13, 25, 16]. Solutions to these problems are similarly varied [24, 23, 17]. Motivated by these differing ideas, in this paper we seek to answer why page loading times are so slow in Ghana.

3. METHODOLOGY

We used standard off-the-shelf tools to collect our traces. We collected HTTP Archive (HAR) browser-level traces using Firefox Version 13 with the Firebug extension and Selenium [7] to automate the process. The browser cache is cleared after each webpage. We also used the Linux dig command-line tool to examine DNS requests in more detail.

Table 1: Experiments details

Time	Type	Link	Location
August 2012	Alexa's top 500 global	Both Wifi & 3G	Accra and Hohoe (3G)
March - July 2013	DNS dig+trace	Wifi	Accra, Abu Dhabi NY and Bremen
August 2014	DNS dig+trace	Wifi	Accra
April 2014	SPDY	Wifi	Accra, Abu Dhabi NY and Bremen
August 2014	Alexa's top 1000 global	Both Wifi & 3G	Accra, Abu Dhabi NY, Bremen and Kumawu (3G)
August 2014	Alexa's top 500 local	Both Wifi & 3G	Accra, Abu Dhabi NY, Bremen and Kumawu (3G)

We ran our experiments from six locations in total: New York City, Bremen (Germany), Abu Dhabi (UAE), Accra (Ghana), Kumawu and Hohoe (both small cities in Ghana). In New York, Bremen, Abu Dhabi, and Accra the machines we used were state-of-the-art with a standard Linux distribution (Ubuntu and CentOS), and the experiments were conducted on university campus networks with over 10Mbps connections using Wifi connectivity and 3G HSPA cellular network connections. In Hohoe/Kumawu, our traces were collected from a 3G HSPA connection. In Hohoe, the fastest wired network was limited to ADSL at a single Internet Cafe and we were not able to collect data from that location. For our experiments, we collected web traces of Alexa's [2] top 1000 global and top 500 local websites, collected results of DNS performance using the "dig +trace" command, and evaluated SPDY performance in Ghana, see Table 1.

4. DISSECTING PAGE LOADS

In this section we focus on identifying problems associated with the webpage download process in Ghana by examining the set of browser-level traces we collected from Ghana in 2012.[1] Some of the timing information we are able to collect from the HAR files include:

- **Blocking**: waiting time of a request in the queue, due to the maximum number of parallel TCP connections that a browser can open per server
- **DNS Lookup**: time required to resolve a host name or an URL
- **Connecting**: TCP connection setup time
- **Sending**: the time required to send HTTP request to the server
- **Waiting**: the time required to receive a response from the server
- **Receiving**: the time required to read the entire response from the server

Figure 1 gives an example of a HAR file visualized as a waterfall chart.

4.1 Domain Name Server (DNS)

From our Ghana traces, the immediate observation is that the dominant contributor to the long page download times is the DNS lookup. Figure 2 shows the statistics taken from our measurements in Ghana 2012. The timing breakdown categories (i.e., "Blocking" and "Waiting") are identical to those defined previously in Section 4. We observe that DNS requests account for 37-40% of the user-perceived latency.[2]

[1]While the issues we observe here serve to highlight the extreme nature of the latency problem in developing countries, Accra actually has one of the fastest Internet infrastructures in Africa. Other developing regions suffer from even worse network conditions, e.g. South Africa has higher latencies [30], East Africa and Southeast Asia have fewer major network cables [10].

[2]A number of these requests occur simultaneously and we removed such overlapping timings. However, these figures do still include timings that do not contribute to the overall page load time, because they are not on the critical path.

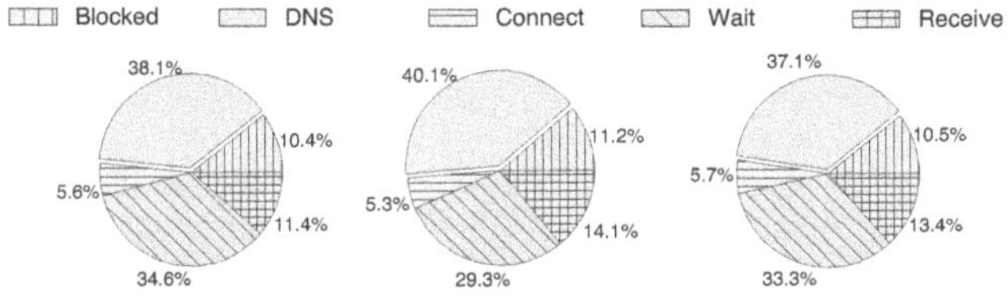

(a) Accra 3G (b) Accra Wifi (c) Hohoe 3G

Figure 2: Web page requests (Alexa's top global 2012)

Although, "Wait" accounts for roughly 30% of the load time in all cases, we do not focus on it because link latency challenges in developing countries like Ghana have already been studied elsewhere [18, 25]. In these studies, the authors suggested several methods to improve the link latencies by investing in local server infrastructure or placing web caches and content on servers within the local service provider.

4.2 HTTP redirects

Looking more closely at the Ghana traces, we find that in about 80% of the cases, the first HTTP GET request actually gets redirected into another page. These redirects are caused either by the HTTP status code response of 301 Moved Permanently or 302 Found. We find that in most cases a redirection is due to directing a browser to a www URL of the same page, i.e. if we look at the example shown in Figure 1, we can see that the client asks for page `craigslist.org` and gets redirected to the domain `www.craigslist.org`.

4.3 HTTP blocking

Another interesting effect that we observe is blocking. In Figure 2 we see that blocking causes more than 10% of the page load time. This is due to the configured maximum number of TCP connections to a server within the web browser. From the example in Figure 3, we see that the browser has already requested six objects simultaneously using six TCP connections (style_splash.css, logo.jpg, etc.), and the next object that has to be requested from the same server (header_left.jpg) now has to wait until one of the previous object is downloaded.

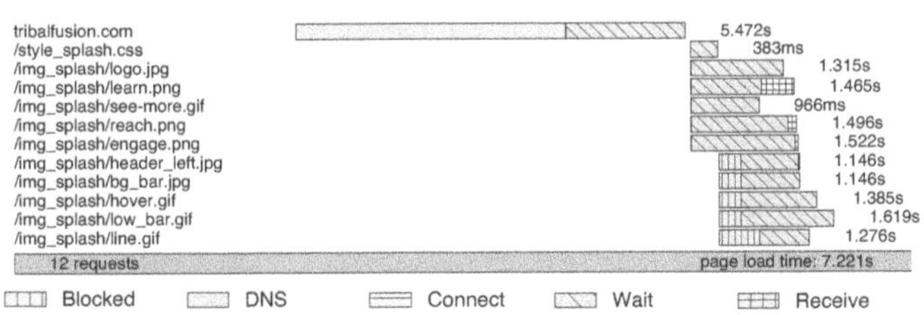

Figure 3: Blocking example of `tribalfusion.com` from Accra, Ghana cellular in 2012

In addition to the maximum number of TCP connections, modern web browsers also use HTTP pipelining with $4-8$ pipelined objects. HTTP pipelining is a way for the client browser to request several objects at the same time within one TCP connection, but Head-Of-Line blocking (HOL blocking) may occur because of this limit as well.

4.4 TLS/SSL

Our 2012 traces from Ghana showed that approx. 8% of the overall object requests require a secure connection. In 2014 this number has nearly doubled to 15%. This corroborates with the trend of increased adoption of secure content exchange on the web. However, in developing regions like Ghana this can severely impact user-perceived latency because establishing a Transport Layer Security (TLS) connection is a lengthy procedure and is severely impacted by latency. The TLS handshake procedure depends on whether only the server is authenticated or both the server and the client are authenticated, but the basic TLS handshake consists of up to 9 round trips [9].

5. SPEEDING UP PAGE LOADS

Here we assess the potential of several straightforward improvements that can cost orders of magnitude less than extending the existing network infrastructure.

5.1 DNS Caching

In order to understand the effect and potential gain of DNS caching, we analyze our traces in more detail. Figure 4 shows an example on long DNS requests of one of the webpages taken from the Accra 2012 cellular traces.

In this example, the page requests objects from *eleven* external domains, where a DNS request must be issued for each single domain. In order to evaluate the ratio of the DNS request to the total page time we calculate the overall delay caused by DNS. This is not a simple summation of all DNS requests, as can be seen in Figure 4. To calculate the potential benefit of DNS caching we leverage the Wprof tool [31] to identify the critical path in the page request and calculate the contribution to that critical path by DNS requests. We find that the ratio of the overall DNS delays to the overall page load time is about 72% of the overall page load time in Figure 4.

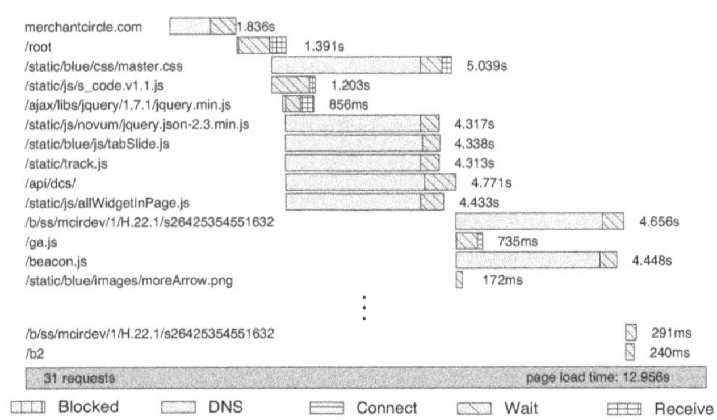

Figure 4: DNS example (`www.merchantcircle.com`) from Accra, Ghana cellular 2012

Figure 5 shows the DNS delays in our traces from Ghana, taken from all embedded domains within Alexa's top websites. The DNS delays are measured at the application layer by means of HAR files, thus they represent the user-perceived performance. These DNS delays also include all DNS retry attempts and redirects. The figure shows how the overall DNS performance in Ghana has changed over the past two years.

In 2012, Ghana's DNS CDFs (Figure 5a Wifi and cellular) split into two regions: a low delay region in the order of milliseconds and a high delay region in the order of seconds. When we examined the websites that belonged to the high delay group, we did not find any distinctive patterns, e.g., all are .com domains etc. However, by cross-referencing the domains behind each region, we found that 15% of the low delay domains were also present in the high delay region. This suggested that the low delay region is likely due to DNS caching at the local ISP DNS server.

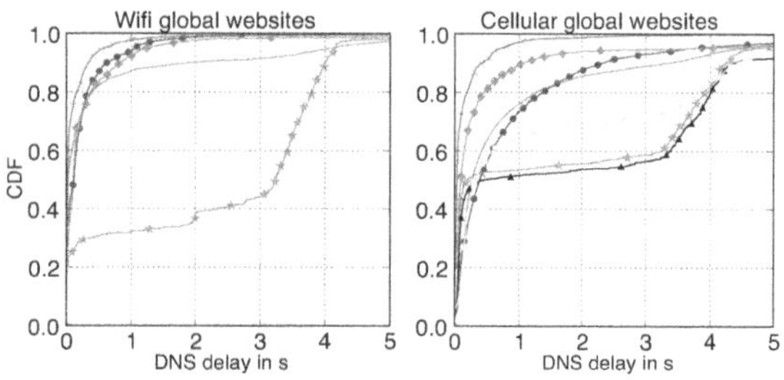

(a) Alexa's top *global* websites

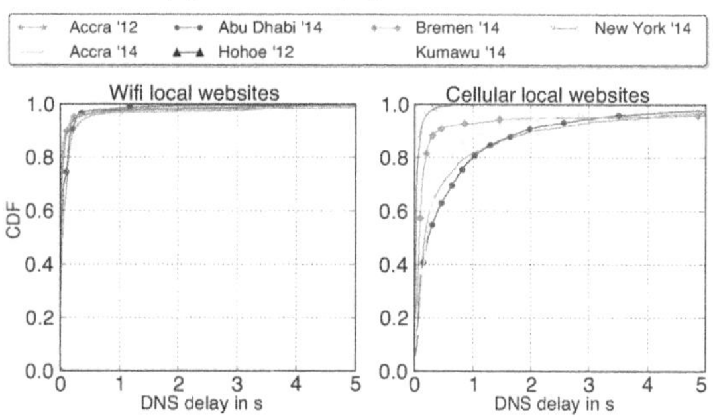

(b) Alexa's top *local* websites

Figure 5: Per location DNS delay (HAR files)

In 2014, we have redone new experiments in Ghana using Alexa's top 1000 global websites and top 500 local websites. We also compare the Ghana results to measurements performed in other locations around the world. We observe a clear improvement in Accra's Wifi DNS performance due to better DNS caching on the university network for both the global and the local measurements. However, the DNS performance over cellular is only improved in Accra's case, but Kumawu's cellular DNS performance is still very poor (Figure 5a right side).

Figure 6 shows the pie chart of the page load time in Ghana for the 2014 measurements. We can see that the DNS response times have improved compared to the 2012 measurements (Figure 2). In contrast, the TCP connection time has increased to 3-4 times in terms of proportion of overall page load time.

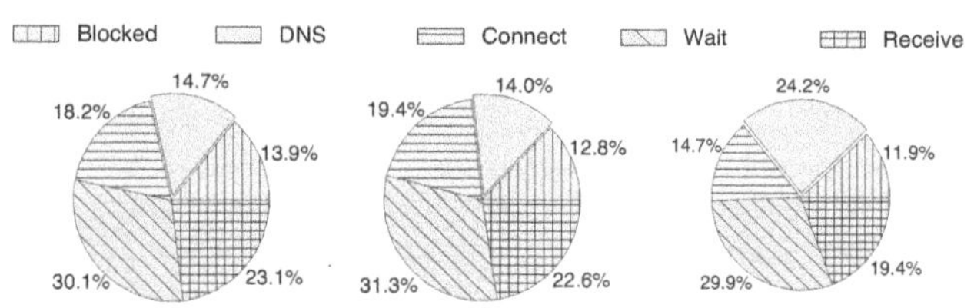

(a) Accra 3G (b) Accra Wifi (c) Kumawu 3G

Figure 6: Web page requests (Alexa's top global 2014)

5.2 DNS Server Placement

Besides caching, DNS server placement plays an important role to reduce DNS latency. There are over 300 root servers scattered around the globe operated by 12 different organizations. Although only 13 root servers appear in response to a request, these servers are reachable with 13 anycast IP addresses [6]. The root DNS servers are not provisioned uniformly around the world or in proportion to population densities. The authoritative DNS servers for Top-level domains (TLDs) is similarly unevenly distributed.

To get a better understanding of the high DNS delay region from Figure 5a, we analyzed the DNS performance using the dig command-line tool. The dig tool is used in Linux to query DNS nameservers. It can be combined with the "+trace" option to follow the full lookup process from the root servers up until getting the IP address of the requested domain while displaying the answer for each involved server.

The "dig +trace" output can be divided into different hierarchical categories starting with the first category where the local DNS server gives back the answer to the root servers (i.e., the '.' domains) all the way to the last category that gives back the IP address of the requested domain. Figure 7 shows the "dig +trace" results for Accra (2013 and 2014) in comparison with New York, Bremen, Abu Dhabi (2013). The total DNS delay depicted in Figure 7 is a combination of several hierarchical requests from the local DNS server, root server, TLD servers, and sub domains servers. Although, the number of categories of the DNS hierarchy can be more than four, we have observed that the most dominant number is four, which is why we only present the first four results. Figures 8a to 8d are CDFs of DNS delays per hierarchy.

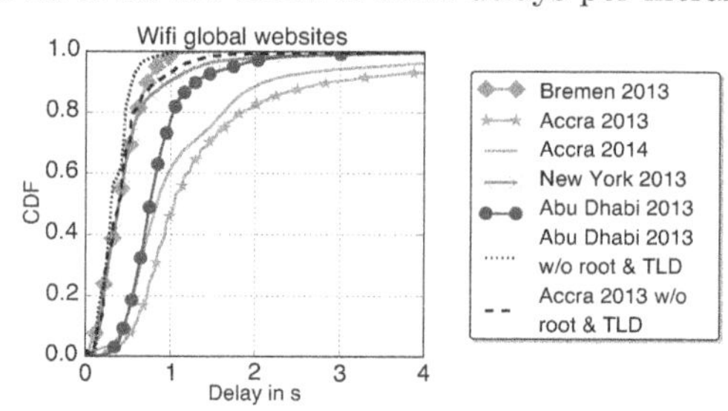

Figure 7: Per location DNS delay on Wifi ("dig +trace")

Figure 8a shows the local DNS server delay (to retrieve the root authoritative servers). Apart from Accra's 2013 upper 30%, the results show that the local DNS server replies back with an answer within milliseconds. For Accra's 2013 upper 30% some network performance issues degrade the performance. Figure 8b and 8c show the DNS delay of the root and TLD servers respectively. The results show that both New York's and Bremen's root and TLD authoritative servers have faster response times compared to Abu Dhabi and Accra. This indicates that these servers are geographically closer to New York and Bremen. Accra has the worst delay profile compared to all other locations. Figure 8d shows the delay CDF for the next DNS hierarchy. The result shows that Abu Dhabi and Accra have slightly higher delays than New York and Bremen. This is due to the increased geographical distance to the DNS resolvers. Although, in the previous section, we have seen better DNS performance for Accra's 2014 over Wifi network; the results depicted in this section show that the physical distance to the DNS resolvers is still a problem.

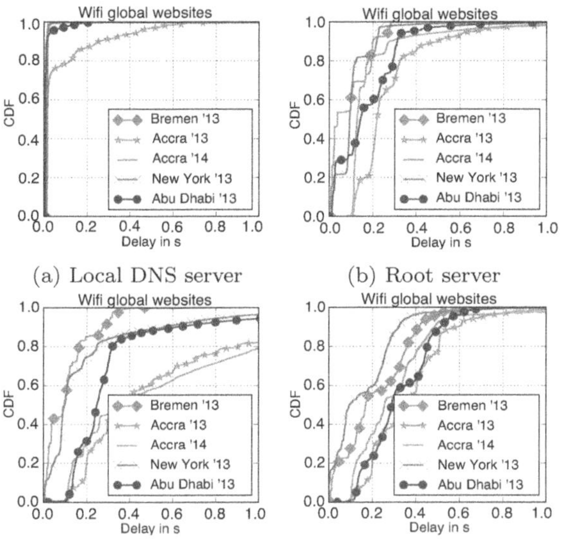

(a) Local DNS server (b) Root server

(c) TLD server (d) Sub-domain server

Figure 8: Per location/hierarchy delay CDFs

In order to evaluate the distance from Ghana to the DNS resolvers, we have performed several experiments using the destination, showing how many hops are in between, and the IP addresses of these hops. We used traceroute against all 13 root domain servers from Accra, recorded the routes, and repeated each experiment about 50 times. We found that nearly all of the traceroutes' first hops were outside Ghana and somewhere in Europe (Switzerland, UK, etc.), from where, the route sometimes diverts to the US or Asia. None of the routes went to DNS root servers that are geographically nearby.

In summary, there are large potential gains for enhancing the overall DNS delay in Ghana in case more root and TLD servers are deployed in that particular region. Figure 7 shows the potential performance gain when root and TLD servers are placed hypothetically with zero latency to Abu Dhabi and Accra. These additional root servers would give very similar performance to what is currently observed for New York and Bremen.

5.3 Caching Redirects

In section 4.2, we discussed the issue of the first HTTP GET redirection. One way to overcome this is to cache redirects, where the client could be informed about the redirection immediately. Caching redirection can enhance the overall page load time by about 20% (see Table 2).

Caching redirects can cause revocation problems since even after removing the redirection, the cached redirections cannot be removed and clients will still be redirected and never reach the new server.

Table 2: Redirects delay to total page load time (2012)

Location	Websites with Redirects	Average Ratio	Standard Deviation
Accra cellular	79%	25%	15%
Accra Wifi	78%	20%	16%
Hohoe cellular	81%	21%	17%

5.4 SPDY vs TCP Optimizations

SPDY [8] is an application layer protocol proposed to enhance the webpage loading time. The SPDY protocol includes header compression and allows servers to send back additional responses without the client asking for them, e.g., the server might send back the style sheet of a page along with the HTML, which can speed up the page load time.

Since blocking was an issue we identified in Section 4.3, we wanted to examine the utility of SPDY, as it offers the potential to reduce the overhead of blocking times. We requested 42 pages from four different locations: Accra, Abu Dhabi, Bremen, and New York.[3] Each experiment was repeated five times to have enough randomness for a better CDF population. Figure 9 shows the overall comparison between SPDY and HTTP for all locations.

For the 42 websites that supported SPDY in our experiments, we have found that SPDY does not show significant performance gain compared to regular HTTP in developed regions (e.g., New York, Bremen). Whereas, in Accra, SPDY shows a performance gain in the upper 40% of the page load times. This is because SPDY reduces the number of TCP connections by multiplexing HTTP requests into a single TCP connection per domain. As found in [32], SPDY reduces the page load times especially for links with less bandwidth and higher RTTs.

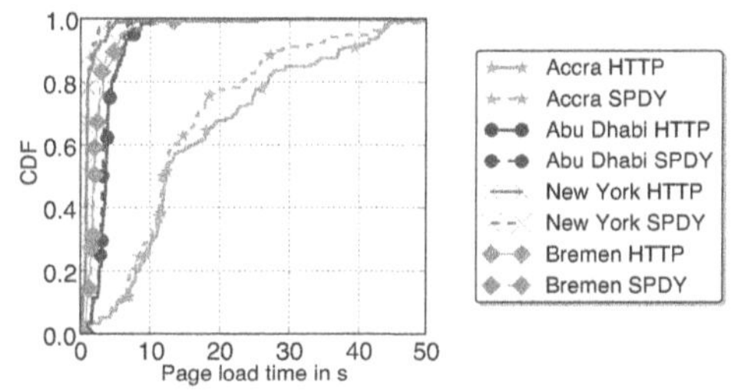

Figure 9: Per location SPDY vs HTTP in 2013

In Ghana where the connections are latency, not bandwidth, constrained (at least for the purposes of web browsing), SDPY is a better solution than multiple TCP connections. Almost all popular browsers are configured by default to use multiple persistent TCP connections when downloading a page over HTTP to avoid HOL blocking, but increasing the number of persistent TCP connections does not always improve the HTTP performance [27]. Furthermore, in developing countries where the bandwidth is scarce and sharing is high, increasing the number of TCP sessions can degrade HTTP performance [16].

5.5 TLS/SSL Speedups

Although the TLS protocol has a resume handshake that significantly reduces the handshake traffic and latency, it requires the server to store the TLS session in its cache. Thus, many servers store the TLS session only for a short period of time resulting in the full handshake being used instead. Approximately 15% of our latest web requests contained a secure connection establishment handshake. Improving handshake procedure can reduce the overall load time, and combining the handshake with SPDY can potentially im-

[3] These were the only websites out of the Alexa's top 500 websites that supported SPDY.

prove the overall page load time without adding significant computational load on the servers [3].

Fast-Track [28] is a proposed mechanism where the server's public and negotiated parameters are cached at the client side, since the server's parameters are nearly static. This helps reduce the overall TLS handshake traffic and the number of RTTs required, thus providing substantial gain in high latency developing countries. Unfortunately, Fast-Track requires modifications to both the client and the server side by means of TLS extensions and not all servers will have the Fast-Track support option implemented. We do not present measurements of the potential of TLS/SSL speedups of these solutions because they require control over the server.

6. OTHER RELATED WORK

There is a wide range of related work in the networking literature and we include in this section only works we have not yet referenced. Stream Control Transmission Protocol (SCTP) is a transport-layer protocol to replace TCP, which provides multiplexed streams and stream-aware congestion control [29]. HTTP 1.1 over SCTP may be used to avoid the HOL blocking problem where when one transport protocol data unit (TPDU) is lost, TCP does not deliver successive TPDUs until the one that is lost is recovered. Structured Stream Transport (SST) is a protocol that uses "structured streams": lightweight, independent streams to be carried over a common transport sharing the same congestion control context [22].

Recent work [32] investigates the conditions under which SPDY provides improvements over HTTP. The work shows that SPDY performs better when few network losses, high RTTs and low bandwidth are given. We corroborate these findings for high RTT conditions in developing countries like Ghana. In [21], the authors propose a simple solution to increase TCP's initial window size to at least ten segments, which may also help for developing regions.

7. CONCLUSIONS

In this paper, we have presented an analysis of the key factors that trigger high end-to-end latency for web page downloads in Ghana. From our measurements over the past two years, we observed that DNS is a critical bottleneck in page load times and even the deployment of simple ideas such as DNS caching can help improve the end-to-end performance. Apart from DNS, we found that because of the lack of server infrastructure within the country, every request needs to be routed to US or European countries thereby incurring a high network latency penalty; hence, even simple operations such as HTTP redirections and TLS/SSL handshakes represent a non-trivial fraction of the page load time. We experimented with a host of well known optimizations and describe the effectiveness of some of the promising approaches including DNS caching, DNS server placement, caching redirects, using SPDY, and TLS/SSL speedups.

8. ACKNOWLEDGEMENTS

We thank Kessir Adjaho and David Hutchful for their help in collecting measurement data from Ghana. We would also like to thank our shepherd Harsha V. Madhyastha and the anonymous reviewers for their valuable feedback. Talal Ahmad was partially supported by the Center for Technology and Economic Development at NYUAD (CTED).

9. REFERENCES

[1] Akamai: State of the Internet. `http://www.akamai.com/stateoftheinternet`. Accessed: 2014-05-04.

[2] Alexa - The top 500 sites on the web. `http://www.alexa.com/topsites`. Accessed: 2014-04-05.

[3] Is TLS Fast Yet? `https://istlsfastyet.com/`. Accessed: 2014-08-15.

[4] Make the Web Faster - Web metrics: Size and number of resources. `http://developers.google.com/speed/articles/web-metrics`. Accessed: 2014-05-04.

[5] Ookla Download Index 2012. `http://www.netindex.com/download/allcountries/`. Accessed: 2013-02-05.

[6] Root Servers. `http://www.root-servers.org/`. Accessed: 2013-03-15.

[7] SeleniumHQ Browser Automation, Version 2.41.0. `http://docs.seleniumhq.org/`.

[8] SPDY: An experimental protocol for a faster web. `http://www.chromium.org/spdy/spdy-whitepaper`. Accessed: 2014-05-04.

[9] SSL Profiles: Part 1 by Jason Rahm. `http://devcentral.f5.com/articles/ssl-profiles-part-1`. Accessed: 2014-04-05.

[10] The World in 2010: ICT Facts and Figures - ITU. `http://www.itu.int/ITU-D/ict/material/FactsFigures2010.pdf`. Accessed: 2014-05-04.

[11] Web Site Optimization: Maximum Website Performance. `http://www.websiteoptimization.com/`. Accessed: 2013-05-04.

[12] World Bank Group - World Development Indicators. `http://data.worldbank.org/country/ghana`. Accessed: 2013-04-30.

[13] E. Brewer, M. Demmer, M. Ho, et al. The challenges of technology research for developing regions. *Pervasive Computing, IEEE*, 5(2):15–23, 2006.

[14] M. Butkiewicz, Z. Wu, S. Li, et al. Enabling the transition to the mobile web with websieve. In *Proc. of the 14th Workshop on Mobile Computing Systems and Applications*, HotMobile, pages 14:1–14:6, New York, NY, USA, 2013.

[15] J. Charzinski. Traffic properties, client side cachability and cdn usage of popular web sites. In B. Müller-Clostermann, K. Echtle, and E. P. Rathgeb, editors, *MMB/DFT*, Lecture Notes in Computer Science, pages 136–150. Springer.

[16] J. Chen, L. Subramanian, J. Iyengar, and B. Ford. TAQ: enhancing fairness and performance predictability in small packet regimes. In *Proc. of the 9th European Conference on Computer Systems*, page 7. ACM, 2014.

[17] J. Chen, L. Subramanian, and J. Li. Ruralcafe: Web search in the rural developing world. In *Proc. of the 18th International World Wide Web Conference*, 2009.

[18] M. Chetty, S. Sundaresan, S. Muckaden, et al. Measuring Broadband Performance in South Africa. In *Proc. of the 4th Annual Symposium on Computing for Development*, pages 1:1–1:10, New York, NY, USA, 2013. ACM.

[19] Sahuquillo J. Pont A. Domenech J., Gil J.A. Ddg: An efficient prefetching algorithm for current web generation. In *Proc. of the 1st IEEE Workshop on Hot Topics in Web Systems and Technologies (HotWeb)*. IEEE, 2006.

[20] B. Du, M. Demmer, and E. Brewer. Analysis of WWW traffic in Cambodia and Ghana. In *Proc. of the 15th International Conference on WWW*, pages 771–780, 2006.

[21] N. Dukkipati, T. Refice, Y. Cheng, et al. An Argument for Increasing TCP's Initial Congestion Window. *SIGCOMM Comput. Commun. Rev.*, 40(3):26–33, June 2010.

[22] B. Ford. Structured streams: A new transport abstraction. In *Proc. of the Conference on Applications, Technologies, Architectures, and Protocols for Computer Communications*, SIGCOMM '07, pages 361–372, New York, NY, USA, 2007. ACM.

[23] S. Guo, MH Falaki, EA Oliver, et al. Very low-cost internet access using KioskNet. *SIGCOMM Comput. Commun. Rev.*, 2007.

[24] B. Hull, V. Bychkovsky, Y. Zhang, et al. CarTel: A distributed mobile sensor computing system. *Sensys*, pages 125–138, 2006.

[25] Z. Koradia, G. Mannava, A. Raman, et al. First impressions on the state of cellular data connectivity in india. In *Proc. of the 4th Annual Symposium on Computing for Development*, Cape Town, South Africa, 2013.

[26] O. Ngwenyama, F. K. Andoh-Baidoo, F. Bollou, and O. Morawczynski. Is There A Relationship Between ICT, Health, Education And Development? An Empirical Analysis of five West African Countries from 1997-2003. *The Electronic Journal of Information Systems in Developing Countries*, 23, 2006.

[27] F. Baker P. Natarajan and P. D. Amer. Multiple TCP Connections Improve HTTP Throughput Myth or Fact? In *Proc. of the IEEE 28th Int'l Performance Computing and Communications Conference*. IEEE, 2009.

[28] H. Shacham and D. Boneh. Fast-track session establishment for TLS. In Mahesh Tripunitara, editor, *Proc. of NDSS 2002*, pages 195–202. Internet Society (ISOC), 2002.

[29] R. Stewart. Stream Control Transmission Protocol, September 2007. RFC4960.

[30] S. Sundaresan, N. Feamster, R. Teixeira, and N. Magharei. Measuring and Mitigating Web Performance Bottlenecks in Broadband Access Networks. In *Proc. of the ACM Internet Measurement Conference*, Barcelona, Spain, 2013.

[31] X. S. Wang, A. Balasubramanian, et al. Demystify Page Load Performance with WProf. In *Proc. of the USENIX conference on Networked Systems Design and Implementation (NSDI)*, 2013.

[32] X. S. Wang, A. Balasubramanian, A. Krishnamurthy, and D. Wetherall. How Speedy is SPDY? In *Proc. of the 11th USENIX Symposium on Networked Systems Design and Implementation (NSDI)*, pages 387–399, Seattle, WA, 2014.

How Much Can We Micro-Cache Web Pages?

Xiao Sophia Wang, Arvind Krishnamurthy, and David Wetherall
University of Washington

ABSTRACT

Browser caches are widely used to improve the performance of Web page loads. Unfortunately, current object-based caching is too coarse-grained to minimize the costs associated with small, localized updates to a Web object. In this paper, we evaluate the benefits if caching were performed at a finer granularity and at different levels (i.e., computed layout and compiled JavaScript). By analyzing Web pages gathered over two years, we find that both layout and code are highly cacheable, suggesting that our proposal can radically reduce time to first paint. We also find that mobile pages are similar to their desktop counterparts in terms of the amount and composition of updates.

Categories and Subject Descriptors

C.4 [**Computer Systems Organization**]: Performance of Systems—*Design studies*

Keywords

Caching, Micro-Caching, Web applications, Web pages

1. INTRODUCTION

Over the years, Web pages have become more complex, making Web page loads notoriously slow even though the underlying network has significantly improved. The situation is worse for the mobile scenario, partly due to the lower compute power available on these devices, and partly due to network inefficiencies. Reports have shown that mobile Web applications[1] are losing the market share to their native counterparts [8, 9].

A significant bottleneck of page load times comes from Web page structures, which do little to minimize updates and maximize caching of unmodified content. For example, reloading a page with minor updates requires fetching the entire HTML object, which often triggers a DNS lookup and a TCP connection setup, taking up one third of the page load time [19]. In contrast, a Web page's native counterpart can render right away, interacting with the network for more resources only when necessary. The result is that the native counterpart offers much faster time to first paint [17] (also user-perceived page load time) than the Web page.

We argue that by restructuring Web pages the performance gap between the Web and native applications can be largely eliminated. The first step is to minimize the impact of page updates by employing *micro-caching*. Different from current object-based caching, micro-caching caches any portion of an object at a much finer granularity, which can be an HTML element, a few lines of JavaScript, or a few CSS rules. Implementing micro-caching is possible given that JavaScript now can control almost every aspect of a page and also has access to browser storage.

The second step is to augment browsers with the ability to distinguish between layout, code, and data. Doing so lets us further cache the computed layout and compiled code, substantially reducing computation that is mostly redundant. Note that caching layout, code, and data contributes differently to improving page load times. Caching layout helps the most because loading HTML is always on the critical path of loading a page, which blocks all subsequent object loads [19]. Caching code also helps since loading and evaluating JavaScript are often on the critical path. But, caching data helps little because only a small portion of data fetches are on the critical path. Therefore, our focus is on caching layout and code.

The idea of micro-caching is not entirely new. Delta encoding was proposed over a decade ago, and it advocates that servers transparently compress pages and send differences between versions of a page [3]. Edge Side Includes (ESI) assembles Web pages at the edge to make use of edge caching [4]. We find the idea of micro-caching worth revisiting given that Web pages have become more dynamic than before. Different from treating every bit equally (as in both delta encoding and ESI), our proposal requires applications to make updates explicit and to make distinctions regarding layout, code, and data. As layout and code are likely on the critical path of a page load, caching them separately is key to improving page load times.

As a first step towards micro-caching, this paper studies its effectiveness — how much can we micro-cache Web pages? To this end, we collect snapshots of hundred Web pages over two years, and perform diff-like analysis that identifies updates from one version of a page to another. To infer whether they are from layout, code, or data, we analyze the context of the updates.

While Web pages are traditionally treated as black boxes by measurement studies, we embrace the opposite approach that lets us uncover the redundant bits in Web traffic, and that treats layout, code, and data differently so as to mit-

[1] In this paper, we use Web pages and Web applications interchangeably since their underlying mechanisms are the same.

IMC'14, November 5–7, 2014, Vancouver, BC, Canada.

http://dx.doi.org/10.1145/2663716.2663739.

igate the bottlenecks of loading modern Web pages. Our main contributions are as follows.

- We propose *micro-caching* that distinguishes portions of a page corresponding to layout, code, and data. We make the case that micro-caching can radically reduce page load times.
- For content-scarce pages, we find that less than 20% (10%) of the HTML page is changed when revisited after a month (day), with updates mostly to code and data, and little to layout. This means that such pages are highly micro-cacheable, especially for layout.
- For content-rich pages, the amount of updates vary across Web pages. In the best (worst) case, 20% (75%) of the HTML page is changed over a month. Most changes are made to data (e.g., links to images, titles) while little is made to layout and code, indicating that layout and code are highly micro-cacheable.
- Mobile pages are similar to desktop counterparts in terms of the amount and composition of updates.
- About half of the object fetches are dynamic and thus the idea of micro-caching is worth revisiting. Unlike CSS and images, most HTML is dynamic. The large amount of dynamic images is also surprising.

2. RELATED WORK

As a key approach to improving page loads, caching has received lots of attention. One related work is delta encoding that advocates compressing HTTP data transparently in the form of differences [3]. Another related work, Edge Side Includes (ESI), assembles Web pages at the edge to exploit edge caching [4]. Unlike delta encoding and ESI that treats every bit equally, we isolate layout and code from data, and cache their evaluated versions separately inside browsers, so as to mitigate the bottlenecks in loading pages, and to remove all the network interactions that block time to first paint in the usual case. Other work focuses solely on object-based caching and treats each object as a black box [14, 21, 16]. We propose micro-caching and are the first to quantitatively and qualitatively study changes in pages at a fine granularity.

There is also a large body of work on measuring other aspects of Web performance. Ihm and Pai [6] presented a longitudinal study of Web traffic, Ager et al. [1] studied Web performance with respect to CDNs, Huang et al. [5] measured the page load times with a slower cellular network, and Wang et al. [18] studied the use of the SPDY protocol to improve page load times. These studies are invaluable for improving our understanding of Web performance.

3. MICRO-CACHING

The case for micro-caching. Web applications are slower than native applications, because Web applications require more steps to launch. Launching a native application requires only executing the code as it has been downloaded beforehand, asking for more data or computation from the server only when necessary (see Figure 1(a)). However, launching a Web application incurs a more complex procedure. It starts with the client asking for the application code from the server, followed by the server running server-side code to generate client-side code and sending it to the client, and finishes with the client running the client-side code, performing layout, and painting (see Figure 1(b)). As

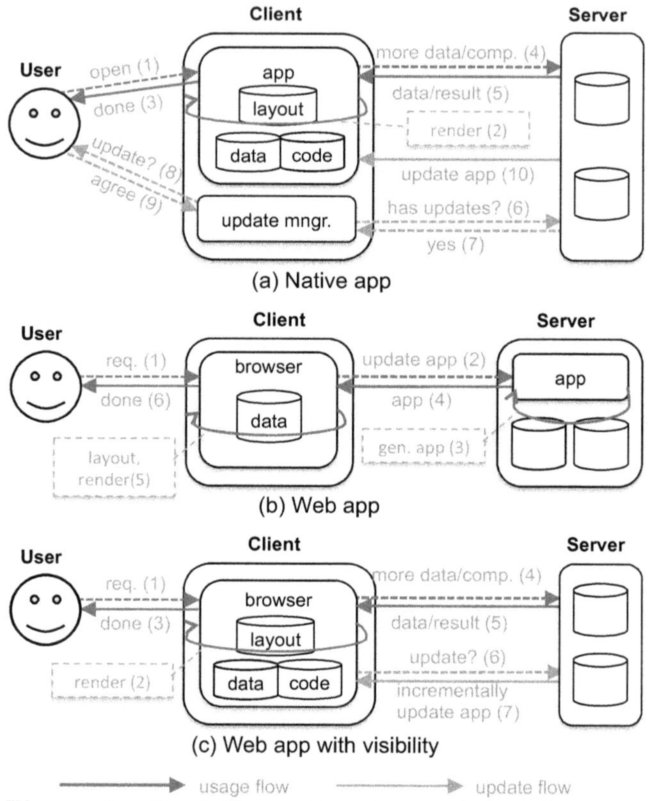

Figure 1: Workflows of native and mobile apps. (solid: data flows; dotted: control flows)

a consequence, Web applications incur much higher time to first paint.

Why do Web applications need more steps to launch? This is because the client side lacks visibility into updates and the model-view-controller (MVC) [10] abstraction of Web applications. The lack of visibility causes three inefficiencies. First, a Web application has to fetch the execution code upon launch even if it hasn't changed, while native applications can explicitly opt in for updates and avoid reloading code. Second, a Web application has to compute the layout from scratch during rendering, while the layout of native applications can be cached. Third, running a Web application always involves JavaScript compilation that happens just in time, while native applications are pre-compiled. Worse for mobile devices, contacting the network sometimes requires a few seconds due to radio interactions, and computation on mobile devices is slower due to the lack of compute power [5, 20]. The result is that Web applications are losing the mobile market to native applications [8, 9].

We argue that, to eliminate these inefficiencies, the client should be provided with enough information — explicit updates and explicit distinctions between layout, code, and data (the MVC abstraction) – both of which are readily available in native applications. The client can then cache not only raw objects but also compiled JavaScript and computed layout, and thus minimize network interactions and computation. We envision the following (as illustrated in Figure 1(c)): both compiled code and computed layout of Web applications are always cached in browsers, incrementally evolving themselves upon updates. When the URL of a Web application is requested, the cached layout is immediately rendered, and the cached code makes the application

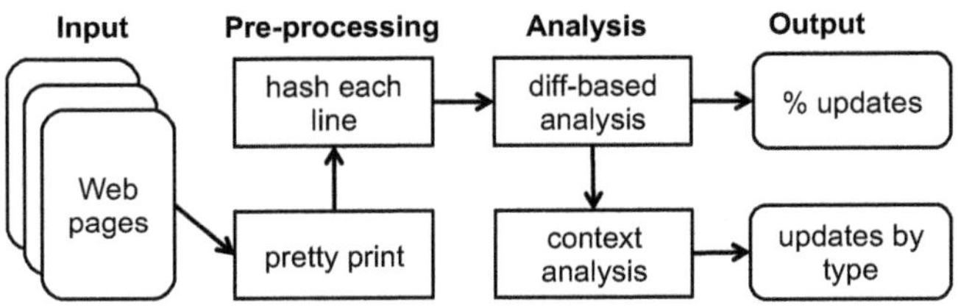

Figure 2: Analysis pipeline.

fully functional including checking the necessity of network interactions, e.g., getting more user data or computation from servers.

This approach removes the entire network interactions that block page loads and portions of computation for the usual case. Therefore, we expect page load times (and time to first paint) to be substantially reduced since our previous study shows that the network time consumes most of the page load time [19].

This approach does not sacrifice any of the existing advantages of Web applications, improves latency, energy consumption, and data usage at the same time, and requires minimal changes to browsers that cache computed layout[2] and compiled code appropriately. Unfortunately, there is no way to provide this visibility automatically without rewriting Web pages because most logics of micro-caching are implemented at the Web page level (e.g., handling versions using HTML5 localStorage). As websites routinely rewrite Web pages, mostly for embracing more efficient architectures (e.g., Groupon and mobile LinkedIn migrated all their pages to node.js [11, 12]), we believe that page rewriting is a viable solution if the benefits are indeed substantial.

Definition of micro-caching. We define micro-caching as caching any portion of an object. Compared to current object-based caching that caches the entire object, micro-caching operates at a much finer granularity. Enabling micro-caching is necessary to provide explicit updates and explicitly distinguish layout, code, and data.

Effectiveness of micro-caching. As a first step towards micro-caching, we study how much we can micro-cache Web pages? We answer this by analyzing the amount of updates from layout, code, and data respectively. This requires us to (i) identify the difference between two versions of a Web page, and (ii) infer whether the difference belongs to data, layout, or code.

4. METHODOLOGY

Figure 2 shows the pipeline of our analysis that we elaborate below.

4.1 Diff-based analysis

We want to study the difference (or similarity) between two versions of a page. A naive approach is to run a `diff` command that identifies the differences at the granularity of lines. As the definition of a line in Web objects is fragile, we pre-process the pages by pretty printing them using the `js-beautify` library [7]. We use the classic dynamic-programming algorithm that matches two versions of a page to maximize the number of matched lines. A matrix $D_{i,j}$ is used to denote the number of matched lines between the first i lines of the first page and the first j lines of the second page. If the i-th line of the first page and the j-th line of the second page are matched, $D_{i,j} = D_{i-1,j-1} + 1$; otherwise, $D_{i,j} = max\{D_{i-1,j}, D_{i,j-1}\}$. We start with $D_{i,0} = 0$ and $D_{0,j} = 0$, and increase the indice until we reach the last lines of both pages. This algorithm incurs a $O(n^2)$ time complexity where n is the number of lines of a page. As some lines can be unexpectedly long and slow down the algorithm, we accelerate this step by calculating an `md5` hash of each line and matching the hash values. Our algorithm outputs the number of unmatched lines, bytes, and unmatched content.

[2]Modern browsers are able to cache computed layout, but use a different policy to control the lifetime of this cache.

Figure 3: Example of inferring context of an HTML document.

We use *similarity*, defined as one minus the fraction of difference in bytes using the above algorithm, to characterize the amount of updates eliminated by micro-caching. *Similarity* provides a lower bound on estimated savings since unmatched lines of two pages are not entirely different.

4.2 Context analysis

We first infer whether a line is one of HTML markup, CSS, and JavaScript, and then infer whether a string belongs to layout, code, or data.

Inferring HTML/CSS/JS. Inferring HTML is straightforward; we infer a line as HTML if it is quoted by <> (pretty printing helps here). However, differentiating between CSS and JavaScript is non-trivial; for example, a CSS property is similar to a property declaration of an object in JavaScript (e.g., Line 5 and 10 in Figure 3). We notice the slight difference that CSS property (JavaScript object property) ends with a semi-colon (comma), and use it to distinguish between CSS and JavaScript. When we are unable to distinguish by looking at the line itself, we search backwards and forwards until hitting a line that allows for inference.

Inferring layout/code/data. Before this inference, we further identify the modified and added content at the granularity of strings. The diff-based analysis gives pairs of unmatched chunks (a few lines) between two pages, indicating that a chunk on the first page is modified into another chunk on the second page. For example, insertions (removals) incur an empty chunk on the first (second) page. Here, we first break up a chunk into strings that are separated by either spaces or the newline character (pretty printing also helps

Page	Content	Country	Category
google.com	scarce	US	Search
baidu.com	scarce	China	Search
wikipedia.org	scarce	–	Information
amazon.com	rich	US	E-Commerce
taobao.com	rich	China	E-Commerce
youtube.com	rich	US	Video
yahoo.co.jp	rich	Japan	News

Table 1: Seven pages for extensive analysis.

here). For each pair of unmatched chunks, we apply the diff-based analysis above to pinpoint the unmatched strings.

Inferring from CSS is trivial since all of CSS maps to layout, but inferring from HTML and JavaScript are not trivial. For HTML, attributes can be layout when they are like CSS properties (e.g., `width`), can be code when they start with `on` (e.g., `onload`), and can be data when they are one of `value`, `name`, and so forth. JavaScript is code by default, but can embed data (e.g., username), and can embed code that is quoted by `document.write()` or `eval()`. To infer from HTML, we pre-classify all known attributes into the appropriate layout, code, or data categories. We are unable to classify self-defined attributes. To infer from JavaScript, we identify strings that are quoted by single or double quotes as data. We do not encounter code that starts with `document.write` or `eval`, and therefore we do not have to handle that case[3]. Figure 3 illustrates the context inference of an HTML document.

4.3 Datasets

We collect our datasets using a measurement node at the University of Washington, starting from April 2012. Our datasets span two years. We extensively take snapshots of top twenty Alexa [2] pages every hour, which is more frequent than page updates. We also take snapshots of top one hundred Web pages every day. To study mobile pages, we collect a month-long dataset of top twenty mobile pages every hour. To take a snapshot of a page, we use both PhantomJS [13] to collect HTTP headers and Web page metadata in the HAR format and `wget` to collect the content of Web objects.

5. RESULTS

We study the benefits of micro-caching and shed light on existing caching schemes.

5.1 Benefits of micro-caching

Filtering Web pages. The set of measured pages are either content-rich pages that provide personalized or up-to-date content (e.g., news, video, e-commerce), or content-scarce pages that provide a single service (e.g., search). In our study, we exclude pages that require logins to provide content (e.g., social network) since these pages without logins are not representative of their real usage. We also exclude pages that are similar to a chosen page (e.g., `google.de` is similar to `google.com`). By excluding such pages, we focus on seven of the top twenty pages for intensive analysis. These pages (shown in Table 1) contain both content-rich

[3] `eval` is considered a bad practice, but was found on half of the top 10,000 pages [15]. We do not find it on our set of pages, likely because the very top pages are optimized.

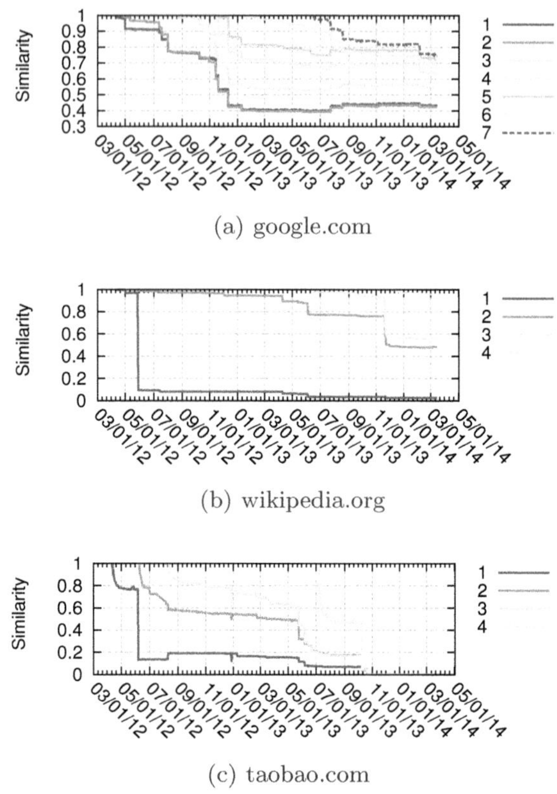

(a) google.com

(b) wikipedia.org

(c) taobao.com

Figure 5: Similarity over time that reflects how websites do updates. Each curve represents similarity between a fixed version and versions after.

and content-scarce pages and span three countries and five categories. We believe that intensively studying a small set of top pages is valuable, because they are often the most dynamic and are thus hardest to be micro-cached.

Estimating benefits. A direct way of estimating benefits of micro-caching would be comparing the page load times before and after micro-caching is applied. However, such comparison is both inaccurate and unfair. It is hard to accurately estimate the page load time benefits without implementing micro-caching since page load times depend on a large number of factors. This includes network parameters, compute power of the browser device, and the dependency model of page load activities. A slight modification to the Web page can result in very different page load times. To enable micro-caching, we propose to modify the entire Web pages so that pages are loaded directly from the browser cache most of the time and are updated asynchronously only when necessary. Comparing page load times of the modified page and the original page would be unfair.

Here, we qualitatively estimate the benefits. Our previous study informs that the network time consumes most of the page load times [19]. For example, contacting remote servers often triggers DNS lookup, TCP connection setup, and SSL handshakes when HTTPS is used; the cascades of latencies make time to first paint slow. Our proposal removes the entire network interactions and portions of computation that block page loads for the usual case. Thus, we expect page load times to be largely reduced.

Instead of quantifying the benefits of page load times, we focus on studying the impact from Web page updates. The

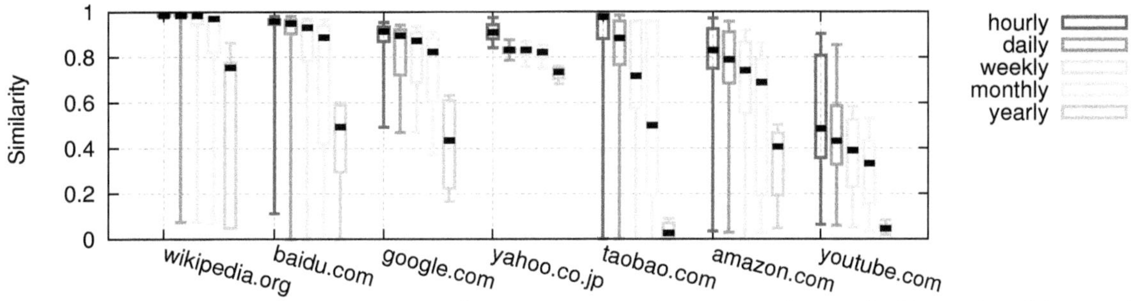

Figure 4: Similarity between two versions of pages by varying access interval. For a fixed interval, we vary the time of accessing the first version and obtain a list of similarities. The candle sticks show minimum, 10-percentile, median, 90-percentile, and maximum.

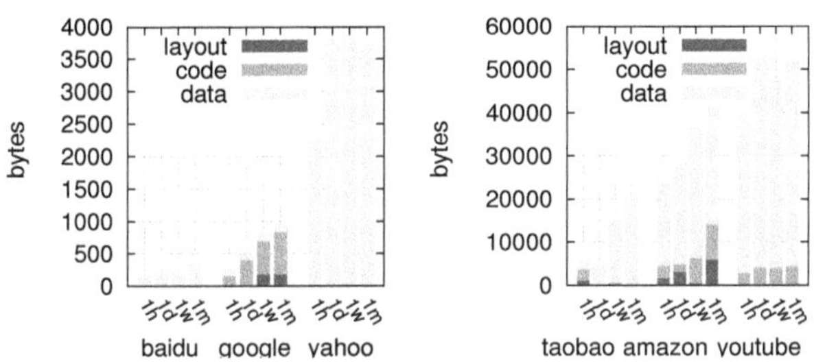

Figure 6: Updated bytes broken down by layout, code, and data. `wikipedia.org` is excluded as little is updated.

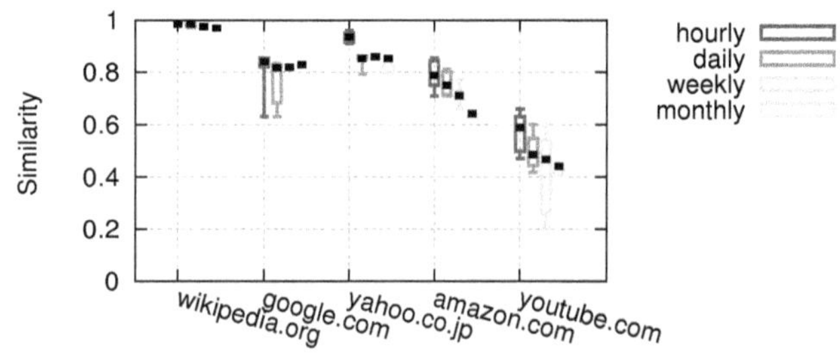

Figure 7: Similarity between two versions of mobile pages by varying access frequency.

less and less often a Web page is updated, the less and less often an asynchronous network fetch needs to be issued, and the more the page can be micro-cached.

5.1.1 *Longitudinal study*

We report on the two-year desktop dataset.

How much is updated. We first look at the amount of updates when visiting a page after a given interval. Here we use *similarity* that indicates an upper bound on the amount of updates. Figure 4 shows the results. For content-scarce pages (left three), less than 20% (10%) of the HTML page is changed when revisited after a month (day), meaning that such pages are highly micro-cacheable. Content-rich pages (right four) have high variance for micro-cacheability: `youtube.com` updates significantly every hour, while `yahoo.co.jp` updates less than 20% even over a month.

How often pages are updated. We further look at how often pages are updated by obtaining similarity over time in Figure 5. Here, we focus on major updates that require reloading a large portion of the page. Updates are indicated by sharp drops in Figure 5 – the more a page is updated, the sharper the drop is. We find that `google.com` updates every few weeks. `wikipedia.org` updates less often; we see one major update at the end of May 2012 and one at the end of November 2013. Unlike content-scarce pages, `taobao.com` updates incrementally between two major updates. These incremental updates are mostly data, but little layout or code. We also plot the graphs for other pages, which we do not show here due to space limits. They together show that major updates are rare and the amount of updates in layout and code between two major updates are moderate, suggesting that micro-caching is practical to mitigate page load bottlenecks.

What is updated. We break down the updated bytes into layout, code, and data. Figure 6 shows that most updates are made to data; `baidu.com` and `yahoo.com` update only data. Updates to data are mostly through HTML attributes (e.g., `href`, `title`) and inner HTML content, while some updates to data are made through JavaScript. Conversely, little update is made to layout; only half of the pages update layout, by a lesser amount. Also, little update is made to code. These results together suggest that layout and code are highly micro-cacheable for both content-scarce and content-rich pages.

To be informative, we manually go through some of the updated content. For example in `google.com`, we find that many updates are random strings/numbers that are generated by servers. Except for security considerations, random string/number generation can be moved to the client side so as to minimize updates. We also find that some pages change CSS that has no visible impact. This CSS is likely being loaded speculatively that will be used when users perform an action. This kind of CSS can be loaded in the background without impairing the cacheability of layout. Some other CSS shows significant visual impact. Because we can cache the previous layout, incremental layout incurs minimal computation.

5.1.2 *Mobile pages*

We report on the month-long mobile dataset. We exclude two pages that provide different functionalities than their desktop counterparts. Figure 7 shows the mobile counterparts of Figure 4. Clearly, the amount of updates in mobile Web pages are similar to their desktop counterparts. The variance is smaller here because the time of measurements

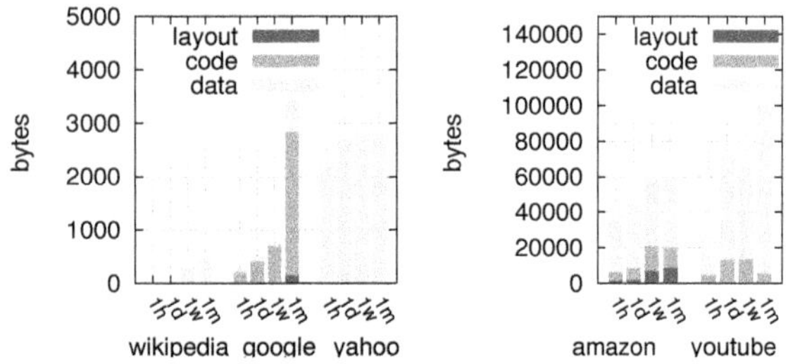

Figure 8: Updated bytes of mobile pages broken down by layout, code, and data.

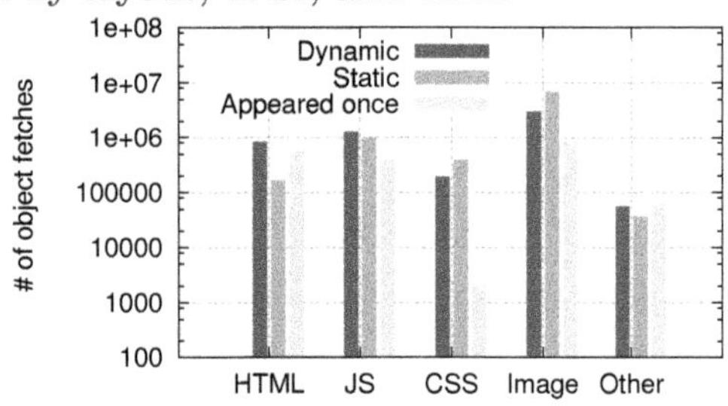

Figure 9: Breakdown the number of static, dynamic, and once objects by mime type.

is shorter. Figure 8 shows the mobile counterpart of Figure 6. They are alike except for some random spikes in Figure 8. We manually look through updates in mobile pages and desktop pages and find that updates in code are similar, indicating that they are likely to share the same code base. However, the format of updated data is different, possibly because of delivering content on a smaller screen.

5.1.3 Practices that undermine micro-caching

We summarize common practices suggested by our measurements that undermine the effectiveness of micro-caching.

- **JavaScript obfuscation.** Websites often obfuscate client-side JavaScript to reduce readability which, however, also reduces micro-cacheability. We find variables in two versions of `google.com` performing the same logic while using different names.
- **CSS reordering.** The order of CSS rules does not matter most of the time and we find some websites reorder their CSS rules. Using consistent ordering would help micro-caching.
- **CSS abbreviation.** We find equivalent CSS rules in different versions of a page. For example, `body,a{rule}` is unfolded to `body{rule} a{rule}`, and `border-top`, `border-bottom`, `border-left`, and `border-right` are condensed into `border`. Using the same level of abbreviation consistently would help micro-caching.
- **Object sharding.** In the HTTP/1.1 era, websites shard JavaScript and CSS objects to exploit concurrent TCP connections. Because sharded objects use random URLs as their keys, they hurt caching.

5.2 Dynamics of Web objects

Our measurements also let us analyze the dynamics at the granularity of a Web object. Static objects can be cached infinitely given enough disk space, while dynamic objects need to evict their cache before updates. Studying the dynamics at the granularity of a Web object sheds light on implementing expiration of object-based caching. Here, we consider all pages we collected.

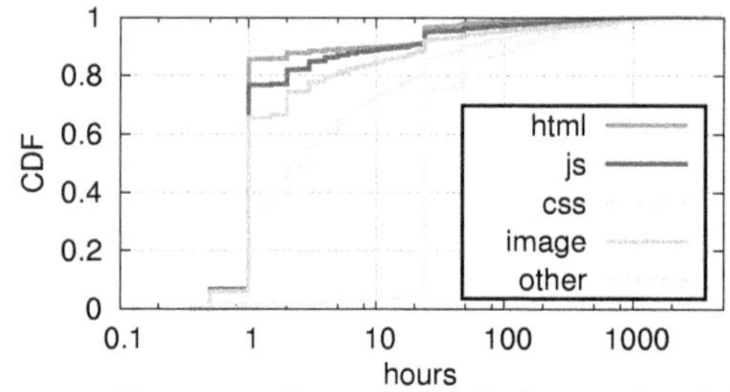

Figure 10: Frequencies at which dynamic objects are updated (breakdown by mime type).

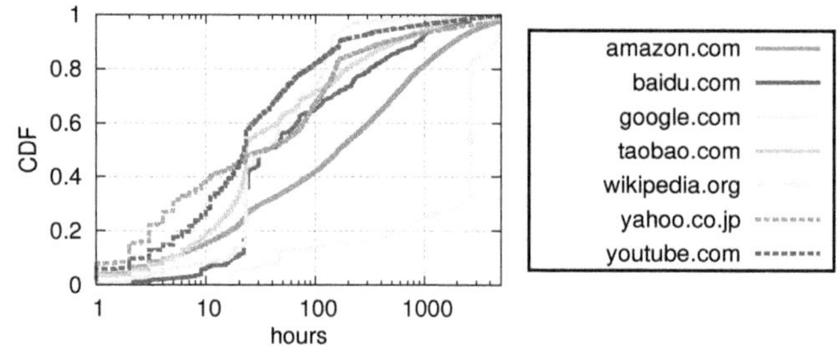

Figure 11: Lifetimes of static objects (breakdowns by popular domain).

We find that about half of the object fetches are dynamic, meaning that the idea of micro-caching is worth revisiting. Figure 9 shows the amount of static and dynamic objects respectively broken down by MIME type. HTML and JavaScript are more dynamic while CSS and images are more static. Images are expected to be identified by a unique URL, but we are surprised to learn that a significant amount of images are dynamic.

Figure 10 shows the frequencies at which dynamic objects are updated. Most dynamic HTML, JavaScript, and images are changing all the time (1 hour is the unit of measurements), likely being backed by server-side scripts. In contrast, less than 40% of CSS is changing all the time. For all kinds of dynamic objects, over 75% of them change within a day, meaning that cache expiration for dynamic objects should be mostly set to just a few hours.

Figure 11 shows the lifetimes of static objects. The median lifetime of static objects is about two days. However, there is high variance in lifetimes regarding different websites. Over 75% of objects in `wikipedia.org` have a lifetime of more than 1,000 hours, suggesting that most static objects in `wikipedia.org` should be cached. But half of the static objects on most other pages have a lifetime of less than a day, suggesting that caching these objects for more than one day is likely to waste disk space.

6. CONCLUSION

This paper proposes to separately cache layout, code, and data at a fine granularity inside browsers to mitigate the bottleneck of loading modern Web pages. By analyzing two years of measurements of Web pages, we find that layout and code that block subsequent object loads are highly cacheable.

Acknowledgements

We thank our shepherd, Andreas Haeberlen, and the anonymous reviewers for their feedback.

7. REFERENCES

[1] B. Ager, W. Muhlbauer, G. Smaragdakis, and S. Uhlig. Web Content Cartography. In *Proc. of the SIGCOMM conference on Internet Measurement Conference (IMC), 2011.*

[2] Alexa - The Web Information Company. http://www.alexa.com/topsites/countries/US.

[3] Delta encoding in HTTP. http://tools.ietf.org/html/draft-mogul-http-delta-07.

[4] ESI Language Specification 1.0. http://www.w3.org/TR/esi-lang.

[5] J. Huang, Q. Xu, B. Tiwana, Z. M. Mao, M. Zhang, and P. Bahl. Anatomizing application performance differences on smartphones. In *Proc. of the international conference on Mobile systems, applications, and services (Mobisys), 2010.*

[6] S. Ihm and V. S. Pai. Towards understanding modern web traffic. In *Proc. of the SIGCOMM conference on Internet Measurement Conference (IMC), 2011.*

[7] JS Beautify. http://jsbeautifier.org/.

[8] The mobile web is still losing out to native apps, by more than 6 to 1. http://venturebeat.com/2014/04/01/the-mobile-web-is-still-losing-out-to-native-apps-six-years-into-the-mobile-revolution/.

[9] Apps Solidify Leadership Six Years into the Mobile Revolution. http://www.flurry.com/bid/109749/Apps-Solidify-Leadership-Six-Years-into-the-Mobile-Revolution#.U2bgha2SzOQ.

[10] Model-view-controller. http://en.wikipedia.org/wiki/Model%E2%80%93view%E2%80%93controller.

[11] Need for Speed: How Groupon Migrated to Node.js. http://www.datacenterknowledge.com/archives/2013/12/06/need-speed-groupon-migrated-node-js/.

[12] Many high-profile companies – node.js. http://nodejs.org/industry/.

[13] PhantomJS. http://phantomjs.org/.

[14] F. Qian, K. S. Quah, J. Huang, J. Erman, A. Gerber, Z. M. Mao, S. Sen, and O. Spatscheck. Web Caching on Smartphones: Ideal vs. Reality. In *Proc. of the ACM Mobisys, 2012.*

[15] G. Richards, C. Hammer, B. Burg, and J. Vitek. The Eval that Men Do. In *Proc. of the 25th European Conference on Object-Oriented Programming (ECOOP), 2011.*

[16] S. Sundaresan, N. Feamster, R. Teixeira, and N. Magharei. Measuring and Mitigating Web Performance Bottlenecks in Broadband Access Networks. In *Proc. of the ACM Sigcomm Internet Measurement Conference (IMC), 2013.*

[17] Transaction Perspective: User Experience Metrics. http://www.keynote.com/products/web_performance/performance_measurement/user-experience-metrics.html.

[18] X. S. Wang, A. Balasubramanian, A. Krishnamurthy, and D. Wetherall. Accelerating the Mobile Web with Selective Offloading. In *Proc. of the USENIX conference on Networked Systems Design and Implementation (NSDI), 2014.*

[19] X. S. Wang, A. Balasubramanian, A. Krishnamurthy, and D. Wetherall. Demystifying page load performance with WProf. In *Proc. of the USENIX conference on Networked Systems Design and Implementation (NSDI), 2013.*

[20] X. S. Wang, H. Shen, and D. Wetherall. Accelerating the Mobile Web with Selective Offloading. In *Proc. of the ACM Sigcomm Workshop on Mobile Cloud Computing (MCC), 2013.*

[21] Z. Wang, F. X. Lin, L. Zhong, and M. Chishtie. How far can client-only solutions go for mobile browser speed? In *Proc. of the international conference on World Wide Web (WWW), 2012.*

Back-Office Web Traffic on The Internet

Enric Pujol
TU Berlin
enric@inet.tu-berlin.de

Philipp Richter
TU Berlin
prichter@inet.tu-berlin.de

Balakrishnan Chandrasekaran
Duke University
balac@cs.duke.edu

Georgios Smaragdakis
MIT / TU Berlin / Akamai
gsmaragd@csail.mit.edu

Anja Feldmann
TU Berlin
anja@inet.tu-berlin.de

Bruce Maggs
Duke / Akamai
bmm@cs.duke.edu

Keung-Chi Ng
Akamai
kng@akamai.com

ABSTRACT

Although traffic between Web servers and Web browsers is readily apparent to many knowledgeable end users, fewer are aware of the extent of server-to-server Web traffic carried over the public Internet. We refer to the former class of traffic as *front-office Internet Web traffic* and the latter as *back-office Internet Web traffic* (or just front-office and back-office traffic, for short). Back-office traffic, which may or may not be triggered by end-user activity, is essential for today's Web as it supports a number of popular but complex Web services including large-scale content delivery, social networking, indexing, searching, advertising, and proxy services. This paper takes a first look at back-office traffic, measuring it from various vantage points, including from within ISPs, IXPs, and CDNs. We describe techniques for identifying back-office traffic based on the roles that this traffic plays in the Web ecosystem. Our measurements show that back-office traffic accounts for a significant fraction not only of core Internet traffic, but also of Web transactions in the terms of requests and responses. Finally, we discuss the implications and opportunities that the presence of back-office traffic presents for the evolution of the Internet ecosystem.

Categories and Subject Descriptors

C.2.3 [**Computer-Communication Networks**]: Network Operations.

Keywords

Network measurement; the Web; content delivery; online advertisements; real-time bidding; crawlers.

1. INTRODUCTION

The Web has not only revolutionized the way people publish, access, and search for content but, some would argue (e.g., [49]), has also evolved to become the new "narrow waist" of the Internet. Indeed, the HTTP protocol provides a common interface that many popular Internet applications rely on, including video, social networking, e-commerce, and software delivery. These applications

IMC '14, November 5–7, 2014, Vancouver, BC, Canada.
Copyright 2014 ACM 978-1-4503-3213-2/14/11 ...$15.00.
http://dx.doi.org/10.1145/2663716.2663756.

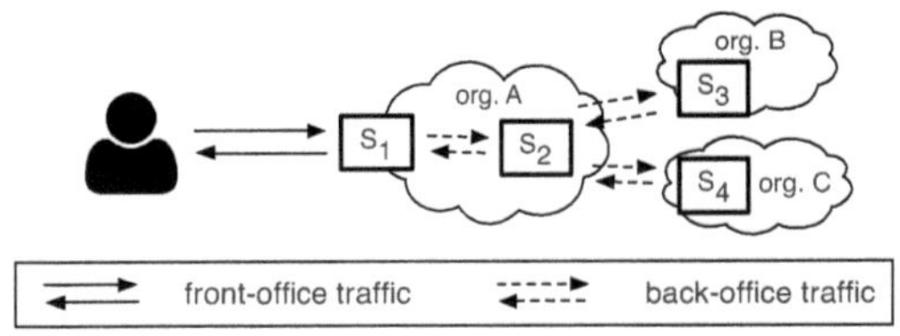

Figure 1: Front- vs. back-office Internet Web traffic.

are often supported by advertisements, which are also delivered via HTTP.

Although an end user typically views a Web page as a unit, recent studies [17, 36] demonstrate that a single Web page often contains links to objects that are delivered by a large and diverse set of servers. For example, the creation of a single Web page may involve several Web companies as, e.g., parts of the Web page may be under the control of a content provider, a Web advertiser, a video streamer, a search engine, and/or a social network. Furthermore, even fetching an individual part of a Web page may involve many parties. For example, when an end user requests Web content, the delivery involves not only the servers that receive HTTP requests from the end user's browser, but also a whole service ecosystem consisting of proxies, content delivery networks (CDNs), adsellers, ad-bidders, back-end servers or databases, crawler bots, etc.

Thus, "there is more to content delivery than is visible to the eye," and, consequently, this paper explores the distinction between *front-office* and *back-office* Web traffic. The first refers to the traffic involving end users directly. The second refers to Web traffic exchanged between machines (e.g., the front-office servers and any other server which is part of the Web service ecosystem). Figure 1 depicts this distinction. Note that not all back-office Web traffic travels over the public Internet. Some is carried over private backbones or within data centers. In this paper, we focus on *back-office Web traffic on the public Internet.* For short, we henceforth use the term "front-office traffic" to refer to front-office Web traffic carried on the public Internet and similarly for "back-office traffic."

In contrast to back-office traffic, front-office traffic has long been studied, e.g., [8, 14, 17, 26, 27, 45, 47]. While there is some related work on Machine-to-Machine traffic in specific environments, e.g., in cellular networks [52] and within data centers [12, 13, 34], we are not aware of studies of back-office Web traffic on the public Internet. Liang et al. studied security-related aspects arising from CDN back-end communication [44] and for some specific other services, e.g., DNS, Gao et al. have characterized the corresponding Machine-to-Machine traffic [31].

The reason why previous work has focused mainly on front-office traffic is that end-user Quality of Experience (QoE) can be analyzed by observing front-office traffic, but back-office traffic is often opaque. Today, more and more Web services also depend on some back-office communication over the public Internet e.g., to assemble Web pages, to perform search queries, to place advertisements, to conduct database transactions, to dynamically generate personalized content, Thus, service QoE now also depends critically on the architecture and performance of the back-office, which relies increasingly on the public Internet. This complexity makes measuring and characterizing back-office traffic challenging.

Among the difficulties faced in studying back-office traffic is that it is rarely present on the network links connecting end users to the Internet. Instead, back-office traffic can generally only be observed on backbone or inter-domain links. However, existing studies of inter-domain and/or backbone traffic [32, 42, 50] have not separated front-office and back-office Web traffic. Indeed, the back-office traffic component for any individual link depends highly on whether the link is on any of the routes between the involved servers. Thus, to observe this traffic requires a variety of vantage points. In this paper we analyze data collected from two IXPs, multiple links of a Tier-1 ISP, and a major CDN.

Web services that involve back-offices include content delivery, search, and advertisements. We focus on these because content delivery is responsible for a significant fraction of all Internet traffic, while advertisements (and in particular those in response to search) are responsible for a significant fraction of Internet revenues.

According to recent studies [32, 42, 48] CDN traffic accounts for more than 50% of Web traffic. This percentage is expected to further increase in part due to the increasing traffic volume attributed to video delivery [23]. Since CDNs operate sophisticated back-offices with distributed server infrastructures, some of this traffic is back-office traffic, which may or may not be routed via the public Internet depending on whether the CDN operates its own backbone [37] or not [54]. The rationale for this distributed infrastructure is the need to improve the end-user experience, react to flash crowds, mitigate attacks, and reduce the cost of content delivery using economies of scale [7, 43, 46]. CDNs are aware of the need to constantly improve communication between their front-end and back-end servers [28, 43, 54].

Search is one of the essential Internet Web services. Without search, the Internet would hardly be usable for most end users as their desired content would be difficult to locate. Search relies on a back-end database which is typically populated by crawling the Internet. For this purpose, search providers including Google and Microsoft operate distributed server infrastructures that crawl the Web. Web crawlers (also known as crawl bots), are orchestrated to partition the Web and index different parts of it to more efficiently cover it. Once the crawler bots have collected their data, they upload it to the back-end where it is processed in large data centers [11], where massively parallel indexing algorithms are used to enable fast search queries [19]. To deliver search results they rely on overlays and/or the above mentioned CDNs [22]. Thus, search engines contribute to back-office Web traffic.

To monetize their content, most Web sites rely on targeted online advertisements. In 2013, online advertising revenues in the United States were estimated to be $42.8 billion [2], an increase of 17% over the previous year. The increasing revenue stream of Web advertisement has given rise to another innovative part of the Web ecosystem: ad-sellers, ad-bidders, and ad-brokers—the ad-networks [10, 59]. These parties negotiate placement of advertisements in today's Web. In many instances, the selection of an advertisement does not take place until an end user visits a Web page where advertisement space is available. At this point, an auctioneer contacts the potential advertisers with information about the visitor's profile and a bidding process is initiated, but hidden from the user. Thus, a visit of an end user to a Web page may trigger a number of back-office connections. Advertisement content is often delivered via a CDN.

Thus, back-office Web Traffic is one of the principle but yet largely unexplored components of today's Web. The contributions of this paper are:

- We introduce the notion of back-office Web traffic and show that its contribution ranges on average from 10% to 30% per vantage point and can even exceed 40% for some time periods. The vantage points include two major IXPs, multiple backbone links from a major ISP, and a number of server clusters from a major CDN. We explore the reasons that different levels of contributions are seen at different vantage points.
- Our methodology allows us to identify and classify different types of back-office traffic including proxy services, crawling, and advertisement bidding.
- Our analysis demonstrates that back-office traffic characteristics differ from front-office characteristics. Moreover, they vary enough by service that individual services can be identified.
- We find, for example, that at one of the IXPs auctioneers have a 22% share of the back-office requests but only 1% of the bytes, while crawlers contribute respectively roughly 10% and 15% to both.
- Our analysis of data from a major CDN confirms what we observe in the wild: CDNs deploy sophisticated back-office infrastructures, and back-office Web traffic is significant.
- Given the volume of back-office traffic on the Internet and its importance for end-user QoE, we identify implications of our analysis on network protocols design and co-location strategies.

2. BACK-OFFICE COMMUNICATION

In this section we provide a brief overview of the typical (i.e., expected) communication patterns of Web services that create back-office traffic. Hereby, we distinguish four different cases: (a) proxies/intermediaries, (b) CDN services, (c) auctioneers, and (d) crawlers. Figure 2 provides an illustration of the expected exchange of HTTP messages. Note, however, that our analysis (Section 7) unveils richer and more complex communication patterns than those shown in the figure.

(a) Proxies/Intermediaries: An intermediary is a network entity that acts as both a client and a server. As shown in Figure 2(a), a Web proxy is an intermediary that acts as a client with the main purpose of forwarding HTTP(S) requests. Thus, Web proxies send and receive requests in a temporally correlated fashion. Forward and reverse Web proxies evaluate requests, check if they can be satisfied locally, and contact a remote server only if necessary. When intermediaries act as clients, they create back-office traffic, but when intermediaries act as servers, the traffic they create can be either front- or back-office traffic. We describe how to differentiate these two cases in Section 6.

(b) CDN Servers: CDNs typically operate front-end servers (i.e., reverse proxies) close to the end user as well as back-end servers. Back-end servers either host the content in data centers or are closer to the origin content server, depending on the CDN's deployment and operation strategy [46, 35, 57, 37, 18, 5, 3]. If the front-end does not have a requested object available locally, it fetches the object from another front-end, a back-end, or the origin server. Since the overall content delivery time has a direct impact on application performance, e-commerce revenue, and end user engagement [39, 23, 41], a number of optimizations for creating

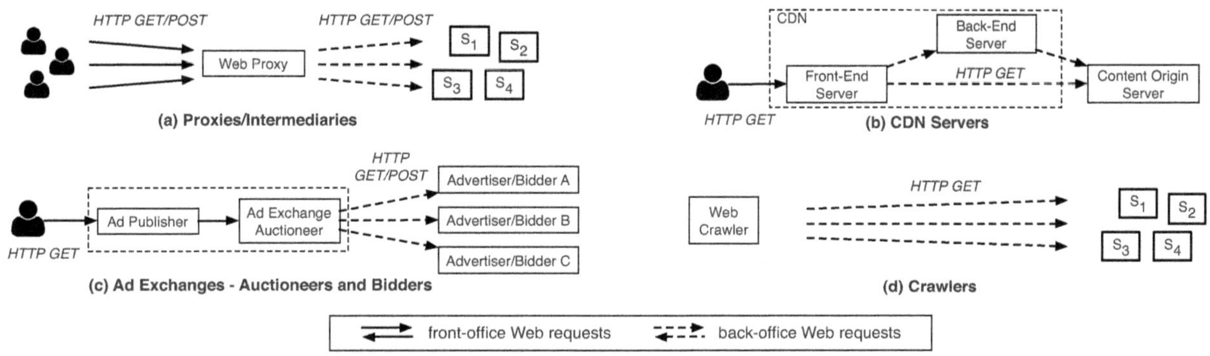

Figure 2: Back-office Web Traffic: typical HTTP requests made by Web proxies, CDNs, ad-exchanges, and crawlers.

overlays to improve end-to-end performance and for task sharing between front-end and back-end servers are deployed by today's CDNs [43, 54, 28, 40, 21].

(c) Ad Exchanges – Auctioneers and Bidders: As shown in Figure 2(c), advertisement exchanges consist of (i) publishers that sell advertisement space (ad space) on their Web pages, as well as (ii) advertisers that buy ad space on these Web pages. An exchange acts as a common platform to bring publishers and advertisers together. The matching between offered ad space on a Web site and interested advertisers is often performed using *real-time bidding* (RTB). Once an end user visits a Web page where ad space is available, the ad exchange auctioneer contacts the potential advertisers (i.e., the bidders), and provides information about the visitor to start a bidding process among the interested parties [10, 59, 55, 9].[1] A number of sophisticated tools together with visitor information suppliers optimize the bidding process for both the advertisers and the publishers. Hence, if RTB is used to place ads on a website, the visit of a Web page by an end user may trigger a large number of requests in the background. The final advertisement content is typically delivered via CDNs [9]. We note that today's Web advertisement ecosystem is complex and may involve many different types of back-office traffic, caused by a variety of different actors. In this paper, we solely focus on RTB-related activity, i.e., back-office traffic as a result of auctioneers interacting with bidders.

(d) Crawlers: Web crawlers continuously index the Web. To optimize crawling, each crawl bot is typically responsible for indexing a small part of the Web [11]. Indexing involves requesting the Web page as well as following embedded links [38, 16]. Web crawlers typically issue an order of magnitude more Web queries than regular end users. Best practices among the major search engines ensure that crawlers have appropriate reverse DNS entries along with well-specified user agents in order to avoid being blocked by Web sites.

Hereafter, we refer to back-office Web traffic as all Web traffic that is not exchanged between end users and servers. This includes traffic exchanged between intermediaries and Web servers (e.g., traffic between a CDN front-end server and a back-end server or between a Web proxy and a Web server), as well as traffic exchanged between automated hosts such as crawlers or auctioneers and any other Web server.

3. DATA SETS

In this work we rely on measurements collected at a diverse set of vantage points.

[1]The bidders may also contact other entities (i.e., *trackers*) to get information regarding the profile of the visitor [33, 59].

IXPs: Packet-sampled traces collected at two Internet eXchange Points (IXPs), which allow us to study back-office traffic in an inter-domain environment, as exchanged between hundreds of networks [6].

ISP: Anonymized packet-sampled traces collected from two transatlantic links from a Tier-1 ISP, providing a view of back-office traffic on long-distance links.

Access network: Anonymized packet dumps collected in a residential network of a Tier-1 ISP, revealing front-office traffic between end users and servers.

CDN: Web server logs from multiple servers in different locations within a large commercial CDN. These logs give us an inside view of back-office traffic created by a CDN.

Active measurements: Probes of IP addresses and DNS reverse lookups to identify Web servers.

This diverse set of traces allows us to study back-office traffic in a variety of locations, including between domains, on backbone links, and within a CDN. Table 1 summarizes the properties of our data sets.

The IXP traces are collected from the public switching infrastructure at two European IXPs. This includes a large IXP (L-IXP) with around 500 members and a medium-sized IXP (M-IXP) with around 100 members. Among the member ASes there are many CDNs, Web hosting services, cloud providers, and large commercial Web sites. We collect sFlow records [51] with a 1 out of 16K sampling rate. sFlow captures the first 128 bytes of each sampled Ethernet frame, providing us access to full network- and transport-layer headers and some initial bytes of the payload, allowing for deep packet inspection (DPI).

The ISP traces are collected from two transatlantic links on the backbone of a large European Tier-1 ISP. These links carry mainly transit traffic. We collect anonymized packet traces with a random packet sampling rate of 1 out of 1K. We also collect unsampled anonymized packet dumps in a residential network with about 20K end users of the same ISP.

The logs from the large commercial CDN encompass the activity of all servers at one hosting location in each of five large cities. Each log entry contains TCP summary statistics including endpoint IPs, number of bytes transferred, and initial TCP handshake round-trip latency. In addition, we received a complete list of all IP addresses used by the CDN infrastructure.

We also use active measurement data from the ZMap Project [25]. This data set contains a list of IPs, i.e., servers, that are responsive to GET requests on port 80 (HTTP) and SSL services on port 443 (HTTPS), spanning the time period from October 2013 to January 2014. In addition, we also make use of the data made public by the

Type	Name	Daily traffic rate	Collection	Period	% TCP	% Web of TCP
Exchanges	L-IXP	11,900 TB	sFlow (1/16K)	37th week 2013	84.40%	78.27%
	M-IXP	1,580 TB	sFlow (1/16K)	4th week 2014	97.22%	92.22%
Transit ISP	BBone-1	40 TB	Packet sampled (1/1K)	5th Feb. - 12th Feb. 2014	86.30%	64.58%
	BBone-2	70 TB	Packet sampled (1/1K)	4th week 2014	73.87%	78.74%
Eyeball ISP	RBN	35 TB	Packet dumps (unsampled)	9th. Jan. 2014	74.83%	79.45%
Server	CDN	350 TB	Server logs (unsampled)	24-25 Apr. 2014	95%	95%

Table 1: Summary of the vantage points and collected traces.

Name	#IPs	Method	C-O (%)	S-O (%)	Dual (%)
L-IXP	45.79M	DPI	96.90	2.74	0.36
		DPI+ZMap	93.85	2.74	3.40
M-IXP	1.9M	DPI	95.15	4.62	0.24
		DPI+ZMap	92.86	4.62	2.52
BBone-1	1.1M	DPI	92.26	7.56	0.18
		DPI+Zmap	86.62	7.56	5.82
BBone-2	4.5M	DPI	95.54	4.36	0.09
		DPI+ZMap	93.97	4.36	1.67

Table 2: Web activity of IPs: client-only (C-O), server-only (S-O), or both (dual) across vantage points.

authors of [18, 56] that disclose the set of IPs used by the Google infrastructure. When combining Google IPs with one of our packet traces, we use the snapshot of the Google IPs that corresponds to the last day of the trace.

4. IDENTIFYING BACK-OFFICE TRAFFIC

Given the above characteristics of back-office Web traffic, we next describe how we identify a significant fraction of it within our data sets. Our methodology involves three steps. First, we classify all IPs based on whether they are involved in any Web activity. Second, we classify their activities as either Web client, Web server, or both—client and server. Finally, we identify auctioneers and crawlers among the clients, bidders among the servers, and Web proxies among those that are acting as both clients and servers.

4.1 Web server endpoints

We focus only on those IPs for which we see Web activity in our traces, meaning either HTTP or HTTPS activity. For this we rely on well-known signatures to detect HTTP requests (`GET`, `POST`) and responses (`HTTP/1.{0,1}`) on any TCP port. For HTTPS we use signatures to match packets to/from port 443 that contain a SSL/TLS hand-shake, i.e., `Client Hello` and `Server Hello` messages [15]. We focus on IPv4, since IPv6 traffic accounts for less than 1% of the traffic across all data sets.

The result is a set of Web server endpoints, i.e., tuples that contain the IP address and the corresponding port number, as identified using the above-mentioned signatures. We then refer to all packets that are sent to/from one of the Web endpoints as Web traffic. Our methodology ensures that in the case of server IPs also hosting other applications on different ports (e.g., email), only their Web-related traffic is considered. Table 1 shows the percentages of Web traffic within our different data sets. As expected, this traffic constitutes a large fraction of the TCP traffic, ranging from 64% to 95% in each data set.

4.2 IP: Client/server/dual roles

Given that we have identified Web server endpoints, we next classify the Web activity of IP addresses to be client-only, server-only, or both (referred to as *dual* behavior in the following). We say that an IP address acts only as server if all of its traffic is related to its previously identified server-endpoint(s) (typically on port 80). If we see this IP address acting only as client, i.e., sending requests and receiving replies from other server-endpoints, it is classified as client only. If we see an IP address both acting as client and as server i.e., it runs a server on a specific port but also issues requests towards other servers, we classify its behavior as dual.[2]

Depending on the vantage point however, one may not see all Web activity a host is involved in. For example, a proxy server might exhibit only client-activity when monitored in the core of the Internet, and only server-activity when monitored in an access network. To tackle this limitation, we rely on a combination of passive and active measurements to uncover more IPs with dual-behavior as follows: we obtain a list of client IPs via DPI from our traces and then use the ZMap data set to check if these IPs respond to HTTP(S) queries. The ZMap data set provides lists of IPs that answer to a `GET` on port 80 or to an SSL handshake on port 443. Thus, if we see an IP address acting only as client, but we find it in the ZMap data set, we classify its behavior as dual.

Table 2 shows the classification of IPs when only relying on DPI (first row for each vantage point), as well as after taking the ZMap data set into account (second row for each vantage point). We make three observations. First, with only DPI, roughly 90% of IPs are classified as client-only across all data sets. Second, a significant fraction of the server IPs also show client behavior e.g., with DPI we see in the L-IXP trace that 11% of the total number of servers also act as clients. Third, adding more information for identifying dual behavior helps e.g., with DPI+ZMap we see in the L-IXP trace that 55% of the servers behave also as clients. Indeed, the fraction of IPs acting both as clients and servers increases significantly across all vantage points when combining active and passive measurements.

There are two main caveats when using this classification approach, which likely result in some overcounting of dual hosts on the one hand, as well as some undercounting on the other hand.

One factor contributing to possibly overcounting dual hosts include the use of dynamically assigned IP addresses. If a dual host is assigned different IP addresses at different times, then each of those IP addresses may be classified as a dual host, even though at other times the same IP addresses act only as servers or, more commonly, only as clients. Dynamically assigned IP addresses are typically found in residential networks. Due to bandwidth limitations, these addresses do not serve a significant fraction of Web traffic or a significant fraction of Web requests. Nevertheless, to minimize the impact of dual hosts with dynamically assigned addresses on our statistics, we only count as servers IP addresses that appear in two consecutive snapshots of the ZMap data set, i.e., they replied to HTTP requests issued two weeks apart.

On the other hand, our methodology may undercount dual hosts because is not able to detect more complex cases of dual behav-

[2]Recall that requests are typically issued with *ephemeral* source port numbers.

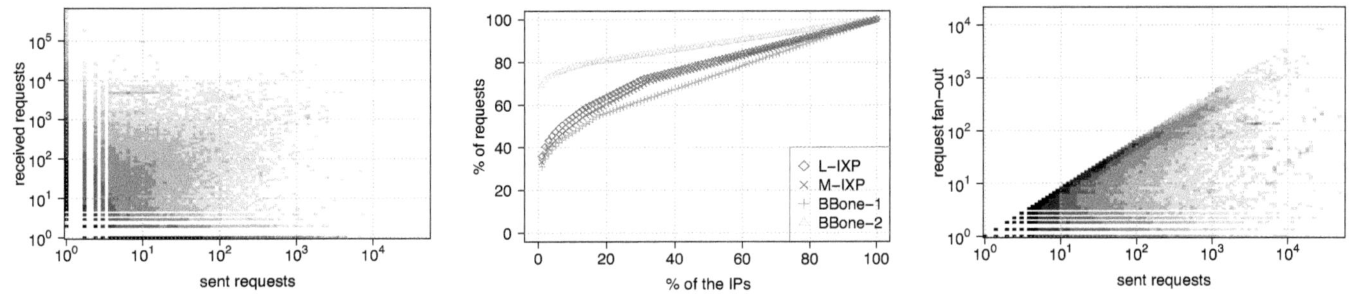

(a) Scatterplot: # sent vs. received requests sampled per IP in the L-IXP trace.

(b) Cumulative sum: # of requests sampled per IP, ranked by activity.

(c) Scatterplot: # sampled sent requests vs. fan-out per IP in the L-IXP trace.

Figure 3: Web IP activity: request frequency and fan-out.

ior, e.g., if a server has multiple interfaces and thus sends/receives traffic from multiple IP addresses, each acting only as a client or server. Furthermore, while we can uncover the server activity of a host that acts only as a client in our traces using the ZMap data set, we lack the tools to uncover the opposite case i.e., to uncover the client activity of a host that acts only as a server in our traces.

Along with the methodology previously described, we also exploit a list of servers provided to us from a large CDN. Henceforth, we distinguish three different classifications of IP addresses, *IPs-CDN*, *IPs-DPI*, and *IPs-ZMap*, based on our confidence in their accuracy. We are most confident in the accuracy of the classifications of the CDN addresses. Based on the DPI performed on a trace, we can also be very sure that an IP at that point in time was used in the identified fashion. The ZMap data set comes with the largest degree of uncertainty, but covers a wide range of IPs. Note that the same IP address may appear in more than one of these sets of classifications.

4.3 IP activity

Figure 3(a) shows a scatter plot for all IPs seen in the L-IXP trace, where we plot each IP according to the number of sampled Web requests it sent vs. received on a log-log scale. This plot highlights the different classes of IPs. The server-only IPs only receive requests and are scattered along the y-axis. The client-only IPs are scattered along the x-axis. The dual-role IPs are scattered across both axes. While the IPs with significant activity in both roles are likely to be intermediaries/proxies, we first take a closer look at some of the other heavy-hitters, i.e., those that only act as clients.

Figure 3(b) shows the cumulative percentage of the number of sampled `GET` and `POST` requests issued per IP, sorted by the number of observed requests. The most striking observation from this plot is that less than 1% of all the IPs are responsible for more than 30% of all requests across the IXP and backbone vantage points. Indeed, we estimate from the sampled data that the IP that contributes most requests at the L-IXP contributes more than 5M requests per hour on average, while at BBone-2 this number is roughly 310K requests per hour. These are unlikely to be humans — rather this behavior points towards a crawler, a proxy, or an auctioneer.

Accordingly, Figure 3(c) shows for each IP the number of sampled requests it sent vs. the number of IPs to which these are sent, namely the *fan-out*, on a log-log scale. While some of these clients contact a huge number of servers, there are also clients that send an enormous number of requests to a rather small set of server IPs (bottom right). As shown in Table 3, when inspecting the types of the requests we find an unexpectedly large number of `POST` requests. These can be attributed to the intensive use of protocols for Web services (e.g., SOAP). Closer inspection shows that for clients with an extraordinary high number of requests the fraction of `POST` requests is larger when compared to clients with low numbers of requests. Based on these observations, we now differentiate between proxies, auctioneers, crawlers, and bidders.

Name	Total	GETs	POSTs	CHellos
L-IXP	76.36M	71.6%	11.5%	16.9%
M-IXP	2.65M	78.9%	3.7%	17.4%
BBone-1	1.81M	88.3%	5.2%	6.5%
BBone-2	2.92M	58.1%	8.2%	33.7%

Table 3: Web IP activity: sampled HTTP/HTTPS requests.

4.4 CDNs, proxies, and other intermediaries

Typical examples of dual-behavior hosts are proxies such as those deployed by some institutions and forward and reverse proxies such as those operated by CDNs and content providers (CPs). However, intermediaries can, in fact, serve many other purposes. For instance, there are many kinds of proxies in the wild that affect a significant number of connections [58] and which are not operated by CDNs or CPs. In addition, intermediaries at hosting or or cloud service provider networks may not necessarily operate for the single purpose of request forwarding. While keeping this in mind, we focus on identifying some of the intermediaries that are operated by CPs or CDNs, which we hereafter refer to as *Content Delivery Proxies* (CDPs).

These are the steps we follow to classify CDPs. Along with the IPs in the *IPs-CDN* set, we select as potential candidates those intermediaries for which we sampled more than 5 requests (heavy-hitters).[3] We then check the origin AS of the corresponding subnet, and manually inspect if the WHOIS information reveals that the address is registered to a known CP or CDN. Since this check is not sufficient to reveal cases in which front-end servers and caches are embedded in ISP networks and use the address space registered to those networks, e.g., Akamai and Google Global Cache, we also check for DNS host-names and use the techniques reported in [18, 56] to attribute IPs to content providers and CDNs.

Based on the previous manual identification, we are able to classify among the list of intermediaries some of the front-ends of 8 well-known organizations such as Google, Akamai, Limelight or EdgeCast. We find more than 36K (15K) IPs in the L-IXP (M-IXP)

[3]Note that 5 sampled requests correspond to an estimated number of roughly 80K requests per week for the IXP traces and to 5K requests per week in the BBone links, respectively.

traces. We also find CDPs that are active on the transatlantic links i.e., 9K and 19K for the BBone-1 and BBone-2 traces.

4.5 RTB: Auctioneers and bidders

The bidding process between auctioneers and bidders is generally done using Web services, such as Google AdExchange or Facebook Exchange. Bidders register with the auctioneer and provide a URI on which they accept offers from the auctioneer and reply with their corresponding bid after a maximum time threshold, often around 100ms [1].

Thus, one of the distinguishing characteristics of auctioneers is that they typically send their offers via `POST` to the potential bidders. The bidders, in turn, receive a large number of `POST` requests from a relatively small number of hosts (the auctioneers). This fits nicely with our earlier observation that there are many more `POST` requests in today's Internet than were observed in the past. In particular, an examination of traces from L-IXP over the past three years shows that the fraction of requests of type `POST` has increased by 80% over that time. Indeed, for each user request which involves an advertisement there may be multiple bidders contacted.

Given that the market for real-time bidding (RTB) is heavily concentrated among a relatively small number of players accounting for the major share of the RTB activity [59], prime candidates for auctioneers are IPs sending large numbers of requests to a comparably small set of IPs (bidders), which in turn receive a large number of requests from a relatively small number of IPs. As bidders can provide customized URIs to auctioneers, we cannot identify auctioneers and bidders in a straightforward manner using payload signatures. Instead, we identify auctioneers and bidders based on partially available URL strings as follows: we first obtain a list of partial URLs sent by the heavy-hitters and select those IPs whose HTTP requests contain in the absolute path and/or query parts of the URL strings such as `ad`, `bid`, or `rtb`. Then, for each of these IPs, we check if its corresponding subset of requests has a fixed structure, i.e., we observe many repetitions of the same partial URL (only the value fields in the query part change), and we mark these IPs as candidates for potential auctioneers. We then manually validate that these IPs are operated by organizations offering RTB services by relying on meta-information such as reverse DNS, WHOIS, and publicly available API documentation of some Ad exchanges. Having a list of auctioneers, we now inspect the corresponding destination IPs, further manually verify the corresponding URL strings to be bidding-related, and mark these IPs as bidders.

With this method we are able to manually identify 316 IPs used by auctioneers and 282 IPs used by bidders in the L-IXP trace. We were not able to identify bidding activity in the M-IXP trace, and also did not identify any ad exchanges co-located at M-IXP. Nor did we find any bidding activity in the backbone traces, perhaps because of the high delay in transatlantic links.

4.6 Web crawlers

One of the distinguishing characteristics of Web crawlers is that they issue many Web queries and then upload their results to the search infrastructure. The queries constitute a large number of `GET` requests sent to a diverse set of servers belonging to different organizations.

For each data set we use the heavy hitters, in terms of `GET` requests, as candidates. Specifically, we pre-select IPs for which we sample at least five queries and then try to verify that they are Web crawlers as follows. It is a best common practice to make crawlers clearly identifiable by setting up reverse DNS entries and including

Name	CDPs	Bidders	Auctioneers	Crawlers	Other
L-IXP	36054	282	316	3920	151095
M-IXP	15116	0	0	541	4417
BBone-1	9330	0	0	81	1214
BBone-2	19890	0	0	894	2669

Table 4: Back-office: IP classification.

an appropriate user-agent with each request.[4] Thus, we search for host-names that include indicative strings such as *bot, crawl, spider* and select those that can be either automatically validated via the user-agent or validated with a manual inspection of the corresponding reverse DNS entry. scp

With this method, we identify 3920 and 541 crawlers in the L-IXP and M-IXP traces. Surprisingly, we also find crawlers in the backbone traces: 81 and 894 for the BBone-1 and –respectively– BBone-2 traces. We see activity from well-known search engines e.g., Google, Bing, Yandex, and Baidu, as well as from smaller search engines and research institutions. To put these numbers into perspective, we use the ZMap reverse DNS data set (i.e., all IPv4 PTR records) and search for host-names of crawlers belonging to three major search engines, which are well-defined in publicly available documents provided by these engines. The percentage of crawler IPs for which we see activity in the L-IXP trace is 7%, 23%, and 51% for three of the major search engines.

Summary

We find that most IPs that are part of the Web ecosystem are clients, but there are a substantial number of Web intermediaries across the vantage points e.g., just by inspecting the L-IXP trace with DPI, we find that 11% of the Web servers also act as Web clients. However, after combining our passive data with active measurements, we discover that many of the client IPs in the traces also act as servers, which is not visible when purely relying on passive data. As a consequence, the number of IPs with dual behavior increases e.g., for the L-IXP trace more than 50% of the server IPs exhibit also client behavior. As shown in Table 4, after we inspect the heavy-hitter IPs, we are able to find activity from content delivery proxies, ad auctioneers, ad bidders, and crawlers in the L-IXP trace, as well as crawling and intermediary activity as seen from the other vantage points.

5. WEB BACK OFFICE: A CLOSE LOOK

To better understand which players are involved in back-office services, we next take a closer look at its components in the L-IXP trace.

Auctioneers and bidders: We identify more than 300 IPs that are auctioneers. These IPs are operated by four different organizations that offer real-time bidding: Two search engines, an online social network, and a major Web portal. Each of these organizations operates at least one AS and the IPs are hosted in the corresponding AS. With regards to the number of IPs per AS we see a rather uneven distribution: The top one hosts 83% of the IPs. The same holds for the distribution of the number of requests: the top organization is involved in 55% of the bids, the others in 32%, 10%, and 3%.

These auctioneers communicate with a rather small set of bidders (282 IPs). The IXP data shows that many of the auctioneers

[4]See, for example Google `https://support.google.com/webmasters/answer/80553?hl=en`, and for Microsoft Bing `http://www.bing.com/webmaster/help/how-to-verify-bingbot-3905dc26`

are co-located with the bidders (both the AS of the auctioneer and the AS hosting the bidder are members of the IXP), with the bidders residing in 42 different ASes. This confirms that bidders are following the recommendations by the auctioneers to locate their servers close by in order to adhere to the strict deadlines of auction-based advertisements. Bidder IPs are typically contacted from all four identified auctioneering organizations. Thus, bidders do not use different IPs for different auctioneers and often cooperate with all of them. The likely motivation is that advertisers try to maximize their bidding opportunities (i.e., receiving offers from all organizations). Moreover, at first glance the number of bidders may appear small but this is mainly due to aggregation. Indeed, most IPs belong to advertisement aggregators.

With regards to the ASes that host the bidders, we find, surprisingly, that a very large hosting service provider dominates with a share of 34%. Indeed, even the remaining bidders are mainly located in the ASes of other Web hosting providers. This finding indicates that today's major players in the Web ecosystem often do not operate their own infrastructure either in terms of an AS or in terms of a data center. They rely instead on cloud services and Web hosting companies. The second AS with the most bidders belongs to, surprisingly, a company that operates a search engine. Indeed, this search engine is involved in all services: it is a search engine, an auctioneer, and even bids on other ad-network auctions. This finding illustrates the complexity of the advertising ecosystem, where different types of business relationships exist between organizations that offer multiple services to both advertisers and publishers, and who may also partner with some of them.[5]

Crawlers: We identify more than 3K crawler IPs from 120 different ASes. Among the ASes, there are two hosting more than 72% of the crawler IPs. These are related to two popular Web search engines. We also see crawlers of 3 other well-known search engines, each with roughly 100 crawlers. Then there is a gap with regards to the number of crawlers per AS as the remaining crawler IPs are hosted in many different ASes. Inspecting the user agent and the reverse DNS entries allows us to conclude that these are mainly associated with specialized search engines.

With regards to the number of requests, the four top contributors all belong to major search engines. The top three/four account for 94/96% of the requests. The fourth accounts for only 2% of the requests. Even though the crawling activity is directed towards more than 4.2K ASes, a single AS receives more than 43% of the requests — a Web hosting provider. The second most popular AS is another hosting provider and both are members of the IXP. Overall, the members account for more than 80% of the received crawling requests. In terms of request popularity, the first AS that is not a member of this IXP is yet another hosting provider and receives roughly 1% of the requests. Overall, the top crawling search engine AS and the top receiving hosting provider AS account for more than 20% of all crawling-related requests.

Content delivery proxies: We identify more than 30K intermediary IPs from 8 well-known CPs and CDNs, scattered across hundreds of different ASes, interacting with IPs from more than 1K different ASes. The CDPs are responsible for roughly 17% of the requests from heavy-hitter IPs. While one expects many of the front ends to be located in ISP networks, a close inspection of destination IPs reveals that some of the back-end servers are also located within the ASes of ISPs, and not in the AS of the CDN. In fact, we observe requests for the content of a major online social network (OSN) where both source and destination IPs are operated by a major CDN, but neither of the endpoints is located within the AS of the CDN or OSN. We also find other more typical scenarios, such as CDNs fetching content directly from OSNs and from large-scale hosting provider ASes.

Other intermediaries: The rest of IPs in the intermediary list (roughly 151K) are located in more than 7K ASes. They contact 399K servers in 10K different ASes. While we strongly suspect that most of these are indeed Web proxies, we cannot be certain. Indeed, on the one hand, one of the heavy-hitters IPs in this set — an oddball — is hosted in an unexpected AS. This oddball IP is serving both ad-related images to a CDN and acting as a Web auctioneer. On the other hand, we see several organizations that use resources from cloud services to set up their own virtual CDNs. A close analysis of which ASes are hosting the heavy hitters shows that most of these ASes are hosting and/or cloud service providers (8 out of 10). There is, however, more diversity in the destination ASes: we find hosting providers, CPs, OSNs and CDNs. We see that a single hosting/cloud service provider is responsible for 21% of the requests issued by IPs in this set. This observation highlights the importance of cloud service providers in the back office of the Web ecosystem once again.

6. BACK-OFFICE TRAFFIC: ESTIMATION

The raw numbers of IPs involved in back-office activity do not tell us much about how much back-office traffic we observe from our vantage points — estimating the volume of this traffic is the topic of this section.

6.1 Across vantage points

The methodology presented in Section 4 allows us to classify IPs as Web crawlers, auctioneers, bidders, and intermediaries such as CDPs. Thus, we can now quantify the amount of back- and front-office Web traffic. For a packet to be classified as back-office traffic, we require that both the source as well as the destination were previously identified as part of the back-office ecosystem. More specifically, we require that the source IP address was previously identified as belonging to an intermediary, crawler, or auctioneer, and the destination IP:port pair matches one of our identified Web server endpoints. We then tag this packet as back-office traffic, issued by the source, namely a crawler, auctioneer, CDP, or other intermediary.

Recall from Section 4 that we rely on passive and active measurements to uncover intermediaries, as well as on manual identification of crawlers and auctioneers, and lastly on a list of CDN servers. To account for the varying degrees of certainty when using these data sets, we distinguish between three different classes when quantifying back-office traffic. In particular, we consider back-office traffic caused by servers in our CDN data set (*IPs-CDN*), caused by servers we identified using DPI and manual inspection (*IPs-DPI+Manual*) and the back-office traffic caused by servers identified using the ZMap data set (*IPs-ZMap*).

Figure 4(a) shows the percentage of back-office traffic of the total Web traffic for each vantage point as a stacked bar plot. Thus, we depict the volume of back-office traffic found with the different methods: (a) information from the CDN only (the bottom bar), (b) information from the *IPs-CDN* and *IPs-DPI+Manual* (the sum of the bottom and the middle bar), (c) all information including ZMap (the sum of all bars). Across all vantage points we see at least 5% back-office Web traffic using the *IPs-CDN* and *IPs-DPI+Manual* set of IPs, confirming that back-office Web traffic is a significant contributor to today's Internet Web traffic. Even when only using the *IPs-CDN* data set, we see at least 4% back-office traffic at all vantage points except for L-IXP. This does not mean that the

[5]For an example of such a complex relationship see `http://ir.yandex.com/releasedetail.cfm?releaseid=828337`

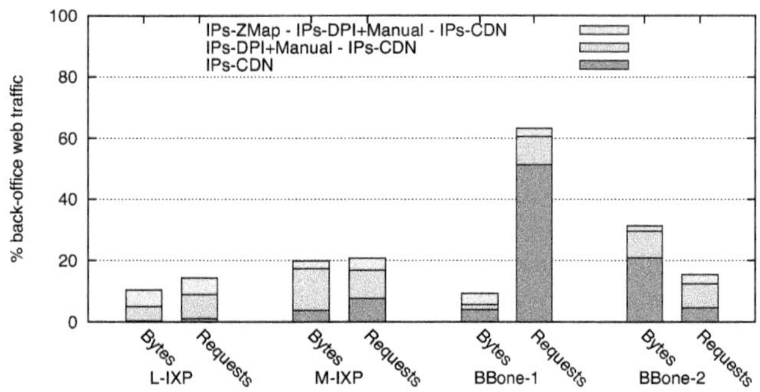

(a) % of Web traffic which is back-office across vantage points.

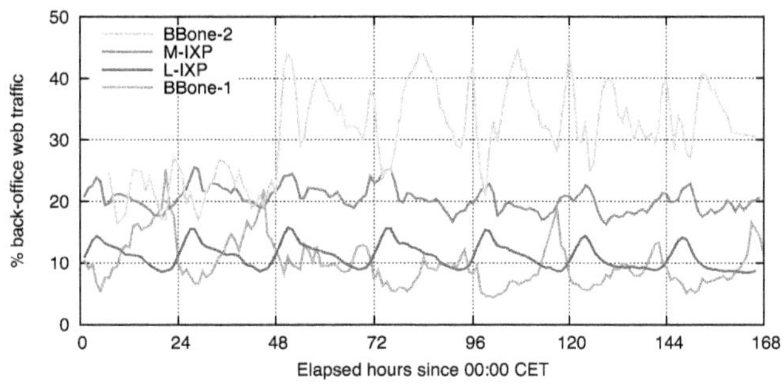

(b) % of Web traffic which is back-office over time (IPs-ZMap).

Figure 4: Fraction of back-/front-office Web traffic across vantage points.

Name	% of	CDPs	Auctioneers	Crawlers	Other
L-IXP	Bytes	12.1%	1.1%	10.3%	76.5%
	Requests	11.8%	22.5%	15.1%	50.6%
M-IXP	Bytes	73.3%	-	1.5%	25.2%
	Requests	65.7%	-	3.2%	31.1%
BBone-1	Bytes	50.7%	-	<0.1%	49.2%
	Requests	95.3%	-	<0.1%	4.6%
BBone-2	Bytes	93.6%	-	<0.1%	6.3%
	Requests	73.7%	-	4.3%	22%

Table 5: Classification of back-office Web traffic.

CDN is not active here but most of its traffic is front-office traffic. In terms of requests, the fraction of requests associated with back-office traffic is even larger with a minimum of 9% when using the *IPs-CDN* and *IPs-DPI+Manual* sets. This points out that some components of back-office traffic are associated with smaller transactions. But asymmetric routing—meaning the forward and return path do not use the same link— are likely the explanation for the extreme difference at BBone-1, where we see a huge number of back-office requests but only a relatively small percentage of back-office bytes. When we include the ZMap server IPs, the percentages of back-office traffic increases to more than 10% across all vantage points.

We next dissect the back-office traffic by type of activity using the *IPs-DPI+Manual* and the *IPs-ZMap* information. We illustrate our findings in Table 5, where we attribute back-office traffic to the entity that acts as client. We find that CDPs contribute 11% and 12% to the back-office requests and bytes in the L-IXP trace. The crawlers contribute 15% and 10% to the back-office requests and bytes, respectively. Surprisingly, the auctioneers are the big contributors to the number of requests with a share of 22% but only 1% of the bytes. The rest of intermediaries contribute more than 76% and 50% of the back-office bytes and requests. The situation differs for the other vantage points, where CDPs clearly dominate the share of bytes and requests with at least 50% of the bytes and 65% of the requests.

Figure 4(b) shows how the percentages of back- and front-office bytes change over time using time bins of one hour. The percentages never decrease below 5% but can even exceed 40%. While some traffic is triggered by end-user action, activities such as crawling and cache synchronization are not. We see that, particularly for the two IXPs, the percentage of back-office traffic increases during the off-hours. The percentage of back-office traffic for BBone-2 increases on the third day of the trace by more than 10%. This increase may be due to (a) a routing change or (b) a change in the operation of the application infrastructure or (c) a change in the popularity of a Web application. In addition, we see more variability for the individual backbone links than for the IXPs. A likely explanation for this is that the IXPs aggregate the information from thousands of different peering links. Similar observations hold for the percentages of back-/front-office requests and responses (not shown).

6.2 Across peering links

The two backbone traces illustrate that there can be notable differences in terms of percentages of back-office bytes and requests on different links, suggesting that links should be examined individually. Hence, we now take advantage of our ability to dissect the traffic seen on hundreds of individual AS-AS links at L-IXP.

Figure 5(a) shows the fractions of back-office traffic per AS-AS link (of the total traffic carried over it), where we sort them by the fraction of back-office Web traffic. We see that the fractions vary drastically from 100% to 0%. Indeed, 18.2% (10.9%) of the peering links carry more than 15% (7%) back-office bytes when relying on the *IPs-ZMap + IPs-DPI+Manual* (*IPs-DPI+Manual*) data set. On the other hand, 25.5% (40.8%) of the peering links carry no back-office traffic at all. In order to get a better understanding of the most important AS-AS links, we inspect more closely the top-10 traffic-carrying links that have a fraction of back-office traffic larger than 95%. We find four links between cloud providers and content providers, three links between search engines and hosting providers, two links between CDNs and content providers, and one link between a content provider and an online advertisement company. This analysis illustrates the diversity of the players contributing to the back-office Web traffic.

If we aggregate the information to the level of IXP member-ASes, the overall observation does change a bit, as shown in Figure 5(b). We do not see member ASes that exchange only back-office Web traffic. They all have at least 20% front-office Web traffic. Nevertheless, most have some fraction of back-office traffic. There are 19.2% (18.0%) of the members with more than 15% (7%) back-office bytes for the *IPs-ZMap + IPs-DPI+Manual* (*IPs-DPI+Manual*) data set. Among the networks with the highest share of back-office traffic are cloud providers, hosting providers, a search engine, and an advertisement company.

Summary

We find a significant percentage of back-office Web traffic in our traces, yet this percentage varies from vantage point to vantage point. Indeed, the back-office traffic carried over the backbone links is mostly dominated by CDPs. The picture differs when looking at IXPs, where we can monitor multiple links at once. While most of the back-office traffic there is also due to CDPs and other intermediaries, real-time-bidding and crawling also contribute a significant share of bytes and Web requests. Our analysis illus-

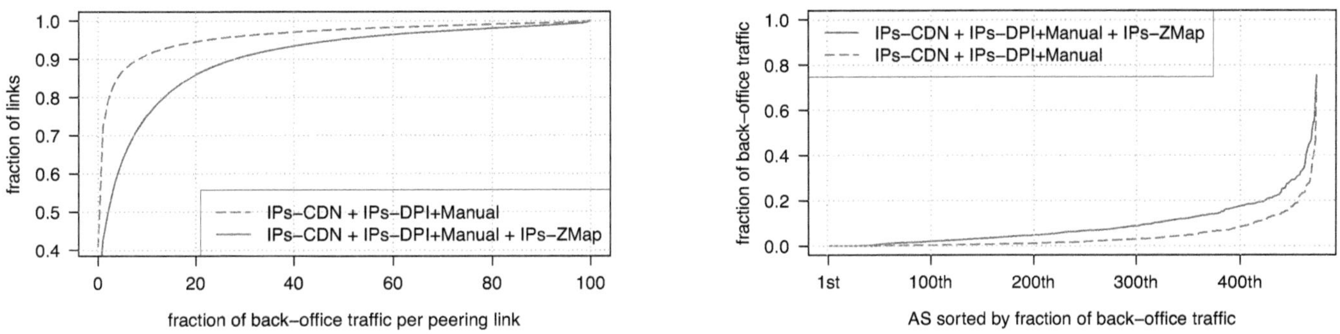

(a) ECDF: fraction of back-office traffic—per link.

(b) Fraction of back-office traffic—per member AS.

Figure 5: Back-office traffic across peering links—L-IXP.

trates that a significant part of the back-office traffic is not triggered by end users. We see that besides the expected players such as CDNs, search-engines and advertisement companies, cloud service providers and Web hosting providers are also responsible for a large fraction of back-office Web traffic. Indeed, they play an important role since they provide the resources necessary to build back-office infrastructure. Thus, back-office traffic is present in multiple links on the AS-level, revealing a complex ecosystem of players in support of the Web.

7. BACK-OFFICE: CHARACTERISTICS

Next, we examine some of the temporal and spatial characteristics of the different types of back-office Web traffic. In this section, we focus exclusively on back-office traffic caused by hosts that we manually identified to be CDPs, crawlers, auctioneers, or bidders.

7.1 Temporal behavior

To illustrate the temporal characteristics of some of the key players in the Web back-office, Figure 6 provides a time series plot of the number of requests seen at L-IXP and issued by content delivery proxies (CDPs), auctioneers, and crawlers, where we normalize the number of issued requests by the average number of crawler requests.

On the one hand, crawlers display rather constant activity throughout the week, which is the reason we use them for normalization. This constancy is to be expected because the request activity is not triggered by humans. The request patterns of the CDPs and auctioneers, on the other hand, display a diurnal pattern due to their connection to end-user activity. Interestingly, the rate of decrease between peak and off hours is larger for the auctioneers than for the CDPs. A possible explanation for the larger decrease is that the bidding process is a multiplicative factor of the end-user activity, i.e., one page visit triggers an auction involving multiple bidders. In terms of traffic volume (not shown), both CDPs and auctioneers exhibit typical diurnal variation while crawlers do not. While crawlers and CDPs dominate in terms of traffic contribution, auctioneers only contribute a tiny share of traffic. This is expected, as the bidding process involves numerous, but small, transactions.

7.2 Spatial behavior: Request forwarding

Noticing that many HTTP requests include the `Via` header, we next take a closer look at Web request forwarding. There are two HTTP header fields that are especially relevant for proxies: `Via` and `X-Forwarded-For`. The former indicates if a request has been forwarded through a proxy or a gateway; multiple `Via` field

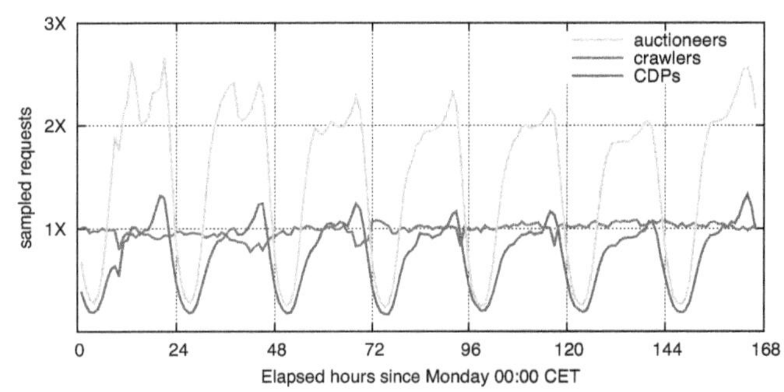

Figure 6: Time series: requests per hour by CDPs, auctioneers, crawlers (normalized by crawler requests).

values represent each host that forwarded the HTTP request. The `X-Forwarded-For` field contains the IP address of the original client, followed by the IP addresses of the proxies on the path to the server. Thus, if present and correctly set, this header includes the original client IP as well as all proxy IPs that forwarded the request. This allows us to elucidate the complexity of the back-office by showing how far requests are forwarded and via how many Web proxies.

Inspecting these headers requires the ability to inspect the complete payload of a packet. We have full payloads for the BBone-1 and BBone-2 traces, and we extract from them the requests according to the previous *IPs-CDN+IPs-DPI+Manual* classification. Recall that a significant fraction of the requests in these traces are issued by IPs in *IPs-CDN*. Thus, the following analysis may be biased by the behavior of this particular CDN.

The `Via` header field indicates that while 12% of the requests traversed one proxy, another 77% traversed two proxies. We even observed a few requests that traversed seven proxies. With the `X-Forwarded-For` header field we now reconstruct the paths of the requests, i.e., for each request we extract the list of proxy IPs and append the destination IP at the end. Perhaps surprisingly, we find many private IP addresses among the IPs in the `X-Forwarded-For` headers, suggesting that either (a) end users use proxies on their premises and/or (b) proxies are located within data-center networks, where private IP address space is used. We argue that the second case dominates as the first IP in the list is typically publicly routable, e.g., belonging to an end user.

Out of the 1M requests we consider, we find 766K different client IPs appearing in the first position of the reconstructed paths.

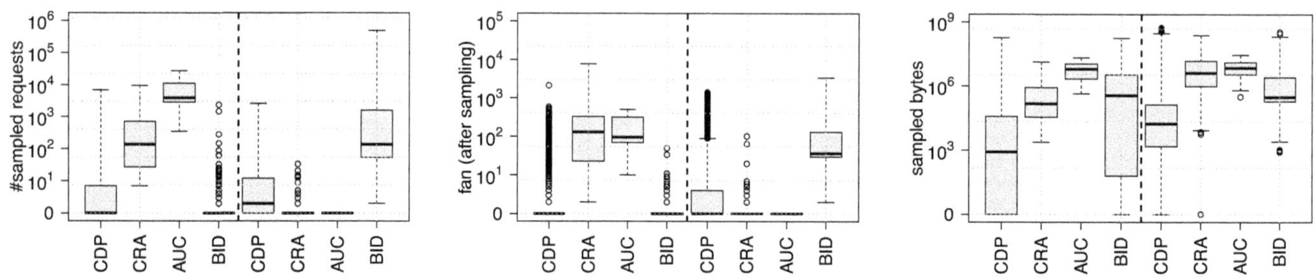

(a) Sampled requests sent/received (left/right). (b) Fan-out/in (left/right). (c) Sampled bytes sent/received (left/right).

Figure 7: IP characteristics: Content delivery proxies (CDPs), crawlers (CRA), auctioneers (AUC), and bidders (BID) — L-IXP.

These IPs map to 7.9K different ASes, and around 94% of these IPs appear only once. The last IP in a reconstructed path may be an origin server or another proxy. We observe 5.9K different IPs appearing in this position, and they map to 350 ASes. Note that an observed request may be further forwarded. Finally, for the subset of IPs that do not appear at the beginning or end of a path (i.e., forwarding proxies), we find 16.5K different IPs scattered across 885 ASes. Notably, around 2.7K of the IPs are not publicly routable, yet they sum up to 40% of the occurrences.

To conclude this section, we take a look at the geographical characteristics of request forwarding. For this exercise we focus on the subset of requests detected via the *IP-CDNs* set. We then use validated information about the geographical coordinates of these CDN servers and rely on this CDN's commercial geolocation product to geolocate end users. We observe the following typical scenario for CDN activity, as seen from these backbone links: an end user issues a request to a front-end server (at 10 to 1000 km distance), this front-end contacts a back-office server within a CDN cluster (0 km distance). This back-office server in turn forwards the request to another back-office server that is still on the same continent (10-1000 km). Then, this proxy forwards the request to an origin server or to another back-office proxy across the Atlantic.

7.3 Communication patterns

Next, we return to examine the activity of the IPs in the L-IXP trace. Figure 7(a) shows, for the crawlers, auctioneers, bidders, and CDPs, a box plot of the number of sampled back-office HTTP/HTTPS requests we observed. Note that we only analyze back-office traffic characteristics here, and do not, for example, consider any requests related to the front-office activity of CDPs. We separate sent and received requests on the left and right sides of the plot. Accordingly, Figure 7(b) shows the observed fan-out (i.e., to how many different hosts were requests sent) and fan-in (i.e., from how many hosts were requests received). Figure 7(c) shows the number of sampled bytes received/sent.

Auctioneers and bidders: Auctioneers are the most active in terms of number of requests sent. From our sampled data we estimate that the average number of bid requests/hour issued by these IPs is roughly 232 million. This estimate implies that an average auctioneer IP issues more than 700K bid requests/hour. Overall, auctioneers also contribute significant numbers of bytes in both directions. Indeed, as Figure 7(c) shows, the number of bytes sent and received are of the same order of magnitude. This balance is reasonable given the underlying bidding protocol (e.g., [1]). Note, that the auctioneers only contact a limited set of servers, as highlighted in Figure 7(b). Correspondingly, the bidders are also contacted only by a limited set of auctioneers. However, in terms of received requests, not all bidder IPs are equally active – some of them receive just a few bidding requests while others see more than 450K sampled requests. Indeed, many bidders receive requests from different organizations simultaneously. Given the sampling ratio of this vantage point, we estimate that the most active bidders receive more than 42 million requests for bids per hour!

Crawlers: Crawler IPs are the second most active group of IPs in terms of requests sent. We estimate that, at this vantage point, crawling accounts for roughly 155 million requests/hour and that the most active crawlers issue up to 910K requests/hour. Naturally, the number of bytes received is larger than the number sent. Overall, we estimate that all together crawlers fetch roughly 3.8 TB per hour. However, not all are equally active, and we even see some fetching content from only a single IP.

Content delivery proxies: On average, the proxies show the lowest activity per individual IP. This observation applies to both bytes and traffic. However, due to their large number, they contribute significantly to back-office traffic. This category of IPs exhibits the largest variation in behavior, and some of the heavy hitters in this category compete with those in the other categories.

Summary

Real-time bidding is very prominent and relies on many small transactions involving a fairly small set of organizations and hosts. As each end-user request may trigger multiple bid requests, RTB significantly contributes to the number of back-office transactions. Crawling, on the other hand, happens on a coarser-grain time scale and is executed by a limited number of organizations that constantly fetch content from a diverse set of mainly Web hosting providers. While CDPs have a diverse profile, our analysis illustrates that a single end-user request to a CDN front-end server can involve a chain of proxies. These connections remain entirely hidden to the end users.

8. A CDN'S PERSPECTIVE

Until now, we have analyzed back-office Web traffic from our vantage points in ISPs and IXPs. In this section, we present a complementary perspective provided by vantage points inside a commercial CDN. A CDN can be viewed as a high-bandwidth low-latency conduit that facilitates data exchanges between end users and different points of origin. As seen in previous sections, they

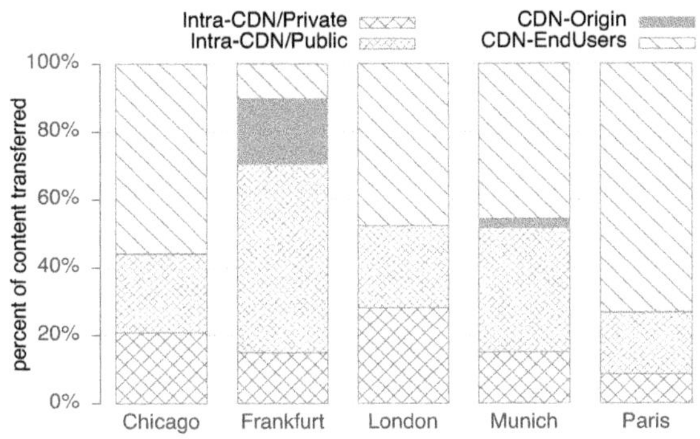

(a) Traffic volumes.

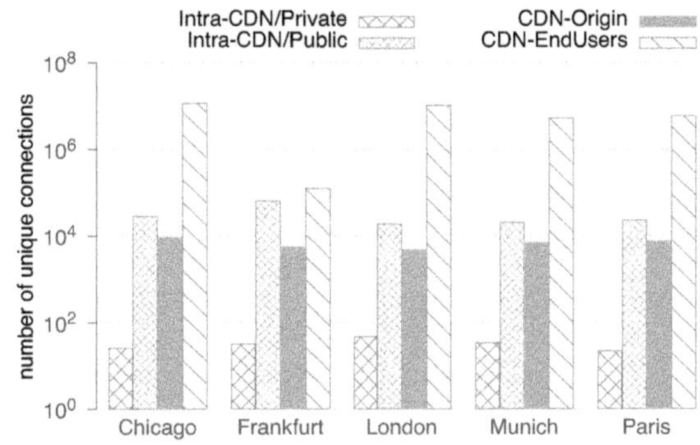

(b) CDN-EndUsers Fan in, Others Fan Out.

Figure 8: Front-office and back-office traffic at a large CDN.

are one of the major contributors to back-office Web traffic. This section delves into the details of the data set provided by a large commercial CDN and highlights a few ways this data can used to characterize back-office Web traffic.

8.1 CDN Dataset

The analysis in this section is based on server logs from the CDN's *edge*, or front-end, servers. Each log line records the details of an exchange of data where the edge server is one of the endpoints. Thus, the logs capture the interactions between the edge server and the end users, i.e., front-office Web traffic, as well as the interactions with other CDN servers and origin servers, i.e., back-office Web traffic.

We obtained the server logs from all servers at one cluster in each of five different cities: Chicago, Frankfurt, London, Munich, and Paris.[6] Note that there may be multiple clusters at each city, and we selected only one of the larger clusters in each city. CDNs also deploy multiple servers at each cluster, e.g., for load-balancing, and servers at each cluster offer a diverse set of services ranging from Web-site delivery to e-commerce to video streaming. We selected clusters of servers configured to handle Web traffic, and our logs measure Web traffic of more than 350TB in volume.

8.2 Front-office vs. back-office CDN traffic

The primary focus of a CDN is to serve content to the user as efficiently as possible. Therefore, one should expect CDN front-office traffic to dominate CDN back-office traffic in volume. As not all content is cacheable [8], up to date, or popular, some content has to be fetched from other servers. Moreover, many CDNs, e.g., Akamai [54], create and maintain sophisticated overlays to interconnect their edge servers and origin servers to improve end-to-end performance, to by-pass network bottlenecks, and to increase tolerance to network or path failures. Hence, a CDN edge server may contact, besides origin servers, other CDN servers located either in the same cluster, with back-office Web traffic routed over a private network, or in a different cluster at the same or different location, with the back-office Web traffic routed over a private or public network.

With the knowledge of the IP addresses used by the CDN's infrastructure, we can differentiate the intra-CDN Web traffic from the traffic between the CDN servers and end users (CDN-EndUsers), and CDN servers and origin servers (CDN-Origin). Furthermore, within the class of intra-CDN Web traffic, we can differentiate the traffic between servers in the same cluster from that between servers in different clusters; traffic between servers in the same

[6]A small fraction of servers at each location did not respond to our requests to retrieve the logs, but this should not affect the analysis.

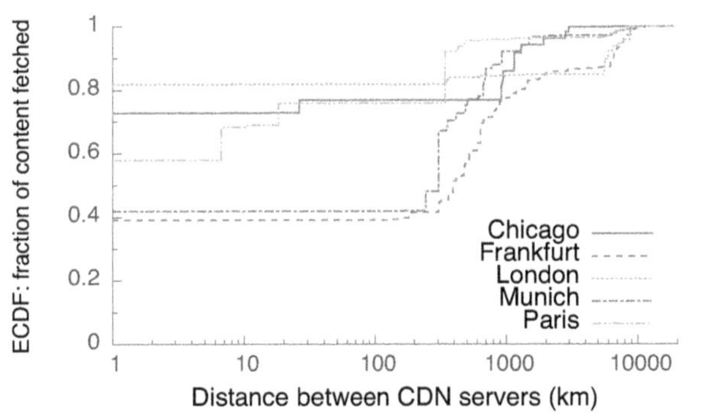

Figure 9: Content volume by distance (Intra-CDN) at a large CDN.

cluster uses high-capacity low-latency links and is routed over a private network (Intra-CDN/Private). We note that this traffic does not qualify as back-office Web traffic routed over the public Internet, which is the main focus of this paper. But in order to properly account for the publicly-routed back-office traffic that we are interested in, we must be able to separate out the Intra-CDN/Private traffic. Note also that since this category of back-office Web traffic is not routed via the public Internet it does not accrue any peering cost or hosting cost. Our classification scheme partitions the Web traffic identified via the logs into four categories: (1) CDN-EndUsers, (2) Intra-CDN/Public, (3) Intra-CDN/Private, and (4) CDN-Origin.

Figure 8(a) shows the proportion of traffic observed in each of the above four categories at the five different locations (or clusters). Not surprisingly, we see that most traffic is, as expected, CDN-EndUsers traffic. We still observe at least 25% back-office traffic at each location. Of the five clusters, Paris is the most efficient from the perspective of the content provider, with more than 70% of the traffic in the CDN-EndUsers category, and CDN-Origin traffic very low (around 1%).

Frankfurt is an oddball. At Frankfurt, the end-user traffic accounts for less than 12%. After discussions with the CDN operator, we learned that servers in the Frankfurt cluster cache content from origin servers for other edge servers in nearby clusters. The high-volume of Intra-CDN/Public traffic (about 55%) is indicative of this role for the servers in the Frankfurt cluster. Besides reducing the latency involved in fetching the content from the origin servers, this practice limits the number of servers that have to fetch content from the origin servers. The traffic at other locations show significant volumes in both the Intra-CDN/Public and Intra-CDN/Private categories. These statistics are indicative of the reliance on cooperative caching with the CDN.

Recall from Section 7.2 that there is a wide range of diversity in the number of hops over which an HTTP request is forwarded, as well as the distances to the final server. Using the actual locations of each CDN server as ground truth, we computed the distances for all Intra-CDN data exchanges. Figure 9 plots the resulting ECDF of the distances for the Intra-CDN/Public traffic weighted by the content size. The cluster in Frankfurt, in addition to serving end-user traffic, acts as a caching hub, as explained previously. Figure 9 provides further evidence of Frankfurt's role as a caching hub. About 20% of the traffic to the cluster in Frankfurt is being transferred over trans-continent links.[7] Contrast this with the cluster in Munich which receives around 2% of it's intra-CDN traffic via trans-continent links; discussion with the CDN operator confirmed that Munich does not serve as a caching hub. Figure 9 also reveals that a substantial fraction of the traffic travels only a short distance. This is expected, since in large metropolitan areas, like those selected for our study, edge servers are located at multiple data centers in the same city.

8.3 CDN back-office: Characteristics

Previously, we observed that the hosts' fan out, i.e., the number of hosts contacted by a host, can vary significantly. Accordingly, we may ask if fan out varies among the different classes of back-office CDN traffic. Not surprisingly, it turns outs that the number of unique end-user addresses to which the edge servers deliver content, i.e., the fan in, is larger than the combined number of CDN and origin servers from which they fetch content, i.e., the fan out.

Figure 8(b) shows the number of unique connections observed in the different traffic categories at each location. From the figure, we see that the number of unique connections in the back-office traffic categories (Intra-CDN/Private, Intra-CDN/Public, and CDN-origin) is two orders of magnitude less than that in the CDN-EndUsers category; note that the y-axis is plotted using a log scale. Moreover, the Intra-CDN/Private category mainly captures intra-cluster data exchanges and thus the fan out is even smaller. Finally, although the number of unique connections in the CDN-Origin category is smaller, it is equivalent in order of magnitude to the connection count in the Intra-CDN/Public category.

Aggregating the traffic volume by server addresses in both the CDN-Origin as well as the Intra-CDN/Public category reveals that the traffic is not uniformly distributed across all servers; rather there are heavy hitters. 20% of the origin servers contribute to more than 96% of the content delivered to the CDN's edge servers. A similar trend manifests in the Intra-CDN/Public category; 20% of the CDN's servers account for over 94% of the traffic volume moved from different servers in the CDN's infrastructure to the front-end, or edge, servers. These figures hint at the impact of the varying popularity and cacheability of content on the traffic patterns within the CDN infrastructure.

9. AN END-USER'S PERSPECTIVE

Improving the end-user experience can lead to a significant increase in revenues [39] and drive up user engagement [23, 41]. These benefits have catalyzed the competition among service companies to offer faster access to content in order to improve the end-user experience. Two "straightforward" ways of improving the end-user experience that can be implemented by ISPs are to (a) upgrade access networks, and to (b) improve the Internet's middle mile (backbones, peering points, and/or transit points); both approaches, however, are expensive.

[7]We assume that distances of 6000 km or more indicate trans-continent links.

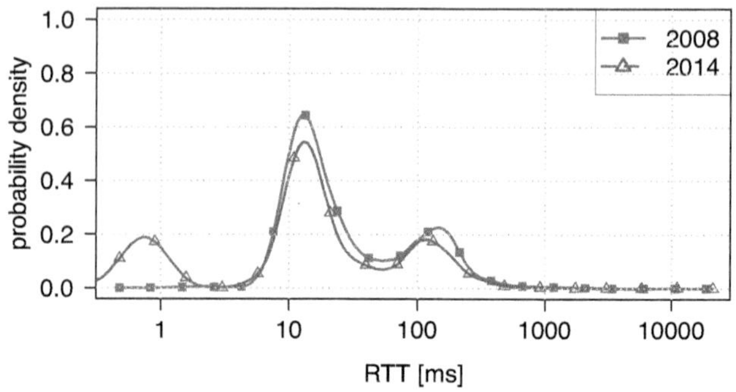

Figure 10: Delay between access aggregation point and front-end servers in 2008 [45] vs. 2014.

Content and application providers, on the other hand, can provide better service by installing servers deep inside ISPs and/or through increased peering at IXPs or colocation facilities. These approaches have been reported in [28, 46, 20] and have led to an increase in back-office Web traffic. Next, we analyze our data sets to see if these approaches have indeed decreased the latencies between end users and front-end servers. The analysis is based on anonymized packet-level traces captured in a residential network within a large European ISP in 2008 and in January 2014. For more details on data capturing, processing and anonymization, we refer to [45].

Figure 10 shows the backbone delay between the aggregation point of the ISP and the front-end servers that end users of the *same* residential network experienced in two different years — 2008, and 2014.[8] While the access technology, and the corresponding delay between end users and the access aggregation point, have not changed over the last six years (not shown), the delay between the aggregation point and servers has seen a significant shift towards shorter delays. A significant fraction of the requests are now terminated by servers within the same city (see the new bell curve around 1 ms delay which was not present in 2008); pushing the content closer to the end users has been successful.

10. IMPLICATIONS

In sections 2 through 4, we defined back-office Web traffic, discussed some methods to identify this traffic from different data sets, and presented some key insights from our analysis. We showed that back-office traffic is responsible for a significant fraction of today's Web traffic, and offered two key reasons to explain this phenomenon: (1) sustained deployment of front-end servers close to end users, and (2) substantial data exchanges conducted by service providers as part of their operations viz., coordination and synchronization of components of their distributed infrastructure. In this section, we discuss a few implications that affect researchers and operators.

This point of view allows us to differentiate the deployed servers into two broad categories, namely front-office and back-office servers that support many of the popular Web applications which run on top of the Internet. The front office is devoted to serving end users, and its performance is mostly influenced by the access technology and, to a different extent, by back-office performance. The back office, in turn, operates on the faster and wider pipes of the Internet backbone, involves multiple organizations and remains invisible to the end-users, yet virtually connected to them via the front-office. However, there is more in the back office than content delivery,

[8]We note that not necessarily all traffic is exchanged with front-end servers e.g., some traffic is due to peer-to-peer applications.

which includes, but is not limited to, real-time bidding and crawling.

With the increasing trend to offload "computations" to the cloud to support enterprise applications [53] or desktop application, e.g., the new release of Microsoft Office, Apple iCloud, and DropBox [24], it is clear that the volume of back-office Web traffic will continue to increase. First, application servers at different data centers will have to exchange data with each other for data synchronization and replication. Second, as edge servers attempt to offer more services [43, 28], viz., personalized Web experiences for end users, they will need to communicate with other edge servers and back-office servers, at different locations, to retrieve relevant content for the end users.

The Web ecosystem as presented in this work, manifesting a rich interplay between front-office and back-office servers, has many *practical* implications that affect not only end users, but also researchers and operators.

For researchers, the implications are two-fold. First, it is of utmost importance to differentiate between back-office and front-office Web traffic as they exhibit different characteristics and operations. Follow-up works may study the correlation of traffic dynamics, topology aspects of the Internet, and performance evaluation with each of the two classes of Web traffic. Second, researchers should be aware that the infrastructure deployed for the back-office presents a unique opportunity to develop and deploy new protocols that are better suited to the characteristics of the front- or the back-office.

For operators, the implications are multi-fold. First, operators should be aware of the importance of links that carry back-office traffic because they may (1) help in monetization of services, or (2) affect the front-office operations, viz., impairing the QoE of more end-users than anticipated. Second, operators should be aware that back-office traffic may have different requirements than front-office traffic. This, in turn, creates new opportunities for operators to provide customized services. In addition, operators may also want to offer different Service Level Agreements (SLAs) for different traffic classes.

10.1 Deployment of new protocols

Deploying new protocols or protocol variants may be very slow or even infeasible if it requires changes in the core infrastructure of the Internet or all end Internet end systems, for instance, consider the adoption of a new TCP variant or IPv6. However, restricting the change to one organization makes this otherwise infeasible effort much easier. Indeed, most Web service companies have the ability to roll out updates to their infrastructure and upgrade it on a regular basis. Thus, if end users connect only to the front-end servers and the front-end and back-end servers are managed by a single entity, it is feasible to rapidly deploy changes and optimize back-office Web communications; these changes are restricted to the servers involved in carrying the back-office traffic. Examples include but are not limited to use of persistent TCP connections between servers, IPv6, multi-path TCP [29], on-the-fly Web page assembly [43], object pre-fetching, compression and delta-encoding, and offloading of computations. Indeed, even the TCP version and parameters can be chosen according to the tasks [28], e.g., the initial window size can be increased. Moreover, it is possible to adopt new networking paradigms, such as Software Defined Networking [37], much more quickly to handle the back-office traffic. As most end-user communication involves some back-office communication, these improvements can directly affect the end-user experience. Lastly, more efficient use of the networking resources can also reduce the cost of content delivery.

10.2 New service opportunities

Network operators i.e., ISPs, can supply CDNs or content providers with the infrastructure that is specifically tailored to handle back-office traffic. For ISPs, this opens up additional opportunities for monetization of services and also provide a better experience to their end users. But, this comes at a cost: ISPs must invest in and enable micro data centers or virtualized services [30, 4] in their networks to harness the opportunity.

On the other hand, ISPs can also customize their traffic engineering policies to better accommodate the two different classes of traffic. They can also offer a different set of SLAs targeted at organizations operating a back office. Along the same line, IXPs can provide value-added services for time-critical applications e.g., bidding and financial applications. IXPs can also incentivize co-location at their peering locations using arguments such as the proximity of third-party servers, the pricing model for exchanging traffic with servers in other networks, and the ability to access the resources that cloud providers offer.

11. CONCLUSION

The Web and its ecosystem are constantly evolving. This paper takes a first step towards uncovering and understanding one component of this ecosystem that is increasing in complexity, but remains understudied: the back-office. The back-office includes the infrastructure necessary to support Web search, advertisements, and content delivery. By using a diverse set of vantage points, we've shown that back-office traffic is responsible for a significant fraction not only of today's Internet traffic but also today's Internet transactions.

Improvement in the back-office has been a major contributor to reducing the delays experienced by end users. Yet the back-office architecture still exposes many opportunities for deploying new protocols or versions of protocols for specialized tasks. The complexity of the back-office, however, also poses new questions. In future work we plan to improve our current methodology and extend it to identify other use-cases for back-office Web traffic, further dissect the interactions of the different services and better understand the performance implications thereof. Finally, we also plan to study the non-Web back-office of the Internet.

Acknowledgments

We would like to thank Oliver Spatscheck (our shepherd), the anonymous reviewers, and Paul Barford for their constructive feedback. This work was supported in part by the EU project BigFoot (FP7-ICT-317858). Georgios Smaragdakis was supported by the EU Marie Curie International Outgoing Fellowship "CDN-H" (PEOPLE-628441).

12. REFERENCES

[1] Google AdExchange. http://developers.google.com/ad-exchange/rtb/getting_started.

[2] Internet Advertising Bureau (IAB). 2013 Internet Advertising Revenue Report. http://www.iab.net/AdRevenueReport.

[3] Netflix Open Connect. https://signup.netflix.com/openconnect.

[4] Network Functions Virtualisation. SDN and OpenFlow World Congress, 2012.

[5] V. K. Adhikari, S. Jain, Y. Chen, and Z. L. Zhang. Vivisecting YouTube: An Active Measurement Study. In *IEEE INFOCOM*, 2012.

[6] B. Ager, N. Chatzis, A. Feldmann, N. Sarrar, S. Uhlig, and W. Willinger. Anatomy of a Large European IXP. In *ACM SIGCOMM*, 2012.

[7] B. Ager, W. Mühlbauer, G. Smaragdakis, and S. Uhlig. Web Content Cartography. In *ACM IMC*, 2011.

[8] B. Ager, F. Schneider, J. Kim, and A. Feldmann. Revisiting Cacheability in Times of User Generated Content. In *IEEE GI*, 2010.

[9] S. Angel and M. Walfish. Verifiable auctions for online ad exchanges. In *ACM SIGCOMM*, 2013.

[10] P. Barford, I. Canadi, D. Krushevskaja, Q. Ma, and S. Muthukrishnan. Adscape: Harvesting and Analyzing Online Display Ads. In *WWW*, 2014.

[11] L. A. Barroso, J. Dean, and U. Holzle. Web Search for a Planet: The Google Clustering Architecture. *IEEE Micro*, 23, 2003.

[12] T. Benson, A. Akella, and D. A. Maltz. Network traffic characteristics of data centers in the wild. In *ACM IMC*, 2010.

[13] T. Benson, A. Anand, A. Akella, and M. Zhang. MicroTE: Fine Grained Traffic Engineering for Data Centers. In *CoNEXT*, 2011.

[14] I. Bermudez, M. Mellia, M. Munafà, R. Keralapura, and A. Nucci. DNS to the Rescue: Discerning Content and Services in a Tangled Web. In *ACM IMC*, 2012.

[15] L. Bernaille and R. Teixeira. Early recognition of encrypted applications. In *PAM*, 2007.

[16] S. Brin and L. Page. The anatomy of a large-scale hypertextual Web search engine. In *WWW*, 1998.

[17] M. Butkiewicz, H. V. Madhyastha, and V. Sekar. Characterizing Web Page Complexity and Its Impact. *IEEE/ACM Trans. Networking*, 22(3), 2014.

[18] M. Calder, X. Fan, Z. Hu, E. Katz-Bassett, J. Heidemann, and R. Govindan. Mapping the Expansion of Google's Serving Infrastructure. In *ACM IMC*, 2013.

[19] F. Chang, J. Dean, S. Ghemawat, W. C. Hsieh, D. A. Wallach, M. Burrows, T. Chandra, A. Fikes, and R. E. Gruber. Bigtable: A Distributed Storage System for Structured Data. 2006.

[20] N. Chatzis, G. Smaragdakis, A. Feldmann, and W. Willinger. There is More to IXPs than Meets the Eye. *ACM CCR*, 43(5), 2013.

[21] Y. Chen, S. Jain, V. K. Adhikari, and Z. L. Zhang. Characterizing Roles of Front-End Servers in End-to-End Performance of Dynamic Content Distribution. In *ACM IMC*, 2011.

[22] Y. Chen, R. Mahajan, B. Sridharan, and Z. L. Zhang. A Provider-side View of Web Search Response Time. In *ACM SIGCOMM*, 2013.

[23] F. Dobrian, A. Awan, D. Joseph, A. Ganjam, J. Zhan, V. Sekar, I. Stoica, and H. Zhang. Understanding the Impact of Video Quality on User Engagement. In *ACM SIGCOMM*, 2011.

[24] I Drago, M. Mellia an M. Munafo, A. Sperotto, R. Sadre, and A. Pras. Inside Dropbox: Understanding Personal Cloud Storage Services. In *ACM IMC*, 2012.

[25] Z. Durumeric, E. Wustrow, and J. A. Halderman. ZMap: Fast Internet-Wide Scanning and its Security Applications. In *USENIX Security Symposium*, 2013.

[26] J. Erman, A. Gerber, M. Hajiaghayi, D. Pei, and O. Spatscheck. Network-aware Forward Caching. In *WWW*, 2009.

[27] A. Feldmann, N. Kammenhuber, O. Maennel, B. Maggs, R. De Prisco, and R. Sundaram. A methodology for estimating interdomain web traffic demand. In *ACM IMC*, 2004.

[28] T. Flach, N. Dukkipati, A. Terzis, B. Raghavan, N. Cardwell, Y. Cheng, A. Jain, S. Hao, E. Katz-Bassett, and R. Govindan. Reducing Web Latency: the Virtue of Gentle Aggression. In *ACM SIGCOMM*, 2013.

[29] A. Ford, C. Raiciu, M. Handley, S. Barre, and J. Iyengar. Architectural guidelines for multipath TCP development. Internet Draft, rfc-6182.

[30] B. Frank, I. Poese, Y. Lin, G. Smaragdakis, A. Feldmann, B. Maggs, J. Rake, S. Uhlig, and R. Weber. Pushing CDN-ISP Collaboration to the Limit. *ACM CCR*, 43(3), 2013.

[31] H. Gao, V. Yegneswaran, Y. Chen, P. Porras, S. Ghosh, J. Jiang, and H. Duan. An Empirical Reexamination of Global DNS Behavior. In *ACM SIGCOMM*, 2013.

[32] A. Gerber and R. Doverspike. Traffic Types and Growth in Backbone Networks. In *OFC/NFOEC*, 2011.

[33] P. Gill, V. Erramilli, A. Chaintreau, B. Krishnamurthy, K. Papagiannaki, and P. Rodriguez. Follow the Money: Understanding Economics of Online Aggregation and Advertising. In *ACM IMC*, 2013.

[34] A. Greenberg, J. R. Hamilton, N. Jain, S. Kandula, C. Kim, P. Lahiri, D. A. Maltz, P. Patel, and S. Sengupta. VL2: A Scalable and Flexible Data Center Network. In *ACM SIGCOMM*, 2009.

[35] C. Huang, A. Wang, J. Li, and K. Ross. Measuring and Evaluating Large-Scale CDNs. In *ACM IMC*, 2008.

[36] S. Ihm and V. S. Pai. Towards Understanding Modern Web Traffic. In *ACM IMC*, 2011.

[37] S. Jain, A. Kumar, S. Mandal, J. Ong, L. Poutievski, A. Singh, S. Venkata, J. Wanderer, J. Zhou, M. Zhu, J. Zolla, U. Holzle, S. Stuart, and A. Vahdat. B4: Experience with a Globally-Deployed Software Defined WAN. In *ACM SIGCOMM*, 2013.

[38] J. Kleinberg. Authoritative sources in a hyperlinked environment. In *ACM/SIAM SODA*, 1998.

[39] R. Kohavi, R. M. Henne, and D. Sommerfield. Practical Guide to Controlled Experiments on the Web: Listen to Your Customers not to the HiPPO. In *ACM KDD*, 2007.

[40] R. Krishnan, H. Madhyastha, S. Srinivasan, S. Jain, A. Krishnamurthy, T. Anderson, and J. Gao. Moving Beyond End-to-end Path Information to Optimize CDN Performance. In *ACM IMC*, 2009.

[41] S. S. Krishnan and R. K. Sitaraman. Video Stream Quality Impacts Viewer Behavior: Inferring Causality using Quasi-Experimental Designs. In *ACM IMC*, 2012.

[42] C. Labovitz, S. Lekel-Johnson, D. McPherson, J. Oberheide, and F. Jahanian. Internet Inter-Domain Traffic. In *ACM SIGCOMM*, 2010.

[43] T. Leighton. Improving Performance on the Internet. *Communications of the ACM*, 52(2):44–51, 2009.

[44] J. Liang, J. Jiang, H. Duan, K. Li, T. Wan, and J. Wu. When HTTPS Meets CDN: A Case of Authentication in Delegated Service. In *IEEE Symp. on Security and Privacy*, 2014.

[45] G. Maier, A. Feldmann, V. Paxson, and M. Allman. On Dominant Characteristics of Residential Broadband Internet Traffic. In *ACM IMC*, 2009.

[46] E. Nygren, R. K. Sitaraman, and J. Sun. The Akamai Network: A Platform for High-performance Internet Applications. *SIGOPS Oper. Syst. Rev.*, 2010.

[47] I. Poese, B. Frank, B. Ager, G. Smaragdakis, and A. Feldmann. Improving Content Delivery using Provider-aided Distance Information. In *ACM IMC*, 2010.

[48] I. Poese, B. Frank, G. Smaragdakis, S. Uhlig, A. Feldmann, and B. Maggs. Enabling Content-aware Traffic Engineering. *ACM CCR*, 42(5), 2012.

[49] L. Popa, A. Ghodsi, and I. Stoica. HTTP as the Narrow Waist of the Future Internet. In *SIGCOMM HotNets*, 2010.

[50] F. Qian, A. Gerber, Z. M. Mao, S. Sen, O. Spatscheck, and W. Willinger. TCP Revisited: A Fresh Look at TCP in the Wild. In *ACM IMC*, 2009.

[51] InMon – sFlow. `http://sflow.org/`.

[52] M. Z. Shafiq, L. Ji, A. X. Liu, J. Pang, and J. Wang. A First Look at Cellular Machine-to-Machine Traffic – Large Scale Measurement and Characterization. In *ACM SIGMETRICS*, 2012.

[53] J. Sherry, S. Hasan, C. Scott, A. Krishnamurthy, S. Ratsanamy, and V. Sekar. Making Middleboxes Someone Else's Problem: Network Processing as a Cloud Service. In *SIGCOMM*, 2012.

[54] R. K. Sitaraman, M. Kasbekar, W. Lichtenstein, and M. Jain. *Overlay Networks: An Akamai Perspective*. John Wiley & Sons, 2014.

[55] K. Springborn and P. Barford. Impression Fraud in Online Advertising via Pay-Per-View Networks. In *USENIX Security Symposium*, 2013.

[56] F. Streibelt, J. Boettger, N. Chatzis, G. Smaragdakis, and A. Feldmann. Exploring EDNS-Client-Subnet Adopters in your Free Time. In *ACM IMC*, 2013.

[57] S. Triukose, Z. Wen, and M. Rabinovich. Measuring a Commercial Content Delivery Network. In *WWW*, 2011.

[58] N. Weaver, C. Kreibich, M. Dam, and V. Paxson. Here Be Web Proxies. In *PAM*, 2014.

[59] S. Yuan, J. Wang, and X. Zhao. Real-time bidding for online advertising: measurement and analysis. In *ADKDD*, 2013.

A Look at the Consequences of Internet Censorship Through an ISP Lens

Sheharbano Khattak[1], Mobin Javed[2], Syed Ali Khayam[3], Zartash Afzal Uzmi[4], Vern Paxson[2,5]
[1]University of Cambridge, [2]UC Berkeley, [3]PLUMgrid, [4]LUMS SBASSE, [5]ICSI

ABSTRACT

Internet censorship artificially changes the dynamics of resource production and consumption, affecting a range of stakeholders that include end users, service providers, and content providers. We analyze two large-scale censorship events in Pakistan: blocking of pornographic content in 2011 and of YouTube in 2012. Using traffic datasets collected at home and SOHO networks before and after the censorship events, we: a) quantify the demand for blocked content, b) illuminate challenges encountered by service providers in implementing the censorship policies, c) investigate changes in user behavior (e.g., with respect to circumvention) after censorship, and d) assess benefits extracted by competing content providers of blocked content.

Categories and Subject Descriptors

C.2.3 [**Network Operations**]: Network monitoring; C.2.0 [**General**]: Security and protection; C.2.2 [**Network Protocols**]: Applications

General Terms

Measurement

Keywords

Censorship; ISP traffic; Content blocking; Video streaming; Porn;

1. INTRODUCTION

Nation-level censorship affects the activities of hundreds of millions of Internet users, with many countries implementing it at different levels and for a variety of reasons [35]. While censorship deployment and technology have seen considerable analysis in previous studies [9, 32], we lack a clear understanding of the *consequences* of censorship: just how does its employment affect different stakeholders? What steps do users, content providers, and ISPs take in response to censorship? How effectively does a given act of censorship achieve the censor's goals, and with what collateral damage?

IMC'14, November 5–7, 2014, Vancouver, BC, Canada.

ACM 978-1-4503-3213-2/14/11 ...$15.00.
http://dx.doi.org/10.1145/2663716.2663750.

While quantifiable answers to these sorts of questions have important socio-economic and policy implications, obtaining fine-grained illumination of these issues has remained largely unexplored due to the lack of datasets collected at appropriate vantage points and at appropriate times (i.e., before and after censorship events). Prior studies instead rely on datasets collected either via active probing [32] or using proxy servers [7]. These datasets cannot characterize individual behavior around censorship events; consequently, prior studies have focused mainly on understanding the mechanics of censorship technology and associated circumvention possibilities, rather than the consequences.

In this work, we seek to provide quantified insights into the impact of censorship on users, content providers, and ISPs, as seen through the lens of traffic datasets captured at a medium-size ISP[1] in a major city in Pakistan. Pakistan provides a useful vantage point for such a study as it recently instituted two large instances of censorship: blocking pornographic content[2] in 2011 [5], and blocking YouTube in 2012 [10].

The datasets we draw upon for this study comprise six residential and SOHO (Small Office / Home Office) traffic traces collected before and after the porn and YouTube censorship events, including one dataset collected on the day when Pakistan blocked YouTube. Trace durations range between 6–16 hours and capture sizes between 200–500GB, comprising traffic from 100–1,000 local IP addresses.[3] We supplement this perspective with a survey we conducted of about 700 Pakistani Internet users.

While analyzing the captured traffic traces, we developed methodologies to establish the ground truth (what was censored and how it was censored). Thus, unlike previous studies, our focus is on the offline analysis of captured data to ascertain the consequences of censorship. Our study develops the following insights:

- We observe a sudden increase in SSL traffic on the day of YouTube blocking, of sufficient volume that we attribute this change to users switching to VPN connections to circumvent the censors. This change persists a year later.

- SOHO users very quickly identified effective circumvention techniques, most of them switching to SSL within hours of the content blocking.

- Competing alternatives to YouTube received considerable benefit from censorship. We observe a sharp increase ($\approx$ 40–80%) in traffic volume towards these websites. Blocked sites

[1]Anonymized at the ISP's request.
[2]Shortened to "porn" henceforth.
[3]Due to NAT usage, one address can potentially correspond to multiple users.

also drop considerably in search-engine page rankings for local content. This change represents a marked regional shift in the economics of video content distributors, who mainly rely upon ad revenue.

- Before to censorship, porn content made up an average of 10% of home and SOHO traffic volume. Post-censorship, this fraction reduces considerably for both types of users. Even after factoring in traffic volume shifted to alternative (unblocked) porn websites, and the contemporaneous increase in SSL (potentially VPN) traffic, porn traffic volume did not return to the same level as before. The apparent reduction of active demand appears to indicate that the censors met their nominal goals.

- The YouTube block has two unintentional, yet significant, consequences: *(i) financial impact on ISP:* as users move to encryption-based circumvention mechanisms, the ISP's bandwidth requirement from the upstream provider increases, since ISPs cannot in general cache encrypted content; and *(ii) financial impact on YouTube:* user demand for YouTube (in terms of video requests observed in unencrypted traffic) eventually becomes half of its pre-censorship magnitude, and shifts to other video content providers.

2. BACKGROUND AND RELATED WORK

This section provides context on the censorship events that we investigate, the issue of determining how censorship is implemented, and the relationship between our work and prior research.

Internet infrastructure and censorship in Pakistan. Our study spans traces collected at a Pakistani ISP between 2011 and 2013—a timeline during which the country's censorship policy evolved considerably. There are ≈ 50 local and regional Internet service providers (ISPs) in Pakistan [25]. Only two of these, Pakistan Telecommunication Company Limited (PTCL) and Transworld Associates (TWA), have direct international connectivity, which they sell to the rest of the providers as well as directly to consumers; note that the majority of CDN servers are located outside of Pakistan. Internet censorship in Pakistan has mostly targeted content hosted outside the country, which Pakistani users access through PTCL or TWA.

The directives to block a particular website originate from the government or the judiciary. The ISPs are directed by the regulator, Pakistan Telecom Authority (PTA), to implement a content-blocking policy. While Pakistan has been intermittently blocking content since 2006 [32], a more persistent blocking policy was implemented in 2011 with the censorship of porn content [5], and then in 2012 with the blocking of YouTube [10]. The porn block in Pakistan was instituted in response to a media report that highlighted Pakistan as the top country in terms of searches for porn content [33], while the YouTube ban arose when a video, deemed blasphemous, appeared on the website. Presently, the country continues to block access to YouTube[4] as well as to sites deemed pornographic, anti-religious, or a general threat to national values and security [34]. A more recent study reports censorship of content related to human rights, independent media, proxy and circumvention tools, and bittorrent file-sharing sites [9].

Determining the implementation of censorship. Prior studies have focussed on inferring technologies for implementing censorship. Most of these studies use active probing to trigger censorship responses and comparing these responses to baseline responses in uncensored regions. These studies seek to detect the manipulation of traffic by intermediate devices [26, 19, 39, 23] and to illuminate the nature of censored content [11, 20] and the corresponding technology and/or mechanisms [14, 4, 43, 13]. Some recent studies apply probe-based approaches to study censorship particularly in Pakistan [32, 9], highlighting ISP-level DNS redirection, along with HTTP-redirection and fake-response injection at the national backbone. While previous work serves to help validate our findings, we cannot directly map it to our three-year dataset because censorship mechanisms can vary *(i)* over time, and *(ii)* across different vantage points. We thus employ passive analysis of each data trace to identify the censorship mechanism(s) in effect at a given time. We are not aware of any prior work that reconstructs censorship mechanisms by passive analysis of network traces, other than within the broader context of detecting forged TCP RST packets [44].

Consequences of Internet censorship. Previous literature has tackled the problem of how different network-level events, particularly in the context of anti-piracy laws, can affect the behavior of users [1] and content providers [22]. In the context of Internet censorship, studies have assessed the (sometimes unintended) impact of Internet censorship on global Internet services. China's injection of forged DNS responses has been reported to cause large scale collateral damage by blocking outside traffic that traverses Chinese links [3]. Upstream filtering can block traffic from outside a censored region due to ISP routing arrangements (for example, users of an ISP in Oman could not access certain content due to filtering regulations in India [27]). Chaabane et al. [7] analyze logs from Syrian censorship proxies to understand censorship methodology and user behaviour. In the latter context, they find that Syrian users employ web/socks proxies, Tor, VPNs, and BitTorrent to circumvent censorship. Labovitz uses a combination of large scale crawling and third-party data sources to investigate how the takedown of MegaUpload servers in North America impacts file-sharing traffic [28]. He finds that the incident caused a very small decrease in MegaUpload's previous traffic share, but makes content delivery inefficient, as files are now fetched from European servers over more expensive transatlantic links. For our purposes, a limitation of these latter studies is that from their own vantage points, they cannot assess the full exchange of traffic between users and providers, and thus cannot analyze the possibility of intermediate censorship (occurring closer to the user). Our study leverages an ISP viewpoint to address this issue and investigates the consequences of Internet censorship on users, content providers and operators. To our knowledge, this last perspective has not seen previous study.

3. DATA SOURCES FOR THE STUDY

Our primary data consists of six network traces captured at a Pakistani ISP[5] between 2011 and 2013. As discussed in Section 2, the government of Pakistan implemented two of the most significant and persistent policies in its censorship history during this period. Figure 1 illustrates the temporal relationship of the capture dates to the censorship events. The traces provide both pre-censorship and post-censorship snapshots of activity seen at an ISP for two major censorship events. We note that our data is not necessarily broadly representative, as it corresponds to just one ISP.

[4]In early 2014, a US court cited copyright issues in forcing YouTube to remove the offending video [36, 18]. As of this writing, Google continues to fight this order.

[5]The ISP requested to treat its name, location and other identifying information as confidential. The ISP originally acquired the data for unspecified purposes, and provided a degree of access out of good will.

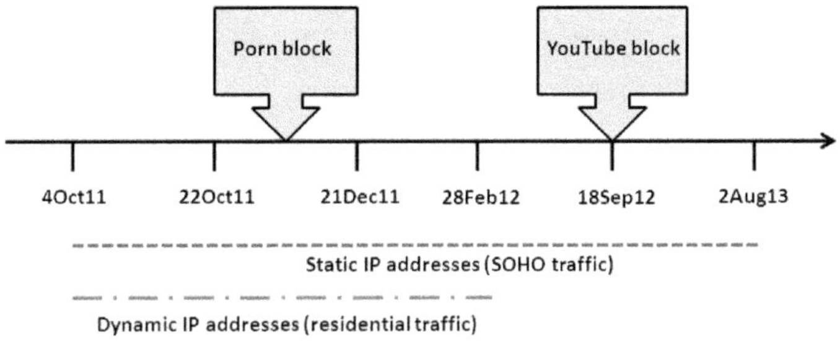

Figure 1: Temporal relationship of data to censorship events.

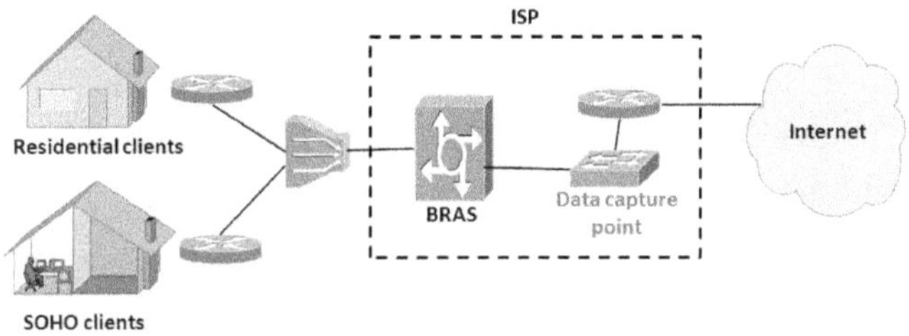

Figure 2: Capture location

Furthermore, it is difficult for us to estimate the actual user population of that ISP due to wide usage of NAT devices.

We supplement this data with a user survey we conducted in the region to explore user behavior post-YouTube censorship [45]. The survey results help shape the scope of our YouTube censorship analysis, and provide additional perspective for our findings from the primary data.

3.1 Capture Location and ISP Overview

Our tier-2 Pakistani ISP peers with a tier-1 provider through the Transworld Associates TWA-1 submarine telecommunications cable in Karachi. The ISP caters to both residential and SOHO customers. Due to our confidentiality agreement, we cannot provide details regarding the scale at which the ISP operates, the magnitude of its customer base, or the address space it uses.

Figure 2 shows the data capture location within the ISP premises. All customer lines terminate at one of several Broadband Remote Access Servers (BRASes) in the ISP's network. Each BRAS connects to the ISP's core Internet-facing router through a switch. The ISP gathered the traces at the BRAS-facing side of this switch. This vantage point captures all of the local ISP-generated traffic (such as redirected DNS traffic) in addition to bi-directional traffic going in or out of the ISP's premises. The ISP assigns each BRAS to a set of addresses. While the allocation remains unchanged for any given trace, across traces the captures correspond to potentially different subsets of the ISP's address space.

Address Pools. The ISP splits its address space into dynamic DHCP and static pools, primarily assigning dynamic IPs to residential customers. The ISP reserves some static IP addresses for hosting its services, such as DNS resolvers, mail and authentication servers, and other web resources. It allocates the bulk of the remainder to SOHO customers. We do not know which IP addresses correspond to particular ISP services; in particular, we have no specifics regarding its censorship apparatus, related IP addresses, or blacklists in effect for different traces. Note that the ISP does not allocate IPv6 addresses to its customers. While we find some

Block Key	Trace	Day	Capture Hour (PKT) + Duration	Size (GB)	Active Local IPs
–	03Oct11	Tue	17:48 + 15h14m	222	1,075
–	22Oct11	Sat	18:49 + 20h42m	460	1,046
P	21Dec11	Wed	22:17 + 16h54m	286	868
P	28Feb12	Tue	18:48 + 11h08m	200	974
PY	18Sep12	Tue	08:54 + 07h19m	500	310
PY	02Aug13	Fri	09:40 + 06h00m	207	136

Table 1: Summary of packet captures. P=Porn, Y=YouTube

IPv6 communication taking place over tunnels, its overall volume is negligible.

Ethical Standards. The authors of this work with direct access to the data signed a contract highlighting the obligations to (*i*) respect user privacy, (*ii*) not share data with third parties (which includes the other co-authors), (*iii*) not move data outside Pakistan, (*iv*) not move data within Pakistan without prior consent, and (*v*) undertake an objective study and refrain from maligning any party involved in the censorship landscape (user, ISP, or government). These restrictions did not affect our study in any respect.

3.2 Data Description

Table 1 characterizes the traces. Capture durations range between 6–16 hours and capture sizes between 200–500GB, comprising traffic from 100–1,000 IP addresses. Some of these IP addresses likely reflect NATs, and thus the effective user population could potentially range larger. Due to a number of variables in the traces, a limitation of our work is that we cannot exclusively attribute cross-trace trends to the consequences of censorship; these might instead arise due to factors introduced by disparate capture days and/or timings. However, some of our results are sharp enough that it appears very likely that they correspond to responses to censorship. Finally, trace characteristics might differ between traces despite similar trace durations and time frames because the IP address prefixes allocated to a BRAS do not necessarily remain consistent across traces.

Protocol Logs. Our analysis relies on protocol logs generated using `Bro` [6]. In particular, we deal with connection, HTTP and DNS logs. The connection log contains one entry per flow, while the protocol logs contain separate entries for each request-response pair. We use *number of connections* to refer to distinct transport-layer flows and *number of requests* for individual request-response pairs as observed in the protocol logs.

3.3 Data Sanitization and Characterization

For soundness of analysis, we first identify measurement ambiguities/inaccuracies (*sanitization*) and then label the data (*characterization*) so as to extract the portion relevant to a given analysis.

Data can include inaccuracies due to various reasons, where a particularly common is the limitation of the capturing device or analysis tool. A large portion of our data reflects connections that did not fully establish (e.g., scanning activity). We remove such connections from the bulk of our analysis (though we include them when assessing evidence of user attempts to access blocked content). We identify unestablished connections based on `Bro`'s connection state field, which captures the sequence of control and data packets seen for a given connection. We only include connections whose state reflects a completed three-way TCP establishment handshake, which reduces our six data sets down to roughly half the original number of connections, as reflected in Table 2.

To characterize our data, we label flows based on the connection direction and the type of local addresses involved, subsequently using only those subsets apt for a particular type of analysis. For

Block Key	Trace	Total conns.	After sanitization (% retained)	Transit	Local	Static IPs		Dynamic IPs	
						Inbound	Outbound	Inbound	Outbound
–	03Oct11	11.53M	5.39M (46.7%)	0.03M	0.68M	1.05M	1.62M	0.54M	1.48M
–	22Oct11	29.19M	12.68M (43.4%)	0.03M	1.24M	3.58M	4.13M	1.25M	2.44M
P	21Dec11	16.06M	8.09M (50.4%)	0.02M	1.21M	1.37M	2.57M	0.50M	2.42M
P	28Feb12	12.12M	5.84M (48.2%)	0.04M	0.59M	0.86M	0.98M	0.99M	2.39M
PY	18Sep12	24.01M	14.93M (62.2%)	0.02M	2.19M	1.13M	11.59M	-	-
PY	02Aug13	8.79M	3.77M (42.9%)	0.01M	0.53M	0.19M	3.03M	-	-

Table 2: Breakdown of data sanitization and characterization. P=Porn, Y=YouTube

example, to gauge the interest of local users in Web content served over the Internet, we only consider outbound connections—see Table 2 for an overview.

With regards to direction, we label a connection as *local* if it has both source and destination IP addresses in the ISP's network block, or *transit* if neither source nor destination belongs to the local network. We consider a connection *inbound* if its originator resides outside the ISP's network and *outbound* if the converse holds.

We further differentiate between residential and SOHO traffic based on the assumption that nearly all static IP addresses correspond to SOHO users, where we determine the set of static IP addresses using information provided by the ISP.

Table 2 summarizes these characterizations. We find that outbound connections predominate, followed by inbound, local and transit, in that order. The small portion of transit traffic agrees with a communication from the ISP that we should expect a small amount of traffic from a sister ISP, along with some IPv6 test traffic.

3.4 Final Datasets

Table 3 summarizes our filtered dataset. We divide our six traces into two datasets corresponding to residential and SOHO users respectively. We use both datasets to study the impact of porn censorship, and the SOHO dataset for YouTube censorship, since the post-YouTube censorship traces contain only small amounts of residential traffic. For a major part of our study, we work with HTTP and DNS logs for outbound and local connections. We include local traffic in our analysis because we expect to find a portion of user traffic redirected to local systems enforcing censorship.

3.5 User Survey

Finally, we carried out an online user survey targeting Pakistani users in order to develop an understanding of their views of and responses to the YouTube block. (We avoided asking about the porn block as it is a culturally sensitive topic in the region.) We disseminated information about the opportunity to take the survey through mailing lists and classroom discussions. The survey asked about: (i) the popularity of blocked content and new players that emerged post-censorship, (ii) user inclinations to circumvent and the corresponding mechanisms, (iii) collateral damage experienced due to the block, and (iv) opinions about Internet censorship in general.

We did not expect many responses because it is hard to get users to respond to surveys without any incentive, especially when the topic is a sensitive one such as Internet censorship. Surprisingly, we received 770 responses (75% male, and 25% female), reflecting a widespread eagerness to comment on the subject. 94% of the responders were young/middle-aged (25-40 years), and resided in major cities, with occupations suggestive of high levels of technological competence. This demographic does not reflect Pakistan's makeup as a whole, and likely skews towards particularly informed and active users. Thus, we do not frame its results as representative, but rather as illuminating of some of the facets of how censorship affects Pakistani users.

4. ESTABLISHING GROUND TRUTH

A significant challenge for our study is that we use historical data for which we lack key contextual information: (*i*) *what* was censored (the blacklist for the porn block), and (*ii*) *how* it was censored (the mechanism of censorship). In this section we discuss the methodology we employed to answer these questions based solely on the information present in the available traces. We do so by analyzing the responses we see from servers in reply to user requests, basing our deductions on the observation that for enforcing censorship, a censor either silently drops requests or sends back false response packets.

4.1 Censorship Indicators

A censor can block HTTP content at any of the layers involved in facilitating an HTTP transaction: DNS, TCP/IP, and HTTP. Across these layers, the censor has an array of choices for how to block, each leaving a trail in the network traces. The presence of such a trail (a sequence of packets not necessarily contiguous, or an absence of expected packets) provides an indicator of censorship. However, some of these indicators can occur in an uncensored environment for legitimate reasons such as measurement loss or excessive server load. We deem censorship indicators that can also occur under uncensored conditions as *ambiguous*, and deal with them as follows: (*i*) If the censored content is *known*, we attribute a high frequency of an ambiguous indicator to censorship (and leverage this information to establish the mechanism of censorship); but (*ii*) if the censored content is *unknown* (that is, we cannot tie any given flow to an attempt to access blocked content), we cannot attribute the occurrence of such an indicator over a short observation window (less than one day for each of our traces) exclusively to censorship. We therefore do not leverage these latter indicators, and rely only on unambiguous indicators to establish (partial) ground truth.

We now discuss assessing censorship indicators at each layer.

DNS Based Censorship. At the DNS level, a censor-controlled resolver (such as one maintained by the present ISP) can effect blocking behavior by sending: (*i*) No Response, (*ii*) False Error (such as NXDOMAIN), or (*iii*) False Response (the RCODE for these responses is NO ERROR). (Clearly, users can bypass these DNS-based censorship mechanisms by using an independent DNS resolver.)

No Response provides an ambiguous indicator because it could occur due to excessive load on the resolver, or network problems. Thus, we do not attribute this scenario to censorship when the censored content is unknown. However, for known censored content, observing a consistent behavior of no response is a strong indicator of censorship.

Block Key	Trace	Active IPs	Conns.	TCP Conns.	UDP Conns.	HTTP Transactions	SSL Conns.	DNS Conns.	Bytes (GB)	Packets
SOHO Traffic (Static IPs)										
–	03Oct11	585	2.02M	1.00M	1.02M	1.44M	0.05M	1.29M	79	119M
–	22Oct11	554	4.84M	1.91M	2.93M	2.18M	0.09M	1.90M	180	276M
P	21Dec11	570	3.24M	1.70M	1.55M	2.52M	0.14M	2.63M	121	182M
P	28Feb12	298	1.16M	0.51M	0.65M	0.62M	0.08M	0.33M	39	61M
PY	18Sep12	298	13.78M	7.53M	6.25M	7.16M	1.05M	4.26M	271	546M
PY	02Aug13	133	3.56M	1.85M	1.71M	1.78M	0.32M	1.57M	143	246M
Residential Traffic (Dynamic IPs)										
–	03Oct11	490	1.76M	0.85M	0.9M	1.14M	0.05M	1.86M	85	149M
–	22Oct11	492	2.97M	1.40M	1.57M	1.84M	0.08M	1.08M	163	237M
P	21Dec11	451	2.96M	1.50M	1.45M	2.11M	0.13M	1.09M	103	176M
P	28Feb12	676	2.80M	1.26M	1.55M	1.46M	0.11M	0.80M	112	176M
PY	18Sep12	-	-	-	-	-	-	-	-	-
PY	02Aug13	-	-	-	-	-	-	-	-	-

Table 3: Final data after preprocessing. P=Porn, Y=YouTube

For the last two cases, we can leverage two public databases to establish the ground truth: *(i)* `dnsdb`, which contains historical information on name-to-IP address mappings [38], and *(ii)* Team Cymru's IP-to-ASN mappings database [40]. We identify false responses as follows:

False Error: We mark the queries that consistently receive an ERROR RCODE response from a resolver for a subsequent `dnsdb` lookup. If there exists a name-to-IP mapping in the database for the domain seen in the trace, we conclude that the censor employed False Error as their mechanism.

False Response: We can detect a DNS resolver including false IP addresses in its responses if we observe consistency in the false answers returned. We identify whether a DNS resolver answers with an IP address belonging to an ISP within the country (either local ISP or an upstream transit provider from within Pakistan) when the domain is actually hosted elsewhere. Let $\text{ASN}_{\text{trace}}$ be the ASN of an IP address returned in a DNS reply recorded in the trace, and ASN_{real} be the ASN for the IP address received in a DNS reply obtained by active testing. If $\text{ASN}_{\text{trace}}$ belongs to an ISP within Pakistan, while ASN_{real} does not, the query received a false response. This technique has the limitation that we cannot detect cases where the censor's redirection points to an IP address that belongs to an AS outside the country. The same problem holds for a censor who employs null-routing. Furthermore, this technique will flag caching servers employed within the country.[6]

TCP/IP blocking. IP-level blocking is an ambiguous indicator of censorship, as it is hard to distinguish from legitimate causes of inaccessibility. However, we can weed out some of the non-censorship cases because censorship generally requires that *all* attempts to establish a connection to a blocked address will fail. To find such IP addresses, we use the heuristic described below.

First, iterate over all the `A` records for queries resolved correctly, and for each connection seen for one of these addresses, label it according to the following three connection states:

- **PARTIAL**: No SYN seen from the connection originator, but packets seen from the responder.
- **EST**: Full TCP establishment handshake observed.
- **BLOCKED**: The originator sent a SYN but either *(i)* receives no response, or *(ii)* receives a TCP RST (potentially injected by the censor).

[6]Indeed we identify the ISP's caching machines using this methodology.

We flag IP addresses for which we never observe EST and for which we observe BLOCKED at least once. We map these IP addresses back to their corresponding domain names in the DNS logs and consider these domains as potentially censored.

HTTP Level Blocking. At the HTTP level, a censor can block via: (i) No HTTP response (for example, by injecting a RST after connection establishment), (ii) return an HTTP-level error response code, or (iii) return a false response such as a block page (either directly or via HTTP-level redirection). We assess these as follows:

- **No Response**: This can occur for legitimate reasons. We do not attribute it to censorship when the censored content is unknown. For known censored content, consistently observing TCP-layer blocking can confirm censorship (for example, the case where the responder always sends a RST in response to an HTTP request).
- **Error Response Codes**: This error can be ambiguous because a client can receive such responses due to resources legitimately not found or forbidden. For known censored content, however, this provides a strong indicator if it is the dominant behavior.
- **Block Page such as via 3XX redirection**: The censor may redirect diverse domains/sub-domains to the same *Location*. We can detect this mechanism by analyzing histograms of the `Location` header in responses. If, however, the censor redirects attempted access for different content to distinct locations (such as by incorporating the request URI into the redirect location), the histogram will not reveal any common redirection target. In this case, the analysis in the next item might reveal blocking.
- **Block Page via 2XX response**: We can detect when the censor sends the same block page for multiple URLs by fingerprinting block pages known to be associated with the censor, or by looking for potential candidates by investigating spikes/modes in a histogram of the number of bytes sent in server reply items.

4.2 Identifying YouTube Censorship

Table 4 shows our findings for deducing the mechanism of YouTube censorship in Pakistan at the two different points in time that are currently under study.

First, we observe DNS redirection in both traces for queries resolved using the ISP's DNS resolvers: all YouTube queries received

	Trace	DNS	IP	HTTP
YouTube	18Sep12	DNS_REDIR	—	HTTP_REDIR
	02Aug13	DNS_REDIR	—	HTTP_NORESP
Porn	21Dec11	DNS_REDIR	—	—
	28Feb12	DNS_REDIR	—	—
	18Sep12	DNS_REDIR	IP_BLOCK	—
	02Aug13	DNS_REDIR	—	HTTP_NORESP

Table 4: Censorship mechanisms for YouTube and porn blocking as observed in our post-censorship traces. "—" indicates that we did not find any concrete evidence of the given mechanism.

Trace	DNS	IP blocking	HTTP blocking
21Dec11	226	3 / 0%	2 / 0%
28Feb12	145	7 / 0%	1 / 0%
18Sep12	105	56 / 41%	6 / 0%
02Aug13	100	0 / 0%	8 / 62%

Table 5: Number of porn domains potentially blocked at each layer. For IP and HTTP blocking, we also show the percentage overlap with DNS blocking. HTTP blocking when present took the form of consistent No Response conditions.

replies with a single ISP-owned address. Queries sent to non-ISP resolvers obtained correct answers. Second, we do not find IP blocking in either trace. We see only one potentially blocked address in 18Sep12, which reverse-maps to a YouTube content server.

Finally, in addition to DNS-based blocking, we also observe HTTP-level blocking in both traces. In 18Sep12, we find blocking of YouTube via 3XX redirection to an IP owned by a large local provider, one of the two with direct international connectivity. In 02Aug13, the blocking shifted from redirection to No Response. In traces before 02Aug13 (including pre-YouTube-censorship traces), the number of YouTube HTTP requests that received no response averaged $\approx 2\%$, whereas in 02Aug13 this number jumps to $\approx 95\%$, with nearly all of these reset by the responder.

These observations confirm the two-layered censorship mechanism for YouTube described by a prior study [32], i.e., ISPs block locally using DNS redirection, and the two large providers in the country with direct international connectivity (PTCL and TWA) employ HTTP-level blocking.

4.3 Identifying Porn Censorship

To accurately identify porn censorship, we characterize all websites recorded in our traces using McAfee's URL categorization service [30] and extract the ones it labels as *Pornography*. We spot-checked a random sample of its decisions (both positive and negative) to confirm its apparent accuracy and lack of any regional lacuna. We did not find any errors.

In recovering the censor's *porn blacklist*, we worked on each trace in turn. Recovered blacklists necessarily represent only a fraction of the censor's true blacklist, since our data-driven approach can only identify the fraction of censored content present in our traces.

Porn domains	Oct11	Dec11	Feb12	Sep12	Aug13
Unblocked	1,313	1,181	1,609	2,210	2,352
Blocked	0	226	145	161	105
New entries	—	0	37	36	0
% overlap	—	8.2%	0.2%	0.5%	0%

Table 6: Evolution of porn blacklist as seen in our traces. % overlap corresponds to the proportion of new entries present (and unblocked) in all previous traces. Oct11 reflects two traces captured during that month.

We aim to recover to blacklists at the granularity of *registered* domains, per the master list kept by Mozilla [31], since later in our analysis we use that granularity for characterizing traffic to blacklisted domains. Where applicable, we mark domains in our blacklist as partially blocked. We consider the possibility of partial blocking of a domain only at IP-level (due to incomplete IP address coverage) and HTTP-level (due to incomplete regex coverage). For DNS, we assume that the true blacklist contains domains at the granularity of *registered* domains. Hence, we only add a domain to our blacklist if we observe consistent blocking behavior for all of its subdomains that appear in the respective trace.

Table 4 summarizes the mechanisms used for censorship for the 4 post-porn censorship traces. Table 5 shows the corresponding development of blacklist. We observe the following:

- We find evidence of DNS redirection in all four traces. All ISP resolvers consistently redirect blocked queries to the same ISP-owned address (the same address as used for YouTube censorship). However, non-ISP resolvers resolve the blocked content queries correctly, indicating that the censor does not employ DNS injection such as discussed by Duan et al. [17]. Table 5 lists the number of blacklisted domains per trace that we recover using this indicator.
- We also observe IP blocking for some porn domains. Since this is an ambiguous indicator, we check for any overlap of potential censored domains we find using IP blocking with those found via DNS blocking. We find significant evidence of IP based blocking only in 18Sep12, with a 41% overlap with our DNS blacklist. The TCP state of these connections indicates that the originator never received any response packet from the responder, consistent with blackholing.
- We did not find any instances of users receiving an HTTP block-page either through injection or redirection. Some domains consistently receive no response, but with negligible overlap with our DNS blacklist, except for the last trace, as shown in Table 5. The TCP states of these connections reveal that in a high percentage of the cases, the responder terminated the connection by sending a RST, indicative of likely censorship.

Based on the above observations, we do not find concrete evidence of extensive IP- or HTTP-level blocking for porn, except for the cases where we observe a high overlap with our DNS blacklist. Accordingly, we do not include these ambiguous domains in our blacklist reconstruction. Doing so omits only a handful of potentially blocked domains.

Table 6 illustrates how the porn blacklist evolved over time. We can in addition consider the question of whether the censoring authority acts in a reactive fashion; that is, do they block porn domains that begin to gain popularity with users? In pre-block traces (03Oct11 and 22Oct11), we see 1,313 unique porn domains. We find that 8.2% of these domains were blocked in 21Dec11. After the initial dissemination of the blacklist in 21Dec11, we see a lull in its updating; we observe only ≈ 35 new domains added in each of 28Feb12 and 18Sep12, and no new ones in the last trace. Moreover, the "new" blocked domains have little overlap with porn domains previously observed and unblocked—reinforcing information unofficially shared with us by local operators that the central regulator disseminates blacklists to ISPs and that their development is independent of the porn browsing trends of users. (Section 2).

Summary. Table 4 summarizes our findings on the mechanism of censorship for YouTube and porn as seen in different traces. We find blocking of both YouTube and porn at the DNS-level using redirection in all of the respective post-block traces. In addition, in 18Sep12 we find YouTube blocked using HTTP redirection, and porn using IP blocking, and in 02Aug13 both are blocked using RST injection.

5. METRICS RELEVANT TO CONTENT PROVIDERS

In this section we discuss two key aspects for our study: (i) what constitutes a "content provider" relative to each censorship event, and (ii) the metrics on which we base our assessment of changes resulting from censorship events (note that we can only apply these metrics to unencrypted traffic).

Censorship events affect both primary and alternate providers of the censored content. For the YouTube event, these relate to the general category of *Video Content Platforms*, for which we focus our analysis on four major players: YouTube, DailyMotion, Tune.pk and Vimeo. These constitute the primary video providers for Pakistan as based on their market share [2] and the results of our user survey [45]. For the porn censorship event, we consider all porn domains seen in our traces as identified by McAfee's URL categorization service in April 2014. Given that our most recent trace was captured in August 2013, some domains might have been inaccurately classified.

The primary metric that we employ is *downstream* traffic (server response bytes) served by blocked and alternate content providers, which we will often abbreviate as "bandwidth" for shorthand. We base this choice on the observation that both the censored categories, video and porn, make heavy use of network downloads—what is censored primarily constitutes images and videos. For these categories, downstream bandwidth reasonably captures the degree of user interest in a content provider. This metric also allows us to readily study shifts in traffic trends in the presence of encryption technologies—a potential response to broad category-based censorship.

In addition, for the video category we assess changes in content *embedded* in other sites in response to censorship.[7] This metric captures the broader ecosystem for users viewing videos sometimes in response to other websites that embed a content provider's videos. (Porn content, on the other hand, is presumably only embedded on other porn sites.) After censorship of a content provider, local websites lack an incentive to embed the provider's videos.

We now discuss computing these two metrics:

(i) Direct vs. embedded video viewing requests: To distinguish between these two types of requests, we need to develop *signatures* that classify a given URL as one or the other (or neither) of these. One approach for developing signatures is to analyze traffic dumps collected by actively downloading video content [24]. However, given we collected our traces over a span of three years, we cannot employ an active approach like this, as signatures can change over the years. To develop signatures that can span our datasets, we use a data-driven methodology: for each video content platform, we examine a histogram of its URI root prefixes and associate them with distinct classes of web content based on inspecting the corresponding content type observed in traffic captures, and in some cases entering the full URL into a browser to see if the video plays. This approach provides us with fingerprints for both *direct* and *embedded* viewing request URLs for each video content platform. We note that direct and embedded video watching requests have a consistent signature across traces, perhaps because these span the same domain.

(ii) Bandwidth per content provider: We could compute downstream bandwidth by accumulating server bytes for all HTTP requests where the content provider domain appears in the `Host` header. However, this approach risks missing traffic because: (*i*) content can be served by CDNs (often the case for videos and images), the domain name of which may have no relationship to the host corresponding to the original video/image request, and (*ii*) CDNs typically serve content on behalf of multiple domains, making it infeasible to exclusively associate a given CDN domain with a specific origin server. We might consider accounting for such traffic by accumulating all response bytes for requests where the content provider appears in `Referer`, but doing so will: (i) include bytes belonging to other websites/providers, since the `Referer` might instead reflect the user clicking on a link on the original content provider page that leads to a *different* content provider's page, and (ii) miss bytes belonging to the content provider in cases where an automatic chain of requests traverses multiple domains in order to ultimately reach the CDN.

Putting the above considerations together, we employ the following approaches for estimating traffic volume:

- *Video Content Platforms:* Because these analyses concern just a handful of content providers, for the video category it remains practical to develop URI signatures for each of the four major players. Note that these signatures are different than the *direct* and *embedded* watch signatures, because the video is in general fetched from a URL different than that of the watch page. Along with analysis of active fetches, we analyze all HTTP requests where either `Host` or `Referer` contains the content provider's domain, and the `Content-Type` header in the response is either `application/octet-stream` or contains the keyword "`video`". It follows that we miss video downloads for content providers whose domain name appears in neither the `Host` nor the `Referer` part of an HTTP request. We find that YouTube transfers video using both `video` and `application/octet-stream`. The other three providers, however, only transfer video using a `video` content-type (and sometimes employ `application/octet-stream` for content such as CSS and fonts).

- *Porn Providers:* Accurately attributing porn bandwidth requires a more generic approach, since there are too many providers ($\approx$ 3,800 seen in our traces) to allow us to craft individual signatures. Since a porn site can embed content from other porn sites, when we see a transfer for which both the `Host` domain and the `Referer` domain are labeled as porn in our dataset, we give priority to the former. Specifically, we use the rule: if `Host` has porn domain X, add the corresponding bytes to X; else if `Referer` exists and has a porn domain Y, add corresponding bytes to Y. Otherwise, do not attribute the transfer to any domain.

6. CHANGES IN USER BEHAVIOR

The intrusive nature of Internet censorship will naturally lead to some users altering their behavior in its aftermath. In this section we quantify several perspectives regarding user demand for

[7]Note that we treat links to a content provider's page returned in search results as a form of direct access, rather than "embedded" access, because we presume that often users navigate to such pages via search engines.

Key	Trace	Total	YouTube(%)	Others (%)	Breakdown of Others		
					DailyMotion (%)	Tune.pk (%)	Vimeo (%)
(a) Video Bandwidth (GB)							
–	03Oct11	26.5 GB	97.9	2.1	2.0	0.0	0.1
–	22Oct11	56.6 GB	97.6	2.4	2.4	0.0	≈ 0.0
P	21Dec11	45.2 GB	98.5	1.5	1.3	0.0	0.2
P	28Feb12	12.6 GB	96.9	3.0	3.0	0.0	≈ 0.0
PY	18Sep12	10.7 GB	15.8	84.2	82.0	0.0	2.2
PY	02Aug13	2.7 GB	0.0	100.0	40.9	57.6	1.5
(b) Number of Direct Watch Requests							
–	03Oct11	2,199	99.5	0.5	0.2	0.0	0.2
–	22Oct11	4,550	99.0	1.0	0.9	0.0	0.0
P	21Dec11	3,254	99.3	0.7	0.6	0.0	0.1
P	28Feb12	878	95.7	4.3	4.3	0.0	0.0
PY	18Sep12	992	71.1	28.9	23.2	0.0	5.7
PY	02Aug13	169	46.1	53.8	37.3	14.2	2.4
(c) Number of Embedded Watch Requests							
–	03Oct11	200	87.0	13.0	10.0	0.0	3.0
–	22Oct11	299	78.9	21.1	14.7	0.0	6.4
P	21Dec11	414	92.5	7.5	2.7	0.0	4.8
P	28Feb12	209	86.1	13.9	11.5	0.0	2.4
PY	18Sep12	2,037	73.0	27.0	19.5	0.0	7.5
PY	02Aug13	647	51.8	48.2	32.6	10.7	4.9

Table 8: Distribution of video bandwidth, number of direct and embedded watch requests across major video content providers over time.

Key	Trace	HTTP GB	% Porn	% Video	HTTP:SSL
(a) SOHO Traffic					
–	03Oct11	58.15	11.5	45.5	40.72
–	22Oct11	105.79	11.6	53.6	38.19
P	21Dec11	90.05	3.7	50.2	23.72
P	28Feb12	23.37	2.0	54.3	17.77
PY	18Sep12	91.60	3.0	11.7	3.20
PY	02Aug13	49.66	3.8	5.5	3.25
(b) Residential Traffic					
–	03Oct11	52.10	9.4	—	20.05
–	22Oct11	100.04	7.4	—	50.30
P	21Dec11	66.70	4.0	—	18.22
P	28Feb12	66.23	3.5	—	14.33

Table 7: Ratio of porn and general video traffic to total HTTP byte volume. The last column shows the ratio of HTTP volume to TLS/SSL volume. "—" indicates datapoint not considered in our study (we only use SOHO traffic for analyzing the YouTube block). P=Porn, Y=YouTube

blocked content before censorship, and their persistence and approaches in accessing blocked content after censorship comes into place. While we cannot rule out other factors leading to some of the changes we have observed, the broad scope of the censorship events we consider makes it quite likely that our observations indeed reflect responses to censorship.

6.1 Changes in Traffic

For video traffic, we observe in Table 7(a) that on average video traffic comprised 50% of HTTP traffic before the YouTube block, consistent with global trends (videos comprised 57% of user-generated traffic in 2012 [8]). The overall (unencrypted) video consumption rate drastically declines after the YouTube block, subsequently comprising only 12% of total HTTP traffic in 18Sep12, and declining further to 5.5% in 02Aug13. The decline in video traffic coincides with a decrease of nearly 90% in the HTTP to SSL[8] ratio in 18Sep12, corresponding to the YouTube block day. The ratio remained fairly consistent on this day as viewed hour-to-hour (on average ≈ 3.25), indicating that SOHO users quickly switched to SSL-based circumvention technologies. The trace for this day does not reflect a clear learning phase, suggesting such had already occurred by the time the capture began. The overall trend for SSL traffic remained consistent 11 months later in 02Aug13. This steep increase in SSL traffic post-YouTube-block highlights that most users likely use encrypted tunnels to watch video content after the block. As we note below, the SSL traffic heavily correlates with the use of proxy services, suggesting that it indeed arises due to employment of circumvention measures. Our user study substantiates this conjecture: 57% of the survey participants state they used SSL-based VPN software (UltraSurf, OpenVPN, Hotspot Shield) to access YouTube content.

If we look at direct video requests (either via user navigation, or mediated by clicking on search results), per Table 8(b) we find that the vast majority of direct video requests prior to the block correspond to YouTube (average 98%). Immediately after block (18Sep12), YouTube still receives the highest portion (though reduced by 27%) of direct requests, but the proportion sharply drops 11 months later in 02Aug13 to 46%, with users dispersing the rest of the requests among alternate providers. The decrease in direct YouTube video requests matches our survey results: 40% of respondents mentioned that they do not bother to click on YouTube links due to the blocking; 39% will access the link using a circumvention mechanism; while 17% access the video via an alternate provider.

Table 7 shows that before the blocking, the average porn bandwidth ranged from 8.4–11.5% for residential and SOHO users, respectively. These numbers lie below global estimates that porn comprises 30% of Internet traffic [21]. That we find more porn bandwidth consumed at SOHOs than at homes likely occurs because of higher bandwidths available in SOHO networks. After

[8]We cannot conclusively say if the SSL traffic corresponds to VPNs or HTTPS.

Resolver ASN shorthand (% of DNS queries)					
–	–	P	P	PY	PY
03Oct11	22Oct11	21Dec11	28Feb12	18Sep12	02Aug13
SOHO Traffic					
39,248	64,269	43,655	10,062	13,025	5,036
Local-ISP (99.89)	Local-ISP (99.58)	Local-ISP (98.23)	Local-ISP (91.93)	Local-ISP (68.75)	Local-ISP (74.12)
Google (0.06)	Google (0.28)	Google (1.46)	Google (5.63)	Google (13.69)	Google (19.32)
LEVEL3 (0.04)	LEVEL3 (0.08)	LEVEL3 (0.12)	VPLSNET (1.37)	LEVEL3 (6.96)	LEVEL3 (2.88)
PKTELECOM-AS-PK (0.01)	IPC Computing (0.03)	VPLSNET (0.10)	HINET (0.96)	SPEEDCAST (5.51)	MULTINET (2.70)
VeriSign (0.01)	DIEGOGARCIA (0.02)	HINET (0.08)	OpenDNS (0.11)	OpenDNS (5.08)	Verizon (0.99)
Residential Traffic					
12,739	15,821	6,767	5,451	—	—
Local-ISP (95.50)	Local-ISP (93.89)	Local-ISP (93.08)	Local-ISP (92.20)	—	—
ASVPSHOSTING (3.73)	OpenDNS (5.49)	Google (6.18)	ASVPSHOSTING (4.59)	—	—
Google (0.69)	ASVPSHOSTING (0.49)	ASVPSHOSTING (0.62)	Google (3.05)	—	-
CELCOMNET (0.06)	LEVEL3 (0.11)	LEVEL3 (0.09)	LEVEL3 (0.13)	—	—
OpenDNS (0.02)	TIGGEE (0.01)	OpenDNS (0.03)	OpenDNS (0.04)	—	—

Table 9: Distribution of DNS A/AAAA queries for blocked categories across top 5 DNS resolvers.

the block, the residential porn bandwidth falls by more than half (averaging 3.7% of HTTP bandwidth post-block).

For SOHO traffic, the average porn bandwidth reduces by a factor of three. In contrast to video, we do not observe a significant increase in the HTTP-to-SSL traffic ratio in response to porn censorship, indicating a subset of users either stopped watching porn or shifted to alternate porn providers.[9].

6.2 Impact on User Behavior

Censorship can potentially modify the network behavior of users or result in new behavior driven by trying to access blocked content. In this section we assess this possibility by examining the usage of DNS resolvers and web proxies over time, along with a look at user browsing activities immediately after encountering the block page.

DNS resolvers. For both censorship events we study, the censor employed DNS redirection by local ISP resolvers as the primary means of censorship enforcement. Circumvention to counter this step only requires using an alternate DNS resolver. Table 9 illuminates the degree to which users pursued this option by examining the top-5 DNS resolvers used to resolve DNS A or AAAA queries across the six traces.[10] We find that prior to censorship, local ISP servers resolved at least 90% of queries for both categories. Post-porn censorship, we observe a small increase ($\approx 5\%$) in queries resolved by Google's public DNS resolvers, with a corresponding decrease in queries resolved by the ISP. This number rises to $\approx 13\%$ in post-YouTube censorship traces. At the same time, the queries resolved by local ISP servers drops to 70%, and we see an increase in queries resolved by OpenDNS and LEVEL-3. The use of alternate DNS resolvers to circumvent censorship has appeared in other censorship incidents [37], and potentially increases user exposure to security risks [12].

Web proxies. For each trace we identify unique domains in HTTP requests labeled by McAfee's categorization service as *Anonymizers*. For SOHO traffic, we observe only 1 web proxy prior to the YouTube block, which rises to an average of 41 proxies post-block, with a striking 114 proxies on the day of the block. Residential traffic shares the same pre-block distribution of web proxies as SOHO traffic, though with a less dramatic increase post-block (11.5% on average). From domains extracted from SSL certificates, we find *no* proxy hosts in traces prior to the YouTube block, but after the block we observe 15 and 8 unique proxy hosts (18Sep12 and 02Aug13, respectively). These hosts either operate encrypted by default or provide an easy option for encryption, as confirmed through manual analysis. For example, the top two, `youtubeproxy.org` and `12345proxy.net`, use HTTPS by default, and another popular one, `4everproxy.com` lists HTTPS-based proxies prominently on its home page. In addition, the respondents to our survey indicated that SSL-based software such as OpenVPN and Hotspot Shield are among the most popular circumvention tools. Apparently these tools grew in popularity during the year between our last trace and our survey, as we did not find dominant usage trends for either in our data.

User behavior after viewing block page. We can also gain insight into how users responded to censorship by analyzing their actions after encountering a block page: in particular, whether they then attempt to access similar unblocked content, attempt to employ circumvention, or apparently give up (shift to some other form of activity).

We assess this as follows: for each user encountering a block page, we analyze their HTTP transactions in the subsequent 5-minute window. To reduce ambiguities due to IP aliasing, we confine this analysis to activity from the same address that also uses the same `User Agent`, which we assume is likely stable over short time intervals. (This approach still suffers from the possibility of multiple users behind a single IP address/NAT who employ the same user agent [29].) We then examine a histogram of the domain names and search keywords[11] in the HTTP requests generated by the users. We observe:

- On average 60% of the users performed a search engine query after encountering a block page for a porn domain, and 75% of users did so after encountering a block page for YouTube. Note that these proportions represent a lower

[9]For SOHO traffic, in our additional traces (18Sep12 and 02Aug13) the SSL ratio increases by several orders of magnitude; however this may instead reflect the YouTube censorship that spans this same timeline.

[10]To eliminate bias due to automated DNS queries that might potentially use a diverse set of DNS resolvers, we limit our analysis to queries for the blocked categories, as these unlikely are due to non-human actors.

[11]We developed signatures to extract keywords from popular search engine queries.

Domain Shorthand (% of total porn bandwidth)					
03Oct11	22Oct11	21Dec11	28Feb12	18Sep12	02Aug13
(a) Residential Traffic (GB)					
4.91	7.37	2.67	2.32	—	—
A / 42.3%	$\underline{A}$ / 26.4%	***I*** / 22.8%	***M*** / 23.2%	—	—
B / 12.1%	$\underline{B}$ / 15.4%	**J** / 16.8%	***R*** / 13.7%	—	—
C / 7.9%	*F* / 9.5%	$\bar{A}$ / 7.9%	*S* / 7.3%	—	—
D / 5.9%	$\underline{D}$ / 7.4%	*K* / 5.5%	***T*** / 4.1%	—	—
E / 3.8%	*E* / 3.2%	**L** / 4.1%	**U** / 3.8%	—	—
(b) SOHO Traffic (GB)					
6.71	12.32	3.37	0.47	2.76	1.90
A / 42.4%	$\underline{A}$ / 46.2%	*M* / 27.4%	**V** / 16.5%	R / 14.0%	X / 71.7%
B / 11.3%	$\underline{D}$ / 12.0%	**N** / 8.3%	**W** / 13.4%	**Z** / 12.5%	S / 13.0%
D / 7.5%	$\underline{B}$ / 8.7%	***O*** / 8.3%	*X* (9.3%	*H* / 11.1%	**BB** / 4.9%
G / 3.5%	C / 5.2%	**P** / 4.8%	**Y** / 7.1%	**AA** / 7.8%	**CC** / 1.6%
E / 3.2%	*H* / 2.7%	**Q** / 4.6%	*F* / 6.6%	$\bar{A}$ / 5.5%	**DD** / 1.4%

Table 10: Top five porn domains sorted by bandwidth over time. The top row in parts (a) and (b) represents the total bandwidth in (GB) per trace. Domains with $\overline{\text{bar}}$ are blocked in the given trace. $\underline{\text{Underlined}}$ domains are blocked in the next trace. **Bold** domains are new domains, not seen in previous traces. *Italic* domains are unblocked in the next trace. Others are currently unblocked cases for which we do not have backward or forward reference.

bound because we lack visibility into encrypted traffic.[12] We find that for porn, content-specific searches heavily dominate these queries, rather than searches for porn domains, which matches previous findings that porn users are flexible about served content as long as it falls into a broad class [42]. For YouTube, we find a diverse range of primarily informational queries.[13].

- For porn, on average 70% of users who hit a block page access another porn domain within the next 5 minutes. For YouTube, on the day of the block 7% of users viewed a video using an alternate video content, rising to 12% in 02Aug13. These figures run slightly lower than those from our survey, where 17% of respondents indicated that they would use an alternate provider to access YouTube videos that they find blocked. Tying this in with our earlier result for search queries being dominated by information-retrieval intent, we speculate that users primarily settle for non-video representations of information, rather than actively searching for alternate/unblocked providers to serve a video.

- Surprisingly, we do not find a wide interest in either searching for circumvention mechanisms or directly accessing non-SSL web proxies within our analysis time window. For porn, this is perhaps because users have a tendency to shift to other unblocked porn providers, resulting in little incentive to try circumvention.

7. IMPACT ON CONTENT PROVIDERS

Upon the imposition of censorship, users have a range of options: (*i*) stop accessing the censored content altogether, (*ii*) access the same or similar content hosted by an alternate content provider, or (*iii*) employ a censorship-bypass mechanism to directly access the censored content. The first two options lead to the censored content provider losing a fraction of its previous traffic, the second of these may have a positive impact on the traffic for alternate content providers. The last option potentially increases costs for content providers from the perspective of content distribution: they will have to serve the blocked content remotely, due to the inability to deploy local servers in the censored region. Additionally, if the chosen circumvention mechanism anonymizes user location, the censored content provider can no longer serve geographically-relevant advertisements, which may reduce revenue. While our current study does not concretely establish the economic implications of censorship on content providers, we highlight where these may manifest with a view to motivate further research.

[12]We find that among popular search engines, `google.com.pk` has a dominating presence in our data, and also appears in top-5 servers in the SSL logs.

[13]Queries that represent user intent to obtain information about an object of interest, with potentially a large number of diverse results.

Trace	Total (GB)	Blocked domains (%)	Unblocked (%)
Residential Traffic			
21Dec11	2.67	9.00	91.00
28Feb12	2.32	3.94	96.06
SOHO Traffic			
21Dec11	3.37	0.16	99.84
28Feb12	0.47	0.29	99.71
18Sep12	2.76	10.70	89.30
02Aug13	1.90	0.01	99.99

Table 11: Distribution of porn bandwidth among blocked and unblocked domains. In 21Dec11 and 28Feb12 the censor only uses DNS for blocking, hence users can still access blocked content by using an alternative name server. In 18Sep12, although the censor uses IP blocking in addition to DNS blocking, its blocking is partial for some domains. In 02Aug13, the censor uses a combination of DNS blocking and HTTP redirection.

7.1 Video Content

Table 8(a) illustrates the distribution of video bandwidth among the four major providers before and after the YouTube block. An overwhelming portion (an average of $\approx$ 97% across four pre-block traces) of video content was provided by YouTube, up until the censorship event concurrent with 18Sep12. On that day, only $\approx$ 15% of video content was fetched from YouTube, half of which was being served by local ISP cache servers, and the other half fetched from servers located outside Pakistan. Recall that on that day, one of the two national service providers (with direct international connectivity) redirected YouTube HTTP traffic to one of its own error pages (Section 4). The residual percentage of YouTube traffic perhaps reflects the providers lacking sufficient capacity to handle the full load, and thus it failed to consistently redirect traffic.

The following two findings support this hypothesis. First, the error page initially appeared only five minutes into the trace, suggesting that the censorship was already taking place at the time traffic was captured. Second, we did not find evidence of any incomplete coverage in blocking YouTube's IP address space: we find sets of IP addresses for which both videos were fetched successfully as well as users were redirected to the error pages (for different HTTP requests). The trace collected 11 months later does not manifest any content served from YouTube. This does not necessarily imply that users stopped accessing the site. Indeed, the percentage of encrypted traffic increased manyfold (see SOHO traffic in Table 7), from about 6% in Feb 2012 to over 30% of total traffic post-YouTube censorship, potentially indicating the use of SSL-based censorship bypass mechanisms, as we discussed in Section 6.

Table 8(b) also indicates that post-censorship, most of the video traffic generated from within Pakistan initially switched to DailyMotion (82% of total traffic in 18Sep12), but 11 months later split between DailyMotion (40.9%) and Tune.pk (57.6%). This traffic distribution is unusual considering the global traffic statistics of DailyMotion ($\approx 23x$ more compared to Tune.pk [2]), thus indicating strong regional popularity. Tune.pk is a Pakistani video portal that essentially provides a censorship-friendly wrapper around YouTube. It downloads inoffensive YouTube videos and serves them from its servers with an option for users to report offensive videos [41]. The case of Tune.pk highlights the benefits reaped by local markets due to blocking of a competitor.

The overall shift in traffic potentially leads to a redistribution of advertisement revenue; the censored content provider loses out in favor of alternate providers, a shift exacerbated by the fact that local content owners tend to provide their content through video sharing sites that remain accessible to their viewers without the use of any circumvention technology. We find such a trend in Table 8(c), which shows more and more embedded links shifting from YouTube to other video sharing sites. Most local content is now served through embedded links of unblocked video providers: embedded links pointing to YouTube drop from an average of around 83% to 73% the day of block (18Sep12), to about 51% 11 months later (02Aug13), with DailyMotion getting $\approx$ 32% of embedded links and Tune.pk jumping from virtually no embedding to nearly 11%.

The drop in the percentage of embedded YouTube links also leads to search engines adjusting their page ranks for localized searches. For example, a manual search (country-specific via `google.com.pk`) for top-5 local television shows reveals that the top results point to Tune.pk and DailyMotion, while a search for non-local content (top-5 television shows in USA) returns top results referencing YouTube.

In summary, the censored video content provider loses traffic and revenue to competing non-censored sites in multiple ways: direct reduction of traffic, local content providers moving their hosted channels to alternate providers, reduced embedded referencing in third-party pages, and lower page rank for localized search. The provider potentially also loses revenue due to the increased expense of serving the content via the distribution channels available to circumventers. For non-censored providers, these considerations may provide an incentive to take long-term control over local content. For example, DailyMotion has recently moved to partner with the largest ISP in the country [15].

7.2 Porn Content

For each trace, we ranked the porn sites in accordance with their traffic served into the country, measured using the methodology described in Section 5. Table 10 shows the top-5 coded porn domains for each trace. We observe that prior to blocking, globally popular domains [2] top the list. After the blocking event, new players emerge and take the top spots. In most cases, these new players were non-existent in previous traces (indicated with bold in the table), and their relative distribution across post-block traces vary inconsistently. (We do see a few domains, such as X, S and R, that appear in the top-5 for more than one trace.) We speculate that users are familiar with a few favorite porn websites, but, after blocking, find out about alternatives through search engines, hence the variety in the top ranked sites. This possibility fits with the finding in Section 6 that after landing on a block page, porn users tend to perform content-specific search queries.

Similar to the non-porn video sharing sites, censoring a porn site also impairs its revenue share from within the censored region. In Table 11 we analyze the bandwidth distribution among blocked and unblocked porn websites. We observe that the bulk of the bandwidth is captured by unblocked porn domains. (An exception to the case is $\bar{A}$, which appears in a subsequent trace despite being blocked in 21Dec11—circumvention is made possible by obtaining correct IP addresses via non-local resolvers.) The popularity of new porn domains can also be explained by the fact that after the initial introduction of the porn blacklist (21Dec11), there seems to be no aggressive strategy by the censor to block new popular porn content.

8. IMPACT ON SERVICE PROVIDERS

In this section we assess the consequences of the censorship events on ISPs. We examine this in terms of analyzing the operator's web caching behavior, focusing on the video content from the four major providers, since our pre-block traces indicate that videos constitute the content ($\approx$ 95%) served by the ISP's cache servers.[14]

Table 12 lists the top-5 ASNs serving video content for each of the traces.[15] Prior to the YouTube blocking, the top ASN is the local ISP—on average its caching servers provided 76% of the video content. On the day of blocking, we still see the ISP's caching servers providing a small fraction of YouTube video content. This leakage indicates that, initially, the ISP's censorship implementation was incomplete; its caching servers had not completely flushed cached YouTube content, and hence still served it upon request. (Recall that the block was put in place on the day of capture; some users could potentially get correct answers for YouTube from their local DNS cache, or by using alternate DNS resolvers as previously discussed.)

Moving forward 11 months, the local ISP completely falls off the charts to be replaced by CDNs serving DailyMotion and Tune.pk videos. Indeed, we find the ISP's cache servers completely absent from 02Aug13, and the ISP confirmed to us that the systems no longer provided any utility. Based on discussions with the ISP operators, we learned two reasons for this. First, Google had provided free caching servers to Pakistani ISPs, infrastructure tailored specifically to YouTube-caching. The other video content providers do not offer such free caching solutions, leaving it difficult for the local ISPs to justify the cost of deploying and maintaining custom solutions for the providers' content. Second, the drastic decrease in unencrypted video content (Table 7) made it hard to justify the benefits of caching, since ISPs cannot in general cache encrypted content. The ISPs instead turned to the option of leasing more upstream bandwidth, rather than buying and maintaining caching servers.

Consequently, today all video content is primarily fetched from the servers of their respective providers. Indeed, the operators we acquired traces from had to purchase additional Internet bandwidth after the block.

9. CONCLUSIONS AND FUTURE WORK

We have studied the impact of Internet censorship on major stakeholders (service providers, content providers, and end users) in the context of two major censorship events in Pakistan, the block of porn content in 2011, and of YouTube in 2012. To this end, we analyzed home and SOHO traffic before, during, and after the censorship events, from the vantage point of a mid-size ISP in a large metropolitan area. As the foundation of our analysis, we de-

[14]We establish this by looking at the distribution of `Content Type` served by the ISP's caching servers.

[15]Labovitz noted that content delivery shifted to European servers after MegaUpload servers in North America were seized [28]. Our study focuses on alternate content providers when the primary has been blocked, and the implications of their infrastructural arrangements on an operator.

ASN (% of total video bandwidth)					
03Oct11	22Oct11	21Dec11	28Feb12	**18Sep12**	**02Aug13**
26.5 GB	56.5 GB	45.2 GB	12.6 GB	10.7 GB	2.7 GB
Local-ISP, PK (78.69)	Local-ISP, PK (82.08)	Local-ISP, PK (70.08)	Local-ISP, PK (76.21)	Dailymotion, FR (45.67)	FIBERRING, NL (58.67)
Google, US (17.85)	Google, US (13.74)	Google, US (24.74)	Google, US (17.62)	TMNET, MY (22.99)	Dailymotion, FR (19.76)
YouTube, IE (1.46)	YouTube, IE (1.68)	YouTube, IE (3.71)	YouTube, IE (3.15)	Local-ISP, PK (7.22)	OMANTEL, OM (14.01)
Dailymotion, FR (1.23)	Dailymotion, FR (1.41)	EdgeCast, US (0.68)	Dailymotion, FR (2.93)	Tinet, DE (4.11)	Akamai, US (7.70)
CCWW, GB (0.80)	Akamai, US (0.84)	Dailymotion, FR (0.62)	EdgeCast, US (0.12)	YouTube, IE (3.98)	Tinet, DE (0.68)

Table 12: Top 5 ASNs serving video, ranked by bandwidth. Bold indicates YouTube blocking. The top row gives the total video bandwidth. In our traces, FIBERRING serves Tune.pk videos, while OMANTEL, TMNET, CCWW, Tinet, Akamai, and EdgeCast primarily serve DailyMotion videos.

veloped methodologies to identify censorship activity within our packet traces with high confidence.

We observed that blocking of porn content caused increases in encrypted traffic (Table 7) but primarily users turned to alternative sites (Table 10). In contrast, YouTube blocking caused a major shift towards increased encrypted traffic, indicating that users resorted to circumvention mechanisms to continue their access. In addition, we find this shift well underway already on the day that the government imposed censorship, indicating that a portion of users can very rapidly adapt to the introduction of new blocking mechanisms.

Censorship of YouTube also affected the financial landscape of video content providers (Table 8). New players emerged and completely took over the video-sharing market that previously was almost wholly owned by YouTube prior to its blocking. This shift also had consequences for ISPs that previously served video content primarily from YouTube caches (freely provided by Google) hosted within their own networks. Post-YouTube blocking, the ISPs must fetch video content through their upstream transit provider, reflecting an increase in bandwidth costs. After the YouTube blocking was implemented at the local-ISP level (using DNS spoofing), we observe a shift away from the use of the local ISP's DNS resolvers, dropping from more than 90% pre-blocking to about 70% post-blocking. We note that such a shift somewhat erodes a nation's overall control over its Internet traffic as users transfer their base of trust (i.e., DNS resolution) to parties outside the country.

Following up on this work, we plan to analyze additional data from a different ISP in another large city in Pakistan to assess trends seen across cities and providers. The expectation in Pakistan is that porn blocking will continue in the future, but YouTube censorship will soon end [16]. If that indeed happens, it will be illuminating to study whether the proportion of encrypted traffic returns to pre-censorship levels; whether users continue to outsource their DNS resolution; and the degree to which video traffic distribution between YouTube and alternate video sharing sites readjusts.

Acknowledgements

This work was supported by the Engineering and Physical Sciences Research Council [grant number EP/L003406/1]; and the US National Science Foundation [grant numbers 1223717, 1237265]. Opinions expressed are solely those of the authors. We thank Jon Crowcroft, Steven Murdoch and Balachander Krishnamurthy for feedback on different parts of this paper. We also thank our shepherd, Olaf Maennel, the anonymous reviewers for their useful comments, and the anonymous ISP for facilitating access to their data.

10. REFERENCES

[1] S. Alcock and R. Nelson. Measuring the impact of the copyright amendment act on New Zealand residential DSL users. In *Proc. ACM Internet Measurement Conference*, 2012.

[2] Alexa. `http://www.alexa.com/topsites`. Online. April, 2014.

[3] Anonymous. The Collateral Damage of Internet Censorship by DNS Injection. *SIGCOMM Comput. Commun. Rev.*, 42(3):21–27, June 2012.

[4] S. Aryan, H. Aryan, and J. A. Halderman. Internet Censorship in Iran: A First Look. In *Free and Open Communications on the Internet*, Washington, DC, USA, 2013. USENIX.

[5] A. Attaa. `http://tinyurl.com/mnw9olp`. Online. Feb, 2014.

[6] Bro. `http://www.bro.org/`. Online. April, 2014.

[7] A. Chaabane, M. Cunche, T. Chen, A. Friedman, E. D. Cristofaro, and M.-A. Kaafar. Censorship in the Wild: Analyzing Web Filtering in Syria. Technical report, Cornell University Library, Feb. 2014.

[8] Cisco. `http://tinyurl.com/mev32z8`. Online. Apr, 2014.

[9] Citizen Lab. O Pakistan, We Stand on Guard for Thee: An Analysis of Canada-based Netsweeper's Role in Pakistan's Censorship Regime. `http://tinyurl.com/oxxap8t`, June 2013.

[10] M. Cooper. `http://tinyurl.com/p7ck76f`. Online. Feb, 2014.

[11] J. R. Crandall, D. Zinn, M. Byrd, E. Barr, and R. East. ConceptDoppler: A Weather Tracker for Internet Censorship. In *Computer and Communications Security*. ACM, 2007.

[12] S. Crocker, D. Dagon, D. Kaminsky, D. McPherson, and P. Vixie. Security and Other Technical Concerns Raised by the DNS Filtering Requirements in the PROTECT IP Bill. `http://domainincite.com/docs/PROTECT-IP-Technical-Whitepaper-Final.pdf`, May 2011.

[13] A. Dainotti, C. Squarcella, E. Aben, K. C. Claffy, M. Chiesa, M. Russo, and A. Pescapé. Analysis of country-wide internet outages caused by censorship. In *Proceedings of the 2011 ACM SIGCOMM Conference on Internet Measurement Conference*, IMC '11, pages 1–18, New York, NY, USA, 2011. ACM.

[14] J. Dalek, B. Haselton, H. Noman, A. Senft, M. Crete-Nishihata, P. Gill, and R. J. Deibert. A Method for Identifying and Confirming the Use of URL Filtering Products for Censorship. In *Proc. ACM Internet Measurement Conference*, 2013.

[15] Dawn. `http://tinyurl.com/n3j22gy`. Online. April, 2014.

[16] Dawn News. `http://tinyurl.com/m7vhg7u`. Online. Apr, 2014.

[17] H. Duan, N. Weaver, Z. Zhao, M. Hu, J. Liang, J. Jiang, K. Li, and V. Paxson. Hold-On: Protecting Against On-Path DNS Poisoning. In *Proc. Workshop on Securing and Trusting Internet Names*, SATIN 2012.

[18] Electronic Frontier Foundation (EFF). `http://tinyurl.com/oklfy29`. Online. Apr, 2014.

[19] ElectronicFrontierFoundation. Switzerland. `http://tinyurl.com/d22vbbq`.

[20] A. M. Espinoza and J. R. Crandall. Automated Named Entity Extraction for Tracking Censorship of Current Events. In *USENIX Workshop on Free and Open Communications on the Internet*, 2011.

[21] ExtremeTech. `http://tinyurl.com/6nabr85`. Online. Apr, 2014.

[22] R. Farahbakhsh, Ã. Cuevas, R. Cuevas, R. Rejaie, M. Kryczka, R. Gonzalez, and N. Crespi. Investigating the reaction of BitTorrent content publishers to antipiracy actions. In *P2P*, pages 1–10. IEEE, 2013.

[23] A. Filastò and J. Appelbaum. OONI: Open Observatory of Network Interference. In *Free and Open Communications on the Internet*. USENIX Association, 2012.

[24] P. Gill, M. Arlitt, Z. Li, and A. Mahanti. Youtube traffic characterization: A view from the edge. In *Proceedings of the 7th ACM SIGCOMM Conference on Internet Measurement*, IMC '07, pages 15–28, New York, NY, USA, 2007. ACM.

[25] Internet Service Providers Association of Pakistan (ISPAK). `http://www.ispak.pk`. Online. Apr, 2014.

[26] C. Kreibich, N. Weaver, B. Nechaev, and V. Paxson. Netalyzr: illuminating the edge network. In *Proc. ACM Internet Measurement Conference*, 2010.

[27] C. Lab. Routing Gone Wild: Documenting upstream filtering in Oman via India. Technical report, Citizen Lab, 2012.

[28] C. Labovitz. The Other 50% of the Internet. North American Network Operators' Group (NANOG) presentation, February 2012.

[29] G. Maier, F. Schneider, and A. Feldmann. NAT Usage in Residential Broadband Networks. In *Proc. Passive and Active Measurement*, 2011.

[30] McAfee. `http://www.trustedsource.org`. Online. Apr, 2014.

[31] Mozilla. `https://wiki.mozilla.org/Public_Suffix_List`. Online. Apr, 2014.

[32] Z. Nabi. The Anatomy of Web Censorship in Pakistan. In *Proc. USENIX Workshop on Free and Open Communications on the Internet*, 2013.

[33] F. News. `http://tinyurl.com/22me5e7`. Online. Feb, 2014.

[34] OpenNet Initiative. Pakistan. Online. April, 2014.

[35] OpenNet Initiative. `https://opennet.net`. Online. Apr, 2014.

[36] P. Reidy. US court orders Google to remove Innocence of Muslims film from YouTube. `http://tinyurl.com/mjd9sjk`. Feb, 2014.

[37] Renesys. Turkish Internet Censorship Takes a New Turn. `http://www.renesys.com/2014/03/turkish-internet-censorship/`, 2014.

[38] Security Information Exchange. `https://www.dnsdb.info/`. Online. Apr, 2014.

[39] A. Sfakianakis, E. Athanasopoulos, and S. Ioannidis. CensMon: A Web Censorship Monitor. In *USENIX Workshop on Free and Open Communications on the Internet*, 2011.

[40] TeamCymru. IP to ASN Mapping. `http://tinyurl.com/5dtp78`. Apr, 2014.

[41] Techniasia. Tune.pk comes up with a way to bypass Pakistan's YouTube block. `http://tinyurl.com/mdgb2ke`. Apr, 2014.

[42] G. Tyson, Y. Elkhatib, N. Sastry, and S. Uhlig. Demystifying porn 2.0: A look into a major adult video streaming website. In *Proceedings of the 2013 Internet Measurement Conference*, IMC '13, pages 417–426, New York, NY, USA, 2013. ACM.

[43] J.-P. Verkamp and M. Gupta. Inferring Mechanics of Web Censorship Around the World. In *Free and Open Communications on the Internet*, Bellevue, WA, USA, 2012. USENIX.

[44] N. Weaver, R. Sommer, and V. Paxson. Detecting Forged TCP Reset Packets. In *Proc. NDSS*, 2009.

[45] YouTube and Blocking in Pakistan. Has it affected you? `http://tinyurl.com/kcvj325`. Online. April, 2014.

Censorship in the Wild: Analyzing Internet Filtering in Syria

Abdelberi Chaabane
INRIA Rhône-Alpes
Montbonnot, France

Terence Chen
NICTA
Sydney, Australia

Mathieu Cunche
University of Lyon & INRIA
Lyon, France

Emiliano De Cristofaro
University College London
London, United Kingdom

Arik Friedman
NICTA
Sydney, Australia

Mohamed Ali Kaafar
NICTA & INRIA Rhône-Alpes
Sydney, Australia

ABSTRACT

Internet censorship is enforced by numerous governments worldwide, however, due to the lack of publicly available information, as well as the inherent risks of performing active measurements, it is often hard for the research community to investigate censorship practices in the wild. Thus, the leak of 600GB worth of logs from 7 Blue Coat SG-9000 proxies, deployed in Syria to filter Internet traffic at a country scale, represents a unique opportunity to provide a detailed snapshot of a real-world censorship ecosystem.

This paper presents the methodology and the results of a measurement analysis of the leaked Blue Coat logs, revealing a relatively stealthy, yet quite targeted, censorship. We find that traffic is filtered in several ways: using IP addresses and domain names to block subnets or websites, and keywords or categories to target specific content. We show that keyword-based censorship produces some collateral damage as many requests are blocked even if they do not relate to sensitive content. We also discover that Instant Messaging is heavily censored, while filtering of social media is limited to specific pages. Finally, we show that Syrian users try to evade censorship by using web/socks proxies, Tor, VPNs, and BitTorrent. To the best of our knowledge, our work provides the first analytical look into Internet filtering in Syria.

Categories and Subject Descriptors

K.5.2 [**Legal Aspects of Computing**]: Governmental Issues—*Censorship*; K.4.1 [**Computers and Society**]: Public Policy Issues—*Privacy*

Keywords

Censorship; Internet Filtering; Measurements

1. INTRODUCTION

As the relation between society and technology evolves, so does censorship—the practice of suppressing ideas and information that certain individuals, groups or government officials may find objectionable, dangerous, or detrimental. Censors increasingly target access to, and dissemination of, electronic information, for instance, aiming to restrict freedom of speech, control knowledge available to the masses, or enforce religious/ethical principles.

Even though the research community dedicated a lot of attention to censorship and its circumvention, knowledge and understanding of filtering technologies is inherently limited, as it is challenging and risky to conduct measurements from countries operating censorship, while logs pertaining to filtered traffic are obviously hard to come by. Prior work has analyzed censorship practices in China [14, 15, 20, 29, 30], Iran [2, 4, 26], Pakistan [18], and a few Arab countries [10], however, mostly based on probing, i.e., *inferring* what information is being censored by generating requests and observing what content is blocked. While providing valuable insights, these methods suffer from two main limitations: (1) only a limited number of requests can be observed, thus providing a skewed representation of the censorship policies due to the inability to enumerate all censored keywords, and (2) it is hard to assess the actual extent of the censorship, e.g., what kind/proportion of the overall traffic is being censored.

Roadmap. In this paper, we present a measurement analysis of Internet filtering in Syria: we study a set of logs extracted from 7 Blue Coat SG-9000 proxies, which were deployed to monitor, filter and block traffic of Syrian users. The logs (600GB worth of data) were leaked by a "hacktivist" group, Telecomix, in October 2011, and relate to a period of 9 days between July and August 2011 [23]. By analyzing the logs, we provide a detailed snapshot of how censorship was operated in Syria. As opposed to probing-based methods, the analysis of actual logs allows us to extract information about processed requests for *both* censored and allowed traffic and provide a detailed snapshot of Syrian censorship practices.

Main Findings. Our measurement-based analysis uncovers several interesting findings. First, we observe that a few different techniques are employed by Syrian authorities: IP-based filtering to block access to entire subnets (e.g., Israel), domain-based to block specific websites, keyword-based to target specific kinds of traffic (e.g., filtering-evading technologies, such as socks proxies), and category-based to target specific content and pages. As a side-effect of keyword-based censorship, many requests are blocked even if they do not relate to any sensitive content or anti-censorship technologies. Such collateral damage affects Google toolbar's queries as well as a few ads delivery networks that are blocked as they generate requests containing the word *proxy*.

Also, the logs highlight that Instant Messaging software (like Skype) is heavily censored, while filtering of social media is limited to specific pages. Actually, most social networks (e.g., Facebook and Twitter) are not blocked, but only certain pages/groups are (e.g., the Syrian Revolution Facebook page). We find that proxies have specialized roles and/or slightly different configurations, as some of them tend to censor more traffic than others. For instance, one particular proxy blocks Tor traffic for several days, while other

IMC'14, November 5–7, 2014, Vancouver, BC, Canada.

http://dx.doi.org/10.1145/2663716.2663720.

proxies do not. Finally, we show that Syrian Internet users not only try to evade censorship and surveillance using well-known web/socks proxies, Tor, and VPN software, but also use P2P file sharing software (BitTorrent) to fetch censored content.

Our analysis shows that, compared to other countries (e.g., China and Iran), censorship in Syria seems to be less pervasive, yet quite targeted. Syrian censors particularly target Instant Messaging, information related to the political opposition (e.g., pages related to the "Syrian Revolution"), and Israeli subnets. Arguably, less evident censorship does not necessarily mean minor information control or less ubiquitous surveillance. In fact, Syrian users seem to be aware of this and do resort to censorship- and surveillance-evading software, as we show later in the paper, which seems to confirm reports about Syrian users enganging in self-censorship to avoid being arrested [3, 5, 19].

Contributions. To the best of our knowledge, we provide the first detailed snapshot of Internet filtering in Syria and the first set of large-scale measurements of actual filtering proxies' logs. We show how censorship was operated via a statistical overview of censorship activities and an analysis of temporal patterns, proxy specializations, and filtering of social network sites. Finally, we provide some details on the usage of surveillance- and censorship-evading tools.

Remarks. Logs studied in this paper date back to July-August 2011, thus, our work is not intended to provide insights to the *current* situation in Syria as censorship might have evolved in the last two years. According to Bloomberg [22], Syria has invested $500K in surveillance equipment in late 2011, thus an even more powerful filtering architecture might now be in place. Starting December 2012, Tor relays and bridges have reportedly been blocked [24]. Nonetheless, our analysis uncovers methods that might still be in place, e.g., based on Deep Packet Inspection. Also, Blue Coat proxies are reportedly still used in several countries [17].

Our work serves as a case study of censorship in practice: it provides a first-of-its-kind, data-driven analysis of a real-world censorship ecosystem, exposing its underlying techniques, as well as its strengths and weaknesses, which we hope will facilitate the design of censorship-evading tools.

Paper Organization. The rest of this paper is organized as follows. The next section reviews related work. Then, Section 3 provides some background information and introduces the datasets studied throughout the paper. Section 4 presents a statistical overview of Internet censorship in Syria based on the Blue Coat logs, while Section 5 provides a thorough analysis to better understand censorship practices. After focusing on social network sites in Section 6 and anti-censorship technologies in Section 7, we discuss our findings in Section 8. The paper concludes with Section 9.

2. RELATED WORK

Due to the limited availability of publicly available data, there is little prior work analyzing logs from filtering devices. A fairly large body of work, which we overview in this section, has focused on understanding and characterizing censorship processes via probing. By contrast, our work is really the first to analyze traffic observed by actual filtering proxies and to provide a detailed measurement-based snapshot of Syria's censorship infrastructure.

Ayran et al. [4] present measurements from an Iranian ISP, analyzing HTTP host-based blocking, keyword filtering, DNS hijacking, and protocol-based throttling, and conclude that the censorship infrastructure heavily relies on centralized equipment. Winter and Lindskog [29] conduct some measurements on traffic routed through Tor bridges/relays to understand how China blocks Tor. Also, Dainotti et al. [9] analyze country-wide Internet outages, in Egypt and Libya, using publicly available data such as BGP inter-domain routing control plane data.

Another line of work deals with fingerprinting and inferring censorship methods and equipments. Researchers from the Citizen Lab [17] focus on censorship/surveillance performed using Blue Coat devices and uncover 61 Blue Coat ProxySG devices and 316 Blue Coat PacketShaper appliances in 24 different countries. Dalek et al. [10] use a confirmation methodology to identify URL filtering using, e.g., McAfee SmartFilter and Netsweeper, and detect the use of these technologies in Saudi Arabia, UAE, Qatar, and Yemen.

Nabi [18] uses a publicly available list of blocked websites in Pakistan, checking their accessibility from multiple networks within the country. Results indicate that censorship varies across websites: some are blocked at the DNS level, while others at the HTTP level. Furthermore, Verkamp and Gupta [26] detect censorship technologies in 11 countries, mostly using Planet Labs nodes, and discover DNS-based and router-based filtering. Crandall et al. [8] propose an architecture for maintaining a censorship "weather report" about what keywords are filtered over time, while Leberknight et al. [16] provide an overview of research on censorship resistant systems and a taxonomy of anti-censorship technologies.

Also, Knockel et al. [15] obtain a built-in list of censored keywords in China's TOM-Skype and run experiments to understand how filtering is operated, while King et al. [14] devise a system to locate, download, and analyze the content of millions of Chinese social media posts, before the Chinese government censors them.

Finally, Park and Crandall [20] present results from measurements of the filtering of HTTP HTML responses in China, which is based on string matching and TCP reset injection by backbone-level routers. Xu et al. [30] explore the AS-level topology of China's network infrastructure, and probe the firewall to find the locations of filtering devices, finding that even though most filtering occurs in border ASes, choke points also exist in many provincial networks.

3. DATASETS DESCRIPTION

This section overviews the dataset studied in this paper, and background information on the proxies used for censorship.

3.1 Data Sources

On October 4, 2011, a "hacktivist" group called Telecomix announced the release of log files extracted from 7 Syrian Blue Coat SG-9000 proxies (aka ProxySG) [23]. The initial leak concerned 15 proxies but only data from 7 of them was publicly released. As reported by the Wall Street Journal [25] and CBS news [28], Blue Coat openly acknowledged that at least 13 of its proxies were used in Syria, but denied it authorized their sale to the Syrian government [6]. These devices have allegedly been used by the Syrian Telecommunications Establishment (STE backbone) to filter and monitor all connections at a country scale. The data is split by proxy (SG-42, SG-43,. . ., SG-48) and covers two periods: (i) July 22, 23, 31, 2011 (only SG-42), and (ii) August 1–6, 2011 (all proxies). The leaked log files are in csv format (comma separated-values) and include 26 fields, such as date, time, filter action, host and URI (more details are given in Section 3.3).

Given the nature of the dataset, one could question the authenticity of the logs. However, Blue Coat *confirmed* the use of its devices in Syria [25, 28] and a few findings emerging from the analysis of the logs actually correspond to events and facts that were independently reported before. Also, this leak is not the first censorship-related project carried out by Telecomix. Thus, we are confident that the datasets studied in this paper provide an accurate snapshot of Syrian censorship activities in Summer 2011.

3.2 Blue Coat SG-9000 Proxies

The Blue Coat SG-9000 proxies perform filtering, monitoring, and caching of Internet traffic, and are typically placed between a monitored network and the Internet backbone. They can be set as *explicit* or *transparent* proxies: the former setting requires the configuration of the clients' browsers, whereas transparent proxies seamlessly intercept traffic (i.e., without clients noticing it), which is the case in this dataset.

Monitoring and filtering of traffic is conducted at the application level. Each user request is intercepted and classified as one of the following three labels (as per the *sc-filter-result* field in the logs):

- `OBSERVED` – request is served to the client.
- `PROXIED` – request has been found in the cache and the outcome depends on the cached value.
- `DENIED` – request is not served to the client because an exception has been raised (might be redirected).

The classification reflects the action that the proxy needs to perform, rather than the outcome of a filtering process. `OBSERVED` means that content needs to be fetched from the Origin Content Server (OCS), `DENIED` that there is no need to contact the OCS, and `PROXIED` – that the outcome is in the proxy's cache. According to Blue Coat's documentation [27], filtering is based on multiple criteria: website categories, keywords, content type, browser type and date/time of day. The proxies can also cache content, e.g., to save bandwidth, in the "bandwidth gain profile" (see page 193 in [1]).

3.3 Datasets and Notation

Throughout the rest of this paper, our analysis will use the following four datasets:

1. ***Full Logs*** (D_{full}): The whole dataset (i.e., extracted from all logs) is composed of 751,295,830 requests.

2. ***Sample Dataset*** (D_{sample}): Most of the results shown in this paper rely on the full extraction of the relevant data from D_{full}, however, given the massive size of the log files (~600GB), we sometimes consider a *random* sample covering 4% of the entire dataset. This dataset (D_{sample}) is only used to illustrate a few results, specifically, for a few summary statistics. According to standard theory about confidence intervals for proportions (see [13], Equation 1, Chapter 13.9.2), for a sample size of n = 32M, the actual proportion in the full data set lies in an interval of ± 0.0001 around the proportion p observed in the sample with 95% probability ($\alpha = 0.05$).

3. ***User Dataset*** (D_{user}): Before the data release, Telecomix suppressed user identifiers (IP addresses) by replacing them with zeros. However, for a small fraction of the data (July 22-23), user identifiers were replaced with the hash of the IP addresses, thus making user-based analysis possible.

4. ***Denied Dataset*** (D_{denied}): This dataset contains all the requests that resulted in exceptions (*x-exception-id* $\neq$ '-'), and hence are not served to the user.

In Table 1, we report, for each dataset, the number of requests in it, corresponding dates, and number of proxies. Then, in Table 2, we list a few fields from the logs that constitute the main focus of our analysis. The *s-ip* field logs the IP address of the proxy that processed each request, which is in the range 82.137.200.42 – 48. Throughout the paper we refer to the proxies as SG-42 to SG-48, according to the suffix of their IP address. The *sc-filter-result* field indicates whether the request has been served to the client. In the rest of the paper, we consider as *denied* all requests

Dataset	# Requests	Period	# Proxies
Full	751,295,830	July 22-23,31, 2011 August 1-6, 2011	7
Sample (4%)	32,310,958	July 22-23, 2011 August 1-6, 2011	7
User	6,374,333	July 22-23 2011	1
Denied	47,452,194	July 22-23,31, 2011 August 1-6, 2011	7

Table 1: Datasets description.

Field name	Description
cs-host	Hostname or IP address (e.g., facebook.com)
cs-uri-scheme	Scheme used by the requested URL (mostly HTTP)
cs-uri-port	Port of the requested URL
cs-uri-path	Path of the requested URL (e.g., /home.php)
cs-uri-query	Query of the requested URL (e.g., ?refid=7&ref=nf_fr&_rdr)
cs-uri-ext	Extension of the requested URL (e.g., php, flv, gif, ...)
cs-user-agent	User agent (from request header)
cs-categories	Categories to which the requested URL has been classified (see Section 4 for details)
c-ip	Client's IP address (removed or anonymized)
s-ip	The IP address of the proxy that processed the client's request
sc-status	Protocol status code from the proxy to the client (e.g., '200' for OK)
sc-filter-result	Content filtering result: `DENIED`, `PROXIED`, or `OBSERVED`
x-exception-id	Exception raised by the request (e.g., *policy_denied*, *dns_error*). Set to '-' if no exception was raised.

Table 2: Description of a few relevant fields from the logs.

that have not been successfully served to the client by the proxy, including requests generating network errors as well as requests censored based on policy. To further classify a denied request, we rely on the *x-exception-id* field: all denied requests which either raise *policy_denied* or *policy_redirect* flags are considered as *censored*.

Finally, we observe some inconsistencies in the requests that have a *sc-filter-result* value set to `PROXIED` with no exception. When looking at requests similar to those that are `PROXIED` (e.g., other requests from the same user accessing the same URL), some are consistently denied, while others are sometimes or always allowed. Since `PROXIED` requests only represent a small portion of the analyzed traffic ($< 0.5\%$), we treat them like the rest of the traffic and classify them according to the *x-exception-id*. However, where relevant, we refer to them explicitly to distinguish them from the `OBSERVED` traffic.

In summary, throughout the rest of the paper, we use the following request classification:

- *Allowed* (*x-exception-id* = '-'): a request that is allowed and served to the client (no exception raised).
- *Denied* (*x-exception-id* $\neq$ '-'): a request that is not served to the client, either because of a network error or due to censorship. Specifically:
  - *Censored* (*x-exception-id* $\in$ {*policy_denied*, *policy_redirect*}): a *denied* request that is censored based on censorship policy.
  - *Error* (*x-exception-id* $\notin$ {'-', *policy_denied*, *policy_redirect*}): a *denied* request not served to the client due to a network error.
- *Proxied* (*sc-filter-result* = `PROXIED`): a request that does not need further processing, as the response is in the cache (i.e., the result depends on a prior computation). The request can

be either allowed or denied, even if *x-exception-id* does not indicate an exception.

3.4 Ethical Considerations

Even though the dataset studied in this paper is publicly available, we are obviously aware of its sensitivity. Thus, we enforced a few mechanisms to safeguard privacy of Syrian Internet users. We encrypted all data (and backups) at rest and did not re-distribute the logs. We never obtained or extracted users' personal information, and we only analyzed aggregated traffic statistics. While it is out of the scope of this paper to further discuss the ethics of using "leaked data" for research purposes (see [12] for a detailed discussion), we argue that analyzing logs of filtered traffic, as opposed to probing-based measurements, provides an accurate view for a large-scale and comprehensive analysis of censorship.[1]

We acknowledge that our work may be beneficial to entities on either side of censorship. However, our analysis helps understand the technical aspects of an actual censorship ecosystem. Our methodology exposes its underlying technologies, policies, as well as its strengths and weaknesses, and can thus facilitate the design of censorship-evading tools.

4. A STATISTICAL OVERVIEW OF CENSORSHIP IN SYRIA

Aiming to provide an overview of Internet censorship in Syria, our first step is to compare the statistical distributions of the different classes of traffic (as defined in Section 3.3), and also look at domains, TCP/UDP ports, website categories, and HTTPS traffic. Unless explicitly stated otherwise, the results presented in this section are based on the full dataset denoted as D_{full} (see Section 3.3).

Traffic distribution. We start by observing the ratio of the different classes of traffic. For each of the datasets D_{sample}, D_{user} and D_{denied}, Table 3 reports how many requests are allowed, proxied, denied, or censored. In D_{sample}, more than 93% of the requests are allowed, and less than 1% of them are censored due to policy-based decisions. The number of censored requests seems relatively low compared to the number of allowed requests. Note, however, that these numbers are skewed because of the request-based logging mechanism, which "inflates" the volume of allowed traffic; a single access to a website may trigger a large number of requests (e.g., for the HTML content, accompanying images, scripts, tracking websites and so on) that will be logged, whereas a *denied* request (either because it has been censored or due to a network error) only generates one log entry. Finally, note that only a small fraction of requests are proxied (0.47% in D_{sample}). The breakdown of *x-exception-id* values within the proxied requests resembles that of the overall traffic.

Denied traffic. Proxies also log requests that have been denied due to network errors: this happens for less than 6% of the requests in our sample. The inability of the proxy to handle the request (identified by the *x-exception-id* field being set to *internal_error*) accounts for 31.15% of the overall denied traffic. Although this could be considered censorship (no data is received by the user), these requests do not actually trigger any policy exception and are not the result of policy-based censorship. TCP errors, typically occurring during the connection establishment between the proxy and the target destination, represent more than 45% of the denied traffic. Other errors include DNS resolving issues (0.41%), invalid HTTP request or response formatting (5.65%), and unsupported protocols (1.46%). The remaining 15.33% of denied traffic represent the actual censored requests, which the proxy flags as denied due to policy enforcement.

[1]Note that we obtained the approval of INRIA's and NICTA's Institutional Review Board (IRB) to publish results of this work.

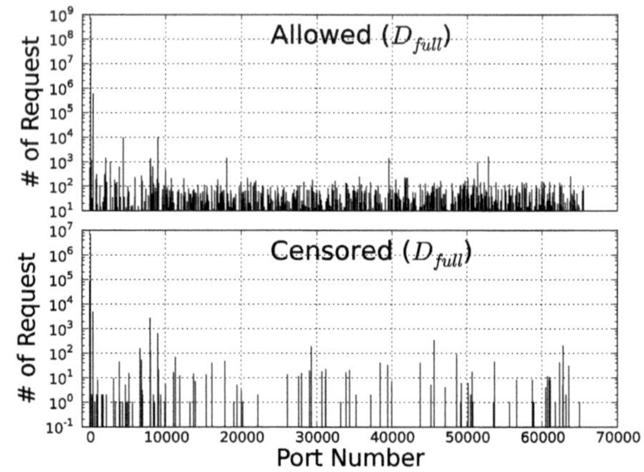

Figure 1: Destination port distributions of allowed and censored traffic (D_{full}).

Ports. We also look at the traffic distribution by port number for both allowed and censored traffic (in D_{full}). We report it in Fig. 1. Ports 80 and 443 (HTTPS) represent the majority of censored content. Port 9001 (usually associated with Tor servers) is ranked third in terms of blocked connections. We discuss Tor traffic in more detail in Section 7.1.

Domains. Next, we analyze the distribution of the number of requests per unique domain. Fig. 2 presents our findings. The y-axis (log-scale) represents the number of (allowed/denied/censored) requests, while each point in the x-axis (also log-scale) represents the number of domains receiving such a number of requests. Unsurprisingly, the curves indicate a power law distribution. We observe that a very small fraction of hosts (10^{-5} for the allowed requests) are the target of between few thousands to few millions requests, while the vast majority are the destination of only few requests. Allowed traffic is at some point one order of magnitude bigger, this happens for at least two reasons: (i) allowed requests target highly popular websites (e.g., Google and Facebook), and (ii) an allowed request is potentially followed up by additional requests to the same domain, whereas a denied request is not.

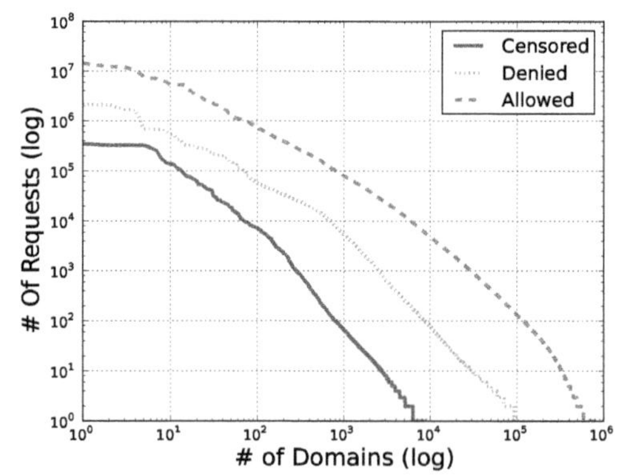

Figure 2: Distribution of # requests per unique domain (D_{full}).

sc-filter-result	x-exception-id	Class	Full (D_{full})	Sample (D_{sample})	User (D_{user})	Denied (D_{denied})
OBSERVED	–	*Allowed*	700,606,503 (93.25%)	30,140,158 (93.28%)	6,038,461 (94.73%)	– –
PROXIED	(total)	*Proxied*	3,504,485 (0.47%)	151,554 (0.47%)	26,541 (0.42%)	267,354 (0.56%)
DENIED	(total)	*Denied*	47,184,840 (6.28%)	2,019,246 (6.25%)	309,331 (4.85%)	47,184,840 (99.44%)
	tcp_error	*Error*	21,499,871 (2.86%)	947,083 (2.93%)	54,073 (0.85%)	21,499,871 (45.30%)
	internal_error		14,720,952 (1.96%)	636,335 (1.97%)	198,058 (3.11%)	14,720,952 (31.02%)
	invalid_request		2,668,217 (0.36%)	115,297 (0.36%)	36,292 (0.57%)	2,668,217 (5.62%)
	unsupported_protocol		719,189 (0.10%)	28,769 (0.09%)	1,348 (0.02%)	719,189 (1.51%)
	dns_unresolved_hostname		141,558 (0.02%)	6,247 (0.02%)	3,856 (0.06%)	141,558 (0.30%)
	dns_server_failure		58,401 (0.01%)	2,235 (0.01%)	396 (0.01%)	58,401 (0.12%)
	unsupported_encoding		269 (0.00%)	6 (0.00%)	0 (0.00%)	269 (0.00%)
	invalid_response		8 (0.00%)	1 (0.00%)	2 (0.00%)	8 (0.00%)
	policy_denied	*Censored*	7,374,500 (0.98%)	283,197 (0.88%)	15,306 (0.24%)	7,374,500 (15.54%)
	policy_redirect		1,875 (0.00%)	76 (0.00%)	0 (0.00%)	1,875 (0.04%)

Table 3: Statistics of different decisions and exceptions in the three datasets in use.

Allowed domains		Censored domains	
Domain	**# Requests (%)**	**Domain**	**# Requests (%)**
google.com	50.36M (7.19%)	facebook.com	1.62M (21.91%)
xvideos.com	23.42M (3.34%)	metacafe.com	1.28M (17.33%)
gstatic.com	23.10M (3.30%)	skype.com	503,932 (6.83%)
facebook.com	17.83M (2.54%)	live.com	441,408 (5.98%)
microsoft.com	16.64M (2.38%)	google.com	420,862 (5.71%)
fbcdn.net	16.46M (2.35%)	zynga.com	379,170 (5.14%)
windowsupdate.com	15.43M (2.20%)	yahoo.com	369,948 (5.02%)
google-analytics.com	12.38M (1.77%)	wikimedia.org	306,994 (4.16%)
doubleclick.net	11.19M (1.60%)	fbcdn.net	264,512 (3.59%)
msn.com	11.01M (1.57%)	ceipmsn.com	135,134 (1.83%)

Table 4: Top-10 Domains (allowed and censored) in D_{full}.

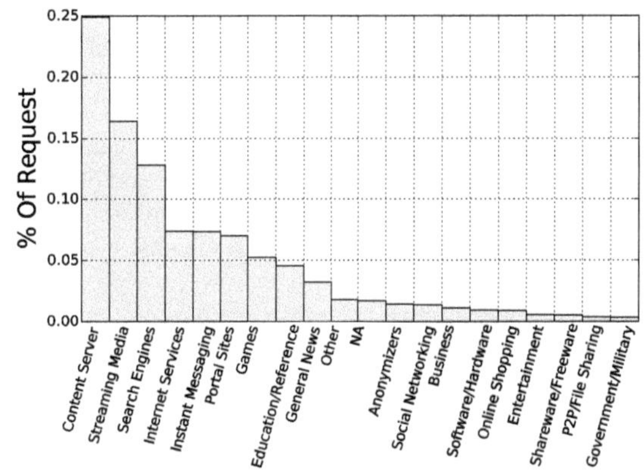

Figure 3: Category distribution of censored traffic (D_{sample}). Categories obtained from McAfee's TrustedSource, 'Other' is used for categories with less than 1K requests.

In Table 4, we report the top-10 allowed (resp., censored) domains in D_{full}. Unsurprisingly, google.com and its associated static/tracking/advertisement components represent nearly 15% of the total allowed requests. Other well-ranked domains include facebook.com (and its associated CDN service, fbcdn.net) and xvideos.com (a pornography-associated website). The top-10 censored domains exhibit a very different distribution: facebook.com (and fbcdn.net), metacafe.com (a popular user-contributed video sharing service) and skype.com account for more than 43% of the overall censored requests. Websites like Facebook and Google are present both in the censored and the allowed traffic, since the policy-based filtering may depend on the actual content the user is fetching rather than the website, as we will explain in Section 6. Finally, observe that mediafire.com is ranked at #9 in the top non-censored domains: according to the Electronic Frontier Foundation (EFF), mediafire.com was actually used to deliver malware targeting Syrian activists.[2]

Categories. The Blue Coat proxies support filtering according to URL categories. This categorization can be done using a local database, or using Blue Coat's online filtering tool.[3] However, according to Blue Coat's representatives [25], the online services are not accessible to the Syrian proxy servers, and apparently the Syrian proxy servers are not using a local copy of this categorization database. Indeed, the *cs-categories* field in the logs, which records the URL categories, contains only one of two values: one value associated with a default category (named "unavailable" in five of the proxies, and "none" in the other two), and another value associated with a custom category targeted at Facebook pages (named "Blocked sites; unavailable" in five of the proxies, and "Blocked sites" in the other two), which is discussed in more details in Section 6.

[2]https://www.eff.org/deeplinks/2012/12/iinternet-back-in-syria-so-is-malware

[3]http://sitereview.bluecoat.com/categories.jsp

Due to the absence of URL categories, we use McAfee's TrustedSource tool (www.trustedsource.org) to characterize the censored websites. Fig. 3 shows the distribution of the censored requests across the different categories. The "Content Server" category ranks first, with more than 25% of the blocked requests (this category mostly includes CDNs that host a variety of websites, such as cloudfront.net, googleusercontent.com). "Streaming Media" are next, hinting at the intention of the censors to block video sharing. "Instant Messaging" (IM) websites, as well as "Portals Sites", are also highly blocked, possibly due to their role in coordination of social activities and protests. Note that both Skype and live.com IM services are always censored and belong to the top-10 censored domains. However, surprisingly, both "News Portals" and "Social Networks" rank relatively low: as we explain in Section 6, censorship only blocks a few well-targeted social media pages. Finally, categories like "Games" and "Education/Reference" are also occasionally blocked.

HTTPS traffic. The number of HTTPS requests is a few orders of magnitude lower than that of HTTP requests. HTTPS accounts for 0.08% of the overall traffic and only a small fraction (0.82%) is censored (D_{sample} dataset). It is interesting to observe that, in 82% of the censored traffic, the destination field indicates an IP address rather than a domain, and such an IP-based blocking occurs at least for two main reasons: (1) the IP address belongs to an Israeli AS, or (2) the IP address is associated with an Anonymizer service. The remaining part of the censored HTTPS traffic actually contains a hostname: this is possible due to the use of the HTTP CONNECT method, which allows the proxy to identify both the destination host and the user agent (for instance, all connections to Skype servers are using the CONNECT method, and thus the proxy can censor requests based on the skype.com domain).

According to the Electronic Frontier Foundation, the Syrian Telecom Ministry has launched man in the middle (MITM) attacks against the HTTPS version of Facebook.[4] While Blue Coat proxies indeed support interception of HTTPS traffic,[5] we do not identify any clear sign of such an activity. For instance, the values of fields such as *cs-uri-path*, *cs-uri-query* and *cs-uri-ext*, which would have been available to the proxies in a MITM attack, are not present in HTTPS requests. However, also note that, by default, the Blue Coat proxies use a separate log facility to record SSL traffic,[6] so it is possible that this traffic has been recorded in logs that were not obtained by Telecomix.

User-based analysis. Based on the D_{user} dataset, which comprises the logs of proxy SG-42 from July 22-23, we analyze user behavior with respect to censorship. We assume that each unique combination of *c-ip* (client IP address) and *cs-user-agent* designates a unique user. This means that a user connecting from several devices with different IP addresses (or a single device with different browsers) is not considered as a single users. Conversely, users behind NAT using browsers with identical user-agent are counted as one user. However, this combination of fields provides the best approximation of unique users within the limits of the available data [31].

We identify 147,802 total users in D_{user}. 2,319 (1.57%) of them generate at least one request that is denied due to censorship. Fig. 4(a) shows the distribution of the number of censored requests per user. We observe that 37.8% of these users have only a single request censored during the observed period. Typically, users do not attempt to access a URL again once it is blocked, but, in some cases, we do observe a few more requests to the same URL. Overall, for 93.87% of the users, all the censored requests (one or more per user) are to the same domain. We also look at the distribution of the number of overall requests per user, for both non-censored and censored users, where a censored user is defined as a user for whom at least one request was censored. Censored users are more active than non-censored users: approximately 50% of the censored users generate more than 100 requests, while only 5% of non-censored users have the same level of activity. This might be explained due to the fact that, as discussed in Section 5.4, many requests are censored since they include a blacklisted keyword (e.g., *proxy*), and active users are more likely to encounter these keywords.

Fig. 4(b) shows the distribution of the number of overall requests per user, for both non-censored and censored users, where a censored user is defined as a user for whom at least one request was censored. We found that the censored users are more active than non-censored users, observing approximately 50% of the censored users have sent more than 100 requests, while only 5% of non-censored users show the same level of activity. As we discuss in Section 5.4, many requests are censored since they happen to contain a blacklisted keyword (e.g., *proxy*), even though they may not be actually accessing content that is the target of censorship. Since active users are more likely to encounter URLs that contain such keywords, this may explain the correlation between the user level of activity and being censored. We also observe that in some cases the user agent field refers to a software repeatedly trying to access a censored page (e.g., skype.com), which augments the user's activity.

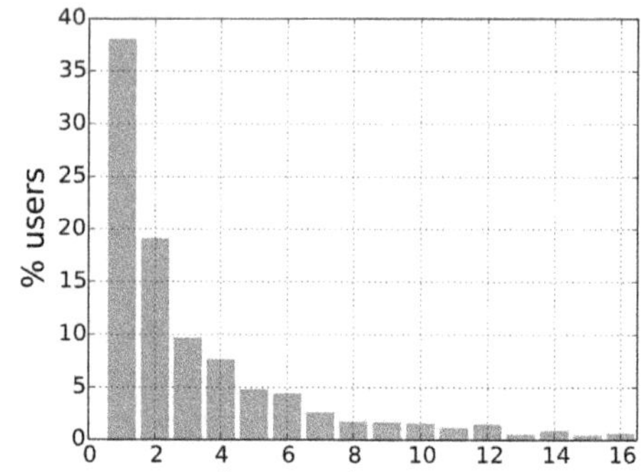

(a)

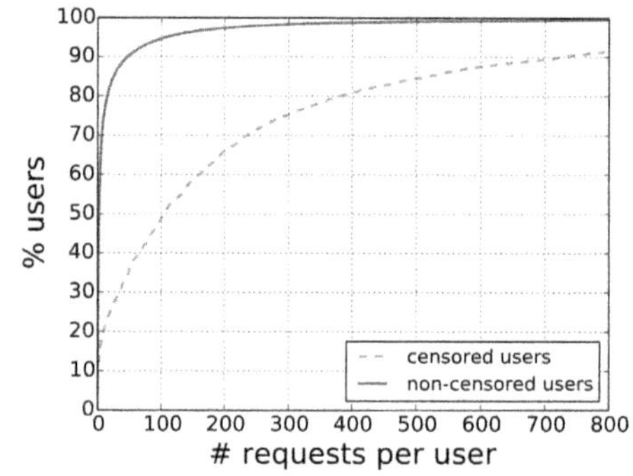

(b)

Figure 4: (a) Number of censored requests per user in D_{user}; (b) The distribution of the overall number of requests per user (both allowed and denied), for censored and non-censored users.

Summary. Our measurements have shown that only a small fraction (<1%) of the traffic is actually censored. Most requests are either allowed (93.28%) or denied due to network errors (5.37%). Censorship targets mostly HTTP content, but several other services are also blocked. Unsurprisingly, most of the censorship activity targets websites that support user interaction (e.g., Instant Messaging and social networks). A closer look at the top allowed and censored domains shows that some hosts are in both categories, thus hinting at a more sophisticated censoring mechanism, which we explore in the next sections. Finally, our user-based analysis has shown that only a small fraction of users are directly affected by censorship.

5. UNDERSTANDING THE CENSORSHIP

This section aims to understand the way the Internet is filtered in Syria. We analyze censorship's temporal characteristics and compare the behavior of different proxies. Then, we study *how* the requests are filtered and infer characteristics on which censorship policies are based.

5.1 Temporal Analysis

We start by looking at how the traffic volume of both censored and allowed traffic changes over time (5 days), with 5-minute granularity. The corresponding time-series are reported in Fig. 5(a): as expected, they roughly follow the same patterns, with an increasing volume of traffic early mornings, followed by a smooth lull during afternoons and nights. To evaluate the overall variation of the cen-

[4]https://www.eff.org/deeplinks/2011/05/syrian-man-middle-against-facebook
[5]https://kb.bluecoat.com/index?page=content&id=KB5500
[6]See https://bto.bluecoat.com/doc/8672, page 22.

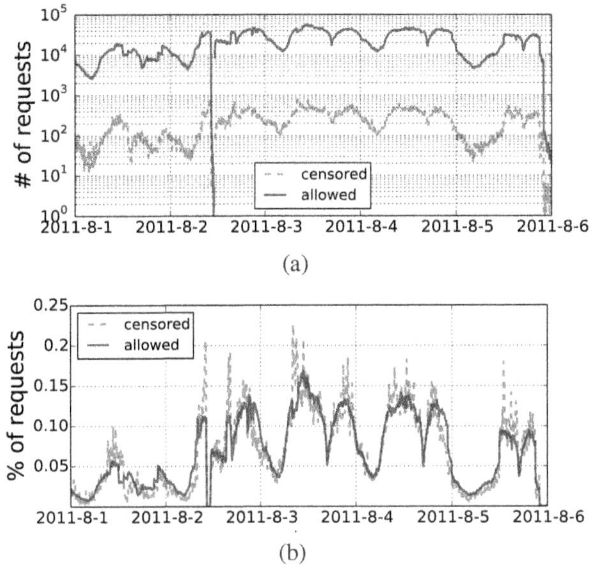

Figure 5: Censored and allowed traffic over 5 days (absolute/normalized).

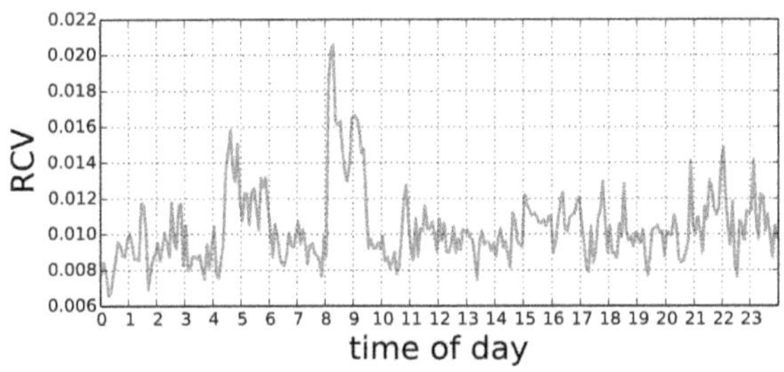

Figure 6: Relative Censored traffic Volume (RCV) for August 3 (in D_{sample}) as a function of time.

sorship activity, we show in Fig. 5(b) the temporal evolution of the number of censored (resp., allowed) requests at specific times of the day, *normalized* by the total number of censored (resp., allowed) requests. Note that the two curves are not comparable, but illustrate the relative activity when considering the overall nature of the traffic over the observation period. The relative censorship activity exhibits a few peaks, with a higher volume of censored content on particular periods of time. There are also two sudden "drops" in both allowed and censored requests, which might be correlated to some protests that day.[7] There is a visible reduction in traffic from Thursday afternoon (August 4) to Friday (August 5), consistent with press reports of Internet connections being slowed almost every Friday "when the big weekly protests are staged" [21].

To further study the activity peaks, we zoom in on one specific day (August 3) that has a particularly high volume of censored traffic. Let RCV (*Relative Censored traffic Volume*) be the ratio between the number of censored requests at a time frame (with a 5-minute granularity) and the total number of requests received on the same time frame; in Fig. 6, we plot RCV as a function of the time of day. There are a few sharp increases in censored traffic, with the fraction of censored content increasing from 1% to 2% of the total traffic around 8am, while, around 9.30am, the RCV variation exhibits a

6am - 8am		8am - 10am		10am -12pm	
Domain	**%**	**Domain**	**%**	**Domain**	**%**
metacafe.com	20.4%	skype.com	29.24%	facebook.com	22.47%
trafficholder.com	16.87%	facebook.com	19.45%	metacafe.com	18.56%
facebook.com	15.08%	live.com	9.59%	live.com	11.93%
google.com	8.15%	metacafe.com	7.59%	skype.com	11.79%
yahoo.com	6.43%	google.com	6.76%	google.com	6.81%
zynga.com	5.14%	yahoo.com	3.57%	zynga.com	3.43%
live.com	3.04%	wikimedia.org	2.47%	ceipmsn.com	2.38%
conduitapps.com	1.45%	trafficholder.com	2.06%	mtn.com.sy	2.13%
all4syria.info	1.44%	dailymotion.com	1.58%	panet.co.il	1.02%
hotsptshld.com	1.18%	conduitapps.com	1.11%	bbc.co.uk	0.91%

Table 5: Top censored domains, August 3, 6am-12pm.

sudden decay. A few other peaks are also observed early morning (5am) and evening (10pm).

We then analyze the distribution of censored content between 8am and 9.30am on August 3 and, in Table 5, we report the top-10 censored domains during this period and the adjacent ones (as well as the corresponding percentage of censored volume each domain represents). It is evident that skype is being heavily blocked (up to 29% of the censored traffic), probably due to the protests that happened in Syria on August 3, 2011. However, 9% of the requests to Skype servers are related to update attempts (for Windows clients) and all of them are denied. There is also an unusually higher number of requests to MSN live messenger service (through msn.com), thus suggesting that the censorship activity peaks might perhaps be correlated to high demand targeting Instant Messaging software websites.[8] In conclusion, censorship peaks might be due to sudden higher volumes of traffic targeting Skype and MSN live messenger websites, which are being systematically censored by the proxies.

5.2 Comparing different proxies

We now compare the behavior of the 7 different proxies whose logs are included in our datasets. In Fig. 7(a), we plot the traffic distribution across proxies, restricted to two days (August 3 and 4) to ease presentation. Note that the load is fairly distributed among the proxies, however, if one only considers censored traffic (Fig. 7(b)), different behaviors become evident. In particular, Proxy SG-48 is responsible for a large proportion of the censored traffic, especially at certain times. One possible explanation is that different proxies follow different policies, or there could be a high proportion of censored (or likely to be censored) traffic being redirected to proxy SG-48 during one specific period of time.

We also consider the top-10 censored domain names in the period of time August 3 (12am)–August 4 (12am) and observe that the domain metacafe.com is *always* censored and that almost all related requests (more than 95%) are processed *only* by proxy SG-48. This might be due to a domain-based traffic redirection process: in fact, we observed a very similar behavior for skype.com during the censorship peaks analysis presented earlier in Section 5.1.

We also look at the categories distribution of all requests across the different proxies and concentrate on two categories, "Unavailable" and "None", which show a peculiar distribution across the proxies (recall that categories have been discussed in Section 4). We note that the "None" category is *only* observed on two different proxies (SG-43 and SG-48), while "Unavailable" is less frequently observed on these two. This suggests either different configuration of the proxies or a content specialization of the proxies.

For more details on the comparison between proxies, and an evaluation of the similarity between censored requests handled by

[7]See http://www.enduringamerica.com/home/2011/8/3/syria-and-beyond-liveblog-the-sights-and-sounds-of-protest.html.

[8]Very similar results also occur for other periods of censorship activity peaks.

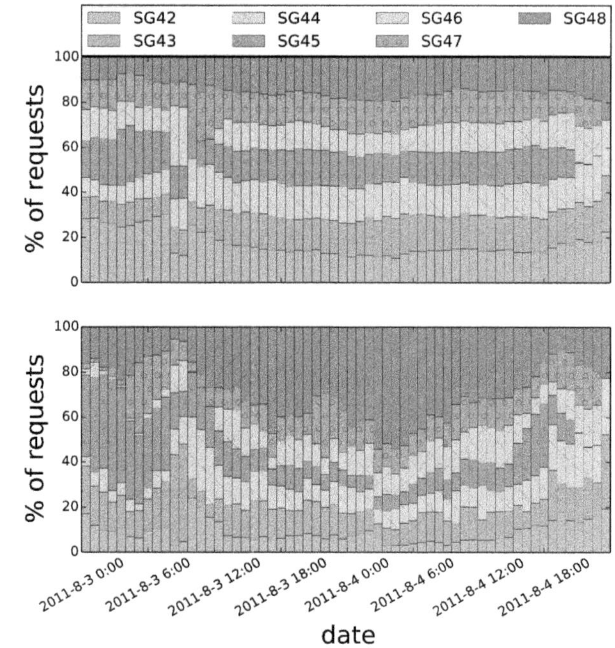

Figure 7: The distribution of traffic load through each proxy and censored traffic over time.

cs_host	# requests	%
upload.youtube.com	12,978	86.79%
www.facebook.com	1,599	10.69%
ar-ar.facebook.com	264	1.77%
competition.mbc.net	50	0.33%
sharek.aljazeera.net	44	0.29%

Table 6: Top-5 hosts for *policy_redirect* requests in D_{full}.

each proxy (using Cosine Similarity), we refer to the extended version of the paper [7].

5.3 Denied vs. Redirected Traffic

Requests are censored in one of two ways: they are either *denied* or *redirected*. If a request triggers a *policy_denied* exception, the requested page is not served to the client. Upon triggering *policy_redirect*, the request is redirected to another URL. For these requests, we only have information from the *x-exception-id* field (set to *policy_redirect*) and the *s-action* field (set to *tcp_policy_redirect*). The *policy_redirect* exception is raised for a small number of hosts – 11 in total. As reported in Table 6, the most common URLs are upload.youtube.com and Facebook-owned domains.

Note that the redirection should trigger an additional request from the client to the redirected URL immediately after *policy_redirect* is raised. However, we found no trace of a secondary request coming right after (within a 2-second window). Thus, we conclude that the secondary URL is either hosted on a website that does not require to go through the filtering proxies (most likely, this site is hosted in Syria) or that the request is processed by proxies other than those in the dataset. Since the destination of the redirection remains unknown, we do not know whether or not redirections point to different pages, depending on the censored request.

5.4 Category, String, and IP-based Filtering

We now study the three main triggers of censorship decisions: URL categories, strings, and IP addresses.

Category-based Filtering. According to Blue Coat's documentation [1], proxies can associate a category to each request (in the *cs-categories* field), based on the corresponding URL, and this category can be used in the filtering rules. In the set of censored requests, we identify only two categories: a default category (named "unavailable" or "none", depending on the proxy server), and a custom category (named "Blocked sites; unavailable" or "Blocked sites"). The custom category targets specific Facebook pages with a *policy_redirect* policy, accounts for 1,924 requests, and is discussed in detail in Section 6. All the other URLs (allowed or denied) are categorized to the default category, which is subject to a more general censorship policy, and captures the vast majority of the censored requests. The censored requests in the default category consist mostly of *policy_denied* with a small portion (0.21% either `PROXIED` or `DENIED`) of *policy_redirect* exceptions. We next investigate the policy applied within the default category.

String-based Filtering. The filtering process is also based on particular strings included in the requested URL. In fact, the string-based filtering only relies on URL-related fields, specifically *cs-host*, *cs-uri-path* and *cs-uri-query*, which fully characterize the request. The proxies' filtering process is performed using a simple string-matching engine that detects any blacklisted substring in the URL.

We now aim to recover the list of strings that have been used to filter requests in our dataset. We expect that a string used for censorship should only be found in the set of censored requests and never in the set of allowed ones (for this purpose, we consider `PROXIED` requests separately from `OBSERVED` requests, since they do not necessarily indicate an allowed request, even when no exception is logged). In order to identify these strings, we use the following iterative approach: (1) Let $\mathcal{C}$ be the set of censored URLs and $\mathcal{A}$ the set of allowed URLs; (2) Manually identify a string w appearing frequently in $\mathcal{C}$; (3) Let $N_{\mathcal{C}}$ and $N_{\mathcal{A}}$ be the number of occurrences of w in $\mathcal{C}$ and $\mathcal{A}$, respectively; (4) If $N_{\mathcal{C}} >> 1$ and $N_{\mathcal{A}} = 0$ then remove from $\mathcal{C}$ all requests containing w, add w to the list of censored strings, and go to step 2.

To mitigate selection of strings that are unrelated to the censorship decision during the manual string identification (step 2), we took a conservative approach by only considering non-ambiguous requests. For instance, we select simple requests, e.g., `HTTP GET new-syria.com/`, which only contains a domain name and has an empty path and an empty query field. Thus, we are sure that the string new-syria.com is the source of the censorship.

URL-based Filtering. Using the iterative process described above, we identify a list of 105 "suspected" domains, for which no request is allowed. Table 7 presents the top-10 domains in the list, according to the number of censored requests. We further categorized each domain in the list and show in Table 8 the top-10 categories according to the number of censored requests. Clearly, there is a heavy censorship of Instant Messaging software, as well as news, public forums, and user-contributed streaming media sites.

Keyword-based Filtering. We also identify five keywords that trigger censorship when found in the URL (*cs-host*, *cs-path* and *cs-query* fields): *proxy*, *hotspotshield*, *ultrareach*, *israel*, and *ultrasurf*. We report the corresponding number of censored, allowed, and proxied requests in Table 9. Four of them are related to anti-censorship technologies and one refers to Israel. Note that a large number of requests containing the keyword *proxy* are actually related to seemingly "non sensitive" content, e.g., online ads content, tracking components or online APIs, but are nonetheless blocked. For instance, the Google toolbar API invokes a call to `/tbproxy/af/query`, which can be found on the google.com domain, and is unrelated to anti-censorship software. Nevertheless, this element accounts for

Domain	Censored	Allowed	Proxied
metacafe.com	1,278,583 (17.33%)	0 (0.00%)	1,164 (0.03%)
skype.com	503,932 (6.83%)	0 (0.00%)	1,313 (0.04%)
wikimedia.org	306,994 (4.16%)	0 (0.00%)	3,379 (0.10%)
.il	112,369 (1.52%)	0 (0.00%)	8,785 (0.25%)
amazon.com	62,759 (0.85%)	0 (0.00%)	345 (0.01%)
aawsat.com	51,518 (0.70%)	0 (0.00%)	5,670 (0.16%)
jumblo.com	23,214 (0.31%)	0 (0.00%)	0 (0.00%)
jeddahbikers.com	21,274 (0.29%)	0 (0.00%)	130 (0.00%)
badoo.com	14,502 (0.20%)	0 (0.00%)	358 (0.01%)
islamway.com	14,408 (0.20%)	0 (0.00%)	329 (0.01%)

Table 7: Top-10 domains suspected to be censored (number of requests and percentage for each class of traffic in D_{full}).

Category (#domains)	Censored requests
Instant Messaging (2)	47,116 (16.63%)
Streaming Media (6)	39,282 (13.87%)
Education/Reference (4)	27,106 (9.57%)
General News (62)	8,700 (3.07%)
NA (42)	6,776 (2.39%)
Online Shopping (2)	4,712 (1.66%)
Internet Services (6)	2,964 (1.05%)
Social Networking (6)	2,114 (0.75%)
Entertainment (4)	1,828 (0.65%)
Forum/Bulletin Boards (8)	1,606 (0.57%)

Table 8: Top-10 domain categories censored by URL (number of censored requests and percentage of censored traffic in D_{sample}).

Keyword	Censored	Allowed	Proxied
proxy	3,954,795 (53.61%)	0 (0.00%)	14,846 (0.42%)
hotspotshield	126,127 (1.71%)	0 (0.00%)	816 (0.02%)
ultrareach	50,769 (0.69%)	0 (0.00%)	68 (0.00%)
israel	48,119 (0.65%)	0 (0.00%)	477 (0.01%)
ultrasurf	31,483 (0.43%)	0 (0.00%)	541 (0.02%)

Table 9: The list of 5 keywords identified as censored (fraction and number of requests for each class of traffic in D_{full}).

4.85% of the *censored* requests in the D_{sample} dataset. Likewise, the keyword *proxy* is also included in some online social networks' advertising components (see Section 6).

IP-based censorship. We now focus on understanding whether some requests are censored based on IP address. To this end, we look at the requests for which the *cs-host* field is an IPv4 address and notice that some of the URLs of censored requests do not contain any meaningful information except for the IP address. As previously noted, censorship can be done at a country level, e.g., for Israel, as all .il domains are blocked. Thus, we consider the possibility of filtering traffic with destination in some specific geographical regions, based on the IP address of the destination host.

We construct D_{IPv4}, which includes the set of requests (from D_{full}) for which the *cs-host* field is an IPv4 address. We geo-localize each IP address in D_{IPv4} using the Maxmind GeoIP database.[9] We then introduce, for each identified country, the corresponding censorship ratio, i.e., the number of censored requests over the total number of requests to this country. Table 10 presents the censorship ratio for each country in D_{IPv4}. Israel is by far the country with the highest censorship ratio, suggesting that it might be subject to an IP-based censorship.

[9]http://www.maxmind.com/en/country

Country	Censorship Ratio (%)	# Censored	# Allowed
Israel	6.69	5,191	72,416
Kuwait	2.02	16	776
Russian Federation	0.64	959	149,161
United Kingdom	0.26	2,490	942,387
Netherlands	0.17	12,206	7,077,371
Singapore	0.13	19	14,768
Bulgaria	0.09	14	14,786

Table 10: Censorship ratio for top censored countries in D_{IPv4}.

	Censored		Allowed		Proxied	
Subnet	# req.	# IPs	# req.	# IPs	# req.	# IPs
84.229.0.0/16	574	198	0	0	4	4
46.120.0.0/15	571	11	5	1	0	0
89.138.0.0/15	487	148	1	1	3	3
212.235.64.0/19	474	5	325	1	0	0
212.150.0.0/16	471	3	6,366	12	1	1

Table 11: Top censored Israeli subnets.

Next, we focus on Israel and zoom in to the subnet level.[10] Table 11 presents, for each of the top censored Israeli subnets, the number of requests and IP addresses that are censored and allowed. We identify two distinct groups: subnets that are almost always censored (except for a few exceptions of allowed requests), e.g., 84.229.0.0/16, and those that are either censored or allowed but for which the number of allowed requests is significantly larger than that of the censored ones, e.g. 212.150.0.0/16. One possible reason for a systematic subnet censorship could be related to blacklisted keywords. However, this is not the case in our analysis since the requested URL is often limited to a single IP address (*cs-uri-path* and *cs-uri-query* fields are empty). We further check, using McAfee smart filter, that none but one (out of 1155 IP addresses) of the censored Israeli IP addresses are categorized as Anonymizer hosts. These results show then that IP filtering targets a few geographical areas, i.e., Israeli subnets.

5.5 Summary

The analysis presented in this section has shown evidence of domain-based traffic redirection between proxies. A few proxies seem to be specialized in censoring specific domains and type of content. Also, our findings suggest that the censorship activity reaches peaks mainly because of unusually high demand for Instant Messaging Software websites (e.g., Skype), which are blocked in Syria. We found that censorship is based on four main criteria: URL-based filtering, keyword-based filtering, destination IP address, and a custom category-based censorship (further discussed in the next section). The list of blocked keywords and domains demonstrates the intent of Syrian censors to block political and news content, video sharing, and proxy-based censorship-circumvention technologies. Finally, Israeli-related content is heavily censored as the keyword *Israel*, the .il domain, and some Israeli subnets are blocked.

6. CENSORSHIP OF SOCIAL MEDIA

In this section, we analyze the filtering and censorship of Online Social Networks (OSNs) in Syria. Social media have often been targeted by censors, e.g., during the recent uprisings in the Middle East and North Africa. In Syria, according to our logs, popular OSNs like Facebook and Twitter are not *entirely* censored and most

[10]The list of IPv4 subnets corresponding to Israel is available from http://www.ip2location.com/free/visitor-blocker.

OSN	Censored	Allowed	Proxied
facebook.com	1,616,174 (21.91%)	17.70M (2.53%)	125,988 (3.60%)
badoo.com	14,502 (0.20%)	0 (0.00%)	358 (0.01%)
netlog.com	9,252 (0.13%)	0 (0.00%)	2,227 (0.06%)
linkedin.com	7,194 (0.10%)	186,047 (0.03%)	1,723 (0.05%)
skyrock.com	3,307 (0.04%)	7,564 (0.00%)	11 (0.00%)
hi5.com	2,995 (0.04%)	210,411 (0.03%)	463 (0.01%)
twitter.com	163 (0.00%)	2.83M (0.40%)	14,654 (0.42%)
ning.com	6 (0.00%)	41,993 (0.01%)	69 (0.00%)
meetup.com	3 (0.00%)	108 (0.00%)	0 (0.00%)
flickr.com	2 (0.00%)	383,212 (0.05%)	3179 (0.09%)

Table 12: Top-10 censored social networks in D_{full} (number and percentage of requests for each class of traffic).

traffic is allowed. However, we observe that a few specific keywords (e.g., *proxy*) and a few pages (e.g., the 'Syrian Revolution' Facebook page) are blocked, thus suggesting a targeted censorship.

We select a representative set of social networks containing the top 25 social networks according to alexa.com as of November 2013, and add 3 social networks popular in Arabic-speaking countries: netlog.com, salamworld.com, and muslimup.com. For each of these sites, we extract the number of allowed, censored and proxied requests in D_{full}, and report the top-10 censored social networks in Table 12.

We find no evidence of systematic censorship for most sites (including last.fm, MySpace, Google+, Instagram, and Tumblr), as all requests are allowed. However, for a few social networks (including Facebook, Linkedin, Twitter, and Flickr) many requests are blocked. Several requests are censored based on blacklisted keywords (e.g., *proxy, Israel*), thus suggesting that the destination domain is not the actual reason of censorship. However, requests to Netlog and Badoo are never allowed and there is only a minority of requests containing blacklisted keywords, which suggests that these domains are always censored. In fact, both netlog.com and badoo.com were identified in the list of domains suspected for URL-based filtering, described in Section 5.4.

Facebook. Recall that the majority of requests to Facebook are allowed, yet facebook.com is one of the most censored domains. As we explain below, censored requests can be classified into two groups: (i) requests to Facebook pages with sensitive (political) content, and (ii) requests to the social platform with the blacklisted keyword *proxy*.

Censored Facebook pages. Several Facebook pages are censored for political reasons and are identified by the proxies using the custom category "Blocked Sites." Requests to those pages trigger a *policy_redirect* exception, thus redirecting the user to a page unknown to us. Interestingly, Reporters Without Borders [21] stated that "the government's cyber-army, which tracks dissidents on online social networks, seems to have stepped up its activities since June 2011. Web pages that support the demonstrations were flooded with pro-Assad messages." While we cannot infer the destination of redirection, we argue that this mechanism could technically serve as a way to show specific content addressing users who access targeted Facebook pages.

Table 13 lists the Facebook pages we identify in the logs that fall into the custom category. All the requests identified as belonging to the custom category are censored. However, we find that not all requests to the facebook.com/<censored_page> pages are correctly categorized as "Blocked Site." For instance, www.facebook.com/Syrian.Revolution?ref=ts is, but www.facebook.com/Syrian.Revolution?ref=ts&__a=11&ajaxpipe=1&quickling[version]=414343%3B0 is not, thus suggesting that the categorization rules targeted a very narrow range of specific *cs-uri-path* and *cs-uri-query* combinations. As shown in Table 13, many requests to targeted Facebook pages are allowed and no allowed request is categorized as "Blocked Site." We also identify successful requests sent to Facebook pages such as Syrian.Revolution.Army, Syrian.Revolution.Assad, Syrian.Revolution.Caricature and ShaamNewsNetwork, which are not categorized as "Blocked Site" and are allowed. Finally, proxied requests are sometimes, but not always, categorized as "Blocked Site" (e.g., all the requests for the Syrian.revolution page).

Facebook page	# Censored	# Allowed	# Proxied
Syrian.Revolution	1461	891	16
Syrian.revolution	0	0	25
syria.news.F.N.N	191	165	1
ShaamNews	114	3944	7
fffm14	42	18	0
barada.channel	25	9	0
DaysOfRage	19	2	0
Syrian.R.V	10	6	0
YouthFreeSyria	6	0	0
sooryoon	3	0	0
Freedom.Of.Syria	3	0	0
SyrianDayOfRage	1	0	0

Table 13: Top blocked Facebook pages in D_{full}.

Social plug-in	Censored	Allowed	Proxied
/plugins/like.php	694,788 (43.04%)	0 (0.00%)	8,919 (7.08%)
/extern/login_status.php	629,495 (38.99%)	0 (0.00%)	3,502 (2.78%)
/plugins/likebox.php	77,244 (4.78%)	0 (0.00%)	3555 (2.82%)
/plugins/send.php	70,146 (4.35%)	0 (0.00%)	272 (0.22%)
/plugins/comments.php	54,265 (3.36%)	0 (0.00%)	331 (0.26%)
/fbml/fbjs_ajax_proxy.php	42,649 (2.64%)	0 (0.00%)	43 (0.03%)
/connect/canvas_proxy.php	40,516 (2.51%)	0 (0.00%)	37 (0.03%)
/ajax/proxy.php	1,544 (0.10%)	0 (0.00%)	6 (0.00%)
/platform/page_proxy.php	1,519 (0.09%)	0 (0.00%)	4 (0.00%)
/plugins/facepile.php	669 (0.04%)	0 (0.00%)	4 (0.00%)

Table 14: Top-10 Facebook social plugin elements in D_{full} (fraction of Facebook traffic and number of requests).

Social plugins. Facebook provides so-called social plugins (one common example is the *Like* button), which is loaded by web pages to enable interaction with the social platform. Some of the URLs used by these social plugins include the keyword *proxy* in the *cs-uri-path* field or in the *cs-uri-query* field, and this automatically raises the *policy_denied* exception whenever the page is loaded.

Table 14 reports, for each of the top-10 social plugin elements, the fraction of the Facebook traffic and the number of requests for each class of traffic. The top two censored social plugin elements (*/plugins/like.php* and */extern/login_status.php*) account for more than 80% of the censored traffic on the facebook.com domain, while the 10 social plugin elements we consider account for 99.9% (1,612,835) of the censored requests on the facebook.com domain. To conclude, the large number of censored requests on the facebook.com domain is in fact mainly caused by social plugins elements that are not related with censorship circumvention tools or any political content.

Summary. We have studied the censorship of 28 major online social networks and found that most of them are not censored, unless requests contain blacklisted keywords (such as *proxy*) in the URL. This is particularly evident looking at the large amount of Facebook requests that are censored due to the presence of *proxy* in the query. Using a custom category, the censors also target a selected number of Facebook pages, without blocking all traffic to the site, thus making censorship and surveillance harder to detect (as independently reported in [19]).

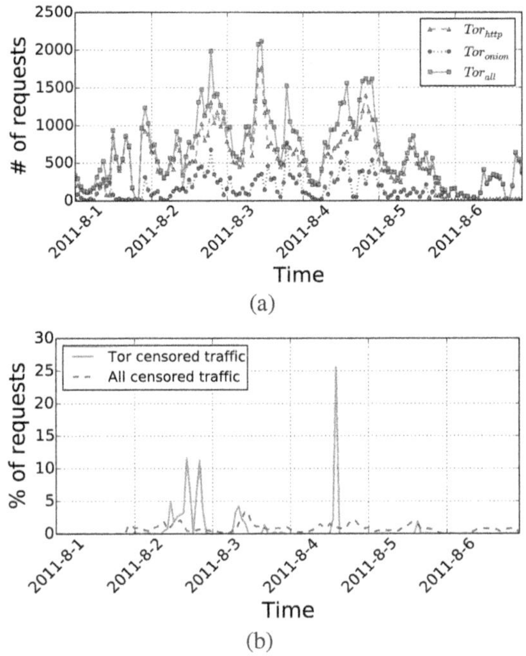

Figure 8: (a) Number of Tor related requests per hour from August 1-6 in D_{full}.; (b) Percentage of all censored traffic and Tor censored traffic by Proxy SG-44.

7. ANTI-CENSORSHIP TECHNOLOGIES

We now investigate the usage (and effectiveness) of censorship-circumvention technologies based on our dataset.

7.1 Tor

According to the logs, access to the Tor project website and the majority of Tor traffic were allowed in July/August 2011. In fact, access to the Tor network was first reported to be blocked on December 16, 2012 [24].

Tor traffic can be classified into two main classes: (1) HTTP signaling, e.g., establishing connections with Tor directories, which we denote as Tor_{http}, and (2) establishing Tor circuits and data transfer, denoted as Tor_{onion}. To identify Tor traffic, we extract Tor relays' IP addresses and port numbers from the Tor server descriptors and network status files (available from https://metrics.torproject.org/formats.html). We then match the extracted <node IP, port, date> triplets to the requests in D_{full} to identify Tor traffic. We further isolate HTTP signaling messages by identifying all HTTP requests to Tor directories, e.g., `/tor/server/authority.z` or `/tor/keys`.[11] This does not take into account the connections via Tor bridges: there is no public list of them (bridges are used to overcome filtering of connections to known Tor relays), however, Tor relays were not filtered in Syria as of 2011, thus users did not actually need to use bridges.

We identify 95K requests to 1,111 different Tor relays, 73% of which belong to Tor_{http}. Only a small fraction (1.38%) of the requests are censored and 16.2% of them generate TCP errors. Figure 8(a) shows the number of requests for August 1-6. The traffic has several peaks, in particular on August 3, when several protests were taking place. We observe that 99.9% of censored Tor traffic is blocked by a single proxy (SG-44), even though the overall traffic

[11] See https://gitweb.torproject.org/torspec.git?a=blob_plain;hb=HEAD;f=dir-spec-v2.txt for a full description.

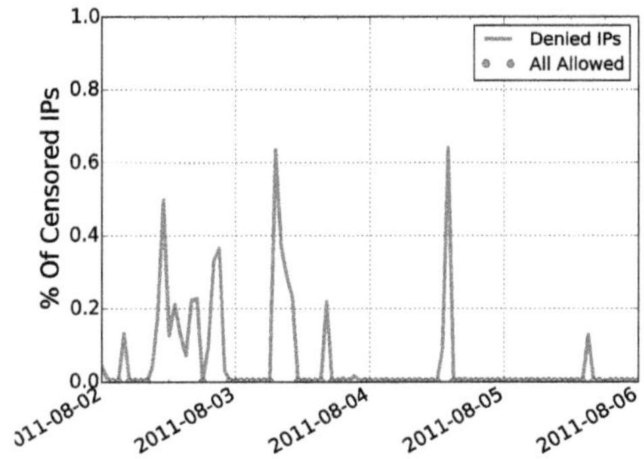

Figure 9: Ratio of (re)censored IPs SG-44.

is uniformly distributed across all the 7 proxies. The other 0.01% of the traffic is censored by SG-48. This finding echoes our earlier discussion on the specialization of some proxies.

We also analyze the temporal pattern of Tor censored traffic and compare it to the overall censored requests of SG-44. As shown in Figure 8(b), Tor censoring exhibits a higher variance. While censoring Tor_{http} is technically simple, as it only requires matching of regular expressions against the HTTP requests, identifying and censoring Tor_{onion} is more challenging, as it involves encrypted traffic. However, only Tor_{onion} traffic is censored according to the logs, while Tor_{http} is always allowed.

Next, we verify whether the Tor censorship is consistent (i.e., whether the blocked Tor relay is re-allowed later). To do so, we proceed as follows: First, we create a set of all censored Tor relay addresses denoted `Censored-IPs`. Then, for each one hour time window considered as a time bin k, we create the set of all Tor relays IP addresses that were allowed, we denote `Allowed-IPs (k)`. For each time bin k, we calculate the relative overlap between the censored Tor relay nodes and the Tor relays allowed at bin k as:

$$R_{filter}(k) = 1 - \frac{|\texttt{Censored-IPs} \cap \texttt{Allowed-IPs(k)}|}{|\texttt{Censored-IPs}|}$$

where $|\cdot|$ denotes the set size. Figure 9 depicts the variation of R_{filter} as a function of time. Note that $R_{filter}(k)$ equals 0 if, at a specific time bin k, all connections to `Censored-IPs` are allowed (line curve) or none of the IPs in Allowed are in Censored (circle curve). $R_{filter}(k)$ equals 1 if none of the connections to `Censored-IPs` have been allowed at a specific time bin k.

The high variance of R_{filter} shows that the censorship is inconsistent. In fact, the beginning of this plot is either dominated by red circles (all traffic is allowed) or few small peaks showing a very mild censorship. Then few successive peaks with a high variance of blockage appear for several hours, followed by a lull at the night of 03 of August. The same scenario is repeated several times, alternating between aggressive censorship and more mild period. This behavior is hard to explain as some IPs are alternating between blocked and allowed status. One explanation might be a testing phase that is carried in a single router and for a short period of time to test a new censorship approach (in this scenario the newly deployed Tor censorship). Or, this censorship is based on fields that are not logged by the appliance and hence inaccessible to us.

7.2 Web Proxies and VPNs

As already mentioned, access to web/socks proxies is censored, as demonstrated by an aggressive filtering of requests including the keyword *proxy*. In the following, we use "proxies" to refer to the Blue Coat appliances whose logs we study in this paper, and "web proxies" to refer to services used to circumvent censorship.

To use web proxies, end-users need to configure their browsers or their network interfaces, or rely on tools (e.g., Ultrasurf) that automatically redirect all HTTP traffic to the web proxy. Some web proxies support encryption, and create a SSL-based encrypted HTTP tunnel between the user and the web proxy. Similarly, VPN tools (e.g., Hotspot Shield) are often used to circumvent censorship, again, by relaying traffic through a VPN server.

We analyze the usage of VPN and web proxy tools and find that a few of them are very popular among Internet users in Syria. However, as discussed in Section 5.4, keywords like *ultrasurf* and *hotspotshield* are heavily monitored and censored. Nonetheless, some web proxies and VPN software (such as Freegate, GTunnel and GPass) do not include the keyword *proxy* in request URLs and are therefore not censored. Similarly, we do not observe any censorship activity triggered by the keyword *VPN*.

Next, we focus on the domains that are categorized as "Anonymizers" by McAfee's TrustedSource tool, including both web proxies and VPN-related hosts. In the D_{sample} dataset, there are 821 "Anonymizer" domains, which are the target of 122K requests (representing 0.4% of the total number of requests). 92.7% of these hosts (accounting for 25% of the requests) are never filtered. Figure 10(a) shows the CDF of the number of requests sent to each of those allowed hosts. Less than 10% of these hosts receive more than 100 requests, suggesting that only a few popular services attract a high number of the requests.

Finally, we look at the 7.3% of the identified "Anonymizer" hosts, for which some of the requests are censored. We calculate the ratio between the number of allowed requests in D_{full} and the number of censored requests in D_{denied}. Figure 10(b) shows the CDF of this censorship ratio. We observe a non-consistent policy for whether a request is allowed or censored, with more than 50% of the proxies showing a higher number of allowed requests than censored requests. This suggests that these requests are not censored based on their IP or hostname, but rather on other criteria, e.g., the inclusion of a blacklisted keyword in the request.

In conclusion, while some services (such as Hotspot Shield) are heavily censored, other, less known, services are not, unless related requests contain blacklisted keywords. This somehow introduces a trade-off between the ability to bypass censorship and promoting censorship- and surveillance-evading tools (e.g., in web searches) by including keywords such as *proxy* in the URL.

7.3 Peer-to-Peer networks

The distributed architecture of peer-to-peer networks makes them, by nature, more resilient to censorship: users obtain content from peers and not from a server, which makes it harder to locate and block content. Shared data is usually identified by a unique identifier (e.g., info hash in BitTorrent), and these identifiers are useless to censors unless mapped back to, e.g., the description of the corresponding files. However, resolving these identifiers is not trivial: content can be created by anyone at any time, and the real description can be distributed in many different ways, publicly and privately.

To investigate the use of peer-to-peer networks as a way to access censored content, we look for signs of BitTorrent traffic. We find a total of 338,168 BitTorrent announce requests from 38,575 users (BitTorrent uses a 20-byte peer_id field to identify peers, which we use to count unique users) for 35,331 unique contents in the D_{full} dataset.[12] Most of these requests (99.97%) are allowed. Censored requests can be explained with the occurrence of blacklisted keywords, e.g., *proxy*, in the request URL. For instance, all announce requests sent to the tracker on *tracker-proxy.furk.net* are censored.

[12]BitTorrent clients send announce requests to BitTorrent servers (aka trackers) to retrieve a list of IP addresses from which the requested content can be downloaded.

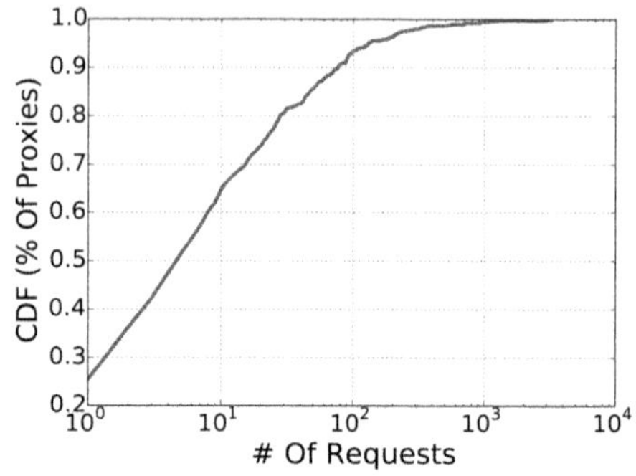

(a)

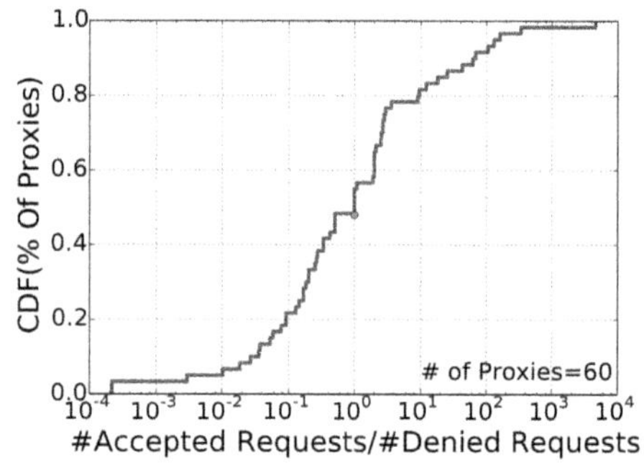

(b)

Figure 10: (a) CDF of the number of requests for identified "anonymizer" hosts; (b) Ratio of Allowed versus Censored number of requests for identified "anonymizer" hosts.

Using the hashes of torrent files provided in the announce messages, we crawl torrentz.eu and torrentproject.com to extract the titles of these torrent files, achieving a success rate of 77.4%. The five blacklisted keywords, reported in Table 9, are actually present in the titles of some of the BitTorrent files, yet the associated announce requests are allowed. We do not find any content that can be directly associated with sensitive topics like "Syrian revolution" or "Arab spring" (these files may still be shared via BitTorrent without publicly announcing the content), however, we identify content relating to anti-censorship software, such as UltraSurf (2,703 requests for all versions), HideMyAss (176 requests), Auto Hide IP (532 requests) and anonymous browsers (393 requests). Our findings suggest that peer-to-peer networks are indeed used by users inside Syria to circumvent censorship to a certain extent. Also note that BitTorrent is used to download Instant Messaging software, such as Skype, MSN messenger, and Yahoo! Messenger, which cannot be downloaded directly from the official download pages due to censorship.

7.4 Google Cache

When searching for terms in Google's search engine, the result pages allow access to cached versions of suggested pages. While Google Cache is not intended as an anti-censorship tool, a simple analysis of the logs shows that it provides a way to access content that is otherwise censored.

We identify a total of 4,860 requests accessing Google's cache on webcache.googleusercontent.com in the D_{full} dataset. Only 12 of them are censored due to an occurrence of a blacklisted keyword in the URL, and a single request to retrieve a cached version of http://ar-ar.facebook.com/SYRIANREVOLUTION.K.N.N has *policy_denied*, although it is not categorized as a "Blocked Site." However, the rest of the requests are allowed. Interestingly, some of the allowed requests, although small in number, relate to cached versions of webpages that are otherwise censored, such as www.panet.co.il, aawsat.com, www.facebook.com/Syrian.Revolution, and www.free-syria.com. While the use of Google cache to access censored content is obviously limited in scope, the logs actually suggest that it is very effective. Thus, when properly secured with HTTPS, Google cache could actually serve as a way to access censored content.

7.5 Summary

The logs highlighted that Syrian users do resort to censorship circumvention tools, with a relatively high effectiveness. While some tools and websites are monitored and blocked (e.g., Hotspot Shield), many others are successful in bypassing censorship. Our study also shows that some tools that were not necessarily designed as circumvention tools, such as BitTorrent and Google cache, could provide additional ways to access censored content if proper precautions are taken, especially considering that Syrian ISPs started to block Tor relays and bridges in December 2012.

8. DISCUSSION

Economics of Censorship. Our analysis shows that Syrian authorities deploy several techniques to filter Internet traffic, ranging from blocking entire subnets to filtering based on specific keywords. This range of techniques can be explained by the cost/benefit tradeoff of censorship, as described, e.g., by Danezis and Anderson [11]. While censoring the vast majority of the Israeli network – regardless of the actual content – can be explained on geo-political grounds, completely denying the access to social networks, such as Facebook, could generate unrest. For instance, facing the "Arab spring" uprisings, the Syrian authorities decided to allow access to Facebook, Twitter, and Youtube in February 2011. Nonetheless, these websites are monitored and selectively censored. Censors might aim at a more subtle control of the Internet, by only denying access to a predefined set of websites, as well as a set of keywords. This shift is achievable as the proxy appliances seamlessly support Deep Packet Inspection (DPI), thus allowing fine-grained censorship in real-time.

Censorship's target. Censored traffic encompasses a large variety of content, mostly aiming to prevent users from using Instant Messaging software (e.g., Skype), video sharing websites (e.g., metacafe.com, upload.youtube.com), Wikipedia, as well as sites related to news and opposition parties (e.g., islammemo.cc, alquds.co.uk). Censors also deliberately block any requests related to a set of predefined anti-censorship tools (e.g., 'proxy'). This mechanism, however, has several side effects as it denies the access to any page containing these keywords, including those that have nothing to do with censorship circumvention.

Censorship Circumvention. We also highlighted that users attempt to circumvent censorship. One interesting way is using BitTorrent to download anti-censorship tools such as UltraSurf as well as Instant Messaging software. Users also rely on known censorship-evading technologies, such as web/socks proxies and Tor.

9. CONCLUSION

This paper presented a measurement analysis of Internet filtering in Syria. We analyzed 600GB worth of logs produced by 7 Blue Coat SG-9000 proxies in Summer 2011 and, by extracting information about processed requests for both censored and allowed traffic, we provided a detailed, first-of-a-kind snapshot of a real-world censorship ecosystem. We uncovered the presence of a relatively stealthy yet quite targeted filtering, which relies on IP addresses to block access to entire subnets, on domains to block specific websites, and on keywords to target specific content. Keyword-based censorship (e.g., denying all requests containing the word 'proxy') also produces collateral damage, as many requests are blocked even if they do not relate to sensitive content. Finally, we showed that Instant Messaging software is heavily censored, that filtering of social media appears to be limited to specific pages, and that Syrian users try to circumvent censorship using web/socks proxies, Tor, VPNs, and BitTorrent.

10. REFERENCES

[1] Blue Coat ProxySG – Configuration and Management Guide. http://wikileaks.org/spyfiles/files/0/226_BLUECOAT-SGOS_CMG_4.1.4.pdf.

[2] C. Anderson. The Hidden Internet of Iran: Private Address Allocations on a National Network. *ArXiv 1209.6398*, 2012.

[3] Arabic Network for Human Rights Information. Online Syria, Offline Syrians. http://old.openarab.net/en/node/1625, 2013.

[4] S. Aryan, H. Aryan, and J. A. Halderman. Internet Censorship in Iran: A First Look. In *FOCI*, 2013.

[5] BBC News. Syrian jailed for Internet usage. http://news.bbc.co.uk/1/hi/world/middle_east/3824595.stm.

[6] Blue Coat. https://www.bluecoat.com/company/news/update-blue-coat-devices-syria, 2011.

[7] A. Chaabane, T. Chen, M. Cunche, E. De Cristofaro, A. Friedman, and M. A. Kafaar. Censorship in the Wild: Analyzing Internet Filtering in Syria (Full Version). http://arxiv.org/pdf/1402.3401.

[8] J. R. Crandall, D. Zinn, M. Byrd, E. T. Barr, and R. East. ConceptDoppler: A Weather Tracker for Internet Censorship. In *CCS*, 2007.

[9] A. Dainotti, C. Squarcella, E. Aben, K. C. Claffy, M. Chiesa, M. Russo, and A. Pescapé. Analysis of country-wide internet outages caused by censorship. In *IMC*, 2011.

[10] J. Dalek, B. Haselton, H. Noman, A. Senft, M. Crete-Nishihata, P. Gill, and R. J. Deibert. A Method for Identifying and Confirming the Use of URL Filtering Products for Censorship. In *IMC*, 2013.

[11] G. Danezis and R. Anderson. The Economics of Censorship Resistance. In *WEIS*, 2004.

[12] S. Egelman, J. Bonneau, S. Chiasson, D. Dittrich, and S. E. Schechter. It's Not Stealing If You Need It: A Panel on the Ethics of Performing Research Using Public Data of Illicit Origin. In *Financial Cryptography*, 2012.

[13] R. Jain. The art of computer systems performance analysis: Techniques for experimental design, measurements, simulation, and modeling. *Wiley*, April 1991.

[14] G. King, J. Pan, and M. Roberts. How censorship in China allows government criticism but silences collective expression. In *APSA Annual Meeting*, 2012.

[15] J. Knockel, J. R. Crandall, and J. Saia. Three Researchers, Five Conjectures: An Empirical Analysis of TOM-Skype Censorship and Surveillance. In *FOCI*, 2011.

[16] C. S. Leberknight, M. Chiang, H. V. Poor, and F. Wong. A Taxonomy of Internet Censorship and Anti-Censorship. Princeton Tech Report, http://www.princeton.edu/~chiangm/anticensorship.pdf, 2012.

[17] M. Marquis-Boire et al. Planet Blue Coat: Mapping Global Censorship and Surveillance Tools. https://citizenlab.org/wp-content/uploads/2013/01/Planet-Blue-Coat.pdf, 2013.

[18] Z. Nabi. The Anatomy of Web Censorship in Pakistan. In *FOCI*, 2013.

[19] Open Net Initiative. Internet Filtering in Syria. https://opennet.net/research/profiles/syria, 2009.

[20] J. C. Park and J. R. Crandall. Empirical Study of a National-Scale Distributed Intrusion Detection System: Backbone-level Filtering of HTML Responses in China. In *ICDCS*, 2010.

[21] Reporters Without Borders. Syria. http://en.rsf.org/syria-syria-12-03-2012,42053.html, 2012.

[22] V. Silver. H-P Computers Underpin Syria Surveillance. http://www.bloomberg.com/news/2011-11-18/hewlett-packard-computers-underpin-syria-electonic-surveillance-project.html, 2011.

[23] Telecomix. #OpSyria: Syrian Censorship Logs (Season 3). http://reflets.info/opsyria-syrian-censoship-log/, 2011.

[24] The Tor Project. Tor's Censorship Wiki – Syria. https://trac.torproject.org/projects/tor/wiki/doc/OONI/censorshipwiki/CensorshipByCountry/Syria, 2013.

[25] J. Valentino-Devries, P. Sonne, and N. Malas. U.S. Firm Acknowledges Syria Uses Its Gear to Block Web. http://preview.tinyurl.com/kvpkeos, 2011.

[26] J.-P. Verkamp and M. Gupta. Inferring Mechanics of Web Censorship Around the World. In *FOCI*, 2012.

[27] VFM Systems & Services Ltd. Blue Coat ProxySG Solution with Web Filter and Reporter. http://www.slideshare.net/vfmindia/vfm-bluecoat-proxy-sg-solution-with-web-filter-and-reporter, 2013.

[28] Whittaker, Z. Surveillance and censorship: Inside Syria's Internet. http://www.cbsnews.com/news/surveillance-and-censorship-inside-syrias-internet/, 2013.

[29] P. Winter and S. Lindskog. How the Great Firewall of China is Blocking Tor. In *FOCI*, 2012.

[30] X. Xu, Z. M. Mao, and J. A. Halderman. Internet censorship in China: Where does the filtering occur? In *PAM*, 2011.

[31] T.-F. Yen, Y. Xie, F. Yu, R. Yu, and M. Abadi. Host Fingerprinting and Tracking on the Web: Privacy and Security Implications. *NDSS*, 2012.

Automated Detection and Fingerprinting of Censorship Block Pages

Ben Jones, Tzu-Wen Lee*, Nick Feamster, Phillipa Gill*
Georgia Tech *Stony Brook University

Abstract

One means of enforcing Web censorship is to return a *block page*, which informs the user that an attempt to access a webpage is unsuccessful. Detecting block pages can provide a more complete picture of Web censorship, but automatically identifying block pages is difficult because Web content is dynamic, personalized, and may even be in different languages. Previous work has manually detected and identified block pages, which is difficult to reproduce; it is also time-consuming, which makes it difficult to perform continuous, longitudinal studies of censorship. This paper presents an automated method both to detect block pages and to fingerprint the filtering products that generate them. Our automated method enables continuous measurements of block pages; we found that our methods successfully detect 95% of block pages and identify five filtering tools, including a tool that had not been previously identified "in the wild".

Categories and Subject Descriptors

C.2.0 [**Computer-Communication Networks**]:[Security and protection (e.g., firewalls)]; C.2.3 [**Network Operations**]: [Network Monitoring]

Keywords

Censorship; Internet Measurement

1 Introduction

Internet censorship is pervasive; for example, the OpenNet Initiative's latest measurements detected censorship in 38 of 74 countries [10]. Censorship mechanisms can take many forms, ranging from injected TCP RST packets or DNS responses, to explicit Web pages notifying users that the content has been blocked, or *block pages*. Previous work has developed mechanisms to automatically detect TCP RST packets and altered DNS responses [13, 1], but a significant share of censorship still consists of block pages. To provide a more complete picture of Internet censorship, we must develop automated methods to detect block pages and identify the filtering tools that create them.

Differentiating accessible content from block pages are difficult for several reasons:

1. *Dynamic Content.* Some sites may update content between requests, returning different versions of the same page. Figures 1a and 1b illustrate this effect for `cnn.com`. Block pages may also change (*e.g.*, to display the blocked URL or category), adding yet more problems. Figure 1c illustrates this problem because the block page includes the URL for `cnn.com`.
2. *Content is personalized.* Web sites may personalize content for an individual or region, thereby decreasing the similarity between versions of the same page.
3. *Content is in different languages.* Languages vary across regions, making keyword matching challenging.

Today, those who wish to measure block pages must manually create regular expressions to detect specific block pages and identify filtering tools. Unfortunately, this approach is too slow and resource-intensive to support consistent, continuous measurements because a person must manually create new regular expressions. This process also cannot identify unknown block page templates *a priori*.

In this paper, we present techniques to automatically detect block pages and identify the products that serve them. Our detection technique is based on the insight that it is easier to detect the *difference* between a block page and legitimate content than the similarity between a block page and known block pages. Based upon this insight, we develop a block page detection method that correctly identifies 95% of block pages and 98.6% of accessible pages.

Our fingerprinting technique is based on the insight that block page templates uniquely identify the filtering tool that generated them. Using this method, we identify five known filtering tools, including one that has not been previously observed "in the wild". We extend the work of Dalek *et al.* [2] by automatically identifying filtering tools where possible, and flagging unidentified templates for researchers to label. Since these methods do not require active probing, we can apply them to archival censorship measurements from the OpenNet Initiative and provide the first glimpse into changes in filtering tools across time.

The rest of this paper describes our methods for detecting block pages; techniques for fingerprinting block pages to uniquely identify block page vendors; the accuracy of these detection and fingerprinting methods; and an application of these techniques to five years of measurements of block pages from 49 countries.

2 Background

In this section, we describe various web filtering mechanisms and survey related work.

2.1 Censorship and Block Pages

A censor may return a block page using a variety of mechanisms, such as injecting DNS responses, redirecting traffic through transparent proxies, and inserting packets directly into a TCP stream. In *DNS redirection*, the censor injects a fake DNS response when the user tries to resolve a hostname that contains blocked content, thereby redirecting the user to a server hosting a block page. *Transparent proxies* can provide more granularity than DNS injection by inspecting the content of HTTP streams for restricted keywords or URLs. If the user tries to access restricted content, the proxy could

IMC'14, November 5–7, 2014, Vancouver, BC, Canada.
ACM 978-1-4503-3213-2/14/11.
http://dx.doi.org/10.1145/2663716.2663722

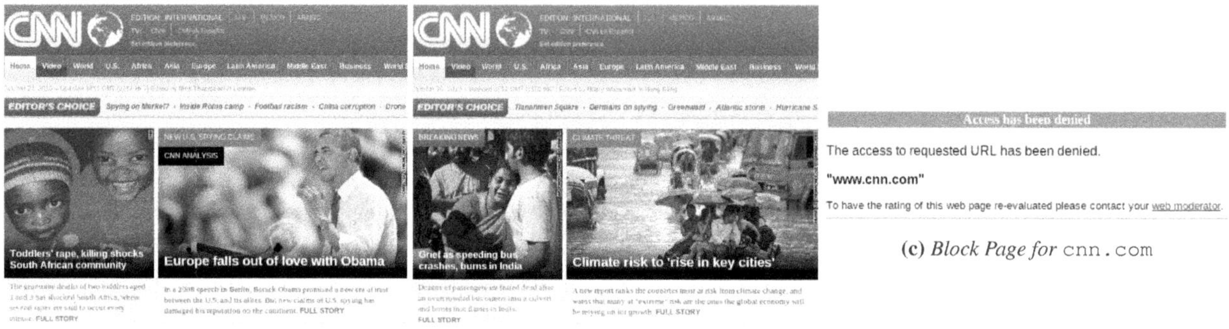

(a) cnn.com *on October 24* (b) cnn.com *on October 30* (c) *Block Page for* cnn.com

Figure 1: *Differences between accessible pages inhibit block page detection. Figure 1a and Figure 1b are structurally similar, but contain different text and links. Both of these versions of the page differ from the block page in Figure 1c. The block page in Figure 1c also shows that block pages can contain custom content, in this case, the blocked URL,* cnn.com *. Variations in block page content make block page detection challenging and time consuming.*

drop the request and return a block page. Because a block page is overt, it is generally safe to assume that a censor who returns a block page to the user is not trying to hide the fact that they are censoring the page and are thus not genearally interested in evading our detection techniques.

2.2 Related Work

OONI [11] is the only other censorship measurement tool that has implemented an automated block page detection method. In Section 4.1, we describe OONI's DOM similarity measure, and in Section 4.2 we compare its method to other block page detection techniques.

Block page detection relates to both document classification and web page classification. *Document classification* aims to classify documents based on features within the documents. The most relevant document classification technique is term-based classification, which clusters pages based on the words in a document [4]. *Web page classification* is a type of document classification that operates on web pages. Web page classification may leverage the semantic content of HTML markup [7], which provides information for visualizing and linking documents. Some classification methods strip the HTML structure from pages and use existing document classification schemes on the stripped content.

Previous work has aimed to identify other types of censorship techniques, such as methods that reset connections or otherwise interfere with connections. Weaver *et al.* detected injected TCP RST packets and tried to isolate the source and purpose of the injected RST packets [13]. They also fingerprinted filtering tools that reset TCP connections. More recently, Weaver *et al.* focus on identifying the existence and purpose of transparent proxies, but did not extend the work to measuring censorship due to user safety concerns [12].

Marqui-Boire *et al.* scanned networks for Blue Coat devices and confirmed the manufacturer by actively probing the devices [5]. Noman *et al.* and the Citizen Lab explored how censorship changes in response to changes in the URL list for a particular product [8, 6]. Dalek *et al.* identified URL filtering tools by network scanning and validated their results with in-network testing [2]. Unfortunately, these methods are time consuming because each measurement requires generating new URLs and inconsistent because network scanning may miss devices that do not have public IPs.

3 Data

We used the OpenNet Initiative (ONI) [10] block page corpus, which has over 500,000 entries. The ONI collected measurements in 49 countries from 2007 to 2012 using locally and globally sensitive URLs as defined by ONI researchers and collaborators around the globe. Each entry in the database corresponds to a single measurement for a URL and contains an uncensored version of the page collected in Toronto, and a test page, collected in the censoring country at approximately the same time. We assume that the Internet in Toronto is not censored and therefore that page represents a known good page. Amongst other data, the dataset has a measurement timestamp, a manually-assigned label indicating whether the test page is blocked or not, the location of the test, and the test network. An anonymized version of the dataset and more information are available online [3].

The ONI dataset has a label for each measurement indicating if the test page was blocked or accessible. To generate this labeling, an ONI staff member generated a regular expression for each block page in each region; about 28,000 test pages were labeled as blocked, and the remaining test pages (about 480,000) were labeled as accessible. We use both sets in our evaluation of detection methods. Because this labeling process created new regular expressions for each new test, the labeling accounts for changes in block pages. Although we identified a few misclassified pages, we have found the labeling to be mostly accurate; these labels have themselves served as a means to identify censorship in previous studies [3] and are thus a reasonable source of an independent label.

4 Block Page Detection

We present methods for detecting block pages based on a simple insight: block pages are less similar to accessible pages than different versions of accessible pages are to one another. Thus, while accessible pages may be non-identical, block pages will exhibit more significant differences. To classify a test page as blocked or not, we compare the test page to a known unblocked version of the page using a similarity measure. Each test page was collected from the region of interest at about the same time as the known unblocked version of the page. To find the best classifier, we evaluated many similarity metrics, including page length, cosine similarity, and DOM similarity (the metric that OONI [11] uses). We evaluated several other document classification methods such as inverse document frequency (IDF), which performed poorly; and

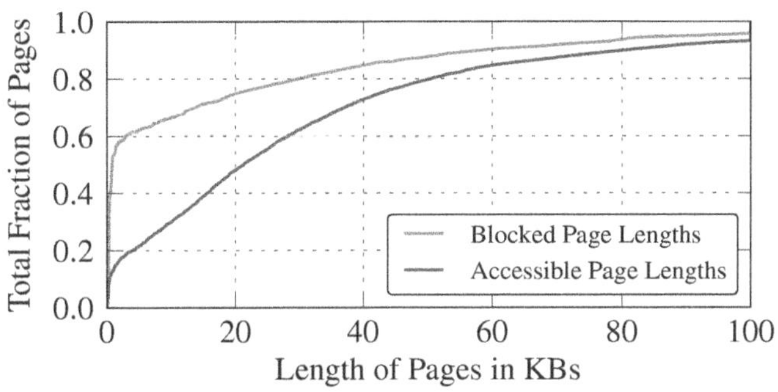

Figure 2: *Block pages are typically smaller than accessible pages. The knee of the blocked page curve is inset.*

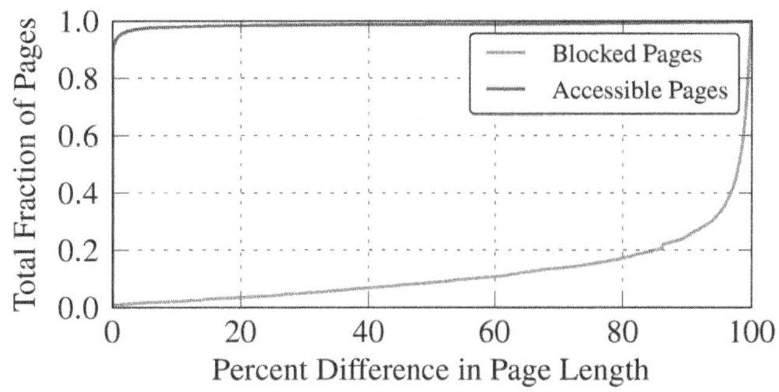

Figure 3: *Differences in page length for blocked and accessible sites imply that the length comparison measure can differentiate between blocked and accessible pages. The knee of the accessible page scores curve is shown inset.*

other methods such as fuzzy hashing. We present the most salient results below.

4.1 Metrics

Length. In the length similarity metric, we compare the sizes of the test page and the known unblocked page. The intuition is that block pages will be smaller than accessible pages, so a test page may be a block page if its size significantly differs from the size of the known good page. This simple approach works well because accessible pages tend to be larger than blocked pages, as Figure 2 illustrates. To compare pages, we compute the page length difference using Equation 1, where $len1$ is the length of the known unblocked page and $len2$ is the length of the test page.

$$\text{Length Percent Diff} = \frac{|len1 - len2|}{max\{len1, len2\}} \tag{1}$$

Cosine Similarity. The cosine similarity metric [4] compares pages based on a term frequency vector, which is a data structure that stores the number of times the words in a document occur. In the context of block page identification, the terms are HTML tags; the term frequency vector stores the number of times each HTML tag appears within a page. Representing a page by its HTML structure allows us to elide most dynamic content, which reduces the variance between accessible pages and (hence) the false positive rate.

DOM Similarity. The developers of OONI [11] proposed comparing the HTML structure of block pages using a DOM similarity measure. The metric creates an adjacency matrix with the probabilities of transitioning between HTML tags. The DOM similarity measure then compresses the adjacency matrix for each page into a vector of its eigenvalues and compares these vectors with a normalized dot product.

4.2 Results

We find that our automated detection methods are accurate, and that the page length similarity measure works best. To evaluate these measures, we compute precision, recall, and false positive rates for each metric using a ten-fold cross-validation and compare precision-recall and ROC curves.

The length comparison measure scored blocked and accessible pages differently, as Figure 3 shows: A threshold that marks any difference in size over 30% as blocked achieves a true positive rate of 95% and a false positive rate of 1.37%. These numbers compare favorably to other similarity measures, as shown in Table 1. Furthermore, the low standard deviation shows that the length comparison metric performed consistently well during cross-validation, implying that these results will generalize to other block pages. Figure 4 shows the precision-recall and ROC curves for each metric, further illustrating that length comparison is the best metric.

5 Block Page Fingerprinting

To fingerprint filtering tools, we identify block page templates and match signatures for each template. Though signature matching for block pages is not new, automated detection of block page templates reduces the effort and increases consistency of filtering product identification.

5.1 Approach

We fingerprint block pages using two features from the block page detection methods: page length and term frequency vectors. Using these features, we cluster the block pages and label each cluster with the filtering tool that generated the template. We assume that filtering tools generate block pages from a template, and that each template is unique to the filtering tool, though a single filtering tool may have many templates. Our analysis of changes in censorship in Section 5.2 and prior work[3] validate this assumption.

We used both term frequency vectors and page length as features for clustering. The intuition behind page length clustering is that block-page templates change at most a few words between different URLs. We used single-link hierarchical clustering to generate clusters on the basis of the block page sizes without knowing the number of clusters *a priori*.

Similarly, the intuition behind term frequency clustering is that the censor will not vary the structure of a block page within the same template. This intuition appears to be accurate because there are only 37 *distinct* term frequency vectors from the 5 years of data. We partitioned the data into different clusters on the basis of unique term frequency vectors.

5.2 Results

To validate the clusters that our algorithm produced, we compared the clusterings to manually labeled block page templates. We manually identified 27 block page templates and computed the longest common subsequences for each template. We used these subsequences to represent the ground truth for distinct clusters and them to calculate precision and recall for each cluster. In this context, precision is the number of pages in the cluster which come from the same block page template. Recall is the number of pages in the cluster which match a block page template out of all the pages that match a block page template. This method may not capture all block page templates, but this should not be a problem because of our evaluation method. Because we are using precision and recall,

Similarity Measure	True Positive/ Recall (%)	False Positive (%)	Precision (%)	Threshold
Page Length	$95.03 \pm 1.128 \cdot 10^{-3}$	$1.371 \pm 1.829 \cdot 10^{-16}$	$79.80 \pm 1.915 \cdot 10^{-4}$	30.19%
Cosine Similarity	$97.94 \pm 2.341 \cdot 10^{-14}$	$1.938 \pm 3.657 \cdot 10^{-16}$	$74.23 \pm 1.170 \cdot 10^{-14}$	0.816
DOM Similarity	$95.35 \pm 1.242 \cdot 10^{-2}$	$3.732 \pm 1.866 \cdot 10^{-3}$	$59.28 \pm 8.929 \cdot 10^{-3}$	0.995
Diff	99.13	30.95	15.44	n/a

Table 1: *Mean detection rates for similarity measures ± standard deviation are much better than a simple diff.*

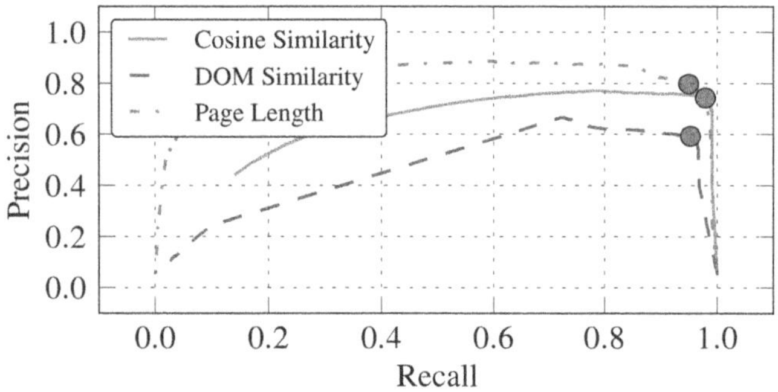

(a) *Precision-recall curve for similarity measures.*

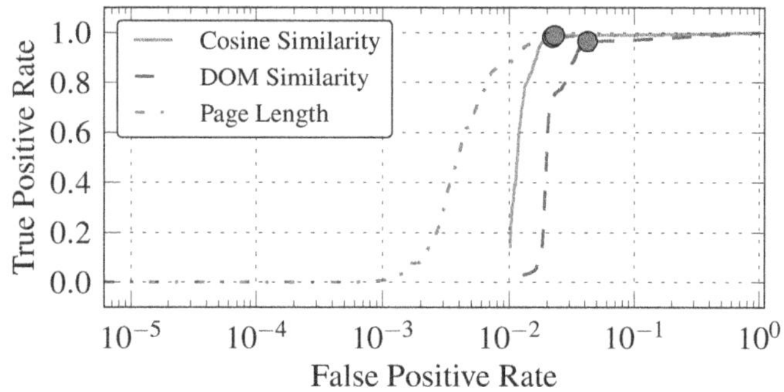

(b) *ROC curve for similarity measures.*

Figure 4: *Precision-recall and ROC curves demonstrate that the length comparison measure is the best similarity measure. Green dots mark the selected threshold values on the graph.*

we are evaluating our clustering based upon how well it identifies the templates *we know about.* Our method may also find templates we did not manually identify, but we do not evaluate the quality of those clusters.

To evaluate the quality of each clustering, we computed an F-1 measure for each cluster. The F-1 measure is a common clustering evaluation measure that combines precision and recall equally: $\frac{2 \cdot precision \cdot recall}{precision + recall}$. Finally, we calculated the overall F-1 measure by summing the maximum F-measure for each subsequence: $\sum_{i \in clusters} \frac{n_i}{N} \cdot max_{j \in subsequences}\{f(i,j)\}$, where N is the total number of block pages, n_i is the number of block pages in the i'th cluster, and $f(i,j)$ is the F-measure for cluster i and subsequence j. By taking the maximum F-measure for each subsequence, we associate the block page template, or template subsequence, with the cluster that best matches the template. We then average the F-measures by weighting the F-measure for each subsequence according to the number of pages using that template. Intuitively, this weighting ensures that an outcome with 20 clusters each with one element and an F-measure of 1 and one cluster with 1000 elements and an F-measure of 0.01 does not score well. The F-1 measure scales between 0 and 1; a higher score correlates with higher precision and recall. When the F-1 measure is higher, the clustering strongly corresponds with the identified common subsequences. Because we generate common subsequences from a random sample of block pages and each page matched at most one subsequence, clusters with a high F-measure also strongly correspond to a single template.

Term frequency clustering performs well, with an F-1 measure of 0.98; clustering based on page length is much worse, with an F-1 measure of 0.64. This result makes sense because block pages are generated from a template. Therefore, they often share the same structure. Term frequency clustering identifies block page templates despite noise introduced by pages mislabeled as blocked and a significant amount of noise introduced by standard HTTP error messages. For instance, the data set included a large number of HTTP 302 and 404 responses. On the other hand, we were surprised that page length produced poor-quality clusters. Block

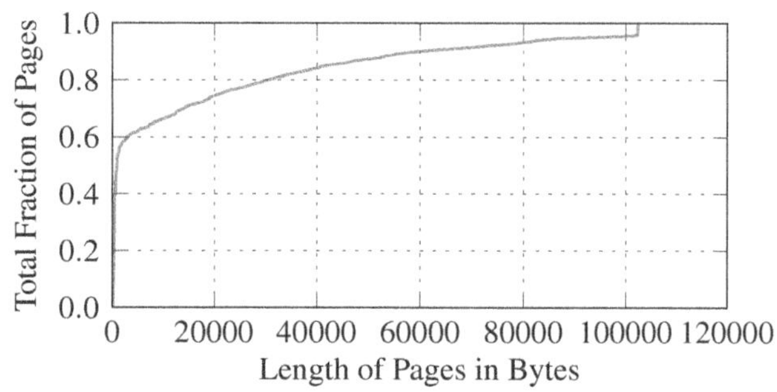

Figure 5: *Block pages have only a few distinct lengths.*

page templates only replace small amounts of text (*e.g.*the URL of the blocked Web site), so we expected similar page lengths within a cluster. Interestingly, Figure 5 shows that block pages have few distinct sizes; there are fewer clusters than templates.

Fingerprinting Filtering Tools. Where possible, we label each cluster according to known signatures (*e.g.*, from previous work [2]); otherwise, we attempt to manually identify the block page vendor based on features of each template. Using this method, we identified five filtering tools that generated 7 out of 36 clusters from the dataset. In these cases, copyright notices within HTML comments, HTTP header fields, or other signatures offered a definitive identification. The remainder of the clusters had no identifying information in the fingerprint, although unique HTTP headers indicated the use of a distinct tool. Table 2 summarizes these results.

6 Case Studies

We now apply our detection and fingerprinting techniques to the ONI dataset to explore how the use of various block page methods has evolved over time. Unfortunately, the ONI did not continuously gather measurements, so we can only explore measurements from small snapshots. Fortunately, each snapshot contains enough measurements to make inferences about the presence of specific filtering tools. Because the censor could always choose to return nothing or

Number of Clusters	Product Manufacturer	Network	Time Frame	Fingerprint
2	FortiGuard	AS 24090 (Malaysia)	2009	Block page contains the text "Powered by FortiGuard"
1	Squid Proxy Server	AS 2609 (Tunisia)	2010	HTTP Headers contain the text "Server: squid/2.6.STABLE16"
1	Netsweeper	AS 12486 (United States), AS 15802 (United Arab Emirates), and AS 12586 (Yemen)	2010-2012	"webadmin/deny" in URL, which indicates that Netsweeper is in use [2]
1	Websense	AS 29584 (Azerbaijan)	2010	Websense copyright disclaimer is included in HTML comments
2	WireFilter	AS 25019 (Saudi Arabia)	2011	HTTP Headers contain the text "Server: Protected by WireFilter"

Table 2: *Filtering tools identified from block page templates*

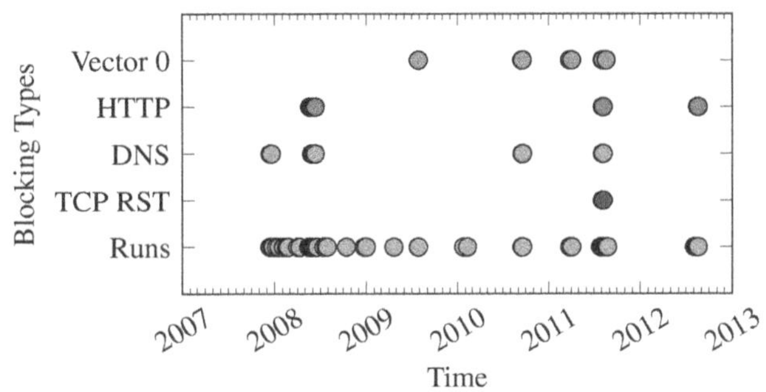

Figure 6: *Filtering mechanisms used in AS 18399 in Burma.*

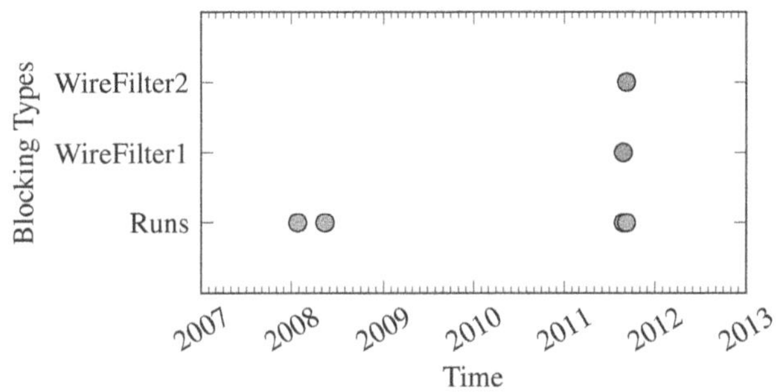

Figure 7: *The appearance of two block page templates in AS 25019 marks the use of WireFilter, a new filtering tool in Saudi Arabia.*

change the block page, the absence of a block page cluster does not indicate that the given filtering tool is no longer in use. To account for this ambiguity, we include other types of blocking to give further insight into changes in filtering tools and capabilities. Specifically, vectors refer to block page templates, HTTP indicates no response to an HTTP request, DNS corresponds to either manipulation by redirection or the lack of a response, TCP RST refers to TCP RST filtering, and runs shows when measurements were taken.

We also extend our analysis by determining if block pages are the result of DNS redirection or not. We assume that the censor can only use a few IP addresses to host block pages, so if DNS redirection is in use, we expect the block pages to resolve to a limited number of IP addresses. Though the number of resolved IP addresses can fluctuate due to CDNs, DNS redirection should return significantly fewer IP addresses than the number of distinct URLs measured.

Political Shifts (Burma). Analyzing changes in filtering mechanisms and block pages in Burma (Myanmar) provides insight into how censorship evolves as filtering tools and regimes change. Figure 6 shows the censorship enforcement mechanisms and block page clusters used in AS 18399 in Burma between 2007 and 2012. Until mid 2009, AS 18399 used DNS redirection as a form of censorship. In mid-2009, a custom block page template for AS 18399, vector 0, appears. Because the block pages in vector 0 resolved 568 URLs to 659 IPs, vector 0 does not appear to be using DNS redirection. Unfortunately, we could not identify the product behind vector 0, but these results indicate that AS 18399 in Burma may have acquired a new filtering tool in mid 2009. In late 2011, Burma underwent a massive political shift and significantly reduced the extent of censorship [9], which may be reflected in the lack of detected block pages after this time.

New Filtering Tools (Saudi Arabia). We observed that Saudi Arabia, like many countries, has upgraded its censorship equipment in recent years. Figure 7 illustrates this shift for AS 25019. Although we do not know what type of filtering equipment was used in AS 25019 prior to 2011, we can conclude that a new filtering tool, WireFilter, begins censoring content in 2011. Oddly, WireFilter appears to be using multiple block page templates concurrently, which implies that multiple devices are in use.

Different Techniques in Different ISPs (Thailand). Different ISPs implement Thailand's censorship mandate differently. Figure 8 illustrates that AS 9737 and AS 17552 use different filtering tools and mechanisms to enforce censorship.

Figure 8a shows that AS 9737 has changed censorship mechanisms over time. The first set of measurements in 2008 show that AS 9737 uses DNS redirection and drops HTTP requests to censor content. In 2010, AS 9737 starts using a new filtering tool, represented by vector 17. We could not identify vector 17, but it appears to be a transparent proxy because the 30 URLS blocked by vector 17 resolved to 48 unique IP addresses, indicating that DNS injection was not used. It appears that AS 9737 is also trying to mask the identity of its filtering software because all HTTP headers for vector 17 contain the string "Server: Apache/2.2.9 (Debian)".

Figure 8b shows that AS 17552 and AS 9737 use different censorship enforcement mechanisms though they have both changed their filtering over time. Our data shows that AS 17552 switched from DNS redirection to a new filtering tool in late 2009, shown by vector 8. Vector 8 does not appear to be the result of DNS redirection because its 19 URLS resolved to 28 IP addresses. AS 17552 also appears to obfuscate the identity of their filtering tool because all HTTP headers for the block page contain the string "Server: Apache".

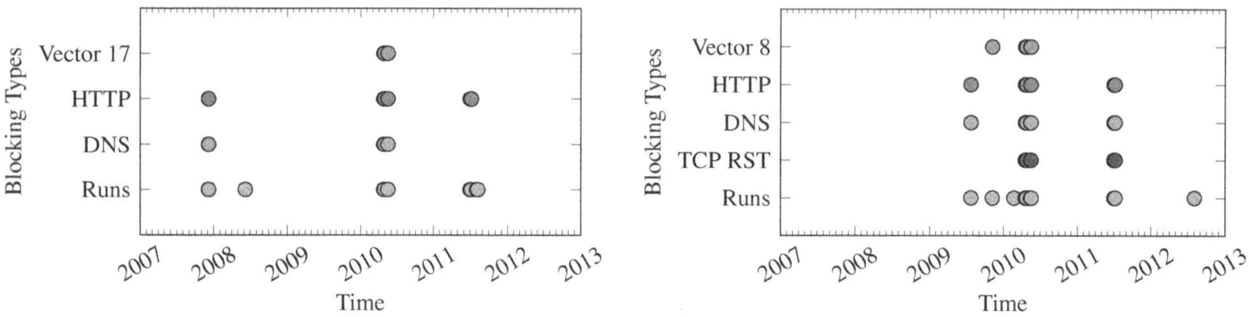

(a) *Filtering mechanisms used in AS 9737 in Thailand* **(b)** *Filtering mechanisms used in AS 17552 in Thailand*

Figure 8: *ASes 9737 and 17552 show that government mandated censorship can vary by ISP*

Though ASes 9737 and 17552 use different block page templates, they may be using different configurations of the same filtering tool. Vectors 8 and 17, the block pages for ASes 9737 and 17552, have different structures, as vector 8 uses tables for layout and is around 6000 bytes in length, whereas vector 17 uses div tags for layout and is around 1000 bytes in length. Despite these differences, the filtering tools both appear to be transparent proxies, the filtering tools return similar HTTP headers, and both block pages contain similar strings such as "The page you are trying to visit has been blocked by the Ministry of Information and Communication Technology" (vector 8) and "This website has been blocked by ICT" (vector 17).

7 Conclusion

We developed block page detection and filtering tool identification techniques to enable scalable, continuous, and accurate censorship measurements. Using these techniques, we built a block page detection method with a 95.03% true positive rate and a 1.371% false positive rate and a block page identification method which correctly identified block page templates for 5 known filtering tools. These methods significantly improve the state of the art in censorship measurement and set the stage for the next generation of censorship measurements. Because the vendor and product behind many clusters remains unidentified, future work could include fingerprinting existing block page products and using the fingerprints to find more template matches.

Acknowledgments

We would like to thank the OpenNet Initiative and the Citizen Lab for the use of their data. This work was supported by a Google Faculty Research Award, a Google Focused Research Award, and NSF awards CNS-1111723 and SaTC-1350720.

References

[1]: J. Crandall, D. Zinn, M. Byrd, E. Barr, and R. East. Conceptdoppler: A weather tracker for internet censorship. In *Proceedings of the 14th ACM Conference on Computer and Communications Security*, CCS '07a, pages 352–365, New York, NY, USA, 2007. ACM. (Not cited.)

[2]: J. Dalek, B. Haselton, H. Noman, A. Senft, M. Crete-Nishihata, P. Gill, and R. J. Deibert. A method for identifying and confirming the use of URL filtering products for censorship. In *IMC '13: Proceedings of the 2013 conference on Internet measurement conference*. ACM Request Permissions, Oct. 2013. (Not cited.)

[3]: P. Gill, M. Crete-Nishihata, J. Dalek, S. Goldberg, A. Senft, and G. Wiseman. Characterizing censorship of web content worldwide: Another look at the opennet initiative data. `http://www.cs.stonybrook.edu/~phillipa/papers/ONIAnaly.html`, 2013. (Not cited.)

[4]: E. H and G. Karypis. Centroid-based document classification: Analysis & experimental results. Technical Report 00-017, University of Minnesota, 2000. (Not cited.)

[5]: M. Marqui-Boire, J. Dalek, S. McKune, M. Carrieri, M. Crete-Nishihata, R. Deibert, S. O. Khan, H. Noman, J. Scott-Railton, and G. Wiseman. Planet blue coat: Mapping global censorship and surveillance tools. Technical report, The Citizen Lab, January 2013. (Not cited.)

[6]: H. Noman and J. C. York. West censoring east: The use of western technologies by middle east censors, 2010-2011. Technical report, The OpenNet Initiative, March 2011. (Not cited.)

[7]: X. Qi and B. D. Davison. Web page classification: Features and algorithms. *ACM Comput. Surv.*, 41(2):12:1–12:31, Feb. 2009. (Not cited.)

[8]: The Citizen Lab. Behind blue coat: Investigations of commercial filtering in syria and burma. Technical report, The Citizen Lab, November 2011. (Not cited.)

[9]: The OpenNet Initiative. Burma (myanmar). `https://opennet.net/research/profiles/burma`. (Not cited.)

[10]: The OpenNet Initiative. The opennet initiative. `https://opennet.net`. (Not cited.)

[11]: The Tor Project. Ooni: Open observatory of network interference. `https://ooni.torproject.org/`. (Not cited.)

[12]: N. Weaver, C. Kreibich, M. Dam, and V. Paxson. Here be web proxies. In M. Faloutsos and A. Kuzmanovic, editors, *Passive and Active Measurement*, volume 8362 of *Lecture Notes in Computer Science*, pages 183–192. Springer International Publishing, 2014. (Not cited.)

[13]: N. Weaver, R. Sommer, and V. Paxson. Detecting forged tcp reset packets. In *Presented as part of 16th Annual Network & Distributed System Security Symposium*, 2009. (Not cited.)

Measuring Price Discrimination and Steering on E-commerce Web Sites

Aniko Hannak
Northeastern University
Boston, MA
ancsaaa@ccs.neu.edu

Gary Soeller
Northeastern University
Boston, MA
soelgary@ccs.neu.edu

David Lazer
Northeastern University
Boston, MA
d.lazer@neu.edu

Alan Mislove
Northeastern University
Boston, MA
amislove@ccs.neu.edu

Christo Wilson
Northeastern University
Boston, MA
cbw@ccs.neu.edu

ABSTRACT

Today, many e-commerce websites personalize their content, including Netflix (movie recommendations), Amazon (product suggestions), and Yelp (business reviews). In many cases, personalization provides advantages for users: for example, when a user searches for an ambiguous query such as "router," Amazon may be able to suggest the woodworking tool instead of the networking device. However, personalization on e-commerce sites may also be used to the user's disadvantage by manipulating the products shown (price steering) or by customizing the prices of products (price discrimination). Unfortunately, today, we lack the tools and techniques necessary to be able to detect such behavior.

In this paper, we make three contributions towards addressing this problem. First, we develop a methodology for accurately measuring when price steering and discrimination occur and implement it for a variety of e-commerce web sites. While it may seem conceptually simple to detect differences between users' results, accurately attributing these differences to price discrimination and steering requires correctly addressing a number of sources of noise. Second, we use the accounts and cookies of over 300 real-world users to detect price steering and discrimination on 16 popular e-commerce sites. We find evidence for some form of personalization on nine of these e-commerce sites. Third, we investigate the effect of user behaviors on personalization. We create fake accounts to simulate different user features including web browser/OS choice, owning an account, and history of purchased or viewed products. Overall, we find numerous instances of price steering and discrimination on a variety of top e-commerce sites.

IMC'14, November 5–7, 2014, Vancouver, BC, Canada.

http://dx.doi.org/10.1145/2663716.2663744 .

Categories and Subject Descriptors

H.3.5 [**Information Systems**]: Online Services—*commercial services, web-based services*; H.5.2 [**Information interfaces and presentation**]: User Interfaces—*evaluation/methodology*

Keywords

Search; Personalization; E-commerce; Price discrimination

1. INTRODUCTION

Personalization is a ubiquitous feature on today's top web destinations. Search engines such as Google, streaming-media services such as Netflix, and recommendation sites such as Yelp all use sophisticated algorithms to tailor content to each individual user. In many cases, personalization provides advantages for users: for example, when a user searches on Google with an ambiguous query such as "apple," there are multiple potential interpretations. By personalizing the search results (e.g., by taking the user's history of prior searches into account), Google is able to return results that are potentially more relevant (e.g., computer products, rather than orchards).

Recently, researchers and Internet users have uncovered evidence of personalization on e-commerce sites [1, 29, 30]. On such sites, the benefits of personalization for users are less clear; e-commerce sites have an economic incentive to use personalization to induce users into spending more money. For example, the travel website Orbitz was found to be personalizing the results of hotel searches [28]. Unbeknownst to users, Orbitz "steered" Mac OS X users towards more expensive hotels in select locations by placing them at higher ranks in search results. Orbitz discontinued the use of this personalization algorithm after one month [7].

At first blush, detecting personalization on e-commerce sites seems conceptually simple: have two users run the same search, and any differences in the results indicate personalization. Unfortunately, this approach is likely to have many false positives, as differences between users' results may exist for a number of reasons not related to personalization. For example, results may differ due to changes in product inventory, regional tax differences, or inconsistencies across data centers. As a result, accurately detecting personalization on e-commerce sites remains an open challenge.

In this paper, we first develop a methodology that can accurately measure personalization on e-commerce sites. We then use this methodology to address two questions: first, *how widespread is personalization on today's e-commerce web sites?* This includes *price discrimination* (customizing prices for some users) as well as *price steering* (changing the order of search results to highlight specific products). Second, *how are e-commerce retailers choosing to implement personalization?* Although there is anecdotal evidence of these effects [46, 48] and specific instances where retailers have been exposed doing so [1,28], the frequency and mechanisms of e-commerce personalization remain poorly understood.

Our paper represents the first comprehensive study of e-commerce personalization that examines price discrimination and price steering for 300 real-world users[1], as well as synthetically generated fake accounts. We develop a measurement infrastructure that is able to distinguish genuine personalization of e-commerce sites from other sources of noise; this methodology is based on previous work on measuring personalization of web search services [17]. Using this methodology, we examine 16 top e-commerce sites covering general retailers as well as hotel and rental car booking sites. Our real-world data indicates that eight of these sites implement personalization, while our controlled tests based on fake accounts allow us to identify specific user features that trigger personalization on seven sites. Specifically, we observe the following personalization strategies:

- Cheaptickets and Orbitz implement price discrimination by offering reduced prices on hotels to "members".
- Expedia and Hotels.com engage in A/B testing that steers a subset of users towards more expensive hotels.
- Home Depot and Travelocity personalize search results for users on mobile devices.
- Priceline personalizes search results based on a user's history of clicks and purchases.

In addition to positively identifying price discrimination and steering on several well-known e-commerce sites, we also make the following four specific contributions. *First*, we introduce control accounts into all of our experiments, which allows us to differentiate between inherent noise and actual personalization. *Second*, we develop a novel methodology using information retrieval metrics to identify price steering. *Third*, we examine the impact of purchase history on personalization by reserving hotel rooms and rental cars, then comparing the search results received by these users to users with no history. *Fourth*, we identify a never-before-seen form of e-commerce personalization based on A/B testing, and show that it leads to price steering. Finally, we make all of our crawling scripts, parsers, and raw data available to the research community.

2. BACKGROUND AND MOTIVATION

We now provide background on e-commerce personalization and overview the terminology used in this paper.

2.1 A Brief History of Personalization

Online businesses have long used personalized recommendations as a way to boost sales. Retailers like Amazon and Target leverage the search and purchase histories of users to identify products that users may be interested in. In some cases, companies go to great lengths to obfuscate the fact that recommendations are personalized, because users sometimes find these practices to be creepy [10].

In several cases, e-commerce sites have been observed performing *price discrimination*: the practice of showing different prices to different people for the same item. Several years ago, Amazon briefly tested an algorithm that personalized prices for frequent shoppers [1]. Although many consumers erroneously believe that price discrimination on the Internet is illegal and are against the practice [8, 36], consumers routinely accept real-world price discrimination in the form of coupons, student discounts, or members-only prices [5].

Similarly, e-commerce sites have been observed performing *price steering*: the practice of re-ordering search results to place expensive items towards the top of the page. For example, the travel web site Orbitz was found to be promoting high-value hotels specifically to Apple users [28]. Although the prices of individual items do not change in this case, customers are likely to purchase items that are placed towards the top of search results [25], and thus users can be nudged towards more expensive items.

2.2 Scope of This Study

Throughout the paper, we survey a wide variety of e-commerce web sites, ranging from large-scale retailers like Walmart to travel sites like Expedia. To make the results comparable, we only consider products returned via *searches*—as opposed to "departments", home page offers, and other mechanisms by which e-commerce sites offer products to users—as searching is a functionality supported by most large retailers. We leave detecting price discrimination and steering via other mechanisms to future work. Additionally, we use *products* and their advertised price on the search result page (e.g., a specific item on Walmart or hotel on Expedia) as the basic unit of measurement; we leave the investigation of effects such as bundle discounts, coupons, sponsored listings, or hidden prices to future work as well.

2.3 Definitions

Personalization on web services comes in many forms (e.g., "localization", per-account customization, *etc.*), and it is not entirely straightforward to declare that an inconsistency between the product search results observed by two users is due to personalization. For example, the two users' search queries may have been directed to different data centers, and the differences are a result of data center inconsistency rather than intentional personalization.

For the purposes of this paper, we define personalization to be taking place *when an inconsistency in product search results is due to client-side state associated with the request.* For example, a client's request often includes tracking cookies, a User-Agent identifying the browser and Operating System (OS), and the client's source IP address. If any of these lead to an inconsistency in the results, we declare the inconsistency to be personalization. In the different-datacenter example from above, the inconsistency between the two results is not due to any client-side state, and we therefore declare it not to be personalization.

More so than other web services [17], e-commerce retailers have a number of different dimensions available to personal-

[1]Our study is conducted under Northeastern Institutional Review Board protocol #13-04-12.

ize on. In this paper, we focus on two of the primary vectors for e-commerce personalization:

Price steering occurs when two users receive different product results (or the same products in a different order) for the same query (e.g., Best Buy showing more-expensive products to user A than user B when they both query for "laptops"). Price steering can be similar to personalization in web search [17], i.e., the e-commerce provider may be trying to give the user more relevant products (or, they may be trying to extract more money from the user). Steering is possible because e-commerce sites often do not sort search results by an objective metric like price or user reviews by default; instead, results can be sorted using an ambiguous metric like "Best Match" or "Most Relevant".

Price discrimination occurs when two users are shown inconsistent prices for the same product (e.g., Travelocity showing a select user a higher price for a particular hotel). Contrary to popular belief, price discrimination in general is not illegal in the United States [13], as the Robinson–Patman Act of 1936 (*a.k.a.* the Anti-Price Discrimination Act) is written to control the behavior of product manufacturers and distributors, not consumer-facing enterprises. It is unclear whether price discrimination targeted against protected classes (e.g., race, religion, gender) is legal.

Although the term "price discrimination" evokes negative connotations, it is actually a fundamental concept in economic theory, and it is widely practiced (and accepted by consumers) in everyday life. In economic theory, *perfect price discrimination* refers to a pricing strategy where each consumer is charged the maximum amount that they are willing to pay for each item [37]. *Elastic* consumers can afford to pay higher prices, whereas *inelastic* (price-constrained) consumers are charged less. In practice, strategies like *direct* and *indirect segmentation* are employed by companies to charge different prices to different segments of consumers [32]. One classic (and extremely popular [5]) example of indirect segmentation is coupons: consumers that take the time to seek out and use coupons explicitly reveal to the retailer that they are price-inelastic. Another accepted form of indirect segmentation is Saturday-night stay discount for airfares. Accepted forms of direct segmentation include discounts for students and seniors.

3. METHODOLOGY

Both price steering and discrimination are difficult to reliably detect in practice, as differences in e-commerce search results across users may be due to factors other than personalization. In this section, we describe the methodology we develop to address these measurement challenges. First, we give the high-level intuition that guides the design of our experiments, and describe how we accurately distinguish personalization of product search results from other causes of inconsistency. Second, we describe the implementation of our experiments. Third, we detail the sites that we choose to study and the queries we select to test for personalization.

3.1 Measuring Personalization

The first challenge we face when trying to measure personalization on e-commerce sites is dealing with the variety of sites that exist. Few of these sites offer programmatic APIs, and each uses substantially different HTML markup to implement their site. As a result, we collect data by visiting the various sites' web pages, and we write custom HTML parsers to extract the products and prices from the search result page for each site that we study. We make these scripts and parsers available to the research community.

The second challenge we face is *noise*, or inconsistencies in search results that are *not* due to personalization. Noise can be caused by a variety of factors:

- **Updates to the e-commerce site:** E-commerce services are known to update their inventory often, as products sell out, become available, or prices are changed. This means that the results for a query may change even over short timescales.
- **Distributed infrastructure:** Large-scale e-commerce sites are often spread across geographically diverse datacenters. Our tests show that different datacenters may return different results for the same search, due to inconsistencies across data centers.
- **Unknown:** As an e-commerce site is effectively a black-box (i.e., we do not know their internal architecture or algorithms), there may be other, unknown sources of noise that we are unaware of.

To control for all sources of noise, we include a *control* in each experiment that is configured identically to one other treatment (i.e., we run one of the experimental treatments twice). Doing so allows us to measure the noise as the level of inconsistency between the control account and its twin; since these two treatments are configured identically, any inconsistencies between them *must* be due to noise, not personalization. Then, we can measure the level of inconsistency between the different experimental treatments; if this is higher than the baseline noise, the increased inconsistencies are due to personalization. As a result, we cannot declare any particular inconsistency to be due to personalization (or noise), but we can report the overall rate.

To see why this works, suppose we want to determine if Firefox users receive different prices than Safari users on a given site. The naïve experiment would be to send a pair of identical, simultaneous searches—one with a Firefox `User-Agent` and one with a Safari `User-Agent`—and then look for inconsistencies. However, the site may be performing A/B testing, and the differences may be due to requests given different A/B treatments. Instead, we run an additional control (e.g., a third request with a Firefox `User-Agent`), and can measure the frequency of differences due to noise.

Of course, running a single query is insufficient to accurately measure noise and personalization. Instead, we run a large set of searches on each site over multiple days and report the aggregate level of noise and personalization across all results.

3.2 Implementation

Except for when we use real users' accounts (our Amazon Mechanical Turk users in § 4), we collect data from the various e-commerce sites using custom scripts for PhantomJS [35]. We chose PhantomJS because it is a full implementation of the WebKit browser, meaning that it executes JavaScript, manages cookies, *etc.* Thus, using PhantomJS is significantly more realistic than using custom code that does not execute JavaScript, and it is more scalable than automating a full web browser (e.g., Selenium [41]). Phan-

Retailer	Site	Category
Best Buy	http://bestbuy.com	Electronics
CDW	http://cdw.com	Computers
HomeDepot	http://homedepot.com	Home-improvement
JCPenney	http://jcp.com	Clothes, housewares
Macy's	http://macys.com	Clothes, housewares
Newegg	http://newegg.com	Computers
Office Depot	http://officedepot.com	Office supplies
Sears	http://sears.com	Clothes, housewares
Staples	http://sears.com	Office supplies
Walmart	http://walmart.com	General retailer

Table 1: The general retailers we measured in this study.

tomJS has been proven to allow large-scale measurements in previous work [17].

IP Address Geolocation. In our experiments, all PhantomJS instances issued queries from a /24 block of IP addresses located in Boston. Controlling the source IP address is critical since e-commerce sites may personalize results based on a user's geolocation. We do not examine geolocation-based personalization in this paper; instead, we refer interested readers to work by Mikians et al. that thoroughly examines this topic [29,30].

Browser Fingerprinting. All of our PhantomJS instances are configured identically, and present identical HTTP request headers and DOM properties (e.g., `screen.width`) to web servers. The only exceptions to this rule are in cases where we explicitly test for the effect of different `User-Agent` strings, or when an e-commerce site stores state on the client (e.g., with a cookie). Although we do not test for e-commerce personalization based on browser fingerprints [34], any website attempting to do so would observe identical fingerprints from all of our PhantomJS instances (barring the two previous exceptions). Thus, personalization based on currently known browser fingerprinting techniques is unlikely to impact our results.

3.3 E-commerce Sites

We focus on two classes of e-commerce web sites: general e-commerce retailers (e.g., Best Buy) and travel retailers (e.g., Expedia). We choose to include travel retailers because there is anecdotal evidence of price steering among such sites [28]. Of course, our methodology can be applied to other categories of e-commerce sites as well.

General Retailers. We select 10 of the largest e-commerce retailers, according to the Top500 e-commerce database [43], for our study, shown in Table 1. We exclude Amazon, as Amazon hosts a large number of different merchants, making it difficult to measure Amazon itself. We also exclude sites like `apple.com` that only sell their own brand.

Travel Retailers. We select six of the most popular web-based travel retailers [44] to study, shown in Table 2. For these retailers, we focus on searches for *hotels* and *rental cars*. We do not include airline tickets, as airline ticket pricing is done transparently through a set of Global Distribution Systems (GDSes) [6]. Furthermore, a recent study by Vissers et al. looked for, but was unable to find, evidence of price discrimination on the websites of 25 major airlines [45].

In all cases, the prices of products returned in search results are in US dollars, are pre-tax, and do not include shipping fees. Examining prices before taxes and shipping are applied helps to avoid differences in pricing that are due to the location of the business and/or the customer.

Retailer	Site	Hotels	Cars
Cheaptickets	http://cheaptickets.com	☑	☑
Expedia	http://expedia.com	☑	☑
Hotels.com	http://hotels.com	☑	☐
Orbitz	http://orbitz.com	☑	☑
Priceline	http://priceline.com	☑	☑
Travelocity	http://travelocity.com	☐	☑

Table 2: The travel retailers we measured in this study.

3.4 Searches

We select 20 searches to send to each target e-commerce site; it is the results of these searches that we use to look for personalization. We select the searches to cover a variety of product types, and tailor the searches to the type of products each retailer sells. For example, for JCPenney, our searches include "pillows", "sunglasses", and "chairs"; for Newegg, our searches include "flash drives", "LCD TVs", and "phones".

For travel web sites, we select 20 searches (location and date range) that we send to each site when searching for hotels or rental cars. We select 10 different cities across the globe (Miami, Honolulu, Las Vegas, London, Paris, Florence, Bangkok, Cairo, Cancun, and Montreal), and choose date ranges that are both short (4-day stays/rentals) and long (11-day stays/rentals).

4. REAL-WORLD PERSONALIZATION

We begin by addressing our first question: *how widespread are price discrimination and steering on today's e-commerce web sites?* To do so, we have a large set of real-world users run our experimental searches and examine the results that they receive.

4.1 Data Collection

To obtain a diverse set of users, we recruited from Amazon's Mechanical Turk (AMT) [3]. We posted three Human Intelligence Tasks (HITs) to AMT, with each HIT focusing on e-commerce, hotels, or rental cars. In the HIT, we explained our study and offered each user $1.00 to participate.[2] Users were required to live in the United States, and could only complete the HIT once.

Users who accepted the HIT were instructed to configure their web browser to use a Proxy Auto-Config (PAC) file provided by us. The PAC file routes all traffic to the sites under study to an HTTP proxy controlled by us. Then, users were directed to visit a web page containing JavaScript that performed our set of searches in an `iframe`. After each search, the Javascript grabs the HTML in the `iframe` and uploads it to our server, allowing us to view the results of the search. By having the user run the searches within their browser, any cookies that the user's browser had previously been assigned would automatically be forwarded in our searches. This allows us to examine the results that the user would have received. We waited 15 seconds between each search, and the overall experiment took ≈45 minutes to complete (between five and 10 sites, each with 20 searches).

[2]This study was conducted under Northeastern University IRB protocol #13-04-12; all personally identifiable information was removed from our collected data.

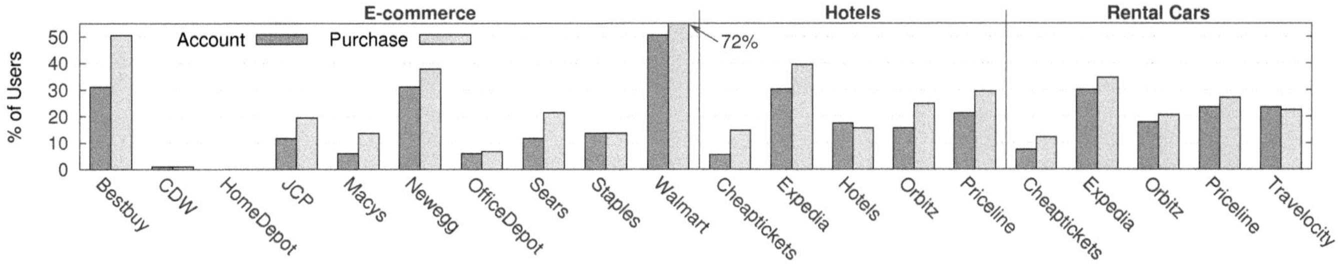

Figure 1: Previous usage (i.e., having an account and making a purchase) of different e-commerce sites by our AMT users.

The HTTP proxy serves two important functions. *First*, it allows us to quantify the baseline amount of noise in search results. Whenever the proxy observes a search request, it fires off *two* identical searches using PhantomJS (with no cookies) and saves the resulting pages. The results from PhantomJS serve as a *comparison* and a *control* result. As outlined in § 3.1, we compare the results served to the comparison and control to determine the underlying level of noise in the search results. We also compare the results served to the comparison and the real user; any differences between the real user and the comparison above the level observed between the comparison and the control can be attributed to personalization.

Second, the proxy reduces the amount of noise by sending the experimental, comparison, and control searches to the web site at the same time and from the same IP address. As stated in § 3.2, sending all queries from the same IP address controls for personalization due to geolocation, which we are specifically not studying in this paper. Furthermore, we hard-coded a DNS mapping for each of the sites on the proxy to avoid discrepancies that might come from round-robin DNS sending requests to different data centers.

In total, we recruited 100 AMT users in each of our retail, hotel, and car experiments. In each of the experiments, the participants first answered a brief survey about whether they had an account and/or had purchased something from each site. We present the results of this survey in Figure 1. We observe that many of our users have accounts and a purchase history on a large number of the sites we study.[3]

4.2 Price Steering

We begin by looking for *price steering*, or personalizing search results to place more- or less-expensive products at the top of the list. We do not examine rental car results for price steering because travel sites tend to present these results in a deterministically ordered grid of car types (e.g., economy, SUV) and car companies (with the least expensive car in the upper left). This arrangement prevents travel sites from personalizing the order of rental cars.

To measure price steering, we use three metrics:

Jaccard Index. To measure the overlap between two different sets of results, we use Jaccard index, which is the size of the intersection over the size of the union. A Jaccard Index of 0 represents no overlap between the results, while 1 indicates they contain the same results (although not necessarily in the same order).

Kendall's τ. To measure reordering between two lists of result, we use Kendall's τ rank correlation coefficient. This metric is commonly used in the Information Retrieval (IR) literature to compare ranked lists [23]. The metric ranges between -1 and 1, with 1 representing the same order, 0 signifying no correlation, and -1 being inverse ordering.

nDGG. To measure how strongly the ordering of search results is correlated with product prices, we use Normalized Discounted Cumulative Gain (nDCG). nDCG is a metric from the IR literature [20] for calculating how "close" a given list of search results is to an ideal ordering of results. Each possible search result r is assigned a "gain" score $g(r)$. The DCG of a page of results $R = [r_1, r_2, \ldots, r_k]$ is then calculated as $DCG(R) = g(r_1) + \sum_{i=2}^{k}(g(r_i)/\log_2(i))$. Normalized DCG is simply $DCG(R)/DCG(R')$, where R' is the list of search results with the highest gain scores, sorted from greatest to least. Thus, nDCG of 1 means the observed search results are the same as the ideal results, while 0 means no useful results were returned.

In our context, we use product prices as gain scores, and construct R' by aggregating all of the observed products for a given query. For example, to create R' for the query "ladders" on Home Depot, we construct the union of the results for the AMT user, the comparison, and the control, then sort the union from most- to least-expensive. Intuitively, R' is the most expensive possible ordering of products for the given query. We can then calculate the DCG for the AMT user's results and normalize it using R'. Effectively, if $nDCG(AMTuser) > nDCG(control)$, then the AMT user's search results include more-expensive products towards the top of the page than the control.

For each site, Figure 2 presents the average Jaccard index, Kendall's τ, and nDCG across all queries. The results are presented comparing the comparison to the control searches (Control), and the comparison to the AMT user searches (User). We observe several interesting trends. *First*, Sears, Walmart, and Priceline all have a lower Jaccard index for AMT users relative to the control. This indicates that the AMT users are receiving different products at a higher rate than the control searches (again, note that we are *not* comparing AMT users' results to each other; we only compare each user's result to the corresponding comparison result). Other sites like Orbitz show a Jaccard of 0.85 for Control and User, meaning that the set of results shows inconsistencies, but that AMT users are not seeing a higher level of inconsistency than the control and comparison searches.

Second, we observe that on Newegg, Sears, Walmart, and Priceline, Kendall's τ is at least 0.1 lower for AMT users, i.e., AMT users are consistently receiving results in a differ-

[3]Note that the fraction of users having made purchases can be higher than the fraction with an account, as many sites allow purchases as a "guest".

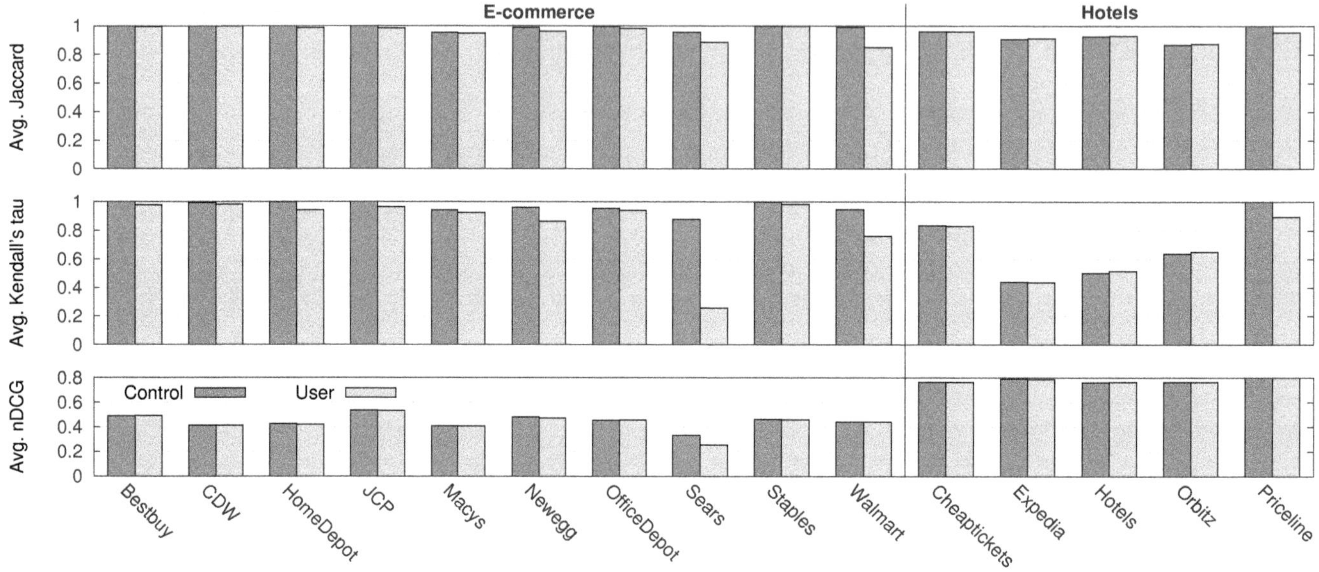

Figure 2: Average Jaccard index (top), Kendall's τ (middle), and nDCG (bottom) across all users and searches for each web site.

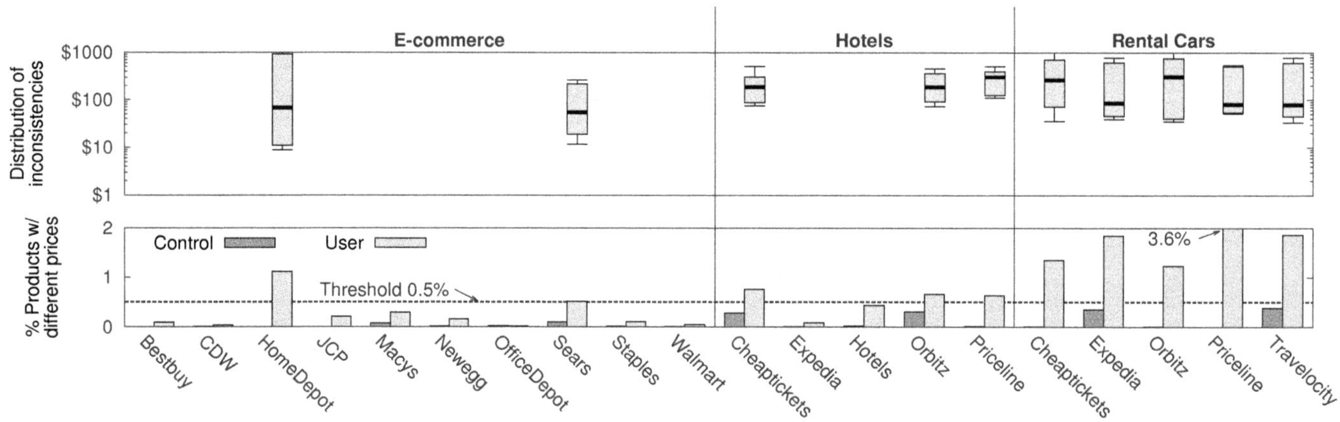

Figure 3: Percent of products with inconsistent prices (bottom), and the distribution of price differences for sites with $\geq$0.5% of products showing differences (top), across all users and searches for each web site. The top plot shows the mean (thick line), 25th and 75th percentile (box), and 5th and 95th percentile (whisker).

ent order than the controls. This observation is especially true for Sears, where the ordering of results for AMT users is markedly different. *Third,* we observe that Sears alone appears to be ordering products for AMT users in a price-biased manner. The nDCG results show that AMT users tend to have *cheaper* products near the top of their search results relative to the controls. Note that the results in Figure 2 are only useful for uncovering price steering; we examine whether the target sites are performing price discrimination in § 4.3.

Besides Priceline, the other four travel sites do not show significant differences between the AMT users and the controls. However, these four sites do exhibit significant noise: Kendall's τ is $\leq$0.83 in all four cases. On Cheaptickets and Orbitz, we manually confirm that this noise is due to randomness in the order of search results. In contrast, on Expedia and Hotels.com this noise is due to systematic A/B testing on users (see § 5.2 for details), which explains why we see equally low Kendall's τ values on both sites for all users. Unfortunately, it also means that we cannot draw any conclusions about personalization on Expedia and Hotels.com from the AMT experiment, since the search results for the comparison and the control rarely match.

4.3 Price Discrimination

So far, we have only looked at the set of products returned. We now turn to investigate whether sites are altering the prices of products for different users, i.e., price discrimination. In the bottom plot of Figure 3, we present the fraction of products that show price inconsistencies between the user's and comparison searches (User) and between the comparison and control searches (Control). Overall, we observe that most sites show few inconsistencies (typically <0.5% of products), but a small set of sites (Home Depot, Sears, and many of the travel sites) show both a significant fraction of price inconsistencies *and* a significantly higher fraction of inconsistencies for the AMT users.

To investigate this phenomenon further, in the top of Figure 3, we plot the distribution of price differentials for all sites where >0.5% of the products show inconsistency. We plot the mean price differential (thick line), 25th and

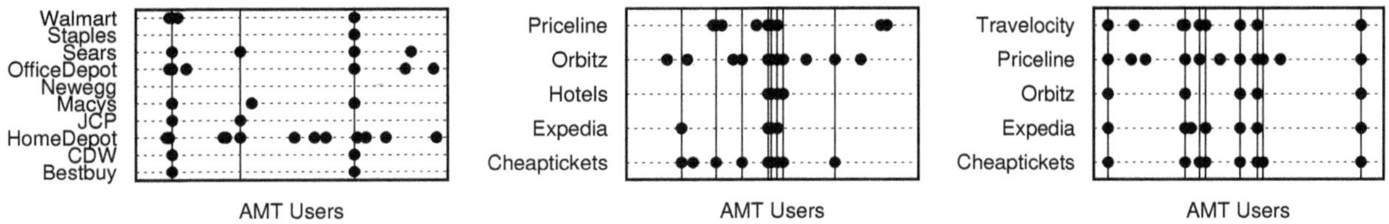

Figure 5: AMT users that receive highly personalized search results on general retail, hotels, and car rental sites.

75th percentile (box), and 5th and 95th percentile (whisker). Note that in our data, AMT users always receive higher prices than the controls (on average), thus all differentials are positive. We observe that the price differentials on many sites are quite large (up to hundreds of dollars). As an example, in Figure 4, we show a screenshot of a price inconsistency that we observed. Both the control and comparison searches returned a price of \$565 for a hotel, while our AMT user was returned a price of \$633.

4.4 Per-User Personalization

Next, we take a closer look at the subset of AMT users who experience high levels of personalization on one or more of the e-commerce sites. Our goal is to investigate whether these AMT users share any observable features that may illuminate why they are receiving personalized search results. We define highly personalized users as the set of users who see products with inconsistent pricing >0.5% of the time. After filtering we are left with between 2-12% of our AMT users depending on the site.

First, we map the AMT users' IP addresses to their geolocations and compare the locations of personalized and non-personalized users. We find no discernible correlation between location and personalization. However, as mentioned above, in this experiment all searches originate from a proxy in Boston. Thus, it is not surprising that we do not observe any effects due to location, since the sites did not observe users' true IP addresses.

Next, we examine the AMT users' browser and OS choices. We are able to infer their platform based on the HTTP headers sent by their browser through our proxy. Again, we find no correlation between browser/OS choice and high personalization. In § 5, we do uncover personalization linked to the use of mobile browsers, however none of the AMT users in our study did the HIT from a mobile device.

Figure 4: Example of price discrimination. The top result was served to the AMT user, while the bottom result was served to the comparison and control.

Finally, we ask the question: are there AMT users who receive personalized results on multiple e-commerce sites? Figure 5 lists the 100 users in our experiments along the x-axis of each plot; a dot highlights cases were a site personalized search results for a particular user. Although some dots are randomly dispersed, there are many AMT users that receive personalized results from several e-commerce sites. We highlight users who see personalized results on more than one site with vertical bars. More users fall into this category on travel sites than on general retailers.

The takeaway from Figure 5 is that we observe many AMT users who receive personalized results across multiple sites. This suggests that these users share feature(s) that all of these sites use for personalization. Unfortunately, we are unable infer the specific characteristics of these users that are triggering personalization.

Cookies. Although we logged the cookies sent by AMT users to the target e-commerce sites, it is not possible to use them to determine why some users receive personalized search results. First, cookies are typically random alphanumeric strings; they do not encode useful information about a user's history of interactions with a website (e.g., items clicked on, purchases, *etc.*). Second, cookies can be set by content embedded in third-party websites. This means that a user with a cookie from e-commerce site S may never have consciously visited S, let alone made purchases from S. These reasons motivate why we rely on survey results (see Figure 1) to determine AMT users' history of interactions with the target e-commerce sites.

4.5 Summary

To summarize our findings in this section: we find evidence for price steering and price discrimination on four general retailers and five travel sites. Overall, travel sites show price inconsistencies in a higher percentage of cases, relative to the controls, with prices increasing for AMT users by hundreds of dollars. Finally, we observe that many AMT users experience personalization across multiple sites.

5. PERSONALIZATION FEATURES

In § 4, we demonstrated that e-commerce sites personalize results for real users. However, we cannot determine *why* results are being personalized based on the data from real-world users, since there are too many confounding variables attached to each AMT user (e.g., their location, choice of browser, purchase history, *etc.*).

Category	Feature	Tested Values
Account	Cookies	No Account, Logged In, No Cookies
User-Agent	OS	Win. XP, Win. 7, OS X, Linux
	Browser	Chrome 33, Android Chrome 34, IE 8, Firefox 25, Safari 7, iOS Safari 6
Account History	Click	Low Prices, High Prices
	Purchase	Low Prices, High Prices

Table 3: User features evaluated for effects on personalization.

In this section, we conduct controlled experiments with fake accounts created by us to examine the impact of specific features on e-commerce personalization. Although we cannot test all possible features, we examine five likely candidates: browser, OS, account log-in, click history, and purchase history. We chose these features because e-commerce sites have been observed personalizing results based on these features in the past [1, 28].

We begin with an overview of the design of our synthetic user experiments. Next, we highlight examples of personalization on hotel sites and general retailers. None of our experiments triggered personalization on rental car sites, so we omit these results.

5.1 Experimental Overview

The goal of our synthetic experiments is to determine whether specific user features trigger personalization on e-commerce sites. To assess the impact of feature X that can take on values $x_1, x_2, \ldots, x_n$, we execute $n + 1$ PhantomJS instances, with each value of X assigned to one instance. The $n + 1$th instance serves as the control by duplicating the value of another instance. All PhantomJS instances execute 20 queries (see § 3.4) on each e-commerce site per day, with queries spaced one minute apart to avoid tripping security countermeasures. PhantomJS downloads the first page of results for each query. Unless otherwise specified, PhantomJS persists all cookies between experiments. All of our experiments are designed to complete in <24 hours.

To mitigate measurements errors due to noise (see § 3.1), we perform three steps (some borrowed from previous work [16, 17]): *first*, all searches for a given query are executed at the same time. This eliminates differences in results due to temporal effects. This also means that each of our treatments has exactly the same search history at the same time. *Second*, we use static DNS entries to direct all of our query traffic to specific IP addresses of the retailers. This eliminates errors arising from differences between datacenters. *Third*, although all PhantomJS instances execute on one machine, we use SSH tunnels to forward the traffic of each treatment to a unique IP address in a /24 subnet. This process ensures that any effects due to IP geolocation will affect all results equally.

Static Features. Table 3 lists the five features that we evaluate in our experiments. In the cookie experiment, the goal is to determine whether e-commerce sites personalize results for users who are logged-in to the site. Thus, two PhantomJS instances query the given e-commerce site without logging-in, one logs-in before querying, and the final account clears its cookies after every HTTP request.

In two sets of experiments, we vary the `User-Agent` sent by PhantomJS to simulate different OSes and browsers. The goal of these tests is to see if e-commerce sites personalize based on the user's choice of OS and browser. In the OS experiment, all instances report using Chrome 33, and Windows 7 serves as the control. In the browser experiment, Chrome 33 serves as the control, and all instances report using Windows 7, except for Safari 7 (which reports OS X Mavericks), Safari on iOS 6, and Chrome on Android 4.4.2.

Historical Features. In our historical experiments, the goal is to examine whether e-commerce sites personalize results based on users' history of viewed and purchased items. Unfortunately, we are unable to create purchase history on general retail sites because this would entail buying and then returning physical goods. However, it is possible for us to create purchase history on travel sites. On Expedia, Hotels.com, Priceline, and Travelocity, some hotel rooms feature "pay at the hotel" reservations where you pay at check-in. A valid credit card must still be associated with "pay at the hotel" reservations. Similarly, all five travel sites allow rental cars to be reserved without up-front payment. These no-payment reservations allow us to book reservations on travel sites and build up purchase history.

To conduct our historical experiments, we created six accounts on the four hotel sites and all five rental car sites. Two accounts on each site serve as controls: they do not click on search results or make reservations. Every night for one week, we manually logged-in to the remaining four accounts on each site and performed specific actions. Two accounts searched for a hotel/car and clicked on the highest and lowest priced results, respectively. The remaining two accounts searched for the same hotel/car and booked the highest and lowest priced results, respectively. Separate credit cards were used for high- and low-priced reservations, and neither card had ever been used to book travel before. Although it is possible to imagine other treatments for account history (e.g., a person who always travels to a specific country), price-constrained (inelastic) and unconstrained (elastic) users are a natural starting point for examining the impact of account history. Furthermore, although these treatments may not embody realistic user behavior, they do present unambiguous signals that could be observed and acted upon by personalization algorithms.

We pre-selected a destination and travel dates for each night, so the click and purchase accounts all used the same search parameters. Destinations varied across major US, European, and Asian cities, and dates ranged over the last six months of 2014. All trips were for one or two night stays/rentals. On average, the high- and low-price purchasers reserved rooms for \$329 and \$108 per night, respectively, while the high- and low-price clickers selected rooms for \$404 and \$99 per night. The four rental car accounts were able to click and reserve the exact same vehicles, with \$184 and \$43 being the average high- and low-prices per day.

Each night, after we finished manually creating account histories, we used PhantomJS to run our standard list of 20 queries from all six accounts on all nine travel sites. To maintain consistency, manual history creation and automated tests all used the same set of IP addresses and Firefox.

Ethics. We took several precautions to minimize any negative impact of our purchase history experiments on travel retailers, hotels, and rental car agencies. We reserved, at most, one room from any specific hotel. All reservations were made for hotel rooms and cars at least one month into the future, and all reservations were canceled at the conclusion of our experiments.

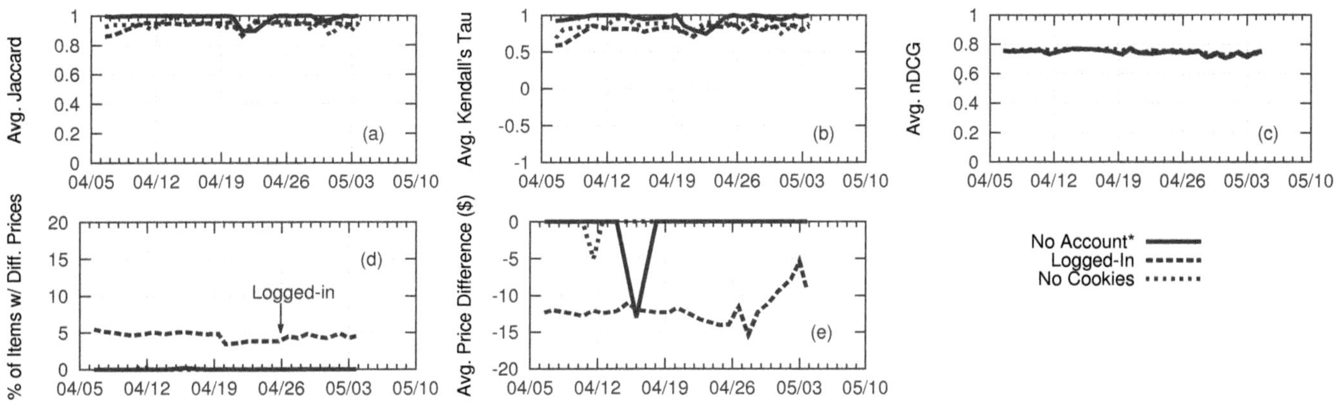

Figure 6: Examining the impact of user accounts and cookies on hotel searches on Cheaptickets.

Analyzing Results. To analyze the data from our feature experiments, we leverage the same five metrics used in § 4. Figure 6 exemplifies the analysis we conduct for each user feature on each e-commerce site. In this example, we examine whether Cheaptickets personalizes results for users that are logged-in. The x-axis of each subplot is time in days. The plots in the top row use Jaccard Index, Kendall's τ, and nDCG to analyze steering, while the plots in the bottom row use percent of items with inconsistent prices and average price difference to analyze discrimination.

All of our analysis is always conducted relative to a control. In all of the figures in this section, the starred (*) feature in the key is the control. For example, in Figure 6, all analysis is done relative to a PhantomJS instance that does not have a user account. Each point is an average of the given metric across all 20 queries on that day.

In total, our analysis produced >360 plots for the various features across all 16 e-commerce cites. Overall, most of the experiments do not reveal evidence of steering or discrimination. Thus, for the remainder of this section, we focus on the particular features and sites where we do observe personalization. None of our feature tests revealed personalization on rental car sites, so we omit them entirely.

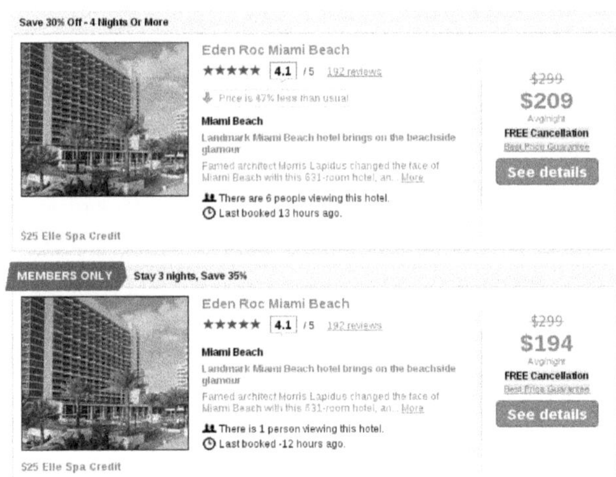

Figure 7: Price discrimination on Cheaptickets. The top result is shown to users that are not logged-in. The bottom result is a "Members Only" price shown to logged-in users.

5.2 Hotels

We begin by analyzing personalization on hotel sites. We observe hotel sites implementing a variety of personalization strategies, so we discuss each case separately.

Cheaptickets and Orbitz. The first sites that we examine are Cheaptickets and Orbitz. These sites are actually one company, and appear to be implemented using the same HTML structure and server-side logic. In our experiments, we observe both sites personalizing hotel results based on user accounts; for brevity we present the analysis of Cheaptickets and omit Orbitz.

Figures 6(a) and (b) reveal that Cheaptickets serves slightly different sets of results to users who are logged-in to an account, versus users who do not have an account or who do not store cookies. Specifically, out of 25 results per page, $\approx$2 are new and $\approx$1 is moved to a different location on average for logged-in users. In some cases (e.g., hotels in Bangkok and Montreal) the differences are much larger: up to 11 new and 11 moved results. However, the nDCG analysis in Figure 6(c) indicates that these alterations do not have an appreciable impact on the price of highly-ranked search results. Thus, we do not observe Cheaptickets or Orbitz steering results based on user accounts.

However, Figure 6(d) shows that logged-in users receive different prices on $\approx$5% of hotels. As shown in Figure 6(e), the hotels with inconsistent prices are $12 cheaper on average. This demonstrates that Cheaptickets and Orbitz implement price discrimination, in favor of users who have accounts on these sites. Manual examination reveals that these sites offer "Members Only" price reductions on certain hotels to logged-in users. Figure 7 shows an example of this on Cheaptickets.

Although it is not surprising that some e-commerce sites give deals to members, our results on Cheaptickets (and Orbitz) are important for several reasons. First, although members-only prices may be an accepted practice, it still qualifies as price discrimination based on direct segmentation (with members being the target segment). Second, this result confirms the efficacy of our methodology, i.e., we are able to accurately identify price discrimination based on automated probes of e-commerce sites. Finally, our results

		Account			Browser				OS			
		In	No*	Ctrl	FX	IE8	Chr*	Ctrl	OSX	Lin	XP	Win7*
OS	Ctrl	0.4	0.4	0.3	0.4	0.4	0.4	0.4	0.4	0.4	0.4	0.4
	Win7*	**1.0**	**1.0**	**1.0**	0.9	**1.0**	**1.0**	0.9	0.9	0.9	0.9	
	XP	0.9	0.9	0.9	**1.0**	0.9	0.9	**1.0**	**1.0**	**1.0**		
	Lin	0.9	0.9	0.9	**1.0**	0.9	0.9	**1.0**	**1.0**			
	OSX	0.9	0.9	0.9	**1.0**	0.9	0.9	**1.0**				
Browser	Ctrl	0.9	0.9	0.9	**1.0**	0.9	0.9					
	Chr*	**1.0**	**1.0**	**1.0**	0.9	**1.0**						
	IE8	**1.0**	**1.0**	**1.0**	0.9							
	FX	0.9	0.9	0.9								
Acct	Ctrl	**1.0**	**1.0**									
	No*	**1.0**										

Table 4: Jaccard overlap between pairs of user feature experiments on Expedia.

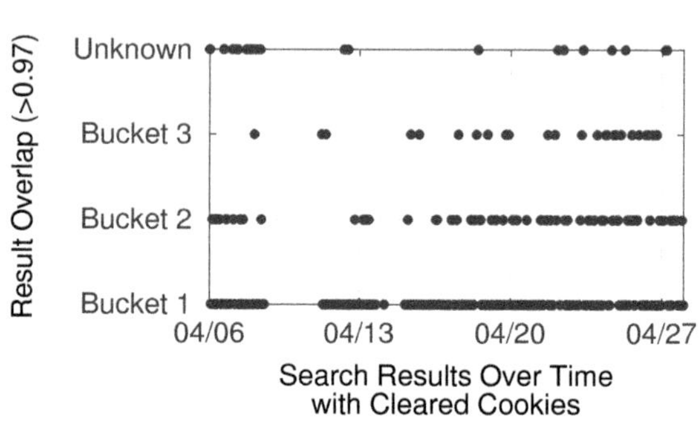

Figure 8: Clearing cookies causes a user to be placed in a random bucket on Expedia.

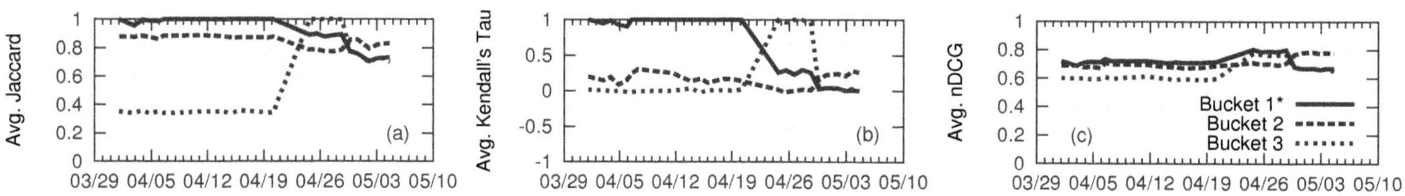

Figure 9: Users in certain buckets are steered towards higher priced hotels on Expedia.

reveal the actual differences in prices offered to members, which may not otherwise be public information.

Hotels.com and Expedia. Our analysis reveals that Hotels.com and Expedia implement the same personalization strategy: randomized A/B tests on users. Since these sites are similar, we focus on Expedia and omit the details of Hotels.com.

Initially, when we analyzed the results of our feature tests for Expedia, we noticed that the search results received by the control and its twin never matched. More oddly, we also noticed that 1) the control results did match the results received by other specific treatments, and 2) these matches were consistent over time.

These anomalous results led us to suspect that Expedia was randomly assigning each of our treatments to a "bucket". This is common practice on sites that use A/B testing: users are randomly assigned to buckets based on their cookie, and the characteristics of the site change depending on the bucket you are placed in. Crucially, the mapping from cookies to buckets is deterministic: a user with cookie C will be placed into bucket B whenever they visit the site unless their cookie changes.

To determine whether our treatments are being placed in buckets, we generate Table 4, which shows the Jaccard Index for 12 pairs of feature experiments on Expedia. Each table entry is averaged over 20 queries and 10 days. For a typical website, we would expect the control (*Ctrl*) in each category to have perfect overlap (1.0) with its twin (marked with a *). However, in this case the perfect overlaps occur between random pairs of tests. For example, the results for Chrome and Firefox perfectly overlap, but Chrome has low overlap with the control, which was also Chrome. This strongly suggests that the tests with perfect overlap have been randomly assigned to the same bucket. In this case, we observe three buckets: 1) {Windows 7, account control, no account, logged-in, IE 8, Chrome}, 2) {XP, Linux, OS X, browser control, Firefox}, and 3) {OS control}.

To confirm our suspicion about Expedia, we examine the behavior of the experimental treatment that clears its cookies after every query. We propose the following hypothesis: if Expedia is assigning users to buckets based on cookies, then the clear cookie treatment should randomly change buckets after each query. Our assumption is that this treatment will receive a new, random cookie each time it queries Expedia, and thus its corresponding bucket will change.

To test this hypothesis we plot Figure 8, which shows the Jaccard overlap between search results received by the clear cookie treatment, and results received by treatments in other buckets. The x-axis corresponds to the search results from the clear cookie treatment over time; for each page of results, we plot a point in the bucket (y-axis) that has >0.97 Jaccard overlap with the clear cookie treatment. If the clear cookie treatment's results do not overlap with results from any of the buckets, the point is placed on the "Unknown" row. In no cases did the search results from the clear cookie treatment have >0.97 Jaccard with more than a single bucket, confirming that the set of results returned to each bucket are highly disjoint (see Table 4).

Figure 8 confirms that the clear cookie treatment is randomly assigned to a new bucket on each request. 62% of results over time align with bucket 1, while 21% and 9% match with buckets 2 and 3, respectively. Only 7% do not match any known bucket. These results suggest that Expedia does not assign users to buckets with equal probability. There also appear to be time ranges where some buckets are not assigned, e.g., bucket 3 in between 04/12 and 04/15. We found that Hotels.com also assigns users to one of three buckets, that the assignments are weighted, and that the weights change over time.

Now that we understand how Expedia (and Hotels.com) assign users to buckets, we can analyze whether users in different buckets receive personalized results. Figure 9 presents

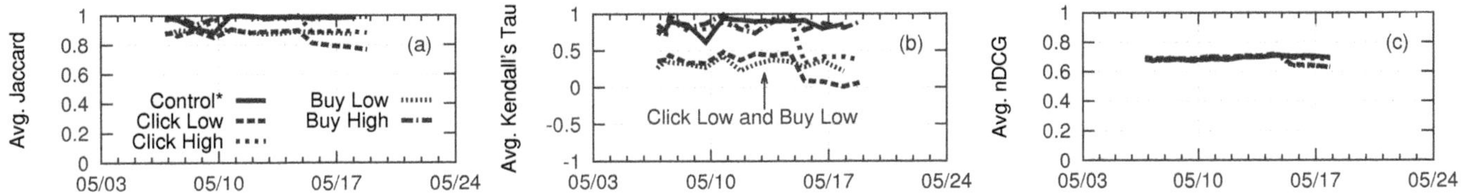

Figure 10: Priceline alters hotel search results based on a user's click and purchase history.

the results of this analysis. We choose an account from bucket 1 to use as a control, since bucket 1 is the most frequently assigned bucket.

Two conclusions can be drawn from Figure 9. First, we see that users are periodically shuffled into different buckets. Between 04/01 and 04/20, the control results are consistent, i.e., Jaccard and Kendall's τ for bucket 1 are $\approx$1. However, on 04/21 the three lines change positions, implying that the accounts have been shuffled to different buckets. It is not clear from our data how often or why this shuffling occurs.

The second conclusion that can be drawn from Figure 9 is that Expedia is steering users in some buckets towards more expensive hotels. Figures 9(a) and (b) show that users in different buckets receive different results in different orders. For example, users in bucket 3 see >60% different search results compared to users in other buckets. Figure 9(c) highlights the net effect of these changes: results served to users in buckets 1 and 2 have higher nDCG values, meaning that the hotels at the top of the page have higher prices. We do not observe price discrimination on Expedia or Hotels.com.

Priceline. As depicted in Figure 10, Priceline alters hotel search results based on the user's history of clicks and purchases. Figures 10(a) and (b) show that users who clicked on or reserved low-price hotel rooms receive slightly different results in a much different order, compared to users who click on nothing, or click/reserve expensive hotel rooms. We manually examined these search results but could not locate any clear reasons for this reordering. The nDCG results in Figure 10(c) confirm that the reordering is not correlated with prices. Thus, although it is clear that account history impacts search results on Priceline, we cannot classify the changes as steering. Furthermore, we observe no evidence of price discrimination based on account history on Priceline.

Travelocity. As shown in Figure 11, Travelocity alters hotel search results for users who browse from iOS devices. Figures 11(a) and (b) show that users browsing with Safari on iOS receive slightly different hotels, and in a much different order, than users browsing from Chrome on Android, Safari on OS X, or other desktop browsers. Note that we started our Android treatment at a later date than the other treatments, specifically to determine if the observed changes on Travelocity occurred on all mobile platforms or just iOS.

Although Figure 11(c) shows that this reordering does not result in price steering, Figures 11(d) and (e) indicate that Travelocity does modify prices for iOS users. Specifically, prices fall by $\approx$\$15 on $\approx$5% of hotels (or 5 out 50 per page) for iOS users. The noise in Figure 11(e) (e.g., prices increasing by \$50 for Chrome and IE 8 users) is not significant: this result is due to a single hotel that changed price.

The takeaway from Figure 11 is that we observe evidence consistent with price discrimination in favor of iOS users on Travelocity. Unlike Cheaptickets and Orbitz, which clearly mark sale-price "Members Only" deals, there is no visual cue on Travelocity's results that indicates prices have been changed for iOS users. Online travel retailers have publicly stated that mobile users are a high-growth customer segment, which may explain why Travelocity offers price-incentives to iOS users [26].

5.3 General Retailers

Home Depot. We now turn our attention to general retail sites. Among the 10 retailers we examined, only Home Depot revealed evidence of personalization. Similar to our findings on Travelocity, Home Depot personalizes results for users with mobile browsers. In fact, the Home Depot website serves HTML with different structure and CSS to desktop browsers, Safari on iOS, and Chrome on Android.

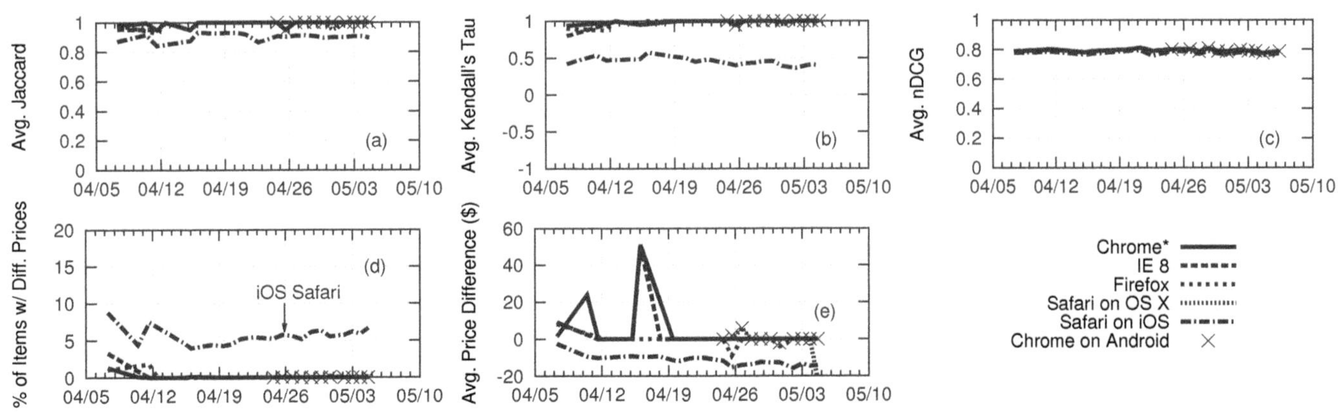

Figure 11: Travelocity alters hotel search results for users of Safari on iOS, but not Chrome on Android.

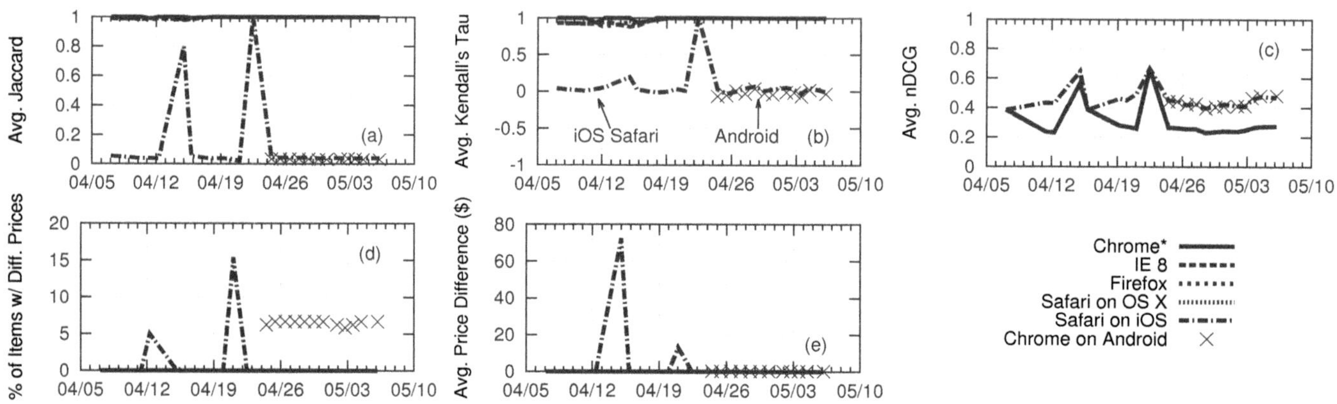

Figure 12: Home Depot alters product searches for users of mobile browsers.

Figure 12 depicts the results of our browser experiments on Home Depot. Strangely, Home Depot serves 24 search results per page to desktop browsers and Android, but serves 48 to iOS. As shown in Figure 12(a), on most days there is close to zero overlap between the results served to desktop and mobile browsers. Oddly, there are days when Home Depot briefly serves identical results to all browsers (e.g., the spike in Figure 12(a) on 4/22). The pool of results served to mobile browsers contains more expensive products overall, leading to higher nDCG scores for mobile browsers in Figure 12(c). Note that nDCG is calculated using the top k results on the page, which in this case is 24 to preserve fairness between iOS and the other browsers. Thus, Home Depot is steering users on mobile browsers towards more expensive products.

In addition to steering, Home Depot also discriminates against Android users. As shown in Figure 12(d), the Android treatment consistently sees differences on $\approx$6% of prices (one or two products out of 24). However, the practical impact of this discrimination is low: the average price differential in Figure 12(e) for Android is $\approx$\$0.41. We manually examined the search results from Home Depot and could not determine why the Android treatment receives slightly increased prices. Prior work has linked price discrimination on Home Depot to changes in geolocation [30], but we control for this effect in our experiments.

It is possible that the differences we observe on Home Depot may be artifacts caused by different server-side implementations of the website for desktop and mobile users, rather than an explicit personalization algorithm. However, even if this is true, it still qualifies as personalization according to our definition (see § 2.3) since the differences are deterministic and triggered by client-side state.

6. RELATED WORK

In this section, we briefly overview the academic literature on implementing and measuring personalization.

Improving Personalization. Personalizing search results to improve Information Retrieval (IR) accuracy has been extensively studied in the literature [33, 42]. While these techniques typically use click histories for personalization, other features have also been used, including geolocation [2, 53, 54] and demographics (typically inferred from search and browsing histories) [18, 47]. To our knowledge, only one study has investigated privacy-preserving personalized search [52]. Dou et al. provide a comprehensive overview of techniques for personalizing search [12]. Several studies have looked at improving personalization on systems other than search, including targeted ads on the web [16,49], news aggregators [9,24], and even discriminatory pricing on travel search engines [15].

Comparing Search Results. Training and comparing IR systems requires being able to compare ranked lists of search results. Thus, metrics for comparing ranked lists are an active area of research in the IR community. Classical metrics such as Spearman's footrule and ρ [11, 38] and Kendall's τ [22] both calculate pairwise disagreement between ordered lists. Several studies improve on Kendall's τ by adding per-rank weights [14,40], and by taking item similarity into account [21,39]. DCG and nDCG use a logarithmic scale to reduce the scores of bottom ranked items [19].

The Filter Bubble. Activist Eli Pariser brought widespread attention to the potential for web personalization to lead to harmful social outcomes; a problem he dubbed The Internet Filter Bubble [31]. This has motivated researchers to begin measuring the personalization present in deployed systems, such as web search engines [17, 27, 50] and recommender systems [4].

Exploiting Personalization. Recent work has shown that it is possible to exploit personalization algorithms for nefarious purposes. Xing et al. [51] demonstrate that repeatedly clicking on specific search results can cause search engines to rank those results higher. An attacker can exploit this to promote specific results to targeted users. Thus, fully understanding the presence and extent of personalization today can aid in understanding the potential impact of these attacks on e-commerce sites.

Personalization of E-commerce. Two recent studies by Mikians et al. that measure personalization on e-commerce sites serve as the inspiration for our own work. The first study examines price steering (referred to as *search discrimination*) and price discrimination across a large number of sites using fake user profiles [29]. The second paper extends the first work by leveraging crowdsourced workers to help detect price discrimination [30]. The authors identify several e-commerce sites that personalize content, mostly based on the user's geolocation. We improve upon these studies by introducing duplicated control accounts into all of our measurements. These additional control accounts are necessary to conclusively differentiate inherent noise from actual personalization.

7. CONCLUDING DISCUSSION

Personalization has become a important feature of many web services in recent years. However, there is mounting evidence that e-commerce sites are using personalization algorithms to implement price steering and discrimination.

In this paper, we build a measurement infrastructure to study price discrimination and steering on 16 top online retailers and travel websites. Our method places great emphasis on controlling for various sources of noise in our experiments, since we have to ensure that the differences we see are actually a result of personalization algorithms and not just noise. *First*, we collect real-world data from 300 AMT users to determine the extent of personalization that they experience. This data revealed evidence of personalization on four general retailers and five travel sites, including cases where sites altered prices by hundreds of dollars.

Second, we ran controlled experiments to investigate what features e-commerce personalization algorithms take into account when shaping content. We found cases of sites altering results based on the user's OS/browser, account on the site, and history of clicked/purchased products. We also observe two travel sites conducting A/B tests that steer users towards more expensive hotel reservations.

Comments from Companies. We reached out to the six companies we identified in this study as implementing some form of personalization (Orbitz and Cheaptickets are run by a single company, as are Expedia and Hotels.com) asking for comments on a pre-publication draft of this manuscript. We received responses from Orbitz and Expedia. The Vice President for Corporate Affairs at Orbitz provided a response confirming that Cheaptickets and Orbitz offer members-only deals on hotels. However, their response took issue with our characterization of price discrimination as "anti-consumer"; we removed these assertions from the final draft of this manuscript. The Orbitz representative kindly agreed to allow us to publish their letter on the Web [7].

We also spoke on the phone with the Chief Product Officer and the Senior Director of Stats Optimization at Expedia. They confirmed our findings that Expedia and Hotels.com perform extensive A/B testing on users. However, they claimed that Expedia does not implement price discrimination on rental cars, and could not explain our results to the contrary (see Figure 3).

Scope. In this study we focus on US e-commerce sites. All queries are made from IP addresses in the US, all retailers and searches are in English, and real world data is collected from users in the US. We leave the examination of personalization on e-commerce sites in other countries and other languages to future work.

Incompleteness. As a result of our methodology, we are only able to identify positive instances of price discrimination and steering; we cannot claim the absence of personalization, as we may not have considered other dimensions along which e-commerce sites might personalize content. We observe personalization in some of the AMT results (e.g., on Newegg and Sears) that we cannot explain with the findings from our feature-based experiments. These effects might be explained by measuring the impact of other features, such as geolocation, HTTP Referer, browsing history, or purchase history. Given the generality of our methodology, it would be straightforward to apply it to these additional features, as well as to other e-commerce sites.

Open Source. All of our experiments were conducted in spring of 2014. Although our results are representative for this time period, they may not hold in the future, as the sites may change their personalization algorithms. We encourage other researchers to repeat our measurements by making all of our crawling and parsing code, as well as the raw data from § 4 and § 5, available to the research community at

`http://personalization.ccs.neu.edu/`

Acknowledgements

We thank the anonymous reviewers and our shepherd, Vijay Erramilli, for their helpful comments. This research was supported in part by NSF grants CNS-1054233 and CHS-1408345, ARO grant W911NF-12-1-0556, and an Amazon Web Services in Education grant.

8. REFERENCES

[1] Bezos calls Amazon experiment 'a mistake'. Puget Sound Business Journal, 2000. http://www.bizjournals.com/seattle/stories/2000/09/25/daily21.html.

[2] L. Andrade and M. J. Silva. Relevance Ranking for Geographic IR. *GIR*, 2006.

[3] Amazon mechanical turk. http://mturk.com/.

[4] F. Bakalov, M.-J. Meurs, B. König-Ries, B. Satel, R. G. Butler, and A. Tsang. An Approach to Controlling User Models and Personalization Effects in Recommender Systems. *IUI*, 2013.

[5] K. Bhasin. JCPenney Execs Admit They Didn't Realize How Much Customers Were Into Coupons. Business Insider, 2012. http://www.businessinsider.com/jcpenney-didnt-realize-how-much-customers-\\were-into-coupons-2012-5.

[6] P. Belobaba, A. Odoni, and C. Barnhart. *The Global Airline Industry*. Wiley, 2009.

[7] C. Chiames. Correspondence with the authors, in reference to a pre-publication version of this manuscript, 2014. http://personalization.ccs.neu.edu/orbitz_letter.pdf.

[8] R. Calo. Digital Market Manipulation. *The George Washington Law Review*, 82, 2014.

[9] A. Das, M. Datar, A. Garg, and S. Rajaram. Google News Personalization: Scalable Online Collaborative Filtering. *WWW*, 2007.

[10] C. Duhigg. How Companies Learn Your Secrets. The New York Times, 2012. http://www.nytimes.com/2012/02/19/magazine/shopping-habits.html.

[11] P. Diaconis and R. L. Graham. Spearman's Footrule as a Measure of Disarray. *J. Roy. Stat. B*, 39(2), 1977.

[12] Z. Dou, R. Song, and J.-R. Wen. A Large-scale Evaluation and Analysis of Personalized Search Strategies. *WWW*, 2007.

[13] J. H. Dorfman. *Economics and Management of the Food Industry*. Routledge, 2013.

[14] R. Fagin, R. Kumar, and D. Sivakumar. Comparing top k lists. *SODA*, 2003.

[15] A. Ghose, P. G. Ipeirotis, and B. Li. Designing Ranking Systems for Hotels on Travel Search Engines by Mining User-Generated and Crowdsourced Content. *Marketing Science*, 31(3), 2012.

[16] S. Guha, B. Cheng, and P. Francis. Challenges in Measuring Online Advertising Systems. *IMC*, 2010.

[17] A. Hannak, P. Sapiezyński, A. M. Kakhki, B. Krishnamurthy, D. Lazer, A. Mislove, and C. Wilson. Measuring Personalization of Web Search. *WWW*, 2013.

[18] J. Hu, H.-J. Zeng, H. Li, C. Niu, and Z. Chen. Demographic Prediction Based on User's Browsing Behavior. *WWW*, 2007.

[19] K. Järvelin and J. Kekäläinen. IR evaluation methods for retrieving highly relevant documents. *SIGIR*, 2000.

[20] K. Järvelin and J. Kekäläinen. Cumulated Gain-based Evaluation of IR Techniques. *ACM TOIS*, 20(4), 2002.

[21] R. Kumar and S. Vassilvitskii. Generalized Distances Between Rankings. *WWW*, 2010.

[22] M. G. Kendall. A New Measure of Rank Correlation. *Biometrika*, 30(1/2), 1938.

[23] W. H. Kruskal. Ordinal Measures of Association. *Journal of the American Statistical Association*, 53(284), 1958.

[24] L. Li, W. Chu, J. Langford, and R. E. Schapire. A Contextual-Bandit Approach to Personalized News Article Recommendation. *WWW*, 2010.

[25] B. D. Lollis. Orbitz: Mac users book fancier hotels than PC users. USA Today Travel Blog, 2012. `http://travel.usatoday.com/hotels/post/2012/05/orbitz-hotel-booking-mac-pc-/690633/1`.

[26] B. D. Lollis. Orbitz: Mobile searches may yield better hotel deals. USA Today Travel Blog, 2012. `http://travel.usatoday.com/hotels/post/2012/05/orbitz-mobile-hotel-deals/691470/1`.

[27] A. Majumder and N. Shrivastava. Know your personalization: learning topic level personalization in online services. *WWW*, 2013.

[28] D. Mattioli. On Orbitz, Mac Users Steered to Pricier Hotels. *The Wall Street Journal*, 2012. `http://on.wsj.com/LwTnPH`.

[29] J. Mikians, L. Gyarmati, V. Erramilli, and N. Laoutaris. Detecting Price and Search Discrimination on the Internet. *HotNets*, 2012.

[30] J. Mikians, L. Gyarmati, V. Erramilli, and N. Laoutaris. Crowd-assisted Search for Price Discrimination in E-Commerce: First results. *CoNEXT*, 2013.

[31] E. Pariser. *The Filter Bubble: What the Internet is Hiding from You*. Penguin Press, 2011.

[32] I. Png. *Managerial Economics*. Routledge, 2012.

[33] J. Pitkow, H. Schütze, T. Cass, R. Cooley, D. Turnbull, A. Edmonds, E. Adar, and T. Breuel. Personalized search. *CACM*, 45(9), 2002.

[34] Panopticlick. `https://panopticlick.eff.org`.

[35] PhantomJS. 2013. `http://phantomjs.org`.

[36] A. Ramasastry. Web sites change prices based on customers' habits. CNN, 2005. `http://edition.cnn.com/2005/LAW/06/24/ramasastry.website.prices/`.

[37] C. Shapiro and H. R. Varian. *Information Rules: A Strategic Guide to the Network Economy*. Harvard Business School Press, 1999.

[38] C. Spearman. The Proof and Measurement of Association between Two Things. *Am J Psychol*, 15, 1904.

[39] D. Sculley. Rank Aggregation for Similar Items. *SDM*, 2007.

[40] G. S. Shieh, Z. Bai, and W.-Y. Tsai. Rank Tests for Independence—With a Weighted Contamination Alternative. *Stat. Sinica*, 10, 2000.

[41] Selenium. 2013. `http://selenium.org`.

[42] B. Tan, X. Shen, and C. Zhai. Mining long-term search history to improve search accuracy. *KDD*, 2006.

[43] Top 500 e-retailers. `http://www.top500guide.com/top-500/`.

[44] Top booking sites. `http://skift.com/2013/11/11/top-25-online-booking-sites-in-travel/`.

[45] T. Vissers, N. Nikiforakis, N. Bielova, and W. Joosen. Crying Wolf? On the Price Discrimination of Online Airline Tickets. *HotPETs*, 2014.

[46] J. Valentino-Devries, J. Singer-Vine, and A. Soltani. Websites Vary Prices, Deals Based on Users' Information. *Wall Street Journal*, 2012. `http://online.wsj.com/news/articles/SB10001424127887323777204578189391813881534`.

[47] I. Weber and A. Jaimes. Who Uses Web Search for What? And How? *WSDM*, 2011.

[48] T. Wadhwa. How Advertisers Can Use Your Personal Information to Make You Pay Higher Prices. *Huffington Post*, 2014. `http://www.huffingtonpost.com/tarun-wadhwa/how-advertisers-can-use-y_b_4703013.html`.

[49] C. E. Wills and C. Tatar. Understanding What They Do with What They Know. *WPES*, 2012.

[50] X. Xing, W. Meng, D. Doozan, N. Feamster, W. Lee, and A. C. Snoeren. Exposing Inconsistent Web Search Results with Bobble. *PAM*, 2014.

[51] X. Xing, W. Meng, D. Doozan, A. C. Snoeren, N. Feamster, and W. Lee. Take This Personally: Pollution Attacks on Personalized Services. *USENIX Security*, 2013.

[52] Y. Xu, B. Zhang, Z. Chen, and K. Wang. Privacy-Enhancing Personalized Web Search. *WWW*, 2007.

[53] B. Yu and G. Cai. A query-aware document ranking method for geographic information retrieval. *GIR*, 2007.

[54] X. Yi, H. Raghavan, and C. Leggetter. Discovering Users' Specific Geo Intention in Web Search. *WWW*, 2009.

Capturing Ghosts: Predicting the Used IPv4 Space by Inferring Unobserved Addresses

Sebastian Zander
CAIA, Swinburne University of Technology
Melbourne, Australia
szander@swin.edu.au

Lachlan L. H. Andrew
Faculty of IT, Monash University
Melbourne, Australia
lachlan.andrew@monash.edu

Grenville Armitage
CAIA, Swinburne University of Technology
Melbourne, Australia
garmitage@swin.edu.au

ABSTRACT

The pool of unused routable IPv4 prefixes is dwindling, with less than 4% remaining for allocation at the end of June 2014. Yet the adoption of IPv6 remains slow. We demonstrate a new capture-recapture technique for improved estimation of the size of "IPv4 reserves" (allocated yet unused IPv4 addresses or routable prefixes) from multiple incomplete data sources. A key contribution of our approach is the plausible estimation of both observed and unobserved-yet-active (ghost) IPv4 address space. This significantly improves our community's understanding of IPv4 address space exhaustion and likely pressure for IPv6 adoption. Using "ping scans", network traces and server logs we estimate that 6.3 million /24 subnets and 1.2 billion IPv4 addresses are currently in use (roughly 60% and 45% of the publicly routed space respectively). We also show how utilisation has changed over the last 2–3 years and provide an up-to-date estimate of potentially-usable remaining IPv4 space.

Categories and Subject Descriptors

C.2.3 [**Computer-Communication Networks**]: Network Operations—*Network Monitoring*; C.4 [**Performance of Systems**]: Measurement Techniques

General Terms

Measurement

Keywords

Used IPv4 space; capture-recapture

1. INTRODUCTION

At the end of June 2014 less than 4% of the IPv4 address space remained unallocated by Regional Internet Registrars (RIRs). RIPE and APNIC have exhausted their supply and the other RIRs (except AfriNIC) will run out of prefixes by the end of 2014 [1]. Understanding the pressures for IPv6 adoption, and the scope of possible IPv4 address markets, requires plausible estimates of actual IPv4 address use – particularly the efficiency with which allocated prefixes are filled with actively-used addresses. Ideally, our estimation techniques should also help the community track progressive exhaustion once all routable IPv4 prefixes are allocated.

Prior studies that, among other things, analysed IPv4 space growth [2–4] and a port scan census from 2012 [5] used mainly active probing ("pinging"). Yet pinging alone will under-count, as many hosts do not respond or their responses are filtered (e.g., by firewalls). Recently, Dainotti *et al.* [6] used IPv4 data from multiple sources to estimate the used /24 networks. Apart from a simple multiplier in [3], previous work did not attempt to correct for under-sampling.

Our key contribution in this work is a new method to estimate the true population of both observed and unobserved (yet still active) IPv4 addresses using a statistical *capture-recapture* (CR) [7–9] model applied over diverse sources of active and passive measurement data. We significantly extend our earlier workshop paper, with refined methodology, additional data sources and greatly extended analysis [10].

Our second contribution is a three-year study of address use using our CR method. We "pinged" the allocated space with ICMP echo requests and TCP port 80 probes, and also gathered IPv4 data from web server logs [11], email spam detector logs [12], Wikipedia edit logs, logs of Valve's Steam online game platform, logs from Measurement Lab [13], and university access router's NetFlow logs. Inevitably, our sources only detect actively used addresses from 80% of the allocated space that is publicly routed (based on [14]). Hence, our analysis is focused on the routed space.

Although our sources provide diverse evidence of active IPv4 address use, there are likely many in-use addresses that we never see. We utilise our CR method to estimate a total population of used IPv4 addresses (and /24 networks) that *includes* these unobserved addresses (ghosts). As many sources obtain measurements over weeks or months, our estimates of the used IPv4 addresses (and /24 networks) are based on observation periods rather than points in time. By cross-validation with our datasets, and comparison with a few samples of ground truth, we show our CR method provides better estimates than prior techniques. We analyse "demand" – growth in address use – over the last 2–3 years relative to factors such as the RIR, country, or prefix size, and estimate the remaining "supply" of unused prefixes.

With just ICMP pinging we observed 4.9 million used /24 subnets and 430 million used IP addresses. Our combined sources observed 5.9 million used /24 subnets and 740 million used IPv4 addresses, yet our CR technique indicates significantly higher actual usage. We estimate 6.3 million /24 subnets and 1.2 billion IPv4 addresses were used by the end of June 2014 (approx. 60% and 45%

IMC'14, November 5–7, 2014, Vancouver, BC, Canada.

http://dx.doi.org/10.1145/2663716.2663718.

of the publicly routed space respectively). From the end of 2011 to June 2014, the growth in used /24 subnets and IPv4 addresses was roughly linear, with an increase of 0.45 million /24 subnets and 170 million IPv4 addresses per year.

These trends mean routed but currently unused space could supply us until 2023. However, supply varies significantly across regions, for example Asia and South America only have supply for another 2–4 years (without reallocations between RIRs). Moreover, if, for example, only 75% of all routed /24 subnets could ever be used, regions with tight supply, like Asia and South America, have less than 1 year of supply left. Unrouted unused space may provide more supply.

The paper is organised as follows. Section 2 discusses related work. Section 3 describes the concept of CR and our log-linear CR models. Section 4 describes our IPv4 address data collection and processing. Section 5 covers the validation of our CR model. In Section 6 we analyse the growth of used IPv4 space over time, and in Section 7 we estimate the space still unused. Section 8 concludes and outlines future work.

2. RELATED WORK

The related measure of *routed* address space has been estimated based on prefixes advertised by BGP [15, 16]. However, estimation of the number of *actively used* addresses began with Pryadkin *et al.* [2], who used ICMP echo and TCP SYN probing to probe the allocated Internet. They discovered 62 million used IPv4 addresses in 2003 and 2004. Pryadkin *et al.* also showed that only a small number of allocated prefixes appeared to be heavily used, while a large part of the IPv4 space appeared unused or underutilized.

Heidemann *et al.* [3] infrequently probed all allocated IPv4 addresses (census) and frequently probed selected address samples (survey) with ICMP echo pinging to study usage, availability and up-time of addresses. The last census in 2007 from [3] accounted for 112 million used addresses. Heidemann *et al.* compared ICMP probing with TCP port 80 probing and passive measurements based on small samples. They proposed a correction factor of 1.86, thus estimating the total number of used IPv4 addresses in mid 2007 was 200–210 million.

Cai *et al.* [4] used ping survey data from [3] and conducted more surveys in 2009–2010 to analyse typical address block sizes and their characteristics. They did not directly estimate the used IPv4 address space, but observed: "most addresses in about one-fifth of /24 blocks are in use less than 10% of the time".

From June to October 2012, anonymous researchers used hacked commodity routers to perform a port scan of the IPv4 Internet [5]. They detected 420 million addresses that responded to ICMP echo, which is broadly consistent with our two ping censuses that detected 360 million addresses between March and September 2012.

In 2013 we initially proposed using a log-linear CR model to estimate the true population of used IPv4 addresses from multiple sources of IPv4 addresses [10]. Our preliminary workshop paper found that our log-linear CR estimate is significantly higher (one billion used IPv4 addresses in mid 2013) than the aggregate number of observed IPv4 addresses from multiple measurement sources.

Dainotti *et al.* [6] developed techniques to filter out spoofed IPv4 addresses from darknet or NetFlow data and showed that the filtered datasets can be used to estimate Internet address space usage. With the filtered darknet data, NetFlow data, and ping census data from USC [3] combined, they estimated 4.8 million used /24 subnets (47% of the routed space) in September 2012. This is broadly consistent with the 5.2 million /24 subnets we observed in the year to September 2012 (c.f. Figure 4). The difference is likely due to the larger number of sources and the longer time window we use.

3. CAPTURE-RECAPTURE

There are many techniques for estimating population sizes from limited samples. Some use problem-specific approaches, but many use CR methods. CR methods have been used in ecology [7, 8], epidemiology [9, 17], and to estimate missing links from observed AS-graphs [18].

First, we discuss general assumptions for CR. Then, to illustrate CR, we discuss the simplest CR technique – the two-sample Lincoln-Petersen (L-P) method. Since we have more than two sources and for our data some assumptions of the L-P method are violated, we do not use this method. Finally, we describe the log-linear CR models that we use. Log-linear models make less restrictive assumptions and work with arbitrarily many sources.

3.1 General assumptions

A prime assumption of CR is that all individuals of the population can be uniquely identified. This assumption obviously holds for IPv4 addresses (we only care if an address was used but not who used it). Another assumption is that the data sources only sample "alive" individuals. We achieve that by filtering out IPs from the data sources that were sampled but not actually used, for example due to address spoofing (see Section 4).

Any individuals with zero sample probability are not part of the CR estimate. In our case these are all used IP addresses in publicly unrouted space, which our sources cannot sample. Hence, our CR estimates are only for the publicly routed space. Furthermore, there may be some specialised devices using public IP addresses, such as printers, that our current data sources also cannot sample. This means our results likely have a downward "bias", but as discussed in Section 4.2 the error may be relatively small.

3.2 Two-sample Lincoln-Petersen method

The Lincoln-Petersen (L-P) method [7, 8] is ideal to illustrate the basic principle behind CR, but has restrictive assumptions that prevent us from using it.

3.2.1 Description

The two-sample L-P method works as follows. Given a first sample, that observes M individuals, the size of the population would be known if we knew what *fraction* of the population had been observed. To estimate this, L-P takes a second sample. Say it contains C individuals, of which R individuals occur in both samples. If the fraction of "recaptured" individuals in the second sample equals the fraction of the total population captured in the first sample, $R/C = M/N$, then the population N is [7, 8]:

$$N = \frac{MC}{R} .$$

In our context, the samples or "sources" are different active and passive measurements (see Section 4). For concreteness, consider Source 1 to result from pinging the entire IPv4 space and Source 2 to be all addresses in a server log. Based on the number of unique addresses observed by Source 1 and Source 2, and the number of unique addresses observed by both sources (Overlap) CR allows to estimate the number of unobserved addresses (Unseen), as illustrated in Figure 1.

3.2.2 Assumptions

The L-P estimate assumes that the probability of an individual being captured in one source does not depend on the probability of being captured in a different source (*independent sources*). It also assumes that, within a sample, each individual has an equal chance of being sampled (*homogenous population*). Furthermore, the L-P

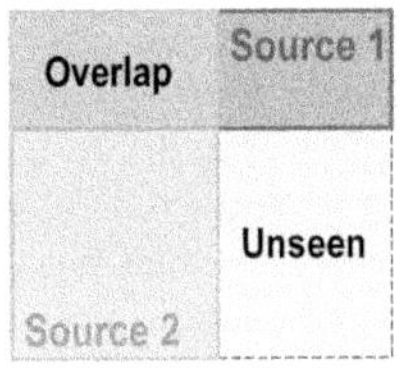

Figure 1: Two-source capture-recapture illustrated

estimate assumes that during measurement no individuals enter or leave the population (*closed population*). However, a violation of the last assumption is just another form of heterogeneity.

Given our data sources (see Section 4.1), there is no significant causal relationship to introduce source dependence. While some samples are dependent, i.e. IPs observed in traffic flows between the two NetFlow-monitored sites or between one NetFlow site and one of the logged sites (e.g. Wikipedia or the gaming site), their number is very small compared to the overall size of the datasets (less than 1%). However, the population is very heterogeneous; for example, servers are more likely to respond to pinging, while client machines may be more likely to appear in certain traffic logs.

Nevertheless, heterogeneity gives rise to what is called *apparent source dependence*. For example, two sources that are biased towards client machines will *appear* to be positively dependent given another source that is less biased towards clients. In fact it is well known that heterogeneity and source dependence are often confounded and cannot be clearly separated [19]. Apparent source dependence must be treated similarly to source dependence.

If there is (apparent) dependence such that two sources are positively correlated, the L-P estimator underestimates the population size: $R/C > M/N$ and so $N > MC/R$. Similarly, if two sources are negatively correlated, the L-P estimator overestimates the population size. If the sign of the correlation is known, then L-P estimates can be used to identify plausible lower or upper bounds [17].

3.3 Log-linear Models

Just as L-P uses a second sample to estimate the fraction of the population of the first sample, a third sample can be used to compensate the correlation between the first two samples. This is the basic idea of log-linear models (LLMs) used for CR [17, 19, 20], which can model (apparent) source dependence among arbitrarily many sources.

3.3.1 *Description*

Let N be the unknown number of distinct individuals of the population. Let t denote the number of sources indexed by $1, 2, \ldots, t$. For each individual, let s_1 to s_t be defined such that $s_i = 1$ if the individual occurs in sample i and $s_i = 0$ otherwise. Then the string $s_1 s_2 \ldots s_t$ is called the "capture history" of the individual. The observed outcome of all measurements can then be represented by variables of the form z_s, which are the numbers of individuals with each capture history $s = s_1 s_2 \ldots s_t$. These are assumed to be instances of random variables Z_s. Note that individuals with the capture history $00\ldots0$ are unobserved, and our goal is to estimate $Z_{00\ldots0}$. Table 1 illustrates the variables Z_s for each possible capture history for three sources ($t = 3$); "yes" means an individual was observed and "no" means an individual was not observed by a source.

For each history s, let $h(s)$ be the set of sources in which the individual occurs; for example, $h(101) = \{1, 3\}$. Define the indicator function $\mathbf{1}_A = 1$ if statement A is true and 0 otherwise. We can now write the following system of equations in 2^t variables

Table 1: Three-source contingency table showing all possible capture histories and number of unseen individuals Z_{000}

		Source 1			
		yes		no	
		Source 2		**Source2**	
		yes	no	yes	no
Source 3	yes	Z_{111}	Z_{101}	Z_{011}	Z_{001}
	no	Z_{110}	Z_{100}	Z_{010}	Z_{000}=?

$u, u_1, u_2, \ldots, u_{12}, \ldots, u_{23}, \ldots$ up to $u_{12\ldots t}$:

$$\log(\mathbb{E}(Z_s)) = \sum_{h \subseteq h(s)} u_h = \sum_h u_h \mathbf{1}_{h \subseteq h(s)} . \quad (1)$$

For example, for $t = 3$, the system is

$$\begin{aligned}\log\left(\mathbb{E}\left(Z_{ijk}\right)\right) =& u + u_1 \mathbf{1}_{i=1} + u_2 \mathbf{1}_{j=1} + u_3 \mathbf{1}_{k=1} \\ &+ u_{12} \mathbf{1}_{i=1 \wedge j=1} + u_{13} \mathbf{1}_{i=1 \wedge k=1} \\ &+ u_{23} \mathbf{1}_{j=1 \wedge k=1} + u_{123} \mathbf{1}_{i=1 \wedge j=1 \wedge k=1} .\end{aligned}$$

The estimate of $Z_{00\ldots0}$ is then $\hat{Z}_{00\ldots0} = \exp(u)$. If we take $\mathbb{E}[Z_s] = z_s$ then this system has 2^t unknowns but only $2^t - 1$ equations, as $Z_{00\ldots0}$ is unknown. Hence it is customary to assume $u_{12\ldots t} = 0$ [17]. As the number of sources t increases, this t-way dependency becomes decreasingly important.

The model with all u_h (the saturated model) is very sensitive to small values of Z_s. For example, a zero count for some capture history may give $\hat{Z}_{00\ldots0} = 0$, regardless of the other Z_s [17]. Furthermore, the larger t is, the higher is the random error for some Z_s. Including "noisy" parameters u_h in a model results in a poor predictive performance of the model (referred to as over-fitting).

Over-fitting is mitigated by "model selection" (see Section 3.3.2), in which some u_h are forced to 0, to reflect assumed independence between certain combinations of sources. For example, setting $u_{12} = 0$ indicates sources 1 and 2 are independent. With such incomplete models, the system of equations is overdetermined, and the maximum likelihood parameters u are typically used, based on the assumption that Z_s result from uniform random sampling and are hence Poisson distributed.

Assuming the Z_s are Poisson distributed is appropriate if the upper limit for the Z_s is unknown. However, we can bound Z_s by the size of the publicly routed IPv4 space. Hence, we use right-truncated Poisson distributions defined over $[0, l] \cap \mathbb{Z}$, where l is the upper limit. These improve estimates substantially for small strata, where the counters are relatively close to the limit (see Section 5.2), but otherwise make little difference.

3.3.2 *Model selection*

Model selection for an LLM consists of selecting which u_h will be assumed *a priori* to be 0. The goal is to select the least complex model with "adequate" fit of the observed (and by assumption) unobserved individuals [20].

A common approach is to minimize an "Information Criterion" (IC). Two common ICs are [21]:

$$\text{AIC} = 2k - 2\log(L), \qquad \text{BIC} = \log(M)k - 2\log(L)$$

where L is the likelihood of the data given the assumed model, k is the number of free parameters of the model and M is the number of observed individuals. AIC is used more often, but each has merits [22]. Section 5 compares the BIC and the AIC for our data. We choose the simplest model m such that no other model n has $\text{IC}_n < \text{IC}_m - 7$ [21].

In our case, k is the number of non-zero u_h, but L is difficult to obtain. AIC and BIC assume that each source samples uniformly and so L is the likelihood of a Poisson model. If the number of samples is large, the central limit theorem indicates that substantial deviations from the mean have very low likelihood. In our case, as in [17, 19], the randomness comes largely from the choice of sources to monitor, which is hard to characterise but has substantially higher variance. Hence the Poisson assumption selects too complex a model.

We mitigate this overfitting using the simple heuristic of dividing all z_s by some integer d when calculating L. It remains to select d. If d is so large that any z_s gets rounded to zero, the LLM breaks down. The further heuristic of selecting d to be the largest number less than $\min_s z_s$ appears to work well (see Section 5.1).

3.3.3 Estimate range

Besides computing point estimates, we also compute estimate ranges (used in Section 5). We use the procedure in [23] to compute a $100(1-\alpha)\%$ profile likelihood "confidence interval" (CI) for $\hat{N}$. Note that this is not a true confidence interval in our case, since it is based on the assumption that each sample is drawn randomly, resulting in a Poisson number of samples with each history. In contrast, our samples arise from different, not completely random sampling procedures. Hence we treat these "confidence intervals" as merely a useful heuristic indication of the sensitivity to modelling variations and we set $\alpha = 10^{-7}$ to obtain wide CIs.

3.3.4 Sampling zeros

Even with appropriate model selection, if the number of samples across all sources is low, we may have a large number of z_s that are near zero leading to unreliable estimates. In our case this only occurs for a few small countries or territories when stratifying by country code (see Section 3.4). Hence, we exclude country codes with fewer than 1000 IP addresses observed by all sources from the results in Section 6.2 (where they are negligible) and in Section 6.7.

3.4 Stratification

We obtain more insight and also initially hoped to mitigate heterogeneity by stratifying the population in different ways. We classified IPv4 addresses as statically or dynamically assigned using the approach described in [10], and based on allocation and whois data we stratified by RIR (e.g. APNIC), country, prefix size, industry[1] and allocation age.

4. DATASETS AND PREPROCESSING

An IPv4 address is considered *used* if it responds to active probes or participates in connections. A *used* /24 subset contains one or more used addresses. This section describes our sources of used IPv4 address data, our data collection and processing, and our handling of both spoofed and dynamically assigned addresses.

4.1 Datasets

Our first two datasets are from actively probing the whole allocated IPv4 Internet using ICMP echo requests (**IPING**) and TCP SYN packets to port 80[2] (**TPING**). Since mid-2011 we probed each allocated IPv4 address (a census) once every 6 months. The first two censuses used ICMP probing and the rest used both ICMP and TCP probing (with TCP probing seeing over 7% more observed IP addresses). We limited the overall ping rate and used reversed bit counting for "traversing" the IP space. On average our prober sent only one packet every two hours to individual /24 networks, to minimise congestion, stay below typical ICMP or TCP rate limit thresholds and avoid triggering monitoring systems (on average we received only 10–20 complaints per census). For the first half of 2011 we use ICMP ping data collected by USC/LANDER [24].

Passively observed IPv4 data includes addresses from Wikipedia's page edit histories[3] (**WIKI**), potential spam email senders from [12] (**SPAM**), addresses of clients tested by Measurement Lab [13] tools (**MLAB**), web clients participating in our IPv6 readiness test [11] (**WEB**), anonymized server logs of game clients connecting to Valve's Steam online gaming platform (**GAME**), and NetFlow records from *incoming* traffic of Swinburne University of Technology's access router (**SWIN**)[4] and Caltech's access router (**CALT**).

We utilise data gathered from 2011 onwards. We generate datasets of unique /24 subnets by processing the IPv4 datasets and setting the last octet of each address to zero and then filtering out the duplicates. Table 2 shows the number of unique IPv4 addresses and /24 subnets per dataset for the years 2011–2013 (IPs for GAME omitted for confidentiality). Note that the numbers in the table cannot be used as growth trends due to sample method variations.

4.2 Host types sampled

We collected data from diverse locations, but CR estimates will only be useful if (1) our datasets sample all types of devices using public IPv4 addresses and (2) a type of device can be sampled by multiple datasets. We now discuss whether this is the case based on grouping devices into routers, servers/proxies, clients (e.g. PCs, smart phones), and specialised devices (e.g. printers, cameras).

ISP routers are sampled by IPING and TPING and may also appear in SWIN and CALT. Home routers are sampled by IPING and TPING (we confirmed that some responses came from Cable/DSL routers by inspecting web pages from IPs responding to TPING) and by all other sources (with NAT packets sent from home networks appear to come from home routers). Servers/proxies are sampled by IPING, TPING, SWIN and CALT. They can also appear in WIKI, SPAM and WEB. Clients are sampled mainly by WIKI, SPAM, MLAB, WEB, GAME, SWIN and CALT, but also appear in IPING. NAT'ed clients also appear in IPING and TPING. Specialised devices may be sampled by IPING and TPING.

Overall, our datasets sample most groups well, especially servers and clients, which we assume are the largest groups. Specialised devices are likely severely under-represented, but these are very hard to sample. The authors of [5] probed the entire IPv4 Internet on several hundred ports and detected 36 million addresses that only responded to TCP SYNs but not to ICMP. In our censuses 15–20 million IPs reacted to port 80 TCP SYNs but not to ICMP. The difference of 15–20 million addresses could be specialised devices listening only on specific ports[5] we missed, but this number is small compared to our total estimate of 1.2 billion used addresses.

4.3 Time windows

We collected data from 1 Jan 2011 until 30 June 2014. To analyse the growth trend of used IPv4 addresses, we split our data into *overlapping* 12-month windows. Windows start every three months, so the first window starts at 1 Jan 2011 and the last window starts at 1 Jul 2013. The last window ends at 30 June 2014. This is a suitable trade-off between temporal resolution and noisy estimates.

[1]"Industry" indicates whether address space is education, military, government, corporate, or ISP. We classified 88% of the allocated address space based on whois information (down to /17 networks).

[2]Initially we probed a sample of the Internet using different commonly used TCP ports and found port 80 to be the most responsive.

[3]Modification time and IPv4 address of edits by unregistered users.

[4]Excluding all traffic flows of our active prober.

[5]E.g., printers responding only on the Internet Printing (IPP) port.

Table 2: Data sources and observed unique IPv4 addresses and /24 subnets per year (SWIN and CALT after spoofed IP filtering)

			2011		2012		2013	
Dataset	**Description**	**Time collected**	**IPs [M]**	**/24 [M]**	**IPs [M]**	**/24 [M]**	**IPs [M]**	**/24 [M]**
WIKI	Wikipedia's page edit histories	Jan 2011 – Jun 2014	5.5	1.69	5.9	1.97	6.8	2.16
SPAM	Potential spam email senders	May 2012 – Jun 2014	-	-	19.2	1.56	17.5	1.73
MLAB	Clients tested by Measurement Lab	Jan 2011 – Jun 2014	30.0	2.66	27.6	2.69	21.5	2.49
WEB	Web clients tested for IPv6	Mar 2011 – Jun 2014	22.0	2.92	88.0	3.89	108.7	4.13
GAME	Game clients logged into Valve's Steam	Jan 2011 – Jun 2014	conf	3.11	conf	3.62	conf	4.32
SWIN	Swinburne access router NetFlow records	Jan 2011 – Jun 2014	150.6	3.13	142.4	3.38	112.9	3.36
CALT	Caltech access router NetFlow records	Jun 2013 – Jun 2014	-	-	-	-	356.8	3.92
IPING	ICMP ping census of IPv4 Internet	Mar 2011 – Jun 2014	320.3	4.24	358.2	4.54	411.1	4.81
TPING	TCP port 80 census of IPv4 Internet	Mar 2012 – Jun 2014	-	-	70.0	3.38	92.7	3.71

Also, for some datasets we cannot have smaller gaps between windows, e.g. we only conducted IPING/TPING censuses every six months and we only collected GAME data every 3+ months.

Overlapping windows smooth out quick changes, but we believe fast transients in the number of used IPv4 addresses are unlikely. In the rest of the paper we associate statistics with the end of time windows. For example, for the first window the observed and estimated used space is associated with 31 December, 2011.

4.4 Data collection and processing

Our goal is to get datasets of publicly routed IPv4 addresses that were actually used. We do not distinguish whether IPs were used legitimately or illegitimately, such as addresses hijacked by spammers. For active probing we assume that positive responses only occur when IP addresses were used – the same assumption made by previous work [2–4].

For IPING we only counted IPv4 addresses that returned ICMP echo replies, "destination protocol unreachable" or "destination port unreachable" messages. We ignored addresses with other ICMP errors or "TTL exceeded" messages, as for these it is unclear if they were actually used. For TPING we only counted addresses that returned SYN/ACKs. We ignored addresses that returned RSTs, as 25% of RSTs cover nearly contiguous /25 or larger networks, suggesting they may have originated from firewalls. Lack of reply indicates an address was truly unused, a host ignored the probe, or the probe or response was filtered or lost.

For the passive datasets we extracted the IPv4 addresses from log files. We filtered out multicast and private addresses (e.g., 10.0.0.0/8), and those in unallocated or unrouted space. We identified the routed space based on the route-views dataset from RouteViews (RVs) [14]. For each time window we downloaded weekly snapshots from RV and then aggregated all the snapshots (excluding a few unallocated but advertised prefixes).

For WIKI, SPAM, MLAB, WEB and GAME (server logs), the addresses are only recorded for successful TCP sessions, so we can be sure the addresses were used. SWIN and CALT contain unused IPs from inside the two networks due to scanning that we cannot filter out, but their number is negligible compared to the sizes of the datasets. More problematically is that SWIN and CALT also contain spoofed IPv4 addresses from outside the two networks that do *not* represent used addresses. We describe our filtering of these in the following section.

4.5 Removal of spoofed IPs

We only have lists of observed IP addresses for SWIN and CALT. We do not have packet or flow data, and we do not know from which IPs flows originated. Hence, instead of using the technique in [6], we needed a new heuristic to remove spoofed addresses.

Our heuristic is based on the assumption that spoofed IP addresses, which were not actively used, are uniformly distributed over the IP space, since there are two main reasons for these:

- Distributed Denial of Service (DDoS) attacks where the attacking machines send traffic from spoofed source addresses selected randomly [25].
- Port scans where the scanner uses decoys. For example, the prominent nmap scanning tool has an option that allows creating additional scans from random spoofed addresses to obfuscate the identity of the scanning host(s).

Note that for CR spoofed addresses only cause errors if *they were not actually used*. DDoS attacks where the attacker spoofs the source address to be the victim's address (reflector attacks) are not a problem, as for these the spoofed addresses are most likely used. Also note that while the autonomous systems (ASs) filtering spoofed source addresses may not be uniformly distributed, this does not affect the overall uniform distribution, since attackers or scanners (or their machines) are usually distributed across the whole Internet *including* ASs that do not filter.

The assumption of uniform distribution is supported by circumstantial evidence from our data. We observed that the unfiltered SWIN and CALT have uniformly random distributed IPv4 addresses in six /8 prefixes that were completely or almost completely unused by other sources (e.g. 53.0.0.0/8 or 55.0.0.0/8).[6] While the number of observed IPs from these 'empty' /8 subnets differs for SWIN and CALT, for a given dataset and time period the number of observed IPs is roughly identical for these /8 – consistent with the assumption that spoofed addresses are uniformly distributed over the IPv4 space.

Our approach works in two stages. First, we estimate which /24 subnets should be removed entirely, and then we remove potentially spoof addresses from used /24s.

From SWIN and CALT we removed all /24 subnets that:

1. have fewer than m observed IPs, *and*
2. have no overlapping IPs that are also in the spoof-free WIKI, WEB, MLAB and GAME datasets.

[6]The number of addresses from these /8 in our non-spoofed sources is negligible (no more than a few tens of addresses) and in some cases we know from the network administrators that these /8 are hardly used. However, for SWIN and CALT we see more than 10,000 addresses in these /8.

We choose m as follows. Treating spoofed IPs as uniformly sampled from a space of s IPs with probability p, the number X of spoofed IPs in the space follows a Binomial distribution. Specifically:

$$\Pr(X > k) = 1 - \sum_{i}^{k} \binom{n}{i} p^i (1-p)^{n-i} .$$

In our case of /24 subnets, $s = 256$ and we estimate p based on the number of spoofed IPs S in each 'empty' /8 prefix, so $p = S/2^{24}$. We then choose $m = k$ where $\Pr(X > k) < 10^{-8}$. Note that for SWIN, S is relatively constant across all time periods (10,000–15,000), but for CALT it increases from 15,000–20,000 until December 2013 to almost 250,000 in March 2014.

Spoofed IP addresses will also fall into /24 subnets that have actually used IP addresses. The second phase is to filter out potentially spoofed IPs in used /24 as follows. Since we assume the spoofed IPs to be uniformly random distributed, the number of spoofed IPs is S for used /8 prefixes as well. Subtracting the number of already removed IPs in spoofed /24 subnets we have S'_i spoofed IPs left in /8 prefix i. Given the observed number of IPs T_i in /8 prefix i in SWIN or CALT the expected number of not-spoofed addresses per /8 prefix (out of 2^{24} addresses) is

$$2^{24} \cdot \frac{T_i - S'_i}{2^{24} - S'_i} .$$

On average the probability that an IP in i is valid (V) is

$$\Pr(V) = \left(\frac{T_i - S'_i}{T_i}\right)\left(\frac{2^{24}}{2^{24} - S'_i}\right) \approx (T_i - S'_i)/T_i .$$

This tells us how many IPs to keep in each /8 prefix, but we must also determine which IPs to keep. To do this we use the fact that the distribution of the final byte B of used addresses is not uniform. We estimate the probability $P(B|V)$ from the IPs observed by all sources except SWIN and CALT. Then assuming that $P(B|\text{not } V) = \frac{1}{256}$ (uniform distribution), Bayes' rule gives that an IP is not spoofed in SWIN or CALT with probability

$$\Pr(V|B) = \frac{\Pr(V)\Pr(B|V)}{\Pr(V)\Pr(B|V) + (1 - \Pr(V))/256} .$$

We then filter SWIN and CALT by independently removing addresses ending with B with probability $1 - P(V|B)$.

We cannot evaluate the true accuracy of our approach, but the following circumstantial evidence shows that it is effective. With filtering, randomly distributed IPs in the 'empty' /8 networks are removed. With filtering, the number of used /24 subnets gradually increases over time and does not show large abrupt increases and decreases anymore. Without filtering the number of /24 subnets in SWIN or CALT is much higher than in any other dataset, e.g. it is up to 30% higher than for our largest dataset (IPING) and up to 60% higher compared to WEB, GAME. After filtering the number of used /24 subnets in SWIN and CALT is lower or similar to that in WEB and GAME.

Figure 2 shows the benefit of filtering spoofed addresses. LLM estimates that include filtered SWIN and CALT are quite consistent with LLM estimates made without SWIN and CALT. LLM estimates using unfiltered SWIN and CALT are much higher (exceeding the possible maximum for March 2014). To save space, we only show this comparison for /24 subnets, as spoofed IPs have less negative impact on the number of observed and estimated used IPv4 addresses due to the uniform random nature and low (10% or less) estimated percentage of spoofed IPs.

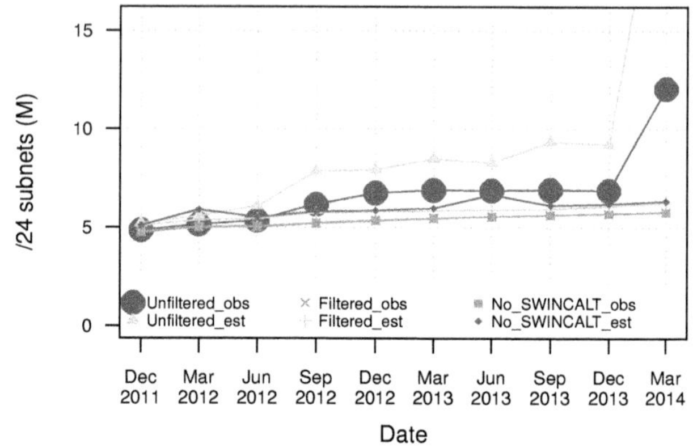

Figure 2: Observed (obs) and estimated (est) /24 subnets with and without spoof filtering compared to observed and estimated /24 subnets without SWIN and CALT

4.6 Dynamic and static addresses

Many IPv4 addresses are (re)assigned dynamically (such as with DHCP or PPPoE). Hence, long passive measurements may observe multiple addresses for a single host, and over-count the number of simultaneously used addresses.

If each assignment uses the lowest/highest unused address of a pool, then the total number of addresses used from the pool is the maximum simultaneous pool utilisation and the LLM estimate would indeed estimate the maximum number of simultaneously used addresses. However, if addresses are drawn uniformly, as our measurements suggest, then all pool addresses could be observed even if at most one address is in use at a time. Similarly, a single host moving between multiple statically assigned addresses may report multiple addresses, even if at most one is in use at a time.

However, addresses assigned to pools cannot be used elsewhere. So we argue that any over-count captures addresses (or /24 subnets) that are on "stand-by" and de facto 'in use' at the time of our measurement. (In the future under-utilised pools may be reduced in size and the freed addresses may be used for other purposes. However, this is the same as re-purposing addresses of de facto unused hosts. We cannot quantify such future optimisations.)

We also study /24 subnets, which are less affected by dynamic addressing [6]. While address reassignments (e.g., host mobility) may cross different /24 subnets, a large fraction of them will be within the same /24 subnets. Evidence for this we found in 16 consecutive days of GAME session data, where we have unique client IDs, client login/logout times and client IP addresses. We selected 9 million distinct clients with multiple sessions and analysed the number of distinct IPv4 addresses and /24 networks used over time. After the first four days all clients had logged in at least once. From this point in time the observed distinct IP addresses increased 2.7 times (from 16 to 42 million), while the observed distinct /24 networks only increased 1.2 times (from 2.3 to 2.8 million).

5. VALIDATION

In this section, we first pick a specific model-selection algorithm from among those described in Section 3.3.2, based on test data. Then, we compare estimated use of addresses against ground truth for a handful of networks, and show that CR gives better estimates than simply summing the observed addresses. Finally, we use *cross-validation* to demonstrate that this also applies to the whole address space, since we have no ground truth for most networks.

Table 3: Cross-validation errors depending on different model selection parameter settings

	IP addresses		/24 subnets	
Setting	RMSE [M]	MAE [M]	RMSE [k]	MAE [k]
AIC-fixed1	28.1	11.9	139.1	57.2
BIC-fixed1	31.7	13.3	136.6	56.4
AIC-fixed10	20.6	9.5	138.4	57.7
AIC-fixed100	11.9	6.6	141.9	59.8
AIC-fixed1000	18.9	9.8	132.5	61.4
AIC-adaptive1000	15.5	7.7	134.9	56.3
BIC-adaptive1000	14.9	7.8	136.6	56.9

To perform cross-validation with our $k = 9$ data sources we consider a particular source i as the "universe" of possible IPv4 addresses. We apply CR to the addresses/subnets in i that are also in the other $k-1$ sources, to estimate the number of individuals unique to source i. Since we know the true number of individuals unique to i, we can evaluate the effectiveness of CR. We do this for each source, to obtain the mean error and mean-square error. We then assume that the CR estimator based on the full k sets is equally accurate at estimating the true number of ghosts, although we do not have confidence intervals for this.

5.1 Model selection

We first investigated how to best select models, as our model selection approach in Section 3.3.2 leaves us with the choice of two ICs and the choice of how to dimension the count pre-processing heuristic. In initial experiments we varied the IC used (AIC, BIC) and we varied d for the count pre-processing heuristic. The variable d was either *adaptive* (starting with $d = 1000$ in each step we halved d, selecting the first d smaller than $\min_s z_s$) or *fixed* to values of 1, 10, 100, or 1000.

For each parameter setting we performed cross-validation for each time window, except the first window for which we have the least data, for both used IPv4 addresses and used /24 subnets. Table 3 shows the different parameter settings we investigated and the Root Mean Square Error (RMSE) and Mean Absolute Error (MAE) averaged over all sources and time windows.

With a fixed divisor using the actual counters (fixed1) results in the highest errors for IPs but provides low errors for /24 subnets. We think this is because (1) there is much more noise in the observed IPs than in the observed /24 subnets and (2) the number of observed /24 subnets is much lower than the number of IPs, and hence even for a small divisor of 10 we already start losing information for /24 subnets, which leads to much reduced accuracy. Choosing a divisor around 100 results in the smallest error for IPs but the largest error for /24 subnets. Effectively, the choice depends on the type of data and it is unclear what choice would be the best for estimating the IP addresses and /24 subnets unseen overall.

In contrast, our adaptive approach (with a maximum divisor of 1000) works quite well for both IPs and /24 subnets, with errors not much larger than the minimum errors. With the adaptive approach, using the BIC instead of the AIC lowers the error for IPs and increases the error for /24 subnets, but the increase for /24 subnets is small and even for /24 subnets the estimates obtained with the BIC are smoother.[7] Hence, in the rest of the paper the estimates presented are based on our adaptive approach with a maximum divisor of 1000 and we use the BIC.

[7]The BIC selects fewer parameters representing interactions of many sources, which have a much lower number of samples than interactions between fewer sources and hence are noisier.

Table 4: Pingable, observed (obs), and estimated (Poisson, right-truncated Poisson) IPv4 addresses vs. peak usage (truth) as percentages of the size of each routed network

Network	Ping [%]	Obs. [%]	Estimated(Error) [%]		Truth [%]
			Poisson	TruncPoisson	
A	0.4	5.7	23.2(-2.7)	26.7(+0.8)	25.9
B	6.7	8.5	13.3(+1.9)	12.3(+0.9)	11.4
C	12.0	13.7	37.6(–)	36.1(–)	30–35
D	24.0	31.8	41.8(-5.8)	51.6(+4.0)	47.6
E	9.4	17.3	52.1(-6.2)	60.5(+2.2)	58.3
F	0.0	15.9	20.2(-2.1)	20.2(-2.1)	22.3

5.2 Comparison with ground truth

We compared our observed and estimated IP addresses with the ground truth for several networks. Our ground truth is estimates of the number of actively used IPv4 addresses at peak times (effectively high watermarks). Since our time windows are very long (12 months), it is appropriate to compare our estimates with high watermarks. We compare the ground truth with the observed and estimated numbers for the time windows where the high watermarks occurred roughly in the middle of the windows.

For privacy reasons we cannot reveal the identity of the networks. We also cannot reveal their sizes, as this would leak information, which allows narrowing down the possible identities (to a very small set in the case of one particular network). The largest network covered is two /16 subnets and the smallest network is roughly one /20 combined from multiple allocations.

For each network Table 4 shows the number of addresses that responded to ping, the number of addresses observed, the number of addresses estimated (for both Poisson and right-truncated Poisson), and the actual number of used addresses as percentages of the sizes of the routed networks. Note that network F blocked our pinger, so we do not have IPING or TPING data for this network.

The results show that the percentage of pingable and observed addresses is much smaller than the ground truth for networks A, C, D, E and F, whereas for the more "open" network B the percentage of observed addresses is relatively close to the truth. However, the CR estimates are always much closer to the truth. Using right-truncated Poisson distributions gives better estimates than using Poisson distributions. The right-truncated Poisson estimates tend to be higher than the truth (except for network F where we do not have IPING and TPING), but the cause may be dynamic addresses (e.g. DHCP) leading to higher estimates due to our long 12-month observation windows in contrast to the short-term peak numbers we use as truth.

5.3 Cross-validation results illustrated

Figure 3 illustrates the results of the cross-validation for addresses and subnets for time window 9 (results for other time windows are largely consistent). The figure shows the number of IPs in each source also observed by IPING (Obs ping), the total number of addresses of a source also observed by any other sources (Obs. all), and the ranges of the CR estimates (confidence interval based on profile likelihood with $\alpha = 10^{-7}$ to get wide intervals). Since the sources are of different sizes we normalised the number of addresses on the total number of addresses observed by each source

Table 5: Observed and estimated used IPv4 addresses and /24 subnets at the end of June 2014 based on different stratifications

Stratification	Estimated total [M] None	RIR	Country	Age	Prefix size	Industry	Stat/Dyn	Ping [M]	Observed [M]	Est. unseen [M]	Routed [M]
IP addresses	1133.3	1167.2	1157.1	1107.0	1091.5	1084.8	1100.4	428.9	739.2	345–455	2725.3
/24 subnets	6.2	6.3	6.3	6.2	6.2	6.3	6.2	4.9	5.9	0.3–0.4	10.7

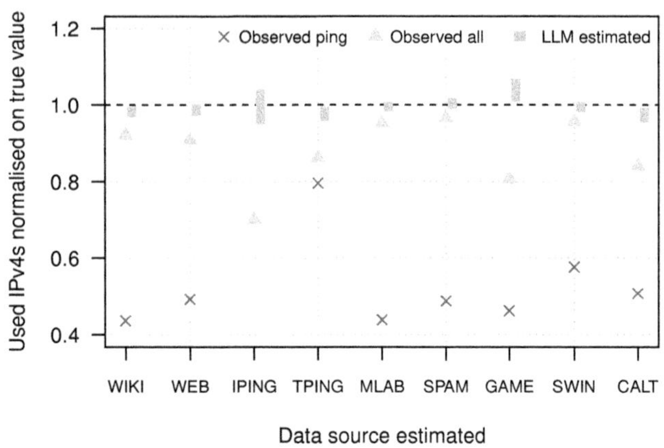

Figure 3: IP addresses observed with ping, observed by any source, and estimated ranges for LLM normalised on the true number of unseen IPs for each data source

(the ground truth). A CR estimate is good, if the normalised range includes 1 and the range is not too large.

Figure 3 shows that for IPv4 addresses all sources other than IPING and GAME have relatively high overlap, but between 10% and 15% of addresses appear only in one source. Only 50–60% of addresses of each source (except TPING) is in IPING, showing that ICMP pinging undercounts significantly. The CR estimates for WIKI, WEB, IPING, MLAB, SPAM, and SWIN are quite good. The estimated ranges for TPING and CALT are slightly too low, and the estimated range for GAME is slightly too high. Nevertheless, the LLM CR estimates are a substantial improvement over just using the number of observed IPs.

For brevity we do not show the figure for /24 subnets. For /24 subnets there is a very high overlap between all data sources. However, for most sources only 90% or less of the /24 subnets appear in IPING, so just using ICMP pinging significantly undercounts even the used /24 subnets. While the difference between CR estimates and observed addresses is much smaller for /24 subnets (in most cases the difference is only 1–2%, except for IPING), our CR estimates are still an improvement.

6. USED SPACE ANALYSIS

Now, we present the results for the estimated used IPv4 addresses and /24 subnets. We present both total estimates as well as estimates for different RIRs, countries, allocation ages, and allocation prefix sizes. We also investigate growth on a longer time scale and whether our estimates are sensible given the reported growth of Internet users.

6.1 Definitions

In most figures we plot one or more of the following metrics:

- *Routed* IPv4 addresses and /24 networks: the total number of addresses/networks that were publicly routed based on RV [14]. For each time window we downloaded and aggregated weekly snapshots (excluding unallocated but advertised prefixes). Gregori *et al.* [26] suggests that while RV data is incomplete for AS-level graph analysis, it does capture the whole routed space.
- *Observed* IPv4 addresses and /24 subnets: the addresses/networks present in one or several of the data sources described in Section 4.1.
- *Estimated* IPv4 addresses and /24 subnets: the total number of addresses/networks estimated with CR, which means the observed addresses/networks plus the unseen estimated addresses/networks. For clarity in the figures we plot the point estimates instead of the estimated ranges.

In the figures with normalised data, we always normalise each series on the first value – the first time window (31 December 2011).

6.2 Used IPv4 space totals

Table 5 shows the estimated used IPv4 addresses and /24 subnets depending on different stratifications (RIR, country, prefix size, industry, allocation age) as introduced in Section 3.4, as well as the pingable, observed and estimated unseen addresses and /24 subnets at the end of June 2014. For each type of stratification we separated each source into the different strata, then used CR to estimate the size of each strata, and finally we summed up the estimates over all strata to get the total estimate.

Only 430 million IPs and 4.9 million /24s responded to ICMP ping, but we observed 740 million IPs and 5.9 million /24s from all sources combined. The estimated used IPs are fairly consistent across stratifications: roughly 1.1–1.2 billion used IPv4 addresses and 6.2–6.3 million used /24 subnets. Based on RV this means we observed only 27% of the routed IPv4 addresses and 55% of the routed /24 subnets, but we estimate that roughly 45% of the routed IPv4 addresses and 60% of the routed /24 subnets were used.

For all stratifications our estimates are always plausible (below the number of routed addresses). The quotient of estimated used addresses divided by the addresses detected only with ICMP echo pinging is 2.6–2.7, larger than the correction factor of 1.86 in [3].

6.3 Used IPv4 space over time

Figure 4 shows the number of estimated used /24 subnets against the number of observed and routed /24 subnets both as absolute numbers and normalised. The dashed line is the actual estimates and the solid line is the estimates smoothed. The total number of observed /24 increased from 4.8 million to 5.9 million, but we estimate that the number of /24 subnets actually increased from 5.1 million to over 6.2 million (an increase of 0.45 million subnets per year). The estimate range is narrow, the minimum and maximum are within ±1% of the point estimates. Whilst the routed space only increased by 7% in two years, the number of observed and estimated used /24 subnets increased by 22% over the same time.

Figure 5 shows the number of estimated used IPv4 addresses against the number of observed and routed IPv4 addresses both as

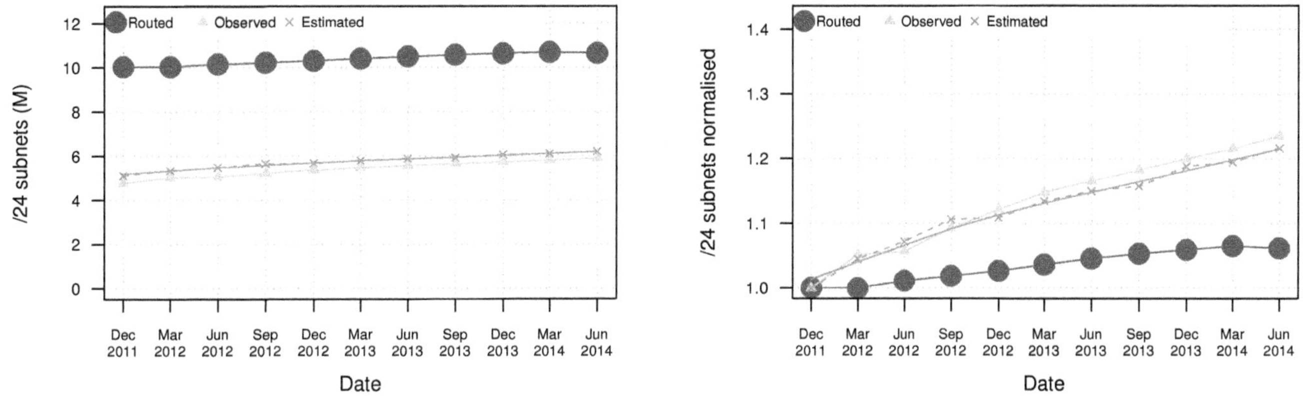

Figure 4: Absolute and relative growth of estimated, observed and routed /24 subnets

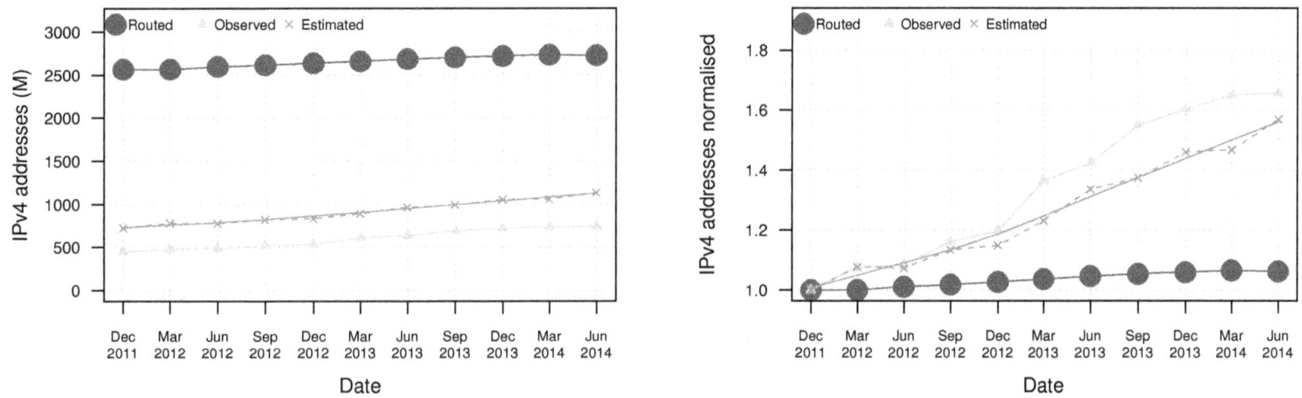

Figure 5: Absolute and relative growth of estimated, observed and routed IPv4 addresses

absolute numbers and normalised. The number of observed IPv4 addresses increased from 450 million to 740 million, but we estimate that the number of addresses actually increased from 720 million to 1.2 billion (an average increase of about 170 million IPv4 addresses per year). Minimum and maximum of the estimate range are within ±3% of the point estimate. As for /24 subnets, the observed and estimated number of IPv4 addresses increased faster than the routed addresses. The difference between estimated and observed relative growth may be in part because of earlier under-counting due to fewer sources and a gap in the GAME data collection.

The number of estimated /24 networks is only 5–10% above the number of observed /24 networks, whereas the number of estimated IPs is 50–60% above the number of observed IPs. Intuitively this makes sense, since a /24 network is observed if *any* of its addresses if observed. The relatively small error for /24s means one could treat the number of observed /24s as relatively good approximation of the number of actually used /24s.

6.4 Used IPv4 space by RIR

Figure 6 shows the estimated number of IPv4 addresses over time depending on the RIR responsible for their allocation both as absolute numbers and normalised. For brevity we omitted the broadly similar statistics for /24 subnets. APNIC has the largest number of used addresses followed by RIPE and ARIN. Looking at relative growth, AfriNIC is growing at the fastest rate, followed by LACNIC. Of the three RIRs with the most allocated space, relatively APNIC and ARIN are growing faster than RIPE.

6.5 Used IPv4 space by prefix size

Figure 7 shows the average yearly growth rate for addresses for different prefix sizes (based on the RIR allocation data). For brevity we do not show the estimates for /24 networks here, as the trends are broadly similar. Absolute growth is strongest in the large prefixes /10 to /16 (/8 and /9 have not grown much). However, if we look at relative growth, growth has been more equally across many prefixes. Exceptions are the old /8 allocations which have not grown and /9, /21 and /22 allocations which show the strongest growth (/9 is driven up by a few ISPs since there are less than ten /9 allocations overall, and /22 is the largest allocation handed out by APNIC since 15 April, 2011, and by RIPE since 14 Sep, 2012).

6.6 Used IPv4 space by allocation age

Figure 8 shows the average yearly growth rate of IPv4 addresses for different allocation ages (based on RIR allocation data) until the end of 2013. For brevity we omitted the results for /24 subnets as the trend is broadly similar. In absolute numbers the more recent allocations made since 2005 are growing the most, with a clear positive correlation between recentness and growth. In relative terms growth is strongest for allocations made in the last three years, but we can also see 20% or higher growth in some old allocations.

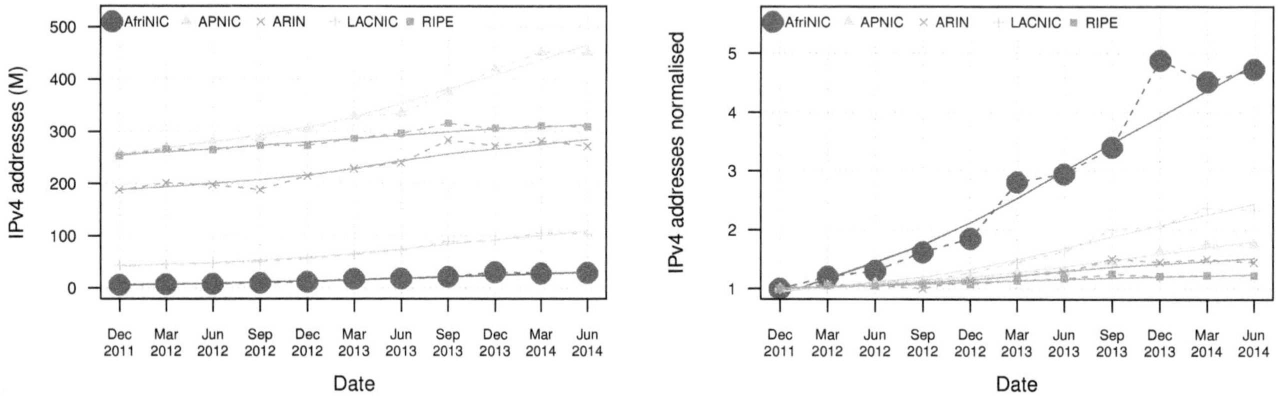

Figure 6: Absolute and relative growth of estimated IPv4 addresses for different RIRs

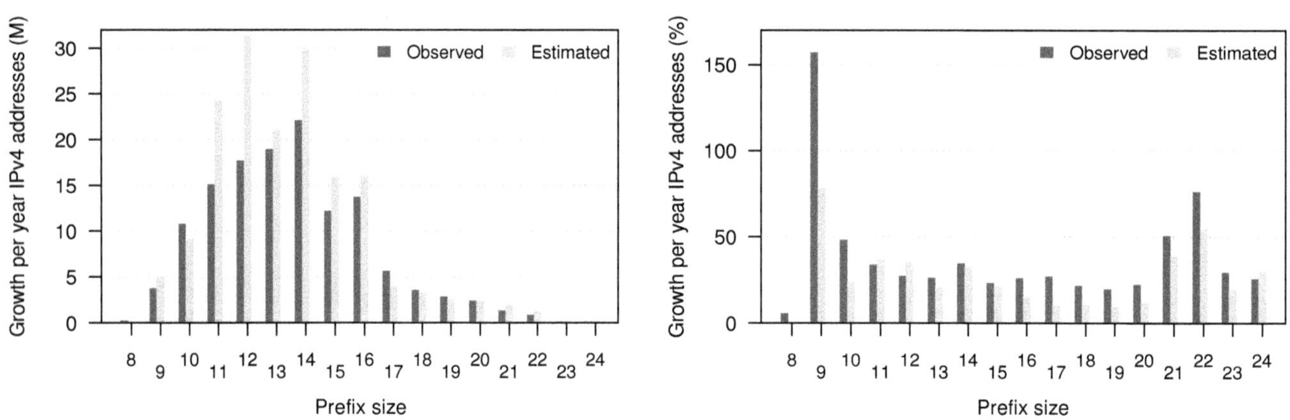

Figure 7: Average absolute and relative yearly growth of observed and estimated IPv4 addresses for different allocation prefixes

6.7 Used IPv4 space by country

Figure 9 shows the absolute and relative growth for IPv4 addresses for the countries with the largest number of observed used IPv4 addresses (at least 1.5 million addresses). Again, we do not show results for /24 subnets as the trends are broadly similar. Absolute growth is strongest in the two nations with the largest allocations (USA, China) followed by Brazil and South Korea. Relative growth is between 10% and 30% for many countries, but Romania and several Asian and South American countries (Brazil, Columbia, Indonesia, India, Vietnam, Argentina, Thailand, Taiwan, and China) have grown faster.

6.8 Long-term growth

Figure 10 shows the number of allocated addresses since 2003 (from RIR data), routed and allocated addresses since 2008 (from RV) and the number of pingable, observed and estimated addresses over time for our 12-month time windows. The ping data from 2003 to 2011 is from USC/LANDER [3]. The ping data since 2012 is the 12-months windows of IPING. Note that allocated and routed addresses are plotted on a different scale (right y-axis).

Two distinct phases are visible for the number of allocated addresses: the last boom 2004–2011, and the slowdown due to running out of unallocated addresses since 2011. The number of allocated addresses increased much faster than the number of pingable addresses until 2011. Even since 2011 the number of allocated addresses increased faster than the number of pingable addresses. On the other hand, the number of estimated used addresses is increasing much faster than the number of pingable addresses with a growth rate similar to the rate of the allocated and routed addresses before their slowdown in 2011 and 2012 respectively.

6.9 Comparison with Internet user growth

We think the growth of the number of used IPv4 addresses is primarily driven by an Internet user population increase, irrespective of the number of devices per user. All home devices are behind NATs and mobile devices are also largely behind NATs. Similarly, if we look at increasingly complex commercial networks, these are also mainly behind NATs (or not even connected to the Internet). In this section we derive a very rough estimate of the IPv4 address growth based on the Internet user growth and compare it with the growth estimated with CR.

According to data from the ITU [27] the number of Internet users has grown from 16 million in December 1995 to 2.75 billion (roughly 39% of the world's population) in December 2013 as shown in Figure 11. The growth rate of Internet users looks exponential at the beginning of the graph, however since 2006/2007 the growth appears roughly *linear*. This is consistent with the roughly linear trend in our results shown in Section 6.3.

Between 2007 and 2012 the number of Internet users grew by roughly 250 million per year (c.f. Figure 11). For private use typ-

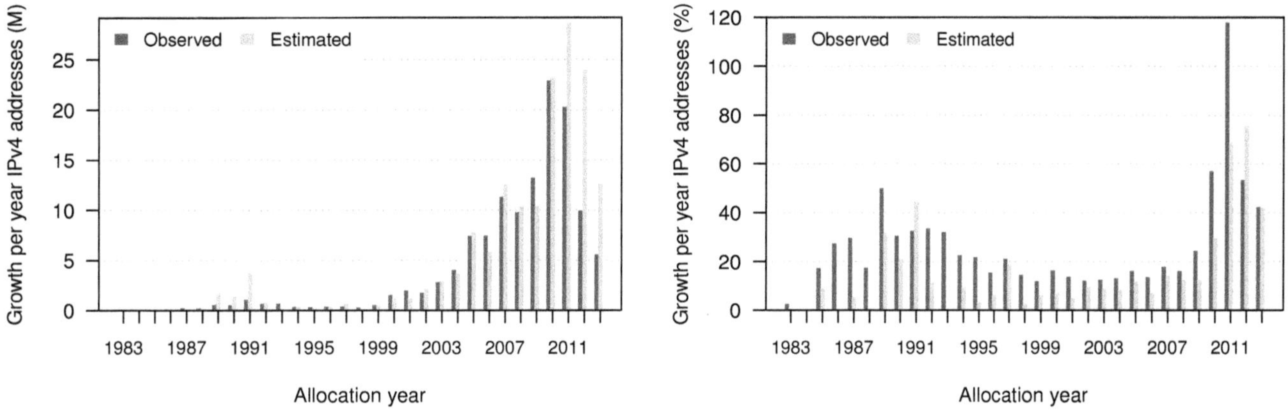

Figure 8: Average absolute and relative yearly growth of observed and estimated IPv4 addresses for different allocation ages

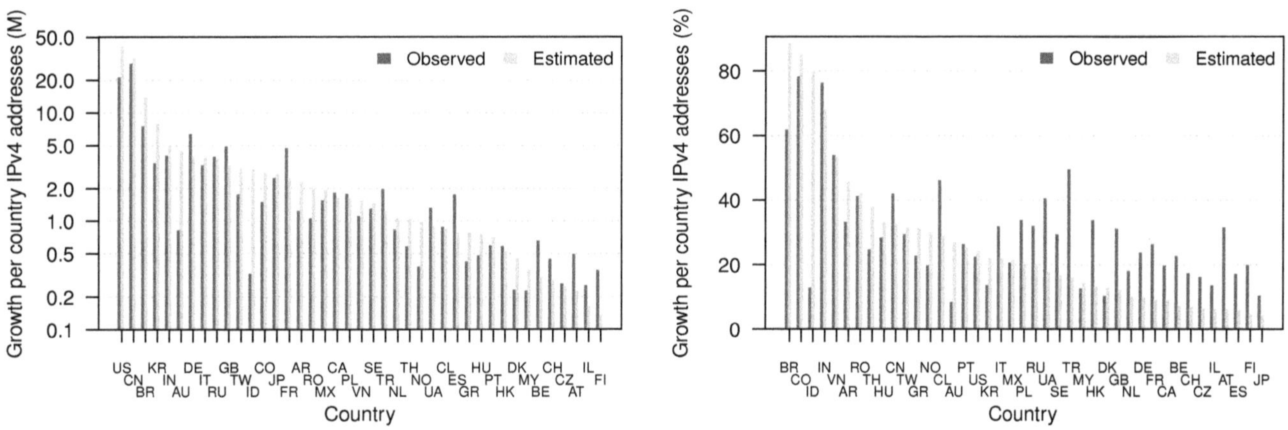

Figure 9: Average absolute and relative yearly growth of observed and estimated IPv4 addresses for different countries sorted by estimated growth (only the largest 42 countries). Note, the absolute numbers are plotted in log scale.

ically a household shares one public IP address. In industrial nations the household size is 2–3, but in developing countries it can be higher, for example it is over 5 in India [28]. We assume the average household size of new Internet users is between 2 and 5.

In addition a fraction of new users will get a public IPv4 address at work. We assume an average employment ratio of 65% [29]. We could not find any data on the number of average public IP addresses used per employee, so we are assuming a wide possible range. As upper limit we assume on average one IPv4 address per two employees, as in reality many employees (especially in developing countries) have no Internet at work, work at home, or share computers with other workers. As a lower limit we assume on average there is one public address per 200 workers.

Let g_U be the user growth per year, H the average household size, p_E the employment ratio, and W the average number of employees sharing an IP at work. Then the IP address growth is $g_I = (1/H + p_E/W)g_U$. Based on the above ranges of H and W, we would expect the IPv4 addresses to grow between 50 million and 205 million per year (plus additional addresses for service and infrastructure growth). Our CR growth estimate from Section 6.3 is 170 million IPv4 addresses per year, which fits within this range.

7. UNUSED SPACE PREDICTION

Our CR technique tells us how many unobserved IPv4 addresses to expect, but says nothing about the distribution of free blocks/prefixes. This is a challenging issue – recipients of newly assigned IPv4 address blocks typically prefer usably-sized contiguous allocations, and forwarding information base (FIB) tables in routers are more efficiently packed if address blocks are allocated hierarchically.

Some information is given by the CR estimate of the used but unobserved /24 networks (in Figure 4). However, this again does not tell us whether these small blocks are isolated or parts of unused larger blocks. In this section, we try to understand how the unseen addresses are distributed among seemingly empty subnets, by observing what happens when data sources are combined sequentially; each new source brings addresses that were unseen by the previous sources, and we can model how those addresses fill the previously empty space.

7.1 Model

Let x_i be the number of observed free /i blocks. Let $Z_{00...0}$ be the total number of new addresses to allocate (given by CR). Let N_i be the number of new addresses assumed to be allocated to vacant /i blocks, assuming sequential allocation. Specifically, if two ad-

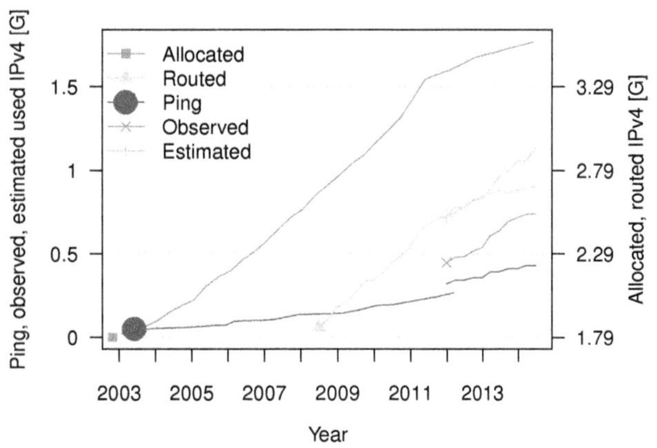

Figure 10: Number of allocated and routed IPv4 addresses (right y-axis), as well as pingable, observed and estimated used IPv4 addresses (left y-axis) over time

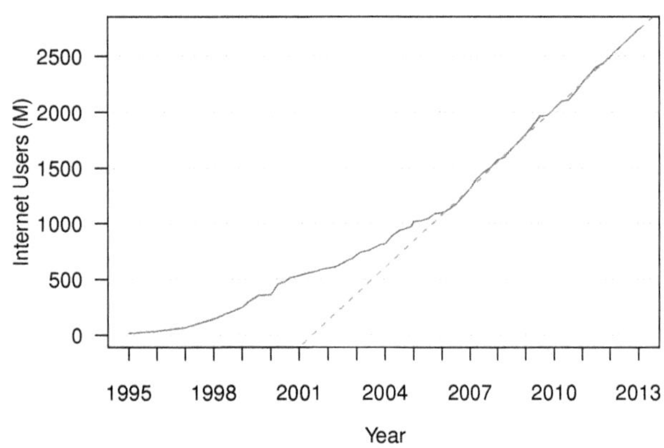

Figure 11: Number of Internet users based on data from ITU

dresses are added to the same vacant $/i$, then only the first of these contributes to N_i , since the block is no longer vacant when the second one is added.

Similarly, let x_i^S be the number of free $/i$ blocks in a set S of addresses, $Z_{00...0}^{S,\Delta}$ be the number of new addresses when a new set Δ is merged with S, and $n_i^{S,\Delta}$ be the number of addresses added to vacant $/i$ blocks in the process. Without the subscript i, the variables x and n denote vectors.

Note that adding an address to a vacant $/i$ will reduce the number of vacant $/i$ blocks by 1, but increase by one the number of $/j$ blocks for each $j > i$, regardless of where within the $/i$ the address is added. That is,

$$x^{S\cup\Delta} - x^S = An^{S,\Delta}, \tag{2}$$

where

$$A = \begin{pmatrix} -1 & 1 & 1 & \cdots & 1 \\ 0 & -1 & 1 & \cdots & 1 \\ \vdots & \vdots & \vdots & \ddots & \vdots \\ 0 & 0 & 0 & \cdots & -1 \end{pmatrix}. \tag{3}$$

A natural approach is to estimate the previous fraction of addresses revealed by each new source that have been allocated to free blocks of a given size, and assume the new $Z_{0,0,...,0}$ addresses will be distributed in the same way. This is not sufficient, because the allocation process changes the number of available blocks. Instead, our model uses the observation that the probability that a

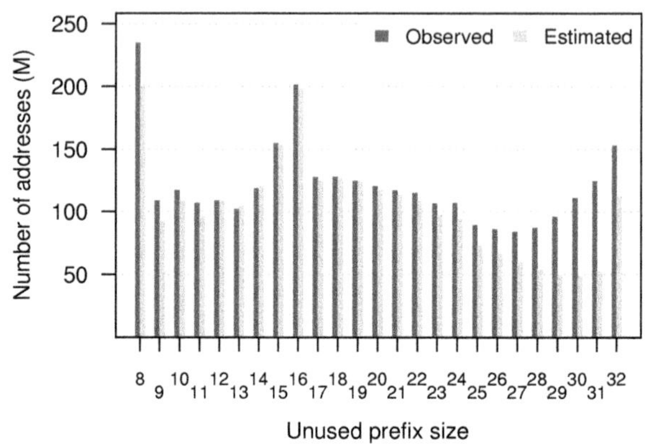

Figure 12: Number of addresses in observed and estimated unused prefixes for different routed prefix sizes

new address is allocated to a free $/i$ block is proportional to x_i, the number of such free blocks. In particular, it assumes that there are $f_1, \ldots, f_{32}$ such that the ratio

$$\frac{N_1}{x_1} : \frac{N_2}{x_2 + N_1} : \cdots : \frac{N_{32}}{x_{32} + \sum_{j=1}^{31} N_j} = f_1 : f_2 : \cdots : f_{32} \tag{4}$$

remains approximately constant as more batches of addresses are discovered.

The model includes subnets larger than /8, even though blocks larger than /8 have not been allocated. Similarly, we consider all vacant subnets down to vacant /32s, even though subnets smaller than a /24 are not routed on the public Internet. However, before computing the remaining unused prefixes we split a few /7 into /8, and we also exclude all private, multicast, experimental and reserved prefixes, such as 224.0.0.0/3 or 10.0.0.0/8. Note that we do not exclude non-publicly routed prefixes.

To determine how the unobserved addresses predicted by CR will affect the distribution of free blocks, it remains to determine f_i. To do this, we observe the change in x when a new data set Δ is added to an existing list S of used IPv4 addresses, and from that calculate n. Since A in (3) is invertible, (2) gives

$$n^{S,\Delta} = A^{-1}(x^{S\cup\Delta} - x^S).$$

The f_i are then found by (4), normalized so that $f_{32} = 1$. Since few large subnets become newly used for each data set, estimates of f_i for $i \lesssim 12$ are noisy. This is unfortunate, since these are the blocks of greatest interest. To reduce this noise, estimates were averaged over four cases: Δ = IPING, GAME, WEB, WIKI; in each case, S is the union of all remaining datasets, except SWIN and CALT.

One concern with this model is that, as the address space fills up, the values of f_i may vary. To check this, we performed tests where datasets were added to S one at a time, in both increasing and decreasing order of the dataset size. The values were reasonably consistent in each case.

7.2 Results

Figure 12 shows the number of addresses in unused prefixes at 30 June 2014, based on all sources except SWIN and CALT. Results are for both direct observation and CR. The majority of empty prefixes are longer than /20 (fewer than 2^{12} addresses), but the unused space is roughly uniformly distributed among prefixes of lengths /9 to /24 (except /15 and /16). The reason for this is unclear.

If the used but unobserved /8 to /24 subnets estimated by the model of Section 7.1 were divided into /24s, there would be 0.3

million /24s. This is consistent with the estimate of 0.26–0.36 million by the independent LLM model for the period ending at 30 June 2014, providing evidence for the validity of both models.

7.2.1 Router FIB limitations

One of the reasons that the distribution of prefix sizes is important is that each routed prefix requires an entry in a router's Forwarding Information Base (FIB), and there is a *prima facie* risk that allocating all unused prefixes could overflow the FIBs. Above we estimated that including the unrouted space there are 0.78 million prefixes that are /24 or larger. Currently, there are more than 0.5 million routed prefixes already (but a substantial fraction is unused). In 2007 Juniper [30] stated that its M120 and MX960 had FIB capacities of about 2 million IPv4 routes, and that IPv4 FIBs with approximately 10 million entries are feasible within a few years if demand exists. In addition, FIB compression techniques can reduce size of FIBs [30]. This suggests that it will be feasible to use and route all less than 1.3 million available prefixes. Even if unused prefixes are subdivided further, it appears feasible to route them all. However, some existing routers may require upgrades.

7.2.2 Estimated years of supply

In July 2014 roughly 5.5 /8 networks of unallocated addresses remained [1] – equivalent to 350,000 /24 networks or 90 million addresses. Even if in addition to these all 4.4 million routed but unused /24 subnets could be prised away from their current owners, /24 networks would be exhausted in 2024 under the current growth trend of 0.45 million /24 subnets per year. Unused routed IPv4 addresses would be exhausted in 2023 given the current growth of 170 million addresses per year.

The overall estimate hides the differences between regions. Table 6 shows the available space (unallocated space plus allocated publicly routed unused space based on our CR estimates), the current average growth rate over our measured time period and the predicted year supply will run out (under the very optimistic assumption that the *whole* unused space could be utilised) for IPs and /24 networks for each RIR. For most RIRs the number of years of IP supply is equal or smaller than the number of years of /24 networks supply. This is because either the IP and /24 growth rates are similar or the IP growth rate is larger, but there are significant numbers of unused IPs in used /24. RIPE is an exception due to similar growth rates for IPs and /24s *and* significant supply in already used blocks. At current growth rates ARIN and RIPE have 14+ years of IP supply left, but AfriNIC has only 8–9 years of supply left, and LACNIC and APNIC have only 2–4 years of supply left. Any future reallocations between RIRs to ease local pressures would change these numbers of course.

However, it appears unlikely that the whole IPv4 space will ever be completely utilised. If the overall utilization of routed /24 subnets remains below, say 75%, the current growth rates suggests four years of remaining supply overall. Moreover, in this case regions with tight supply, such as APNIC and LACNIC, would be exhausted within one year. APNIC stands out, because its IP growth rate is much larger than its /24 growth rate with unused IPs in used /24s depleted soon. We expect a slowdown shortly – in fact Figure 6 suggests it may have begun already. An open question is the large amount of unrouted IPv4 space, much of which has not been routed for years. Unused parts of the unrouted space might provide a short-lived increase in IPv4 supply.

Over the next one to two years, we expect IPv4 exhaustion to be increasingly felt, resulting in a brief growth in the IPv4 address market. Most organizations holding unused addresses do so for operational reasons – to allow expansion or flexibility, or in one case as a /8 darknet – but some may be holding them to sell if the market price rises sufficiently. The numbers in this paper may guide how long they can expect to be held for, assuming that the market will collapse once IPv6 is widely adopted. However, this is complicated by the fact that the very act of selling a large block of IPv4 addresses will delay the implementation of IPv6, and hence prolong the IPv4 market.

8. CONCLUSIONS AND FUTURE WORK

Our key contribution is describing and demonstrating a new statistical *capture-recapture* technique for improved estimation of the true population of both observed and unobserved (yet still active) IPv4 addresses from diverse sources of active and passive measurement data. This technique refines our community's understanding of IPv4 address space exhaustion and consequent incentives for IPv6 adoption.

Data from nine sources over the past three years suggests 5.9 million used /24 subnets and 740 million used IPv4 addresses. Yet our CR technique indicates a significantly higher 1.2 billion IPv4 addresses in use across 6.3 million /24 subnets, with usage growing at around 0.45 million /24 subnets and 170 million IPv4 addresses per year. Asia and Europe have the highest numbers of used IP addresses, while Africa and South America show the fastest growth. Based on the overall estimates, at the very best unallocated plus routed but unused addresses will last until 2023. More likely, if say only 75% of routed /24 subnets could ever be used, supply will be exhausted in 2018. Moreover, Asia and South America are the two "pressure points" that will experience a shortage of addresses within the next one or two years.

Previous sales of IP addresses saw prices of US$8–17 per IP depending on the sizes of the blocks sold [31, 32]. At an average price of US$10 per IP address, the 4.4 million routed unused /24 subnets have a value of over US$11 billion. However, probably only a small fraction of those will be sold, so even if prices rise substantially, the eventual market value is likely to be smaller.

Our ability to collect more IP data for validating or improving our estimates, or potentially detecting more hosts (e.g. private servers), is limited by common privacy restrictions. We plan to explore an enhanced method [33] for securely applying CR to multi-source measurement data without revealing which IPv4 addresses each source contains.

Acknowledgements

This research was supported by Australian Research Council grants LP110100240 (with APNIC Pty Ltd) and FT0991594. We thank Geoff Huston, George Michaelson, Valve Corporation, A. Reynolds, Swinburne ITS, Caltech IMSS, D. Buttigieg, C. Tassios, R. Bevier, B. Mattern, USC/ISI and J. Heidemann for providing data. We thank our shepherd X. Dimitropoulos and the anonymous reviewers for their helpful comments.

9. REFERENCES

[1] G. Huston. IPv4 Address Report. `http://www.potaroo.net/tools/ipv4/index.html`.

[2] Y. Pryadkin, R. Lindell, J. Bannister, R. Govindan. An Empirical Evaluation of IP Address Space Occupancy. Technical Report ISI-TR 598, USC/ISI, 2004.

[3] J. Heidemann, Y. Pradkin, R. Govindan, C. Papadopoulos, G. Bartlett, J. Bannister. Census and Survey of the Visible Internet. In *ACM Conference on Internet measurement (IMC)*, pages 169–182, 2008.

Table 6: Available IPv4 addresses and /24 networks (unallocated plus publicly routed but unused), growth rate and years where supply will run out (under the very optimistic assumption that all currently unused space will be used) by RIR

RIR	Available IPs [M]	Growth IPs [M/year]	Year runout IPs	Available /24s [M]	Growth /24s [M/year]	Year runout /24s
AfriNIC	75	9	2022–2023	0.29	0.03	2023–2024
APNIC	310	80	2017–2018	1.04	0.11	2023–2024
ARIN	830	35	2037–2038	2.39	0.08	2043–2044
LACNIC	65	25	2016–2017	0.15	0.09	2015–2016
RIPE	370	25	2028–2029	0.87	0.11	2021–2022
World	1650	170	2023–2024	4.7	0.45	2024–2025

[4] X. Cai, J. Heidemann. Understanding Block-level Address Usage in the Visible Internet. In *ACM SIGCOMM Conference*, pages 99–110, 2010.

[5] Internet Census 2012 – Port scanning /0 using insecure embedded devices, 2012. `http://internetcensus2012.bitbucket.org`.

[6] A. Dainotti, K. Benson, A. King, kc claffy, M. Kallitsis, E. Glatz, X. Dimitropoulos. Estimating Internet Address Space Usage Through Passive Measurements. *ACM Computer Communication Review (CCR)*, 44(1):42–49, Jan. 2014.

[7] C. G. J. Petersen. The Yearly Immigration of Young Plaice into the Limfjord from the German Sea. *Rept. Danish Biol. Sta.*, 6:1–77, 1895.

[8] F. C. Lincoln. Calculating Waterfowl Abundance on the Basis of Banding Returns. *U.S. Dept. Agric. Circ.*, 118:1–4, 1930.

[9] A. Chao. An Overview of Closed Capture-Recapture Models. *Journal of Agricultural, Biological, and Environmental Statistics*, 6(2):158–175, 2001.

[10] S. Zander, L. L. H. Andrew, G. Armitage, and G. Huston. Estimating IPv4 Address Space Usage with Capture-Recapture. In *7th IEEE Workshop on Network Measurements (WNM)*, Oct. 2013.

[11] S. Zander, L. L. H. Andrew, G. Armitage, G. Huston, and G. Michaelson. Mitigating Sampling Error when Measuring Internet Client IPv6 Capabilities. In *ACM Internet Measurement Conference (IMC)*, Nov. 2012.

[12] DNS-based Blacklist of NiX Spam. `http://www.dnsbl.manitu.net/`.

[13] Measurement Lab. `http://www.measurementlab.net/`.

[14] University of Oregon Route Views Project. `http://www.routeviews.org/`.

[15] X. Meng, Z. Xu, B. Zhang, G. Huston, S. Lu, L. Zhang. IPv4 Address Allocation and the BGP Routing Table Evolution. *ACM Computer Communication Review (CCR)*, 35(1):71–80, 2005.

[16] A. Sriraman, K. R. B. Butler, P. D. McDaniel, P. Raghavan. Analysis of the IPv4 Address Space Delegation Structure. In *IEEE Symposium on Computers and Communications (ISCC)*, pages 501–508, Jul. 2007.

[17] E. B. Hook, R. R. Regal. Capture-Recapture Methods in Epidemiology: Methods and Limitations. *Epidemiologic Reviews*, 17(2):243–264, 1995.

[18] M. Roughan, J. Tuke, O. Maennel. Bigfoot, Sasquatch, the Yeti and other missing links: what we don't know about the AS graph. In *8th ACM Internet Measurement Conference (IMC)*, pages 325–330, Oct. 2008.

[19] A. Chao, P. K. Tsay, S. H. Lin, W. Y. Shau, D. Y. Chao. The Applications of Capture-Recapture Models to Epidemiological Data. *Statistics in Medicine*, 20:3123–3157, Oct. 2001.

[20] S. E. Fienberg. The Multiple Recapture Census for Closed Populations and Incomplete 2k Contingency Tables. *Biometrika*, 59(3):591–603, Dec. 1972.

[21] E. Cooch, G. C. White. *Program MARK: A Gentle Introduction*. Cornell University, 2009.

[22] K. P. Burnham, D. R. Anderson. Multimodel Inference - Understanding AIC and BIC in Model Selection. *Sociological Methods & Research*, 33:261–304, 2004.

[23] S. Baillargeon, L.-P. Rivest. Rcapture: Loglinear Models for Capture-Recapture in R. *Journal of Statistical Software*, 19(5):1–31, Apr. 2007.

[24] Internet Addresses Census dataset, PREDICT ID: USC-LANDER/internet_address_census_it40c-20110406. Provided by the USC/LANDER project. `http://www.isi.edu/ant/lander`.

[25] D. Moore, G. M. Voelker, S. Savage. Inferring Internet Denial-of-Service Activity. In *Usenix Security Symposium*, August 2001.

[26] E. Gregori, A. Improta, L. Lenzini, L. Rossi, L. Sani. On the Incompleteness of the AS-level Graph: a Novel Methodology for BGP Route Collector Placement. In *Internet Measurement Conference (IMC)*, 2012.

[27] ITU key 2006-2013 ICT data for the world, 2013. `http://www.itu.int/en/ITU-D/Statistics/Documents/statistics/2013/ITU_Key_2005-2013_ICT_data.xls`.

[28] Wikipedia. List of countries by number of households, Oct. 2013. `http://en.wikipedia.org/w/index.php?title=List_of_countries_by_number_of_households&oldid=576467223`.

[29] Wikipedia. Employment-to-population ratio, Mar. 2014. `http://en.wikipedia.org/w/index.php?title=Employment-to-population_ratio&oldid=598945003`.

[30] J. Scudder. Router Scaling Trends. Presentation at RIPE-54, May 2007. `http://meetings.ripe.net/ripe-54/presentations/Router_Scaling_Trends.pdf`.

[31] B. Edelman and M. Schwarz. Pricing and Efficiency in the Market for IP Addresses. Working Paper Number: 12-020, Nov. 2011. `http://hbswk.hbs.edu/item/6849.html`.

[32] S. Brown. IPv4 Trading in Review, Jan. 2014. `http://ipv4marketgroup.com/blog/`.

[33] S. Zander, L. L. H. Andrew, and G. Armitage. Estimating the used IPv4 address space withsecure multi-party capture-recapture. In *INFOCOM (poster)*, Turin, Italy, 15-18 Apr 2013.

A QoE Perspective on Sizing Network Buffers

Oliver Hohlfeld
RWTH Aachen University

Enric Pujol
TU Berlin

Florin Ciucu
University of Warwick

Anja Feldmann
TU Berlin

Paul Barford
UW Madison

ABSTRACT

Despite decades of operational experience and focused research efforts, standards for sizing and configuring buffers in network systems remain controversial. An extreme example of this is the recent claim that excessive buffering (*i.e.*, *bufferbloat*) can severely impact Internet services. In this paper, we systematically examine the implications of buffer sizing choices from the perspective of factors impacting *end user experience*. To assess user perception of application quality under various buffer sizing schemes we employ Quality of Experience (QoE) metrics. We evaluate these metrics over a wide range of end-user applications (*e.g.*, web browsing, VoIP, and RTP video streaming) and workloads in two realistic testbeds emulating access and backbone networks. The main finding of our extensive evaluations is that *network workload*, rather than buffer size, is the primary determinant of end user QoE. Our results also highlight the relatively narrow conditions under which bufferbloat seriously degrades QoE, *i.e.*, when buffers are oversized and sustainably filled.

Categories and Subject Descriptors

C.2.6 [**Internetworking**]: Routers

Keywords

Buffer size; bufferbloat; QoE

1. INTRODUCTION

Packet buffers are widely deployed in network devices to reduce packet loss caused by transient traffic bursts. Surprisingly, even after decades of research and operational experience, 'proper' buffer sizing remains challenging due to inherent trade-offs in performance metrics applied to the problem and different application requirements. While queueing theory suggests that large buffers improve transfer throughput at the expense of larger delays, there exists real-time applications requiring low and consistent delay, and thus preferring little to no buffering. Responding to the need to address such orthogonal objectives, the community has been involved in a decades-long struggle to identify general rules for both sizing and managing buffers that tries to match both ends of the spectrum (*i.e.*, low delay and high performance).

Traditionally, router buffer sizing is proportional to the bandwidth of the linecards *i.e.*, bandwidth-delay product (BDP). This rule-of-thumb emerged in the mid 1990s based on studies of the dynamics of TCP flows [25, 44]. A decade later, Appenzeller et al. reexamined buffer sizing and argued that throughput can be maintained using much smaller buffer sizes in core routers [9]. This reignited interest in the research community with regards to buffer dimensioning schemes, however the issue continues to remain far from resolved.

Recently, the buffer sizing debate has focused on the *existence* of large buffers in the network edge (bufferbloat [6]) and stimulated a debate on its potential negative effects. Excessive buffering *can* cause excessive queuing delays, *e.g.*, in the order of seconds), in phases of congestion when the buffer capacity is fully utilized. Resulting excessive delays *can* degrade the performance from a users' perspective [6], *e.g.*, by adversely effecting TCP due to increased round trip times or unnecessary timeouts. While the *existence* of large buffers has been observed, little is known on how often queues are *utilized* to degrade performance in practice. Also, the evaluation of the bufferbloat problem has so far focused on evaluating influence on QoS metrics. In the absence of a solid understanding, buffer sizes are currently used to drive engineering changes in Internet standards (see *e.g.*, [18]) and motivate new AQM approaches (*e.g.*, CoDeL [32]). We posit that a deeper understanding of buffering effects is needed before altering important engineering aspects.

This paper describes the first comprehensive study on the impact of buffer sizes on *end-user quality*. The goal of our work is to elucidate the sizing issues empirically and to pave the way for more informed sizing decisions. Unlike previous studies that consider Quality of Service (QoS) metrics (*e.g.*, packet loss or throughput) our study focuses on end-user *Quality of Experience (QoE)*. The use of standardized QoE metrics enables *estimation* of end-user perceived quality *without involving human subjects*. By using QoE metrics rather than conducting user studies, we are able to assess quality in an extensive sensitivity study involving a broad range of buffer size and workload configurations. Identified experimental scenarios pave the way for controlled user studies conducted in a scaled down fashion in the future.

Concretely, we evaluate QoE metrics for relevant user applications (*i.e.*, web browsing, VoIP, and RTP video streaming) in two realistic laboratory-based testbeds: access and backbone networks. Each application type is analyzed over Internet-like traffic scenarios—without isolation in separate QoS classes—and over a range of buffer sizes.

IMC'14, November 5–7, 2014, Vancouver, BC, Canada.

ACM 978-1-4503-3213-2/14/11 ...$15.00.
http://dx.doi.org/10.1145/2663716.2663730.

Our main observations are as follows:

1. We mainly find *network workload*, rather than buffer size, to be the primary determinant of end-user QoE. As intuitively expected, sustainable congestion impacts both QoS and QoE metrics by keeping the queue of the bottleneck buffer filled. This effect is amplified by large (bloated) buffers. In the absence of congestion, however, (even bloated) buffer sizes impact QoS metrics, as observed by previous studies, *e.g.*, [11], but impact QoE metrics only marginally. The good news for network operators is that limiting congestion, *e.g.*, via QoS or over-provisioning, can yield more immediate QoE improvements than efforts to optimize buffering.

2. We show the perceptual (QoE) perspective on buffering to differ from the known QoS perspective. This further emphasizes the use of application specific and perceptual metrics in Internet measurements. In this regard, this paper serves as an example on the use of QoE metrics for measurement studies.

2. RELATED WORK

The rule-of-thumb [25, 44] for dimensioning network buffers relies on the bandwidth-delay-product (BDP) $RTT * C$ formula, where RTT is the round-trip-time and C is the (bottleneck) link capacity. The reasoning is that, in the presence of *few* TCP flows, this ensures that the bottleneck link remains saturated even under packet loss. This is not necessary for links with a large number of concurrent TCP flows (*e.g.*, backbone links). It was suggested in [44] and convincingly shown in [9, 11] that much smaller buffers suffice to achieve high link utilizations. The proposal is to reduce buffer sizes by a factor of $\sqrt{n}$ as compared to the BDP, where n is the number of concurrent TCP flows [9]. Much smaller buffer sizes have been proposed, *e.g.*, drop-tail buffers with $\approx 20 - 50$ packets for core routers [17]. However, these come at the expense of reduced link utilization [11]. This problem has been addressed by a modified TCP congestion control control scheme that aims to maintain high link utilizations in small buffer regimes [20]. For an overview of existing buffer sizing schemes we refer the reader to [45].

While the above discussion focuses on backbone networks, more recent studies focus on access networks, *e.g.*, [13, 28, 30, 42], end-hosts [1], and 3G networks [22]. These studies find that excessive buffering in the access network exists and can cause excessive delays (*e.g.*, on the order of seconds). This has fueled the recent bufferbloat debate [6, 19] regarding a potential degradation in Quality of Service (QoS).

Indeed, prior work has shown that buffer sizing impact QoS metrics. Examples include *network-centric* aspects such as per-flow throughput [33], flow-completion times [29], link utilizations [11], packet loss rates [11], and fairness [46]. Sommers *et al.* studied buffer sizing from an operational perspective by addressing their impact on service level agreements [37]. However, QoS metrics and even SLAs do not necessarily reflect the actual implications for the end-user. A first step towards investigating the impact of buffering on gaming QoE has been made in simulations for Poisson traffic [36]. In this paper, we present the first *QoE centric* study that broadly investigates the impact of buffering and background traffic by using realistic testbed hardware and Internet like traffic scenarios.

3. BUFFERING IN THE WILD

Before investigating the *impact* of buffering on QoE, we first motivate our study by investigating the *occurrence* of buffering in the wild. Our analysis is based on snapshots of Linux kernel level TCP statistics for 430 million randomly selected TCP/HTTP connections captured at a major Content Distribution Network (CDN). The data was collected at different vantage points, located primarily in central Europe, over a period of five months in 2011. All flows were established by end-users to retrieve content from the respective CDN caches, thus they capture typical web browsing activity. This data corpus represents a significant sample of Internet users. It includes 81 million unique IP addresses originating from 22,490 autonomous systems (roughly 60% of the total advertised ASes when capturing the trace), located in more than 220 countries. Due to the vantage point locations, 56% of the IPs are located in central Europe.

We build our evaluation on smoothed RTT (sRTT) information reported in the data set. Smoothed RTT values are estimated by the TCP stack using Karn's algorithm and are provided by the kernel level TCP statistics. For each TCP connection, the data set reports *(i)* the minimum sRTT, *(ii)* the average sRTT, *(iii)* the maximum sRTT, and *(iv)* the number of samples. To evaluate the variability due to queueing, we focus on flows that have at least 10 RTT samples. The distribution (PDF) of the logarithm of the minimum, average, and maximum RTT is shown in Figure 1a. The plot highlights that the average and maximum RTT deviate significantly from the minimum RTT, which is one indicator of possible queueing. Figure 1b underlines this intuition by showing the relationship of minimum and maximum RTT per flow in a 2D histogram. The figure shows that the maximum RTT significantly differs from the minimum RTT per flow, which further suggests the presence of queuing.

We estimate the queueing delay by evaluating the sRTT range (*i.e.*, max-min) for each connection with at least 10 RTT samples. The implicit assumption is that the minimum RTT accounts for an empty queue and that queueing is the only source of delay variations. In general, additional factors such as route changes and layer 2 delays—particularly prominent in wireless networks—also contribute to delay variations. Since we cannot distinguish these factors from queuing delays, our estimation overestimates queueing and thus yields an *upper bound* on the magnitude of queueing.

We show the PDF of the logarithm of the estimated queueing delay in Figure 1c. Based on whois and DNS information, we split the complete data set into ADSL, Cable, and FTTH users and show their respective queuing delay distribution. Using this scheme, we associate 70% the flows to ADSL users, 1.4% to Cable users, and 0.02% to FTTH users. Most of the user flows experience a modest amount of queueing; 80% of all the flows experience less than 100ms of delay variation. Only 2.8% (1%) experience excessive queueing delays of more than 500ms (1000ms). This corresponds to only 2.5% (2%) of the observed hosts. We also consider user proximity to the CDN caches. Specifically, we consider flows with minimum RTT $\leq$ 100ms. In this setting, even more flows experience modest amounts of queueing: 95% (99.9%) of all connections have a queuing delay of less than 100ms (1sec), respectively.

Recently, the issue of *buffer bloat* has attracted significant attention. The debate is based on observations (*e.g.*, [28]) showing that bufferbloat *can* happen, rather than it *does* happen. Despite this lack of empirical evidence, the bufferbloat argument has been used to motivate engineering changes in Internet standards (*e.g.*, see [18]) and to motivate new AQM approaches (*e.g.*, CoDeL [32]). Two very recent studies examined the magnitude of the problem based on data from 118K [8] and 25K hosts [12], respectively and concluded that the magnitude of bufferbloat is modest.

Our results, based on a much large data set of 80M hosts that is representative for a significant body of Internet users, further

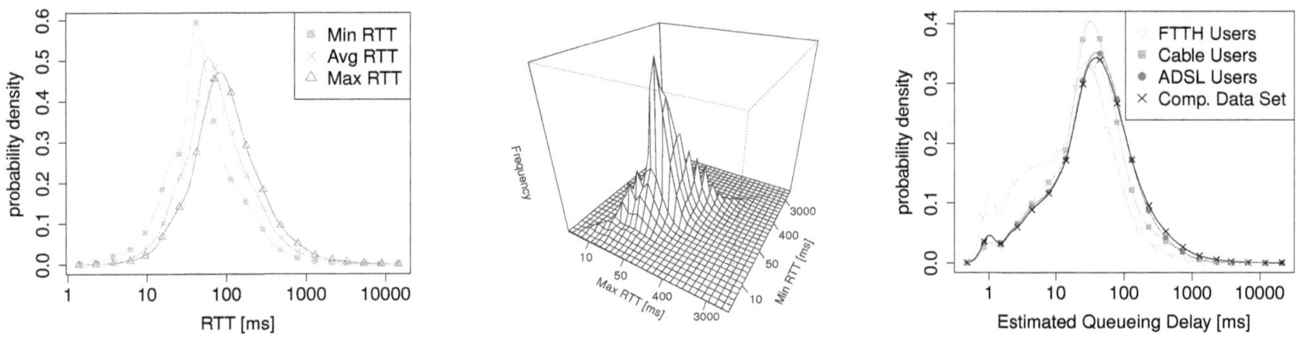

(a) Min, Avg, and Max RTT Distribution

(b) Min vs. Max RTT per Flow

(c) Queueing Delays

Figure 1: Occurrence of queueing in the wild

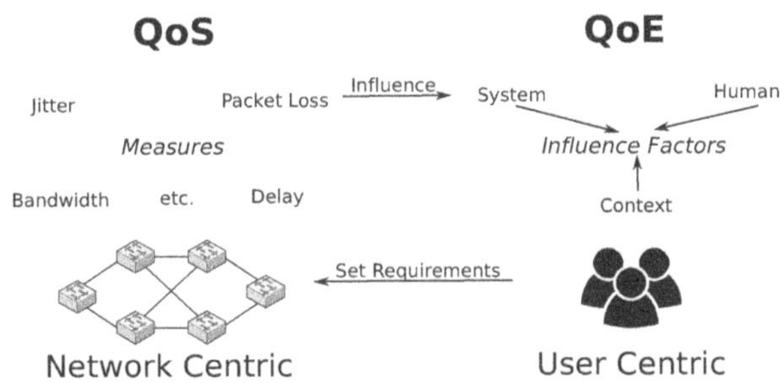

Figure 2: Conceptual difference of QoS and QoE

substantiate these findings. We empirically study whether Internet users at large experience excessive delays and we conclude that excessive delays do occur, but only for a small number of flows and hosts. Thus—despite what is often claimed by the bufferbloat community—our findings further confirm the modest magnitude of excessive queueing delays. One explanation is that uplink capacity in the access, where bufferbloat has been found, is seldom utilized.

Our study of buffering in the wild is the starting point for our evaluation of the impact of buffering on QoE, including the case of excessive buffering (bufferbloat). While we estimate the magnitude of bufferbloat to be modest, its implications on QoE are largely unknown. For instance, a single delayed flow can severely degrade the QoE of an entire HTTP transaction. To shed light on the QoE impact of buffering, we first briefly introduce QoE, and then conduct a multi-factorial testbed study covering a wide range of end-user applications, buffer configurations, and traffic scenarios.

4. QOS $\neq$ QOE

Assessing human quality perception is challenging due to its subjective nature. This challenge is addressed by research on Quality of Experience (QoE) which aims at capturing the "degree of delight of the user of a service. In the context of communication services, it is influenced by content, network, device, application, user expectations and goals, and context of use." [7].

While network performance is typically expressed by QoS metrics, QoS and QoE represent fundamentally different concepts that can influence each other; QoS represents a *network centric* view whereas QoE represents a *user centric* view (see Figure 2). QoE depends on a multidimensional perceptual space that includes *i)* system influence factors (*e.g.*, QoS measures, transport protocols, or device specific parameters), *ii)* human influence factors (*e.g.*, mood, personality traits, or expectations), and *iii)* contextual factors (*e.g.*, location, task, or costs). For an extensive discussion on factors influencing QoE, we refer to [7]. These features are not necessarily independent of each other and do not always have clear mappings, *e.g.*, users tend to give different opinion scores for the same stimulus, *e.g.*, depending on mood, expectation, and memory. While some QoE influence factors include QoS metrics (*e.g.*, packet loss), QoE depends on a larger set of influence factors that cannot be derived from QoS metrics and requires new measures.

To quantify the users' perception of the quality of (network) applications, QoE metrics have been defined and standardized for applications such as VoIP, Video, Web, etc. These metrics are rooted in psychological tests that involved human subjects in the metric *construction phase*. In the *application phase*, however, they allow automatic quality assessments without user involvement; *i.e.*, conclusions on user-experience can be drawn from testbed evaluations *without costly user involvement*. This is an appealing property as it enables the automatic exploration of a large state space that involves a significant number of different workload and buffer size configurations in *controlled experiments*. While desired, involving human subjects is time intensive and thus requires only a small set of conditions to be tested in order to be economically feasible. However, insights obtained in this paper allow sub-sampling of this large state space and therefore enable subjective tests to be conducted in future work.

We base our QoE evaluation on standardized and widely used QoE metrics for quality assessment. Since the metrics depend on the applications, we refer the reader to the corresponding section for a discussion of the used metrics.

5. METHODOLOGY

We use a testbed driven approach to study the impact of buffer sizes on the user perception (QoE) of common types of Internet applications: *i)* Voice over IP, *ii)* RTP/UDP video streaming as used in IPTV networks, and *iii)* web browsing.

5.1 Testbed Setup

We consider two scenarios: *i)* an access network and *ii)* a backbone or core network. Each scenario is realized in a dedicated testbed as shown in Figure 3 (a) and (b). We use a testbed setup to have full control over all parameters including buffer sizes and generated workload.

As most flows typically experience only a single bottleneck link, both testbeds are organized as a dumbbell topology with a single bottleneck link, configurable buffer sizes, and a client and a server network. The hosts within the server (client) network on the left (right) side act as servers (clients), respectively. In the backbone

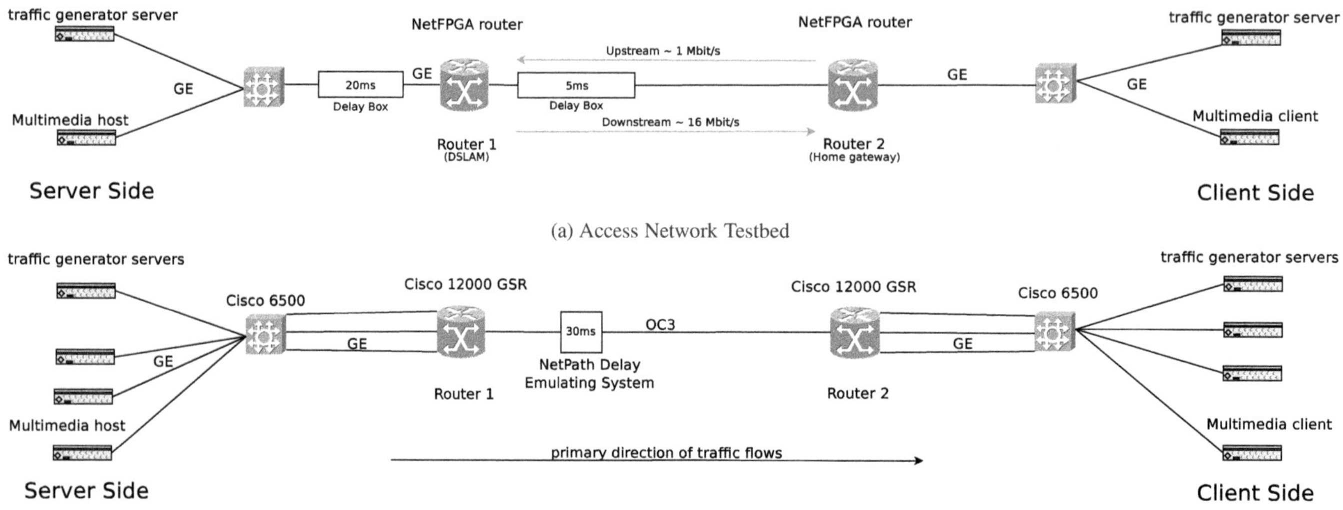

(a) Access Network Testbed

(b) Backbone Network Testbed

Figure 3: Access and backbone network testbeds used in the study

case we configured the bandwidth and the delays of all links symmetrically. For the access network we use an asymmetric bottleneck link. In the backbone case we only consider data transfers from the servers to the clients. For the access network we also include data uploads by the clients—as they mainly triggered the bufferbloat debate [19].

The access network testbed, see Figure 3a, consists of two Gigabit switches, four quadcore hosts equipped with 4 GB of RAM and multiple Gigabit Ethernet interfaces. Moreover, two hosts are equipped with a NetFPGA 1 Gb card each. The hosts are connected via their internal NICs to the switch to realize the client/server side network. The NetFPGA cards run the Stanford Reference Router software and are thus used to realize the bottleneck link. Thus the NetFPGA router and the multimedia hosts are located on the same physical host. As the NetFPGA card is able to operate independent of the host, it does not impose resource contention. The right NetFPGA router acts as the home router, aka DSL modem, whereas the left one acts as the DSLAM counterpart of the DSL access networks. To capture asymmetric bandwidth of DSL we use the hardware capabilities of the NetFPGA card to restrict the uplink and downlink capacities to approximately 1 respectively 16 Mbit/s. We use hardware to introduce a 5 ms respectively 20 ms delay between the client (server) network and the routers. The 5 ms delay corresponds to DSL with 16 frame interleaving or to the delays typical for cable access networks [10]. The 20 ms account for access and backbone delays. While we acknowledge that delays to different servers vary according to a network path, a detailed study of path delay variation is beyond the scope of this paper. This is also the reason we decided to omit WiFi connectivity which adds its own variable delay characteristics due to layer-2 retransmissions. Instead, we focus on delay variations induced by buffering.

To be able to scale up the background traffic to the backbone network, see Figure 3b, we include eight hosts, four clients and four servers. Each has again a quadcore CPU, 4 GB of RAM, and multiple Gigabit Ethernet network interfaces. The client/server networks are connected via separate Gigabit switches, Cisco 6500s, to backbone grade Cisco 12000GSR routers. Instead of using 10 Gbit/s and soon to be 100 Gbit/s interfaces for the bottleneck link, we use an OC3 (155 Mb/s nominal) link. The reason for this is that we wanted to keep the scale of the experiments reasonable, this includes, *e.g.*, the tcpdump files of traffic captures. Moreover, scaling down allows us to actually experience bufferbloat given the available memory within the router. We use multiple parallel links between the hosts, the switch, and the router so that it is possible for multiple packets to arrive within the same time instance at the router buffer. With regards to the delays we added a NetPath delay box with a constant one-way delay of 30 ms to the bottleneck link. 30 ms delay roughly corresponds to the one-way delay from the US east to the US west coast. We again note, that the path delays in the Internet are not constant. However, variable path delays are beyond the scope of this paper. Instead we focus on delay variability induced by buffering. Moreover, we eliminate most synchronization potential by our choice of workload (see § 5.2).

To gather statistics and to control the experiments we always use a separate Ethernet interface on the hosts as well as a separate physical network (not shown).

5.2 Traffic Scenarios

We use the Harpoon flow level network traffic generator [38] to create a number of congestion scenarios which range from no background traffic (noBG) to fully overloading (short-overload) the bottleneck link. Congestion causes packets from both the background traffic as well as the application under study to be queued or dropped just before the bottleneck link. Depending on the fill grade of the buffer, the size of the buffer, and the link speed, this will increase the RTT accordingly (see Table 2). Overall, we use 12 scenarios for the access testbed and 6 for the backbone. We consider more for the access to distinguish on which links (*i.e.*, upstream, downstream, or both) the congestion is subjected to.

In terms of traffic that imposes the congestion we distinguish two different kinds of scenarios (see Table 1): (*i*) long-lived TCP flows (long) and (*ii*) long-tailed file sizes to be able to resemble self-similar traffic as seen in today's networks (e.g., in core networks). For the latter, we choose Weibull distributed file sizes with a shape of 0.35 as their mean and standard deviation are finite as opposed to those of the often used Pareto distributions with a shape > 2. The generated traffic results in a mixture of bursty short-lived and long-lived flows with a mean of 50 KB. As the number of short flows dominates the number of long flows we refer to these scenarios as "short".

Testbed	Name	Flow Interarrival Distribution	File Size Distribution	# Sessions Up	# Sessions Down	Concurrent Flows	Link Utilization [%] Mean Up	Mean Down	Sd Up	Sd Down	Packet Loss [%] Up	Packet Loss [%] Down	Description
Access	noBG	—	—	—	—	—	—	—	—	—	—	—	No bg. traffic
	short-few	exp-a	weibull	1	—		98.9	0.3	0.7	0.1	34.7	0	Upstream
				1	8		95	8.5	5.6	15.2	58.6	0.7	Bidirectional
				—	8		27.8	44.1	13.7	25.1	1.4	3	Downstream
	short-many	exp-a	weibull	1	—		98.9	0.3	0.7	0.1	33.1	0	Upstream
				1	16		93.3	10.7	4.3	20.1	60.9	1.3	Bidirectional
				—	16		53.8	78.7	12.8	23.5	4	4.5	Downstream
	long-few	—	infinite	1	—		99	0.2	0.7	0.0	1	0	Upstream
				1	8		71.9	83.1	8.9	12.6	41.7	0.6	Bidirectional
				—	8		39.5	99.9	1.9	0.6	0.1	0.5	Downstream
	long-many	—	infinite	8	—		98.9	0.3	0.7	0.0	14.4	0.0	Upstream
				8	64		83.8	61.8	11.2	26.4	60.7	0.2	Bidirectional
				—	64		68.5	99.6	3.9	4.9	0.03	9.3	Downstream
Backbone	noBG	—	—	—	—	—	—		—		—		No bg. traffic
	short-low	exp-b	weibull	—	$3 * 10$	18	16.5		11.6		0		
	short-medium	exp-b	weibull	—	$3 * 30$	49	49.5		18.8		0		
	short-high	exp-b	weibull	—	$3 * 60$	206	98		6.5		0.2		
	short-overload	exp-b	weibull	—	$3 * 256$	2170	99.7		2.2		5.2		
	long	—	infinite	—	$3 * 256$	675	99.7		0.1		3.8		

Table 1: Workload configuration for both testbeds, where the flow interarrival time distributions are specific to the access and backbone testbed; exp-a has a mean of 2 sec and exp-b a mean of 1 sec. The file size distribution is defined as weibull(shape=0.35, scale=10039), resulting in a mean flow size of 50 KB. The number of parallel flows at the bottleneck link is shown by their mean. Link utilization and loss measures are obtained for buffers configured according to the BDP.

For scenarios with long-lived flows (long) we use flows of infinite duration. In this case the link utilization is almost independent of the number of concurrent flows. For long-tailed file sizes the workload of each scenario is controlled via the number of concurrent sessions that Harpoon generates. A session in Harpoon is supposed to mimic the behaviour of a user [38] with a specific interarrival time, a file size distribution, and other parameters. We used the default parameters except for the file size distribution. In addition, we rescaled the mean of the interarrival time for the access network, as Harpoon's default parameters are geared towards core networks with a larger number of concurrent flows. To impose different levels of congestion we adjusted the number of sessions for the backbone scenario to result in low, medium, high, and overload scenarios which correspond to link utilizations as shown in Table 1. For the access network we distinguish between few and many concurrent flows which results in medium and high load for the downstream direction and high load for the upstream, see Table 1.

We checked that all hosts are using a TCP variant with window scaling. Due to the Linux version used the background traffic uses TCP-Reno in the backbone and TCP BIC/TCP CUBIC for the access. However, note that this does not substantially impact the QoE results as the applications VoIP and video rely on UDP and the Web page is relatively small. Moreover, since the results are consistent it suggests that using a TCP variant optimized for high latency does not change the overall behavior even when the buffers are large.

5.3 Buffer Configurations

One key element of our QoE study is the buffer size configurations. Buffers are everywhere along the network path including at the end-hosts, the routers, and the switches. The most critical one is at the bottleneck interface, the only location where packet loss occurs. Therefore we focus on these and rely on default parameters for the others. For the bottleneck we choose a range of different buffer sizes, some reflect existing sizing recommendations, some are chosen to be small other large in order to capture extremes. Table 2 summarizes the buffer size configuration in terms of number of packets and shows the corresponding queuing delays.

For the access network we choose buffer sizes of powers of two, ranging from 8 to 256 packets. 256 is the maximum supported

Access					Backbone		
Buffer Size (Pkts)	Uplink Delay (ms)	Uplink Scheme	Downlink Delay (ms)	Downlink Scheme	Buffer Size (Pkts)	Delay (ms)	Scheme
8	98	≈ BDP	6	min	8	0.6	≈ TinyBuf
16	198		12		28	2.2	Stanford
32	395		24		749	58	BDP
64	788		49	≈ BDP	7490	580	$10 \times$ BDP
128	1,583		97				
256	3,167	max	195	max			

Table 2: Buffer size configurations and corresponding maximum queuing delays for both testbeds (full sized packets).

buffer size by the Stanford Reference Router software. For our choice of an asymmetric link (recall 1 Mbps uplink/16 Mbps downlink) the bandwidth-delay product (BDP) corresponds to roughly 8 and 64 packets, respectively. Since this set of buffer sizes yields delays up to buffer bloat, we consider the buffer configurations to approximate home router behaviour.

For the backbone network we use *i)* the same minimum buffer size of 8 packets, which resembles the TinyBuffer scheme [17], depending on the largest congestion window achieved by the workloads. In addition, we use *ii)* 749 full-sized packets which corresponds to the BDP formula given an RTT of 60 ms, *iii)* 28 packet which corresponds to the Stanford scheme [9], *i.e.*, BDP/$\sqrt{n}$, where $n = 3 * 256$ is the maximum number of concurrent for short-low, short-medium, short-high, and long (see Table 1), and *iv)* $10 \times$ BDP packets an excessive buffering scheme.

6. QOS: BACKGROUND TRAFFIC

To highlight the potential importance of the buffer configuration on latencies, network utilization, and packet loss—the typical QoS values—we start our study with a detailed look at the background traffic. While the story is relatively straight forward for the backbone scenario, and captured in Table 1, it is more complicated for the access network as the number of concurrent flows is smaller and there are subtle interactions between upstream and downstream.

To illustrate how the workloads and buffer sizes effect real-time applications, we conducted experiments to measure the latency introduced by the buffers. For this purpose we use the detailed buffer utilization statistics of the FPGA cards. Figure 4 shows the corresponding mean delays as heatmaps. We use three different heatmaps: one each for downstream/upstream workload only and one for combined up- and downstream workload. Each heatmap has two subareas—one for upstream at the top and one for downstream at the bottom. Each heatmap cell show the mean delay for a specific buffer size configuration and workload scenario, measured over two hours. The color of the heatmap cells correspond to categories of the ITU-T Recommendation G.114 which classifies delays based on their potential to degrade the QoE of interactive applications: green (light gray) is acceptable, orange (medium gray) problematic, and red (dark gray) causes problems.

In principle, we see that larger buffers sizes can increase the delays significantly independent of the workload. For the downlink direction the maximum delay is less than 200 ms. However, this can differ for the uplink direction. In particular, we observe delays of up to three seconds for larger–over-sized–buffers when the upstream is used for the uplink direction. This is almost independent of the workload! Overall, these delays are consistent with observations by Gettys [6] which started the bufferbloat discussion.

Given these high latencies, we investigate the link utilization. Figure 5 shows a boxplot of the link utilization for the various buffer sizes in the scenario with simultaneously downloads and uploads (bidirectional workloads). The left/right half focuses on the downlink/uplink utilization. The uplink utilization is almost 100% while the downlink utilization ranges from 20% to 100%. Consistent with related work, we see that very small buffers can lead to underutilization while very large buffers can lead to large delays.

Comparing these link utilizations to those with no upstream workload (not shown) we find that, for bidirectional workloads, the buffer configurations below the BDP do not always fully utilize the downlink direction. Buffer sizes that correspond to the BDP yield full downlink utilization in the absence of upload workload, but not with concurrent download and upload activities. This phenomena can be explained by the queuing delay introduced by bloated uplink buffers that *virtually* increase the BDP thus rendering the downlink under-buffered. Related work coined the problem of bidirectional TCP flows that influence each other *data pendulum* [23]. In contrast to related work, our analysis highlights interdependencies between buffers and suggests that buffers should not be sized independent of each other.

The phenomena of low link utilization can be mitigated by counter-intuitively "bloating" the downlink buffer. Considering the delays observed in Figure 4b, the BDP increases beyond the initial buffer size of 64 to 835 full sized packets. Note, that we can get full link utilization for buffers of smaller than 835 packets as we have a sufficient number of concurrent flows active.

In summary, the latency introduced by the buffers in home routers, aka, the uplink, might not only i) harm real-time traffic applications (due to excessive buffering), but also ii) drastically reduce TCP performance (due to insufficient buffering) in case of bidirectional workloads in asymmetric links. In effect it invalidates the buffer dimensioning assumptions due to the increase in RTT.

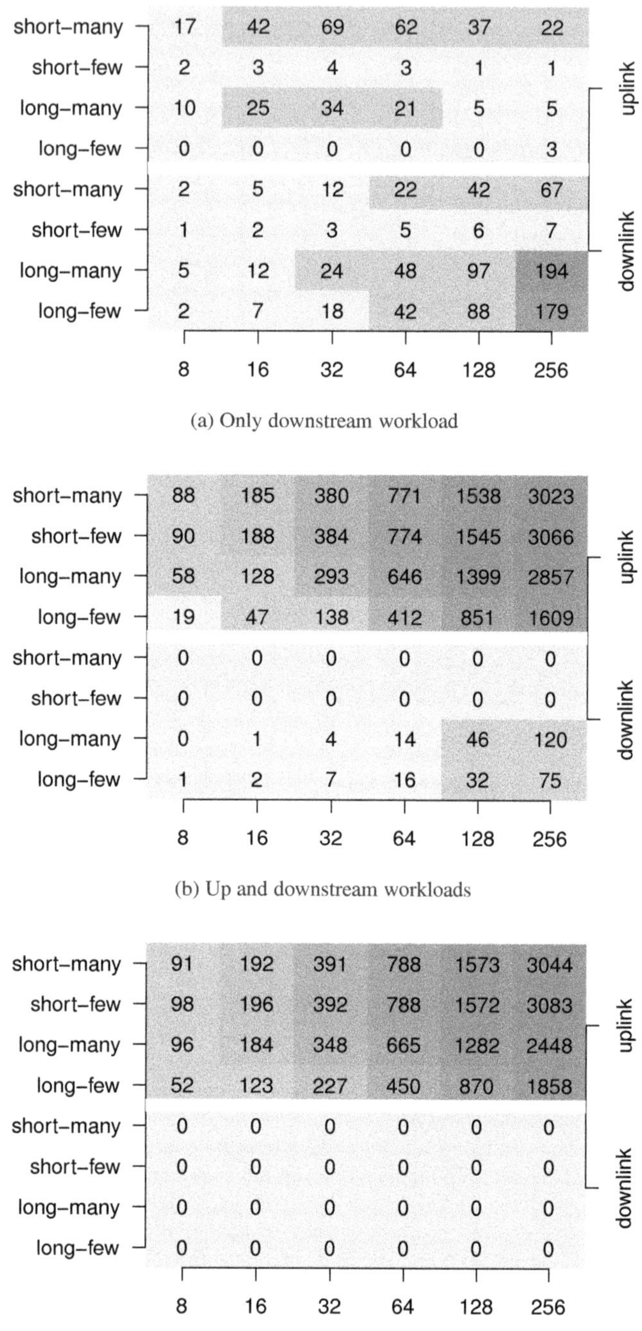

(a) Only downstream workload

(b) Up and downstream workloads

(c) Only upstream workload

Figure 4: Mean queuing delay (in ms) for the access networks testbed with different buffer size (x-axis) and workload (y-axis) configurations. Delays that significantly degrade the QoE of interactive applications (ITU-T Rec. G.114) are colored in red.

7. VOICE OVER IP

We start our discussion of application QoE with Voice over IP (VoIP). In IP networks speech signals can be impaired by QoS parameters (*e.g.*, packet loss, jitter, and/or delay), talker echo, codec and audio hardware related parameters, etc. Regarding QoS parameters, packet losses directly degrade speech quality as long as forward error correction is not used as is typical today. Network jitter can result in losses at the application layer as the data arrives after its scheduled playout time. Moreover, excessive delays impairs any bidirectional conversation as it changes the conversational dynamics in turn taking behavior.

7.1 Approach

We use a set of 20 speech samples recommended by the ITU [4] for speech quality assessment. Each sample is an error-free

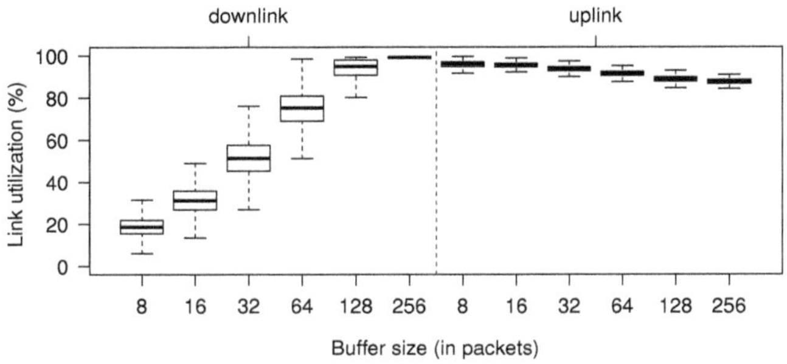

Figure 5: Link utilization for an asymmetric access link with various buffer sizes. The uplink and the downlink are simultaneously congested by 8 and 64 long-lived TCP flows, respectively.

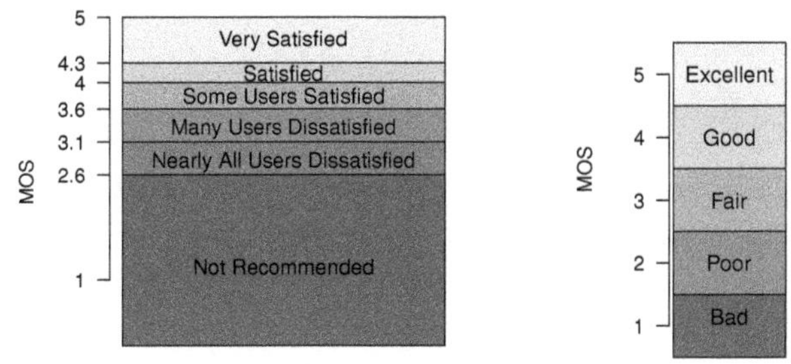

(a) G.711 (PCMA audio codec). (b) Video & Web

Figure 6: MOS scales used in this paper

recording of a male or female Dutch speaker, encoded with G.711.a (PCMA) narrow-band audio codec, and lasts for eight seconds. Each of the 20 samples is automatically streamed, using the PjSIP library, over our two evaluation testbeds, see § 5 and subjected to the various workloads. PjSIP uses the typical protocol combination of SIP and RTP for VoIP. We remark that we do not consider other situational factors such as the users' expectation (*e.g.*, free vs. paid call) [31] which can also affect the perceived speech quality (see § 4). For the VoIP QoE assessment, we separately evaluate speech signal degradations and conversational dynamics, using two widely used and standardized QoE models: PESQ and E-Model. Individual scores are combined to the final QoE score.

Speech signal degradations. To assess the speech quality of each received output audio signal, relative to the error-free sample signal, we use the Perceptual Speech Quality Measure (PESQ) [2] as standardized model. PESQ takes as input both the error-free audio signal and the perturbed audio signal, and computes the QoE score z_1. Note that while z_1 is *influenced* by loss and jitter, the QoE estimation is *signal based* and *not a function of QoS parameters*. The influence of loss and jitter on z_1 can therefore not be quantified.

Conversational dynamics. The PESQ model only accounts for the perceived quality when listening to a remote speaker but does not account for conversational dynamics, *e.g.*, for humans taking turns and/or interrupting each other. This can be impaired by excessive delays and thus can degrade the quality of the conversation significantly [31, 26, 34, 35]. Thus, according to the ITU-T recommendation G.114 one-way delays should be below 150 ms (or at most 400 ms).

Therefore, we measure the packet delay during the VoIP calls. We now use the delay impairment factor of the ITU-T E-Model [3] to get a score z_2. We remark that even though z_2 is computed using a standardized and widely used model, it is subject to an intense debate within the QoE literature as there is a dispute about the impact of delay on speech perception [26, 34, 16]. Among the reasons is that the delay impact depends on the nature of the conversational task (e.g, reading random numbers vs. free conversation) as well as the level of interactivity required by the task [26]. Thus, there can be mismatches between the quality ratings of the E-Model and tests conducted with subjects.

Overall score. The range of the score z_1, which captures loss and jitter, is $[1, 5]$. We remap it to $[0, 100]$ according to [41]. The range of the score z_2, capturing the delay impairment, is $[0, 100]$. Note, the semantics of z_1 and z_2 are reversed: a large value for z_1 reflects an excellent quality; however, a large value for z_2 reflects a bad quality, and vice-versa. We combine the two scores to an overall one as follows: $z = \max\{0, z_1 - z_2\}$. Thus, if z_1 is good (*i.e.*, due to negligible loss and jitter), but the z_2 is bad (*i.e.*, due to large delays), then the overall score z is low, reflecting a poor quality and vice-versa. Finally, we map z to the MOS scale $[1, 5]$ according to the ITU-T recommendation P.862.2, see Figure 6a; in the end, low values correspond to bad quality and high values to excellent quality.

7.2 Access networks results

Figures 7a and 7b show heatmaps of the median call quality (MOS) for the access networks. Each cell in the heatmap shows the median MOS of 200 VoIP calls (each speech sample is send 10 times) per buffer size (x-axis) and workload scenario (y-axis) combination. The heatmap is colored according to the color scheme of Figure 6a. The heatmap is divided into two parts (i) when user talks (upper part) and (ii) when the user listens to the remote speaker (bottom part).

The baseline results, namely the ones without background traffic are shown in the bottom row of each heatmap part, labeled noBG. They reflect the achievable call quality of the scenarios. As all of them are green, we can conclude that in principle each scenario supports excellent speech quality and that any impairment is due to congestion and not due to the buffer size configuration per se.

Download activity. Figure 7a focuses on the scenarios when there is congestion in the downlink. As there is no explicit workload in the uplink, one may expect that only the "user listens" part is effected but not the "user talks" part. This is only partially true as the "user talks" part of the heatmap shows deviations of up to 0.8 MOS points from the baseline score. These degradations are explained by the substantial number of TCP ACK packets, reflected by higher link utilizations (not shown). Recall, the uplink capacity is 1/16th only of the downlink capacity.

The degradations in "user listens" part of the heatmap are, as expected, more pronounced then for the "user talks" part. However, there are also significant differences according to the workload and the buffer configurations. For instance, with buffers sizes of 64 packets the long-many workload yields a median MOS of 2.8, whereas the long-few workload yields a median MOS of 3.5. Interestingly, even though the short-few workload does not fully utilize the downlink, *i.e.*, less than 50% (not shown), it gets scores worse than a workload with higher link utilization, *e.g.*, long-few. This is due to the higher jitter that is imposed by the large changes in link utilization and thus in the buffer utilization. With regards to buffer sizes we in general observe the worst scores for the larger buffer configurations, *i.e.*, 256 packets due to the added delays. However, the best scores only deviate by 0.7 MOS points from this worst score (*e.g.*, for the 8 packets buffer), suggesting that smaller buffers do not significantly improve audio quality.

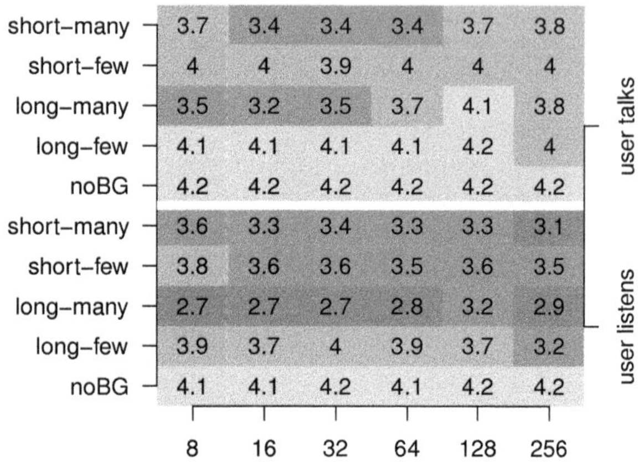

(a) Access: download activity

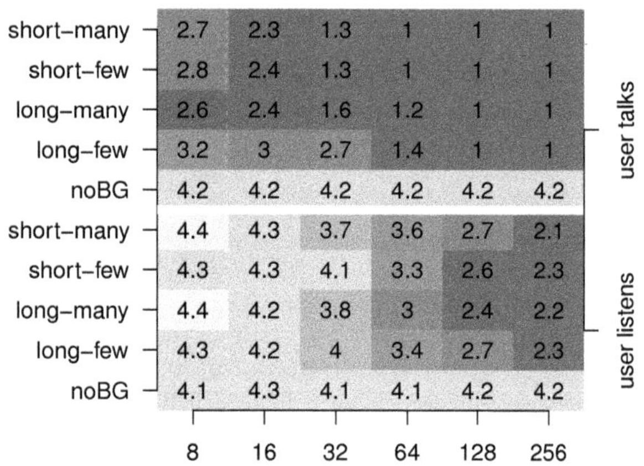

(b) Access: upload activity

Figure 7: VoIP Access: Median Mean Opinion Scores (MOS) for voice calls with different buffer size (x-axis) and workload (y-axis) configurations. The heatmaps for the access networks include inbound calls (user listens) and outbound calls (user talks).

We conclude that the level and kind of workload has a more significant effect than buffer size.

Upload activity. Figure 7b focuses on the scenarios when there is congestion on the uplink. According to the above reasoning one would therefore only expect degradations for the "user talks" part. This is not the case. The MOS in the "user listens" part of the heatmap decreases by 0.5 to 2 from the baseline results for all scenarios with buffer sizes ≥ 64. The reason for this is that the delays added by the excessive buffering in the uplink also degrade the overall score due to the delay impairment factor z_2. Since this factor expresses the conversational quality, it does not only effect the "user talks" but also the "user listen" part sent over the (non-congested) downlink.

Excessive delays added by the buffers also explain the significant degradation of MOS values from 4.2 to $1 - 1.4$ for the "user talks" part. Due to the congestion, packet loss is also significant for all scenarios. This is why the best MOS value is limited to 3.2 even for short buffer configurations.

In the context of the bufferbloat discussion, Figure 7b corroborates that excessive buffering in the uplink yields indeed bad quality scores. Reducing the buffer sizes results in better MOS and contributes to mitigate the negative effects of the large delays introduced by the uplink buffer, *e.g.*, the difference in the MOS for an inbound audio can be as high 2.5 points (long-many workload).

Combined upload and download activity. Scenarios (plot not shown) with upload and download congestion show similar results to scenarios with only uploads. Here as well the delays introduced by the uplink buffer dominate in both "user talks" and "user listens" parts. However, with combined upload and download activity, the "user listens" is slightly more degraded than with only upload activity. The reason for this is additional background traffic in the downlink that interacts with the voice call. For instance, with buffers configured to 16 packets, the long-few shows an additional degradation of 0.8 MOS points (thus mapping to a different rating scale).

Limiting access congestion by isolating VoIP calls in a separate QoS class—as often implemented for ISP internal services but not Internet-wide—is therefore a good strategy.

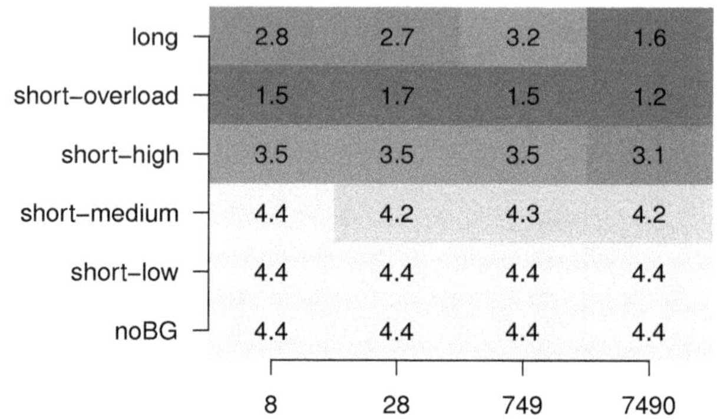

Figure 8: VoIP Backbone: Median Mean Opinion Scores (MOS) for voice calls with different buffer size (x-axis) and workload (y-axis) configurations.

7.3 Backbone networks results

Similar to the access network scenario, we show the voice quality in the backbone network scenario as a heatmap in Figure 8. The heatmap shows the median MOS for unidirectional audio from the left to the right side of the topology per buffer size (x-axis) and workload scenario (y-axis). Each cell in the heatmap is based on 2000 VoIP calls. Here, each speech sample is send 100 times which is possible as the total number of scenarios is smaller. As in the access network scenario, the bottom row label noBG shows the baseline results for an idle backbone without background traffic.

While the effects of the buffer size are less pronounced, the nature of the background traffic (long vs. short-*) and the link utilization (short-low to short-overload) are more significant. The type of workload can drastically degrade the quality score. Concretely, low to medium utilization levels as imposed by the scenarios short-low and short-medium, respectively, are close to the baseline results. In contrast, more demanding workloads such as the scenarios short-high and long, leading to higher link utilizations, and result in more than 1 point reductions in the MOS scale. Further, the aggressiveness of the workload further decrease the quality; the median MOS for the short-overload workload is 1.5 and thus significantly lower than for short-high and long that also lead to high link utilizations.

In general, the quality scores are, on a per workload basis, fairly stable across buffer-configurations below the BDP (749 packets). In these cases, we only observe small degradation of 0.4 points for the scenario long workload for the smallest buffer configuration. However, buffer configuration larger than the BDP, i.e, 7490 packets, lead to excessive queueing delays. As in the access network scenario, excessive delays lead to significant quality degradations of the z_2 delay impairment component. For example, the scores corresponding to the scenarios long and short-overload workloads have MOS values of almost half of their counterpart with the BDP configuration.

7.4 Key findings for VoIP QoE

We find that VoIP QoE is substantially degraded when VoIP flows have to compete for resources in congested links. This is particularly highlighted in the backbone network scenario, where low to medium link utilizations yields good QoE and high link utilization ($> 98\%$) degrade the QoE. In the case of the latter, the congestion leads to insufficient bandwidth on the bottleneck link that affects the VoIP QoE.

For access networks we show that, due to the asymmetric link capacities, the different audio directions can yield different QoE scores. For instance, in one direction (*e.g.*, user talks) the speech quality might be acceptable, while it is impaired for the other (*e.g.*, remote speaker talks) or vice-versa. Moreover, the speech quality is much more sensitive to congestion on the upstream direction than the downstream one. Due to the light queueing delays introduced by bloated buffers in the uplink, maintaining a conversation can be challenging in the presence of uplink congestion.

For both access and backbone networks, configuring small buffers can results in better QoE. However, our results highlight that this may not suffice to yield "excellent" quality ratings. Thus, we advocate to use QoS mechanisms to isolate VoIP traffic from the other traffic. This is already common for ISP internal services but not for ISP external services.

8. RTP VIDEO STREAMING

Next, we explore the quality of video streaming using the Real-time Transport Protocol (RTP) which is commonly used by IPTV service providers. RTP streaming can be impaired by packet loss, jitter, and/or delay. Again packet losses directly degrades the video as basic RTP-based video streaming *typically* does not involve any means of error recovery. Network jitter and delays result in similar impairments as with voice and include visual artifacts or jerky playback. However, they depend on the concrete error concealment strategy applied by the video decoder.

8.1 Approach

We chose three different video clips from various genres as reference. Each video has a length 16 seconds. They are chosen to be representative of various different kinds of TV content and vary in level of detail and movement complexity. Thus, they result in different frame-level properties and encoding efficiency; *A)* an interview scene, *B)* a soccer match, and *C)* a movie. Each video is encoded using H.264 in SD (4 Mbps) as well as HD (8 Mbps) resolution. Each frame is encoded using 32 slices to keep errors localized. This choice of our encoding settings is motivated by our experiences with an operational IPTV network of a Tier-1 ISP.

We use VLC to stream each clip using UDP/RTP and MPEG-2 Transport Streams. Without any adjustment VLC tries to transmit all packets belonging a frame immediately. This leads to traffic spikes exceeding the access network capacity. In effect VLC and other streaming software propagate the information bursts directly to the network layer. As our network capacity, in particular for the access, is limited we configured VLC to smooth the transmission rate over a larger time window as is typical for commercial IPTV vendors. More specifically, we decided to use a smoothing interval

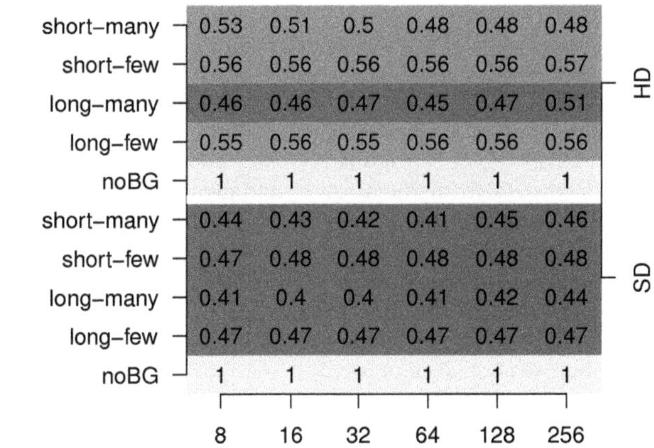

(a) Access: download activity

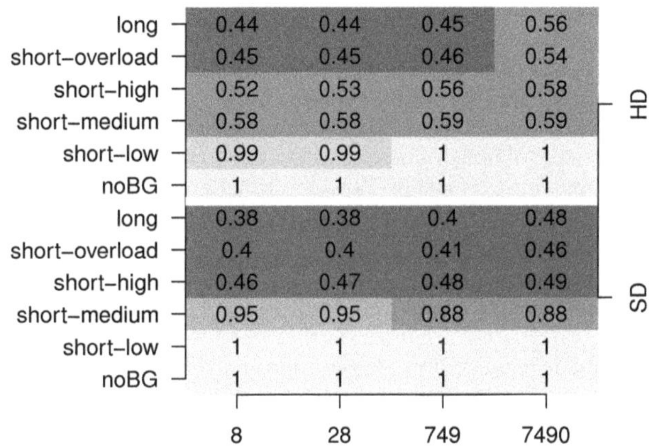

(b) Backbone

Figure 9: Median MOS (color) and SSIM (text) for HD and SD RTP video streams with different buffer size (x-axis) and workloads (y-axis).

(1 second) that ensures that the available capacity is not exceeded in the absence of background traffic. The importance of smoothing the sending rate is often ignored in available video assessment tools such as EvalVid, making them inapplicable for this study.

We note that Set-top-Boxes in IPTV networks often use proprietary retransmission schemes that request lost packets once [24]. Due to the unavailability of exact implementation details we do not account for such recovery. Our results thus present a baseline in the expected quality; however, systems deploying active (retransmission) or passive (FEC) error recovery can achieve higher quality.

We use two different full-reference metrics, PSNR and SSIM, to compute quality scores from the original and the perturbed video stream. While not considered as QoE metric, PSNR (Peak Signal Noise Ratio) enables a quality ranking of the same video content subject to different impairments [43, 27]. However, it does not necessarily correlate well with human-perception in general settings. SSIM (Structural SIMilarity) [47] has been shown to correlate better with human perception [48]. We map PSNR and SSIM scores to quality scores according to [49].

8.2 Access network results

We show our results as heatmap in Figure 9a. The heatmap shows the quality score for video C sent 50 times per buffer size (x-axis) and workload (y-axis) combination. Each cell shows the median SSIM score and is colored according to the corresponding MOS score (see Figure 6b); a SSIM score of 1 expresses excellent video quality, whereas 0 expresses bad quality. The upper and the bottom parts of the heatmap correspond to the results of HD and SD video streams, respectively. We omit quality scores obtained for the PSNR metric as they yield predicted scores similar to those obtained by SSIM. Also, as we focus on IPTV networks where the user consumes TV streams, no video traffic is present in the upstream. For this reason, we only show results for workloads congesting the downlink.

To show the achievable quality for all buffer size configurations in the absence of background traffic, we show baseline results in rows labeled noBG. In these cases, the video quality is not degraded due to the absence of congestion.

In the presence of congestion, however, the SD video quality is severely degraded, expressed by a "bad" MOS score. This holds regardless of the workloads and the buffer configuration; the link utilization by all of the workloads cause video degradation due to packet loss in the video stream. We observe that even a low packet loss rate can yield low MOS estimates. Moreover, much higher loss rates (one order of magnitude bigger) can yield the same estimates. For instance, although both scenarios, long-few and long-many, have a similar SSIM and MOS score for buffers sized to 256 and 8 packets respectively, they show different packet loss rates of 0.5% and 12.5%.

In comparison to the SD video, degradations in HD videos are less pronounced although, in some cases, the packet loss rate is higher. For instance, the packet loss rate for HD and SD video streaming is, with the long-few workload and buffers sized to 256 packets, 2.6% and 1.3% respectively. However, the HD video stream obtains a better MOS score. This interesting phenomena can be explained by the higher resolution and bit-rate of HD video streams, which reduce the visual impact of artifacts resulting from packet losses during video streams.

In the case of UDP video streaming in access networks, what matters is the available bandwidth, not the buffer size. Moreover, even though buffers regulate the trade-off between packet losses and delay, they have limited influence on the quality from the perspective of an IPTV viewer.

8.3 Backbone network results

Similar to the previous access network scenario, we show the video quality scores obtained for the same video C as a heatmap in Figure 9b, both for SD and HD resolution. Each cell of the heatmap shows the median SSIM score and is colored according to the corresponding perceptive MOS score (see Figure 6b). As in the previous scenario, the video was sent 50 times per buffer size (x-axis) and workload (y-axis) configuration. We omit PSNR quality scores as they are similar to the SSIM quality scores.

As in the access network scenario, the bottom row labeled noBG shows the baseline results for an idle backbone without background traffic. Similarly, workloads that do not fully utilize the bottleneck link, *i.e.*, short-low, lead to optimal video quality, as expressed by an SSIM score of 1. The reason is that the available capacity in the bottleneck link allows streaming the video without suffering from packet losses.

First quality degradations are observable in the short-medium scenario, where the quality decreases with increasing link utilization. In this scenario, workloads achieve full link utilization for 749/7490 buffers more often than for the 8/28 buffer configurations. It results in higher loss rates for the video flows lowering the quality and is more pronounced for the HD videos which have higher bandwidth requirements.

Workloads that sustainably utilize the bottleneck link, *i.e.*, short-high, short-overload, and long, yield bad quality scores due to high loss rates. These scenarios provide insufficient available bandwidth to stream the video without losses. Increasing the buffer size helps to decrease the loss rate, leading to slight improvements in the SSIM score.

Comparing the obtained quality scores among the three different videos leads to minor differences in quality scores. These differences result from different encoding efficiencies that cause different levels of burstiness in the streamed video. However, the quality scores of all video clips lead to the same primary observation: quality mainly depends on the workload configuration and decreases with link utilization. Increasing the buffer size helps to lower the loss rate and therefore to marginally improve the video quality.

8.4 Key findings for RTP video Quality

Our results indicate a roughly binary behavior of video quality: *i)* when the bottleneck link has sufficient available capacity to stream the video, the video quality is good, and *ii)* otherwise the quality is bad. In between, if the background traffic utilizes the link only temporarily, the video quality is sometimes degraded. This results in an overall degradation that increases with link utilization. Using HD videos yields marginally better quality scores even though they use higher bandwidth. We find that the influence of the buffer size is marginal as delay does not play a major role for IPTV. What mainly matters is the available bandwidth. We did not include quality metrics relevant for interactive TV or video-calls. We further note that our results represent a baseline quality achievable without error recovery. Error recovery (e.g., retransmissions) will increase the overall quality.

9. WEB BROWSING

We next move to web browsing, our last application under study. The web browsing experience (WebQoE) can be quantified by two main indicators [14]. One is the *page loading time* (PLT), which is defined as the difference between a Web page request time and the completion time of rendering the Web page in a browser. Another is the time for the first visual sign of progress. In this paper we consider PLT of information retrieval tasks, for which there exists an ITU QoE model (*i.e.*, G.1030 [5]) to map page loading times to user scores.

We note that WebQoE does not directly depend on packet loss artifacts, but rather on the completion time of underlying TCP flows. Thus, factoring in various workloads and buffer sizing configurations—which influence the TCP performance—is particularly relevant for understanding WebQoE from a network only perspective. Given that the PLT as measured in a browser can be approximated from flow completion times as parameter, is sometimes considered as a QoS parameter. Since the applied G.1030 model logarithmically maps PLT to QoE, it can be misbelieved QoS parameters can (always) be mapped to QoE. We therefore note that other QoE models are of higher complexity as different input parameter are used that cannot be directly derived from a QoS parameters, e.g., speech signals as used in Section 7.

9.1 Approach

To evaluate the WebQoE, we map the PLT to a user score z by using the ITU Recommendation G.1030 [5] specified for web information retrieval tasks. We consider the one-page version of the ITU model, which logarithmically maps *single* PLT's to scores in the range $z \in [1, 5]$ (*i.e.*, 5:excellent, 4:good, 3:fair, 2:poor, 1:bad, as shown in Figure 6b). This mapping uses six seconds as the maximum PLT, *i.e.*, mapping to a "bad" QoE score. The minimum PLT—mapping to "excellent"—is set to 0.56 (0.85) seconds for access (backbone) scenario, due to different RTTs.

We remark that WebQoE research has advanced beyond factors captured in the applied ITU G.1030 [5] model. This concerns the impact of distraction factors such as noise or traffic on quality perception [21], task and content dependent factors [39], or task completion times and loading pattern [40]. These advances have, however, not yet converged to an revised model that is applicable in this study. Beyond additional factors, WebQoE research addresses the need for interactive web use that goes beyond information retrieval tasks which follow request response pattern [15]. We remark that no QoE models fully addresses interactive web usage (such as AJAX requests), which is why we must leave this aspect for future work. For the information retrieval scenario considered in this section, however, recent findings suggest the logarithmic dependency of waiting time and QoE [15, 40]—as used in applied G.1030 model—to remain valid. We thus stick to using ITU Recommendation G.1030 [5] as the current standard for assessing WebQoE.

To measure the PLT's, we consider a single static web page, located in one of the testbed servers, and consisting of: one html file, one CSS file, and two medium JPEG images (sized to 15, 5.8, 30, and 30 KB, respectively). The web page is loaded within 14 RTTs, including the TCP connection setup and teardown. Choosing a relatively small web page size was inspired by the frequently accessed Google front page designed to quickly load. To retrieve this web page we use the *wget* tool which measures the transfer time. *wget* is configured to sequentially fetch the web page and all of its objects in a single persistent HTTP/1.0 TCP connection without pipelining. We point out that, as static web pages have constant rendering times, it suffices to rely on *wget* rather than on a specific web browser.

To further analyze the page retrieval performance, we rely on full packet traces capturing the HTTP transactions. We analyze the loss process of the captured TCP flows using the *tcpcsm* tool estimating retransmission events. We further measure the RTT during each experiment. We denote PLTs as RTT dominated if a significant portion of the PLT consists of the RTT component expressed by $14 * RTT$. Similarly, we denote PLTs as loss dominated if the increase in PLT can be mainly attributed to TCP retransmissions.

9.2 Access network results

Figures 10a and 10b show heatmaps of the median web browsing quality (MOS) for the access network. Each cell in the heatmap shows the median PLT of 300 web page retrievals per buffer size (x-axis) and workload scenario (y-axis) combination. The heatmap is colored according to Figure 6b.

The baseline results, namely the ones without background traffic, are shown in the bottom row of each heatmap part, labeled noBG. The fastest PLT that can be achieved in this testbed is $\approx$ 0.56s. As all of the cells are green (light gray), we can conclude that in principle each scenario almost supports excellent browsing quality and that any impairment is due to congestion. In this respect, it turns out that, even without background traffic, the WebQoE can be degraded by (too) small buffers, *e.g.*, 8 packets. Due to packet losses causing retransmissions, the PLT is increased to 1 second thereby changing the user perceived quality.

Download activity. Figure 10a focuses on the scenarios when there is congestion on the downlink. For the short-few scenario the downlink is not fully utilized, thus most scores do not deviate much from the baseline results. With this type of moderate workload browsing can benefit from the capacity of large buffers

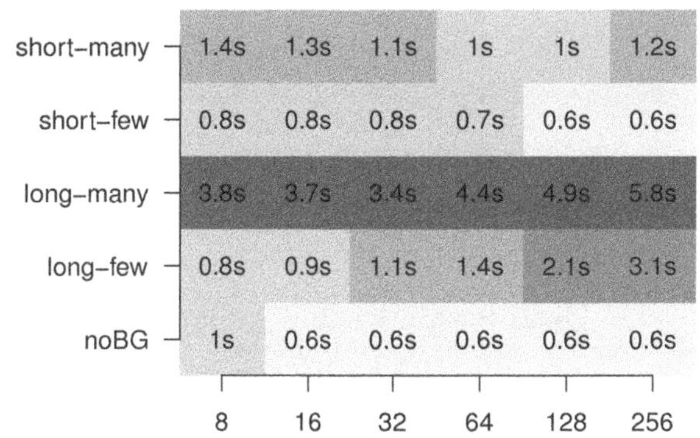

(a) Access: only download activity

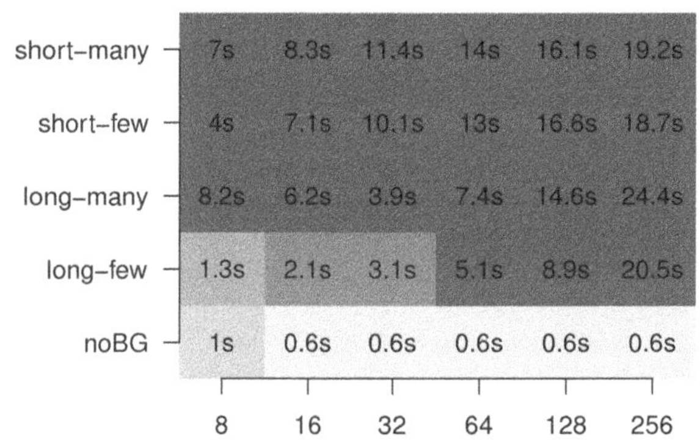

(b) Access: only upload activity

Figure 10: WebQoE Access: Median MOS (color) and page loading times (text) with different buffer size (x-axis) and workloads (y-axis).

to absorbe transient bursts and reduce packet losses. For instance, configuring the buffers size to 256 packets reduces the PLTs to the baseline results (as opposed to PLTs of 0.8s for the smallest buffer configuration). Likewise, for the short-many scenario, which involves more competing flows and imposes a higher link utilization, big buffers generally reduce PLTs. As the queueing delays for these scenarios are not excessive, *i.e.*, they are bounded by 192 ms, see Table 2, large buffers do in fact improve the QoE by limiting the loss rate.

Bufferbloat is visible for the long-few scenario, where the median PLT increases with the buffer size, as the PLT is dominated by RTTs caused by large queueing delays. As for the previous scenario, the effects of various buffer sizes are clearly perceived by the end-user (yet in a different manner).

In contrast, the buffer size does not change the WebQoE in the long-many scenario. The larger number of competing flows reduces the per-flow capacity and lets the PLT increases beyond the users' acceptance threshold. Therefore, the perceived QoE, in contrast to the previous configuration, can not be improved by adjusting the buffer size. Nevertheless, from a QoS perspective, configuring an appropiate buffer size can let web pages to load 2 seconds faster. This is not as straightforward since it involves considering the tradeoff between small buffers (packet losses) and large buffers (combined effect of packet losses and large RTTs).

Upload activity. Figure 10b focuses on the scenarios when there is congestion on the uplink. As expected, congesting the uplink seriously degrades the link overall performance and thereby also the WebQoE. The perceived quality is degraded to the min-

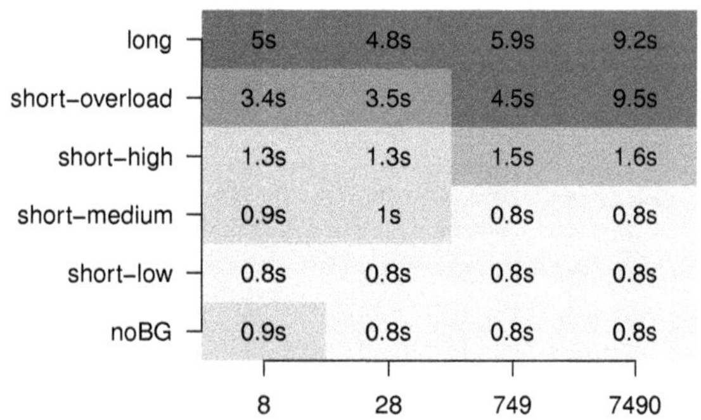

Figure 11: WebQoE Backbone: Median MOS (color) and page loading times (text) with different buffer size (x-axis) and workloads (y-axis).

imum for every buffer size configuration of the scenarios short-many, short-few, and the long-many. The only scenario where the browsing experience is slightly more acceptable is the long-few scenario if buffers are small. Such configuration reduces the median PLT from 20 to 1.3 seconds, which maps to a *fair* quality rating.

From a QoS perspective, the figure shows that the PLT and the buffer size are strongly correlated to the QoE. A wise decision on the dimensioning of the buffers can reduce the PLT from 24.4 to 3.8 seconds (long-many). However, and in line with the previous observations, such reductions do not generally suffice to change the user perceived (*bad*) quality.

Combined upload and download activity. In the case of workloads in both, the uplink and downlink direction (not shown), the QoE is dominated by the upload activity. However, due to lower *overall* link utilization and shorter queueing delays (see § 6), the median PLT are less than for the scenarios involving only uploads. The resulting scores generally map to *bad* quality scores; only the long-few workload shows better QoE for buffers ≤ 128 packets.

9.3 Backbone networks results

The median PLT and the corresponding QoE scores in the backbone setup are shown as a heatmap in Figure 11. As in the access scenario, the heatmap shows buffer sizes on the x-axis and the workload configuration on the y-axis. Each cell is colored according to the MOS scale from Figure 6b and displays the median PLT of 500 web page retrievals.

The baseline results (noBG) show median page loading times of ≈ 0.8 seconds. These loading times are mainly modulated by $14 \times$ RTT (RTT $= 60$ ms (see § 5.1)) needed to fully load the page (RTT component), making them higher than in the access network scenarios that has lower RTTs. In this scenario, the distribution of page loading times generally yields a slightly better performance for buffer sizes greater than or equal to the BDP; for these buffer configurations web pages load up to 200 ms faster (80th percentile not shown in the figure). The short-low scenario yields similar results despite the existence of background traffic.

We observe the first PLT degradations in the short-medium scenario for the 8 and 28 packets buffer configurations. In these cases, PLTs are affected by packet losses causing TCP retransmissions, while the 749 (BDP) and 7490 packet buffers absorb bursts and prevent retransmissions. As in the previous case, web pages load up to 200 ms faster (80th percentile not shown in the figure). The degradations in PLT are, however, small and only marginally affect the QoE score.

Degradations in the short-high scenario are twofold; while packet losses mainly affect the QoE for the 8 and 28 packets buffers, queuing delays degrade the QoE for the larger buffers. This effect is more pronounced in the short-overload and long scenarios that impose a higher link load. In these scenarios, the degradations for the 8 and 28 buffers are mainly caused by packet losses. The 749 and especially the large 7490 buffer affected flow by introducing significant queueing delays; while the RTT doubles for the 749 buffer configuration, it increases by a factor of 10 for the 7490 buffer. Comparing short-overload to long for the 8, 28 and 749 buffer size yields a higher number of retransmissions in the long scenario, degrading the PLT. Concerning the PLT, short buffers of 8 and 28 packets show faster PLT for the short-high, short-overload, and long scenarios. However, improvements in the PLT do not help to generally improve the QoE as the PLTs are already high, causing bad QoE scores.

Our findings highlight the trade-off between packet loss and queueing delays. While larger buffers prevent packet losses and therefore improve the PLT in cases of less utilized queues/links, the introduced queuing delays degrade the performance in scenarios of high buffer/link utilization. In the latter, shorter buffers improve the PLT by avoiding large queueing delays, despite the introduced packet losses. The "right" choice in buffer size therefore depends on the utilization of the link and the buffer.

9.4 Key findings for WebQoE

Our observations fall into two categories: *i)* When the link is low to moderately loaded, larger buffers (*e.g.*, BDP or higher) help minimizing the number of retransmissions that prolong the page transfer time and thus degrade WebQoE. *ii)* When the link utilization is high, however, this increases RTT and thus the page transfers become RTT dominated. Also, loss recovery times increase. Therefore, smaller buffers yield better WebQoE despite a larger number of losses.

However, the impact of the buffer size on the QoE metric page loading time is ultimately marginal, although the QoS metric page loading time sees significant improvements. While this may seem weird at first, let us consider a twofold improvement of the page loading time from 9 seconds to 5 seconds. This improvement is large for the QoS metric, but it is insignificant for the QoE metric, as both 9 and 5 seconds map to "bad" QoE scores regardless the QoS performance.

10. SUMMARY & DISCUSSION

The goal of our work is to elucidate the open problem of proper buffer sizing and to pave the way for more informed sizing decisions. In this respect, this paper presents the first comprehensive study of the impact of buffer sizes on *Quality of Experience*. By this we complement a large body of related work on buffering with a first look at factors relevant to end-user experience. This is a relevant view since it has implications for network operators and service providers, and by extension, device manufacturers.

To tackle this problem, we first evaluate the impact of buffering in the wild using a large data set from a major CDN that serves for a large number of Internet users (80M IPs from 235 countries). Our analysis shows that buffering is likely to be prevalent on a large scale. We also observe a rather modest amount of potential buffer bloat. This motivates our further evaluation of buffer sizing including the impact of very large buffers, *i.e.*, buffer bloat.

The main contribution of this paper is an extensive sensitivity study on the impact of buffer sizing on Quality of Experience. This is based on a testbed-driven approach to study three standard application classes (voice, video, and web) in two realistic testbeds emulating access and backbone networks. Our evaluation considers a wide range of traffic scenarios and buffer size configurations, including buffer bloat.

Our main finding is that the *level of competing network workload* is the primary determinant of user QoE. It is generally known and understood that buffer sizing impacts QoS metrics. In particular, it is not surprising that sustainable congestion degrades network performance. Surprisingly, our results show that in the absence of congestion, buffer sizing has a significant impact on QoS metrics, whereas it only marginally impacts QoE metrics. The good news of this novel observation for network operators is that limiting congestion, *e.g.*, via QoS mechanisms or over-provisioning, may actually yield more immediate improvements in QoE than efforts to reduce buffering. There are, however, several subtle issues that complicate buffer sizing.

Concretely, application characteristics and the level of congestion determine the potential impact of buffer sizing choices. In the case of Web browsing, large buffers yield better QoE for moderate network loads, while smaller buffers improve QoE for high network loads. This suggests load-dependent buffer sizing schemes. Despite the potential for optimization, the impact of reasonable buffer sizes on QoE metrics is marginal, while the impact on QoS metrics can be significant. This is relevant for network operators, as it indicates that as long as buffers are kept to a reasonable size their impact is of marginal relevance. Concerning the ongoing bufferbloat debate, our main claim is that only relatively narrow conditions seriously degrade QoE, *i.e.*, when buffers are over-sized and sustainably filled. Such conditions indeed occur in practice, as our empirical evaluation and other recent studies confirm, but their occurrence is relatively rare.

We remark that emulations are by definition an abstraction of live networks and that predictive QoE models are abstractions of end-users. Thus our results should not be interpreted as representative of any specific network deployment or specific end-user quality ratings. We do, however, argue that our results accurately reflect the key interactions between buffer sizes and network traffic, which is the objective of our study.

We envision future work to extend our first step towards the QoE-driven buffer size evaluation in the following directions: 1) including more applications, 2) going beyond testbed studies by verifying the results of our testbed-driven evaluations in operational (wireless) networks, and 3) verifying selected scenarios in user studies. While our UDP video quality assessment did not involve retransmissions for error recovery, initial work on HTTP video streaming is consistent with our results.

Observed discrepancies among network-centric QoS metrics and application/user centric QoE metrics advocate a stronger use of application centric metrics in measurement and performance evaluation studies. This is challenging since QoE is an application-specific measure and thus needs to be evaluated individually for every application. To reduce the complexity of QoE assessment in network design and network measurement, it appears appealing to aim for a general mapping of network performance (e.g., QoS metrics) to QoE. We believe this is possible for some QoE indicators, e.g., page-loading time in specific scenarios. However, since QoS and QoE represent fundamentally different concepts that depend on different parameters despite of common misconceptions QoE cannot be generally derived from QoS metrics. Examples used in this paper include speech QoE assessment based on audio signals or video quality assessment based on decoded video frames. To simplify future QoE evaluations, this paper exemplifies the use of QoE metrics for measurement studies.

11. ACKNOWLEDGEMENTS

Oliver Hohlfeld was supported in part by DFG SFB 1053 and Telekom Innovation Laboratories project OMAR. We thank Mark Allman and Dennis Guse for their insightful comments and Michael Blodgett for maintaining the WAIL backbone testbed. We also thank the anonymous IMC reviewers and our shepherd Rodrigo Fonseca for their valuable comments and suggestions to improve this manuscript.

12. REFERENCES

[1] Bufferbloat. `http://www.bufferbloat.net/`.

[2] ITU-T Recommendation P.862: Perceptual Evaluation of Speech Quality (PESQ): An Objective Method for End-To-End Speech Quality Assessment of Narrow-Band Telephone Networks and Speech Codecs, 2001.

[3] ITU-T Recommendation G.107: The E-Model, a computational model for use in transmission planning, 2003.

[4] ITU-T Rec. P.862 annex a: Reference implementations and conformance testing for ITU-T Recs P.862, P.862.1 a. P.862.2, 2005.

[5] ITU-T Recommendation G.1030: estimating end-to-end performance in IP networks for data applications, 2005.

[6] Bufferbloat: What's wrong with the internet? *Queue*, 9(12):10:10–10:20, Dec. 2011.

[7] Qualinet white paper on definitions of Quality of Experience. European Network on Quality of Experience in Multimedia Systems and Services (COST Action IC 1003), Patrick Le Callet, Sebastian Möller and Andrew Perkis, eds., Version 1.1, June 2012.

[8] M. Allman. Comments on bufferbloat. *ACM CCR*, 43(1):31–37, Jan. 2013.

[9] G. Appenzeller, I. Keslassy, and N. McKeown. Sizing router buffers. In *ACM SIGCOMM*, 2004.

[10] N. Barakat and T. E. Darcie. Delay characterization of cable access networks. *IEEE Communications Letters*, 11(4):357–359, 2007.

[11] N. Beheshti, Y. Ganjali, M. Ghobadi, N. McKeown, and G. Salmon. Experimental study of router buffer sizing. In *ACM IMC*, 2008.

[12] C. Chirichella and D. Rossi. To the moon and back: are Internet bufferbloat delays really that large. In *IEEE INFOCOM TMA Workshop*, 2013.

[13] M. Dischinger, A. Haeberlen, K. P. Gummadi, and S. Saroiu. Characterizing residential broadband networks. In *ACM IMC*, 2007.

[14] S. Egger, T. Hossfeld, R. Schatz, and M. Fiedler. Tutorial: Waiting Times in Quality of Experience for Web based Services. In *IEEE QoMEX*, 2012.

[15] S. Egger, P. Reichl, T. Hosfeld, and R. Schatz. "time is bandwidth"? narrowing the gap between subjective time perception and Quality of Experience. In *IEEE ICC*, 2012.

[16] S. Egger, R. Schatz, K. Schoenenberg, A. Raake, and G. Kubin. Same but different? - using speech signal features for comparing conversational voip quality studies. In *IEEE ICC*, 2012.

[17] M. Enachescu, Y. Ganjali, A. Goel, N. McKeown, and T. Roughgarden. Routers with very small buffers. In *IEEE INFOCOM*, 2006.

[18] J. Gettys. IW10 considered harmful. IETF Internet-Draft, 2011.

[19] J. Gettys and K. Nichols. Bufferbloat: Dark buffers in the internet. *ACM Queue*, 9:40:40–40:54, Nov. 2011.

[20] Y. Gu, D. F. Towsley, C. V. Hollot, and H. Zhang. Congestion control for small buffer high speed networks. In *IEEE INFOCOM*, 2007.

[21] D. Guse, S. Egger, A. Raake, and S. Möller. Web-QoE under real-world distractions: Two test cases. In *IEEE QoMEX*, 2014.

[22] K. L. Haiqing Jiang, Yaogong Wang and I. Rhee. Tackling bufferbloat in 3G/4G networks. In *ACM IMC*, 2012.

[23] M. Heusse, S. A. Merritt, T. X. Brown, and A. Duda. Two-way TCP connections: old problem, new insight. *ACM CCR*, 41(2):6–15, 2011.

[24] O. Hohlfeld, B. Balarajah, S. Benner, A. Raake, and F. Ciucu. On revealing the ARQ mechanism of MSTV. In *IEEE ICC*, 2011.

[25] V. Jacobson. Modified TCP congestion control algorithm. End2end-interest mailing list, Apr. 1990.

[26] N. Kitawaki and K. Itoh. Pure delay effects on speech quality in telecommunications. *IEEE Journal on Selected Areas in Communications*, 9(4):586–593, 1991.

[27] J. Korhonen and J. You. Peak signal-to-noise radio revised: Is simple beautiful? In *IEEE QoMEX*, 2012.

[28] C. Kreibich, N. Weaver, B. Nechaev, and V. Paxson. Netalyzr: Illuminating the edge network. In *ACM IMC*, 2010.

[29] A. Lakshmikantha, C. Beck, and R. Srikant. Impact of file arrivals and departures on buffer sizing in core routers. *IEEE/ACM ToN*, 19(2):347–358, Apr. 2011.

[30] J. Martin, J. Westall, T. Shaw, G. White, R. Woundy, J. Finkelstein, and G. Hart. Cable modem buffer management in docsis networks. In *IEEE conference on Sarnoff*, 2010.

[31] S. Möller, W.-Y. Chan, N. Côté, T. H. Falk, A. Raake, and M. Wältermann. Speech quality estimation: Models and trends. *IEEE Signal Process. Mag.*, 28(6):18–28, 2011.

[32] K. Nichols and V. Jacobson. Controlling queue delay. *ACM Queue*, 10(5), May 2012.

[33] R. S. Prasad, C. Dovrolis, and M. Thottan. Router buffer sizing for tcp traffic and the role of the output/input capacity ratio. *IEEE/ACM ToN*, 17(5):1645–1658, Oct. 2009.

[34] A. Raake. Predicting speech quality under random packet loss: Individual impairment and additivity with other network impairments. *Acta Acustia*, 90:1061–1083, 2004.

[35] B. Sat and B. W. Wah. Analyzing voice quality in popular voip applications. *IEEE MultiMedia*, 16(1):46–59, 2009.

[36] L. Sequeira et al. The influence of the buffer size in packet loss for competing multimedia and bursty traffic. In *SPECTS*, 2013.

[37] J. Sommers, P. Barford, A. Greenberg, and W. Willinger. An SLA perspective on the router buffer sizing problem. *SIGMETRICS Perf. Eval. Review*, 35:40–51, March 2008.

[38] J. Sommers, H. Kim, and P. Barford. Harpoon: a flow-level traffic generator for router and network tests. *SIGMETRICS Perf. Eval. Review*, 32(1):392–392, June 2004.

[39] D. Strohmeier, S. Jumisko-Pyykko, and A. Raake. Toward task-dependent evaluation of web-QoE: Free exploration vs. "who ate what?". In *IEEE Globecom Workshops*, 2012.

[40] D. Strohmeier, M. Mikkola, and A. Raake. The importance of task completion times for modeling web-QoE of consecutive web page requests. In *IEEE QoMEX*, 2013.

[41] L. Sun. *Speech Quality Prediction for Voice over Internet Protocol Networks*. PhD thesis, Univ. of Plymouth, 2004.

[42] S. Sundaresan, W. de Donato, N. Feamster, R. Teixeira, S. Crawford, and A. Pescapè. Measuring home broadband performance. *Commun. ACM*, 55(11):100–109, Nov. 2012.

[43] Q. H. Thu and M. Ghanbari. Scope of validity of PSNR in image/video quality assessment. *Electronics Letters*, 44(13):800–801, June 2008.

[44] C. Villamizar and C. Song. High performance tcp in ansnet. *ACM CCR*, 24(5):45–60, Oct. 1994.

[45] A. Vishwanath, V. Sivaraman, and M. Thottan. Perspectives on router buffer sizing: recent results and open problems. *ACM CCR*, 39(2):34–39, Mar. 2009.

[46] M. Wang and Y. Ganjali. The effects of fairness in buffer sizing. In *IFIP-TC6 conference on Ad Hoc and sensor networks, wireless networks, next generation internet*, 2007.

[47] Z. Wang, A. C. Bovik, H. R. Sheikh, and E. P. Simoncelli. Image quality assessment: From error visibility to structural similarity. *IEEE Trans. on Image Processing*, 13:600–612, 2004.

[48] Z. Wang, L. Lu, and A. Bovik. Video quality assessment based on structural distortion measurement. *Signal Processing: Image Communication*, 19(1), Jan. 2004.

[49] T. Zinner, O. Abboud, O. Hohlfeld, T. Hossfeld, and P. Tran-Gia. Towards QoE management for scalable video streaming. In *21st ITC-SS*, 2010.

Handcrafted Fraud and Extortion: Manual Account Hijacking in the Wild

Elie Bursztein† Borbala Benko† Daniel Margolis† Tadek Pietraszek†
Andy Archer† Allan Aquino† Andreas Pitsillidis* Stefan Savage*

†Google, Inc *University of California, San Diego

{elieb, bbenko, dmargolis, tadek, archer, aaquino}@google.com {apitsill, savage}@cs.ucsd.edu

ABSTRACT

Online accounts are inherently valuable resources—both for the data they contain and the reputation they accrue over time. Unsurprisingly, this value drives criminals to steal, or hijack, such accounts. In this paper we focus on manual account hijacking—account hijacking performed manually by humans instead of botnets. We describe the details of the hijacking workflow: the attack vectors, the exploitation phase, and post-hijacking remediation. Finally we share, as a large online company, which defense strategies we found effective to curb manual hijacking.

1. INTRODUCTION

Online accounts are inherently valuable resources—both for the data they contain and the reputation they accrue over time. With the advent of the cloud, the most intimate details of our lives are contained on remote servers in a single account. This makes account theft, or *account hijacking*, a lucrative monetization vector for miscreants. Criminals leverage millions of hijacked credentials to send spam [5, 10], tap into the social connections of victim's to compromise additional accounts [24], or alternatively liquidate a victim's financial assets using malware such as Zeus or SpyEye [12].

While significant research attention has focused on wide-spread automated hijacking facilitated via botnets, we explore a second class of attacks we refer to as *manual hijacking*. Manual hijackers spend significant non-automated effort on profiling victims and maximizing the profit—or damage—they can extract from a single credential. In contrast to automated hijacking, manual hijacking is exceedingly rare. We observe an average of 9 incidents *per million* Google users per day. However, the damage manual hijackers incur is far more severe and distressing to users [22] and can result in significant financial loss [4]. These needle-in-a-haystack attacks are very challenging and represent an ongoing threat to Internet users.

IMC'14, November 5–7, 2014, Vancouver, BC, Canada.

ACM 978-1-4503-3213-2/14/11 ...$15.00.
http://dx.doi.org/10.1145/2663716.2663749.

In this paper, we explore the manual hijacking lifecycle as gleaned from incidents that occurred at Google between 2011–2014. Our study consists of three components: we explore how criminals acquire a victim's credentials (Section 4); examine how criminals monetize account credentials (Section 5); and finally highlight the process Google used to ultimately restore control back to the victim (Section 6). Based on our findings, we offer a set of best practices for others to defend against manual hijacking and discuss many of the corner cases that exacerbate the problem (Section 8).

In particular, we link manual hijacking with phishing and provide evidence supporting the hypothesis that phishing is the main way manual hijackers steal user credentials. We found that phishing requests target victims' email (35%) and banking institutions (21%) accounts, as well as their app stores and social networking credentials. Of the hijacking case samples we analyzed, we found that most of the hijackers appear to originate from five main countries: China, Ivory Coast, Malaysia, Nigeria, and South Africa.

Injecting decoy credentials in phishing pages targeting Google users reveals that criminals' response time is surprisingly fast. We found that criminals attempted to access 20% of the accounts within 30 minutes. Looking at real hijacking cases, we observed that, once logged in, manual hijackers profile the victim's account and spend an average of 3 minutes to assess the value of the account before exploiting it or abandoning the process. This step entails searching through the victim's email history for banking details or messages that the victim had previously flagged as important. We also see attackers scanning through email contacts which are then either solicited for funds or targeted with a salvo of targeted phishing emails.

Restoring a victim's account access is a non-trivial problem. We found that SMS is the most reliable out-of-band channel, where users that provided a phone number recover their account 81% of the time. Providing a secondary email address is also fruitful, succeeding 75% of the time. Absent these two mechanisms, we must rely on secret questions or manual review where our success rate falls to 14%.

Ethics We acknowledge that most of the results in the paper depend on proprietary data. As a result, we attempted to clearly explain how we reached our conclusions while balancing our need to protect the security and privacy of our users.

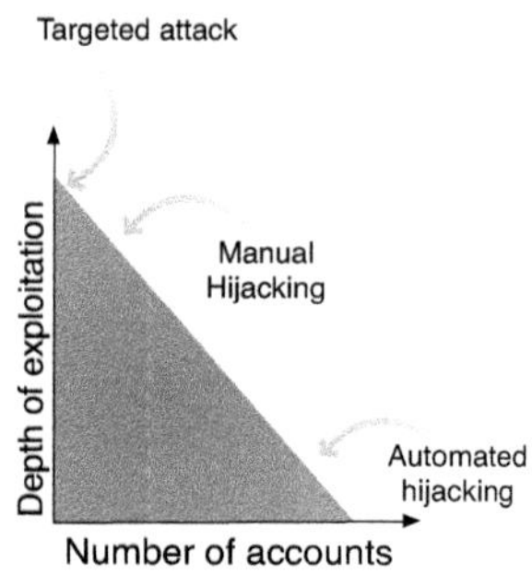

Figure 1: Hijacking trade-off: the depth of exploitation versus the number of accounts compromised.

2. HIJACKER TAXONOMY

Account hijacking stems from a multitude of attack vectors and underlying incentives. At Google, we categorize hijacking campaigns based on the depth of exploitation (e.g. the damage incurred to each victim) and the number of accounts impacted, as depicted in Figure 1. We currently observe three classes of attacks:

Automated hijacking: An automated hijacking attack attempts to compromise large quantities of accounts using botnets or other professional spamming infrastructure [11]. This type of attack is carried out entirely by automated tools that monetize the most common resources across all compromised accounts (e.g. spamming via a victim's email).

Targeted attacks: Targeted attacks [23] include industrial espionage and state-sponsored break-ins. In our experience, these attacks are carried out by highly sophisticated parties who have the resources to extensively profile targets and launch tailored attacks. These include using dedicated 0-day exploits [20], less expensive readily-available exploits, or highly targeted phishing campaigns.

Manual hijacking: Manual hijacking consist of attack that opportunistically select victims with the intent of monetizing the victim's contacts or personal data; any sufficiently lucrative credential will suffice. These attacks are carried manually rather than automatically. As a result, we observe orders of magnitude fewer instances compared to automated hijacking. However, criminals heavily abuse victim's information, making such attacks highly distressing to the impacted parties [22].

In this paper, we choose to focus on manual hijacking. While automated hijacking impacts the most users, manual hijacking incurs significantly more damage to the victims involved and represents an ongoing pertinent threat to Google. We restrict our analysis of manual hijacking to cases where the attacker does not know the victim personally. Similarly, we also exclude hijacking instances where an attacker leverages physical access to a victim's devices. These personalized attacks represent their own area of focus [2, 17], and while they are of serious importance, combating such threats relies on individual insights that benefit little from large-scale measurement.

Figure 2: Overview of the account hijacking cycle.

3. METHODOLOGY

We provide a high-level workflow of the account hijacking lifecycle, depicted in Figure 2, along with our methodology for studying each component.

In total, we rely on 14 distinct datasets collected between 2011–2014, outlined in Table 1. Each dataset originates from various system logs that we aggregate via map-reduce computation. For privacy and storage reasons, Google sanitizes or entirely erases many authentication-related logs within a short time window. Consequently, some of our datasets are drawn over a period of only a few weeks despite the three year span of our study. Similarly, as many of our datasets rely on user reports, we are forced to manually curate data points sampled from a much larger, noisy source to have precise ground truth. This problem originates from the fact that both computers and humans alike are imprecise at distinguishing phishing or similar attacks from scams and other bulk spam.

To offer some perspective on sample size, we observed an average of 9 case of manual hijacking per million active users per day in 2012 and 2013. This number includes those our abuse detection mechanisms detected before the hijacker fully exploits the account, and those for which the victim had to file a recovery claim. An account is considered active if it has been accessed within the past 30 days. In term of phishing page, SafeBrowsing detected between 16,000 and 25,000 page per week on the Internet for the period 2012–2013 [9] [Dataset 2 and 3 in Table 1].

Credential acquisition [Section 4]: Account hijacking begins when a hijacker steals a user's credentials. This can occur in a multitude of ways: phishing a user's credentials; installing malware on the victim's machine to steal credentials; or guessing a victim's password. Overall we find corroborating evidence throughout our measurements that phishing is likely to be the main way hijackers compromise user accounts. We argue that phishing is the attack vector of choice for manual hijackers as it is easier and cheaper to perform than other mean to compromise accounts: e.g using 0-day exploits to install malwares. This is why for this part of the study dedicated to the attack vectors used by manual hijackers we decided to focus on phishing emails and phishing pages targeting Google users.

Datasets used: In this section we use a manually curated sample of 100 phishing emails selected from a random sample of 5000 emails reported by our users to understand how email phishing is structured and what type of accounts are targeted[1] [Dataset 1 in Table 1]. Next we use a manually reviewed random sample of 100 phishing pages detected by the SafeBrowsing anti-phishing pipeline [26] while indexing the web for our search engine to understand what type of accounts are phished [Dataset 2 in Table 1].

[1] we only have access to the emails the users manually reported as spam and phishing.

Id	Data type	Samples	Date	Used in section
1	Phishing emails	100	Jan 2014	4.1
2	Phishing pages detected by SafeBrowsing	100	Jan 2014	4.1
3	Google Forms taken down for phishing	100	Nov 2012	4.2
4	Decoy credentials injected in phishing pages	200	Nov 2012	5.1
5	Login attempts from IPs belonging to hijackers	300 IPs/day	Nov 2012	5.1
6	Keywords searched by hijackers	Top 10	Jan 2014	5.2
7	High-confidence hijhacked accounts	575	Nov 2012	5.2
8	Mail sent from hijhacked accounts from dataset 7 and reported as spam by users	200	Nov 2012	5.3
9	Hijacked account contacts and active users random sample hijacking rate	3000 / 3000	Nov 2011	5.3
10	High-confidence hijhacked accounts	600	Oct 2011	5.4
11	Hijacked accounts recovery cases	5000	Nov 2012	6.2
12	Accounts recovery	1 month	Feb 2013	6.3
13	IP used by hijackers	3000 hijacking cases	Jan 2014	7
14	Phone numbers used by hijackers	300	Mid-2012	7

Table 1: List of dataset used throughout this study.

The manual review was used to identify what type of account are targeted by phishers (e.g Bank, Social Network). Finally we look at the HTTP logs of a random sample of 100 Google Drive forms that were used as phishing pages before we detected and took them down [Dataset 3 in Table 1]. This dataset is used to understand the conversion rate of phishing pages, the victims targeted, and the methods for luring victims to the pages.

Account exploitation [Section 5]: If the hijacker is able to log into the victim's account, then a second phase begins that we call the exploitation phase. We observe that this phase consists of two distinct parts: The *account profiling* part where the hijacker decides on a concrete exploitation plan and the *exploitation* itself.

The existence of this profiling phase is one of the most surprising insights we gained by fighting manual hijackers. Instead of blindly exploiting every account, hijackers take on average 3 minutes to assess the value of the account before deciding to proceed. This profiling phase and the fact that hijackers decide to not exploit certain accounts is consistent with our claim that this type of hijacking is manual rather that automated. Similarly, we observe that most manual hijackers use semi-personalized scams as the main exploitation vector, e.g. to trick the victim's contacts into transferring money to the hijacker. We have also observed other more opportunistic approaches such as holding the account for ransom. We note that this type of exploitation is very different from the one we observe for automated hijacking, which mainly focuses on abusing the hijacked account's good reputation to send email spam that will bypass spam filters.

Datasets used: In this section we start by using a dataset of 200 fake credentials injected into various phishing pages targeting Google to measure a hijacker's responsiveness [Dataset 4 in Table 1]. Those pages were detected while indexing the web by the SafeBrowsing anti-phishing pipeline. Then we look at 200 IPs that were used to access stolen accounts to understand hijackers' access patterns [Dataset 5 in Table 1]. Next we analyze a set of 575 accounts that were hijacked to characterize how hijackers are exploiting accounts [Dataset 6 in Table 1]. Those accounts were selected based on their account recovery claims, which clearly indicate that they were manually hijacked.

Next we look at 200 phishing emails sent by those accounts during the hijacking period to understand what type of attack the hijackers conducted [Dataset 7 in Table 1]. We also examine the likelihood that a victim's contacts will become compromised compared to a random sample of users, using a sample of 3,000 contacts and 3,000 random accounts [Dataset 8 in Table 1]. Our analysis confirms that a contact's victims are heavily targeted by hijackers as their hijacking rate is 36 times higher than our random sample. Finally we study how hijackers' tactics to retain control of the hijacked accounts evolved over time by comparing the tactics used on our 2012 dataset with the tactics used on a set of hijacked accounts from 2011 [Dataset 9 in Table 1]. The accounts used in datasets 8 and 9 have no overlap.

Hijacking remediation [Section 6]: This last phase of the cycle starts when the exploitation is over or is interrupted by our defense mechanisms. The goal of this phase is to give the account back to its real owner and revert all the account changes made by the hijacker.

Datasets used: We analyze a set of 5000 hijacked accounts that were successfully recovered to estimate how long hijackers retained control of each account [Dataset 11 in Table 1]. We note that there is no overlap between dataset 7 and dataset 11. We next examine a month's worth of account recovery claims (Feb. 2013) to determine the most successful method for recovering account ownership [Dataset 12 in Table 1].

Hijacking attribution[Section 7] Stepping back from the manual hijacking workflow, we shed light on the origin of hijackers. Of the hijacking case samples we analyzed, we found that most of the hijackers appears to originate from five main countries: China, Ivory Coast, Malaysia, Nigeria and South Africa.

Datasets used: Our analysis relies on the geolocation of IPs used to access 3000 hijacked accounts selected at random in January 2014. Independently, we examine the country code of a set of 300 phones that hijackers used in a attempt to lock out their victims by turning on two-factor authentication for hijacked accounts in 2012. We lack more recent data on phone numbers as hijackers abandoned this tactic after realizing it was unsuccessful.[Dataset 13 and 14 in Table 1].

Account type	Phishing emails	Phishing pages
Mail	35	27
Bank	21	25
App Store	16	17
Social network	14	15
Other	14	15

Table 2: Number of phishing emails and pages targeting a specific type of account.

4. ATTACK VECTORS

Manual hijacking begins with acquiring a victim's credentials.

Phishing is a natural attack vector of choice for manual hijackers. It requires less infrastructure than operating a botnet and allows attackers to target specific victims, especially an existing victim's contacts.

Although phishing as an attack mechanism is well studied [1, 6, 16, 27, 13], little is known about its victims or effectiveness.

To understand what types of accounts are targeted by phishers and the relation of phishing to manual hijacking, we looked at what type of accounts are targeted by email-based phishing and website-based phishing. We start by analyzing email-based phishing attacks, in which phishers send email that pretends to come from a legitimate source and requests user credentials under a false pretext, such as impending account deactivation. We then turn to web-based phishing, in which an attacker sets up a webpage which looks like a traditional sign-in page for a web service and attempts to get users to input their login credentials. Finally, to understand phishing effectiveness and how users are lured to phishing pages, we look at the traffic of a random sample of phishing pages that were inadvertently hosted on Google Drive.

4.1 Phishing targets

We generated a manually curated sample of the phishing emails from January, 2014 [Dataset 1 in Table 1] This dataset was constructed by first extracting a random sample of 5,000 phishing emails and then manually reviewing the sample to find 100 emails that explicitly phish for users credentials or point to phishing webpages. This manual curation is necessary to reliably distinguish spam emails from phishing emails.

We found that 62 of those emails contain URLs, which were likely to point to phishing pages designed to impersonate well known site login pages in order to trick users into submitting their credentials. The remaining 38 did not contain URLs and instead asked users to reply to the email with their credentials. By manually categorizing the type of account each phishing email targets, we found that email account credentials were by far the most popular target, followed by bank credentials (Table 2). The result of a similar analysis for phishing pages reported on the same table reveals a mirrored distribution in terms of which type of credentials were phished for. This analysis was conducted by manually reviewing 100 phishing pages detected while indexing the web [26].

The target distribution consistency between our two distinct datasets suggests that phishing is mainly used by the group of attackers that focuses on acquiring email and financial institution credentials.

This focus is consistent with manual hijackers priorities, as this group primarily monetize victim's accounts by running emails and financial scams as detailed in section 5.

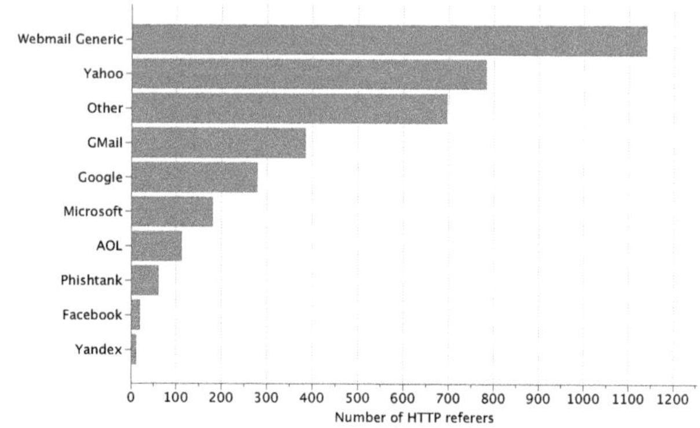

Figure 3: Non-Blank HTTP referrers breakdown.

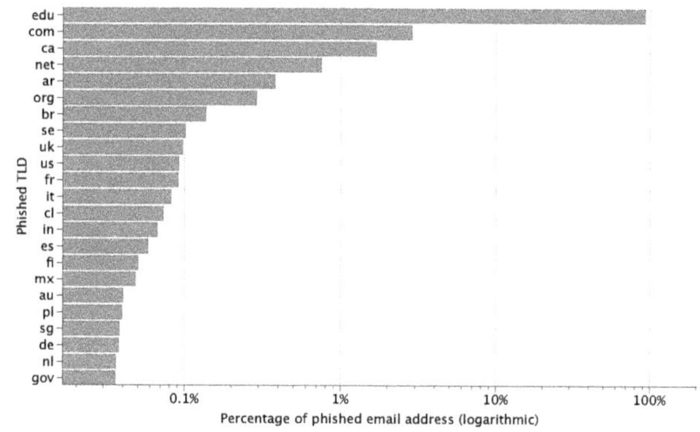

Figure 4: Phished email TLD breakdown

4.2 Phishing effectiveness

Using a separate dataset, we analyzed traffic to a random sample of 100 Google Forms that Google later flagged as phishing and disabled for abuse [Dataset 3 in Table 1]. We used this dataset to understand how users were lured to phishing pages, what domains were targeted most often by phishers, how many credentials hijackers could collect per hour/page, and what success rates phishing pages had. We caution that the behaviors we observed on Google Forms may not be representative of all phishing pages, but no other studies exist on the topic to offer comparison.

Origin of Phished Users: We looked at the HTTP referer of the requests made to phishing pages to understand how users are lured onto those pages. We were surprised to observe that above 99% of those referrers were blank. We hypothesize that it is due to the fact that most traffic toward phishing pages is driven via emails as this source of traffic don't have HTTP referer. Traffic from desktop email clients don't have HTTP referer as it come from an application, and major webmails, including Gmail, ensure the HTTP referer is not set by opening links in a new tab. The hypothesis that most victims are lured via emails is further supported by the fact that most of the remaining 1% of visitors arrived from various webmail providers (Figure 3). The Gmail referrers oddity can be traced back to one of our old HTML frontends used by legacy phones.

The TLDs of the email addresses phished, reported in Figure 4, reveal that the vast majority (> 99%) of the emails address phished come from .edu domains.

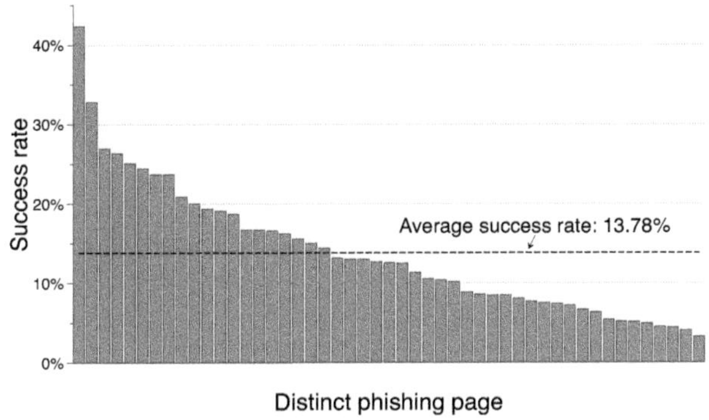

Figure 5: Credential submission rate for phishing pages. Ratio between the number of submitted credential and the number of page views

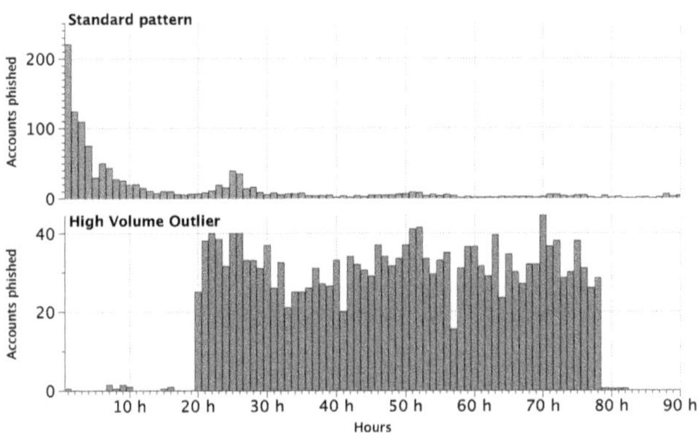

Figure 6: Average number of submitted credentials over time.

A possible explanation, behind the overwhelming prevalence of .edu emails address is that self-hosted emails, e.g by universities, have less robust spam filters than large mail providers and social networks. This explanation is supported by previous work [14] that observed that the spam delivery rate was 10 times higher for webmail protected by commodity spam filtering than by large mail provider such as Gmail, Yahoo, and Hotmail. This explanation is also consistent with our hypothesis that most phishing victims are lured to phishing pages via email.

Phishing Submission Rates: Using the submission rate of visitors to phishing forms, we can estimate the success rate of phishing campaigns. The phishing page success rate is computed by dividing the number of page submissions (HTTP POST requests) by the number of page views (HTTP GET requests). We observe that 13.7% of visitors complete the form (which we assume indicates users submitted accurate credentials); much higher than we anticipated. Broken down by individual page,s we observe a huge variance in success rate, with the highest page having a 45% success rate and the lowest only 3% (Figure 5).

We visually inspected a sample of pages and found that those with low submission rates were very poorly executed and contained only a form asking for a username and password.

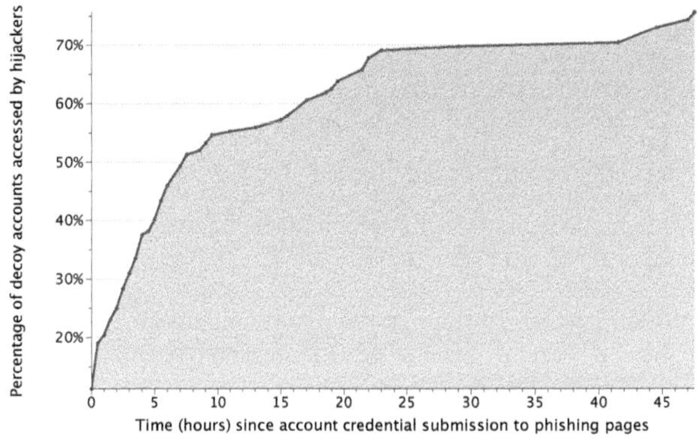

Figure 7: Speed of compromised account access.

Arrival Rate of Phishing Victims: Finally we looked at the average hourly volume of credential submissions for a phishing page, calculated from the time when the page was first visited (first entry in the HTTP request log) until it was taken down (Figure 6) as determined by our logs. The pattern exhibits a clear decay, from the moment the webpage receives its first visitors until it is taken down. This pattern is consistent with a mass mailed email, with clicks centered around the initial delivery time.

We note that while analyzing our phishing page set, we found a single outlier (Figure 6, bottom) that received a huge number of submissions after a step function following a gentle diurnal pattern through several days. This is a prime example of a successful large-scale phishing campaign—starting when the first email went out and ending abruptly when the phishing page was taken down. The initial 15 hour quiet period is, upon a closer investigation, best explained by the attackers testing the page themselves before launching the campaign.

Overall our analysis supports our hypothesis that phishing is a key vector of attack used by manual hijackers and that email is the primary vector by which victims are phished or lured to phishing pages.

5. ACCOUNT EXPLOITATION

Once hijackers obtain access to a victim's login credentials, we observe a multitude of monetization vectors. We find that criminal activities are well-structured, efficient, and savvy at taking advantage of human psychology. A typical hijacker's method adheres to the following playbook: access the account, assess its value, exploit it, and make efforts to delay account recovery in order to increase the chances of successful exploitation. We present our findings about each of these steps.

5.1 Logging Into Accounts

Rapid response time: In order to measure the hijacker response time—the delta between a victim submitting an account's login credentials to a hijacker and the account being accessed by the hijacker—we manually submitted 200 fake credentials into a random sample of 200 phishing pages that explicitly ask for Google credentials (each credential was submitted to exactly one phishing page)[Dataset 4 in Table 1]. We recorded the time when each credential was submitted to a phishing page, and used our logs to observe when the hijacker first attempted to access each account. We found that 20% of the decoy accounts were accessed within 30 minutes of credential submission, and 50% within 7 hours.

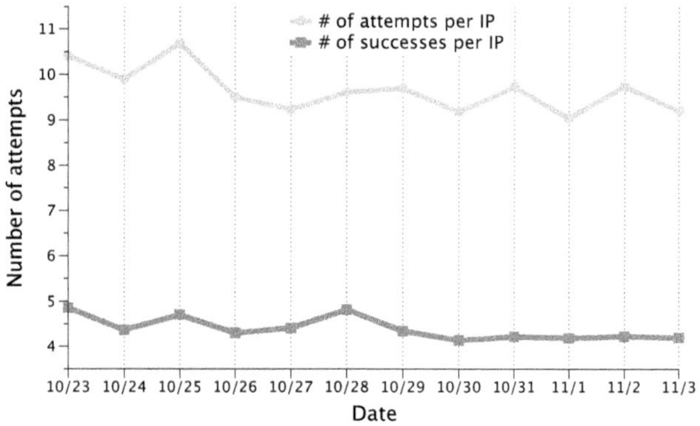

Figure 8: Average hijacker activity per IP.

Figure 7 describes this relationship in more detail. Although not all of the decoy accounts were accessed, possibly due to the suspension of either the phishing website or the email account used by the hijacker to collect credentials [19], the speed with which decoy accounts were accessed was astonishing. Our findings suggest that in order to prevent a hijacked account's exploitation, the reaction time to the credential compromise needs to be even faster than previously thought [18]. Hijhackers' extreme reactivity emphasizes the need to perform an accurate, real-time login risk analysis (Sec 8.2) at the time of log-in in order to detect hijacking attempts since it is unreasonable to expect both the user and the service provider to reliably react within a time window as short as 30 minutes. How we implemented such real time hijacking detection system is discussed in Section 8.

Efforts to Blend in With Organic Traffic: Our next surprising finding is the systematic effort the manual hijackers make in order to avoid detection. Studying the log-in activity of a random sample of 300 IPs used by hijackers, selected daily over a period of two weeks in October/November 2012, reveals that on average, the hijackers attempted to access only 9.6 distinct accounts from each IP, which makes their activity extremely difficult to distinguish from organic traffic [Dataset 5 in Table 1].

The average number of account access attempts per IP is consistently under 10 during the entire two week period studied (Figure 8), suggesting that the manual hijackers may have established guidelines to avoid detection. We observe that hijackers have the correct password for an account 75% of the time (including retries with trivial variants).

5.2 Account Value Assessment

A surprising finding is that hijackers spend 3 minutes on average assessing the value of the account and will not attempt to exploit accounts that they deem not valuable enough. This systematic assessment phase and the fact that certain accounts are not exploited suggest that manual hijackers are "professional" and follow a well established playbook designed to maximize profits. The assessment phase ends when the hijacker performs an active action (e.g sending an email) or logs out of the account. The remaining results in this section are based on a study of 575 randomly sampled accounts that were compromised by manual hijackers [Dataset 7 in Table 1].

We analyze which features of Gmail were accessed by hijackers and find that the most common way for them to assess an account's value is via the Gmail search feature. We also observe that beside familiarizing themselves with the contents of the victim's account via the search terms, hijackers often also open content folders of special significance, such as *Starred* (viewed by 16% of hijackers) *Drafts* (11% of hijackers), *Sent Mail* (5% of hijackers), or *Trash* (less than 1%). The hijackers also look at the user contacts to estimate the number of potential scam and phishing victims.

To better understand how the search feature is abused, we set up a temporary experiment that collected and analyzed the search terms hijackers used for exploring the contents of the victim's mailbox. We found out that hijackers mainly look for financial data (including the victim's financial status and images of signatures to be used for future impersonation), linked account credentials (e.g., usernames and passwords for the victim's other accounts), and personal material that might be sold or used for blackmail (e.g., adult pictures). Table 3 summarizes the frequency of hijackers' top 10 search keywords [Dataset 6 in Table 1]. We find that searches are overwhelmingly for financial data as opposed to other account credentials or content.

The fact that some searches were performed in Spanish and Chinese suggests that certain hijackers target specific regions the world. This observation is consistent with our hijacking attribution analysis (section 7), which shows that besides Africa, hijackers seem to come from Asia (China, Malaysia) and South America (Venezula).

We believe few hijackers look for account credentials because most websites will not send them in clear and instead favor a password reset process. We note that searches for credentials for e-commerce and gaming sites are most prominent among the account searches. Confirming how any of these searches yield an actual financial attack or blackmail is beyond the capabilities of our datasets.

Although, as discussed in Section 8, detection of account hijacking at the initial log-in stage is the most effective way to prevent harm due to hijacking, the systematic approach hijackers use to assess the value of accounts opens another possibility for rapid account hijacking detection. Namely, an approach that models manual hijacker initial activity on hijacked accounts and compares a logged-in user's activity to this model in order to flag those that exhibit excessive similarity to hijacker activity.

5.3 Account's contacts exploitation

If the brief account value exploration using the above techniques yields promising results, the hijackers spend an additional 15 to 20 minutes per account sifting through emails and finding ways to monetize the account. We now discuss how hijackers use this time to exploit the victim's contacts through scams and phishing.

Scam Schemes: Among the exploitations that we can observe, the most common one employed by the manual hijackers is to scam the contacts of the hijacked account owner. A typical scam consists of an email describing a reasonably credible story of how the account owner got into a difficult situation and a plea for money to help get out of the situation. We observe that scams are semi-personalized, e.g take into account the victim gender and location, appeal to human emotions, and systematically exploit known psychological principles [3] to maximize their success rate as discussed below.

Finance		Account		Content	
wire transfer	14.4%	password	.6%	jpg	.2%
bank	11.9%	amazon	.4%	mov	.2%
transfer	6.2%	dropbox	.1%	mp4	.2%
bank transfer	5.2%	paypal	.3%	3gp	.1%
wire	4.7%	match	.1%	passport	.1%
transferencia	4.6%	ftp	.1%	sex	.1%
investment	3.4%	facebook	.1%	filename:(jpg or jpeg or png)	.1%
banco	3.0%	skype	.1%	is:starred	.1%
账单 (account statement)	1.9%	username	.1%	zip	.1%

Table 3: Top search terms used by hijackers for the various type of information searched.

A prominent example of such a scam scheme is the *Mugged-In-"City"* scheme, in which, according to the story told by the hijacker, the account owner was robbed during his or her trip to a faraway city and is asking for a temporary emergency loan to help settle bills and get out of the situation:

...My family and I came down here to West Midlands, UK for a short vacation...

...we were mugged last night in an alley by a gang of thugs on our way back from shopping, one of them had a knife poking my neck for almost two minutes and everything we had on us including my cell phone, credit cards were all stolen, quite honestly it was beyond a dreadful experience...

...I'm urgently in need of some money to pay for my hotel bills and my flight ticket home, will payback as soon as i get back home...

Besides the *Mugged-In-"City"* scheme, there is a large variety of scam schemes with different stories that appeal to the same human emotions and exploit the same psychological principles. For example, the following excerpt presents an example where the reason for the plea is a sick relative with a sudden need for a medical procedure:

Sorry to bother you with this. I am presently in Spain with my ill Cousin. She's suffering from a kidney disease and must undergo Kidney Transplant to save her life. ...

Over time, we realized that scam schemes share a set of core principles that we were then able to formalize as follow:

- A story with credible details to limit the victim suspicion.
- Words or phrases that evoke sympathy and aim to persuade. E.g apologizing and providing distressing details such as "had a knife poking my neck for almost two minutes".
- An appearance of limited financial risk for the plea recipient, as financial requests are typically requests for a loan with concrete promises of speedy repayment.
- Language that discourages the plea recipient from trying to verify the story by contacting the victim through another means of communication, often through claims that the victim's phone was stolen.
- An untraceable, fast and hard-to-revoke yet safe-looking money transfer mechanism. The payment also needs to be picked up anywhere and somewhat anonymously as the scammers might not be from the country they claim the victim what mugged in.

  For example, a request to transfer money to the victim by name via Western Union/MoneyGram helps the request appear credible, and enables the recipient to reclaim money anywhere in the world. [28].

Thus, despite the appearance of simplicity, in reality, the scam emails are well-formed and thought-out in a way to maximize efficiency by preying on known human physiological principles [3]. The potentially high level of financial and psychological distress due to scam emails [22], explains why detecting and filtering out such emails is a high priority for us.

The volume of scam emails sent from hijacked accounts is relatively low and supports our earlier claim that they are likely a result of manual work. For 65% of the victims, the hijacker sends at most five messages, each with a high number of recipients We further analyze the 6% of the cases in which the number of recipients is less than 10, and conclude that those tend to contain a more customized message.

We hypothesize that although message customization comes at an additional (time) cost for the hijackers, certain hijacker groups anticipate higher returns on those messages, thus making the trade-off worthwhile.

Phishing: Another common exploitation pattern is to use the hijacked account for email-based phishing. We reached this conclusion by observing 2 key facts: First the number of outgoing emails for our sample accounts was only 25% higher on average on the suspected day of the hijacking compared with the previous day's volume, the number of distinct recipients of that traffic was 630% higher than on the previous day. This suggests that hijackers generate traffic by sending the same message to many recipients.

Secondly the traffic generated on the suspected day of the hijacking received 39% more user spam/phishing reports than the previous day's traffic. This sharp increase of reports confirms that malicious emails were sent from stolen account and corroborate our hypothesis that manual hijackers attempt to scam and phish the victim's contacts. To further confirm this, we performed a manual analysis of 200 randomly selected phishing messages sent from one of the hijacked accounts on the day of the suspected hijacking [Dataset 8 in Table 1]. This analysis reveals that 35% of them were phishing messages and the remaining 65% were attempts to scam the recipients, as described earlier in this section. These results also support our hypothesis that hijacked accounts are used for phishing.

We were able to confirm that hijackers favor the use of the victim's contacts to select their next set of phishing victims and to improve the attack's chances of success using a second measurement. For this second analysis we measured the number of account hijacked for two account sets: The first set consisted of random sample of 3000 accounts that belonged to the contact list of accounts that were hijacked [Dataset 9 in Table 1]. The second set consisted of 3000 randomly sampled 7-day active users[Dataset 9 in Table 1] We found that the number of manual hijackings over the next 60 days among the users of the first set was 36 times higher than among the users of the second set. This supports our hypothesis that hijackers use victim's contacts as their next targets.

These results are consistent with our first experiment observations and support the hypothesis that phishing is manual hijackers' main way to compromised accounts. We hypothesize that the rationale behind phishing people in the social circle of previous victims is that hijackers try to leverage the sometimes more lenient and trusting treatment given by automated mail classifiers and humans to emails originating from a person's regular contact. This observation is consistent with previous studies on the subject [24].

5.4 Account Retention Tactics

In order for the scam attempts to succeed, the hijacker needs to control the account for a sufficiently long period of time. For example, the *Mugged-In-"City"* scams typically require at least two rounds of emails – one with the call for help and one with the money transfer details, meaning that even the shortest process may take one or two days, depending on the responsiveness of the contact. In this section, we present our analysis of the account-level tactics deployed by the hijackers in order to increase the chances of their scam's success. This longitudinal study was performed by comparing the retention tactics used for 600 high confidence hijacking cases from October 2011 [Dataset 10 in Table 1] with the retention tactics used for the 575 high confidence hijacking cases from November 2012 that are used in throughout this section [Dataset 7 in Table 1]. The most popular tactics during this period were: *locking out the victim from his account* and *delaying account recovery*, *minimizing the chances of account hijacking discovery*, and *redirecting future communications from the plea recipients to a "doppelganger" account*. These tactics are often combined with each other or alternated between.

Locking out the Victim and Delaying Recovery: The intent behind locking out the account owner is to separate him from his contacts. Most people do not have a copy of their contact list offline, so by losing access to the account the victim also loses the ability to warn his contacts about the scam. The lockout can be as simple as changing the account's password. Most victims are not experts in manual hijacking, so even if they realize that they cannot log in to their account they may not conclude that their contacts are at risk of being scammed. As a result, they are unlikely to warn their contacts of a potential scam via an alternate channel. Locking out the victim is, however, a double-edged sword. While it helps the hijacker in delaying the victim's counter-actions, it also provides a very clear signal for abuse detection and account recovery purposes.

Besides locking out the user, the hijackers also often invest effort in delaying account recovery by changing the account's recovery options, including the secondary email, recovery phone number, and secret question. Finally, they often delete the user's emails and contact lists, so even after the recovery, the victim cannot easily warn his contacts.

Acting in the Shadow: Hijackers sometimes find it more beneficial to remain unnoticed and carry out the scam while the victim remains in control of the account. However, operating in the background is risky for the hijacker: his direct actions (e.g., marking a mail as read) as well as the service provider's countermeasures (e.g., suspicious activity notifications) can easily reveal his presence. In order to remain undetected, hijackers try to separate their emails from the victim's communications. A common tactic for doing so is to set up an email filter and redirect all hijacker-initiated communication to the Trash or to the Spam folder.

In a sample from November 2012, ,15% of the accounts had hijacker-initiated email forwarding rules and 26% had a hijacker-configured Reply-To address.

"Doppelganger" Accounts: Given that the exploitation window can close rapidly, it is advantageous for the hijacker to divert the communication to a separate email account that he owns. That way the hijacker has all the time in the world to scam its victim. In order to accomplish this, the hijacker creates and uses a duplicate ("*doppelganger*") email account that looks reasonably similar from the point of view of the victims. The exact choice of the account name depends on the available usernames and on the personal taste of the hijacker. Some hijackers prefer to set up the doppelganger with the same provider as the victim's account, and introduce a difficult-to-detect typo to the username. Other hijackers prefer to host the doppelganger with a different email provider, preferably, but not necessarily, with a similar-looking domain name [15]. For example *johndoe@example.com* is a doppelganger account for *johndoe@gmail.com* that retain the same username but use a different mail provider.

We observe that the methods of choice for attackers to divert subsequent emails to their doppelganger accounts are to either populate the *Reply-To* email field with it when sending the first email or to use the *Gmail email filters* to forward all victim's email to his own accounts. To efficiently counter those doppelganger tactics it is essential during the account recovery process to have these settings reviewed by the legitimate account owner or automatically cleared.

Retention tactics evolution: It is interesting to note that hijacker's tactics are constantly evolving in response to the new defenses we put in place. For example, in October 2011, for *46%* of the manual hijacking cases in which the hijackers initiated a password-change, the user also suffered a mass deletion of their emails. We believe hijackers deleted emails in attempt to make harder for the victims to reach their contacts when they got their accounts back. By November 2012 this probability was down to *1.6%*, since hijackers realized that this tactic was no longer effective after we improved our account recovery process by allowing users to optionally restore the emails, contacts, and settings added/modified/deleted by hijackers. Following this change we also saw the ratio of hijacker-initiated recovery option changes dropping from 60% (October 2011) to 21% (November 2012).

5.5 Manual Hijacking – an Ordinary Office Job?

We present further circumstantial evidence that manual hijackers may work in organized groups that follow a playbook based on an opportunity that we had to (retrospectively) monitor the activities of five individual hijackers for a short period of time.

We did observe the following:

- The individuals seemed to work according to a tight daily schedule. They started around the same time every day, and had a synchronized, one hour lunch break. They were largely inactive over the weekends.
- All individuals followed the same daily time table, defining when to process the newly gathered password lists, and how to divide time between ongoing scams and new victims.
- They were operating from different IPs, on different victims, and in parallel with each other, but the tools and utilities they used were the same. They also shared certain resources such as phone numbers.

We note that these observations support the results of the analysis presented throughout this paper.

6. HIJACKING REMEDIATION

In this section we discuss how our remediation process works. In particular, we study how long it takes for users to recover their account after being hijacked and analyze what is the success rate of the various options (SMS, email, knowledge test) that can be used by user to recover their accounts.

6.1 Remediation Workflow

The account hijacking remediation process consists of two parts. The first part, the recovery process, typically starts when the user realizes that his account is not accessible and submits an account recovery claim. The exact trigger may be a notification (e.g. an SMS notification about the password change on the account), or the user may just notice by himself that the password does not work or that the account was disabled by our anti-abuse systems to prevent further damage. The recovery part ends with Google verifying ownership and restoring exclusive access to the account to its rightful owner. The second part of the process is the cleanup and mitigation phase. This is triggered either by the account recovery system itself, or at the user's explicit request. At the end of it, all the changes made by the hijacker are ideally reverted.

6.2 ETA until recovery

From the anti-hijacking standpoint, a core metric is *latency*, which is the time elapsed between the hijacking and when the victim regains exclusive control over the account. The lower the latency, the less opportunity the hijacker has for exploitation, and the lower the cost for the victim. To encourage users to reclaim their accounts quickly, we keep users informed about key settings changes and potential suspicious activity via notifications over independent channels (e.g. SMS or secondary email address) whenever possible.

Figure 9 shows the distribution of the end-to-end recovery latencies for a random sample of 5000 accounts that were returned to the rightful owner after hijacking in Nov 2012 [Dataset 11 in Table 1]. In 22% of the cases, the victim successfully reclaimed the account within one hour after the hijacking, and in 50% of the cases the account was returned in less than 13 hours. The recovery time is calculated by taking the delta between the time our risk analysis

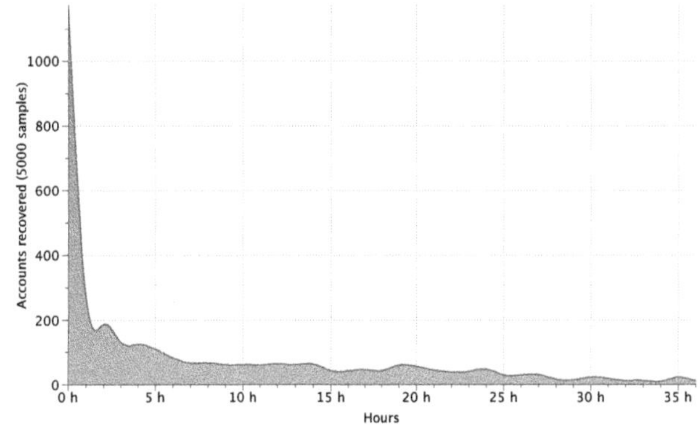

Figure 9: Hijacking recoveries by time. Sample of 5000 recoveries.

system flagged the account as hijacked and the time the user started the recovery process. The fastest recoveries are best explained by the proactive notifications we send, enabling the user to recognize the hijacking and act immediately. Enabling more users to react quickly in case of hijacking is one of the main reason why we ask our users to keep their contact information up to date and give us their mobile phone number.

6.3 Recovery methods

Providing a secure and efficient account recovery process is a complex problem for two main reasons. First, we need to accommodate varying levels of user comfort towards sharing information for recovery (e.g. a phone number). Secondly, the recovery process needs to include contingency plans for the cases where an existing recovery option is inaccurate, outdated, or is itself compromised. This is particularly problematic for the secondary email recovery option as several providers, including Microsoft [25], expire email addresses after some period of inactivity and allows anyone, including the hijacker, to register them again. As of 2014, we estimate that 7% of the secondary emails our users provided for recovery have since been recycled. This email recycling problem makes recovery emails address a somewhat unreliable medium.

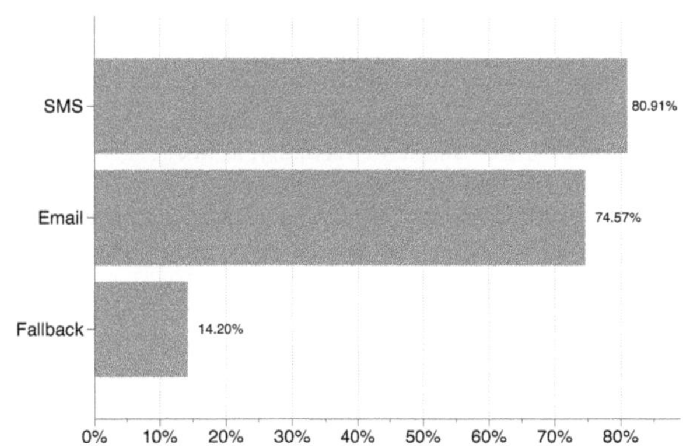

Figure 10: Success rate for various recovery methods.

Figure 11: Top countries for the IPs involved in hijacking.

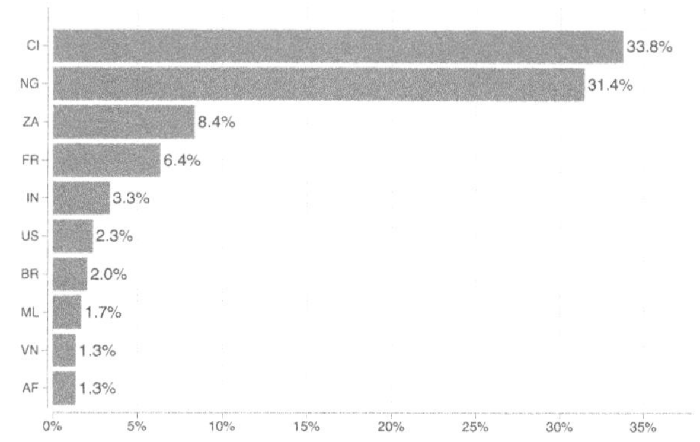

Figure 12: Top countries for the phone numbers involved in hijacking.

Figure 10 depicts the recovery success rate, based on a random sample of a month worth of account recovery claims, broken down by the method used to recover the account. Given the low volume of hijacking cases, this sample contains all the claims that were made in Feb. 2013 to avoid sample bias issues [Dataset 12 in Table 1].

We note that, while we always offer multiple recovery options to our users, the choice that we offer depends on our risk analysis and the recovery options that the account owner selected.

SMS: SMS verification, which has an over 80% success rate, is the most reliable recovery option for multiple reasons. First, users tend to keep their phone number up-to-date, which make non-existent phone numbers a non-issue. Secondly, it provides a very good user experience. Users find it easy to type in the code they receive via SMS. Finally, it is hard to fake. Failures can be traced back to the unreliability of SMS gateways in certain countries, and to confused users who did not really mean to use this option.

Email: Email is our most popular account recovery option and has a success rate of 74.57%. Email based recovery provides a good cross-device user experience as the user simply has to click on the link contained in the email. However as we explained earlier, email is a weaker recovery channel than SMS both in terms of security and reliability. The main source of failures is that users mistype their recovery emails, causing the password reset link to go to a wrong address or to a non-existing email address. We saw email bounces in approximately 5% of the cases. We are actively mitigating this issue by encouraging our users to verify their recovery addresses, but we do not enforce this step. Secondly, as also discussed above, the ownership of the secondary email is easier to lose, and users tend to not keep this recovery option up-to-date. We encourage our users to update their recovery email by showing reminder when they use our services. Furthermore to mitigate the risk of returning the account to an impostor, we do not offer this option if there is any indicatios that the secondary email address has been recycled.

Fallback options: We offer industry standard fallback options (security questions, knowledge tests and manual review) to our users when the account has no other recovery option available. For these fallback options, both the user experience and the success rate are significantly worse than for email or SMS.

We are constantly encouraging our users to upgrade to other options to improve their experience. Sadly a large portion of our users still hasn't upgraded, which force us to rely upon those less reliable options when they need to recover their accounts [21].

We also deemed security questions insecure and unreliable, and stopped allowing new users to use them as they have poor user recall and would-be hijackers may succeed by guessing the answer. However secret questions answering is still the only available method for a non-negligible portion of our user base. This is why, we only offer the ability to recover an account via security questions under certain limited circumstances, and repeatedly ask our users to give us better means to help them restore access to their accounts if needed. We only support knowledge-based options as a last resort.

6.4 Remission

After hijacking, regardless of whether the victim was locked out or has retained access, hijacker-initiated changes must to be reverted. This is very important because, as discussed in section 5.4, hijackers used to change the account settings and delete users' emails and contacts before we added this step to our account recovery flow. The remission process include restoring hijacker-deleted content, removing the hijacker-added content, and resetting all account options to their original state.
We found out by experimenting with various alternatives, that making content recovery an optional last step rather than having a fully automated process was user preferred behavior.

7. HIJACKERS' ORIGIN

Attributing accounts hijacking to specific groups of actors is very difficult as we have at best incidental proof. This section discuss hijacking attribution based on a sample of IPs used by hijackers in January 2014 [Dataset 13 in Table 1] and a set phone numbers used by hijackers sometime in 2012 [Dataset 14 in Table 1].

Figure 11 summarizes the geo-location of the IPs involved in 3000 hijacking cases that occurred in January 2014. As visible on the map, most of the traffic comes from China and Malaysia. We don't know if this traffic come from proxies or represent the true origin of the hijackers. However we do note that having Chinese traffic is consistent with the fact that hijackers search for Chinese terms.[2] Similarly having traffic originating from south america, mainly Venezuela, is consistent with hijackers search in spanish.

[2]While some Google services such as YouTube are completely blocked in China, Gmail on the other hand is not systematically blocked

The other source of data we have is a set of phone numbers that hijackers briefly used in 2012 to try to lock out users out of their accounts by enabling the two step authentication as an account retention tactic.

They quickly gave up after realizing it was not effective and we haven't seen this tactic used in the last 2 years which explain why we don't use a more recent dataset. The mapping of those 300 phone numbers to country using phone country code is summarized in figure 12. From this dataset two major groups of hijackers emerge: the Nigerian one (NG) and the Ivory Coast (CI) one. We believe those two groups to be different as their native language differs, French vs English, and they are 2000km apart. Anecdotal evidence suggest that the Ivory Coast specialize in scamming French speaking countries where as the Nigeria focus on English speaking countries. The volume of phone numbers involved in this type of attack is small enough to corroborate our hypothesis that is manual work and large enough to point to organized groups that are dedicated to monetize hijacked accounts. Finally we note that South Africa (ZA) account for 10% of both datasets which suggest that South Africa is also one of the largest home of hijackers. The fact that neither China or Malaysia show up in the phone dataset might be explained by the fact that the hijacking groups from those countries didn't try to use second factor enabling as a retention tactic.

8. DISCUSSION

In this section we discuss why it is difficult to defend against manual hijackers. In particular we summarize the defenses strategies that we found to work well, and those that did not work out so well.

8.1 Detecting manual hijackers is challenging

In our experience the greatest challenges in detecting manual hijacking is that it is extremely low volume, that hijackers are very versatile, and that it is difficult to strike the right balance between false positives (challenging legitimate users) and false negative (letting a hijacker in) when it come to detection.

Low volume: The volume of successful manual hijacking Google sees is extremely low. The exact rate varies with time, but its average is around 9 hijacks per day per million active accounts. This make the use of any large statistical model at best very difficult.

Hijacker versatility: Manual hijackers, as the name suggests, are human beings with all the flexibility and intelligence that comes with it. Our observations indicate that they are likely to have average technical ability, plus some additional knowledge of using IP cloaking services and browser plugins. Accordingly, what manual hijackers do when interacting with Google's services is not very different from what normal users do. Normal users also search their inboxes and read emails, set up email filters, and change their password and their recovery options. Thus the rules or models derived from those behaviors are not crystal clear and are certainly not high enough confidence to act upon easily. Furthermore, as we have emphasized throughout this paper, manual hijacking is an ever-moving target. The actions of the hijacker, while following certain patterns, are by no means deterministic or static.

Striking the right balance: A key challenge is handling the base error rate of our detection systems. Although we have invested a great deal in minimizing the error rate, our systems are not perfect. We have to carefully tune the aggressiveness of our system to balance acting upon signals that *might* indicate manual hijacking (but potentially inconveniencing legitimate users) against the risk of harm done by allowing hijackings to occur. This is especially difficult in light of the extreme low volume of manual hijacking; the vast majority of users are not hijacked this way. We concluded that a certain error rate, which we call the *false positive rate*, is a fair price to pay for greatly reducing the number of successful hijackings, e.g., temporarily not being able to access the account or being asked to answer additional verification questions.

8.2 Defense strategies

Second factor: Using a second authentication factor, such as a phone, has proven the best client-side defense against hijacking. While second factor authentication has some drawbacks, we believe that it is the best way to curb hijacking long term. The main issue with second factor authentication is that it is incompatible with legacy applications, such as mail clients. We work around this by authorizing our users to generate an application-specific password for those type of apps. However, this is far from ideal since those passwords can be phished. Consequently, we also work with vendors to move their apps to a better authentication technology, such as OAuth. An additional drawback of second factor authentication is usability. While phones provide a good user experience, we are exploring alternatives [7] for people who don't have a smartphone (e.g emerging countries) or want a separated physical device. We hope to see more research done in this space as there is a clear need of innovation in term of usability and accessibility.

Login time risk analysis is for us the best defense strategy that an identity provider can implement server-side since it stops the hijacker before getting into the account. Over the years we have built a complex login risk analysis system that assess for each login attempt whether it is the legitimate owner or not. Our system uses many signals (that we can't disclose for obvious reasons) to evaluate how anomalous a login attempt is. If the login attempt is deemed suspicious the user is redirected to an additional verification step before begin allowed to access his account: the login challenge [8]. Our login challenge asks the user to answer knowledge test questions or to verify their identity by proving he has access to the phone that was registered with the account earlier. e.g. by receiving an SMS. We view the proof of having access to the phone associated with the account as a safer challenge than knowledge question answers that the hijacker may just guess by researching the user's background. We spend a lot of time ensuring that our login challenge is easy to pass for our users, but hard for hijackers. This allows us to aggressively block hijacking in exchange for a small fraction of false positives as the "annoyance" cost associated of being mistakenly challenged is marginal for legitimate users.

Account behavioral risk analysis is important and needed, but we argue that it should be viewed as a last resort as it is already too late from the victim perspective. By that time any behavioral detector reports an anomaly the hijacker already had accessed the account data (emails / contact lists), and even might have setup means to continue his attack by setuping a "doppelganger" account for example.

User notifications is another tool that as proven to be essential to fight hijackers. Triggering notifications on critical events is very effective to thwart hijacking attempts and speed up the recovery process. We found out that is is important to being mindful about the keeping the volume of notification low so users know they are important when they see them. We notify our users upon account settings changes, blocked suspicious logins, and unusual in-product activity for which we have high confidence.

Iron tight Account recovery Finally we can't stress enough how important it is to invest into having a very secure and reliable *account recovery system*. We continuously improve our recovery process to ensure that it is easy for legitimate users to get their account back while keeping hijackers out. Developing novel ways to validate user identity both for login challenge and account recovery purpose is something that we view as critical and we would love to see more research done in this space.

9. REFERENCES

[1] APWG. Global phishing survey: Trends and domain name use in 1h2011. http://www.antiphishing.org/reports/, 2011.

[2] A. J. Aviv, K. Gibson, E. Mossop, M. Blaze, and J. M. Smith. Smudge attacks on smartphone touch screens. In *Proceedings of the 4th USENIX conference on Offensive technologies*, pages 1–7. USENIX Association, 2010.

[3] R. B. Cialdini. Influence: The psychology of persuasion. 1993.

[4] FBI. 2013 internet crime report. Technical report, FBI, 2013.

[5] H. Gao, J. Hu, C. Wilson, Z. Li, Y. Chen, and B. Y. Zhao. Detecting and characterizing social spam campaigns. In *SIGCOMM*. ACM, 2010.

[6] S. Garera, N. Provos, M. Chew, and A. D. Rubin. A framework for detection and measurement of phishing attacks. In *WORM '07*, 2007.

[7] Google. Google's internet identity research. https://sites.google.com/site/oauthgoog/gnubby.

[8] Google. Login challenge for suspicious sign-ins. https://support.google.com/a/answer/6002699?hl=en.

[9] Google. Transparency report: Safe browsing. http://www.google.com/transparencyreport/safebrowsing/?hl=en.

[10] C. Grier, K. Thomas, V. Paxson, and M. Zhang. @spam: The Underground on 140 Characters or Less. In *Proceedings of the ACM Conference on Computer and Communications Security (CCS)*, 2010.

[11] M. Hearn. An update on our war against account hijackers. http://bit.ly/1qfMckD, 2013.

[12] IOActive. Reversal and analysis of zeus and spyeye banking trojans. http://www.ioactive.com/pdfs/ZeusSpyEyeBankingTrojanAnalysis.pdf.

[13] T. Jagatic, N. Johnson, M. Jakobsson, and F. Menczer. Social phishing. *Communications of the ACM*, 50(10):94–100, 2007.

[14] C. Kanich, C. Kreibich, K. Levchenko, B. Enright, G. Voelker, V. Paxson, and S. Savage. Spamalytics: An empirical analysis of spam marketing conversion. *Proceedings of the 15th ACM conference on Computer and communications security*, pages 3–14, 2008.

[15] J. Leyden. Typo-squatting domains can harvest corporate emails. http://bit.ly/1o8dx6d, 2011.

[16] C. Ludl, S. McAllister, E. Kirda, C. Kruegel, and C. Kruegel. On the effectiveness of techniques to detect phishing sites. In *DIMVA '07: Proceedings of the 4th International Conference on Detection of Intrusions, Malware, and Vulnerability Assessment*, pages 20–39, 2007.

[17] S. Maggi, A. Volpatto, S. Gasparini, G. Boracchi, and S. Zanero. Poster: Fast, automatic iphone shoulder surfing. In *Proceedings of the 18th ACM conference on Computer and communications security*, pages 805–808. ACM, 2011.

[18] T. Moore and R. Clayton. Examining the impact of website take-down on phishing. In *Proceedings of the anti-phishing working groups 2nd annual eCrime researchers summit*, pages 1–13. ACM, 2007.

[19] T. Moore and R. Clayton. Discovering phishing dropboxes using email metadata. In *eCrime Researchers Summit (eCrime), 2012*, pages 1–9. IEEE, 2012.

[20] R. Naraine. Zdnet security blog: 'state-sponsored attackers' using ie zero-day to hijack gmail accounts, Jun. 2012.

[21] S. Schechter, A. B. Brush, and S. Egelman. It's no secret. measuring the security and reliability of authentication via "secret" questions. In *Security and Privacy*, pages 375–390. IEEE, 2009.

[22] R. Shay, I. Ion, R. W. Reeder, and S. Consolvo. "my religious aunt asked why i was trying to sell her viagra": Experiences with account hijacking. In *CHI*, 2014.

[23] Symantec. Industrial espionage: Targeted attacks and advanced persistent threats (apts). http://bit.ly/RsGkV7.

[24] K. Thomas, F. Li, C. Grier, and V. Paxson. Consequences of connectivity: Characterizing account hijacking on twitter. In *Proceedings of the 21st Annual Conference on Computer and Communications Security*, 2014.

[25] T. N. Web. Microsoft can recycle your outlook.com email address if your account becomes inactive. http://tnw.co/1sWsNAU, 2013.

[26] C. Whittaker, B. Ryner, M. Nazif, and M. Nazif. Large-scale automatic classification of phishing pages. In *NDSS*, 2010.

[27] Y. Zhang, S. Egelman, L. Cranor, J. Hong, and J. Hong. Phinding phish: Evaluating anti-phishing tools. In *NDSS*, 2007.

[28] Embassy of the Unites States warning on West African advanced fee scams, http://abidjan.usembassy.gov/art_of_scam.html.

Search + Seizure: The Effectiveness of Interventions on SEO Campaigns

David Y. Wang Matthew Der Mohammad Karami[†]
Lawrence Saul Damon McCoy[†] Stefan Savage Geoffrey M. Voelker

University of California, San Diego George Mason University[†]

Abstract

Black hat search engine optimization (SEO), the practice of abusively manipulating search results, is an enticing method to acquire targeted user traffic. In turn, a range of interventions—from modifying search results to seizing domains—are used to combat this activity. In this paper, we examine the effectiveness of these interventions in the context of an understudied market niche, *counterfeit luxury goods*. Using eight months of empirical crawled data, we identify 52 distinct SEO campaigns, document how well they are able to place search results for sixteen luxury brands, how this capability impacts the dynamics of their order volumes and how well existing interventions undermine this business when employed.

1. INTRODUCTION

Every new communications medium inevitably engenders a new form of abuse — telephones led to unsolicited "robocalls", email begat spam, and so on. In turn, new mechanisms and policies are invariably brought to bear to restrict such activities (e.g., spam filters or, in the U.S., the national do-not-call registry). Today, one of the most dynamic such conflicts is playing out in the medium of online search.

In particular, as online marketing has become the leading mechanism by which sellers of goods and services engage potential consumers online, search engines, such as Google and Bing, have become the primary platform of this engagement. Because search engine results are presented directly in response to user queries, they offer the opportunity to precisely target consumers at the moment of their interest. As a testament to this, search engines received over $16B in revenue in 2012 (46% of the total online advertising expenditures) for clicks on sponsored advertisements appearing in their search engine result pages (SERPs) [29].

However, while criminal use of sponsored advertisements occurs, the more fertile ground for abuse is the so-called "organic" search results, which are unpaid. These results are generated and ranked automatically based on the content and structure of the visible Web (e.g., based on the PageRank algorithm, the presence of user-generated content, etc.) and produce far more click traffic than sponsored ads. Unsurprisingly, techniques for improving the ranking of particular Web sites in these organic search results — termed search engine optimization (SEO) — are extremely popular. While some SEO techniques are completely benign (e.g., keyword friendly URLs), quite a few are actively abusive (e.g., the use of compromised Web sites as "doorway" pages, "cloaking", farms of "back links", etc.). As a result, such "black hat" SEO campaigns are frequently able to poison search results so that one or more highly-ranked results for key search terms will direct traffic to their sites. This traffic can then be monetized by infecting the user with malware [11, 14, 30], defrauding the user via phishing [38], or through the marketing of counterfeit or illegal goods (e.g., pharmaceuticals [25]).

In this paper, we focus on a range of such SEO campaigns that are the principal means of marketing for organizations selling counterfeit luxury and lifestyle fashion goods. To wit, at the time of this writing, typing "cheap louis vuitton" into Google produces a list of ten results. Fully seven of these are fraudulent and ultimately direct user clicks to storefronts selling counterfeit knockoffs of Luis Vuitton products. This is no exception and similar search result poisoning is evident for a range of luxury brand names. Indeed, the combination of both high demand and high margins (a counterfeit of a handbag that might retail for $2400 will sell for $250, but will typically cost as little as $20 to produce) make this a vibrant and profitable scam; we have evidence that a *single* fulfillment organization delivered over 250,000 such items over a nine-month period. However, such actors are not unopposed and there are a range of interventions they must contend with including labeling and deranking of their sites by search engine operators, and site or domain takedowns driven by brand holders. It is understanding the interplay of SEO campaigns and these interventions that motivates our research.

Concretely, our paper makes three contributions. First, we provide the first large-scale empirical characterization of SEO abuse for luxury brands. In particular, we explain how such scams work (identifying how they differ from existing markets technically and operationally), analyze their search placement success over time and, using the prior "purchase pair" technique [16], gather indicators of order flow volumes. Second, we develop a methodology for using this data to evaluate the impact of interventions on the effectiveness of these SEO campaigns. Finally, we apply our methodology to a range of existing anti-counterfeiting actions, identify why these prior efforts have had limited impact and make suggestions for improving their utility in the future.

The remainder of the paper is structured as follows. We begin by describing the background of search engine optimization and prior research in Section 2. In Section 3, we describe the technical details of how SEO campaigns are structured in the counterfeit luxury market as well as how current interventions by search engines and brand holders operate and the rationale behind them. Section 4 describes our data set and data collection methodology. Finally,

IMC'14, November 5–7, 2014, Vancouver, BC, Canada.

http://dx.doi.org/10.1145/2663716.2663738.

in Section 5 we present our findings and their implications, while summarizing the most significant in the conclusion.

2. BACKGROUND

The term search engine optimization (SEO) covers a broad array of techniques, all designed to improve the ranking of organic search results in popular search engines. Given that the goal of search engines is to provide high-quality results, only the subset of these techniques that explicitly aid in search quality are viewed as benign by search companies. For example, in their "Search Engine Optimization Starter Guide", Google suggests things such as using accurate page titles and the use of the "description" meta tag, which Google's ranking algorithms view positively [8]. However, these benign techniques do not change the underlying Web link structure, and are insufficient to produce the large-scale changes in rankings required to capture significant traffic for popular queries.

Thus, "black hat" SEO campaigns will typically orchestrate thousands of Web sites operating in unison to achieve their goals. Each site will present the targeted keywords when visited by a search engine crawler.[1] However, when a visitor arrives at such a site via a targeted search, entirely different content will be revealed (this is one case of a general technique called "cloaking"). This content may be native to the site, may be proxied from a third site or, most commonly, will arise from a redirection to the true site being advertised. The popularity of this third approach is why such sites are commonly called "doorways" in the SEO vernacular. Doorways in turn obtain high-ranking either by mimicking the structure of high reputation sites (typically by creating backlinks to each other) or by compromising existing sites and exploiting the positive reputation that they have accrued with the search engine.

Poisoned search results (PSRs), or search results promoted by an attacker using black hat SEO with the intent of surreptitiously amassing user traffic, have been studied for a decade, with one of the best-known early empirical analyses due to Wang et al. [37]. More modern analyses have covered advances in detecting cloaking and poisoning techniques [19, 22, 27, 35] as well as deeper studies of the particular campaigns and their operational behavior [15, 36]. These efforts, which identify a range of technical behaviors implicated in abusive SEO, serve as the foundation for our own measurement work. However, our goals differ considerably from previous work as we are focused on understanding the overall business enterprise and through this lens evaluate the efficacy of existing interventions. In this, our work is similar to prior efforts to understand particular underground economies [16, 17, 18, 25, 34] and the economic issues surrounding various defenses and interventions [3, 12, 20, 21, 24, 26].

However, the ecosystem around luxury SEO abuse is quite distinct from these others and, as we will show, there are large differences in the underlying techniques, business structure, stakeholders and the kinds of interventions being practiced. Thus, we believe that our findings both serve to advance our understanding of how to best address search abuse, but also to expand our broader understanding about the interplay between technical countermeasures and the structure of online criminal enterprises.

3. LUXURY SEO AND INTERVENTIONS

Abusive SEO campaigns, by definition, can victimize two groups, users and search engine providers. The former because they may be convinced to purchase goods or services that are of low quality or illegal, the latter because their ability to provide high quality search results is imperiled. However, within the niche of counterfeit luxury goods another potential victim is the luxury brands themselves (both in terms of lost potential sales and brand damage). Consequently, in addition to interventions from search engines (driven by general concerns about search quality), brands also drive interventions to protect their economic interests. In this section we discuss what makes this market distinct, both in terms of how counterfeit luxury SEO campaign are structured and the kinds of interventions used in response.

3.1 SEO Campaigns

The SEO campaigns funded by the counterfeit luxury goods market operate similarly to other SEO campaigns (see [36] for one such example), with a couple of noteworthy differences. First, they introduce distinct cloaking and evasion techniques designed to undermine existing defenses. Second, the businesses that ultimately fund these campaigns appear to be organized differently than the open affiliate marketing programs that have been endemic in prior studies of underground economics (e.g., counterfeit pharmaceuticals [25], software [24] or FakeAV [34]). We discuss each of these in turn.

3.1.1 Cloaking

At its essence, cloaking refers to any mechanism for delivering different content to different user segments. For the purposes of SEO, cloaking's primary objective is to deceive search engines by providing different content to the search engine crawler than to users clicking on search results. For example, the most widely-used cloaking technique, called *redirect cloaking*, arranges that search engine crawlers (e.g., Googlebot) receive content crafted to rank well for targeted query terms, while normal users who access the site are instead redirected to another site hosting a particular scam (e.g., a storefront selling counterfeit goods). In some cases, particularly when the doorway is on a compromised site, a visitor will only be redirected after arriving via a search results page. Otherwise, the original legitimate site content is returned, enabling compromised sites to remain compromised longer by appearing unchanged to normal visitors.

However, cloaking is a violation of most search engine's content guidelines and, when such activity is discovered, the cloaked sites are typically deranked automatically in search results. As with any adversarial process, though, attackers adapt to new defenses. In contrast to cloaking techniques we have previously observed [35, 36], we have identified a new method of cloaking, which we call *iframe cloaking*, which bypasses traditional means of detection. In particular, iframe cloaking does not redirect the user and frequently returns the same content to both search engines and users.[2] Instead of redirecting a user to a landing store site, the store is simply loaded within an iframe element on top of the existing doorway page content. Typically the iframe visually occupies the entire height and width of the browser to provide the illusion that the user is browsing the store (Figure 1 shows a simple example of iframe cloaking using JavaScript). The JavaScript implementation is frequently obfuscated to further complicate analysis and in some cases the iframe itself is dynamically generated. Taken together, these countermeasures require any detection mechanism to run a com-

[1]This is commonly done using the User-Agent string which self-identifies popular crawlers, but some SEO kits also include IP address ranges they have associated with the major search engines.

[2]A complementary feature of iframe cloaking is that it reduces the requirements for cloaking on compromised sites. Traditional cloaking uses network features (e.g., IP address or user agent) to identify crawlers, requiring specialized server side code. In contrast iframe cloaking runs entirely on the client, relying on the assumption that crawlers do not fully render pages at scale.

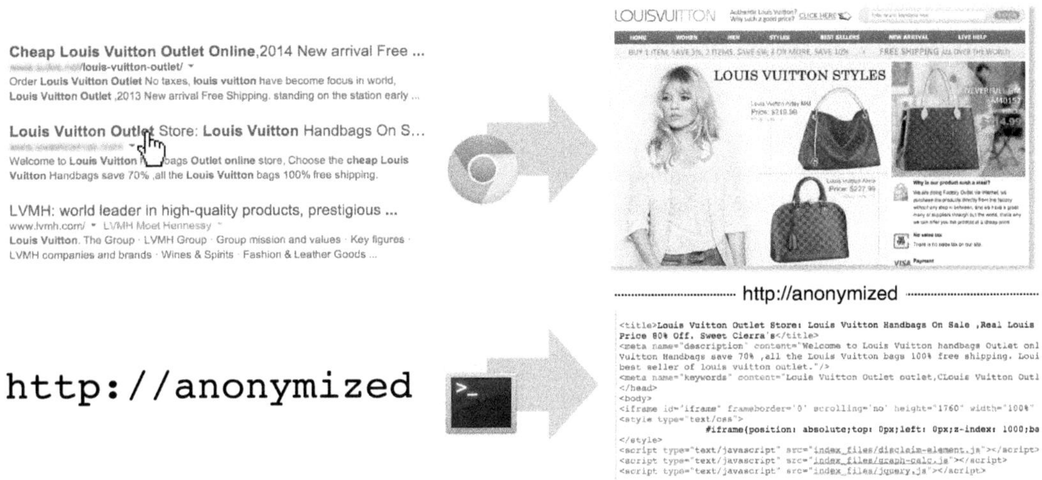

Figure 1: An example of iframe cloaking where the same URL returns different content for different visitor types. Above, a user clicks through a search result and loads a counterfeit Louis Vuitton store. While, below, a search engine crawler visits the same URL directly, receiving a keyword-stuffed page because the crawler does not render the page. Our crawlers mimic both types of visits.

plete browser that evaluates JavaScript and fully renders a page (a set of requirements that greatly increase the overhead of detection at scale).[3] We found the use of iframe cloaking to be pervasive within the domain of counterfeit luxury, but a more comprehensive study of the use of iframe cloaking for other domains remains an open question.

3.1.2 Business structure

Traditionally, a broad range of online scams have been organized around an affiliate marketing model in which an affiliate program is responsible for creating site content, payment processing and fulfillment, while individual affiliates are responsible for delivering the user to storefronts (e.g., via email spam, SEO, etc.). Core to this business model is the notion that affiliates are independent contractors agents paid on a commission basis, and thus affiliate programs work to attract a diverse set of affiliates. This model is commonly used today in a broad range of scams with a nexus in Eastern Europe and Russia including pharmaceuticals, pirated software, books, music and movies, herbal supplements, e-cigarettes, term paper writing, fake anti-virus and so on [32].

However, there are many indications (albeit anecdotal) that the structure of organizations in the counterfeit luxury market are distinct.[4] First, the marketing portion of these scams can span both an array of brands and types of merchandise. For example, from infiltrating their command and control (C&C) infrastructure using the same approach as described in previous work [36], we find a single SEO campaign may shill for over ninety distinct storefronts selling thirty distinct brands ranging from apparel (Abercrombie), luxury handbags (Louis Vuitton), and electronics (Beats By Dre). Moreover, the same campaign will commonly host localized sites catering to international markets (e.g., United Kingdom, Germany, Japan, and so forth). Unlike other kinds of counterfeit sales, which centralize payment processing within the affiliate program [16, 25, 34], we find each counterfeit luxury storefront allocates order numbers independently and engages directly with payment processors (merchant identifiers exposed directly in the HTML source on storefront pages allowed us to confirm). Finally, in the traditional affiliate program model, fulfillment is managed internally by the program, but in our investigations we have found at least one fulfillment site for luxury goods that appears to be designed to support outside sales on an *á la carte* basis (i.e., the site is designed to support wholesale ordering and allows each member to track the order status of their customer's shipments). Overall, we suspect the counterfeit luxury ecosystem does not use an affiliate program and instead the ecosystem is composed of several independent advertisers (SEO campaigns) contracting with third parties for fulfillment and payment processing.

3.2 Interventions

As we have observed, the two groups with natural incentives to disrupt SEO campaigns targeting counterfeit luxury goods are search engine providers and luxury brand holders. Search engines maintain the value of their page views (and hence the pricing they can charge for advertising) by providing consistently high quality search results for their users. Thus, all major search engines have active anti-abuse teams that try to reduce the amount of search spam appearing in their results. When an SEO campaign is detected, search engines attempt to disrupt the campaign by either demoting their doorway pages in search results or even removing those pages from the search index entirely. Brand holders have a far less privileged technical position and they are neither able to analyze the Web at scale nor directly influence search results. However, as brand and trademark holders they have unique legal powers that allow them to target particular pieces of infrastructure from SEO campaigns. These two techniques, search and seizure, represent the de facto standard methods of intervention against SEO campaigns, with pressure applied at different strata in the business model.

3.2.1 Search Engine

In addition to allowing the search ranking algorithm to demote doorways performing black hat SEO, search engines commonly

[3]Even after rendering a page, the ubiquity of iframes in online advertising make distinguishing benign from malicious content a challenge.

[4]There is a range of evidence suggesting that the big counterfeit luxury organizations have a nexus in Asia, unlike the Eastern European origin of many other scams. Our evidence includes the use of Asian language comments in SEO kit source code, the choice of Asian payment processors, fulfillment and order tracking from Asia and direct experience interviewing an Asian programmer working for one of these organizations. We surmise that a distinct cybercrime ecosystem has evolved separately in East Asia with its own standard practices and behaviors.

have special handling for certain classes of malicious content. For example, starting in 2008, Google's Safe Browsing service (GSB) has detected and blacklisted sites leading to malware or phishing sites with the aim of preventing users from being defrauded through search. GSB labels search results leading to malware or phishing pages as *malicious*, appends the subtitle "This site may harm your computer" to the result, and prevents the user from visiting the site directly by loading an interstitial page rather than the page linked to by the result.

In 2010, Google instituted a similar effort to detect compromised Web sites and label them as *hacked* by similarly appending the subtitle "This site may be hacked" in the result [9]. The motivation is to curb the ability of compromised sites to reach unsuspecting users, while simultaneously creating an incentive for innocent site owners to discover their site has been compromised and clean it. In principle, this notification could undermine black hat SEO since users may be wary to click on links with a warning label.

However, there are important differences between these two seemingly similar efforts, which more likely reflect policy decisions rather than technical limitations. First, contrary to malicious search results, users can still click through hacked search results without an interstitial page. Second, typically only the root of a site is labeled as hacked; e.g., while `http://anonymized` may be labeled as a hacked site, `http://anonymized/customize.php` will not. Unfortunately, often only the non-root search results are compromised and redirect users, while the root search result is clean. In Section 5.2 we examine the implications and limitations of these policy decisions on search interventions against SEO campaigns.

3.2.2 Seizure

As the name suggests, seizures reflect the use of a legal process to obtain control of an infringing site (typically by seizing their domain name, but occasionally by seizing control of servers themselves) and either shut it down or, more commonly, replace it with a seizure notification page. In the context of counterfeit luxury, seizures prevent users from visiting seized domains, thereby hindering the store's ability to monetize traffic. Although we have witnessed brand holders performing seizures directly, typically they contract with third party legal counsel or with companies who specialize in brand protection, such as MarkMonitor [23], OpSec Security [28] and Safenames [31], to police their brand.

However, there are significant asymmetries in this approach. For example, a new domain can be purchased for a few dollars, but the cost to serve a legal process to seize it can cost 50–100 times more. Similarly, while a new domain name can be allocated within a few minutes and effectively SEO'ed in 24 hours [36], a seizure first requires finding the site, filing a legal claim and then waiting (from days to weeks) for the docket to be picked up by the federal judge to whom the case has been assigned. Presumably to amortize these costs, a manual review of court documents shows that domain name seizures commonly occur in bulk (hundreds or thousands at a time) and are not performed on a reactive basis. Finally, it is worth noting that doorway sites based on compromised Web servers present their own challenges since seizing the domain of an innocent third party can carry liability. Thus, while brands sometimes seize doorway pages, it is more common for them to target the storefront advertised. Section 5.3 explores these asymmetries in greater depth.

4. DATA SETS

The basis of our study relies upon extensive crawls of Google search results to discover poisoned search results that lead to counterfeit storefront sites. We then use a combination of manual labeling and supervised learning to map storefront sites into the different SEO campaigns that promote them. On a subset of storefront sites, we also use a combination of test orders and actual purchases to reveal information about customer order volume and payment processing. Finally, we crawl the site of a supplier to provide insight into the scale of order fulfillment and high-level customer demographics. This section describes each of these efforts in detail.

Vertical	# PSRs	# Doorways	# Stores	# Campaigns
Abercrombie	117,319	2,059	786	35
Adidas	102,694	1,275	462	22
Beats by Dre	342,674	2,425	506	16
Clarisonic	10,726	243	148	6
Ed Hardy*	99,167	1,828	648	31
Golf	11,257	679	318	20
Isabel Marant	153,927	2,356	1,150	35
Louis Vuitton*	523,368	5,462	1,246	34
Moncler	454,671	3,566	912	38
Nike	180,953	3,521	1,141	32
Ralph Lauren	74,893	1,276	648	27
Sunglasses	93,928	3,585	1,269	34
Tiffany	37,054	1,015	432	22
Uggs*	405,518	4,966	1,015	39
Watches	109,016	3,615	1,470	35
Woolrich	55,879	1,924	888	38
Total	2,773,044	27,008	7,484	52

Table 1: A breakdown of the verticals monitored highlighting the number of poisoned search results, doorways, stores, and campaigns identified throughout the course of the study. Note that the KEY campaign targeted all verticals except those with an '*'.

4.1 Google Search Results

Our primary data set comes from daily crawls of Google search results using a system that we previously developed for detecting search cloaking [35]. Each day we issue queries to Google using search terms targeted by counterfeit sites, crawl the sites listed in the search results, and identify sites using cloaking as depicted in Figure 1. We repeat this process for five months from November 13, 2013 through July 15, 2014.

In the rest of this section we define the notion of counterfeit luxury *verticals* for organizing search queries, and describe our methodology for selecting the search terms that comprise the verticals, the implementation of our crawlers and the information they collect, and our heuristics for detecting counterfeit stores in poisoned search results.

Note that we search exclusively using Google for a couple of reasons. In prior work we found that Google is the most heavily targeted search engine by attackers performing search poisoning and black hat SEO [35]. Furthermore, Google is the leading search engine for the United States and many European countries, the preeminent markets receiving counterfeit products (based on shipping data from a large supplier as discussed in Section 4.5).

4.1.1 Search Terms

Any work measuring search results is biased towards the search terms selected because the selected terms represent just a subset of the entire search index. In our study, we monitor search results for counterfeit luxury *verticals*, a set of search terms centered around a single brand (e.g., Ralph Lauren) or a category composite of several brands (e.g., Sunglasses is a composite of Oakley, Ray-Ban, Christian Dior, etc.). For our study, each vertical consists of a static set of 100 representative terms that we determined were targeted by SEO campaigns.

Due to the early prominence of the KEY campaign, a large SEO botnet responsible for most of the PSRs manually observed in September 2013, we initially compiled terms for each of the 13 verticals it targeted as listed in Table 1. Similarly, we followed the KEY campaign's approach in determining whether to center a verticals' terms around a single brand or a composite. To select these terms we extracted keywords from the URLs of the doorway pages of the KEY campaign. For a given vertical, we manually queried Google to find ten KEY doorways redirecting to the same store selling counterfeit merchandise (related to the vertical). Then we issued site queries (e.g., "site:doorway.com") for each doorway to collect all search results originating from the doorway. And for each search result we extracted search terms from the URL path (e.g., "cheap beats by dre" from `http://doorway.com/?key=cheap+beats+by+dre`) to assemble a large collection of terms. We then randomly selected 100 unique terms as a representative set for each vertical.

To extend the scope of our study to other campaigns, we included three additional verticals that we saw counterfeiters targeting: Ed Hardy, Louis Vuitton, and Uggs. Since the KEY campaign does not target these brands, we adopted a different approach in selecting search terms by using Google Suggest, a keyword autocomplete service. We first fetched suggestions for a targeted brand (e.g., "Louis Vuitton wallet"). Then we recursively fetched suggestions for the suggestions. In addition, we fetched suggestions for the concatenation of a commonly used adjective (e.g., cheap, new, online, outlet, sale or store) and the brand name to form search strings (e.g., "cheap Louis Vuitton"). From the combined set of these various search strings, we randomly selected 100 unique strings as our search set for each vertical.

To evaluate any bias introduced from these two different approaches, we take the ten original KEY verticals that are not composites, generate alternate search terms using the Google Suggest approach, and run the crawlers using those alternate terms for one day on April 25, 2014. Among the ten verticals, we find four out of a thousand total terms overlap. Additionally, when comparing the percentange of PSRs detected after crawling, for both classified and unknown, and the distribution of PSRs associated to specific campaigns, we find no significant difference between results from the original and alternate terms over the same time range. Despite using two different approaches for selecting search terms, in the end we find the same campaigns poisoning search results. This overlap highlights both the pervasiveness of these campaigns and the representativeness of terms selected in spite of the KEY campaign's early influence on our methodology.

4.1.2 Crawling Search Results

For each search term, we query Google daily for the top 100 search results. For each search result, we crawl each page link using an updated version of the Dagger cloaking detection system from previous work [35]. Dagger uses heuristics to detect cloaking by examining semantic differences between versions of the same page fetched first as a user and then as a search engine crawler (distinguished by the User-Agent field in the HTTP request).

A previous limitation of Dagger was that it did not render the page and, as a consequence, did not follow JavaScript (JS) redirects. Thus, we extended Dagger by rendering each cloaked search result detected using HtmlUnit [13], essentially a headless browser complete with a JavaScript interpreter. (Since rendering a page is an expensive operation, we only render pages we detect as cloaked.)

To detect iframe cloaking (Section 3.1.1), we implemented a second crawler, VanGogh. VanGogh also uses HtmlUnit to render pages. To detect iframe cloaking, it identifies any iframes attempting to occupy the entire page visually (hiding the original content). Specifically, we classify pages as using iframe cloaking if they load iframes where the height and width attributes are both either set to 100% or larger than 800 pixels.

And again, due to the high overhead of rendering pages, we only crawl a subset of search results using VanGogh. In particular, for each measurement we crawl at most three randomly selected pages from the same doorway domain to reduce the crawling workload. We further trim the workload by not crawling domains previously seen and not detected as poisoned by either VanGogh or Dagger. This approach has proved reasonable due to the low daily churn in search results for each vertical (on average 1.84% newly seen domains are found in search results each day).

4.1.3 Store Detection

Ultimately we want to identify counterfeit luxury storefronts advertised through PSRs. We detect stores by applying two heuristics to the set of PSRs discovered from crawling. First, we inspect cookies from each landing site (the page eventually loaded in a user's browser after redirection through the doorway page) to look for cookies commonly used by counterfeit luxury storefronts such as those related to payment processing (e.g., Realypay, Mallpayment), e-commerce (e.g., Zen Cart, Magento), and Web analytics (e.g., Ajstat, CNZZ). Second, we search for either of the substrings "cart" or "checkout" on the landing pages. If either of the heuristics succeed, we treat the landing site as a counterfeit luxury store advertised through search poisoning. Note that this approach identifies stores from the search results within a vertical irrespective of brand. For example, we may identify a counterfeit Christian Louboutin store within Louis Vuitton search results.

We validate our detection methodology by manually inspecting sampled search results from three popular verticals, Beats By Dre, Isabel, and Louis Vuitton. For each vertical, we randomly chose three search terms, and compared the search results for those terms from two measurements taken at least two months apart (e.g., one from November 23, 2013 and one from February 24, 2014). In total we examined 1.8K search results and detected 532 storefronts advertised using cloaked search results. Among these we found no false positives (instances where a benign page is mistakenly labeled as a doorway to a storefront) and 21 (1.2%) false negatives (instances where a doorway to a storefront is not labeled). These results are reassuring because errors are likely skewed towards underrepresenting the number of storefronts.

4.2 Campaign Identification

Our targeted crawls of Google search results produce a large collection of doorway pages and counterfeit storefronts. We know that behind these thousands of doorways and storefronts lurk a much smaller number of distinct SEO campaigns, and the goal of our work is to understand the full ecosystem of campaigns operating in this counterfeit luxury market rather than focus on a singular campaign, e.g., the KEY campaign.

A brute-force approach to this understanding would require a domain expert to examine each Web page in our collection and use domain-specific heuristics to infer the SEO campaign behind it. The manual labeling of Web pages, however, is a time-consuming and laborious endeavor that does not scale well to the many thousands of examples in our collection. Instead we take a statistical approach, and the rest of this section describes an automated, data-driven method to identify the SEO campaigns behind individual doorway and storefront Web pages.

To build a statistical model, we need a data set of *labeled examples*. Though manual labeling is tedious, we created such a data set by identifying the SEO campaigns behind a small subset of 491

Web pages in our much larger collection of crawled results. From this small data set, we learned a classifier that mapped the remaining thousands of doorway and storefront Web pages to the 52 SEO campaigns for which we had manually labeled examples. The results of this analysis (discussed in later sections) provide a comprehensive understanding of the ecosystem of SEO campaigns in the counterfeit luxury market.

Our classifier makes its predictions by extracting textual features of HTML content and analyzing the statistics of these features that distinguish Web pages from different campaigns. The following subsections describe the classifier in more detail, focusing in particular on the individual stages of feature extraction, model estimation, and model validation.

4.2.1 Feature Extraction

The premise of our statistical approach is that doorway and storefront Web pages contain predictive signatures of the SEO campaigns behind them. Motivated by previous work [2], we looked for these signatures in their HTML source. We expect HTML-based features to be predictive in this domain for two reasons: first, because SEO campaigns use highly specialized strategies to manipulate the search rankings of doorways [36], and second, because campaigns often develop in-house templates for the large-scale deployment of online storefronts (e.g., customized templates for Zen Cart or Magento providing a certain look and feel).

To extract HTML features, we follow a conventional "bag-of-words" approach. In particular, we construct a dictionary of all terms that appear in the HTML source code, and for each Web page, we count the number of times that each term appears. In this way, each Web page is represented as a sparse, high-dimensional vector of feature counts. We implemented a custom bag-of-words feature extractor based on tag-attribute-value triplets [5] for the Web pages in our data set.

One might also expect to find predictive signatures of SEO campaigns in network-based features (e.g., IPv4 address blocks, ASes). However, we found that such features were ill-suited to differentiate SEO campaigns due to the growing popularity of shared hosting and reverse proxying infrastructure (e.g., CloudFlare). Therefore, after a brief period of experimentation, we did not pursue the use of such features.

4.2.2 Model Estimation

We learned linear models of classification from our data set of labeled examples. Specifically, we used the LIBLINEAR package [7] to learn L1-regularized models of logistic regression. The L1-regularization encourages sparse linear models in which the predictions of SEO campaigns are derived from only a handful of HTML features. Thus the resulting models are highly interpretable: for each campaign, the regularization serves to identify the most strongly characteristic HTML features from the tens of thousands of extracted ones.

We evaluated the predictive accuracy of the classifier by performing 10-fold cross-validation on the data set of labeled examples. The average accuracy on held-out data was 86.8% for multi-way classification of Web pages into 52 different SEO campaigns. (Note that uniformly random predictions would have an accuracy of 1/52 = 1.9%.) Our model's high accuracy on held-on examples gave us confidence to classify the remaining (unlabeled) Web pages that we collected from poisoned search results.

4.2.3 Model Validation and Refinement

We used the above models, trained on a small subset of labeled Web pages, to infer the SEO campaigns behind the remaining unlabeled Web pages. To do so, we extracted HTML features from the unlabeled Web pages and used the classifiers to predict the most likely campaign behind each example. To validate these predictions, we manually inspected additional subsets of unlabeled examples. This step can be done efficiently by first validating the top-ranked predictions for each SEO campaign (as reflected by the probabilities that the logistic regressions attach to each prediction).

We briefly describe how we validated the classifier's predictions on unlabeled Web pages. Primarily we assume that distinct SEO campaigns are unlikely to share certain infrastructure such as SEO doorway pages and C&Cs, payment processing, and customer support. We also consider less robust indicators such as unique templates, WHOIS registrant, image hosting, and Web traffic analytics (e.g., `51.la`, `cnzz.com`, `statcounter.com`, etc.).

A final stage is to refine the model, using the manually verified predictions to expand the set of labeled Web pages, retraining the classifier on this expanded set, and repeating this process in rounds. With each iteration of this process we obtain a more accurate classifier and also one with greater coverage of distinct SEO campaigns. Though some manual labeling is unavoidable, this overall approach (of repeated human-machine interaction) is far more efficient than a brute-force expert analysis.

4.3 Purchases

From previous work studying email spam advertising illicit pharmaceutical and software storefronts [16, 20], we found that making orders on sites can shed light on normally opaque facets of underground businesses: order volume, payment processing, and order fulfillment. This information serves two important roles. First, it reveals the interplay between the various actors in the counterfeit luxury ecosystem (SEO campaigns, payment processors, and suppliers). Second, the estimated order volume serves as a vital metric in measuring the effectiveness of interventions (e.g., does labeling doorway search results as "hacked" lead to lower campaign order volume?). Similar to this prior work, we created test orders on counterfeit stores to estimate their order volume over time, and made actual purchases to reveal the payment processors used by these storefronts and the quality of the merchandise they sell.

4.3.1 Order Volume

We use the "purchase pair" technique [16] to estimate the order volume of individual stores over time. This technique exploits the fact that stores use monotonically increasing order numbers, where the difference between order numbers represents the total number of orders created over the time delta between orders.

Note that stores give users an order number before processing their credit cards, and users still have an opportunity to back out. Therefore this metric represents an upper bound on orders placed and overestimates the absolute number of orders at a given store. However, it is still useful to quantify the rate at which orders are created, as well as the changes in order rate over time when correlated with interventions.

Using this technique, we created 1,408 orders from 290 stores touching 24 distinct campaigns and 13 verticals, between November 29, 2013 and July 15, 2014. We created 343 orders by hand and 1,065 orders using scripts. Operationally, for both manual and automated orders, we visit each store using via TOR and create orders at weekly intervals, and we limit orders to three per day per campaign to reduce the chance of being detected by the store or payment processor. We take the orders all the way to the payment processing page, which requires credit card details, before finally leaving the site. The order and customer information we provide

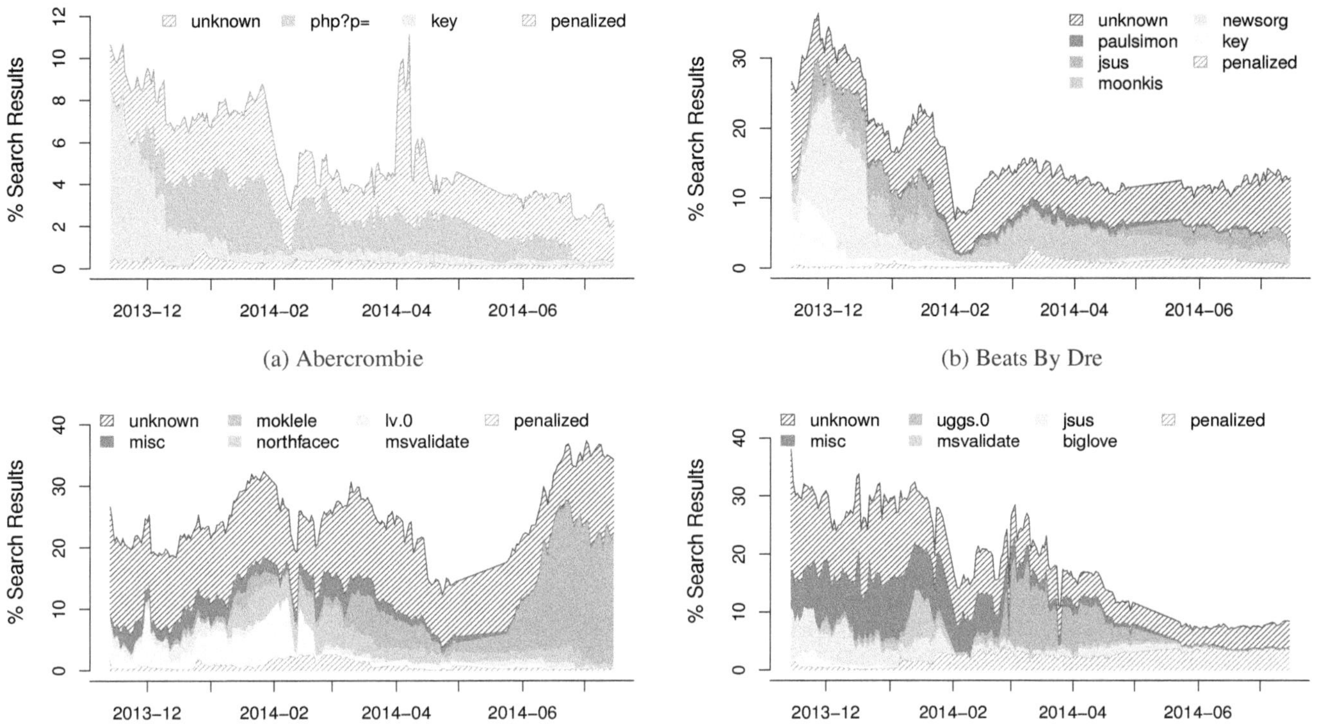

(a) Abercrombie

(b) Beats By Dre

(c) Louis Vuitton

(d) Uggs

Figure 2: Stacked area plots attributing PSRs to specific SEO campaigns within the labeled vertical. The red area represents the percentage penalized, either through search or seizure. The remainder of the areas represents active PSRs, where the filled areas are attributed to specific campaigns and the unfilled area is the remainder unclassified.

are semantically consistent with real customers, but fictional and automatically generated [6].

4.3.2 *Transactions*

To shed light on payment processing and order fulfillment in the counterfeit luxury ecosystem, we successfully placed product orders from 16 unique stores covering 12 different campaigns. In total, we received 12 knock offs of low to medium quality, all shipped from China. From the bank identification numbers (BINs) in our transactions, we found that our purchases were processed through three banks (two in China, one in Korea). This concentration suggests payment processing is another viable area for interventions as in [24], but investigating such an intervention remains future work.

4.4 User Traffic

As surveyed in Section 2 and described in depth in our previous study [36], SEO campaigns poison search results to acquire user traffic that can then be monetized through scams — in this case, counterfeit luxury stores. The order volume data shows that counterfeit luxury stores do successfully convert user traffic into sales, and indirectly measures an SEO campaign's effectiveness in attracting traffic via PSRs.

For a small number of stores, we were also able to collect user traffic data that directly measures an SEO campaign's effectiveness in attracting customers to their stores. Specifically, we were able to periodically collect AWStats data for 647 storefronts in 12 campaigns. AWStats is a Web analytics tool [1] that uses a Web site's server logs to report aggregated visitor information (e.g., the number of visitors, visitor durations, visitor geolocations, referrers of visitors, etc.). From our crawled data, we discovered that these stores left their AWStats pages publicly accessible, and we were able to fetch visitor data for each store by visiting the publicly accessible default AWStats URL (e.g., `http://<site>/awstats/awstats.pl?config=<site>`).

4.5 Supply Side Shipments

To better understand the suppliers, customers, and operational relationship among storefronts and suppliers, we collected longitudinal shipment data from a supplier partnering with MSVALIDATE, one of largest SEO campaigns peddling counterfeit Louis Vuitton.

We discovered the supplier site from the packing slip of two of our purchases. Upon visiting the site, we noticed it contains a scrolling list of fulfilled orders and a mechanism to lookup shipping records for valid order numbers in bulk (20 orders at a time). Each record contains a timestamp and information regarding current location and delivery status.

Using this mechanism, we collected over 279K shipping records for nine months of orders placed through the supplier between July 5, 2013 and March 28, 2014. In summary, 256K orders successfully reached their destination, 4K were seized at the source (China), 15K were seized at the destination, and of the delivered, 1,319 were returned by the customer. From country data listed in the records, the three largest destinations are the United States, Japan, and Australia, with 90k, 57K, and 39K orders, respectively. If we combine these with the countries from Western Europe (41K), these regions account for over 81% of orders.

5. RESULTS

In this section we use our crawler data to characterize the activities of SEO campaigns that use search to promote stores selling counterfeit luxury goods, and we further use our order data to study the effects of both search engine and domain seizure interventions on these SEO activities. In short, we find instances where both can have the desired effect of disrupting counterfeit sites, but they need to be far more reactive in time and comprehensive in coverage to undermine the entire ecosystem of SEO campaigns exploiting search engines for customers.

5.1 Ecosystem

We start with classifying poisoned search results into campaigns, how those campaigns target verticals, and what the PSRs reveal about the operations of the campaigns.

In terms of raw data, we crawled search results for eight months from November 13, 2013 through July 15, 2014 and detected 2.7M PSRs, across all verticals, using 27K doorways from unique domains and sending users to 7,404 different stores selling counterfeit luxury merchandise. Applying the classifier described in Section 4.2 to this data, we identified 52 distinct SEO campaigns that account for 828 stores, 11K doorway domains, and 1.6M PSRs. Table 2 lists the campaigns using a name we derived from a pattern in their URLs, the domain names used for their C&C, or some other telltale aspect of their operation. For each campaign, the table lists the number of doorway domains, storefronts, and brands targeted. Note that, although we ascribed more than half (58%) of all PSRs to their respective campaigns, these PSRs only account for 11% of all stores. This disparity suggests that the ecosystem has a skewed distribution where a handful of large campaigns account for the majority share of PSRs that redirect users to a concentrated set of storefronts.

From the perspective of brands, we attributed 16% to 69% of PSRs in each vertical to known campaigns. Figure 2 visualizes our classification results for four verticals: Abercrombie (64.2% of PSRs classified to campaigns), Beats By Dre (62.2%), Louis Vuitton (66%), and Uggs (58%). We chose these verticals for their diversity in merchandise, campaigns, and search term selection methodology. For each vertical, the filled areas in the stacked area plots show the fraction of search results poisoned by the major campaigns targeting the vertical; note that the "misc" label collapses multiple campaigns into a single category to reduce clutter.

Each graph presents the PSRs detected, classified, and penalized over time at the granularity of a day. For example, in Figure 2b on December 1, 2013, 34.6% of search results for the Beats By Dre vertical were poisoned. Of these PSRs, 85.3% redirect users to counterfeit stores operated by five campaigns: KEY (16.8%), NEWSORG (53.8%), MOONKIS (5.8%), JSUS (8.0%), and PAULSIMON (0.3%). The remaining 14.7% PSRs redirect users to counterfeit stores we have yet to classify. The bottom shaded area shows that just 0.6% are penalized either through Google labeling the search result as "hacked" (Section 5.2.2) or a brand has seized the storefront domain name (Section 5.3).

5.1.1 *Verticals*

Figure 3 shows the percentage of search results that were poisoned for each vertical as pairs of sparklines. Each sparkline is a time series showing relative values over the five-month time span of the study at the granularity of days. The left number is the minimum value across time and the right is the maximum (also shown as dots on the line). Each column of lines shows the percentage of PSRs among top 10 search results (left) or top 100 (right). For example, in the Abercrombie vertical in the top left, at most 13% of the top 10 search results in the vertical were poisoned, while at least 2% were poisoned. The sparkline shows that the first three months were closer to the 13%, while the latter five months were much lower.

Figure 3: Percentage of search results poisoned for each brand vertical, shown as sparklines. Each sparkline is a daily time series showing relative values over five months. The left number is the minimum value across time and the right is the maximum (also shown as dots on the line).

Overall, heavily targeted verticals are particularly vulnerable to poisoned search results. In 13 out of 16 verticals, about 5% of search results are poisoned at some point in time. But for the five verticals most vulnerable to search poisoning, at different points in time 31–42% of the top 100 search results in those verticals were poisoned. Also, as expected, it is easier in general to poison search results from outside the top 10; Beats By Dre, for instance, had at most 23% of its top 10 results poisoned while at one point 37% of its top 100 results were poisoned.

Brands face multiple "adversaries". Whether targeted by many campaigns (14 and 17 for Louis Vuitton and Uggs, respectively) or just a few (three and six for Abercrombie and Beats By Dre), all verticals are targeted by multiple campaigns all competing to SEO their doorway pages into search results to lure customers for their counterfeit goods.

5.1.2 *SEO Campaigns*

SEO campaigns employ considerable infrastructure to maintain their businesses. As shown in Table 2, SEO campaigns use hundreds to thousands of doorway sites to redirect users to dozens of storefronts (similar in scale to other abusive SEO botnets [36]). Interestingly, we do not find a strong correlation between the num-

Campaign	# Doorways	# Stores	# Brands	Peak
171760	30	14	7	44
ADFLYID	100	18	4	66
BIGLOVE	767	92	30	92
BITLY	190	40	15	89
CAMPAIGN.02	26	4	3	61
CAMPAIGN.10	94	18	5	99
CAMPAIGN.12	118	5	1	59
CAMPAIGN.14	39	8	2	67
CAMPAIGN.15	364	10	10	8
CAMPAIGN.17	61	8	3	44
CHANEL.1	50	10	4	24
G2GMART	916	28	3	53
HACKEDLIVEZILLA	43	49	9	56
IFRAMEINJS	200	2	1	39
JAROKRAFKA	266	55	3	87
JSUS	439	59	27	68
KEY	1,980	97	28	65
LIVEZILLA	420	33	16	70
LV.0	42	3	1	62
LV.1	270	12	9	90
M10	581	35	8	30
MOKLELE	982	15	4	36
MOONKIS	95	7	4	99
MSVALIDATE	530	98	6	52
NEWSORG	926	7	5	24
NORTHFACEC	432	2	1	60
NYY	29	14	5	40
PAGERAND	122	7	4	43
PARTNER	62	9	5	33
PAULSIMON	328	33	12	128
PHP?P=	255	55	24	96
ROBERTPENNER	56	7	12	50
SCHEMA.ORG	46	17	7	54
SNOWFLASH	271	14	1	48
STYLESHEET	222	9	6	63
TIFFANY.0	26	1	1	4
UGGS.0	428	6	5	30
VERA	155	38	12	156

Table 2: Classified campaigns along with # doorways seen redirecting on behalf of a specific campaign, # stores monetizing traffic from the campaign, # brands whose trademarks are abused by the campaign, and # days of peak poisoning duration, for campaigns with 25+ doorways.

ber of doorways and the campaign's efficacy in poisoning search results. For example, as shown in Figure 2b, MOONKIS poisoned search results for Beats By Dre from the start of 2014 onwards with 95 doorways, while two larger campaigns, JSUS and NEWSORG, used 439 and 926 doorways, respectively, in the same time period.

The operators of the campaigns successfully SEO their doorways in concentrated time periods. Although we observe campaigns poisoning search results for multiple months, their SEO effectiveness varies over time as exemplified by the campaigns targeting Beats By Dre in Figure 2b. To capture this notion of bursty SEO behavior, we compute a "peak range" for each campaign defined as the shortest contiguous time span that includes 60% or more of all PSRs from the campaign. For example, NEWSORG's peak range lasts 24 days from November 23 to December 17, 2013, with a daily average of 1676 PSRs during this span. Table 2 summarizes the peak duration in terms of number of days for each campaign. Using this metric, we find campaigns run at their peak for 51.3 days on average.

The campaign operators also run a diversified business that gives them flexibility in the face of disruption. A single campaign, for example, will use its doorways to poison search results from multiple verticals simultaneously. For instance, the MSVALIDATE and BIGLOVE campaigns both successfully poison search results for Louis Vuitton (Figure 2c) and Uggs (Figure 2d). As a result, campaigns possess multiple revenue streams, giving them flexibility in the event a setback disrupts one revenue stream (e.g., domain seizures from one brand, problems with a supplier for Beats By Dre headphones, etc.). The campaign can adjust and continue monetizing traffic by simply reallocating resources towards stores selling counterfeit merchandise from other verticals.

Moreover, campaigns often operate multiple storefronts targeting the same vertical and selling the same merchandise. Sometimes the goal is to localize for a market, such as a Japanese Uggs storefront catering to Japanese consumers. More often, though, these redundant stores can serve as backups in the event of interventions, which we explore further in Section 5.3.

5.2 Search Engine Interventions

Since poisoned search results manipulate and degrade user experience, search engines have an incentive to identify and penalize PSRs used by the SEO campaigns that lead users to counterfeit sites. Two options available to search engines for reacting to PSRs are to demote them in search rank, and to add warning labels to search results to alert users before clicking through.

5.2.1 Search Result Demotion

Figure 4 shows the prevalence of poisoned search results for four SEO campaigns over time, and the corresponding order activity at storefront sites gleaned from creating test orders as described in Section 4.3.1. The bottom two rows of graphs show the number of PSRs per day for each SEO campaign: the lowest row focuses on PSRs in just the top 10 search results, and the row above focuses on the full top 100 search results. The dark portion of the bars at the bottoms of the graphs corresponds to PSRs labeled by Google as "hacked".

The top two rows show the results of sampling order numbers from a handful of representative stores promoted by each campaign; the stores that are both visible in PSRs and have high order activity relative to other stores from within the same campaign. The top "Volume" row shows the actual samples over time for the handful of representative stores and reflects the combined cumulative volume of order numbers created (recall that these numbers are an upper bound of actual orders made by customers). As another way of looking at the same data, the lower "Rate" row shows the order data as a histogram: we bin the number of estimated orders per week, interpolating in regions where we lack samples. The number at the top of each graph is the maximum value across the time series.

In all four campaigns, we see correlation between PSR prevalence and order activity, which suggests that search penalizations can be effective. This is most evidedent with the KEY campaign. The rate of orders (slope of the line in the "volume" graph) decreases in mid-December, soon after its PSR activity drops precipitously. We do not know the actual cause of the drop in PSRs: whether the KEY campaign stopped actively performing SEO on its doorway sites, Google aggressively demoted its doorways in search result rank, or the "hacked" warning added to its PSRs dissuaded users from clicking on search results. However, it appears that the penalization pressure from Google—demoting most of the PSRs out of the top 100 and labeling half of the remaining as hacked—did have an effect. From attempts to actually purchase items, the stores promoted by the KEY campaign stopped processing orders after the drop in PSRs.

Penalizing PSRs by demoting them in search rank follows the conventional SEO wisdom that highly-ranked results are by far the

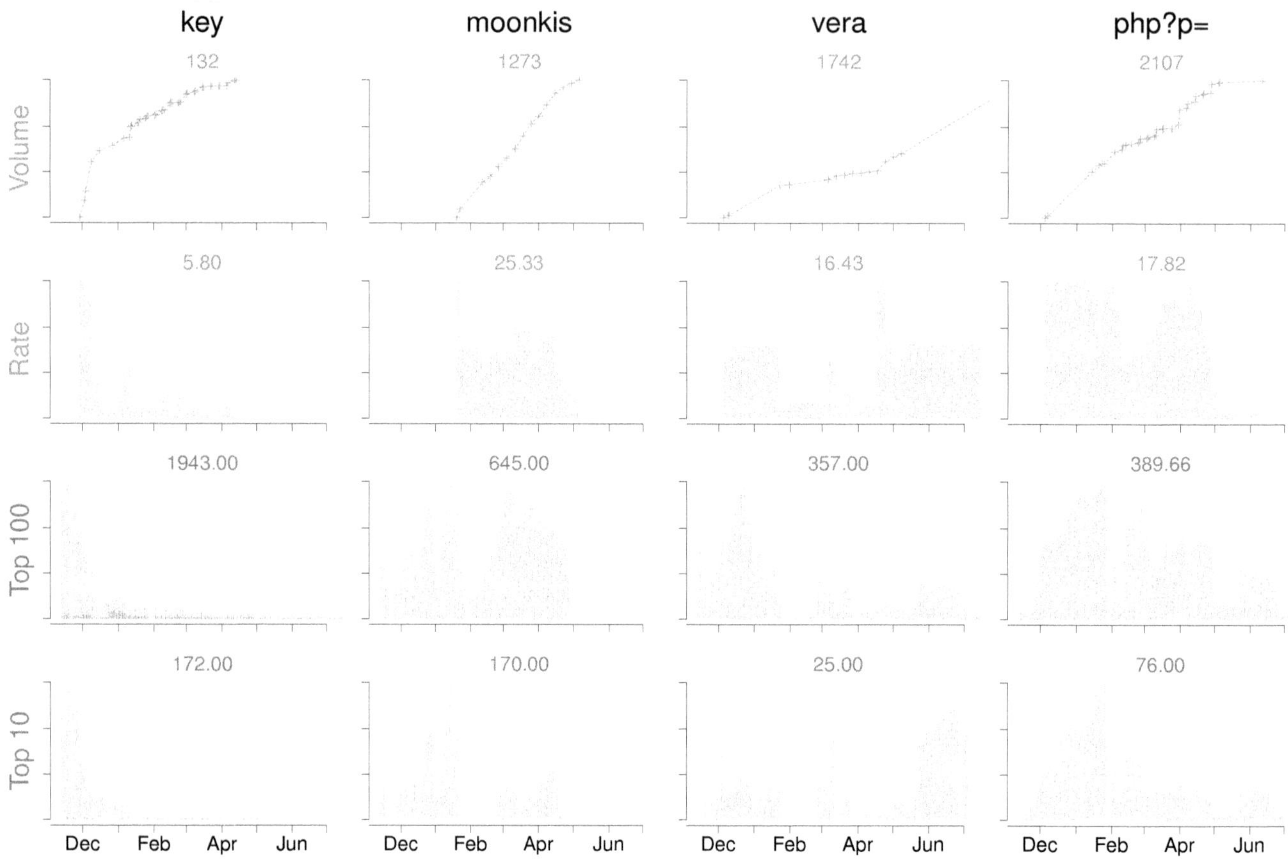

Figure 4: Correlation between a store's visibility in PSRs and order activity for four SEO campaigns. Each column of graphs is associated with an SEO campaign. Bottom two rows of graphs depict the prevalence of PSRs among the top 100 and top 10 search results, respectively. Top two rows reveal cumulative changes in sampled order numbers, as well as histograms binning order number changes into extrapolated daily rates, respectively.

most valuable. On this topic, the bottom two rows of Figure 4 show the prevalence of PSRs in the top 10 and top 100 results. For the most part, the shapes of both histograms are similar: campaigns are successful in SEOing poisoned search results throughout search page ranks, and it is difficult to conclude whether order volumes seen at stores are primarily due to the much smaller number in the top 10 or the much larger number across the top 100. One example, though, suggests that there is value in having PSRs across the full top 100. For the MOONKIS campaign, during most of March 2014 it had negligible PSRs in the top 10 but hundreds in the top 100. Nonetheless, order volumes seen at its stores remained high and steady. In this instance at least, search rank penalization would need to be even more aggressive to demote the PSRs from the top 100.

5.2.2 *Warning Labels*

Google uses the "hacked" label on search results to warn users about suspicious sites. This form of intervention faces two key challenges—coverage and reaction time—and, based upon our crawling results, overall appears to be ineffective for this type of abusive SEO activity.

Although most doorways are hacked sites, Google only penalizes 2.5% of the PSRs we crawled with a "hacked" label. From the perspective of brands, Figure 2 showed that penalized PSRs labeled with the "hacked" warning were a small fraction of all PSRs at any point in time for four large brand verticals. From the perspective of campaigns, Figure 4 shows a similar result: except for the KEY campaign, both the absolute number and fraction of penalized PSRs are quite small.

One issue that undermines coverage is that Google only labels the root of a Web site as "hacked", and does not label search results that link to sub-pages within the same root domain. In the PSR data set, we found 68,193 "hacked" search results. When counting the number of PSRs that share the same root as a penalized site, Google could have labeled 102,104 search results (an additional 49%).

A second challenge is reaction time. A key metric of any reactive intervention is the time delay between when a campaign starts SEOing a doorway and when the search provider detects and penalizes the doorway with a label. This delta represents the window of opportunity for an SEO campaign to monetize traffic obtained through PSRs without any warnings to users.

For doorways penalized with a label, campaigns have multiple weeks in which to monetize traffic through PSRs. Of the 1,282 "hacked" doorways in the PSRs data, 588 doorways were already labeled when we first saw them and we cannot determine when they were first labeled. The remaining 694 have lifetimes between 13–32 days on average until Google labeled them as "hacked".

Note that the variance in the lifetime is due to the difficulty in determining exactly when Google penalizes a site. Using crawled search results, we know when we last saw a doorway prior to the

Company	# Cases	# Brands	# Seized	# Stores	# Classified Stores	# Campaigns
Green, Burns, & Crain	69	17	31,819	214	40	17
SMGPA	47	11	8,056	76	20	12

Table 3: Summary of domain seizures initiated by brand holders from Feb. 2012 – Jul. 2014, aggregating the following per seizing entity: number of court cases initiating seizures (# Cases), number of brands protecting their trademarks through such cases (# Brands), and total number of store domains seized as reported in cases (# Seized). For overlap with the eight months of our crawled data set (Nov. 2013 – Jul. 2014), we also list the subset of store domains seized and directly observed in our crawled PSRs (# Stores), the number of those stores we classified into campaigns (# Classified Stores), and the number of SEO campaigns affected by seizures (# Campaigns).

penalty and when we first saw a doorway after the penalty. However we cannot always determine when the penalty occurred because it may be the case the doorway does not appear in our results for an extended period of time. As a result, we present two numbers, the smaller of which is the lifetime ending when we last saw the doorway actively redirecting, while the larger number is the lifetime when we first observed the labeling.

5.2.3 *User Traffic*

The correlation between search result visibility and order volume, observed in Figure 4, is an indirect measure of the ability of campaigns to attract and convert traffic via PSRs. Combining the AWStats data described in Section 4.4 with the crawled data and test purchases, we are able to examine this relationship in greater detail with a case study of a counterfeit Chanel store run by the BIGLOVE campaign that rotates across three storefront domains over time (`cocoviphandbags.com`, `cocovipbags.com`, and `cocolovebags.com`).

As above, in Figure 5 we present both the prevalence of PSRs attributable to this store and the corresponding extrapolated order activity from June 10, 2014 to August 31, 2014. Using the AWStats data, in the bottom-most graph we also present the daily user traffic seen by the store in terms of the number of HTML pages fetched by users each day. We use color gradients in the PSRs and traffic graphs of Figure 5 to distinguish separate instances of `coco*.com`, where each instance represents a different domain name used for the storefront. As seen by the change in gradients, the BIGLOVE campaign rotated domains for this storefront twice, at the end of June and the middle of August, updating its doorways found in PSRs to redirect to the new instances. We see similar changes in traffic coinciding with each of the domain name changes.

Although there is not sufficient evidence to discern the campaign's intent, one possibility is that these domain name changes are a proactive countermeasure against domain name seizures. As discussed in Section 3.2.2, luxury brand holders frequently seize domain names to curtail counterfeit sales. However, as we will show in Section 5.3, SEO campaigns are well aware of the ongoing seizures and oftentimes react within days of the initial seizure by simply redirecting to another domain. And being proactive ensures that there is no downtime: the first domain `cocoviphandbags.com` was seized on July 11, yet by that time the doorways were already redirecting users to the second domain `cocovipbags.com`.

Inspecting the detailed user traffic data from AWStats, we make rough estimates on conversion metrics from `coco*.com` that are consistent with those reported by marketers [4]. During the months of July and August 2014, `coco*.com` combined received 93,509 visits, 60% of which properly set the HTTP referrer header.[5] Extracting the referrers reveals the complete set of doorways supplying traffic for this store, and we find 83 out of 174 doorway domains (47.7%) were seen in our crawled PSRs data (recall that we limit the number of terms we search for a given vertical, and so it is not surprising that we do not capture all doorways). Examining user visits more closely, we find each visit generates 5.6 HTML page fetches on average. And when combining the traffic data with the order data from test purchases, we estimate this store had a 0.7% conversion rate, roughly a sale every 151 visits.

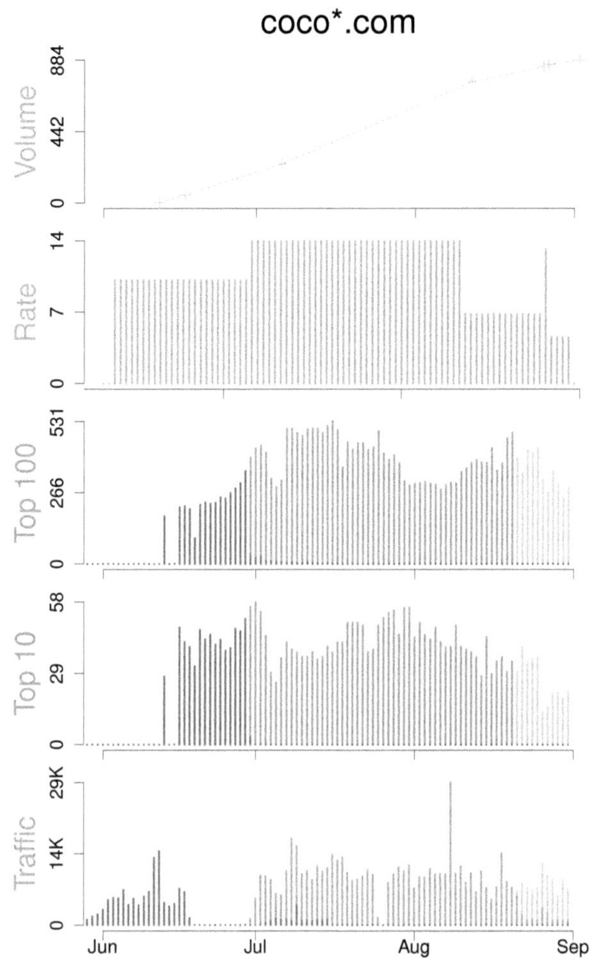

Figure 5: A detailed example of the correlation between a store's prominence in search results (Top 100, Top 10), the resulting user traffic seen by the store (Traffic), and the monetization of user traffic through orders (Volume, Rate), for a counterfeit Chanel store run by the BIGLOVE campaign from June – September 2014. Each color gradient in the PSRs and traffic graphs is associated with separate instances of coco*.com, where each instance used a different domain name.

[5]The HTTP referrer header is not properly set in many situations, including transitioning from HTTPS to HTTP, visiting through an email client, visiting through a proxy that strips the header, or simply typing the URL directly into the browser.

5.3 Domain Seizure Interventions

As discussed in Section 3.2.2, brands have the most incentive for undermining online counterfeiters, and a highly visible intervention they can use is to seize the domains of counterfeit storefronts. With this intervention, brands use legal means to seize domain names of stores violating brand holder trademarks, thereby preventing users from visiting sites selling counterfeit merchandise.[6]

We use two sources of data for studying domain seizure by brand holders. The first is the set of PSRs from our crawled search data. Mechanistically, it is straightforward to determine whether a store is seized by checking whether the site redirects users to a serving notice provided by one of the third-party brand protection services (e.g., Greer, Burns & Crain [10], SMGPA [33]) or the brand holders themselves. The second is a set of seized domains listed in court documents embedded in the serving notice pages; these documents list all domains involved in a seizure, and enable us to obtain a broader view of domain seizure activity by brand holders spanning up to two years.

By extracting the brand holders and the timestamps from seizure notices, we can also infer how brands use brand protection services. For both GBC and SMGPA, we find brand holders initiate domain name seizures on a periodic basis, typically on the order of months between rounds of seizures. Although a handful of brands seized domains more frequently—Oakley issued 6 court cases at monthly intervals, Uggs issued 19 court cases at bi-weekly intervals, and Chanel issued 18 court cases also at bi-weekly intervals—they tend to be the exception.

To assess the completeness of observing domain seizures using PSRs, we compared the court cases seen in PSRs against ground truth we collected by enumerating all court orders from GBC, which are publicly available through their Web site. During the time frame of our study (November 2013 to July 2014), we observe 47 cases in PSRs out of the 50 total cases initiated by GBC (94%) during the same time frame. This overlap indicates that our crawled search data captures the bulk of seizure activity by brand holders.

5.3.1 Coverage

Brand holders have been aggressive in seizing storefront domains. Table 3 shows a breakdown of seized domains across brands, storefronts, and campaigns. From manually examining the court documents embedded in seizure notice pages, brands arranged to have almost 40,000 domains seized over two years. Specifically, while representing 17 brand holders GBC seized 31K domains using 69 court orders from December 2012 to June 2014. Similarly, while representing 11 brand holders SMGPA seized 8K domains using 47 court orders from February 2012 to July 2014.

Seizing domains can disrupt online counterfeit stores. For example, Figure 6 shows order numbers over time for four stores promoted by the PHP?P= campaign. The domain for its Abercrombie UK store was seized on February 9, 2014 (vertical dotted line), and its rate of new order numbers declined immediately (it did not stop completely due to reaction by the SEO campaign, as discussed below in Section 5.3.2).

Despite their aggressiveness, though, brand holders must be far more aggressive when seizing domains. From the PSRs crawled, we directly observed 290 seizures over our eight-month period: 214 seized by GBC and 76 by SMGPA. Compared with the total number of storefronts we observed (7,484), though, these domain seizures represent just a small percentage (3.9%) of stores used by SEO campaigns. As a result, unless brands comprehensively seize domains, stores promoted by SEO campaigns remain unaffected and they continue to attract traffic and customers via search. Referring back to the example in Figure 6, the orders remained steady at other stores whose domains were not seized and the SEO campaign remained effective overall.

[6]Another option would be to seize doorway domains, but doing so presents two obstacles: there are two orders of magnitude more doorway domains than stores (Table 2), and the doorways are often compromised sites.

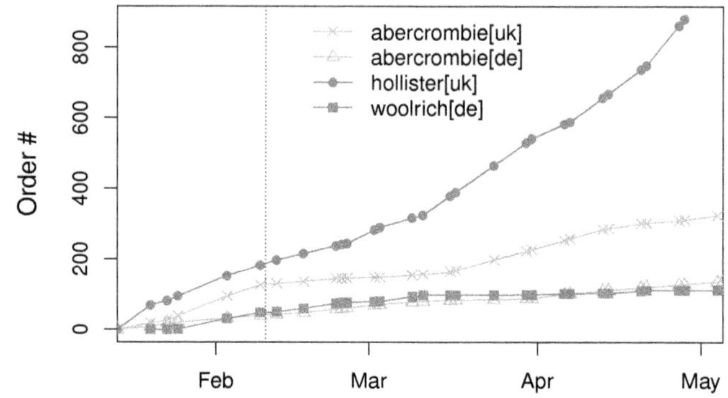

Figure 6: Order number samples over time in early 2014 for the PHP?P= campaign. Each curve corresponds to one of four international stores, where three sell Abercrombie (United Kingdom, Germany) while the remaining sells Woolrich (Italy).

5.3.2 Reaction Time

Even if brands eventually seize all storefront domains, though, they take such a long time to seize domains, and attackers respond so quickly to having domains seized, that the current environment still strongly favors the attackers.

As with labeling sites as "hacked", the time from when a storefront goes live and when a brand seizes the store domain represents the window of opportunity for a counterfeit store to monetize traffic. As in Section 5.2.2, we can compute the lifetime of seized stores to measure their earning potential before seizure. We define the lifetime of seized stores as the delta between the first time that the storefront appears in PSRs to the time the domain was seized.

We find the average lifetime of seized stores lies between 58–68 days for GBC and 48–56 days for SMGPA. Again, due to the nature of our data collection, we can only observe seizures when crawling search results redirects our crawlers to seized stores. Therefore, we cannot determine exactly when a seizure takes place. Instead, we present two bounded numbers approximating the true lifetime. The smaller is the duration ending when we last saw the store actively poisoning search results, while the larger is the lifetime ending when we first definitively observed the seizure.[7]

However, even when brands seize storefront domains, the SEO campaigns possess backup domains in anticipation of such an intervention and can quickly react to continue to monetize traffic without significant interruption. Returning to the example in Figure 6, when the Abercrombie UK domain was seized, the PHP?P= campaign changed their doorways to forward to a new store domain within 24 hours. This domain agility represents a critical weakness of seizures: even though a store domain is seized, SEO campaigns

[7]Given how quickly campaigns react to domain seizures, it is also possible for campaigns to redirect doorways to new store domains faster than our crawler can detect that the initial domain was seized.

can easily modify their doorways to redirect users to their backups rather than the seized domains.

Indeed, we found widespread evidence of attackers exploiting this weakness as a countermeasure to domain seizures. Specifically, of the 214 seized stores from GBC, 130 were redirected to new stores (59 of which were subsequently seized) and, among the 76 seized from SMGPA, 57 were redirected to new stores (22 of which were subsequently seized). These responses by the counterfeiters happened on average within 7 and 15 days of the initial seizure, respectively, for GBC and SMGPA. Such domain agility suggests the counterfeiters are well prepared for domain seizures, and as a result such interventions are not likely to undermine their business.

6. CONCLUSION

Online business in counterfeit luxury goods is brisk: from the site of just one supplier, we saw over 250,000 successfully delivered orders in nine months. Such businesses prosper by poisoning search results for popular luxury goods to attract customers to their online storefronts; for heavily-targeted brands, a third of the top 100 search results are so poisoned for months at a time.

In this paper we presented techniques for detecting poisoned search results that lead users to counterfeit stores, and a classification approach for mapping the Web sites of these stores into distinct SEO campaigns that promote these sites. From eight months of crawled search results for 16 brand verticals, we detected 2.7 million PSRs using 27 thousand doorway pages that redirect users to 7,484 storefronts, and classified over half of the PSRs into 52 distinct SEO campaigns. Simultaneously, we created test orders on stores to sample their order number sequence space to estimate their order volume over time.

Finally, we used our crawler and order data to study the effects of both search engine and domain seizure interventions on these abusive SEO activities. Although we find instances where both can have the desired effect of disrupting counterfeit sales activity, overall neither are currently employed with the level of coverage or responsiveness necessary to be broadly effective against the actors in this market. Search engines and brand holders should take into account that these activities are organized as business campaigns, that effective interventions should target their infrastructure at the granularity of these campaigns, and that they are being targeted by dozens of campaigns. Otherwise campaigns have shown great agility in adapting to partial intervention, and in filling in gaps left by the disappearance of other campaigns. We believe that the measurement and classification techniques we describe in this paper for identifying campaigns and their infrastructure could provide the improved targeting required for more robust intervention.

7. ACKNOWLEDGMENTS

We are grateful to Aaron Hurtado and Kelsey Ma, supported by the National Science Foundation Research Experience for Undergraduates (REU) program, for scripting the process of gathering order volume data. We also thank Andreas Haeberlen and the anonymous reviewers for their valuable feedback. This work was supported in part by National Science Foundation grant NSF-1237264, by the Office of Naval Research MURI grant N00014-09-1-1081, and by generous support from Yahoo, Google, Microsoft, and the UCSD Center for Networked Systems (CNS).

8. REFERENCES

[1] AWStats — Free log file analyzer for advanced statistics (GNU GPL). `http://awstats.sourceforge.net/`.

[2] BANNUR, S. N., SAUL, L. K., AND SAVAGE, S. Judging a site by its content: learning the textual, structural, an d visual features of malicious Web pages. In *Proceedings of the ACM Workshop on Artificial Intelligence and Security (AISEC)* (Chicago, IL, Oct. 2011).

[3] CHACHRA, N., MCCOY, D., SAVAGE, S., AND VOELKER, G. M. Empirically Characterizing Domain Abuse and the Revenue Impact of Blacklisting. In *Proceedings of the Workshop on the Economics of Information Security (WEIS)* (State College, PA., June 2014).

[4] CHAFFEY, D. Ecommerce conversion rates. `http://www.smartinsights.com/ecommerce/ecommerce-analytics/ecommerce-conversion-rates/`, March 2014.

[5] DER, M. F., SAUL, L. K., SAVAGE, S., AND VOELKER, G. M. Knock It Off: Profiling the Online Storefronts of Counterfeit Merchandise. In *Proceedings of the ACM SIGKDD Conference* (New York, NY, August 2014).

[6] Generate a Random Name — Fake Name Generator. `http://www.fakenamegenerator.com/`.

[7] FAN, R. E., CHANG, K. W., HSIEH, C. J., WANG, X. R., AND LIN, C. J. LIBLINEAR: A Library for Large Linear Classification. `http://www.csie.ntu.edu.tw/~cjlin/liblinear/`.

[8] Google Search Engine Optimization Starter Guide. `http://www.google.com/webmasters/docs/search-engine-optimization-starter-guide.pdf`.

[9] GOOGLE. Results labeled "This site may be hacked". `http://support.google.com/websearch/answer/190597`.

[10] GREER, BURNS, & CRAIN. Anti-counterfeiting legal strategies, enforcement and remedies. `http://gbclaw.net/practiceareas/anti-counterfeiting`.

[11] GRIER, C., BALLARD, L., CABALLERO, J., CHACHRA, N., DIETRICH, C. J., LEVCHENKO, K., MAVROMMATIS, P., MCCOY, D., NAPPA, A., PITSILLIDIS, A., PROVOS, N., RAFIQUE, M. Z., RAJAB, M. A., ROSSOW, C., THOMAS, K., PAXSON, V., SAVAGE, S., AND VOELKER, G. M. Manufacturing Compromise: The Emergence of Exploit-as-a-Service. In *Proceedings of the ACM Conference on Computer and Communications Security* (Raleigh, NC, October 2012).

[12] HERLEY, C., AND FLORENCIO, D. Nobody Sells Gold for the Price of Silver: Dishonesty, Uncertainty and the Underground Economy. In *Proceedings of the Workshop on the Economics of Information Security (WEIS)* (London, UK, June 2009).

[13] HtmlUnit — Welcome to HtmlUnit. `http://htmlunit.sourceforge.net/`.

[14] INVERNIZZI, L., BENVENUTI, S., COVA, M., MILANI-COMPARETTI, P., KRUEGEL, C., AND VIGNA, G. EvilSeed: A Guided Approach to Finding Malicious Web Pages. In *Proceedings of the IEEE Symposium and Security and Privacy* (San Francisco, CA, May 2012).

[15] JOHN, J. P., YU, F., XIE, Y., KRISHNAMURTHY, A., AND ABADI, M. deSEO: Combating Search-Result Poisoning. In *Proceedings of the USENIX Security Symposium* (San Francisco, CA, August 2011).

[16] KANICH, C., WEAVER, N., MCCOY, D., HALVORSON, T., KREIBICH, C., LEVCHENKO, K., PAXSON, V., VOELKER, G. M., AND SAVAGE, S. Show Me the Money: Characterizing Spam-advertised Revenue. In *Proceedings of the USENIX Security Symposium* (San Francisco, CA, August 2011).

[17] KARAMI, M., GHAEMI, S., AND MCCOY, D. Folex: An Analysis of an Herbal and Counterfeit Luxury Goods Affiliate Program. In *Proceesings of the eCrime Researchers Summit (eCRS)* (San Francisco, CA., September 2013).

[18] LEONTIADIS, N., MOORE, T., AND CHRISTIN, N. Pick Your Poison: Pricing and Inventories at Unlicensed Online Pharmacies. In *Proceedings of the ACM Conference on Electronic Commerce* (Philadelphia, PA., June 2013).

[19] LEONTIADIS, N., MOORE, T., AND CHRISTIN, N. A Nearly Four-Year Longitudinal Study of Search-Engine Poisoning. In *Proceedings of the ACM Conference on Computer and Communications Security* (Scottsdale, AZ, Nov. 2014).

[20] LEVCHENKO, K., PITSILLIDIS, A., CHACHRA, N., ENRIGHT, B., FÉLEGYHÁZI, M., GRIER, C., HALVORSON, T., KANICH, C., KREIBICH, C., LIU, H., MCCOY, D., WEAVER, N., PAXSON, V., VOELKER, G. M., AND SAVAGE, S. Click Trajectories: End-to-End Analysis of the Spam Value Chain. In *Proceedings of the IEEE Symposium and Security and Privacy* (Oakland, CA, May 2011).

[21] LIU, H., LEVCHENKO, K., FELEGYHAZI, M., KREIBICH, C., MAIER, G., VOELKER, G. M., AND SAVAGE, S. On the Effects of Registrar-level Intervention. In *Proceedings of the USENIX Workshop on Large-scale Exploits and Emergent Threats (LEET)* (Boston, MA, March 2011).

[22] LU, L., PERDISCI, R., AND LEE, W. SURF: Detecting and Measuring Search Poisoning. In *Proceedings of the ACM Conference on Computer and Communications Security* (Chicago, IL, October 2011).

[23] MarkMonitor Brand Protection. `https://www.markmonitor.com/services/brand-protection.php`.

[24] MCCOY, D., DHARMDASANI, H., KREIBICH, C., VOELKER, G. M., AND SAVAGE, S. Priceless: The Role of Payments in Abuse-advertised Goods. In *Proceedings of the ACM Conference on Computer and Communications Security* (Raleigh, NC, October 2012).

[25] MCCOY, D., PITSILLIDIS, A., JORDAN, G., WEAVER, N., KREIBICH, C., KREBS, B., VOELKER, G. M., SAVAGE, S., AND LEVCHENKO, K. PharmaLeaks: Understanding the Business of Online Pharmaceutical Affiliate Programs. In *Proceedings of the USENIX Security Symposium* (Bellevue, WA, August 2012).

[26] MOORE, T., AND CLAYTON, R. The consequence of non-cooperation in the fight against phishing. In *Proceesings of the eCrime Researchers Summit (eCRS)* (Atlanta, GA., October 2008).

[27] MOORE, T., LEONTIADIS, N., AND CHRISTIN, N. Fashion Crimes: Trending-Term Exploitation on the Web. In *Proceedings of the ACM Conference on Computer and Communications Security* (Chicago, IL, October 2011).

[28] OPSEC. Brand protection from manufacturing to retail. `http://www.opsecsecurity.com/brand-protection`.

[29] PRICEWATERHOUSECOOPERS. IAB Internet Advertising Revenue Report, 2012 Full Year Results. `http://www.iab.net/media/file/IABInternetAdvertisingRevenueReportFY2012POSTED.pdf`.

[30] RAJAB, M. A., BALLARD, L., MARVROMMATIS, P., PROVOS, N., AND ZHAO, X. The Nocebo Effect on the Web: An Analysis of Fake Anti-Virus Distribution. In *Proceedings of the USENIX Workshop on Large-scale Exploits and Emergent Threats (LEET)* (San Jose, CA, April 2010).

[31] SAFENAMES. Mark Protect. `http://www.safenames.net/BrandProtection/MarkProtect.aspx`.

[32] SAMOSSEIKO, D. The Partnerka – What Is It, And Why Should You Care? In *Proceedings of the Virus Bulletin Conference* (September 2009).

[33] SMGPA. `http://smgpa.net/`.

[34] STONE-GROSS, B., ABMAN, R., KEMMERER, R., KRUEGEL, C., STEIGERWALD, D., AND VIGNA, G. The Underground Economy of Fake Antivirus Software. In *Proc. of the 10th Workshop on the Economics of Information Security (WEIS)* (Washington D.C., 2011).

[35] WANG, D. Y., SAVAGE, S., AND VOELKER, G. M. Cloak and Dagger: Dynamics of Web Search Cloaking. In *Proceedings of the ACM Conference on Computer and Communications Security* (Chicago, IL, October 2011).

[36] WANG, D. Y., SAVAGE, S., AND VOELKER, G. M. Juice: A Longitudinal Study of an SEO Campaign. In *Proceedings of the Network and Distributed System Security Symposium* (San Diego, CA, February 2013).

[37] WANG, Y.-M., MA, M., NIU, Y., AND CHEN, H. Spam Double-Funnel: Connecting Web Spammers with Advertisers. In *Proceedings of the International World Wide Web Conference (WWW)* (Banff, Alberta, May 2007).

[38] WHITTAKER, C., RYNER, B., AND NAZIF, M. Large-Scale Automatic Classification of Phishing Pages. In *Proceedings of the Network and Distributed System Security Symposium* (San Diego, CA, February 2010).

The Dark Alleys of Madison Avenue: Understanding Malicious Advertisements

Apostolis Zarras
Ruhr-University Bochum
apostolis.zarras@rub.de

Alexandros Kapravelos
UC Santa Barbara
kapravel@cs.ucsb.edu

Gianluca Stringhini
University College London
g.stringhini@ucl.ac.uk

Thorsten Holz
Ruhr-University Bochum
thorsten.holz@rub.de

Christopher Kruegel
UC Santa Barbara
chris@cs.ucsb.edu

Giovanni Vigna
UC Santa Barbara
vigna@cs.ucsb.edu

ABSTRACT

Online advertising drives the economy of the World Wide Web. Modern websites of any size and popularity include advertisements to monetize visits from their users. To this end, they assign an area of their web page to an advertising company (so called *ad exchange*) that will use it to display promotional content. By doing this, the website owner implicitly trusts that the advertising company will offer legitimate content and it will not put the site's visitors at risk of falling victims of malware campaigns and other scams.

In this paper, we perform the first large-scale study of the safety of the advertisements that are encountered by the users on the Web. In particular, we analyze to what extent users are exposed to malicious content through advertisements, and investigate what are the sources of this malicious content. Additionally, we show that some ad exchanges are more prone to serving malicious advertisements than others, probably due to their deficient filtering mechanisms. The observations that we make in this paper shed light on a little studied, yet important, aspect of advertisement networks, and can help both advertisement networks and website owners in securing their web pages and in keeping their visitors safe.

Categories and Subject Descriptors

K.4.4 [**Computers and Society**]: Electronic Commerce; C.2.0 [**Computer-Communication Networks**]: General; H.3.5 [**Information Storage and Retrieval**]: Online Information Services

General Terms

Measurement; Security

Keywords

Online Advertising; Malware; Malvertising

IMC'14, November 5–7, 2014, Vancouver, BC, Canada.

http://dx.doi.org/10.1145/2663716.2663719.

1. INTRODUCTION

The online advertising industry is constantly growing. A recent report showed that this industry generated a revenue of 42.8 billion dollars in 2013, which is 17% higher than what had been reported in the previous year [14]. In the World Wide Web, where most online services are free of charge, advertisements constitute the main revenue for website administrators, and it is very common to see promotional content alongside the actual information contained in such sites.

Given the profitability of online advertising, many big players have entered the arena. Such players, known as *ad exchanges*, put in contact the *advertisers*, who want their content to be displayed, with the *publishers*, who want to show promotional content on their web pages, and make sure that the most suitable advertisement will be displayed to the visitors of that site at all times. Recent research showed that Google's *Doubleclick* ad exchange service is the largest on the Internet, being present on 80% of the websites that provide advertisements [12]. A publisher looking to generate some revenue can easily subscribe with one of these companies, dedicate a part of her web pages to advertisements, and start serving promotional content to that page's visitors. Publishers are paid either by *impression*, meaning that they get a sum of money every time a visitor watches an advertisement on their site, or by *click*, meaning that they get paid every time a user shows interest in the advertisement and clicks on it, visiting the advertiser's website.

Because of their pervasiveness, online advertisements are not only used by legitimate parties, but also by miscreants. A common scam linked to online advertisements is *click fraud* [29]. In this scheme, cyber-criminals first set up web pages and become publishers. Then, they instruct a *botnet*, which is a network of compromised computers acting under the cyber-criminal's control, to visit the web page and click on the advertisements displayed on it [3]. By doing this, the cyber-criminal will get paid by the ad exchange and make a revenue. Click fraud is a big concern for ad exchanges, and a wealth of research has been conducted to detect and block suspicious clicks on online advertisements [6, 7, 25].

Besides click frauds, online advertisements provide a convenient platform for infecting web users with malware. Attackers can set up malicious advertisements that attempt to automatically exploit the user's browser and install malware with a *drive-by download* attack [23], or they can display an advertisement that lures the victim into installing malware through social engineering, making the advertisement look appealing to the user [24].

Leveraging advertisements to spread malware has many advantages for attackers. Since advertisements are displayed on very popular websites, miscreants have a chance of infecting a larger number of victims in a short amount of time. Without the use of advertisements, the only way that an attacker would reach a similar goal is by compromising the home page of a popular site, which is a challenging task due to its security mechanisms. In addition, publishers usually trust the advertisement network (*ad network*) that they entertain business with, and are unaware that such networks could actually end up serving malicious content.

Previous research showed that malicious advertisements are fairly common in the wild [18, 20, 22, 26]. Similarly, recent news showed the feasibility of having malicious advertisements going undetected by major ad exchanges, and being served to users [11]. However, no comprehensive research has been conducted on understanding the ecosystem surrounding malicious advertisements. The prevalence of malicious advertisements on the Web, the number of ad networks that serve these malvertisements, and the quality of the defense systems deployed by ad exchanges are still open questions.

In this paper, we study the ecosystem of malicious advertisements. We crawled more than 600,000 real-world advertisements, and checked them against multiple detection systems to assess their maliciousness. We show that certain ad exchanges are serving more malicious content than others, probably because they have insufficient detection systems. We also show that, because of the arbitration process, it is common for ad exchanges to serve a malicious advertisement provided by another ad exchange.

In summary, we make the following main contributions:

- We collect a corpus of more than 600,000 real-world advertisements from various web pages and describe the misbehaving advertisements that we discovered.
- We analyze different ad exchanges and show that some of them are more prone to serving malicious advertisements than others.
- We demonstrate that due to the arbitration process, every website that serves advertisements and that does not have an exclusive agreement with the advertiser is a potential publisher of malicious advertisements.
- We show that the vast majority of publishers tend to trust their advertisers not to serve malicious advertisements and thus they do not apply any additional filters to protect their users.

2. MALICIOUS ADVERTISING

Malicious advertising, known as *malvertising*, is the cybercriminals' practice of injecting malicious or malware-laden advertisements into legitimate online advertising networks and syndicated content. It can occur through deceptive advertisers or agencies running advertisements or compromises to the ad-supply chain including ad networks, ad exchanges, and ad servers. Different types of malicious advertisements exhibit different behaviors and in the following sections we briefly describe them.

2.1 Drive-by Downloads

A drive-by download advertisement is an advertisement that hosts one or more exploits that target specific vulnerabilities in web browsers. More precisely, attackers target vulnerabilities in web browsers or in browser plugins, such as Flash or Java, that enable users to experience rich media content within the browser environment. In some cases, the browser vendor pre-installs these plugins. The user may not even use the vulnerable plugin or be aware that it is installed. Users with vulnerable computers can be transparently infected with malware by visiting a website that serves a drive-by download, even without interacting with the malicious part of the page.

2.2 Deceptive Downloads

Deceptive downloads try to lure their victims to download and install a specific software component that is malicious. The main difference from drive-by downloads is that attackers do not try to find a vulnerability in the victim's browser or browser plugins to download and install a piece of malware, but instead they try to trick the users into performing that procedure voluntarily. This happens by having the user believe that there is some desirable content on the visited web page. More specifically, the victims get informed that, in order to gain access to specific content of the page, they need to install a particular software component or to upgrade their supposedly outdated plugins. Of course, the updating/installing procedure installs malware on the user's hosts instead of the advertised software.

2.3 Link Hijacking

Link hijacking allows an advertisement to automatically redirect users to websites that they have not decided to visit. The advertisements are included in iframes, and the advertising scripts cannot access the Document Object Model (DOM) of the publisher's web page due to the Same-Origin Policy (SOP) restrictions [2]. However, a malicious script contained in an advertisement can redirect the entire page to a preselected destination by setting Browser Object Model's (BOM) `top.location` variable [22]. This way, the victim is redirected to an arbitrary location and not to the one she has initially selected.

3. METHODOLOGY

In this section, we present the methodology we used to generate and evaluate a large corpus of advertisements. Our process includes two steps. First, we extract the advertisements from a variety of websites. Second, we use a number of oracles to classify the advertisements as malicious or legitimate. We describe both steps in detail.

3.1 Data Collection

In the first phase, we performed a large web crawl to create a corpus of advertisements. For this purpose, we used two different data feeds. First, we leveraged a data feed obtained from an antivirus company (already used in our previous work [26]). This feed contains web pages that in the past appeared to have a malicious behavior, and was generated by users who installed a browser security product to voluntarily share their data with the company for research purposes. For the second feed, we used Alexa's one million top-ranked websites list. To have a certain degree of diversity in our data, we selected the top and the bottom 10,000 websites, the top and the bottom 1,000 websites from selected top-level domains, and also 20,000 randomly selected websites from Alexa's ranked websites.

Due to the fact that the content of the advertisements is dynamically generated, we periodically crawled each web page in an attempt to obtain different advertisements. More specifically, our crawler visited each website once per day, and refreshed a web page five times. Our crawler was based on `Selenium`, which is a software-testing framework for web applications that has the ability to programmatically control a real web browser (Mozilla Firefox in our experiments). This approach allowed us to retrieve the whole content of a rendered advertisement, which would not be possible if we used a simple command-line tool like `wget`. Additionally, we captured all the HTTP traffic during crawling for further investigation.

In most of the cases, the advertisements were included in an *iframe*. An iframe is an HTML document embedded inside another HTML document. This allows the iframe to be rendered in a consistent way even if it is included by different websites. We leveraged this fact and we created HTML documents based on the contents of the iframes. These iframes included both statically- and dynamically-generated HTML elements. It is important to note that not all the iframes included in a web page contain advertisements. Thus, to distinguish the advertisement-related iframes, we utilized *EasyList*[1]. EasyList include domains and URL patterns for ad-related hosts, and is used by the browser plugin `Adblock Plus` [1] to block advertisements.

After a period of three months, we have created a corpus of 673,596 unique advertisements. We then analyzed this dataset searching for misbehaving advertisements.

3.2 Oracles

To classify if an advertisement exhibits malicious behavior, we utilized an oracle. The oracle constitutes an essential part of our study. It gets as an input the initial request for advertisements from a publisher's website, and by monitoring several behavioral features, it can effectively determine the maliciousness of the advertisement. The lifeblood of our oracle constitutes by three main components: `Wepawet` [4], malware and phishing blacklists, and `VirusTotal`. We describe the contribution of each component in the classification process in the next paragraphs.

3.2.1 Wepawet

As advertisements are included in pages with dynamic content that often changes over time, they are also dynamically-generated. The dynamic nature of advertisements is achieved with the use of JavaScript or Flash. Miscreants can unleash their nefarious activities (drive-by download attacks, phishing attempts, etc.) to victims through advertisements. Therefore, we need to analyze the advertisements' embedded code, which is often dynamically loaded, to detect if there exist any kind of malicious behavior.

To do so, we utilized `Wepawet` [4], a honeyclient that uses an emulated browser to capture the execution of JavaScript code on web pages. `Wepawet` uses anomaly-based techniques to identify signs of maliciousness that are typical of a drive-by download attack.

We submitted the iframes that contained advertisements to `Wepawet`, which executed all the JavaScript code and captured all the network traffic. Finally, with the use of specific heuristics, such as the download of malicious executables or machine learning models, `Wepawet` classified the advertisements as malicious or not.

3.2.2 Malware and Phishing Blacklists

Blacklists are one of the most widespread techniques to protect users against malicious websites. In a domain-based blacklist, a domain is added to the list as soon as it is discovered to host malicious content. Additionally, the domain is classified based on its behavior, such as malware distribution, phishing attempts, stealing users' credentials, and others. In this study, we used a tracking system that constitutes a collection of 49 antivirus, spam and phishing blacklists [17]. We utilized these blacklists by checking against them all the domains we monitored to serve advertisements. Note that it is fairly common for the blacklists to produce false positives. In our study, we wanted to minimize the risk of false classification of an advertisement. To do so, we use an empirically calculated threshold. More precisely, to increase the accuracy of our results, we considered domains as malicious only if they were contained in more than five different blacklists at the same time.

3.2.3 VirusTotal

Among the malicious advertisements, there exist some that try to lure users to install software in their machines. They disguise the software as a media player or an up-to-date browser plugin required to display specific content. Most of the time, this software contains malware that tries to infect the user. Nevertheless, there will be some cases in which a benign plugin is required by the browser to display the content. For instance, a browser could not display Flash content due to Flash plugin absence. Hence, we need a way to decide whether the downloaded software is benign or malicious.

Antivirus products are the best solution for this classification. However, not all vendors can recognize the same malware. Additionally, having access to multiple antivirus products is a time and resource consuming process. Fortunately, `VirusTotal` can solve this problem. `VirusTotal` is an online service[2] that analyzes files using 51 different antivirus products and scan engines to check for malware. One can submit samples to `VirusTotal` and get a report with the classification of these samples by different antivirus companies. We consider `VirusTotal` as a key component of our oracle. Whenever an advertisement tried to force a user to download software, we forward this software to `VirusTotal` and retrieve its classification. This way, we can accurately decide if the downloaded software is benign of malicious.

4. ANALYZING MALVERTISEMENTS

In this section, we analyze the malicious advertisements that we discovered. In particular, we study various aspects of malvertising and try to understand what types of websites are more prone to malvertisements. Furthermore, we investigate whether a website is more secure by selecting a trusted ad network to serve the advertisements. Finally, we examine if the publishers take the users' security into their consideration and thus, take actions to protect their visitors from being infected.

[1] `https://easylist.adblockplus.org`

[2] `http://virustotal.com`

Type of maliciousness	#Incidents
Blacklists	4,794
Suspicious redirections	1,396
Heuristics	309
Malicious executables	68
Malicious Flash	31
Model detection	3

Table 1: Classification of malvertisements.

4.1 Type of Maliciousness

To investigate to what extent cyber-criminals utilize advertisements to promote their nefarious activities, we analyzed the collected advertisements. For this purpose, we used the following procedure: Initially, we retrieved all the analysis reports from `Wepawet`. Then, we examined the reports looking for the existence of specific heuristics like redirects to NX domains or benign websites like Google and Bing, which suggest the utilization of cloaking techniques. Additionally, we looked for behaviors (models) that are similar to previously-known malicious behaviors. Next, all the executables and Flash files were validated against `VirusTotal`. Finally, we used the previously-mentioned blacklists to monitor if the content of the advertisement was served by a blacklisted domain. Table 1 shows the results of all the misbehaving advertisements that we detected. In general, we identified 6,601 incidents in which the advertisements triggered our detection framework. Surprisingly, we observed that about 1% of all the collected advertisements show a malicious behavior.

4.2 Identifying Risky Advertisers

In the next experiment, we wanted to investigate if there is any preference from the side of the malicious advertisers to specific ad networks. In other words, we wanted to measure if some ad networks are more prone to serving malicious advertisements than others. As we already mentioned, each ad network applies its own policy regarding the acceptance of an advertisement. For instance, some of the biggest ad networks do not allow the promotion of websites infected with malware while others, usually smaller in size, are more tolerant to this. Figure 1 illustrates the proportion of malvertisement in the total advertisements served by an ad network. The ad networks are sorted based on the ratio of malicious ads compared to the legitimate ones served. As we can observe, there are some ad networks that are preferred by cyber-criminals, and therefore show more malicious ads. Interestingly, there are ad networks in which the malvertisements underlie more than a third of their global traffic. Note that in this figure we only display the ad networks that contain at least one malvertisement and omit all these that are able to successfully filter them.

Although the existence of ad networks that serve malvertisements constitute a threat for the users of the Web, the size of this threat can only be quantified if we measure the proportion that these ad networks have in the total served advertisements. Figure 2 shows that most of these ad networks send only a small degree of malicious advertisements. This verifies our initial statement that the bigger ad networks tend to perform a more accurate filtering of the advertisements they serve compared to smaller networks. Nevertheless, we spotted a specific ad network that served almost

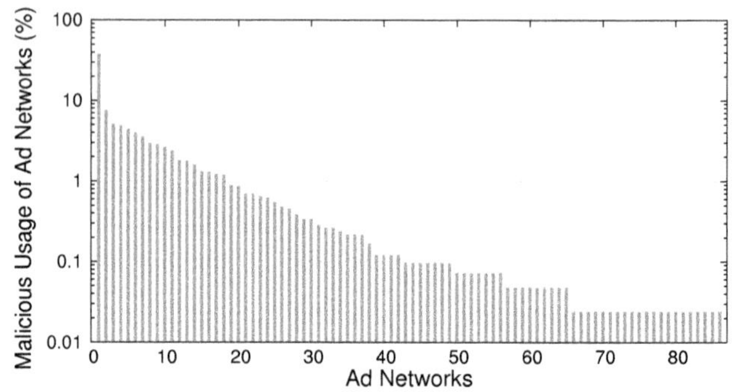

Figure 1: Malvertising distribution from selected ad networks.

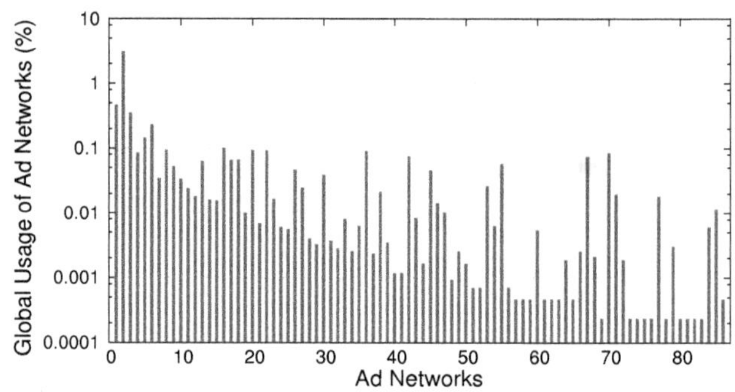

Figure 2: Distribution of advertisements from selected ad networks.

3% of the total advertisements and was responsible for a significant amount of the detected malvertisements. This gave us a significant insight on the ad network filtering mechanisms, which is that no matter how sophisticated the filters used by the ad networks are, there exists a possibility that the cyber-criminals can successfully evade them.

Next, we created three major clusters of websites. The first cluster contained the top 10,000 websites from Alexa's one million top-ranked websites, the second cluster the bottom 10,000, and the third more than 23,000 websites that existed in our advertisement dataset and did not belong to the previous clusters. We wanted to measure from which websites we observe the majority of the malvertisements. We discovered that the first cluster served 82.3% of the whole malvertisements, while the second 6.2%, and the third 11.5%. One can consider that the more famous a website is, the better techniques are applied to protect its visitors. However, the recent event occurred in Yahoo! confirm our hypothesis [11]. In detail, when users visited Yahoo!'s website between 31 December 2013 and 4 January 2014, they were served with malvertisements. Given a typical infection rate of 9%, this incident likely resulted in around 27,000 infections every hour.

In order to discover if the top websites receive more malvertisements because they display more advertisements on their web pages compared to the bottom websites, or whether they are simply preferred by cyber-criminals, we measured the number of the total advertisements (both benign and malicious) the previous clusters displayed. The results revealed that the first cluster served 76.6% of the total advertisements, the second 11.6%, and the third 11.8%. These

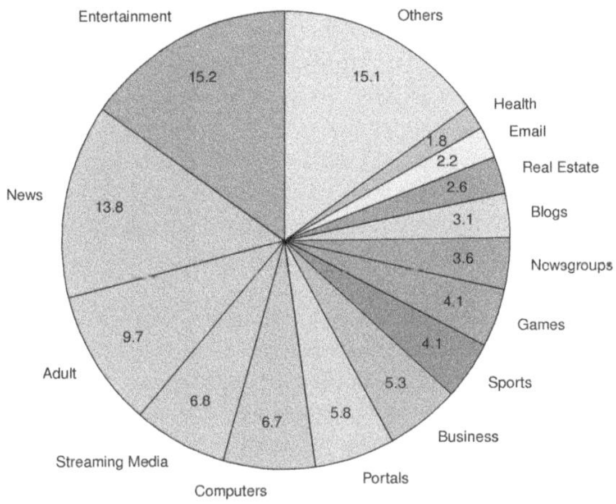

Figure 3: Websites categorization that served malvertisements.

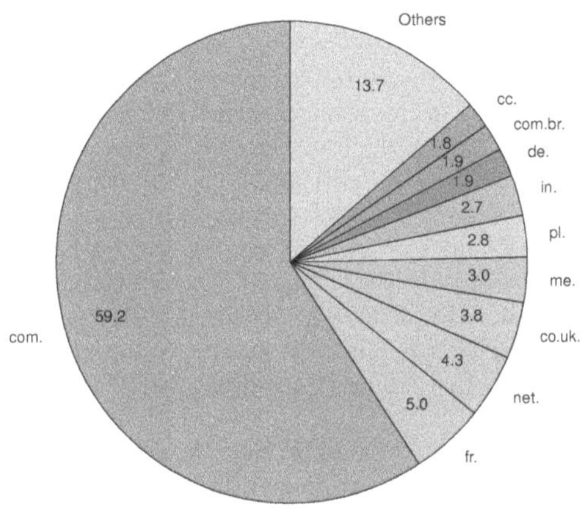

Figure 4: Malvertisement distribution based on top level domains.

results are close to the previously-mentioned malvertising results. Consequently, we believe that miscreants are not interested from which website their malicious code will be delivered, but they are actually concerned about the total amount of infections they will earn from malvertising.

To understand the type of websites that malvertisements are usually targeting, we clustered all the websites we spotted with malvertisement into major categories. Figure 3 shows this categorization. Websites that contain entertainment and news content constitute almost one third of the total websites targeted by malvertisement. Interestingly, the websites that contain adult material are ranked third in the preference of miscreants. This fact conflicts with previous studies, which showed that adult content is tied to increased maliciousness [30].

Finally, we wanted to see the quota of top-level domains that serve malvertisements. Figure 4 shows that the `.com` domains constitute the majority of the websites serving malicious advertisements. Additionally, we noticed that the generic top-level domains (mainly `.com` and `.net`) compose more than 66% of the malvertising traffic. Given the fact that most of the `.com` domains have an American-driven orientation, we believe that malvertising are primarily designed to target United States citizens.

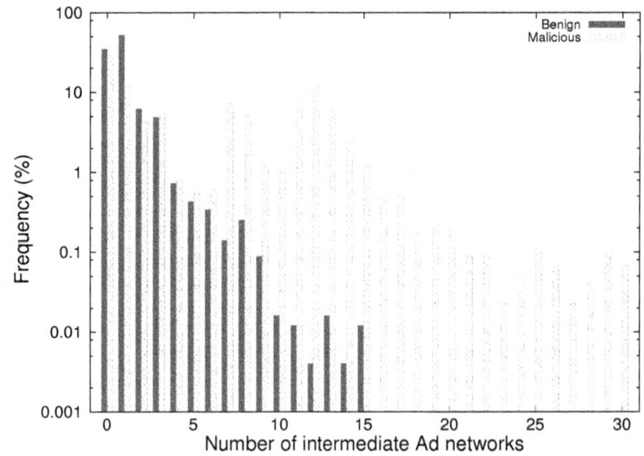

Figure 5: Ad networks involved in ad arbitration for malicious and benign advertisements.

4.3 Ad Arbitration

Website administrators might assume that by using only advertisements from major networks, which are considered trustworthy, they can protect their visitors from potential malvertisements. Unfortunately, this is not the case. There is a practice called *ad arbitration*, which is widely used by ad networks to increase their revenue. During the ad arbitration process, the ad networks buy impressions from publishers as if they were advertisers, and then start a new auction for these ad slots as if they were publishers [25]. Hence, even if an administrator delegates a portion of her website to a specific ad network, she cannot be sure that the advertisements will be only provided by that particular ad exchange.

Although we expected to see a similar behavior in both benign and malicious advertisements, we discovered some cases in which the ad arbitration chain had a much higher length when it came to malvertisements. As we see in Figure 5, in some cases, both benign and malicious advertisements were served directly from the initial ad network. Nevertheless, there were cases in which a specific ad slot participated in up to 15 auctions for benign advertisements and up to 30 auctions for malvertisements. Even though the ad slots that participate in more than 15 auctions constitute only 2% of the malvertisements, we further investigated this phenomenon. Our results revealed that in the initial phases of the auction process, the participants are both popular ad networks and ad networks that we found out being involved in malvertising. However, once the auction process gets longer the last auctions typically happen only among those ad networks that we found to serve malvertisements. An explanation for this could be that smaller and less reputable ad exchanges come into play only when the larger ones failed to obtain an ad slot for a particular arbitration.

Interestingly, we observed ad networks to repeatedly participate in the auctions for the same ad slot. Specifically, we noticed that the same ad networks buy and sell the same slot multiple times. Another interesting fact is the distribution of the ad arbitration chains. Regarding the benign advertisements, the arbitration chain follows a decreasing trend, while, when it comes to malvertisements, it follows a slightly different model. In absolute numbers, the chain follows the same decreasing trend, however, we observe an increase in the frequency of chains in the middle of our graphs.

4.4 Secure Environment

Publishers tend to trust the ad networks that they provide benign advertisements. Hence, they do not secure the environment where the advertisements are displayed. Nikiforakis et al. [22] described the problem of link hijacking, in which advertisements that are contained in iframes redirect the entire web page to an arbitrary destination. This is a serious attack, given the fact that most users open multiple tabs in their browsers for later reading. Hence, the users can be redirected to phishing websites without even noticing that. This problem can be solved in modern browsers with the utilization of the *sandbox* attribute of iframes in HTML5. Unfortunately, none of the websites that we crawled utilized this attribute to protect its users.

5. COUNTERMEASURES

We have shown that malvertising poses a problem to the security of Internet users. In this section, we therefore discuss proactive and reactive countermeasures against malicious advertisements.

5.1 Ad Networks Filtering

Ad networks are the primary mean used by miscreants to deliver their malicious advertisements. Many ad networks have detection mechanisms that successfully filter malvertisements. Yet, there exist others that have poor filtering processes, which are unable to completely eliminate this threat. We believe that collaboration among the ad networks can bring better results in defending against malvertisements compared to individual actions. For instance, the existence of a common blacklist where all the malicious advertisements will be submitted can prevent attackers from submitting their malvertisements to a different network if they get rejected from a former one. Another, more drastic, solution will be penalizing of the ad networks which are inefficient to detect the malicious code embedded in advertisements. For instance, forbidding from participating in ad arbitrations for a certain amount of time, or the application of similar penalties, when an ad network is found delivering malvertisements, can boost the ad networks to invest in better detection algorithms.

5.2 Last Line of Defense

In the case that a malicious advertisement can successfully bypass the filtering mechanisms deployed by ad networks, there should exist reactive countermeasures to protect the users from being infected. Li et al. [18] proposed a browser-based protection mechanism, which can utilize the knowledge of malicious ad paths and their topological features to raise an alarm when a user's browser starts visiting a suspicious ad path, protecting the user from reaching an exploit server. SCARECROW [31], on the other hand, triggers false alarms in a user's browser causing to malicious code, which wants to remain hidden from detection systems, not to be executed. Finally, the safest way for users to protect themselves against malvertisements is to utilize solutions like `Adblock Plus` [1] to prevent advertisements from being delivered to their browsers. Although these solutions appear as the most secure way for the users to protect themselves, and it is already being used by a significant portion of the Web population, a universal adoption of this approach can cause a domino effect in the Internet's economy.

6. RELATED WORK

Detecting malvertisements falls under the category of detecting drive-by downloads. Stringhini et al. [26] and Mekky et al. [20] used the properties of HTTP redirections to identify malicious behavior. Provos et al. [23] introduced *Google Safebrowsing* with the use of high-interaction honeypots. Ford et al. [10] focused on malicious flash-based advertisements by using dynamic and static analysis techniques. A more ad-specific approach was followed with MADTRACER, a tool that inspects the advertisement delivery processes and detects malicious activities with machine learning.

Instead of detecting malicious advertisements, ADJAIL [27] focuses on content restriction policies against third-party advertisements. ADSANDBOX [8] infers maliciousness by executing the suspected JavaScript in an isolated environment and observing the performed actions. ADSENTRY [9] works in a similar way, by executing advertisements in a sandboxed JavaScript engine with control over the interactions with the user's visited page.

Regarding the malvertising detection techniques, previous works focused on various aspects of detecting click-fraud. Majumdar et al. proposed a content delivery system to verify broker honesty under standard security assumptions [19]. Metwally et al. [21] and Zhang et al. [32] on the other hand proposed algorithms to efficiently detect duplicate clicks. Additionally, Daswani and Stoppelman [5] investigate the ways that malware can exploit ad networks. Immorlica et al. [15] studied fraudulent clicks and presented a click-fraud resistant method for learning the click through rate of advertisements. Finally, Kintana et al. [16] created a system designed to penetrate click-fraud filters to discover detection vulnerabilities.

Studying the operations of ad networks is recent in the literature. Guha et al. [13] explored different classes of advertising, like search, contextual, and social networks. Vallina-Rodriguez et al. [28] studied the mobile advertisement ecosystem and how mobile ads introduce energy and network overhead. A financial aspect of advertising was also studied in works of Gill et al. [12]. We differ from these studies as we focus on malvertisements and how these reach the end users.

7. CONCLUSIONS

In this paper, we performed the first large-scale study of ad networks that serve malicious advertisements. We studied various aspects of the advertising ecosystem and observed how malicious advertisements differ from benign ones. In addition, we found that none of the websites that serve advertisements take advantage of new HTML5 features to protect its visitors. Despite any server-side efforts employed by the ad networks, malicious advertisements still reach the end users.

Acknowledgements

This material is based upon work supported by the German Federal Ministry of Education and Research under grant BMBF-01BY1111 (MoBE), by the ARO under Award No. W911NF-09-1-0553, by the ONR under Award No. N00014-09-1-1042, by the Air Force under Award No. FA8750-12-2-0101, and by the NSF under Award CNS-1408632. Any opinions, findings, and conclusions or recommendations expressed in this publication are those of the authors and do not necessarily reflect the views of the funding agencies.

8. REFERENCES

[1] Adblock Plus. Surf the web without annoying ads! https://adblockplus.org, 2014.

[2] A. Barth. RFC 6454: The Web Origin Concept. http://tools.ietf.org/html/rfc6454, 2011.

[3] E. Cooke, F. Jahanian, and D. McPherson. The Zombie Roundup: Understanding, Detecting, and Disrupting Botnets. In *USENIX Workshop on Steps to Reducing Unwanted Traffic on the Internet (SRUTI)*, 2005.

[4] M. Cova, C. Kruegel, and G. Vigna. Detection and Analysis of Drive-by-Download Attacks and Malicious JavaScript Code. In *International Conference on World Wide Web (WWW)*, 2010.

[5] N. Daswani and M. Stoppelman. The Anatomy of Clickbot. A. In *USENIX Workshop on Hot Topics in Understanding Botnets (HotBots)*, 2007.

[6] V. Dave, S. Guha, and Y. Zhang. Measuring and Fingerprinting Click-Spam in Ad Networks. In *ACM SIGCOMM Conference on Data Communication*, 2012.

[7] V. Dave, S. Guha, and Y. Zhang. ViceROI: Catching Click-Spam in Search Ad Networks. In *ACM Conference on Computer and Communications Security (CCS)*, 2013.

[8] A. Dewald, T. Holz, and F. C. Freiling. ADSandbox : Sandboxing JavaScript to fight Malicious Websites. In *ACM Symposium on Applied Computing (SAC)*, 2010.

[9] X. Dong, M. Tran, Z. Liang, and X. Jiang. AdSentry: comprehensive and flexible confinement of JavaScript-based advertisements. In *Annual Computer Security Applications Conference (ACSAC)*, 2011.

[10] S. Ford, M. Cova, C. Kruegel, and G. Vigna. Analyzing and Detecting Malicious Flash Advertisements. In *Annual Computer Security Applications Conference (ACSAC)*, 2009.

[11] Fox-IT. Malicious advertisements served via Yahoo. http://blog.fox-it.com/2014/01/03/malicious-advertisements-served-via-yahoo/, Jan 2014.

[12] P. Gill, V. Erramilli, A. Chaintreau, B. Krishnamurthy, K. Papagiannaki, and P. Rodriguez. Follow the Money: Understanding Economics of Online Aggregation and Advertising. In *ACM SIGCOMM Conference on Internet Measurement (IMC)*, 2013.

[13] S. Guha, B. Cheng, and P. Francis. Challenges in Measuring Online Advertising Systems. In *ACM SIGCOMM Conference on Internet Measurement (IMC)*, 2010.

[14] IAB. Internet Advertising Revenue Report. http://www.iab.net/media/file/IAB_Internet_Advertising_Revenue_Report_FY_2013.pdf, 2014.

[15] N. Immorlica, K. Jain, M. Mahdian, and K. Talwar. Click Fraud Resistant Methods for Learning Click-Through Rates. *Internet and Network Economics*, pages 34–45, 2005.

[16] C. Kintana, D. Turner, J.-Y. Pan, A. Metwally, N. Daswani, E. Chin, and A. Bortz. The Goals and Challenges of Click Fraud Penetration Testing Systems. In *International Symposium on Software Reliability Engineering*, 2009.

[17] M. Kührer and T. Holz. An empirical analysis of malware blacklists. *Praxis der Informationsverarbeitung und Kommunikation*, 35(1):11–16, 2012.

[18] Z. Li, K. Zhang, Y. Xie, F. Yu, and X. Wang. Knowing Your Enemy: Understanding and Detecting Malicious Web Advertising. In *ACM Conference on Computer and Communications Security (CCS)*, 2012.

[19] S. Majumdar, D. Kulkarni, and C. V. Ravishankar. Addressing Click Fraud in Content Delivery Systems. In *IEEE Conference on Computer Communications (INFOCOM)*, 2007.

[20] H. Mekky, R. Torres, Z.-L. Zhang, S. Saha, and A. Nucci. Detecting Malicious HTTP Redirections Using Trees of User Browsing Activity. In *IEEE Conference on Computer Communications (INFOCOM)*, 2014.

[21] A. Metwally, D. Agrawal, and A. El Abbadi. Duplicate Detection in Click Streams. In *International Conference on World Wide Web (WWW)*, 2005.

[22] N. Nikiforakis, F. Maggi, G. Stringhini, M. Z. Rafique, W. Joosen, C. Kruegel, F. Piessens, G. Vigna, and S. Zanero. Stranger Danger: Exploring the Ecosystem of Ad-based URL Shortening Services. In *International Conference on World Wide Web (WWW)*, 2014.

[23] N. Provos, P. Mavrommatis, M. Rajab, and F. Monrose. All Your Iframes Point to Us. In *USENIX Security Symposium*, 2008.

[24] B. Stone-Gross, R. Abman, R. Kemmerer, C. Kruegel, D. Steigerwald, and G. Vigna. The Underground Economy of Fake Antivirus Software. In *Workshop on Economics of Information Security (WEIS)*, 2011.

[25] B. Stone-Gross, R. Stevens, A. Zarras, R. Kemmerer, C. Kruegel, and G. Vigna. Understanding Fraudulent Activities in Online Ad Exchanges. In *ACM SIGCOMM Conference on Internet Measurement (IMC)*, 2011.

[26] G. Stringhini, C. Kruegel, and G. Vigna. Shady Paths: Leveraging Surfing Crowds to Detect Malicious Web Pages. In *ACM Conference on Computer and Communications Security (CCS)*, 2013.

[27] M. Ter Louw, K. T. Ganesh, and V. Venkatakrishnan. AdJail: Practical Enforcement of Confidentiality and Integrity Policies on Web Advertisements. In *USENIX Security Symposium*, 2010.

[28] N. Vallina-Rodriguez, J. Shah, A. Finamore, Y. Grunenberger, K. Papagiannaki, H. Haddadi, and J. Crowcroft. Breaking for Commercials: Characterizing Mobile Advertising. In *ACM SIGCOMM Conference on Internet Measurement (IMC)*, 2012.

[29] K. C. Wilbur and Y. Zhu. Click Fraud. *Marketing Science*, 28(2):293–308, 2009.

[30] G. Wondracek, T. Holz, C. Platzer, E. Kirda, and C. Kruegel. Is the Internet for Porn? An Insight Into the Online Adult Industry. In *Workshop on Economics of Information Security (WEIS)*, 2010.

[31] A. Zarras. The Art of False Alarms in the Game of Deception: Leveraging Fake Honeypots for Enhanced Security. In *IEEE International Carnahan Conference on Security Technology (ICCST)*, 2014.

[32] L. Zhang and Y. Guan. Detecting Click Fraud in Pay-Per-Click Streams of Online Advertising Networks. In *International Conference on Distributed Computing Systems*, 2008.

Layer 1-Informed Internet Topology Measurement

Ramakrishnan Durairajan
University of Wisconsin-Madison
rkrish@cs.wisc.edu

Joel Sommers
Colgate University
jsommers@colgate.edu

Paul Barford
University of Wisconsin-Madison
pb@cs.wisc.edu

ABSTRACT

Understanding the Internet's topological structure continues to be fraught with challenges. In this paper, we investigate the hypothesis that physical maps of service provider infrastructure can be used to effectively guide topology discovery based on network layer TTL-limited measurement. The goal of our work is to focus layer 3-based probing on broadly identifying *Internet infrastructure that has a fixed geographic location* such as POPs, IXPs and other kinds of hosting facilities. We begin by comparing more than 1.5 years of TTL-limited probe data from the Ark [25] project with maps of service provider infrastructure from the Internet Atlas [15] project. We find that there are substantially more nodes and links identified in the service provider map data versus the probe data. Next, we describe a new method for probe-based measurement of physical infrastructure called *POPsicle* that is based on careful selection of probe source-destination pairs. We demonstrate the capability of our method through an extensive measurement study using existing "looking glass" vantage points distributed throughout the Internet and show that it reveals 2.4 times more physical node locations versus standard probing methods. To demonstrate the deployability of POPsicle we also conduct tests at an IXP. Our results again show that POPsicle can identify more physical node locations compared with standard layer 3 probes, and through this deployment approach it can be used to measure thousands of networks world wide.

Categories and Subject Descriptors

C.2.1 [**Network Architecture and Design**]: Network topology; C.2.3 [**Network Operations**]: Public networks

General Terms

Algorithms, Design, Measurement

Keywords

Physical Internet, POPsicle probing heuristic

IMC'14, November 5–7, 2014, Vancouver, BC, Canada.
Copyright 2014 ACM 978-1-4503-3213-2/14/11 ...$15.00.
http://dx.doi.org/10.1145/2663716.2663737.

1. INTRODUCTION

Studies that aim to map the Internet's topological structure have been motivated for many years by a number of compelling applications including the possibilities of improving performance, security and robustness (e.g., [19]). While these motivations remain as compelling as ever, the ability to accurately and comprehensively map the Internet has, for the most part, remained beyond our grasp.

The primary challenges to thoroughly mapping the Internet stem from its enormous size, distributed ownership, and constantly changing characteristics. Faced with these challenges, the most widely used approach to Internet mapping has been based on gathering data from network-layer measurements using TTL-limited probes[1]. Great progress has been made on solving some of the specific problems related to using these network layer measurements for understanding Internet topological characteristics. However, the fact remains that layer 3 data are inherently tied to the management policies and operational objectives of service providers, which may be at odds with comprehensive and accurate mapping of the Internet.

So, just what do we mean by an "Internet map"? At the lowest level, the Internet is composed of physical conduits that contain bundles of optical fiber, and that terminate at buildings that house routing and switching equipment. We refer to the collection of these data and their geographic locations as "physical maps" of the Internet. Several recent projects have begun to assemble repositories of physical Internet maps [15, 29]. These maps are valuable because they reflect a ground truth perspective of service provider infrastructure. These are in contrast with maps that have been generated based on layer 3 probes (*e.g.,* [45]), which we refer to as "network-layer maps". Ideally, network-layer maps reflect a timely representation of network topology as well as the dynamic aspects of management and configurations.

In this paper we investigate the hypothesis that physical maps can be used to guide and reinforce the process of collecting layer 3 probe data toward the goal of expanding the scope of physical infrastructure captured in network-layer maps. This conjecture leads directly to two key research questions that are the focus of our work: *(i)* how do physical layer maps compare and contrast with network-layer maps? and *(ii)* how can probe methods used by projects like Ark [25] be improved to reveal a larger portion of physical infrastructure? We contend that some of the challenges

[1] Maps can also be created using BGP updates or application-layer data, however those are not the focus of this paper.

inherent in generating maps from layer 3 probes can be overcome by using the constructive approach of first identifying key infrastructure (POPs, etc.) and then identifying nodes (identified by disambiguating IP addresses or using DNS names) that reside in those locations.

Our study begins by considering physical map data from the Internet Atlas (or Atlas) project and network-layer map data from the Ark project. We focus specifically on infrastructure in North America. The Atlas repository includes data from 78 Internet service providers with over 2600 nodes and over 3580 links. Nodes in the Atlas data refer to hosting centers or points of presence (POPs), with links referring to physical connections between those locations. We use Ark measurements collected from September 2011 to March 2013 (approximately the same period over which the Atlas repository has been assembled). We resolve the IP addresses from this corpus to DNS names and then use location hints to associate these with physical locations (*e.g.*, cities), which becomes the basis for our comparisons.

Several characteristics are immediately evident in the data. Most prominent is the fact that among the 50 networks that are the focus of our comparison study, we observe many more nodes and links in the physical maps. There can be a number of explanations for this observation, including *(i)* the limitations of exploiting DNS naming conventions, *(ii)* the use of tunneling protocols (*e.g.*, MPLS) or the lack of layer 3 services which can render nodes invisible to probes, *(iii)* the limited perspective of the network mapping infrastructure and *(iv)* the fact that layer 3 routing configurations may simply obviate the ability to observe all networks, nodes and links. This supposition is supported by the observation that all Ark probes are confined to a minority subset of networks, with the majority of probes traversing an even smaller subset of networks. Despite this, there are still some nodes/locations/links that appear in the network-layer map but are not indicated in the physical map. This can be explained by physical maps that are out of date or are either intentionally or erroneously incomplete.

The differences between the physical and network-layer maps suggests opportunities for *reinforcement* between the data sets. First, networks observed in Ark that do not appear in Atlas offer clues for searching for new maps that would expand the repository. Second, nodes or links in Atlas that do not appear in Ark can become targets for additional probing that could expand the scope of resulting network-layer maps, thereby making them more useful in target applications. We focus specifically on the possibility of identifying new nodes in layer 3 measurements through targeted probing in the second component of our study.

We define the *targeting problem* as identifying source-destination pairs for layer 3 probes that reveal nodes indicated in the physical maps[2]. Probing sources (or Vantage Points—VPs) are publicly available infrastructure such as looking glass and traceroute servers and PlanetLab nodes from which probes can be sent. Destinations are simply IP addresses that may respond to probes. We began our targeting analysis by identifying a subset of 596 POPs from the physical maps across 25 networks as our target set. We then conducted extensive probe-based measurements using 266 unique sources and 742 destination addresses in the target networks using two core ideas: *(i)* source-destination pairs should be proximal to the target geographically and in address space, and *(ii)* verification of measurements using multiple sources is required. We verify the identification of infrastructure using location hints in DNS names and using records available in PeeringDB [5]. Our analysis shows that probing between sources and destinations that are both *within the same autonomous system as the target(s)* reveals the most physical infrastructure.

The results of our targeting experiments motivate a new heuristic algorithm for probe targeting that we call *POPsicle.* We show that POPsicle finds 2.4 times as many nodes as are identified by Ark. We compare the number of POPs found by POPsicle with POPs found using Rocketfuel [45] and in all cases POPsicle performs better. We also found that IXPs play a critical role in the way probes traverse a given network. Specifically, sources that are co-located with IXPs have the advantage of appearing—from a layer 3 perspective—as being internal to any/all of the networks that are connected at that location. Thus, a single source that is co-located within an IXP may enhance the identification of infrastructure across all networks that connect to the IXP. This has the effect of significantly broadening the scope of the infrastructure that can be identified using our approach. To validate this idea, we deployed POPsicle at the Equinix IXP in Chicago, USA, and measured the number of POPs for 10 ISPs and found that POPsicle reveals almost all POPs compared to Atlas and extra POPs (in certain cases) compared to Ark. We also find through a case study of Cogent network that POPsicle identifies over 90% of the nodes identified in Atlas or by the reverse DNS technique of [21], compared with about 65% of the POPs identified through Ark, and only 25% identified in the most recently available Rocketfuel data.

To summarize, the key contributions of our work are as follows. First, we perform a first-of-its-kind comparison of large repositories of physical and network maps and find that physical maps typically reveal a much larger number of nodes (*e.g.,* POPs and hosting infrastructure). Next, we consider the targeting problem and find that using sources and destinations within the same autonomous system for probing reveals the most physical infrastructure. We develop a layer 1-informed heuristic algorithm for probe source-destination selection called POPsicle that identifies 2.4 times as many nodes as standard probing methods. Finally, we identify the fact that sources co-located as IXPs can be used to amplify POPsicle-based probing broadly throughout the Internet resulting in layer 3 maps that can be more effectively applied to problems of interest. To that end, we deployed our method at a real IXP and found that our method finds almost all POPs compared to Atlas and additional POPs compared to Ark for the ISPs studied.

2. RELATED WORK

Creating maps of the Internet's topology has been of interest to the research community since the early days of the Internet, and its predecessor, the ARPAnet [37]. Just as maintaining a `hosts.txt` file was feasible in the Internet's infancy, so was the capability of identifying *all* nodes and links in the network [32]. After the privatization and commercialization of the Internet, it became well accepted and understood that the Internet's rapid growth implied that the cataloging efforts of earlier years were no longer possible.

[2] *Efficient targeting* is a related problem that seeks to identify infrastructure with a minimal number of probes. We do not directly consider minimizing probe budget in this study.

Since then, there has been a great deal of effort made to harness layer 3 TTL-limited probes for network mapping since the introduction of the `traceroute` tool [26]. Some efforts (*e.g.*, [40, 45]) have focused on the goal of developing a comprehensive network-layer view of the Internet *i.e.*, unique identification of nodes and links. Other efforts have focused on developing new probing techniques that expand the ability to collect data and thereby improve accuracy and mapping coverage, *e.g.*, [9, 10, 41]. More recent efforts have focused on analyzing and addressing various inaccuracies inherent in probe-based network mapping [43,49]. For example, Roughan, *et al.* and Eriksson, *et al.* develop inferential techniques to quantify the nodes and links that are missed through network-layer mapping [18, 38]. Other researchers have looked closely at the rise of Internet Exchange Points (IXPs) and the effects of IXPs on inaccuracies of network-layer mapping, *e.g.*, [8, 10]. Concurrent with the rise of IXPs has come a "flattening" of the Internet's peering structure [13,22,30], which affects the very nature of end-to-end paths through the Internet. Still other researchers have observed that increased use of network virtualization techniques such as MPLS have led to additional inaccuracies in layer 3 mapping, and which are likely to continue to thwart probe-based mapping efforts [14,40,42]. We posit that layer 3 mapping efforts will continue to be important sources of Internet topology information and that complementary efforts to build repositories of physical Internet maps (*e.g.*, [15,29]) will result in representations of Internet topology that are more accurate and applicable to problems of interest than either representation in isolation.

The targeting problem that is a focus of our work is informed by prior studies that analyze the intrinsic importance of measurement infrastructure in Internet topology mapping. Barford *et al.* were among the first to quantify the value of vantage points in discovery of nodes and links in core and edges of the Internet [11]. More recently, Shavitt and Weinsberg consider the problem of bias in measurements based on vantage point distributions and show that a broad distribution of vantage points reduces bias in resulting maps [39]. Our work differs from these studies in that we are focused on using layer 3 probes to identify specific infrastructure targets.

Identifying the geographic location of nodes that have been assigned specific IP addresses (*i.e.*, *IP geolocation*) is a challenging problem that is highly relevant to our study. Some of the earliest work on this problem was done by Paxson, who developed the idea of using DNS hints to identify the geographic locations of nodes that were responding to TTL-limited probes [35]. We use similar methods in our study. Since then, many studies have addressed the problem of IP and POP geolocation using a variety of measurement techniques (*e.g.*, [17,20,23,28,34,36,46,47]). The fact that POP locations in physical maps are often given at the street address level offers the possibility to improve IP geolocation estimates using standard measurement-based methods. We are also investigating another possibility of leveraging state-of-the-art geolocation techniques (*e.g.*, [24,46]) to enhance the accuracy of our location extraction approach.

3. DATASETS

In this section we describe the datasets used in our study. One of the key contributions of our work is the comparison of physical topology data from primary sources and network-layer topology data extracted from layer 3 TTL-limited probes, as described below. In the case of physical infrastructure data, we use the latest maps from service providers collected as part of Internet Atlas project [15]. For network-layer topology data, we rely on traceroute data collected as part of CAIDA's Archipelago (Ark) project [25].

3.1 Physical Topology Data

In this study, we rely on the publicly available physical topology data from the Internet Atlas project. Internet Atlas is a visualization and analysis portal for diverse Internet measurement data. The starting point for Internet Atlas is a geographically anchored representation of the physical Internet including *(i)* nodes (*e.g.*, hosting facilities and data centers), *(ii)* conduits/links that connect these nodes, and *(iii)* relevant meta data (*e.g.*, source provenance). The approach for building the repository is to use targeted search to identify maps and other listings of physical Internet infrastructure that are published on the web by ISPs. Though there is no guarantee as to their timeliness or completeness, we use this data as ground truth of service provider infrastructure in this study. Since these data come from primary sources, they also reflect a ground truth perspective of service provider infrastructure. The current repository contains geocoded physical infrastructure data of over 425 ISPs around the world. From this online repository, we obtain detailed geographic information of 7 Tier-1 networks and 71 non-Tier-1/regional networks with a presence in North America consisting of 2611 POPs and 3588 links.

3.2 Network-layer Topology Data

We seek to improve the state-of-the-art in Internet topology mapping by investigating structural characteristics revealed by layer 3 probes. Our goal is to broaden the understanding of Internet topology by investigating how topological characteristics as revealed by layer 3 traceroute probes compare to and contrast with physical structure derived from service provider maps.

The network-layer probe data that we use are collected as part of the Ark project, and include traceroute measurements from a set of 77 monitoring systems distributed around the globe to all routed /24 prefixes in the IPv4 Internet. We used the traceroute data gathered by the Ark project since it represents a canonical system for large-scale Internet topology measurement. We note, however, that the measurements collected in Ark are subject to a variety of network management policies, including blocking or limiting responses to TTL-limited probes, routing configurations and MPLS tunnels, each of which can limit the scope of the measurement data.

Ark is the canonical example of what we might call a *generalized topology probing system*. POPsicle, on the other hand, has a specific goal, which is to discover unique nodes based on guidance from physical maps. Given the difference in goals, the comparisons of the number of unique nodes identified by Ark vs. POPsicle should be interpreted as a comparison between a generalized and a purpose-built system, *i.e.*, POPsicle can be implemented as an extension to Ark or as the basis for designing an entirely new *coordinated large-scale traceroute-based topology measurement system.*

3.3 DNS Data

The DNS data we use are also collected as part of the IPv4 Routed /24 DNS Names Dataset [4], and provide fully-qualified domain names for IP addresses seen in the Ark traces. In this work, our consideration of network-layer topology data is limited by the scope and placement of Ark monitors. However, that project has taken pains to include a broad spectrum of network types (*e.g.*, research, commercial, and educational networks) as vantage points for their monitoring systems, and it provides a widely-used view of the Internet's topology.

Leveraging *location hints* present in domain names to classify IP addresses into POPs is fraught with challenges as described in Section 4. We believe that the accuracy of our results could be improved further either with better techniques of handling DNS naming hints, *e.g.,* using the techniques of Huffaker *et al.* [24], or by using non-DNS-based techniques to classify IP addresses to their corresponding POPs [44].

3.4 Scope of Comparison Study

In this study, we restrict our analysis of Ark data to a period of 19 months, from September 2011 to March 2013, which is contemporaneous with data collection in Atlas. Our focus is on understanding the composite views of networks offered by both data sets over this period. From each individual traceroute in the source data, we extract all the *internal* network IP addresses and links. That is, after processing each traceroute, there is a corresponding interface list (*e.g.*, IP1, IP2, IP3, IP4, *etc.*) and link list (*e.g.*, IP1-IP2, IP3-IP4, *etc.*). For instance, if the traceroute contains a probe of the form A-B-C-D-E (where A, B, C, D and E are IP addresses), we ignore the end point IP addresses (A and E) and extract only the network IP addresses (B, C and D). The interface list thus contains IP addresses B, C and D, and the link list contains B-C and C-D. We merge all the interface/link lists after removing all the duplicate entries to produce a final list of interface IP addresses and links. We then use the corresponding DNS dataset and join the list of interface IPs to their corresponding DNS entries.

4. DATA ANALYSIS

In this section, we describe the methods we use to analyze the network-layer topology data. We begin with discussing results from processing the network-layer data followed by associating geographic locations to the network-layer data.

4.1 Network-layer Data Analysis

In this section, we describe the two-step mapping algorithm that we use to associate a physical location to the IP address interface list obtained from processing network-layer traceroute data, as described above.

Key Idea. One of the aspects of this algorithm is to translate location-based patterns in DNS names that refer to router interfaces to physical (geographic) locations. The influential topology mapping work of Spring *et al.* [45] used such "hints" in their `undns` tool as part of the Rocketfuel project in order to infer locations of network POPs. Many network service providers employ naming conventions that include geographically relevant information such as airport codes, city names, or other location information. By exploiting these conventions and developing rules to infer geographic locations from them, we can build a network-layer topology map.

Challenges. Leveraging naming conventions in DNS entries has two important challenges. The first is that these names may be out-of-date or misconfigured, which would lead to invalid geographic inferences. The work of Zhang *et al.* [48] quantified the prevalence such problems and found them to occur infrequently, but to have potentially large impact on topology mapping studies that rely on DNS information. They developed a set of heuristics to avoid such problems, including the detection of POP-level loops within a single provider (which should not occur, assuming that the ISP's intra-domain routing protocols are configured properly). We also use such techniques in our work to avoid problems with exploiting DNS naming conventions. A second challenge with using DNS entries is that there are inherent ambiguities associated with them, *e.g.*, a single string may be used by two different ISPs to refer to two *different* physical locations. To cope with these problems, a set of regular expression patterns can encode different rules to disambiguate location hints from different providers. This approach was also taken in the earlier `undns` tool [45]. Table 1 shows several example patterns and how they are used to resolve ambiguities in naming.

Algorithm. The algorithm for developing a network-layer map from raw traceroute data takes four inputs:

- *regular expression patterns* to extract the location code from DNS entries. The location code is that part of the hostname that contains location data. For example, for `A.B.C.LAX2.D.NET`, the location code is LAX, which is the airport code for Los Angeles, CA, USA;
- *mapping codes* [12] to translate location code obtained from DNS entries to physical location (a latitude/longitude pair);
- the *list of nodes* (along with each corresponding DNS entry) obtained by parsing the traceroute data from Ark as described above;
- and the *list of links* obtained by parsing the traceroute data from Ark, also as described above.

Using these inputs, we associate physical locations to the IP addresses in the interface list using the following steps:

- First, we match the domain names against the regular expression location patterns and extract a location code from every entry.
- Next, we translate the location code to an actual physical location using the mapping codes. The result of this second step is that we have location information associated with every interface IP address that has a DNS entry with location hints embedded in it. We also use Team Cymru's IP-to-ASN mapping service [3] to classify the list of nodes and links into different ISPs based on the Autonomous System (AS) Numbers.

At the end of applying this algorithm we have network-layer maps for different autonomous systems in which the nodes refer to geographic locations of POPs, and links refer to the fact that packets can be forwarded between a pair of POPs. Note that we do not consider intra-POP links, or individual routers in POPs. The result is that we have a network-layer map that can be equitably compared with the physical map available from Internet Atlas.

Table 1: Examples of regular expressions used for extracting location hints from DNS entries.

Regular expression	Explanation
/\.(birmingham)\d*\.(level3)\.net$/i	`birmingham` could refer to a city like Birmingham, UK, but means Birmingham, AL, USA to Level3.
/\.(manchester)\d*\.(level3)\.net$/i	`manchester` could refer to a city like Manchester, NH, USA, but it means Manchester, UK to Level3.
/\.(mad)\.(verizon\-gni)\.net$/i	`mad` could refer to a city like Madrid, Spain, but it means Madison, NJ, USA to Verizon.
/\.(ham)\d*\.(alter)\.net$/i	`ham` could refer to a city like Hamburg, Germany, but it means Hamilton, Canada to alter.net
/\.(cam)\-bar\d*\.(ja)\.net$/i	`cam` could refer to a city like Cambridge WI, USA, but it means Cambridge, MA, USA to bbnplanet, and Cambridge, UK to ja.net

4.2 How are POPs in the same city identified?

To identify POPs located within the same city, we leverage three types of information: *(1)* Personal email communication with network operators and administrators who run the ISPs, *(2)* IP address allocation information from publicly available databases like PeeringDB, and *(3)* naming conventions recorded from ISP websites. In what follows, we give a list of examples for all three cases.

- Tinet (now Intelliquent) has multiple POPs at multiple cities. To identify those POP locations, we contacted one of the network operators [16] from Tinet and identified the naming convention followed by them — the first three letters are city code, and next digit is location code. For instance, `ams10` and `ams20` are two different POPs in Amsterdam.
- Another reliable source of information that is frequently updated and maintained by network operators is PeeringDB. Apart from providing the list of peers at a particular facility (or an IXP), PeeringDB also provides information like address space allocation, network operator contacts, etc. For instance, GTT has multiple POP locations in New York. One of them peers at NYIIX and has `198.32.160.0/24` as its address space, and one another POP peers at Coresite NY with `206.51.45.0/24` as its address space.
- ISPs routinely publish their naming conventions in their websites along with inter-city POP details. For instance, Lumos Networks and Atlantic Metro Communications publicly list all inter-city POP naming conventions [6,7].

4.3 Associating Geographic Locations with Traceroute Data

We first provide details on results from processing the traceroute data used for building network-layer topologies. Over the 19 months of Ark data considered in our study, we identified 14,593,457 unique interface IP addresses, comprising 31,055 unique ASes. On these traceroute measurements, we applied the algorithm described above to construct network-layer topologies for comparison with the physical networks chosen for our study. Table 2 shows several statistics resulting from applying our algorithm.

As shown in Table 2, there were a number of situations in which we could not reliably use the traceroute data for building network-layer topologies. In particular, over 13M IP addresses did not have an associated DNS name with any (obvious) location information embedded in it[3], which represents 95.16% of all IP addresses observed in our data. Of these, over 6M were unusable because of DNS resolution failures, *e.g.*, `fail.non-authoritative.in-addr.arpa`, which represented 40.31% of all IP addresses observed in our data. While these results certainly limit our ability to compare physical and network-layer topologies for *all* networks, the remaining "usable" trace information represents 4,135 separate autonomous systems, which we argue still represents a significant slice of the Internet.

Table 2: Basic results from processing 19 months of Ark traceroute data using the algorithm described in Section 3

Total traceroutes processed	2,674,959,041
Number of unique interface IP addresses	14,593,457
Number of unique ASes	31,055
Valid DNS entries found	6,936,146
No associated DNS name found	7,657,311
DNS entries with location hints	704,935
Number of ASes with at least one geographically identifiable interface address	4,135

An issue we encountered when applying the algorithm of Section 4.1 was that, in some cases, there were no associated AS numbers indicated by the Team Cymru IP-to-AS mapping service or available in other whois databases. For such networks, we used a manual keyword search (*e.g.*, layer42.net refers to the Layer42 ISP), which was effective for subnets with at least one associated DNS entry.

5. COMPARING LAYER 1 MAPS WITH LAYER 3 PROBE DATA

In this section, we analyze the physical and network-layer topology data. We begin with comparing the two views of Internet topology by considering how each view intersects and differs from one another, and also how the two views of network topology reinforce each other. We focus our discussion on 50 regional and national ISPs with footprints in North America. We focus on these particular networks be-

[3]For example, the DNS naming conventions may not be oriented around physical node location and thus be unusable for our purposes, *e.g.*, entries such as `216-19-195-15.getnet.net` and `173-244-236-242.unassigned.ntelos.net`.

cause there is significant detail within the Internet Atlas data regarding POPs and inter-POP links for these ISPs.

5.1 Comparison of Physical and Network-layer Nodes and Links

We now compare the physical and network-layer topologies obtained from the Atlas data and the Ark data, respectively. Again, the basic entities we compare are *nodes*, which represent city-level points of presence or data centers, and *links*, which represent physical and/or logical connectivity between two city-level POPs.

Table 6 in Appendix A shows the number of nodes and links observed in each topology type, for each of the 50 networks under study. We first see that while all physical networks have non-zero nodes and links, there are some network-layer topologies for which there are zero nodes and/or links observed. There are two reasons for this. First, an interface IP address for a given network may have no clear location information embedded in its associated DNS entry. For example, for 21 out of 50 networks, there were no location hints observable in the related DNS records. This result may be because of non-obvious naming conventions, or simply that there are no name records available. We note that although some ISPs in our list of 50 have been acquired by other companies, the AS number and address blocks assigned to these companies still refer to the original ISP [4].

The second reason we may observe zero nodes and/or links for a given network is that we may simply not have observed *any* interface addresses for a given network in 19 months of traceroute data. This observation was true for 16 out of the 50 networks included in our study. Considering the fact that the Ark project targets *every* routable /24 in the IPv4 Internet, this is a surprising result. Still, there may be a variety of reasons for this observation. First, some ISPs may configure their routers not to respond to hop-limited probes with ICMP time exceeded messages (resulting in "stars" in the traceroute output). Second, some networks may use tunneling protocols such as MPLS, and configure these tunnels to be completely hidden. Third, there may be interfaces controlled by an ISP under study that are configured with IP addresses from a third party, *e.g.*, an IXP. In the end, we were left with 13 networks that had DNS entries for which we could identify a physical location.

To assess how the physical and network-layer views of a network compare, we consider node and link *intersection*, as well as the number of nodes and links *only* observed in one or other other topology. To determine the intersection, we consider a node to intersect each topology if we identify the same POP location in each one. We consider a link to intersect each topology if there are POPs identified in the same two locations in each topology and there is a link identified between them. For example, if we observe nodes in Chicago and Kansas City in both the physical and network-layer topologies for a given ISP, and a link between those two cities, we say the link and two nodes intersect.

Table 6 in Appendix A shows results from the intersection analysis. We also show in the table nodes or links that *only* appear in one or the other topology. We see that, in general, there are more nodes and links observed in the physical topologies than are seen in the network-layer topologies. For the networks for which this observation holds, the number of nodes and links observed is, in some cases, *significantly* larger than those seen using the traceroute data. These results strongly suggest that sole reliance on layer 3 probes to generate physical network maps is likely to result in an incomplete view of Internet topology. On the other hand, the table shows that there are a small number of networks in which we observe *more* nodes and links in the network-layer topology. In particular, we see this for AT&T, Tinet, NTT, Sprint, Layer42, and Hurricane Electric (abbreviated as HE in the table). This observation suggests that while published physical maps *usually* offer an authoritative view of physical infrastructure, the published maps may lag recent deployments which can be observed through layer 3 probing.

More broadly, analysis of the Ark traces shows that there are at least 448 distinct networks in North America (that are not part of Atlas). This number is identified by first searching for all North American location DNS hints and then identifying unique service providers in the DNS names. This compares to the 320 distinct networks in the Atlas repository, which have been identified through extensive search-based methods. An implication for this difference is that measurements from Ark can be used as guidance for identifying service provider networks that could be included in Atlas. For example, many small/regional networks like Adera Networks (CA), Grande Communications (TX) and Atala T (NY) were found in the traces of Ark and such networks could be incorporated into future search-based campaigns.

Of the 448 distinct networks identified through Ark measurements, the vast majority of probes pass through tier-1 and major ISPs, as shown in Figure 1. Thus, while it is likely that the POP-level topology of well-connected ISPs can be largely identified through general probing techniques, smaller ISPs are unlikely to be well-mapped. This observation is supported by prior studies on sampling bias in network topology measurements (*e.g.,* [39]). An implication for this observation is that *targeted probing methods* may be necessary to obtain a more comprehensive topological picture of physical Internet infrastructure.

Lastly, we consider one form of *validation* of physical node locations when we observe the same location for nodes in more than one network. We define the metric N_{Index} as the percentage of nodes identified for a given network that have the same physical location as a node in another network. The right-most column of Table 6 in Appendix A shows the N_{Index} for each network. The intuition for why this metric provides some level of validation of the physical location has to do with common industry practices of using co-location facilities and telecom hotels. While this observation may not hold universally, we believe that co-location practices are generally observed for small regional networks in geographically isolated areas since the costs associated with setting up new facilities is high. For instance, larger national ISPs like Layer42, Napnet, Navigata and Netrail show an N_{Index} of 100 (complete overlap with nodes in other networks), whereas smaller regional cariers such as NetworkUSA, RedBestel and Syringa[5] show an N_{Index} less than 20 (mostly their own locations). The combination of

[4]For example, although BellSouth was acquired by AT&T in 2006, the name BellSouth is still referred to in `whois` databases and appears in recent address block usage reports (`http://www.cidr-report.org/as2.0/`).

[5]NetworkUSA is a regional carrier serving Louisiana, RedBestel operates in the Guadalajara region of Mexico, and Syringa is a regional carrier in Idaho.

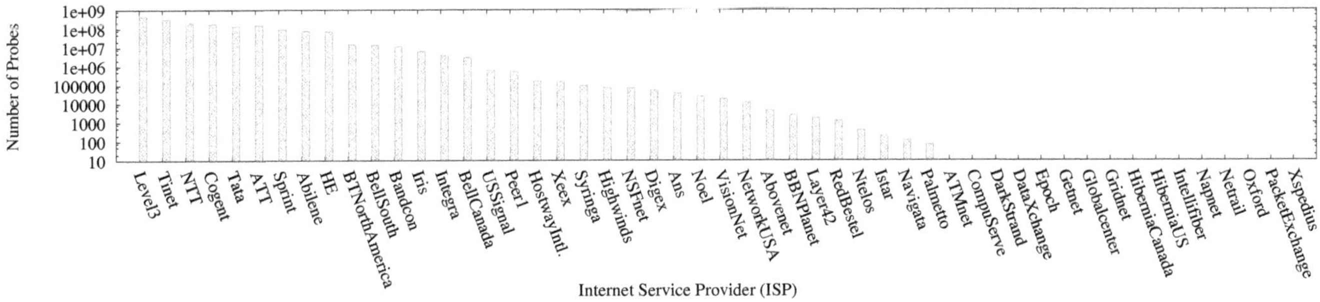

Figure 1: Number of probes sent out by Ark across Internet Service Providers

a high N_{Index} and overlap with traceroute probes provides perhaps the best validation of node locations.

5.2 Case study: Tinet

Tinet represented an interesting special case: the physical topology contained nodes not present in the network-layer topology, and the network-layer topology also contained nodes not present in the physical topology. In particular, there were 65 nodes only present in the physical topology, and 7 nodes that were only observed in the Ark data and network-layer topology. For example, the Tinet physical network map shows four nodes for Amsterdam, Netherlands, one node in San Jose, CA, two nodes in Milan, Italy and two nodes in Washington, DC. However, the network-layer topology revealed additional nodes for these locations. The missing nodes from the physical network may be due to Tinet's network maps not reflecting the most up-to-date deployments. Missing nodes and links in the network-layer view may be due to a variety of reasons, including the inability to gain a broad perspective on Tinet's network from Ark vantage points. What these results indicate is that to gain a *complete* view of a network's topology, multiple data sources must be considered.

5.3 Main findings and implications

The main findings of our comparison of physical and network-layer topologies are as follows.

- We observe many more nodes and links in the physical maps, which may be due to a variety of reasons, but is most critically due to the fact that layer 3 routing configurations simply eliminate the possibility to observe all networks, nodes, and links through end-to-end probing. This likelihood is supported by the fact that all Ark probes are limited to a relatively small subset of networks, with the majority of probes passing through an even smaller set of networks.
- There are still some nodes, locations, and links that appear in the network-layer map but are not observed in physical maps. The likely reason is that the physical maps are out of date or incomplete.
- The observed differences between the physical and network-layer maps suggest opportunities for using one to *reinforce* the other. In particular, networks observed in Ark that do not appear in Atlas offer clues for searching for new maps to expand Atlas. Similarly, nodes or links in Atlas that do not appear in Ark can become targets for additional probing in order to broaden the scope of the resulting network-layer maps.

Indeed, in the next section we focus specifically on how to emit targeted layer 3 probes in order to confirm the existence of nodes identified in physical maps, as well as to identify additional physical nodes.

6. EFFECTS OF VANTAGE POINTS ON NODE IDENTIFICATION

In this section, we examine the effects of source-destination selection on the ability to identify POPs within a service provider using targeted layer 3 probes. Specifically, we examine the differences between using vantage points (probing sources) internal or external to an ISP containing target POP(s), and destinations either internal or external to the ISP. Furthermore, we examine the effects that IXPs may have on probe-based POP identification and how IXP placement may be exploited to aid in node identification by providing a larger set of internal vantage points.

6.1 Effects of vantage point and destination selection

To examine the impact of vantage point and destination IP address selection for identifying all target POPs in an ISP, we leverage publicly available traceroute servers, looking glass servers and Planetlab nodes as VPs[6], and select different combinations of them located within or external to different service providers. In particular, we use three combinations: probing from VPs outside an ISP to destinations inside (denoted VP_{out} to t_{in}), from VPs inside an ISP to destinations outside (denoted VP_{in} to t_{out}) and from VPs inside an ISP and destinations inside (denoted VP_{in} to t_{in}). For each directional modality ($VP_{out} \rightarrow t_{in}$, $VP_{in} \rightarrow t_{out}$, $VP_{in} \rightarrow t_{in}$), we use a greedy approach to identify probe source-destination pairs based on geographic proximity. We choose the VP geographically closest to a target POP, then successively choose from the set of destinations that are also geographically proximal to the target until the target is identified. For instance, a probe from `planet-lab4.wail.wisc.edu` to 184.105.184.158[7] with the aim to identify Hurricane Electric's POP in Los Angeles identified two additional POPs (in Chicago and Denver) in addition to identifying the Los Angeles POP. If we can not identify

[6]We followed principles established in prior work, *e.g.*, [45], to avoid burdening these public servers with excessive load.

[7]`lightower-fiber-networks.gigabitethernet4-10.core1.lax2.he.net`

the POP from a given vantage point, we choose the next closest VP, and so forth (specific details of this method are provided in Section 7).

Using a subset of 25 ISP networks that assign DNS names with location hints and that contain 596 target POPs, we analyze the source-destination combinations. Figure 2 shows the fraction of target POPs discovered by these three probing modalities relative to the number of POPs identified in Atlas. The figure shows clearly that the most effective strategy is to send probes from vantage points located *within* an ISP to destinations that are *also within the ISP* (VP_{in} to t_{in}). We further observe that using a VP located within an ISP is more effective than choosing one external to the ISP. We hypothesize that these differences are due to the effects of interdomain versus intradomain routing on probes. In the case of both VP and destination located within an ISP, there is a greater chance for a diversity of paths to be observed due to ECMP, the fact that more information about shortest paths is available, and the greater degree of flexibility that a service provider has in routing packets within its own infrastructure. In the case of either VP or destination being external to the ISP that contains a target POP, interdomain routing protocol effects come into play, such as hot-potato routing and the forced choice of a single best path.

Lastly, we note that in absolute numbers, we observed a total of 188 POPs using VP_{in} to t_{in}, 157 POPs via VP_{in} to t_{out}, and 93 with VP_{out} to t_{in}. For 11 networks we observed zero POPs. Similar to our earlier observations in which we do not see POPs identified in physical maps, this may be due to MPLS deployments, traffic management policies, or routing policies. We intend to further investigate the reason for the invisibility of POPs in future work.

6.2 Using IXPs to expand perspective

Given the result that the most effective probing strategy for identifying physical infrastructure is to choose source-destination pairs that are within an ISP, it is important to recognize that broad deployment of such targeted measurements is inherently limited by the availability of VPs within provider networks. Indeed, the 266 VPs used in this paper are restricted to 248 separate networks, which is substantially less than the total number of networks identified in North America by Ark in Section 5.

Recent work in [10] has highlighted the enormous amount of layer 2 peering that is taking place at IXPs. This leads us to posit that VPs co-located with IXPs might be leveraged to dramatically expand our ability to identify physical infrastructure. Indeed, there is anecdotal evidence that much of the rapid growth in peering at IXPs is being driven by local and regional ISPs and that Tier-1 ISPs have been slower to connect [27]. This offers a tantalizing opportunity since it is generally the smaller networks that are more difficult to map and those networks often do not deploy looking glass servers that are necessary for mapping physical infrastructure.

To consider this possibility, we begin by looking for VPs that are co-located with IXPs in North America. We find that 14 out of 65 IXPs have co-located VPs. Using PeeringDB [5] we find that the total number of unique ISPs that peer at these 14 IXPs is 642. A comparison between these ISPs and those in with VPs used in our study shows that an additional 625 unique networks could be measured from these 14 IXPs alone. This suggests that deployment of VPs in other IXPs could be the starting point for comprehensive mapping of physical Internet infrastructure.

6.3 Main findings and implications

In summary, we consider how to choose sources and destinations for probing in order to identify POPs within a service provider, as well as to discover new POPs. Specifically, we examine whether it is better to use vantage points (probing sources) internal or external to an ISP containing the target POP(s) and destinations either internal or external to the ISP. Our results show that it is best to choose both source and destination to be *within* the ISP that contains the targeted POP(s), which we hypothesize is largely due to intradomain versus interdomain route selection. Further, we observe that co-locating a probing vantage point at an IXP may be particularly useful in that the VP can effectively appear as being internal to all ISPs that peer at the IXP.

7. ENHANCING NODE IDENTIFICATION

In this section, we build on the observations and experiments of Section 6 to describe a new targeted probing algorithm called *POPsicle*. We evaluate POPsicle's effectiveness for reinforcing and confirming information available in physical maps. We deploy POPsicle at an IXP in Chicago, and describe results of experiments carried out at the IXP.

7.1 POPsicle algorithm

POPsicle is designed to send traceroute-like probes toward a target with a known geographic location based on information from a physical map. The objective is to detect the target *at the network layer*. POPsicle is based on the insight that vantage points co-located with IXPs can be used to launch probes in many different networks, and that probe-based detection of target physical infrastructure is most effective when both VP and destination are located within the same service provider network.

Algorithm 1 shows the key steps of POPsicle. The inputs to the algorithm are (1) the name and address prefix(s) of the ISP within which physical targets are to be identified, (2) the specific list of targets (*e.g.*, POPs) to be identified, including their geographic locations according to physical mapping information, and (3) a list of VPs and their known geographic coordinates. The algorithm proceeds by first scanning the target network to identify which hosts are accessible[8]. This step is performed to collect a set of hosts that can be used as probe destinations. The geographic locations of these hosts are then inferred using DNS location hints. Another option at this step would be to use IP geolocation algorithms or tools. However, the accuracy of these techniques is a subject of ongoing research (*e.g.*, [17]) so we do not use them in POPsicle, but they could be easily incorporated.

Next, POPsicle iterates through the list of target nodes to be identified. For each target, we obtain a list of VPs for initiating probes in step 4, ordered by proximity in Euclidean space (using the Haversine formula [1]) to the target. For each VP, we then select a set of destinations that are also ordered by proximity to the target. Destinations, compiled from a variety of sources like Internet Atlas portal and PeeringDB, are IP addresses of infrastructure, like looking glass

[8]We employ the `nmap` tool for this step with the command line `nmap -Pn -sn` *prefix*. Even though `nmap` is considered bad, we only did a passive scan without causing any trouble to ISPs

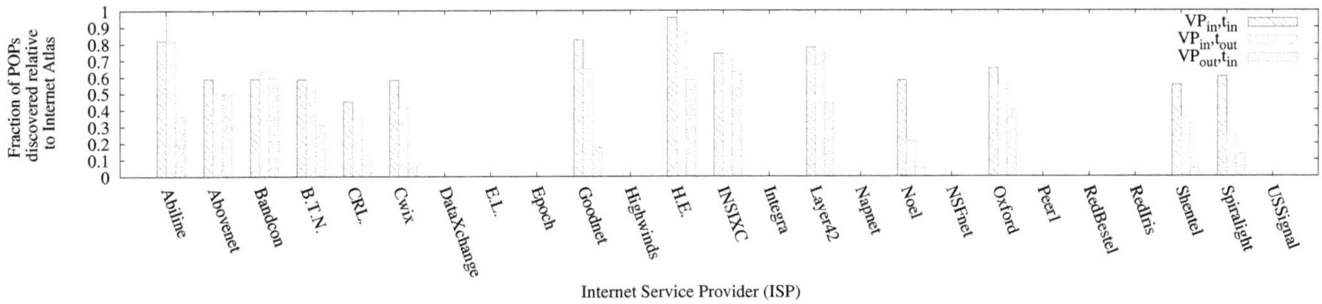

Figure 2: Number of POPs discovered by different probing modalities.

servers, traceroute servers, telecom hotels, and other entities that may simply respond to probes. From this set, we sub-select the destinations such that the square of the Euclidean distance between the VP and destination is greater than the sum of the squares of the distance between VP and target and VP and destination. This has the effect of creating a "measurement cone" centered at the VP and directed toward the target node (step 6). These destinations are then iteratively probed using traceroute. For each completed trace we determine whether the target has been found using location hints. If it has, the algorithm completes. If not, we continue until we have exhausted all VPs and their corresponding destination sets. Figure 3 depicts the targeting process of POPsicle.

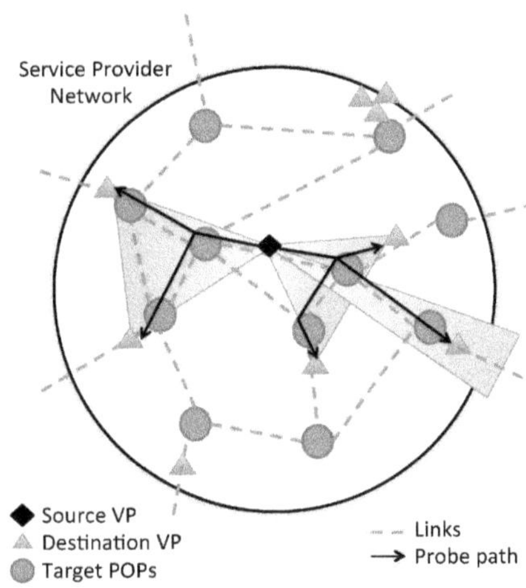

Figure 3: POPsicle targeting process. VPs within the ISP that are geographically closest to the target are selected along with destinations that are geographically closest to the target and "on the other side" of the VP.

POPsicle is based on the notion that target POPs will be part of routes that connect sources and destinations located on either side (from a Euclidean perspective) of the target. We argue that this is likely due to shortest path intra-domain routing. POPsicle is also currently dependent on location hints from DNS for both destination identification and to identify when a target has been discovered. IP geolocation could be used to address the former, while the latter could be addressed through publicly available data (*e.g.*, PeeringDB) by associating IP address ranges with POP locations.

Algorithm 1: POPsicle algorithm

input: $targetNet$ = target network
input: L^T = list of targets to be identified
input: L^S_{vp} = list of source VPs with known coordinates

`// Scan target network to find reachable hosts`
1 $scanResults$ = scan($targetNet$);
2 L^D_{vp} = inferLocations($scanResults$);
3 **foreach** t *in* L^T **do**
  `// Choose destination VPs that are closest to reachable hosts`
4 S^t_{vp} = geographicallyNearest(t, L^S_{vp});
5 **foreach** vp *in* S^t_{vp} **do**
   `// Greedily choose probing destinations within a cone extending from vp to t`
6   D^t_{vp} = searchCone(vp, t);
7   **foreach** dst *in* D^t_{vp} **do**
8   send probe from vp to dst;
9   **if** *t found* **then**
10   record success for t;
11   goto step 3;

7.2 POPsicle Evaluation

We selected 30 looking glass servers from the Atlas database that satisfied the following criteria: (1) the server is co-located with an IXP in North America, and (2) the ground truth information of the POPs is available either from Internet Atlas or in PeeringDB [5]. The vast majority of providers we selected for analysis are regional providers since we found them to be poorly represented in Ark probing results and thus prime candidates for detailed study. In terms of the number of networks used in this study, the coverage of our technique can appear limited. We had to remove several networks from our study due either to the incompleteness of the physical or network maps, or due to the lack of DNS locations hints.

The selection of these 30 looking glass servers resulted in 13 service provider networks that were the focus for our evaluation. We began by examining Internet2, which we consider a special case since complete ground truth for all the layer1, layer2, and layer3 devices is available [2]. POPsicle-directed probing found 10 out of the 10 POPs in Internet2 that house layer 3 infrastructure.

We initiated probing on the remaining set of 12 ISPs using POPsicle-directed probing to verify and map the POPs for

Table 3: **Summary results of network POPs identified with POPsicle, Atlas, Ark, and Rocketfuel for POPsicle deployed at publicly accessible looking glass servers.**

	POPsicle	Atlas	Ark	Rocketfuel
Abovenet	13	22	13	13
BellCanada	34	48	30	29
Centauri	7	14	3	—
Cyberverse	2	2	2	—
Data102	2	2	2	—
HopOne	4	4	4	—
HE	23	24	23	8
Inerail	3	25	3	—
Internet2	10	10	10	10
Interserver.net	2	2	1	—
Steadfast.net	3	3	3	—
Towardex	7	8	6	—
XO	42	80	42	39

each of those networks. Table 3 shows the results from all of our probing experiments. Overall, for 8 out of 13 ISPs, we see all or almost all of the POPs identified in physical maps. These 8 ISPs include Cyberverse, data102, HopOne, Hurricane Electric (HE), Inerail, Interserver.net, Steadfast.net, and Towardex. For several ISPs, we also observed additional POP locations which we verified using PeeringDB. We also compare with the most recently available measurements from Rocketfuel. Although the Rocketfuel measurements are not especially recent, we note that it is likely that POP deployments are fairly stable. We observe, for example, that POPsicle and Rocketfuel identify the same number of POPs for 3 out of 5 ISPs. Lastly, we note that Rocketfuel data were unavailable for 8 ISPs.

In the following we discuss various special cases and observations related to results for each ISP:

- For BellCanada, POPsicle identified significantly more POPs than were revealed in Ark data. Additional locations identified were in New York, Palo Alto, Seattle, and Woodbridge. We confirmed these locations with Equinix Palo Alto, NYIIX, and SIX exchange points in PeeringDB. The Woodbridge location could not be confirmed in PeeringDB.
- For Centauri Communications, POPsicle identified four additional POP locations in comparison with Ark, including Palo Alto, San Francisco, San Jose, and Sunnyvale. These locations were all confirmed by SFIX and SFMIX in PeeringDB.
- For cyberverse, data102, Steadfast.net, Inerail, Internet2, Hurricane Electric and XO Communications POPsicle identified the same POPs as were observed using the Ark data.
- For HopOne, POPsicle found one extra POP location in Palo Alto (which is not seen in either Ark or physical topology maps), which was confirmed in PeeringDB. POPsicle did *not* observe a node in Mclean, VA, which was seen in the Ark data.
- For Interserver.net, POPsicle identified one additional POP location in New Jersey which is confirmed by Equinix New York IX.
- For Towardex, POPsicle found an extra POP in Boston which is confirmed in PeeringDB (Boston IX).

In addition to mapping POPs of the 13 ISPs described above, we evaluated POPsicle's effectiveness for mapping and confirming additional *infrastructural* nodes that have known/published physical locations. This test set included data centers, DNS root servers, NTP servers (both stratum 1 and stratum 2), and IXPs. Table 4 shows results of these experiments, as well as summary results of the POP-identification experiments. We can see from the table that POPsicle is able to identify network-layer locations for this larger and much more diverse set of devices. In total, it finds 1.04 times more POPs, 1.54 times more data centers, 9 times more DNS servers, over 11 times more NTP servers, and 1.48 times more IXPs[9] (in North America) compared to nodes found by standard end-to-end layer 3 probing campaigns. Overall, POPsicle reveals and confirms 2.4 times more physical node locations versus standard probe-based topology measurement methods.

7.3 IXP deployment of POPsicle

We observe in Section 6 that a VP co-located with an IXP can provide what appears to be an *internal* probing source for *any* ISP that peers at the IXP as depicted in Figure 4. From such a vantage point, a tool implementing the POPsicle algorithm could be employed to map and identify POPs and other nodes of interest in any one of the adjacent ISPs.

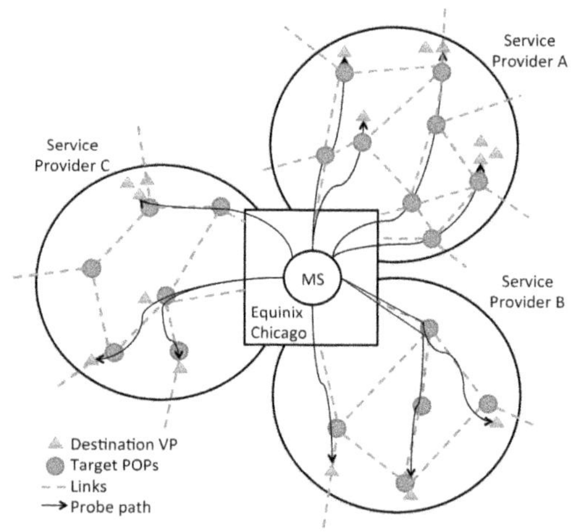

Figure 4: "Multiplexing" an IXP-based measurement server across multiple ISPs using POPsicle.

To substantiate this idea, we deployed a tool implementing POPsicle on a server at the Equinix Chicago Internet Exchange with the help of network operators, and we conducted a week-long measurement study. We chose 10 ISPs that peer at Equinix Chicago for targeted probing. These ISPs were chosen because (1) there was information available in PeeringDB, or we had operator contacts who could verify our inferences, and (2) location hints were available in DNS for IP addresses within the ISP. Unfortunately, the vast majority of ISPs that peer at Equinix Chicago do not have publicly available ground truth information and/or location hints available via DNS thus we could not include

[9] We expect our result to coincide with [10] if we have access to more vantage points.

Table 4: Summary of results from mapping infrastructural nodes.

	POPs (for 13 ISPs)	Datacenters	DNS Servers	NTP Servers	IXPs	Total locations
POPsicle	149	487	9	627	37	1309
Ark	143	315	1	55	25	539
Atlas	244	641	13	827	65	1790
POPsicle compared to Atlas	61.07%	75.98%	69.23%	75.82%	56.92%	73.13%
Ark compared to Atlas	54.60%	49.14%	7.69%	6.65%	38.46%	30.11%
Improvement	1.04x	1.54x	9x	11.40x	1.48x	2.42x

them in this initial study. Also, we note that the ISPs we considered in our POPsicle deployment have, unfortunately, little overlap with the ISPs we consider in Section 5 (and which appear in Table 3) due to our requirement that we have ground truth and location hint information available — only Hurricane Electric and HopOne are in common.

Table 5 shows the results of our IXP-based POPsicle deployment. We observe from the table that POPsicle finds all nodes for 8 out of the 10 ISPs (as compared with the Atlas physical topology data). In the Ark measurements, 6 out of 10 ISPs are fully mapped. For the two ISPs the POPsicle is not able to fully map, a very likely possibility is that the unobserved POPs are invisible to layer3 probes due to configured router policies [31], thus the results we show may be the best that can be achieved through active probing. Overall, our results suggest that POPsicle could be deployed more broadly to accurately map (to the extent possible) ISPs for which we do not have ground truth.

Special Cases. *(1)* The number of POPs found for HE in Table 3 is 23 but in Table 5 the number of POPs found for HE is 24. That is, POPsicle deployed at Equinix Chicago saw an extra node in Calgary, Canada (YYC) which is verified with Datahive IX. One possible implication of this result is that such probe-based measurements are biased towards the vantage points selected. *(2)* For 2 ISPs (PaeTec and Atlantic Metro) some POPs were not visible to our probes, which we intend to investigate further in future work. There is anecdotal evidence that ISPs typically do not expose certain locations to traceroute probes (or any access methods from outside) even when layer 3 services are available at that particular location due to security reasons [31].

Case Study: Cogent. In [21], Ferguson *et al.* present an analysis of Cogent Communication's network based on using reverse DNS records, as well as location-based naming hints. We used the dataset made public by these authors to evaluate, compare and validate POPsicle's probe-based measurement of Cogent's network. We processed the DNS names from Ferguson *et al.*'s dataset using the modified version of location inference technique developed by Chabarek *et al.* [12] and identified 187 POP locations. We then used POPsicle deployed at the Equinix Chicago IXP to target routers within Cogent's network, and it identified 173 POPs. In Appendix A, we see that there are 186 POP locations identified in the Atlas physical topology; it is likely that the additional POP identified in the Ferguson *et al.* dataset is a more recent deployment than was found in Atlas. Also in the table of Appendix A, we see that there are 122 POPs identified through the Ark probes. Lastly, we note that in the most recent Rocketfuel data, there are only 45 POP locations identified. Altogether, these results show that POPsicle's probing technique is very effective for discovering locations of physical infrastructure like POPs, is much better than existing probe-based techniques, and nearly as good as exhaustive use of reverse DNS records.

Table 5: Summary results of network POPs identified with POPsicle deployed at the Equinix Chicago IXP.

ISP Name	POPsicle	Atlas	Ark
BTN	29	29	28
HE	24	24	23
Internet2	10	10	10
PaeTec	54	61	54
Nexicom	9	9	9
HopOne	3	3	3
Indiana Gigapop	2	2	2
MOREnet	4	4	4
Atlantic Metro	9	12	8
Steadfast.net	3	3	3

7.4 Main findings and implications

We describe a new targeted probing technique called POPsicle that is designed to reveal and confirm the presence and location of physical infrastructure such as POPs. To evaluate our method, we used publicly accessible looking glass servers deployed at IXPs, and made a custom deployment of POPsicle at the Equinix Chicago IXP. POPsicle finds 2.4x more physical nodes than Ark probes, and in our custom deployment in Chicago, POPsicle finds nearly all POPs identified in the Atlas physical topologies. In a case study of Cogent's network, POPsicle identified more than 90% of the POPs known through Atlas as well as through the recently described technique based on using reverse DNS records [21]. Moreover, it found many more POPs than Ark probes, or the most recent Rocketfuel measurements.

Overall, our results show that an IXP deployment provides a prime location from which to launch targeted topology discovery probes. Since Rocketfuel maps are commonly used in networking studies that require realistic and representative network topologies, we view this deployment paradigm as having significant potential for generating machine-readable topological information on an on-going basis. We plan to investigate the possibility for additional IXP deployments and a full-fledged system for generating up-to-date network topology data in future work.

The peering model in which IXPs operate is different across different continents. For instance, an IXP in Europe is completely different from an IXP in North America. On one hand the peering model in North America typically involves a commercial colo-operator who also operates the peering equipment. On the other hand, the exchange points in Europe tend to be non-profit, community-based organizations, and the colocation and peering equipment operators are different [8]. We believe that such a peering model will lead to differences on the results that we observe for networks in our study compared to networks in Europe.

8. CONCLUSIONS AND FUTURE WORK

The high level objective of this paper is to move closer to the goal of having comprehensive and accurate maps of the Internet's topology that can be applied to a wide range of problems. The starting point of our study is to understand how physical and network-layer maps differ. To that end, we compare large repositories of physical and network maps and find that physical maps typically reveal a much larger number of nodes (*e.g.,* POPs and hosting infrastructure). For the selected networks, we find that: *(i)* the physical maps typically show many more nodes/links than the network-layer maps, *(ii)* there is often a high amount of overlap in nodes/links that appear in both data sets, and *(iii)* network-layer maps sometimes include some nodes/links that are not in physical maps due to incomplete or out-of-date published topologies.

These results motivate the development of probing techniques for targeting the identification of nodes with known or suspected physical locations. We develop a layer 1-informed heuristic algorithm for probe source-destination selection called POPsicle that identifies 2.4 times as many nodes as standard probing methods. Finally, we identify the fact that sources co-located as IXPs can be used to amplify POPsicle-based probing since an IXP-based vantage point can be considered to reside within all of the service providers that peer at the IXP. To that end, we deployed POPsicle at a real IXP and found that it finds almost all POPs compared to Atlas, and additional POPs compared with Ark.

In future work, we plan to use POPsicle to more broadly confirm and map network-layer nodes by exploiting additional available IXP-based VPs and by deploying it to new IXPs. We also intend to examine potential efficiency gains in POPsicle's algorithm by more aggressively pruning the search space of destination VPs. Future efforts will include benchmarking versus simple probing methods and more targeted approaches (like iPlane [33]) that will enable us to reason about and quantify the efficiency and effectiveness of the tool in a broader deployment. Lastly, we are considering how to fully automate and integrate POPsicle with the Internet Atlas in order to accurately and quickly assemble multi-layer maps of network service providers.

9. ACKNOWLEDGMENTS

We thank our shepherd, Michael Bailey, and the anonymous reviewers for their invaluable feedback. We also thank Michael Blodgett, Peter Helmenstine (Telx), Sven Engelhardt (GTT), and Adam Eaglestone (Integra) for their feedback and helpful discussions. We also thank Jeff Bartig (Equinix Chicago and Mad-IX), Michael Hare (DoIT) and Bruce LaBuda (DoIT) for helping us run the POPsicle experiments at Equinix Chicago.

This material is based upon work supported by the National Science Foundation under grants CNS-1054985, CNS-0905186, ARL grant W911NF1110227, DHS BAA 11-01 and AFRL grant FA8750-12-2-0328. Any opinions, findings, and conclusions or recommendations expressed in this material are those of the author and do not necessarily reflect the views of the NSF, ARL, DHS or AFRL.

10. REFERENCES

[1] Haversine formula. http://en.wikipedia.org/wiki/Haversine_formula.

[2] Internet2 Network Map. http://www.internet2.edu/media/medialibrary/2013/07/31/Internet2-Network-Infrastructure-Topology.pdf.

[3] Team Cymru IP-to-ASN service. http://www.team-cymru.org/Services/ip-to-asn.html.

[4] The CAIDA UCSD IPv4 Routed /24 DNS Names Dataset - September 2011–March 2013. http://www.caida.org/data/active/ipv4_dnsnames_dataset.xml.

[5] The PeeringDB. https://www.peeringdb.com/.

[6] Atlantic Metro Communications. http://www.atlanticmetro.net/resources/maps.php, Accessed February 2013.

[7] Lumos Networks. https://www.lumosnetworks.com/sites/default/files/POP-Colocation-List-Feb2013.xlsx, Accessed February 2013.

[8] B. Ager, N. Chatzis, A. Feldmann, N. Sarrar, S. Uhlig, and W. Willinger. Anatomy of a large European IXP. In *Proceedings of ACM SIGCOMM conference*, 2012.

[9] B. Augustin, X. Cuvellier, B. Orgogozo, F. Viger, T. Friedman, M. Latapy, C. Magnien, and R. Teixeira. Avoiding traceroute anomalies with Paris traceroute. In *Proceedings of ACM SIGCOMM Internet measurement conference*, 2006.

[10] B. Augustin, B. Krishnamurthy, and W. Willinger. IXPs: mapped? In *Proceedings of ACM Internet measurement conference*, 2009.

[11] P. Barford, A. Bestavros, J. Byers, and M. Crovella. On the Marginal Utility of Network Topology Measurements. In *Proceedings of ACM Internet Measurement Workshop*, 2001.

[12] J. Chabarek and P. Barford. What's in a Name? Decoding Router Interface Names. In *Proceedings of ACM HotPlanet*, 2013.

[13] A. Dhamdhere and C. Dovrolis. The Internet is flat: modeling the transition from a transit hierarchy to a peering mesh. In *Proceedings of ACM CoNEXT*, 2010.

[14] B. Donnet, M. Luckie, P. Mérindol, and J.-J. Pansiot. Revealing MPLS tunnels obscured from traceroute. *ACM SIGCOMM Computer Communication Review*, 2012.

[15] R. Durairajan, S. Ghosh, X. Tang, P. Barford, and B. Eriksson. Internet Atlas: A Geographic Database of the Internet. In *Proceedings of ACM HotPlanet*, 2013.

[16] S. Engelhardt. Personal communication, 2014.

[17] B. Eriksson, P. Barford, B. Maggs, and R. Nowak. Posit: A Lightweight Approach for IP Geolocation. *ACM SIGMETRICS Performance Evaluation Review*, 2012.

[18] B. Eriksson, P. Barford, J. Sommers, and R. Nowak. Inferring Unseen Components of the Internet Core. *IEEE Journal on Selected Areas in Communications*, 2011.

[19] B. Eriksson, R. Durairajan, and P. Barford. Riskroute: A framework for mitigating network outage threats. In *Proceedings of ACM CoNEXT*, 2013.

[20] D. Feldman, Y. Shavitt, and N. Zilberman. A structural approach for PoP geo-location. *Computer Networks*, 56(3), February 2012.

[21] A. D. Ferguson, J. Place, and R. Fonseca. Growth analysis of a large isp. In *Proceedings of ACM SIGCOMM Internet Measurement Conference*, 2013.

[22] P. Gill, M. Arlitt, Z. Li, and A. Mahanti. The flattening Internet topology: Natural evolution, unsightly barnacles or contrived collapse? In *Proceedings of PAM*. 2008.

[23] B. Gueye, A. Ziviani, M. Crovella, and S. Fdida. Constraint-Based Geolocation of Internet Hosts. *IEEE/ACM Transactions on Networking*, 2006.

[24] B. Huffaker, M. Fomenkov, and K. Claffy. DRoP:DNS-based Router Positioning. *ACM SIGCOMM Computer Communication Review (CCR)*, Jul 2014.

[25] Y. Hyun, B. Huffaker, D. Andersen, E. Aben, M. Luckie, kc claffy, and C. Shannon. The IPv4 Routed /24 AS Links Dataset: September 2011–March 2013. `http://www.caida.org/data/active/ipv4_routed_topology_aslinks_dataset.xml`.

[26] V. Jacobson and S. Deering. Traceroute, 1989.

[27] A. Kapela. Personal communication, 2014.

[28] E. Katz-Bassett, J. John, A. Krishnamurthy, D. Wetherall, T. Anderson, and Y. Chawathe. Towards IP Geolocation Using Delay and Topology Measurements. In *Proceedings of ACM Internet Measurement Conference*, 2006.

[29] S. Knight, H. X. Nguyen, N. Falkner, R. A. Bowden, and M. Roughan. The Internet Topology Zoo. *IEEE Journal on Selected Areas in Communications*, 2011.

[30] C. Labovitz, S. Iekel-Johnson, D. McPherson, J. Oberheide, and F. Jahanian. Internet inter-domain traffic. In *Proceedings of ACM SIGCOMM Conference*, 2010.

[31] B. LaBuda. Personal communication, 2014.

[32] M. Lottor. RFC 1296: Internet Growth (1981-1991). `http://www.ietf.org/rfc/rfc1296.txt`, January 1992.

[33] H. Madhyastha, T. Isdal, M. Piatek, C. Dixon, T. Anderson, A. Krishnamurthy, and A. Venkataramani. iPlane: An Information Plane for Distributed Services. In *Proceedings of the USENIX Symposium on Operating Systems Design and Implementation(OSDI '06)*, November 2006.

[34] V. Padmanabhan and L. Subramanian. An Investigation of Geographic Mapping Techniques for Internet Hosts. In *Proceedings of ACM SIGCOMM Conference*, 2001.

[35] V. Paxson. *Measurement and Analysis of End-to-end Internet Dynamics*. PhD thesis, University of California at Berkeley, 1997.

[36] A. Rasti, N. Magharei, R. Rejaie, and W. Willinger. Eyeball ASes: from geography to connectivity. In *Proceedings of ACM Internet Measurement Conference*, 2010.

[37] L. Roberts. The Arpanet and computer networks. In *Proceedings of the ACM Conference on the HPW*, 1986.

[38] M. Roughan, S. J. Tuke, and O. Maennel. Bigfoot, sasquatch, the yeti and other missing links: what we don't know about the AS graph. In *Proceedings of ACM Internet measurement conference*, 2008.

[39] Y. Shavitt and U. Weinsberg. Quantifying the Importance of Vantage Points Distribution in Internet Topology Measurements. In *Proceedings of IEEE INFOCOM*, 2009.

[40] R. Sherwood, A. Bender, and N. Spring. Discarte: a disjunctive internet cartographer. In *Proceedings of ACM SIGCOMM conference*, 2008.

[41] R. Sherwood and N. Spring. Touring the Internet in a TCP Sidecar. In *Proceedings of ACM Internet Measurement Conference*, 2006.

[42] J. Sommers, P. Barford, and B. Eriksson. On the prevalence and characteristics of MPLS deployments in the open Internet. In *Proceedings of ACM Internet measurement conference*, 2011.

[43] L. Spinelli, M. Crovella, and B. Eriksson. AliasCluster: A Lightweight Approach to Interface Disambiguation. In *Proceedings of the Global Internet Symposium*, 2013.

[44] L. Spinelli, M. Crovella, and B. Eriksson. AliasCluster: A lightweight approach to interface disambiguation. In *Proceedings of the Global Internet Symposium*, 2013.

[45] N. Spring, R. Mahajan, and D. Wetherall. Measuring ISP topologies with Rocketfuel. *ACM SIGCOMM conference*, 2002.

[46] Y. Wang, D. Burgener, M. Flores, A. Kuzmanovic, and C. Huang. Towards Street-Level Client-Independent IP Geolocation. In *Proceedings of USENIX NSDI*, 2011.

[47] B. Wong, I. Stoyanov, and E. Sirer. Octant: A Comprehensive Framework for the Geolocation of Internet Hosts. In *Proceedings of USENIX NSDI*, 2007.

[48] M. Zhang, Y. Ruan, V. Pai, and J. Rexford. How DNS misnaming distorts internet topology mapping. In *Proceedings of USENIX ATC*, 2006.

[49] Y. Zhang, R. Oliveira, Y. Wang, S. Su, B. Zhang, J. Bi, H. Zhang, and L. Zhang. A framework to quantify the pitfalls of using traceroute in AS-level topology measurement. *IEEE Journal on Selected Areas in Communications*, 2011.

APPENDIX

A. COMPARISON RESULTS

Table 6: Summary comparison of nodes and links observed in physical and network-layer topologies for networks with a footprint in North America.

ISP	Physical		Network-layer		Nodes			Links			N_{Index}
	Nodes	Links	Nodes	Links	Intersection	Only in P	Only in N	Intersection	Only in P	Only in N	
AT&T	25	57	39	72	25	0	14	51	6	21	100
Cogent	186	245	122	172	122	64	0	171	74	1	63
NTT	47	216	65	229	47	0	18	189	27	40	57
Tinet	122	132	64	79	57	65	7	79	53	0	37
Sprint	63	102	67	108	63	0	4	98	4	10	54
Level3	240	336	129	237	129	111	0	237	99	0	63
Tata	69	111	0	0	0	69	0	0	111	0	40
Abiline	11	14	8	13	8	3	0	13	1	0	100
Ans	18	25	0	0	0	18	0	0	25	0	94
ATMnet	21	22	0	0	0	21	0	0	22	0	100
Bandcon	22	28	14	22	14	8	0	22	6	0	100
BBNPlanet	27	28	0	0	0	27	0	0	28	0	100
BellCanada	48	65	22	0	22	26	0	0	65	0	56
BellSouth	50	66	0	0	0	50	0	0	66	0	76
BTNorthAmerica	33	76	0	0	0	33	0	0	76	0	85
CompuServe	11	17	0	0	0	11	0	0	17	0	100
DarkStrand	28	31	0	0	0	28	0	0	31	0	96
DataXchange	6	11	0	0	0	6	0	0	11	0	100
Digex	31	38	0	0	0	31	0	0	38	0	97
Epoch	6	7	0	0	0	6	0	0	7	0	100
Getnet	7	8	0	0	0	7	0	0	8	0	100
Globalcenter	9	36	0	0	0	9	0	0	36	0	89
Gridnet	9	20	0	0	0	9	0	0	20	0	100
HiberniaCanada	10	14	0	0	0	10	0	0	14	0	60
HiberniaUS	20	29	0	0	0	20	0	0	29	0	100
Highwinds	18	53	0	0	0	18	0	0	53	0	80
HostwayIntl.	16	21	0	0	0	16	0	0	21	0	94
HE	24	37	23	41	23	1	0	34	3	7	100
Integra	27	36	0	0	0	27	0	0	36	0	74
Intellifiber	70	97	0	0	0	70	0	0	97	0	77
Iris	51	64	0	0	0	51	0	0	64	0	27
Istar	19	23	0	0	0	19	0	0	23	0	84
Layer42	9	12	10	6	9	0	1	4	8	2	100
Napnet	6	7	0	0	0	6	0	0	7	0	100
Navigata	13	17	0	0	0	13	0	0	17	0	100
Netrail	7	10	0	0	0	7	0	0	10	0	100
NetworkUSA	35	39	0	0	0	35	0	0	39	0	34
Noel	19	25	2	0	2	17	0	0	25	0	16
NSFnet	13	15	0	0	0	13	0	0	15	0	92
Ntelos	48	61	0	0	0	48	0	0	61	0	48
Oxford	20	26	0	0	0	20	0	0	26	0	50
PacketExchange	21	27	0	0	0	21	0	0	27	0	100
Palmetto	45	70	0	0	0	45	0	0	70	0	49
Peer1	16	20	0	0	0	16	0	0	20	0	100
RedBestel	82	101	0	0	0	82	0	0	101	0	9
Syringa	66	74	0	0	0	66	0	0	74	0	9
USSignal	61	79	0	0	0	61	0	0	79	0	46
VisionNet	22	23	0	0	0	22	0	0	23	0	23
Xeex	24	34	4	3	4	20	0	3	31	0	96
Xspedius	34	49	0	0	0	34	0	0	49	0	100

WireCAP: a Novel Packet Capture Engine for Commodity NICs in High-speed Networks

Wenji Wu
Fermilab
Batavia IL, USA
wenji@fnal.gov

Phil DeMar
Fermilab
Batavia IL, USA
demar@fnal.gov

ABSTRACT

Packet capture is an essential function for many network applications. However, packet drop is a major problem with packet capture in high-speed networks.

This paper presents WireCAP, a novel packet capture engine for commodity network interface cards (NICs) in high-speed networks. WireCAP provides *lossless zero-copy packet capture and delivery services* by exploiting multi-queue NICs and multicore architectures. WireCAP introduces two new mechanisms—*the ring-buffer-pool mechanism* and *the buddy-group-based offloading mechanism*—to address the packet drop problem of packet capture in high-speed network. WireCAP is efficient. It also facilitates the design and operation of a user-space packet-processing application. Experiments have demonstrated that WireCAP achieves better packet capture performance when compared to existing packet capture engines.

In addition, WireCAP implements a packet transmit function that allows captured packets to be forwarded, potentially after the packets are modified or inspected in flight. Therefore, WireCAP can be used to support middlebox-type applications. Thus, at a high level, WireCAP provides a new packet I/O framework for commodity NICs in high-speed networks.

Categories and Subject Descriptors

D.4.4 [**Operating Systems**]: Communications Management; C.2.3 [**Network Operations**]: Network monitoring

General Terms

Measurement, Performance

Keywords

Linux kernel; network packet capture; multi-core system

1. INTRODUCTION

Packet capture is an essential function for many network applications, including intrusion detection systems (IDS) [1, 2, 3], and packet-based network performance analysis applications [4]. Packets are typically captured from the wire, temporarily stored at a *data capture buffer*, and finally delivered to the applications for processing. Because these operations are performed on a per-packet basis, packet capture is typically computationally and I/O throughput intensive. In high-speed networks (10 Gbps and above), packet capture faces significant performance challenges.

Packet drop is a major problem with packet capture in high-speed networks. There are two types of packet drop: *packet capture drop* and *packet delivery drop*. Packet capture drop is mainly caused by the inabilities of packet capture to keep pace with the incoming packet rate. Consequently, packets may be dropped because they cannot be captured in time. Packet delivery drop is mainly caused by the inability of the application to keep pace with the packet capture rate. Consequently, the data capture buffer overflows, and packet drops occur even when 100% of the network traffic is captured from the wire. Any type of packet drop will degrade the accuracy and integrity of network monitoring applications [2, 5]. Thus, avoiding packet drops is a fundamental design goal in packet capture tools.

There are two approaches to performing packet capture. The first approach is to use a dedicated packet capture card to perform the function in hardware [6, 7]. This approach requires the least amount of CPU intervention, thus saving the CPU for packet processing. A dedicated packet capture card can ensure that 100% of the network packets are captured and delivered to applications without loss. However, this approach demands custom hardware solutions, which tend to be more costly, relatively inflexible, and not very scalable.

An alternative approach is to use a commodity system with a commodity NIC to perform packet capture. In this approach, the commodity NIC is put into promiscuous mode to intercept network packets. A packet capture engine (a software driver) receives the intercepted packets and provides support to allow user-space applications to access the captured packets. This capture solution depends mainly on the software-based packet capture engine, which is flexible and cost-effective, but requires significant system CPU and memory resources. Therefore, this solution is not suitable for resource-limited systems where resource competition between packet capture and packet processing might lead to drops. However, with recent technological advances in multicore platforms and multi-queue NICs, this approach becomes more appealing due to the availability of ample system CPU resources and I/O throughputs, and paves the way for a new paradigm in packet capturing and processing [8, 9, 10].

The new paradigm typically works as follows. A multi-queue NIC is logically partitioned into n receive queues, with each queue tied to a distinct core of a multicore system (Figure 1). Packets are distributed across the queues using a hardware-based traffic-steering mechanism, such as receive-side scaling (RSS) [11]. A thread (or process) of a packet-processing application runs on each core that has a tied queue. Each thread captures packets via a packet capture engine and handles a portion of the overall traffic. On a multicore system, there are several programming models (e.g., the run-to-completion model and the pipeline model [12]) for a packet-processing application. Here, the application

IMC'14, November 5–7, 2014, Vancouver, BC, Canada.
Copyright 2014 ACM 978-1-4503-3213-2/14/11...$15.00.
http://dx.doi.org/10.1145/2663716.2663736.

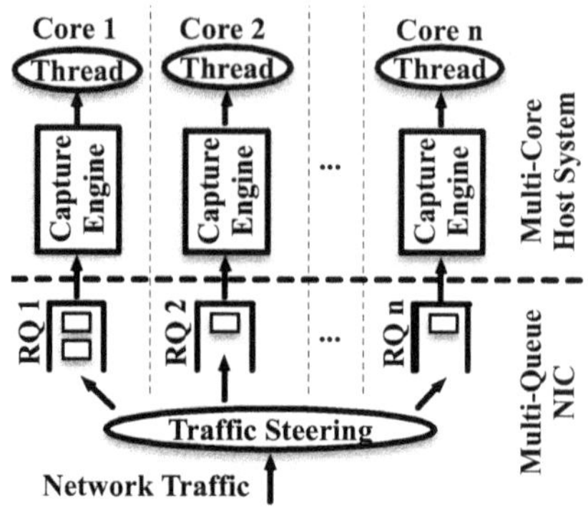

Figure 1. A new packet capturing and processing paradigm

may be of any type. This new paradigm essentially exploits the computing parallelism of multicore systems and the inherent data parallelism of network traffic to accelerate packet capturing and processing. A basic assumption associated with this approach is that the hardware-based balancing mechanism is capable of evenly distributing the incoming traffic among cores. Thus, each core would handle *1/n* of the overall traffic and the packet rate at each core would be reduced to *1/n* of the overall packet rate from the network, with a significantly reduced chance of causing a packet drop. However, this assumption is often not the case in practice [8]. Typically, a NIC's traffic-steering mechanism distributes packets to cores based on a per-flow policy that assigns packets of the same flow to the same core. A flow is defined by one or more fields of the IP 5-tuple. Such a traffic-steering mechanism maintains core affinity in network processing [11], helping to preserve application logic (i.e., packets belonging to the same flow must be delivered to the same application). However, this method of traffic steering can lead to a load imbalance condition in which certain cores become overloaded while others remain idle. In the worst-case scenario, a single core will be flooded with all the network traffic at wire speed.

There are two types of load imbalance. The first type is a short-term load imbalance on one or several cores. In this situation, an overloaded core experiences bursts of packets on a short scale. Here, "short" typically refers to time intervals up to 100 – 500 ms [13]. The second type is a long-term load imbalance, which may be due to an uneven distribution of flow groups in the NIC. Our research reveals that (1) load imbalance of either type occurs frequently on multicore systems; and (2) existing packet capture engines (e.g., PF_RING [14], NETMAP [15], and DNA [16]) can suffer significant packet drops when they experience load imbalance of either type in a multicore system, due to one or several of the following limitations: inability to capture packets at wire speed, limited buffering capability, and lacking of an effective offloading mechanism to address long-term long imbalance.

In order to avoid packet drops, load imbalances on multicore systems must be handled properly. There are several approaches for solving this problem. A first approach is to apply a round-robin traffic steering mechanism at the NIC level to distribute the traffic evenly across the queues. However, this approach cannot preserve the application logic (see Section 2.3). A second approach is to use existing packet capture engines (e.g., DNA) and handle load imbalance in the application layer. But an application in user space has little knowledge of low-level layer conditions, and cannot effectively handle load imbalance (see Section 2.3). A third approach is to design a new packet-capture engine that addresses load imbalance at the packet-capture level. A packet-capture engine has full knowledge of low-level layer conditions, placing it in a better position to deal with load imbalance. In addition, this approach simplifies the design of a packet-processing application. In this paper, we focus on the third approach.

This paper presents WireCAP, a novel packet capture engine for commodity NICs in high-speed networks. WireCAP is designed to support the packet capturing and processing model shown in Figure 1. It has several salient features.

(1) WireCAP provides lossless packet capture and delivery services by exploiting multi-queue NICs and multicore architectures. We have designed two new mechanisms to handle load imbalance in order to avoid packet drops.

For short-term load imbalance, we design and implement a *ring-buffer-pool* mechanism. A ring buffer pool, which consists of chunks of packet buffers*, is allocated for each receive queue in kernel. Through *dynamic packet buffer management*, each chunk of packet buffers can be used to receive packets flowing through the network, and temporarily store received packets. A ring buffer pool's capacity is configurable. When a large pool capacity is configured, a ring buffer pool can provide sufficient buffering at the NIC's receive ring level to accommodate short-term bursts of packets.

To handle long-term load imbalance, we apply a *buddy-group-based offloading* mechanism. The basic idea is simple: a busy packet capture engine offloads some of its traffic to less busy or idle queues (cores) where the traffic can be processed by other threads. However, the challenge of our design is how to preserve application logic—traffic belonging to the same flow must be delivered to the same application when multiple applications are running in the system. We introduce a *buddy group* concept: the receive queues accessed by threads (or processes) of a single application can form a *buddy group*. Traffic offloading is only allowed within a *buddy group*.

(2) WireCAP is efficient. WireCAP employs several optimization techniques—including pre-allocated large packet buffers, packet-level batching processing, and zero-copy—to reduce the packet capture and delivery costs. These optimization techniques have been used in the past and are well understood [14—16, 23]. The challenge in designing WireCAP was to understand how to combine these techniques with our *ring-buffer-pool* and *buddy-group-based offloading* mechanisms in an effective solution to achieve high performance.

In high-speed networks, excessive data copying results in poor performance [15, 17, 18, 19]. Zero-copy is widely used in our design. WireCAP can achieve *zero-copy packet capture and delivery* (i.e., a network packet can be captured and delivered to an application with zero-copy), and *zero-copy forwarding* (i.e., a captured packet can be forwarded with zero-copy).

We specifically separate short-term load imbalance from long-term load imbalance and address them appropriately. When only short-term load imbalance occurs, WireCAP not only avoids packet drops but also ensures that packets belonging to the same flow are handled in the same core. This design improves performance.

(3) With WireCAP, the design of a packet-processing application can be simplified. WireCAP addresses load imbalance in the packet-capture engine level to avoid packet drops. Therefore, an application need not implement its own mechanism to handle load imbalance in the application layer.

---

* A chunk of packet buffers is a group of packet buffers that typically occupy physically contiguous memory.

(4) With WireCAP, the performance of a packet processing application can be improved. WireCAP provides large ring buffer pools in the kernel to accommodate captured packets and supports *zero-copy packet capture and delivery*. Therefore, an application need not copy captured packets from low-level ring buffer pools and store them into its own set of buffers in user space. Instead, the application can use ring buffer pools as its own data buffers, and process the captured packets directly from there. This strategy helps to improve application performance.

(5) WireCAP implements a packet transmit function that allows captured packets to be forwarded, potentially after being analyzed in flight. Thus, WireCAP can be used to support middlebox-type applications.

Ultimately, WireCAP is intended to advance the state-of-the-art for packet capture engines on commodity multicore systems. Our design is unique in the sense that we seek to *address off-the-wire packet capture concerns in conjunction with packet delivery issues to the application.* WireCAP potentially paves the way for advancement of packet analysis tools to deal with emerging high-speed networks.

We implemented WireCAP in Linux. It consists of a kernel-mode driver and a user-mode library. The optimized kernel-mode driver manages commodity NICs and provides WireCAP's low-level packet capture and transmit services. The user-mode library is Libpcap-compatible [20], which provides a standard interface for low-level network access and allows existing network monitoring applications to use WireCAP without changes. We evaluated WireCAP with several experiments. Experiments have demonstrated that WireCAP achieves better performance compared with existing packet captures engines. For example, in our packet capture experiments, WireCAP can capture and deliver 100% of the network traffic to applications without loss while existing packet capture engines (e.g., PF_RING, NETMAP, and DNA) suffer a packet drop rate ranging from 20% to 40% under the same conditions.

2 Background and Motivation

2.1 Problems with existing packet capture engines

When a commodity system with a commodity NIC is used for packet capture, the NIC is put into promiscuous mode to capture network packets. A packet capture engine manages the NIC and provides packet capture services to user-space applications.

Capturing packets from the wire. Packet capture is a special case of packet reception [21]. Typically, a commodity NIC can be logically partitioned into one or multiple receive queues. For each receive queue, the NIC maintains a ring of receive descriptors, called a receive ring. The number of receive descriptors in a ring is device-dependent. For example, an Intel 82599-based 10 GigE NIC has 8192 receive descriptors [22]. Assuming that the NIC is configured with n receive queues, each receive queue will have, at most, a ring size of $\lfloor 8192/n \rfloor$. A receive descriptor must be initialized and pre-allocated with an empty ring buffer in host memory—in the ready state—to receive a packet. Before packet capture begins, the packet capture engine performs this receive ring initialization. When network packets arrive, the NIC moves packets from the wire to the ring buffers via direct memory access (DMA). Subsequently, applications can access the received packets through the OS services provided by the packet capture engine. Receive descriptors are used circularly and repeatedly. The packet capture engine needs to reinitialize a used receive descriptor and reload it with an empty ring buffer as quickly as possible because incoming packets will be dropped if the receive descriptors in the ready state aren't available.

Existing packet capture engines. The protocol stack of a general purpose OS can provide standard packet capture services through raw sockets (e.g., PF_PACKET). However, because the protocol stack is designed to support a wide range of network applications, it is not optimized for packet capture. Consequently, the performance is inadequate for packet capture in high-speed networks. A number of packet capture engines, such as PF_RING [14], NETMAP [15], and DNA [16], have been developed. These packet capture engines essentially bypass the standard protocol stack and achieve improved performance through techniques such as pre-allocated large packet buffer, packet-level batch processing, and zero-copy [15, 23]. Existing packet capture engines can be classified into two types, depending on how captured packets are delivered from ring buffers to applications:

Type-I Packet Capture Engine, represented by PF_RING, pre-allocates a large packet buffer in kernel space for each receive ring. The large packet buffer consists of fixed-size cells. Each cell corresponds to a ring buffer and is assigned to a receive descriptor in the ring. A receive descriptor and its assigned ring buffer are 1-to-1 mapped to one another. The ring buffers are used circularly and repeatedly; a used receive descriptor is refilled with the same assigned ring buffer. In addition, PF_RING allocates an intermediate data buffer, termed *pf_ring*, within the kernel and uses it as *data capture buffer* for each receive ring. When the network packets arrive, the NIC moves the packets from the wire to the ring buffers via DMA. Subsequently, the packet capture engine copies packets from the ring buffers to *pf_ring* (for example, using NAPI polling in Linux [21]). Finally, a user-space application accesses captured packets from *pf_ring*. To improve performance, *pf_ring* is memory-mapped into the address space of the user-space application to avoid copying.

Type-II Packet Capture Engine, represented by DNA and NETMAP. Like PF_RING, DNA and NETMAP implement a similar pre-allocated large packet buffer scheme for ring buffer operations. DNA and NETMAP expose shadow copies of receive rings to user-space applications. The ring buffers of a receive ring are memory-mapped into the address space of a user-space application. The ring buffers not only are used to receive packets but are also employed as *data capture buffer* to temporarily store the packets. When network packets arrive, the NIC moves packets from the wire to the ring buffers via DMA. A user-space application accesses packets directly from the memory-mapped ring buffers. The advantage of this design is that it avoids the costs of unnecessary data movement.

The problems. A Type-I packet capture engine requires at least one copy to move a packet from the NIC ring into the user space. At high packet rates, excessive data copying results in poor performance. In addition, it may suffer the receive livelock problem in user context [24].

A Type-II packet capture engine has limited buffering capability. For DNA or NETMAP, a received packet is kept in a NIC ring buffer until it is consumed. During this period, the ring buffer and its associated receive descriptor cannot be released and reinitialized. Because a NIC ring has a limited number of receive descriptors, the receive descriptors in the ready state can be rapidly depleted if the received packets are not consumed in a timely manner. Consequently, subsequent packets would be dropped.

Neither type of packet capture engine has an effective offloading mechanism to address the long-term load imbalance problem.

2.2 Experimental proof

We conduct two experiments to support our claims. In the first, we demonstrate that load imbalance occurs frequently in multicore systems. In the second, we demonstrate the deficiencies of existing packet capture engines, including PF_RING, DNA, and NETMAP.

Experiment tools. The first tool is called *queue_profiler.* It is a single-threaded application that captures packets from a specific receive queue and counts the number of packets captured every 10 *ms*.

The second tool is called *pkt_handler* and is single-threaded. It captures and processes packets from a specific queue and executes a repeating *while* loop. In each loop, a packet is captured and applied with a Berkeley Packet Filter (BPF) [25] *x* times before being discarded. By varying *x*, we simulate different packet-processing rates of real applications during monitoring. In our experiments, the BPF filter "131.225.2 and UDP" is used, and *x* is set to 0 and 300, respectively. With x=0, no packet-processing load is actually applied. We use this value to evaluate whether a packet capture engine can capture packets at wire speed with no loss. With x=300, the packet-processing rate of a single 2.4 GHz CPU is 38,844 p/s. The value 300 was selected to emulate a heavy load application such as snort [1], which is capable of sustaining similar packet-processing rates [26].

Experiment data. To ensure that the evaluations are practical and repeatable, we capture traffic from the Fermilab border router for use as experiment data. The experiment data includes 5 million packets and lasts for approximately 32 seconds.

Experiment configuration. The experiment system is depicted in Figure 2. It is a non-uniform memory access (NUMA) system with two NUMA nodes—node 0 and node1. Each NUMA node features an Intel E5-2690 processor (P0 or P1*)*. The system has 32 GB of system memory and the system I/O bus is PCIE-Gen3. In additional, two Intel 82599-based 10 GigE NICs—*NIC1* and *NIC2*—are installed in NUMA node 0. A traffic generator capable of generating traffic at wire speed or replaying captured traffic at the speed exactly as recorded is connected directly to *NIC1*. *NIC2* is not used in this experiment.

The system runs a 64-bit Scientific Linux 6.0 server distribution. For packet capture engines, we use driver *pf_ring_5.5.2* (PF_RING) [14], *ixgbe-3.10.16-DNA* (DNA) [16], and *20131019-netmap* (NETMAP) [15].

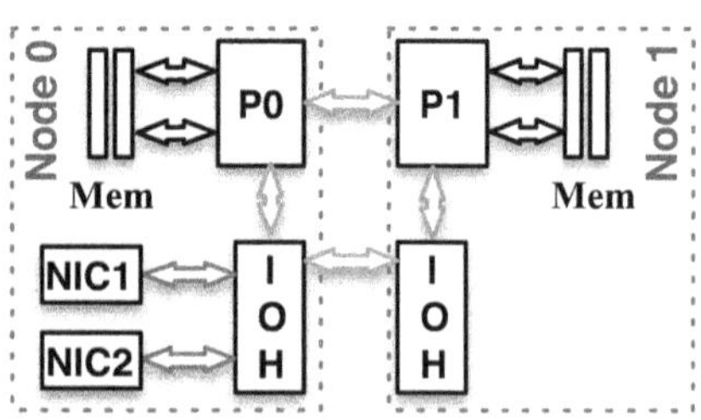

Figure 2. Experiment system

Experiment 1. The traffic generator replays the captured data at the speed exactly as recorded. *NIC1* is configured with six receive queues (*queue 0 – 5*), with each queue tied to a distinct core (*core 0 – 5*). A separate *queue_profiler* is launched to profile traffic for

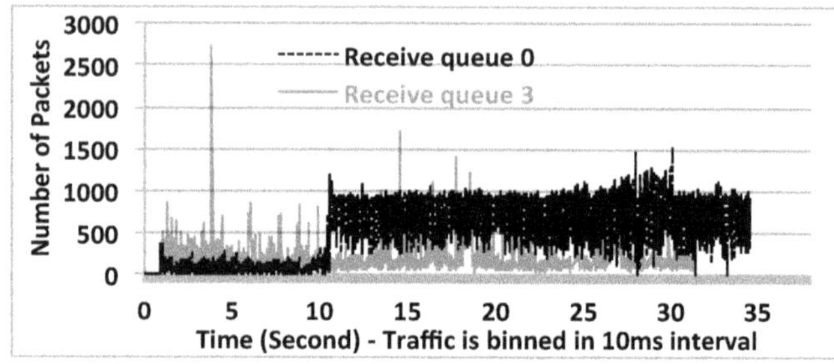

Figure 3. Load imbalance

each queue. We use DNA as the packet capture engine. No packet drops occur in the experiment. Figure 3 presents the time-series of the number of packets received during a short time interval for queue 0 and 3, respectively. The figure shows that a load imbalance can occur routinely in a multicore system because the Intel NIC distributes packets to cores based on a per-flow policy that assigns packets of the same flow to the same core [22]. We observed both short-term load imbalance (short-term bursts of packets) and long-term load imbalance (*queue 0* receives much more traffic than *queue* 3). Because network traffic is bursty by nature and TCP is the dominant transport protocol, a short-term load imbalance occurs more frequently in practice. When we vary the number of receive queues, similar load imbalance patterns are observed.

Experiment 2. The traffic generator replays the same captured data as in experiment 1. Again, *NIC1* is configured with six receive queues (*queue 0 – 5*), and each queue tied to a distinct core (*core 0 – 5*) on which a separate *pkt_handler* is launched to capture and process the traffic for each queue. For *pkt_handler*, *x* is set to 0 and 300, respectively. The CPU speed is set at 2.4 GHz. We vary the packet capture engines in the experiments, using PF_RING (mode 2), DNA, and NETMAP, respectively. Each NIC receive ring is configured with a size of 1,024. For PF_RING, the size of *pf_ring* buffer is set to 10,240. We calculate the *packet capture drop rate* and the *packet delivery drop rate.* Note: because PF_PACKET's performance is too poor compared with these packet capture engines, we do not include PF_PACKET in our experiments. Readers can refer to [9] for PF_PACKET evaluation.

With x=0, each *pkt_handler* does not incur any packet-processing load. In the experiments, we did not observe any packet drops for DNA or NETMAP. However, we observed that PF-RING suffers small packet capture drops at queue 3.

With x=300, pkt_handler emulates a heavy load application. Table 1 lists the packet drop rates for queue 0 and 3, respectively. At queue 0, the incoming packet rate sustains approximately 80,000 p/s from 10s to 35s (Figure 3, Note: the traffic is binned in 10ms interval), which far exceeds the packet-processing speed of a 2.4 GHz CPU (38,844 p/s). Because the *pkt_handler* at queue 0 is over-flooded by incoming packets, all packet capture engines suffer substantial packet drops. DNA and NETMAP suffer substantial packet capture drops because they use ring buffers as *data capture buffers*, which has a limited buffering capability. PF_RING avoids packet capture drops but suffers substantial packet delivery drops due to both the inability of the application to keep pace with the packet capture rate and the receive livelock problem [24]. In addition, because PF_RING requires at least one copy to move a packet from the NIC ring into the user space, PF_RING incurs higher packet capture costs than DNA and NETMAP. Consequently, PF_RING suffers higher overall packet drops than DNA and NETMAP. Table 1 demonstrates that the existing packet capture engines lack an offloading capability to migrate traffic to less busy or idle cores, where other thread would process it.

At queue 3, the incoming packet rate sustains approximately 20,000 p/s between 1s and 32s (Figure 3). While this rate is less than the packet processing speed of a 2.4 GHz CPU (38,844 p/s), DNA and NETMAP still suffer significant packet capture drops due to the limited buffing capability for dealing with short-term bursts of packets. For example, during the time interval [3.86s 3.97s], 2724 packets are sent to queue 3. Because *pkt_handler* can process only 10ms * 38,844 p/s = 388 packets during the interval and because the ring buffers can temporarily buffer 1024 packets at most, packet capture drops inevitably occur. PF-RING also suffers small packet capture drops.

Table 1. Packet drop rates

	NETMAP	DNA	PF_RING
Receive Queue 0:			
Packet Capture Drops	46.5%	50.1%	0%
Packet Delivery Drops	0%	0%	56.8%
Receive Queue 3:			
Packet Capture Drops	33.4%	9.3%	0.8%
Packet Delivery Drops	0%	0%	0%

2.3 How to avoid packet drops that are caused by load imbalance?

The experiments reveal that existing packet-capture engines suffer significant packet drops when they experience load imbalance in a multicore system. To avoid packet drops, we must handle load imbalance. There are several possible approaches.

A first approach is to apply a round-robin traffic steering mechanism at the NIC level to distribute the traffic evenly across the queues. However, this approach cannot preserve the application logic because packets belonging to the same flow can be delivered to different applications when multiple applications are running in the system.

A second approach is to use existing packet capture engines (e.g., DNA) and to address load imbalance in the application layer. For example, an application thread can read packets from a queue, and store them into its own set of buffers, and then process a fixed number of packets before reading again. When load imbalance occurs, the application thread can move packets in some flows over to other threads if its own buffers were filling up. However, this approach has several limitations:

- An application in user space has little knowledge of low-level layer conditions. If the application thread cannot read data from a queue in time, bursts of network packets would overrun low-level packet buffers and cause packet drops.
- Because existing packet capture engines have a limited buffering capability, this approach must involve copying captured packets into user space. At high packet rates, excessive data copying leads to poor performance [15, 17, 18, 19].
- This approach would make the application complex and difficult to design.

Our approach is to design a new packet-capture engine that addresses load balance in the packet-capture level. We believe a packet capture engine is in a better position to address load imbalance because it has full knowledge of low-level layer conditions. WireCAP is our solution.

3 The WireCAP Design & Implementation

3.1 Design goals

WireCAP is designed to support the packet capturing and processing paradigm as shown in Figure 1. We have several design goals:

- Providing lossless packet-capture services in high-speed networks is our primary goal. WireCAP aims to provide lossless packet capture services in high-speed networks by exploiting multicore architecture and multi-queue NICs. Therefore, WireCAP must handle load imbalance that frequently occurs in multicore systems.
- Providing efficient packet delivery.
- WireCAP must be efficient. In a multicore system, core affinity on network processing can significantly improve performance. Therefore, when short-term load imbalance occurs, WireCAP must not only avoid packet drops but also ensure core affinity on network processing. However, when long-term load imbalance occurs, WireCAP has to perform traffic offloading to avoid packet drops. We believe this is an appropriate tradeoff.
- WireCAP must facilitate the design and operation of a packet-processing application in user space.
- WireCAP must have wide applicability and can be easily adopted.
- WireCAP should implement a transmit function that allows captured packets to be forwarded. Such a function would allow WireCAP to support middlebox-type applications.

3.2 WireCAP design

We begin by describing our *ring-buffer-pool* and *buddy-group-based offloading* mechanisms. Then, we discuss the WireCAP architecture.

3.2.1 The mechanisms

Ring-buffer-pool. Figure 4 illustrates the ring-buffer-pool concept. Assume each receive queue has a ring of N descriptors. Under WireCAP, each receive ring is divided into *descriptor segments*. A descriptor segment consists of M receive packet descriptors (e.g., 1024), where M is a divisor of N. In kernel space, each receive ring is allocated with R *packet buffer chunks*, termed the *ring buffer pool*. In this case, R is greater than N/M, which is meant to provide a large ring buffer pool. A *packet buffer chunk* consists of M fixed-size cells, with each cell corresponding to a ring buffer. Typically, the M ring buffers within a packet buffer chunk occupy physically contiguous memory. Both M and R are configurable. Within a pool, a packet buffer chunk is identified by a unique *chunk_id*. Globally, a packet buffer chunk is uniquely identified by a {*nic_id*, *ring_id*, *chunk_id*} tuple. Here, *nic_id* and *ring_id* refer to the NIC and to the receive ring that the packet buffer chunk belongs to.

When an application *opens* a receive queue to capture packets, the ring buffer pool for the receive queue will be mapped into the application's process space. Therefore, a packet buffer chunk has three addresses, *DMA_address*, *kernel_address*, and *process_address*, which are used by the NIC, the kernel, and the application, respectively. These addresses are maintained and translated by the kernel. A cell within a chunk is accessed by its relative address within the chunk.

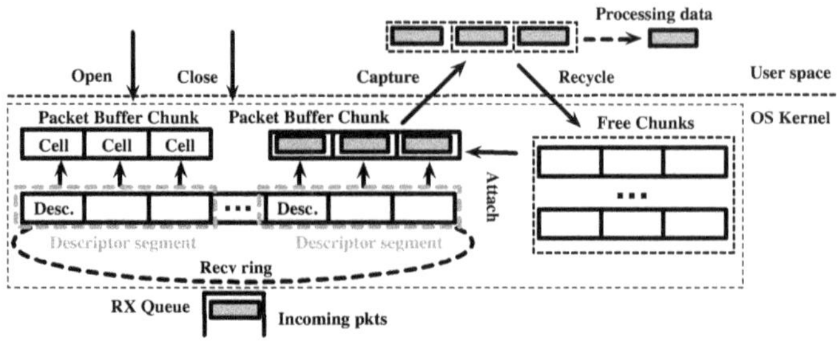

Figure 4. The ring-buffer-pool concept

A packet buffer chunk can exist in one of three states: "free", "attached", and "captured". A "free" chunk is maintained in the kernel, available for (re)use. In the "attached" state, the chunk is attached to a descriptor segment in its receive ring to receive packets. Each cell in the chunk is sequentially tied to the corresponding packet descriptor in the descriptor segment. A "captured" chunk is one that has been filled with received packets and captured into the user space.

A ring-buffer-pool provides operations to allow a user-space application to capture packets. These operations can be accessed through the *ioctl* interface:

Open. Opens a specific receive queue for packet capture. It maps its ring buffer pool into the application's process space and attaches each descriptor segment in the receive ring with a "free" packet buffer chunk.

Capture. Captures packets in a specific receive queue. The capture operation is performed in the units of the packet buffer chunk; a single operation can move multiple chunks to the user space. To capture a packet buffer chunk to user space, only its metadata {{*nic_id*, *ring_id*, *chunk_id*}, *process_address*, *pkt_count*} is passed. The chunk itself is not copied. Here, *pkt_count* counts the number of packets in the chunks. When a packet buffer chunk attached to the receive ring is captured to the user space, the corresponding descriptor segment must be attached with a new "free" chunk to receive subsequent packets. Because the NIC moves incoming packets to the empty ring buffers without CPU intervention, a packet buffer chunk cannot be safely moved unless it is *full*. Otherwise, packet drops might occur. Thus, our capture operation works as follows. (1) If no packet is available, the capture operation will be blocked until incoming packets wake it up. (2) Else if full packet buffer chunks are available, the capture operation will return immediately, with one or multiple full chunks moved to the user space. The corresponding descriptor segment will be attached with a new "free" chunk. (3) Else, the capture operation will be blocked with a timeout. The process will continue as stated in (2) if new full packet buffer chunks become available before the timeout expires. If the timeout expires and the incoming packets only partially fill an attached packet buffer chunk, we copy them to a "free" packet buffer chunk, which is moved to the user space instead. This mechanism avoids holding packets in the receive ring for too long.

Recycle. In the user space, once the data in a "*captured"* packet buffer chunk are finally processed, the chunk will be recycled for future use. To recycle a chunk, its metadata are passed to the kernel, which will be strictly validated and verified; the kernel simply changes the chunk's state to "free".

Close. Closes a specific receive queue for packet capture and performs the necessary cleaning tasks.

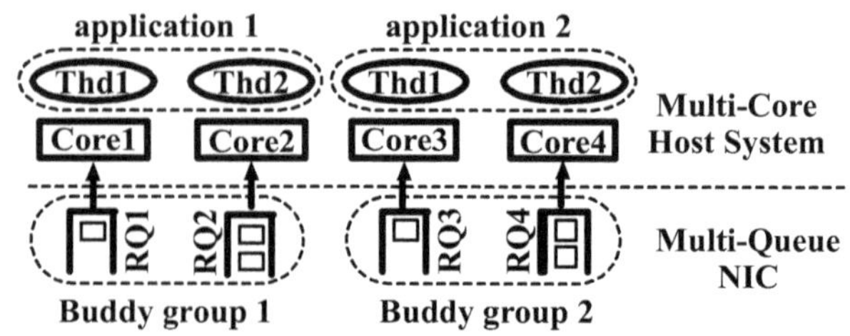

Figure 5. The buddy-group concept

Through the *capture* and *recycle* operations, each chunk of packet buffers can be used to receive packets flowing through the network, and temporarily store received packets. A ring buffer pool's capacity is configurable. When a large pool capacity is configured, a ring buffer pool can provide sufficient buffering at the NIC's receive ring level to accommodate short-term bursts of packets. Thus, it helps to avoid packet drops.

Buddy-group-based offloading. The basic concept is simple: a busy packet capture engine offloads some of its traffic to less busy or idle queues (cores) where it can be processed by other threads. However, the challenge is how to preserve application logic—traffic belonging to the same flow must be delivered to the same application when multiple applications are running in the system. Therefore, we introduce a *buddy group* concept: the receive queues accessed by a single application can form a *buddy group*. Traffic offloading is only allowed within a *buddy group*.

We illustrate the buddy group concept in Figure 5. In the system, each receive queue (RQ1—RQ4) is tied to a distinct core. Application 1's threads are running at core 1 and 2 while application 2's threads are running at core 3 and 4. In this scenario, RQ1 and RQ2 can form a buddy group to implement the offloading mechanism for application 1. Similarly, RQ3 and RQ4 can form a buddy group to implement the offloading mechanism for application 2.

3.2.2 The WireCAP architecture

Figure 6 shows the WireCAP architecture. It consists of a kernel-mode driver and a user-mode library.

- The kernel-mode driver manages NICs and provides low-level packet capture and transmit services. It applies the *ring-buffer-pool* mechanism to handle short-term load imbalance.

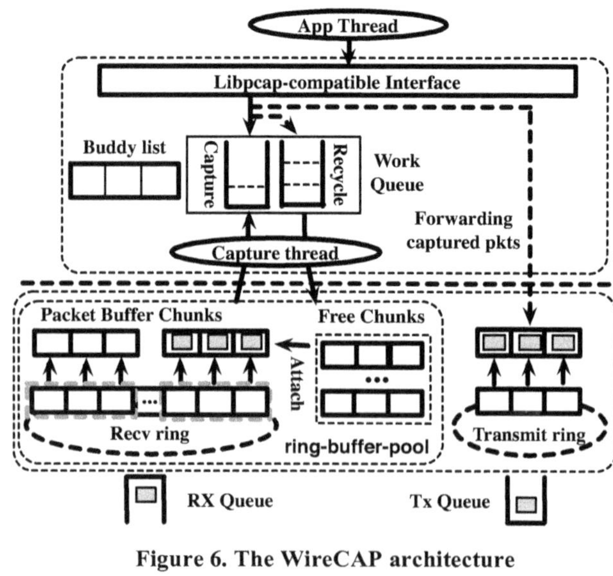

Figure 6. The WireCAP architecture

- The user-mode library extends and builds upon the services provided by the kernel-mode driver and executes several mechanisms: it provides a Libpcap-compatible interface for low-level network access, and it applies the *buddy-group-based offloading* mechanism to handle long-term load imbalance.

a. Lossless zero-copy packet capture and delivery

WireCAP captures packets on a per-receive-queue basis. When a user-space application opens a receive queue to capture packets, the kernel-mode driver maps the ring buffer pool associated with the receive queue into the application's process space, and the use-mode library creates and assigns three key entities in the user space for the receive queue:

- *A capture thread* performs the low-level *capture* and *recycle* operations, and implements the offloading mechanism. Typically, a *capture thread* and an application thread do not run in the same core. The system can dedicate one or several cores to run all *capture threads*.
- *A work-queue pair* consists of a capture queue and a recycle queue. A capture queue keeps the metadata of captured packet buffer chunks, and a recycle queue keeps the metadata of packet buffer chunks that are waiting to be recycled.
- *A buddy list* keeps the buddies of a receive queue in a buddy group. It is used to implement the *buddy-group-based offloading* mechanism. The receive queues in a buddy group are buddies. The user-mode library provides functions to allow an application to populate the buddies of a receive queue.

WireCAP captures packets in two modes—the basic mode and the advanced mode.

In the basic mode, WireCAP handles each receive queue independently. Figure 7a illustrates how this process works. (1) For each receive queue, its dedicated *capture thread* executes the low-level *capture* operations to move filled packet buffer chunks into the user space. The packet buffer chunks captured from a particular receive queue are placed into its capture queue in the user space. (2) To ingest packets from a particular receive queue, a packet-processing thread accesses the receive queue's capture queue in the user space through a Libpcap-compatible API such as *pcap_loop()* or *pcap_dispatch()*. Packet buffer chunks in the capture queue are processed one by one; a used packet buffer chunk is placed into the associated recycle queue. (3) A *capture thread* executes the low-level *recycle* operations to recycle used packet buffer chunks from its associated recycle queue.

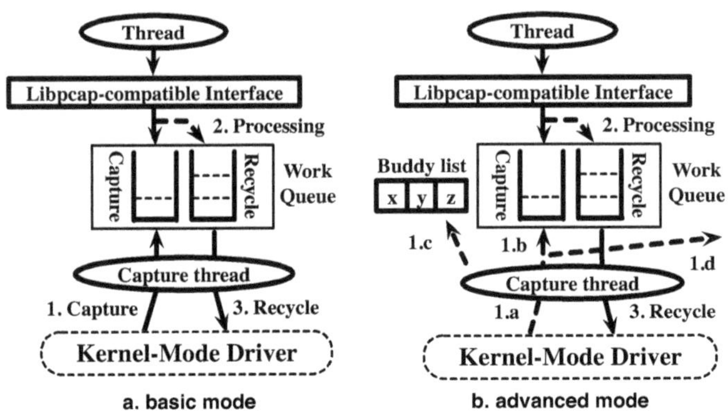

Figure 7. WireCAP packet-capturing operations

A ring buffer pool can temporarily store $R*M$ packets. Assuming P_{in} is the maximum incoming packet burst rate at a receive queue and P_p is the processing rate of the corresponding packet-processing thread. WireCAP in the basic mode can handle a maximum burst of $P_{in}*(R*M)/(P_{in}-P_p)$ packets without loss at the receive queue. However, WireCAP in the basic mode cannot handle long-term load imbalance. When one core is over-flooded by incoming packets, the corresponding capture queue in the user space will soon be filled. Because the captured packet buffer chunks cannot be processed and recycled in time, the free packet buffer chunks in the corresponding ring buffer pool become depleted, causing packet capture drops.

In the advanced mode, WireCAP updates the basic mode operation (1) with the *buddy-group-based offloading* mechanism to handle long-term load imbalance. Figure 7b illustrates how this process works: (1.a) For each receive queue, its dedicated *capture thread* executes the low-level *capture* operations to move filled packet buffer chunks into the user space. (1.b) When a *capture thread* moves a chunk into the user space, the thread examines its associated capture queue in the user space. If the queue length does not exceed an *offloading percentage threshold* (T), WireCAP's indicator of long-term load imbalance, the thread will place the chunk into its own capture queue. (1.c) When the threshold T is exceeded, the thread will query the associated buddy queue list and (1.d) place the chunk into the capture queue of an idle or less busy receive queue. The assumption is that, when a capture queue is empty or shorter, the corresponding core is idle or less busy.

In our design, a ring buffer pool is mapped into an application's process space. Thus, a network packet can be captured and delivered to the application with zero-copy.

b. Zero-copy packet forwarding

A multi-queue NIC can be configured with one or multiple transmit queues for outbound packets. For each transmit queue, the NIC maintains a ring of transmit descriptors, called a transmit ring. To transmit a packet from a transmit queue, the packet should be attached to a transmit descriptor in the transmit ring of the queue. The transmit descriptor helps the NIC locate the packet in the system. After that, the NIC transmits the packet.

With WireCAP, an application can use ring buffer pools as its own data buffers and handle captured packets directly from there. Therefore, the application can forward a captured packet by simply attaching it to a specific transmit queue, potentially after the packet has been analyzed and/or modified. Attaching a packet to a transmit queue only involves metadata operations. The packet itself is not copied.

c. Safety considerations

Two aspects of WireCAP would raise safety concerns: (1) the sharing of memory between the kernel and the user-space applications and (2) the offloading mechanism. However, WireCAP should not cause any safety problems. A misbehaving application will not crash the kernel. WireCAP only maps ring-buffer pools, which do not involve critical kernel memory regions, into the address space of user-space applications. In addition, when a used packet buffer chunk is to be recycled, its metadata will be strictly validated and verified by the kernel. Similarly, a misbehaving application will not crash other applications. The offloading mechanism is implemented across the receive queues of a buddy group belonging to the same application. Different applications do not interfere with one another.

d. Supporting multiple NICs

Because WireCAP operates on a per-receive-queue basis, WireCAP naturally supports multiple NICs. In Section 4, we run experiments to demonstrate that WireCAP supports multiple NICs.

e. Application support

Upon work-queue pairs, WireCAP supports a Libpcap-compatible interface. Packets can be read with APIs such as *pcap_dispatch ()* or *pcap_loop ()*. Both blocking and non-blocking modes can be supported.

3.3 Implementation

WireCAP was developed on Linux. The kernel-mode driver was implemented on the Intel 82599-based 10GigE NIC. We modified the *ixgbe* driver to implement the WireCAP functions, and the modifications involve a few hundred lines of code. We also implemented a user-mode library. The current version supports a simple Libpcap-compatible interface. We plan to release WireCAP for public access soon.

4 Performance evaluations

We evaluate WireCAP using the experiment tools and configuration described in Section 2.2. In addition, we develop a third tool for our experiments. It is a multi-threaded version of *pkt_handler,* called *multi_pkt_handler,* which can spawn one or multiple *pkt_handler* threads that share the same address space.

We evaluate WireCAP from different perspectives. The descriptor segment size *M*, the ring buffer pool size *R*, and the offloading percentage threshold *T* are variables in the experiments. A simple name convention is used in the following sections. *WireCAP-B-(M, R)* represents WireCAP in the basic mode with a descriptor segment size of *M* and a ring pool size of *R*, while *WireCAP-A-(M, R, T)* represents WireCAP in the advanced mode with a descriptor segment size of *M*, a ring pool size of *R*, and an offloading threshold of *T*.

We compare WireCAP with existing packet capture engines (PF_RING, DNA, and NETMAP). The performance metric is packet drop rate. In the experiments, these packet capture engines suffer different types of packet drops: (1) WireCAP suffers only packet capture drops, which can occur when the free packet buffer chunks in a ring buffer pool are depleted; (2) DNA and NETMAP suffer only packet capture drops; and (3) PF_RING suffers both packet capture drops and packet delivery drops. To make the comparison easier, we only calculate the overall packet drop rate. Each NIC receive ring is configured with a size of 1,024 for all packet capture engines. PR_RING is set to run at mode 2, and the size of *pf_ring* buffer is set to 10,240. The CPU frequency is set to 2.4 GHz.

Packet capture in the basic mode. The traffic generator transmits *P* 64-Byte packets at the wire rate (14.88 million p/s). *P* varies, ranging from 1,000 to 10,000,000. *NIC1* is configured with a single receive queue, tied to a core, on which a *pkt_handler* is launched to capture and process traffic for that queue. For *pkt_handler*, *x* is set to 0 and 300.

With x=0, *pkt_handler* does not incur any packet-processing load. We test WireCAP with various *R* and *M* values. No packet drops are observed (Figure 8), indicating that WireCAP can capture packets at wire speed without loss. No packet drops were observed for NETMAP and DNA. However, PF-RING suffers significant packet drops (both packet delivery drops and packet capture drops).

With x=300, *pkt_handler* emulates a heavy load application. Because the incoming packet rate (14.88 million p/s) far exceeds the packet-processing speed of *pkt_handler* on a 2.4 GHz CPU (38,844 p/s), the maximum *P* that a packet capture engine can handle without packet loss reflects its buffering capability for short-term bursts of packets. As shown in Figure 9, WireCAP demonstrates superior buffering capability for short-term bursts of packets. For example, DNA suffers a 15% packet drop at *P=6,000*, while *WireCAP-B-(256, 500)* has no packet drops even at *P=100,000.* WireCAP's resilient buffering capability comes from its unique ring-buffer-pool design and is proportional to the ring-buffer pool capacity *R*M. WireCAP-B-(256, 500)* clearly has a higher buffering capability than *WireCAP-B-(256,100).* At *P=100,000, WireCAP-B-(256,500)* has no packet drops, whereas *WireCAP-B-(256, 100)* has a packet drop rate of 71%.

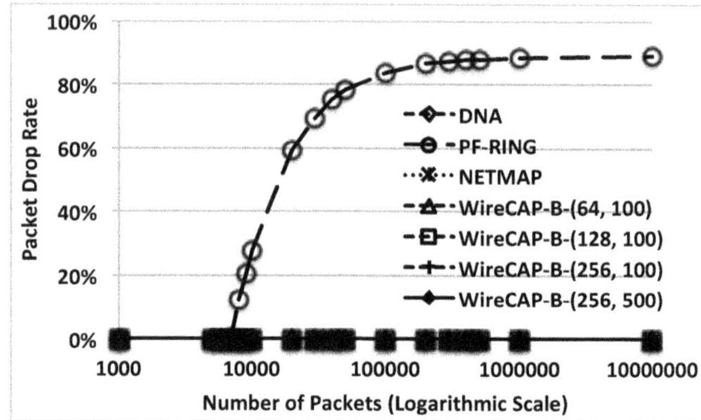

Figure 8. WireCAP packet capture in the basic mode, with no packet processing load (x=0)

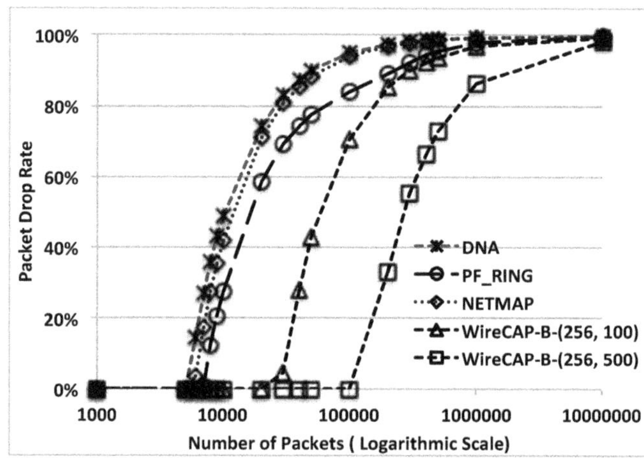

Figure 9. WireCAP packet capture in the basic mode, with a heavy packet-processing load (x=300)

Figure 10 illustrates that WireCAP's buffering capability is proportional to the overall ring buffer capacity *R*M.* The individual *R* or *M* does not affect the overall performance. In the experiment, *R* and *M* are varied, but *R*M* is fixed. The results indicate that *WireCAP-B-(64, 400)*, *WireCAP-B-(128, 200)*, and *WireCAP-B-(256, 100)* have approximately the same packet drop rates at different *P* values.

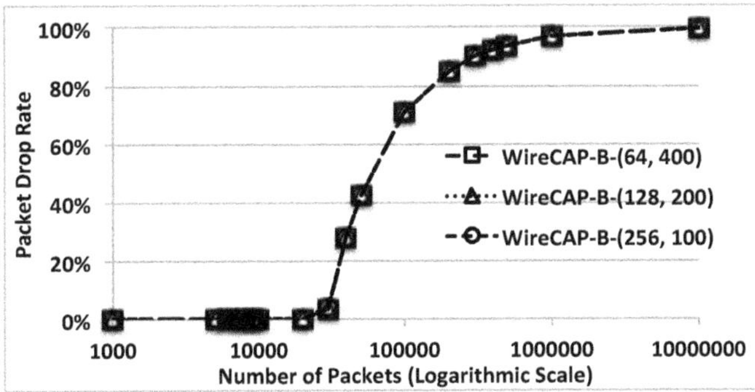

Figure 10. WireCAP packet capture in the basic mode (R and M are varied, R*M is fixed)

Packet capture in the advanced mode. The traffic generator replays the captured data at the speed exactly as recorded. *NIC1* is configured with *n* receive queues, with each queue tied to a distinct core. A *multi_pkt_handler* runs at the system and spawns *n pkt_handler* threads. Each thread runs on a core that has a tied receive queue. It captures and processes traffic from its queue. For *pkt_handler*, *x* is set to 300. We vary the packet capture engines in the experiments, using PF_RING, DNA, NETMAP, and WireCAP in the basic mode and WireCAP in the advanced mode, respectively. For WireCAP in the advanced mode, the *n* queues form a single buddy group.

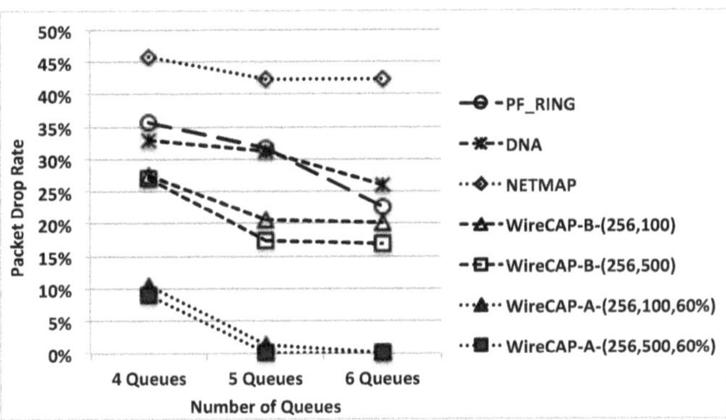

Figure 11. WireCAP packet capture in the advanced mode, with a heavy packet-processing load (x=300)

In the basic mode, WireCAP can capture packets at wire speed and effectively handle short-term bursts of packets. Although WireCAP in the basic mode achieves better performance than existing packet capture engines, it still suffers significant packet losses, due to long-term load imbalance (Figure 11). WireCAP in the advanced mode implements the *buddy-group-based offloading* mechanism to address that problem. When a long-term load imbalance occurs, the offloading mechanism will offload some traffic from a busy core (receive queue) to less busy or idle cores (receive queues) where other threads can process it. This mechanism allows the system resources to be better utilized. It is evident that the offloading mechanism achieves a significantly improved performance (Figure 11). For WireCAP in the advanced mode, the offloading mechanism is triggered when the queue length of a capture queue exceeds the offloading percentage threshold (*T*). In general, WireCAP performs better when *T* is set to a relatively lower value (Figure 12).

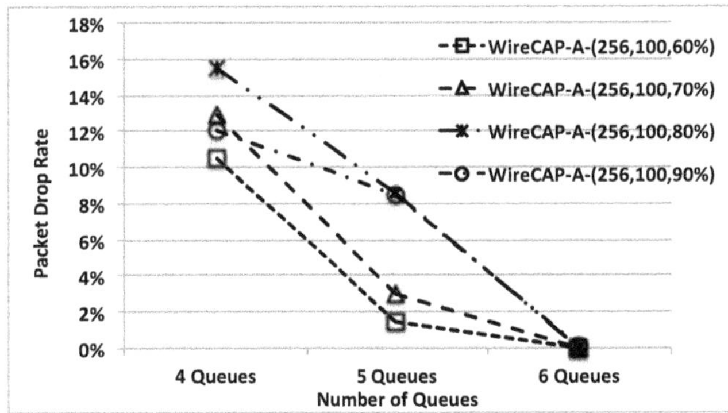

Figure 12. WireCAP packet capture in the advanced mode (R and M are fixed, T is varied)

Packet forwarding. We repeated the above experiments with a small modification to *pkt_handler:* a processed packet is forwarded through *NIC2* (Figure 2) instead of being discarded. *NIC2* is directly connected to a packet receiver. By counting the number of packets that the traffic generator sends and the number of packets the traffic receiver receives, we calculate the packet drop rate. Figure 13 illustrates the experiment results.

The experiments demonstrate that WireCAP's packet forwarding function is capable of supporting middlebox applications. Again, the experiments reveal that the *buddy-group-based offloading* mechanism can achieve a significant improved performance.

We cannot make *multi_pkt_handler* work under NETMAP in this experiment. Under NETMAP, a *pkt_handler* thread cannot synchronize between receiving and transmitting because NETMAP's NIOCTXSYNC (or NIOCRXSYNC) operations do not work on a per-receive-queue (or per-transmit-queue) basis.

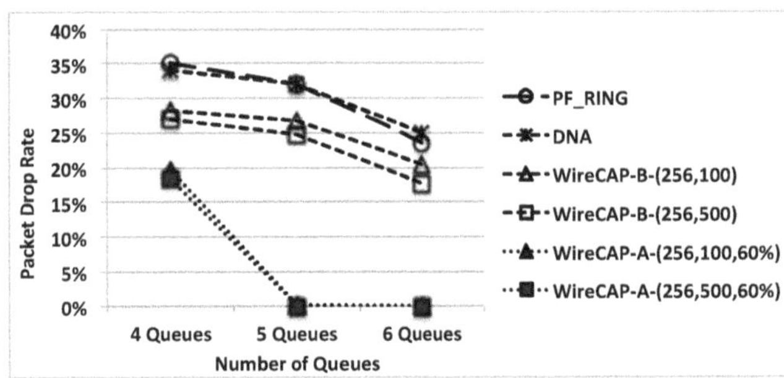

Figure 13. WireCAP packet forwarding

WireCAP scalability. We now evaluate and discuss WireCAP's scalability performance. In the experiments, each of *NIC1* and *NIC2* is connected directly to a traffic generator. The generators transmit 1×10^9 64-Byte or 100-Byte packets at the wire rate. Each NIC is configured with *n* receive queues, with each queue tied to a distinct core.

- For *NIC1*, a *multi_pkt_handler* is launched, which spawns *n* pkt_handler threads. Each thread runs on a core that has a tied receive queue of *NIC1*. It captures and processes traffic from its queue. For pkt_handler, *x* is set to *0*, with processed packet forwarded on through *NIC2*.
- For *NIC2*, a *multi_pkt_handler* is similarly launched except that captured packets are forwarded on through *NIC1*.

In this experiment, we only compare DNA and WireCAP in the advanced mode because PF_RING's performance is too poor and we cannot make *multi_pkt_handler* work under NETMAP. With WireCAP in the advanced mode, *NIC1's* queues form a buddy group and *NIC2's* queues form another buddy group. Each of *NIC1* and *NIC2* is directly connected to a packet receiver. By counting the number of packets that the traffic generators send and the number of packets that the traffic receivers receive, we calculate the packet drop rate. Figure 14 illustrates the experiment results.

When the generators transmit 100-Byte packets, *NIC1* and *NIC2* in together receive approximately 20 million p/s. We did not observe any packet loss for WireCAP and DNA. The experiment indicates that WireCAP scales well with multiple NICs. Please note: *NIC1* and *NIC2* are installed in a single NUMA node on our experiment system (Figure 2)

When the generators transmit 64-Byte packets, the system needs to handle an approximate rate of 30 million p/s. Under such conditions, the experiment system bus becomes saturated, causing both DNA and WireCAP to suffer significant packet drops. Compared with DNA, WireCAP requires extra I/O operations and memory accesses to implement its *ring-buffer-pool* and *buddy-group-based offloading* mechanisms. When the system bus is saturated, the I/O operations and memory accesses become costly. As a consequence, WireCAP suffers a higher packet drop rate than DNA @ queues/NIC=1. WireCAP-A-(256,100,60%) performs similar to DNA with the number of queues per NIC increased. Again, the experiments reveal that the *buddy-group-based offloading* mechanism can achieve a significant improved performance. WireCAP-A-(256,500,60%) performs poorly @ queues/NIC=5 or 6. With the number of receive queues per NIC increased, WireCAP-A-(256,500,60%) requires larger memory use. A "big-memory" application typically pays a high cost for page-based virtual memory [27]. However, WireCAP is designed to use additional system resources to address the packet drop problem. Certainly WireCAP of such a design will lose some scalability performance. We believe this is an appropriate tradeoff.

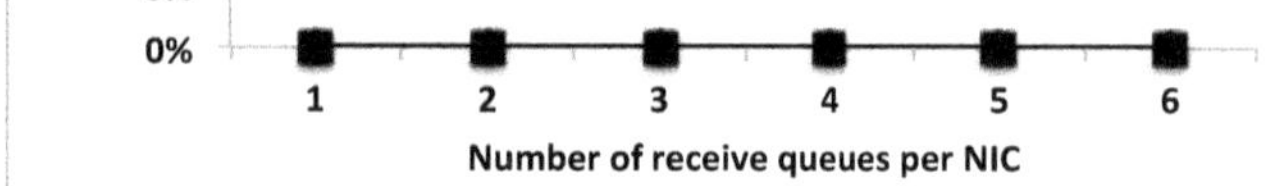

Figure 14. Scalability experiment

5 Discussions

a. The use of additional resources

Our experiments have demonstrated that WireCAP achieves better packet capture performance than that of the existing packet capture engines through the use of additional resources. WireCAP employs additional computing resources by dedicating a capture thread to perform low-level *ioctl* operations for each receive queue. A modern multicore system can provide sufficient computing resources to support WireCAP operations.

WireCAP utilizes large amounts of kernel space memory to support its ring-buffer-pool mechanism. For *WireCAP-B-(M, R)* or *WireCAP-A-(M, R, T)*, a single pool requires $R*M*2K$ bytes of memory (Note: a cell is two Kbytes in the current implementation). If n receive queues are configured, then $n*R*M*2K$ *bytes* are required. Because WireCAP's buffering capability is proportional to the ring buffer capacity $R*M$, there is a tradeoff between WireCAP's buffering capability and its memory consumption.

b. The choice of T

Determining an optimal value for T in WireCAP's advanced mode operation also presents tradeoff challenges. Offloading is necessary to prevent packet drops due to a long-term load imbalance. However, redirecting packets to different, less busy capture queues can result in a degraded CPU efficiency caused by a loss of the core affinity on packet processing [11]. Therefore, a simple guideline for configuring T is as follows: When avoiding packet drops is critical to the application, T should be set to a relatively lower value (e.g., 50%); otherwise, T should be set to a relatively higher value (e.g., 80%).

c. Delay and accurate timestamping

WireCAP uses batch processing to reduce packet capture costs. Applying this type of technique may entail side effects, such as latency increases and inaccurate time-stamping [28].

On Windows and Linux, timestamp can be obtained from two sources, OS jiffy and CPU time stamp counter (TSC). The OS jiffy resolution is on the order of milliseconds, which cannot provide accurate timestamp support in high-speed networks. CPU time stamp counter (TSC) can provide finer resolution. However, the overheads will be too high if TSC is accessed on a per-packet basis, especially in high-speed networks. Therefore, almost all software-based packet capture engines suffer the timestamp accuracy problem and the uniqueness of timestamp problem if NIC does not provide high-resolution timestamp support in hardware.

d. How to address load imbalance in a multicore system?

Because networks are getting faster (e.g., 10/40 GE) and CPU cores are not [29], it is increasingly difficult for a single core to keep up with the high-speed link rates. Multicore and multi-queue NIC technologies have been introduced to allow host systems to keep up with high-speed networks. However, existing per-flow based traffic-steering mechanisms (e.g., RSS) can easily lead to load imbalance across cores. Because of *network traffic fluctuating significantly*, *the need to preserve application logic*, and *the necessity of maintaining core affinity in network processing*, we believe:

- It is difficult to apply a pure NIC-based solution to address load imbalance in a multicore system;
- Traffic offloading in an application-aware manner is an indispensible function for packet capturing and processing in a multicore system;
- Accordingly, an application has to be able to deal with flows being distributed over multiple threads.

e. WireCAP can support different packet capturing and processing paradigms

Ideally, WireCAP is designed to support the packet capturing and processing paradigm as shown in Figure 1. Within a multi-queue NIC, packets are distributed across receive queues using a hardware-based traffic-steering mechanism. And each receive queue is handled by a thread (or process) of a packet processing application. Because this paradigm uses NIC hardware, instead of CPU, to classify and steer packets across cores, it helps to save CPU for packet capturing and processing. On the other hand, modern NICs are becoming more powerful, and typically feature advanced traffic filtering, classification, and steering mechanisms. We believe this packet capturing and processing paradigm is a promising approach.

However, WireCAP is flexible and robust enough to support other types of packet capturing and processing paradigms:

- Multiple threads (or processes) of a packet-processing application can access a single NIC receive queue, through the queue's corresponding work-queue pair in user space. Certainly, this approach incurs extra synchronization overheads across these threads.
- Upon WireCAP work-queue pairs, a packet-processing application can implement its own traffic steering and classification mechanisms to create packet queues at the application level, in the cases of the NIC hardware-based traffic classification and steering mechanism cannot meet the application requirements; or there are not enough physical queues in the NIC.

In these paradigms, a simple approach is to copy captured packets from WireCAP into the application's own set of buffers. This approach simplifies WireCAP's *recycle* operations while the benefit of zero-copy delivery will not be available. However, WireCAP still provides lossless packet capture and delivery services.

WireCAP can be configured to switch between supporting different packet capturing and processing paradigms.

6 Related work

Receive-side scaling and Flow Director [11, 22, 30] are advanced NIC technologies that enable the efficient distribution of packets across receive queues in a multi-queue NIC. RSS uses a hash function in the NIC. The NIC computes a hash value for each incoming packet. Based on hash values, the NIC assigns packets of the same flow to a single queue. Flow Director maintains a flow table in the NIC to assign packets across queues. Each flow has an entry in the table. The entry tracks which queue a flow should be assigned to. The flow table is established and updated by traffic in both the forward and reverse directions. Flow Director is typically not used in a packet capture environment because the traffic is unidirectional.

The protocol stack of a general purpose OS can provide standard packet capture services through raw sockets (e.g., PF_PACKET). However, research [9] show that the performance is inadequate for packet capture in high-speed networks.

Several packet I/O engines have been proposed to boost the performance of commodity NICs in packet capture, such as NETMAP [15], DNA [16], PF_RING [14], and the PacketShader I/O engine (PSIOE) [23], These packet capture engines essentially bypass the standard protocol stack and achieve improved performance. Table 2 compares WireCAP and the existing packet-capture engines.

PacketShader I/O engine (PSIOE) is similar to PF_RING, except that PSIOE uses a user-space thread, instead of Linux NAPI polling, to copy packets from receive ring buffers to a consecutive user-level buffer (*user buffer*). For PacketShader, the copy operation in packet capture makes little impact on performance and does not consume additional memory bandwidth because the user buffer likely resides in CPU cache [23]. *However, this result does not have wide applicability.* If a network application that uses PSIOE to capture packets has a large working set, the *user buffer* is not likely to reside in CPU cache. Under such condition, copying will have a significant impact on performance. PSIOE was specifically designed and optimized for PacketShader. It provides only a limited buffering capability for the incoming packets. PSIOE is not suitable for a heavy-load application.

Table 2. WireCAP vs. existing packet-capture engines

WireCAP	**Goal**: avoiding packet drops. **Deficiency**: requiring additional resources.
DNA **NETMAP**	**Goal**: minimizing packet capture costs. **Deficiency:** limited buffering capability, no offloading mechanism.
PSIOE	**Goal**: maximizing system throughput. **Deficiency**: limited buffering capability; copying in packet capture.
PF_RING	**Goal**: minimizing packet capture costs. **Deficiency:** copying in packet capture; receive livelock problem; no offloading mechanism.

At a high level, WireCAP provides a new packet I/O framework for commodity NICs in high-speed networks. Therefore, there are some similarities between WireCAP and Intel DPDK [31]. Both WireCAP and DPDK can provide large packet buffer pools at each receive queue to accommodate packet bursts, support dynamic packet buffer management capabilities, employ flexible zero-copying, and receive (or capture) packets from each receive queue through polling. However, WireCAP and DPDK differ in two major aspects. First, they have different packet buffer allocation approaches. WireCAP allocates packet buffer pools in kernel. Each packet buffer pool is mapped into an application's process space. By contrast, DPDK handles an NIC device in user space through UIO [32]. It allocates packet buffer pools in user space. Second, DPDK does not provide an offloading mechanism as WireCAP. To avoid packet drops, a DPDK-based application must implement an offloading mechanism in the application layer to handle long-term load imbalance. However, implementing an application-specific offloading mechanism is complex and involves several considerations, including:

- When load imbalance occurs, how to steer packets from overloaded core(s) to idle (less busy) core(s)? Should packets be steered on a per-packet basis or in burst? Should packets be steered in push or pull mode?
- How to synchronize the related threads?
- How to recycle used packet buffers?
- ...

These issues will significantly affect the overall performance. Therefore, a DPDK-based application is complex and difficult to design.

7 Conclusion & future work

In this paper, we have described our architectural approach in developing a novel packet capture engine for commodity NICs in high-speed networks. Experiments have demonstrated that WireCAP achieves better packet capture performance than that of existing packet captures engines. Our design is unique in the sense that we seek to *address off-the-wire packet capture concerns in conjunction with packet delivery issues to the application.* WireCAP potentially paves the way for advancement of packet analysis tools to deal with emerging high-speed networks.

Although our current work has been with 10 GE technology, our objective is to support 40 GE and, eventually, 100 GE technologies. In the near future, we will apply WireCAP for 40 GE networks.

Comparing WireCAP with DPDK (with offloading) will be our future research areas. However, a fair comparison can only be achieved when DPDK provides its own version of offloading mechanism.

8 References

[1] M. Roesch, Snort: Lightweight Intrusion Detection for Networks. In *USENIX LISA* (Nov. 1999), pp. 229-238.

[2] A. Papadogiannakis, M. Polychronakis, and E. P. Markatos, Improving the accuracy of network intrusion detection systems under load using selective packet discarding. In *ACM ERUOSEC* (2010), pp. 15-21.

[3] M. Jamshed, J. Lee, S. Moon, I. Yun, D. Kim, S. Lee, Y. Yi, and K. Park, Kargus: a highly-scalable software-based intrusion detection system. In *ACM CCS* (Oct. 2012), pp. 317-328.

[4] V. Paxson, Automated packet trace analysis of TCP implementations. *ACM SIGCOMM CCR* 27, 4 (1997).

[5] S. A. Crosby and D. S. Wallach. Denial of service via algorithmic complexity attacks. In *USENIX Security* (Aug. 2003), pp. 29-44.

[6] http://www.endace.com/endace-dag-high-speed-packet-capture-cards.html.

[7] http://www.napatech.com/.

[8] F. Fusco, and L. Deri, High speed network traffic analysis with commodity multi-core systems. In *ACM IMC* (2010), pp. 218-224.

[9] L. Braun, A. Didebulidze, N. Kammenhuber, and G. Carle, Comparing and improving current packet capturing solutions based on commodity hardware. In *ACM IMC* (2010), pp. 206-217.

[10] N. Bonelli, A. Di Pietro, S. Giordano, and G. Procissi, On multi–gigabit packet capturing with multi–core commodity hardware. In *PAM* (2012), pp. 64-73.

[11] W. Wu, P. DeMar, and M. Crawford, A transport-friendly NIC for multicore/multiprocessor systems. Parallel and Distributed Systems, IEEE Transactions on, 23(4), 607-615.

[12] C. F. Dcumitrescu, Models for packet processing on multi-core systems. http://www.intel.com/content/www/us/en/intelligent-systems/intel-technology/ia-multicore-packet-processing-paper.html.

[13] T. Benson, A. Akella, and D. A. Maltz, Network traffic characteristics of data centers in the wild. In *ACM IMC* (2010), pp. 267-280.

[14] PF_RING. www.ntop.org/products/pf_ring/.

[15] L. Rizzo, netmap: a novel framework for fast packet I/O. In *USENIX ATC* (2012).

[16] DNA. www.ntop.org/products/pf_ring/dna/.

[17] H. K. J. Chu, Zero-copy TCP in Solaris. In Proceedings of the 1996 annual conference on USENIX Annual Technical Conference (pp. 21-21). Usenix Association.

[18] P. Druschel, and G. Banga, Lazy receiver processing (LRP): A network subsystem architecture for server systems. In OSDI (Vol. 96, pp. 261-275).

[19] A. Foong, T. Huff, H. Hum, J. Patwardhan, and G. Regnier, TCP performance re-visited. In Performance Analysis of Systems and Software, 2003. ISPASS. 2003 IEEE International Symposium on (pp. 70-79). IEEE.

[20] TCPDUMP and LIBPCAP public repository. http://www.tcpdump.org/.

[21] W. Wu, M. Crawford, and M. Bowden, The performance analysis of Linux networking–packet receiving, Computer Communications, 30(5), 1044-1057.

[22] Intel 82599 10GbE Controller Datasheet. http://www.intel.com/content/www/us/en/ethernet-controllers/82599-10-gbe-controller-datasheet.html.

[23] S. Han, K. Jang, K. Park, and S. Moon, PacketShader: a GPU-accelerated software router. ACM SIGCOMM Computer Communication Review, 41.4 (2011), 195-206.

[24] J. Mogul, and K. K. Ramakrishnan, Eliminating receive livelock in an interrupt-driven kernel. In *ACM Transactions on Computer Systems* 15.3 (1997): 217-252.

[25] S. McCanne and V. Jacobson, The BSD packet filter: A new architecture for user-level packet capture. In *Winter USENIX Conference*, 1993.

[26] J. S. White, T. Fitzsimmons, and J. N. Matthews, Quantitative analysis of intrusion detection systems: Snort and Suricata. In SPIE Defense, Security, and Sensing, pp. 875704-875704.

[27] A. Basu, J. Gandhi, J. Chang, M. D. Hill, and M. M. Swift, (2013, June). Efficient virtual memory for big memory servers. In *ACM ISCA* (2013): pp. 237-248.

[28] V. Moreno, P. Santiago del Rio, J. Ramos, J. Garnica, and J. Garcia-Dorado, Batch to the future: Analyzing timestamp accuracy of high-performance packet I/O engines, *IEEE Communications letters*, 16(11): 1888-1891, 2012.

[29] D. Geer, Chip makers turn to multicore processors. Computer, 38(5), 11-13, 2005.

[30] W. Wu, P. DeMar, and M. Crawford, Why can some advanced Ethernet NICs cause packet reordering?. *IEEE Communications Letters*, 15(2): 253-255, 2011.

[31] Intel DPDK website. http://dpdk.org.

[32] H. J. Koch, "Userspace I/O drivers in a realtime context", [Online], Available: https://www.osadl.org/fileadmin/dam/rtlws/12/Koch.pdf.

Timing is Everything: Accurate, Minimum Overhead, Available Bandwidth Estimation in High-speed Wired Networks

Han Wang[1]
hwang@cs.cornell.edu

Ki Suh Lee[1]
kslee@cs.cornell.edu

Erluo Li[1]
erluoli@cs.cornell.edu

Chiun Lin Lim[2]
cl377@cornell.edu

Ao Tang[2]
atang@ece.cornell.edu

Hakim Weatherspoon[1]
hweather@cs.cornell.edu

[1]Department of Computer Science
Cornell University
Ithaca, NY 14850

[2]Department of Electrical and Computer Engineering
Cornell University
Ithaca, NY 14850

ABSTRACT

Active end-to-end available bandwidth estimation is intrusive, expensive, inaccurate, and does not work well with bursty cross traffic or on high capacity links. Yet, it is important for designing high performant networked systems, improving network protocols, building distributed systems, and improving application performance. In this paper, we present minProbe which addresses unsolved issues that have plagued available bandwidth estimation. As a middlebox, minProbe measures and estimates available bandwidth with high-fidelity, minimal-cost, and in userspace; thus, enabling cheaper (virtually no overhead) and more accurate available bandwidth estimation. MinProbe performs accurately on high capacity networks up to 10 Gbps and with bursty cross traffic. We evaluated the performance and accuracy of minProbe over a wide-area network, the National Lambda Rail (NLR), and within our own network testbed. Results indicate that minProbe can estimate available bandwidth with error typically no more than 0.4 Gbps in a 10 Gbps network.

1. INTRODUCTION

Active end-to-end available bandwidth estimation is intrusive, expensive, inaccurate, and does not work well with bursty cross traffic or on high capacity links [13, 33]. Yet, it is important [17, 43, 45]. It is necessary for designing high performant networked systems, improving network protocols, building distributed systems, and improving application performance.

The problems associated with available bandwidth estimation stem from a simple concept: Send a train of probe packets through a network path to momentarily congest the bottleneck link, then infer the available bandwidth at the receiving end from probe packet timestamps [20, 36, 40, 46]. There are three significant problems with current bandwidth estimation approaches. First, such approaches are intrusive since load is being added to the network. Current measurement methods require creating explicit probe packets that consume bandwidth and CPU cycles. Second, current approaches often do not have enough fidelity to accurately generate or timestamp probe packets. By operating in userspace to maximize programming flexibility, precise control and measurement of packet timings is sacrificed. As a result, the probe packet timings are often perturbed by operating systems (OS) level activities. Without precise timestamps, accurate estimation becomes very challenging, especially in high-speed networks. Finally, Internet traffic is known to be bursty at a range of time scales [22], but previous studies have shown that existing estimation approaches perform poorly under bursty traffic conditions [48].

In this paper, we present a middlebox approach that addresses the issues described above. MinProbe performs available bandwidth estimation in real-time with minimal-cost, high-fidelity for high-speed networks (10 Gigabit Ethernet), while maintaining the flexibility of userspace control and compatibility with existing bandwidth estimation algorithms. MinProbe minimizes explicit probing costs by using application packets as probe packets whenever possible, while generating explicit packets only when necessary. MinProbe greatly increases measurement fidelity via software access to the wire and maintains wire-time timestamping of packets before they enter the host. Finally, a userspace process controls the entire available bandwidth estimation process giving flexibility to implement new algorithms as well as reuse existing estimation algorithms. Importantly, minProbe operates in real-time, such that it is useful as a networked systems building block.

MinProbe was designed with commodity components and achieves results that advance the state of the art. It can be built from a commodity server and an FPGA (field programmable gate array) PCIe (peripheral component interconnect express) pluggable board, SoNIC [26]. As a result, any server can be turned into a minProbe middlebox. Indeed, we have turned several nodes and sites in the GENI (global environment for networking innovations) network into minProbe middleboxes. It has been evaluated on a

IMC'14, November 5–7, 2014, Vancouver, BC, Canada.

http://dx.doi.org/10.1145/2663716.2663746.

	Low Fidelity Timestamping	High-Fidelity Timestamping
Active Probe	Pathload [20], Pathchirp [40], Spruce [46], TOPP [36]	minProbe
Passive Monitor	tcpdump	DAG [1]

Table 1: Bandwidth Estimation Design Space

testbed that consists of multiple 10 Gigabit Ethernet (10 GbE) switches and on the wide-area Internet via the National Lambda Rail (NLR). It achieves high accuracy: Results illustrate available bandwidth estimation with errors typically no more than 0.4 Gbps in a 10 Gbps network. It estimates available bandwidth with minimal overhead: Available bandwidth estimates use existing network traffic as probes. Overall, minProbe allows software programs and end-hosts to accurately measure the available bandwidth of high speed, 10 gigabit per second (Gbps), network paths even with bursty cross traffic, which is a unique contribution.

Our contributions are as follows:

- **High performance:** We are the first to demonstrate a system that can accurately estimate available bandwidth in 10 Gbps network.
- **Minimal overhead:** Albeit not the first middlebox approach to available bandwidth estimation(e.g. MGRP [37]), our system performs accurate bandwidth estimation with minimal overhead.
- **Ease of use:** Our system provides flexible userspace programming interface and is compatible with existing algorithms.
- **Sensitivity study:** We conduct a sensitivity study on our estimation algorithm with respect to internal parameter selection and network condition.

2. BACKGROUND

Available bandwidth estimation is motivated by a simple problem: What is the maximum data rate that a user could send down a network path without going over capacity? This data rate is equal to the available bandwidth on the *tight link,* which has the minimum available bandwidth among all links on the network path. While the problem sounds simple, there are four main challenges to available bandwidth estimation—timeliness, accuracy, non-intrusiveness, and consistency. In particular, an available bandwidth estimation methodology and tool would ideally add as little overhead as possible and return timely and accurate estimation on the available bandwidth consistently across a wide range of Internet traffic conditions.

In this section, we first discuss many of the key ideas and assumptions underlying existing available bandwidth estimation methods and tools. Then, motivate the development of minProbe by illustrating the limitations faced by these current methods and tools.

2.1 Methodology

Many existing available bandwidth estimation tools take an end-to-end approach. A typical setup sends probe packets with a predefined interval along the path under measurement, and observe change in certain packet characteristics

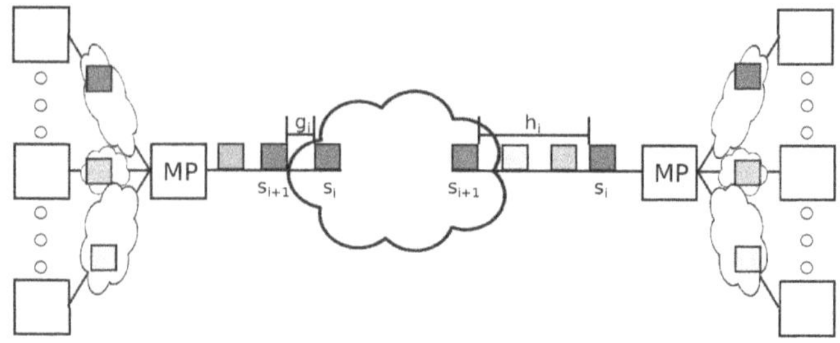

Figure 1: Usage of bandwidth estimation

at the receiver to infer the amount of cross traffic in the network. The key idea to such inferences: When the probing rate exceeds the available bandwidth, the observed packet characteristics undergo a significant change. The turning point where the change occurs is then the estimated available bandwidth. See Figure 9, for example, the turning point where queuing delay variance increases is the available bandwidth estimate. Most existing available bandwidth estimation tools can be classified according to the packet characteristics and metrics used to observing a turning point.

Bandwidth estimation tools such as Spruce [46] and IGI [16] operate by observing the change in the output probing rate. The idea is that when the probing rate is below the available bandwidth, probe packets should emerge at the receiver with the same probing rate. However, once the probing rate exceeds the available bandwidth, the gap between packets will be stretched due to queuing and congestion, resulting in a lower output probing rate. On the other hand, bandwidth estimation tools such as Pathload [20], PathChirp [40], TOPP [36], and Yaz [42] operate by observing the change in one-way delay (OWD), i.e. the time required to send a packet from source to destination. OWD increases when the probing rate exceeds the available bandwidth, as packets have to spend extra time in buffers.

An alternative methodology to the end-to-end approach would be to query every network element (switch/router) along a network path. A network administrator could collect the statistical counters from all related ports, via protocols such as sFlow [5]; or infer from Openflow control messages such as `PacketIn` and `FlowRemoved` messages [50]. However, obtaining an accurate, consistent, and timely reading from multiple switches in an end-to-end manner can be very difficult [2]. Further, collecting counters from switches is done at per-second granularity and requires network administrative privileges, which makes the approach less timely and useful for building distributed systems, improving network protocols, or improving application performance. As a result, we assume and compare to other end-to-end approaches for the rest of this paper.

2.2 Current Limitations

While useful, the end-to-end approach for available bandwidth estimation has inherent issues that limit its applicability, especially in high-capacity links. We outline a few of these challenges.

- **High-fidelity measurements require high-fidelity instruments.** Generating packet trains in userspace typically require a CPU-intensive busy-wait loop, which is prone to operating system level noise, such as OS scheduling, interrupt coalescing, and batching. As a result, generated interpacket gaps of a packet train rarely match the interpacket gaps specified by the userspace program. Moreover, timestamping in user or kernel space adds considerable error to the available bandwidth estimation. Even timestamping in hardware adds noise when timestamping packet (albeit, less noise than kernel space, but still enough to make available bandwidth estimation unusable in many situations [27]). The takeaway: Without high-fidelity capabilities, available bandwidth estimation lacks accuracy.

• **Non-negligible overhead.** Bandwidth estimation tools add traffic to the network path under measurement. This may adversely affect application traffic and measurement accuracy [37]. The amount of probe traffic is proportional to the rate of sampling and the number of concurrent measurement sessions. As a result, the effect of probe packets on cross traffic exacerbates with traffic increase.

• **Traffic burstiness impacts measurement results.** Bandwidth estimation results are sensitive to traffic burstiness. However, existing tools typically ignore the burstiness of cross traffic in favor of simple estimation algorithms. Limitations of batching and instrumentation further mask burstiness to some degree to userspace tools. As a result, existing tools may not be able to reflect true available bandwidth with bursty traffic.

In this paper, we introduce a new tool that can be applied to existing available bandwidth estimation algorithms and tools while overcoming the limitations discussed above. Indeed, we demonstrate that we can accurately estimate available bandwidth in high-speed networks with minimal overhead with existing algorithms. In the next section, we discuss the details of the design and implementation of our methodology.

3. MinProbe DESIGN

MinProbe measures the available bandwidth with high-fidelity, minimal-cost and in userspace; thus, enabling cheaper (virtually no overhead) and more accurate available bandwidth estimation. It achieves these goals through three main features:

First, minProbe is a middlebox architecture that uses application network traffic as probe traffic to eliminate the need for explicit probe packets. When an application packet arrives at minProbe, minProbe decides whether the packet should be used as a probe; if so, minProbe modulates the timings between application packets chosen as probe packets before forwarding them to their destination. A programmable flow table accessible from userspace controls the selection of an application packet as a probe packet. Thus, by using application traffic implicitly as available bandwidth probes, we are able to remove all the traditional costs and overheads. A similar idea was proposed in MGRP [37], which has the same goal of lower overhead, but MGRP lacks high-fidelity measurement capability.

Second, minProbe is a high-fidelity network measurement substrate that is capable of modulating and capturing traffic timings with sub-nanosecond precision. The high-precision is achieved by enabling software access to the physical layer of the network protocol stack. When minProbe modulates probe packets (application packets), it adds and removes minute spacings between packets through direct access to the physical layer.

Finally, minProbe is accessible from userspace. From userspace, users can control sub-nanosecond modulations between packets to generate probes and obtain sub-nanosecond timings between received packets to estimate available bandwidth. Further, all probes can be generated and timing measurements can be received in real-time from userspace.

We envision minProbe to be deployed in an architecture where a separate control plane manages a rich set of middlebox functionalities with event trigger support(e.g [9]). In particular, we believe the separation of measurement hardware and production hardware enables high-fidelity measurement in high-speed networks (and in real-time) that is difficult to achieve otherwise.

3.1 Precise Probe Control

MinProbe offers enhanced network measurement capabilities: High-fidelity packet pacing to generate probe packets and high-fidelity packet timestamping to measure received packet times. We achieve high-fidelity capabilities via direct access to the physical layer from software and in real-time. To see how minProbe works, we first describe the physical layer of 10 Gigabit Ethernet (GbE). Then, we describe how minProbe takes advantage of the software access to the physical layer to achieve high-fidelity network measurement.

3.1.1 10 GbE Physical Layer

According to the IEEE 802.3 standard [3], when Ethernet frames are passed to the physical layer (PHY), they are reformatted before being sent across the physical medium. On the transmit path, the PHY encodes every 64bits of an Ethernet frame into a 66bit *block*, which consists of a two bit *synchronization header* (sync-header) and a 64bit *payload*. As a result, a 10 GbE link actually operates at 10.3125 Gbaud ($10G \times \frac{66}{64}$). The PHY also scrambles each block before passing it down the network stack to be transmitted. The entire 66bit block is transmitted as a continuous stream of *symbols*, which a 10 GbE network transmits over a physical medium. As 10 GbE always sends 10.3125 gigabits per second (Gbps), each bit in the PHY is about 97 pico-seconds wide. On the receive path, the PHY layer removes the two-bit header and de-scrambles each 64bit block before decoding it.

Idle symbols (`/I/`) are special characters that fill the gaps between any two packets in the PHY. When there is no Ethernet frame to transmit, the PHY continuously inserts `/I/` symbols until the next frame is available. The standard requires at least twelve `/I/`s after every packet. Depending on Ethernet frame and PHY alignment, an `/I/` character can be 7 or 8 bits, thus it takes about 700~800 pico-seconds to transmit one `/I/` character [3]. Importantly, controlling or simply counting the number of `/I/`s between packets is what enables high-fidelity. However, before the SoNIC [26] platform was created, `/I/` characters were typically inaccessible from higher layers (L2 or above), because they are discarded by hardware, and definitely were not accessible in software.

3.1.2 High-Fidelity Measurement

The key insight and capability of how minProbe achieves high-fidelity is from its direct access to the `/I/` characters in the physical layer. In particular, minProbe can measure (count) and generate (insert or remove) an exact number of `/I/` characters between each subsequent probe packet to measure the relative time elapsed between packets or generate a desired interpacket gap. Further, if two subsequent probe packets are separated by packets from a different flow

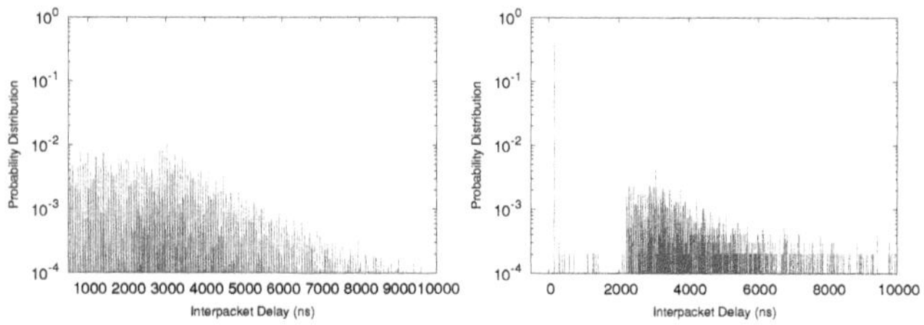

(a) original traffic (b) modulated traffic

Figure 2: Comparison of traffic pattern before and after passed through middlebox

(*cross traffic*), the gap between probe packets will include /I/ characters as well as data characters of the cross traffic packets, but the measurement will still be exact (i.e. /I/ and data characters represent time with sub-nanosecond precision). This level of access from software is unprecedented. Traditionally, however, an end host may timestamp packets in userspace, kernel, or network interface hardware which all add significant noise. None of these methods provide enough precision for high-fidelity network measurements; consequently, many existing bandwidth estimation tools report significant estimation error (large variation and low accuracy) [27].

In a similar fashion to measuring the space between packets, minProbe generates probe packets through high-fidelity pacing, by inserting an exact spacing between packets. By accessing the physical layer of 10 GbE in software in real-time, minProbe can insert or remove /I/ characters from application traffic as needed. In particular, two variables of the probe traffic are of interest: The gap between packets and the overall rate of packet trains. Users can program minProbe via command line calls or API calls to specify the number of /I/ characters (i.e. the number of 100s of pico-seconds) to be maintained between subsequent probe packets, allowing userspace programs to perform high-fidelity pacing.

Direct access to /I/ characters from software and in real-time differentiates minProbe from other measurement tools. Specifically, minProbe is able to characterize and generate an *exact* spacing (interpacket gap) between probe packets.

3.1.3 Probing without a Probe

Explicit probes are not necessary for minProbe. Similar to MGRP [37], minProbe can use application traffic as probe packets. It has a programmable flow table that performs flow matching on pass-through traffic. Users can insert entries into the flow table to specify which flows are probes. Traffic that have a match in the flow table are modulated before they are forwarded. Other flows that do not have a match are simply forwarded without any change in timing. With minProbe, we are able to perform line-rate forwarding at 10 Gbps, even for the minimum size packets. Moreover, minProbe has the ability to generate explicit probe packets, especially when there is insufficient application traffic. Dummy probing packets are padded with zero bytes and transmitted at pre-defined intervals as programmed by the users.

Figure 2 illustrates minProbe's ability to perform high-fidelity measurement and pacing as a middlebox with only application packets as probes. Figure 2a shows the distribution of incoming application traffic to a minProbe middlebox. The x-axis is the distance in time between the first byte of subsequent packets (or *interpacket delay*), and y-axis is the frequency of occurrences. We generated two flows of application traffic at 1 Gbps, and a minProbe middlebox was configured to only modulate one of the flows. As can be seen in Figure 2b, after minProbe, the packets of the probing flow have minimal spacing (interpacket delay) between subsequent packets, and exhibit a much higher probe rate: The peak just to the right of 0 ns interpacket delay was the modulated probing traffic. Even though the overall application traffic rate was 1 Gbps, we were able to increase the instantaneous probe rate up to 10 Gbps for short periods of time by creating short packet trains with minimal interpacket delay. The packets of the other flows, on the other hand, were forwarded as-is, with no changes in timing.

How would minProbe impact the application traffic performance? Obviously, if any traffic were paced, then minProbe would change the pacing. But, for general TCP traffic, the minute modulation that minProbe causes does not affect the rate or TCP throughput. Similar results have been demonstrated in prior art MGRP [37]. One problem may occur when a TCP cwnd (congestion window) is small, e.g., when cwnd = 1. In this case, the application does not create enough traffic and dummy probe needs to be created.

3.2 Generalized Probe Model

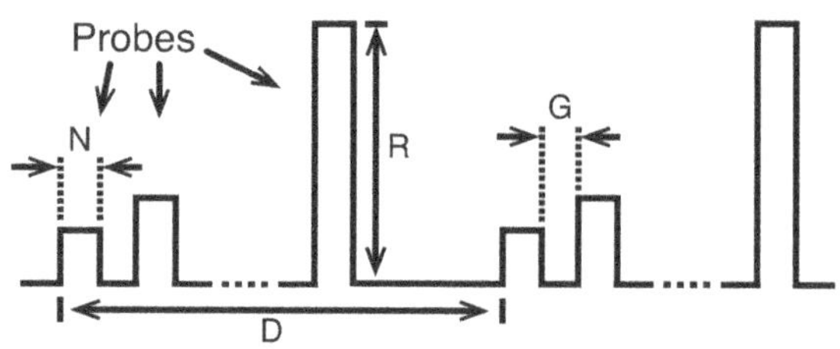

Figure 3: Generalized probe train model

Figure 3 shows a generalized probe train model we developed to emulate a number of existing bandwidth estimation algorithms and used for the rest of the paper. The horizontal dimension is time. The vertical dimension is the corresponding (instantaneous) probe rate. Each pulse (we call it a *train*) contains multiple probe packets sent at a particular rate, as depicted by the height. In particular, the parameter N represents the number of packets in each train and parameter R represents the (instantaneous) probe rate of the train (i.e. we are able to change the interpacket gap between N packets to match a target probe rate R). Packet sizes are considered in computing the probe rate. For a mixed-size packet train, minProbe is able to adjust the space between all adjacent packets within the train to achieve the desired probe rate R. The gaps between successive probe trains are specified with parameter G (gap). Finally, each measurement *sample* consists of a set of probe trains with increasing probe rate. The distance in time between each measurement sample is identified with parameter D (distance). With these four parameters, we can emulate most probe traffic used in prior work, as shown in Table 2 and discussed in Section 2.1. For example, to emulate Spruce probes, we can set the parameters (N, R, G, D) to the values (2, 500Mbps, 1.2ns, 48us), which would generate a pair of probe packets every 48 us with minimal inter-packet gap (12 /I/ characters or 1.2ns) at 500Mbps (5% of the capacity of a 10Gbps link), as in-

Algorithm	N	R	G	D
Pathload	20	[0.1:0.1:9.6] Gbps	Variable	Variable
Pathchirp	1	[0.1:0.1:9.6] Gbps	Exponential decrease	Variable
Spruce	2	500Mbps	1.2ns	48us
IGI	60	[0.1:0.1:9.6] Gbps	30s	30s

Table 2: Parameter setting for existing algorithms. G is the gap between packet trains. R is the rate of probe. N is the number of probe packets in each sub-train. D is the gap between each sub-train.

tended by the original Spruce Algorithm [46]. Similarly, to reproduce the IGI experiment results [16], we set the parameters (N, R, G, D) to the values (60, [0.1:0.1:9.6]Gbps, 30s, 30s) to generate probe trains of 60 packets every 30 seconds with rate ranging from 100Mbps to 9.6Gbps at 100Mbps increments. In summary, most types of existing probe trains can be emulated with the generalized model we developed for minProbe, where different points in the parameterization space can represent different points in the entire design space covering prior art and possibly new algorithms.

In the following sections, we use a parameterization that is similar to Pathload, which estimates available bandwidth based on the increasing one-way delay (OWD) in probe trains. If the rate of a probe train is larger than the available bandwidth of the bottleneck link, the probe train will induce congestion in the network. As a result, the last packet of the probe train will experience longer queuing delays compared to the first packet of the same probe train. The difference between the OWD of the last packet and the first packet of the same probe train can be used to compute the increasing OWD in the probe train. On the other hand, if a probe train does not induce congestion, then there will be no change in the OWD between the first and last packet. Thus, if an available bandwidth estimation algorithm sends probe trains at different rates R, it will estimate the available bandwidth to be the lowest probe train rate R where the OWD (queuing delay) increases.

A bandwidth estimation algorithm based on Pathload needs to measure the change (increase) in OWD between the first and last packet in a probe train. Since we can measure the gaps between subsequent packets, we show that the interpacket gap information is sufficient to compute the increase in the OWD of a probe packet train.

PROOF. Consider sending a train of n packets with packet sizes $s_1, s_2, \ldots, s_n$ and interpacket gaps $g_1, g_2, \ldots, g_{n-1}$ from host A to host B through a network path. The received packets at host B experiences one-way delays of q_1, q_2, ..., q_n through the network and now have interpacket gaps h_1, h_2, ..., h_{n-1}. Assume no packet losses due to network congestion, and no packet reordering in the network. Then we want to show that the difference in one-way delay of the first and last packets is equal to the total increase in interpacket gaps, i.e. $q_n - q_1 = \sum h_i - \sum g_i$.

Initially, the length of the packet train measured from the first bit of the first packet to the last bit of the nth packet is given

$$l^A = \sum_{i=1}^{n-1} g_i + \sum_{j=1}^{n} s_j \tag{1}$$

Similarly at the receiving end

$$l^B = \sum_{i=1}^{n-1} h_i + \sum_{j=1}^{n} s_j \tag{2}$$

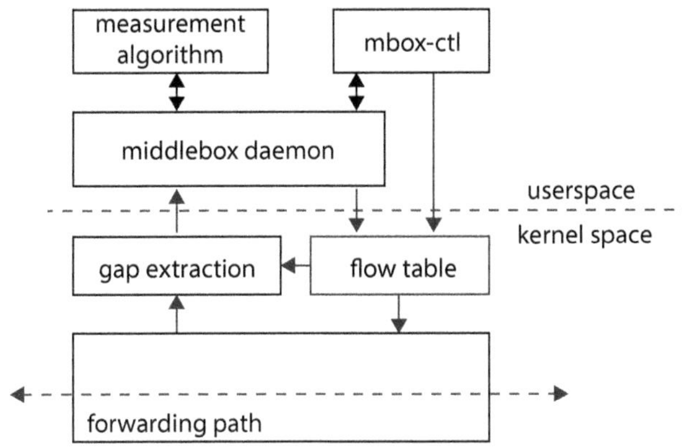

Figure 4: MinProbe Architecture

Additionally, the difference in one-way delay tells us that

$$l^B = l^A + (q_n - q_1) \tag{3}$$

Substitute the relationship for l^A and l^B and we can see that the difference in one-way delay is equivalent to the difference of interpacket gap. □

3.3 Implementation

We built a prototype of minProbe on the software network interface, SoNIC, platform with two 10 GbE ports [26]. The detailed design of the SoNIC platform has been described in prior work [26]. Here, we briefly recount the main features of SoNIC. SoNIC consists of two components: a software stack that runs on commodity multi-core processors, and a hardware PCIe pluggable board. The software implements all of the functionality in the 10GbE physical layer that manipulates bits to enable access to `/I/` in software. The hardware performs line-speed data transfer between the 10 GbE transceiver and the host. To enable the high-fidelity network measurements required by minProbe, we extended SoNIC's capabilities with three new features:

Packet Filtering and Forwarding: We extended SoNIC to support packet forwarding and filtering at line rate. Packet forwarding preserves the timing characteristics of the pass-through traffic exactly: Data is copied from an incoming port to an outgoing port, including the exact number of `/I/` characters in between each packet. To filter for probe packets, we use an in-kernel flow table that matches on the 5-tuples of a packet IP header. The packets that have a match are temporarily buffered in a queue, interpacket gap modulated, and sent once enough packets have been buffered for a single packet train (a measurement sample).

Packet Gap Extraction and Manipulation: MinProbe has two operational modes: a modulation mode for sending probes and an extraction mode for receiving probes. In the modulation mode, we extended SoNIC with additional packet queues for temporarily buffering of probe packets, and modified the amount of `/I/` characters in front of the buffered packet to change the packet spacing. If `/I/` characters are removed from the probe packet trains to increase the probe rate, we compensate for the loss of `/I/` characters at the end of the probe packet train to conform to the 10 GbE standard, and vice versa. In the extraction mode, the number of `/I/` characters are extracted from the matched probe packet trains and sent to the userspace programs via kernel upcalls.

Function	Description	Example
set_mode	set middlebox mode	set_mode
set_gap	set gap between probes	set_gap(120,120,120)
flow_add	add flow used as probes	flow_add(srcip,dstip)

Table 3: Application Programming Interface

Application Programming Interface: The last feature we added was the userspace accessibility. Users can insert/remove flow entries, dynamically adjust probe packet gaps, and retrieve probe packet gap counts from minProbe. It is required to implement a flexible user and kernel space communication channel for passing measurement data and control messages between user and kernel space. We used the *netlink* [4] protocol as the underlying mechanism and implemented the exchange of information using netlink messages. For example, we encapsulate the interpacket gaps in a special netlink message, and transmitted it from kernel to userspace, and vice versa.

Userspace daemons control minProbe. Userspace daemons provide a programmable interface for the kernel-to-user datapath. Table 3 presents a few API calls that are supported by minProbe. For example, as shown in Figure 4, users can program the flow table through the daemon or directly by `flow-add` commands. In addition, users can retrieve information from the kernel through the userspace daemon. In particular, a kernel module captures the interpacket gap `/I/` counts from the probe traffic and passes the information to userspace through the userspace daemon. All communication consumes a reasonably small amount of bandwidth. For instance, the most expensive action is the transfer of interpacket gap `/I/` counts from kernel to userspace, which requires a few hundred mega-bytes per second of bandwidth for minimum sized 64 byte packets at 10 Gbps.

4. EVALUATION

MinProbe can accurately estimate the available bandwidth in high-speed networks with minimal overhead. To demonstrate its capabilities and accuracy, we evaluated minProbe over three different physical networks: Two topologies in our controlled environment and the National Lambda Rail (NLR). We used a controlled environment to study the sensitivity of estimation accuracy to various network conditions. We also evaluated minProbe on NLR to study its performance in wide area networks. To highlight the accuracy minProbe is capable of, Figure 8 in Section 4.2 shows that minProbe can accurately estimate the available bandwidth within 1% of the actual available bandwidth in a 10Gbps network with topology shown in Figure 6a.

In the remainder of this section, we evaluate minProbe in depth and seek to answer the following questions:

- How *sensitive* is minProbe to application and cross traffic characteristics (Section 4.3 and 4.4)?
- Does minProbe work in the wild (Section 4.5)?
- Can other software middleboxes accurately measure available bandwidth (Section 4.6)?

4.1 Experimental setup

Our evaluation consists of two parts: Controlled environment experiments and wide area network (WAN) experiments. For the WAN experiments, we evaluate minProbe over the National Lambda Rail (NLR). NLR is a transcontinental production 10Gbps Ethernet network shared by research universities and laboratories with no restriction on usage or bandwidth. As a result, traffic in the NLR is typically bursty, yet persistent, and similar to the Internet. We provisioned a dedicated virtual route that spans nine routing hops over 2500 miles, as shown in Figure 5. Since the underlying physical network is also shared with other provisioned routes, we observed persistent cross traffic between 1 Gbps to 3.5 Gbps.

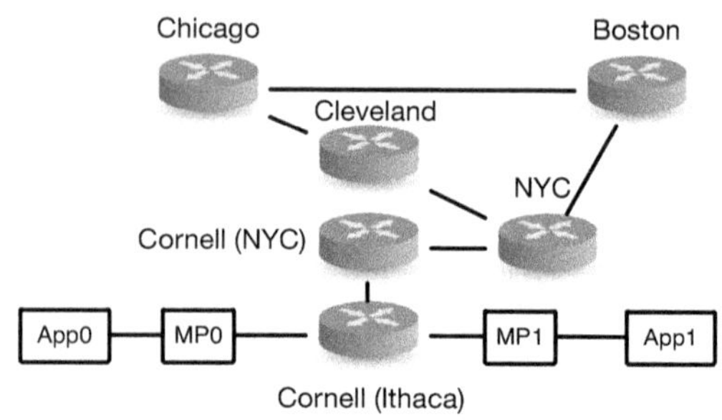

Figure 5: National Lambda Rail Experiment

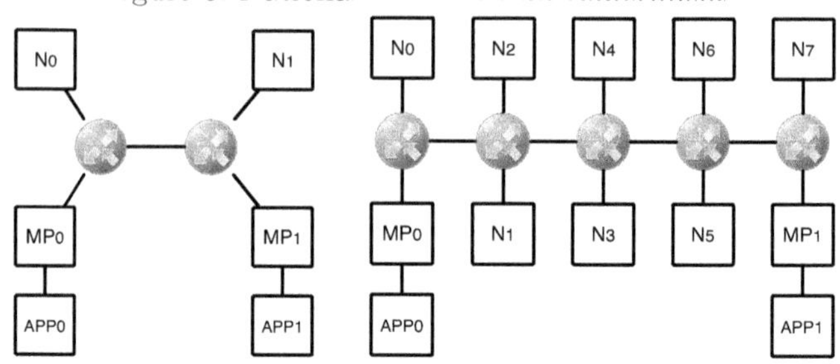

(a) Dumb-bell (b) Parking lot

Figure 6: Controlled Experiment Topologies

For the controlled environment experiments, we set up two different network topologies in a 10 Gbps network testbed: Dumb-bell (DB) and parking-lot (PL), as illustrated in Figure 6 and described in [49]. We used one minProbe middlebox (MP_0) to modulate the application traffic generated from a server directly connected to MP_0 . We used the other minProbe middlebox (MP_1) as the receiver of the modulated probes to capture the timing information from the application traffic. A network of one or more hops separated the two middleboxes, where one link was a bottleneck link (i.e. a tight link with the least available bandwidth). Our experiments attempted to measure and estimate the available bandwidth of this bottleneck (tight) link. The testbeds were built with commercial 10 GbE switches, represented by circles in Figure 6. MinProbe middleboxes and hosts that generated cross traffic were separately connected to the switches using 10 GbE links, illustrated with the solid line. In the DB topology, the link between the two switches is the bottleneck (tight) link. In the PL topology, the bottleneck (tight) link depends on the pattern of the cross traffic.

MP_0 and MP_1 were Dell PowerEdge T710 servers. Each server had two Intel Xeon Westmere [19] X5670 2.93GHz processors, with six cores in each CPU and a total of 24 GB RAM. The Westmere architecture of the processor is well-known for its capability of processing packets in a multi-threaded environment [11, 14, 35]. The switches used in the environment consisted of an IBM G8264 RackSwitch and

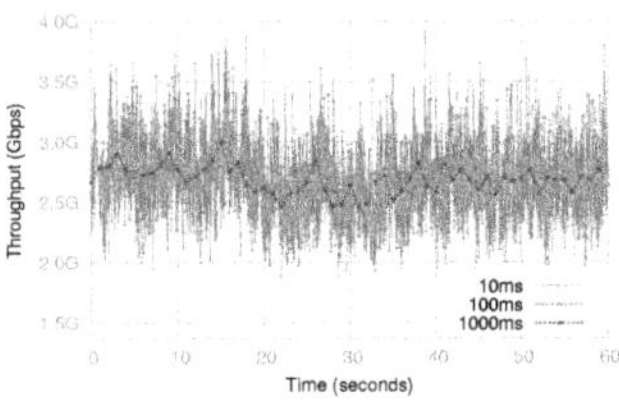

(a) CAIDA OC-192 trace

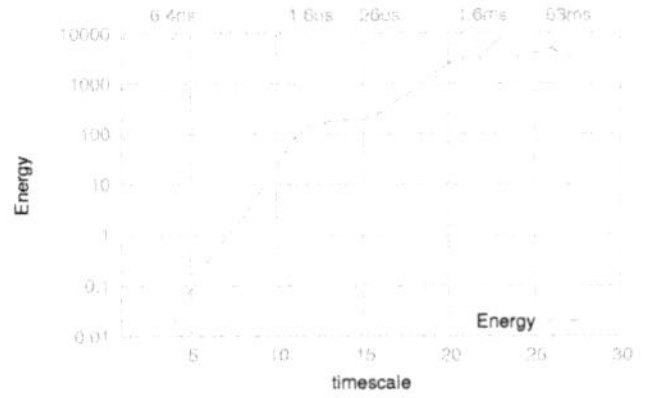

(b) Energy plot for CAIDA trace

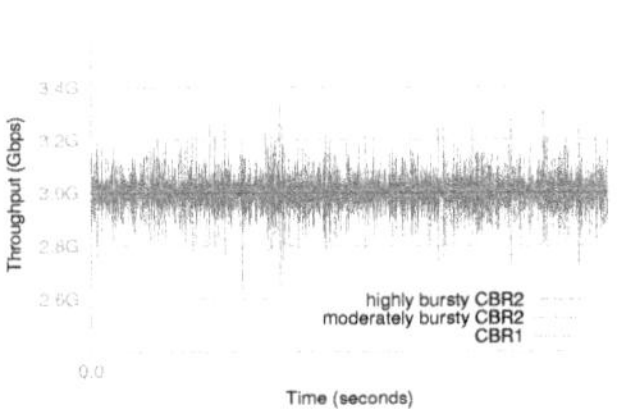

(c) Synthesized traffic

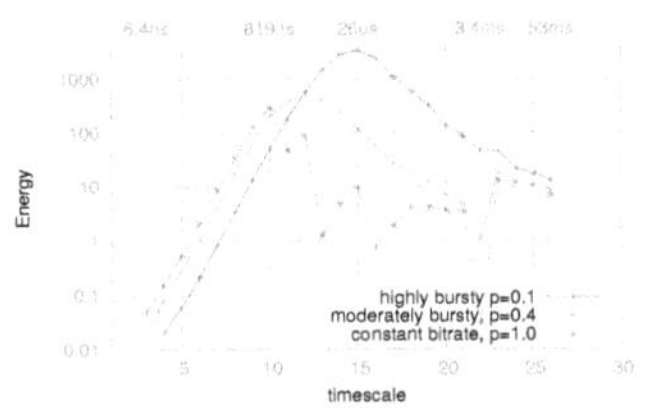

(d) Energy plot for synthesized traffic

Figure 7: The time series and wavelet energy plots for cross traffic used in controlled experiments. Figure 7a shows a time series of a CAIDA trace in three different time scales: 10ms, 100ms and 1s. Coarser time scale means longer averaging period, hence less burstiness. Figure 7b shows the corresponding wavelet energy plot for the trace in Figure 7a. Figure 7c shows three different traces with different traffic burstiness of the same time scale. Figure 7d shows the corresponding wavelet energy plot, with higher energy indicating more burstiness.

a Dell Force10 switch, with network divided into separate logical areas using VLANs.

We used three different classes of cross traffic for our controlled experiments. Figure 7 illustrates the time series characteristics of all three traffic classes. The different classes of cross traffic are also described below.

Constant bit rate cross traffic (CBR1): CBR1 cross traffic consists of fixed-sized and uniformly distributed packets. In particular, CBR1 traffic is a stationary traffic with constant average data rate over long time scale (milliseconds), and interpacket gaps are uniform (i.e., variance is zero).

Stationary, but bursty cross traffic (CBR2): The second class of cross traffic was generated from stationary but bursty distributions, CBR2. CBR2 is created by varying both the packet size and packet chain length distributions with two parameters $\mathcal{D}_{size}$ and $\mathcal{D}_{len}$. Both parameters range from 0.0 (zero variance) to 1.0 (high variance). We draw the packet size from a log-normal distribution which has been demonstrated to closely resemble the distribution of Internet traffic in [28]. The mean of the log-normal distribution is fixed, while the variance is controlled by the parameter $\mathcal{D}_{size}$ to be $\mathcal{D}_{size} \cdot \mathcal{V}_{size}$, where $\mathcal{V}_{size}$ is a fixed high variance value. A packet chain is a series of consecutive packets with minimal interpacket gap in between, and from [12], we know its length takes on a geometric distribution. The parameter of the geometric distribution is taken to be $1 - \mathcal{D}_{len}$. Thus, CBR1 is a special case of CBR2 where both $\mathcal{D}_{size}$ and $\mathcal{D}_{len}$ equals 0.0.

Packet size [Bytes]	Data Rate [Gbps]	Packet Rate [pps]	IPD [ns]	IPG [/I/]
792	1	156250	6400	7200
792	3	467814	2137	1872
792	6	935628	1068	536
792	8	1250000	800	200

Table 4: IPD and IPG of uniformly spaced packet streams.

CAIDA: In the third scheme, we generated cross traffic from a real internet trace. In particular, we used the CAIDA OC-192 [6] trace which was recorded using a DAG card with nano-second scale timestamps.

While there is not one commonly accepted definition for traffic burstiness in the literature, burstiness generally refers to the statistical variability of the traffic. In other words, high variability in traffic data rates implies very bursty traffic. Variability, and by extension, traffic burstiness could be captured by wavelet-based energy plot [47]. Specifically, the energy of the traffic represents the level of burstiness at a particular timescale (e.g. at the microsecond timescale). The higher the energy, the burstier is the traffic. Figure 7b and 7d illustrate this wavelet-based energy plot when applied to the byte arrivals for CAIDA Internet traces and synthetically generated traffic, respectively. The x-axis represents different time scale, ranging from nano-second to second in log scale. The y-axis represents the abstracted energy level at a particular time scale. We were mostly interested in the micro-second timescale, which correspond to x-axis values around 15. Notice that the synthetic traffic behave very much like CAIDA internet traces for energy levels for these values.

For most experiments, we used 792 bytes as the application traffic packet size, which according to [6], is close to the average packet size observed in the Internet. We adjusted the traffic data rate by varying interpacket gaps (IPG). In particular, we insert a specific number of `/I/`'s between packets to generate a specific data rate. We controlled the exact data rate of CBR1 and CBR2 since we control the exact number of `/I/`'s inserted between packets. However, for the CAIDA traces, we selected portions of the trace recording times to obtain different average data rates. In addition, when we replay a trace, we only need to preserve the timing information of the trace, not the actual payload. We used SoNIC to replay the CAIDA trace. As described in [26], SoNIC can regenerate the precise timing characteristics of a trace with no deviation from the original.

4.2 Baseline Estimation

How does available bandwidth estimation perform using minProbe in a base case: A simple topology with a couple to several routing hops (Figure 6.a and b) and uniform cross traffic (uniform packet size and interpacket gaps)? We illustrate the result with the following experiments.

In the first experimental network setup, we use a dumbbell topology with two routing hops and a single bottleneck link (Figure 6a). Cross traffic is generated with a constant bit rate that has uniform packet sizes and interpacket gaps (CBR1). Node N_0 sends cross traffic to node N_1 according to the CBR1 uniform distribution.

The second experimental setup is similar to the first except that we use a parking-lot topology (Figure 6b). Further, cross traffic is generated with the CBR1 uniform distribution between neighboring nodes: N_{even} to N_{odd} (e.g. N_0 to

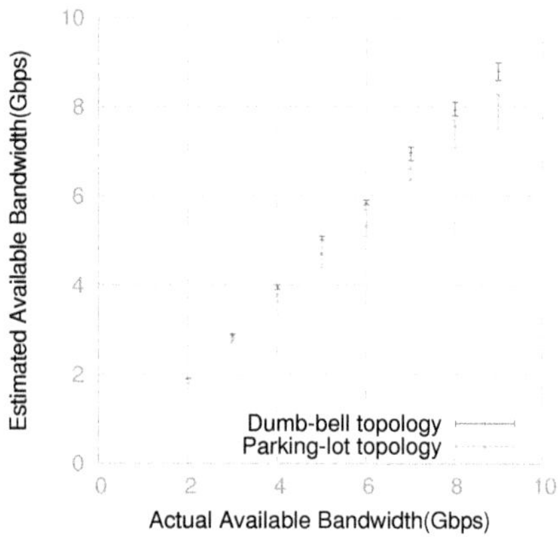

Figure 8: Available bandwidth estimation in a dumb-bell and parking-lot topology under CBR traffic. Both cross traffic and probe traffic share one bottleneck with the capacity of 10Gbps. The x-axis represents the actual available bandwidth of the bottleneck link. The y-axis represents the estimation by minProbe. This evaluation demonstrates minProbe's ability to accurately measure the available bandwidth and achieve the estimation with minimal probing overhead.

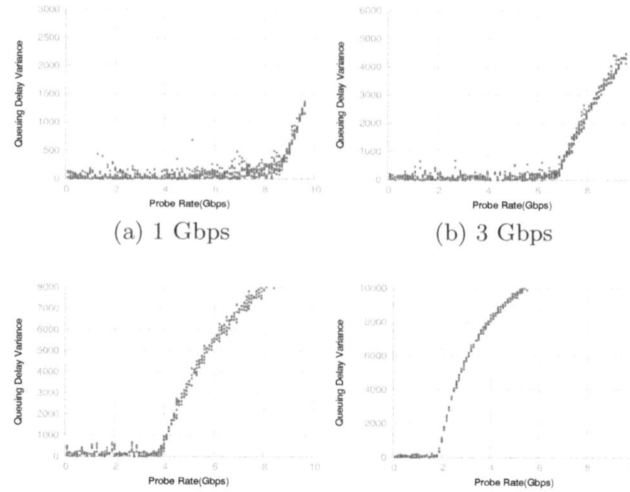

(a) 1 Gbps (b) 3 Gbps (c) 6 Gbps (d) 8 Gbps

Figure 9: Scatter-plot showing the queuing delay variance of probe packets versus the probe rate. The cross traffic rate are constant at 1Gbps, 3Gbps, 6Gbps and 8Gbps. We used probe with N=20, R=[0.1:0.1:9.6]Gbps, G=10us, D=4ms.

N_1, N_2 to N_3, etc). Thus, we can control the cross traffic separately on each link.

In all experiments, we varied the data rate of the CBR1 cross traffic from 1 Gbps to 8 Gbps with an increment of 1 Gbps each time. We configured MP_0 to modulate application traffic from APP_0 destined to APP_1 to create probe packet samples. Note that there is no overhead since we are not introducing any new packets. Further, we configured MP_1 to capture the timing information of the probe packet samples (i.e. application traffic destined to APP_1 from source APP_0). The probe packets modulated by MP_0 were parameterized using the model introduced in Section 3.2. We used the parameters (N, R, G, D) = (20, [0.1 : 0.1 : 9.6] Gbps, 10 us, 4 ms) where MP_0 sends a probe packet sample every 4 ms enabling us to collect 250 samples per second. Each probe sample consists of 96 constant bit rate (CBR) trains with a 10 us gap between trains. Each train runs at an increasing data rate ranging from 0.1 Gbps to 9.6 Gbps, with an increment of 0.1 Gbps. Recall that we are able to precisely control the data rate of trains by controlling the interpacket gap between probe packets within the train (e.g. See Table 4). We assume node APP_0 generates enough application traffic to create probe packet samples.

Figure 8 shows the result. It shows the actual available bandwidth on the x-axis and estimated available bandwidth on the y-axis for the the dumb-bell and parking-lot topologies. We estimated the available bandwidth with the mean of 10 measurement samples. The estimations in the dumb-bell topology were within 0.1 Gbps of the actual available bandwidth. The estimations in parking-lot topology tended to under-estimate the available bandwidth, due to the multiple bottleneck links in the network path. Higher available bandwidth scenarios were more difficult to measure as accurately in a multiple-hop network path. Alternatively, the maximum value of a measurement could be used to estimate available bandwidth if the estimation was always overly conservative; this would actually increase the estimation accuracy.

Figure 9 shows the raw probe sample data that was used to estimate the available bandwidth of different cross traffic rates in the dumb-bell topology. The x-axis is the rate (R) at which the probe trains were sent. The y-axis is the variance of the queuing delay, which was computed from the one-way delay (OWD) experienced by the packets within the same probe train. We kept the cross traffic rate constant at 1Gbps, 3Gbps, 6Gbps and 8Gbps. The available bandwidth was estimated to be the turning point where the delay variance shows an significant trend of increasing.

4.3 Impact of Application Traffic

Next, we study whether minProbe is impacted by characteristics of application traffic. In particular, we focus on two characteristics that matter the most for available bandwidth estimation: the length of a probe train and the distribution of probe packet sizes. The length of a probe train affects the delay experienced by application traffic (See the description of probe train length in Section 3.2 and equation 1). The longer the probe train, the longer the application traffic has to be buffered in the middlebox, resulting in longer delays the application traffic experiences. Typically, a probe train consists of around 100 or more packets [20,40]. A probe train of two packets is essentially similar to the packet pair scheme described by Spruce [46].

Creating probe packet trains from variable sized packets is difficult because packets with different sizes suffer different delays through a network. Because minProbe does not have control over the application traffic that is used as packet probes, it is important to understand how the accuracy of minProbe changes with different distributions of probe packet sizes. Another consideration is that many estimation algorithms prefer large probe packets to small packets [20,40].

We evaluate the effect of the length of a probe packet train (i.e. the number of packets in a train) to the accuracy of available bandwidth estimation in Section 4.3.1 and the effect of the distributions of probe packet sizes in Section 4.3.2 and 4.3.3. For these experiments, we always used CBR1 as cross traffic.

	Available Bandwidth [Gbps]							
	Dumb-bell				Parking-lot			
Actual	1.9	3.9	6.9	8.9	1.9	3.9	6.9	8.9
Length	Estimated Available Bandwidth [Gbps]							
5	2.57	5.57	8.54	9.5	1.99	4.41	6.57	8.59
20	2.07	3.96	6.97	8.8	1.80	3.80	6.90	8.30
40	1.9	3.87	6.94	8.68	1.80	3.86	6.70	8.50
60	1.85	3.79	6.79	8.70	1.80	3.80	6.76	8.56
80	1.86	3.79	6.90	8.70	1.80	3.75	6.78	8.44
100	1.83	3.96	6.79	8.55	1.80	3.70	6.56	8.02

Table 5: Estimation with different probe train length.

	Available Bandwidth [Gbps]							
	Dumb-bell				Parking-lot			
	1.9	3.9	6.9	8.9	1.9	3.9	6.9	8.9
Size [B]	Estimated Bandwidth [Gbps]							
64	9.47	9.50	9.50	9.50	9.50	9.50	9.50	9.50
512	2.06	4.51	7.53	8.9	1.85	3.76	6.64	8.09
792	2.07	3.96	6.97	8.8	1.80	3.80	6.90	8.30
1024	1.90	3.97	7.01	8.83	1.80	3.75	6.72	8.54
1518	1.81	3.88	6.91	8.84	1.80	3.81	6.83	8.48

Table 6: Estimation results with different probe packet size.

4.3.1 Impact of Varying Probe Train Length

In order to understand how the number of packets in a probe packet train affects the accuracy of minProbe, we varied the number of packets in each train while using the same parameters as the baseline experiment (Section 4.2). In particular, we used $(N, [0.1 : 0.1 : 9.6]$ Gbps, 10 us, 4 ms) while increasing N from 5 to 100. Table 5 illustrates the estimated available bandwidth when different train lengths were used. The actual available bandwidth is shown in the row marked "Actual" and the estimated available bandwidth is in the rows below "Length" in Table 5. As shown in the table, increasing the number of probe packets per flow yields diminishing returns. A probe train with five packets is not as accurate as the baseline experiment with 20 packets regardless of the actual available bandwidth. However, trains with larger than 20 packets result in similar estimation accuracy. The take-away: Increasing the number of packets in a probe packet train does not necessarily result in more accurate estimation. The minimum number of packets to obtain accurate estimation results was about 20 packets. More packets in a probe train elongate the delay of applications traffic due to buffering, but do not improve estimation accuracy.

What happens when there is not enough packets between a source and destination pair? This highlights the fundamental trade-off between application latency and probing overhead. MinProbe has a timeout mechanism to deal with this corner case. If the oldest intercepted packet has exceeded a pre-defined timeout value, minProbe will generate dummy probe packets to fulfill the need for probe packets and send out the probe train. Since minProbe requires much shorter probe trains compared to existing tools, opportunistically inserting additional dummy packets add minimal overhead.

4.3.2 Impact of Varying Probe Size

Next, we evaluated minProbe with different packet sizes for probes. All the parameters were the same as in the baseline experiment except that we varied the size of packets for probes from 64 bytes to 1518 bytes (the minimum to maximum sized packets allowed by Ethernet). In particular, we used $(20, [0.1 : 0.1 : 9.6]$ Gbps, 10 us, 4 ms) while increasing probe packet sizes from 64 to 1518 bytes. As can be seen from Table 6, larger packet sizes (more than 512 bytes) perform better than smaller packet sizes in general. Note that we used 792 byte packets in our baseline experiment, which resulted in similar available bandwidth estimate accuracy as 1518 byte probe packets. On the other hand, smaller probe packets, such as 64 byte packets resulted in poor accuracy. This result and observation is consistent with the previous results from literature such as [40]. The take-away is that probe trains with medium to large packet sizes perform better than trains of smaller packet sizes.

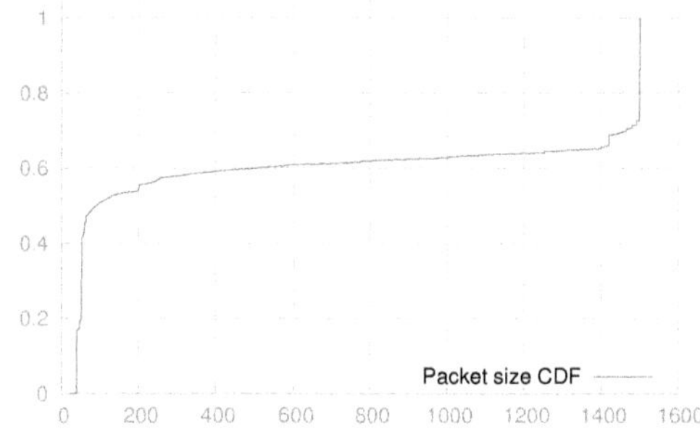

Figure 10: The distribution of probe packet sizes from the CAIDA trace.

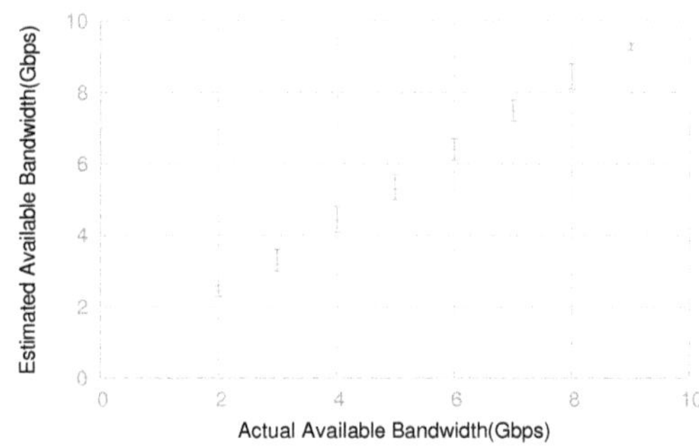

Figure 11: Estimation with probe packets drawn from the CAIDA trace.

4.3.3 Mixed Probe Packet Sizes

In a real network, the distribution of packet sizes is usually mixed with large and small packets. Figure 10 shows the distribution of packet sizes in a recorded Internet trace. We repeat the previous experiment using the baseline setting, except that in this case, we use APP_0 to replay the Internet trace. We let MP_0 modulate the probe train in presence of mixed-sized probe traffic. For each rate $R \in [0.1, 9.6]$, MP_0 ensures that the interpacket gaps between packets of the same flow are uniform. Figure 11 shows the result for CBR1 cross traffic. As can be seen, even though a probe train has mixed packet sizes, the estimation result is still accurate. The reason is that small packets only take a small fraction of total probe train length with respect to large packets. The estimation accuracy is largely determined by the large packets, thus remains accurate.

4.4 Impact of Cross Traffic Characteristics

So far, we have evaluated minProbe under the assumption of constant bit-rate cross traffic. In this section, we no longer make this assumption and instead examine minProbe under bursty cross traffic. In particular, we evaluate minProbe using modeled synthetic bursty traffic (CBR2) and realistic Internet traces.

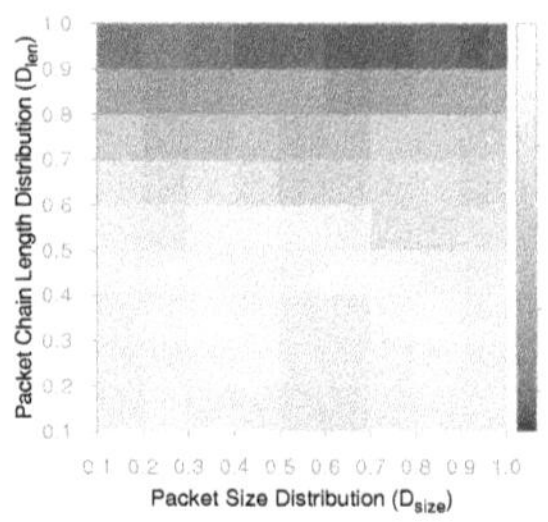

(a) 1 Gbps

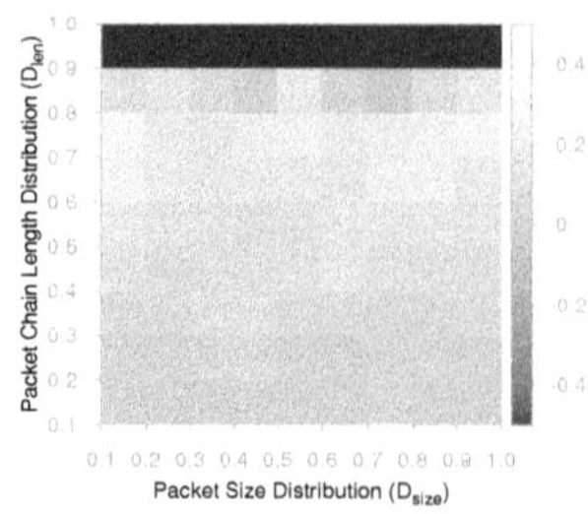

(b) 3 Gbps

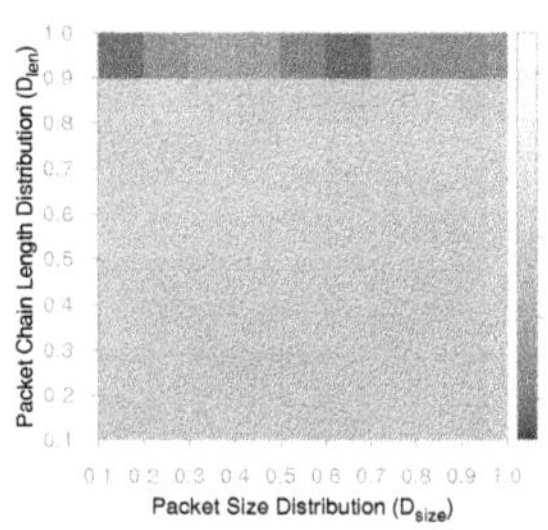

(c) 6 Gbps

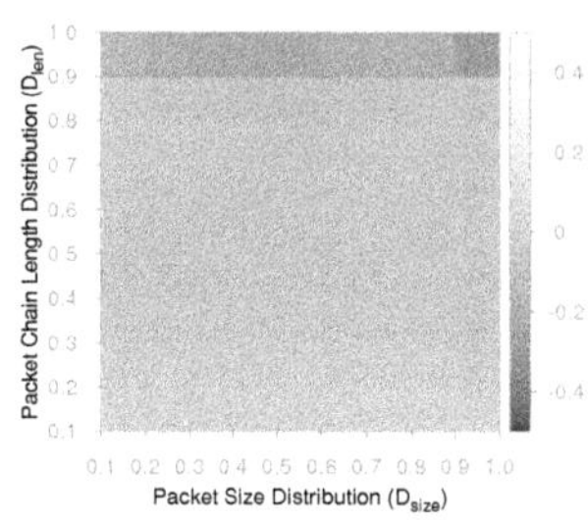

(d) 8 Gbps

Figure 12: Bandwidth estimation accuracy with different cross traffic burstiness. On y-axis, we turn the knob from no clustering to batching. On x-axis, we turn the knob on cross traffic packet size distribution from uniform distribution to log-normal distribution. We plot the graph for different cross traffic rate: 1Gbps, 3Gbps, 6Gbps and 8Gbps.

4.4.1 Cross Traffic Burstiness

Synthesized Traffic: We first show the results of synthesized bursty cross traffic (CBR2). We generated CBR2 with rate $\in [1, 3, 6, 8]$ Gbps. We set $\mathcal{V}_{size}$ to be a fixed large variance value, e.g. 8×10^4 bytes^2, as specified in [28]. Next, we varied the distribution $\mathcal{D}_{size}$ of packet sizes in CBR2 from 0 to 1 with 0.1 step size. 0 means uniform distribution, 1 means distribution with large variance. Similarly, we varied the distribution $\mathcal{D}_{len}$ of packet chain length in CBR2 from between 0 to 1 with 0.1 step size. Note that even though CBR2 is bursty in terms of the variation of packet distribution, the long term average data rate of CBR2 remains constant.

Figure 12 shows the estimation error (in Gbps) over a range of cross traffic burstiness for four different cross traffic data rates. In each figure, we plot the difference between the actual available bandwidth and the estimated available bandwidth for the cross traffic burstiness identified by the $(\mathcal{D}_{size}, \mathcal{D}_{len})$ parameters. Traffic close to the bottom left corner was more uniformly distributed in both packet sizes and train lengths. Traffic on the top right corner was burstier. Dark gray colors mean under estimation, and light gray colors mean over estimation. As shown in the figure, the estimation error by minProbe is typically within 0.4 Gbps of the true value except when the link utilization is low, or the cross traffic is bursty.

Real Internet Trace: Next, we evaluate minProbe with traces extracted from CAIDA anonymized OC192

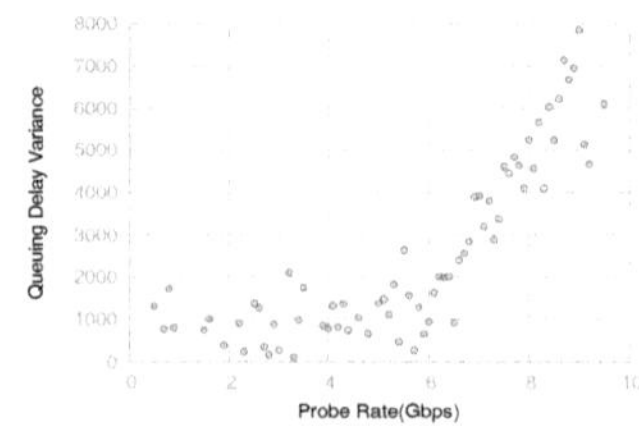

(a) raw measurement

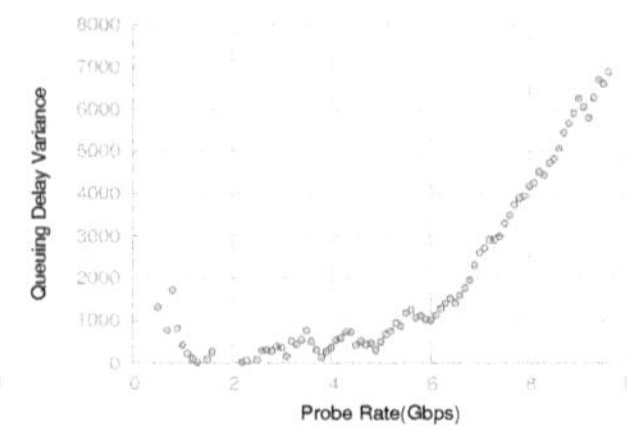

(b) after moving average

Figure 13: Bandwidth estimation of CAIDA trace, the figure on the left is the raw data trace, the figure on the right is the moving average data.

dataset [6], and replayed by SoNIC as a traffic generator. Figure 13a shows an example of the raw data captured by minProbe. We observed that real the traffic traces were burstier than the synthesized traffic in the previous section. To compensate, we used standard exponential moving average (EMA) method to smooth out the data in Figure 13a. For each data points in Figure 13a, the value was replaced by the weighted average of the five data points preceding the current data point. Figure 13b shows the result. Similar to the highly bursty synthesized cross traffic, we achieved a similarly accurate estimation result for the real traffic trace via using the EMA. The estimation error was typically within 0.4Gbps of the true available bandwidth.

In summary, while bursty cross traffic resulted in noisier measurement data than CBR, we were able to compensate for the noise by performing additional statistical processing in the bandwidth estimation. Specifically, we found using the EMA smoothed the measurement data and improved the estimation accuracy. As a result, we observed that cross traffic burstiness had limited impact on minProbe.

4.5 MinProbe In The Wild

In this section, we demonstrate that minProbe works in a wide area Internet network, the National Lambda Rail (NLR). Figure 5 illustrates the experimental network topology. We setup a dedicated route on the NLR with both ends terminating at Cornell University. Node APP_0 generated application traffic, which was modulated by MP_0 using parameter $(N, R, G, D) = (20, [0.1 : 0.1 : 9.6]$ Gbps, 10 us, 4 ms). The traffic was routed through the path shown in Figure 5 across over 2500 miles. Since it was difficult to obtain accurate readings of cross traffic at each hop, we relied on the router port statistics to obtain a 30-second average of cross traffic. We observed that the link between Cleveland and NYC experienced the most cross traffic compared to other links, and was therefore the bottleneck (tight) link of the path. The amount of cross traffic was 1.87 Gbps on average, with a maximum of 3.58 Gbps during the times of our experiments.

Figure 14 shows the result of minProbe in the wild. We highlight two important takeaways: First, the average of our estimation is close to 2 Gbps, which was consistent with the router port statistics collected every 30 seconds. Second, we observed that the readings were very bursty, which means the actual cross traffic on NLR exhibited a good deal of burstiness. In summary, minProbe performed well in the wild, in the wide area. The available bandwidth estimation by minProbe agreed with the link utilization computed from switch port statistical counters: The mean of the minProbe estimation was 1.7Gbps, which was close to the 30-second

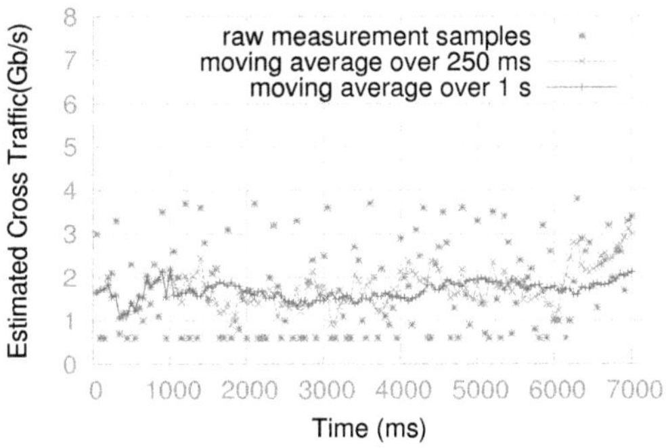

Figure 14: Measurement result in NLR.

average 1.8Gbps computed from switch port statistical counters. Moreover, minProbe estimated available bandwidth at higher sample rate and with finer resolution.

Many cloud datacenters and federated testbeds enforce rate limits on their tenants. For example, the tenants are required to specify the amount of bandwidth to be reserved at the time of provisioning. However, many bandwidth estimation algorithms need to send probe traffic at high data rates to temporarily saturate the bottleneck link. As a result, rate limiting may affect the applicability of the algorithms. We tested the minProbe middlebox inside a federated testbed, ExoGENI, with a virtual network provisioned at 1Gbps on a 10Gbps physical network. We used minProbe to send probe packet trains with different lengths at line rate to find the maximum length of packet train that could be sent before throttled by rate limiters. We found that, in the provisioned 1Gbps virtual network, if the probe train was less than 1200 packets, then there was no observable packet loss. As has been shown in Section 4.3, minProbe only uses probe trains with less than 100 probe packets. As a result, and interestingly, rate limiters do not impact the applicability of minProbe in federate testbed environments.

4.6 Software Router and Other Hardware

Finally, we evaluate whether other middleboxes, such as software routers, can be used to perform high-fidelity network measurements required to accurately estimate available bandwidth without any overhead. In particular, we evaluated two software routers, one based on the Linux kernel network datapath, and another based on the Intel DPDK driver [18]. We configured the software routers to perform L2 forwarding from one port to another. Again, we used the baseline setup, with the exception that software routers were placed between minProbe and the switch. The network path started at the application. After minProbe modulated the application traffic to create packet probe trains, the probe trains were passed through a software router before being sent to a 10 GbE switches.

The experiment was generated from probe packet trains with data rates ranging according to (N, R, G, D) = (20, [0.5 : 0.5 : 9.5] Gbps, 10 us, 4 ms). We show two figures from the this experiment to illustrate the result. First, Figure 15a shows the CDF of the measured instantaneous data rate of probe packet pairs passing through a software router (i.e. we measured the interpacket gap of probe packet pairs after passing through a software router). We configured each software router to forward each packet as soon as it received the packet to minimize any batching. Since we generated an equal number of probe packets (20) for a probe train and

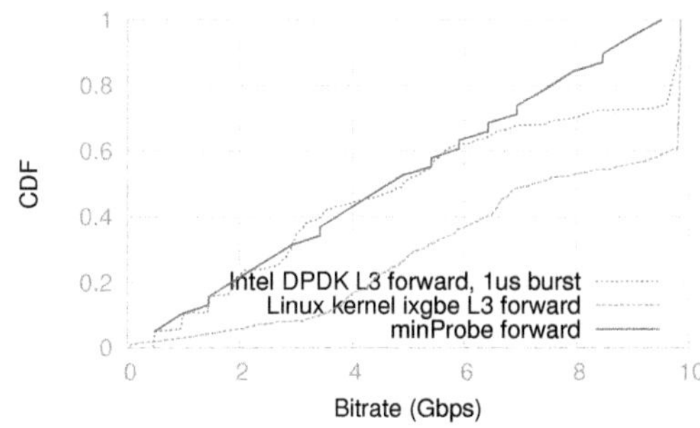

(a)

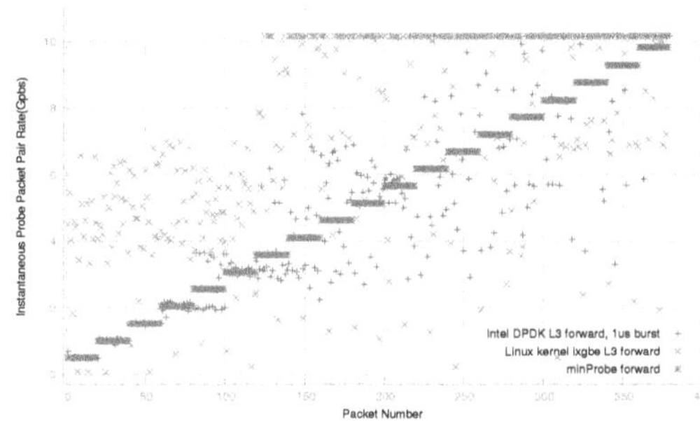

(b)

Figure 15: Software Routers do not exhibit the same fidelity as minProbe

increased the probe packet train data rate by 0.5 Gbps, the ideal CDF curve should increase along a diagonal frp, 0.5 Gbps to 9.5 Gbps at 0.5 Gbps increments (the red line). However, as seen in the figure, over 25% of the probe packet pairs in the Intel DPDK-based software router were batched with minimum interpacket gap: Batching can be seen via the large increase in the CDF near the highest data rate close to 10 Gbps. Worse, the vanilla kernel datapath (with ixgbe kernel driver) batched over 40% of packets. These results were consistent with the existing research findings that show that network interface cards (NICs) generate bursty traffic at sub-100 microsecond timescale. [25]

Second, Figure 15b highlights the same result but slightly differently. The x-axis is the packet number and the y-axis is the measured instantaneous probe packet pair rate (in Gbps). The figure shows that minProbe was able to modulate interpacket gaps to maintain the required probe data rate (all 20 packets in a probe train exhibited the target data rate), while the software routers were not able to control the probe rate at all. To summarize, due to batching, software routers are not suitable for performing the required high-fidelity available bandwidth estimation on high-speed networks.

Next, we investigated the question if prior work such as MGRP [37] could perform on high-speed networks? To answer this, we setup MGRP to perform the same baseline estimation experiment in Figure 8. Unfortunately, the result was consistent with our findings above and in Figures 15a and 15b. In particular, we found that MGRP could not report valid results when it was used in high-speed networks (10Gbps Ethernet). The accuracy of MGRP was limited by its capability to precisely timestamp the received probe packets and its ability to control the probe packet gaps. Both of these capabilities were performed at kernel level in MGRP and were prone to operating system level noise. The accu-

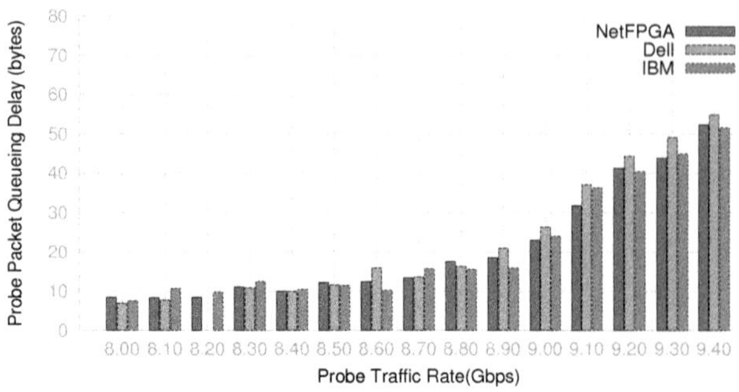

Figure 16: Estimating Available Bandwidth on different switches

racy of MGRP was better than Pathload [20], it eliminated the overhead of extra probing traffic, but the fundamental accuracy was still constrained by the measurement platform.

Finally, we studied the sensitivity of bandwidth estimation with respect to network hardware. In particular, we experimented with three different 10 GbE switches: IBM G8264T, Dell S4810, and NetFPGA-10G reference switch design [31]. We used the baseline setup for all experiments and configured all three switches to perform L2 forwarding. Figure 16 illustrates an example of captured queuing delay after each hardware. As can be seen from the figure, the three switches can be used nearly interchangeably since there was no significant difference in queuing delay. As a result, we have found that the underlying hardware itself may not contribute to the available bandwidth estimation. Instead, as earlier results in the paper indicate, the fidelity of the available bandwidth estimation depend more on the ability to control generated interpacket gaps and measure received interpacket gaps.

5. DISCUSSION

In this section, we discuss the issues regarding the deployment of minProbe, the applications of available bandwidth estimation, and whether minProbe can be generalized to measure bandwidth in 1GbE and 40GbE.

5.1 Deployment

Middleboxes are widely deployed in datacenter networks to perform a wide spectrum of advanced network processing functions ranging from security (firewalls, intrusion detection), traffic shaping (rate limiters, load balancers), to improving application performance (accelerators, proxies, caches), to name a few. Similarly, minProbe deployment scenarios include middleboxes with enhanced measurement capabilities potentially located in the same rack as other servers, or even integrated into each server directly, possibly using hypervisor-based network virtualization, provided that there exists proper support for accessing the physical layer of the network in software. In the future, we will explore the possibility of deploying minProbe as a platform for providing high-fidelity network measurement as a service (NMaaS).

5.2 Virtualization and Availability Bandwidth Estimation

Because of virtualization, datacenter tenants no longer have direct access to the underlying physical network. The extra layer of indirection makes it hard to optimize application performance. MinProbe could potentially bridge the gap. It can measure the underlying network and provide performance metrics to the virtualized applications to optimize tasks such as VM placement and route selection.

5.3 Generalization to 1GbE and 40GbE

At the time of writing, minProbe operated only in 10 GbE networks. However, the high-fidelity capability of minProbe can be extended to support 1GbE and 40GbE networks as well. The architecture of the PHY for 40GbE networks is very similar to the PHY in a 10GbE network. As a result, as future work, we intend to extend minProbe to support 40GbE. Support for 40GbE networks will require parallelizing the processing the PHY layer functionality using modern multi-core architecture. Moreover, as future work, we intend to extend minProbe to support 1GbE networks. The PHY for 1GbE networks are less complicated than 10GbE PHY, which makes it possible to port minProbe to 1GbE. For example, the encoding and decoding schemes at physical coding layer in 1GbE is simpler than the 10GbE physical coding layer.

5.4 GENI

MinProbe is available on ExoGENI [10]. Users can provision compute nodes that has SoNIC cards installed and use it as a minProbe to run network measurement experiments. Currently, at the time of writing, minProbe was enabled at two ExoGENI sites: RENCI (Renaissance Computing Institute) and University of California, Davis. We are in the process of expanding to more sites in the near future.

6. RELATED WORK

Prior work in MAD [43], MGRP [37] and Periscope [15] provide a thin measurement layer (via userspace daemon and kernel module) for network measurement in a shared environment. These works complement minProbe. MinProbe is applicable in a shared environment. We also advance the conversation of available bandwidth estimation to 10Gbps, unlike most of the prior work, which were only demonstrated to operate in 1Gbps or less.

We use an algorithm similar to Pathload [20] and Pathchirp [40] to estimate available bandwidth. There are many related works on both theoretical and practical aspect of available bandwidth estimation [7,20,23,29,30,32,38,40, 42,44]. Our work contributes more on the practice of available bandwidth estimation in high speed network (10Gbps). We found that existing probing parameterizations such as probe trains are sound and still applicable in high-speed networks when supported by the appropriate instrumentation. Furthermore, [21,48] mentioned that burstiness of the cross traffic can negatively affect the accuracy of estimation. While we found that bursty traffic introduces noise into the measurement data, the noise can be filtered out using simple statistical processing, such as the moving average.

Middleboxes are popular building blocks for current network architecture [41]. MinProbe, when operating as a middlebox, is similar to software routers in a sense that minProbe consists of a data forwarding path and programmable flow table. Unlike software routers, which typically focus on high throughput, minProbe has the capability to precisely control the distance between packets; this capability is absent in most existing software routers. From the system design perspective, ICIM [34] has proposed a similar inline network measurement mechanism as our middlebox approach. However, ICIM has only simulated their proposal, while we implemented a prototype and performed experiment in real network. Others have investigated the effect of interrupt coalescence [39] and memory I/O subsystem [24], but they are orthogonal to our efforts. MinProbe, albeit a software tool, avoids the noise of OS and network stack completely by operating at the physical layer of the network stack.

Another area of related work is precise traffic pacing and precise packet timestamping. They are useful system building blocks for designing a high-fidelity network measurement platform. Traditionally, traffic pacing [8] is used to smooth out the burstiness of the traffic to improve system performance. In minProbe, we use traffic pacing in the opposite way to generate micro-burst of traffic to serve as probe packets. Precise timestamping has been used widely in passive network monitoring. Typically, this is achieved by dedicated hardware platform, such as Endace Data Acquisition and Generation (DAG) card [1]. With minProbe, we achieve the same nanosecond timestamping precision, and we are able to use the precise timestamp for active network measurement, which the traditional hardware platform are incapable of.

7. CONCLUSION

Available bandwidth estimation as a research topic has been studied extensively, but there still lacks an accurate and low cost solution in high-speed networks. We present minProbe, which is a high-fidelity, minimal-cost and userspace accessible network measurement approach that is able to accurately measure available bandwidth in 10 gigabit-per-second (Gbps) networks. We provided a systematic study of minProbe's performance with respect to various cross traffic and probe traffic conditions and patterns. We found that minProbe performs well even under bursty traffic, and the estimation is typically within 0.4 Gbps of the true value in a 10 Gbps network.

8. AVAILABILITY

The *minProbe* and SoNIC source code is published under a BSD license and is freely available for download at `http://sonic.cs.cornell.edu`. SoNIC nodes are available for experimentation as bare-metal nodes at the following ExoGENI sites: RENCI and UCDavis.

9. ACKNOWLEDGMENTS

This work was partially funded and supported by an Intel Early Career and IBM Faculty Award received by Hakim Weatherspoon, DARPA (No. D11AP00266), DARPA MRC (No. FA8750-11-2-0256), NSF CAREER (No. 1053757), NSF TRUST (No. 0424422), NSF FIA (No. 1040689), NSF CiC (No. 1047540), and NSF EAGER (No. 1151268). We would like to thank our shepherd, Oliver Spatsch, and the anonymous reviewers for their comments. We further recognize the people helped establish and maintain the network infrastructure on which we performed our experiments: Eric Cronise and Laurie Collinsworth (Cornell Information Technologies); Scott Yoest, and his team (Cornell Computing and Information Science Technical Staff). We also thank the people who provided support for us to perform experiments on GENI and ExoGENI: Ilya Baldin (RENCI) and his team (RENCI Network Research and Infrastruture Program), Jonathan Mills (RENCI), and Ken Gribble (UC Davis).

10. REFERENCES

[1] Endace DAG Network Cards. `http://www.endace.com/endace-dag-high-speed-packet-capture-cards.html`.

[2] High Frequency sFlow v5 Counter Sampling. `ftp://ftp.netperf.org/papers/high_freq_sflow/hf_sflow_counters.pdf`.

[3] IEEE Standard 802.3-2008. `http://standards.ieee.org/about/get/802/802.3.html`.

[4] Linux programmer's manual. `http://man7.org/linux/man-pages/man7/netlink.7.html`.

[5] sflow, version 5. `http://www.sflow.org/sflow_version_5.txt`.

[6] The CAIDA UCSD Anonymized Internet Traces. `http://www.caida.org/datasets/`.

[7] Ahmed Ait Ali, Fabien Michaut, and Francis Lepage. End-to-End Available Bandwidth Measurement Tools : A Comparative Evaluation of Performances. *arXiv.org*, June 2007.

[8] Mohammad Alizadeh, Abdul Kabbani, Tom Edsall, Balaji Prabhakar, Amin Vahdat, and Masato Yasuda. Less is more: Trading a little bandwidth for ultra-low latency in the data center. In *Procs. NSDI*, 2012.

[9] Bilal Anwer, Theophilus Benson, Nick Feamster, Dave Levin, and Jennifer Rexford. A slick control plane for network middleboxes. In *HotSDN*, 2013.

[10] Mark Berman, Jeffrey S. Chase, Lawrence Landweber, Akihiro Nakao, Max Ott, Dipankar Raychaudhuri, Robert Ricci, and Ivan Seskar. Geni: A federated testbed for innovative network experiments. *Comput. Netw.*, 61:5–23, March 2014.

[11] Mihai Dobrescu, Norbert Egi, Katerina Argyraki, Byung-Gon Chun, Kevin Fall, Gianluca Iannaccone, Allan Knies, Maziar Manesh, and Sylvia Ratnasamy. Routebricks: exploiting parallelism to scale software routers. In *Proc. SOSP*, 2009.

[12] Daniel A. Freedman, Tudor Marian, Jennifer H. Lee, Ken Birman, Hakim Weatherspoon, and Chris Xu. Exact temporal characterization of 10 gbps optical wide-area network. In *Proc. IMC*, 2010.

[13] Cesar D. Guerrero and Miguel A. Labrador. On the applicability of available bandwidth estimation techniques and tools. *Comput. Commun.*, 33(1):11–22, January 2010.

[14] Sangjin Han, Keon Jang, KyongSoo Park, and Sue Moon. Packetshader, a gpu-accelerated software router. In *Proc. SIGCOMM*, 2010.

[15] Khaled Harfoush, Azer Bestavros, and John Byers. Periscope: An active internet probing and measurement api. Technical report, Boston University Computer Science Department, 2002.

[16] Ningning Hu, Li Erran Li, Zhuoqing Morley Mao, Peter Steenkiste, and Jia Wang. Locating internet bottlenecks: algorithms, measurements, and implications. In *Proc. SIGCOMM, 2004*, 2004.

[17] Péter Hága, Attila Pásztor, Darryl Veitch, and István Csabai. Pathsensor: Towards efficient available

bandwidth measurement. In *Proc. IPS-MoMe 2005*, 2005.

[18] Intel DPDK. `http://www.dpdk.com`.

[19] Intel Westmere. `http://ark.intel.com/products/codename/33174/Westmere-EP`.

[20] M Jain and C Dovrolis. Pathload: A Measurement Tool for End-to-End Available Bandwidth. 2002.

[21] Manish Jain and Constantinos Dovrolis. Ten fallacies and pitfalls on end-to-end available bandwidth estimation. In *Proc. IMC*, 2004.

[22] Hao Jiang and Constantinos Dovrolis. Why is the internet traffic bursty in short time scales? In *Proc. SIGMETRICS*, 2005.

[23] Guojun Jin and Brian L. Tierney. System capability effects on algorithms for network bandwidth measurement. Proc. IMC, 2003, New York, NY, USA, 2003. ACM.

[24] Guojun Jin and Brian L. Tierney. System capability effects on algorithms for network bandwidth measurement. In *Proc. IMC*, 2003.

[25] Rishi Kapoor, Alex C. Snoeren, Geoffrey M. Voelker, and George Porter. Bullet trains: A study of nic burst behavior at microsecond timescales. In *Proc. CoNEXT*, 2013.

[26] Ki Suh Lee, Han Wang, and Hakim Weatherspoon. Sonic: Precise realtime software access and control of wired networks. In *Proc. NSDI*, 2013.

[27] Ki Suh Lee, Han Wang, and Hakim Weatherspoon. Phy covert channels: Can you see the idles? In *Proc. NSDI*, 2014.

[28] ChiunLin Lim, KiSuh Lee, Han Wang, Hakim Weatherspoon, and Ao Tang. Packet clustering introduced by routers: modelling, analysis and experiments. In *Proc. CISS*, 2014.

[29] Xiliang Liu, Kaliappa Ravindran, Benyuan Liu, and Dmitri Loguinov. Single-hop probing asymptotics in available bandwidth estimation: sample-path analysis. In *Proc. IMC*, 2004.

[30] Xiliang Liu, Kaliappa Ravindran, and Dmitri Loguinov. Multi-hop probing asymptotics in available bandwidth estimation: stochastic analysis. In *Proc. IMC*, October 2005.

[31] John W. Lockwood, Nick McKeown, Greg Watson, Glen Gibb, Paul Hartke, Jad Naous, Ramanan Raghuraman, and Jianying Luo. NetFPGA–An Open Platform for Gigabit-Rate Network Switching and Routing. In *Proceedings of Microelectronics Systems Education*, 2007.

[32] Sridhar Machiraju. *Theory and Practice of Non-Intrusive Active Network Measurements*. PhD thesis, EECS Department, University of California, Berkeley, May 2006.

[33] Sridhar Machiraju and Darryl Veitch. A measurement-friendly network (mfn) architecture. In *Proc. SIGCOMM INM*, Pisa, Italy, 2006.

[34] Cao Le Thanh Man, G. Hasegawa, and M. Murata. Icim: An inline network measurement mechanism for highspeed networks. In *Proceedings of the 4th IEEE/IFIP Workshop on End-to-End Monitoring Techniques and Services*, April 2006.

[35] Tudor Marian, Ki Suh Lee, and Hakim Weatherspoon. Netslices: scalable multi-core packet processing in user-space. In *Proc. ANCS*, 2012.

[36] B. Melander, M. Bjorkman, and P. Gunningberg. A new end-to-end probing and analysis method for estimating bandwidth bottlenecks. In *IEEE Global Telecommunications Conference*, 2000.

[37] Pavlos Papageorge, Justin McCann, and Michael Hicks. Passive aggressive measurement with mgrp. *SIGCOMM Comput. Commun. Rev.*, 39(4):279–290, August 2009.

[38] R Prasad, C Dovrolis, M Murray, and K Claffy. Bandwidth estimation: metrics, measurement techniques, and tools. *Network*, 2003.

[39] Ravi Prasad, Manish Jain, and Constantinos Dovrolis. Effects of interrupt coalescence on network measurements. In *Proceedings of Passive and Active Measurements Workshop*, 2004.

[40] V Ribeiro, R Riedi, R Baraniuk, and J Navratil. pathchirp: Efficient available bandwidth estimation for network paths. In *Proc. PAM*, 2003.

[41] Vyas Sekar, Sylvia Ratnasamy, Michael K. Reiter, Norbert Egi, and Guangyu Shi. The middlebox manifesto: Enabling innovation in middlebox deployment. In *Proc. HotNet*, 2011.

[42] J Sommers, P Barford, and W Willinger. Laboratory-based calibration of available bandwidth estimation tools. *Microprocessors and Microsystems*, 31(4):222–235, 2007.

[43] Joel Sommers and Paul Barford. An active measurement system for shared environments. In *IMC*, 2007.

[44] Joel Sommers and Paul Barford. An active measurement system for shared environments. In *Proc. IMC, 2007*, October 2007.

[45] Joel Sommers, Paul Barford, and Mark Crovella. Router primitives for programmable active measurement. In *In Proc. PRESTO*, 2009.

[46] Jacob Strauss, Dina Katabi, and Frans Kaashoek. A Measurement Study of Available Bandwidth Estimation Tools. In *Proc. SIGCOMM*, 2003.

[47] Kashi Venkatesh Vishwanath and Amin Vahdat. Realistic and responsive network traffic generation. In *Proc. SIGCOMM*, 2006.

[48] Kashi Venkatesh Vishwanath and Amin Vahdat. Evaluating distributed systems: Does background traffic matter? In *Proc. USENIX ATC*, 2008.

[49] Yong Xia, Lakshminarayanan Subramanian, Ion Stoica, and Shivkumar Kalyanaraman. One more bit is enough. *SIGCOMM Comput. Commun. Rev.*, 35(4):37–48, August 2005.

[50] Curtis Yu, Cristian Lumezanu, Yueping Zhang, Vishal Singh, Guofei Jiang, and Harsha V. Madhyastha. Flowsense: Monitoring network utilization with zero measurement cost. In *In Proc. PAM*, 2013.

Identifying and Analyzing High Impact Routing Events with PathMiner

Giovanni Comarela
Boston University
Boston, USA
gcom@bu.edu

Mark Crovella
Boston University
Boston, USA
crovella@bu.edu

ABSTRACT

Understanding the dynamics of the interdomain routing system is challenging. One reason is that a single routing or policy change can have far reaching and complex effects. Connecting observed behavior with its underlying causes is made even more difficult by the amount of noise in the BGP system. In this paper we address these challenges by presenting PathMiner, a system to extract large scale routing events from background noise and identify the AS or link responsible for the event.

PathMiner is distinguished from previous work in its ability to identify and analyze large-scale events that may re-occur many times over long timescales. The central idea behind PathMiner is that although a routing change at one AS may induce large-scale, complex responses in other ASes, the *correlation* among those responses (in space and time) helps to isolate the relevant set of responses from background noise, and makes the cause much easier to identify. Hence, PathMiner has two components: an algorithm for mining large scale coordinated changes from routing tables, and an algorithm for identifying the network element (AS or link) responsible for the set of coordinated changes.

We describe the implementation and validation of PathMiner. We show that it is scalable, being able to extract significant events from multiple years of routing data at a daily granularity. Finally, using PathMiner we study interdomain routing over past 9 years and use it to characterize the presence of large scale routing events and to identify the responsible network elements.

Categories and Subject Descriptors

C.2.3 [**Network Operations**]: Network monitoring; C.2.5 [**Local and Wide-Area Networks**]: Internet – BGP

General Terms

Measurement

Keywords

BGP, Interdomain Routing, Boolean Tensor Factorization

IMC'14, November 5–7, 2014, Vancouver, BC, Canada.
ACM 978-1-4503-3213-2/14/11.
http://dx.doi.org/10.1145/2663716.2663754

1. INTRODUCTION

The state of the interdomain routing system – that can be seen as the set of next-hops chosen by each AS (Autonomous System) toward each prefix – is driven by constant change, both automated (by the rules of BGP path selection) and human-mediated (by policy changes). Each routing change made by an individual AS is in response to some discrete event, such as a link failure or addition, a peer's route announcement or withdrawal, or a policy change. However the complexity of the resulting dynamics means that the causal relationship between routing changes in different parts of the system is notoriously difficult to tease out.

In this paper we present PathMiner, a system for identifying large-scale changes to the state of the routing system that are caused by individual events, and for narrowing down network elements (ASes or links) responsible for the set of changes. By 'large-scale' we mean routing changes that involve many ASes and prefixes, and may re-occur at multiple times.

The central idea behind PathMiner is that when a set of ASes change their next-hop decisions to a set of prefixes in a coordinated fashion, especially when those same changes are repeated at multiple points in time, then it is very likely that the coordinated activity is ultimately caused by actions taken by a single AS or link. This is an application of Occam's Razor: when a large set of ASes all change their next-hop decisions for a large set of prefixes, it is unlikely to be a coincidence. Rather, the simplest explanation is that all the changes were ultimately triggered by the action of a single 'actor' (AS or link). Furthermore, as the size of the AS set and prefix set involved grows, causation by a single actor becomes even more likely. Hence, PathMiner looks for significant spatio-temporal patterns in BGP routing, extracts them from background noise, and identifies the network element most likely to be responsible for generating the pattern.

We start by formalizing the concept of high impact routing events, and showing how to translate the discovery of such events into the Boolean Tensor Factorization problem. The first component of PathMiner is a new algorithm for Boolean Tensor Factorization that is well suited for the kind of data that is derived from network routing changes.

The second component of PathMiner identifies the single actor that is responsible for each event. This second step crucially depends on the fact that the first step extracts a set of coordinated routing changes. The key insight is that over the set of all paths that participate in the routing changes, the network element having highest precision and recall as a classifier for changed paths is most likely the single actor responsible for the event.

We validate PathMiner by manually inspecting the extracted events and actors. For this we developed an automated tool for graphical reconstruction of the event, which depicts the changes made to the subgraph that is induced by the set of ASes and prefixes involved in the event. While manual inspection is time consuming and imperfect, we know of no alternative, since existing systems for root-cause analysis are not capable of working with historical data, nor with sets of large-scale routing changes. Our validation finds that the actors identified for each event almost always agree with manual analysis.

Using PathMiner we perform an initial analysis of the last 9 years of interdomain routing data, sampled at a daily granularity. We show that PathMiner is capable of extracting large events, some of which involve over 100,000 coordinated routing changes. Taken together, these events constitute between 10% and 20% of all visible routing changes over time in the datasets we analyzed. Individual events can involve tens to hundreds of ASes and prefixes, and occur tens to hundreds of times in our data. For most of these events, PathMiner is able to identify a single actor (or a small set of actors) that is likely responsible for ultimately causing this coordinated activity.

One of the main contributions of our work is to provide evidence that large-scale events do exist and they also re-occur over long periods of time. Specifically, PathMiner exposes the existence of regions of the AS-level Internet that have similar dynamics towards sets of prefixes. To the best of our knowledge PathMiner is the first tool capable of exposing such facets of the Internet at a global scale. From an engineering point of view, such information may be valuable for network administrators, when making changes in their systems, by providing historical view of events related to similar actions.

A high-level view laying out the main stages in PathMiner is shown in Figure 1. In the rest of this paper, we describe each of the stages shown in the figure. First, Section 2 uses an example to motivate the development of PathMiner. Section 3 presents a formal definition for our problem. In Section 4 we present and describe how to process raw BGP data (corresponding to the first two stages in Figure 1). In Sections 5 and 6 we describe and present results of our event detection methodology (the next two stages in Figure 1). Section 7 describes our single actor identification strategy (the last stage of the figure). Finally, we discuss related work in Section 8 and present concluding remarks and future work directions in Section 9.

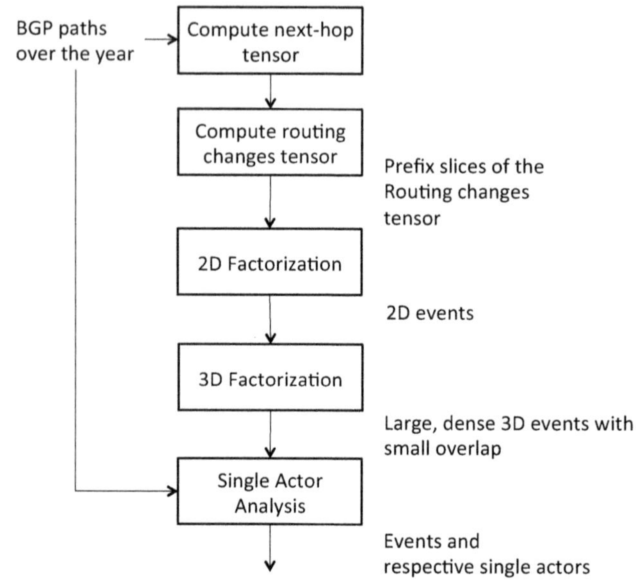

Figure 1: Stages of PathMiner.

2. AN EXAMPLE

Before diving into the details of PathMiner, it is helpful to examine a typical example to provide intuition and motivate our approach.

Figure 2 shows a small subgraph representing the dynamics of a portion of the network with respect to routing towards two prefixes (hosted at AS42381 and AS44173, and shown in gray at the bottom). The figure captures routing dynamics over two consecutive days (April 30, 2013 and May 1, 2013).

This subgraph is a portion of an event extracted by PathMiner. The ASes along the top row of the figure and the prefixes at the bottom of the figure constitute the output of the first step of PathMiner. From the first to the second day, all of the ASes at the top change their next-hops toward all of the prefixes at the bottom. In fact, the full event is quite large, involving dozens of ASes that all change their next-hops; we have extracted these ASes which show behavior that is typical of all the others.

A directed edge in the graph denotes the fact that the first AS uses the second AS as its next-hop for (each of) the two prefixes. Black (solid) edges refer to edges seen in both days, red (dashed) edges refer to edges seen just in the first day and green (dotted) edges refer to those seen only in the second day. Inside each node, the negative (positive) number shows the number of paths passing through the node in the first (second) day of the event (Note that the path counts reflect the full event, which involves many ASes not shown.)

Figure 2 shows that on April 30, most of the paths towards prefixes 1 and 2 were passing through AS6939 (Hurricane Electric). In the next day however paths are more dispersed; some pass through AS3549 (Global Crossing), some through AS3257, some only through AS174 (Cogent), and some pass only through other ASes, not in the figure, which connect directly to AS29632. In other words, ASes are switching from AS6939 to other ways to reach AS29632. We can conclude that either (a) AS6939 made its routes to the subject prefixes unattractive or unavailable, or (b) AS29632, as well the others mentioned above, took actions to make their routes more attractive or available.

This is interesting as a single event, as it shows a large-scale reorganization of the network with regard to two prefixes hosted by different ASes. However, it becomes even more interesting when we note that the same event (or its reverse) happened 28 times during 2013. From these 28 days PathMiner identified AS6969 and AS29632 as responsible by the event in 18 and 10 days respectively.

To illustrate how PathMiner finds such event, consider Figures 3(a) and 3(b). These plots show all points in time during 2013 (on the x axis) where each AS (on the y axis) changes its next-hop towards one prefix. We treat each plot as a binary matrix, in which element (j, k) is 1 if the AS represented by row j changes it next-hop towards the subject prefix between the days k and $k + 1$.[1] It is clear that each matrix consists of noise plus a strong signal; that signal is extracted and shown in Figures 3(c) and 3(d). Because Figures 3(c) and 3(d) are very similar, they together represent the fact that a group of many ASes changed their next-hops towards both prefixes synchronously, multiple times in 2013.

[1] A change is related to the observed next-hops at two instants of data collection, the first on day k, and the second on day $k + 1$. Transient changes, between the two data collection points, are not considered in this work. Details in Sections 3.2 and 4.

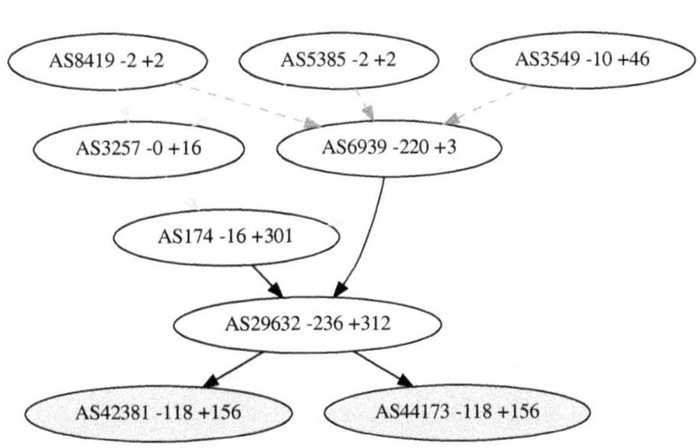

Figure 2: Path changes summary in the network towards two prefixes (hosted at gray nodes) from Apr-30-2013 to May-01-2013.

This simple example shows the nature of the kinds of events captured by PathMiner. It also illustrates the key challenges that PathMiner must overcome: *i)* how can we extract signal from noise (e.g., going from Figure 3(a) to 3(c))? *ii)* next, how can we find prefixes with similar signal matrices (e.g., matching Figure 3(c) with 3(d))? and *iii)* once multi-AS/prefix/time events are extracted, how can we identify the AS or link most likely to have triggered all of the routing changes captured in the event (as shown in Figure 2)? In the following sections we present the solutions taken by PathMiner to these challenges.

3. NOTATION AND DEFINITIONS

In this section we present the mathematical notation/definitions (Section 3.1) used throughout the paper and a formal definition of the problem we aim at solving (Section 3.2).

3.1 Notation

In this paper scalars will be denoted by lower-case letters (a), sets by upper-case letters (A), vectors by lower-case bold-face letters ($\mathbf{v}$), and matrices by upper-case bold-face letters ($\mathbf{M}$). We will also work extensively with 3-dimensional arrays, or *tensors*,[1] which we denote by upper-case calligraphic letters ($\mathcal{T}$).

A tensor may be seen as a collection of slices (matrices), fibers (vectors) or elements. More specifically, for the n-by-m-by-l tensor $\mathcal{X}$, we use $\mathbf{X}_{i::}$, $\mathbf{X}_{:j:}$ and $\mathbf{X}_{::k}$ respectively to denote horizontal, lateral and frontal slices. In the same way, $\mathbf{x}_{:jk}$, $\mathbf{x}_{i:k}$ and $\mathbf{x}_{ij:}$ denote column, row and tube fibers respectively. Finally, x_{ijk} (and with same meaning $x_{i,j,k}$, $\mathcal{X}_{ijk}$ or $\mathcal{X}_{i,j,k}$ depending on convenience) denotes the element (i, j, k) of $\mathcal{X}$. In all cases above, $i = 1, \ldots, n$, $j = 1, \ldots, m$ and $k = 1, \ldots, l$.

Tensor $\mathcal{Y}$ is an induced tensor from $\mathcal{X}$ if there exist sets $A = \{a_1, \ldots a_{n'}\}$, $B = \{b_1, \ldots, b_{m'}\}$ and $C = \{c_1, \ldots, c_{l'}\}$ such that $y_{ijk} = x_{a_i,b_j,c_k}$. In this case we say that sets A, B and C induce $\mathcal{Y}$ in $\mathcal{X}$ and we write $\mathcal{Y} = \mathcal{X}(A, B, C)$. The same meaning holds if we use vectors instead of sets (with the provision that when using vectors, the ordering of indices matters, which is not the case when using sets).

Unless otherwise stated, operations over tensors are defined analogously as operations over matrices. Specifically, for a n-by-m-by-l tensor $\mathcal{X}$, we denote its size as (n, m, l), its volume as $vol(\mathcal{X}) = n \times m \times l$, and its Frobenius norm as $||\mathcal{X}|| = \sqrt{\sum_{i,j,k} x_{ijk}^2}$. We will also frequently refer to the *density* of a tensor, which is the fraction of its entries that are nonzero. In the particular case of binary tensors, this is $den(\mathcal{X}) = \frac{\sum_{i,j,k} x_{ijk}}{vol(\mathcal{X})}$.

[1]The word tensor is in general used to refer to N-dimensional arrays. In this paper we deal only with $N = 3$. More details about tensors can be found at [8].

3.2 Problem definition

Our starting point is the path-based nature of BGP (Border Gateway Protocol), in which ASes keep information about the preferred paths to each reachable prefix [19]. From a perspective of ASes and prefixes, at a given time t the global state of the system can be defined as: a set of ASes A, a set of prefixes P, and for each $a \in A$ a set of AS-paths, each of which allows a to reach a prefix in P. Another representation that we will also use is based on next-hops. In this representation, the state of the system consists of a set of tuples (a, b, p) where $a \in A$ uses $b \in A$ as the next-hop to reach $p \in P$. The next-hop representation of the system contains less information than the preferred-paths representation, so they are not equivalent, but each will be more convenient for certain parts of PathMiner.

To formalize the next-hop representation, at a given time t let $\mathbf{N}$ be a multivalued n-by-m matrix of next-hops in the network, where $\mathbf{N}_{ij}$ denotes the set of next-hops used by AS j to reach prefix i. Observing $\mathbf{N}$ over a discrete set of l points in time yields a n-by-m-by-l multivalued tensor $\mathcal{N}$, where $\mathcal{N}_{ijk}$ is the set of next-hops used by AS j to reach prefix i at time k. Tensor $\mathcal{N}$ represents the complete dynamics of the network over the set of measurements.

By comparing (frontal) slices of $\mathcal{N}$, we can identify next-hop changes in the network. This results in a binary tensor $\mathcal{C}$, which is the n-by-m-by-$(l-1)$ tensor of *routing changes*, defined as:

$$\mathcal{C}_{ijk} = \begin{cases} 1, & \text{if } \mathcal{N}_{i,j,k} \neq \mathcal{N}_{i,j,k+1}, \\ 0, & \text{otherwise.} \end{cases} \tag{1}$$

Given these definitions, we can define a *high impact event* in the global routing system as: sets I (of prefixes), J (of ASes) and K (of points in time) such that the sub-tensor $\mathcal{C}(I, J, K)$ has large volume and high density. Because $\mathcal{C}(I, J, K)$ has large volume, it has potential for high impact – many routing changes might be involved. The fact that $\mathcal{C}(I, J, K)$ has high density means that it is likely to be a singular event – that is, most ASes are changing their next-hops toward most prefixes at most timepoints, and as argued above, such unusually coordinated activity is likely due to the actions of a single network element.

To make this definition concrete, we introduce the concept of a (λ, ν)-event:

DEFINITION 1. *((λ, ν)-event) A binary tensor $\mathcal{B}$ is a (λ, ν)-event with regard to binary tensor $\mathcal{X}$ if there exist sets I, J and K such that $\mathcal{B} = \mathcal{X}(I, J, K)$; $den(\mathcal{B}) \geq \lambda$; and $vol(\mathcal{B}) \geq \nu$.*

Definition 1 still is not enough to fully characterize the events we are seeking. For instance, two distinct (λ, ν)-events $\mathcal{B}$ and $\mathcal{B}'$ may be such that $\mathcal{B}$ is a sub-tensor of $\mathcal{B}'$ and hence, the former can be viewed just as redundant information when compared with the latter. Therefore, it is also necessary to put constraints on the set of (λ, ν)-events we want to find. Thus, the final description of our problem, which we call Boolean Tensor (λ, ν)-Factorization (or (λ, ν)-BTF) is:

PROBLEM 1. *(Boolean Tensor (λ, ν)-Factorization) Given a binary tensor $\mathcal{X}$, integers r and ν and a real λ, the Boolean Tensor (λ, ν)-Factorization problem consists of finding r triples of sets (I_h, J_h, K_h), $h = 1, \ldots, r$ such that:*

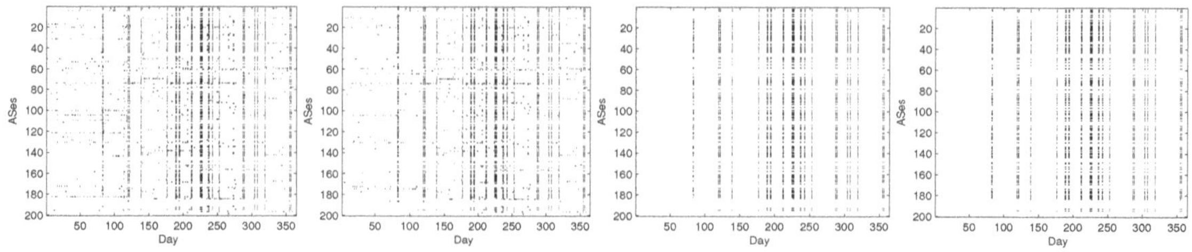

(a) Prefix 1, all changes (b) Prefix 2, all changes (c) Prefix 1, signal (d) Prefix 2, signal

Figure 3: Next-hop changes towards the two prefixes of Figure 2 during 2013. An observed next-hop change, by AS j, towards the subject prefix at day k implies value 1 for the element (j, k).

i) $\mathcal{X}(I_h, J_h, K_h)$ *is a* (λ, ν)*-event in* $\mathcal{X}$, *for* $h = 1, \ldots, r$; *and*

ii) $\left\| \mathcal{X} - \bigvee_{h=1}^{r} \mathcal{X}^{(h)} \right\|$ *is minimized, where:* $\mathcal{X}^{(h)}$ *is a binary tensor with same size as* $\mathcal{X}$, *and* $x_{ijk}^{(h)} = 1$ *iff* $(i, j, k) \in I_h \times J_h \times K_h$; *and* $\bigvee_{h=1}^{r} \mathcal{X}^{(h)}$ *is defined as the elementwise logical* or *of* $\mathcal{X}^{(1)}, \ldots, \mathcal{X}^{(r)}$.

The intuition behind the definition of Problem 1 is to find a set of r binary tensors that best approximate $\mathcal{X}$ as blocks of 1's. Moreover, we are only interested in tensors related to (λ, ν)-events. More formally, $\bigvee_{h=1}^{r} \mathcal{X}^{(h)}$ is the best approximation for $\mathcal{X}$ that can be obtained with a rank-r binary tensor, when each $\mathcal{X}(I_h, J_h, K_h)$ is a (λ, ν)-event.

Unfortunately, easy ways to solve Problem 1 exactly are not known. Setting $\lambda = 0$ and $\nu = 0$, the problem is equivalent to the Boolean Tensor Factorization problem studied in [9], which is known to be NP-hard [18]. Therefore, the more general problem of (λ, ν)-BTF is also NP-hard.

In summary, this section sets out a definition that translates the general notion of *identifying high impact events in the global routing* into a specific problem. Unfortunately this definition highlights two difficulties: *i)* complete topologies of the global interdomain routing system over time are not available; and *ii)* computing an exact solution to Problem 1 is hard in general. In the next section we discuss the available data we used and how we address its incompleteness, and then in Section 5 we describe our heuristic algorithms for finding solutions to Problem 1.

4. DATASET DESCRIPTION

In this section we present the dataset we used, how we processed it, and its limitations. Our source of data consisted of BGP RIBs (Routing Information Bases) made available by RIPE [2] and the Route Views project [4].

We obtained data from 9 years, from the beginning of 2005 until the end of 2013, at a daily timescale. For each day and repository we obtained the RIB made available at 8am (or, if not available, the closest one). We made the arbitrary choice of 8am in order to have approximately 24 hours between routing information collected for each day. From the RIBs we extracted all records of the form *route dumping date*, *prefix* and *AS-path* (only data related to IPv4 prefixes). We stored this data on a 12-node cluster in a Hadoop Distributed File System (HDFS) and, for the most data intensive computations, we used Hadoop [1] and Spark [3]. Table 1 presents a summary of our dataset.

As described in Section 3, our first step is to obtain the next-hop tensor $\mathcal{N}$. To this end, for each entry of the form [date, prefix p, AS-path], where AS-path is given by $[AS_1, \ldots, AS_q]$, we computed the $q - 1$ 4-tuples [date, p, AS_i, AS_{i+1}], for $i = 1, \ldots, q - 1$. Each 4-tuple means that at time *date*, in order to reach prefix p, the source AS_i uses as next-hop AS_{i+1}.

Table 1: Dataset summary

Year	Prefixes	ASes	Size (GB)
2005	286723	23157	340
2006	331421	26188	470
2007	400784	29382	640
2008	438730	32929	806
2009	506978	36336	845
2010	543868	39339	939
2011	626312	43151	1154
2012	879730	46262	1397
2013	850997	49502	1745

Referring to Table 1, it is important to remark that we do not have routing information from every source to every destination at every point in time. In this context, missing data can arise mainly for two reasons: (a) data collection issues and (b) visibility problems (the RIPE and Route Views RIBs do not capture the complete AS-topology of the Internet). Note as well that the datasets considered are large – for recent years, over 1TB each in size.

Fortunately, both of these problems (missing data, and dataset size) can be significantly lessened by carefully selecting a representative subset of the data. Accordingly, we selected our data subset by greedily choosing ASes and prefixes with most of the next-hop changes in the network. To that end, using big data tools, we computed the tensor $\mathcal{C}$ ($\mathcal{C}_{ijk} = 1$ iff AS j changed next-hop towards prefix i from day k to $k + 1$) for each of the nine datasets in full. Next, we computed the total number of changes over the year for each prefix i (as a destination), each AS j (as a source) and for each pair (i, j). Figures 4(a) and 4(b) present the log-log complementary CDFs of the total number of changes for prefixes and ASes, respectively. It can be seen that for ASes there is a distinct subset of heavy-hitters that account for the majority of routing changes.

Going further, Figure 4(c) shows the cumulative number of changes for a pair (i, j) for the year of 2011. That is, value at row i and column j of the heat map represents the fraction of changes corresponding to the i prefixes and j ASes with most changes in the dataset. This figure provides information about how to greedily, with respect to the number of routing changes, obtain a sample of ASes and prefixes. With regard to ASes it is possible to see that including more than the top 200 ASes in the sample does not increase significantly the fraction of changes captured.

On the other hand, there are hundreds of thousands of prefixes that experience significant levels of routing changes. At the same time, it is also important to recognize that there exist many sets of prefixes for which routing information is essentially redundant. In

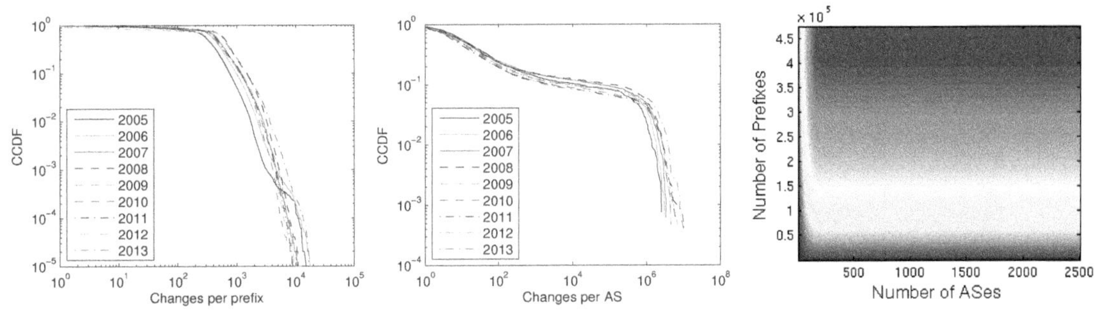

(a) (b) (c)

Figure 4: Distributions of the total number of next-hop changes: (a) per prefix; (b) per AS; and (c) per pair (AS, prefix), for 2011 only. In (c) value at (i, j) indicates the total number of next-hop changes from the first j ASes towards first i prefixes (ASes and prefixes are sorted, in decreasing order, by their number of changes).

Table 2: Summary of the sampled routing changes tensors

Year	Density (%)	Missing (%)
2005	0.9	7.4
2006	1.2	8.7
2007	1.5	6.7
2008	1.9	6.3
2009	1.7	8.1
2010	1.6	7.0
2011	1.7	5.9
2012	1.8	7.4
2013	2.3	5.5

particular, in many cases prefixes originated by the same AS are routed similarly [6]. For our problem, such sets of prefixes add no additional information about coordinated routing changes.

Hence, in our data subset we chose the top 20000 prefixes in terms of volume of changes, but only allowing at most one prefix hosted in each AS.[1] Since the 20000 prefixes come from 20000 distinct ASes, and there are only about 50000 ASes active in total, we expect that this subset captures a large fraction of the distinct and observable routing changes in our data. That is, the intuition behind our sampling strategy was to obtain a set of prefixes responsible for many changes, and at the same time avoiding the discovery of blocks with many prefixes belonging to the same AS and hence having identical routing changes.

Table 2 presents statistics about tensor $\mathcal{C}$ projected only over the samples; each sample tensor is of size 20000-by-200-by-364. Note that because the set of active ASes and prefixes has changed over the 9 year timespan, the sampling procedure was done independently for each year. Therefore, the sets of prefixes and ASes considered vary from year to year, in order to capture the maximum amount of routing changes, and hence results in the remaining of this work were computed independently for each sample.

Table 2 also shows the percent of missing data, i.e., missing next-hop entries in the tensor $\mathcal{N}$ (projected over the samples). Since these percentages were reasonably small, we handled missing data as follows. Suppose that at some point in time k we have $\mathcal{N}_{ijk} \neq \emptyset$ for some i, j and $\mathcal{N}_{i,j,k+1} = \emptyset$. Because data at time $k+1$ is missing, we cannot know for certain whether: *i)* AS j cannot reach prefix i at time $k+1$ (which would imply that $\mathcal{C}_{ijk} = 1$), or *ii)* AS j can reach i at time $k+1$ but our data set does not contain that information (which implies that $\mathcal{C}_{ijk}$ can be either 0 or 1). In light of this limitation we took a conservative approach and defined $\mathcal{C}_{ijk}$ to be 0. Therefore, a 1 in the tensor $\mathcal{C}$ means that we definitely observe a next-hop change in the data, but a 0 can either imply that a change did not happen, or that we simply do not know what happened. Choosing to set these entries to 0 also reflects that fact that zeros comprise the vast majority of known values in our data.

Note that the amount of uncertainty in the routing changes tensors ($\mathcal{C}$) is thus bounded by the 5 to 10% of missing data. This has implications in the next section for our event extraction. In particular, we should expect that even when a set of ASes all change their next-hops for a set of prefixes, our data may only show a portion (e.g., 90%) of those changes – i.e., the observed density of a valid event may be less than 100%.

Another aspect worth mentioning about the dataset is the presence of more than one next-hop from some ASes towards some prefixes. In fact, that was the motivation for our definition of next-hop change, given in Equation 1, where one can see that we compare sets, instead of elements. Other possible approach would be to use a finer granularity of the network, where the issue of more than one next-hop never arises. For instance, such granularity could be obtained by considering quasi-routers. Unfortunately, the use of quasi-routers would introduce problems hard to be addressed in our analyses. For example, which quasi-router observed at a day k corresponds to the quasi-routers observed at day $k+1$?

In order to provide means to understand how much the issue of more than one next-hop may affect our results, we computed the fraction of cases in which $|\mathcal{N}_{ijk}| > 1$ or $|\mathcal{N}_{i,j,k+1}| > 1$, during the computation of $\mathcal{C}_{ijk}$, in our nine datasets (before sampling). In all cases this fraction was below 8%. Furthermore, from the cases where $\mathcal{C}_{ijk} = 1$ we have that the same fraction is below 30% (in all datasets).

5. EXTRACTING EVENTS

As previously discussed, at a high level PathMiner consists of two main steps: (1) finding high-impact events, and (2) identifying the most likely network element causing the event. In this section, we describe our solution to step (1), which is an algorithm for finding good solutions to the (λ, ν)-BTF problem.

An attractive solution to the (λ, ν)-BTF problem would be to start from an existing algorithm for standard Binary Tensor Factorization. Unfortunately, the large size (combined with the density) of our binary tensors was too much for existing algorithms (e.g., in [9]) to handle. As a result, we developed a scalable heuristic to find (λ, ν)-events in the routing changes tensor $\mathcal{C}$.

[1]We considered the *host* of a prefix to be the AS advertising the prefix for the first time in each year.

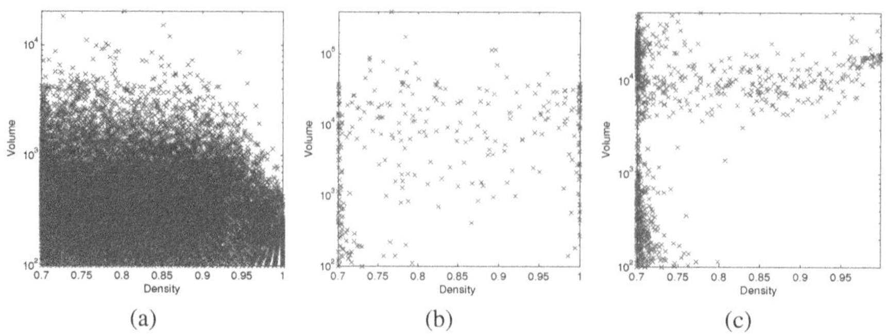

Figure 5: Density *versus* Volume for 2D (λ, ν)-events obtained from slices of tensor $\mathcal{C}$, 2013 only. Prefix (horizontal) slices in (a), AS (lateral) slices in (b) and time (frontal) slices in (c). Experiments performed using Algorithm 1 with $\lambda = 0.7$, $\nu = 100$ and $\epsilon = 1\%$.

Our approach has two steps. First we look at individual slices of $\mathcal{C}$ and extract (λ, ν)-events within slices (Section 5.1). Then, we aggregate similar slice events in order to form events that span multiple slices (Section 5.2).

The algorithmic approach we adopt is well suited to the case where significant large, dense events exist in the data (as those presented in Figure 3). Thus it is well suited to the current problem, while other algorithms (including [9]) may be more appropriate when events are smaller and rarer. For the sake of brevity and due to space limitations we present only a high level description of our algorithms.[1]

5.1 2D Factorization

Let $\mathbf{X}$ be a slice of $\mathcal{C}$. It can be a prefix (horizontal), AS (lateral) or a time (frontal) slice. For example, $\mathbf{X}$ may be the prefix slice shown in Figure 3(a). The goal of 2D Factorization is to extract from $\mathbf{X}$ a set of large volume, high density patterns such as shown in Figure 3(c). For simplicity of notation we assume from now on that $\mathbf{X}$ is a prefix slice of $\mathcal{C}$ for prefix i. Description for AS and time slices proceeds analogously.

To start, we define a rank-1 binary matrix: given binary vectors $\mathbf{a}$ and $\mathbf{b}$, a rank-1 binary matrix $\mathbf{X}$ is given by $\mathbf{X}_{ij} = \mathbf{a}_i \times \mathbf{b}_j$. That is, a rank-1 binary matrix is the outer product of two binary vectors and can be thought of as a 'block' of 1s (after reordering of rows and columns).

The 2D Factorization step repeats the following as long as a significant fraction of 1s can be obtained from $\mathbf{X}$: Find a good rank-1 binary approximation for $\mathbf{X}$, denoted $\mathbf{M}$. If the set of rows J (representing ASes) and columns K (representing days) with non zero elements of $\mathbf{M}$ induces a submatrix $\mathbf{B}$ with volume at least ν and density at least λ, then label the triple $(\{i\}, J, K)$ as a (λ, ν)-event. Next, independently of volume and density of $\mathbf{B}$, remove all ones captured by the set of rows J and the set of columns K. This strategy is described more precisely in Algorithm 1.

The key challenge is to obtain the rank-1 approximation $\mathbf{M}$ (Line 5). In fact, this is equivalent to the Frequent Itemset Mining problem, which currently has not a known easy way to be exactly solved. Furthermore, the tensor $\mathcal{C}$ may have many thousands of slices, so the algorithm we use must run quite quickly. Hence we use the strategy of *relaxing* the discrete problem into a continuous one, solving the continuous problem, and thresholding the result to find an approximate discrete solution.

[1]Our implementation is publicly available and can be obtained at `http://cs-people.bu.edu/gcom/bgp/imc2014` or by direct request to the authors.

Algorithm 1: 2D-FACTORIZATION

Data: n by m binary matrix $\mathbf{X}$ related to prefix i, λ, ν and convergence parameter ϵ

1 $F \leftarrow \{\}$
2 $\mathbf{Z} \leftarrow \mathbf{X}$
3 **repeat**
4 $\quad \mathbf{Z}' \leftarrow \mathbf{Z}$
5 $\quad \mathbf{M} \leftarrow$ RANK-1-APPROXIMATION$(\mathbf{X}, \mathbf{Z}, \lambda, \nu)$
6 $\quad J \leftarrow \{j : m_{jk} = 1\}$
7 $\quad K \leftarrow \{k : m_{jk} = 1\}$
8 $\quad \mathbf{B} \leftarrow \mathbf{X}(J, K)$
9 $\quad$ **if** $den(\mathbf{B}) \geq \lambda$ **and** $vol(\mathbf{B}) \geq \nu$ **then**
10 $\quad\quad F \leftarrow F \cup \{(\{i\}, J, K)\}$
11 $\quad$ **for** $(j, k) \in J \times K$ **do**
12 $\quad\quad z_{jk} \leftarrow 0$
13 **until** $\|\mathbf{Z}\| = 0$ **or** $\frac{\|\mathbf{Z} - \mathbf{Z}'\|^2}{\|\mathbf{Z}\|^2} < \epsilon$;
14 **return** F

Our relaxation seeks a real-valued rank-1 approximation to $\mathbf{Z}$ (which initially is a copy of $\mathbf{X}$). For this we use Non-Negative Matrix Factorization (NNMF) [5]. Using NNMF we find real nonnegative vectors $\mathbf{w}$ (n-by-1) and $\mathbf{h}$ (1-by-m) such that $\mathbf{wh}$ is a real nonnegative rank-1 matrix approximating $\mathbf{Z}$. We then threshold $\mathbf{w}$ and $\mathbf{h}$ independently, obtaining the binary vectors $\mathbf{w}'$ and $\mathbf{h}'$, such that $\mathbf{M} = \mathbf{w}'\mathbf{h}'$ minimizes $\|\mathbf{X} - \mathbf{M}\|$ (see that the error is computed considering the original matrix). We note that once $\mathbf{w}$ and $\mathbf{h}$ are computed, computing $\mathbf{M}$ (by finding the optimal thresholding) can be performed in time $O(mn)$.

For the results in this paper, we ran Algorithm 1 for each of the 9 datasets with $\lambda = 0.7$, $\nu = 100$ and $\epsilon = 1\%$. We considered as input three different sets of slices: prefix slices, AS slices and time slices. Figure 5 summarize the results by presenting a scatterplot of density *versus* volume for the year of 2013 (same general comments apply for other datasets). While prefix slices give us events with a wide range of density and volume, AS and time slices behave differently. Basically, most of the AS and time events have low density or volume close to 10^4. The explanation is twofold: first, AS and time slices are harder to mine, since their size is significantly larger than the size of prefix slices; and second, many of the events on AS and time slices consist of one AS changing its next-hop towards all (or almost all) prefixes in the network. Hence, because prefix slices offer the best quality results (in terms of density) and reveal the most interesting structure in the data, we use only prefix slices to generate the (λ, ν)-events used in the next stage of the algorithm.

5.2 3D Factorization

The next step is to find 3 dimensional (λ, ν)-events in the tensor $\mathcal{C}$. The input S, obtained using the method in the last section, is a set of triples of the form $(\{i\}, J, K)$, where i represents a prefix, J a set of ASes and K a set of points in time. The basic idea is to find triples having similar blocks (given by sets J and K) and to group them to create 3D events.

We consider that there may be two ways of combining a pair of blocks. First, they may be nearly identical – that is, their intersection may be nearly as large as their union. In that case, we merge them by constructing the block that contains them both. Second, their intersection may be much smaller than their union, but still sufficiently large in terms of absolute volume. In that case, we merge them by constructing the block that is their intersection.

To evaluate these two cases, we define two functions over pairs of triples $x = (I, J, K)$ and $x' = (I', J', K')$ as:

$$d_B(x, x') = 1 - \frac{|J \cap J'| \times |K \cap K'|}{|J \cup J'| \times |K \cup K'|} \quad (2)$$

and

$$s_B(x, x') = |J \cap J'| \times |K \cap K'|. \quad (3)$$

The distance function d_B measures the volume of the intersection of two blocks divided by the volume of their union. If close to zero, then J is similar to J' and K is similar to K'. Hence, it is natural to assume that $(I \cup I', J \cup J', K \cup K')$ is a larger event. We extend this strategy to merge multiple triples in a single step as follows: given a triple x, look for a set S' (which contains x) such that $\max_{y,z \in S'} d_B(y, z) \leq \gamma$, for some $0 \leq \gamma \leq 1$. Once S' is found we combine all of its elements at once using the following operator:

$$\text{COMBINE-UNION}(S') = \left(\bigcup_{y \in S'} y_1, \bigcup_{y \in S'} y_2, \bigcup_{y \in S'} y_3 \right),$$

where y_1, y_2 and y_3 represent, for triple y, the sets of prefixes, ASes and points in time respectively.

The similarity function s_B captures the case when the intersection of two blocks is large enough by itself to merit merging the blocks. That is, it may be the case that triple x is not nearly the same as any other triple in S, but there still exists x' such that $s_B(x, x')$ is significantly large (larger than some threshold β). In this case, we may conclude that $(I \cup I', J \cap J', K \cap K')$ is an event. In fact, the second part of the algorithm looks for elements $x' \in S$ such that $s_B(x, x') \geq \beta$ and then combines them using the following operator:

$$\text{COMBINE-INTER}(x, x') = (I \cup I', J \cap J', K \cap K').$$

Alternating the test for maximum distance and minimum similarity and using COMBINE-UNION and COMBINE-INTER operators iteratively yields the discovery of new triples (possible representing new (λ, ν)-events) and is the core of our strategy to find 3 dimensional blocks in $\mathcal{C}$. The procedure is summarized in Algorithm 3 (presented in Appendix A).

One may note that Algorithm 3 does not check the density of new formed 3D blocks. This is because extracting the relevant portions of $\mathcal{C}$ for this check is so time consuming as to be prohibitively expensive for our datasets. Of course this absence of verification may lead to triples that induce blocks with low density. A second problem that may arise is that the extracted 3D blocks may still show significant overlap. In order to address these two issues we added a final stage that discards blocks with low density and blocks that do not add new information to the results because it overlaps with many others. This process is described in Algorithm 2, which greedily (by decreasing order of volume) selects only triples with a minimum density and that captures significant information not contained in blocks previously selected. Results and parameters set up related to the methodology presented in this section will be discussed in Section 6.

Algorithm 2: EVENT-SELECTION

Data: Tensor $\mathcal{C}$, S, set of triples of sets of the form (I, J, K) and thresholds λ and ν

$L \leftarrow$ sort triples $(I, J, K) \in S$ in decreasing order of volume $(|I| \times |J| \times |K|)$
$S' \leftarrow \emptyset$
for $i = 1$ **to** $|L|$ **do**
  $(I, J, K) \leftarrow L_i$
  $\mathcal{B} \leftarrow \mathcal{C}(I, J, K)$
  if $vol(\mathcal{B}) \geq \nu$ **and** $den(\mathcal{B}) \geq \lambda$ **then**
    foreach $(i, j, k) \in I \times J \times K$ **do**
      $\mathcal{C}_{ijk} \leftarrow 0$
    $S' \leftarrow S' \cup \{(I, J, K)\}$
return S'

6. CHARACTERIZING EVENTS

After the execution of the set of algorithms presented in the previous section, we have a collection of 3D events extracted from from the routing changes tensor $\mathcal{C}$, each one with large volume and high density. In this section, we briefly pause to characterize the events found by PathMiner in the 9 years of routing data.

After experimentation we settled on the following parameters for the algorithms presented in Section 5.2: $\lambda = 0.8$, $\nu = 100$, $\gamma = 0.1$ and $\beta = 100$.[1] Table 3 summarizes the overall performance of PathMiner when using these parameter settings on our data. The column '# 1's Retrieved' is the total number of routing changes that were contained in events, and the 'Percent' column is the fraction of all routing changes in our data that were contained in events.

Table 3: Summary of (λ, ν)-events

Dataset	#Events	#1's Retrieved	Percent
2005	5255	1107109	8.2
2006	6823	1689299	9.5
2007	8252	2504558	11.1
2008	7996	2411041	8.3
2009	8602	2466807	9.7
2010	9646	2952688	12.6
2011	12042	3991264	16.3
2012	13910	4611049	17.8
2013	13992	5880885	17.7

The table shows that PathMiner is able to find many blocks, comprising a significant fraction of the routing changes contained in the datasets, ranging from 8.2% in 2005 up to 17.8% in 2012. Figures

[1] For instance, using $\beta = 200$ and $\gamma \in \{0.2, 0.05\}$ did not change the results significantly in terms of percentage of retrieved next-hop changes, average volume or average density. Tests performed with 2013 dataset.

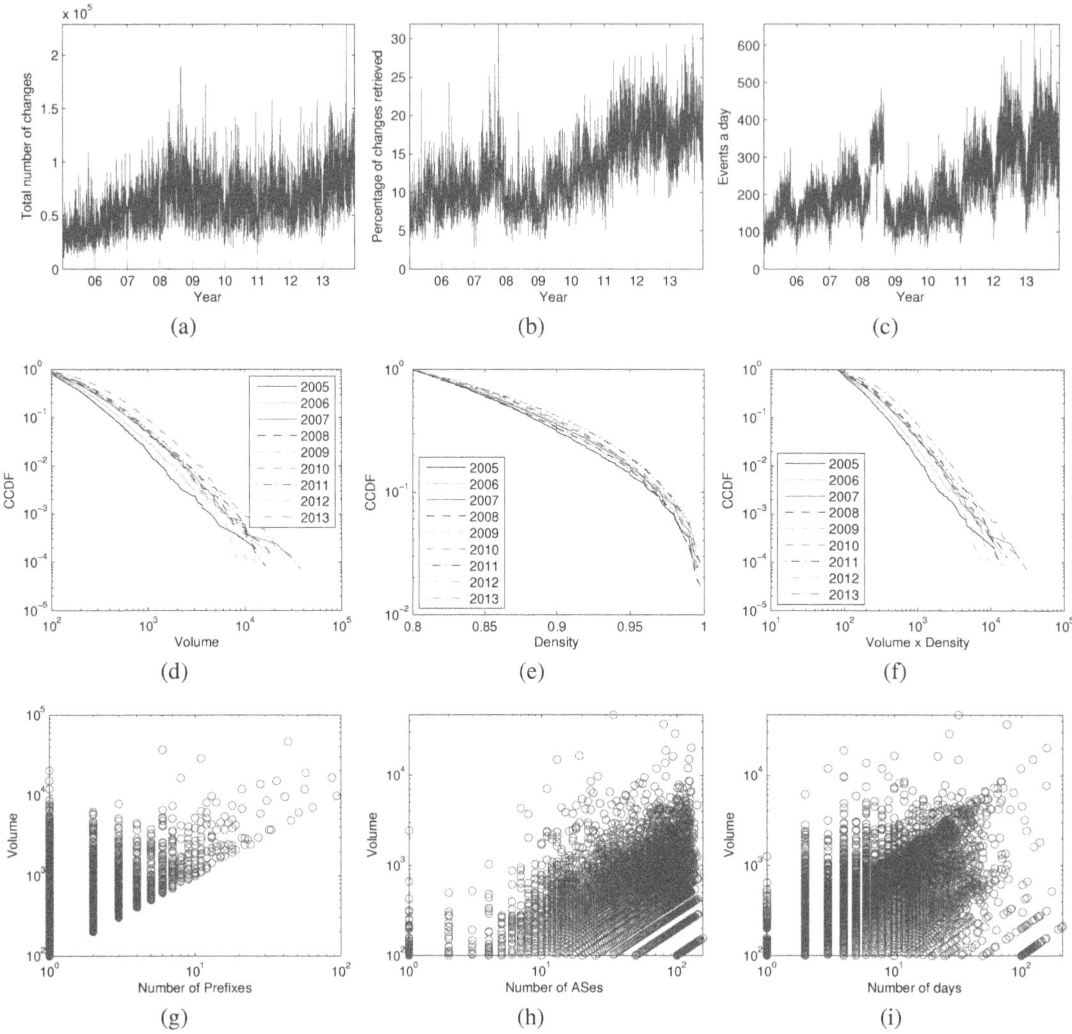

Figure 6: Basic statistics about (λ, ν)-events found by PathMiner (λ = 0.8 and ν = 100). Time series of: (a) total number of next-hop changes in each yearly sample; (b) percentage of these changes captured in events by PathMiner; (c) number of events found in each day. Complementary CDFs of: volume of events – volume is defined as the product of the number of prefixes, ASes and days in a event; (e) density of events – density is the number of changes captured by an event over its volume; (f) product volume $\times$ density of events. Event scatterplots (2013 only): (g) number of prefixes *versus* volume; (h) number of ASes *versus* volume; (i) number of days *versus* volume.

6(a), 6(b) and 6(c) present the same statistics on a daily basis as a time series over the 9 years of data. Note that the samples for each year are distinct so trends should not be inferred across years. From Figures 6(b) and 6(c) we can see that PathMiner performs better in tensors with higher density and that overall, the shape of the time series related to the fraction of changes and the number of events a day is similar to the shape of the time series related to the total number of changes (higher values in 2008 and in the last three years, 2011, 2012 and 2013).

Next, we move to analyzing density and volume of events. As an algorithmic constraint we have that each block has density higher than 0.8 and volume greater than 100. But, in general, how large and dense are the events? Figures 6(d), 6(e) and 6(f) present the log-log complementary CDF for volume, density and their product, respectively, for all 9 datasets. In general the distributions are long-tailed, with many small events and a few very large events. In terms of volume we can see that for 2005 more than 10% of all blocks have volume greater than 500 and that this number goes up to 1000 in 2013. In the tail of the curves we can see some huge events with volume greater than 10^4. Similar comments can be made for Figure 6(f). In terms of density, although 0.8 can be considered a high threshold, there are many blocks that are much denser. For instance, approximately 30% of all events (in all datasets) have density higher than 0.9 and 10% are higher than 0.95 in density.

We also explore the relationship between the volume of events and the number of prefixes, ASes and days that the event contains. Figures 6(g), 6(h) and 6(i) present the results for the year of 2013 (results for other years follow the same trend). It can be seen that the extracted events include large numbers of days and ASes (obtained via the 2 dimensional factorization algorithm) and that events with many prefixes are formed as a result of the 2D event aggregation step.

Finally, Table 4 presents the 5 largest events, in terms of volume for each year. Columns 2 to 4 represent the number of prefixes, ASes and days in each event (thus the volume of the event can be obtained by their product). The table shows that PathMiner was able to find events of remarkable scope, some of which involve dozens of ASes, prefixes, and days. The largest events (in

2007 and 2008) involve over 100,000 individual routing changes. In this respect it is important to recall as well that each prefix in our datasets is originated in a distinct AS, so the actual number of routing changes per event in the full data is much larger because of the similar routing behavior of co-originated prefixes.

Table 4: Description of top-5 events over 9 years

Dataset	#Prefixes	#ASes	#Days	Density
	2	54	200	0.90
	2	60	109	0.88
2005	1	59	138	0.83
	1	57	95	0.87
	2	52	48	0.91
	3	68	168	0.86
	82	11	19	0.83
2006	1	66	183	0.86
	3	58	61	0.91
	1	65	156	0.85
	140	49	20	0.80
	13	52	44	0.81
2007	75	8	35	0.89
	77	5	28	0.80
	45	37	6	0.91
	156	28	25	0.88
	79	41	6	0.85
2008	15	44	23	0.83
	22	37	13	0.83
	10	103	10	0.88
	45	102	2	0.80
	1	90	91	0.87
2009	13	51	11	0.81
	6	89	13	0.80
	14	48	10	0.83
	49	38	16	0.90
	28	41	11	0.97
2010	60	101	2	0.88
	98	15	8	0.94
	17	43	13	0.80
	81	23	16	0.80
	37	23	19	0.90
2011	21	43	14	0.88
	46	53	5	0.90
	47	20	11	0.95
	1	87	152	0.82
	4	65	44	0.86
2012	1	98	101	0.90
	1	94	96	0.90
	31	36	8	0.87
	43	34	32	0.82
	6	80	77	0.82
2013	11	92	27	0.81
	1	128	158	0.80
	57	83	4	0.86

7. SINGLE ACTOR ANALYSIS

In this section we present the second component of PathMiner, an algorithm to identify the network element that is most likely to have caused a large event, given that the ASes, prefixes and days involved in the event are known. We start by explaining our identification methodology, and then we present results.

7.1 Algorithm

We start with some basic observations. Consider an action taken by some network element a (say, an AS) that causes a path from AS b towards prefix p to change. We observe that a is, in general, either on the path from b to p before the change, or after [10]. For example, if a link fails or comes up, or an AS announces a new route and/or withdraws an existing route, these events can cause changes to many paths, but the paths involved will all pass through the link or AS either before or after the change.[1]

Thus, if we are interested in some event that happened on day k, then we may want to compare the set of paths seen in the network on day k with those seen on day $k+1$. Counting paths in order to identify (or narrow down) a root cause for a routing change has been explored before, e.g. [16]. However, PathMiner differs from such previous work in terms of goals (since it particularly focuses on large events that may re-occur over time) and in methods (since it carefully chooses the set of paths to analyze).

PathMiner takes advantage of the fact that starting from a collection of (λ, ν)-events, found by its first component, is an effective way of isolating the set of paths to study, thus avoiding interference of paths that are changing for unrelated reasons. Specifically, when analyzing an event that on day k has set of ASes J and set of prefixes I, we consider only paths seen on days k and $k+1$ passing through ASes in J towards prefixes in I. If one of such path start at an AS which is not in J and passes through $a \in J$, then PathMiner takes such path in account, but it ignores the portion before a. Accordingly, we define P_k to be the multiset of all paths that are found starting at an element of J and ending at an element of I on day k.

Considering the above observations we have that a good candidate for the single network element responsible for the entire set of observed path changes has the following properties: on either day k or day $k+1$, (a) most of the changed paths pass through the network element and (b) most the paths going through the network element change. We call these rules *single actor rules* and the network element so identified the *single actor.*

For concreteness, assume that network element e is the single actor, and the changed paths go through e on day k but not on day $k+1$. Among all the paths being considered, define $D = P_k \setminus P_{k+1}$ as the paths that disappeared; D_e as the paths in D passing through e; and $P_{k,e}$ as the paths in P_k that pass through e. If e is the single actor, by the single actor rules one concludes that $r_e^D = \frac{|D_e|}{|D|}$ should be close to 1, and $p_e^D = \frac{|D_e|}{|P_{k,e}|}$ should be close to 1. In other words, r_e^D captures the fraction of disappeared paths passing through e (rule (a)) and p_e^D captures the fraction of paths passing through e that disappeared (rule (b)).

For intuition, we note that p_e^D and r_e^D correspond respectively to the definitions of *precision* and *recall* for a particular classifier. This classifier is the one that declares that a path will disappear if the path passes through e on day k. In other words, maximizing p_e^D and r_e^D with regard to e yields the network element that best classifies the paths as changing versus unchanging. Following common practice in machine learning, we combine precision and recall into the F-score. In fact, in our case we use the F_2 score defined by $F_2^D(e) = \frac{5p_e^D r_e^D}{4p_e^D + r_e^D}$ to place higher emphasis on the role of recall.

We can make analogous definitions covering the set of paths that appear on day $k+1$. In that case, we define $A = P_{k+1} \setminus P_k$, and A_e as the paths in A that pass through e. Hence, $p_e^A = \frac{|A_e|}{|P_{k+1,e}|}$, $r_e^A = \frac{|A_e|}{|A|}$, $F_2^A(e) = \frac{5p_e^A r_e^A}{4p_e^A + r_e^A}$ and the same interpretation given above is valid here as well.

In practice one does not know a priori whether e will be found using the single actor rules applied to disappeared paths on day k, or appearing paths on day $k+1$. To overcome this problem we

[1]The assumption that the cause of the event will be in the new or old path is not always true [14]. However, PathMiner is built under such assumption because it deals with large-scale events, where the likelihood of observing paths passing through the cause increases.

define the candidate single actor to be the network element (or set of elements) that maximizes $\Delta F(e) = \max\{F_2^D(e),\ F_2^A(e)\}$. From this analysis we exclude AS-links that are seen on days k and $k+1$ and ASes which all incoming and outgoing AS-links are also seen on days k and $k+1$. This decision is justified by the fact that an AS-link that has not been disrupted and an AS that, explicitly, has not changed its local preference and/or export policies are unlikely the element that triggers a large-scale event.

This algorithm is effective, but can some times return multiple elements as candidate single actors for any given day k in an event. However, one can bring one more observation to bear: the single actor should be the same over all days k in the event. This offers an additional opportunity to winnow the set of candidate single actors. So the final step of the single actor analysis is: for events that reoccur over a set of days K, repeat the single-day strategy for every $k \in K$. Then, define as the final single actor of the event the element (or elements) that is observed in the candidate single actors set in at least the majority of the days in K. If such element is not found (no element is a candidate single actor in the majority of days) the algorithm declares that it was not able to identify the cause of the event.

7.2 Performance

PathMiner is able to identify the actors responsible for most of the events presented in Table 4. Table 5 shows the ASes identified as the single actor for each event, and the number of days that the element was classified as single actor (note that in the table we present only the most frequent one and that other elements, present in the majority of days, also have to be considered as possible actors). The boldface numbers indicate the cases where PathMiner identified the same element(s) as cause(s) for a majority of days in the event. It can be seen that PathMiner has more difficulty identifying single actors for events spanning many days and/or involving few ASes.

In order to validate the actors identified by PathMiner for events in Table 4 we performed a visual inspection of each event as follows[4]: for each day of each event we looked at the network element identified as actor, the graphical representation of the event, and asked two questions. First, "would an action of that network element (e.g. an AS changing its local preferences and/or its export policies) explain the occurrence of the event?" Second, "Do the actions of this network element provide the simplest explanation among all elements involved in the event?" If the answers for those question were affirmative in the majority of days of the event we considered such event validated.

We also conducted analyses to understand how often PathMiner is able to identify a single actor as cause of an event. Our first analysis is related to the maximum value of $\Delta F(e)$ obtained for each day in an event and for all events that PathMiner found in the 9 datasets. The results, presented in Figure 7(a) by a CDF, indicate that large values are the predominant case. For instance, the figure shows that the maximum $\Delta F(e)$ is equal to 1 in 40% of the cases and is greater than 0.8 in more than 80%. These numbers suggest that in most of the days within events PathMiner is capable of finding a network element (or a set of) that, in fact, can explain the massive amount of changes related to the event.

These results are promising, but note that they refer to individual days within events. It is important to also ask how consistent the identification is over the days of an event, and how often PathMiner is able to find the same actor over the set of days of the event. To answer those questions we identified for each event the element that appears as cause of the event most frequently over the days of the event and the fraction of days this single actor has been identified. Figure 7(b) presents the results. It can be seen (with exception of 2005) that in more than 40% of the events a single network element has been observed by PathMiner as an event cause over all days of the event. Furthermore, we can see that in more than 90% of the events there is a single actor that is present over the majority of days. For the cases where majority has not been found we refer to Figure 7(c) to show that in some of them the event contains many days, which naturally increases the complexity of the problem. However, there are many small (in terms of days) events for which PathMiner was not able to identify a single actor. Initial

[4]Graphical representations for these events and actor identification summary are available at `http://cs-people.bu.edu/gcom/bgp/imc2014`. We also make available the same representation and summary for another 500 randomly selected events for the year of 2013.

Table 5: Single actor analysis of Top-5 events of each year

Dataset	Most Frequent Actor	Days
2005	31050	76
	23918	38
	1299	38
	8342	**57**
	20485	**30***
2006	23918	50
	3257	**13**
	33697	**103**
	20485	**58**
	33697	**93**
2007	174	**14**
	1273	18
	4637	**35**
	3257	**16***
	7575	**6**
2008	9121	**16***
	25462	3
	174	**12**
	25462	5
	3303	**8**
2009	3216	**2***
	15412	**62**
	3216	**7**
	8359	**10**
	29049	5
2010	30890	**14**
	3491	**11**
	21219	**2**
	5588	**8***
	13249	**8**
2011	5588	**16**
	3549	**17**
	3491	**13**
	12989	**4***
	174	**10**
2012	38312	**142**
	29632	**37**
	4755	**96**
	56209	**91**
	4651	**8**
2013	7713	**28**
	12880	**52**
	8529	**19**
	10029	**116**
	21219	**4**

* The actor found by PathMiner provides a simple explanation for the event. However, other elements providing a simple explanation could be identified by visual inspection.

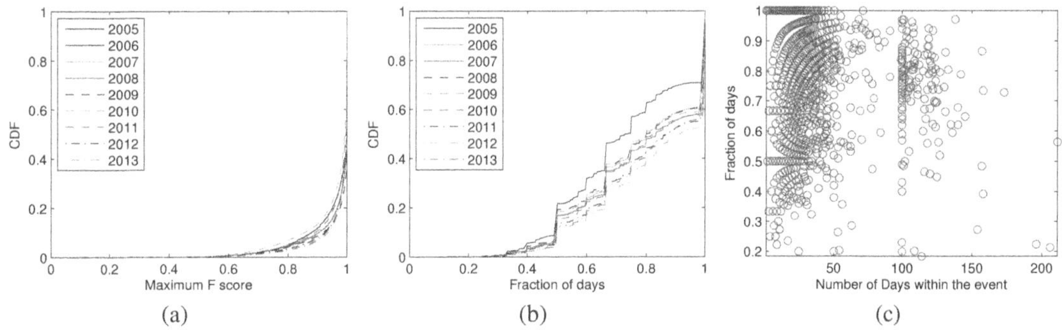

Figure 7: Summary of our methodology for Single Actor identification: (a) CDF of ΔF, computed over each day of each event; (b) CDF of the fraction of days that the same AS (or AS-link) is reported as actor (has maximum ΔFscore) over all days of the event; (c) scatterplot of the number of days within an event *versus* the fraction of days that the same AS (AS-link) is reported as actor – same variable as in (b).

investigation reveals that those events are related to a small number of ASes, and as consequence to a small number of paths, which is not an ideal situation to work with measures such as precision and recall. We emphasize that further investigation is necessary in that direction as future work.

As a final analysis, we list the ASes which, as actors had the greatest impact on the network. We considered the year of 2013, for all events that PathMiner was able to identify a single actor and that involved at least 50 ASes (to avoid the problem of few paths mentioned previously). Table 6 shows the top-20 ASes ranked in three different ways: first, by the number of events that the AS is an actor; second, by the aggregate volume of all events that the AS is an actor; and third, by the aggregate number of days of all events that the AS is an actor. In all three cases, if more than one AS was identified as actor, or if there was an AS-link, we counted each AS involved individually. Therefore, events with more than one AS as actor are counted more than once in Table 6.

Table 6: Three different rankings for the Top-20 Single Actors

#Events	Total volume	Total days
AS174	AS9498	AS9498
AS9498	AS4755	AS4755
AS9002	AS6453	AS6453
AS3356	AS12880	AS174
AS6939	AS6939	AS3549
AS3549	AS9002	AS3216
AS12389	AS174	AS6939
AS3216	AS3549	AS3356
AS20485	AS3216	AS20485
AS6453	AS12389	AS15412
AS31133	AS15412	AS12389
AS7018	AS20485	AS9002
AS701	AS3356	AS701
AS4755	AS3491	AS3491
AS12880	AS55410	AS18101
AS8167	AS10029	AS8167
AS6461	AS12989	AS12880
AS209	AS4651	AS7018
AS3491	AS197556	AS18881
AS8359	AS8167	AS55410

First, it can be seen that the way we ranked the ASes change the order in the three columns of the table, but there is a significant overlap between the top-20 of each rank, showing that, in general, there are heavy-hitter actors that trigger many large, re-occurring events. Second, in all three ranks, it is possible to identify some large ASes, which peer other large ASes and are important parts of the Internet core. For example, AS174 (Cogent), AS6939 (Hurricane Electric), AS3549 (GBLX) and AS3356 (Level3) are in the top-20 of each list. This suggests that some ASes in the core are responsible for a large amount of the reorganization that happens in the network. However, it is important to remember that our strategy to sample ASes may have influence in this result, and ultimately that our original dataset does not cover the complete AS-level topology of the Internet (which in fact motivated our sampling strategy).

7.3 Case studies

In this section we present three case studies in order to show the ability of PathMiner to identify actors of high impact events. Case studies I and II were chosen to illustrate typical scenarios where PathMiner is able to identify a network element (or set of elements) whose actions would explain, in a simple way, the occurrence of the event. We remark that many events share the same structure (this can be seen in the online supplementary material). Case study III, on the other hand, shows that PathMiner is not guaranteed to always work. In that case, we discuss the reason and show that the assumptions under which PathMiner was build are not satisfied.

In the representation of each case study, Figures 8, 9 and 10, ASes in gray hosts a destination prefix. Red (dashed) edges are those present only at day k, green (dotted) edges are present only at day $k+1$ and black (solid) edges are present in both days. Inside each node we have: the AS identifier; the number of paths passing through the AS at day k, with a negative sign; and the number of paths passing through the AS at day $k+1$, with a positive sign. Only paths passing through an AS in the event towards a prefix in the event are counted.

7.3.1 Case study I

Our first case study is related to the second event for the year of 2009 presented in Table 4. In this event we have 90 ASes changing their next-hops towards one prefix over 91 days during the year. Among those, we picked 2 pairs of consecutive days in order to illustrate the nature of the event. Following the same convention used in Section 2, Figures 8(a) and 8(b) picture the most important part of the network for our needs. From Feb-08 to Feb-09 many ASes stopped using AS15412 as next-hop and started using

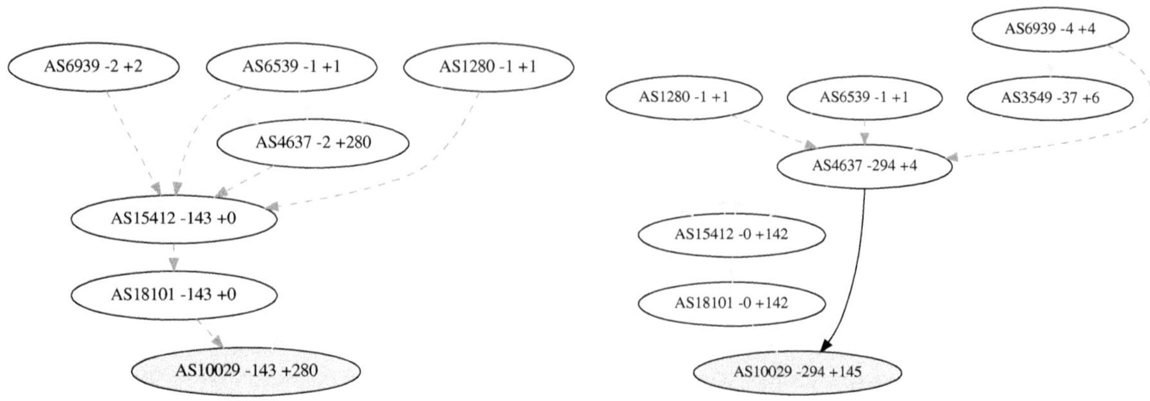

(a) Path changes between Feb-08-2009 and Feb-09-2009 (b) Path changes between Feb-10-2009 and Feb-11-2009

Figure 8: Representation of case study I.

AS4637 instead. Just from that observation it is possible to conjecture that one of these two ASes was responsible for the changes, and in fact, considering Feb-08 and Feb-09, both ASes have the same ΔF value. On the next day almost the reverse event happens, with ASes leaving AS4637 and starting to use AS15412 as next-hop. But it can be seen that AS4637 still has a path towards the prefix and it still is used by some ASes as next-hop. This fact indicates that AS4637 is probably not the actor responsible for the event.

It is also necessary to observe that AS15412 and AS18101 are not seen in our dataset at Feb-09 and Feb-10 (no paths passing through them). Hence we cannot say exactly if the cause is one or the other or even a link leaving one of them, narrowing down the set of candidates to AS15412, AS18101 and AS10029 (and links). However, in other days of the event the same structure of the figures was observed, but there were paths passing through AS15412 and AS18101. This indicates that in fact many paths left (preferred) AS15412 as next-hop due its actions, not AS18101 or AS10029.

Following the majority rule, PathMiner selected AS15412 as single actor of the event and therefore, it was able to capture the discussion presented above.

7.3.2 *Case study II*

In this case study we explore the second event for the year of 2012 shown in Table 4. The event involves 4 prefixes, 65 ASes, and occurs on 44 days during the year. Figures 9(a) and 9(b) present the simplified dynamics of the changes for 2 days, Jan-10-2012 and Jan-11-2012. This case study seems similar to the previous one, since we can observe that over the time ASes are alternating their next-hops (towards the four prefixes) between AS35320 and AS29632. Simply looking at those figures it is possible to narrow down the cause to one of these two ASes (or the links between them and AS42418). The question that arises is: why did PathMiner chose AS29632? It turns out that for many of the 44 days of the event, some of ASes leaving next-hop AS29632 started reaching two of the four destinations by paths not passing through AS35320. Therefore, either AS29632 or two other ASes (at the same time) are the causes. PathMiner identifies AS29632 as actor, capturing the idea that the simplest explanation is the most likely one.

7.3.3 *Case study III*

Our last case study discusses an event for which PathMiner was not able to identify a single network element responsible for the whole event. The event is the one on the first row of Table 4 for the year of 2005. The event involves 2 prefixes, 54 ASes and it happens on 200 days of the year. However PathMiner was not able to find a single network element responsible for changes in at least 100 days. Why did that happen? A closer look at the event shows us that the assumptions over which PathMiner is built are not valid. In fact, this is a strange case. Figures 10(a) and 10(b) present two typical subgraphs describing the changes over the days of the event. First, we note that the structure of the graph is completely different of our two previous case studies. The second, and key, fact is that the event contains only two prefixes, but we can see three gray nodes in the figures (gray nodes are those hosting the prefixes of the event). Denoting those two prefixes by prefix 1 and prefix 2, through data examination it was possible to see that: *i)* at Jan-11 prefixes 1 and 2 were being hosted at AS23918 and AS29257 respectively; *ii)* at Jan-12 prefix 1 was being hosted at AS29257 and at AS31050 (which does not seem to be a normal situation) and prefix 2 was being hosted at AS23918; and *iii)* at Jan-13 prefixes are hosted as at Jan-11.

Over the 200 days of the event this alternating state was repeated. In summary, it can be seen that is hard to find one network element that can be responsible for these changes. More specifically, our assumption of a single actor causing the event does not seem to be valid here – it appears that a set of coordinated changes is being implemented through actions of multiple ASes.

8. RELATED WORK

There is a considerable amount of literature about BGP due to its importance to the global Internet. In this section we discuss how PathMiner differs from existing work.

BGP event detection: BGP event detection has been studied in a variety of ways. Most work on event detection relies on BGP update messages in order to analyze path changes. For example, the authors in [20] proposed a methodology to identify high impact BGP routing changes. However their scope is different from ours, since in their context the term *high impact* is related to the impact in the network traffic leaving a specific ISP and not in terms of changes propagating throughout the network.

In [17, 16] the authors propose a way to identify temporal event boundaries in the stream of update messages and a visualization tool that allows users to narrow down and infer root causes. Our work, on the other hand, does not rely on inferring the state of the routing system by using update messages (in fact this is a hard task, since in most cases internal AS policies are unknown). Instead, we

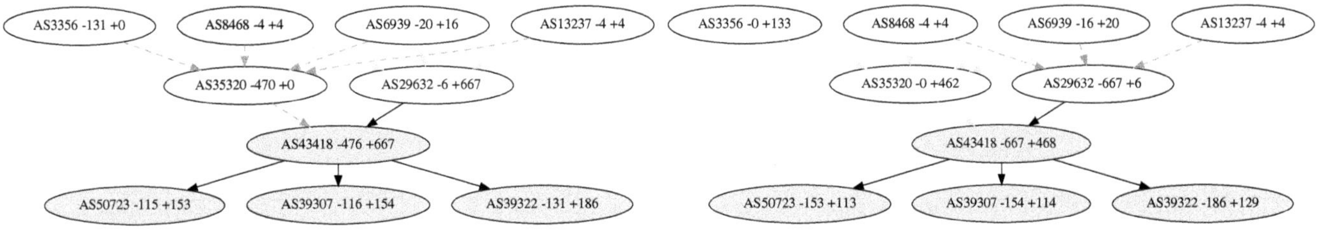

(a) Path changes between Jan-10-2012 and Jan-11-2012 (b) Path changes between Jan-11-2012 and Jan-12-2012

Figure 9: Representation of case study II.

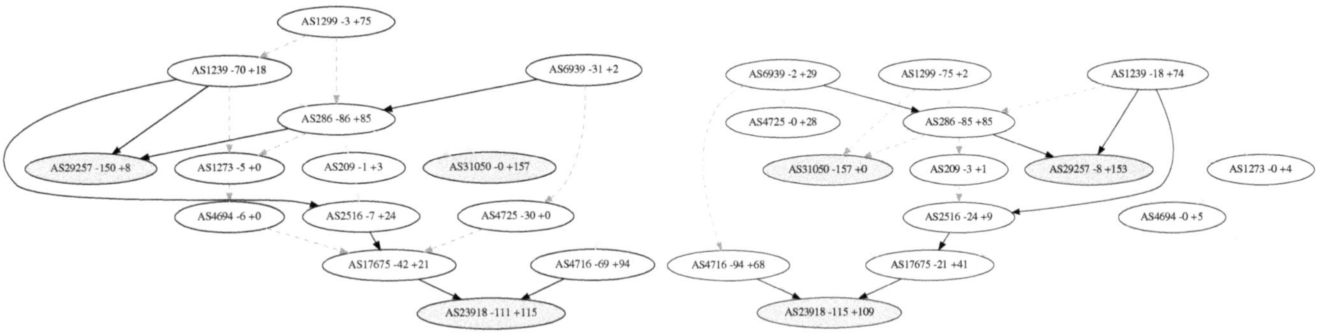

(a) Path changes between Jan-11-2005 and Jan-12-2005 (b) Path changes between Jan-12-2005 and Jan-13-2005

Figure 10: Representation of case study III.

use real daily snapshots of the network to perform a large scale event identification.

The authors of [11] use tensor factorization techniques (real, not boolean) to infer events in the stream of BGP updates. However, since they use a path-based representation they are restricted to a small set of monitors. Moreover, since they work with data obtained at the granularity of minutes their strategy is not able to identify large scale events involving hundreds of sources, possibly months apart.

Finally, it is important to mention that working with BGP updates demands extra processing in order to clean the data. In our approach we use BGP RIBs, i.e., snapshots of the interdomain routing system , which avoids the complex process of update messages cleaning and allows PathMiner to scale over long timescales.

Root cause analysis: the second component of PathMiner, described in Section 7, consists of a technique to identify (or at least narrow down) possible ASes (or links) triggering large scale events. Although sounding related to root cause analysis, as in [14] and [10], it is important to remark that our requirements and assumptions differ significantly. On one hand, general root cause identification systems are real time, work with BGP update messages (sometimes with information coming from external sources) and are interested at identifying causes of any path changes. On the other hand, differently of PathMiner, those systems are not capable, of identifying large events and narrowing down causes using just routing tables.

BGP path discovery: as mentioned in Section 8 our datasets do not contain paths from every source to every destination and even for those we have, the issue of missing data arises. Therefore, we note that PathMiner could benefit from techniques that allow it to have better snapshots of the global interdomain routing system. Among recent works on this direction are [15], [13] and [12].

Boolean Tensor Factorization: in this work we did not aim at a general approach for solving instances of the BTF problem coming from an abitrary application. In fact, among recent works trying to solve the general BTF problem are [7] and [9]. The former is designed to find blocks of closed relations (i.e., equivalent to blocks with density 1), which is too strong a requirement for our application. The latter would suit our needs, but although it does not impose any formal requirement for volume and density, unfortunately the available implementation did not scale for our datasets due to the amount of data analyzed by PathMiner.

9. CONCLUSIONS AND FUTURE WORK

In this work we presented PathMiner, a system capable of identifying and analyzing high impact events in the interdomain routing system of the Internet. We started by giving a formal definition of the problem and discussing how to prepare the data and how to deal with missing data. In its first phase PathMiner has the advantage of working with a next-hop representation of the AS-level Internet, which allows PathMiner to naturally combine paths obtained from multiple sources.

In order to identify events we proposed a new heuristic to solve the Boolean Tensor Factorization problem, since algorithms currently available in the literature were not scalable to our datasets. Using datasets spanning 9 years of routing in the Internet we showed that PathMiner is able to find many large and dense events.

Next, we addressed the challenge of discovering network elements (ASes or AS-links) that were likely the actors responsible for the event occurrence. Our methodology, based on concepts borrowed from classification theory, was able to identify possible event causes in most of the events we found. One key aspect of PathMiner is its ability to look at the same event re-occurring many times, which helps the process eliminating event cause candidates. Finally, we presented 3 case studies, for large events, exemplifying all these aspects of PathMiner.

To the best of our knowledge, PathMiner is the first system capable of exploring the amount of information we analyzed, finding daily large routing events and recognizing that such events re-occur many times during the period of one year, in some cases months apart.

In future work we intend to address the need to better understand cases where PathMiner is not capable of finding a single actor responsible for an event (as exemplified in our third case study). Moreover, we are interested in the possibility of using PathMiner to explore persistent routing changes, i.e., considering only changes that were not quickly undone in the system. Such studies might have the potential to expose interesting structural reorganization of the AS-level Internet.

10. ACKNOWLEDGEMENTS

This material is based upon work supported by the National Science Foundation under grant numbers CNS-0905565, CNS-1018266, CNS-1012910, and CNS-1117039, and supported by the Army Research Office under grant W911NF-11-1-0227. We are grateful to the anonymous reviewers and to our shepherd, Alex Snoeren, for their valuable comments. We also thank Evimaria Terzi and Dora Erdos for the helpful discussions.

11. REFERENCES

[1] Hadoop. `http://hadoop.apache.org`.

[2] Ripe's routing information service raw data project. `http://www.ripe.net/data-tools/stats/ris/ris-raw-data`.

[3] Spark. `http://spark.apache.org`.

[4] University of oregon route views project. `http://www.routeviews.org`.

[5] Michael W. Berry, Murray Browne, Amy N. Langville, V. Paul Pauca, and Robert J. Plemmons. Algorithms and applications for approximate nonnegative matrix factorization. *Computational Statistics & Data Analysis*, 52(1):155–173, September 2007.

[6] A. Broido and kc claffy. Analysis of RouteViews BGP data: policy atoms. In *NRDM*, 2001.

[7] Loïc Cerf, Jérémy Besson, Céline Robardet, and Jean-François Boulicaut. Closed Patterns Meet n-ary Relations. *ACM Trans. Knowl. Discov. Data*, 3(1), 2009.

[8] Andrzej Cichocki, Rafal Zdunek, Anh Huy Phan, and Shun-ichi Amari. *Nonnegative Matrix and Tensor Factorizations: Applications to Exploratory Multi-way Data Analysis and Blind Source Separation*. Wiley Publishing, 2009.

[9] Dóra Erdös and Pauli Miettinen. Walk 'n' Merge: A Scalable Algorithm for Boolean Tensor Factorization. In *Proceedings of the 13th International Conference on Data Mining*, ICDM '13, pages 1037–1042. IEEE, 2013.

[10] Anja Feldmann, Olaf Maennel, Z. Morley Mao, Arthur Berger, and Bruce Maggs. Locating Internet Routing Instabilities. In *Proceedings of SIGCOMM Conference*, SIGCOMM '04, pages 205–218. ACM, 2004.

[11] K. Glass, R. Colbaugh, and M. Planck. Automatically identifying the sources of large Internet events. In *Intelligence and Security Informatics (ISI), 2010 IEEE International Conference on*, pages 108–113, 2010.

[12] Enrico Gregori, Alessandro Improta, Luciano Lenzini, Lorenzo Rossi, and Luca Sani. On the incompleteness of the as-level graph: A novel methodology for bgp route collector placement. In *Proceedings of the 2012 ACM Conference on Internet Measurement Conference*, IMC '12, pages 253–264. ACM, 2012.

[13] Yihua He, Georgos Siganos, Michalis Faloutsos, and Srikanth Krishnamurthy. Lord of the Links: A Framework for Discovering Missing Links in the Internet Topology. *IEEE/ACM Trans. Netw.*, 17(2):391–404, April 2009.

[14] Umar Javed, Italo Cunha, David Choffnes, Ethan Katz-Bassett, Thomas Anderson, and Arvind Krishnamurthy. PoiRoot: Investigating the Root Cause of Interdomain Path Changes. In *Proceedings of SIGCOMM Conference*, SIGCOMM '13, pages 183–194. ACM, 2013.

[15] Akmal Khan, Taekyoung Kwon, Hyun-chul Kim, and Yanghee Choi. AS-level Topology Collection Through Looking Glass Servers. In *Proceedings of the 2013 Internet Measurement Conference*, IMC '13, pages 235–242. ACM, 2013.

[16] Mohit Lad, Dan Massey, and Lixia Zhang. Visualizing Internet Routing Changes. *IEEE Transactions on Visualization and Computer Graphics*, 12(6):1450–1460, November 2006.

[17] Mohit Lad, Lixia Zhang, and Daniel Massey. Link-rank: A Graphical Tool for Capturing BGP Routing Dynamics. In *Proceedings of the Network Operations and Management Symposium*, NOMS '04, pages 627–640. IEEE, 2004.

[18] Pauli Miettinen. Boolean Tensor Factorizations. In *Proceedings of the 11th International Conference on Data Mining*, ICDM '11, pages 447–456. IEEE, 2011.

[19] Y. Rekhter and T. Li. *A Border Gateway Protocol (BGP-4)*. RFC Editor, 1995.

[20] Jian Wu, Zhuoqing Morley Mao, Jennifer Rexford, and Jia Wang. Finding a Needle in a Haystack: Pinpointing Significant BGP Routing Changes in an IP Network. In *Proceedings of the Symposium on Networked Systems Design & Implementation*, NSDI'05, pages 1–14. USENIX Association, 2005.

Appendix A - 3D-FACTORIZATION Algorithm

Algorithm 3: 3D-FACTORIZATION

Data: S, set of triples of the form (I, J, K), and thresholds γ and β

$F \leftarrow \emptyset$
while $S \neq \emptyset$ **do**
  $s \leftarrow$ pick and **do not** remove an element of S
  $S' \leftarrow \{x : x \in S \text{ and } d_B(x, s) \leq \gamma\}$
  find maximal $S'' \subseteq S'$ such that $\max_{x,y \in S''} d_B(x, y) \leq \gamma$
  if $|S''| > 1$ **then**
    $y \leftarrow$ COMBINE-UNION(S'')
    $S \leftarrow S \backslash S''$
    $S \leftarrow S \cup \{y\}$
  else
    $F \leftarrow F \cup \{s\}$
    $S \leftarrow S \backslash \{s\}$
    $S' \leftarrow \{x : x \in S, s_B(x, s) \geq \beta$ and COMBINE-INTER$(s, x) \neq s\}$
    if $|S'| > 0$ **then**
      $s' \leftarrow \arg\max_{x \in S'} s_B(s, x)$
      $y \leftarrow$ COMBINE-INTER(s, s')
      $S \leftarrow S \cup \{y\}$
return F

Taming the 800 Pound Gorilla: The Rise and Decline of NTP DDoS Attacks

Jakub Czyz
University of Michigan

Michael Kallitsis
Merit Network, Inc.

Manaf Gharaibeh
Colorado State University

Christos Papadopoulos
Colorado State University

Michael Bailey
University of Michigan
University of Illinois

Manish Karir
Merit Network, Inc.

ABSTRACT

Distributed Denial of Service (DDoS) attacks based on Network Time Protocol (NTP) amplification, which became prominent in December 2013, have received significant global attention. We chronicle how this attack rapidly rose from obscurity to become the dominant large DDoS vector. Via the lens of five distinct datasets, we characterize the advent and evolution of these attacks. Through a dataset that measures a large fraction of global Internet traffic, we show a three order of magnitude rise in NTP. Using a large darknet, we observe a similar rise in global scanning activity, both malicious and research. We then dissect an active probing dataset, which reveals that the pool of amplifiers totaled 2.2M unique IPs and includes a small number of "mega amplifiers," servers that replied to a single tiny probe packet with gigabytes of data. This dataset also allows us, for the first time, to analyze global DDoS attack victims (including ports attacked) and incidents, where we show 437K unique IPs targeted with at least 3 trillion packets, totaling more than a petabyte. Finally, ISP datasets shed light on the local impact of these attacks. In aggregate, we show the magnitude of this major Internet threat, the community's response, and the effect of that response.

Categories and Subject Descriptors

C.2.3 [**Computer-Communication Networks**]: Network Operations—*Network management, Network monitoring*

General Terms

Measurement, Networking, Security

Keywords

DDoS; NTP; Darknet

1. INTRODUCTION

Though Distributed Denial of Service (DDoS) attacks have become increasingly commonplace, the scope and magnitude of the firepower that can now be unleashed on a target is unprecedented. A comprehensive recent study described various DDoS amplification attack vectors and their attack potential, predicting the rise of Network Time Protocol (NTP) [23] as one of the most potent [32]. In the weeks since, data published by efforts such as the OpenNTPProject.org [2] painted a bleak picture of millions of devices that were readily available to facilitate these attacks. Indeed, in the first quarter of 2014, 85% of DDoS attacks larger than 100 Gbps were using NTP reflection [24]. Used for everything from a gaming edge [18] to extortion [28], DDoS attacks have been a scourge for years, but this new attack vector has made them even more powerful.

We study the dramatic rise of NTP-based DDoS attacks, in a span of just a few months, from a mere trickle to rapidly become the primary DDoS vector for large attacks. We show who the amplifiers are, what they are capable of, who they attack, and what attacks looked like. We present findings from the vantage points of five unique datasets: a global traffic profile and attack dataset from a large analytics and DDoS mitigation vendor; a global probing dataset that sheds light on potential amplifiers, their victims, and attacks; a large darknet that observes Internet-scale scanning activities; and, finally, two regional Internet service providers that give us a local perspective on attack mechanics and evolution.

NTP DDoS Mechanics: Much has been written on the general ideas of reflection and amplification (e.g., [27], [32]), so, we discuss attack mechanics only briefly. For these attacks, the first step is the identification of vulnerable *amplifiers*, which attackers can accomplish via large-scale scanning. An amplifier is simply a host running a protocol (e.g., NTP, DNS) which, when sent a query packet, responds with one or more packets whose aggregate size is larger than the query it received. Once suitable amplifiers have been identified, an attacker, directly or via intermediate hosts he controls, sends small UDP packets with the spoofed *source* address set to the IP of the intended attack victim and the destination address a vulnerable amplifier. Such spoofing is possible because many networks do not follow best security practices (e.g., BCP 38/84) [36]. In turn, as is the goal of these *volumetric* DDoS attacks, large amounts of traffic from amplifiers may saturate bandwidth at the victim. We say these attacks are *reflected* as they are executed via an intermediate host (the amplifier); attacks are *amplified* in that more bandwidth is used at the victim than the attacker (or its bots) need to expend. In the case of NTP, the protocol feature that has been used in large attacks is the *monlist* command. A command intended only for diagnostics, it returns the last 600 clients of the amplifier, producing a typically very large, multi-packet reply to a single small query packet—an ideal amplification attack vector.

The rest of our paper and highlighted findings are as follows. In § 2 we describe a rapid rise of NTP traffic to become the most potent DDoS attack vector. Only constituting 0.001% of traffic four months earlier, by mid-February NTP had climbed to use up 1% of global

IMC'14, November 5–7, 2014, Vancouver, BC, Canada.

http://dx.doi.org/10.1145/2663716.2663717.

Internet traffic, surpassing even the ubiquitous DNS. Simultaneously, the majority of large DDoS attacks observed globally were now using the NTP vector, one not even on the radar in November. In § 3 we explore the amplifier pool that enabled this rapid rise in traffic and attacks—a pool of 2.2M vulnerable NTP servers. In this pool we find several surprises: first, while a typical server provides just 4x amplification, we find a subset we term "mega amplifiers," who respond to a single packet with gigabytes of data; second, we find that a large fraction of amplifiers are not infrastructure servers but end hosts; comically, we also discover that nearly a fifth of NTP servers do not serve the correct synchronized time.

As for target victims, in § 4 we seek to answer the questions of who is being DDoSed, when, and how badly. We find tens of thousands of victim IPs across thousands of autonomous systems, and discover that many appear to be gamers. The 437K unique victims we saw were hit over fifteen weeks with at least 3 trillion packets, which is, at median amplifier response, over 1.2 petabytes. Luckily, things are improving, which we begin to outline in § 5 and § 6 where we first show a dramatic increase in scanning for NTP over eight months as attackers scramble to build lists of vulnerable IPs. Then, we discuss how the pool of NTP monlist amplifiers being scanned for has itself decreased rapidly, especially relative to other amplifier pools.

Zooming in from the global perspective to the local, in § 7 we highlight the effect on and mitigation at two regional networks that actively worked to respond to attacks, including local confirmation of some of our global dataset findings and several new insights. Finally, in § 8 we describe some related work, and in § 9 we summarize key conclusions and future work.

2. GLOBAL NTP TRAFFIC AND ATTACKS

2.1 Global Internet NTP Traffic

In late 2013 and early 2014, public attack disclosures suggested that NTP-based DDoS attacks were very large and increasingly common (e.g., [12], [18], and [30]) . To gauge the global prevalence of these types of attacks, we obtained traffic statistics from Arbor Networks, a provider of network analytics and attack mitigation services [9]. Arbor Networks collects traffic data, via appliances that export network flow statistics, from a global set of over 300 generally large and typically global network operators, including tier-1 ISPs, tier-2/regional ISPs, mobile service providers, as well as two dozen large enterprise customers. Arbor Networks estimates that their netflow traffic dataset represents between a third and a half of all Internet traffic.

In Figure 1 we show the relative fraction of all measured Internet traffic that NTP and DNS represent, observed by Arbor over six months, between November 1st, 2013 and May 1st, 2014. The data lines are the ratio of each protocol's daily bits-per-second averages to all Internet traffic seen. The overall daily average of Internet traffic represented in this dataset is 71.5 Tbps. As the figure shows, NTP starts this period off at a level that constitutes only about 0.001% of daily bits per second transferred. By March 1st, NTP had grown to use up about 1% of of global Internet traffic, surpassing even DNS, which hovers at around 0.15% of traffic throughout this period. The dramatic three order of magnitude rise of NTP traffic in both absolute and relative terms, translates to noticeable financial impact, even at service providers who host not only victims but the NTP amplifiers used in attacks. It is possible that this impact is part of the reason for rapid remediation, which we discuss in § 6. After peaking on February 11th, NTP traffic appears to have begun a decline and is at around 0.1% of Internet traffic at the beginning of May, still two orders of magnitude higher than at the start of November 2013, but a tenth of what it was at peak.

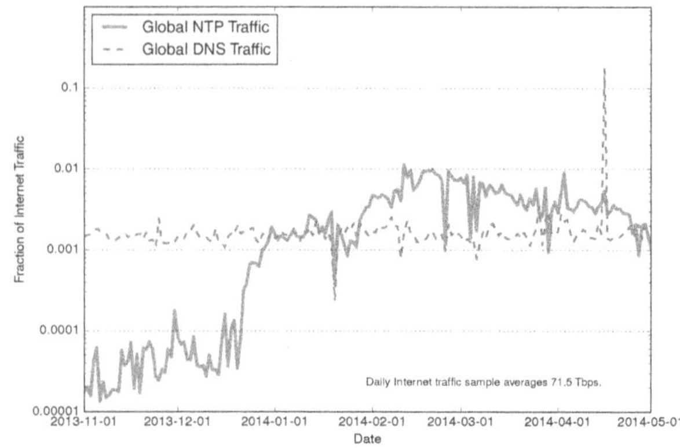

Figure 1: Fraction of Internet traffic that is NTP and DNS for November 2013 – April 2014. There is a nearly three order of magnitude growth in the fraction of global traffic that is NTP, peaking at 1% of all traffic in mid-February, but then dropping, to around 0.1%.

2.2 Global NTP DDoS Attacks

In addition to the traffic statistics described in § 2.1, the Arbor Networks devices also collect labeled attack counts, which detail the types of attacks that are being seen by Arbor Networks' customers, including the prevalent protocols used in the attacks (e.g., ICMP flooding, TCP SYN flooding, bandwidth exhaustion using DNS, etc.). The exact mechanism for labeling a traffic spike as an attack is proprietary, and any method is likely to miss some attacks—especially small ones—but our aim here is merely to show the relative trend in attack categories.

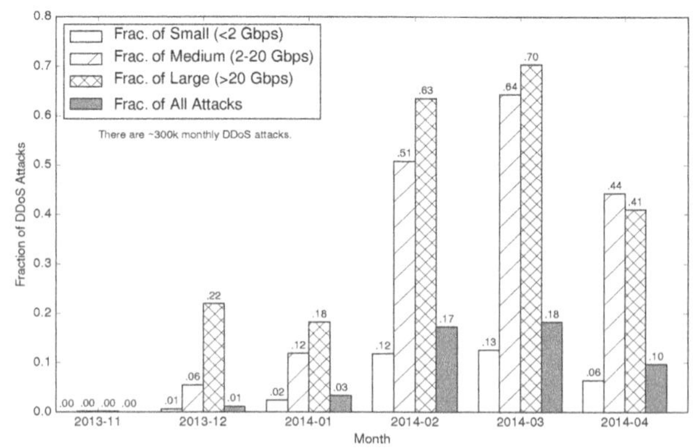

Figure 2: Fraction of all monthly global DDoS attacks in three size ranges and overall that are NTP-based. Note that NTP quickly rises from obscurity to dominate medium and large attacks. Mitigation appears to have had an impact with NTP-based attacks declining substantially in April.

In Figure 2 we show the attacks seen by Arbor Networks' customers in the six months starting in November 2013. For each month, we bin attacks into three size categories: *Small*, consisting of aggregate bandwidth less than 2 Gbps ; *Medium*, which are attacks that are between 2 and 20 Gbps; and *Large*, which are any attacks larger than 20 Gbps. In the figure, a different bar represents the fraction of all DDoS attacks in each category as well as of all attacks that were NTP-based. We do not show the frequency of attacks in each category, but there are approximately 300K monthly attacks seen globally by Arbor Networks, and approximately 90% of them are Small, 10% Medium, and 1% Large. While the raw number of attacks was never dominated by NTP, the majority of Medium and Large DDoS attacks in February and March were, a dramatic change from just three months earlier, when only 0.07% of attacks involved NTP. The first quarter 2014 attack fractions were confirmed by Prolexic, who reported NTP used in 17% of attacks [31] (also see Goodin, [18], who quotes a third DDoS protection vendor that reported a majority of attacks in January were via NTP). In the first quarter of 2014, 85% of attacks exceeding 100 Gbps were using NTP reflection [24]. Fortunately, as evidence that the community's mitigation efforts are starting to pay off, the fraction of attacks using NTP has started to decline in April and is now below February levels.

These traffic and attack statistics point to NTP-based DDoS as a major new vector and as another reminder of the power of reflected amplification DDoS attacks. This was a category of attacks that have been seen for some time but gained notoriety in recent years when unsecured open DNS resolvers started being used to amplify attackers' ability to exhaust targets' bandwidth. To better understand the amplifiers that miscreants are using to generate the NTP traffic, we next delve into the vulnerable NTP server population.

3. GLOBAL NTP AMPLIFIERS

The linchpin in NTP-based reflected amplification attacks is a large pool of globally-reachable NTP servers that are configured in a way that allows them to serve as reflectors and amplifiers.

3.1 The Amplifier Population

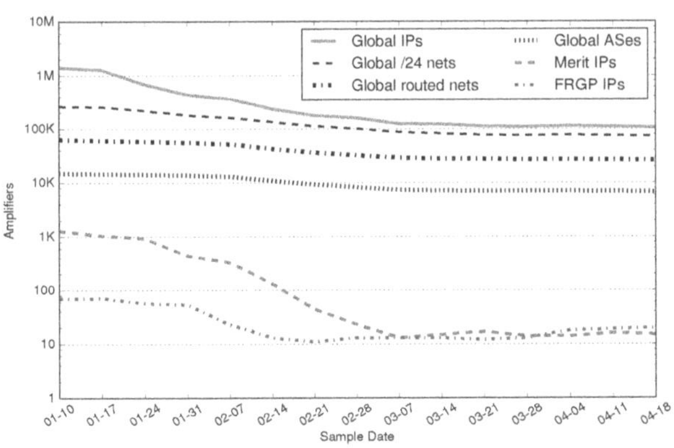

Figure 3: Count of NTP monlist amplifiers, including aggregations at the /24, routed block, and AS level, and subsets of IPs under Merit and CSU/FRGP address space. Remediation at IP levels has been swift, though many networks and nearly half of ASes still have some amplifiers.

Since January 10th, 2014, the OpenNTPProject.org [2] has been conducting weekly Internet-wide scans of the entire IPv4 address space in an effort to estimate and identify the global population of NTP servers that are vulnerable to being used as reflectors and amplifiers in DDoS attacks. These measurements entail simply sending a single NTP packet that requests a target server return the results of a *monlist* query, as described in § 1, and capturing all response packets. Since the size of the single query packet is known, when servers reply with their packets of monlist table data, we are able to determine if each server can be used for attacks, and we can measure its amplification factor. We analyzed the response data that the OpenNTPProject.org shared with us (*ONP data*) in order to learn about the amplifier population as well as other facets of the NTP DDoS phenomenon. We report on fifteen weekly measurements through April 18th 2014, except where noted.

Before continuing, we discuss several limitations of this data. First, we note that one important source of error in the ONP dataset has to do with the type of monlist query packet that was issued. There are several implementations of the NTP service, and they do not all respond to the same packet format. The Linux `ntpdc` tool for example, when used to query a server with the monlist command, tries each of two implementation types, one at a time, before failing. The ONP monlist scans in the dataset shared with us only used one of the two implementation values in the one NTP packet they send each IP. However, the implementation used appears to be more commonly present in the attacker scripts and darknet scanning data we have observed. Further, the raw numbers we report match those published by an independent scanning effort, reported in Kührer *et al.* [20]. Although the same error might affect both datasets. We also note that Internet-wide scans conducted from a single source IP, as the ONP scans were, are prone to be affected by some networks eventually blocking or filtering the scanning IP over time. The ONP data was not measured for this effect, but in their study, Kührer found an additional 9% amplifiers when scanning from a secondary network versus repeated scans from their main network. For these reasons, our numbers likely under-represent the full population of amplifiers. Finally, we note that the data only speaks to the amplifiers that respond to *monlist* and *version* (discussed later) queries, and not other NTP queries. Although these two are most commonly discussed in literature, there are other commands. Those others have typically lower amplification than monlist, however.

In Figure 3 we show the number of global NTP monlist amplifiers, and include aggregation at network levels, which underlines the global dispersion and varying remediation rates. The figure also shows amplifier count lines labeled Merit and CSU(FRGP), which we will elaborate on later. As can be seen, the global Amplifier population starts at approximately 1.4M in the first half of January and, as the Internet community begins to patch servers and block certain NTP requests, the population begins a mostly steady decline through mid-March, when it levels off at around 110K amplifiers. We discuss operator mitigation and amplifier remediation in § 6.

We were next interested in measuring the churn in the amplifier population. Over the course of the 15-week measurement period, we learn 2,166,097 unique amplifier IPs. We found that the first weekly sample only sees about 60% of these unique IPs seen, and that some new amplifiers are discovered on every scan conducted. About half of the amplifiers are only seen during one of the fifteen weekly scans, which is partly due to the rapid remediation of the amplifier population. A second factor is that a non-trivial fraction (13% – 35%) of these NTP servers are running on end-user (i.e., residential) machines and, thus, may be subject to DHCP churn. The left half of Table 1 shows the percentage of each sample's IPs that are "end hosts" according to the Spamhaus Policy Block List (PBL) [34], taken on April 18th, 2014. The PBL identifies end-user IP addresses, and there is independent evidence that PBL-labeled IPs are, indeed, residential [7]. Finally, we calculate the average number of IPs per routed block, which starts at a peak of 22 and declines toward 4. This tells us that, initially, the pool of vulnerable servers included many large groups of closely-addressed (and, thus, likely managed together) server machines, whereas the population left in

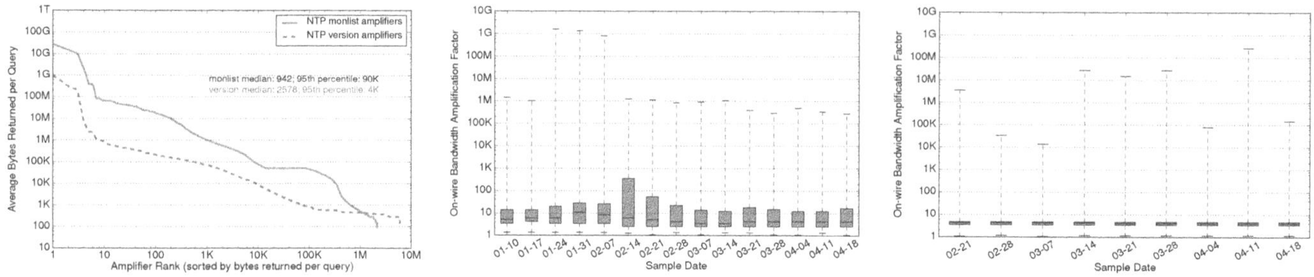

(a) Bytes returned by monlist amplifiers

(b) BAF of monlist amplifiers

(c) BAF of version amplifiers

Figure 4: (a) Average on-wire bytes returned by monlist and version amplifiers. Boxplots of the resultant bandwidth amplification factors (BAF) for monlist (b) and version (c). Boxplots show the minimum, first quartile, median, third quartile, and maximum BAF. There are a small number of very large outliers in both types.

Table 1: For both amplifiers and victims seen in the fifteen weeks of ONP data, the IP counts, unique routed blocks, unique origin AS numbers, percentage of IPs that are end hosts, and number of IPs per routed block.

	Global Amplifiers						Global Victims					
Date	IPs	Blocks	ASNs	End Hosts	End Host %	IPs per Block	IPs	Blocks	ASNs	End Hosts	End Host %	IPs per Block
2014-01-10	1405186	63499	15131	260252	18.5	22.13	49979	16233	4797	15571	31.2	3.08
2014-01-17	1276639	61070	14671	207647	16.3	20.90	59937	18722	5373	19321	32.2	3.20
2014-01-24	677112	58519	14339	90889	13.4	11.57	66373	19690	5334	25504	38.4	3.37
2014-01-31	438722	56376	13903	74781	17.1	7.78	68319	20561	5351	28614	41.9	3.32
2014-02-07	365724	52229	13095	70053	19.1	7.00	81284	23062	5624	36765	45.2	3.52
2014-02-14	235370	42719	10961	63164	26.8	5.51	94125	25302	6154	42070	44.7	3.72
2014-02-21	176931	36411	9335	54578	30.9	4.86	121362	28235	6261	60866	50.1	4.30
2014-02-28	159629	32376	8241	51551	32.3	4.93	156643	31802	6702	83178	53.1	4.93
2014-03-07	123673	29159	7403	43531	35.2	4.24	153541	31111	6435	81684	53.2	4.94
2014-03-14	121507	27849	7115	40934	33.7	4.36	169573	32533	6585	88840	52.4	5.21
2014-03-21	110565	27590	7036	38870	35.2	4.01	167578	32748	6700	87550	52.2	5.12
2014-03-28	108385	27003	6997	37808	34.9	4.01	160191	31485	6512	82881	51.7	5.09
2014-04-04	112131	26947	7000	37880	33.8	4.16	143422	28656	5975	69340	48.4	5.00
2014-04-11	108636	26514	6925	36493	33.6	4.10	108756	24425	5272	52371	48.1	4.45
2014-04-18	106445	25976	6751	35683	33.5	4.10	107459	23264	5009	53233	49.5	4.62

April tends to be sparse, helping explain remediation slow-down, perhaps.

3.2 NTP monlist Amplifier Power

To begin to characterize the threat that this amplifier pool posed, we first aggregated the on-wire bytes of all monlist responses from each queried amplifier over the course of the ONP data collection weeks. As shown in Figure 4a, which plots the average per-sample on-wire bytes (i.e., packet bytes plus all Ethernet framing and overhead), there is a large range of data returned for the single monlist query packet. We find a median of 942 bytes for monlist responses, and maximum sizes for a given sample were typically in the tens to a hundred megabytes. Surprisingly, however, a small fraction of amplifiers responded with much more data than the monlist command should ever return; in one case, this was as high as 136 Gigabytes. We discuss these "mega amplifiers" in § 3.4. The figure also shows the response sizes to the *version* command, discussed in § 3.3.

A key feature of a good candidate service for use in amplification attacks is that it has a high asymmetry of responses to queries, (i.e., a high *packet- or bandwidth amplification factor (BAF)*). Thus, the servers that return the most packets or bytes for every packet or byte sent are the most powerful weapons for attacks. For simplicity, we focus just on bandwidth amplification in our analyses. We also caution that attackers may "prime" their amplifiers by first making connections from various IPs in order to make sure that the monlist table returns the maximum number of entries (600) when later sending traffic to victims. Thus, actual effects on victims may be larger when attackers make this effort.

To measure this relative power of the global population of vulnerable amplifiers over time, we calculated the aggregate on-wire bytes from each amplifier in the ONP data and divided that by the on-wire bytes of a minimum monlist query packet. We used the 64 byte minimum Ethernet frame plus preamble and inter-packet gap, which total 84 bytes, to obtain the "on-wire" bandwidth amplification factor (BAF). Note that with respect to using all UDP, IP, and Ethernet frame overhead (including all bits that take time on the wire), our BAF calculations are lower than [32] but more accurately represent real bandwidth exhaustion effects via the most common (Ethernet) data links, as the actual load on the wire in both directions is considered. Figure 4b shows boxplots for the BAFs seen in each of the fifteen ONP monlist query response samples. As we can see, there is a wide range of BAFs in any sample, but the median is fairly steady across samples at around 4 (4.31 in the last five samples), and the maximum is generally around 1 million, except for the three samples starting on January 24th, when the maximum is around 1 billion. The third quartile BAF is typically around 15, except for the middle two samples in February, when it spikes to between 50 and 500. This suggests that, while the typical monlist-responding NTP server can provide an on-wire amplification of just 4x, a quarter of the amplifiers still seen in the wild can provide at least a 15x amplification. Using just one or a handful of such amplifiers, an attacker with a 100 Mbps Internet connection can easily overwhelm a service with a 1000 Mbps connection.

3.3 Threat of the Version Command

Our main focus in this paper is on the threat posed by the NTP *monlist* command, as it is known to have a high BAF, is of low utility for normal NTP operation, and has been used in high-profile DDoS attacks. However, NTP supports other commands that return more data than is sent (e.g., *version*, *showpeers*) though these have not been as widely reported in attacks. As of February 21st 2014, the ONP data also includes separate Internet-wide NTP mode 6 *version* command probes. These are conducted in the same fashion as the monlist scans, in that every IP in the IPv4 address space is sent a single packet with the NTP version command and all response packets are stored. As of the April 18th ONP sample, the global pool of version responders is around 4M unique IPs. In Figure 4c we show the version BAFs observed. The measurements reveal several noteworthy differences between the version command and the monlist command threat. First, the pool of NTP server IPs that respond to the version query is much larger (4M vs 110K). Second, the version pool has not reduced substantially over the nine weeks that it has been measured. Third, there is much less variance in the BAF, (the 25th, 50th, and 75th percentiles are almost exactly the same at around 3.5, 4.6, and 6.9 throughout the nine samples). Fourth, there are still some outliers, as with monlist, with the maximum BAF as high as 263M, possibly due to the same routing loop-like behavior seen for the largest monlist amplifiers discussed in § 3.4. This all means that, while the threat from NTP DDoS using monlist may be starting to wane, the amplifier pool available for amplification and reflection using the version command is much larger and the median BAFs are comparable (though the higher end, 75 or 95 percentile, are much lower for version).

We were curious to know what fractions of scanning host or victim attack packets involved the version versus monlist command. To measure this, we tabulated the mode flag for likely victim or scanning NTP clients listed in the monlist tables that ONP-probed amplifiers return (detailed in § 4.1). We found that interest in the version command (mode 6) by both scanners and attackers relative to monlist (mode 7) appears to have grown somewhat since mid-February, with both showing the highest fraction of scanner or victim IPs contacting the sampled amplifiers in the final, April 18th sample (19% of scanners and 0.3% of victims). These values, especially for victims, should be interpreted with caution, since the global pool of NTP servers responding to the version command is nearly 40 times the size of the current monlist pool (4M vs 110K), and shrewed attackers may simply be using the former for version-based attacks and the latter for monlist. However, as monlist remediation reduces the pool of those amplifiers, this ratio may change.

Global NTP Versions and Systems: We parsed the responses to version command probes included in the ONP data between February 21st and March 28th. We aggregated version information for the samples, which include the OS, system, and version strings, as well as the NTP *stratum* of each server [23]. Table 2 shows the strings most commonly found in the OS field. No other systematic patterns in the data were prominent. We did make one surprising finding, however; of the 5.8M unique IPs returning data, nearly a fifth, 19%, reported stratum 16, which indicates that the NTP server is unsynchronized to the correct time [23]. This suggests poor management, as providing the correct time is the reason for an NTP server's existence. We also extracted the compile time year from all version strings, which was present in 1.1M of the server samples. Only 21% had compile dates in 2013 or 2014; We found that 59% were compiled before 2012, 48% before 2011, and 23% before 2010. Surprisingly, 13% were compiled before 2004, over ten years ago. Such poor state of updates and management is perhaps one reason vulnerabilities can have impact long after they are discovered.

3.4 The Case of the Mega Amplifiers

The maximum number of table entries that the monlist command returns (which we've confirmed empirically) is 600, and each entry includes just a handful of small fields, which we discuss in § 4.1. The expected maximum amount of data returned for a query is under 50K. Indeed, as Figure 4a shows (note the log scale), the vast majority of amplifiers (99%) return less than 50K in aggregate.

However, as previously shown in Figures 4a and 4b, there is a small set of amplifiers that, at least in one or more of the fifteen weekly samples, behaves in an unusual and most devastating way. These "mega amplifiers," when sent a single packet of size less than 100 bytes, reply with megabytes or gigabytes of aggregate response packets. We found six amplifiers that responded with more than a gigabyte of aggregate packets, and the largest amplifier returned over 136 Gigabytes in a single day sample. In total, about 10 thousand amplifiers responded with more than 100KB of data, double or more than the command should ever return.

Since April, we have also been conducting twice-daily probes of a set of 250K IPs that were monlist amplifiers in any of the March 2014 ONP data samples. Between 60K and 15K of these IPs (decreasing over time) have been responding with monlist tables. Between April 2nd and June 13th, a set of nine IPs from seven ASNs had, on at least one occasion replied with more than 10,000 packets (at least 5MB). In parallel to monlist probes, we have been running packet captures to identify the amplifiers that exhibit this mega amplifier behavior. Several of these amplifiers did so on multiple samples, including the largest of the nine, which replied with more than 20M packets on each of at least a dozen samples during this period. This indicates that the behavior was not briefly transient but likely a systematic misconfiguration or bug. On May 31st, a single of these amplifiers sent 23M packets totalling over 100 gigabytes in just the first hour after our probe. Traffic data shows that this IP continued replying for hours afterwards. These mega amps often caused a steady stream of $\approx$50Mbps of traffic, and spikes above 150Mbps were common, with the largest peak around 500Mbps, likely when more than one such mega amplifier was triggered. Strangely, all nine of these amplifiers were located in Japan, according to GeoIP information. We contacted JPCERT about these IPs and the operators were notified. After several weeks, these IPs no longer responded with excessive volume. However, we never received confirmation as to the root cause of the phenomenon.

If an attacker was lucky enough to either identify an amplifier or, by chance, happen to trigger an amplifier into behaving this way, he would hit the DDoS jackpot. Even a single host sending a small number of packets to a handful of such amplifiers could theoretically use up gigabits of victim bandwidth, and a single such amplifier would be enough to effectively knock a home Internet user, such as a gamer, offline, possibly for hours.

To understand what could cause this unusual behavior, returning to the 15-week ONP data, we first examined the *monlist* and *version* responses from both normal and unusually-large amplifiers, and found that these mega amplifiers did not differ systematically from the overall pool of 6M NTP servers or other amplifiers, with perhaps the exception of system strings, which we show in Table 2. We observe that in the overall pool, nearly half of the systems responding to the version command list their system as "Cisco," followed by 31% that list "Unix" (some Cisco devices running the IOS-XR OS apparently also report system as "UNIX"). In the mega amplifier (top 10k) pool (of which about half responded to the version command, allowing labeling) the reported system is most likely to be Linux (44%) or Junos (36%). In spite of this systematic difference, there is a large variety of systems represented in this mega amplifier pool, suggesting that a single bug or common configuration is likely not the cause of the behavior. For a second clue, we turned to the contents of the replies, whose parsing we detail in § 4.2.

Briefly, we looked at the monlist tables that the probed servers replied with, reconstructing the table from the packet payloads just as the NTP tools would do. We found that the mega amplifiers were

Table 2: **Mega amplifier operating system strings, versus all amplifiers and all NTP servers reporting version information.**

	Mega (10k)		All Amplifiers		All NTP	
Rank	OS	%	OS	%	OS	%
1	linux	44.18	linux	80.22	cisco	48.39
2	junos	35.85	bsd	11.08	unix	30.64
3	bsd	9.18	junos	3.43	linux	18.97
4	cygwin	4.82	vmkernel	1.42	bsd	0.97
5	vmkernel	2.41	darwin	0.92	junos	0.33
6	unix	2.01	windows	0.84	sun	0.21
7	windows	0.42	unix	0.56	darwin	0.13
8	sun	0.37	secureos	0.49	OTHER	0.14
9	secureos	0.25	sun	0.25	vmkernel	0.10
10	isilon	0.23	qnx	0.22	windows	0.07
11	OTHER	0.21	cisco	0.17	secureos	0.03
12	cisco	0.06	OTHER	0.41	qnx	0.02

incrementing the count for the ONP scanning server and resending an updated monlist table, continuously, up to thousands of times. Since we know that the ONP probe server only sent one packet, this behavior is consistent with a routing or switching loop or a similar networking stack flaw, which resulted in the ONP query packet being re-transmitted along the path or re-processed by these mega amplifiers' ntpd processes. Other entries in these repeating (re-sent) tables showed that different clients of these servers had previously also seen the same multiple response behavior. These repeated responses typically occurred on a single sample week, but, in several cases, the same behavior was observed more than one week in a row for the same amplifier, suggesting something other than a brief transient failure. We are unable to definitively confirm that a network loop was to blame, but evidence points in that direction.

4. VICTIMOLOGY

NTP DDoS attacks involve at least three categories of systems: victims, amplifiers, and the attacker-controller nodes that spoof source addresses and trigger amplifiers to generate attack traffic. Our perspectives do not shed much light on the third category, but, in addition to the amplifiers described above, thanks to monlist for the first time we have insight into the population of NTP *victims*. This is because the monlist command used to conduct attacks can itself be used to gain an understanding of who the attacked targets are. Recall that the command returns the most recent set of clients that communicated with the NTP service, up to 600 (the median we saw was 6, the mean 70). Since NTP attacks use the NTP service by spoofing victim IPs, this list of "clients" will also include the IPs and other characteristics of actual DDoS victims and attacks.

4.1 Understanding the monlist Table

Table 3 shows two truncated examples of tables returned by an NTP server in response to a monlist query with IPs obfuscated. We have also eliminated three unrelated columns for clarity (the local address, client version, and restricted field). Thus, the columns of interest to us are: (*i.*) remote address (client or victim IP); (*ii.*) client source port; (*iii.*) count of packets; (*iv.*) client request mode; (*v.*) average inter-arrival time; and (*vi.*) last seen time (seconds ago).

In monlist table 3a, we first observe that the ONP scanning IP appears as the topmost address in the table. This is typically but not always the case, perhaps because some implementations may only update the table after replying to the probe. The *last seen* for the ONP IP is thus 0, and the *inter-arrival time* is typically around 600 thousand, since ONP probes IPs once a week. Second, we note that the count field for our probe is in the single digits, and that the mode column shows 7, which, along with mode 6, are the special NTP modes that include commands such as monlist and version. In

Table 3: **Partial monlist table examples, showing the ONP probe, normal clients, as well as apparent NTP DDoS victims and the fields used to identify each.**

(a) monlist Table A

Address	Src. Port	Count	Mode	Inter-arrival	Last Seen
ONP-IP	57915	6	7	526929	0
client.a1	10151	19	6	154503	310
client.a2	123	3281	4	1024	345
client.a3	54660	2	7	823	20795
client.a4	36008	1	3	0	104063

(b) monlist Table B

Address	Src. Port	Count	Mode	Inter-arrival	Last Seen
ONP-IP	47188	1	7	0	0
client-b1	59436	3358227026	7	0	0
client-b2	43395	25361312	7	0	0
client-b3	50231	158163232	7	0	0
client.b4	80	2189	7	0	2

addition to the ONP IP, we see four other clients, with request modes 3,4,6 and 7, that have also communicated with this server between 29 hours and five minutes ago (*last seen*). Client 1a sent 19 packets up to this point, about once every 43 hours, using mode 6; so, it is likely another probe. Checking the hostname of that IP confirms that it is indeed a research project. Client a3 is also a benign Internet survey host. Clients a2 and a4 appear to be normal NTP clients, contacting the server over mode 3 and 4 (normal operational modes) and using expected source ports and *inter-arrival times* (the time for a4 is 0, because it only sent one packet).

Moving to the second example table, 3b (assembled from entries in two actual tables for illustration), we again see the ONP probe packet. We also see four client IPs, each using mode seven, some with average inter-arrival times of 0 seconds and last seen within the last second. Further, the packet count sent by some clients is very high, with the largest of the four clients showing a count of over 3 billion packets. These all appear to be victims of the example amplifier. What is more, one of the clients is using source port 80, which, for UDP, is not a well-known service port but, as our victim port analysis (section 4.3.2) reveals, is commonly targeted.

4.2 monlist Table Analysis

For each of the weeks of ONP data, we parsed the responses to ONP monlist probes from each amplifier, 5M amplifier-week pairs. We applied the protocol logic found in the NTP `ntpdc` tool to rebuild the monlist tables present in the packets captured for each probed amplifier. If an amplifier sent repeated copies of the table (i.e., was a "mega-amplifier" discussed in § 3.4) we used the final table received that sample day. For each client IP in each table parsed, we use a filter we describe next to bin each client into one of three categories: a *non-victim*, a *scanner/low-volume victim*, or an actual apparent *victim* of that amplifier.

Identifying Victims: While the normal NTP modes could conceivably be used for reflection, there is little reason for attackers to do so, as no amplification is provided. Thus, if the mode value was less than 6, we classified the client as a *non-victim*. For clients that were using modes 6 or 7, we applied the following thresholds: if a client sent less than three packets to this amplifier (via the *count* field) or the average *inter-arrival* time was greater than 3600, indicating that it had received no more than one packet per hour from the amplifier, on average, we categorized the client as a *scanner/low-volume victim*, otherwise it was labeled a *victim*. We only report results for *victims*. This limits our reporting of victims to those above a low threshold of packets. Again, when a client received more than three packets from an amplifier *and* averaged more than one packet per hour, we labeled it a victim of that amplifier. While this may seem like a low threshold, note that no legitimate NTP client would send these mode packets in the course of normal operation, and that individual researchers scanning the IP address space are not likely to re-scan a given IP more than once per hour.

For each victim seen by an amplifier, we extracted the *count* of packets it received, the average *inter-arrival* time, and the *last seen* time that the amplifier saw the victim, which is the attack end time for that amplifier/victim pair. We also estimated the duration of attacks, using simply the packet *count* multiplied by the average *inter-arrival* time. As the start time is not part of the monlist table, we estimate it using the duration and *last seen* time values, via similarly simple arithmetic including this calculated duration and time the table was received by the ONP scanner.

View Provided By Tables: Across all ONP weekly samples, the median largest *last seen* time in the monlist tables is about 44 hours. Thus, the median window within which we see attacks is approximately the previous two days. Arguably, this suggests that our samples will underestimate the number of victims, packets, or attacks by roughly a factor of 3.8 (i.e. there are 168 hours per week and we see 44). We don't show a plot, but, as expected, the largest *last seen* time in tables shrinks between the first sample in January and the peak of attacks in mid-February as the volume of attacks increases (thus shrinking the view of the 600-entry-capped monlist tables), and then increases again; following the same pattern seen in our other measurements (e.g., Internet NTP traffic). For this reason, our February peaks are likely underestimating attacks more than in the lower-volume months before or since.

4.3 Victims and Attacks

We next seek to understand who is the target of NTP DDoS attacks, when attacks occurred, how long the attacks lasted, and whether we see evidence for any of the public attacks.

4.3.1 Victim Locations and Networks

Our victim list includes victims from 184 countries in six continents, and, as Table 1 shows, the victim population in our samples spans up to 33K routed blocks and 6700 ASes at peak. We find that about half of victims are end host IPs, though this has grown from 31% on January 10th. The average number of IPs attacked in routed blocks is between 3–5, suggesting most attacks target a very small number of selected hosts in targeted organizations. Together with the fraction of target hosts that are end-hosts, this adds evidence to the idea that many DDoS attacks are launched against individuals.

We plot a CDF of the contribution of victim packets by autonomous system in Figure 5 for both amplifier and victim ASes. *Just 100 amplifier ASes are responsible for 60% of the victim packets measured.* Victim ASes are even more concentrated, with the *top 100 ASes receiving three quarters of all attack packets*. In examining top ASes with victims, we note that, out of the top ten ASes, eight are hosting providers and two are telecom companies. The top attacked AS is French hosting firm OVH, the purported target of large NTP DDoS attacks in mid-February (see § 4.4).

4.3.2 Attacked Ports

We were interested in seeing what services or ports were being attacked at these victim networks. For each victim seen at each amplifier, we tallied the source port used. Table 4 shows the top twenty attacked ports, along with the count of amplifier/victim pairs and fraction of all. We also include a column describing common use of each port, where known.

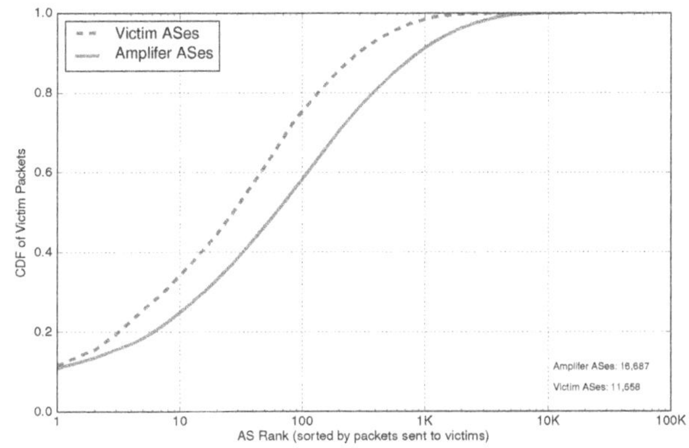

Figure 5: CDF of aggregate victim packets sent or received by autonomous systems. Just 100 amplifier ASes are responsible for 60% of the victim packets measured. Victims are even more concentrated, with 75% in the top 100 ASes.

Table 4: Top 20 ports seen in victims at amplifiers. Note prevalence of ports known to be associated with games, marked with *(g)*, which add up to at least 15% of the victim ports attacked in the top 20 (we did not manually label ports above rank 20). Port 80 is also used by game systems, though over TCP.

Rank	Attacked Port	Fraction	Common UDP Use
1	80	0.362	None. via TCP:HTTP *(g)*
2	123	0.238	NTP server port
3	3074	0.079	XBox Live *(g)*
4	50557	0.062	Unknown
5	53	0.025	DNS; XBox Live *(g)*
6	25565	0.021	Minecraft *(g)*
7	19	0.012	chargen protocol
8	22	0.011	None. via TCP:SSH
9	5223	0.007	Playstation *(g)*; other
10	27015	0.006	Steam/e.g. Half-Life *(g)*
11	43594	0.004	Runescape *(g)*
12	9987	0.004	TeamSpeak3 *(g)*
13	8080	0.004	None. via TCP:HTTP alt.
14	6005	0.003	Unknown
15	7777	0.003	Several games *(g)*; other
16	2052	0.003	Star Wars *(g)*
17	1025	0.002	Win RPC; other
18	1026	0.002	Win RPC; other
19	88	0.002	XBox Live *(g)*
20	90	0.002	DNSIX (military)

The top port attacked is port 80. Since port 80 in UDP is not a well-known application port (unlike in TCP, where it is the most used port, supporting HTTP), we speculate that perhaps attackers hoped that port 80 packets might be less likely to be filtered or blocked, enabling a more effective attack; this attack pattern has been reported by others [33]. Other ports prominently seen in attack traffic, include port 123 itself, which is the NTP *server* port (we also find this in our local impact datasets, described in § 7).

Game Wars: In addition to 80 and 123, other notable ports that show up in the top 20 list include at least 10 associated with gaming (e.g., ports for Xbox Live, Playstation, and specific games, such as Minecraft, Half-Life, and Counter-Strike). If we include port 80, which in TCP is used by many games (and non-games, of course) and may be mistakenly targeted, the total fraction possibly related to games may be even higher; likewise many of the ports above the top-20 list are also used by games. Along with the end-host fraction mentioned earlier, this targeting of game ports adds evidence to our conclusion that *a large fraction of NTP DDoS attacks are perpetrated against gamers*, as previously reported in press and industry reports (e.g., Goodin [18], Prolexic [31], and

Arbor Networks [8]). Minecraft (6th highest), in particular, was a confirmed large attack target, according to Goodin's sources.

4.3.3 Attack Volume

Having discussed the target networks and ports, we turn to the volume of attacks. The aggregate attack packet count across all amplifiers over fifteen weeks is 2.92 trillion packets. The median bytes on the wire seen in the ONP response data is 420 bytes, thus, assuming each packet had that size, 1.2 petabytes may be a reasonable estimate of the aggregate data these particular attack numbers represent. However we believe that these samples underestimate the size of the victim population; this is because we do not see version victims from non-monlist-returning NTP servers, we only sample once per week, we only see the last 600 victims, and some amplifiers have been seen to attack thousands of victims at a time (e.g., see Table 5). As discussed in § 4.2, we under-sample by a median factor of 3.8. Thus, the likely actual volume of traffic to victims is probably closer to 3.8 times 1.2 petabytes. Of course, we caution that our data is lossy and sourced from often mis-manged devices, so these estimates may be considerably off. In general, we believe our numbers underestimate the amplifier population, victim population, attack counts, and attack sizes, because of the limitations discussed here and earlier.

Figure 6 shows the total number of packets that observed victims receive. We see that median attacks are quite small, at around 300-1000 packets, but the average is high at 1-10M, driven by a relatively small number of heavily-attacked victims. The 95th-percentile had been in the range of 400K to 6M until mid February, but since then has been in the 110k-200k range, suggesting the effect of remediation.

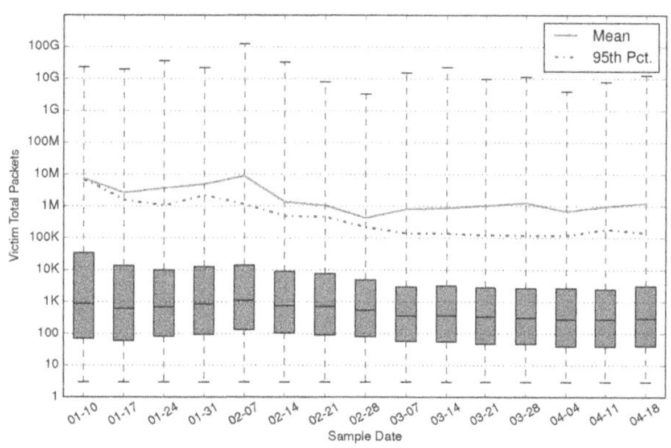

Figure 6: Total packets victims received from amplifiers. The mean packets are skewed by mega-amplifiers, but the 95th percentile has gone down by two orders of magnitude and median by a factor of 3.

4.3.4 Attack Counts and Durations

Because of the noise and lossy nature of our data, we make some simplifying assumptions when discussing attack counts and durations. First, we count each unique IP targeted in a given weekly sample as a single victim and attack. Of course, this is a simplification because: *(i.)* a given attack campaign may involve several IPs in a network block or several autonomous systems (ASes); *(ii.)* a single IP may be a host to multiple websites or users that are targets of independent attacks; and, *(iii.)* multiple attacks launched by one or more attackers may be targeting the same IP in small time frames that are too fine-grained for our data to disambiguate. Second, to determine start time of an attack, we use the median start time calculated across all amplifiers seen attacking the victim. In § 4.2 we explained how we derive start times from the monlist tables.

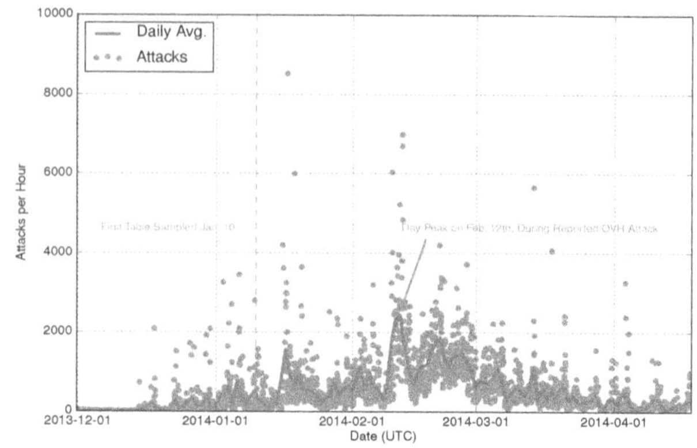

Figure 7: Time series of attack counts seen in ONP monlist table data, including some time before first table. Attack counts are a lower bound. Mean: 514/hr; median: 280/hr.

In Figure 7 we use these derived median attack start times to show a time series of attack counts per hour seen in the ONP data. The attack counts are a lower bound, because, as discussed previously, the tables only show a median of 44 hours of amplifier activity every week. Samples start on January 10th, but some tables include evidence of older activity by virtue of not yet flushing older victims. Our calculations thus allow us to partially identify attacks with start and end times prior to our first sample, indicated with a vertical dashed line. We plot the attacks seen binned by hour as well as a daily average line. Note that the daily average peaks on February 12th, which is the time of the largest publicly-disclosed CloudFlare and OVH attacks (discussed in § 4.4), that started on February 10th. This peak corresponds to the same daily peak in NTP traffic observed in the Arbor Networks Internet traffic graph in Figure 1; likewise, the general trend up through mid-February and down afterwards matches the trajectory of global NTP traffic, suggesting that the attacks indeed drove global NTP traffic. Median attacks over our sample period only lasted approximately 40 seconds in the samples since mid February, and about half or a quarter of that in previous samples. On the other hand, the 95th percentile duration attacks lasted about six and a half hours in the January 10th sample and have been declining since, with 50 minutes being the 95th percentile duration in the later April samples.

4.4 Validation

One of the early massive NTP-based DDoS attacks that was observed in the wild occurred in early February and was disclosed by CloudFlare [30]. The attack started on February 10th, and was reportedly near 400Gbps in size, a record for NTP DDoS at the time. Purportedly, the attack targeted servers at OVH, a French-based hosting firm that was protected by CloudFlare [13]. The firm is one of the largest hosting providers in the world, and includes services targeting game servers [6]. In our rankings of networks that have been the targets of attacks, out of 11,558 ASes, OVH (AS number 16267) is the top AS (Cloudflare itself ranks 18th). Our data shows the OVH AS getting hit with over 170Bn aggregate packets from the amplifiers we studied, nearly 6% of all attack packets. OVH also features prominently in the Colorado State University (CSU) top-10 victims list (see § 7), accounting for five of the top 10 most attacked IPs. The attack campaign against it appears to be long-lasting; for example, OVH is the top AS in at least one weekly sample during each of the four months in our dataset, and shows up as one of the top ten ASes that are attacked in 13 of the 15 weeks. Attackers target multiple unique IPs at OVH, peaking at nearly 4K in March.

CloudFlare also published the list of 1,297 ASes that hosted vulnerable NTP servers used as amplifiers in this attack. Of these 1,297, 1,291 were also seen in the ONP data, which totals 16,687 total amplifier-hosting ASes. The 1,291 that overlapped were, in aggregate, responsible for 60% of all victim packets. In addition to cross-dataset confirmation discussed throughout, this example supports the validity of our approach and gives us greater confidence.

5. ATTACKERS AND DARKNET SCANNING

5.1 View from a Darknet

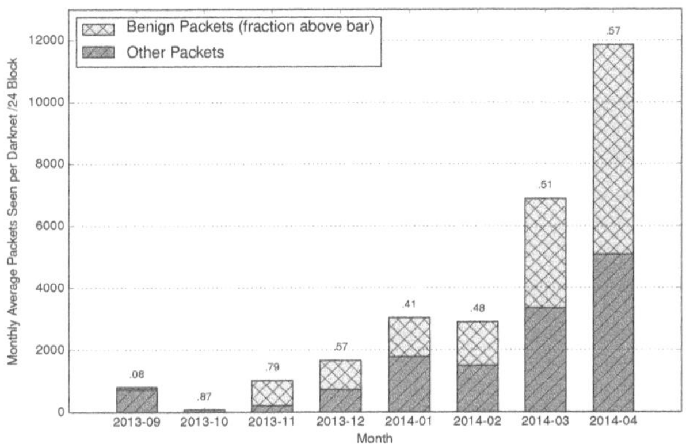

Figure 8: NTP scanning packet volume (in avg. packets per destination /24) detected by an ≈/9 darknet over eight months, broken down by known benign (e.g., academic research projects) and other, which are from suspected malicious scanners.

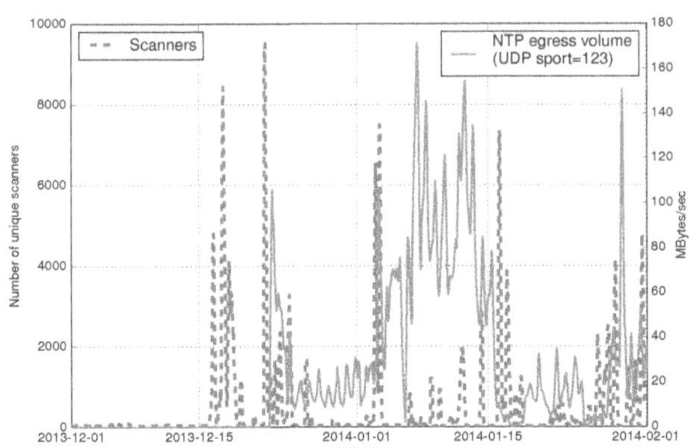

Figure 9: Darknet scanning activity increased a week before the NTP attacks became significant.

Darknet or network telescope based observations of unused portions of the Internet IP address space (e.g., [35]) have often been used to detect the impact of large-scale phenomenon. The core idea behind such observations is that any large-scale significant physical or network event will ultimately have some spillover into unused address space (e.g., by not seeing expected noise packets from some remote network). Such analyses have, for example, been used to observe the impact of earthquakes on the Internet infrastructure, worm propagation, DDoS backscatter, misconfigurations, and censorship, among other events (e.g., [10, 11, 15]).

Based on the scale of the NTP events, we expected to find significant evidence of attacker activity (i.e., scanning) in darknets. Our darknet dataset consists of full packet captures for roughly 75% of an IPv4 /8 address block[1] operated by Merit Network.

Figure 8 shows the volume of NTP traffic observed at the darknet by an average /24 network block equivalent. We notice a 10-fold increase in NTP related scanning activity starting from December 2013 to April 2014. It is interesting to note that we observe not just an increase in malicious scanning, but also scanning from various research efforts that were attempting to track the vulnerable NTP population (we identified these by their hostnames). Roughly half of the increase in scanning can be attributed to research efforts.

Figure 9 shows a time series of NTP scanning activity in terms of the number of unique IP addresses observed in our darknet. We are clearly able to pinpoint the onset of large-scale NTP scanning in mid December 2013. The figure also shows aggregate NTP traffic volume on the operational (non-dark) portions of Merit's network (details in § 7). We observe that the rise in scanning activity precedes actual NTP attack traffic increases by roughly a week. This highlights the importance of using darknets to build active early warning systems of new and emerging threats [10]. It should also be noted that scanning traffic volumes continue to be high even as the global vulnerable NTP population has seen a dramatic decline. This indicates a continuing interest in finding vulnerable NTP servers.

Since at least one study reported seeing some UDP amplifiers (it is unclear if these were NTP) in the IPv6 space, we were curious to see if there was scanning activity observable in IPv6 [32] . We examined collected packets to dark (unused) address space in a large IPv6 darknet we operate, which includes covering prefixes for four of the five Regional Internet Registrars, including the RIRs for North America, South America, Asia, and Africa [14]. We searched for evidence of NTP scanning in the IPv6 darknet data in Nov. 2013, Dec. 2013, and Feb. 2014, but saw mostly errant point-to-point NTP connections, and no evidence of broad scanning. Likewise, the Arbor Networks netflow data for IPv6 does not list NTP within the top 200 UDP ports (it was 12th in IPv4), and, thus, did not show a noticeable level of NTP traffic.

5.2 Attacker Ecosystem and Motivations

The concept of "attacker" in this type of DDoS activity is both nebulous to define and difficult to measure. Unfortunately, most of the available datasets shed very little light on who the actual attackers are that perpetrate these NTP-based DDoS attacks or what their motivations may be. However, there are a few small clues that public reports have revealed as well as a few tidbits in our data.

Dissecting the DDoS ecosystem and understanding attackers is complicated by the fact that several types of actors are involved in launching attacks. We've reserved the term "amplifier" for the vulnerable or misconfigured boxes that are leveraged in attacks to flood victims with traffic. These are part of the problem, but they are more enablers than aggressors. The attack ecosystem has several other entities that better fall under the umbrella of "attacker." First, there are the nodes that send spoofed-source packets to amplifiers in order to elicit the large responses that flood victims. These may or may not be the machines that are owned by the humans launching attacks. In many cases, they are actually compromised Internet user machines ("zombies" or "bots") that can be remotely commanded to perform such actions on behalf of a "botmaster." Thus, the second entity we might label an attacker is the botmaster himself. Certainly, this person or group and the system they use can be

[1] We typically have around 75% coverage for the darknet /8 in terms of effective unique /24 that are advertised and can receive traffic. However, the size of the darknet varies over time due to routing changes and suballocations. To account for this, we normalize the data to average packets per effective dark /24s that month.

labeled culpable. But, blame might not stop there. These botmasters could be individuals acting on behalf of a black market DDoS ("booter") service, many of which are advertised on underground forums (e.g. [5]) [19]. They or the service may have been hired by the party that is actually motivated to cause damage to the victim.

So, while a botmaster or booter service is likely to be motivated by money, the person that actually wants the attack to happen could be motivated by anything that normally motivates people to attack others. This, of course, includes money (e.g., via extortion [28]), revenge, political reasons, competitive advantage (see Poulsen for an early example [29]), etc. According to a large 2014 survey of global network operators, political/idealogical reasons top the list of perceived motivations for being attacked [8].

We discuss several clues about attackers and their motives that appear in our own data where that data is presented. For instance, in § 4.3.2 we mentioned that a significant amount of victims were targeted on game-related ports. This is congruent with the idea that many DDoS attacks are perpetrated against gamers, by rivals or for financial gain, as reported previously (e.g., [4, 18, 19, 26, 31]). Another clue is discussed briefly in § 7.2, where we found that packet TTLs of scanning packets indicate they are mostly Linux, while packets sent by nodes generating traffic to amplifiers indicates they run Windows. As botnet nodes are often Windows machines, while individual miscreants with enough sophistication to conduct broad Internet scans may be Linux users, this clue fits the story that attackers are using botnet hosts to indirectly launch attack traffic.

6. REMEDIATION

One of the most encouraging observations regarding the NTP DDoS attacks has been the community response. Community response to the NTP amplifier threat has been swift [17], with the number of vulnerable monlist NTP servers dropping dramatically from a high of 1.4M when first measured on January 10th, down to less than half (678K) just two weeks later and continuing to fall to around 110K, where it has held steady since March 21st. Some interesting facets of how remediation occurred are presented next.

6.1 Subgroup Remediation Rates

One interesting aspect of how monlist amplifier remediation is proceeding is its varying nature across several axes.

Network Levels: First, we look at network granularity. We already noted that the overall set of amplifier IPs has been reduced in cardinality from approximately 1.4M in early January to 110K by April 18th; a reduction of 92%. However, when we aggregate amplifier IPs by /24 subnets, we find that the reduction is from 264K to 73K, or 72%. There are at least two possible reasons for this discrepancy; given IPs in a /24 might be managed by different operators (e.g., because they are home PCs in a residential ISP), or the individual hosts may be more or less difficult to patch, for example, due to their role. When we aggregate up to the routed block level, the percentage reduction falls again, from 64K routed blocks to 26K, or 59% reduction. At the autonomous system level, it is only 55%, from 15k origin ASes to 6.8K. These trends highlight the difficulty in completely eliminating a vulnerability from all of a single network, let alone such a large number of independently-managed networks.

Regional Levels: The second axis along which remediation differs is the regional one. When we aggregate the amplifiers according to their continent, we find that North America has remediated 97% of its amplifiers, Oceania 93%, Europe 89%, Asia 84%, Africa 77%, and South America 63%. These differences in the speed to remediate amplifiers across region may be caused by various socio-economic factors, by the relative regional impact that these amplifiers have caused, and by network management practices or norms.

End Host Composition: A third axis is the relative composition of amplifiers that are end hosts. We again used the PBL [34] to label each IP seen in the weekly samples as either an end host or not. As Table 1 showed, as the pool of amplifiers was remediated, the fraction of amplifiers that are end hosts approximately doubled from 17% in the first two weeks to 34% in the last, suggesting that perhaps remediation was more likely to happen at servers that are professionally managed versus at workstations.

6.2 Comparison to Open DNS Resolvers

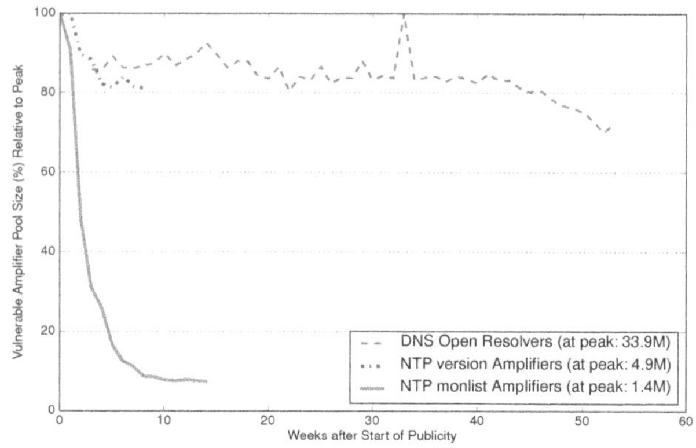

Figure 10: Size of vulnerable NTP (and, for comparison) DNS amplifier pools, relative to peak, versus weeks since the OpenNTPProject.org and OpenResolverProject.org, respectively, began publicizing vulnerable server counts. (We ablate the first three DNS samples and a single DNS outlier, artificially low due to collection and methodology issues.) Monlist amplifiers have been remediated dramatically faster than the other two pools.

The initial rapid remediation of over 90% of vulnerable servers is remarkable in how it compares to another, related, Internet threat, DNS-based DDoS amplifiers. In Figure 10 we show the fraction of amplifiers seen in the wild versus the number of weeks since the OpenNTPProject began collecting data and raising awareness of the threat. For comparison, we show the counts of open DNS resolvers, which are susceptible to use in amplification/reflection attacks for the same reasons that NTP servers are attractive. The OpenResolverProject.org [3], which is run by the same people as the NTP project, has been conducting identical IPv4-wide surveys of the size of the vulnerable DNS server population for about a year. As the figure shows, that pool has not decreased much in relative terms. A possible key difference is that open DNS resolvers are often found on customer premises equipment, which is much more difficult to update or replace than are infrastructure servers, like those that typically run NTP. We measured the intersection between the NTP monlist amplifier IP pool and the corresponding open DNS recursive resolver pool. It is about 7K out of 107K monlist amplifiers in the latest sample. The aggregate unique IPs seen over 15 ONP samples and the DNS IPs over the same period show an overlap of 199K or 9.2%. These badly mis-manged IPs may remain vulnerable for some time to come given the length of time since the open resolver threat has been known and that a non-trivial fraction of networks are mis-managed for reasonable metrics of management [36].

6.3 The Effect of Remediation

The drastic amplifier reduction we saw was also evident in the number of amplifiers seen per each victim IP, which also decreased by an order of magnitude across the ONP samples. On the other hand, we don't show this in a figure, but the number of packets that the average amplifier sends all victims has actually gone up by about an order of magnitude, to somewhat compensate for the reduced number of amplifiers. In other words, remaining amplifiers are being put to more use. Likewise, as Table 1 showed, more victims are being attacked over time, though this stopped increasing in April. As shown in Figure 6, the average number of packets that a victim sees has decreased by about an order of magnitude (from 10M in January to 1M starting in mid-February), and the median has decreased to about a third.

It is possible, and, as discussed in § 3.3, likely, that other NTP commands may be used by attackers as the pool of monlist amplifiers is reduced. Figure 10 also shows the size of the version command amplifier pool, which only decreased 19% since peak.

Because our victim and attack counts come from a parsing of the monlist tables, as our view of the global NTP population is reduced when the command is blocked or patched, we will see fewer victims, attacks, and packets. Thus, our estimates of these populations and the attack traffic are a lower bound. Finally, those small number of mega amplifiers, if they are being exploited by more attackers, might increase actual overall attack traffic seen by victims.

6.4 Operator Motivation and Notification

We learned that part of the reason that monlist amplifiers were remediated more quickly than other amplifier populations may be due to an aggressive notification effort that was conducted via CERTs and direct operator contact, as recently reported by Kührer *et al.* [20] just as we were going to press. While it is plausible and likely that communication had an impact on remediation, causality, unfortunately, can not be determined. Our discussions with experts in DDoS at Arbor Networks and with one global ISP operator also suggested that operator motivation to remediate amplifiers or otherwise mitigate NTP traffic in other ways was likely increased by the large impact that this traffic was having on the operators' own networks. Understanding the reasons and mechanisms for the dramatic reduction in the NTP monlist population was beyond our scope, but we mention these two possible causes as it is important for the community to work to understand what encourages beneficial operator response to such global Internet threats. Clearly, remediation and mitigation of amplifiers have positive externalities—they are behaviors that not only help the operator's own network but help the Internet at large be more secure.

7. A VIEW FROM REGIONAL NETWORKS

In the previous sections we have focused on the global view of the NTP DDoS phenomenon. We now turn our attention to how these events appeared at individual networks and the commonalities between them.

7.1 Local Impacts

The two local views include Merit Network and Front Range Gigapop (FRGP). Merit [22] is a large regional ISP serving multiple educational and non-profit institutions via a state-wide fiber backbone in Michigan while FRGP [1] is the major ISP serving Colorado State University (CSU).

Overall aggregate Merit traffic ranges from 15-25 Gbps. On a normal day, NTP constitutes a negligible fraction of this traffic. The NTP attacks first became visible at Merit on the third week of December 2013. Figure 11 shows an almost instantaneous increase in both inbound and outbound aggregate NTP volume with peaks exceeding 200MB/sec. At FRGP/CSU, however, we see the first sign of NTP attacks almost a month later. Figure 12 shows the aggregate NTP volume at CSU and FRGP. Due to network size differences and the limited FRGP vantage points, the attack volumes observed were an order magnitude less than at Merit. The CSU NTP servers were secured on January 24th, 2014. This is the point at which the NTP traffic volumes returned to pre-attacks levels. We do however, note that other networks within FRGP were not nearly as proactive. A number of vulnerable NTP servers within FRGP were used to launch attacks throughout the month of February. NTP traffic volume continues to grow throughout our observation window of 3 months. The distinctive spikes in FRGP ingress traffic in Figure 12 were NTP reflection attacks directed at specific hosts within FRGP prefixes. The largest one on the 10th of February lasted for just under 23 minutes with an attack rate of close to 3GBps and a total of 514 GB of attack traffic.

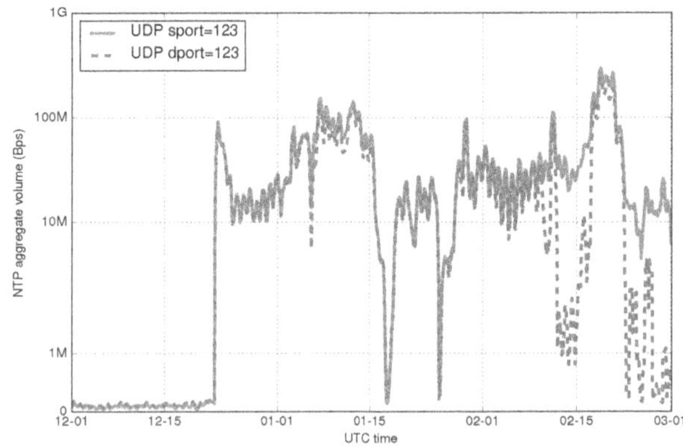

Figure 11: Merit NTP traffic (3 months).

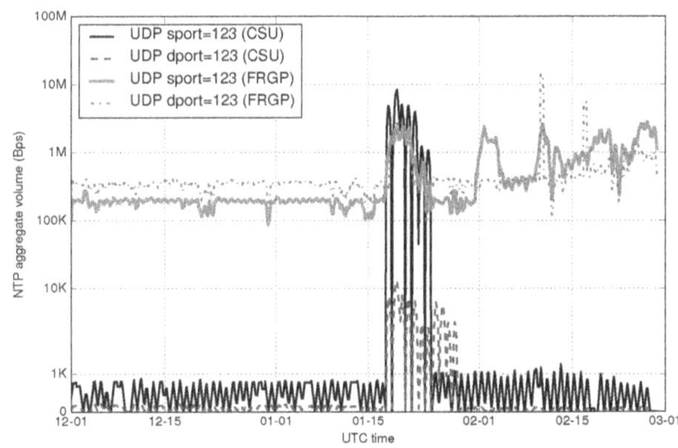

Figure 12: CSU/FRGP NTP traffic (3 months).

For the purposes of conducting detailed forensics we focused our attention on a 12-day period for the Merit dataset, and a 19-day period for CSU and FRGP datasets starting January 25th and January 18th, 2014 respectively. During the corresponding periods, we identified 50 NTP amplifiers inside Merit with an average amplification factor of 187, nine amplifiers at CSU with an average amplification factor of 436, and 48 amplifiers at FRGP[2]. Note that, as both Merit and FRGP are ISPs that each encompass multiple independent networks, these numbers of NTP servers are larger than a single enterprise would typically run. Further, depending on configuration, potentially any server or high-end router can act as an NTP server.

Table 5 shows the five worst amplifiers at Merit and CSU and their BAF, unique victims contacted over the periods studied, and the total volume sent in gigabytes[3]. Our analysis shows the extent to which

[2] BAF was not computed for FRGP due to incomplete picture of egress and ingress volume of the dataset.

[3] In this section, amplifiers, victims and the BAF are defined similar to [32]. Here, a *victim* is a client receiving at least 100KB from

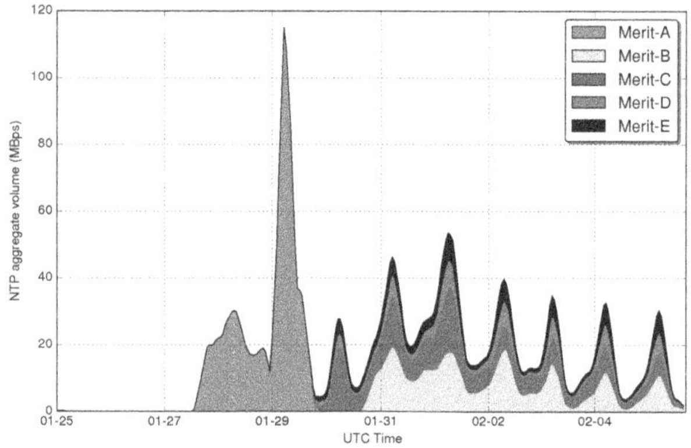

Figure 13: Time series of top-5 affected victims (Table 6).

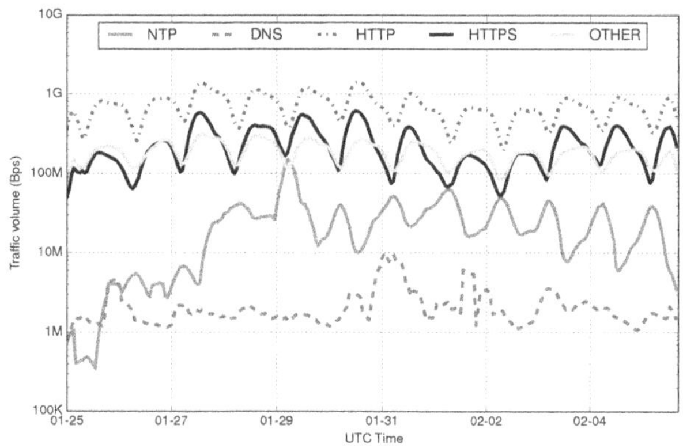

Figure 14: Time series of all traffic at Merit.

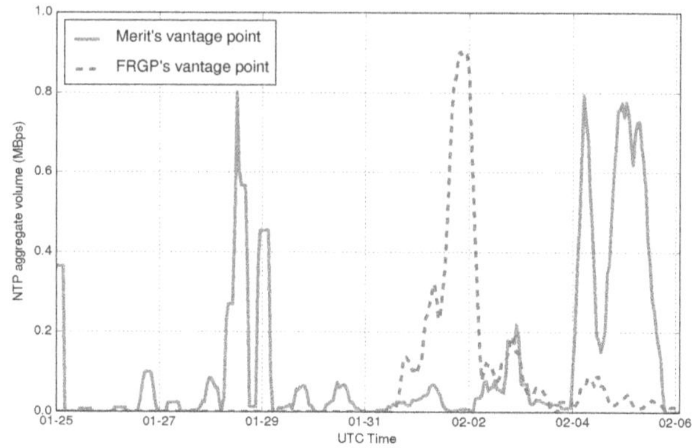

Figure 15: Common Merit/FRGP victims volume.

Table 5: Top-5 amplifiers at Merit and CSU

Amplifier	BAF	Unique victims	GB sent
Merit-A	1297	1966	375
Merit-B	1148	1626	4697
Merit-C	1004	3072	5808
Merit-D	993	1801	316
Merit-E	948	2740	4369
CSU-F	805	38	162
CSU-G	797	33	163
CSU-H	796	33	163
CSU-I	469	238	223
CSU-J	465	236	222

some of the NTP amplifiers in these networks participated in this global phenomenon. Notice, for example, that the five amplifiers alone identified in Merit were abused to target thousands of victims generating terabytes of data over a short time span.

Overall, we identified 13,386 unique victims at Merit and 5,659 at FRGP and CSU. There were 291 victims common between the two sites. We identified target networks and countries to which these systems belong. Table 6 shows a characterization of the top 5 victims at Merit and at CSU. Our data also clearly shows signs of coordination in these attacks as we frequently see several amplifiers being used to target the same victim at each site (Figure 15). All of the 9 CSU amplifiers were observed to attack many victims in a coordinated fashion. Further, in several cases at Merit, more than 35 of the identified amplifiers were used in a coordinated manner in attacks that lasted multiple days. Figure 13 provides a stacked-graph visualization of these victims. Interestingly, we observe a diurnal pattern of traffic destined to the victims perhaps suggesting a manual element in the attacks. Note that the larger attacks that used the most amplifiers also lasted longer (e.g., see top half of Table 6).

Since the attack volume constitutes a significant amount of ISP traffic, we investigate whether these attacks had monetary impact. Figure 14 shows the aggregate NTP traffic volume at Merit, along with other traffic, illustrating NTP's steep rise. We estimate that attacks resulted in over 2% additional traffic at Merit, overall, which would incur extra transit costs. Whether it did or would at another ISP depends on the billing model used (e.g., a 95*th* percentile model, which Merit uses with its upstream), the aggregation window size, and *when* the extra traffic was transited [16]. For example, if the extra traffic resulted in a higher billed traffic level after removing the 5% of peak traffic in a 95th percentile model, it might have produced more transit cost at the ISP, which was the case at Merit.

Remediation: Figure 3 showed the rate at which remediation efforts at both these networks progressed. At Merit, trouble tickets were used to track the status of each identified amplifier, and customer notifications were used to encourage prompt patching of systems. During the early stages of the attacks, Merit also put in place traffic rate limits on NTP traffic to minimize the impact of these attacks to its customers. At CSU, due to the small set of servers, patching happened rapidly, within a single day, though remediation in the rest of FRGP is ongoing. Likewise, some holdouts remain under Merit.

7.2 Individual Attacker/Victim Activity

One of the unique aspects of our datasets from these two sites is that they offer us a level of detail that is not present in some of our higher level global datasets. In particular, we are able to examine flow and packet level details that offer additional insight about the activity of individual attackers and victims as well as validate our global datasets.

The attack volume to common targets is shown in Figure 15. We plot the traffic volume to common targets as recorded from our two vantage points, Merit and FRGP. We found 291 common targets attacked by amplifiers at both sites. However, the attack

Table 6: Top-5 victims at Merit and CSU

Victim	ASN	Country	BAF	Amplifiers	Dur. Hours	GB
Merit-A	AS4713	Japan	105	42	114	5887
Merit-B	AS4837	China	1380	4	143	4542
Merit-C	AS30083	USA	202	7	166	4017
Merit-D	AS8972	Germany	165	7	166	1703
Merit-E	AS8972	Germany	147	7	166	1595
CSU-F	AS16276	France	730	9	31	17
CSU-G	AS39743	Romania	658	9	143	14
CSU-H	AS28666	Brazil	670	9	30	12
CSU-I	AS12390	UK	670	9	51	10
CSU-J	AS16276	France	669	9	74	10

an amplifier with a ratio of amplifier's bytes received to bytes sent of at least 100. An *amplifier* sent at least 10MB and had a ratio of sent/received traffic greater than 5. BAF is UDP payload ratio.

volumes were fairly low. We also find that the overlap in target ports between attack traffic at Merit and the global data shown in Table 4 is remarkable. The ports shown in that table constitute 98.91% of the total traffic destined to victims identified with Merit's flow data.

The information we obtained from the local views confirms some of our observations from the global ONP data in terms of attack magnitude and attack occurrences. For example, the BAFs reported via traffic analysis of the local datasets Tables 5 and 6 confirms those depicted in Figure 4b after allowing for differences due to packet headers. Additionally we also note that FRGP data shows servers in that network actively participated in the attacks on OVH servers described in section 4.4. Furthermore, the remediation efforts at each site were clearly visible in the ONP datasets giving us increased confidence in the completeness of the ONP data.

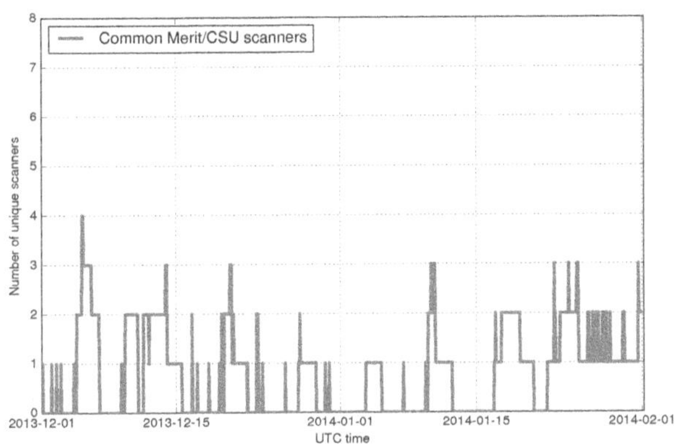

Figure 16: Common scanners Merit/CSU.

We also attempted to identify common scanning activity that might have been visible from both sites. However, we find little evidence of this in our datasets from Merit and CSU. Figure 16 shows a timeline of the trickle of activity from these common scanners. Though we identify 42 IP addresses in common, most of these were determined to be a result of research scanning. We speculate that true malicious scanning activity may be well distributed in time, and, therefore, the likelihood of two distinct sites observing synchronized scans is relatively low—whereas research scanning is being conducted in the open and at much more aggressive rates.

Another attacker behavior of interest is whether it is possible to estimate if scanning activity (to find amplifiers) and attack traffic (for amplifiers to reflect) is sourced from the same systems. To study this, we analyzed TTL values from the CSU dataset corresponding to both scanning activity as well as spoofed attacks. Surprisingly, we find that while the scanning activity appears to be largely sourced from Linux-based systems (mode TTL:54), the attack traffic appears to be originating from Windows-based systems (mode TTL: 109), perhaps botnet nodes.

8. RELATED WORK

The threat of DDoS attacks leveraging reflection has been well-known for many years (e.g., [27]), and the 2014 study by Rossow [32] is the latest and most comprehensive example of work examining the potential vectors for amplification in these reflected attacks. The Rossow paper characterized how 14 UDP protocols, including SNMP, chargen, and NTP with the monlist command, may be used for reflection/amplification DDoS attacks. For each of these protocols, broad and multifaceted passive and active measurements of a limited scale (e.g., scanning a random sample of 1M IPv4 addresses, partial crawling of P2P networks, and measurements of scanning in a medium-sized (/17) and small (/27) darknet over four weeks) were conducted. In contrast to that comprehensive examination of amplification in general, we instead focus just on the threat and actual harm caused by attacks leveraging NTP. Further, our measurements of this particular amplification vector are much broader, over a longer timespan, and include a deep analysis of the actual attack and victim characteristics seen in the wild, and at Internet-scale. At the time Rossow's paper was written, no major attacks using NTP had been reported. Since then, NTP had became the dominant attack vector for large DDoS attacks, and our work aims to chronicle that rise, explore who was attacked and how, and show how the mitigation of the vector has impacted the threat.

As our manuscript was undergoing final preparation for publication, new work by Kührer *et al.* [20] was published exploring several DDoS attack vectors and aspects. Pertinent to our work here, the study examined the size of the NTP amplifier populations via global scanning, conducted a notification campaign that may have (though causality can not be shown) speeded remediation of monlist amplifiers, and reported on several aspects of the amplifier population over 13 weeks, starting in November 2013. The numbers reported in Internet scans for NTP amplifiers match our numbers closely, as expected. In addition, characterizations of the amplifier pool (e.g., that nearly half of the version command amplifiers are Cisco), likewise match our analysis. The study also examined two interesting but unrelated to our work facets of DDoS in general, one being a TCP attack vector and the other a technique for remotely identifying networks that allow IP spoofing. Unlike the Kührer *et al.* study, our work digs deeper into who NTP attacks target and with what force, as well as explores other features of the attacks (e.g., attacked ports). We also bring to bear a dataset on NTP scanning from a large ($\approx$ /8) darknet, large global traffic and attack data, and data from local ISPs impacted by these attacks.

While DDoS attacks in general and mitigation strategies in particular have seen much work, reports on large-scale measurements of DDoS attacks are few. We are not aware of any studies characterizing DDoS attacks at-scale since 2006, aside from proprietary industry reports based on commercial deployments (e.g., [31], [30]), whereas the DDoS threat landscape has evolved significantly in the ensuing years. The 2006 measurement studies examining DDoS attack activity focused on backscatter (e.g., [25]) and flow analysis (e.g., [21]). Backscatter is evident in random spoofed-source flood attacks (esp. SYN-flood), which makes it inapplicable to the specific type of attack we focus on, NTP-based reflection/amplification attacks. The relative fraction of attacks based on NTP is similar to that using SYN floods [31], though it is unclear what fraction of modern SYN floods utilize random spoofed source addresses, which are required for detection in darknets, as done by [25], and [21]. To address some of the limitations of backscatter, Mao et al. [21], argued for direct measurement of DDoS attacks (e.g., flow data), which is one of the approaches we take here.

To our knowledge, ours is also the first study to measure amplification-type DDoS attack activity via a direct global survey of records on the amplification hosts themselves. In addition, we bring to bear passive datasets with both global and local perspective.

9. CONCLUSION

Using data from a variety of vantage points, we chronicle the rapid rise and steady decline of the NTP DDoS attack phenomenon. Our analyses serve to characterize the global scale of attacks, both in terms of amplifiers as well as victims. We confirm the value of actively monitoring darknet address space, as it can help detect attack precursors, such as large-scale scanning and probing, observed prior to the onset of the first large-scale attacks. We demonstrate that, in addition to countless hours spent by engineers worldwide to install patches and filters, these events had direct measurable costs in terms of increased bandwidth loads as measured at example edge networks. Though this paper documents the lethal power of the largest DDoS attacks observed to date, our conclusions include a positive one. The network research and operations community worked to actively mitigate the effects of these attacks and these efforts have had a visible impact in diminishing the vulnerable amplifier population and reducing attack traffic. There are, however, limits to the effectiveness of such remediation efforts, as the tapering of mitigation shows. Since rapid remediation is how such attack vectors are thwarted, we are interested in future work examining why some networks remediate faster than others.

Acknowledgments

This work was supported in part by the Department of Homeland Security Science and Technology Directorate under contract numbers D08PC75388, FA8750-12-2-0314, FA8750-12-2-0235, and N66001-13-C-3001; the National Science Foundation under contract numbers CNS 1111699, CNS 091639, CNS 08311174, CNS 0751116, CNS 1330142, and CNS 1255153; and the Department of the Navy under contract N000.14-09-1-1042. We would like to thank Jared Mauch for sharing the OpenNTPProject.org dataset as well as Kirk Soluk and team at Arbor Networks for sharing traffic and attack statistics. Finally, we are grateful to Roland Dobbins, Christian Rossow, Denis Foo Kune, anonymous reviewers, and our shepherd, Sharon Goldberg, for valuable feedback on earlier drafts.

10. REFERENCES

[1] Front Range GigaPop. http://www.frgp.net/frgp-overview-2014-03-27.pdf.

[2] Open NTP Project. http://openntpproject.org/.

[3] Open Resolver Project. http://openresolverproject.org/.

[4] Arbor Networks Solution Brief: DDoS Attacks in the Gaming Industry, 2013. www.arbornetworks.com/docman-component/doc_download/687-gaming-company-defends-against-ddos-attacks.

[5] Hack Forums "Server Stress Testing" marketplace forum, Aug. 2014. http://www.hackforums.net/forumdisplay.php?fid=232.

[6] The OVH offering expands with new lines of dedicated serers., Feb 2014. https://www.ovh.com/us/newsroom/cp1355.the_ovh_offering_expands_with_new_lines_of_dedicated_servers.

[7] M. Allman. Comments on Bufferbloat. *ACM Computer Communication Review*, 43(1), Jan. 2013.

[8] D. Anstee, A. Cockburn, G. Sockrider, and C. Morales. Arbor Networks Worldwide Infrastructure Security Report, 2014. http://pages.arbornetworks.com/rs/arbor/images/WISR2014.pdf.

[9] Arbor Networks. www.arbornetworks.com.

[10] M. Bailey, E. Cooke, F. Jahanian, J. Nazario, and D. Watson. The internet motion sensor: A distributed blackhole monitoring system. In *Proceedings of Network and Distributed System Security Symposium (NDSS '05)*, pages 167–179, 2005.

[11] K. Benson, A. Dainotti, k. Claffy, and E. Aben. Gaining Insight into AS-level Outages Through Analysis of Internet Background Radiation. In *Proceedings of the 2012 ACM Conference on CoNEXT Student Workshop*, CoNEXT Student '12, 2012.

[12] S. O. Blog. Hackers Spend Christmas Break Launching Large Scale NTP-Reflection Attacks, Dec 2013. http://www.symantec.com/connect/blogs/hackers-spend-christmas-break-launching-large-scale-ntp-reflection-attacks.

[13] L. Constantin. OVH's Own NTP Servers Used in Attack, Feb 2014. http://news.techworld.com/security/3501549/attackers-use-ntp-reflection-in-huge-ddos-attack/.

[14] J. Czyz, K. Lady, S. G. Miller, M. Bailey, M. Kallitsis, and M. Karir. Understanding IPv6 Internet Background Radiation. In *Proceedings of the ACM SIGCOMM Internet Measurement Conference (IMC'13), Barcelona, Spain*, 2013.

[15] A. Dainotti, C. Squarcella, E. Aben, K. C. Claffy, M. Chiesa, M. Russo, and A. Pescapé. Analysis of Country-wide Internet Outages Caused by Censorship. In *Proceedings of the 2011 ACM SIGCOMM Internet Measurement Conference (IMC'11)*, pages 1–18. ACM, 2011.

[16] X. Dimitropoulos, P. Hurley, A. Kind, and M. P. Stoecklin. On the 95-percentile billing method. In *Proceedings of the Passive and Active Network Measurement Conference (PAM'09)*, 2009.

[17] J. Fleury. Good News: Vulnerable NTP Servers Closing Down, Feb 2014. http://blog.cloudflare.com/good-news-vulnerable-ntp-servers-closing-down.

[18] D. Goodin. New DoS attacks taking down game sites deliver crippling 100Gbps floods, Jan 2014. http://arstechnica.com/security/2014/01/new-dos-attacks-taking-down-game-sites-deliver-crippling-100-gbps-floods/.

[19] M. Karami and D. McCoy. Understanding the Emerging Threat of DDoS-as-a-Service. In *Presented as part of the 6th USENIX Workshop on Large-Scale Exploits and Emergent Threats*. USENIX, 2013.

[20] M. Kührer, T. Hupperich, C. Rossow, and T. Holz. Exit from Hell? Reducing the Impact of Amplification DDoS Attacks. In *Proceedings of the 23rd USENIX Security Symposium*, August 2014.

[21] Z. M. Mao, V. Sekar, O. Spatscheck, J. Van Der Merwe, and R. Vasudevan. Analyzing Large DDoS Attacks Using Multiple Data Sources. In *Proceedings of the 2006 SIGCOMM workshop on Large-scale attack defense*, pages 161–168. ACM, 2006.

[22] Merit Network, Inc. www.merit.edu.

[23] D. Mills, J. Martin, J. Burbank, and W. Kasch. Network Time Protocol Version 4: Protocol and Algorithms Specification. RFC 5905, 2010.

[24] M. Mimoso. Volume of NTP Amplification Attacks Getting Louder, Apr 2014. http://threatpost.com/volume-of-ntp-amplification-attacks-getting-louder/105763.

[25] D. Moore, C. Shannon, D. J. Brown, G. M. Voelker, and S. Savage. Inferring internet denial-of-service activity. *ACM Transactions on Computer Systems (TOCS)*, 24(2):115–139, 2006.

[26] K. Orland. Multiple gaming platforms hit with apparent DDoS attacks, Jan 2014. http://arstechnica.com/gaming/2014/01/multiple-gaming-platforms-hit-with-apparent-ddos-attacks/.

[27] V. Paxson. An analysis of using reflectors for distributed denial-of-service attacks. *ACM SIGCOMM Computer Communication Review*, 31(3):38–47, 2001.

[28] N. Perlroth. Tally of Cyber Extortion Attacks on Tech Companies Grows, Jun 2014. http://bits.blogs.nytimes.com/2014/06/19/tally-of-cyber-extortion-attacks-on-tech-companies-grows/.

[29] K. Poulsen. FBI busts alleged DDoS Mafia, Aug. 2004. http://www.securityfocus.com/news/9411.

[30] M. Prince. Technical Details Behind a 400Gbps NTP Amplification DDoS Attack, Feb 2014. http://blog.cloudflare.com/technical-details-behind-a-400gbps-ntp-amplification-ddos-attack.

[31] Prolexic. Prolexic Quarterly Global DDoS Attack Report: Q1 2014, Apr. 2014. http://www.prolexic.com/knowledge-center-ddos-attack-report-2014-q1.html.

[32] C. Rossow. Amplification Hell: Revisiting Network Protocols for DDoS Abuse. In *Proceedings of the 2014 Network and Distributed System Security Symposium, NDSS*, San Diego, CA, 2014.

[33] C. Systems. Cisco Event Response: Network Time Protocol Amplification Distributed Denial of Service Attacks, Feb. 2014. http://www.cisco.com/web/about/security/intelligence/ERP-NTP-DDoS.html.

[34] The Spamhaus Project - PBL. http://www.spamhaus.org/pbl/.

[35] E. Wustrow, M. Karir, M. Bailey, F. Jahanian, and G. Houston. Internet Background Radiation Revisited. In *Proceedings of the 10th ACM SIGCOMM Conference on Internet Measurement (IMC '10)*, Melbourne, Australia, November 2010.

[36] J. Zhang, Z. Durumeric, M. Bailey, M. Karir, and M. Liu. On the Mismanagement and Maliciousness of Networks. In *Proceedings of the Network and Distributed System Security Symposium (NDSS '14)*, San Diego, CA, February 2014.

DNSSEC and Its Potential for DDoS Attacks

A Comprehensive Measurement Study

Roland van Rijswijk-Deij
University of Twente and SURFnet bv
r.m.vanrijswijk@utwente.nl

Anna Sperotto
University of Twente
a.sperotto@utwente.nl

Aiko Pras
University of Twente
a.pras@utwente.nl

ABSTRACT

Over the past five years we have witnessed the introduction of DNSSEC, a security extension to the DNS that relies on digital signatures. DNSSEC strengthens DNS by preventing attacks such as cache poisoning. However, a common argument against the deployment of DNSSEC is its potential for abuse in Distributed Denial of Service (DDoS) attacks, in particular reflection and amplification attacks. DNS responses for a DNSSEC-signed domain are typically larger than those for an unsigned domain, thus, it may seem that DNSSEC could actually worsen the problem of DNS-based DDoS attacks. The potential for abuse in DNSSEC-signed domains has, however, never been assessed on a large scale.

In this paper we establish ground truth around this open question. We perform a detailed measurement on a large dataset of DNSSEC-signed domains, covering 70% (2.5 million) of all signed domains in operation today, and compare the potential for amplification attacks to a representative sample of domains without DNSSEC. At first glance, the outcome of these measurements confirms that DNSSEC indeed worsens the DDoS phenomenon. Closer examination, however, gives a more nuanced picture. DNSSEC really only makes the situation worse for one particular query type (ANY), for which responses may be over 50 times larger than the original query (and in rare cases up to 179×). We also discuss a number of mitigation strategies that can have immediate impact for operators and suggest future research directions with regards to these mitigation strategies.

Categories and Subject Descriptors

C.2 [**Computer-Communication Networks**]: Miscellaneous; C.4 [**Performance of Systems**]: Measurement Techniques

Keywords

DNS; DNSSEC; DDoS; amplification attack; reflection attack; measurements; denial-of-service; attack

IMC'14, November 5–7, 2014, Vancouver, BC, Canada.
Copyright 2014 ACM 978-1-4503-3213-2/14/11 ...$15.00.
http://dx.doi.org/10.1145/2663716.2663731.

1. INTRODUCTION

Since they were first seen at scale at the turn of the century [1], Distributed Denial of Service (DDoS) attacks have become one of the biggest threats to the Internet's security and stability. The scale of DDoS attacks keeps growing; the "biggest DDoS ever" of 300 Gbit/s in early 2013[1] has already been surpassed this year by an attack that was 25% larger in volume[2].

These large volume attacks usually rely on the same basic principles. First, they use *spoofing*. Spoofing allows the attacker to falsify the source IP in a request to some network service, resulting in the response to this request being sent to the falsified source IP (this is known as *reflection*). Second, attackers leverage *amplification*, the principle that some network protocols return a large answer to a relatively small request. Amplification is of particular interest to an attacker since a small investment in attack traffic results in large attack volumes.

A commonly used DDoS attack is *DNS amplification* (as e.g. Arbor Networks' annual security report [2] shows). As the name suggests, this attack relies on bandwidth amplification using the DNS protocol, where amplification is defined as $\frac{response\ size}{query\ size}$. Typical DNS requests are in the order of magnitude of $20-60$ bytes in size. The classic DNS protocol [3] limits responses to at most 512 bytes; assuming a request size of 40 bytes this already yields an amplification factor of $\frac{512}{40} \approx 12.8$. More recent extensions to DNS that allow for larger responses easily result in amplification factors of 100 or more.

Over the past six years, since Dan Kaminsky disclosed a serious vulnerability in the DNS protocol [4], a major overhaul of the DNS has been underway: the introduction of the DNS Security Extensions (DNSSEC) protocol. This deployment is now bearing fruit; where in 2008 there were a handful of DNSSEC-signed domains, the total number now tops 3.5 million[3]. One of the key features of the DNSSEC protocol is the introduction of digital signatures in DNS responses. Consequently, the size of DNS responses increases. Many experts consider this a major drawback of DNSSEC (e.g. Cowperthwaite & Somayaji [5]) and noted opponents of DNSSEC cite this as one of the reasons why they feel DNSSEC should not be used (e.g. Bernstein [6]).

Although the DDoS potential keeps coming up time and again in discussions about DNSSEC, very little ground truth

[1] `http://www.bbc.com/news/technology-21954636`

[2] `http://www.bbc.com/news/technology-26136774`

[3] based on statistical sources listed at `http://www.internetsociety.org/deploy360/dnssec/statistics/`

exists about the actual DDoS potential of the millions of DNSSEC-signed domains that are online today. This leads us to the main question we will answer in this paper: *How bad is DNSSEC really?*

Contribution.

In this paper, we provide the first comprehensive measurement of the DDoS potential of DNSSEC. Our measurements encompass 70% of all DNSSEC-signed domains in operation today and is based on data from six major top-level domains (TLDs) each with a significant number (> 10K) of signed domains. We compare the DDoS potential of DNSSEC-signed domains to a representative sample of domains without DNSSEC. Analysis of our measurements shows that the average amplification of DNSSEC exceeds that of regular DNS many times (by a factor of 6× - 12×). At first glance, this is worrying. Looking deeper, however, it becomes evident that extreme amplification only occurs for a certain type of query (ANY) that is often abused for amplification attacks. For "normal" DNS queries, the picture is much more nuanced and does not warrant some claims that DNSSEC should not be deployed [5, 6]. Next to that, a number of measures can be taken to dampen the DDoS potential of DNSSEC significantly, although further work in this area is required.

To encourage further study we make the data collected for our measurements available as open data to the Internet measurement community (see Sec. 8).

Organization of this paper.

This paper is organized as follows: Sec. 2 provides background material on DNS amplification as an attack method. Sec. 3 describes our methodology and measurement setup. In Sec. 4 we discuss the data sets collected during our measurements. Sec. 5 gives a detailed analysis of the data we obtained. Sec. 6 provides an overview of current countermeasures based on the literature and calls for the introduction of additional countermeasures. We discuss related work in Sec. 7. Finally, we draw conclusions and suggest future research directions in Sec. 8.

2. BACKGROUND

2.1 DNS amplification: a brief primer

2.1.1 Attacks using open resolvers

Fig. 1 shows how DNS amplification attacks work. Attacks are initiated from a swarm of machines (left-hand side of the figure) under the control of the attacker. The attacker uses this swarm to send large numbers of DNS queries in which the sender IP address is spoofed to be the victim's IP address (bottom middle of the figure). Queries are sent ① to so-called *open DNS resolvers*. These are misconfigured DNS resolvers that do not restrict which clients are allowed to send them queries. In turn, the open resolvers will – if the query result is not cached – contact the appropriate authoritative DNS servers ② to resolve the query. Finally, the open resolvers will send the responses ③ to the victim. In general, the queries ① are small whereas the responses ③ are large, hence achieving amplification.

Unfortunately, open resolvers are plentiful on the Internet. Kührer et al. [7] report observing between 23 and 25.5 million open resolvers during weekly Internet-wide scans over a

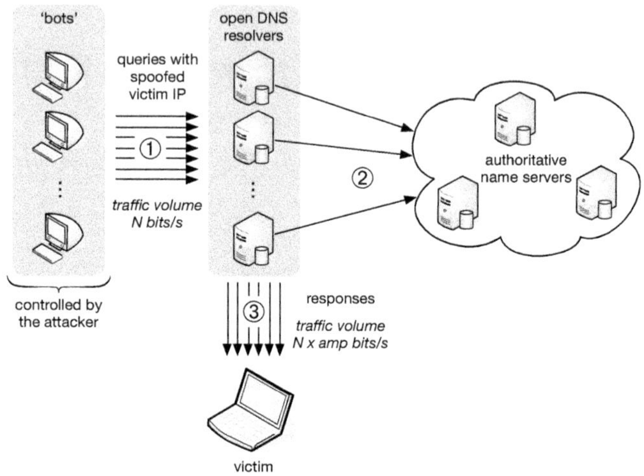

Figure 1: DNS amplification attack

period of 4 months between November 2013 and February 2014. This makes this attack easy to carry out and thus attractive for attackers.

2.1.2 DNS extensions (EDNS0)

Typically, the goal of an attacker is to achieve a high amplification factor. This gives him the best return on investment where he only needs to generate a small amount of traffic for a large attack. With the introduction of the EDNS0 extension [8] larger DNS responses (than the original 512 bytes) become possible. EDNS0 allows clients and servers to specify the maximum response size they support. Fig. 2 shows whether clients to one of SURFnet's[4] authoritative name servers use EDNS0. As the figure shows, about two thirds of clients use EDNS0; earlier research (e.g. [9]) shows that this figure is similar for other name servers across the Internet. The prevalent configuration for EDNS0 is to set the maximum response size to approximately 4Kbytes. Fig. 3 shows the maximum response size reported by clients of the same name server as in Fig. 2, with around 90% advertising a size over 4000 bytes. Again, this matches earlier results reported by Kreibich et al. [9].

[4]The National Research and Education Network in the Netherlands, `http://www.surf.nl/en/about-surf/subsidiaries/surfnet`

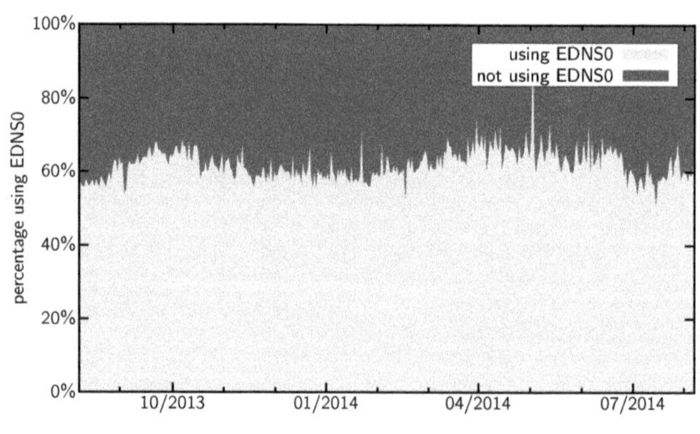

Figure 2: EDNS0 use for `ns1.surfnet.nl`

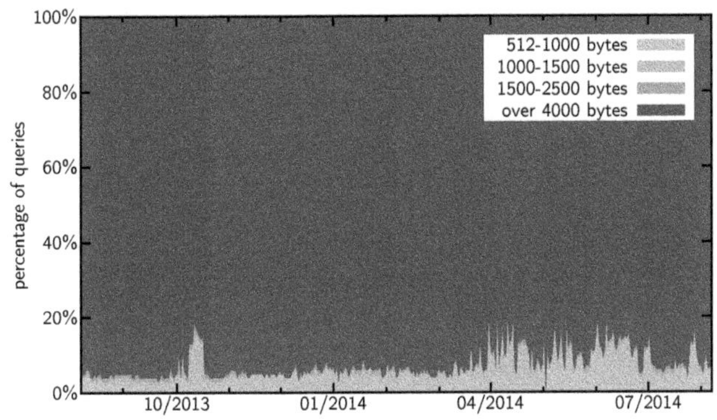

Figure 3: Advertised EDNS0 maximum response size for `ns1.surfnet.nl`

In theory, given a query size of 40 bytes, an amplification of $\frac{4096}{40} \approx 102.4$ is achievable. Table 1 gives some examples of the theoretical attack volumes that can be achieved if the attacker generates 100Mbit/s in queries for various amplification factors.

Q-size (bytes)	R-size (bytes)	Ampl. (factor)	Attacker (bits/s)	Victim (bits/s)
40	512	12.8	100M	1.28G
40	1472	36.8	100M	3.68G
40	4096	102.4	100M	10.24G

Table 1: Theoretical effect of DNS amplification

As the table shows, when using EDNS0's expanded maximum response size, significant attack results can be achieved with a relatively small investment in bandwidth on the side of the attacker.

2.1.3 *Crafted domains*

Also of interest is how attackers select the DNS query to use in the attack. One current practice is that attackers craft special domains for which certain DNS queries are guaranteed to return large responses. Vaughn & Evron [10], for instance, analyse a case where an attacker crafted a domain with a large `TXT` record that guaranteed a large response to certain queries. A particularly interesting query type for attackers to abuse is the `ANY` query; when faced with such a query, name servers are supposed to return all record types for the name specified in the query. In practice, a combination of both a crafted domain as well as the use of `ANY` queries are often observed. In our own research group, as part of another project in which we are investigating "DDoS-for-hire" services [11] we have observed a number of DNS amplification attacks, most of which used EDNS0, `ANY` queries and crafted domains.

2.2 Benefits DNSSEC offers to the attacker

There are a number of "hinderances" for attackers given the attack methodology described in the previous subsections:

- bandwidth on the open resolvers that are abused for the attack may be scarce (for instance because the open resolver is on a DSL CPE device), necessitating the use of large numbers of amplifiers;
- creating crafted domains makes the attacker vulnerable to prosecution since domain registrations can – sometimes – be traced back to the attacker;
- crafted domains may be taken down when discovered;
- filtering of responses for crafted domains can be a possible mitigation strategy for victims.

DNSSEC-signed domains offer an attractive alternative to attackers since they help avoid the hinderances described above. Given the high number of signed domains, it gets more interesting to directly abuse authoritative name servers for DNSSEC-signed domains, instead of open resolvers; it is more likely that authoritative name servers have sufficient bandwidth available than e.g. open resolvers on DSL CPE devices. Also, instead of crafting a dedicated domain, attackers can now choose from a wide range of DNSSEC-signed domains for which the answers to e.g. `ANY` queries are most likely quite large due to the inclusion of DNSSEC key material and signatures. This makes attackers less vulnerable to discovery, prosecution and take-down of the crafted domains. Finally, DNS responses for legitimate DNSSEC-signed domains are much harder to filter since filtering is likely to also impact legitimate queries and responses.

These benefits to attackers underline the necessity of establishing ground truth about the actual DDoS potential of the already large and growing number of DNSSEC-signed domains. With this data in hand, it becomes possible to develop targeted strategies to address this potentially dangerous side effect of deploying DNSSEC.

The importance of studying this topic now is also emphasised by the fact that there have already been attacks that abuse DNSSEC-signed domains for amplification. In mid-2012 many organizations across the Internet saw their DNSSEC-signed domains being abused directly on authoritative name servers for amplification attacks. Documentation about these attacks is, unfortunately, not available as they were mainly discussed in private by large operators, on mailing lists and at meetings such as RIPE and the IETF. The lead author of this paper, however, was involved in many of these discussions. An indirect discussion of these attacks was written up by Cisco in their security blog[5].

We note that the DNS and DNSSEC community (consisting of network engineers, DNS software developers and organisations concerned with online security) has already started to take steps to mitigate the dangers of DNSSEC-based amplification attacks by introducing Response Rate Limiting (RRL), which is discussed in Sec. 6.

3. METHODOLOGY

3.1 High-level goals

Our high-level goal, as stated in Sec. 1, is to gauge the DDoS potential of DNSSEC-signed domains in comparison to unsigned domains. In order to achieve this goal, we perform a large scale measurement of all DNSSEC-signed domains in six top-level domains (TLDs) that have large numbers of signed domains. We compare these against a representative sample of unsigned domains in the same TLDs.

[5]Case study 2 in `http://blogs.cisco.com/security/real-world-dns-abuse-finding-common-ground/`

3.2 Acceptable upper limit for amplification

An important question to ask – and one that is difficult to answer – is what is an acceptable upper limit on the amplification possible for a particular domain on a particular server. The simple answer is that any amplification is bad, but such an answer is too simple, since the DNS protocol already inherently has some amplification effect.

As we outlined in the previous section, EDNS0 vastly increases the amplification potential in DNS. Since – other than combating open resolvers – no large scale action has been taken to reduce the amplification potential in pre-EDNS0 classic DNS, we take the maximum amplification achievable using classic DNS as an upper limit. We calculate[6] this maximum achievable amplification by 1) assuming a query for the shortest name in a domain (e.g. "`x.com`"), which will consequently result in the smallest query and 2) a response that uses the maximum allowed size for regular DNS (512 bytes). For our example (`x.com`) this yields an amplification of $\frac{response\ size}{query\ size} = \frac{512}{23} \approx 22.3$.

3.3 Query types

We selected a number of queries to perform for each domain. These queries are specified below, together with a rationale for why we selected this particular query type:

- `ANY` – as explained in Sec. 2.1.2 this query results in the largest possible response since it includes all resource records for the queried name.
- `MX` – returns the names of mail exchangers for the domain; domains usually have more than one mail exchanger hence the answer to this query may be relatively large.
- `NS` – returns all authoritative name servers for a domain; again, domains usually have more than one authoritative name server, thus the answer to this query may also be relatively large.
- `A` – returns the IPv4 address(es) for the queried name and is typically the most common DNS query performed for a domain.
- `AAAA` – returns the IPv6 address(es) for the queried name and is another common query type since most modern software will look for both the IPv4 and the IPv6 address of a host.
- `TXT` – returns textual information for the queried name; this can, for instance, be information about mail handling for the domain (used by spam filters). Additionally, as mentioned in Sec. 2.1.3 this query type is sometimes used by attackers in domains especially crafted for amplification attacks.

For the latter three query types (`A`, `AAAA` and `TXT`) we perform multiple queries. One for the so-called apex record (denoted by `@`), one for the name `www` under the domain and one for the name `mail`. We expect that at least one of these names exists in most domains.

For DNSSEC-signed domains we also measure the answer to two DNSSEC-specific query types:

- `DNSKEY` – returns the set of public keys required to validate signatures in a domain. The answer is usually large as there is often more than one key and individual key records are large as RSA keys of sizes 1024- and 2048-bits are commonly used (as suggested in [12] and because these are default values for many DNSSEC implementations).
- `NSEC(3)` – this is not a query type as such, but is the record type that is returned when the queried name does not exist; `NSEC(3)` is also known as *authenticated denial of existence* and proves with a digital signature that the queried name does not exist. Especially responses of the newer variant `NSEC3` are likely to be quite large.

Each individual query is performed once using classic DNS and once using EDNS0 with the EDNS0 maximum response size set to 32768[7]. For DNSSEC-signed domains we also perform the query with EDNS0 and the DNSSEC OK (DO) flag set to `true`, to get DNSSEC-signed responses.

3.4 Metrics

The metrics we record for each query are:

- the query size (DNS UDP datagram size);
- the response size (DNS UDP datagram size, possibly reassembled from multiple UDP fragments);
- the amplification factor (defined as $\frac{response\ size}{query\ size}$);
- the EDNS0 maximum response size reported by the authoritative name server (puts an upper bound on the maximum amplification that can be achieved using this particular name server);
- whether or not the response was truncated (this indicates that the authoritative name server was unable or unwilling to return all requested data in the response), and indicates that the querying host should fall back to TCP to get the full response;
- the number of answers in the response;
- the number of authority records in the response (in most responses including this information is optional and indicates which name servers are authoritative for the queried name);
- the number of additional records in the response (these optional records can for instance specify IP addresses for name servers included in the authority section);
- the number of distinct resource record types in the response.

[6]Note that this is not just a theoretical value; analysis of our measurements shows that each measured TLD has a non-negligible number of domains that meet this pattern (small query, maximum size response) when queried using classic DNS.

[7]We chose this value to also register results that exceed the commonly used maximum response size of 4KB; we decided not to use the maximum value (65535) since we did not want to risk running into possible boundary conditions in DNS software implementations.

To ensure that we are not inadvertently including domains of one kind in the other data set, we check for each domain whether it is DNSSEC-signed or not (by checking the presence of `DNSKEY` records). If the domain turns out to belong to another category than expected, we exclude this domain from the measurement. Equally, those domains for which we are unable to determine the set of authoritative name servers or for which none of the authoritative name servers responds to queries are excluded from the data sets. We note that, for reasons of efficiency, we attempt each query only once, since authoritative name servers are generally always online.

3.5 Measurement software

To perform the measurements we developed two applications. The first is a zone file parser, which given the size of the DNS zones for TLDs, we needed specially tailored software for. The parser application is able to extract DNSSEC secure delegations, i.e. DNS delegations for which a DNSSEC chain of trust is established by including one or more `DS` records in the TLD (see Sec. 5 of [13]). It is also able to extract regular domains from the zone. The parser stores the extracted domain names in a SQLite database. Optionally, the application can take a random sample of domains.

The second application is a scanner application. This application operates on the database created by the zone file parser and for each domain in the database will perform the queries outlined in Sec. 3.4. The application is massively parallel and launches several hundreds of threads to perform the scan. Scanning takes place in two phases. In phase one, the application determines the set of authoritative name servers for each domain in the database and the corresponding IPv4 and IPv6 addresses for these name servers. In phase two, the application sends the queries described in Sec. 3.4 to each individual IP address for each name server of each domain. After each set of queries to a single IP address, the domain is placed back at the end of the queue until no more IP addresses remain for the domain to be scanned in which case it is marked as completed. This design choice ensures that no excessive amounts of queries for a single domain are sent in bursts while keeping the amount of state the scanner needs to maintain manageable. We found that this strategy strikes an optimal balance between the load imposed on the scanning system as well as the scanned systems.

Both applications make extensive use of the LDNS library by NLnet Labs[8], a popular software package that provides a comprehensive set of DNS-related functions.

Note that the SQLite database schema was designed such that the data can easily be anonymized. This was done on purpose because the resulting data sets will be shared as open data with the research community.

3.6 Ethical considerations

As mentioned in the previous section, we took particular care to ensure that our measurements do not impose an undue burden on authoritative name servers we scan. To this end we made deliberate design choices as discussed in Sec. 3.5. In addition to this, we monitored our experiment while it was running to check if the design worked as foreseen. Additionally, we only performed legitimate queries that are expected to be part of day-to-day traffic to authoritative name servers.

With respect to the data sets for the TLDs we used, we obtained these through specific processes established by the TLD operator or under a specific contract with individual TLDs. In both cases, we took care to inform the TLDs about the purpose for which we were going to use the data and obtained their consent.

[8]`http://www.nlnetlabs.nl/projects/ldns/`

4. DATA SETS

4.1 Source data

TLD	Data obtained	#domains	#DNSSEC	
.com	Full zone	113.1M	326.5k	(0.3%)
.net	Full zone	15.2M	69.5k	(0.5%)
.org	Full zone	10.3M	37.6k	(0.4%)
.nl	Selection	5.4M	1696.1k	(31.2%)
.se	Full zone	1.4M	334.9k	(24.8%)
.uk	Selection	10.6M	10.2k	(0.1%)

Table 2: Overview of source data

We obtained data covering 70% of all 3.5 million DNSSEC-signed domains from six different top-level domains. Tab. 2 lists the TLDs from which we obtained data. The table lists the type of data obtained (either the full zone or a selection containing all secure delegations and a random sample of unsigned domains), the total number of domains in the TLD and the number of secure delegations (as an absolute value and a percentage).

4.2 Collected data

TLD	#domains	#failed	#skipped	#queried	#queries	#auth ns
.com	326504	7416	471	318576	54.6 M	2550
.net	69552	2672	55	66814	11.0 M	2476
.org	37621	555	19	37024	6.7 M	2073
.nl	1696103	12304	1002	1682770	233.3 M	1316
.se	334880	8696	100	326067	43.3 M	3681
.uk	10225	314	10	9894	1.6 M	570

Table 3: Overview of DNSSEC data sets

TLD	#domains	#failed	#skipped	#queried	#queries	#auth ns
.com	498502	55909	2231	436593	37.6 M	72168
.net	99564	13904	355	84882	7.4 M	26396
.org	100000	11031	277	88372	7.5 M	27761
.nl	1000000	69092	6812	921441	69.3 M	31108
.se	499999	37361	149560	311871	21.5 M	23756
.uk	26131	3883	92	21858	1.6 M	7091

Table 4: Overview of non-DNSSEC data sets

We ran two scans for each TLD in the source data set. The first scan covered all DNSSEC-signed domains in the TLD. The second scan examined a representative uniformly random sample of unsigned domains with a size in the same order of magnitude as the number of DNSSEC-signed domains in the TLD.

For each scan type Tab. 3 and Tab. 4 show the total number of domains for which queries were attempted, the number of domains for which we failed to obtain the list of authoritative name servers, the number of domains that were skipped (because they were DNSSEC-signed whereas they were expected not to be or vice versa), the actual number of domains that were successfully queried, the total number of queries included in the data set and the number of distinct authoritative name servers observed during the scan. We note that there may be a slight difference between the total number of domains for which queries were attempted (col. 2) and the number of failed, skipped and successfully queried domains added up (col. 3 + 4 + 5). This is because for a small number of domains although we were able to determine the set of authoritative name servers none of these responded to queries. Since for both the regular as well as the DNSSEC data sets this difference is very small (0.52% and 0.03% on average over all TLDs respectively) it is not shown in the table.

4.3 General observations

If we look at the result data sets in Tab. 3 and Tab. 4 three observations stand out.

1. The fraction of domains for which the set of authoritative name servers could not be determined is significantly larger for unsigned domains (on average 10.9% for unsigned domains versus 2.3% for DNSSEC-signed domains). This seems to imply that DNSSEC-signed domains are generally configured better and are more likely to have functioning delegations.
2. The ratio of distinct authoritative name servers versus the number of domains in the data set is much higher for unsigned domains (by more than a factor of 10). This is probably due to the fact that a number of large DNS operators enabled DNSSEC for all domains they manage stimulated by TLDs like .nl, .se and .org offering financial incentives for deploying DNSSEC.
3. A very high number of domains in the .se TLD were skipped in the non-DNSSEC data set because they turned out to be DNSSEC-signed after all; a random sampling of the skipped domains shows that this is very likely due to one large DNS operator having enabled DNSSEC without creating secure delegations in the parent TLD.

5. ANALYSIS

5.1 Introduction

In this section, we provide a detailed analysis of our measurements and examine the differences between regular and DNSSEC-signed domains. Rather than looking at the exact response size in bytes for different queries, we use the amplification factor as main metric. We do this because it allows for a non-biased comparison between queries for different domains independent of the length of the domain name. To illustrate this with an example, the shortest scanned domain name in `.com` is 1 character long; the query size for this domain is 34 bytes, the response size for an `ANY` query with DNSSEC enabled is 3549 bytes. This gives an amplification factor of 104.4, which is very high as we will see later. The query size for the longest name (63 characters) scanned in `.com` is 96 bytes and the response size is 3805 bytes. That only yields an amplification factor of 39.6 (around average as we will see later). If we had compared these two domains on the basis of the response size then the second domain would have been classified as "worse" than the first domain,

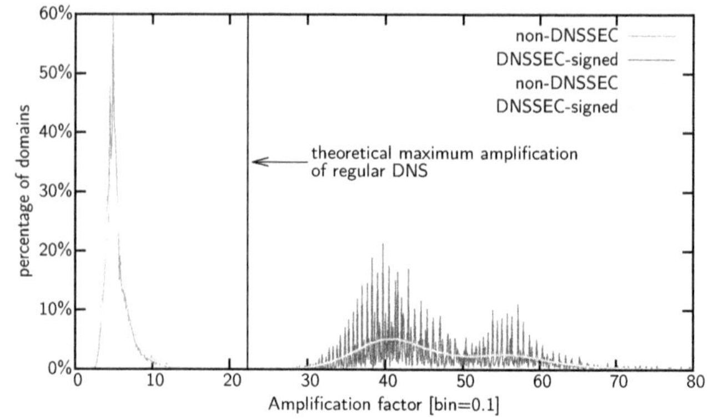

Figure 4: Amplification of `ANY` queries for `.net`

whereas in fact it is not. We also note that the amplification factor more accurately reflects the return on investment for attackers. A certain amount of traffic n sent by an attacker results in an attack that is $n \times amplification$ in size. Note that we calculate the amplification factor using the UDP datagram size for both query and response rather than using the full packet size. This prevents noise from varying packet sizes caused by differences in the underlying network technology.

Another general remark concerns the selection criteria for the graphs we plot. In most of our analyses, we only include responses we consider valid, defined as those responses that include at least one answer in the answer section and that have a response code (`RCODE`) that indicates success (`NOERROR`). We do this to exclude as many authenticated denial-of-existence answers as possible from the data sets used to plot the graphs since these may skew the data in the graphs (as especially the `A` and `AAAA` queries we perform may result in authenticated denial-of-existence as the name we query for may not exist). We cover authenticated denial-of-existence itself in a separate graph, which of course does include responses with no answers and with response codes that indicate that the name does not exist.

In our analysis, we look at three areas of interest. First we examine the main vehicle for DNS amplification attacks, `ANY` queries. Next, we look at query types for which we expect large answers. We finish by examining the bread and butter of the DNS, address queries.

5.2 ANY amplification increase

Since `ANY` queries are the most interesting for attackers, we start our analysis by looking at these in more detail. To compare the amplification factor that is achievable with an `ANY` query for regular domains and DNSSEC-signed domains we plot this factor for both types of domains in a single graph. In order to do this, we distribute the data across bins of size 0.1; plotting the actual data results in a graph as shown in Fig. 4, which shows the `ANY` amplification factor for the `.net` TLD. As can be seen, graphing the original data (thin red and blue lines) leads to a jagged graph. This is due to the fact that the amplification factor is derived from discrete values (query and response size) resulting in a bias for certain bins. To mitigate this, we have chosen to represent the data using a Bézier curve that follows the average fill of the bins (thicker cyan and green lines).

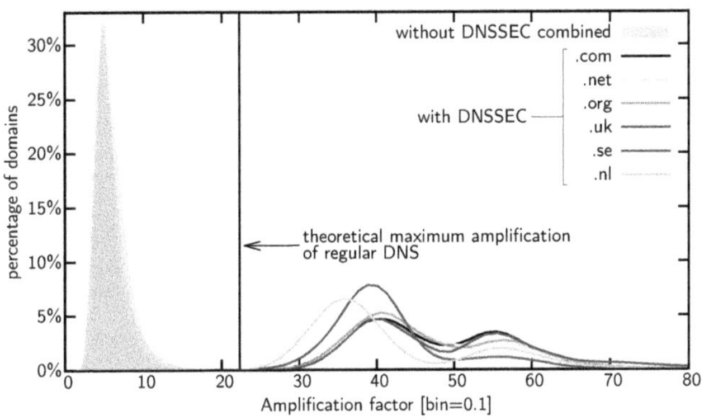

Figure 5: Amplification of ANY queries (all TLDs)

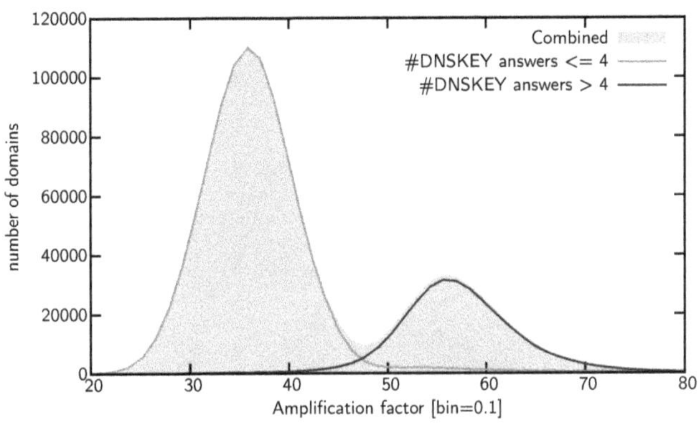

Figure 6: Examining the two peaks in .nl

The graph in Fig. 5, plotted as described above, compares the ANY amplification factor for all TLDs for which we performed measurements. Regular domains are represented by filled grey curves whereas DNSSEC-signed domains are represented using coloured lines. This approach to plotting is repeated in all other graphs that compare amplification of regular versus DNSSEC-signed domains. The vertical black line (indicated with an arrow) represents the theoretical maximum achievable amplification factor using regular DNS, which we set as an acceptable upper limit to amplification in Sec. 3.2.

Looking at Fig. 5 we see that, as expected, the amplification factor for DNSSEC-signed domains is significantly higher than for unsigned domains. On average, the amplification for unsigned domains is around 5.9 whereas for DNSSEC-signed domains the average lies around 47.2 (about 8× higher). We also note that – apart from outliers not visible in the graph – the amplification factor for ANY queries for DNSSEC-signed domains always exceeds the acceptable upper limit we set.

Next, the distribution of the amplification factors observed is much more spread out for DNSSEC-signed domains. This is as expected; a DNSSEC-signed answer includes a separate signature (RRSIG record) for each resource record set (all records of a certain type for a name). Thus, the more different resource record types in an answer the more signatures. Signature records are large (> 150 bytes for a 1024-bit signature) and contribute significantly to the amplification factor.

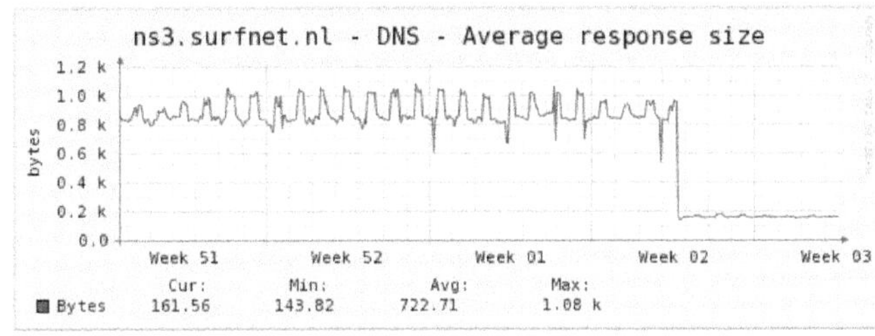

Figure 7: Effect of disabling optional response sections on ns3.surfnet.nl

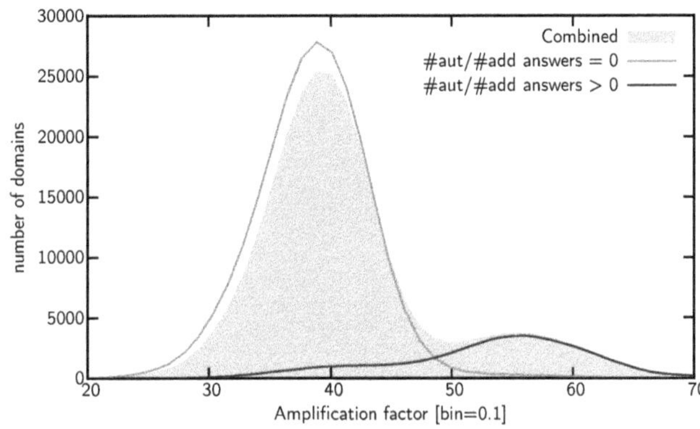

Figure 8: Examining the two peaks in .se

Finally we note that the distribution of amplification factors for DNSSEC-signed domains shows two peaks for each TLD, one around 40 and a lower peak around 55. We found two effects that play a role in this.

The first effect occurs for the majority of the TLDs we measured (.com, .net, .org, .nl and .uk). For these TLDs, the two peaks can be explained by looking at the number of DNSKEY records in the zone. The first peak coincides with having 2 DNSKEY records in the zone, the second peak coincides with having 3 or more DNSKEY records in the zone. Fig. 6 shows this correlation for the .nl TLD (the blue line in Fig. 6 corresponds to the data for .nl as graphed in Fig. 5 in orange). Note that we do not have direct data for the number of DNSKEY records per scanned domain. Rather, we derive this from the number of answers in the DNSKEY query for a domain. If this number is 4 or below (red line in Fig. 6), then there are 2 or less DNSKEYs present (4 answers means 2 DNSKEY records and 2 signatures in the answer, one signature with each key). If this number is higher than 4 (blue line in Fig. 6) then there are 3 or more DNSKEYs present. The reason for having different numbers of DNSKEY records in a domain is simple: different software implementations that use different key rollover strategies (a discussion of which is outside of the scope of this paper, for more information on DNSSEC key rollovers see e.g. [14]).

The second effect occurs for one TLD (.se) only. Interestingly, in this case the two peaks show no relation to the number of DNSKEY records. Rather, the peaks are related to whether or not the additional and authority sections in a DNS answer are filled. These sections are optional in most DNS responses (see Sec. 4 of [3]). Most DNS software implementations have a configuration option that allows administrators to disable filling of these optional sections of a DNS answer[9]. Disabling these optional responses can have a dramatic effect on the response size. Fig. 7 shows the change in average response size (a reduction of ±80%) for an authoritative name server. Especially for DNSSEC-signed domains, the difference in size can be dramatic since signatures will be included in these optional sections. In Fig. 8 we graphed the amplification for DNS responses that did not include the optional authority and additional sections (red line), the amplification for responses that did include optional sections (blue line) and the original data for `ANY` responses in `.se` (blue filled curve) corresponding to the brown line in Fig. 5.

5.2.1 *Outliers*

Fig. 5 shows the distribution in amplification factor for the majority of domains measured. There are, however, outliers that have much higher amplification factors. Tab. 5 gives an overview of the outliers. Per TLD, it shows the number of domains with an amplification factor higher than 100 as well as the absolute maximum amplification factor of any domain measured.

TLD	#amp. > 100	%	maximum amplification with DNSSEC	maximum amplification w/o DNSSEC
.com	144	(0.05%)	119.2	75.0
.net	168	(0.25%)	178.6	51.0
.org	139	(0.38%)	143.1	33.6
.nl	145	(0.01%)	131.0	80.9
.se	211	(0.06%)	120.0	63.7
.uk	26	(0.26%)	148.6	26.7

Table 5: Outliers per TLD

The table shows some staggering outliers, especially keeping in mind that an amplification factor of 100 means an attacker can mount an attack of 1Gbit/s by sending only 10Mbit/s. For comparison, the rightmost column of Tab. 5 shows the maximum amplification factor for the unsigned domains we measured. These are clearly a lot lower, with none exceeding 80.9.

5.3 Other large queries (DNSKEY, NSEC3, MX, NS, TXT)

First, we analyse two DNSSEC-specific query types, the `DNSKEY` query and authenticated denial-of-existence. As explained in Sec. 3.4, the answer to a `DNSKEY` query for a domain is likely to be large. Fig. 9 shows the amplification factor for `DNSKEY` queries for all TLDs we measured. On average 37.8% of `DNSKEY` queries yield an amplification factor that exceeds the acceptable upper limit we set in Sec. 3.2. We observe that most TLDs have two peaks in the graph; this is again caused by varying numbers of `DNSKEY` records per domain as described in the analysis of `ANY` queries in Sec. 5.2.

The other query type likely to result in large responses when DNSSEC is used, is a query that has no answer. Just like in regular DNS, a special response is returned when the name and/or record type queried for does not exist. The difference is that in DNSSEC a proof is included that the name and/or record type does not exist. This is called authenticated denial-of-existence and relies on two special record types, `NSEC` and `NSEC3`. These record types are two protocol variants that achieve the same goal. The difference between the two is that `NSEC` uses names in proofs whereas `NSEC3` uses hash values in proofs (a detailed discussion of the protocol differences is out of scope for this paper). Depending on the protocol and the type of proof required a number of `NSEC` or `NSEC3` records are included in an authenticated denial-of-existence proof, each accompanied by a signature. Fig. 10 shows the amplification factor for `NSEC(3)` responses for all TLDs measured. As the graph shows, except for some outliers, the majority of responses fall within the acceptable upper limit we set. The graph contains multiple peaks for each TLD. Analysis of the data shows that the peaks are related to the number of `NSEC(3)` records in a response.

[9]For instance, the popular DNS implementation BIND has the `minimal-responses` option, for more information see `ftp://ftp.isc.org/isc/bind9/cur/9.10/doc/arm/`

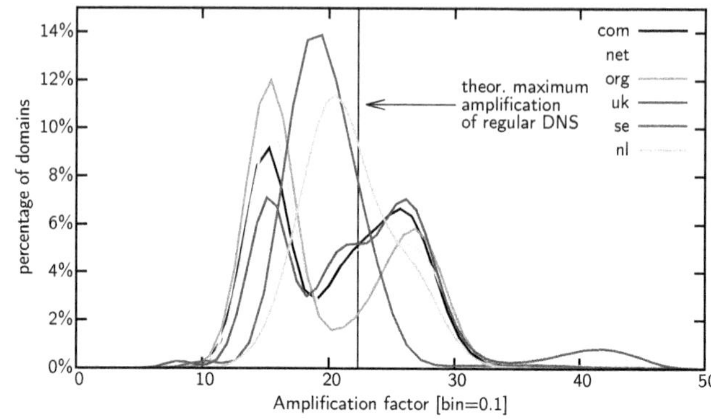

Figure 9: Amplification factor of `DNSKEY` queries

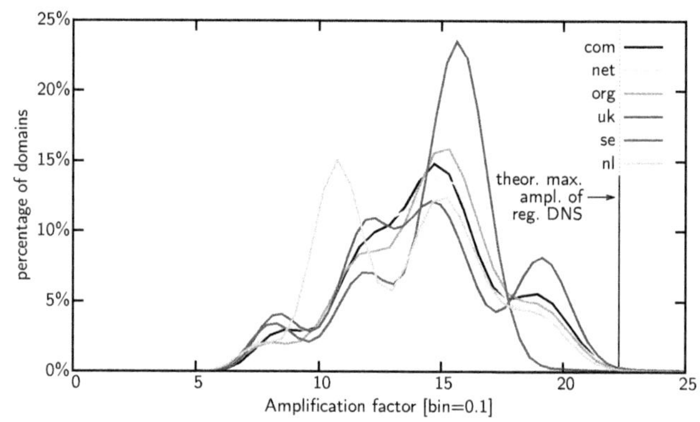

Figure 10: Amplification factor of authenticated denial-of-existence

In Sec. 3.4 on metrics we said that we expected two other types of queries, the `MX` and `NS` query types, to also yield potentially large answers. Our measurements show, however, that this is not the case. Fig. 11 and Fig. 12 respectively show a comparison between the amplification factors we measured for regular domains versus DNSSEC-signed domains for `MX` and `NS` queries. As both graphs illustrate, the increase in amplification is low (between a 2× and 3×) and – outliers excepted – remains well below the acceptable maximum upper limit we set in Sec. 3.2. This is in line with other regular queries that will be discussed in the next section.

Similarly, we discussed that the `TXT` query type, that is for instance commonly used to convey information about spam filtering, is sometime abused by attackers in specially crafted

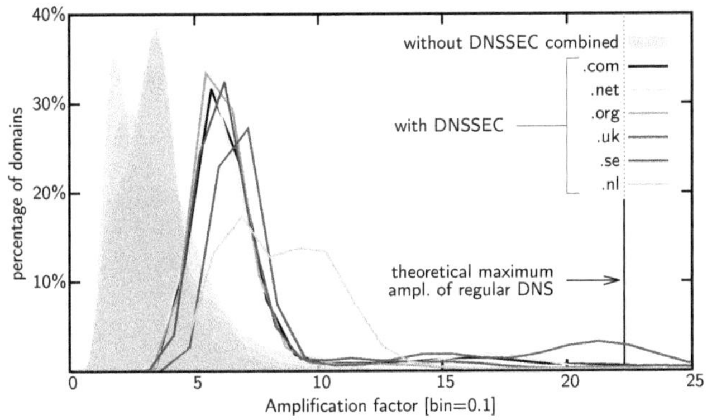

Figure 11: Amplification of MX queries

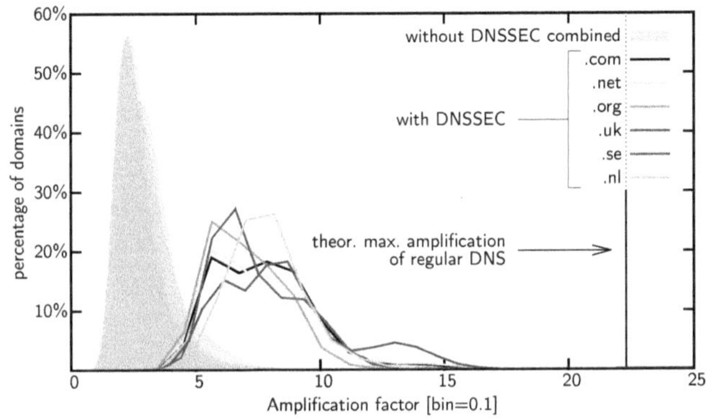

Figure 12: Amplification of NS queries

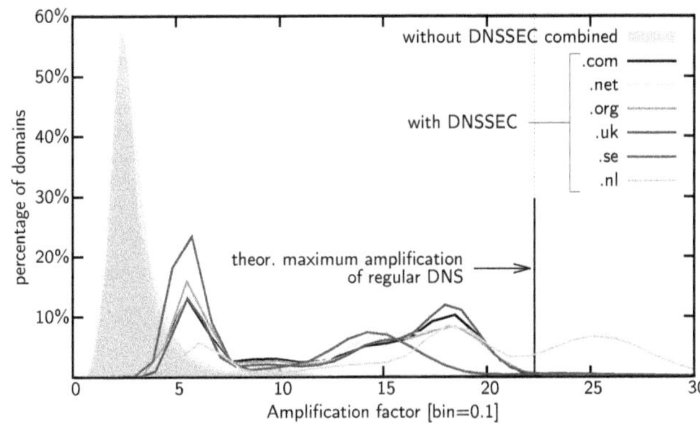

Figure 13: Amplification of TXT queries

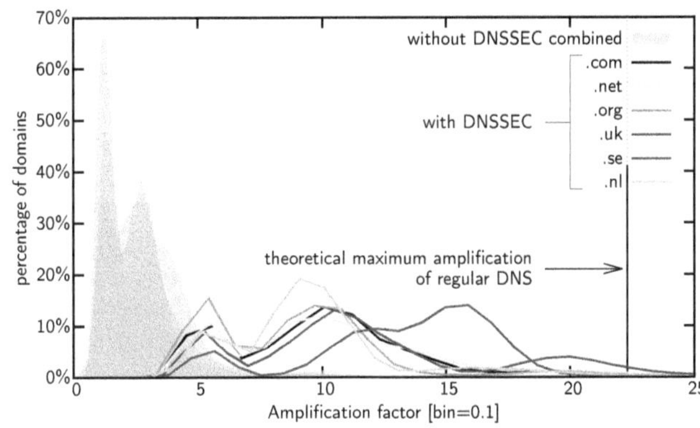

Figure 14: Amplification of A queries

domains created to perform DDoS attacks (see Sec. 2.1.3). Fig. 13 shows the comparison in amplification for `TXT` queries. As the graph shows, the majority of responses is below the acceptable upper limit. We note that for the `.nl` domain there is a small peak in responses just beyond the acceptable upper limit. Closer examination shows that this peak is caused by authenticated denial-of-existence answers. Recall from Sec. 5.1 that we only include responses in the data set that is plotted that have one or more actual answers in them. It turns out that the responses that make up this peak are `CNAME` responses. In DNS, a `CNAME` functions like an alias that refers to another name. The DNS server will attempt to expand a `CNAME` answer to include the actual record that the `CNAME` refers to. If this is not possible (because no record of the queried type exists) then it will return only the `CNAME` answer together with an authenticated denial-of-existence (`NSEC(3)`) proof in the authority section of the response. We examined the data set used to plot Fig. 13 and compared the average number of answers in the authority section for responses both below as well as above the acceptable upper limit. For responses below the limit there are about 2.98 answers in the authority section whereas for responses above the upper limit this number is 7.75. Examination of a random sample of domains combined with this information provides a clear indication that this peak is caused by authenticated denial-of-existence answers related to `CNAME` expansion. We repeated this analysis for the other TLDs and saw a similar pattern albeit with peaks at slightly lower amplification factors (between 15 and 20).

5.4 Regular queries (A, AAAA)

We end with queries for the IPv4 (`A`) and IPv6 (`AAAA`) addresses of a name, which are the bread and butter of DNS. We start with the first, `A` queries. Fig. 14 shows the comparison in amplification factor between regular and DNSSEC-signed domains. As the graph shows, the vast majority of responses to `A` queries is well below the acceptable upper limit defined in Sec. 3.2. Generally speaking, the increase in amplification for DNSSEC-signed domains is between $2\times$ and $4\times$. We examined the higher amplification factors, above 12.5 present in the graph, to find out why these responses are larger. We believe that this is caused by a configuration difference in the name servers. Responses with an amplification factor above 12.5 include significantly more answers in the authority and additional section (3.90 and 3.46 for responses with amplification > 12.5, 0.16 and 0.02 for responses with amplification < 12.5). This indicates that answers with an amplification > 12.5 come from name servers that fill the optional authority and additional sections, whereas answers with a lower amplification come from name servers configured to give minimal responses (see also Sec. 5.2).

Fig. 15 shows the situation for `AAAA` queries. The graph shows strong similarities with the graph for `TXT` records, with the majority of responses falling within the acceptable upper limit and with a small peak for the `.nl` domain just beyond the upper limit around an amplification factor of 26. Repeating the analysis we applied to `TXT` and `A` records shows that the cause of this peak is the same as for `TXT` records, namely authenticated denial-of-existence answers for `CNAME`

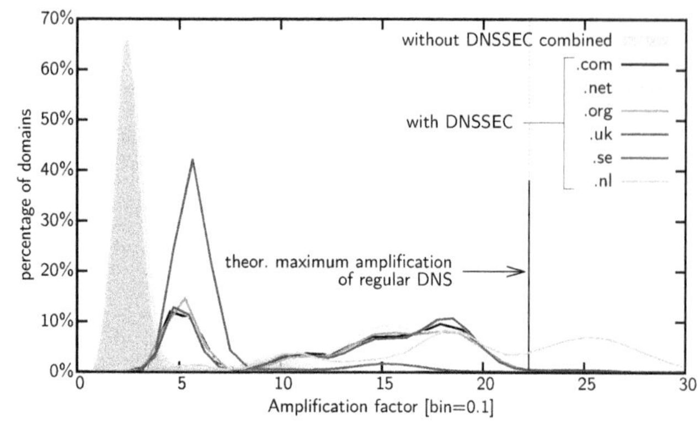

Figure 15: Amplification of AAAA queries

expansions. Again, this also proved to be the case for the other TLDs which have a similar peak around the somewhat lower amplification factor of 18.

6. COUNTERMEASURES

In Sec. 5 we showed that certain queries for DNSSEC-signed domains yield amplification factors that allow attackers to attain high attack volumes with a relatively small investment in bandwidth on their side. In this section we discuss a number of mitigation strategies to address this problem.

6.1 Ingress filtering

The root cause of any type of amplification attack is attackers having the ability to spoof source IP addresses in connectionless protocols (e.g. UDP). This problem has been known for a long time and the obvious solution is to stop source address spoofing. The solution is known as ingress filtering and is described in BCP 38 [15]. The basic premise behind ingress filtering is that network operators only allow traffic to enter their network if the source IP address is a legitimate address within their network. Although this solution is highly effective, it only works if deployed Internet-wide. Unfortunately, that is not the case. NPS runs a project that measures deployment of BCP 38[10]. Although their statistics indicate that the majority of networks implement ingress filtering, a large number still do not, making this mitigation strategy ineffective.

6.2 Response Rate Limiting

As mentioned briefly in Sec. 2.2, Response Rate Limiting (RRL) was introduced in 2012 after a slew of DNS amplification attacks that abused DNSSEC-signed domains. The idea behind RRL is that authoritative name servers rate limit outgoing responses, when responses to the same query are sent repeatedly to the same IP block[11]. At first glance, RRL can significantly dampen the impact of DNS amplification attacks. A closer examination, however, shows a number of problems:

- RRL only works for authoritative name servers; since most attacks do not directly use authoritative name servers but instead abuse open DNS resolvers (see also Sec. 2.1) its mitigating effect is limited. Especially if an attack uses queries that are cached by an open resolver, RRL on the authoritative name server for the domain abused for the attack will have little or no effect.
- As Paul Vixie's memorandum on RRL[11] mentions in Sec. 5, attackers can craft an attack that circumvents RRL by using a spread of queries in the attack rather than one single query.
- RRL can affect legitimate queries. Resolvers that do not (properly) cache results will suffer from RRL, which results in service degradation for clients behind these resolvers. Additionally, RRL can be turned into a denial-of-service weapon. By flooding authoritative name servers that use RRL with queries in which the source address is spoofed to be that of a legitimate resolver (e.g. the resolver of a large ISP) this legitimate resolver can experience service degradation in resolving specific queries on the authoritative name server under attack.

Thus, although RRL can certainly play a role in mitigation, it is not the definitive solution to name servers being abused for DNS amplification attacks.

6.3 EDNS0 cookies

Before EDNS0 was introduced the potential for amplification attacks using DNS was limited by the hard upper response size limit of 512 bytes. As we have shown in Sec. 2.1.2, EDNS0 is now in wide-spread use across the Internet. Because it allows for much larger responses, DNS amplification attacks have gained much more potential. As mentioned before, the root cause that allows for these attacks is source address spoofing. A potential solution to this is some form of source address authentication, that allows the recipient of a packet to establish that the source address has not been spoofed. An effective way to implement this is by using cookies, as proposed by Eastlake in [16]. In short, the idea is that a name server does not send large responses to a client using EDNS0 unless the client proves its authenticity using an authentication cookie established during an initial interaction between client and server. We believe that this can be a particularly effective solution to the DNS amplification attack problem.

6.4 Response size limiting

Another mitigation strategy is to limit the size of DNS responses such that no answer exceeds the acceptable upper limit for amplification we set in Sec. 3.2. The results of our analysis in Sec. 5 show that doing this would not affect most regular queries, but would probably only impact `ANY` queries. A beneficial side effect of this mitigation strategy is that it also prevents IP fragmentation of DNS responses, which is a serious stability problem affecting DNSSEC-signed domains, as described in [17]. If applied, DNS responses over UDP are restricted to a certain maximum size. Answers exceeding that size result in truncated DNS responses, forcing clients to retry the query over TCP. This effectively stops attackers from using responses larger than the chosen maximum size as TCP is connection-oriented and thus immune to source address spoofing.

[10] `http://spoofer.cmand.org/summary.php`

[11] A detailed discussion of RRL by its designer can be found at `http://ss.vix.su/~vixie/isc-tn-2012-1.txt`

6.5 Restricting or blocking ANY queries

The biggest amplification problem – if we do not consider crafted domains – is ANY queries. This begs the question whether this query type should be severely restricted or even blocked. Restricting ANY queries can be done using response size limiting (Sec. 6.4) and is automatically done by RRL (Sec. 6.2). A more extreme measure would be to block ANY queries altogether. This can only be done, however, if no legitimate use cases depend on ANY queries. We know, however, that certain software, such as qmail[12], uses ANY queries. Blocking ANY queries might thus affect some legitimate users.

Assessing the full impact of blocking ANY queries is outside the scope of this work but definitely warrants further investigation. We note that – just like RRL – blocking ANY queries is not a complete solution as other query types, such as DNSKEY queries, can still result in a significant amount of amplification.

7. RELATED WORK

Geva et al. [18] discuss DDoS attacks in a general sense. They performed simulations that illustrate the damage that attacks can cause and describe a spectrum of different DDoS attack mechanisms and various mitigation strategies against these attacks. They conclude that many defense mechanisms are problematic to deploy and that they may struggle to protect against the increasing threat level of today. A similar, but more practical and elaborate overview of DDoS attacks and defense mechanisms is given by Zargar et al. [19].

On the measurement side, Casalicchio et al. [20] describe a highly detailed reference architecture for measuring the stability and security of the DNS. They argue that the DNS is the most important infrastructure underpinning the Internet and that there is a great need to assess the health of the DNS on a continuous basis.

Rossow [21] performed measurements for 14 protocols that can be abused for amplification attacks. Where we focus on DNSSEC, Rossow covers amplification in its breadth. For DNS, Rossow considers amplification through open resolvers and directly abusing authoritative name servers. In the latter category he examines ANY queries for DNSSEC-signed domains. We corresponded with him and his data set covers 25K domains distributed over more than 70 TLDs. Rossow finds ANY amplification factors in the same range as we do, although the outliers in our data set exceed his findings and the distribution of amplification factors differs. We believe that this difference in distribution can be explained by the difference in sample size and composition; we use a much larger sample in which groups of domains hosted by a single operator may dominate. If such an operator has configured their servers such that they are less amenable to amplification then this will be reflected in the distribution of amplification factors in our results.

Highly relevant is work by Anagnostopoulos et al. [22]. They also perform extensive measurements to assess the potential impact of DNS amplification attacks. Where their work differs from our approach is that they focus on open resolvers. They measure numbers of open resolvers for three European countries and assess their capabilities (i.e. what amplification factor can be achieved by abusing them). This makes their work complementary to our study.

[12]http://fanf.livejournal.com/122220.html

8. CONCLUSIONS AND FUTURE WORK

We set out to answer the question how bad DNSSEC really makes DNS amplification. The simple conclusion from our measurements is that it is quite bad. If we only consider ANY queries, then DNSSEC-signed domains yield high amplification factors, averaging between 40 and 55. This exceeds the average amplification of regular DNS by a factor of 6×-12×. Looking deeper, however, the picture is more nuanced. For many common DNS queries, using DNSSEC results in larger responses but the amplification factor mostly stays within the acceptable upper limit (based on the maximum amplification of classic DNS) set in Sec. 3.2. Nevertheless, an attacker needs only one or a few domains with large amplification factors, and by carefully choosing a signed domain attackers can achieve significant amplification using e.g. DNSKEY queries. It is clear then that this needs to be addressed, both by mitigating the risk of carrying out a successful amplification attack as well as by improving the DNSSEC protocol, for instance by using cryptographic signature schemes with more favourable key and signature sizes that reduce the size of DNSSEC responses, such as elliptic curve digital signatures (ECDSA) [23]. We also bring back to mind that attacks with large amplification factors were already feasible without DNSSEC. Attackers already use crafted domains and can continue to do so regardless of whether DNSSEC is implemented. DNSSEC does, however, give attackers more options, such as directly abusing authoritative name servers instead of open resolvers and foregoing the use of crafted domains.

There are a number of countermeasures that can be deployed to mitigate the effect of DNS amplification attacks. The first two we discussed (BCP 38 and RRL) are already in active (albeit not universal) use. The other three, however, require further work. We consider EDNS0 cookies to be a particularly promising strategy for combating DNS amplification attacks but note that work on this approach is still at an early stage. We intend to investigate the effectiveness of this approach in a future project. Response size limiting, also requires more study. Before such a solution can become a recommended best practice the impact of this approach on legitimate DNS traffic will need to be assessed to ensure that it does not adversely affect DNS functionality. We have already looked at this on a small scale while working on [17] but a more extensive assessment is required. Blocking ANY queries, finally, also warrants further investigation as it may be a good stopgap measure against the worst amplification attacks. We note again, however, that it is certainly not a panacea as other query types can still lead to significant amplification.

As mentioned in Sec. 3.5, we will share the data sets resulting from our measurements as open data and do so on http://traces.simpleweb.org.

9. ACKNOWLEDGEMENTS

We would like to thank Siôn Lloyd (Nominet, .uk), Marco Davids (SIDN, .nl) and Patrik Wallström (IIS, .se) for helping out with DNS data for their TLDs. Additionally, we thank VeriSign for sharing data on .com and .net and the Public Interest Registry (PIR) for sharing data on .org.

We would also like to thank Christian Rossow for reviewing the draft camera-ready version of our paper.

Finally, we would like to thank Shobha Venkataraman for shepherding our paper and the anonymous reviewers for their valuable feedback on our work.

Part of this work has been supported by the EU-FP7 FLAMINGO Network of Excellence Project (318488) and by the GigaPort3 programme funded by the Dutch Economic Structure Enhancing Fund (FES).

10. REFERENCES

[1] L. Garber. Denial-of-service attacks rip the Internet. *Computer*, 33(4):12–17, April 2000.

[2] D. Anstee, A. Cockburn, and G. Sockrider. Worldwide Infrastructure Security Report. Technical report, Burlington, MA, USA, 2014.

[3] P. Mockapetris. RFC 1035 - Domain Names - Implementation and Specification, 1987.

[4] D. Kaminsky. Black Ops 2008: It's the End of the Cache As We Know It. In *Black Hat USA*, 2008.

[5] A. Cowperthwaite and A. Somayaji. The futility of DNSSec. *5th Annual Symposium on Information Assurance (ASIA10)*, page 28, 2010.

[6] D.J. Bernstein. High-speed high-security cryptography: encrypting and authenticating the whole Internet. In *27th Chaos Communication Congress (27C3)*, Berlin, 2010.

[7] M. Kührer, T. Hupperich, C. Rossow, and T. Holz. Exit from Hell? Reducing the Impact of Amplification DDoS Attacks. In *Proc. of the 23rd USENIX Security Symposium*, August 2014.

[8] J. Damas, M. Graff, and P. Vixie. RFC 6891 - Extension Mechanisms for DNS (EDNS(0)), 2013.

[9] C. Kreibich, N. Weaver, B. Nechaev, and V. Paxson. Netalyzr: Illuminating the Edge Network. In *Proceedings of IMC 2010*, pages 246–259, New York, USA, 2010. ACM Press.

[10] R. Vaughn and G. Evron. DNS Amplification Attacks (preliminary release). 2006.

[11] J.J. Santanna and A. Sperotto. Characterizing and Mitigating The DDoS-as-a-Service Phenomenon. In *8th International Conference on Autonomous Infrastructure, Management and Security (AIMS)*, LNCS, Brno, Czech Republic, 2014. Springer.

[12] O. Kolkman and R. Gieben. RFC 4641 - DNSSEC Operational Practices, 2006.

[13] R. Arends, R. Austein, M. Larson, D. Massey, and S. Rose. RFC 4034 - Resource Records for the DNS Security Extensions, 2005.

[14] O. Kolkman, W. Mekking, and R. Gieben. RFC 6781 - DNSSEC Operational Practices, Version 2, 2012.

[15] P. Ferguson and D. Senie. BCP 38 - Network Ingress Filtering: Defeating Denial of Service Attacks which employ IP Source Address Spoofing, 2000.

[16] D. Eastlake. Domain Name System (DNS) Cookies (Internet Draft), 2014.

[17] G. van den Broek, R. van Rijswijk-Deij, A. Sperotto, and A. Pras. DNSSEC Meets Real World: Dealing with Unreachability Caused by Fragmentation. *IEEE Communications Magazine*, 52(4):154–160, 2014.

[18] M. Geva, A. Herzberg, and Y. Gev. Bandwidth Distributed Denial of Service: Attacks and Defenses. *IEEE Security & Privacy*, 2013.

[19] S.T. Zargar, J. Joshi, and D. Tipper. A Survey of Defense Mechanisms Against Distributed Denial of Service (DDoS) Flooding Attacks. *IEEE Communications Surveys & Tutorials*, 15(4):2046–2069, January 2013.

[20] E. Casalicchio, M Caselli, and A Coletta. Measuring the global domain name system. *IEEE Network*, 27(1):25–31, January 2013.

[21] C. Rossow. Amplification Hell: Revisiting Network Protocols for DDoS Abuse. In *Proceedings of the 2014 Network and Distributed Systems Security Symposium (NDSS 2014)*, number February, pages 23–26, San Diego, 2014. Internet Society.

[22] M. Anagnostopoulos, G. Kambourakis, P. Kopanos, G. Louloudakis, and S. Gritzalis. DNS amplification attack revisited. *Computers & Security*, 39(February 2012):475–485, 2013.

[23] P. Hoffman and W.C.A. Wijngaards. RFC 6605 - Elliptic Curve Digital Signature Algorithm (DSA) for DNSSEC, 2012.

HILTI: An Abstract Execution Environment for Deep, Stateful Network Traffic Analysis

Robin Sommer
ICSI / LBNL
robin@icir.org

Matthias Vallentin
UC Berkeley
vallentin@icir.org

Lorenzo De Carli
University of Wisconsin-Madison
lorenzo@cs.wisc.edu

Vern Paxson
ICSI / UC Berkeley
vern@icir.org

ABSTRACT

When developing networking systems such as firewalls, routers, and intrusion detection systems, one faces a striking gap between the ease with which one can often describe a desired analysis in high-level terms, and the tremendous amount of low-level implementation details that one must still grapple with to come to a robust solution. We present HILTI, a *platform* that bridges this divide by providing to application developers much of the low-level functionality, without tying it to a specific analysis structure. HILTI consists of two parts: *(i)* an *abstract machine model* that we tailor specifically to the networking domain, directly supporting the field's common abstractions and idioms in its instruction set; and *(ii)* a *compilation strategy* for turning programs written for the abstract machine into optimized, natively executable code. We have developed a prototype of the HILTI compiler toolchain that fully implements the design's functionality, and ported exemplars of networking applications to the HILTI model to demonstrate the aptness of its abstractions. Our evaluation of HILTI's functionality and performance confirms its potential to become a powerful platform for future application development.

Categories and Subject Descriptors

C.2.0 [**Computer-Communication Networks**]: General—*Security and protection*; C.2.3 [**Computer-Communication Networks**]: Network Operations—*Network monitoring*

General Terms

Measurement; Security

Keywords

Real-time monitoring; deep packet inspection; intrusion detection

1. INTRODUCTION

Deep, stateful network packet inspection represents a crucial building block for applications that analyze network traffic. However, when developing systems such as firewalls, routers, and network intrusion detection systems (NIDS), one faces a striking gap between the ease with which one can often describe the desired analysis in high-level terms ("search for this pattern in HTTP requests"), and the tremendous amount of low-level implementation details that one must still grapple with to come to an efficient and robust implementation. When applications reconstruct a network's high-level picture from zillions of packets, they must not only operate efficiently to achieve line-rate performance under real-time constraints, but also deal securely with a stream of untrusted input that requires conservative fail-safe processing. Despite such implementation challenges, our community sees little reuse of existing, well-proven functionality across applications. While individual projects invest significant resources into optimizing their particular implementation, new efforts can rarely leverage the accumulated experience that such systems have garnered through years of deployment. Not only do they end up building much of same functionality from scratch each time, but they also tend to fall into the same pitfalls that others had to master before.

In this work we set out to overcome this situation. We present a novel *platform* for building network traffic analysis applications that provides much of the standard low-level functionality without tying it to a specific analysis structure. Our system consists of two parts: *(i)* an *abstract machine model* that we tailor specifically to the networking domain, directly supporting the field's common abstractions and idioms in its instruction set; and *(ii)* a compilation strategy for turning programs written for the abstract machine into optimized, natively executable code. Our abstract machine model has at its core a *high-level intermediary language for traffic inspection (HILTI)* that provides rich data structures, powerful control flow primitives, extensive concurrency support, a secure memory model protecting against unintended control and data flows, and potential for domain-specific optimizations that include transparent integration of non-standard hardware capabilities. Conceptually, HILTI provides a *middle-layer* situated between the operating system and a *host application*, operating invisibly to the application's end-users who do not directly interact with it. An application leverages HILTI by *compiling* its analysis/functionality from its own high-level description (like a firewall's rules or a NIDS's signature set) into HILTI code. HILTI's compiler then translates it further down into native code.

We have developed a prototype of the HILTI compiler toolchain that fully supports all of the design's functionality, and we have ported a set of example networking applications to the HILTI machine model that demonstrate the aptness of its abstractions, including the BinPAC protocol parser generator [36] and Bro's scripting language [37]. Even though performance does not yet represent a particular focus of the prototype's code generator, our evaluation with real-world network traffic shows that already the compiled code executes with generally similar performance as native imple-

IMC'14, November 5–7, 2014, Vancouver, BC, Canada.

ACM 978-1-4503-3213-2/14/11 ...$15.00.
http://dx.doi.org/10.1145/2663716.2663735.

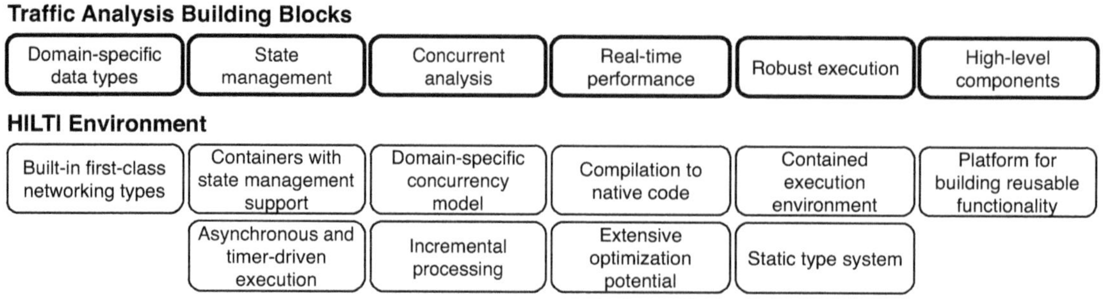

Figure 1: Building blocks of network traffic applications and how HILTI supports them.

mentations, with the potential to significantly outperform them in the future as we further optimize the toolchain. We are releasing both HILTI and our example applications as open-source software to the community [6].

As one of HILTI's overarching objectives we aim to build a platform that integrates much of the knowledge that the networking community has collected over decades into a single framework for applications to build upon. While in this work we focus on the low-level machine model, we envision HILTI to eventually ship with an extensive library of reusable higher-level components, such as packet reassemblers, session tables with built-in state management, and parsers for specific protocols. By providing both the means to implement such components as well as the glue for their integration, HILTI can allow application developers to focus on their core functionality, relieving them from low-level technical work that others have previously implemented.

We structure the remainder of this paper as follows. We motivate our work in §2 by examining the potential for sharing functionality across networking applications. We present HILTI's design in §3 and showcase four example applications in §4. We discuss our implementation in §5, and then evaluate HILTI in §6. We discuss some broader aspects in §7, and summarize related work in §8. We conclude in §9.

2. SHARING FUNCTIONALITY

Internally, different types of networking applications—packet filters, stateful firewalls, routers, switches, intrusion detection systems, network-level proxies, and even OS-level packet processing—all exhibit a similar structure that builds on a common set of domain-specific idioms and components.[1] Implementing such standard functionality is not rocket science. However, experiences with developing robust and efficient monitoring systems reveal that coming to correct and memory-safe code quickly proves challenging—much more than one might intuitively expect. It is, hence, unfortunate that in contrast to other domains, where communities have developed a trove of reusable standard functionality (e.g., HPC or cryptography), we find little sharing across networking systems—not even in the open-source world. We examined the code of three open-source networking applications of different types: iptables (firewall), Snort (NIDS), and XORP (software router). All three implement their own versions of standard data structures with state management, support for asynchronous execution, logic for discerning IPv4 and IPv6 addresses, and protocol inspection. We also compared the source code of the three major open-source NIDS implementations (Bro, Snort, and Suricata), and we found neither any significant code reuse across these systems, nor leveraging of much third-party functionality. `libpcap` and `libz` are the only external libraries to which they all link. In addition, Snort and Suricata both leverage `PCRE` for regular expression matching, while Bro implements its own engine. Indeed, in a panel discussion at RAID 2011 all three projects acknowledged the lack of code reuse, attributing it to low-level issues concerning program structures and data flows.

From our source code analysis we identify a number of common building blocks for networking applications, as illustrated in Figure 1:

Domain-specific Data Types. Networking applications use a set of domain-specific data types for expressing their analysis, such as IP addresses, transport-layer ports, network prefixes, and time. HILTI's abstract machine model provides these as first-class types.

State Management. Most applications require long-lived state, as they correlate information across packet and session boundaries. However, managing that state in real-time requires effective expiration strategies [16]. HILTI provides container types with built-in state management, and timers to schedule processing asynchronously into the future, e.g., for customized cleanup tasks or time-driven logic.

Concurrent Analysis. High-volume network traffic exhibits an enormous degree of inherent parallelism [38], and applications need to multiplex their analyses across potentially tens of thousands of data flows, either inside a single thread or parallelized across multiple CPUs. High-performance applications employ the latter only sparingly today, as it remains challenging to parallelize stateful analysis efficiently across threads while maintaining linear scaling with the workload size. HILTI supports both forms of parallelism by *(i)* enabling transparent incremental processing, and *(ii)* providing a concurrency model that employs cooperative multitasking to supply applications with a large number of lightweight threads with well-defined semantics.

Real-time Performance. With 10 Gbps links now standard even in medium-sized environments, applications deal with enormous packet volumes in real-time. In addition to supporting parallel processing, HILTI compiles analyses into native executables with the potential for extensive domain-specific code optimization.

Robust & Secure Execution. Networking applications process untrusted input: attackers might attempt to mislead a system, and—more mundanely— real-world traffic contains plenty "crud" [37] not conforming to any RFC. While writing robust C code remains notoriously difficult, HILTI's abstract machine model provides a contained, well-defined, and statically typed environment that, for example, prevents code injection attacks.

[1] To simplify terminology, throughout our discussion we use the term "networking application" to refer to a system that processes network packets directly in wire format. We generally do not consider other applications that use higher-level interfaces, such as Unix sockets. While these could benefit from HILTI as well, they tend to have different characteristics that exceed the scope here.

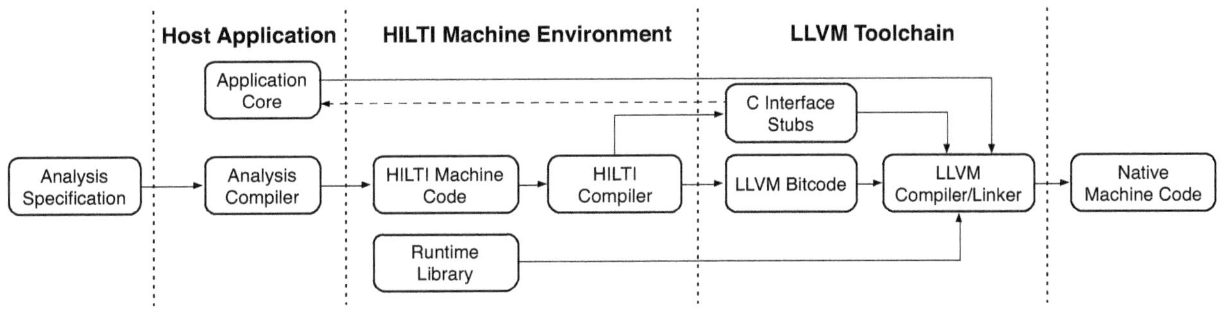

Figure 2: Workflow for using HILTI.

```
# cat hello.hlt
module Main

import Hilti

void run() { # Default entry point for execution.
    call Hilti::print("Hello, World!")
}

# hilti-build hello.hlt -o a.out && ./a.out
Hello, World!
```

Figure 3: Building a simple HILTI program.

High-level Standard Components. HILTI facilitates reuse of higher-level functionality across applications by providing both *(i)* a *lingua franca* for expressing their internals, and *(ii)* extensive interfaces for integration and customization across both host applications and other HILTI-based components.

3. HILTI ABSTRACT MACHINE MODEL

The heart of HILTI consists of an abstract machine model that we tailor to network traffic analysis. In the following we discuss HILTI's design in more detail. For brevity we will use the name HILTI for both the abstract machine model itself as well as for the framework that implements it, i.e., the compiler toolchain and runtime library.

3.1 Workflow

Figure 2 shows the overall workflow when using HILTI. A *host application* leverages HILTI for providing its functionality. Typically, the host application has a user-supplied *analysis specification* that it wants to instantiate; e.g., the set of filtering rules for a firewall, or the set of signatures for a NIDS. The application provides a custom *analysis compiler* that translates its specifications into HILTI machine code, either in the form of text files or, more conveniently, as an in-memory AST representation it creates via a corresponding C++ API that HILTI provides. In either case the *HILTI compiler* then compiles that input into *bitcode* for *LLVM* (the Low-Level Virtual Machine [30]), which we leverage for all target-specific code generation. The HILTI compiler also generates a set of *C stubs* for the host application to interface with the resulting code. Finally, LLVM combines compiled code, stubs, runtime library, and the host application into a single unit of native machine code for execution, either statically or just-in-time at startup (JIT). Our prototype includes two tools, `hiltic` and `hilti-build`, which employ this workflow to compile HILTI code into native objects and executables, respectively. Figure 3 shows an example compiling a trivial HILTI program into a static binary. Alternatively, `hiltic` can JIT-execute the source directly.

Generally, there are two ways to structure a host application. First, the HILTI code can be the main entry point to the execution, with the application providing additional functionality via further C-level functions called out to as necessary as if using an external library; Figure 3 demonstrates this model by defining the `Main::run()` as the entry point. Alternatively, the host application itself can drive execution and leverage HILTI-based functionality by calling the generated C stubs on demand (e.g., a NIDS might feed payload into a HILTI-based protocol parser; see §4).

3.2 Execution Model

Syntax. To keep the syntax simple we model HILTI's instruction set after register-based assembler languages. A program consists of a series of instructions of the general form `<target> = <mnemonic> <op1> <op2> <op3>`, with target/operands omitted where not needed. In addition, there exist primitives to define functions, custom data types, and local and thread-local variables (but no truly global; see below). By convention, mnemonics have the form `<prefix>.<operation>`, where the same `prefix` indicates a related set of functionality; Table 1 summarizes the available groups. For data types in particular, `<prefix>` refers to the type and the first operand to the manipulated instance, e.g., `list.append l 42`, appends the integer 42 to the specified list `l`. In total HILTI currently offers about 200 instructions (counting instructions overloaded by their argument types only once). Generally, we deliberately limit syntactic flexibility to better support compiler transformations because HILTI mainly acts as compiler *target*, and not a language that users write code for directly.

Rich Data Types. While being parsimonious with syntax, we equip HILTI with a rich set of high-level data types relevant to the networking domain. First, HILTI features standard atomic types such as integers, character sequences (with separate types for Unicode strings and raw bytes), floating-point, bitsets, enums, and statically typed tuples. In addition, HILTI comes with domain-specific types such as IP addresses (transparently supporting both IPv4 and IPv6), CIDR-style subnet masks, transport-layer ports, and timestamp / time interval types with nanosecond resolution. All these types provide crucial context for type checking, optimization, and data flow/dependency analyses. Second, HILTI offers a set of high-level container types (lists, vectors, sets, maps) that come with built-in support for state management that automatically expires elements according to a given policy. Iterators, along with overloaded operators, provide type-safe generic access to container elements. Further domain-specific types include *overlays* for dissecting packet headers into their components; *channels* for transferring objects between threads; *classifiers* for performing ACL-style packet classification; *regular expressions* supporting incremental matching and simultaneous matching of multiple expressions; *input sources* for accessing external input (e.g., network interfaces and trace files); *timer managers* for maintaining multiple independent notions of time [43]; and *files* for interacting with the file system.

Memory Model. HILTI's memory model is statically type-safe, with containers, iterators, and references parameterized by type. A `new` instruction makes dynamic allocations explicit. The HILTI runtime automatically garbage-collects objects that have become no longer accessible.

Control Flow and Concurrency. For flexible control flow, HILTI provides *timers* to schedule function calls to the future; *closures* for capturing function calls; *exceptions* for robust error handling; and *hooks* for allowing host applications to provide non-intrusive callbacks that run synchronously at well-defined times.

HILTI also supports two styles of concurrency. First, within a single hardware thread, one can multiplex analyses by switching arbitrarily between stacks using co-routines. Consider protocol analysis where the host application incrementally feeds chunks of payload into the parsing code, switching between different sessions as their packets arrive. When the host's C code calls for the first time the HILTI parsing function for a session, HILTI internally instantiates a *fiber* object for the call's execution that can capture its state, and then proceeds with processing the data. Once parsing reaches the end of the currently available chunk, it suspends execution by freezing the stack and copying the CPU's registers into the fiber. Later, when new payload arrives for that session, the application resumes parsing by reactivating the fiber, leading HILTI to reinstate the frozen stack and continue where it left off. Compared to traditional implementations—which typically maintain per-session state machines manually that record the current state—this model remains transparent to the analysis code and hence simplifies its structure.

Second, HILTI provides threads for distributing an analysis concurrently across CPU cores. We employ an Erlang-style threading model that provides an application with a large supply of lightweight *virtual threads*, which a runtime scheduler then maps to a small number of hardware threads via cooperative multitasking. HILTI identifies threads with 64-bit integer IDs: The instruction `thread.schedule foo("abc") 123456` schedules an asynchronous invocation of the function `foo` with one string argument `abc` to thread number `123456`. The ID-based model maps directly to hash-based load-balancing schemes that networking applications commonly deploy for parallel traffic analysis (e.g., Suricata [5] and Bro [44]). For example, to distribute flow processing across threads, one would hash the flow's 5-tuple into an integer and then interpret that value as the ID of the virtual thread to assign the corresponding analysis to. As processing within each virtual thread proceeds sequentially, this approach implicitly serializes all computation relating to a single flow and thus obviates the need for further intra-flow synchronization. We find typical analysis tasks amenable to this model [43].

HILTI's execution model prevents data races and low-level deadlocks by design: virtual threads cannot share state directly. In particular, HILTI does not provide global variables visible across threads. Instead, each virtual thread receives its own set of *thread-local* variables for recording state related to its processing. Exchanging global state requires explicit message passing, either by connecting threads with HILTI's thread-safe channel data type, or by scheduling tasks to a target thread and passing the relevant information as arguments.[2] In either case, the runtime deep-copies all mutable data so that the sender will not see any modifications that the receiver may make. This strict model of data isolation enables reliable concurrent execution because it encourages value semantics as opposed to complicated data dependencies that would require locks to synchronize access.

Functionality	Mnemonic	Functionality	Mnemonic
Bitsets	`bitset`	Packet i/o	`iosrc`
Booleans	`bool`	Packet classification	`classifier`
CIDR masks	`network`	Packet dissection	`overlay`
Callbacks	`hook`	Ports	`port`
Closures	`callable`	Profiling	`profiler`
Channels	`channel`	Raw data	`bytes`
Debug support	`debug`	References	`ref`
Doubles	`double`	Regular expressions	`regexp`
Enumerations	`enum`	Strings	`string`
Exceptions	`exception`	Structs	`struct`
File i/o	`file`	Time intervals	`interval`
Flow control	(No joint prefix)	Timer management	`timer_mgr`
Hashmaps	`map`	Timers	`timer`
Hashsets	`set`	Times	`time`
IP addresses	`addr`	Tuples	`tuple`
Integers	`int`	Vectors/arrays	`vector`
Lists	`list`	Virtual threads	`thread`

Table 1: HILTI's main instruction groups.

3.3 Profiling & Debugging

A key challenge for high-volume traffic analysis is assessing and optimizing runtime performance [16]. HILTI supports measuring CPU and memory properties via *profilers* that track attributes such as CPU cycles, memory usage, and cache performance for arbitrary blocks of code. During execution the HILTI runtime records measured attributes to disk at regular intervals, e.g., enabling tracking of CPU time spent per time interval [16, 17]. The HILTI compiler can also insert instrumentation to profile at function granularity.

3.4 Host Application API

HILTI comes with an extensive C API that offers host applications direct access to its data types. In addition, control flow can transfer bi-directionally between applications and HILTI. C programs call HILTI functions via the C stubs, and HILTI code can invoke arbitrary C functions. The API integrates exception handling, timer management, fiber resumption, and thread scheduling between HILTI and application.

A second part of HILTI's API is a C++ AST interface for constructing HILTI programs in memory. `hiltic` and `hilti-build` are in fact just wrappers around this API, which host applications can likewise employ to compile their analysis specifications into HILTI code. Combining AST and JIT interfaces enables applications to go all the way from user-level specification to native code on the fly.

4. APPLICATION EXEMPLARS

We now develop four applications as examples to illustrate HILTI's ability to accommodate a wide range of common network processing tasks: *(i)* a BPF-style packet filter engine; *(ii)* a stateful firewall; *(iii)* a parser generator for network protocols; and *(iv)* a compiler for Bro scripts. We have implemented all four as prototypes. While we consider the former two primarily proof-of-concepts, the latter two represent realistic and fully functional applications that we intend to further improve as HILTI matures.

[2]Note that the interpretation of HILTI's `global` keyword in code examples below is "a variable global to the current virtual thread".

```
type IP::Header = overlay {
  # <name>: <type> at <offset> unpack <format> [(bits)]
  version: int<8> at 0 unpack UInt8InBigEndian (4, 7),
  hdr_len: int<8> at 0 unpack UInt8InBigEndian (0, 3),
  [...]
  src:     addr   at 12 unpack IPv4InNetworkOrder,
  dst:     addr   at 16 unpack IPv4InNetworkOrder
}

bool filter(ref<bytes> packet) { # Input: raw data.
  local addr a1, a2
  local bool b1, b2, b3

  # Extract fields and evaluate expression.
  a1 = overlay.get IP::Header src packet
  b1 = equal a1 192.168.1.1
  a1 = overlay.get IP::Header dst packet
  b2 = equal a2 192.168.1.1
  b1 = or b1 b2
  b2 = equal 10.0.5.0/24 a1
  b3 = or b1 b2
  return b3
}
```

Figure 4: Generated HILTI code for the BPF filter `host 192.168.1.1 or src net 10.0.5.0/24`.

Berkeley Packet Filter.

As an initial simple application to explore, we implemented a compiler for BPF [32]. BPF traditionally translates filters into code for its custom internal stack machine, which it then interprets at runtime. Compiling filters into native code via HILTI avoids the overhead of interpreting, enables further compile-time code optimization, and facilitates easy extension of the filtering capabilities in the future.

Figure 4 shows HILTI code that our compiler produces for a simple BPF filter. The generated code leverages a HILTI *overlay type* for parsing IP packet headers. Overlays are user-definable composite types that specify the layout of a binary structure in wire format and provide transparent type-safe access to its fields while accounting for specifics such as alignment and endianness. While our proof-of-concept BPF compiler supports only IPv4 header conditions, adding further `BPF` features would be straight-forward. The compiler could also go beyond standard BPF capabilities and, for example, add stateful filtering [25].

Stateful Firewall.

Our second proof-of-concept host application is a basic stateful firewall, implemented as a Python host application that compiles a list of rules into corresponding HILTI code. To simplify the example, our tool supports only rules of the form `(src-net, dst-net)` → `{allow,deny}`, applied in order of specification. The first match determines the result, with a default action of `deny`. In addition, we provide for a simple form of stateful matching: when a host pair matches an `allow` rule, the code creates a temporary dynamic rule that will permit all packets in the *opposite direction* until a specified period of inactivity has passed.

Figure 5 shows the code generated for a simple rule set, along with additional static code that performs the matching. The code leverages two HILTI capabilities: *(i)* the *classifier* data type for matching the provided rules; and *(ii)* a *set* indexed by host pair to record dynamic rules, with a timeout set to expire old entries. While we have simplified this proof-of-concept firewall for demonstration purposes, adding further functionality would be straightforward. In practice, the rule compiler could directly support the syntax of an existing firewall system, like `iptables`.

```
### Compiled rule set (net1 -> net2) -> {Allow, Deny}.
### Generated by the application's analysis compiler.

void init_rules(ref<classifier<Rule, bool>> r) {
  # True -> Allow; False -> Deny.
  classifier.add r (10.3.2.1/32,  10.1.0.0/16) True
  classifier.add r (10.12.0.0/16, 10.1.0.0/16) False
  classifier.add r (10.1.6.0/24,  *) True
  classifier.add r (10.1.7.0/24,  *) True
}

### The host application also provides the following
### static code.

# Data type for a single filter rule.
type Rule = struct { net src, net dst }

# The classifier storing the rules.
global ref<classifier<Rule, bool>> rules

# Dynamic rules: address pairs allowed to communicate.
global ref< set< tuple<addr, addr> > > dyn

# Function to initialize classifier at startup.
void init_classifier() {
  rules = new classifier<Rule, bool> # Instantiate.
  call init_rules(rules)             # Add rules.
  classifier.compile rules           # Freeze/finalize.

  # Create set for dynamic state with timeout of 5 mins
  # of inactivity.
  dyn = new set<tuple<addr, addr>>
  set.timeout dyn ExpireStrategy::Access interval(300)
}

# Function called for each packet, passing in
# timestamp and addresses. Returns true if ok.
bool match_packet(time t, addr src, addr dst) {
  local bool b

  # Advance HILTI's global time. This will expire
  # inactive entries from the state set.
  timer_mgr.advance_global t

  # See if we have a state entry for this pair.
  b = set.exists dyn (src, dst)
  if.else b return_action lookup

lookup: # Unknown pair, look up rule.
  try { b = classifier.get rules (src, dst) }
  catch ( ref<Hilti::IndexError> e ) {
      return False # No match, default deny.
  }

  if.else b add_state return_action

add_state: # Add dynamic rules to allow both sides.
  set.insert dyn (src, dst)
  set.insert dyn (dst, src)

return_action: # Return decision.
  return b
}
```

Figure 5: HILTI code for firewall example.

A Yacc for Network Protocols.

To provide a more complete example, we reimplemented the BinPAC parser generator [36] as a HILTI-based compiler. BinPAC is a "yacc for network protocols": given a protocol's grammar, it generates the source code of a corresponding protocol parser. While the original BinPAC system outputs C++, our new version targets HILTI. As we also took the opportunity to clean up and extend syntax and functionality, we nicknamed the new system BinPAC++.

```
const Token      = /[^ \t\r\n]+/;
const NewLine    = /\r?\n/;
const WhiteSpace = /[ \t]+/;

type RequestLine = unit {
    method:  Token;
    :        WhiteSpace;
    uri:     URI;
    :        WhiteSpace;
    version: Version;
    :        NewLine;
};

type Version = unit {
    :       /HTTP\//; # Fixed string as regexp.
    number: /[0-9]+\.[0-9]+/;
};
```

(a) BinPAC++ grammar excerpt for HTTP.

```
struct http_requestline_object {
    hlt_bytes* method;
    hlt_bytes* uri;
    struct http_version_object* version;
    [... some internal fields skipped ...]
};

extern http_requestline_object*
  http_requestline_parse(hlt_bytes *,
                         hlt_exception **);
```

(b) C prototypes generated by HILTI compiler. The host application calls `http_requestline_parse` to parse a request line.

```
[binpac] RequestLine
[binpac]   method = 'GET'
[binpac]   uri = '/index.html'
[binpac]   Version
[binpac]     number = '1.1'
```

(c) Debugging output showing fields as input is parsed.

Figure 6: BinPAC++ example (slightly simplified).

Figure 6 (a) shows an excerpt of a BinPAC++ grammar for parsing an HTTP request line (e.g., `GET /index.html HTTP/1.1`). In Figure 6 (b) we show the C prototype for the generated parsing function as exposed to the host application, including a struct type corresponding to the parsed protocol data unit (PDU). At runtime, the generated HILTI code allocates instances of this type and sets the individual fields as parsing progresses, as the debugging output in Figure 6 (c) shows for an individual request. When the parser finishes with a field, it executes any callbacks (hooks) that the host application specifies for that field. If the grammar does not include hooks, the host application can still extract the parsed data from the returned struct (as Figure 6 (b) exemplifies) after HILTI finishes processing the type.[3]

BinPAC++ provides the same functionality as the original implementation, and we converted parsers for HTTP and DNS over to the new system. Internally, however, we could structure BinPAC++ quite differently by taking advantage of HILTI's abstractions. While the original BinPAC provides its own low-level runtime library for implementing domain-specific data types and buffer management, we now use HILTI's primitives and idioms, which results in higher-level code and a more maintainable parser generator. Leveraging HILTI's flexible control-flow, we can now generate fully incremental LL(1)-parsers that postpone parsing whenever they run out of input and transparently resume once more becomes available. In contrast, the C++ parsers of the original BinPAC need to manually manage the parsing process and further rely on an additional PDU-level buffering layer that often requires additional hints from the grammar writer to work correctly. Finally, while the original BinPAC requires the user to write additional C++ code for any logic beyond describing basic syntax layout, BinPAC++ extends the grammar language with semantic constructs for annotating, controlling, and interfacing to the parsing process, including support for keeping arbitrary state, by compiling them to corresponding HILTI code.

BinPAC++ remains independent of a specific host application because HILTI generates external C interfaces for the compiled parsers. We demonstrate this functionality by extending Bro to both drive the parsing and use the results, just as it does with its built-in protocol parsers. As Bro decodes protocols, it executes *event handlers* written in Bro's custom scripting language. For example, the internal TCP parser generates a `connection_established` event for any successful three-way handshake, passing along metadata about the corresponding connection as the event's argument. Similarly, Bro's HTTP parser generates `http_request` and `http_reply` events for client and server traffic, respectively. To define the events that BinPAC++ will generate for Bro, we add additional "event configuration files". Figure 7 showcases the interaction between the two systems: (a) shows a basic BinPAC++ grammar to parse SSH banners; the event configuration file in (b) tells Bro to trigger an `ssh_banner` event whenever the generated code finishes parsing an `SSH::Banner` unit; and (c) shows corresponding Bro script code that implements a simple handler for that event. Finally, (d) demonstrates the usage: Bro loads the event configuration file from the command line, pulls in the corresponding BinPAC++ grammar, compiles the grammar into HILTI parsing code, and generates internal HILTI glue code that at runtime interfaces back to Bro's event engine for triggering the defined events.

Bro Script Compiler.

Our final application implements a compiler for Bro scripts [37]. Unlike purely signature-based NIDSs, Bro's domain-specific, Turing-complete scripting language decouples the system from any specific analysis model. In addition to detection tasks, Bro uses its language also for higher-level analysis logic in the form of library functionality that ships with the distribution. For example, most protocol-specific scripts perform per-session state-tracking, such as the HTTP analysis correlating replies with earlier requests.

To demonstrate that HILTI can indeed support such a complex, highly stateful language, we developed a Bro plugin that translates all loaded scripts into corresponding HILTI logic, mapping Bro constructs and data types to HILTI equivalents as appropriate. The plugin executes the HILTI toolchain just-in-time, generating native code at startup. When Bro generates events, it triggers the HILTI code instead of going through its standard script interpreter.

With HILTI's rich set of high-level data types we generally found mapping Bro types to HILTI equivalents straightforward. While Bro's syntax is complex, the compiler can generally directly convert its constructs to HILTI's simpler register-based language. Figure 8 shows a simple example compiling two event handlers tracking the server addresses of all established TCP connections. As the example shows, the compiler translates Bro's event handler into HILTI hooks (which are, roughly, functions with multiple bodies that all execute upon invocation).

[3] An advantage of using hooks is that HILTI could optimize away the parsing of unused fields and also avoid further unnecessary data copying (not implemented yet).

```
module SSH;

export type Banner = unit {
    magic   : /SSH-/;
    version : /[^-]*/;
    dash    : /-/;
    software: /[^\r\n]*/;
};
```

(a) BinPAC++ grammar for SSH banners in `ssh.pac2`.

```
grammar ssh.pac2; # BinPAC++ grammar to compile.

# Define the new parser.
protocol analyzer SSH over TCP:
    parse with SSH::Banner, # Top-level unit.
    port 22/tcp,            # Port to trigger parser.

# For each SSH::Banner, trigger an ssh_banner() event.
on SSH::Banner
    -> event ssh_banner(self.version, self.software);
```

(b) Event configuration file in `ssh.evt`.

```
event ssh_banner(version: string, software: string) {
    print software, version;
    }
```

(c) Bro event handler in `ssh.bro`.

```
# bro -r ssh.trace ssh.evt ssh.bro
OpenSSH_3.9p1, 1.99
OpenSSH_3.8.1p1, 2.0
```

(d) Output with a single SSH session (both sides).

Figure 7: Bro/BinPAC++ interface example.

Our prototype compiler supports most features of the Bro scripting language.[4] Specifically, it supports running Bro's default HTTP and DNS analysis scripts, which we use as representative case studies in our evaluation (see §6). The HTTP and DNS scripts generate extensive logs of the corresponding protocol activity, correlating state across request and reply pairs, plus (in the case of HTTP) extracting and identifying message bodies.

5. IMPLEMENTATION

We now discuss our prototype HILTI implementation, which consists of a C++-based compiler along with a C runtime library. In addition, we have implemented the four application scenarios we discuss in §4 in the form of *(i)* Python scripts for the two proof-of-concepts (BPF and Firewall); *(ii)* a C++ compiler to translate BinPAC++ grammars into HILTI; and *(iii)* a Bro plugin in C++ that (a) provides a runtime interface to BinPAC++ parsers and (b) compiles Bro script code into HILTI and executes it. HILTI, BinPAC++, and the Bro plugin come with a total of about 850 unit tests ensuring correctness. Unless indicated otherwise, our implementation implements all functionality discussed in this paper, and we release it to the community as open-source software under a BSD-style license [6]. As a large part of the implementation represents an application of well-known compiler techniques, we focus on some of the more interesting aspects in the following.

[4]We currently exclude some rarely used constructs as well as a small set of advanced functionality that does not have direct HILTI equivalents yet. In particular, the compiler lacks support for Bro's `when` statement, which triggers script code asynchronously once a specified global condition becomes true. We plan to add watchpoints to HILTI to support that functionality. Only few scripts make use of that capability, most commonly for resolving DNS names.

```
global hosts: set[addr];

event connection_established(c: connection) {
    add hosts[c$id$resp_h]; # Record responder IP.
    }

event bro_done() {
    for ( i in hosts ) # Print all recorded IPs.
        print i;
}
```

(a) Bro event handlers in `track.bro`.

```
global ref<set<addr>> hosts = set<addr>()

[... Definitions for "connection" and "conn_id" ...]

hook void connection_established(ref<connection> c) {
  local addr __t1
  local ref<conn_id> __t2

  __t2 = struct.get c id
  __t1 = struct.get __t2 resp_h
  set.insert hosts __t1
}

hook void bro_done() {
    for ( i in hosts ) {
        call Hilti::print (i)
    }
}
```

(b) Compiled HILTI code (slightly simplified for readability).

```
# bro -b -r wikipedia.pcap compile_scripts=T track.bro
208.80.152.118
208.80.152.2
208.80.152.3
```

(c) Output with a small sample trace containing 3 servers.

Figure 8: Bro compiler example.

Code Generation. The compiler `hiltic` receives HILTI machine code for compilation, as illustrated in Figure 2, which it then compiles into LLVM's instruction set. LLVM is an industrial-strength, open-source compiler toolchain that models a low-level but portable register machine. We also compile HILTI's runtime library into LLVM's representation, using the accompanying C compiler *clang*. We then link all of the parts together, first with a custom linker (see below), followed by LLVM's linker; and finally compile the result into native machine code. Besides generating machine code, LLVM also implements domain-independent code optimizations. All parts of the code generation can either take place statically, producing a native binary to execute; or just-in-time inside a host application.

Linker. We add a specialized linker to our toolchain to support the HILTI compiler through custom transformations at the LLVM-level, enabling HILTI features that require a global view of all compilation units. For example, we maintain thread-local state per *virtual* thread and hence cannot leverage the corresponding pthread-style functionality directly because it only separates the underlying hardware threads. HILTI's runtime associates with each virtual thread a separate array that contains a copy of all thread-local variables. However, as one compilation unit might access thread-locals defined in another, only the link stage has the global view necessary to determine the final layout of that array. Accordingly, our custom linker first merges all thread-locals across units into a single array structure, and then adapts all instructions to that aggregate layout. We use a similar link-time mechanism to support hooks across compilation units.

Runtime Model. With each virtual thread HILTI's runtime associates a context object that stores all its relevant state, including the array of thread-locals discussed above, the currently executing fiber (for suspending execution; see §3.2), timers scheduled for execution inside the thread, and exception status. Internally, we use a custom calling convention for compiled functions (as well as the runtime library) that passes the context object as an additional hidden object. HILTI currently propagates exceptions up the stack with explicit return value checks after each function call, which incurs a slight overhead. In the future we might switch to C++-style DWARF exceptions, which come with zero costs when not raising any exception.

HILTI garbage-collects dynamically allocated memory via reference counting—a technique Bro has proven a good match for the domain. While generally considered less efficient than mark-and-sweep collectors [26], reference counting is not only less complex to implement, but its incremental operation and short deallocation times also fit better with real-time constrains. The HILTI compiler emits reference count operations transparently during code generation as necessary. It does so rather freely at the moment, but we plan to add an optimization pass that removes redundant counter operations and also applies further optimizations similar to those that ARC [3] deploys. Our implementation currently lacks a cycle detector (as does Bro).

When implementing fibers, we considered several alternatives, including CPS-conversion [10] and manually copying the stack on demand. We settled on a `setcontext`-based scheme that proves both simple and efficient for supporting the large number of context switches that HILTI relies upon for implementing both incremental processing and virtual threads. The `setcontext` primitive allows a program to temporarily switch its stack over to a self-allocated memory segment, saving and later restoring processor registers to continue at the original location. A challenge with that approach lies in sizing the custom stacks correctly: if they remain too small, they will overflow; if too large, they will waste memory. While LLVM's code generator offers "segmented stacks" [12] as a mechanism to start with a small stack and then grow dynamically, this feature turns out complex, non-portable, and rather inefficient. Instead we follow the lead of Rust [8] and leverage the MMU: we request large worst-case-sized memory segments with `mmap()` and rely upon the MMU to not actually allocate physical memory pages until it sees accesses. That approach performs well in practice: using libtask's optimized `setcontext` implementation [2] along with a custom free-list for recycling stacks, a micro-benchmark shows that the HILTI runtime can perform about 18 million context switches per second between existing fibers on a Xeon 5570 CPU. It furthermore supports about 5 million cycles per second of creating, starting, finishing, and deleting a fiber. We also confirmed that the memory usage indeed corresponds to the space in use, versus the amount allocated. We hence conclude that our fiber implementation provides the necessary performance.

Runtime Library. The runtime library implements the more complex HILTI data types—such as maps, regular expressions, and timers—as C functions called out to by the generated LLVM code. LLVM can inline function calls across link-time units and thus may eliminate the extra overhead of these invocations. The runtime library also implements the threading system with a corresponding scheduler, mapping virtual threads to native threads and scheduling jobs on a first-come, first-served basis. For functionality that requires serial execution, the runtime provides a command queue to send operations from arbitrary threads to a single dedicated manager thread. HILTI uses this mechanism, for example, for file output occurring from multiple threads concurrently. Generally, all runtime functionality is fully thread-safe, 64-bit code. However, we have not yet focused on efficiency when implementing runtime functionality. For example, we currently implement the `classifier` type as a linked list internally, which does not scale with larger numbers of rules. It will be straightforward to later transparently switch to a better data structure for packet classification [22].

Bro Interface. When adding the Bro interface for compiling BinPAC++ and scripts, we faced two main challenges: *(i)* we had to hook the generated code into Bro's processing at a number of points across its code base; and *(ii)* execution needs to translate back and forth between Bro's internal representation of data types and those of HILTI. For the former, we started with a Bro development version based on release 2.2 that comes with an early version of a new plugin interface, which enables us to load additional Bro functionality at runtime in the form of shared libraries. We extended that interface to provide further hooks into the script infrastructure and then implemented all HILTI-specific code as a plugin.

The translation between data types turned out to be more difficult. Internally, Bro represents all script values as instances of classes derived from a joint `Val` base class (e.g., there is an `EnumVal`, a `TableVal`, etc.). Unfortunately these instances are not only used by the script interpreter itself, but also passed around to most other parts of Bro's code base. Therefore, even when we replace the interpreter with our compiled code, to interface to the rest of Bro—e.g., for feeding data into the logging system—we still need to create instances of these value classes. Similarly, we also need to convert Val's into the corresponding HILTI representation when generating events. Consequently, our HILTI plugin needs to generate a significant amount of glue code, which comes with a corresponding performance penalty as we discuss in §6. In practice, one would avoid this overhead by tying the two systems together more directly.

6. EVALUATION

We now evaluate the HILTI environment by assessing the functionality and performance of the applications discussed in §4. We begin by summarizing our data and setup.

6.1 Data and Setup

To drive our applications with realistic workloads, we captured two full-payload packet traces at the border gateway of the UC Berkeley campus, exclusively containing HTTP and DNS traffic, respectively. The HTTP trace comprises a total of 30 GB of data in libpcap format, spanning 52 minutes of TCP port 80 traffic during a recent weekday morning and representing a sample of 1/25 of the link's total connections on port 80 during that time.[5] The trace contains about 340K HTTP requests/replies between 35K distinct pairs of hosts. The DNS trace comprises 1 GB in libpcap format, spanning about 10 minutes of UDP port 53 traffic during a recent weekday afternoon. Due to the lower overall volume of DNS, we could capture *all* of the campus' DNS during that interval. The trace contains about 65M DNS requests/replies between 435K distinct host pairs. We captured both traces with tcpdump, which reported no packet loss in either case. We chose the trace durations as a trade-off between including significant diversity and keeping their volume manageable for repeated offline measurements. We note that in particular for DNS, the number of requests/replies constitutes the primary driver for analysis performance, not raw packet volume. We conduct all measurements on a 64-bit Linux 3.12.8

[5] We captured the trace on a backend system behind a front-end load-balancer that splits up the total traffic on a per-flow basis [44].

system with two Intel Xeon 5570 CPUs, 24GB of RAM, and CPU frequency scaling disabled.

For the applications involving Bro we slightly adapt some of Bro's default scripts—which generate all of Bro's output files—by backporting a few recent bugfixes to the version we used. We also remove some minor dependencies on specifics of the built-in parsers. For DNS we furthermore disable per-request expiration timers, and for Bro's standard HTTP parser we disable recovering from content gaps; both features are not yet supported by our BinPAC++ versions. We use the modified Bro versions for all runs so that results are comparable across configurations. When measuring execution performance (in contrast to validating correct operation), we disable Bro's logging to avoid its I/O load affecting the results; Bro still performs the same computation but skips the final write operation. To measure CPU performance, we instrument Bro to also record the time spent inside four different components of the code base: protocol analysis, script execution, HILTI-to-Bro glue code (see §5), and all remaining parts excluding initialization and finalization code (which we refer to as "other" below).[6] We measure time in CPU cycles as retrieved via the PAPI library. Out of necessity these measurements remain somewhat approximate: *(i)* control flow within Bro is complex and one cannot always precisely attribute which subsystem to charge; and *(ii)* PAPI comes with overhead and fluctuations that affect the results [46]. However, after performing a number of cross-checks, we are confident that these measurements give us a solid qualitative understanding on how HILTI performs relative to standard Bro.

6.2 Berkeley Packet Filter

We first verify that running the compiled filter from Figure 4 on the HTTP trace performs correctly. Instead of the private addresses we use real ones from the trace that trigger the filter for about 2% of the packets. We link a basic libpcap-based driver program written in C with the compiled HILTI code. The driver reads the trace file inside a loop, calls the filter successively for each packet and increases a counter for every match. We then implement a second version of the driver that instead uses BPF to perform the same filtering, and we find that both applications indeed return the same number of matches. To understand the relative performance of the two filter implementations, we measure the CPU cycles spend inside the filtering code, finding that the HILTI version spends 1.70 times more cycles than BPF. A closer looks reveals that the HILTI-generated C stub is responsible for 20.6% of the difference, leaving an increase of 1.35 times when ignoring that (the runtime functionality that the stub facilitates remains unnecessary in this case, and the compiler could indeed just skip it). We deem the remaining difference acceptable, considering the HILTI's higher-level model in comparison to BPF's internal representation.

6.3 Stateful Firewall

We confirm the functionality of the stateful firewall application by comparing it with a simple Python script that implements the same functionality independently. We drive both instances with the DNS trace, configuring them with a small example rule set and feeding them with timestamp, source, and destination address for each packet, as extracted by `ipsumdump`. Both HILTI and Python versions parse the `ipsumdump` output into its components and then pass them as input into their rule matching logic. We confirm that the HILTI version produces the same number of matches vs. non-matches. It also performs the task orders of magnitude faster; however, given the slow nature of the Python interpreter, comparing times does not reveal much here.

[6] This also excludes compiling HILTI code at startup. While that can take noticeable time, one could cache the machine-code for reuse on later invocations.

#Lines	`http.log`		`files.log`		`dns.log`	
	Std	Pac	Std	Pac	Std	Pac
Total	338K	338K	273K	273K	2573K	2573K
Normalized	338K	338K	273K	273K	2492K	2492K
Identical	98.91%		98.36%		>99.9%	

Table 2: Agreement HILTI (Pac) vs. standard (Std) parsers.

6.4 Protocol Parsing

We next examine BinPAC++ protocol parsers, using Bro as the driver to feed them packet data. We take the HTTP and DNS parsers as case-studies and compare their results with Bro's standard, manually written C++ implementations.[7] We confirm correctness by running both BinPAC++ and standard parsers on the corresponding input trace and comparing the relevant Bro log files. For HTTP, `http.log` records all HTTP sessions along with extensive meta information such as requested URL, server response code, and MIME types of the message; and `files.log` records further information on the message bodies, including a SHA1 hash of their content. For DNS, `dns.log` records all DNS requests with queries, types, responses, and more.

Our BinPAC++ parsers attempt to mimic Bro's standard parsers as closely possible, however small discrepancies in analysis semantics remain hard to avoid for protocols as complex as HTTP and DNS. Before comparing the log files, we hence first normalize them to account for a number of minor expected differences, including unique'ing them so that each entry appears only once.[8]

Table 2 summarizes the remaining differences. We find that for the normalized versions of `http.log`, 98.91% of all of the standard parser's log entries correspond to an identical instance in the BinPAC++ version; 98.36% for `files.log`. About half of the HTTP mismatches are due to a small number of "Partial Content" sessions, for which the BinPAC++ version often manages to extract more information. The remaining discrepancies reflect further semantic differences, often leading to different (or no) MIME types for an HTTP body. These mismatches then transfer over to the `files.log`, and we find neither parser consistently right in these cases. The (low) number of mismatches remains on the order of what we would expect for any two independent HTTP implementations. For `dns.log` we find almost perfect agreement, with >99.9% of the entries matching, and the remaining deviations being due to minor semantic differences (e.g., Bro's parser extracts only one entry from TXT records, BinPAC++ all; the BinPAC++ parser does not abort as easily for traffic on port 53 that is not in fact DNS). Overall, we conclude that the BinPAC++ results closely match those of Bro's standard parsers, which means we can proceed to meaningfully compare their performance, as they indeed perform essentially the same work.

Figure 9 summarizes CPU times. The plot breaks down the time spent inside Bro components when using its standard parsers vs. the HILTI-based versions. The time for "Protocol Parsing" con-

[7] Note that we indeed compare against manually written C++ implementations, *not* code generated by the classic BinPAC discussed in [36]. While Bro uses BinPAC for some of its protocols, it does not do so for HTTP and DNS.

[8] The normalization further includes adjustments for slight timing and ordering differences, a few fields with size information that the BinPAC++ parsers cannot easily pass on to Bro for technical reasons, and formatting differences in field content.

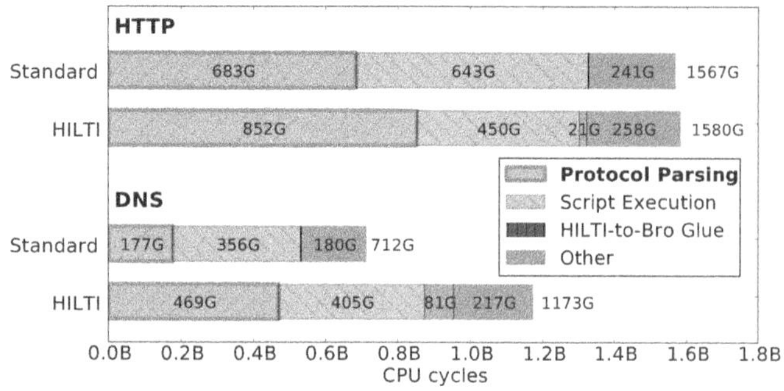

Figure 9: Performance of HILTI-based protocol parsers.

stitutes the key metric: the BinPAC++ parsers need 1.28 times and 3.03 times more CPU cycles, respectively, when running on the HTTP and DNS traces than the standard implementations. For HTTP that means HILTI already comes close to the performance of manually written C++ code. For DNS, the slowdown is more significant, though we argue still acceptable given the current prototype state of our compiler implementation with its potential for further optimization and tuning. We profiled the DNS analysis in more detail on a trace excerpt and found two particular opportunities for improvement. First, BinPAC++ parsers perform more memory allocations, and the effect is particularly pronounced for DNS: when using the BinPAC++ parser Bro performs about 47% more memory allocations (19% more for HTTP). The increase comes from frequent instantiation of dynamic objects during the parsing process—likely a similar overhead as classic BinPAC exhibits as well, and with similar solutions [41]. Second, currently the BinPAC++ compiler always generates code supporting incremental parsing, even though it could optimize for UDP where one sees complete PDUs at a time (as Bro's standard parser indeed does).

Figure 9 also shows the time spent inside the HILTI-to-Bro data conversion glue: 1.3%/6.9% of the total cycles, respectively—an overhead that would disappear if HILTI were more tightly integrated into the host application. Interestingly, we also see in Figure 9 that for HTTP, Bro spends less time in script execution when using the BinPAC++ analyzer, even though it follows the same code path. We tracked down this difference to the standard parser generating a large number of redundant events related to file analysis, which the BinPAC++ parser omits (about 30% more in total). While the impact of these events on parsing and output remains negligible, they lead to more load on the script interpreter. Recent Bro versions have fixed this problem.

6.5 Bro Script Compiler

Turning to the script compiler application, we again first verify its correct operation. Using the same methodology as with the protocol parsers, we compare the log files that the compiled HILTI versions of the HTTP and DNS scripts produce with the output of Bro's standard script interpreter. Table 3 summarizes the differences running on the corresponding traces. We see an excellent fit in all three cases. Inspecting the few cases where the two versions do not agree, we find that for `http.log` and `files.log` almost all differences are due to fully insignificant output ordering when logging sets of values—which our normalization cannot easily account for. For `dns.log` the only differences come from an IPv6 address logged in a slightly different output format. Overall, we conclude that the compiled HILTI code produces the same output as Bro's standard interpreter, and we thus confirm that HILTI's model can indeed capture a complex domain-specific language.

#Lines	`http.log`		`files.log`		`dns.log`	
	Std	Hlt	Std	Hlt	Std	Hlt
Total	338K	338K	273K	273K	2573K	2573K
Normalized	338K	338K	273K	273K	2492K	2492K
Identical	>99.99%		99.98%		>99.99%	

Table 3: Output of compiled scripts (Hlt) vs standard (Std).

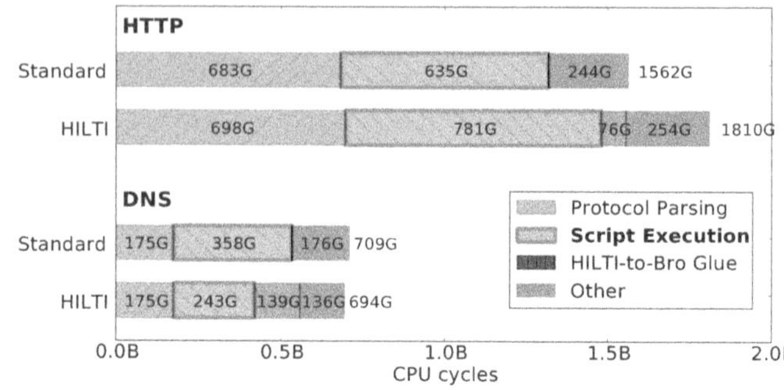

Figure 10: Performance of scripts compiled into HILTI.

Next we turn to execution performance. As a simple baseline benchmark, we first execute a small Bro script that computes Fibonacci numbers recursively. The compiled HILTI version solves this task orders of magnitude faster than Bro's standard interpreter, which demonstrates the potential for compiling scripts into machine code. However, this example represents the best case for HILTI: it requires hardly any interaction between HILTI and Bro's C++ core, and it allows LLVM's code generation to shine by producing optimal machine code. As more realistic examples, Figure 10 compares execution performance with the HTTP and DNS scripts, respectively. For HTTP, the HILTI version remains slightly slower, requiring 1.30 times the cycles. For DNS, HILTI proves 6.9% faster. As with the protocol parsers, the glue code adds further overhead—4.2% and 20.0% of total cycles, respectively—which a fully integrated host application would not incur. Overall we conclude that the compiled HILTI scripts exhibit performance similar to Bro's existing scripting system. One could argue that compiled scripts should decrease execution times more, compared to Bro's standard interpretation. While indeed we expect that further improvements of our toolchain will achieve that, we also point out that it remains challenging to quantify the potential: with a high-level scripting language, operations on data structures (e.g., hash maps) and other runtime library functionality, including dynamic memory management, account for a significant share of the work load that can only improve to a certain extent. Furthermore, even when interpreted, Bro's statically typed language can execute much faster than dynamically typed environments such as Python or Perl, which would be infeasible to use for real-time network traffic analysis in the first place.

6.6 Summary

We have shown that *(i)* HILTI correctly captures the semantics of all four application scenarios, from low-level protocol parsing to complex high-level analyses; and *(ii)* its runtime performance generally aligns with that of the existing systems. While sometimes slower, it remains on the order of what we expect for the current state of the implementation, i.e., a 4-stage compilation process (host application, HILTI, LLVM, machine code) only partially optimized (LLVM) versus manually written production code. Indeed, our toolchain does not yet exploit HILTI's optimization potential: it lacks support for even the most basic compiler optimizations, such as constant folding and common subexpression elimination at the HILTI level (e.g., the LLVM-level lacks the semantics to identify subsequent lookups for the same map element, which however would be easy to compress before compiling them down).

We have not yet pursued parallelizing the presented applications inside HILTI, as that would involve a number of further aspects in terms of analysis structure and evaluation, exceeding the scope of this paper. However, we have verified HILTI's thread-safety guarantees, as well as correct operation of the scheduler, by load-balancing DNS traffic across varying numbers of hardware threads, each processing their input with the corresponding HILTI-based parser. As expected, we found the same HILTI parsing code to support both the threaded and non-threaded setups.

7. DISCUSSION

Safe Execution Environment. As a key design aspect, HILTI provides a safe runtime execution environment that prevents unintended data and control flows when facing unexpected input. For example, HILTI's instructions generally validate their operands to avoid undefined behavior, such as out-of-bounds iterators; and the memory management prevents dangling references. Furthermore, by separating state between threads, HILTI provides a well-defined setting for concurrent analysis: HILTI code is always safe to execute in parallel. While some of these safety properties come with performance penalties, we deem them well worth their cost, compared to the traditional alternative of writing C code that parses untrusted input, potentially concurrently, in real-time.

Performance via Abstraction. We designed HILTI's machine model to preserve high-level domain semantics that offer extensive potential for global, transparent optimization. While not yet a focus of our prototype implementation, we expect HILTI to eventually facilitate a range of powerful code enhancements. Consider our two Bro-based applications, protocol parsing and script analysis: taken together, they effectively port the core part of Bro over to the HILTI platform. While today parsing and analysis remain separate Bro subsystems, HILTI allows us to reason about them simultaneously inside a single model, with the opportunity to then optimize functionality across their boundaries. For example, if a user does not configure any Bro scripts that inspect bodies of HTTP messages, HILTI could simply remove the code for parsing them in depth.

Generally, we see opportunities for automatic optimization in four main areas. First, HILTI facilitates *improving individual functionality* by tuning the implementation. As a simple example, we plan to better adapt HILTI's `map` type to real-time usage by avoiding CPU spikes during hash table resizes [16]. Likewise, we are considering JIT compilation of regular expressions, similar to `re2c` [4]. HILTI allows to perform such fine-tuning "under the hood" while transparently benefiting any host application.

Second, HILTI's abstractions enable *transparent integration of non-standard hardware capabilities*. Traditionally, integrating custom hardware elements (e.g., FPGA pattern matchers, dedicated lookup modules, fast packet classification) into a networking application requires significant effort to manually adapt the code. HILTI, however, can switch to a different code path as suitable, either at compile-time or dynamically during execution, without changing the interface to the host application. For example, preliminary simulations show that HILTI's hash tables map well to PLUG [13].

Third, HILTI's execution model facilities *compiler-level code optimization* by providing context for control and dataflow analyses [27]. For example, state management can benefit from grouping memory operations for improved cache locality, according to access patterns that the HILTI representation suggests (e.g., containers could structure memory operations with element expiration times in mind). Also, optimizations can help remove overhead coming with HILTI's runtime model, such as skipping unnecessary exception checks, moving bounds-checking from runtime to compile time where statically safe, and optimizing memory management and garbage collection (e.g., BinPAC++-style parsers could often move intermediary heap objects to less expensive stack storage). Another powerful technique concerns elimination of unneeded code at link-time, as in the Bro example we sketch above: the HILTI linker can remove any code (as well as state) that it can statically determine as unreachable with the host application's parameterization.

Fourth, HILTI has sufficient context available to *automatically infer suitable parallelization strategies* for many networking applications. By analyzing data flows, potentially augmented with feedback from runtime profiling, it can leverage the typical unit-based structure of network analysis tasks for scheduling them scalably across CPUs; see below.

Global State. By design, HILTI does not provide truly global state that concurrent threads can access directly—a choice that enables safety guarantees and optimizations we deem worth the restriction. As a substitute, host applications can generally deploy message passing for communication between threads, and potentially designate a single "master" thread for managing state that requires global visibility across the entire system.

In practice, however, we expect the need for global state to remain rare in HILTI's target domain, as typical analyses tend to structure their logic around inherent units of analysis—such as connections, or IP addresses—with little need for correlation across independent instances. As a simple example, consider a scan detector that counts connection attempts per source address. As each individual counter depends solely on the activity of the associated source, one can parallelize the detector by ensuring, through scheduling, that the same thread carries out all counter operations associated with a particular address. That thread can then keep a local variable to record the current value. We envision such *scoped scheduling* to become HILTI's primary concurrency model, and we refer to [14] for more exploration of this topic.

Porting Legacy Applications. We consider HILTI primarily a platform for implementing novel host applications, for which it significantly reduces the barrier for developing an efficient and robust system. However, legacy applications can benefit from HILTI as well, as long as the porting effort remains tenable. Generally, we expect that existing systems will prove most amenable to leveraging HILTI if they already represent their analyses in a structured, customizable way. Indeed, all four of our example applications fall into this category: they express their functionality in terms of expressions, rules, grammars, and scripts, respectively. Traditionally, such applications compile their inputs into custom internal representations before beginning their processing—a step that could now target HILTI instead. We deem HILTI less promising, however, for porting efforts that involve significant hard-coded, low-level logic, such as a manually written TCP stream reassembler. While HILTI can certainly express such functionality—indeed, we envision eventually providing this particular example in the form of a HILTI library—it remains unclear if porting such code would provide significant benefit, as to a large degree it simply reflects translating code from one language into another.

8. RELATED WORK

By their very nature, existing abstract machine implementations focus on specifics of their respective target domains, and to our knowledge none fits well to the requirements of flexible, high-performance network traffic analysis. This includes machine models underlying typical programming languages (e.g., JVM, Parrot VM, Lua VM, Erlang's BEAM/HiPE [39]). Despite raising the level of abstraction, these machines do not offer high-level primitives to efficiently express problems of the domain. Consequently, we leverage an existing *low-level* abstract machine framework, LLVM, in our implementation.

In the networking domain, we find a range of efforts that share aspects with our approach, yet none provides a similarly comprehensive platform for supporting a wide range of applications. Many could however benefit from using HILTI internally. For example, the C library libnids [1] implements basic building blocks commonly used by NIDS, paying particular attention to a design robust when facing adversaries and evasion [24]. We envision such libraries to eventually use HILTI for their implementation. Doing so would relieve them from low-level details (e.g., libnids is not thread-safe and has no IPv6 support), and also benefit from a tighter semantic link between host applications and library. NetShield [31] aims to overcome the fundamentally limited expressiveness of regular expressions by building a custom NIDS engine on top of BinPAC to match more general vulnerability signatures. However, implementing the low-level parts of the engine accounts for a significant share of the effort. Using HILTI primitives would be less time-consuming and also enable other applications to share the developed functionality. The Click modular router [28] allows users to compose a software router from elements that encapsulate predefined primitives, such as IP header extractors, queues, and packet schedulers. Rather than mapping the custom configuration language to the underlying C++ engine, Click configurations could alternatively compile into HILTI. RouteBricks [18] is a multi-Gbps distributed software router which uses techniques akin to HILTI's concurrency model: per-core packet queues enable a lock-free programming scheme with good cache performance. HILTI can easily express such per-flow analysis (within a single system) by routing related analysis to the same thread, and its threading model allows for other scheduling strategies as well. NetPDL [40] is an XML-based language to describe the structure of packet headers. It decouples protocol parsing code from protocol specifics. The language supports fixed and variable-length protocol fields as well as repeated and optional ones. While NetPDL takes a conceptually different approach than BinPAC, it uses similar building blocks and would nicely map to HILTI. Xplico [7] is a network forensic tool written in C that ships with protocol analyzers and manipulators.The HTTP analyzer, for example, reassembles HTTP payload by writing the packet contents into per-flow files on disk, which higher-level analyzers (such as webchat) then re-read for further analysis. HILTI's incremental and suspendable stream parsing makes it easier to implement such functionality efficiently. Software-defined networking (SDN) separates a network's device control and data planes, allowing operators to program routers and switches; OpenFlow [33] provides a vendor-agnostic interface to such functionality, and a number of higher-level languages [21, 29, 19, 34] use it to control compatible hardware devices. By adding an OpenFlow interface to HILTI, it could become a corresponding backend to drive the software component of such systems and dynamically control network policies based on traffic analysis. NetVM [35] compiles Snort rules into a custom intermediary representation, and from there just-in-time into native code. It routes packets through a graph of connected network elements, each of which features a stack-based processor, private registers, and a memory hierarchy. NetVM's functionality has a lower-level focus than HILTI because it primarily attempts to achieve portability of signature matching. Contrary to the VM isolation model of NetVM, HILTI's compilation into LLVM code enables late and global optimizations, whereas it appears difficult to optimize across NetVM elements. Similar to our example in §4, Linux has added support for JIT compiling BPF expressions into native assembly [11]. FreeBSD 7 also includes experimental BPF JIT support. Finally, there is a large body of work on accelerating parts of the network traffic analysis pipeline with custom hardware elements, targeting for example pattern matching (e.g., [42, 20]), parallelization on GPUs (e.g., [45, 9, 23]), robust TCP stream reassembly [15], and high-speed lookup tables such as PLUG [13]. HILTI's design allows to transparently offload specific computations to such specialized hardware when available.

9. CONCLUSION

We present the design and implementation of HILTI, a platform for deep, stateful network traffic analysis. HILTI represents a middle-layer located between a host application and the hardware platform that executes the analysis. We argue that while networking applications tend to share a large set of common functionality, they typically reimplement it from scratch each time, raising the possibility of falling into pitfalls that others have previously mastered. HILTI bridges that gap by providing a common substrate to applications to support their implementation while facilitating reuse of high-level components built on top of the platform. We developed a prototype compiler that implements all of HILTI's functionality, including rich domain-specific data types, automatic memory management, flexible control flow, concurrent execution, profiling and debugging support, and an extensive API for host applications. We further built four example applications on top of HILTI that demonstrate its ability to support a range of typical network analyses. We plan to advance HILTI further into a platform suitable for operational deployment in large-scale network environments by exploiting its full performance potential through transparent optimization and integration of non-standard hardware elements. We also envision HILTI to become a platform for networking research by facilitating rapid prototyping of novel network functionality.

Acknowledgments

This work was supported by the US National Science Foundation under grants CNS-0831535, CNS-0915667, CNS-1228792, and CNS-1228782. Any opinions, findings, and conclusions or recommendations expressed in this material are those of the authors or originators, and do not necessarily reflect the views of the National Science Foundation.

10. REFERENCES

[1] libnids. `http://libnids.sourceforge.net`.
[2] libtask. `http://swtch.com/libtask`.
[3] Objective-C Automatic Reference Counting (ARC). `http://clang.llvm.org/docs/AutomaticReferenceCounting.html`.
[4] re2c. `http://re2c.org`.
[5] Suricata source code - `src/flow-hash.c`. `https://github.com/inliniac/suricata/blob/master/src/flow-hash.c`.
[6] Web site and source code for HILTI and BinPAC++. `http://www.icir.org/hilti`.
[7] Xplico. `http://www.xplico.org`.
[8] B. Anderson. Abandoning Segmented Stacks in Rust. `https://mail.mozilla.org/pipermail/rust-dev/2013-November/006314.html`.

[9] M. B. Anwer, M. Motiwala, M. b. Tariq, and N. Feamster. SwitchBlade: A Platform for Rapid Deployment of Network Protocols on Programmable Hardware. In *Proc. ACM SIGCOMM*, 2010.

[10] A. W. Appel. *Compiling with Continuations*. Cambridge University Press, 1992.

[11] J. Corbet. A JIT for packet filters. `http://lwn.net/Articles/437981/`.

[12] S. Das. Segmented Stacks in LLVM. `http://www.google-melange.com/gsoc/project/google/gsoc2011/sanjoyd/13001`.

[13] L. De Carli, Y. Pan, A. Kumar, C. Estan, and K. Sankaralingam. PLUG: Flexible Lookup Modules for Rapid Deployment of New Protocols in High-Speed Routers. *ACM SIGCOMM Computer Communication Review*, 39:207–218, 2009.

[14] L. De Carli, R. Sommer, and S. Jha. Beyond Pattern Matching: A Concurrency Model for Stateful Deep Packet Inspection. In *Proc. ACM Computer and Communications Security (CCS)*, 2014.

[15] S. Dharmapurikar and V. Paxson. Robust TCP Stream Reassembly in the Presence of Adversaries. In *USENIX Security*, 2005.

[16] H. Dreger, A. Feldmann, V. Paxson, and R. Sommer. Operational Experiences with High-Volume Network Intrusion Detection. In *Proc. ACM Computer and Communications Security (CCS)*, Oct. 2004.

[17] H. Dreger, A. Feldmann, V. Paxson, and R. Sommer. Predicting the Resource Consumption of Network Intrusion Detection Systems. In *Proc. Recent Advances in Intrusion Detection (RAID)*, 2008.

[18] K. Fall, G. Iannaccone, M. Manesh, S. Ratnasamy, K. Argyraki, M. Dobrescu, and N. Egi. RouteBricks: Enabling General Purpose Network Infrastructure. *SIGOPS Operating Systems Review*, 45:112–125, February 2011.

[19] N. Foster et al. Frenetic: A High-Level Language for OpenFlow Networks. In *Proc. PRESTO*, 2010.

[20] R. Franklin, D. Carver, and B. Hutchings. Assisting Network Intrusion Detection with Reconfigurable Hardware. In *Proc. FCCM*, 2002.

[21] N. Gude, T. Koponen, J. Pettit, B. Pfaff, M. Casado, N. McKeown, and S. Shenker. NOX: Towards an Operating System for Networks. *ACM SIGCOMM Computer Communication Review*, 38:105–110, 2008.

[22] P. Gupta and N. McKeown. Algorithms for Packet Classification. `http://yuba.stanford.edu/~nickm/papers/classification_tutorial_01.pdf`, 2001.

[23] S. Han, K. Jang, K. Park, and S. Moon. PacketShader: A GPU-accelerated Software Router. In *Proc. ACM SIGCOMM*, 2010.

[24] M. Handley, C. Kreibich, and V. Paxson. Network Intrusion Detection: Evasion, Traffic Normalization, and End-to-End Protocol Semantics. In *Proc. USENIX Security*, 2001.

[25] S. Ioannidis, K. Anagnostakis, J. Ioannidis, and A. Keromytis. xPF: Packet Filtering for Lowcost Network Monitoring. In *Proc. IEEE HPSR*, pages 121–126, 2002.

[26] R. Jones, A. Hosking, and E. Moss. *The Garbage Collection Handbook: The Art of Automatic Memory Management.* Cambridge University Press, 2011.

[27] K. Kennedy and J. R. Allen. *Optimizing Compilers for Modern Architectures*. Morgan Kaufmann, 2002.

[28] E. Kohler, R. Morris, B. Chen, J. Jannotti, and M. F. Kaashoek. The Click Modular Router. *ACM Transactions on Computer Systems*, 18:263–297, August 2000.

[29] T. Koponen et al. Onix: A Distributed Control Platform for Large-Scale Production Networks. In *USENIX OSDI*, 2010.

[30] C. Lattner and V. Adve. LLVM: A Compilation Framework for Lifelong Program Analysis & Transformation. In *Proc. Symposium on Code Generation and Optimization*, 2004.

[31] Z. Li et al. NetShield: Massive Semantics-Based Vulnerability Signature Matching for High-Speed Networks. In *Proc. ACM SIGCOMM*, 2010.

[32] S. McCanne and V. Jacobson. The BSD Packet Filter: A New Architecture for User-level Packet Capture. In *Proc. USENIX Winter 1993 Conference*.

[33] N. McKeown et al. OpenFlow: Enabling Innovation in Campus Networks. *ACM SIGCOMM Computer Communication Review*, 38:69–74, 2008.

[34] C. Monsanto, N. Foster, R. Harrison, and D. Walker. A Compiler and Run-time System for Network Programming Languages. In *Proc. POPL*, 2012.

[35] O. Morandi, G. Moscardi, and F. Risso. An Intrusion Detection Sensor for the NetVM Virtual Processor. In *Proc. ICOIN*, 2009.

[36] R. Pang, V. Paxson, R. Sommer, and L. Peterson. binpac: A yacc for Writing Application Protocol Parsers. In *Proc. ACM Internet Measurement Conference (IMC)*, 2006.

[37] V. Paxson. Bro: A System for Detecting Network Intruders in Real-Time. *Computer Networks*, 31(23–24), 1999.

[38] V. Paxson, K. Asanovic, S. Dharmapurikar, J. Lockwood, R. Pang, R. Sommer, and N. Weaver. Rethinking Hardware Support for Network Analysis and Intrusion Prevention. In *Proc. USENIX Hot Security Workshop*, August 2006.

[39] M. Pettersson, K. Sagonas, and E. Johansson. The HiPE/x86 Erlang Compiler: System Description and Performance Evaluation. In *Proc. FLOPS*, 2002.

[40] F. Risso and M. Baldi. NetPDL: An Extensible XML-based Language for Packet Header Description. *Computer Networks*, 50:688–706, April 2006.

[41] N. Schear, D. Albrecht, and N. Borisov. High-Speed Matching of Vulnerability Signatures. In *Proc. Recent Advances in Intrusion Detection (RAID)*, 2008.

[42] R. Sidhu and V. K. Prasanna. Fast Regular Expression Matching using FPGAs. In *Proc. IEEE FCCM*, Apr. 2001.

[43] R. Sommer, V. Paxson, and N. Weaver. An Architecture for Exploiting Multi-Core Processors to Parallelize Network Intrusion Prevention. *Concurrency and Computation: Practice and Experience*, 21(10):1255–1279, 2009.

[44] M. Vallentin, R. Sommer, J. Lee, C. Leres, V. Paxson, and B. Tierney. The NIDS Cluster: Scalable, Stateful Network Intrusion Detection on Commodity Hardware. In *Proc. Recent Advances in Intrusion Detection (RAID)*, 2007.

[45] G. Vasiliadis, S. Antonatos, M. Polychronakis, E. P. Markatos, and S. Ioannidis. Gnort: High Performance Network Intrusion Detection Using Graphics Processors. In *Proc. Recent Advances in Intrusion Detection (RAID)*, 2008.

[46] D. Zaparanuks, M. Jovic, and M. Hauswirth. Accuracy of Performance Counter Measurements. In *IEEE ISPASS*, 2009.

The Matter of Heartbleed

*Zakir Durumeric[1], James Kasten[1], David Adrian[1], J. Alex Halderman[1], Michael Bailey[1,2]
[1] University of Michigan
[2] University of Illinois, Urbana Champaign
{zakir, jdkasten, davadria, jhalderm}@umich.edu, mdbailey@illinois.edu

*Frank Li[3], Nicholas Weaver[3,4], Johanna Amann[4], Jethro Beekman[3], Mathias Payer[3,5], Vern Paxson[3,4]
[3] EECS, University of California, Berkeley
[4] International Computer Science Institute
[5] Purdue University
{frankli, nweaver, jbeekman, vern}@cs.berkeley.edu, johanna@icir.org, mpayer@purdue.edu

ABSTRACT

The Heartbleed vulnerability took the Internet by surprise in April 2014. The vulnerability, one of the most consequential since the advent of the commercial Internet, allowed attackers to remotely read protected memory from an estimated 24–55% of popular HTTPS sites. In this work, we perform a comprehensive, measurement-based analysis of the vulnerability's impact, including (1) tracking the vulnerable population, (2) monitoring patching behavior over time, (3) assessing the impact on the HTTPS certificate ecosystem, and (4) exposing real attacks that attempted to exploit the bug. Furthermore, we conduct a large-scale vulnerability notification experiment involving 150,000 hosts and observe a nearly 50% increase in patching by notified hosts. Drawing upon these analyses, we discuss what went well and what went poorly, in an effort to understand how the technical community can respond more effectively to such events in the future.

1. INTRODUCTION

In March 2014, researchers found a catastrophic vulnerability in OpenSSL, the cryptographic library used to secure connections in popular server products including Apache and Nginx. While OpenSSL has had several notable security issues during its 16 year history, this flaw—the *Heartbleed* vulnerability—was one of the most impactful. Heartbleed allows attackers to read sensitive memory from vulnerable servers, potentially including cryptographic keys, login credentials, and other private data. Exacerbating its severity, the bug is simple to understand and exploit.

In this work, we analyze the impact of the vulnerability and track the server operator community's responses. Using extensive active scanning, we assess who was vulnerable, characterizing Heartbleed's scope across popular HTTPS websites and the full IPv4 address space. We also survey the range of protocols and server products affected. We estimate that 24–55% of HTTPS servers in the Alexa Top 1 Million were initially vulnerable, including 44 of the Alexa Top 100. Two days after disclosure, we observed that 11% of HTTPS sites in the Alexa Top 1 Million remained vulnerable, as did 6% of all HTTPS servers in the public IPv4 address space. We find that vulnerable hosts were not randomly distributed, with more than 50% located in only 10 ASes that do not reflect the ASes with the most HTTPS hosts. In our scans of the IPv4 address space, we identify over 70 models of vulnerable embedded devices and software packages. We also observe that both SMTP+TLS and Tor were heavily affected; more than half of all Tor nodes were vulnerable in the days following disclosure.

Our investigation of the operator community's response finds that within the first 24 hours, all but 5 of the Alexa Top 100 sites were patched, and within 48 hours, all of the vulnerable hosts in the top 500 were patched. While popular sites responded quickly, we observe that patching plateaued after about two weeks, and 3% of HTTPS sites in the Alexa Top 1 Million remained vulnerable almost two months after disclosure.

In addition to patching, many sites replaced their TLS certificates due to the possibility that the private keys could have been leaked. We analyze certificate replacement and find that while many of the most popular websites reacted quickly, less than a quarter of Alexa Top 1 Million sites replaced certificates in the week following disclosure. Even more worryingly, only 10% of the sites that were vulnerable 48 hours after disclosure replaced their certificates within the next month, and of those that did, 14% neglected to change the private key, gaining no protection from certificate replacement.

We also investigate widespread attempts to exploit Heartbleed, as seen in extensive bulk traffic traces recorded at four sites. We find no evidence of exploitation prior to the vulnerability's public disclosure, but we detect subsequent exploit attempts from almost 700 sources, beginning less than 24 hours after disclosure. Comparing attack attempts across sites, we observe that despite the large number of sources and scans, only a handful appear to reflect exhaustive Internet-wide scans.

Finally, starting three weeks after disclosure, we undertook a large-scale notification effort and contacted the operators responsible for the remaining vulnerable servers. By contacting the operators in two waves, we could conduct a controlled experiment and measure the impact of notification on patching. We report the effects of our notifications, observing a surprisingly high 47% increase in patching by notified operators.

We draw upon these observations to discuss both what went well and what went poorly in the aftermath of Heartbleed. By better understanding the lessons of this security disaster, the technical community can respond more effectively to such events in the future.

*These authors contributed equally to this work.

IMC'14, November 5–7, 2014, Vancouver, BC, Canada.
ACM 978-1-4503-3213-2/14/11.
http://dx.doi.org/10.1145/2663716.2663755 .

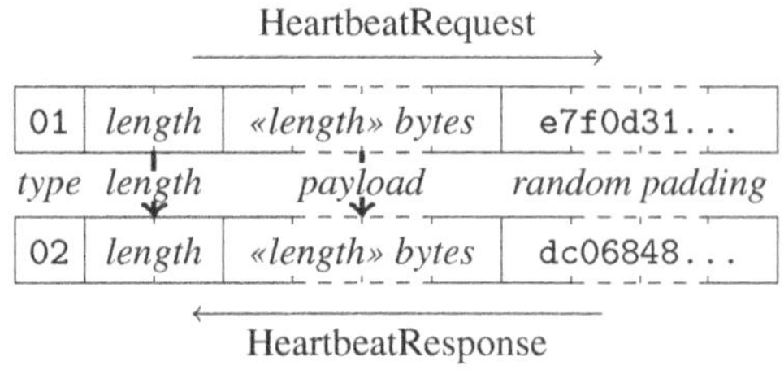

Figure 1: **Heartbeat Protocol.** Heartbeat requests include user data and random padding. The receiving peer responds by echoing back the data in the initial request along with its own padding.

2. BACKGROUND

On April 7, 2014, the OpenSSL project publicly disclosed the Heartbleed vulnerability, a bug in their implementation of the TLS Heartbeat Extension. The vulnerability allowed attackers to remotely dump protected memory—including data passed over the secure channel and private cryptographic keys—from both clients and servers. In this section, we provide a brief history of OpenSSL, the Heartbeat Extension, and details of the vulnerability and its disclosure.

2.1 OpenSSL: A Brief History

OpenSSL is a popular open-source cryptographic library that implements the SSL and TLS protocols. It is widely used by server software to facilitate secure connections for web, email, VPN, and messaging services. The project started in 1998 and began tracking vulnerabilities in April 2001.

Over the last 13 years, OpenSSL has documented six code execution vulnerabilities that allowed attackers to compromise private server data (e.g., private cryptographic keys and messages in memory) and execute arbitrary code. The project has faced eight information leak vulnerabilities, four of which allowed attackers to retrieve plaintext, and two of which exposed private keys. Two of the vulnerabilities arose due to protocol weaknesses; the remainder came from implementation errors.

The Heartbleed bug reflects one of the most impactful vulnerabilities during OpenSSL's history for several reasons: (1) it allowed attackers to retrieve private cryptographic keys and private user data, (2) it was easy to exploit, and (3) HTTPS and other TLS services have become increasingly popular, resulting in more affected services.

2.2 TLS Heartbeat Extension

The Heartbeat Extension allows either end-point of a TLS connection to detect whether its peer is still present, and was motivated by the need for session management in Datagram TLS (DTLS). Standard implementations of TLS do not require the extension as they can rely on TCP for equivalent session management.

Peers indicate support for the extension during the initial TLS handshake. Following negotiation, either end-point can send a `HeartbeatRequest` message to verify connectivity. The extension was introduced in February 2012 in RFC 6520 [66], added to OpenSSL on December 31, 2011, and released in OpenSSL Version 1.0.1 on March 14, 2012.

`HeartbeatRequest` messages consist of a one-byte type field, a two-byte payload length field, a payload, and at least 16 bytes of random padding. Upon receipt of the request, the receiving endpoint responds with a similar `HeartbeatResponse` message, in which it echoes back the `HeartbeatRequest` payload and its own random padding, per Figure 1.

Date	Event
03/21	Neel Mehta of Google discovers Heartbleed
03/21	Google patches OpenSSL on their servers
03/31	CloudFlare is privately notified and patches
04/01	Google notifies the OpenSSL core team
04/02	Codenomicon independently discovers Heartbleed
04/03	Codenomicon informs NCSC-FI
04/04	Akamai is privately notified and patches
04/05	Codenomicon purchases the `heartbleed.com` domain
04/06	OpenSSL notifies several Linux distributions
04/07	NCSC-FI notifies OpenSSL core team
04/07	OpenSSL releases version 1.0.1g and a security advisory
04/07	CloudFlare and Codenomicon disclose on Twitter
04/08	Al-Bassam scans the Alexa Top 10,000
04/09	University of Michigan begins scanning

Table 1: **Timeline of Events in March and April 2014.** The discovery of Heartbleed was originally kept private by Google as part of responsible disclosure efforts. News of the bug spread privately among inner tech circles. However, after Codenomicon independently discovered the bug and began separate disclosure processes, the news rapidly became public [36, 53].

2.3 Heartbleed Vulnerability

The OpenSSL implementation of the Heartbeat Extension contained a vulnerability that allowed either end-point to read data following the payload message in its peer's memory by specifying a payload length larger than the amount of data in the `HeartbeatRequest` message. Because the payload length field is two bytes, the peer responds with up to 2^{16} bytes (~64 KB) of memory. The bug itself is simple: the peer trusts the attacker-specified length of an attacker-controlled message.

The OpenSSL patch adds a bounds check that discards the `HeartbeatRequest` message if the payload length field exceeds the length of the payload. However, while the bug is easy to conceptualize and the fix is straight-forward, the potential impact of the bug is severe: it allows an attacker to read private memory, potentially including information transferred over the secure channel and cryptographic secrets [31, 59, 67].

2.4 Heartbleed Timeline

The Heartbleed vulnerability was originally found by Neel Mehta, a Google computer security employee, in March 2014 [36]. Upon finding the bug and patching its servers, Google notified the core OpenSSL team on April 1. Independently, a security consulting firm, Codenomicon, found the vulnerability on April 2, and reported it to National Cyber Security Centre Finland (NCSC-FI). After receiving notification that two groups independently discovered the vulnerability, the OpenSSL core team decided to release a patched version.

The public disclosure of Heartbleed started on April 7, 2014 at 17:49 UTC with the version 1.0.1g release announcement [53], followed by the public security advisory [52] released at 20:37 UTC; both announcements were sent to the OpenSSL mailing list. Several parties knew of the vulnerability in advance, including CloudFlare, Akamai and Facebook. Red Hat, SuSE, Debian, FreeBSD and ALT Linux were notified less than 24 hours before the public disclosure [36]. Others, such as Ubuntu, Gentoo, Chromium, Cisco, and Juniper were not aware of the bug prior to its public release. We present a timeline of events in Table 1.

3. THE IMPACT OF HEARTBLEED

Heartbleed had the potential to affect any service that used OpenSSL to facilitate TLS connections, including popular web, mail, messaging, and database servers (Table 2). To track its damage, we performed regular vulnerability scans against the Alexa Top 1 Million domains [1] and against 1% samples of the public, non-reserved IPv4 address space. We generated these samples using random selection with removal, per ZMap's existing randomization function [30]. We excluded hosts and networks that previously requested removal from our daily HTTPS scans [29]. In this section, we analyze the impact on those services—particularly HTTPS. We have publicly released all of the data used for this analysis at https://scans.io/study/umich-heartbleed.

3.1 Scanning Methodology

We tested for the Heartbleed bug by modifying ZMap [30] to send Heartbeat requests with no payload nor padding, and the length field set to zero. Per the RFC [66], these requests should be rejected. However, vulnerable versions of OpenSSL send a response containing only padding, rather than simply drop the request. The patched version of OpenSSL—as well as other popular libraries, including GnuTLS, NSS, Bouncy Castle, PolarSSL, CyaSSL and MatrixSSL—correctly discard the request (or do not support the Heartbeat Extension).

We emphasize that this approach does not exploit the vulnerability or access any private memory—only random padding is sent back by the server. While it was later found that Heartbleed scanning caused HP Integrated Lights-Out (iLO) devices to crash [11], we received no reports of our scans disrupting these devices—likely because our approach did not exploit the vulnerability. We have publicly released our scanner at https://zmap.io.

3.2 False Negatives

Our Heartbleed scanner contained a bug that caused vulnerable sites to sometimes appear safe due to a timeout when probing individual hosts. The root cause was that the scanner labelled each host's vulnerability as false by default, rather than null or unknown. If a Heartbleed test timed out, the scanner returned the host's vulnerability status as the default false, providing no indication of a failed test. The result is a potential false negative, where the scan reports the system as immune. Note that our scanner does not however err when reporting a system as vulnerable. As we develop in this section, the likelihood of a given scan exhibiting such as false negative fortunately does not appear to depend on the particular address being scanned, and this allows us to estimate the false negative rate.

We first assessed whether some addresses were more prone to manifest false negatives than others. To do so, we compared three complete IPv4 scans and examined systems reported as vulnerable in one scan but immune in previous scans. Since the scanner does not err in reporting a host as vulnerable, any prior report of immunity reflects a false negative (assuming no one unpatches systems). We found the IP addresses associated with such false negatives spread evenly across the address space, without any apparent correlations. This observation leads us to believe the false negatives manifest in an address-independent manner.

Although our initial scanner did not fetch the web page itself, a subsequent change in the comprehensive scan (but not the incremental scans) attempted to fetch the server's home page. As the home page fetch occurred after the Heartbleed check, any reported home page data implicitly indicates that the Heartbleed test successfully completed without a timeout.

To investigate the false negative rate, we use two full scans of the IPv4 address space, one with and one without home page fetching. The full scan conducted on April 24 did not grab server home pages, while the May 1 scan did, hence we know the validity of scan results from the May 1 scan. To soundly conduct this comparison we need to remove servers that may have switched IP addresses between the two scans. To do so, we only considered servers that presented identical TLS certificates between the two scans. While this restriction potentially introduces a bias because some sites will have both patched and changed their TLS certificates, the address-independent nature of the false negatives should cause this effect to even out.

Our scanner failed to grab the server home page for 24% of the hosts in the May scan. Of these 24% of hosts, we observe 44% appear immune. False negatives could only have occurred when testing these hosts. The remaining 56% of hosts appeared vulnerable (and hence are correctly labelled). From this, we conclude that at most $(0.24 \cdot 0.44) = 0.105$, or 10.5%, of hosts were incorrectly labelled in the May 1 scan.

For the April scan, the only observable signal of a false negative is if a host was reported immune and then reported vulnerable in the May scan. We find 6.5% of hosts exhibit this behavior. Assuming that people do not unpatch their systems, this provides an estimated lower bound of 6.5% for the April scan false negative rate. This estimate represents a lower bound because we cannot determine the vulnerability in April of a host that appears immune in both scans. In that case, a false negative is a host vulnerable in April but reported as immune, and patched by May. However, we do observe that of hosts reported as vulnerable in the April scan and successfully tested in May (so the server page was retrieved), only 0.36% appeared immune in May, indicating a very modest overall patching rate between the two scans (which accords with Figure 3 below). Given that our false negatives are address-independent, we expect a similarly low patch rate for all vulnerable April hosts. Thus, while a 6.5% false negative rate is a lower bound for the April scan, the true rate should not be significantly higher.

Given the similarity of these two false negative estimates using two different scans, ultimately we conclude that the scanner exhibited a false negative rate between 6.5% and 10.5%, but that these manifest independently of the particular server scanned. Due to this address-independent behavior, we can assume a similar false negative rate for sampled scans. We attempt to account for this error whenever possible. In particular, the bias implies that any population-based survey based on a single scan underestimates the vulnerable population. Finally, for our assessment of the impact of notifications (Section 7), we only consider a given server as non-vulnerable when it consistently reports as immune in repeated scans, which would require multiple (presumably independent) false negatives to occur before introducing a bias.

3.3 Impact on Popular Websites

Determining which websites were initially vulnerable poses significant difficulties. Little attention was paid to the Heartbeat Extension prior to the vulnerability announcement, and many popular sites patched the vulnerability within hours of the disclosure. Codenomicon, one of the groups that discovered Heartbleed, speculated that 66% of HTTPS sites were vulnerable [45]. However, this number represented the Apache and Nginx market share and may well reflect an overestimate, because some operators may have disabled the extension, deployed dedicated SSL endpoints, or used older, non-vulnerable versions of OpenSSL.

Web Servers		Mail Servers		Database Servers		XMPP Servers		Other Servers	
Apache (mod_ssl) [45]	Yes	Sendmail [62]	Yes	MySQL [62]	Yes	OpenFire [12]	No	OpenVPN [54]	Yes
Microsoft IIS [46]	No	Postfix [62]	Yes	PostgreSQL [62]	Yes	Ejabberd [5]	Yes	OpenLDAP [63]	Yes
Nginx [14]	Yes	Qmail [62]	Yes	SQL Server [46]	No	Jabberd14 [70]	Yes	Stunnel [65]	Yes
Lighttpd [62]	Yes	Exim [35]	Yes	Oracle [55]	No	Jabberd2 [41]	Yes	Openswan [49]	Yes
Tomcat [17]	Yes	Courier [37]	Yes	IBM DB2 [38]	No			Telnetd-ssl [4]	Yes
Google GWS [50]	Yes	Exchange [46]	No	MongoDB [47]	Yes			OpenDKIM [3]	Yes
LiteSpeed [42]	Yes	Dovecot [35]	Yes	CouchDB [32]	No			Proftpd [64]	Yes
IBM Web Server [38]	Yes	Cyrus [48]	Yes	Cassandra [6]	No			Bitcoin Client [24]	Yes
Tengine [13]	Yes	Zimbra [56]	Yes	Redis [35]	No				
Jetty [51]	No								

Table 2: **Vulnerable Server Products.** We survey which server products were affected by Heartbleed.

3.3.1 Top 100 Websites

All of the Alexa Top 100 websites were patched within 48 hours of disclosure—prior to the start of our scans. To document the impact on these websites, we aggregated press releases, other's targeted scans, and quotes provided to Mashable, a news site that hosted one of the popular lists of sites for which users should change their passwords due to possible exposure via Heartbleed [10].

Al-Bassam completed a vulnerability scan of the Alexa Top 10,000 domains on April 8, 2014 at 16:00 UTC (22 hours after the vulnerability disclosure) [20]. His scan found 630 vulnerable sites, 3,687 supporting HTTPS but not vulnerable, and 5,683 not supporting HTTPS. Several prominent sites, including Yahoo, Imgur, Stack Overflow, Flickr, Sogou, OkCupid, and DuckDuckGo, were found vulnerable. We investigated other sites in the Alexa Top 100 and found that half made a public statement regarding vulnerability or provided information to Mashable [8, 10, 18–21, 23, 26, 28, 33, 39, 40, 50, 58, 61, 68, 69, 71, 73, 74]. Combining these press releases, Mashable's report, and Al-Bassam's scan, we find that at least 44 of the Alexa Top 100 websites were vulnerable. However, this figure reflects a lower bound, as we were unable to find information for some sites. Table 3 lists the vulnerability status of the top 30 HTTPS-enabled sites in the US.

Site	Vuln.	Site	Vuln.	Site	Vuln.
Google	Yes	Bing	No	Wordpress	Yes
Facebook	No	Pinterest	Yes	Huff. Post	?
Youtube	Yes	Blogspot	Yes	ESPN	?
Yahoo	Yes	Go.com	?	Reddit	Yes
Amazon	No	Live	No	Netflix	Yes
Wikipedia	Yes	CNN	?	MSN.com	No
LinkedIn	No	Instagram	Yes	Weather.com	?
eBay	No	Paypal	No	IMDB	No
Twitter	No	Tumblr	Yes	Apple	No
Craigslist	?	Imgur	Yes	Yelp	?

Table 3: **Vulnerability of Top 30 US HTTPS-Enabled Websites.** We aggregate published lists of vulnerable sites, press releases, and news sources to determine which of the top sites were vulnerable before the discovery of Heartbleed.

3.3.2 Estimating Broader Impact

Within 48 hours of the initial disclosure, we conducted our first vulnerability scan of the Alexa Top 1 Million. At that point, we found that 45% of all sites supported HTTPS. 60% of those supported the Heartbeat Extension, and 11% of all HTTPS sites were vulnerable. While 60% of HTTPS sites supported the extension, 91% of these were powered by known vulnerable web servers (e.g., Nginx or Apache Web Server), as shown in Table 4. If all of these servers were initially vulnerable and operators installed a patched OpenSSL version (rather than rebuilding OpenSSL with Heartbeat disabled), at most about 55% of the HTTPS sites in the Alexa Top 1 Million were initially vulnerable.

While disabling the largely unused extension would appear to provide an obvious solution, it is not possible to disable the extension through a configuration file. Instead, this change requires recompiling OpenSSL with a specific flag—an option likely more laborious than updating the OpenSSL software package.

Some sites may possibly have used an older version of OpenSSL that was not vulnerable. To estimate a lower bound for the number of vulnerable sites, we considered sites that used vulnerable web servers and supported TLS 1.1 and 1.2—features first introduced in OpenSSL 1.0.1 along with the Heartbeat Extension. Such sites would have been vulnerable unless administrators had recompiled OpenSSL to explicitly disable the extension.

To estimate the number of sites that supported TLS 1.1 and 1.2 prior to the Heartbleed disclosure, we analyzed the data collected by the Trustworthy Internet Movement's SSL Pulse [16], which provides monthly statistics of SSL-enabled websites within the Alexa Top 1 Million. We find that 56,019 of the 171,608 (32.6%) sites in the SSL Pulse dataset supported TLS 1.1 or 1.2. Of these sites, 72.7% used known vulnerable web servers, yielding an estimated lower bound of 23.7% of the sites being vulnerable.

In summary, we can reasonably bound the proportion of vulnerable Alexa Top 1 Million HTTPS-enabled websites as lying between 24–55% at the time of the Heartbleed disclosure.

Web Server	Alexa Sites	Heartbeat Ext.	Vulnerable
Apache	451,270 (47.3%)	95,217 (58.4%)	28,548 (64.4%)
Nginx	182,379 (19.1%)	46,450 (28.5%)	11,185 (25.2%)
Microsoft IIS	96,259 (10.1%)	637 (0.4%)	195 (0.4%)
Litespeed	17,597 (1.8%)	6,838 (4.2%)	1,601 (3.6%)
Other	76,817 (8.1%)	5,383 (3.3%)	962 (2.2%)
Unknown	129,006 (13.5%)	8,545 (5.2%)	1,833 (4.1%)

Table 4: **Alexa Top 1 Million Web Servers.** We classify the web servers used by the Alexa Top 1 Million Sites, as observed in our first scan on April 9, 2014. Percentages represent the breakdown of server products for each category. We note that while Microsoft IIS was not vulnerable to Heartbleed, a small number of IIS servers used vulnerable SSL terminators.

3.4 Pre-Disclosure Patching

Google, Akamai, and other sites disabled the Heartbeat Extension prior to public disclosure. To detect when services disabled the Heartbeat Extension, we examined data from the ICSI Certificate Notary, which passively monitors TLS connections from seven research and university networks (approximately 314K active users) [22].

The Notary data shows that Google disabled Heartbeat starting at least 12 days prior to public disclosure, with all servers Heartbeat-disabled by April 15. While some servers still had Heartbeat enabled after disclosure, they may not have been exploitable. Google may have already patched those servers, and decided afterwards to disable the Heartbeat Extension as a company-wide policy. Similarly, Akamai began disabling Heartbeat at least 4 days prior to disclosure, completing the process by April 18.

3.5 Internet-Wide HTTPS Vulnerability

We began performing daily 1% scans of the IPv4 address space on April 9, 48 hours after the disclosure. Our first scan found that 11.4% of HTTPS hosts supported the Heartbeat Extension and 5.9% of all HTTPS hosts were vulnerable. Combining these proportions from random sampling with our daily scans of the HTTPS ecosystem [29] (which do not include Heartbleed vulnerability testing), we estimate that 2.0 million HTTPS hosts were vulnerable two days after disclosure.

Surprisingly, 10 ASes accounted for over 50% of vulnerable HTTPS hosts but represented only 8.6% of all HTTPS hosts (Figure 2). With the exception of Comcast Cable Communications, the ASes all belonged to web hosting companies or cloud providers (Table 5). The vulnerable hosts in the Comcast AS were Fortinet devices. In the case of Strato Hosting, vulnerable addresses were hosting Parallels Plesk Panel, a web hosting management software. The vulnerable addresses of Minotavar Computers, ZeXoTeK IT-Services, Euclid systems, Vivid Hosting, and ACCESSPEOPLE-DE all served the default Apache page, likely reflecting named-based virtual hosts. In the case of the two Amazon ASes and Hetzner Online, a large number of the vulnerable hosts served public facing websites, and used Apache or Nginx.

AS	% of Vulnerable	% of HTTPS
Minotavar Computers EOOD	18.5%	1.7%
ZeXoTeK IT-Services GmbH	13.0%	0.9%
ACCESSPEOPLE-DE ISP-Service	7.4%	0.7%
Amazon.com, Inc.	4.6%	0.8%
Amazon.com, Inc.	4.1%	0.9%
Hetzner Online AG	2.6%	0.4%
Comcast Cable Communications	2.3%	2.8%
Vivid Hosting	2.0%	0.1%
Euclid Systems	1.5%	0.1%
Strato Hosting	1.4%	0.1%
Total	57.4%	8.6%

Table 5: **Top ASes with Most Vulnerable Hosts.** We aggregate hosts by AS and find that 57% of vulnerable hosts in the April 9 scan were located in only 10 ASes.

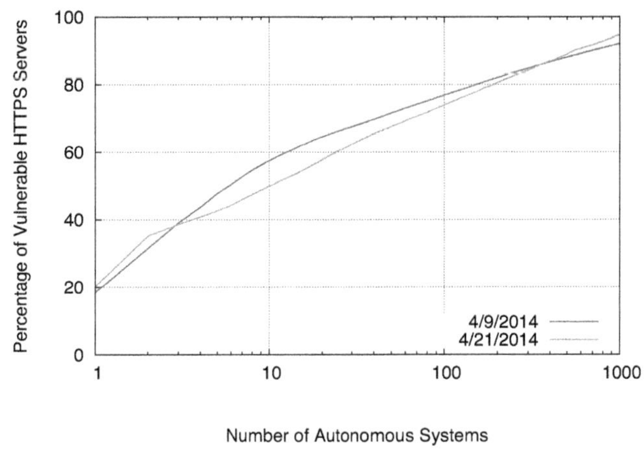

Figure 2: **Vulnerable Servers by AS.** We aggregate vulnerable hosts by AS and find that over 50% of vulnerable hosts are located in ten ASes.

3.6 Vulnerable Devices and Products

Heartbleed also affected many embedded systems, including printers, firewalls, VPN endpoints, NAS devices, video conferencing systems, and security cameras. To understand the embedded systems that were affected, we analyzed the self-signed certificates employed by vulnerable hosts. We clustered these by fields in the certificate Subject and manually inspected large clusters. From this, we developed device "fingerprints". We took a conservative approach and chose the most restrictive fingerprints in order to minimize false positive identifications. This, and the manual effort required, means that our fingerprints lack comprehensive coverage. However, we still identified 74 distinct sets of vulnerable devices and software packages that fall into a number of broad categories:

Communication Servers: IceWarp messaging, Zimbra collaboration servers, iPECS VoIP systems, and Polycom and Cisco video conference products.

Software Control Panels: Puppet Enterprise Dashboard, IBM System X Integrated Management Modules, Kloxo Web hosting control panel, PowerMTA, Chef/Opscode management consoles, VMWare servers, and Parallels control panels for Plesk and Confixx.

Network Attached Storage: QNAP, D-Link, ReadyNAS, LaCie, Synology, and Western Digital NAS devices.

Firewall and VPN Devices: Devices from Barracuda Networks, Cisco, SonicWALL, WatchGuard, OpenVPN, pfSense, TOPSEC Network Security (a Chinese vendor), and Fortinet.

Printers: Dell, Lexmark, Brother, and HP printers.

Miscellaneous: Hikvision and SWANN security cameras, AcquiSuite power monitors, IPACCT (a management tool used by Russian ISPs), Aruba Networks WiFi login portals, INSYS VPN access for industrial controllers, and SpeedLine Solutions (the "#1-rated Pizza POS System").

3.7 Other Impacts

While our study focuses on Heartbleed's impact on public HTTPS web services, Heartbleed also affected mail servers, the Tor network, Bitcoin, Android, and wireless networks, as we briefly assess in this section.

Mail Servers. SMTP, IMAP, and POP3 can use TLS for transport security via use of a `StartTLS` directive within a plaintext session. As such, if mail servers used OpenSSL to facilitate TLS connections, they could have been similarly vulnerable to Heartbleed. On April 10, we scanned a random 1% sample of the IPv4 address space for vulnerable SMTP servers. We found that 45% of those providing SMTP+TLS supported the Heartbeat Extension, and 7.5% were vulnerable to Heartbleed.

These estimates only provide a lower bound, because similar to HTTPS, our scanner sometimes timed out, causing false negatives. (We also scanned for IMAP and POP3 servers, but later analysis of the data found systematic flaws that rendered the results unusable.)

Tor Project. Tor relays and bridges use OpenSSL to provide TLS-enabled inter-relay communication. In our April 10 scan, we found that 97% of relays supported Heartbeat and could have been vulnerable. 48% of the relays remained vulnerable at that time, three days after announcement of the vulnerability. The vulnerability could have allowed an attacker to extract both short-term onion and long-term identity keys, ultimately allowing an attacker to intercept traffic and impersonate a relay. In the case of a hidden service, the bug could have allowed an entry guard to locate a hidden service. The Tor client was similarly affected, potentially allowing entry guards to read sensitive information from a client's memory, such as recently visited websites [27].

Bitcoin Clients. Heartbleed affected both Bitcoin clients and exchanges, and in the most severe case, allowed an attacker to compromise the accounts on a popular exchange, BTCJam [15]. The value of Bitcoin did not change drastically on April 7, the date of public disclosure, falling only 3.1% from the previous day (a figure within its regular volatility) and returned to its April 6 value by April 14.

All versions of the Bitcoin software from May 2012 to April 2014 used a vulnerable OpenSSL version [2]. Immediately after Heartbleed's disclosure, a new Bitcoin version was released linking to the newly patched OpenSSL version. Because clients were also affected by the bug, attackers could potentially compromise wallets or retrieve private keys if a susceptible user followed a payment request link [24]. However, we have not found any reports of the theft of Bitcoins from local wallets.

Several companies, including Bitstamp and Bitfinex, temporarily suspended transactions on April 8 until they could patch their servers. In the most severe case, 12 customers had a total of 28 BTC ($\approx$ \$6,500) stolen from BTCJam after account credentials were compromised, though with all funds subsequently reinstated by the exchange [15].

Android. Heartbleed only affected Android version 4.1.1 [50]. It is unclear how many devices currently run the affected version, but Google recently estimated that 33.5% of all Android devices currently run Android 4.1.x [7]. A vulnerable device would have been susceptible to having memory read by a malicious server.

Wireless Networks. Several variants of the Extended Authentication Protocol, a commonly used framework for wireless network authentication, use TLS, including EAP-PEAP, EAP-TLS, and EAP-TTLS. For implementations based on OpenSSL, Heartbleed would have allowed attackers to retrieve network keys and user credentials from wireless clients and access points [34]. We do not know of any statistics regarding what sort of vulnerable population this potentially represents.

4. PATCHING

In Section 3, we estimated the initial impact of Heartbleed. In this section, we discuss the patching behavior that occurred subsequent to the disclosure.

4.1 Popular Websites

Popular websites did well at patching. As mentioned above, only five sites in the Alexa Top 100 remained vulnerable when Al-Bassam completed his scan 22 hours after disclosure. All of the top 100 sites were patched by the time we started our scans, 48 hours after disclosure. As discussed in Section 3, our first scan of the Alexa Top 1 Million found that 11.5% of HTTPS sites remained vulnerable. The most popular site that remained vulnerable was `mpnrs.com`, ranked 689th globally and 27th in Germany. Similarly, all but seven of the vulnerable top 100 sites replaced their certificate in the first couple of weeks following disclosure. Most interestingly, `godaddy.com`, operator of the largest commercial certificate authority, did not change their certificates until much later. The other six sites are `mail.ru`, `instagram.com`, `vk.com`, `sohu.com`, `adobe.com`, and `kickass.to`.

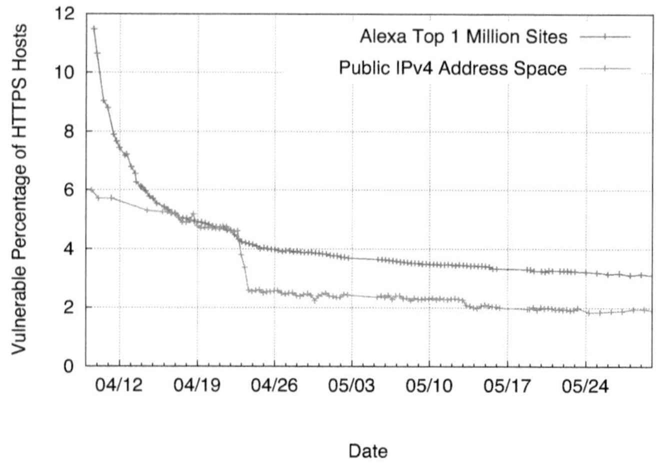

Figure 3: **HTTPS Patch Rate.** We track vulnerable web servers in the Alexa Top 1 Million and the public IPv4 address space. We track the latter by scanning independent 1% samples of the public IPv4 address space every 8 hours. Between April 9 and June 4, the vulnerable population of the Alexa Top 1 Million shrank from 11.5% to 3.1%, and for all HTTPS hosts from 6.0% to 1.9%.

As shown in Figure 3, while many Alexa Top 1 Million sites patched within the first week, the patch rate quickly dropped after two weeks, with only a very modest decline between April 26 and June 4, 2014. While top sites in North America and Europe were initially more vulnerable than Asia and Oceania (presumably due to more prevalent use of OpenSSL-based servers), they all followed the same general patching pattern visible in Figure 3.

4.2 Internet-Wide HTTPS

As can be seen in Figure 3, the patching trend for the entire IPv4 address space differs from that of the Alexa Top 1 Million. The largest discrepancy occurs between April 22, 14:35 EDT and April 23, 14:35 EDT, during which the total number of vulnerable hosts fell by nearly a factor of two, from 4.6% to 2.6%. This dropoff occurred because several heavily affected ASes patched many of their systems within a short time frame. The shift from 4.6% to 3.8% between 14:35 and 22:35 on April 22 reflects Minotavar Computers patching 29% of their systems, ZeXoTeK IT-Services patching 60%, and Euclid Systems patching 43%. Between April 22, 22:35 and April 23, 06:35, Minotavar Computers continued to patch systems. The last major drop from 3.4% to 2.6% (06:35–14:35 on April 23) was primarily due to Minotavar Computers patched remaining systems, and to a lesser extent, Euclid Systems and Vivid Hosting.

4.3 Comparison to Debian Weak Keys

In 2008, a bug was discovered in the Debian OpenSSL package, in which the generation of cryptographic keys had a severely limited source of entropy, reducing the space of possible keys to a few hundred thousand. The lack of entropy allowed attackers to fully enumerate the SSL and SSH keys generated on Debian systems, thus making it vital for Debian OpenSSL users to generate fresh replacement keys.

Yilek et al. measured the impact of the vulnerability and patching behavior by performing daily scans of HTTPS servers [72]. Given the similarities in the severity and nature of remediation between

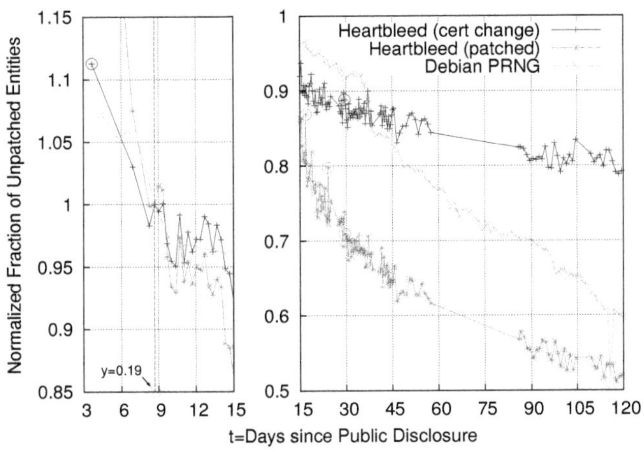

Figure 4: **Comparison of the Patch Rates of the Debian PRNG and Heartbleed Vulnerabilities.** The y-axis is normalized at 8.7 days, indicated by the vertical striped line. Thus, the fraction of unpatched entities at a given time is relative to the fraction at 8.7 days after disclosure, for each dataset. Except for the points marked by ○, for each measurement the size of the Debian PRNG entity population was $n = 41{,}200 \pm 2{,}000$, and for Heartbleed, $n = 100{,}900 \pm 7{,}500$. Due to a misconfiguration in our measurement setup, no Heartbleed data is available days 58–85.

this event and Heartbleed, we compared the community's responses to both disclosures.

A key methodological issue with conducting such a comparison concerns ensuring we use an "apples-to-apples" metric for assessing the extent of the community's response to each event. The comparison is further complicated by the fact that our Heartbleed measurements sample a different 1% of the Internet each scan. We do the comparison by framing the basic unit of "did an affected party respond" in terms of aggregate entities very likely controlled by the same party (and thus will update at the same time). To do so, we define an entity as a group of servers that all present the same certificate during a particular measurement. This has the potential for fragmenting groups that have partially replaced their certificates, but we argue that this effect is likely negligible since the number of entities stays roughly constant across our measurements. Note that this definition of entity differs from the "host-cert" unit used in [72], in which groups were tracked as a whole from the first measurement.

Figure 4 shows for both datasets the fraction of unfixed entities to the total number of entities per measurement. We consider an entity as "fixed" in the Debian PRNG dataset if the certificate now has a strong public key (and previously did not), otherwise "unfixed". For our Heartbleed IPv4 dataset (labelled "patch"), we deem an entity as "fixed" if *all* servers presenting the same certificate are now no longer vulnerable, "unfixed" otherwise.

This data shows that entities vulnerable to Heartbleed patched somewhat more quickly than in the Debian scenario, and continue to do so at a faster rate. It would appear that aspects of the disclosure and publicity of Heartbleed did indeed help with motivating patching, although the exact causes are difficult to determine.

Note that for the Debian event, it was very clear that affected sites had to not only patch but to also issue new certificates, because there was no question that the previous certificates were compromised. For Heartbleed, the latter step of issuing new certificates was not as pressing, because the previous certificates were compromised only if attackers had employed the attack against the site prior to patching *and* the attack indeed yielded the certificate's private key.

Given this distinction, we also measured whether entities changed their certificates after patching Heartbleed.* To do so, we now define an entity as a group of servers that all present the same certificate during both a particular measurement and all previous measurements. We regard an entity as "unfixed" if *any* server presenting that certificate is vulnerable at any time during this time frame and "fixed" otherwise. Again, we argue that fragmentation due to groups having their servers only been partially patched is likely negligible. We label this data as "cert change" in Figure 4. We see that while entities patched Heartbleed faster than the Debian PRNG bug, they replaced certificates more slowly, which we speculate reflects a perception that the less-definitive risk of certificate compromise led a number of entities to forgo the work that reissuing entails.

5. CERTIFICATE ECOSYSTEM

Heartbleed allowed attackers to extract private cryptographic keys [67]. As such, the security community recommended that administrators generate new cryptographic keys and revoke compromised certificates [35]. In this section, we analyze to what degree operators followed these recommendations.

5.1 Certificate Replacement

To track which sites replaced certificates and cryptographic keys, we combined data from our Heartbleed scans, Michigan's daily scans of the HTTPS ecosystem [29], and ICSI's Certificate Notary service [22]. Of the Alexa sites we found vulnerable on April 9 (2 days after disclosure), only 10.1% replaced their certificates in the month following disclosure (Figure 5). For comparison, we observed that 73% of vulnerable hosts detected on April 9 patched in that same time frame, indicating that most hosts who patched did not replace certificates. In addition, it is striking to observe that only 19% of the vulnerable sites that did replace their certificates also revoked the original certificate in the same time frame, and even more striking that 14% *re-used the same private key*, thus gaining no actual protection by the replacement.

We find that 23% of all HTTPS sites in the Alexa Top 1 Million replaced certificates and 4% revoked their certificates between April 9 and April 30, 2014. While it may seem inverted that fewer vulnerable sites changed their certificates compared to all HTTPS sites in the Alexa Top 1 Million, our first scan was two days after initial disclosure. We expect that diligent network operators both patched their systems and replaced certificates within the first 48 hours post disclosure, prior to our first scan.

The ICSI Certificate Notary (see Section 6.1) provides another perspective on changes in the certificate ecosystem, namely in terms of Heartbleed's impact on the sites that its set of users visit during their routine Internet use. In Figure 6, we show the difference in certificate replacement between March and April 2014. For the first four days after public disclosure on April 7, we observed a large drop in the number of servers with the same certificate as on April 6, indicating a spike in new certificates. After that, certificate changes progressed slowly yet steadily for the rest of the month. This matches our expectations that a number of operators patched their systems prior to our scans and immediately replaced certificates.

Ultimately, while popular websites did well at patching the actual vulnerability, a significantly smaller number replaced their

*See Section 5.1 for a discussion on the replacement of public/private key pairs in addition to certificates.

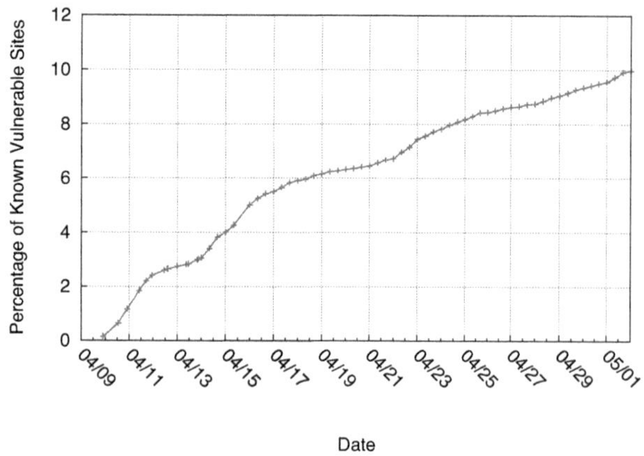

Figure 5: **Certificate Replacement on Vulnerable Alexa Sites.** We monitored certificate replacement on vulnerable Alexa Top 1 Million sites and observe only 10% replaced certificates in the month following public disclosure.

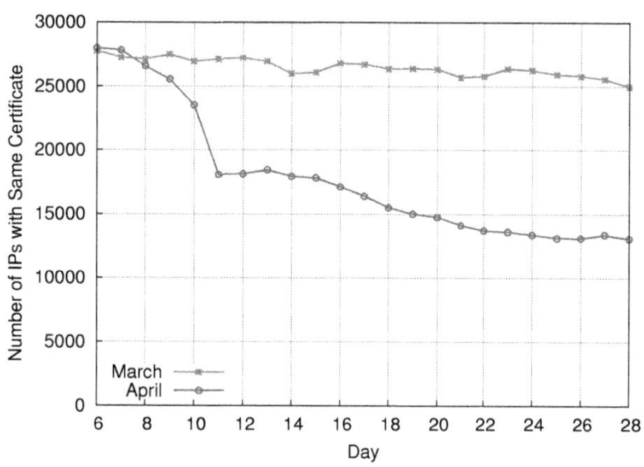

Figure 6: **ICSI Notary Certificate Changes.** Over both March and April, we track the number of servers who have the same certificate as on the 6th of each month. We only include servers that served the same certificate for the previous month.

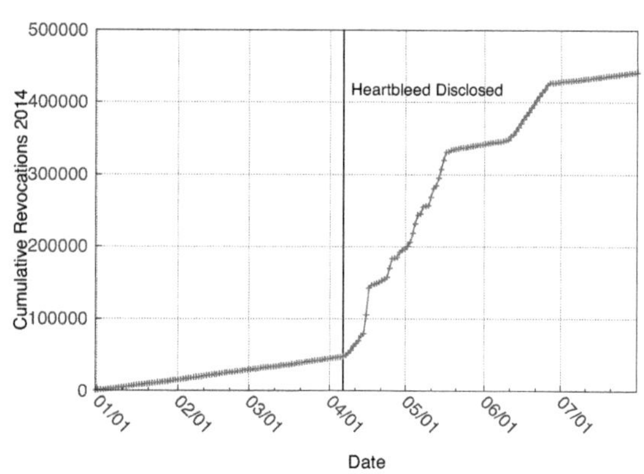

Figure 7: **Revocations after Heartbleed.** Certificate revocations dramatically increased after the disclosure. The jumps reflect GlobalSign (first) and GoDaddy (rest). However, still only 4% of HTTPS sites in the Alexa Top 1 Million revoked their certificates between April 9 and April 30, 2014.

certificates, and an even smaller number revoked their vulnerable certificates.

5.2 Certificate Revocation

When a certificate or key can no longer be trusted, sites can request the issuing CA to *revoke* the certificate. CAs accomplish this by publishing certificate revocation lists (CRLs) and supporting the Online Certificate Status Protocol (OCSP) for live queries. Even though most vulnerable hosts failed to revoke old certificates, we observed about as many revocations in the three months following public disclosure as in the three previous years.

Prior to the vulnerability disclosure, we saw on average 491 (σ=101) revocations per day for certificates found in our scans. As seen in Figure 7, in the days following disclosure, the number of revocations dramatically increased. The sudden increases were due to individual CAs invalidating large portions of their certificates. Most notably, GlobalSign revoked 56,353 certificates over two days (50.2% of their visible certificates), and GoDaddy, the largest CA, revoked 243,823 certificates in week-long bursts over the following three months. GlobalSign's large number of revocations were precipitated by a major customer, CloudFlare, revoking all of their customers' certificates [60].

Revoking such a large number of certificates burdens both clients and servers. Clients must download large CRLs, which CAs must host. GlobalSign's CRL expanded the most, from 2 KB to 4.7 MB due to CloudFlare's revocations. CloudFlare hesitated to revoke their certificates, citing its significant cost, which they estimated would require an additional 40 Gbps of sustained traffic, corresponding to approximately $400,000 per month [60]. StartCom, a CA that offers free SSL certificates, came under fire for continuing their policy of charging for revocation after the Heartbleed disclosure [44]. However, revocation places a sizable financial strain on CAs due to bandwidth costs [9,60].

5.3 Forward Secrecy

Heartbleed highlights the importance of using *forward secret* cipher suites in TLS. Without forward secrecy, the compromise of a server's private key, such as due to Heartbleed, allows an attacker who recorded previous communications encrypted with TLS to recover the session key used to protect that communication, subverting its confidentiality. Thus, we might expect operators to respond to Heartbleed by ensuring that at least in the future their servers will support forward secrecy.

Unfortunately, we find that only 44% of the connections observed by the ICSI Notary in May 2014 used forward secrecy. There has been a slow increase in adoption between December 2013 and April 2014, a gain of 1.0–4.3% each month. We observe a 4.2% increase between March and April 2014, but no larger than that between January and February. Surprisingly, this trend stagnated from April to August; the percentage of connections using forward secrecy stayed virtually the same. Currently, we are not sure why the increase in forward secrecy cipher use ceased. However, it appears clear that Heartbleed did not spur adoption of forward secrecy.

6. ATTACK SCENE

In addition to tracking vulnerable servers, we analyzed who was scanning for the Heartbleed vulnerability by examining network traffic collected from passive taps at Lawrence Berkeley National Laboratory (LBNL), the International Computer Science Institute (ICSI), and the National Energy Research Scientific Computing Center (NERSC), as well as a honeypot operated by a colleague on Amazon EC2.

To detect Heartbleed scanning, we extended the Bro's SSL/TLS analyzer to recognize Heartbeat messages [25,57]. Note that this approach parses the full TLS protocol data stream, including the TLS record layer which remains unencrypted throughout the session, and thus achieves an accuracy significantly better than that provided by simple byte pattern matching. We have released our Bro modifications along with our detection script via the Bro git repository.

6.1 Pre-Disclosure Activity

LBNL's network spans two /16s, one /20 and one /21. The institute frequently retains extensive packet traces for forensic purposes, and for our purposes had full traces available from February–March 2012, February–March 2013, and January 23–April 30 2014. ICSI uses a /23 network, for which we had access to 30-days of full traces from April 2014. NERSC has a /16 network, for which we analyzed traces from February to April 2014. The EC2 honeypot provided full packet traces starting in November 2013.

For all four networks, over these time periods our detector found no evidence of any exploit attempt up through April 7, 2014. This provides strong evidence that at least for those time periods, no attacker with prior knowledge of Heartbleed conducted widespread scanning looking for vulnerable servers. Such scanning however could have occurred during other time periods.

6.2 Post-disclosure Activity

To detect post-disclosure scanning, we similarly examined packet traces from LBNL, ICSI, and the EC2 honeypot. The first activity we observed originated from a host at the University of Latvia on April 8, starting at 15:18 UTC (21 hours 29 minutes after public disclosure), targeting 13 hosts at LBNL. This first attack was unusual in that it sent both unencrypted (pre-handshake) and encrypted (post-handshake) Heartbleed exploit packets to each host, likely trying to gauge the effectiveness of both approaches. We observed scanning of the other two networks within a few more hours.

In total, we observed 5,948 attempts to exploit the vulnerability from 692 distinct hosts (Table 7). These connections targeted a total 217 hosts. 7 attackers successfully completed 103 exploit attempts against 12 distinct hosts (excluding the intentionally vulnerable honeypot). Figure 8 presents the temporal behavior of scanning as seen at each location.

We detected several different types of exploit attempts, which we list in Table 6. In types (1) and (2), attackers sent exploit attempts prior to completely establishing the TLS session, which allowed us to directly inspect the attack payload. After establishment of the TLS session, the only pieces of information we can retrieve are the message type and size, which are both transferred in the clear. To detect scanning conducted in a fashion similar to our own, we checked the length of the encrypted message (3). We also consider all Heartbeat messages that we see prior to the first transmission of application data (4) to reflect exploit attempts.* We identify attacks as successful when the destination server responds with more data than included in the original request (5), though as noted above we do not consider attacks on the EC2 honeypot as "successful".

The sixteen most aggressive probe sources (by number of scans) reside in Amazon address space. The scans originating from these hosts share many characteristics, including the use of encryption, the same packet length, and identical cipher suites. Closer examination reveals that these hosts belong to two popular Heartbleed scan services: `filippio.io` (3,964 attempts from 40 hosts) and `ssllabs.com` (16 attempts from 5 hosts).

Examining connection attempts across each site, we find only three sources that attempted to scan all three networks. However, LBNL aggressively blocks scan traffic, so most hosts scanning it were likely blocked before they could locate a server against which to attempt Heartbleed exploits. Considering only the EC2 honeypot and the ICSI network (neither of which block scanning), we find 11 sources that scanned both.

Apart from our scans at the University of Michigan and another research group at TU Berlin, we found four sources that targeted more than 100 addresses at ICSI. Two of the sources were located in CHINANET, one at Nagravision, and one at Rackspace. The remaining Heartbleed exploit attempts only targeted smaller numbers of hosts without performing widespread scanning.

Hosts performing widespread scans exclusively targeted port 443 (HTTPS). We observed a small number of exploit against ports 993 (IMAPS), 995 (POP3S), 465 (SMTPS), as well as GridFTP. We also found a small number of exploit attempts against services running on other ports.

While we observed Heartbleed attacks originating from a large number of sources, we find that most hosts did not target more than one of our sites and likely do not represent Internet-wide scanning. Given the low volume of widespread scanning, the 201 sources attempting to exploit the EC2 honeypot appears surprisingly high. Our hypothesis is that attackers may preferentially scan denser address spaces, such as those of Amazon EC2, as they will likely yield a greater number of vulnerable targets.

*Heartbeat messages should never precede application data. We verified this does not happen in real-world traffic by manually reviewing traces prior to the Heartbleed disclosure. We observed no such instances.

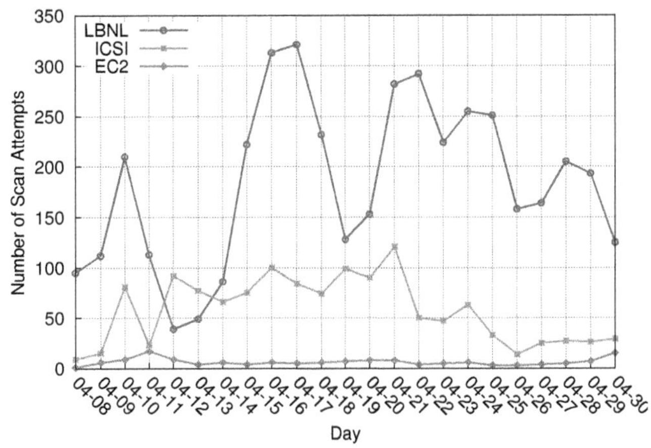

Figure 8: **Incoming Attacks.** We track the number of incoming connections containing Heartbleed exploit messages seen at ICSI, LBNL, and the EC2 honeypot per day.

Type	Sources	Targets	Connections
(1) Cleartext attacks	628	191	1,691
(2) Successful cleartext attacks	4	10	26
(3) Short Heartbeats	8	10	187
(4) Heartbeats before data	61	132	4,070
(5) Successful attacks after encryption	5	6	77
Total	692	217	5,948

Table 6: **Attack Types.** We list different stages of attacks observed against LBNL, ICSI and the EC2 honeypot.

AS Name	ASN	Scans	Hosts
Amazon.com	14618	4,267	206
China Telecom	4812	507	139
China169 Backbone	4837	147	34
Chinanet	4134	115	23
University of Michigan	36375	92	3
SoftLayer	36351	85	2
University of Latvia	8605	50	1
Rackspace	19994	47	11
GoDaddy.com	26496	34	15
OVH	16276	30	9
ViaWest	13649	30	1
Guangdong Mobile	9808	29	1
New York Internet Company	11403	29	1
ServerStack	46652	27	1
Comcast	7922	20	5
Global Village Telecom	18881	19	4
China Telecom	4816	16	1
Turk Telekomunikasyon	9121	15	8
DFN	680	15	2
Amazon.com	16509	12	5
TekSavvy Solutions	5645	11	2
Oversun	48172	11	2
HKNet	4645	11	1
CariNet	10439	10	8
PowerTech	5381	10	1
Nagravision	42570	10	1
CYBERDYNE	37560	10	1

Table 7: **ASes Responsible for Attacks.** We list the ASNs/ISPs that sent 10 or more Heartbleed exploit attempts to LBNL, ICSI, and our EC2 honeypot.

7. NOTIFICATION

Three weeks after the initial disclosure a large number of hosts remained vulnerable, and we began notifying the system operators responsible for unpatched systems. This endeavor provided us with an opportunity to study the impact of large-scale vulnerability notification. In this section we describe our notification methodology and analyze the reactions to our notifications and its impact on patching.

7.1 Methodology

In order to find the appropriate operators to contact, we performed WHOIS lookups for the IP address of each vulnerable host appearing in our April 24, 2014 scan of the full IPv4 address space. We used the "abuse" e-mail contact extracted from each WHOIS record as our point of notification. We chose to use WHOIS abuse emails because they struck us as more reliable than emails from other sources. There also appeared to be less risk in offending a network operator through contacting the abuse contact. For example, many emails extracted from certificate Subject fields were not valid emails, and we observed several WHOIS records with comments instructing anything related to spam or abuse be sent to the abuse contact rather than the technical contact.

Our scan found 588,686 vulnerable hosts. However, we excluded embedded devices—which accounted for 56% of vulnerable hosts—because administrators likely had no avenue for patching many of these devices at the time. These devices were detected using the fingerprints described in Section 3.6. The remaining 212,805 hosts corresponded to 4,648 distinct abuse contacts. Approximately 30,000 hosts belonged to RIPE and Amazon each. Because neither of these organizations directly manage hosts, we omitted them from our notifications.

To measure the impact of our notifications, we randomly split the abuse contacts into two groups, which we notified in stages.

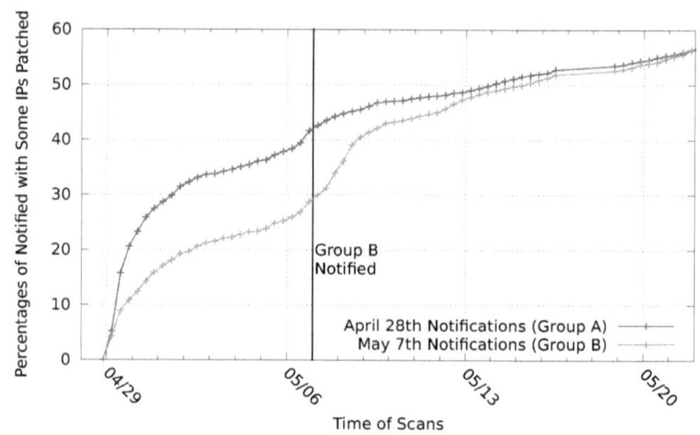

Figure 9: **Patch Rates of Group A vs Group B.** The patch rates for our two notification sets show that notification had statistically significant impact on patch rate.

We sent notifications to the first half (Group A) on April 28, 2014, and the second half (Group B) on May 7, 2014. Our notification e-mail introduced our research and provided a list of vulnerable hosts, information on the vulnerability, and a link to the EFF's Heartbleed recovery guide for systems administrators.

7.2 Patching Behavior

To track patching behavior, we conducted regular scans of the known vulnerable hosts every eight hours. We considered a contact as having reacted and begun patching if we found at least one host in the list we sent to the contact as patched. Figure 9 shows a comparison of the patch rates between the two groups. Within 24 hours of the initial notification, 20.6% of the Group A operators had begun to patch, whereas only 10.8% of Group B contacts (not yet notified) had reacted. After eight days (just before the second group of notifications), 39.5% of Group A contacts had patched versus 26.8% in Group B. This is a 47% increase in patching for notified operators.

Fisher's Exact Test yields a one-sided p-value of very nearly zero for the null hypothesis that both groups reflect identical population characteristics. We thus conclude that our notification efforts had a statistically significant positive effect in spurring notified sites to patch. Our second round of notifications followed a similar pattern as the first. As Group A's rate of patching had decreased at that point, Group B caught up, resulting in both converging to around 57% of contacts having reacted within a couple of weeks of notification.

We also investigated the relationship between the reactions of network operators (per Section 7.3) and their patching behavior. First, we sent our notification message in English, possibly creating a language barrier between us and the contact. We analyzed the Group A responses and found that email responses entirely in English had no statistically significant difference in the corresponding patching rate than for responses containing non-English text (Fisher's Exact Test yielded a two-sided p-value of 0.407).

We did, however, find statistically significant differences between each of the categories of responses framed below in Section 7.3, as shown in Figure 10, with human responders patching at the highest rate. Within the first day post-notification, 48% of human responders had begun patching, while none of the other categories had a patch rate higher than 32%.

The second strongest reactions came from contacts configured to send automated responses. 32% had reacted after one day, and 75% had reacted after three weeks. This indicates that operators using a

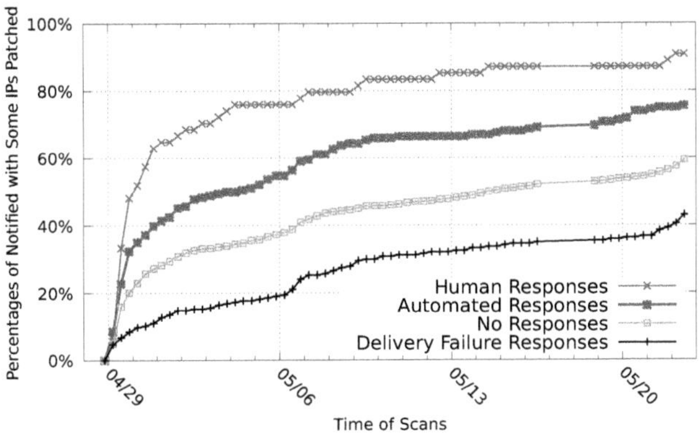

Figure 10: **Patch Rates for Different Response Types.** Conditioning on the sort of reply we received for a given notification reveals statistically significant differences.

system to automatically process notifications and complaints will still often react appropriately.

Over 77% of the contacts never responded. After one day, 20% of such contacts had conducted some patching; after three weeks, 59% had. Right before Group B's notifications, the patch rate of these contacts was statistically significantly higher than Group B's patch rate. This shows that even when system operators do not respond when notified, they often still patch vulnerable systems.

7.3 Responses

In our first group of notifications, on April 28, 2014, we contacted 2,308 abuse contacts and received email responses from 514 contacts. Of these 59 (11%) were clearly human-generated, 197 (38%) were automated, and 258 (50%) were delivery failures. We received 16 automated emails where we subsequently received a human response; these we classified as human (thus, in total we received 530 emails). The vast majority of responses (88%) were in English; other common languages included Russian, German, Portuguese, and Spanish.

We classified a positive response as one that thanked us or stated their plan to remedy their vulnerable hosts. The human-generated responses were overall very positive (54/59), with only three that we deemed neutral, and two negative. The two negative responses questioned the legality of our scan despite our explicit explanation that we did not exploit the vulnerability.

Automated messages came in four forms: confirmations (24%), tickets (44%), trackers (23%), and miscellaneous bounces (9%; primarily out-of-office notices and "no longer working here" messages). Confirmation emails confirmed the receipt of our notification; tickets provided a reference or ticket identifier to associate with our notification message; and trackers were tickets that also explicitly provided a link to a support site to track progress on opened tickets. Curiously, 21 of the 45 trackers did not provide the credentials to log into the support website, 2 provided invalid credentials, and 3 did not have our ticket listed on their support site. In the week following our notification, we were informed that 19 tickets were closed, although only 4 provided any reasoning.

Out of the 258 delivery failure replies, 197 indicated the recipient did not receive our notification. Other error messages included full inboxes or filtering due to spam, and several did not describe a clear error. We observed 30 delayed and retrying emails, but all timed-out within three days.

7.4 Network Operator Survey

We sent a brief survey to positive human responders, where all questions were optional, and received anonymous submissions from 17 contacts. Surprisingly, all 17 expressed awareness of the vulnerability and stated their organizations had performed some remediation effort prior to our notification, typically through informing their clients/customers and patching machines if accessible. When we asked why might the hosts we detected still be vulnerable, the most common responses were that they did not have direct control over those servers, or their own scans must have missed those hosts. It appears ignorance of the vulnerability and its threat did not play a factor in slow patching, although our sample size is small. When asked if they replaced or revoked vulnerable certificates, nine said yes, two said no, and one was unaware of the recommendation. Finally, we asked if these contacts would like to receive notifications of similar vulnerabilities in the future. Twelve said yes, two said no, and the others did not respond. This again demonstrates that our notifications were in general well-received.

8. DISCUSSION

Heartbleed's severe risks, widespread impact, and costly global cleanup qualify it as a security disaster. However, by analyzing such events and learning from them, the community can be better prepared to address major security failures in the future. In this section, we use our results to highlight weaknesses in the security ecosystem, suggest improved techniques for recovery, and identify important areas for future research.

HTTPS Administration. Heartbleed revealed important shortcomings in the public key infrastructure that underlies HTTPS. One set of problems concerns certificate replacement and revocation. As discussed in Section 5, only 10% of known vulnerable sites replaced their certificates, and an astounding 14% of those reused the existing, potentially leaked, private key. This data suggests that many server administrators have only a superficial understanding of how the HTTPS PKI operates or failed to understand the consequences of the Heartbleed information leak. This underscores the importance for the security community of providing specific, clear, and actionable advice for network operators if similar vulnerabilities occur in the future. Certificate management remains difficult for operators, highlighting the pressing need for solutions that enable server operators to correctly deploy HTTPS and its associated infrastructure.

One of the ironies of Heartbleed was that using HTTPS, a protocol intended to provide security and privacy, introduced vulnerabilities that were in some cases more dangerous than those of unencrypted HTTP. However, we emphasize that HTTPS is ultimately the more secure protocol for a wide variety of threat models. Unfortunately, only 45% of the Top 1 Million websites support HTTPS, despite efforts by organizations such as the EFF and Google to push for global HTTPS deployment.

Revocation and Scalability. Even though only a small fraction of vulnerable sites revoked their certificates, Heartbleed placed an unprecedented strain on certificate authorities and revocation infrastructure. In the three months following public disclosure, about as many revocations were processed by CAs as in the three years proceeding the incident. Wholesale revocation such as required by an event like Heartbleed stresses the scalability of basing revocation on the distribution of large lists of revoked certificates. As a result, CAs were backlogged with revocation processing and saddled with unexpected financial costs for CRL distribution—CloudFlare alone paid $400,000 per month in bandwidth [60]. The community needs to develop methods for scalable revocation that can gracefully accommodate mass revocation events, as seen in the aftermath of Heartbleed.

Support for Critical Projects. While not a focus of our research, many in the community have argued that this event dramatically underscores shortcomings in how our community develops, deploys, and supports security software. Given the unending nature of software bugs, the Heartbleed vulnerability raises the question of why the Heartbeat extension was enabled for popular websites. The extension is intended for use in DTLS, an extension unneeded for these sites. Ultimately, the inclusion and default configuration of this largely unnecessary extension precipitated the Heartbleed catastrophe. It also appears likely that a code review would have uncovered the vulnerability. Despite the fact that OpenSSL is critical to the secure operation of the majority of websites, it receives negligible support [43]. Our community needs to determine effective support models for these core open-source projects.

Vulnerability Disclosure. With the exception of a small handful, the most prominent websites patched within 24 hours. In many ways, this represents an impressive feat. However, we also observed vulnerability scans from potential attackers within 22 hours, and it is likely that popular sites were targeted before the onset of large, indiscriminate scans.

Several factors indicate that patching was delayed because the Heartbleed disclosure process unfolded in a hasty and poorly coordinated fashion. Several major operating system vendors were not notified in advance of public disclosure, ultimately leading to delayed user recovery. As discussed in Section 3, a number of important sites remained vulnerable more than 24 hours after initial disclosure, including Yahoo, the fourth most popular site on the Internet. The security community needs to be better prepared for mass vulnerability disclosure before a similar incident happens again. This includes addressing difficult questions, such as how to determine which software maintainers and users to notify, and how to balance advance disclosure against the risk of premature leaks.

Notification and Patching. Perhaps the most interesting lesson from our study of Heartbleed is the surprising impact that direct notification of network operators can have on patching. Even with global publicity and automatic update mechanisms, Heartbleed patching plateaued two weeks after disclosure with 2.4% of HTTPS hosts remaining vulnerable, suggesting that widespread awareness of the problem is not enough to ensure patching. However, as discussed in Section 7, when we notified network operators of the unpatched systems in their address space, the rate of patching increased by 47%. Many operators reported that they had intended to patch, but that they had missed the systems we detected.

Although Internet-wide measurement techniques have enabled the mass detection of vulnerable systems, many researchers (including us) had assumed that performing mass vulnerability notifications for an incident like Heartbleed would be either too difficult or ineffective. Our findings challenge this view. Future work is needed to understand what factors influence the effectiveness of mass notifications and determine how best to perform them. For instance, was Heartbleed's infamy a precondition for the high response rate we observed? Can we develop systems that combine horizontal scanning with automatically generated notifications to quickly respond to future events? Can we standardize machine-readable notification formats that can allow firewalls and intrusion detection systems to act on them automatically? What role should coordinating bodies such as CERT play in this process? With additional work along these lines, automatic, measurement-driven mass notifications may someday be an important tool in the defensive security arsenal.

9. CONCLUSION

In this work we analyzed numerous aspects of the recent OpenSSL Heartbleed vulnerability, including (1) who was initially vulnerable, (2) patching behavior, and (3) impact on the certificate authority ecosystem. We found that the vulnerability was widespread, and estimated that between 24–55% of HTTPS-enabled servers in the Alexa Top 1 Million were initially vulnerable, including 44 of the Alexa Top 100. Sites patched heavily in the first two weeks after disclosure, but patching subsequently plateaued, and 3% of the HTTPS Alexa Top 1 Million sites remained vulnerable after two months. We further observed that only 10% of vulnerable sites replaced their certificates compared to 73% that patched, and 14% of sites doing so used the same private key, providing no protection.

We investigated the attack landscape, finding no evidence of large-scale attacks prior to the public disclosure, but vulnerability scans began within 22 hours. We observed post-disclosure attackers employing several distinct types of attacks from 692 sources, many coming from Amazon EC2 and Chinese ASes. We also conducted a mass notification of vulnerable hosts, finding a significant positive impact on the patching of hosts to which we sent notifications, indicating that this type of notification helps reduce global vulnerability. Finally, we drew upon our analyses to frame what went well and what went poorly in our community's response, providing perspectives on how we might respond more effectively to such events in the future.

Acknowledgments

The authors thank Ivan Ristic for providing historical data on TLS support, as well as Elie Bursztein, Paul Pearce, Hovav Shacham, Aashish Sharma, and Matthias Vallentin. We similarly thank the exceptional sysadmins at the University of Michigan for their help and support throughout this project.

This work was supported in part by the Department of Homeland Security Science and Technology Directorate under contracts D08PC75388, FA8750-12-2-0235, and FA8750-12-2-0314; the National Science Foundation under contracts CNS-0751116, CNS-08311174, CNS-091639, CNS-1111699, CNS-1255153, and CNS-1330142; DARPA award HR0011-12-2-005; and the Department of the Navy under contract N000.14-09-1-1042.

10. REFERENCES

[1] Alexa Top 1,000,000 Sites. http://s3.amazonaws.com/alexa-static/top-1m.csv.zip.

[2] Bitcoin Core Version History. https://bitcoin.org/en/version-history.

[3] Installing OpenDKIM. http://www.opendkim.org/INSTALL.

[4] Telnet Server with SSL Encryption Support. https://packages.debian.org/stable/net/telnetd-ssl.

[5] Install Ejabberd, Oct. 2004. http://www.ejabberd.im/tuto-install-ejabberd.

[6] Cassandra Wiki - Internode Encryption, Nov. 2013. http://wiki.apache.org/cassandra/InternodeEncryption.

[7] Android Platform Versions, Apr. 2014. https://developer.android.com/about/dashboards/index.html#Platform.

[8] Apple Says iOS, OSX and "Key Web Services" Not Affected by Heartbleed Security Flaw, Apr. 2014. http://recode.net/2014/04/10/apple-says-ios-osx-and-key-web-services-not-affected-by-heartbleed-security-flaw/.

[9] Heartbleed F.A.Q., 2014. https://www.startssl.com/?app=43.

[10] The Heartbleed Hit List: The Passwords You Need to Change Right Now, Apr. 2014. http://mashable.com/2014/04/09/heartbleed-bug-websites-affected/.

[11] HP Support Document c04249852, May 2014. http://goo.gl/AcUG8I.

[12] Is Openfire Affected by Heartbleed?, Apr. 2014. https://community.igniterealtime.org/thread/52272.

[13] June 2014 Web Server Survey, 2014. http://news.netcraft.com/archives/2014/06/06/june-2014-web-server-survey.html.

[14] NGINX and the Heartbleed Vulnerability, Apr. 2014. http://nginx.com/blog/nginx-and-the-heartbleed-vulnerability/.

[15] Official BTCJam Update, Apr. 2014. http://blog.btcjam.com/post/82158642922/official-btcjam-update.

[16] SSL Pulse, Apr. 2014. https://www.trustworthyinternet.org/ssl-pulse/.

[17] Tomcat Heartbleed, Apr. 2014. https://wiki.apache.org/tomcat/Security/Heartbleed.

[18] Wikimedia's Response to the "Heartbleed" Security Vulnerability, Apr. 2014. https://blog.wikimedia.org/2014/04/10/wikimedias-response-to-the-heartbleed-security-vulnerability/.

[19] Adobe. Heartbleed Update, Apr. 2014. http://blogs.adobe.com/psirt/?p=1085.

[20] M. Al-Bassam. Top Alexa 10,000 Heartbleed Scan—April 14, 2014. https://github.com/musalbas/heartbleed-masstest/blob/94cd9b6426311f0d20539e696496ed3d7bdd2a94/top1000.txt.

[21] Alienth. We Recommend that You Change Your Reddit Password, Apr. 2014. http://www.reddit.com/r/announcements/comments/231hl7/we_recommend_that_you_change_your_reddit_password/.

[22] B. Amann, M. Vallentin, S. Hall, and R. Sommer. Extracting Certificates from Live Traffic: A Near Real-Time SSL Notary Service. Technical Report TR-12-014, ICSI, Nov. 2012.

[23] AWeber Communications. Heartbleed: We're Not Affected. Here's What You Can Do To Protect Yourself, Apr. 2014. http://blog.aweber.com/articles-tips/heartbleed-how-to-protect-yourself.htm.

[24] Bitcoin. OpenSSL Heartbleed Vulnerability, Apr. 2014. https://bitcoin.org/en/alert/2014-04-11-heartbleed.

[25] Bro Network Security Monitor Web Site. http://www.bro.org.

[26] N. Craver. Is Stack Exchange Safe from Heartbleed?, Apr. 2014. http://meta.stackexchange.com/questions/228758/is-stack-exchange-safe-from-heartbleed.

[27] R. Dingledine. Tor OpenSSL Bug CVE-2014-0160, Apr. 2014. https://blog.torproject.org/blog/openssl-bug-cve-2014-0160.

[28] Dropbox Support. https://twitter.com/dropbox_support/status/453673783480832000, Apr. 2014. Quick Update on Heartbleed: We've Patched All of Our User-Facing Services & Will Continue to Work to Make Sure Your Stuff is Always Safe.

[29] Z. Durumeric, J. Kasten, M. Bailey, and J. A. Halderman. Analysis of the HTTPS Certificate Ecosystem. In *Proc. ACM Internet Measurement Conference*, Oct. 2013.

[30] Z. Durumeric, E. Wustrow, and J. A. Halderman. ZMap: Fast Internet-Wide Scanning and its Security Applications. In *Proc. USENIX Security Symposium*, Aug. 2013.

[31] A. Ellis. Akamai heartbleed Update (V3), Apr. 2014. https://blogs.akamai.com/2014/04/heartbleed-update-v3.html.

[32] A. S. Foundation. CouchDB and the Heartbleed SSL/TLS Vulnerability, Apr. 2014. https://blogs.apache.org/couchdb/entry/couchdb_and_the_heartbleed_ssl.

[33] GoDaddy. OpenSSL Heartbleed: We've Patched Our Servers, Apr. 2014. http://support.godaddy.com/godaddy/openssl-and-heartbleed-vulnerabilities/.

[34] L. Grangeia. Heartbleed, Cupid and Wireless, May 2014. http://www.sysvalue.com/en/heartbleed-cupid-wireless/.

[35] S. Grant. The Bleeding Hearts Club: Heartbleed Recovery for System Administrators, Apr. 2014. https://www.eff.org/deeplinks/2014/04/bleeding-hearts-club-heartbleed-recovery-system-administrators.

[36] B. Grubb. Heartbleed Disclosure Timeline: Who Knew What and When. Apr. 2014. http://www.smh.com.au/it-pro/security-it/heartbleed-disclosure-timeline-who-knew-what-and-when-20140415-zqurk.html.

[37] L. Haisley. OpenSSL Crash with STARTTLS in Courier, May 2014. http://sourceforge.net/p/courier/mailman/message/32298514/.

[38] IBM. OpenSSL Heartbleed (CVE-2014-0160), May 2014. https://www-304.ibm.com/connections/blogs/PSIRT/entry/openssl_heartbleed_cve_2014_0160.

[39] Infusionsoft. What You Need to Know About Heartbleed, Apr. 2014. http://blog.infusionsoft.com/company-news/need-know-heartbleed/.

[40] Internal Revenue Service. IRS Statement on "Heartbleed" and Filing Season, Apr. 2014. http://www.irs.gov/uac/Newsroom/IRS-Statement-on-Heartbleed-and-Filing-Season.

[41] W. Kamishlian and R. Norris. Installing OpenSSL for Jabberd 2. http://www.jabberdoc.org/app_openssl.html.

[42] Litespeed Technologies. LSWS 4.2.9 Patches Heartbleed Bug, Apr. 2014. http://www.litespeedtech.com/support/forum/threads/lsws-4-2-9-patches-heartbleed-bug.8504/.

[43] S. Marquess. Of Money, Responsibility, and Pride, Apr. 2014. http://veridicalsystems.com/blog/of-money-responsibility-and-pride/.

[44] M. Masnick. Shameful Security: StartCom Charges People To Revoke SSL Certs Vulnerable to Heartbleed, Apr. 2014. http://www.techdirt.com/articles/20140409/11442426859/shameful-security-startcom-charges-people-to-revoke-ssl-certs-vulnerable-to-heartbleed.shtml.

[45] N. Mehta and Codenomicon. The Heartbleed Bug. http://heartbleed.com/.

[46] Microsoft. Microsoft Services unaffected by OpenSSL Heartbleed vulnerability, Apr. 2014. http://blogs.technet.com/b/security/archive/2014/04/10/microsoft-devices-and-services-and-the-openssl-heartbleed-vulnerability.aspx.

[47] MongoDB. MongoDB Response on Heartbleed OpenSSL Vulnerability, Apr. 2014. http://www.mongodb.com/blog/post/mongodb-response-heartbleed-openssl-vulnerability.

[48] K. Murchison. Heartbleed Warning - Cyrus Admin Passowrd Leak!, Apr. 2014. http://lists.andrew.cmu.edu/pipermail/info-cyrus/2014-April/037351.html.

[49] E. Ng. Tunnel Fails after OpenSSL Patch, Apr. 2014. https://lists.openswan.org/pipermail/users/2014-April/022934.html.

[50] M. O'Connor. Google Services Updated to Address OpenSSL CVE-2014-0160 (the Heartbleed Bug), Apr. 2014. http://googleonlinesecurity.blogspot.com/2014/04/google-services-updated-to-address.html.

[51] P. Ondruska. Does OpenSSL CVE-2014-0160 Effect Jetty Users?, Apr. 2014. http://dev.eclipse.org/mhonarc/lists/jetty-users/msg04624.html.

[52] OpenSSL Project Team. OpenSSL Security Advisory, Apr. 2014. http://www.mail-archive.com/openssl-users@openssl.org/msg73408.html.

[53] OpenSSL Project Team. OpenSSL Version 1.0.1g Released, Apr. 2014. http://www.mail-archive.com/openssl-users@openssl.org/msg73407.html.

[54] OpenVPN. OpenSSL Vulnerability—Heartbleed. https://community.openvpn.net/openvpn/wiki/heartbleed.

[55] Oracle. OpenSSL Security Bug—Heartbleed / CVE-2014-0160, Apr. 2014. http://www.oracle.com/technetwork/topics/security/opensslheartbleedcve-2014-0160-2188454.html.

[56] L. Padron. Important Read – Critical Security Advisory And Patch for OpenSSL Heartbleed Vulnerability, Apr. 2014. http://blog.zimbra.com/blog/archives/2014/04/important-read-critical-security-advisory-patch-openssl-heartbleed-vulnerability.html.

[57] V. Paxson. Bro: A System for Detecting Network Intruders in Real-Time. *Computer Networks*, 31(23-24):2435–2463, 1999.

[58] PayPal. OpenSSL Heartbleed Bug—PayPal Account Holders are Secure, Apr. 2014. https://www.paypal-community.com/t5/PayPal-Forward/OpenSSL-Heartbleed-Bug-PayPal-Account-Holders-are-Secure/ba-p/797568.

[59] W. Pinckaers. http://lekkertech.net/akamai.txt.

[60] M. Prince. The Hidden Costs of Heartbleed, Apr. 2014. http://blog.cloudflare.com/the-hard-costs-of-heartbleed.

[61] Publishers Clearing House. Stay Smart About The "Heartbleed" Bug With PCH!, Apr. 2014. http://blog.pch.com/blog/2014/04/16/stay-smart-about-the-heartbleed-bug-with-pch/.

[62] Rackspace. Protect Your Systems From "Heartbleed" OpenSSL Vulnerability, Apr. 2014. http://www.rackspace.com/blog/protect-your-systems-from-heartbleed-openssl-vulnerability/.

[63] Red Hat. How to Recover from the Heartbleed OpenSSL vulnerability, Apr. 2014. https://access.redhat.com/articles/786463.

[64] T. Saunders. ProFTPD and the OpenSSL "Heartbleed" Bug, May 2014. http://comments.gmane.org/gmane.network.proftpd.user/9465.

[65] B. Say. Bleedingheart Bug in OpenSSL, Apr. 2014. http://www.stunnel.org/pipermail/stunnel-users/2014-April/004578.html.

[66] R. Seggelmann, M. Tuexen, and M. Williams. Transport Layer Security (TLS) and Datagram Transport Layer Security (DTLS) Heartbeat Extension. IETF Request for Comments (RFC) 6520, February 2012. https://tools.ietf.org/html/rfc6520.

[67] N. Sullivan. The Results of the CloudFlare Challenge. Apr. 2014. http://blog.cloudflare.com/the-results-of-the-cloudflare-challenge.

[68] Tumblr. Urgent Security Update, Apr. 2014. http://staff.tumblr.com/post/82113034874/urgent-security-update.

[69] United States Postal Service. Avoiding Heartbleed, May 2014. https://ribbs.usps.gov/importantupdates/HeartbleedArticle.pdf.

[70] M. Wimmer. Removed Support for OpenSSL, 2007. https://jabberd.org/hg/amessagingd/rev/bcb8eb80cbb9.

[71] WordPress. Heartbleed Security Update, Apr. 2014. http://en.blog.wordpress.com/2014/04/15/security-update/.

[72] S. Yilek, E. Rescorla, H. Shacham, B. Enright, and S. Savage. When Private Keys Are Public: Results from the 2008 Debian OpenSSL Vulnerability. In *Proc. ACM Internet Measurement Conference*, Nov. 2009.

[73] ZDNet. Heartbleed Bug Affects Yahoo, OKCupid Sites, Apr. 2014. http://www.zdnet.com/heartbleed-bug-affects-yahoo-imgur-okcupid-convo-7000028213/.

[74] ZEDOinc. https://twitter.com/ZEDOinc/status/456145140503957504, Apr. 2014. Customers and partners: none of the ZEDO sites or assets are affected by Heartbleed.

Analysis of SSL Certificate Reissues and Revocations in the Wake of Heartbleed

Liang Zhang
Northeastern University
liang@ccs.neu.edu

David Choffnes
Northeastern University
choffnes@ccs.neu.edu

Dave Levin
University of Maryland
dml@cs.umd.edu

Tudor Dumitraş
University of Maryland
tdumitra@umiacs.umd.edu

Alan Mislove
Northeastern University
amislove@ccs.neu.edu

Aaron Schulman
Stanford University
aschulm@stanford.edu

Christo Wilson
Northeastern University
cbw@ccs.neu.edu

ABSTRACT

Central to the secure operation of a public key infrastructure (PKI) is the ability to *revoke* certificates. While much of users' security rests on this process taking place quickly, in practice, revocation typically requires a human to decide to reissue a new certificate and revoke the old one. Thus, having a proper understanding of how often systems administrators reissue and revoke certificates is crucial to understanding the integrity of a PKI. Unfortunately, this is typically difficult to measure: while it is relatively easy to determine when a certificate is revoked, it is difficult to determine whether and when an administrator *should have* revoked.

In this paper, we use a recent widespread security vulnerability as a natural experiment. Publicly announced in April 2014, the Heartbleed OpenSSL bug, potentially (and undetectably) revealed servers' private keys. Administrators of servers that were susceptible to Heartbleed should have revoked their certificates and reissued new ones, ideally as soon as the vulnerability was publicly announced.

Using a set of all certificates advertised by the Alexa Top 1 Million domains over a period of six months, we explore the patterns of reissuing and revoking certificates in the wake of Heartbleed. We find that over 73% of vulnerable certificates had yet to be reissued and over 87% had yet to be revoked three weeks after Heartbleed was disclosed. Moreover, our results show a drastic decline in revocations on the weekends, even immediately following the Heartbleed announcement. These results are an important step in understanding the manual processes on which users rely for secure, authenticated communication.

IMC'14, November 5–7, 2014, Vancouver, BC, Canada.

ACM 978-1-4503-3213-2/14/11 ...$15.00.
http://dx.doi.org/10.1145/2663716.2663758.

Categories and Subject Descriptors

C.2.2 [**Computer-Communication Networks**]: Network Protocols; C.2.3 [**Computer-Communication Networks**]: Network Operations; E.3 [**Data Encryption**]: Public Key Cryptosystems, Standards

Keywords

Heartbleed; SSL; TLS; HTTPS; X.509; Certificates; Reissue; Revocation; Extended validation

1. INTRODUCTION

Secure Sockets Layer (SSL) and Transport Layer Security (TLS)[1] are the de-facto standards for securing Internet transactions such as banking, e-mail and e-commerce. Along with a public key infrastructure (PKI), SSL provides trusted identities via certificate chains and private communication via encryption. Central to these guarantees is that private keys used in SSL are not compromised by third parties; if so, certificates based on those private keys must be reissued and revoked to ensure that malicious third parties cannot masquerade as a trusted entity.

Importantly, the PKI uses a default-valid model where potentially compromised certificates remain valid until their expiration date or until they are revoked. Revocation, however, is a process that requires manual intervention from certificate owners and cooperation from clients that use these certificates. As a result, the practical security of the PKI is dependent on the speed with which certificate owners and SSL clients update their revocation lists, operations that occur at human timescales (hours or days) instead of computer ones (seconds or minutes). An important open question is: when private keys are compromised, how long are SSL clients exposed to potential attacks?

In this paper, we address this question using a recent widespread security vulnerability as a natural experiment. In mid-April 2014, an OpenSSL security vulnerability, Heartbleed, made it possible for attackers to inspect servers' memory contents, thereby potentially (and undetectably) revealing servers' private keys. Administrators of

[1]TLS is the successor of SSL, but both use the same X.509 certificates. Throughout the paper, we refer to "SSL clients" and "SSL certificates," but our findings apply equally to servers using both protocols.

servers that were susceptible to Heartbleed should have operated under the assumption than an attacker had already obtained their private keys, and therefore should have revoked their certificates and reissued new ones [5], ideally as soon as the vulnerability was publicly announced.

The scope of this vulnerability—it is estimated that up to 17% of all HTTPS web servers were vulnerable [22]—makes it an ideal case study for evaluating large-scale properties of SSL security in the face of private key compromise. While previous studies have measured how quickly and thoroughly administrators patch software vulnerabilities [25, 27, 35], we are, to the best of our knowledge, the first to study administration of certificates in the wake of a vulnerability. In particular, this paper focuses on certificate revocation and reissues in response to the public announcement of Heartbleed, both in terms of how quickly certificates are reissued and whether or not the certificates are eventually revoked.

Toward this goal, we make the following key contributions. First, we conduct a large-scale measurement study of SSL certificates in the wild using both data collected from public archives and through custom measurements conducted after Heartbleed was publicized. We focus on the Alexa Top 1 Million (Top-1M) domains, for which we find a total of 628,692 valid SSL certificates from 166,124 unique domains.

Second, we conduct measurements to determine which servers remain vulnerable to Heartbleed and which ones were previously vulnerable but are now patched. We develop a new SSL implementation fingerprinting technique that is able to determine if a host is running a version of OpenSSL that was vulnerable in the past. We cross-validate with direct measurements of the vulnerability (we find our technique has a false positive rate of only 1.9%) and conduct scans to compose a list of previously vulnerable hosts. We find that the most popular web sites were more likely to have at least one host vulnerable to Heartbleed, likely because they often have more hosts.

Third, we develop novel heuristics to identify which certificates have been reissued in direct response to Heartbleed, as opposed to other reasons such as certificate expiration or periodic reissues. This allows us to understand how administrators do (or do not) react to potential private key compromise. We observe that while vulnerable sites with a higher Alexa rank were more likely to reissue their certificates, the vast majority (73.3%) of vulnerable certificates had not been reissued fully three weeks after the vulnerability was announced. These vulnerable certificates come from more than 55,000 unique domains.

Fourth, we analyze certificate revocation behavior over time and across certificate owners. We find a sharp (up to 40-fold) increase in revocations per day after the Heartbleed announcement, but for the majority (60%) of reissued certificates, the previous (vulnerable) certificate was not revoked. For those that are revoked due to Heartbleed, we find more revocations in certificate revocation lists (CRLs) to have explanations (reason codes) than revocations unrelated to Heartbleed, and they appear in the CRLs more quickly than revocations not due to Heartbleed. Further, we examine the update frequency of CRLs to determine if Certificate Authorities (CAs), the entities that issue certificates, serve as a "bottleneck" for revocations (as it is the CA who maintains the CRL). We find that CRLs appear to be updated frequently, with over 95% of them being updated within the previous 24-hour period.

The remainder of this paper is organized as follows. In the next section, we provide background about SSL/TLS, PKIs, and the Heartbleed vulnerability. In §3 we describe our dataset and methodology for extracting valid certificates and determining Heartbleed vulnerability at servers. §4 presents the results of our analysis, where we identify the behavior of certificate reissuing and revocation on a large dataset of Alexa's Top-1M web sites. We summarize related work in §5 and conclude in §6.

2. BACKGROUND

Secure Sockets Layer (SSL) and Transport Layer Security (TLS) offer application-layer confidentiality and integrity, and are the basis of the vast majority of secure online communication. Through the use of a public key infrastructure (PKI), these protocols also allow clients to authenticate the servers with whom they communicate. In this section, we provide a brief background of SSL/TLS and PKIs relevant to our study, and describe the recent Heartbleed vulnerability.

2.1 Certificates

A certificate is, at its core, a signed attestation binding a *subject* to a public key. Certificates are signed by a Certificate Authority (CA), who in turn has its own certificate, and so on, terminating at self-signed *root certificates.* There is a logical *chain* of certificates—leading from a root certificate through zero or more *intermediate* certificates, to a *leaf* certificate—wherein the certificate at level i is signed with the private key corresponding to the certificate at level $i-1$, with the exception of the self-signed certificate at the root. In practice, the topology of certificates can be somewhat complex, with CAs signing one another's certificates [17], but such details are not pertinent to the study performed in this paper.

When a client visits a site that supports, say, HTTPS, that site sends its certificate chain to the client, who verifies the signatures from leaf to root. If the client can successfully validate each signature, and if the client trusts the root certificate—for instance by checking it against a set of certificates pre-installed in the browser or operating system—then the client infers that the subject in the leaf certificate truly is the owner of the public key.

The predominant format of certificates is X.509 [6], which includes considerably more information than just subject and public key, including a unique (for that CA) serial number, an expiration date, the key's cipher suite, acceptable uses of the key, and information on how to check whether the certificate has been *revoked.*

2.2 Certificate Revocation

In addition to issuing certificates, CAs are also responsible for making available a list of certificates it has issued that have been *revoked*, after which clients should no longer consider those certificates valid. Note that, if a CA's (intermediate or root) certificate is revoked, all leaf certificates signed by that CA will fail to validate.

There are many reasons a site can decide to revoke a certificate. One critically important example is that of a compromised certificate. A certificate is *compromised* if someone other than its original owner learns the corresponding private key, allowing that person to generate signatures and thus impersonate the owner. In the case of a CA certificate, release of the private key may allow an attacker to generate new certificates for arbitrary subjects. In such an event, it is important that the owner revokes the compromised certificate as quickly as possible to mitigate the set of users affected by the compromise.

Certificate Revocation Lists (CRLs) are by far the most common means of disseminating revocations. CRLs consist of a list of (serial number, time stamp of revocation, reason for revocation) triples, all of which are collectively signed by the CA. CAs include in the certificates that they issue a URL pointing to the CRL that would contain that certificate's serial number, if it were to become revoked. Clients periodically download and cache CRLs, and use them when validating a certificate chain. Ostensibly to reduce the communication overhead for CAs and for users, clients typically download CRLs infrequently (on the order of hours or days), potentially leaving many users with outdated information on the validity of their certificates. This has spurred several studies into more efficient means of revocation [12, 21, 23, 29, 36], and general doubt as to the overall efficacy of revocations [28]. Yet, CRLs remain the de facto means of disseminating revocation information, and thus they factor heavily in our study.

2.3 Certificate Reissues

When a site ceases to use a certificate—for instance because they found that the certificate has been compromised, or because the certificate expired—they must use a new certificate instead. This process is referred to as *reissuing* the certificate. To do so, the system administrator must contact the CA who signed their certificate and request a new signature; this is typically done by sending the CA a Certificate Signing Request (CSR). In the case where the private key may have been compromised, the administrator should also choose a new public/private key pair to be signed (as reissuing the certificate with the same key does nothing to mitigate the leaked private key).

While it seems natural to assume that certificates are reissued at precisely the moment the old certificate is revoked, in fact today's PKI protocols make no such requirement. As our study will demonstrate, reissues can happen before, during, or after a revocation—or even without revoking the old certificate at all. To the best of our knowledge, we are the first to correlate revocations with reissues.

2.4 Heartbleed

Heartbleed is a buffer over-read vulnerability discovered in OpenSSL [24] that was present in versions 1.0.1 (released March 14, 2012) through 1.0.1f. The vulnerability stems from a bug in OpenSSL's implementation of the TLS Heartbeat Extension [30]. The intended functionality of TLS Heartbeat is to allow a client to test a secure communication channel by sending a "heartbeat" message consisting of a string and the 16-bit `payload_length` of this string. Unfortunately, vulnerable OpenSSL versions fail to check that the `payload_length` supplied by the client matches the length of the provided string. This allows a malicious client to craft a heartbeat message containing a 1-byte string and $2^{16} - 1$ as the `payload_length`. In this case, OpenSSL will allocate a 64KB block of heap memory, `memcpy()` 64KB of data into it, starting with the 1-byte string, and finally send the contents of the entire buffer to the client. In effect, this allows the malicious client to read up to $2^{16} - 2$ bytes of the server's heap memory. Note that while the malicious client can choose the amount of memory to read, it has no control over the location of the memory that is copied, and therefore cannot choose *which* memory to read.

By repeatedly exploiting Heartbleed, an attacker can extract sensitive data from the server (e.g., SSL private keys [32], user data [13], etc.). The severity of Heartbleed is exacerbated by the fact that OpenSSL does not log heartbeat messages, giving attackers free reign to undetectably exploit Heartbleed. Given the severity and undetectable nature of malicious users exploiting Heartbleed, site operators were urged to immediately update their OpenSSL software and revoke and reissue their certificates [5].

Timeline. Heartbleed was first discovered by Neel Mehta from Google on March 21, 2014. Google immediately wrote a patch and applied it to their own OpenSSL deployments. On April 2, researchers at Finnish security company Codenomicon independently discovered the bug and dubbed it Heartbleed. On April 4, Akamai patched their servers. On April 7, the bug became public and the OpenSSL project released a patched version (1.0.1g) of the OpenSSL library [15].

Why study Heartbleed? The significance of this timeline, and of Heartbleed in general, is that it represents a point in time after which *all* vulnerable servers *should have* taken three critical steps to ensure the security of their service and their users: they should have patched their code, revoked their old certificate, and reissued a new one. As a result, Heartbleed acts as a sort of natural experiment, allowing us to measure how completely and quickly administrators took steps to secure their keys. While such events are (sadly) not terribly uncommon for general security vulnerabilities [25, 27, 35], it remains rare that such a large fraction of the certificate ecosystem must reissue and revoke their SSL certificates.

3. DATA AND METHODOLOGY

We now describe the data sets that we collected and our methodology for determining a host's SSL certificate, when it was in use, if and when the certificate was revoked, and if the host was (or is still) vulnerable to the Heartbleed bug.

3.1 Certificate Data Source

We obtain our collection of SSL certificates from (roughly) weekly scans of the entire IPv4 address space made available by Rapid7 [26]. In this paper, we use scans collected between October 30, 2013 and April 28, 2014. There are a total of 28 scans during this period, giving an average of 6.7 days (with a minimum of 3 days and maximum of 9 days) between successive scans.

The scan data includes *all certificates* advertised by each host (including intermediate and root certificates) in the scans up through February 5, 2014, and includes *only the first advertised certificate* by each host in the later scans. For example, suppose that a host is advertising a chain of three certificates: a certificate for `example.com`, a certificate for GeoTrust, and self-signed root certificate, where each certificate signs the previous. The earlier scans would include all three certificates, whereas the later scans would include only the certificate for `example.com`. The lack of full certificate chains in the later scans presents challenges for validation, which we address in §3.2.

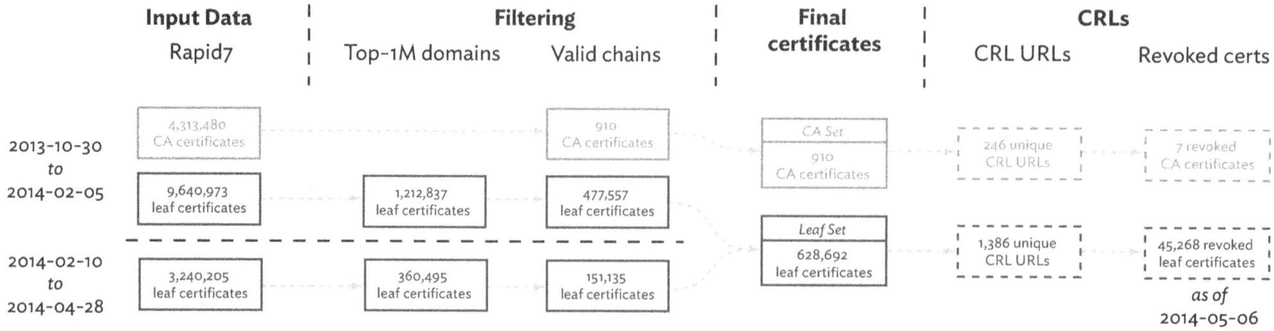

Figure 1: Workflow from raw scans of the IPv4 address space to valid certificates (and corresponding CRLs) from the Alexa Top-1M domains. The Rapid7 data after February 5, 2014 did not include the intermediate (CA) certificates, necessitating additional steps and data to perform validation.

The scans found an average of 26.9 million hosts responding to SSL handshakes on port 443 (an average of 9.12% of the entire IPv4 address space). Across all of the scans, we observed a total of 19,438,865 unique certificates (including all leaf and CA certificates). In the sections below, we describe how we filtered and validated this data set; an overview of the process is provided in Figure 1.

3.2 Filtering Data

To focus on web destinations that are commonly accessed by users, we use the Alexa Top-1M domains [2] as observed on April 28, 2014. We first extract all leaf (non-CA) certificates that advertise a *Common Name* (CN) that is in one of the domains in the Alexa list (e.g., we would include certificates for `facebook.com`, `www.facebook.com`, as well as `*.dev.facebook.com`). This set represents 1,573,332 certificates (8.1% of all certificates). In order to remove invalid and self-signed certificates from this list, we then extract all advertised chains for these certificates (which are only present in the scans through February 5, 2014).

Reconstructing chains. The lack of full certificate chains for the post-February 5, 2014 scans (see §3.1) presents a challenge at this point, as we need the full certificate chains in order to properly validate the leaf certificates. To verify new certificates observed in these later scans, we construct a list of all 4,509 intermediate (CA), non-self-signed certificates observed in previous scans.[2] From these certificates, we use two types of X.509 fields to help with chain reconstruction [6]:

- The *Subject Key Identifier* and *Authority Key Identifier* are two fields included in most certificates, and uniquely identify the public key the certificate represents (*Subject Key Identifier*) and the public key that signed this certificate (*Authority Key Identifier*). The value is typically implemented as a hash of the public key.

- The *Subject Name* and *Issuer Name* are text fields that represent the name of the entity this certificate represents (*Subject Name*) and the name of entity that signed this certificate (*Issuer Name*).

We construct a database of all four of these fields across all 8,954 CA certificates.

Using this database, we attempt to reconstruct a leaf certificate's chain based first on the certificate's *Authority Key ID* and, failing that, the certificate's *Issuer Name*. In other words, given a leaf certificate, we look for a CA certificate whose *Subject Key Identifier* is the same as our leaf's *Authority Key Identifier*. Should we not find one (or should the *Subject Key Identifier* not be present), we instead look for a CA certificate whose *Subject Name* is the same as our leaf's *Issuer Name*. We then recursively apply this technique until we cannot find a parent key, we hit a trusted root certificate, or we hit a self-signed CA certificate. Should we find multiple CA keys that match at any stage, we include them all as potential chains.

Verifying chains. We then unify our set of potential chains, consisting of both host-advertised chains (for the data collected through February 5, 2014) and reconstructed-chains (for the data collected post-February 5, 2014). Unfortunately, despite the leaf certificate having a *Common Name* in the Alexa list, many of our chains may not be valid (e.g., expired certificates, forged self-signed certificates, certificates signed by an invalid root, etc.). One common source of invalid certificates is home routers/DSL modems provided by ISPs (e.g., FRITZ!Boxes) or cloud-accessible storage devices (e.g., Western Digital's My Cloud), both of which advertise self-signed SSL certificates in the `fritz.net` and `wd2go.com` domains.

We removed these invalid chains by running `openssl verify` on each certificate (and its corresponding chain), and only kept the certificates that OpenSSL could verify. Because the scans occurred at different points of time, we used the `faketime` library [14] to have OpenSSL validate the certificate as of the time of the scan. We also configure OpenSSL to trust the set of root CA certificates included by default in the OS X 10.9.2 root store [20]; this includes 222 unique root certificates.

After validation, we are left with 628,692 leaf certificates (40.0% of all certificates advertising Alexa domains and 3.2% of all certificates) from Alexa Top-1M domains that were advertised by some IP address and could be validated; we refer to this set of certificates as the *Leaf Set*. Each of these

[2] We also conduct our own crawl (see §3.4) of hosts advertising certificates in the Alexa list, and included all 4,445 additional non-self-signed CA certificates that we discovered in this list as well. However, we found that none of the additional CA certificates were necessary for validation.

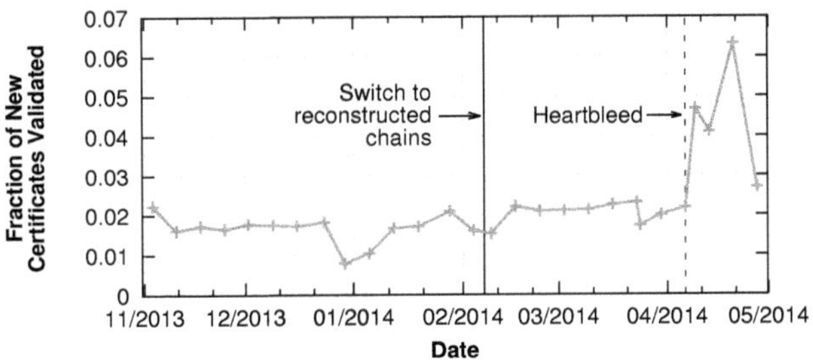

Figure 2: Fraction of new certificates that we could verify for provided (February 5, 2014 and before) and reconstructed (post February 5, 2014) chains.

certificates has a valid chain; we refer to the collection of all CA certificates on these chains (not including the leaf certificates) as the *CA Set*; the CA Set contains 910 unique certificates. The Leaf Set certificates cover 166,124 (16.6%) of the Alexa Top-1M domains. This is the set of certificates (and certificate chains) that we use in the remainder of the paper.

Validation of reconstruction. Finally, we briefly validate our certificate chain reconstruction mechanism on the post-February 5, 2014 certificates. In Figure 2, we present the fraction of new certificates discovered over time for which we were able to find a valid chain, both for the pre- and post-February 5, 2014 data. We make two interesting observations: *First*, the fraction of certificates that we could validate is relatively stable at 2% both before and after the switch to using reconstructed chains, suggesting that our mechanism for chain reconstruction does not miss many chains. *Second*, we see a large uptick in the fraction of newly-appearing certificates that we could validate after Heartbleed; as we discuss in the following section, this is due to many certificates being reissued in the wake of Heartbleed.

3.3 Collecting CRLs

To determine if and when certificates were revoked, we extracted the CRL URLs out of all Leaf Set certificates. We ignored invalid URLs, including `ldap://` protocols and non-routable addresses. We found 626,659 (99.7%) of these certificates to include at least one well-formed, reachable CRL URL; for certificates that included multiple CRL URLs, we included them all. We found a total of 1,386 unique CRL URLs (most certificates use a unified CRL provided by the signing CA, so the small number of CRLs is not surprising). We downloaded all of these CRLs on May 6, 2014, and found 45,268 (7.2%) of the Leaf Set certificates to be revoked.

We also collected the CRL URLs for all certificates in the CA set. We found that 884 (97.1%) of the certificates in the CA Set included a reachable CRL; the union of these URLs comprised 246 unique reachable URLs. We downloaded these CRLs on May 6, 2014, as well. We found a total of seven CA certificates that were revoked, which nullified the validity of 60 certificates in the Leaf Set (< 0.01%).

3.4 Inferring Heartbleed Vulnerability

Finally, we wish to determine if a site was ever vulnerable to the Heartbleed OpenSSL vulnerability (and if it continued to be vulnerable at the end of the study). Doing so allows us to reason about whether the site operators should have reissued their SSL certificate(s) and revoked their old one(s). Determining if a host is currently vulnerable to Heartbleed is relatively easy, as one can simply send improperly-formatted SSL heartbeat messages to test for vulnerability.

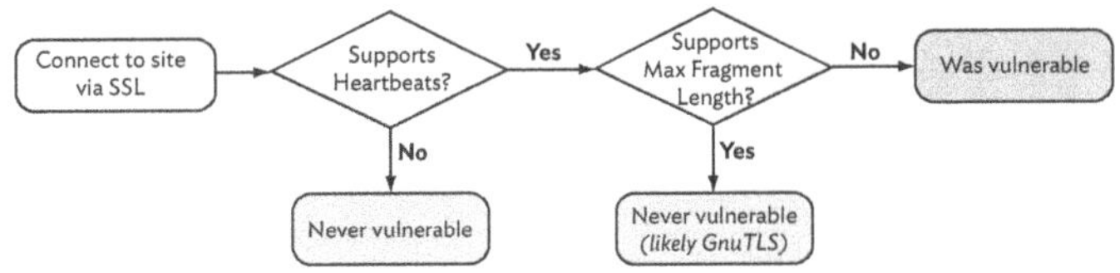

Figure 3: Flowchart of inference of previous Heartbleed vulnerability of hosts based on our SSL scan.

However, determining if a site *was* vulnerable at some point in the past—but has since updated their OpenSSL code—is more challenging. We observe that only three of the common TLS implementations have ever supported SSL Heartbeats [30]: OpenSSL [24], GnuTLS [33], and Botan [4]. Thus, if a host supports the SSL Heartbeat extension, we know that it is running one of these three implementations. Botan is a library that is targeted for client-side TLS, and we know of no popular web server that is able to use the Botan TLS library. GnuTLS has support for the SSL Heartbeat extension, but it is not enabled by default.[3] To determine if the host is using GnuTLS, we observed that GnuTLS supports the Max Fragment Length SSL extension [1], which *is* enabled by default, while OpenSSL has never supported this extension. Thus, if we observe a host that supports the SSL Heartbeat extension but *not* the Max Fragment Length extension, we declare that host to have been running a version of OpenSSL that was vulnerable (see Figure 3 for a graphical representation).

To collect the list of sites that were ever vulnerable to Heartbleed, we first extracted the set of IP addresses in the April 28, 2014 Rapid7 scan that were advertising a certificate with a *Common Name* in the Alexa Top-1M list. We found 5,951,763 unique IP addresses in this set. We then connected to these IP addresses, performed the TLS negotiation, determined the SSL extensions that the host supported, and determined whether the host was still vulnerable to the Heartbleed vulnerability. We also downloaded the set of CA certificates that the host advertised, which we used to aid certificate validation (see §3.2).

Limitations. Our methodology for inferring a host's vulnerability to Heartbleed has the following limitations. Because we did our scan three weeks after Heartbleed was announced, we may have both false positives and false negatives in detecting whether a host was ever vulnerable to Heartbleed. For false positives, hosts that were upgraded *directly* from OpenSSL 0.9.8 to OpenSSL 1.0.1g (i.e., bypassing the Heartbleed bug) would be incorrectly flagged as being vulnerable in the past. We suspect this fraction is small, as this would have had to have happened between April 7th (the release of OpenSSL 1.0.1g) and April 28th (our scan), but we are unable to estimate the fraction of hosts this covers.

For false negatives, administrators who responded to Heartbleed by either recompiling OpenSSL with

[3] In fact, in our scan, we did not discover *any* hosts that were running GnuTLS with SSL Heartbeats enabled.

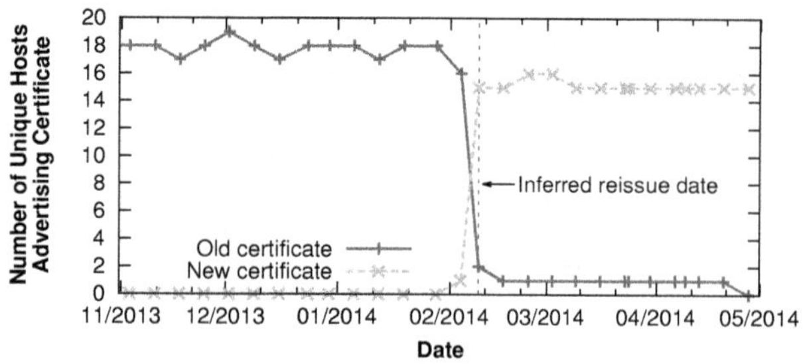

Figure 4: Example of lifetime, for certificates for `m.scotrail.co.uk`. All hosts except one switch to a new certificate after February 10, 2014.

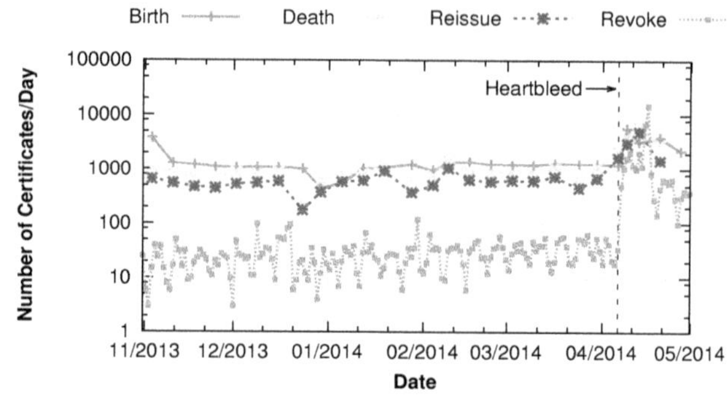

Figure 5: Number of certificate birth, deaths, reissues, and revocations over time. Note the log scale on the y-axis.

`-DOPENSSL_NO_HEARTBEATS` or who downgraded their OpenSSL implementation to version $\leq$0.9.8 would have their hosts incorrectly flagged as never having been vulnerable. We are similarly unable to determine the fraction of hosts in our data set that this applies to; we suspect it is small as well, as many operating systems vendors (e.g., Ubuntu) pushed out a Heartbleed security update that is usually automatically applied.

Verification of vulnerability detection. We performed a brief experiment to estimate the false negative rate of our Heartbleed vulnerability detection mechanism. We use a vulnerability scan of the Alexa Top-1M domains conducted by the authors of ZMap [37] on April 9, 2014, which contains a list of hosts they confirmed to be vulnerable to Heartbleed. In our scan on April 28, 2014 (19 days after the ZMap scan), we found that 8,651 of these hosts were still advertising a certificate with the same *Common Name*. Of these, 1,737 (20.1%) were *still* vulnerable; the remainder were likely patched in the meantime. Using our fingerprinting methodology above, we would have inferred that 8,483 (98.1%) of the hosts were running a version of OpenSSL that was vulnerable at some point (despite the fact that the majority of these were actually no longer vulnerable). This high rate of recall, coupled with the unlikelihood of false negatives, leads us to conclude that our methodology for inferring previous vulnerability is highly accurate.

4. ANALYSIS

We now turn to examine the collected SSL certificate data. We first present a few definitions we use in the analysis before proceeding.

4.1 Definitions

We are concerned with the evolution of SSL certificates (i.e., when are new certificates created, old ones retired, etc.). To aid in understanding this evolution, we define the following notions:

Certificate birth: We define the birth of an SSL certificate to be the date of the first scan where we observed any host advertising that certificate. For hosts that we observed advertising a certificate on the very first scan (October 30, 2013), we define these certificates to have no birth date, since we do not know when they were first advertised.[4]

Certificate death: Defining the death of a certificate is more complicated, as we observe a number of instances where many hosts advertise a given certificate, and then all but one or a few of the hosts switch over to a new certificate (presumably, the site intended to retire the old certificate, but missed some of the hosts). To handle these cases, we calculate the *maximum* number of hosts that were ever advertising each certificate. We then define the death of an SSL certificate to be the last date that the number of hosts advertising the certificate was above 10% of that certificate's maximum. The 10% threshold prevents us from incorrectly classifying certificates that are still widely available as dead, even if the certificate has been reissued. Note that certificates may not have a death date if the certificate is still advertised by many IP addresses on our last scan.

An example of certificate lifetime is shown in Figure 4, for the certificates for `m.scotrail.co.uk`. All hosts except one switch to a new certificate after February 10, 2014; this lone host finally switches on April 28, 2014. In this case, we would consider the death date of the old certificate to be February 10, 2014 (as indicated in the figure), and we would consider the new certificate to have no death date.

Based on these definitions, we can now define the notion of a certificate reissue and revocation:

Certificate reissue: We consider a certificate to be reissued if the following three conditions hold: (a) we observe the certificate die, and (b) we observe a new certificate for the same *Common Name* born during a scan within 10 days[5] of the certificate's death, and (c) we observe at least one IP address switch from the old certificate to the new between the two scans. We define the date of the certificate reissue to be the date of the certificate's death. For the sake of clarity, we refer to the old certificate that was replaced as the *retired certificate*.

Certificate revocation: We consider a certificate to be revoked if the certificate's serial number appears in any of the certificate's CRLs. The date of revocation is provided in the CRL entry.

[4]Of course, some certificates may have been missed on the first scan if the host was down; these certificates would likely show up in the second scan (and would have a birth date of the next scan). This is the cause of the small spike in births on November 2, 2013 in Figure 5.

[5]We choose 10 days as a threshold as this is the maximum difference between two successive scans.

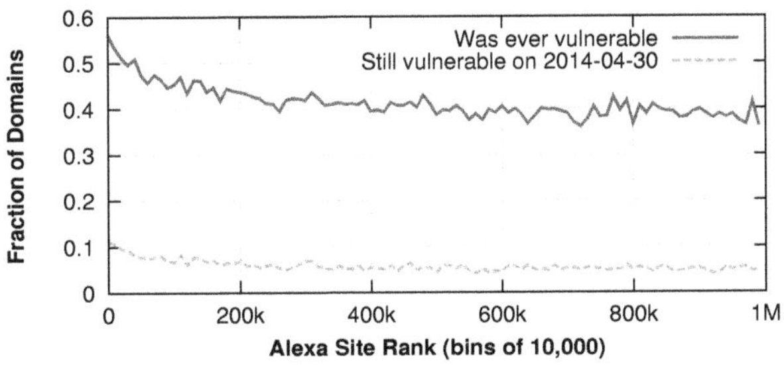

Figure 6: Fraction of domains that have at least one host that was ever vulnerable to Heartbleed as a function of Alexa rank, as well as domains that continued to be vulnerable at the end of the study.

In Figure 5, we present the number of certificate births, deaths, reissues, and revocations per day over time. The number of births is almost always larger than the number of deaths, meaning that the total number of certificates in-the-wild is increasing over time. Furthermore, we observe a large spike in all four events in the wake of Heartbleed, with an especially large increase in the number of revocations. For example, we see an average of 29 certificate revocations per day before Heartbleed; after Heartbleed, this jumps to an average of 1,414 revocations per day.

4.2 Heartbleed Prevalence

We present a brief analysis on the number of certificates hosted by machines that were ever vulnerable to Heartbleed. Of the 428,552 leaf certificates that were still alive on the last scan, we observe 122,832 (28.6%) of them advertised by a host that was likely vulnerable to Heartbleed at some point in time.[6] These certificates are for 117,112 unique *Common Names* and come from 70,875 unique Alexa Top-1M domains. Of these certificates, 11,915 certificates (from 10,366 unique domains) were on hosts that were *still* vulnerable at the time of our crawl (April 30, 2014, over three weeks after the announcement of Heartbleed). This result demonstrates that even in the wake of a well-publicized, severe security vulnerability, around 10% of vulnerable sites have not yet addressed the underlying issue three weeks after the fact.

In Figure 6, we present the fraction of domains that have at least one SSL host that was ever vulnerable to Heartbleed (or still was as of April 30, 2014). We can observe a slight increase in likelihood of ever being vulnerable for the most popular sites, but the distribution quickly stabilizes. Again, the increased likelihood of being vulnerable is likely because these sites have larger numbers of hosts. This trend is mirrored in the hosts that are still vulnerable on April 30, 2014.

4.3 Certificate Reissues

We now examine the reissuing of SSL certificates in the wake of Heartbleed. Not all SSL certificate reissues that we observe following Heartbleed's announcement are due to the Heartbleed vulnerability. In particular, reissues can happen

[6]This fraction is somewhat higher than the 17% of sites that Netcraft found to be vulnerable [22], but we note that we are measuring *certificates* from the Alexa Top-1M while Netcraft is measuring all SSL-enabled *sites* on the Internet.

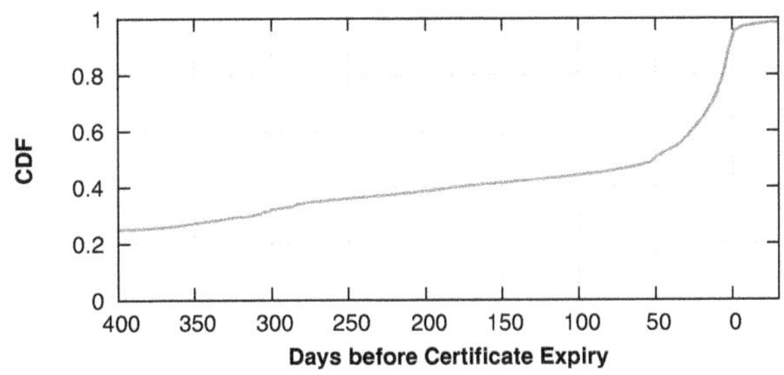

Figure 7: Cumulative distribution of the number of days before expiration that certificates are reissued.

for at least two other reasons: *First*, the old certificate could be expiring soon, and the organization reissues the certificate as it would normally. In Figure 7, we present the cumulative distribution of the number of days before expiry that we observe certificates being reissued. We see that over 50% of certificates are reissued within 60 days of their expiry date (with a long tail).

Second, a site may periodically reissue certificates as a matter of policy (even if the old certificate was not near expiration). For example, Figure 8 presents a graph showing the prevalence of the `www.google.com` certificates over time, with each line representing the number of hosts advertising a different certificate. Google typically reissues this certificate every two weeks, despite the fact that the certificates are typically valid for more than three months.

In this study, we would like to be able to distinguish a *Heartbleed-induced* certificate reissue from a reissue that would otherwise have happened anyway. We define the reissue of a certificate to be Heartbleed-induced if all three of the following conditions hold:

1. The date of reissue was on or after April 7, 2014 (the day Heartbleed was announced). We note that a small number of organizations were informed about Heartbleed before the public announcement; as this list is not fully known, we do not consider them separately.

2. The certificate that is reissued was going to expire more than 60 days after the reissue. This eliminates certificates that were very likely to be reissued in the near future anyway.

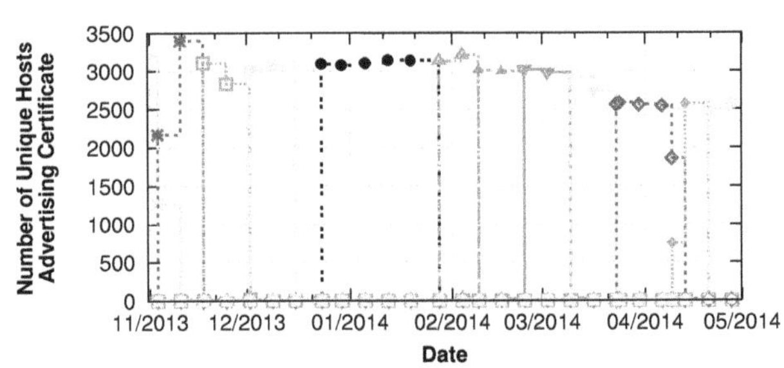

Figure 8: Example of certificate birth and death for certificates for `www.google.com`. Google reissues this certificate about once every two weeks (each impulse represents a different certificate).

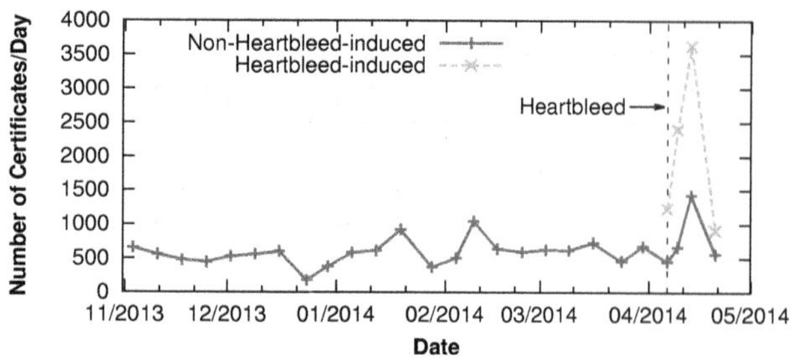

Figure 9: Number of Heartbleed-induced and non-Heartbleed-induced certificate reissues over time.

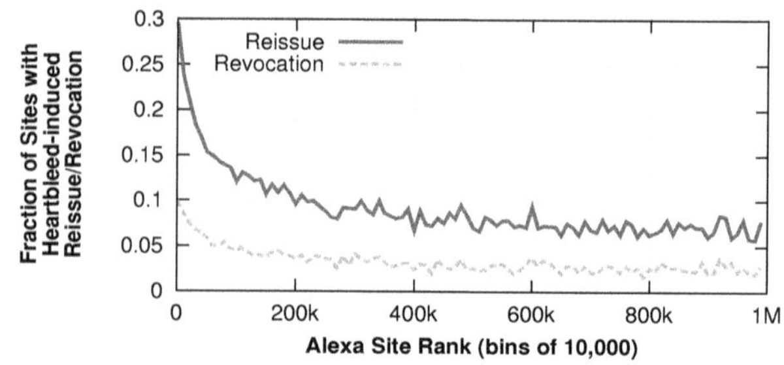

Figure 10: Fraction of domains that have at least one Heartbleed-induced reissue/revocation as a function of Alexa rank.

3. We do not observe more than two other reissues for certificates with that *Common Name* in the time before Heartbleed. This implies that certificates with that name do not typically get reissued more than once every 3 months (as far as we can observe from our dataset), as our data set begins on October 30, 2013 (slightly over 5 months before the announcement of the Heartbleed vulnerability).

Thus, for the examples shown so far, we would not have considered the reissue of the retired certificate in Figure 4 to be Heartbleed-induced (as it happened before Heartbleed), and we would also have not considered any of Google's reissues in Figure 8 to be Heartbleed-induced (because we observed a total of 12 reissues of certificates with that *Common Name* prior to Heartbleed). It is important to note that Heartbleed-induced reissues can happen for certificates that we never observed on a vulnerable host, either because we falsely declared the certificate to not be vulnerable (see §3.4) or because the site reissued out of an abundance of caution, even though they were not actually vulnerable. Given these three conditions, we expect that our estimate of Heartbleed-induced reissues is a strict *lower bound.*

Heartbleed-induced reissues. Overall, we observe 36,781 certificate reissues that we declare to be Heartbleed-induced in the three weeks following the announcement; this is 8.9% of all certificates that were alive at the time Heartbleed was announced. In Figure 9, we present the number of Heartbleed-induced and non-Heartbleed-induced certificate reissues over time. We observe that the number of non-Heartbleed-induced reissues is relatively stable—even after Heartbleed—suggesting our designation of Heartbleed-induced reissues is likely accurate. The slight spike in non-Heartbleed-induced reissues after April 7 may reflect that our approach yields a conservative underestimate of the number of Heartbleed-induced reissues.

Next, we examine the fraction of sites that have at least one Heartbleed-induced certificate reissue, as a function of Alexa rank. Figure 10 presents these results; we can observe a strong correlation with Alexa rank. Higher-ranked sites are much more likely to have reissued at least one certificate due to Heartbleed (even though they are only slightly more likely to have been vulnerable, as observed in Figure 6). This result complements previous studies' findings that more popular websites often exhibit more sound administrative practices [8, 17].

Vulnerable certificates. Next, we examine the certificates that *should have* been reissued (regardless of whether they actually were); we refer to these certificates as *vulnerable certificates.* We declare a certificate to be vulnerable if the following three conditions hold:

1. Its date of birth was before April 7, 2014,
2. It has not expired as of April 30, and
3. It was advertised by at least one host that was (or is) vulnerable to Heartbleed.

In other words, these certificates are vulnerable because their associated private keys could have been stolen by attackers.

Overall, we find 107,712 vulnerable certificates. Of these, we observe that only 28,652 (26.7%) have been reissued as of April 30. The remaining 79,060 (73.3%) vulnerable certificates that have not been reissued come from 55,086 different Alexa Top-1M domains. Thus, the vast majority of SSL certificates that were potentially exposed by the Heartbleed bug remain in-use over three weeks after the vulnerability was announced.

Reissues with same key. System administrators who believe that their SSL private key may have been compromised should generate a new public/private key pair when reissuing their certificate. We now examine how frequently this is done, both in the case of normal certificate reissues and for Heartbleed-induced reissues.

We first observe that, in general, reissuing a certificate using the same public/private key pair is quite common. Figure 11 presents the fraction of all new certificates that use the same key as the one they are replacing; up to 53% of all reissued certificates do so. This high level of key reuse is

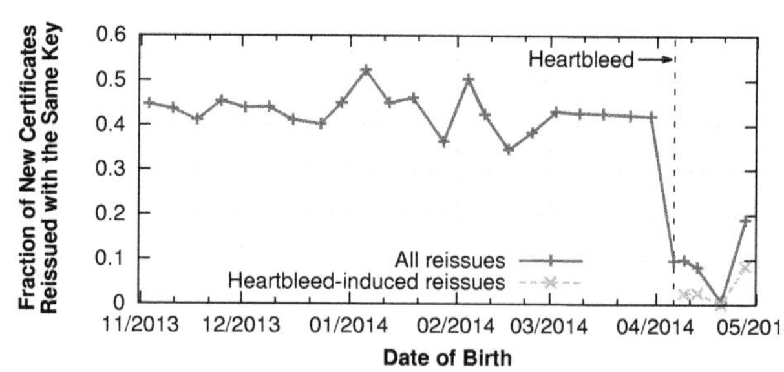

Figure 11: Fraction of new certificates that use the same public/private key pair as the key they are replacing.

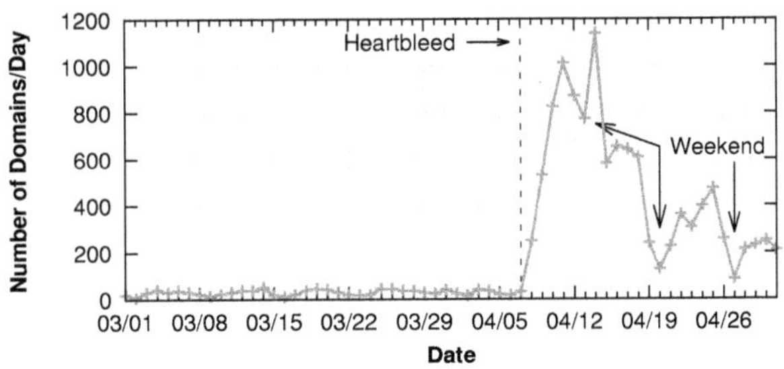

Figure 12: Number of domains that revoked at least one certificate over time for the month before and after Heartbleed.

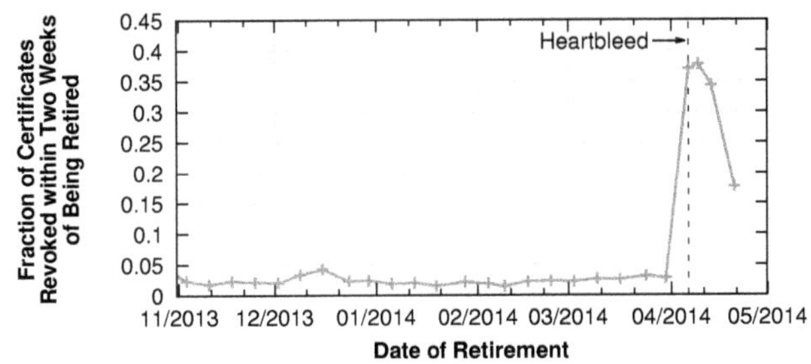

Figure 13: Fraction of reissued certificates that are revoked within two weeks of being retired. A significant increase in revocation probability is observed after Heartbleed.

at least partially due to system administrators re-using the same Certificate Signing Request (CSR) when requesting the new certificate from their CA.

In the wake of Heartbleed, we observe a significant drop in the frequency of reissuing certificates with the same key; this result indicates that sites are generating a new key pair more frequently. However, if we focus on the Heartbleed-induced reissues, we observe that a non-trivial fraction (4.1%) of these certificates are reissued with the same key (thereby defeating the purpose of reissuing the certificate). In fact, we observe a total of 912 such certificates coming from 747 distinct Alexa domains.

4.4 Certificate Revocation

We now turn to investigating certificate revocation before, during, and after the revelation of Heartbleed. Recall that it is critical that a vulnerable certificate be revoked: even if a site reissues a new certificate, if an attacker gained access to the vulnerable certificate's private key, then that attacker will be able to impersonate the owner until either the certificate expires or is revoked.[7] We study both revocation and expiration here, and correlate them with rates of reissue. Contrary to standard assumptions, we find that revocation and reissues do not happen simultaneously.

Overall revocation rates. Figure 5 shows the number of certificate revocations over time; as noted above, the average jumps from 29 certificates revoked per day to 1,414 post-Heartbleed. However, the spike on April 16, 2014 is somewhat misleading, as it was largely due to the mass-revocation of 19,384 CloudFlare certificates of the form `ss-1XXXXX.cloudflare.com` [31].

To mitigate this issue, we plot in Figure 12 the number of unique *domains* that revoked at least one certificate over time. We make three interesting observations: *First*, the magnitude of the Heartbleed-induced spike is greatly reduced, but we still observe an up-to-40-fold increase in the number of domains issuing revocations per day. *Second*, we observe that the number of domains issuing revocations falls closer to its pre-Heartbleed level by April 28th, suggesting that *most of the domains that will revoke their certificate in direct response to Heartbleed already have.*

Third, we observe three "dips" in the post-Heartbleed revocation rate on April 13th, April 20th, and April 27th—all weekends, indicating that far fewer revocations occur on the weekend relative to the rest of the week. This periodicity can also be (less-easily) observed in the pre-Heartbleed time frame. It is reasonable to assume revocations dip on weekends because humans are involved in the revocation process, however it is not clear who is responsible for the delays: is it site administrators or CRL maintainers at CAs (or both) who are not working on weekends? Regardless of who is responsible, these weekend delays are problematic for online security, since vulnerabilities (and the attackers who exploit them) do not take weekends off.

Revocation of reissued certificates. We now examine the fraction of retired certificates (i.e., old certificates that have been superseded by a reissued cert) that are revoked within two weeks of being retired. Figure 13 plots this fraction over time. For example, the point on March 3, 2014 shows that 2.2% of the certificates retired on that day were revoked by March 17, 2014. Overall, we see that between 2% and 3% of certificates being retired are eventually revoked. This probability increases by an order of magnitude after Heartbleed, with almost 40% of retired certificates being revoked quickly afterwards. This result suggests that the reason many certificates were reissued just after April 7 was because of Heartbleed, since the retired certificates were also revoked. This contrasts with certificates that are reissued due to impending expiration, in which case the retired certificate does not need to be revoked.

Heartbleed-induced revocations. Similar to certificate reissues, not all certificate revocations after April 7, 2014 are necessarily due to Heartbleed (e.g., the site could have exposed their private key due to a different vulnerability). We therefore define a *Heartbleed-induced revocation* to be a certificate revocation where the certificate had a Heartbleed-induced reissue (see §4.3).

Overall, we observe 14,726 Heartbleed-induced revocations; this corresponds to 40% of all Heartbleed-induced reissued certificates. Thus, 60% of all certificates that were reissued due to Heartbleed were *not* revoked, implying that, if the certificate's private key was actually stolen, the attacker would be able to impersonate the victim without any clients being able to detect it.

Figure 10 presents the fraction of sites that have at least one Heartbleed-induced certificate revocation, as a function of Alexa rank. Revocations follow a similar trend to reis-

[7] We note that revocation alone is often insufficient to prevent impersonation, as an attacker may be able to prevent the client from accessing the CRL. In this case, many web browsers still accept the certificate as valid [18].

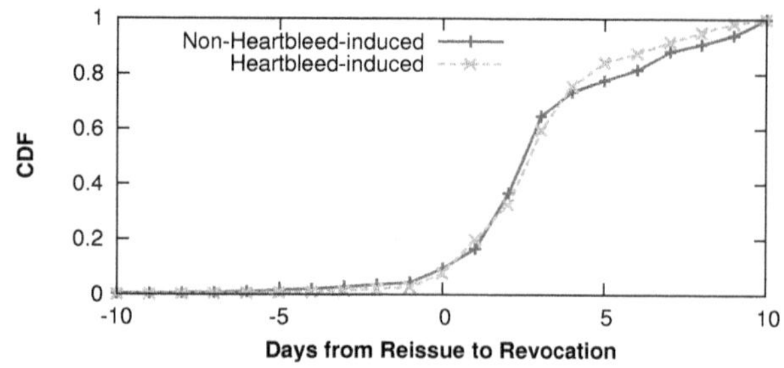

Figure 14: Cumulative distribution of the number of days between when a certificate is reissued and when it is revoked. Positive values indicate the certificate is reissued before it is revoked; negative values indicate the opposite.

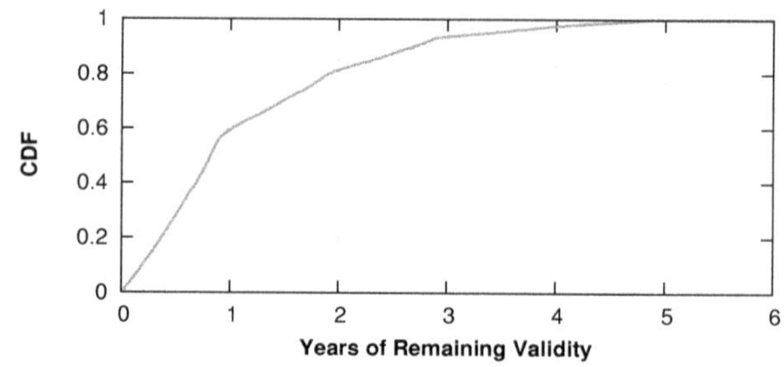

Figure 15: The distribution of time-until-expiry for vulnerable, reissued, but not revoked certificates. If these certificates are never revoked, this figure shows how long they will persist.

sues, i.e., sites with high rank are slightly more likely to revoke. Ideally, the two lines in Figure 10 should be coincident, i.e., all sites reissuing certificates due to Heartbleed should also have revoked the retired certificates (the only exception to this rule is if the retired certificate was about to expire anyway, but we account for this in our definitions of Heartbleed-induced reissues and revocations). This result highlights a serious gap in security best-practices across all of the sites in the Alexa Top-1M.

Finally, we examine the *revocation speed*, or the number of days between when a certificate is reissued and it is revoked. Figure 14 presents the cumulative distribution of the revocation speed for both Heartbleed-induced and non-Heartbleed-induced revocations. To make the distributions comparable, we only look at differences between -10 and 10 days (recall that Heartbleed-induced reissues and revocations can only occur after April 7, 2014, limiting that distribution). We observe that Heartbleed-induced revocations appear to happen slightly more quickly, thought not to the extent one might expect, given the urgent nature of the vulnerability. We also observe that revocation almost always happens *after* reissue, which is likely explained by the more manual process that revocation often entails. This result contradicts previous assumptions [8] that revocations and reissues occur simultaneously. Finally, it is worth noting that the granularity of our scans makes generalizing these results difficult, since we cannot tell exactly when a certificate was reissued; however, the two distributions are comparable to each other.

Expirations are not enough. To demonstrate how long the effects of this vulnerability could be felt if sites do not revoke their vulnerable certificates, we analyze certificates that, by the end of our data collection, were found to be vulnerable (and alive) when Heartbleed was announced, reissued thereafter, but never revoked. Figure 15 presents the distribution of how much longer such certificates will continue to live if their sites do not revoke them. Note that this CDF appears to be piecewise linear at intervals of 1 year: this is because expiration dates are typically set at intervals of a year—that the distribution is roughly uniform within these year intervals indicates that certificates are issued mostly uniformly throughout the year. This figure shows that, without revoking, the vulnerability introduced in 2014 could affect clients through 2020. We conclude from this that, given the meager rates of revocation, it would be helpful for CAs to shift to shorter expiry times in their certificates.

CRL reason codes. The CRL specification allows the maintainers of CRLs to include a *reason* for why a certificate was revoked along with the revocation in the form of a small set of *reason codes*. The reason code is optional, and the options range from "Unspecified" to "Key Compromised" to "Privilege Withdrawn" [6]. Note that the CRL reason codes are not necessarily verified by the certificate authorities, and they may be incorrect.

For all of the certificates that we observed to be revoked, we extracted the reason code (if one existed); we present the distribution of these reason codes for both Heartbleed-induced and non-Heartbleed-induced certificate reissues in Figure 16. Note the log-scale on the x-axis.

We make two key observations. *First*, we see a significant increase in the probability of a reason code being provided at all for Heartbleed-induced revocations: only 19.2% of non-Heartbleed-induced revocations provide any reason code (*including* the "Unspecified" reason code), while 27.1% on Heartbleed-induced revocations provide a reason code. *Second*, we observe a large increase in the "Key Compromise" reason code (from 0.40% to 1.18% of all CRL entries); given that Heartbleed certificates are likely being reissued

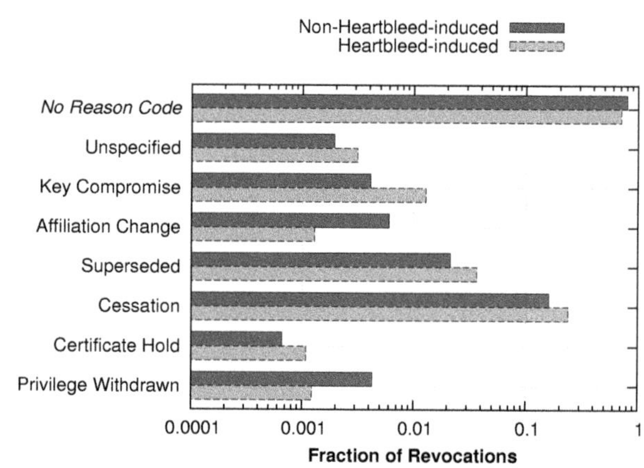

Figure 16: Distribution of CRL reason codes given for both Heartbleed-induced and non-Heartbleed-induced certificate reissues. Note the log scale on the x-axis. We observe an increase in reasons for revocations being given for Heartbleed-induced reissues, especially for the "Key Compromised" reason code.

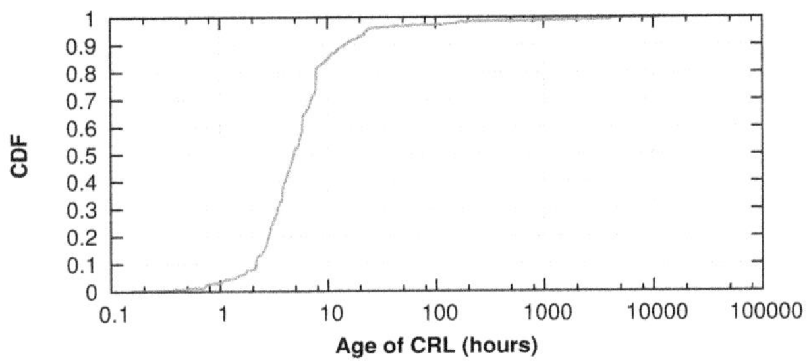

Figure 17: Cumulative distribution of the time between when we downloaded the CRLs (6:00pm EST) and the time of issue recorded in the CRL (and signed by the CA). Most CAs have a chance to revoke certificates at least once a day, as 95% of the CAs updated their CRLs within 24 hours of when we downloaded them.

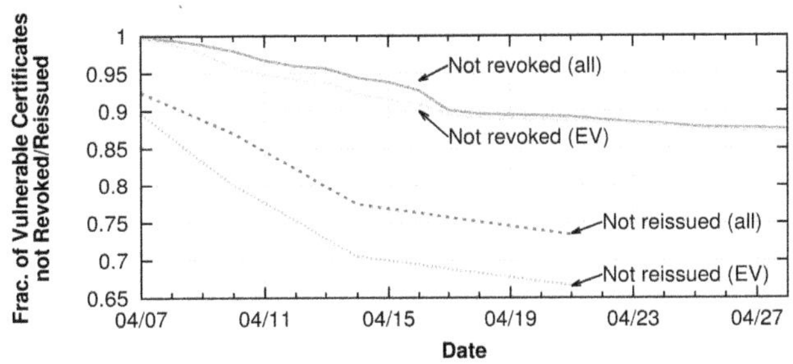

Figure 18: The rate at which vulnerable certificates were reissued and revoked after Heartbleed's announcement. (Note that the y-axis does not begin at zero.)

due to concerns that the private key may have been compromised, this increase is not unexpected. However, it still appears that vast majority of CRL entries are mis-coded. Prior work has also noted that CRLs are usually mis-coded [8], although the snapshot we present in Figure 16 is even more stark, given that we know Heartbleed-induced revocations should have been revoked with a reason code of "Key Compromise".

CRL update intervals. The general lack of site administrators revoking certificates when they should (e.g., after Heartbleed) could be attributed to the CAs only updating their CRLs on very long timescales. For example, one reason for this would be if CAs kept their private keys on offline hosts that would have to be powered on every time to sign CRLs. Another reason would be so clients do not need to download new CRLs very often.

Figure 17 indicates that neither of these reasons are true. This figure shows the cumulative distribution of the difference between the time we downloaded a CRL and the time it was issued. We see that 95% of CAs signed a fresh CRL within 24 hours of 6:00pm EST (when we downloaded the CRLs). When CAs sign a fresh CRL, they have the opportunity to revoke more certificates. These results suggest that CAs could revoke certificates as often as every few hours. Thus, any delays in the revocation of certificates are due to humans in the loop: either certificate owners who are not reporting potentially compromised keys, or CA personnel who are not manually adding new entries to CRLs before they are signed and shipped.

Another important factor in the context of client impact is when (and whether) clients obtained the list of revocations. Unfortunately, we are unable to answer this question given our data collection methodology (it would require instrumenting end-hosts to see when precisely their browsers and operating systems fetched CRLs or issued OCSP queries). Such a study is an interesting area of future work. However, there is one aspect of this problem to which we may be able to lend insight; it was recently reported that many browsers do not even bother to check certificates' CRLs, with the exception of extended validation (EV) certificates [7]. We next turn to an analysis of how these EV certificates are reissued and revoked in comparison to the entire corpus of certificates.

4.5 Extended Validation Certificates

Recall that one of the major roles of a CA is to validate the identity of the subjects for whom it issues certificates. *Extended Validation* (EV) certificates are a means by which CAs can express that this identity-verification process has followed a set of (presumably stringent) established criteria. EV certificates are standard X.509 certificates, and offer no additional security per se, but the rationale is that with a more thorough verification process by the CAs, these certificates can be more readily verified and trusted by users.[8] That said, there remains concern as to whether or not this trust is well-placed. We close this section by investigating the rate at which vulnerable EV certificates were revoked and reissued as compared to the entire aggregate of certificates.

Figure 18 shows the fraction of vulnerable certificates that have yet to be reissued or revoked over time. In this figure, the initial y values do not all start at 1.0 for reissues: this is because, with coarse granularity of our data, we cannot be certain whether some certificates were reissued immediately after the scan on April 7, 2014, immediately before the scan on April 10, 2014, or in between. We therefore provide the *most optimistic* possibility: if we know a certificate was reissued between days d and $d + k$, then we plot it as having been reissued on day d. The coarse granularity of the scans also explains why the reissue lines do not advance beyond April 21.

Regardless, one trend that remains clear is that sites are more proactive in reissuing new certificates than in revoking old ones. This contradicts prior assumptions that revocations and reissues occur simultaneously [8]. Indeed, it is not yet clear to us *why* a site would reissue a vulnerable certificate without revoking it, but these trends demonstrate that it is a common practice, even for those with EV certificates.

This figure shows a generally bleak view of how *thoroughly* sites revoke and reissue their certificates when necessary. Note that the y-axis begins at 0.65: three weeks after the revelation of Heartbleed, over 87% of all certificates we found to be vulnerable have yet to be revoked, and over 73% of them have yet to be reissued. Of those that *did* revoke their certificates, we find that the speed at which they did so matches that of earlier studies on the spread of patches [25, 27]: there is an exponential drop-off, followed by a gradual decline. Specifically, the "Not revoked (all)" line fits the

[8]Many browsers present EV certificates with a green box in the address bar, while non-EV certificates are often just represented with a gray lock icon.

curve $0.179e^{-0.073x} + 0.830$, while the "Not revoked (EV)" line fits the curve $0.144e^{-0.118x} + 0.859$.

Overall, EV certificates follow similar trends to the entire corpus, with a slightly faster and more thorough response. Interestingly, while EV certificates were revoked more quickly, their non-EV counterparts caught up within ten days; however, EV certificates were reissued both more quickly and more thoroughly. We expect that the underlying cause of this observation is a self-selection effect, i.e., security-conscious sites are more likely to seek out EV certificates in the first place. We doubt that the additional identity verification steps required to obtain an EV certificate play a large role in this (slightly) improved reaction to Heartbleed. Nonetheless, there are still many vulnerable EV certificates that have not been reissued two weeks after the event (67%) and that have not been revoked three weeks after (87%).

5. RELATED WORK

Our work lies at the intersection of two general areas of prior work: studies of how effectively administrators react to widely publicized vulnerabilities, and measurements of the TLS/SSL certificate ecosystem. To the best of our knowledge, we are the first to look specifically at how potentially compromised certificates are replaced and revoked.

Vulnerability patching. There have been several studies of how quickly and effectively administrators patch well-known software vulnerabilities. Rescorla measured the response to a 2002 buffer overflow vulnerability in OpenSSL [27], and Ramos investigated how the fraction of vulnerable systems changes after various security holes from 2000–2005 had been published [25]. Both of these studies found an exponential decrease in the fraction of vulnerable hosts shortly after public revelation of the vulnerability, followed by a gradual decline thereafter. Interestingly, in Rescorla's study, another sharp decline in the number of vulnerable hosts occurred after the release of the Slapper worm which exploited the buffer overflow.

Closely related to our study is that of Yilek et al., who measured the aftermath of a 2008 vulnerability in Debian's OpenSSL key generation that resulted in predictable RSA keys [35]. What makes this work particularly related to ours is that fixing the vulnerability required not only patching OpenSSL, but also reissuing new keys. They found that this process resulted in a gradual decline in the fraction of vulnerable hosts, as opposed to the sharp exponential decay when only patching the software is necessary. However, because their data collection only began several days after the vulnerability was released, the sharp decline may have occurred but gone unnoticed. Our data covers months leading up to and weeks after Heartbleed, allowing us more confidence in the initial drop-off of vulnerabilities.

Our work broadly builds on these prior studies in that we focus on a different, though equally important, aspect of the vulnerability fixing cycle: when potentially compromised certificates were not only replaced, but explicitly *revoked*. The connection between patching software, reissuing new certificates, and revoking old ones has, to the best of our knowledge, not been explicitly studied. Though it had been previously believed that revocations and reissues occur simultaneously [8], our results demonstrate that revocations are often offset in time, or simply never occur at all.

The certificate ecosystem. In focusing on vulnerability fixing as it pertains to certificates, our work is also related to recent studies of the certificate ecosystem at large. Holz et al. [17] performed passive and active measurements on HTTPS certificates from the Alexa Top-1M domains. Durumeric et al. [8] performed active measurements using ZMap [10] that yielded nearly 40× more certificates than prior studies [11, 16, 17]. Broadly, these studies exposed several grim properties of today's certificate ecosystem, including weaker key lengths than suggested by NIST [3], longer certificate chains than necessary, invalid subject names, and so on. Comparing these studies to one another, it appears that the Alexa Top-1M sites—though still far from perfect—do manage certificates more appropriately on average, with a slight weight to higher-ranked domains. Like Holz et al., our work focuses solely on the Alexa Top-1M; we expect that expanding to more domains would, as Durumeric et al. found [8], result in less effective certificate management, though this is an area of future work.

While these studies have shed considerable light on the certificate ecosystem (and found it to be surprisingly bleak), our study is the first to explicitly consider reissues and revocations, particularly in the wake of a widespread vulnerability. Durumeric et al. [8] briefly investigated certificate revocations, and found that a mere 2.5% of the certificates they encountered were ever revoked—of these, the majority gave no reason code. By using Heartbleed as a wide-scale correlated event, we complement this prior work by investigating which certificates *should* have been revoked, and *when* the revocations should have taken place. In the context of the certificate ecosystem, we believe this to be novel.

Heartbleed. The recent nature of the Heartbleed vulnerability means little scientific work has yet to come out studying the vulnerability itself and the community's reaction to it. The most closely related work—a study performed concurrently with our own—presents a comprehensive study of the breadth of the vulnerability, the clean-up, and surveys of administrators who failed to patch their servers [9]. Interestingly, the study leverages historic packet traces [19] to look for evidence of Heartbleed exploitation *before* the announcement and finds no evidence that the vulnerability was exploited beforehand. This study and our own are complementary—theirs briefly examines SSL certificate reissues and revocations, and the results of their analysis are in agreement with ours.

6. CONCLUDING DISCUSSION

In this paper, we study how SSL certificates are reissued and revoked in response to a widespread vulnerability, Heartbleed, that enabled undetectable key compromise. We conducted large-scale measurements and developed new methodologies and heuristics to determine how the most popular 1 million web sites reacted to this vulnerability in terms of certificate management, and how this impacts security for clients that use them.

We found that the vast majority of vulnerable certificates have not been reissued; further, of those domains that reissued certificates in response to Heartbleed, 60% do not revoke their vulnerable certificates—if they do not eventually become revoked, 20% of those certificates will remain valid (not expire) for two or more years. The ramifications of this findings are alarming: modern Web browsers will remain potentially vulnerable to malicious third parties using stolen keys to masquerade as a compromised site for a long time to come. We analyzed these trends with vulnerable EV certificates, as well, and have found that, while they exhibit better security practices, they still remain largely not reissued (67%) and not revoked (88%) even weeks after the vulnerability was made public.

To the best of our knowledge, our focused study on certificate reissues and revocations is the first of its kind. Our results are, in some ways, in line with previous studies on the rates at which administrators patched vulnerable software—for instance, revocation rates followed a sharp exponential drop-off shortly after the vulnerability was made public, and tapered off relatively soon thereafter. However, unlike with software patches, we find the vast majority of certificates have still not been reissued or revoked. These findings indicate quite simply that the current practices of certificate management are misaligned with what is necessary to ensure a secure PKI.

Surveying system administrators. To help better understand the reasons behind the lack of prompt certificate reissues and revocations, we informally surveyed a few systems administrators. We asked what steps they had taken in response to Heartbleed: did they patch, reissue, and revoke, and if not, then why not? We received seven responses. Most reported patching their systems, typically in direct response, but some relied on managed servers or automatic updates and therefore took no Heartbleed-specific steps. There was some variance in when patches were applied, due to a combination of scheduled reboots and delayed responses from some vendors, but the majority of patches were applied quickly.

For revoking and reissuing, however, we saw a wide spectrum of behavior. Few both revoked and reissued, but among them, they did so within 48 hours. Many neither revoked nor reissued; a common reason provided was that the vulnerable hosts were either not hosting sensitive data or were not running services that were deemed sensitive enough to warrant it. Along similar reasons, others reported having reissued the certificate but not revoking, explaining that the certificate is only for internal use. Finally, others reported that they did not perceive reissuing and revoking as important because they had patched quickly after the bug was publicly announced (recall, however, that the vulnerability was introduced over two years prior).

Our results from this small survey should be viewed anecdotally—a more extensive survey on certificate administration is an interesting area of future work—but they do shed light on some of the root causes of why revoking and reissuing are not on equal footing with patching. While administrators almost universally understand the importance of patching after a vulnerability, many do not appreciate or know about the importance of revoking and reissuing certificates with new keys. Of those administrators who do understand the importance, even some of them reported pushback from others who perceived the process as being overly complex. In sum, this points to the need for broader education on the treatment of certificates, and perhaps more assistance from CAs to help ensure that all the prescribed steps are taken.

Lessons learned. Our results suggest several changes to common PKI practices that may improve security in practice. First, the practices of low revocation rates and long expiration dates form a dangerous combination. Techniques that automate revocation would vastly reduce the period during which clients are vulnerable to malicious third parties. Similarly, setting reasonably short certificate expiration dates (as suggested by Topalovic et al. [34]) by default will significantly reduce the period during which vulnerable certificates are valid. Second, mechanisms that enable a simultaneous reissue-and-revoke for a certificate will make it less likely that invalid certificates are accepted by clients. Third, we have found that many domains, when they reissue a certificate, continue to offer the old, vulnerable certificate, as well. Given the large number of certificates and hosts using them per domain in our dataset, we believe administrators would benefit from tools that more easily track and validate the set of certificates they are using.

Future work. This paper is, we believe, the first step towards understanding the manual process of reissuing and revoking certificates in the wake of a vulnerability. Several interesting open problems remain. Because our data focuses on the server and CA side of the PKI ecosystem, we are unable to draw any direct conclusions as to what clients experience. A host-centered measurement study would, for instance, allow us to understand not only when revocations were added to CRLs, but when clients actually received the CRLs. Moreover, our study opens many questions as to *why* the certificate reissue and revocation processes are so extensively mismanaged. Our results reinforce previous findings that site popularity is correlated with good security practices, but even the highest ranked Alexa websites show relatively anemic rates of reissues and revocations. Understanding the root causes is an important step towards developing secure infrastructures that effectively incorporate (or mitigate) the end-user administrators.

Open source. Our analysis relied on both existing, public sources of data and those we collected ourselves. We make all of our data and our analysis code available to the research community at

`https://ssl-research.ccs.neu.edu`

Acknowledgments

We thank the anonymous reviewers and our shepherd, Jelena Mirkovic, for their helpful comments. We also thank Rapid7 for collecting the SSL certificate data, the authors of ZMap for collecting the Heartbleed vulnerability data, and for making it publicly available. Finally, we thank our survey respondents for their candid responses. This research was supported in part by NSF grants CNS-1054233, CNS-1319019, and CNS-1150177, and an Amazon Web Services in Education grant.

7. REFERENCES

[1] D. E. 3rd. Transport Layer Security (TLS) Extensions: Extension Definitions, Jan. 2011. IETF RFC-6066.

[2] Alexa Top 1 Million Domains. `http://s3.amazonaws.com/alexa-static/top-1m.csv.zip`.

[3] E. Barker, W. Barker, W. Burr, W. Polk, and M. Smid. Recommendation for Key Management – Part 1: General (Revision 3), 2012. NIST Special Publication 800-57.

[4] Botan SSL Library. http://botan.randombit.net.

[5] CERT Vulnerability Note VU#720951: OpenSSL TLS heartbeat extension read overflow discloses sensitive information. http://www.kb.cert.org/vuls/id/720951.

[6] D. Cooper, S. Santesson, S. Farrell, S. Boeyen, R. Housley, and W. Polk. Internet X.509 Public Key Infrastructure Certificate and Certificate Revocation List (CRL) Profile. IETF RFC-5280, May 2008.

[7] R. Duncan. How certificate revocation (doesn't) work in practice, 2013. http://news.netcraft.com/archives/2013/05/13/how-certificate-revocation-doesnt-work-in-practice.html.

[8] Z. Durumeric, J. Kasten, M. Bailey, and J. A. Halderman. Analysis of the HTTPS certificate ecosystem. In *ACM Internet Measurement Conference (IMC)*, 2013.

[9] Z. Durumeric, J. Kasten, F. Li, J. Amann, J. Beekman, M. Payer, N. Weaver, J. A. Halderman, V. Paxson, and M. Bailey. The matter of Heartbleed. In *ACM Internet Measurement Conference (IMC)*, 2014.

[10] Z. Durumeric, E. Wustrow, and J. A. Halderman. ZMap: Fast Internet-wide Scanning and Its Security Applications. In *USENIX Security Symposium*, 2013.

[11] P. Eckersley and J. Burns. An observatory for the SSLiverse. In *Defcon 18*, 2010. https://www.eff.org/files/DefconSSLiverse.pdf.

[12] F. F. Elwailly, C. Gentry, and Z. Ramzan. QuasiModo: Efficient certificate validation and revocation. In *Public Key Cryptography (PKC)*, 2004.

[13] P. Evans. Heartbleed bug: RCMP asked Revenue Canada to delay news of SIN thefts, 2014. http://www.cbc.ca/news/business/heartbleed-bug-rcmp-asked-revenue-canada-to-delay-news-of-sin-thefts-1.2609192.

[14] Faketime library. http://www.code-wizards.com/projects/libfaketime/.

[15] B. Grubb. Heartbleed disclosure timeline: who knew what and when, 2014. http://www.smh.com.au/it-pro/security-it/heartbleed-disclosure-timeline-who-knew-what-and-when-20140415-zqurk.html.

[16] N. Heninger, Z. Durumeric, E. Wustrow, and J. A. Halderman. Mining your Ps and Qs: Detection of widespread weak keys. In *USENIX Security Symposium*, 2012.

[17] R. Holz, L. Braun, N. Kammenhuber, and G. Carle. The SSL landscape – A thorough analysis of the X.509 PKI using active and passive measurements. In *ACM Internet Measurement Conference (IMC)*, 2011.

[18] Revocation doesn't work. https://www.imperialviolet.org/2011/03/18/revocation.html.

[19] S. Kornexl, V. Paxson, H. Dreger, A. Feldmann, and R. Sommer. Building a time machine for efficient recording and retrieval of high-volume network traffic. In *ACM Internet Measurement Conference (IMC)*, 2005.

[20] Mac OS X 10.9.2 Root Certificates. http://support.apple.com/kb/HT6005.

[21] S. Micali. NOVOMODO: Scalable certificate validation and simplified PKI management. In *PKI Research Workshop*, 2002.

[22] P. Mutton. Half a million widely trusted websites vulnerable to heartbleed bug, 2014. http://news.netcraft.com/archives/2014/04/08/half-a-million-widely-trusted-websites-vulnerable-to-heartbleed-bug.html.

[23] M. Naor and K. Nissim. Certificate revocation and certificate update. In *USENIX Security Symposium*, 1998.

[24] OpenSSL Project. https://www.openssl.org.

[25] T. Ramos. The laws of vulnerabilities. In *RSA Conference*, 2006. http://www.qualys.com/docs/Laws-Presentation.pdf.

[26] Rapid7 SSL Certificate Scans. https://scans.io/study/sonar.ssl.

[27] E. Rescorla. Security holes... Who cares? In *USENIX Security Symposium*, 2003.

[28] R. L. Rivest. Can we eliminate certificate revocation lists? In *Financial Cryptography (FC)*, 1998.

[29] S. Santesson, M. Myers, R. Ankney, A. Malpani, S. Galperin, and C. Adams. X.509 Internet Public Key Infrastructure Online Certificate Status Protocol - OCSP, June 2013. IETF RFC-6960.

[30] R. Seggelmann, M. Tuexen, and M. Williams. Transport Layer Security (TLS) and Datagram Transport Layer Security (DTLS) Heartbeat Extension, Feb. 2012. IETF RFC-6520.

[31] N. Sullivan. The Heartbleed Aftermath: all CloudFlare certificates revoked and reissued, 2014. http://blog.cloudflare.com/the-heartbleed-aftermath-all-cloudflare-certificates-revoked-and-reissued.

[32] N. Sullivan. The Results of the CloudFlare Challenge, 2014. http://blog.cloudflare.com/the-results-of-the-cloudflare-challenge.

[33] The GnuTLS Transport Layer Security Library. http://www.gnutls.org.

[34] E. Topalovic, B. Saeta, L.-S. Huang, C. Jackson, and D. Boneh. Toward short-lived certificates. In *Web 2.0 Security & Privacy (W2SP)*, 2012.

[35] S. Yilek, E. Rescorla, H. Shacham, B. Enright, and S. Savage. When private keys are public: Results from the 2008 Debian OpenSSL vulnerability. In *ACM Internet Measurement Conference (IMC)*, 2009.

[36] P. Zheng. Tradeoffs in certificate revocation schemes. In *ACM Computer Communication Review (CCR)*, 2013.

[37] ZMap Vulnerable Hosts. https://zmap.io/heartbleed/vulnerable.html.

Forced Perspectives

Evaluating an SSL Trust Enhancement at Scale

Adam Bates
University of Florida
adammbates@ufl.edu

Joe Pletcher
University of Oregon
pletcher@cs.uoregon.edu

Tyler Nichols
University of Oregon
tnichols@cs.uoregon.edu

Braden Hollembaek
iSEC Partners
bhollembaek@isecpartners.com

Kevin R. B. Butler
University of Florida
butler@ufl.edu

ABSTRACT

The *certificate authority (CA)* PKI system has been used for decades as a means of providing domain identity verification services throughout the Internet, but a growing body of evidence suggests that our trust in this system is misplaced. A recently proposed CA alternative, *Convergence*, extends the *Network Perspectives* system of multi-path probing to perform certificate verification. Unfortunately, adoption of Convergence and other SSL/TLS trust enhancements has been slow, in part because it is unknown how these systems perform against large workloads and realistic conditions.

In this work we ask the question "*What if all certificates were validated with Convergence?*" We perform a case study of deploying Convergence under realistic workloads with a university-wide trace of real-world HTTPS activity. By synthesizing Convergence requests, we effectively *force perspectives-based verification* on an entire university in simulation. We demonstrate that through local and server caching, a single Convergence deployment can meet the requirements of millions of SSL flows while imposing under 0.1% network overhead and requiring as little as 108 ms to validate a certificate, making Convergence a worthwhile candidate for further deployment and adoption.

Categories and Subject Descriptors

C.2.0. [**Computer-Communication Networks**]: General — *Security and protection*

Keywords

SSL, TLS, HTTPS, public-key certificates

1. INTRODUCTION

Establishing identity is one of the fundamental challenges on the Internet. To provide an identity verification mechanism for the virtually ubiquitous SSL/TLS communications protocols, the world has adopted a PKI-based *certificate authority (CA)* system where *trusted third parties* attest the identity of remote destinations visited by clients using the web, email, and other applications where assurance of site legitimacy are critical. CAs provide digital signatures for the certificates of the individual domains that they attest, and these certificates can form a transitive chain of trust.

While widely deployed, numerous serious issues have been found with the traditional CA systems. The risks of the CA-based system have been well known for well over a decade [12][1] but recent serious compromises have readily exposed these fundamental and systemic limitations. Security breaches where a CA's private key is hijacked have taken place with alarming frequency [14, 25], and an incident last year with the TURKTRUST CA has shown that flawed business practices can lead to the unauthorized issue of intermediate certificates that can create valid certificates for any domain [8]. A recent study of over 48,000 valid certificates recommended that 61% of these not be trusted due to the lack of CA verification [33]. These lapses in security procedure lead to the threat of a Man-in-the-Middle (MitM) attack, in which an attacker intercepts and reads supposedly-secure SSL traffic bound to or from a target website[2]. In the case of the Comodo CA [25], several breaches occurred over a span of months but little could be done as punishment; revoking Comodo's certificate would have been tantamount to denying SSL access to approximately 25% of the Internet [22], indicating an underlying problem of *trust lock-in* plaguing the current CA system.

In response to this crisis, countless proposals in the literature have attempted to patch, trash, and re-architect the CA model [7]. Amongst these are Marlinspike's *Convergence* [22], an extension to Wendlandt et al. *Perspectives* [34] multi-path probing system that provides enhanced privacy and performance. However, trust enhancements like Convergence have been slow to be deployed in practice, in part due to a lack of understanding of their impact on large networks. Convergence was released without a performance evaluation, and Perspectives' evaluation does not investigate server performance at scale under bursty, realistic workloads.

IMC'14, November 5–7, 2014, Vancouver, BC, Canada.

http://dx.doi.org/10.1145/2663716.2663759.

[1] The Mozilla employee responsible for CAs has since acknowledged that the proposal was a "bit of a handwave".

[2] In the case of TURKTRUST, the issued intermediate certificate was used precisely for this reason in a decryption/re-encryption proxy mechanism within an organization.

To investigate the implications of global support for CA alternatives, we perform a comprehensive performance evaluation of the Convergence architecture. A key insight of our approach is that real-world SSL traffic can be mapped to certificate validation attempts in alternate trust models. We apply this insight to a university traffic capture of over 2 million SSL flows. Our contributions can thus be summarized as follows:

- **Synthesized traffic for CA Alternatives:** We map a university-wide trace of HTTPS traffic into a realistic workload for a Convergence Notary. Our approach can be generalized to other SSL trust enhancements such as DANE [18], AKI [19], Certificate Transparency [20], and Sovereign Keys [10].
- **Benchmark Convergence Architecture:** We apply this traffic in real time to a Convergence notary. We analyze the results for general performance, cache utilization, and network overhead, discovering that a single notary scales to upwards of 300 requests per second in the general case, and 1000 requests per second using fully cached results.
- **Costs to End Users:** We benchmark client costs on both continental and globally distributed notary distributions, and find that the average time to validate a certificate with a continental notary deployment is 260 ms, and as little as 108 ms on a return visit to the same domain.

The rest of this paper is organized as follows. In Section 2 we provide background on SSL, Certificate Authorities, and recently proposed CA alternatives. In Section 3, we perform a rigorous performance analysis of a Convergence notary deployment, and in Section 4 we consider the performance of convergence from the perspective of an end user. We summarize our findings in Section 5. In Section 6, we introduce libraries for the development of Convergence-aware applications, and in Section 7 we conclude.

2. BACKGROUND & RELATED WORK

Establishing destination identity on the Internet is a surprisingly difficult problem. In 1995, Netscape introduced the SSL protocol family (Secure Socket Layer) [17] to provide confidentiality, integrity, and identity to network communications. Identity assurance is a critical property in SSL, as its absence leaves communications vulnerable to impersonation and Man-in-the-Middle (MitM) attacks. As a solution to the identity problem, SSL introduced the Certificate Authority (CA) system, an industry that facilitates the verification of website certificates (public keys) through a Public Key Infrastructure (PKI). The CA business model is a domain identity service. Using a protected private key, CAs sign the certificates of customers that wish to prove their identity on the Internet. CA public keys, which are distributed in browsers and operating systems, can then be used to verify the authenticity of the server certificate presented when an SSL connection is established.

Independent of the known difficulties of SSL use and development [2, 4, 5, 13, 15, 32], the CA trust model introduces many additional problems. First, Vendor CA selection is largely an opaque process. Browser and operating system

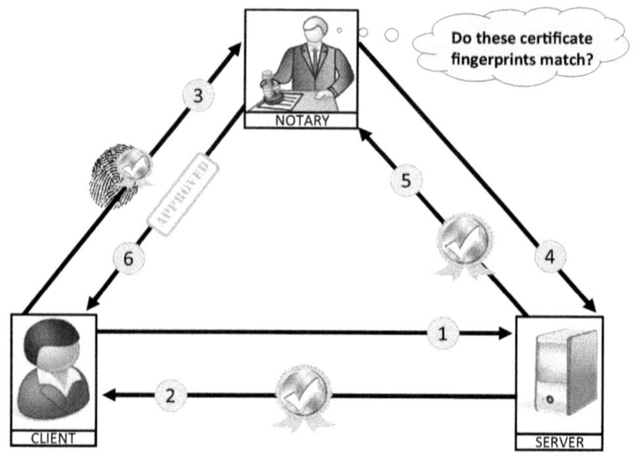

Figure 1: Multipath Probing (e.g., Convergence) leverages network path diversity to verify SSL certificates.

vendors do not justify the CAs they include in their products, and even well meaning agents (e.g., Mozilla) accept the vast majority of CAs to ensure compatibility with Internet services [11], while end users are limited to their ability to override vendor trust decisions. Second, CAs are not sufficiently incentivized to protect their customers. Even in cases where a CA is subject to a catastrophic security breach, it may still avoid serious repercussions [6, 22]. Third, each CA has unlimited scope, meaning that any CA can certify any certificate. As a result, conscientious businesses that certify with reputable CAs are just as at-risk for attack [33]. Additionally, CAs have a history of losing and licensing their private keys. DigiNotar, Comodo, and VeriSign have all had their private keys stolen or hijacked [22]. There is even evidence of certificate authorities that provide wiretap services or license their private keys [16, 29, 30, 31], creating a conflict of interest regarding customers' security needs.

Proposed CA enhancements and alternatives were extensively surveyed by Clark and van Oorschot [7], who identify *families* of proposals based on their underlying fundamental principles of operation. These alternatives vary widely in terms of both their advantages and limitations, reflecting differences of opinion on the fundamental problems with the CA trust model. An important subset of these security enhancements possess the property that they require no server side changes in order to be adopted; primitives such as multipath probing [3, 22, 34], client-based key pinning [27, 10, 23, 31], and certificate revocation lists [26, 28, 9, 20] are eligible for immediate deployment by individual users, providing tangible security enhancements to today's Internet threats. This aspect of multi-path probing motivated our selection of Convergence for this study.

2.1 Convergence

Convergence, based largely on Perspectives, is a method of using multi-path probing to establish a domain identity [22, 34]. Convergence clients verify a site's certificate by comparing it to the certificates obtained by trusted *notaries* that have accessed the target site via different network paths. By comparing the certificates, Convergence can probabilistically detect the presence of a MitM attack, with increasing confidence as the notary set's network path diversity increases. This procedure *replaces* traditional signature verification in multi-path probing systems; hence, even when a site's certificate was issued by a CA, Convergence need not trust that CA's public key in order to validate the certificate. Convergence offers the property of *trust agility* for the end user. Trust agility is comprised of two properties: first, the ability to re-evaluate trust decisions at anytime without repercussion; second, an ability for each individual to select their own trust anchors [22].

While Convergence Notaries can actually be extended to make use of a variety of verification methods [24], in this work we use the term "Convergence" to succinctly refer to the `NetworkPerspectivesVerifier` of the Convergence System. A simplified example of this verifier is pictured in Figure 1: The `Client` attempts to initiate an SSL session with the `Server` (1), and receives a certificate as part of the SSL handshake (2). Rather than verifying the CA signature on the certificate, the `Client` sends a request to the `Notary` containing the domain, port, and certificate hash of the `Server` (3). The `Notary` contacts the `Server` via a different network path (4) and receives another copy of the certificate (5). If the certificate hashes match, the `Notary` endorses the certificate to the `Client` (6). If the certificates do not match, the `Client` is alerted to the possibility of a MitM attack. Convergence draws its strength from network path diversity, so in practice a client queries many notaries before deciding whether to trust a certificate.

Convergence's primary improvements over Perspectives are performance and privacy. Convergence eliminates a *notary lag* problem by maintaining certificate fingerprint caches at both the notary and client. When a fingerprint is already present in the notary's cache, the target domain need only be contacted in the event of a mismatch between the cache entry and the client-presented fingerprint. When a fingerprint is present in the client's cache and the cache entry matches the site-presented certificate, the client need not contact a notary at all. Since mismatches provide a natural cue for refreshing stale cache entries, the lifespan of a cached fingerprint can be set on the order of months [24]. Convergence also enhances user privacy through use of a request-bouncing scheme that prevents a malicious notary from discovering the browsing habits of clients.

3. BENCHMARKING NOTARY SERVICES

We now investigate the costs of running a Convergence notary service. The primary question we wished to answer was: *Can the Convergence architecture efficiently validate the majority of SSL connections in a large network?* To answer this question, we made use of a Convergence workload that was synthesized from actual HTTPS traffic from a major university. We then ran the workload against a notary service in real time, benchmarking the notary for general performance, cache utilization, and network overhead.

3.1 Finding Convergence Usage Data

An ideal investigation of any alternate CA proposal would include an empirical study of its usage in the wild, but this is presently impossible for Convergence due to a lack of users and infrastructure. However, through consultation with a major university's network services, we overcame this obstacle – we obtained anonymized netflow data of HTTPS traffic from the university's network gateway, which we then used to synthesize a realistic Convergence workload at university scale. The traffic trace was from a link that was connected to three outbound networks: a third party Internet service provider, an in-state inter-university network, and Internet 2. Aggregated on this link was all of the outbound IPV4 HTTPS traffic for the entire university, including the campus wireless network, department buildings, and residence halls. The capture occurred on Monday, April 21st, 2013, starting at noon local time. Source IP addresses in our dataset were deterministically anonymized before we received the data. Destination IP addresses were left unchanged. Our use of this data was in accordance with university policy, and their network services department approved this paper before submission.

Our method for mapping SSL traffic into a Convergence workload was as follows. Using `nfdump`, we filtered for TCP traffic with destination port 443, giving us per-flow statistics for duration, bytes per second, and packets per second. In total, there were 3,922,967 flows in the trace. We then performed reverse DNS lookups on the destination IP addresses. Flows with destination IP addresses that were not resolvable were at this point discarded. This left a total of 2,139,632 flows, 54% of the original dataset. We performed `whois` lookups on the unresolvable IP addresses and found that the vast majority belonged to content distribution networks; 33% of the addresses were registered to Apple.com, but presented certificates with canonical names of the form `*.apple.com.akadns.net`, indicating that Akamai was proxying the SSL connection. We attribute the failed reverse DNS lookups to the request-routing techniques used by CDN-managed domains. We note also that Liang et al.'s recent study details the systemic conflicts between the end-to-end nature of HTTPS and the man-in-the-middle nature of CDN [21].

The full workload is visualized in Figure 2. The generated traffic lagged behind observed traffic in requests per second during the first 3 minutes, after which the simulator was able to accurately model the workload for the remainder of the trial. The traffic reflected a great diversity of SSL usage, including content distribution network domains such as Akamai (24%), cloud services like Amazon AWS (9%), and personal use domains such as Facebook (14%), Twitter (4%), and Spotify (0.2%).

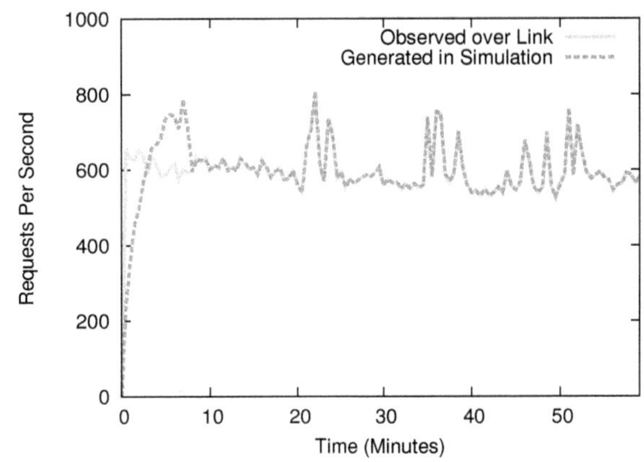

Figure 2: Convergence requests per second during synthesized university workload.

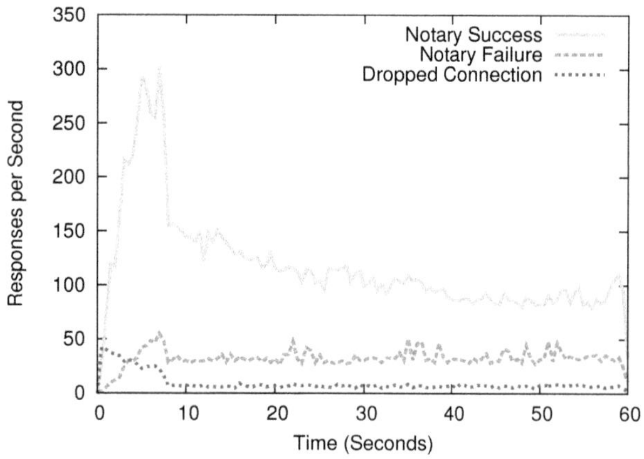

Figure 3: Notary performance against workload.

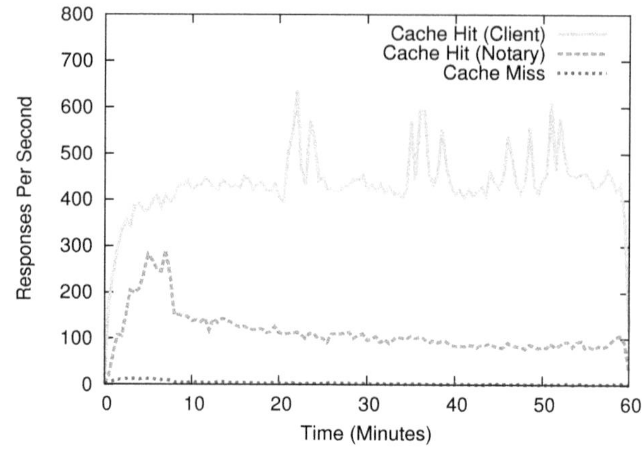

Figure 4: Caching frequency at Client and Notary.

Notary Response/Result	Count	Percent
Notary: 202 Accepted	423,438	74%
Notary: 503 Service Unavailable	116,000	20%
Client-Notary Connection Error	33,837	6%
Client Timeout	803	<1%

Table 1: Results for every Notary request in our workload, grouped by response code.

Event	Count	Perc.
Client: Cached Domain	1580087	77%
Notary: Cached Domain	436085	21%
Cache Miss	38704	1%

Table 2: Cache utilization breakdowns for University workload. This table considers only successful requests, as failed requests cannot be cached.

3.2 Testbed

We ran a series of benchmarking tests against a Convergence 0.4 notary. The notary was deployed on a Dell PowerEdge R610 server with two 4-core Intel Xeon E5606 processors and 12 GB RAM. The operating system used the Red Had Linux 2.6.32 kernel and was connected to a university network using twisted-pair copper transmitting in 1000 BaseT. The notary exclusively made use of the `NetworkPerspectiveVerifier` method. Several small changes were made to the convergence-0.4 source before launching the server. Convergence–0.4 is implemented in Python's Twisted library as a multithreaded web server, but is not multicore as implemented. We inserted `fork` commands during initialization such that there were two Convergence processes per core, all of which were listening on the same ports; we found that this did not introduce instability or corrupt the shared cache database. Convergence-0.4 is also configured to have a 10 second timeout on its outbound connections; however, many of the requests in our dataset were to bad domains that were no longer running an HTTPS service, creating excessive delay. To account for this, we reduced the timeout to 2 seconds. We did not find that reducing the timeout decreased the number of successful requests.

Elsewhere in the same subnet, we deployed several VMs to represent several thousand Convergence users, issuing hundreds of requests per second to the notary. VMs were provisioned sufficiently to ensure that any delay was the result of a bottleneck at the notary; in practice, we found that 3 VMs were sufficient for this task. For each request, the VM recorded the status code returned by the notary and the length of time between the request and response timestamps. The VMs simulated the client-side caching mechanism by maintaining a separate cache for each source IP address (*src_ip*); when the VM found a (*src_ip*, *dst_domain*) cache hit, it moved on without issuing a new notary request for domain *dst_domain*.

3.3 General Performance

Distributing synthesized Convergence requests across our client VMs, we simulated a full hour of university SSL traffic. As noted above, we also simulated a client-side caching mechanism that reduced the number of requests issued to the notary from 2,139,632 to 574,078; we discuss cache performance in greater depth in Section 3.4. Over the course of the entire trial, the average number of notary requests per second was 160.

The breakdown of notary responses from the university tests are found in Table 1. **202** codes indicate that the Notary successfully contacted the target domain and validated the certificate fingerprint. **503** codes indicate that the Notary-Target connection failed because the domain no longer ran an HTTPS service on port 443; many of these codes were from cloud services' VMs (e.g. Akamai, Amazon AWS) whose domains still resolved, but presumably had been transferred to new customers that were not using port 443. Overall notary performance is summarized in Figure 3. A number of connections were dropped by the notary due to sudden bursts of requests, the majority of which occurred in the first 7 minutes of the workload. A few connections were also cancelled due to a client-side timeout.

Over the course of the trial, the notary reached upwards of 300 correctly handled requests per second. To arrive at a tighter upper bound for the performance of our deployment, we ran a series of Apache bench trials [1] in which the notary targeted a web server in the same LAN. We found that our notary could field up to 1051 requests per second with its caching enabled, and up to 199 requests per second with caching disabled.

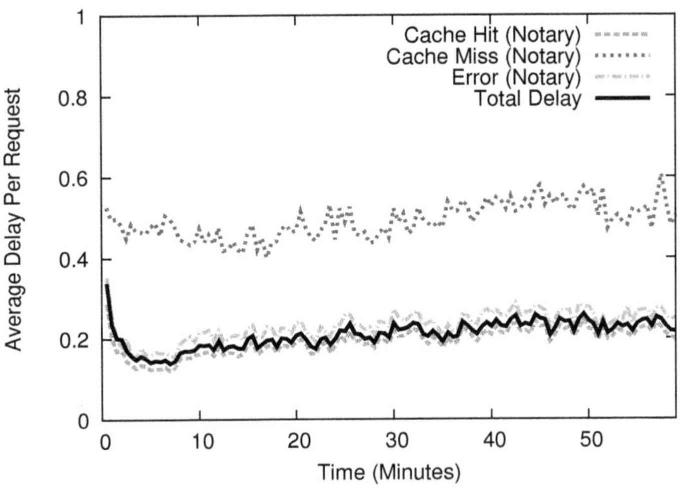

Figure 5: Average delay per minute for requests under different caching conditions.

Cache Utilization	Average Time
65%	16 sec
70%	25 sec
75%	27 sec
80%	35 sec
85%	122 sec
90%	271 sec

Table 3: Time required to reach various notary cache utilization levels, starting from the beginning of the trial.

3.4 Cache Utilization

The proportion of client cache hits, notary cache hits, and cache misses from the university workload can be seen in Figure 4 and Table 2. 79% of the requests triggered our simulated client-side cache mechanism, and hence did not require communication with the notary. For the requests that did reach the notary, almost all of them used a cached result. Only 0.7% of requests in the workload actually required the notary to contact the target domain. Figure 5 shows the performance improvement of the notary caching mechanism – for a cache miss, the notary took approximately 0.5 seconds to respond, whereas only 0.2 seconds were required to respond when a cached fingerprint was found.

We also recorded the speed with which the notary reached various levels of cache utilization. For each second of the trial, we calculated the number of cache hits per second as a ratio of the total number of successful requests. We considered the cache to have reached a certain utilization only once it maintained a given hit rate for the remainder of the trial; that is, the cache hits per second rate did not drop below that level later in the trial. As shown in Table 3, the notary reached 90% cache utilization in under 5 minutes, meaning that notaries rarely need to contact the target domain in order to validate certificate fingerprints.

3.5 Network Overhead

As Convergence replaces a cryptographic signature check with additional network activity, another important consideration is the potential impact on the network. We can express this impact as a measure of the overhead imposed on each SSL session:

$$Overhead = \frac{Notary\ Bytes}{SSL\ Bytes} \quad (1)$$

In order to discover *Notary Bytes*, we performed packet captures at the notary using *tcpdump* while running the university workload. The capture filtered for packets that were both inbound and outbound for port 443. We then summed together the length of each captured frame at a per-second granularity. *SSL Bytes* was approximated from the original netflow data, which provided us with a start time, duration, and bits per second for each captured flow. For each second, we discovered the flows that were currently active, then summed their bits per second. If a flow ended during a given second, only a fraction of the bits per second was summed. This resulted in a bandwidth overhead of 0.06% for Convergence: the total amount of SSL traffic during the trial was 2.77 TB, while the corresponding Convergence traffic was calculated to be 1.73 GB.

Figure 6: Notary services run on EC2 instances. Red squares mark a continental notary (size 3). Our global set used both the red dots and blue circles (size 8).

4. ESTABLISHING END USER COSTS

We now consider the performance of Convergence from the client perspective. In multi-path probe systems, domain identity assurances stem from the use of multiple, geographically disparate notaries.[3] As the number of network vantage points increases, the likelihood of an undetected MitM attack becomes vanishingly small. This claim is based on a threat motel in which persistent large-scale MitM attacks are not practical [34]. To arrive at a performance cost estimate for the end user, we created two notary sets (Figure 6); the first was a continental set of 3 notaries in the United States, and the second was a global set of 8 notaries. Notaries were run from Ubuntu server micro instances at Amazon EC2 sites in the United States, Ireland, Singapore, Japan, Australia, and Brazil. To simplify the benchmarking process, we did not use the available Firefox Plug-In, but instead issued Convergence API requests to the notaries via `wget`, caching results locally in a `sqlite3` database. Our client was an Ubuntu desktop that repeatedly attempted to validate a domain that was at a fixed location in North America.

[3]Clients reconcile conflicting results from different notaries by specifying a consensus policy.

Event	Notaries	Real Time	
Local Cache Hit	N/A	108 ms	[107, 110]
Notary Cache Hit	Continental	743 ms	[742, 744]
Notary Cache Hit	Global	1,508 ms	[1503, 1513]
Notary Cache Miss	Continental	1,006 ms	[996, 1017]
Notary Cache Miss	Global	1,790 ms	[1762, 1818]

Table 4: Benchmarks for Convergence client usage. 95% confidence intervals are included in brackets.

The results, displayed in Table 4, show the real time in milliseconds for the request to return. The minimum cost of Convergence usage was 108 ms, which occurred when a domain's certificate fingerprint had previously been cached on the client machine. We attribute this relatively high baseline cost to the fact that our benchmarking client re-loaded the cache database for each execution. The remaining four rows of the table show the cost of Convergence when a request was issued to the notaries. At worst, when both local and notary caches miss, the cost of a request using a global set was approximately 1.8 seconds. These benchmarks establish upper and lower bounds for the cost of Convergence during normal operation.

An additional cost to consider is the storage size of the client cache. Each cache entry requires 20 bytes of space for a cache fingerprint, plus a small character string to represent the associated domain and port. For example, google.com's entire cache entry would require just 34 bytes. This means that a Convergence cache can store 100,000 records in approximately 3.2 MB. Cache records remain usable forever unless the cached domain changes its certificate, at which point the client contacts the notaries to refresh the record.

5. REMARKS

Based on the findings of Sections 3 - 4, we conclude that Convergence is an efficient means of certificate validation, in spite of additional network communication over traditional signature verification. Our deployment was able to handle over 1000 requests per second. Based on the fact that a single server was able to validate the SSL certificates of an entire university, we feel that Convergence has many strengths as a candidate for widespread deployment. A summary of the security properties of Convergence and other multi-path probing systems can be found in [7].

Convergence's high throughput is due in large part to the effectiveness of its client and notary caches. The notary caching mechanism quickly became saturated during a more realistic SSL workload, and the local caching mechanism proved highly effective, dramatically reducing the cost of system usage to the end user. 75% of all validated domains used locally cached fingerprints, requiring no request to a Convergence notary. Of the remaining requests, 92% made use of the notary's cache.

Based on the frequency of cache utilization from Section 3.4, and the benchmarks from Section 4, we can arrive at an expected validation delay for the end user. We estimate that the average time per certificate validation during our trial was 260 ms. When visiting a locally cached domain, validation required just 108 ms.

6. DEVELOPMENT LIBRARIES

We recognize the long-term importance of developer support to the widespread deployment of Convergence. Convergence usage is currently specified as a REST API whose only implementation is as a Firefox plug-in. This is problematic because the Convergence Client API exposes the application developer to low-level artifacts, creating inconvenience and the opportunity for configuration errors. To address this, we are releasing 7 new Convergence clients for development in C, Java, PHP, Python, Perl, Ruby, and Lua. Through the C implementation, Convergence can also be embedded in C++, Objective-C, and other C runtimes. Each library contains a `converge(host, port, sha1sum)` that can be used in place of a `SSL_get_verify_result()` call, masking the complexity of Convergence's local cache and API. All configuration for the Convergence notaries are stored in flat files in `/usr/local/etc/converge`, making adding and managing notaries a simple process.

7. CONCLUSION

Widespread adoption of SSL trust enhancements like Convergence have in part been hampered by a lack of understanding of their performance characteristics under realistic conditions. We have performed a thorough case study of the Convergence architecture, evaluating its performance in simulation as the sole certificate validation service of a major university. Under realistic conditions, we found that Convergence was able to handle up to 300 requests per second. Under those same conditions end users would experience a barely perceptible average performance delay of 260 ms, and only a 108 ms delay on return trips to a domain. Our methodology is generalizable to the majority of recently proposed Certificate Authority alternatives and enhancements, allowing for a more objective and informed discussion on the future of authenticity on the Internet.

Acknowledgments

We would like to thank Paul van Oorschot, Jeremy Clark, Patrick Traynor, and Boyana Norris for their valuable comments and insight, and Abdul Alkhelaifi for his assistance with the development libraries. This work is supported in part by the US National Science Foundation under grant numbers CNS-1118046 and CNS-1254198. Braden Hollembaek was funded in part through an NSF REU supplement.

8. REFERENCES

[1] ab - Apache HTTP server benchmarking tool. Available: http://httpd.apache.org/docs/2.2/programs/ab.html.

[2] D. Akhawe, B. Amann, M. Vallentin, and R. Sommer. Here's My Cert, So Trust Me, Maybe? Understanding TLS Errors on the Web. In *Proceedings of the 22nd International World Wide Web Conference (WWW 2013)*, Rio de Janeiro, Brazil, May 2013.

[3] M. Alicherry and A. D. Keromytis. Doublecheck: Multi-path verification against man-in-the-middle attacks. In *Computers and Communications, 2009. ISCC 2009. IEEE Symposium on*, pages 557–563. IEEE, 2009.

[4] B. Amann, R. Sommer, M. Vallentin, and S. Hall. No Attack Necessary: The Surprising Dynamics of SSL Trust Relationships. In *ACSAC '13: Proceedings of the 29th Annual Computer Security Applications Conference*, Dec. 2013.

[5] C. Brubaker, S. Jana, B. Ray, S. Khurshid, and V. Shmatikov. Using Frankencerts for Automated Adversarial Testing of Certificate Validation in SSL/TLS Implementations.

[6] R. Carly. Internet Security provider Comodo's CEO Named "Entrepreneur of the Year" by Info Security Products Guide. Available: `http://www.comodo.com/news/press_releases/2011/02/comodo-CEO-entrepreneur-of-the-Year-infosecurity-global-excellence-award.html`, February 2011.

[7] J. Clark and P. C. van Oorschot. SoK: SSL and HTTPS: Revisiting Past Challenges and Evaluating Certificate Trust Model Enhancements. In *Proceedings of the 2013 IEEE Symposium on Security and Privacy*, San Francisco, CA, May 2013.

[8] P. Ducklin. The TURKTRUST SSL Certificate Fiasco – What Really Happened, and What Happens Next? Available: `http://nakedsecurity.sophos.com/2013/01/08/`Available: `the-turktrust-ssl-certificate-fiasco-what-happened-and-what-happens-next/`, January 2013.

[9] D. Eastlake et al. Transport Layer Security (TLS) Extensions: Extension Definitions. 2011.

[10] P. Eckersley. Sovereign Key Cryptography for Internet Domains, 2011.

[11] J. Edge. Mozilla and CNNIC. Available: `http://lwn.net/Articles/372386/`, February 2010.

[12] C. Ellison and B. Schneier. Ten Risks of PKI: What You're Not Being Told About Public Key Infrastructure. *Comput Secur J*, 16(1):1–7, 2000.

[13] S. Fahl, M. Harbach, H. Perl, M. Koetter, and M. Smith. Rethinking SSL Development in an Appified World. In *Proceedings of the 2013 ACM SIGSAC Conference on Computer & Communications Security*, CCS '13, pages 49–60, New York, NY, USA, 2013. ACM.

[14] D. Fisher. Microsoft Revokes Trust in Five Diginotar Root Certs. Wired. Available: `http://threatpost.com/microsoft-revokes-trust-five-diginotar-root-certs-mozilla-drops-trust-staat-der-nederland-cert`, September 2011.

[15] M. Georgiev, S. Iyengar, S. Jana, R. Anubhai, D. Boneh, and V. Shmatikov. The most dangerous code in the world: validating SSL certificates in non-browser software. In *Proceedings of the 2012 ACM conference on Computer and communications security*, CCS '12, pages 38–49, Raleigh, NC, USA, 2012. ACM.

[16] I. Grigg. VeriSign's Conflict of Interest Creates New Threat. *Financial Cryptography*, 1, September 2004.

[17] K. Hickman and T. Elgamal. The SSL protocol. *Netscape Communications Corp*, 501, 1995.

[18] P. Hoffman and J. Schlyter. The DNS-Based Authentication of Named Entities (DANE) Transport Layer Security (TLS) Protocol: TLSA. Technical report, RFC 6698, August, 2012.

[19] T. H.-J. Kim, L.-S. Huang, A. Perring, C. Jackson, and V. Gligor. Accountable Key Infrastructure (AKI): A Proposal for a Public-Key Validation Infrastructure. In *WWW '13: Proceedings of the 22nd International World Wide Web Conference*, Rio de Janeiro, Brazil, May 2013. International World Wide Web Conferences Steering Committee.

[20] B. Laurie, A. Langley, and E. Kasper. Certificate Transparency. *Available: ietf. org-Certificate Transparency (06.01. 2013)*, 2013.

[21] J. Liang, J. Jiang, H. Duan, K. Li, T. Wan, and J. Wu. When HTTPS Meets CDN: A Case of Authentication in Delegated Service. In *Proceedings of the 2014 IEEE Symposium on Security and Privacy*, San Jose, CA, May 2014.

[22] M. Marlinspike. SSL and the Future of Authenticity. *Black Hat USA*, 2011.

[23] M. Marlinspike. Trust Assertions for Certificate Keys. 2013.

[24] Marlinspike, M. Convergence – Running a Notary. Available: `https://github.com/moxie0/Convergence/wiki/Running-a-Notary`.

[25] E. Mills. Comodo: Web Attack Broader Than Initially Thought. CNET. Available: `http://news.cnet.com/8301-27080_3-20048831-245.html?part=rss&tag=feed&subj=InSecurityComplex`, March 2011.

[26] M. Myers. Revocatoin: Options and challenges. In *Financial Cryptography*, pages 165–171. Springer, 1998.

[27] Psyced.org. Certificate Patrol. Available: `http://patrol.psyced.org/`.

[28] R. L. Rivest. Can We Eliminate Certificate Revocation Lists? In *Financial Cryptography*, pages 178–183. Springer, 1998.

[29] R. Sandvik. Security Vulnerability Found in Cyberoam DPI Devices (CVE-2012-3372). Available: `https://blog.torproject.org/blog/security-vulnerability-found-cyberoam-dpi-devices-cve-2012-3372`, July 2012.

[30] R. Singel. Law Enforcement Appliance Subverts SSL. Available: `http://www.wired.com/threatlevel/2010/03/packet-forensics`, March 2010.

[31] C. Soghoian and S. Stamm. Certified Lies: Detecting and Defeating Government Interception Attacks Against SSL. In *Financial Cryptography and Data Security*, pages 250–259. Springer, 2012.

[32] D. Sounthiraraj, J. Sahs, G. Greenwood, Z. Lin, and L. Khan. SMV-HUNTER: Large Scale, Automated Detection of SSL/TLS Man-in-the-Middle Vulnerabilities in Android Apps. In *Proceedings of the 19th Network and Distributed System Security Symposium.*, 2014.

[33] N. Vratonjic, J. Freudiger, V. Bindschaedler, and J.-P. Hubaux. The Inconvenient Truth About Web Certificates. In B. Schneier, editor, *Economics of Information Security and Privacy III*, pages 79–117. Springer New York, 2013.

[34] D. Wendlandt, D. G. Andersen, and A. Perrig. Perspectives: Improving SSH-style Host Authentication with Multi-Path Probing. In *USENIX 2008 Annual Technical Conference*, ATC'08, pages 321–334, Boston, MA, 2008.

Author Index

www.ingramcontent.com/pod-product-compliance
Ingram Content Group UK Ltd.
Pitfield, Milton Keynes, MK11 3LW, UK
UKHW051415290926
15471UKWH00009B/1618

9 781450 33385